CADOGAN

A Chelsea Family

BY TAMSIN PERRETT

Edited by Camilla Mountain
Unicorn in association with Cadogan

Published in 2024 by Unicorn,
an imprint of Unicorn Publishing Group
Charleston Studio
Meadow Business Centre
Lewes BN8 5RW
www.unicornpublishing.org

© Cadogan Estates Ltd
Text © Tamsin Perrett
Foreword © Charles Moore, Baron Moore of Etchingham
Afterword © Edward Cadogan, 9th Earl Cadogan

The author has asserted her moral right under the Copyright, Designs and Patents Act 1988 to be identified as the author of this work.

All rights reserved. No part of the contents of this book may be reproduced, stored in or introduced into a retrieval system, or transmitted, in any form or by any means (electronic, mechanical, photocopying, recording or otherwise), without the prior written permission of the copyright holder and the above publisher of this book.

Every effort has been made to trace copyright holders and to obtain their permission for the use of copyrighted material. The publisher apologises for any errors or omissions and would be grateful to be notified of any corrections that should be incorporated in future reprints or editions of this book.

ISBN 978-1-912690-90-9
10 9 8 7 6 5 4 3 2 1

Picture research by Pauline Hubner
Designed by Karin Fremer
Printed by Gomer

For Charles Gerald John,
8th Earl Cadogan KBE DL

CONTENTS

—

FOREWORD Charles Moore … 7

EARLY BEGINNINGS … 10

1. Princes of Fferllys & Monmouthshire Farmers: Roman Britannia to the Middle Ages … 12
* The First Millennium, from Roman Britannia to Cadwgan ab Elystan Glodrydd … 32
* The Middle Ages, from Rhodri Mawr to the last Welsh Princes … 34

THE STUARTS … 36

2. Opportunity in Ireland: Major William Cadogan (1601–1661) and his son Henry (1642–1715) … 38
3. Marlborough's Right-hand Man, Multilingual Spy: General Sir William Cadogan, the first 1st Earl (1672–1726) … 58
* The Early Modern era, from the Tudors to the first Earls Cadogan … 86

THE GEORGIANS … 88

4. Custodians of Caversham & Chelsea: Charles, 2nd Baron Cadogan of Oakley (1685–1776), his wife Elizabeth Sloane (1701–1768) and their son Charles Sloane Cadogan (1728–1807) … 90
5. Family Affairs: Charles Sloane Cadogan, 3rd Baron Cadogan, 1st Viscount Chelsea and 1st Earl Cadogan (New Creation) (1728–1807) … 112
* Churchill and Walpole connections … 116
6. Evangelists & Educators: Reverend William Bromley Cadogan (1751–1797) and his wife Jane (d.1827) … 138
7. Adventure & Affliction: Charles Henry, 2nd Earl (1749–1832) … 152
* Sloane and Stanley connections; children of the second 1st Earl Cadogan (NC) … 170

NAPOLEONIC WARS & THE WELLINGTON CONNECTION — 172

8. Made in the Royal Navy: Captain George Cadogan (1783–1864) — 174
9. Pistols at Dawn: Scandalous Lady Charlotte (1781–1853) — 194
10. Wellington's Aide-de-Camp: Colonel Henry Cadogan (1780–1813) — 214
11. Greatness Thrust Apon Him: George, 3rd Earl (1783–1864) — 236
* Wellesley and Paget connections; children of the 3rd Earl Cadogan — 256

THE VICTORIANS — 258

12. Palaces, Parliament & Postings: Henry, 4th Earl (1812–1873) — 260
13. Art & Europe: Ladies Augusta (1811–1882) and Honoria (1813–1904), and General Sir George Cadogan (1814–1880) — 280
14. Politics & Property: George Henry, 5th Earl (1840–1915), creator of modern Chelsea — 304
15. Court & Countryside: George Henry, 5th Earl, and the Crown — 328
* Children of the 4th & 5th Earls Cadogan onwards — 354

THE TWENTIETH CENTURY — 356

16. Society & Succession: Henry 'Haggy' Cadogan (1868–1908) and the 'Cadogan Square' — 358
17. Brothers in Arms: Captain Gerald (1869–1933), Majors William (1879–1914) and Sir Edward Cadogan (1880–1960) — 382
18. The Sporting Life: Gerald, 6th Earl (1869–1933) — 404
19. Riding the Whirlwind: Sir Alexander Cadogan (1884–1968) — 426
20. Military Man & Modernizer: William, 7th Earl (1914–1997) — 446

AFTERWORD Edward, 9th Earl Cadogan — 468

Notes — 472
Select Resources & Bibliography — 487
Acknowledgements — 492
Picture Credits — 492
Index — 495

Foreword

—

CHARLES MOORE

I am not the right person to write this foreword. Its intended author was Charles Cadogan. From its genesis, the 8th Earl had warmly supported the project of a family history, but he did not live to see it finished. He died in June 2023, aged eighty-six. I cannot match Charles's famously direct style or, of course, his knowledge of the subject, but I can say with some confidence that this is the book he had hoped for.

Walking through London SW3 about a week before these words were written, I looked up and saw I was in Elystan Street. Thanks to this book, I knew that Elystan was a tenth-century Celtic chieftain known, in Wales, as 'the Renowned'. Although his original renown may have slipped a bit in the intervening millennium, it has taken a different form in modern times. Elystan's son was called Cadwgan, and that is why Elystan's name adorns a Chelsea street in 2024 – and why his lion rampant appears on the badge of Chelsea Football Club.

The Cadwgan/Cadogan story runs from wild Wales, for several centuries, to mutinous Ireland in the seventeenth. There, Major William Cadogan managed adroitly to serve Charles I, Oliver Cromwell, and the Restoration of Charles II, picking up 665 acres in County Meath on the way. His grandson was also William. (You need to bear in mind that almost every man in this saga is called William, George, Edward, Henry or Charles – none of the quirky names often popular with the aristocracy.) This William, the first (and only) Earl Cadogan of the first creation, was a brave soldier and brilliant quarter- and spymaster in the Duke of Marlborough's wars. His achievements and his marriage made him very rich, though he was as good at spending as at getting. A critic called him 'a big, bad, bold, blustering, bloody, blundering booby', a backhanded tribute to the fact that he and his family had well and truly arrived.

Perhaps the real turning point, however, was when the 1st Earl's brother, Charles, married Elizabeth Sloane. Her prodigious father was Sir Hans Sloane, explorer, physician, naturalist, and later co-founder, with his vast collection, of the British Museum. He also owned 166 acres of Chelsea, half of which passed to Elizabeth. In her will, the Sloane and Cadogan interests were united. The rest is this history.

Their son, Charles Sloane Cadogan, began the great development of 'Hans Town' and was made the 1st Earl Cadogan of the new creation. George Henry, the 5th Earl, as well as being a statesman, was the creator of modern Chelsea, with such Victorian gems as the Rossetti Studios, Cadogan Square, the Cadogan Hotel (where Oscar Wilde was arrested) and the matchless Holy Trinity Sloane Street, which John Betjeman called 'the cathedral of the Arts and Crafts movement'. He was a great improver and donated many parcels of land to the borough, including the site upon which stands Chelsea Old Town Hall (scene of so many glamorous weddings). In 1890, George Henry also set up the Cadogan Estate office, a key development in the professionalization, and therefore the prosperity, of the family property empire.

But the 5th Earl had also bought, in 1889, the great Suffolk house Culford Hall, with fifty-one bedrooms and over 11,000 acres. Thanks to death duties and the ravages of World War I, Culford became an incubus. Well advised, the young 7th Earl ('Bill') ignored those who advocated getting out of London, deciding to sell the unmanageable Culford in the early 1930s and to keep the Chelsea estate.

Many Cadogans have been countrymen, yet their counter-cultural commitment to London over so many generations has been the secret of their success. As so many grand families retreated from the capital to their country seats, the Cadogans could see that their fortunes lay the other way.

I say 'to London', but of course I ought to say Chelsea. That is where the entire metropolitan estate – currently ninety-three acres – is to be found, and it is where the Cadogan heart is. In their collective memory, Chelsea is their village. As recently as two hundred years ago, it still encompassed some farms. Today it still contains churches which they help look after, and residential streets, commercial property and public spaces that they have helped plan. It has a coherent character that residents and visitors love. It would not have that coherence today without the Cadogans.

As this book entertainingly reveals, they were not all heroes or geniuses. There were a few renegades, failures, debtors and one lunatic. But the great majority shared the following valuable qualities – courage in war, loyalty to king and country, a respect for how money works, a devotion to family that enabled them to take a long view, and a sense of place. Almost no Cadogan was an intellectual. In most cases, that led them to see truth and speak as they found. Last, which is perhaps surprising in a family with such possessions, many of them have been serious though undemonstrative Christians. They have understood what 'stewardship' means, which is why they are still there.

It was a condition of Charles Cadogan's that his own time as earl, which began in 1997, should not appear in this book. But it should be noted here that he expressed in his own character most of the qualities I have just noted. He also contributed greatly to the innovations of his time, of which Duke of York Square is the most notable.

He was big man in physical stature and personal presence. He was kind, funny, ribald, and could be gruff. He had strong loves – music, wild birds (for whom he created such a sanctuary at Glenquaich in Perthshire), White's, racing and the Church – and when he did not love something, he would say so. He also had a practical turn of mind, giving short, clear advice on small things, as he did to me about how to bring back house martins to our eaves. To all good causes, he gave generously, often and without fuss.

Those who walked with Charles Cadogan round Chelsea were amazed by how often people came up to greet him, and even more amazed that he usually knew who they were. Both literally and metaphorically, Chelsea was his. So he did his best for it. For him, it was both a duty and a pleasure.

Some people with great inherited wealth fritter it away. Others feel guilty about it. Charles did neither. He was unembarrassed by his great fortune, but he did feel a lifelong sense of obligation – not lifelong, actually, but longer still, felt towards generations yet to come. He had great family pride, but he also liked the unvarnished truth. This history offers both.

Map of Wales (detail), Christopher Saxon, 1580

EARLY BEGINNINGS

CHAPTER 1

Princes of Fferllys & Monmouthshire Farmers

—

ROMAN BRITANNIA TO THE MIDDLE AGES

We begin a thousand years ago, with a king. Elystan Glodrydd (*c.* AD 975–1010), progenitor of the 5th Royal Tribe of Wales, was a Celtic chieftain. A misty figure from the *Brut y Tywysogion* – the Welsh equivalent of the *Anglo-Saxon Chronicle* – he inherited rule of Buellt and Gwrtheyrion, and more than doubled his territory by conquering Fferllys/Ferlix to create the realm of Rhwng Gwy a Hafren ('between Wye and Severn').[1] The landscape of his kingdom has changed little in a millennium: a contrasting mix of highland moor and fertile valleys, unified by sheep and rain. Along its eastern edge runs Offa's Dyke, built by a Mercian (Anglo-Saxon) king two hundred years before Elystan to delineate the border between competing genealogies, languages and cultures. The earth was soaked in blood. Over in Wessex, King Æthelred (r.978–1013; 1014–16) was paying Danegeld to a fresh wave of Viking raiders and earning himself the epithet 'the Unready'. By contrast, the Briton Elystan, who today is commemorated in Elystan Street and Elystan Place in London's Chelsea, was dubbed 'Glodrydd' – 'the Renowned'. Tales of how he came by this sobriquet have been lost. But his true legacy is alive in his illustrious descendants, whose name is an anglicized form of his son Cadwgan's: the Cadogan family.[2]

The Cadogans' lineage through Elystan Glodrydd embodies the complex early history of Britain. The Celts were Plato's 'warlike' peoples whose

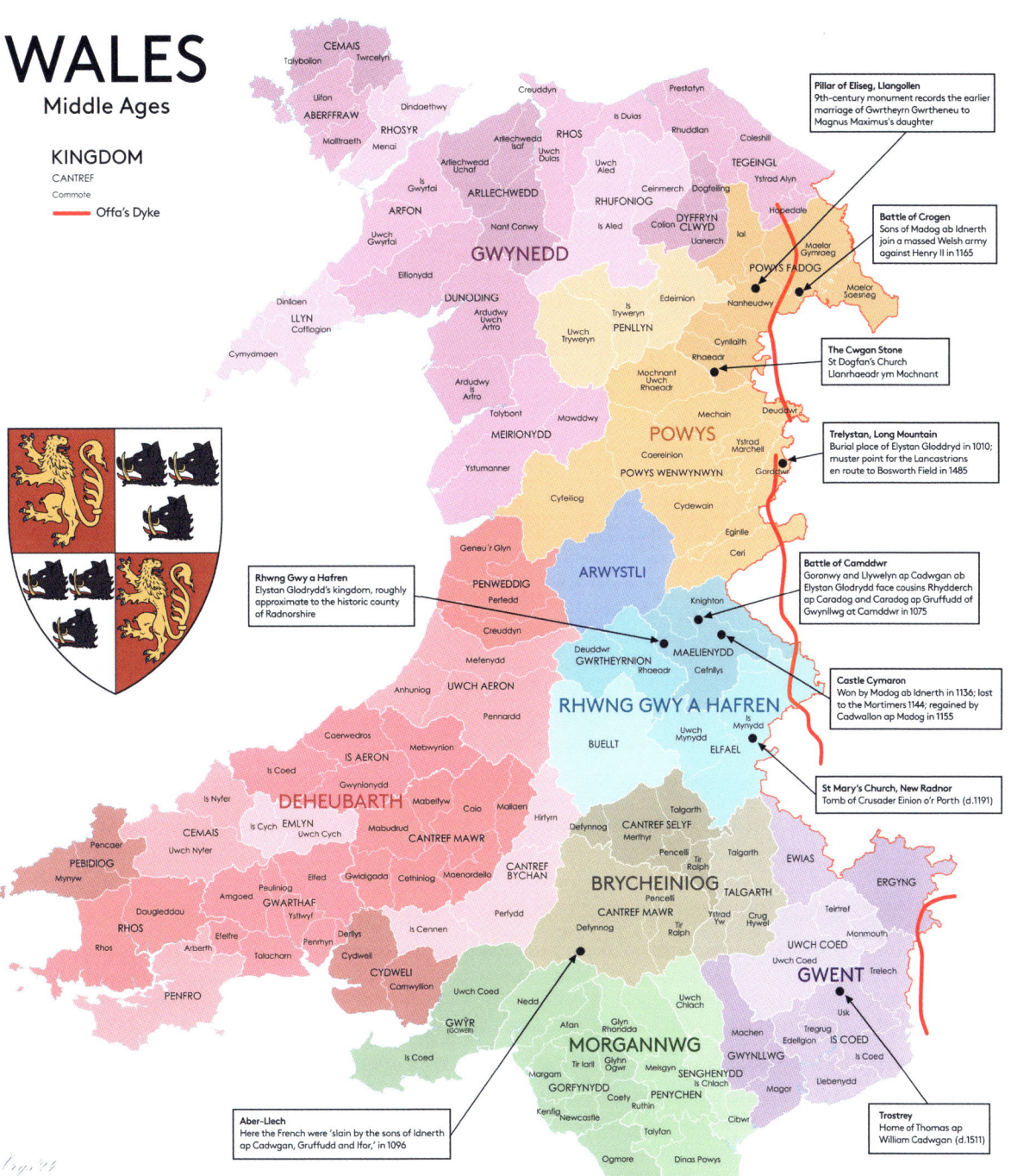

Map of the land divisions of medieval Wales (source: RCAHMW). The golden lion rampant regardant on a red shield is the coat of arms retrospectively attributed to Elystan Glodrydd; the three boars' heads attributed to his son Cadwgan. Together they form the arms of the 5th Royal Tribe of Wales, central to the Cadogan family's coat of arms.

culture came to dominate the island during the Iron Age (*c.* 800–100 BC), commonly known as the Ancient Britons.[3] They adapted to Roman occupation two millennia ago and flourished in the mountainous west and north of the British Isles while the south and east faced tides of Germanic tribes (Jutes, Angles, Saxons) and flaxen-haired Vikings. By Elystan's time, a handful of interwoven indigenous royal dynasties had emerged from the sparse population.[4]

Before we come to tales from the modern age, of well-known military masterminds, spies, diplomats and surprisingly scandalous ladies, first let us indulge briefly in the few family stories we can tease out from a largely unwritten history. Dates and spellings are not the fixed points on which we rely today, emerging from an oral, poetic and embellishing tradition. But, by following the linguistic chains of patronymic convention – ab or ap (meaning 'son of') and ferch ('daughter of') in Brythonic Old Welsh – a direct line of reverse begats emerges that provides a reasonable family tree. In Elystan's case, naturally this includes many individuals of note, staging posts along the way back to the past, who are identified by their evocative nicknames.

FIRST, ELYSTAN'S PATERNAL LINE. His father Cuhelyn ab Ifor (said in English: Kai-helin son of Ivor), Lord of Buellt, was, to give him the full flourish, Cuhelyn ab Ifor ap Severus ap Cadwr ap Cadwr Wenwyn ab Idnerth ab Iorwerth Hirflawdd. Six generations run together in a link back to Iorwerth Hirflawdd (Iorwerth of the Long Struggle, born *c.* AD 770). Elystan's 'tall and grey'[5] great(x5)-grandfather was ruler of Arwystli, just north of Buellt in the heart of Wales, surrounded on all sides by competing tribes. As a local chieftain he would have kept a band of retainers, who he feasted in the hall while his bard recited the heroic legends of his ancestors, as well as serfs who worked the land. Together they set out in battle. 'Hirflawdd' perhaps refers not to the man but more broadly to the long struggles of his people, throughout the seventh and eighth centuries, against the Anglo-Saxons of Northumbria and Mercia. This was significant warfare that culminated in construction of the massive earthwork defining the Welsh–English border. Iorwerth certainly deserves our sympathies.

Through him we follow the line back to legendary sixth-century leader Casnar/Kasnat/Casanauth Wledig (Casnar the Ruler, active around AD 500) of Powys. His qualities are self-evident in his name. Not only was Casnar a synonym for 'famous warrior', 'proud warlike man',[6] additionally:

> 'Wledig' is...derived from the Welsh for 'land'[;] it seems to mean an army commander who attains a more or less legitimized power – a 'land-holder'. Four or five men are styled so who flourished during the last phase of the [Roman] Western Empire. All but Maximus are native to the island, so the bestowal of the title on him is another token of his adoption as a compatriot.[7]

Magnus Maximus (Great the Greatest, not lacking in self-confidence), known to the Welsh as Macsen Wledig, was the last Roman Emperor of Britannia and briefly ruler of much of Western Europe (r. AD 383–88). He too can be claimed as an august ancestor of Elystan and the Cadogans. Buoyed by victory over the Picts and Scots, the ambitious general and his loyal legionaries swept over the Channel to take Gaul from Emperor Gratian and usurp the imperial crown. Eventually, Maximus overextended himself trying to take Italy and was executed. Before his death, however, the man from Hispania Gallaecea (modern Spain) married his daughter Severa into the Welsh royal family, and here comes the link: the couple's granddaughter Thewer became Casnar's wife. A record of the union between Severa and the powerful native king Gwrtheyrn 'Gwrtheneu' ('the Thin') is engraved in Latin on the ninth-century Pillar of Eliseg, which still stands near Llangollen.

RIGHT Gold solidus coin of Emperor Magnus Maximus, struck AD 383–88, minted in London. The last Roman Emperor of Britannia is linked to the Cadogan family by marriage.

Both Macsen Wledig and Casnar Wledig (as Kasnat) feature in *The Mabinogion*, a fourteenth-century collection of the earliest native prose texts in Welsh. These tales contain folkloric kernels of truth, however, rather than delineating strict biography: an Irish king is transformed into a boar, for example, and heroic quests are undertaken with the help of a band of knights led by King Arthur. Hold that last thought. Gwrtheyrn – Elystan's great(x15)-grandfather – appears in early literature on both sides of Offa's Dyke. Up in Jarrow, Northumbria, the Venerable Bede wrote him into both *De temporum ratione* (AD 725) and his more famous *Historia ecclesiastica* (AD 731).[8] A century later, Welsh monk Nennius of Bangor included him in the *Historia Brittonum* (completed *c*. AD 830). The story goes that it was Gwrtheyrn who invited the Saxons to settle in Kent, welcoming exiled warlords Horst and Hengist in exchange for fealty and thus changing the human landscape of the British Isles. Today, Gwrtheyrn has broken through into common consciousness via Geoffrey of Monmouth's reimagining,[9] as Arthur's nemesis Vortigern, King of Gwent and later King of the Britons (*fl*. AD 425–50), who the *Encyclopædia Britannica* decrees 'may probably be safely regarded as an actual historical figure.'

The Pillar of Eliseg, also known as the Valle Crucis pillar, 9th century. An inscription relating to its re-erection after the Civil War is clearly visible. Now largely obliterated by time and weather, the original inscriptions recorded a genealogy of the kings of Powys through King Vortigern and Magnus Maximus.

ELYSTAN GLODRYDD'S MOTHER GWEN was also of royal descent. Her paternal grandmother was Angharad ferch Hywel Dda (Angharad daughter of Howell the Good). Hywel (*c*. AD 880–950) was King of Deheubarth and later Ruler of Wales – though not following modern borders, as this excluded Morgannwg and Gwent in the far south-east. He was a man of peace who engaged in diplomacy, completing a pilgrimage to Rome in AD 928 and attending the court of the English King Æthelstan (r. AD 927–39). Most famously, he set in train the codification of the ancient Laws of Wales.

'King Vortigern and Merlin watch two dragons fight', *The St Albans Chronicle*, English school, 15th century. The Celtic king (Gwrtheyrn 'Gwrtheneu') is shown the red Celtic dragon fighting the white Saxon dragon by the boy wizard. The victorious red dragon of Wales sleeps still under the mountain of Dinas Emrys.

Few modern Acts of Parliament can match the style of a law defining the penalty for killing or stealing the cat which guards a royal barn. The thief must pay a fine which is assessed by measurement of the cat. 'Its head is to be held downwards on a clean, level floor, and its tail is to be held upwards; and after that, wheat must be poured over it until the tip of its tail is hidden, and that is its value.'[10]

Hywel Dda reigned over a golden age that was literate and law-abiding, if lived in subjugation to the English. His laws were seen as just, and perhaps that was the essence of their 'goodness': they were visible and defined. His achievement is remembered today in the Welsh parliament building named after him, Tŷ Hywel.

Hywel's grandfather – Elystan's great(x4)-grandfather – is another towering figure of Welsh history: Rhodri Mawr (Roderick the Great, c. AD 820–878). Rhodri was a warrior-king, defending the coast against marauders with mixed success. One notable victory is the mid-career trouncing of 'Viking leader, Gormr or Ormr, [who] was represented as Horm in the Irish and Welsh annals' report of his death at the hands of Rhodri Mawr during a raid on Anglesey in the 850s.'[11] Horm is interesting as the possible inspiration for the earliest romance written in Middle English, *King Horn* (c.1250).[12]

King Hywel Dda (Howell the Good) enthroned, illustration from a Latin copy of the Laws of Hywel Dda, Peniarth MS 28, f. 1v, 13th century. Elystan's maternal great(x2)-grandfather.

Back on the battlefields of first-millennial Wales, Rhodri Mawr's power and kingdom grew. He assumed the protectorate of Powys when his uncle died and annexed Seisyllwyg when his brother-in-law drowned – no comment on the circumstances – enabling him to stage a united Welsh defence against the Norse raiders. Such was his influence that Rhodri Mawr is cited as a common ancestor among almost all of the Royal Tribes of Wales. Across the Irish Sea, the medieval *Annals of Ulster* called him King of the Britons. It was trouble on his eastern border that brought about his death in battle, at the hands of the Mercians.

Rhodri Mawr inherited the kingdom of Gwynedd from his marvellously named father Merfyn Frych (Mervyn the Freckled, d. AD 844). Through Merfyn's mother Esyllt, the Cadogan family can look right back to the founder of the Gwynedd dynasty, Cunedda Wledig (King

Kenneth, *c.* AD 386–460). He rose to power during the great fifth-century migration of the Votadini tribe from the Old North of Roman Britannia (Northumberland and the Scottish Borders) south over Hadrian's Wall and into north Wales, perhaps under Vortigern's auspices.[13] It should come as no surprise that in those times, this was no caravan of love; they fought their way down. 'And with great slaughter they drove out from those regions the Scotti [decendants of the Picts who had taken Ireland] who never returned again to inhabit them,' wrote Nennius.[14] The Votadini were immortalized by Welsh bard Aneirin in the elegiac poem *Y Gododdin*, a commemoration of the Battle of Catraeth (present-day Catterick, North Yorkshire), which they fought against the Angles in *c.* AD 600. And what of Cunedda himself? He may have had Roman blood. His paternal grandfather, who governed from a powerbase in Edinburgh, was Padarn Beisrudd (Paternus of the Red Cloak or Tunic, around AD 300), whose epithet likely refers to the *paludamentum* of a Roman military commander. We can infer that Padarn was either a Roman on an imperial posting or a local chieftain who had been handed devolved power – a fairly common occurrence by the third century of imperial rule. Medieval attempts to create a sketchy lineage for Padarn went back nine possible generations through his father, conjured up as Tegid (Tacitus) ap Cain ap Gwrgain ap Doli ap Gwrddoli ap Dwfn ap Gwrddwfn ap Goruc ap Meirchion Fawdfilwr…at which point even the tenacious and authoritative historian P.C. Bartrum inserts '(fictitious)' and the fog descends on an impenetrable, vowel-phobic pre-history.[15] What emerges with clarity is that in a world of shifting political and territorial landscapes, by the turn of the first millennium both sides of Elystan's family – the Cadogan family – had claimed rule for several hundred years.

ELYSTAN GLODRYDD MARRIED WELL, uniting royal tribes and cementing regional power. He may even have had two wives. Genealogist and deputy herald Lewys Dwnn (*c.*1550–1616) found references to both Gwenllian (Gwen) ferch Einon ab Owain ap Hywel Dda (he of the good laws), and Gwladys (Gladys) ferch Rhûn ab Ednowain Bendew, Lord of Tegaingl (modern-day Flintshire). Of the two, Gwenllian – a distant cousin on his mother's

The Cwgan Stone at St Dogfan's Church, Llanrhaeadr ym Mochnant. A 9th-century Celtic cross with later inscription, it has been linked to Cadwgan ab Elystan Glodrydd.

side – has more frequent mention, and she is the sole wife charted by Bartrum in his colossal eight-volume work *Welsh Genealogies AD 300–1400*.[16] Elystan's legacy was secured with the arrival of children; no other details of his life survive. An early heraldic pedigree records that he met a sudden end in the year 1010 at Long Mountain, near Welshpool in Montgomeryshire, where he was 'slain in a civil broil' and buried on the mountain's south-eastern slope.[17] Today a medieval chapel stands on top of a remote burial mound said to mark the spot, above a hamlet called Trelystan.

His son Cadwgan/Cadwgon ab Elystan Glodrydd, Lord of Radnor, is the heir through whom the Cadogan family is descended.[18] Like his father, he probably married more than once.[19] Efa (Eva) ferch Gwrgant ab Ithel was Cadwgan's most prominent wife – her brother was Iestyn ap Gwrgant, Prince of Morgannwg (Glamorgan) and founder of the 4th Royal Tribe of Wales. Iestyn married Cadwgan's sister Angharad, further entwining these two royal families. Their lives are shrouded in mystery, though a nineteenth-century discovery may hold the key to Cadwgan's fate. Built into the wall of a Montgomeryshire church is an intricately carved stone slab, incorporating a Celtic cross and lettering that reads: '+Co(corg)om/ Cwgan Filiu(s) Edelstan'. Historians have speculated that if Edelstan is Elystan, his *filius* (son) Cwgan could well be Cadwgan.[20] Christianity survived in Wales throughout the rather misleadingly termed Dark Ages and it was not unknown for Welsh leaders to retire into holy orders. A cross before the name on 'the Cwgan Stone' may designate a convert. The Caldey Stone, on Caldey Island off the southern coast of Wales, is a similarly repurposed Celtic stone, inscribed both with sixth-century Ogham and ninth-century Latin script, and marked with a cross. Scholars have suggested that the Latin instruction to 'pray for the soul of Catuoconus' is probably to be identified with 'Cadwgan', though its dating places it too early for the son of Elystan Glodrydd.[21]

Efa and Cadwgan had several sons, whose lives were lived far from quiet contemplation. Battles were bloody; grudges intergenerational; punishments gruesome. King Cnut/Canute (r.1016–35), Viking ruler of Denmark, England and Norway, was succeeded by Edward the Confessor (r.1042–66), who took an aggressive stance against the Welsh and Scots. A scion and distant cousin of the Gwynedd dynasty, Rhys brother of Gyffudd ap Rhydderch, met a grisly end:

> ...a man of bold and enterprising spirit, having committed frequent depredations in the English marches, had become, on that account, the object of particular resentment...he was put to death at Bulundune, by the command of King Edward the Confessor, who in this instance assumed a sovereign authority; and his head was sent to that prince, who then kept his court at Gloucester.[22]

The Welsh also fought among themselves: Wales was a contested territory of fragmented principalities. Inheritance passed from the eldest son to the next brother in line, exhausting each generation (with the perfect motive for fratricide) before doubling back to the eldest son's sons. Wider family loyalties often demanded that cousins join the fight – a look at the family trees is strongly recommended. At the end of the eleventh century Cadwgan's sons were involved in a chaotic series of turf wars that resulted from the regicide of Bleddyn ap Cynfyn, King of Gwynedd and Powys and founder of the 3rd Royal Tribe of Wales, in 1074. The *Brut* records that brothers Goronwy and – importantly for Cadogan family history – Llewelyn ap Cadwgan took to the field twice against their cousins from Gwynllwg (relations of the unfortunate, headless Rhys), at Camddwr in 1075 and at Gweunotyll two years later.[23]

It is Llewelyn ap Cadwgan (d.1099) who is the Cadogan family's ancestor. In 1911, the discovery of a rare silver penny stamped 'Lewillen Rex' and dating by style from 1090–93, suggested a rather grand coda for him. British Numismatic Society founder P.W.P. Carlyon-Britton's research led him to conclude:

> Although the circumstance is not recorded in the meagre chronicles of the period, I suggest that it was immediately after the death of William Fitz Baldwin that the castle of Rhyd y Gors was taken possession of by Llywelyn, son of Cadwgan, and that he thereupon issued a coinage copied from that type of William II, which was probably still current amongst the Norman soldiery engaged in the campaign against the Britons.[24]

This was a pinnacle for Llewelyn's line. His eldest brother Idnerth ap Cadwgan was the man born to rule Rhwng Gwy a Hafren. By contrast, Llewelyn's son Sitsylt was Lord of Buellt, a *cantref* within the kingdom; his grandson Howell ap Sitsylt, through whom the Cadogan line continues, became Lord of Penbualt, a smaller commote within Buellt. Family landholdings were reduced by ever-decreasing circles and younger sons. It would be five hundred years before the descendants of Llewelyn ap Cadwgan would rise again to prominence. Meanwhile, the exploits of their close cousins in the 5th Royal Tribe of Wales glittered for at least a further century.

ABOVE Silver penny of King Llywelyn ap Cadwgan, 11th century, struck at Rhydygors (Carmarthen) by the mint of regional King William Rufus (r.1087–1100). The coin bears the inscription 'Llywelyn ap Cadwgan, Rex'.

Bayeux Tapestry, 11th century, wool thread on linen. A vivid depiction of what war would have looked like to the Cadogans' ancestors at this point in history: grisly hand-to-hand fighting.

THE WELSH FACED A NEW COMMON ENEMY: the Normans. In 1066 William the Conqueror had defeated King Harold at the Battle of Hastings and swiftly set about establishing rule across England. Wales was invaded in waves, with varying success. The Conqueror himself visited St David's (Cardiff) in 1081, extracting payment in fealty of £40 from Rhys ap Tewdwr, founder of the 2nd Royal Tribe of Wales and King of Deheubarth (Hywel Dda's old kingdom), as recorded in the *Domesday Book* (1085).[25] In that feat of administration and accounting, Rhwng Gwy a Hafren is largely undescribed – only Pilleth and Cascob on its eastern fringes had been taken – possibly because it was seen as of little value, being so sparsely populated, largely with sheep; possibly because it was so difficult to police.[26] The Normans kept trying. Of the many motte-and-bailey castles built in the Middle Marches at this time, only their impressive earthworks remain – occasionally the ruins of a stone circular keep (fortress) are visible on top of a man-made hill (motte), with a larger encircled area (the bailey) at the foot.

Elystan's family fought back. Two of Idnerth ap Cadwgan's sons scored a victory over the French recorded by the *Brut*:

> 1092–96 And the French [Normans] moved a host to Gwent; but they returned empty-handed having gained naught.

> And as they were returning they were slain by the Britons at a place called Celli Carnant. And after that the French moved a host to Brycheiniog and thought to ravage the whole land, but, having failed to accomplish their thoughts, as they were returning they were slain by the sons of Idnerth ap Cadwgan [ab Elystan], Gruffudd and Ifor, in the place called Aber-Llech. And the inhabitants stayed in their houses unafraid although the castles were still intact and the garrisons in them.[27]

A few years later, King Henry I (r.1100–35) tried a new tactic, granting a form of viceroyalty to favoured Welshmen. Hywel ap Goronwy ap Cadwgan ab Elystan Glodrydd (d.1106, a son of Goronwy who had fought alongside Llewelyn ap Cadwgan in the 1070s), was given Ystrad Tywi and Cydweli and Gower, a large kingdom in the south. Not surprisingly, the previous rulers of the area objected. Hywel was set up by a man he considered a friend, Gwgan ap Merig, whose supporters half-strangled him before he was turned over to the Normans and beheaded.[28]

Maelienydd and neighbouring Elfael were the last bastions of power in Wales for Elystan's descendants. The family had arch enemies in the powerful de Mortimers, who became neighbours when they were granted the Earl of Hereford's Wigmore estate, following his unsuccessful rebellion in 1075.[29] The battles for Castle Cymaron/Cwm Aran (in present-day Radnorshire) are emblematic of the ensuing back-and-forth over border territory. 'It seems likely that the castle was founded during the [de] Mortimer conquest of the *cantref* of Maelienydd in the late eleventh century.'[30] In 1136 Llewelyn ap Cadwgan's nephew Madog ab Idnerth (d.1140), the last King of Rhwng Gwy a Hafren, drove them out. It was a good year: he joined forces with two Princes of Gwynedd, Owain and Cadwalader, burning the castle of Caerwedros in Ceredigion before setting out for Cardigan with 'a numerous force of picked warriors, about six thousand fine-footed soldiers and two thousand mailed horsemen most brave and ready for battle.'[31] They had learned cavalry skills and armour from their conquerors. Four years after Madog's death, however, the *Brut* tells us that Hugh de Mortimer 'for the second time subjugated Malienedd', before murdering Madog's son Maredudd (Meredith, meaning redhead), in 1146.[32] Redheads, freckles… in the absence of physical portraits, we can tell from their names that the early Cadwgans certainly looked Celtic. Another son, Cadwallon ap Madog, Prince of Maelienydd (d.1179), led multiple assaults on Cymaron, the last of which, in 1155, kept the castle in Cadogan hands for twenty-five years. He made a strategic marriage to Efa (Eva) the daughter of the Prince of Powys.

In 1165 Cadwallon ap Madog and another brother, Einion Clud, Prince of Elfael, joined a massed Welsh army to defend themselves against invasion by Henry II (r.1154–89):

> Not all Welsh rulers joined the coalition which gathered in the region of Corwen, but enough did to give some support to the [*Brut y Tywysogion*] chronicler's assertion that Henry was opposed by 'the host of Gwynedd…the host of Deheubarth… and the host of all Powys', together with the forces of the sons of Madog ab Idnerth [ap Cadwgan], the rulers of the land between Wye and Severn.[33]

The struggle has become distilled in the legendary Battle of Crogen, from which the Plantagenet withdrew.[34] Concessions to the Welsh in the years that followed included recognition of ancestral land claims. Cadwallon ap Madog and Einion Clud both travelled to Henry II's court at Gloucester in 1175, under protection of their first cousin Rhys ap Gruffydd (1132–1197), Prince of Deheubarth, today known as The Lord Rhys.[35] Two years after the Gloucester meeting, Einion Clud (d.1177) was murdered by supporters of their old enemy de Mortimer while on his way back

ABOVE Battle of Crogen commemorative plaque, Castle Mill Bridge, Bronygarth, near Chirk. Cadwgan's grandsons joined massed Welsh forces to defeat King Henry II of England in 1165. Einion Clud is named.

from a Christmas Eisteddfod. They came for Cadwallon (d.1179) as he returned from the English court. This time they had overstepped the mark: he was carrying a royal letter of safe conduct. King Henry II was unamused and threw Roger de Mortimer, Lord of Wigmore, into prison for three years.

Loyalty to the Church was as important as fealty to the Crown. Einion Clud's son Einion o'r Porth (d.1191) and Cadwallon's son Maelgwyn (d.1197) both took the cross in 1188 while Henry II was still on the throne, joining the Crusades for which his successor is chiefly remembered.[36] The Archbishop of Canterbury toured Wales on a recruitment drive, recorded by the monk Giraldus who accompanied him, in his *Itinerarium Cambriae* (1191):

> The archbishop proceeded to Radnor, on Ash Wednesday... where a sermon being preached by the archbishop, upon the subject of the Crusades, and explained to the Welsh by an interpreter, the author of this Itinerary, impelled by the urgent importunity and promises of the king, and the persuasions of the archbishop and the justiciary, arose the first, and falling down at the feet of the holy man, devoutly took the sign of the cross. His example was instantly followed by Peter, bishop of St. David's, a monk of the abbey of Cluny, and then by Eineon [Einion o'r Porth], son of Eineon Clyd, prince of Elvenia, and many other persons. Eineon rising up, said to [the Lord] Rhys, whose daughter he had married, 'My father and lord! with your permission I hasten to revenge the injury offered to the great father of all.' ...Malgo [Maelgwyn], son of Cadwallon, prince of Melenia, after a short but efficacious exhortation from the archbishop, and not without the tears and lamentations of his friends, was marked with the sign of the cross.[37]

Investitures of the Prince of Wales, at Caernarfon Castle. The heraldic emblems of the Royal Tribes of Wales, including the lion of Elystan Glodrydd, are on prominent display.

LEFT The future King Edward VIII, on 13 July 1911, with his parents King George V and Queen Mary. Major the Hon. William 'Willie' Cadogan, MVO (1879–1914), was his private equerry at Magdalen College, Oxford, in the lead-up to World War I.

BELOW The future King Charles III, with his mother Queen Elizabeth II (in yellow), on 1 July 1969.

OPPOSITE Stone effigy of Einion o'r Porth, Prince of Elfael, St Mary's Church, Radnor Castle. Einion is shown wearing the armour of close combat: a chain-mail coif and hauberk, with a fabric surcoat. The surcoat was a recent development that aided identification on the battlefield and protected the crusader from the heat of the sun. His circular shield is unusual for the period, one of only two such depictions in the Welsh Marches – shields were usually large and triangular.

Einion o'r Porth, 'who was much addicted to the chase', returned unscathed from the Holy Land only to be murdered by another brother, Gwalter, in 1191.[38] And King Richard I ('the Lionheart', r.1189–99) backed the de Mortimers; Roger retook Cymaron Castle in 1195.

Cadwallon's grandson Madog ap Maelgwyn retained some regional power, though the lines between Welsh and Anglo-Norman were beginning to blur, at least among the nobility. 'It is quite probable – and an early example of political accommodation between marchers and native Welsh dynasts – that Madog ap Maelgwyn had succeeded in recovering some territory in Maelienydd as a result of an agreement with the then lord of that land, Roger [de] Mortimer,'[39] notes early Welsh historian Dr David Stephenson. De Mortimer's death in 1214 seems to have polarized old loyalties. The sons of Maelgwyn ap Cadwallon joined a grand coalition of forces under Llywelyn Fawr (Llywelyn the Great, *c*.1173–1240), who swept through south Wales driving out the Anglo-Normans the following year.[40] A period of relative stability dawned. King John (r.1199–1216) had enough problems at home to deal with, forced to sign the *Magna Carta* before his ignominious death; the increasingly powerful English barons kept his successor Henry III (r.1216–72) occupied with the first stirrings of Parliament. King Henry, who was crowned at the age of nine, was more interested in the new style of English Gothic architecture and refounding Westminster Abbey. Wales was somewhat left to its own devices. Sixteen years after his father's death, Ralph de Mortimer married Gwladus Ddu, Llywelyn's daughter: if you can't beat them, join them. The legitimacy of rule by Llywelyn Fawr and his line was recognized by the Crown in the 1267 Treaty of Montgomery. It was short-lived.

In 1277 Wales was annexed to England. King Edward I of England (r.1272–1307) invaded Wales with a fifteen-thousand-strong army, on the grounds that Llywelyn ap Gruffudd, Fawr's grandson (*c*.1223–1282), who swiftly surrendered, had failed to attend his coronation. In 1301 Edward proclaimed his son Prince of Wales, a title bestowed upon the heir apparent to the English throne ever since.

THE CADOGANS' POWER RECEDED and they drop from the view of history. They survived the Hundred Years' War (1337–1453), which took thousands of Welsh archers to the battlefields of France; and its interruption by the Black Death, which wiped out a quarter of the population on its arrival in 1348. They remained landowners through the end of feudalism that resulted, bringing higher wages and lower rents, forcing many to sell. We cannot know if they joined a brief rebellion against English rule during which Owain Glyndŵr, of the ancient royal house of Gwynedd and Powys, was crowned Prince of Wales (r.1404–15). Curiously, the family's old enemies, the anglicized Mortimers, now the first Earls of March, were allies to the Welsh in this. (Not to be confused with the fourth Earls of March three centuries later, the Lennox family, later Gordon-Lennox – Dukes of Richmond – whose tree would join the Cadogans' twice.)

The name Elystan Glodrydd echoed once more in the Welsh hills, at a pivotal moment in British history. In the second week of August 1485, Long Mountain, Elystan's burial place, was the muster point for the Lancastrian army before they marched to Bosworth Field.[41] Rhys ap Thomas (1449–1525), descended from the Princes of Deheubarth (the line of Elystan's great-great-grandfather Hywel Dda), had travelled from the south coast up through the old Cadogan lands of Buellt and the Wye Valley, recruiting up to two thousand warriors along the way, to join Henry Tudor and his French and Scots forces. The Welsh claimed Henry as a kinsman. His paternal grandfather was Owain (Owen) ap Maredudd ap Tudur

Illustrated page of heraldry, Harleian MSS (detail), early 1500s. According to *The Great Chronicle of London* (c.1439–1512), Henry Tudor carried a 'Red fiery dragon peyntid upon white and Grene Sarcenet' at Bosworth Field, making a conscious link to Cadogan ancestor Cadwaladr ap Cadwallon (d. AD 664) and the folkloric resurgence of the Cymry (Welsh people). The red dragon appears on today's flag of Wales.

EARLY BEGINNINGS

(*c*.1400–1461), a young squire from Anglesey who had caught the eye of Catherine de Valois, Dowager Queen Consort to King Henry V:

> Many later legends developed to explain their remarkable romance: that Owen had been in Henry V's service in the wars in France or in the royal household, that he had first attracted attention by falling into the queen's lap in an inebriated state at a dance or when she and her ladies had espied him swimming…[42]

…naked, we might presume. If there were Cadogans on the battlefield at Bosworth, armed with swords, daggers, maces – or perhaps halberds, such as dispensed with Shakespeare's villain, Richard III – they were surely on the side of victory. Henry Tudor himself was in the fray, the last king of England to win his crown in battle, leading his men under the red dragon standard of Cadwaladr ap Cadwallon (another ancient Cadogan ancestor, between Cunedda Wledig and Merfyn Frych's wife Esyllt). King Henry VII (r.1485–1509) founded a new ruling dynasty, ended the Wars of the Roses, married the opposition (Elizabeth of York) and brought the Middle Ages

ABOVE Chelsea Place, the old Tudor manor house acquired by Henry VIII. Inherited by the Cadogan family, it stood on what is now Cheyne Walk. OPPOSITE Trostrey marked on a map of Wales (detail), Christopher Saxton, 1580. The Cadogans were living in relative obscurity in the village of Lower Trostre.

to a close. Rhys ap Thomas became Sir Rhys, rewarded with more land and titles including Governor of All Wales, Knight of the Garter and (in 1505) privy counsellor. He accompanied Henry's son to the Field of the Cloth of Gold in 1520.

The second Tudor king, Henry VIII (r.1509–47), needs no introduction: a big personality with six wives, a gammy leg and a love of hunting, who installed himself as head of the Church of England. In 1536 he acquired Chelsea Place (sometimes called Old Chelsea Manor House), one of many summer palaces that had sprung up along the river. He granted the royal residence to his last queen, Katherine Parr, in 1543, who lived there with two of her charges, Elizabeth I and Lady Jane Grey; his fourth wife Anne of Cleves reputedly ended her days there in 1557. The house would still be standing, if much altered, when the manor passed into Cadogan hands two hundred years later.

Meanwhile, the descendants of Llewlyn ap Cadwgan ab Elystan Glodrydd were living quietly as gentlemen farmers in Monmouthshire. Thomas Cadwgan ap William (d.1511) is recorded in Burke's peerages with his wife Catherine (née Kemeys) and sons in a farmhouse at Trostrey Fach. So peaceful obscurity continued for the next two generations: Thomas's son William Cadwgan and his wife Anne (née Arnold); and their son Henry Cadogan and his wife Catherine (née Stradling) of St Donat's Castle and Merthyr Mawr, Glamorgan. Their lives passed unremarked during the brief and turbulent reigns of King Edward VI and the Roman Catholic Queen 'Bloody' Mary I. No Cadogans were burned at the stake or accused of witchcraft. Queen Elizabeth I (r.1558–1603) ruled over a golden age of stability, artistic flowering and geographical exploration. As the first Elizabethan era drew to a close at the turn of a new century, Henry and Catherine welcomed a son, a great(x15)-grandson of Elystan Glodrydd: William Cadogan would be one to watch.

The First Millennium, from Roman Britannia to Cadwgan ab Elystan Glodrydd

MACSEN WLEDIG
Roman Emperor Magnus Maximus
d. AD 388, general commanding the Army in Britannia

SEVERA ferch Macsen Wledig ~~~~ **GWRTHEYRN GWRTHENEU**
'Vortigern the Thin', fl. AD 425–50
King of Gwent and King of the Britons
nemesis of King Arthur

BRYDW

CASNAR WLEDIG ~~~~ THEWER ferch Brydw
'Casnar the Ruler', fl. c. AD 500 ferch Gwrtheyrn Gwrtheneu
appears in the *The Mabinogion* as Kasnat Wledig

LLARY ap Casnar

RHUN RHUDD BALADR

BYWDEG

BYWYR LEW

GWINEU DEUFREUDDWYD

TEON ap Gwineu

TEGONWY ap Teon

IORWERTH HIRFLAWDD
'Iorwerth of the Long Struggle'
b.c. AD 770, Ruler of Arwystli

CYNOG MAWR | IDNERTH ab Iorwerth Hirflawdd

BLEDRUS | CADWR WENWYN ab Idnerth

BLEDDYN | CADWR ap Cadwrn Wenwyn

EDNYWAIN | SEVERUS ap Cadwr | TUDUR TREFOR ~~~~
 | | Lord of both the Maelors
GOLLWYN | IFOR ap Severus | GRONO ap Tudur Trefor

GWYN | CUHELYN ab Ifor
 | (Kai-helin, son of Ivor)
 | Lord of Buellt ~~~~ GWEN
 | ferch Grono

a dau. of Gwerystan ~~~~ CARADOG
(aunt of Bleddyn ap Cynfyn)

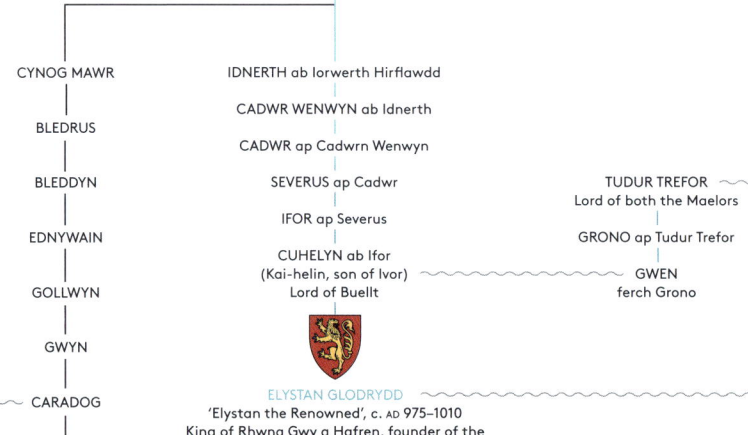

ELYSTAN GLODRYDD ~~~~
'Elystan the Renowned', c. AD 975–1010
King of Rhwng Gwy a Hafren, founder of the
5th Royal Tribe of Wales

GWRGANT ab Ithel
of Morgannwg

NEST ferch ~~~~ TRAHAEARN ap Caradog
Gruffudd ap Prince of Arwystli,
Llywelyn succeeded Bleddyn ap
Cynfyn as King of
Gwynedd & Powys

CADWGAN ab Elystan Glodrydd ~~~~ EFA
Lord of Radnor ferch Gwrgant

ANGHARAD
ferch Elystan Glodrydd ~~~~ IESTYN ap Gwrgant
Cadwgan's sister King of Morgannwg,
founder of the
4th Royal Tribe of Wales

Abridged family tree

EARLS CADOGAN

PADARN BEISRUDD
'Paternus of the Red Cloak' fl. AD 300
ruler of Edinburgh

CUNEDDA WLEDIG
'King Kenneth', c. AD 386–460
founder of the dynasty of Gwynedd,
migration retold in *Y Goddodin*

BROCHWEL YSGITHROG
'Brockwel of the Tusks'
King of Powys

ELISE ap Gwylog
King of Powys
Pillar of Eliseg is named after him by his
great-grandson Cyngen ap Cadell

CADWALADR ap Cadwallon
d. AD 664, whose legendary dragon standard was
carried by his descendant Henry Tudor

IDWAL ap Cadwaladr

RHODRI MOLWYNOG

CYNAN DINDAETHWY

GWRIAD ab Elidyr ～～～ ESYLLT ferch Cynan Dindaethwy

BROCHWEL ab Elise
King of Powys

CADELL ap Brochwel
King of Powys

MERFYN FRYCH ～～～ NEST
'Mervyn the Freckled', d. AD 844 ferch Cadell
King of Gwynedd ap Brochwel

CYNGEN ap Cadell
last King of Powys
of the dynasty Brochwel Ysgithrog

RHODRI MAWR
'Roderick the Great', c. AD 820–878
King of Gwynedd, Powys & Deheubarth, Prince of Wales

CADELL ap Rhodri Mawr

CAENOG

HYWEL DDA
'Howell the Good', c. AD 880–950
King of Deheubarth, Ruler of Wales

ANGHARAD
ferch Hywel Dda

OWAIN ap Hywel Dda

CORF

CEIDIO

GWYNNOG FARFSYCH

GWYNNAN

GWAITHFOED of Powys

EINION ab Owain

MAREDUDD ab Owain
'Redhead'
King of Deheubarth

GWERYSTAN

～～～ GWENLLIAN
ferch Einion

1. LLYWELYN ap Seisyll ～～～ ANGHARAD ～～～ 2. CYNFYN ap
King of Gwynedd & Deheubarth ferch Maredudd Gwerystan of Powys

BLEDDYN ap Cynfyn
King of Powys & (later) Gwynedd,
founder of the
3rd Royal Tribe of Wales

EALDGYTH dau. of ～～～ GRUFFUDD ap Llywelyn
Aelfgar, Earl of Mercia Ruler of All Wales

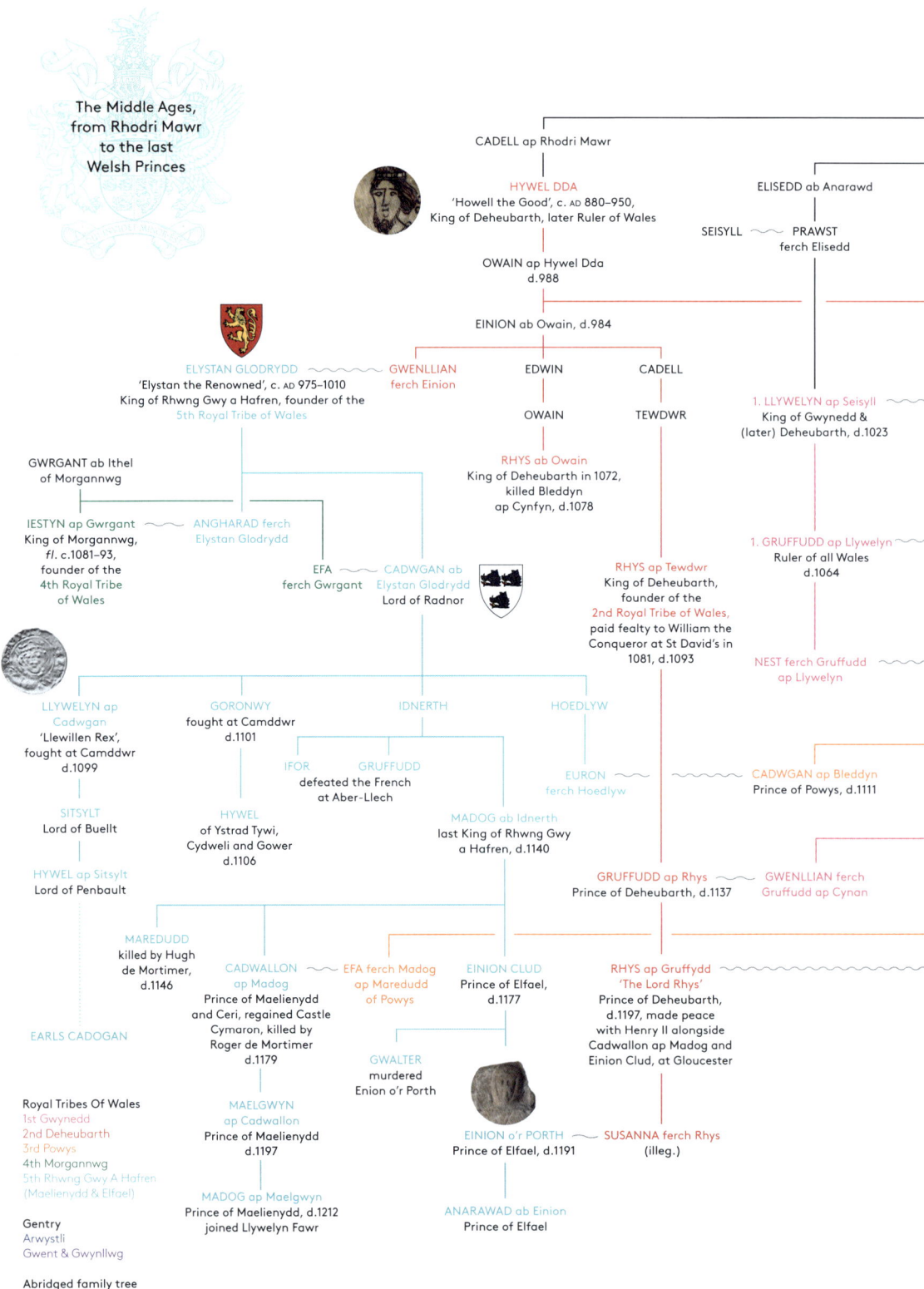

Welsh Royal Genealogy

Welsh Rulers

RHODRI MAWR
'Roderick the Great', c. AD 820–878,
King of Gwynedd, Powys & Deheubarth
later Prince of Wales

ANARAWD ap Rhodri Mawr

IDWAL FOEL
'Idwal the Bold',
King of Gwynedd, d. AD 942

MEURIG ab Idwal Foel

- **MAREDUDD ab Owain** — 'Redhead', King of Deheubarth, d.999
- **GWERYSTAN**
- **RHYS ab Owain** — King of Deheubarth (after Maredudd)
- **IESTYN**
- **IDWAL ap Meurig**

RHYDDERCH of Gwynllwg, d.1033

IAGO ab Idwal — King of Gwynedd, d.1039

- **ANGHARAD** ferch Maredudd
- **2. CYNFYN ap Gwerystan** of Powys
- a daughter
- **CARADOG** descendant of **IORWERTH HIRFLAWDD**
- **CARADOG ap Rhydderch** d.1035
- **GRUFFUDD ap Rhydderch** d.1055, took Deheubarth in 1044
- **RHYS ap Rhydderch** lost his head at Bulundune

CYNAN ab Iago d.c.1060

EALDGYTH (Edith) dau. of Earl of Mercia

BLEDDYN ap Cynfyn — King of Powys & (later) Gwynedd, d.1075, founder of the 3rd Royal Tribe of Wales

RHYDDERCH ap Caradog d.1076, fought sons of Cadwgan ab Elystan at Camddwr

TRAHAEARN ap Caradog — Prince of Arwystli, King of Gwynedd (seized power at Bleddyn's death), d.1081

GRUFFUDD ap Cynan c.1055–1137, King of Gwynedd (defeated Trahaearn), founder of the 1st Royal Tribe of Wales

- **MAREDUDD ap Bleddyn** d.1132
- **LLYWARCH ap Trahaern**
- **GWENLLIAN ferch Bleddyn ap Cynfyn** — **CARADOG ap Gruffudd** d.1081, fought sons of Cadwgan ab Elystan at Camddwr

SUSANNA ferch Gruffudd ap Cynan — **MADOG ap Maredudd** King of Powys, d.1160

GWLADUS ferch Llywarch

OWAIN GWYNEDD c.1100–1170, King of Gwynedd, led rebellious Welsh including Madog ab Idnerth in 1136 and Cadwallon ap Madog and Einion Clud in 1165

- **GWENLLIAN ferch Madog ap Maredudd**
- **GRUFFUDD MAELOR** of Powys Fadog, d.1191
- **MARARED ferch Madog ap Maredudd**
- **IORWERTH DRWYNDWN** 'Iorwerth the Flat-nosed' Prince of Gwynedd, d.c.1174

JOAN PLANTAGENET dau. of King John (illeg.) Lady of Wales, d.1237 — **LLYWELYN FAWR** 'Llywelyn the Great', 1173–1240, Prince of Gwynedd, Ruler of All Wales

- **DAFYDD ap Llywelyn Fawr** Prince of Gwynedd, d.1246
- **GWLADUS DDU ferch Llywelyn Fawr** — **Ralph de Mortimer**
- **GRUFFUDD ap Llywelyn Fawr (illeg.)**

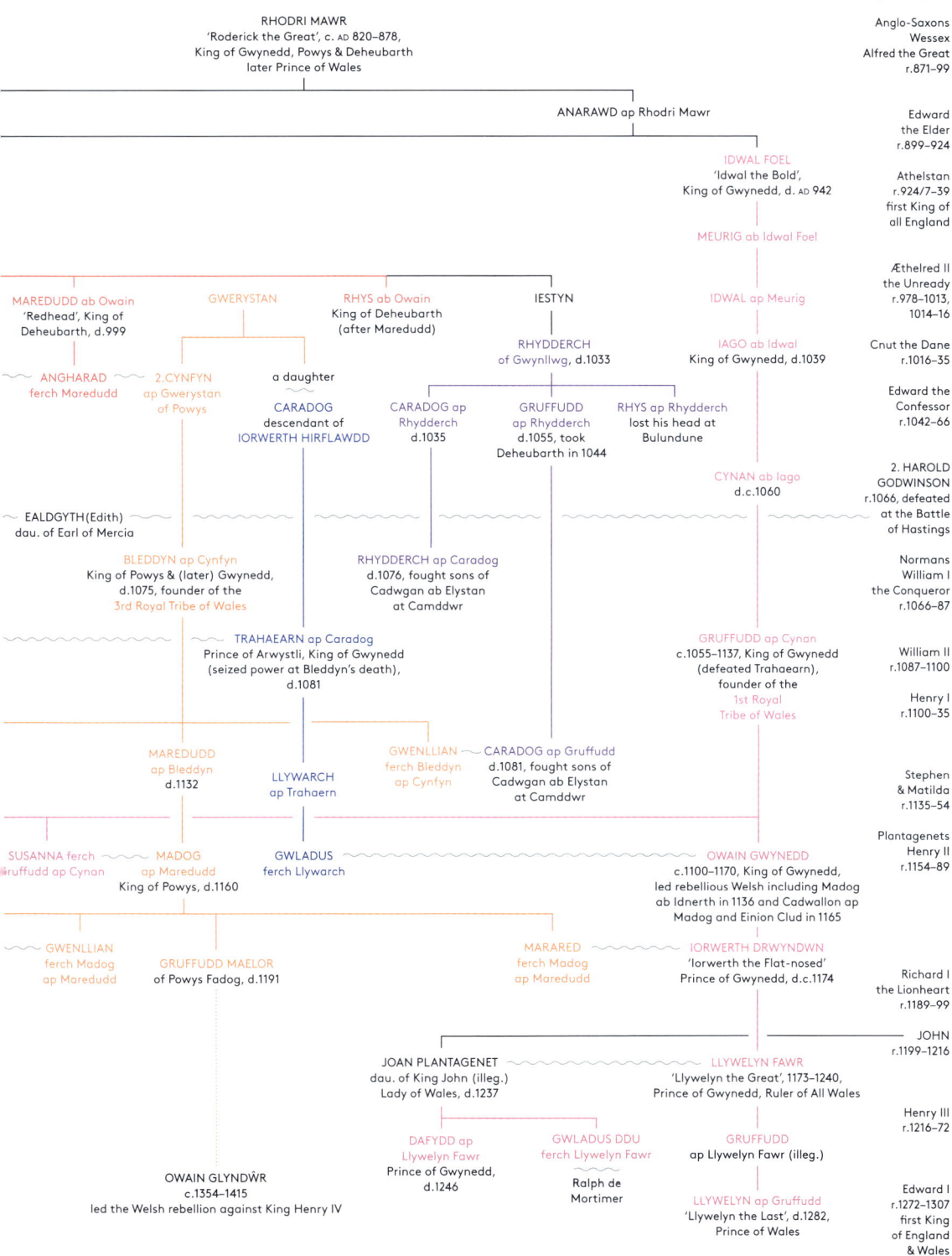

OWAIN GLYNDŴR c.1354–1415 led the Welsh rebellion against King Henry IV

LLYWELYN ap Gruffudd 'Llywelyn the Last', d.1282, Prince of Wales

Kings of England

Anglo-Saxons
Wessex
Alfred the Great r.871–99

Edward the Elder r.899–924

Athelstan r.924/7–39 first King of all England

Æthelred II the Unready r.978–1013, 1014–16

Cnut the Dane r.1016–35

Edward the Confessor r.1042–66

2. HAROLD GODWINSON r.1066, defeated at the Battle of Hastings

Normans
William I the Conqueror r.1066–87

William II r.1087–1100

Henry I r.1100–35

Stephen & Matilda r.1135–54

Plantagenets
Henry II r.1154–89

Richard I the Lionheart r.1189–99

JOHN r.1199–1216

Henry III r.1216–72

Edward I r.1272–1307 first King of England & Wales

The Battle of Hochstet or Blenheim..., attr. Adolf van der Laan, 1704, etching on paper

THE STUARTS

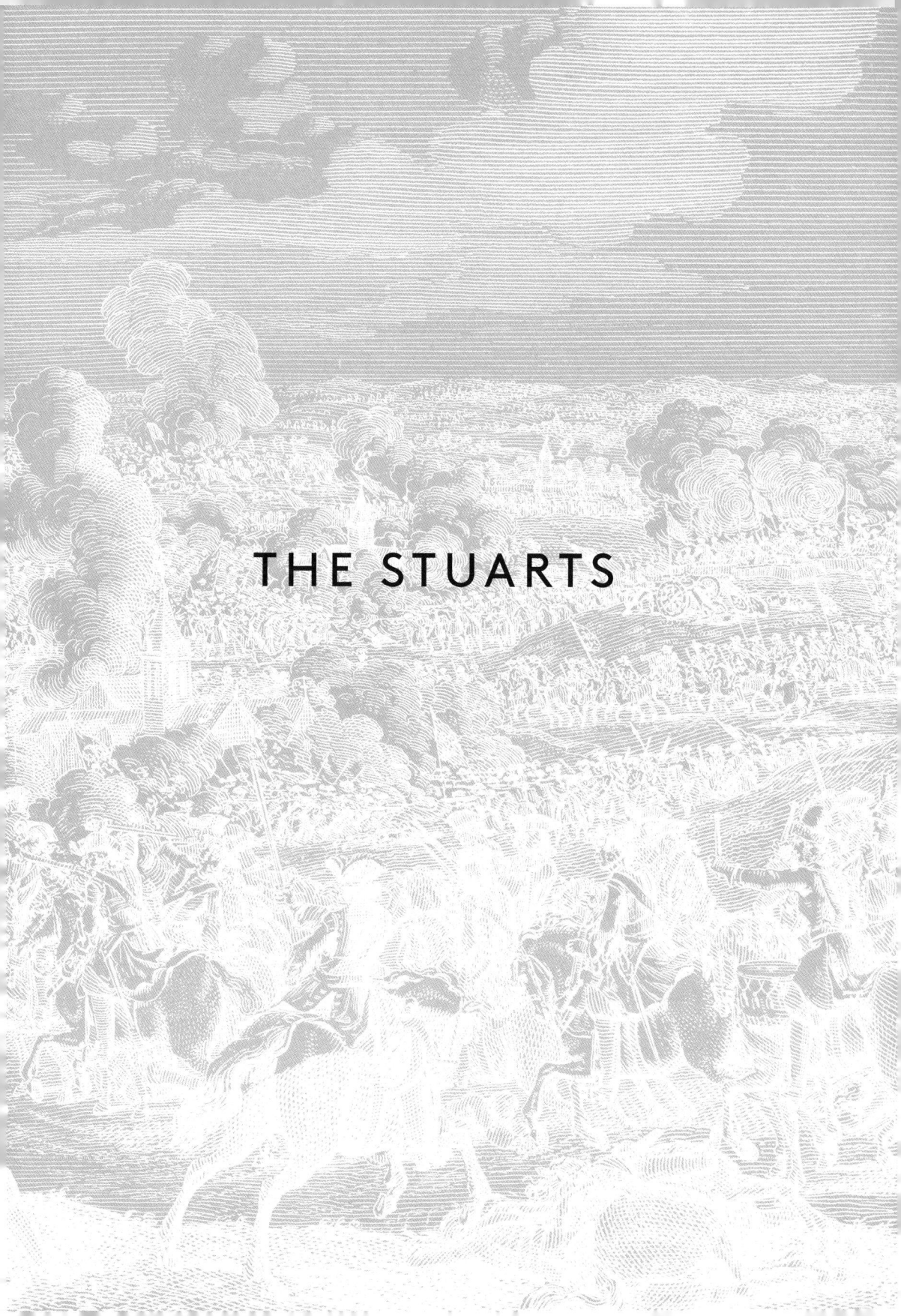

CHAPTER 2

Opportunity in Ireland

—

MAJOR WILLIAM CADOGAN (1601–1661)
AND HIS SON HENRY (1642–1715)

William Cadogan, grandfather of the first 1st Earl Cadogan, was a man who seized opportunity with both hands. It was in his genes. His father, a younger son bypassed for inheritance of the modest farmhouse in Lower Trostre, had bagged a bride from a family of local grandees, the Stradlings of St Donat's Castle, and William (born in Cardiff on 5 February 1601, NS) was raised a gentleman. Not much is known about his early years, but from his later life we can conclude that he received a classical education and picked up some irregular military experience. William surfaces in his mid-thirties as a Private Secretary to the Lord

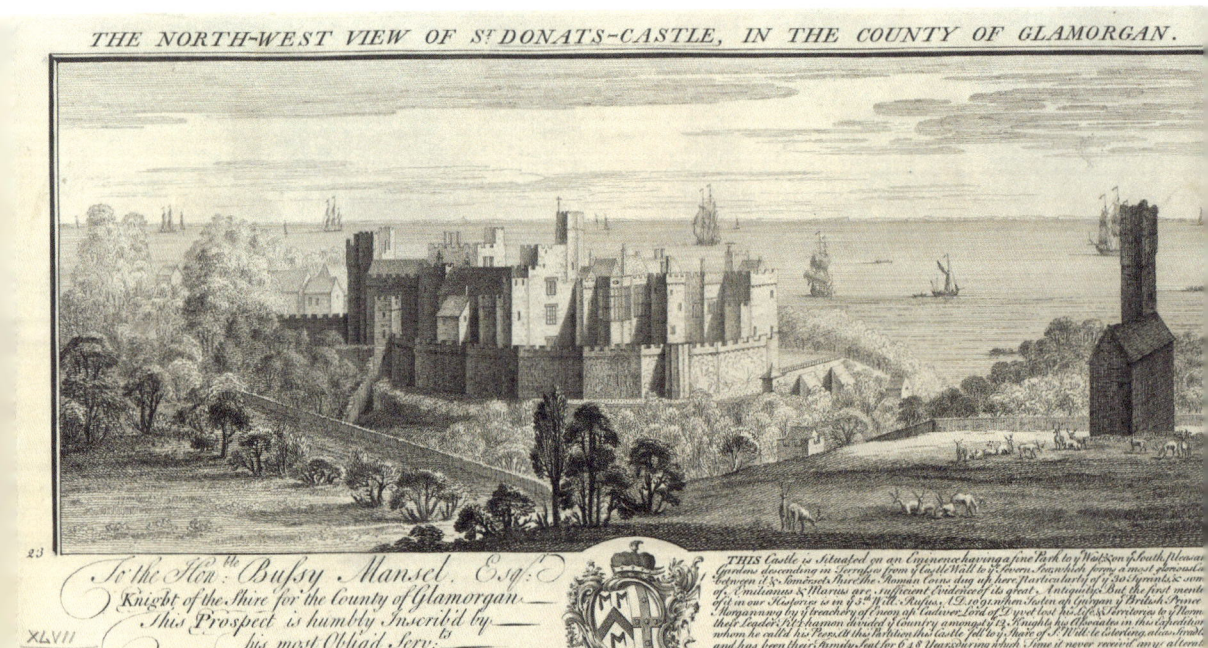

ABOVE *The Gunpowder Plotters and their Execution in February 1606*, after Heinrich Ulrich, late 18th century, etching. The Jacobean era was defined by civil unrest and peacocking fashions. OPPOSITE *St Donat's Castle...*, Samuel Buck, engraving published London 1740

Lieutenant of Ireland. Quite how he came to that position is a mystery. But that is where his story truly begins, the man of 'rare mental endowments'[1] whose adventurous spirit and ambition would take the Cadogans across the Irish Sea from Wales to power and wealth in another Celtic land.

William's life spans a dramatic period of British history; he evaded the fabled curse of living in interesting times. In his infancy the Stuarts took the throne, uniting the crown of Scotland with that of England and Ireland in King James VI and I (r.1603–25). There were positives. The arts flourished as they had under Good Queen Bess – Ben Jonson's comedies and the most famous Shakespearean tragedies were written at the behest of the new king and his queen consort Anne of Denmark; fashions reached a peacocking apex of lace, silk and pom-pommed shoes. But the Jacobean era was marked from the start by civil unrest and religious friction. 'Remember, remember, the fifth of November/ Gunpowder, treason and plot': Guy Fawkes and his co-conspirators of 1605 convinced James to take harsh measures against both Roman Catholics and Puritans who would not swear an oath of allegiance placing the monarch above the Pope. He went as far as commissioning his own 'Authorized Version' of the Bible – the King James Bible (KJV, 1611), the poetic thees and thous of which were uttered in Church of England services as standard until well into the twentieth century.

Wales, land of Cadogan fathers, was by now considered a relatively quiet annexe to England. Henry VIII had formally declared Wales to be a part of the English realm in the Acts of Union (1536 and 1543). Where once Elystan Glodrydd had been king there was a new county called Radnorshire. Legislation not only did away with the power of the Marcher lords, supplanting them with English MPs, but – with a message of unity – included the explicit intention to 'utterly extirpe alle and singular sinister [Welsh] usages and customs' and to suppress the Welsh language in public office, 'a speche nothing like ne consonaunt to the naturall mother tonge used within this Realme.'[2] (Tempting as it may be to read 'ne consonaunt' as relating to opaque spellings, its meaning is 'not harmonious with'.) Thus, although William's grandfather had delighted in the surname Cadwgan, his father became Cadogan; and William Cadogan himself grew up speaking English. Culturally, he would have been encouraged to look not back to his royal Celtic ancestors but to London as the seat and source of power. It was in London that the brightest and best had been able to find promotion regardless of their status at birth since at least the days of two Thomases, Wolsey and Cromwell (both reputedly sons of butchers). By the turn of the seventeenth century, the colonizing impulse was taking Englishmen halfway across the world, capitalizing on advances in seafaring to expand into

RIGHT *The Mariner's Mirrour*, Theodor de Bry, 1588, hand-coloured etching. Frontispiece from Anthony Ashley's English translation of Lucas Janszoon Waghenaer's *Speighel der Zeevaerdt* (Sea Atlas, 1583–84). Adventure across the water was the order of the 17th century: note the blank globe to be mapped; lead-lines to gauge depth; dividers and compass for drawings; and astrolabes and quadrants for astronomical measurements.

both North and South America. Jamestown, Virginia, was founded in 1607 on the king's commercial charter; the Pilgrims arrived on the Mayflower in 1620. Opportunity for William Cadogan would present itself across the Irish Sea, where the Crown Act of Ireland (1542), and its familiar subjugating intention, had lit the spark of Counter-Reformation and resistance that continued to smoulder. By the time he arrived on Irish shores, a policy of sending English lords to settle and govern the land 'beyond the pale' (outside English control) had long been in place. The defeat of the Gaelic princes in the Nine Years' War had been followed by King James's official policy of seeding the land with Englishmen: the Plantation of Ulster. Many Scots were also making their own way there, their numbers peaking in 1635.[3]

IN 1636 WILLIAM LANDED AT DUBLIN as a member of the secretariat of Sir Thomas Wentworth, who had been installed as Lord Deputy of Ireland by James's son – and William's close contemporary – King Charles I (r.1625–49). From Wentworth he learned the arts, weaponry and rewards of a successful courtier: a quick mind and strategic diplomacy could result in money, titles and land. Sir Thomas's early rise had been rapid. Born on Friday the thirteenth – Good Friday, in fact – 1593 to North Yorkshire gentry, he was educated by the clergy, entered the Inner Temple at fourteen and matriculated at St John's College, Cambridge, at sixteen. He was knighted at eighteen, six weeks after having married a daughter of the 4th Earl of Cumberland. Two years of travel in Europe left him fluent in French, with a dusting of Spanish and Italian, before he returned to inherit his father's baronetcy at twenty-one, when he entered the House of Commons. The *History of Parliament* records:

> Some of his successes can be ascribed to fortunate circumstances, but he was also possessed of what Clarendon termed 'a piercing judgment both into things and persons', which he consistently turned to his best advantage. This can be seen both during his parliamentary career in 1628, when he laboured to dispel the mutual suspicion which existed between Crown and Commons,

IRELAND
17th Century

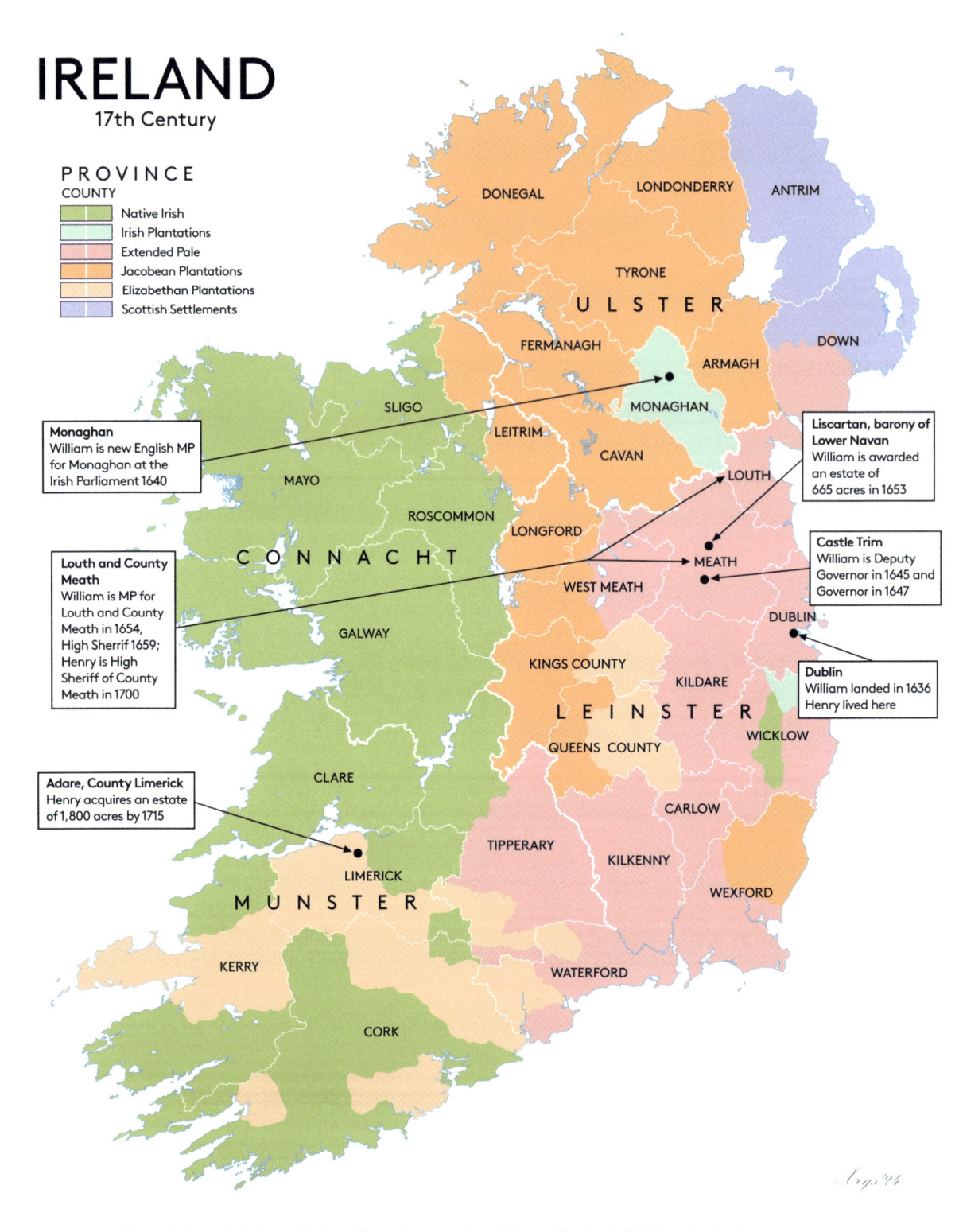

PROVINCE
COUNTY

- Native Irish
- Irish Plantations
- Extended Pale
- Jacobean Plantations
- Elizabethan Plantations
- Scottish Settlements

Monaghan
William is new English MP for Monaghan at the Irish Parliament 1640

Louth and County Meath
William is MP for Louth and County Meath in 1654, High Sherrif 1659; Henry is High Sheriff of County Meath in 1700

Adare, County Limerick
Henry acquires an estate of 1,800 acres by 1715

Liscartan, barony of Lower Navan
William is awarded an estate of 665 acres in 1653

Castle Trim
William is Deputy Governor in 1645 and Governor in 1647

Dublin
William landed in 1636 Henry lived here

Map of the land divisions of Ireland from the ascension of Queen Elizabeth (1558) to the Act for the Settlement of Ireland (1652) (sources: OSI, OSNI, NUI Galway Barony Maps; Stanford, *Ireland 1558–1652*, Cambridge University Press, 1912). The Cadogan family were in Ireland before and after Cromwell.

and also during the 1630s, when he juggled factional rivalries in Ireland, Yorkshire and Whitehall in order to secure his own position and effect administrative reforms.[4]

The diarist 1st Earl Clarendon knew Wentworth personally; his *History of the Rebellion and Civil Wars in England* (published posthumously in 1702 and 1704) was an eyewitness account. During that important year of 1628, Wentworth – now thirty-five – was first elevated to baron and, six months later, created viscount. His second wife was also an earl's daughter; the double widower had married again by the time he left for Dublin in 1633. William Cadogan – bright, ambitious, keen to improve his position and his fortune – had found a mentor and kindred spirit.

William's job was to assist Wentworth in assimilating Irish law and customs into English ones, creating a well-run Protestant country that served an English king. As a Welshman, he was familiar with the ideology that had governed his homeland for a hundred years. In practical terms, this meant ruthless efficiency in raising taxes for the exchequer to fund the whims of an autocrat. By tradition, the Crown asked Parliament to approve new taxes in return for an opportunity for the Commons to air their grievances. But Charles I had been anointed by God; whose permission did he need? In England he had imposed forced loans on landowners, throwing those who refused to pay in jail, and following one such summary judgment in the Star Chamber, Wentworth had spent six months incarcerated. Not surprisingly, the last parliamentary session of 1628 had seen heated debates about royal prerogative as the Commons attempted to confirm the rights afforded to the king's subjects. *Magna Carta* was cited, to no avail: the following year, the king embarked on a period of personal rule. Wentworth was appointed to the Privy Council – a pragmatic *volte face* that startled even some of his closest friends.

William had a ringside seat in the build-up to the English Civil War. It was as special advisor to the king that his boss was recalled to England in 1639, created 1st Earl of Strafford in 1640, and put in charge of quelling a Scottish uprising against the imposition of Anglican worship.

Illuminated initial membrane with portrait of King Charles I, *Coram Rege Rolls*, Court of the King's Bench, 1643

The Short Parliament called on Strafford's advice to raise more money, for England's defence and Scotland's return, lasted only three weeks before once more descending into arguments about abuses of power. The king tried again, summoning his MPs that autumn. It would be the last time: the Long Parliament sat for twenty years. Strafford had become deeply unpopular. After a failed impeachment for attempting to consolidate sovereign power, Parliament passed a bill of attainder against him. Charles I reluctantly signed his death warrant and Strafford was executed on 12 May 1641.

William Cadogan had stayed on in Ireland. He was elected as a 'New English' MP for the borough of Monaghan in the Irish Parliament in 1640. It seems that while the Lord Lieutenant had become ever-more embedded with the authoritarian monarchy, perhaps William had taken the earlier lesson, stepped back from the brink, and been careful to back the winners. Indeed, he sat on the June 1641 committee seeking to impeach Strafford's associates. Life on committees was about to come to an abrupt end, however. The Irish Catholics, whose land had been confiscated, whose customs had been quashed, whose religion had been called heresy, unleashed their anger on 23 October. An estimated quarter of the forty thousand English Protestants in Ulster were massacred; Irish nationalists would later cite a loss of half their population in the ensuing rebellion.[5] The numbers may be muddy, but it is clear that there were huge losses on both sides.

William took a commission in the king's Army, directing defence of the area north of Dublin before moving to the city itself 'about his Majesty's special service'.[6] A contemporary report describes him bringing news of a successful *ruse de guerre*:

2. OPPORTUNITY IN IRELAND

The Arch-Prelate of St Andrews...assaulted, Wenceslaus Hollar, 1642, etching. In 1637 the introduction of the new *Booke of Common Prayer* in Scotland sparked rioting that led to the Bishops' Wars (1639, 1640). Efforts to quell the Scottish rebellion led to Strafford's downfall and execution, and to the Civil War.

Sir Thomas Wentworth, Earl of Strafford (1593–1641) and his Secretary, Sir Philip Mainwaring (1589–1661), Sir Anthony Van Dyck, c.1634, oil on canvas. William Cadogan was a member of Wentworth's secretariat in Ireland 1636–39.

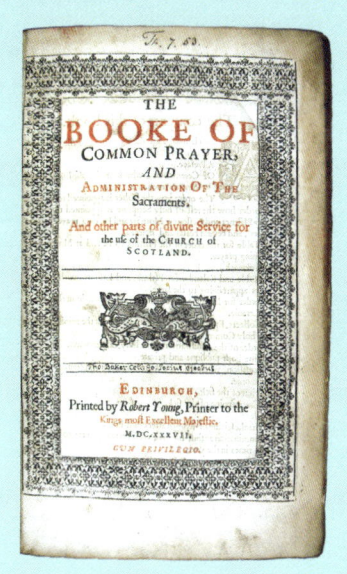

The Booke of Common Prayer, published in Edinburgh by Robert Young, 1637

> The fifth of May [1642]. Newes came from Dundalk to the Lords Justices by Captaine Cadogan (who came thence through Maday with ten horse-men only) that the Newry was not only retaken by the Lord Conway, and Munroe the Scots Commander, from the rebels, but also that the towne and castle of Carlingford was taken by a ship that came from Knockfergus[;] their pollicy was to put up the Spanish colours, which the rebels discerning, sent a fisher-boate, with ten or twelve of their commanders to goe aboard the ship, supposing that some ammunition was come unto them; but the captaine of the ship instead of shewing them any such commodities, clapt them up under decks, and so landing his musketiers, they took the towne, which they of the castle soone perceiving, fled away, and left both unto our forces.[7]

William crops up the following year in a deposition by the Reverend George Creichtonn. Here he is the mouthpiece of the Crown:

> And in a letter to the Lord Marquesse of Ormond, the Deponent sett downe the names of all the Brittish Protestants that were with him at this tyme. Upon the receipt of theis letters, Sir Pawle Davis was pleased (in his care of him this Deponent) to speake some sharpe words to Friere Anthony Newgent, that if the Deponent should miscarry, he would revenge his death upon all priests that should be found in and about Dublin. The like words were spoken in the Deponents behalf, and to the same frier, by Captain William Cadogan, as the frier hath since told the Deponent.[8]

We might imagine that such a warning, even whispered, from the lips of a military commander, would achieve the desired effect with ease. On 15 September 1643 a fragile cessation of arms was agreed.

2. OPPORTUNITY IN IRELAND

By early 1645, William had taken up an appointment in County Meath as Deputy Governor of Trim Castle, the largest Anglo-Norman fortification in Ireland. He had the unenviable job of the steadying hand during a truce. 'The humble petition of Jarcoke Wilkinson, Corporall', written in August 1646, describes an infringement – a fight – that took place eight miles north-west of Trim 'within the English quarter'. Sent outside the castle walls on William's orders to keep the peace at a seemingly innocuous village fair, at Athboy, a small troop of the king's men was set upon as they returned to their garrison. They were outnumbered more than six to one:

> ...your petitioner and the 10 troopers under his commaund performing their charge, repaired to their garrison aboute 3 or 4 of the clock in the afternoon of the said 24th day of July last, and in the way to their garrison mett the under named persons accompanied with above 60 horse more belonging to Gennerall Owen Roe O Neales regiment, who in a hostile and most inhumane manner fell on your petitioner and his 10 troopers under

Castle Trim, County Meath. A military stronghold, it is a twenty-sided, three-storeyed, cruciform keep protected by a ditch, curtain wall and water-filled moat. Captain William Cadogan was its Governor during the Irish Rebellion.

his command, dismounted them, tooke away their horses and armes, and wounded most of the troopers very dangerously, there being small hope of their recovery.[9]

The petition was to Lord Ormonde, Lieutenant General of the English Army in Ireland, asking for restitution. Ormonde sent it on to O'Neill, commander of the Ulster Army. Whatever the niceties of ceasefire, plans were underway for a restart, with William at the heart of them. Just a month later, on 12 September, Captain Cadogan wrote to Ormonde with an intelligence report and a plan:

> There are some six gentlemen of good quality in a county in the Pale, who (if they may have your Excellence's commissions dormant to raise foote and horse) will drawe a considerable force to the field, under the pretence to be of Owen Roes [O'Neill's] party, but when once assembled will declare for his Majesty. These comissions they desire further warrant in the future, being not willing otherwise to appear in the doeing thereof, least it might be expounded in an ill sence. The Sheriff of the county is very earnest in the buisnes, and some other that are really affected to the service. The commissions (if your Excellence soe think fitt) may be sent, with blankes for the captaines names, unto my Lord of Roscomon, and hee to deliver them. Noe county in the Pale (if this be don) will or can prove soe usefull. The county and the gentlemen's names I dare not mention, least this my letter should micarry.[10]

All very cloak-and-dagger: an enclosure details names and numbers of troops from his network of spies. William was shrewd enough to see that the cessation was a sham, writing to Ormonde in October that 'every man is able to discern how the Irish, to gain time to provide themselves arms and ammunition, have played poltrons with a good king'.[11] He upheld the law. When the Parliamentarians arrived in Dublin, in June 1647, they promoted him almost immediately to Governor of Trim, and the following year advanced him to major. In July 1649 William 'showed great courage' during the infamous battle at Drogheda. A few weeks later, the chief Roundhead, General Oliver Cromwell, defender of the English Commonwealth, landed his New Model Army in Ireland. After nine months of fighting, the uprising – and Major William Cadogan's military career – drew to a close.

WILLIAM RETURNED TO POLITICS and governance. In 1654 he was elected MP for Meath and County Louth; four years later he was the High Sheriff of County Meath and by 1659 he commanded its militia. William also spent much of the 1650s working with surveyors on land redistribution. English soldiers who had fought in Ireland were offered acreage in lieu of backpay – presumably including the major himself.

William was assigned £400-worth of 'adventurers' shares', their translation into land to be determined by lottery. As early as 1642, an Act 'for the speedy and effectual reducing of the rebels in His Majesty's Kingdom of Ireland' was passed, better known as the Act for Adventurers. Everyone was invited – just four shillings would buy one English acre of Ulster, though it would take twelve to buy the same in Leinster – in a fundraising scheme to support the war. Its initial target was £1 million in exchange for 2.5 million acres, roughly one eighth of the land area of Ireland. MPs and merchants of the City of London were among the first to sign up, followed by private investors encouraged by pamphlets and handbooks claiming: 'He that hath many children may raise his

Oliver, British Hero, William Faithorne, engraving, plate from *Parallelum Olivae nec non Olivarii...Protectoris*, published in London, 1656

younger sons to as great a fortune by £200 purchase in…[Irish land] as £2,000 in trade.'[12] In January 1643 the government opened the scheme even wider, to those who had no money for investment but could lend arms, ammunition or even food rations and clothing to the war effort. This still failed to raise the required funds and the government eventually resorted to taxation.

> …the final settlement of Ireland was worked out not primarily for the benefit of those who had leapt, in 1641, at the opportunity to acquire Irish land, but for the fiscal benefit of the heavily burdened Cromwellian state. It was not zealous colonists but rather reluctant creditors of the state who constituted the new English planter class in Ireland.[13]

The first lottery draw took place at 8 am on 20 July 1653 at the Grocers' Hall in London. Major William Cadogan became the new owner of an estate of 665 acres (411 Irish acres) in Liscartan Parish, in the barony of Navan,

Grocers' Hall, Poultry, London, c.1730, engraving. In the building that had already stood for over two hundred years, and which would go on to house the fledgling Bank of England (est. 1694), William was awarded 665 acres of Irish land in 1653.

County Meath, where he was later elected portreeve (mayor).[14] Baronies – the land, though not the titles – were divided into equal moieties (halves) between adventurers and ex-soldiers, so that the military settlers might provide a sense of bodily safety to their merchant neighbours. In total, the Cromwellian Settlement disposed of seven million acres, thirty-five per cent of the surface of the emerald isle; between 1641 and 1688 the Protestant share of Ireland increased from forty-one to seventy-eight per cent.[15]

William lived in County Meath until his death at Trim on 14 March 1661. He was buried at Christ Church Cathedral, Dublin, as his commemorative plaque records, 'having first witnessed what he had so earnestly desired – the safe return of His Most Gracious Majesty, Charles II, from his unjust exile.' No mention is made of his time in Cromwell's army. The Interregnum had ended with a whimper: a Protectorate led by Cromwell's son had lost the support of Parliament, the Army and the people through the no-fun policies of the Puritan Commonwealth. The popular Restoration of the Stuarts released a joyful renaissance of the arts. Bawdy satire on the stage – the Restoration comedies of William Wycherley and, later, John Vanbrugh – openly mocked the foppish court and its manners as King Charles II (r.1660–85), the merry monarch, was careful not to take himself too seriously. His choice of mistresses included 'pretty witty Nell' Gwynn

ABOVE Memorial to William Cadogan, Christ Church Cathedral, Dublin. William's dates are recorded here as 1600–1660 using the Julian Calendar (Old Style) of the time, which began the year on 25 March. Today we use the Gregorian Calendar (New Style), adopted by law in 1752, which starts on 1 January. For clarity, this book uses New Style dates throughout.

(as Samuel Pepys described her),[16] one of the first women allowed on the stage, set a new tone of possibility and confidence. The Cadogans carved William's loyalty to the monarch in Dublin stone.

OVER THE WATER IN ENGLAND, work was being carried out on two estates that would become hugely significant in the family's story. In London, the bridge over the River Westbourne was widened and strengthened – a medieval plank footbridge replaced with stone – to bear the weight and width of Charles's carriage as it rattled across the fields between St James's Palace and Hampton Court, along the route that would become the King's Road, Chelsea. (Happily, the story goes, it also passed Nell's house at Sands End, Sands Manor.) Chelsea's rural character – recorded in Lord Macaulay's *History of England* as 'a quiet country village, with about a thousand inhabitants,'[17] – saw it spared during the Great Fire of London in September 1666. However, the area was not so fortunate during that other disaster of Charles's reign, the Great Plague Year of 1665. Pepys again:

Charles II, John Michael Wright, c.1671–76, oil on canvas

> ...thinking to have been merry at Chelsey; but, being almost come to the [public] house by coach near the waterside, a house alone, I think the Swan, a gentleman walking by called out to us that the house as shut up because of the sicknesse. So we with great affright turned back...[18]

To the west, another kind of restoration was taking place at Caversham, later significant to the Cadogans. Confiscated from the 1st Earl Craven during the Civil War, the estate had been used to hold the doomed king. A century later, diarist Mrs Lybbe Powys, who kept a weather eye on comings and goings, was delighted to record:

> In one of the memorandum books of the Lybbes is this entry: 'King Charles the First was prisoner at Causham [Caversham] Lodge, and bowled in Collin's End Green, 19th July 1648, attended by a troop of horse of Colonel Rossiter's. Collin's End is on the top of the hill at the back of Hardwick, and belonged to the Lybbe estate. There was a bowling-green attached to an inn there, afterwards called the "King's Head".'[19]

In 1660 the Elizabethan manor house, which had fallen into disrepair and bad memories, was demolished, and rebuilt as Caversham Park.

For now, the Cadogan estates were Irish. The family's County Meath lands were confirmed to Major William's son in the Act of Settlement of 1662. The Claims of Court appointed to administer the Act in 1663 show a failed attempt to reclaim the land: 'Edward Geoghan, Mary Geoghan alias Misseret, his wife, claim parish Liscartan, Barony Navan; the towns and lands of Liscartan, possession of Mr. Cadogan, held from some unknown adventurer.'[20] Mr Cadogan was well-placed to dismiss a legal claim.

Chelsea Riverside near the Physic Gardens in 1871, William Aschroft, watercolour.
The Old Swan, frequented by Samuel Pepys two hundred years earlier, is seen on the left.

HENRY CADOGAN (1642–1715) WAS BORN to William and his second wife, a Cardiff lass called Elizabeth Roberts (1602–1665), the year of their marriage. (William's first wife, Elizabeth Thring, had died childless in 1641.) We can imagine that Henry enjoyed a comfortable upbringing as the only child of a late-in-life father who had found his position at the heart of the Irish establishment. He embarked upon a career as a barrister. Henry spent some time as a law student in London, which since the 1540s had been a formal requirement for any lawyers wishing to practise in the Dublin Inn of Court (the King's Inns).[21] He also studied at Trinity College, Dublin. Far from making glamourous, grandstanding speeches on human rights or the defence of the innocent, however, he is more likely to have made detailed arguments about land ownership:

> A few crude gauges show how the business of the Dublin courts grew in the late seventeenth and early eighteenth centuries. This growth testified to the government's success in persuading landowners to settle their disputes at law rather than by violence – a changed attitude vital to the transformation of Irish society...The heydays of Protestant interest and of litigation coincided...[22]

Those 'crude gauges' include a tripling in fines issued in the Dublin courts during Henry's career: the law was a burgeoning business. Indeed, by the 1690s, successful lawyers were also involved in political arguments about the anglicization of Irish law and customs. We might say Henry was continuing his father's work. Henry lived in the family town house in St George's Lane, Dublin, at the heart of the old medieval city (now replaced by South Great George's Street).[23] On 1 August 1671, at the church of St Peter and St Kevin, he married Bridget Waller (1638–1721).

Bridget's father Sir Hardress Waller, MP, born in Kent, had been ennobled by King Charles I and acquired a large 'Old English' estate at Castletown

OPPOSITE *A coloured exact survey of the city of Dublin, and part of the harbour, anno 1685, shewing the 'citadel designed' to be built near Stephen's Green; drawn on a scale of 1010 feet to 1 5/8 inch*, attr. Thomas Philips, 1685

AN EXACT SUR=
=VEY OF THE CIT=
=TY OF DUBLIN AND
PART OF THE HAR=
=BOUR ANNO: 1685
Dublin
Strand
Strand
Clontarf Island
Clontarf Head
Kings End

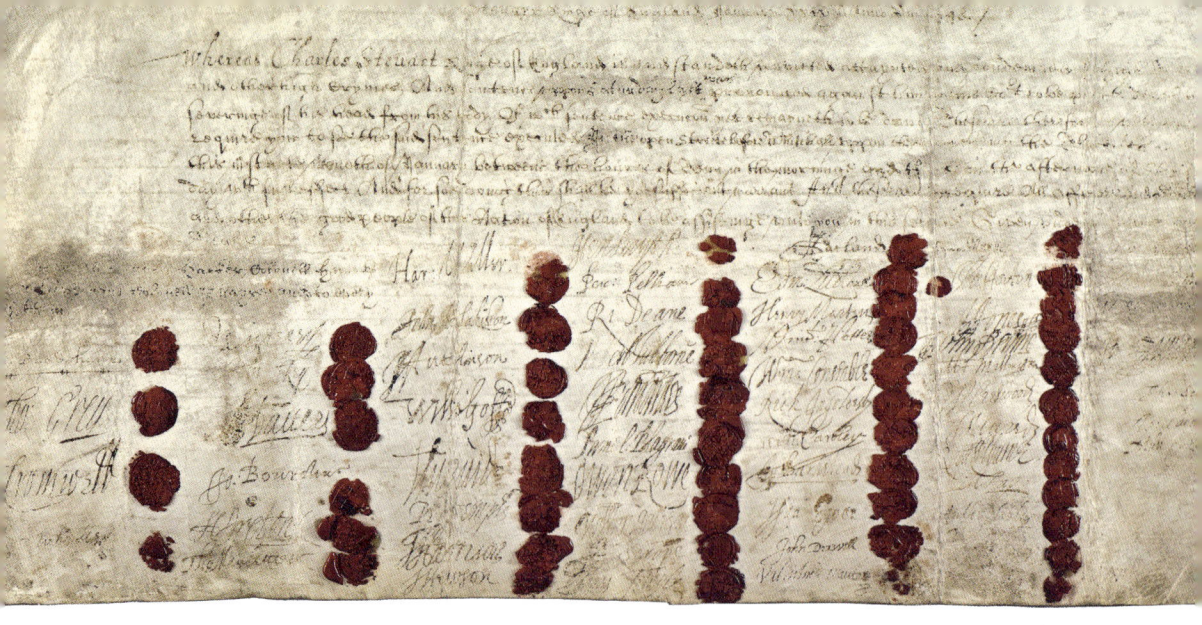

Death Warrant of King Charles I, 29 January 1649. The signature of Henry Cadogan's father-in-law, Sir Hardress Waller, is visible at the top of the second column of fifty-nine names. Following the Restoration of the monarchy in 1660, the Death Warrant was used to identify the commissioners who had signed it (the 'regicides') and prosecute them for treason.

in County Limerick by marriage. He opposed many of the policies of Sir Thomas Wentworth at the time when Henry's father worked with him during the 1630s, although he spent the early 1640s first at the king's court, then as Deputy Governor of Munster. Like William Cadogan, however, he swapped hats from Cavalier to Roundhead. Waller fought at Naseby in June 1645 as colonel of a regiment of foot in the New Model Army and in January 1649 he inked his name on the parchment document that legally sanctioned regicide. Waller returned to Ireland in the 1650s, as a major general, later becoming Governor of Limerick and working on the settlement of land. Things went badly wrong for him in 1660. Thanks to a cousin's intervention, he was spared the grim traitor's execution meted out to his fellow signatories – even, ritualistically, on the bodies of those already deceased – and had his sentence commuted to life imprisonment in Jersey, where he died in 1666.

Happily, Henry and Bridget Cadogan seem to have been outwardly unaffected by the scandal of her father's fate. The year before, Henry was in receipt of all goods and chattels belonging to his parents – bar a few heifers and ewes for the servants, and small bequests to friends outlined in his mother's will 'to buy…a Ring to wear in memory of me'. (Mourning jewellery, while associated with the Victorians, has a much longer history.) He became High Sheriff of County Meath (in 1700), like his father before him. At his death in January 1715 (NS), Henry had increased the Cadogans' landholdings by eighteen-hundred acres, adding an estate in County Limerick with its own castle, near Adare.[24]

The couple had five children: two girls and three boys. Ambrose, their eldest son, took a commission in the Army as a second lieutenant but 'to the extreme sorrow of his parents, and all good men',[25] died in 1693. He was buried in Dublin cathedral, alongside Major William. Youngest son Charles also joined up. One of the girls, Frances, died aged only nine. Penelope (1676–1746) lived her biblical three-score years and ten. She made a rather glamorous match. On 10 August 1697 she married Thomas Prendergast, fifteen years her senior, a dispossessed landowner and former highwayman, who had been granted the Gort estate in County Galway that April by the grateful survivor of attempted regicide:

> Late on 14 February 1696, the eve of the attempt, Prendergast secretly went to Whitehall, where he broke the news of the plot to William's confidential advisor Hans Willem Bentinck, Earl of Portland. He told him that William must be prevented from hunting next day, but that the same honour and conscience which made him, a Catholic Jacobite, give the warning prevented him from testifying against, or even naming, his fellow conspirators, particularly one of them (Porter).[26]

Prendergast converted to Protestantism and was rewarded with more lands and, in 1699, created Sir Thomas Prendergast, 1st Baronet. The British Isles were two kings on from Charles II. But we are getting ahead of ourselves. There had been a changing of the guard and, once again, the Cadogans were in the thick of it: Henry and Bridget's second son William, the first 1st Earl Cadogan, marshalled the charge.

CHAPTER 3

Marlborough's Right-hand Man, Multilingual Spy

—

GENERAL SIR WILLIAM CADOGAN,
THE FIRST 1ST EARL (1672–1726)

William Cadogan, 'the King's favourite Englishman',[1] could hardly have avoided leaving his mark on history. A physically imposing soldier and exceptional logistician, he possessed an equally natural flair for languages and diplomacy: a round peg in a round hole at a time when these skills were a key to rapid social advancement and huge wealth. His champions were John Churchill, 1st Duke of Marlborough, to whom he was an ingenious and energetic Quartermaster General, acting as chief of staff and intelligence during the War of the Spanish Succession, and ultimately the Hanoverian monarchs themselves, whose cause he advanced. William amassed two baronies and an earldom; town houses in Piccadilly and St James's; estates in Oxfordshire; and a large fortune. Not all of these would survive his passing: he had also acquired vast debts and powerful enemies. The first 1st Earl Cadogan was quite a character.

William spent his formative years as a Westminster schoolboy, boarding in London during the 1680s. His father Henry had sent him over the Irish Sea from his birthplace in Liscartan, County Meath, to receive a classical education. It was brutal. Hoary headmaster Dr Richard Busby (in post 1638–95) was old-school in every way: conversation among the boys was strictly in Ancient Greek or Latin, learning was by rote, and reprimands were delivered via enthusiastic floggings. William, being both bright and 'exceptionally tall, broad and strong',[2] apparently found it character-forming.

William Cadogan, first 1st Earl Cadogan, studio of Hans Hysing, c.1726, oil on canvas

Frost Fair on the Thames, with Old London Bridge in the distance, formerly attr. Jan Wyck, 1684, oil on canvas. Food ran short; there was rioting.

At school he met James Brydges, future 1st Duke of Chandos, who, as Paymaster General of the forces abroad, would facilitate some of William's wealth accumulation.

It is unlikely that William made it beyond the school's walls very often. Perhaps he was grateful to be indoors; the winter of 1683/84 was one of the frostiest in recorded British history, quickly labelled – as is the English way – the Great Frost.[3] Upriver in a small town outside the city limits, work had begun on the Royal Hospital Chelsea, founded in 1682. Today, the landmark has seen more than three centuries of continuous use 'as a place of refuge and shelter for such Land Soldiers as are or shall be old, lame or infirm in the service of the Crown.'[4] Following Charles II's sudden illness and death in 1685, Westminster boys were allowed across the road to attend the coronation of his brother King James VII and II (r.1685–89). The new monarch would prove deeply divisive; the fall-out from his toppling would decide William's path in life.

3. MARLBOROUGH'S RIGHT-HAND MAN, MULTILINGUAL SPY

IN 1687 WILLIAM RETURNED to Ireland, where on 28 March, at the age of fifteen, he enrolled at his father's alma mater, Trinity College Dublin. Trinity was approaching its centenary, providing an educated professional class to run the Protestant civil infrastructure of largely Catholic Ireland. But his student days were to be cut short by constitutional upheaval. Following the Glorious Revolution, William of Orange, Stadtholder of Holland, became King William III (r.1689–1702), jointly crowned with Queen Mary II (1689–94), who undertook to reign by consent of Parliament, signing one of the most important pieces of legislation in British history, the Bill of Rights (1689). In Ireland, however, there was still widespread support for the exiled ex-king James. That September, William and his fellow students and faculty were summarily turfed out of Trinity College by the Jacobites, who commandeered it for a barracks and prison after James landed on the coast. Three generations of Cadogan lands in Ireland were now under growing threat.

William had taken a work hard, play hard approach to student life. He was perhaps more like his grandfather than his father. Young William found a friend in the Wentworth family, as old Major William had:

> He befriended another young tearaway, his contemporary Lord Raby (later...Earl of Strafford), who was to be a lifelong companion...they frolicked and drank and wenched together to their hearts' delight.[5]

Landing of William III at Carrickfergus, 14 June 1690, English school, 17th century, oil on canvas

In 1688 Raby joined up as a cornet in William III's Army. Now, in early 1689, the teenage William did the same, taking a commission as a cornet in Colonel Wynn's Dragoons. His first major engagement was the Battle of the Boyne, on 11 July 1690. Pushed back to the river just north of Dublin, the former King James II again fled to the court of the Sun King. Three months later, William played his part in the successful sieges of Cork and Kinsale. That operation was the brainchild of Lieutenant General Lord Churchill, then 1st Earl of Marlborough. Pearman notes in *The First Earl Cadogan* (1988), 'It was during the attacks upon the two ports that the merits of William Cadogan as a solider first attracted the attention of Marlborough.'

William had found his calling. During several years' fighting in Flanders against France and her allies – the Nine Years' War (1688–97) – he progressed to captain in General Erle's Regiment of Foot. In 1698 he returned to his old regiment as quartermaster, buying a promotion (as was the way) to major. A brief spell of peace was then broken by the death in November 1700 of the last Habsburg King of Spain and its colonies, and the discovery of a deathbed will, the stuff of modern whodunnits. The resulting international race for dominance brought two rapid promotions for William Cadogan. On 1 June he was awarded a brevet promotion to colonel of foot by Marlborough, who had been appointed commander of English forces in Holland just the day before. Marlborough was then advanced to Ambassador Extraordinary and Plenipotentiary, with the rather extraordinary licence to 'conceive treaties without reference, if needs be, to King or Parliament' and on 1 July appointed William his Quartermaster General. They headed out to Holland together. Their royal commission had not long been in place, however, when the king was fatally injured in a riding accident and, Queen Mary having already perished from the pox in 1694, the Crown went to his sister-in-law, Queen Anne (r.1702–14). Anne was a friend of the Churchill family (Marlborough's wife Sarah was her closest friend and lady-in-waiting) and William, aged only thirty, was in with the in crowd.

THE WAR OF THE SPANISH SUCCESSION (1701–14) was a showcase for William's extraordinary talents. England declared war on France on 15 May

1702, allied with the other great maritime power of the day, the United Provinces (the Netherlands), together with the Austro-Hungarian Empire (excluding Bavaria). France teamed up with Spain, Portugal, Bavaria and Savoy – the great continental land powers. The first campaign, in and around the Bishopric of Liège, was an early triumph of William's logistics: sixty-seven 24-pounders (cannon) and 140 mortars were kept busy battering the French and Spanish. Queen Anne elevated Marlborough to a dukedom and he in turn requested a bonus for William, of £175 4s, roughly a year's wages, for 'his extraordinary charge, care and pains in the execution of his said office of Quartermaster General during the last campaign.'[6]

Thomas Wentworth, 1st Earl of Strafford NC (Lord Raby), Paul Carl Leygebe, 1711, oil on canvas

On 2 March of the following year, William was appointed to full colonelcy of the 6th Horse (later the 2nd Irish Horse, the 5th Dragoon Guards), which became known as Cadogan's Horse: 'Big men mounted on big horses,' according to Burke's. William stood head and shoulders above his peers, a commanding figure at a time when the average height for an Englishman was hovering around five-foot-five (169 centimetres).[7]

Still, William was far more than just brawn; he was a fixer and an indispensable aide. In September 1703, during the build-up to the siege of Limburg, he wrote to his old friend Lord Raby, now – rather usefully – envoy to Prussia:

> I have been till now on the road of all posts, being employed to find horses in the country from drawing the cannon from Liège to Limburg; those whose business it properly was having so wholly neglected it that there wanted above 1,000 which with much ado I have got at last…[8]

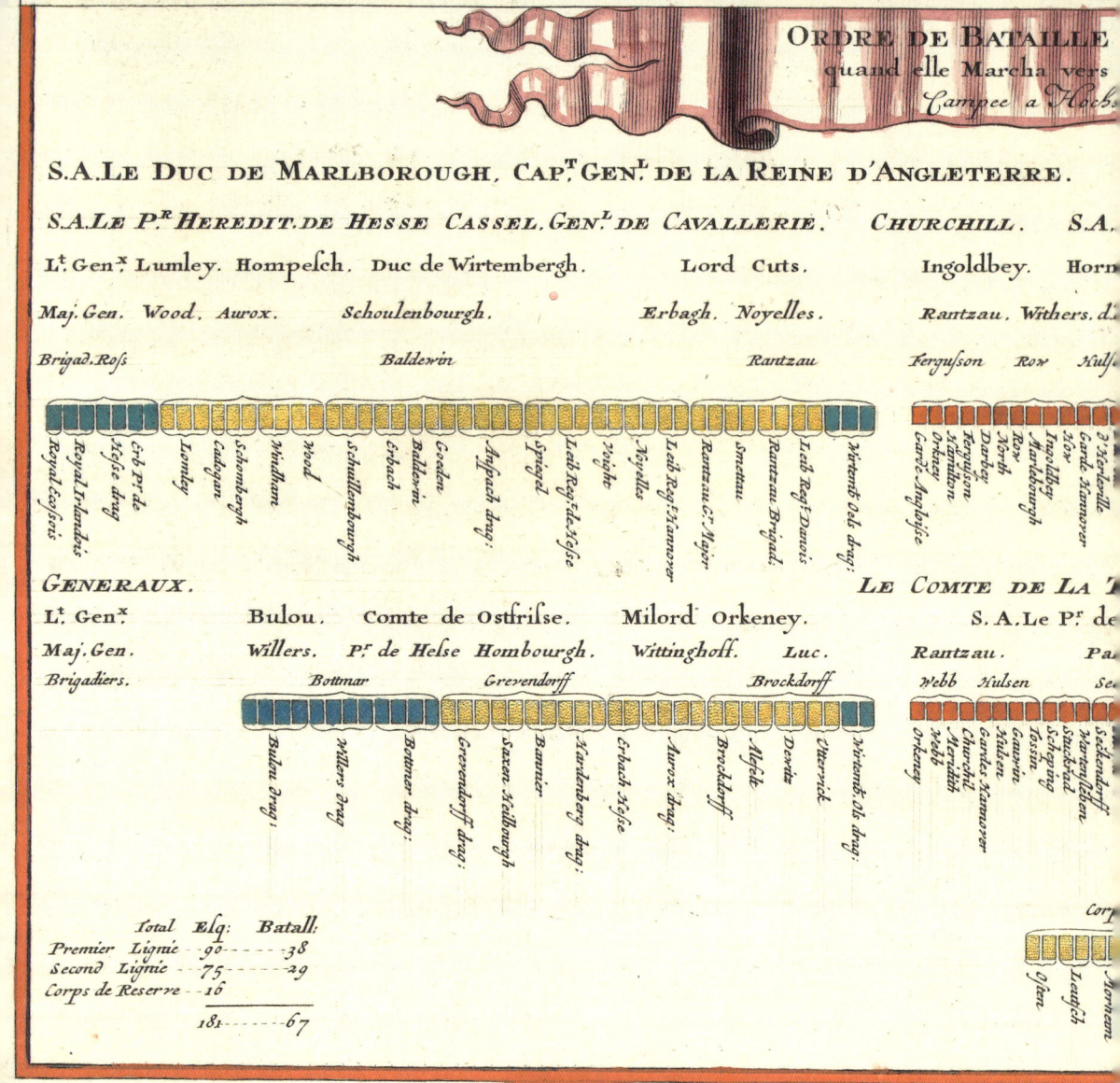

Order of Battle of the Allies Before the Battle of Blenheim, Jan van Vianen, 1704, etching. William's is the second name from left among the cavalry on the front line: Cadogan.

One thousand horses found, victory at Limburg came before the month was out. After the winter break, at the beginning of March, William sailed for England carrying papers for Marlborough on a paquet boat that was attacked by a privateer. As shots were fired, quick-thinking William, rather than risk the great general's secrets, threw the papers overboard into the North Sea.

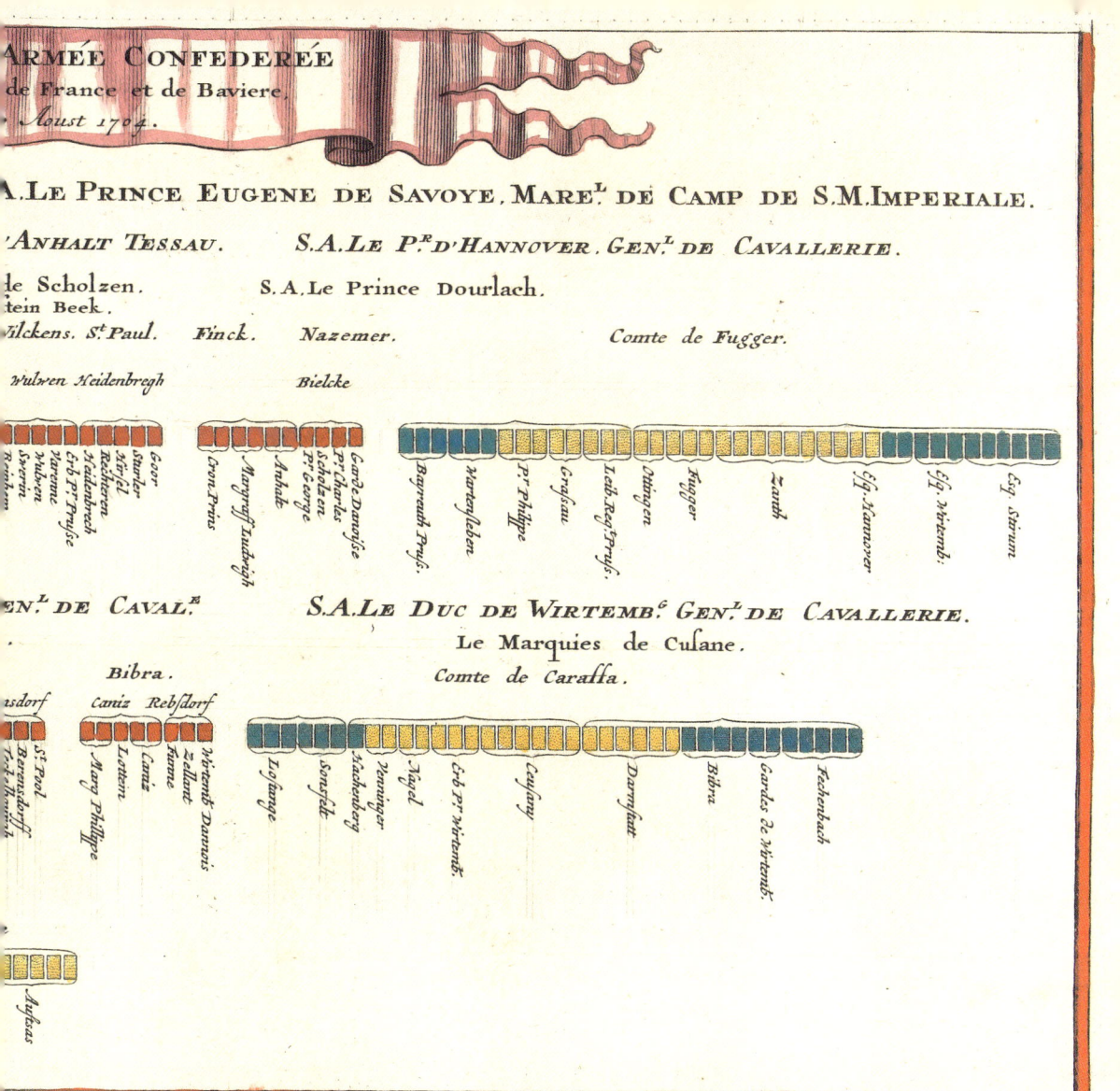

ARMÉE CONFEDERÉE
de France et de Baviere.
Aoust 1704.

A. LE PRINCE EUGENE DE SAVOYE, MARE.ˡ DE CAMP DE S.M. IMPERIALE.

'ANHALT TESSAU.   S.A. LE P.ʀ D'HANNOVER. GEN.ˡ DE CAVALLERIE.

de Scholzen.   S.A. Le Prince Dourlach.
tein Beek.
Vilckens. S.ᵗ Paul.   Finck.   Nazemer.   Comte de Fugger.

Wulven Heidenbregh   Bielcke.

EN.ˡ DE CAVAL.ᴱ   S.A. LE DUC DE WIRTEMB.ᴳ GEN.ˡ DE CAVALLERIE.
                                   Le Marquies de Cusane.
     Bibra.   Comte de Caraffa.
sdorf   Caniz Rebsdorf

IN MAY 1704 MARLBOROUGH'S ARMY left Maastricht, embarking on the epic journey that would confirm William's reputation as a quartermaster – a logistician – of genius. He marched them from first light until midday, every day, but no more. The great 'scarlet caterpillar' was thus spared the heat of the long summer days as it trooped across the flat plains of the Low Countries and into the foothills of Germany.⁹ Infantrymen wore heavy, pocketed coats over waistcoats, shoes with stockings, and tricorn hats; and each man carried nearly sixty pounds of increasingly lethal kit. Cavalrymen wore breeches and sweaty thigh-high boots astride their steeds. They and William himself also wore full-bottomed wigs – even into battle.

William's remit included all aspects of soldiers' welfare: ensuring portable ovens baked fresh bread daily, setting up field hospitals and establishing discipline. The latter he did surprisingly well, given that the infantry of the early eighteenth century comprised men variously press-ganged or conscripted at the Savoy Garrison, 'a parcel of mercenary, fawning, lewd, dissipated creatures, the dregs and scum of mankind.'[10] Fines, floggings and hangings – or the threat of them – kept the men honest. Cavalrymen were less problematic, being largely volunteers. William ensured morale received the occasional boost. 'At least 200 Ladies come to see us on the march, some of them very much handsomer than we expected to find,' wrote one cavalry troop leader.[11]

As they climbed into the Taunus Mountains, they encountered hailstorms that frightened the horses, endless rain and flooding that ruined the roads and risked their feet, but still the Army was maintained in good health and good spirits. Doubtless the flow of English gold to suppliers *en route* smoothed the way. Prince Eugène of Savoy inspected the cavalry on 11 June, declaring:

> My lord, I never saw better horses, better clothes, finer belts and accoutrements...money, which you don't want in England, will buy fine clothes and fine horses, but it can't buy that lively air I see in every one of these troopers' faces.[12]

William wrote to Raby that he hardly had time to eat or sleep. The friendship between the two old schoolfriends had already provided vital intelligence that the Allies should switch their supply lines and focus their minds on securing Schellenberg.

On 2 July 1704, at 2 am, William set out with several squadrons of horse and dragoons, an advance party leading the attack on the Schellenberg fortress. Marlborough had chosen to strike immediately, based on William's

The Brabant Tapestry/Victories Series (detail), commissioned for Blenheim Palace, designed by Lambert de Hondt and woven by Judocus de Vos, Brussels, c.1720. William Cadogan accompanies Marlborough as he accepts Marshal Tallard's surrender at Blenheim.

reconnaissance of the previous day. An army that had just completed a long, forced march – a journey of 260 miles completed by 21,000 men in seven weeks – was ready to fight. The French were taken by surprise and surrendered by 8.30 pm. It was hellish, as a French officer recalled:

> We were all fighting hand-to-hand, hurling them back as they clutched the parapet; men were slaying, or tearing at the muzzles of guns and the bayonets which pierced their entrails; crushing under their feet their own wounded comrades, and even gouging out their opponents' eyes with their nails, when the grip was so close that neither could make use of their weapons.[13]

The cavalry fared no better. William's horse was shot from under him and he was hit in the thigh. Five thousand men on each side were killed or wounded, and while the Allies' victory secured the town, it afforded only a temporary respite. A month later the opposing armies squared up again, fifteen miles east at Blenheim.

The Battle of Blenheim, on 13 August 1704, was William's first set-piece open battle – his previous engagements were almost all sieges – and he was chief of staff. The duke was trying out new strategies of mutual infantry and cavalry support; clear communication was paramount, placing the pair close enough to the action that a cannonball fell at their feet as they observed the field. William's personal bravery was remarkable. As colonel of Cadogan's Horse, he led his regiment into the decisive charge to the centre of the enemy's line: a full-frontal attack. Contemporary French practice was to stop the charge short for a pistol barrage before the final dash. By contrast, the English crashed into the enemy at full speed: that takes some nerve, and an unwavering command of men and mounts. Indeed, William's 'valour greatly contributed to the success of the cavalry'.[14] He was rewarded with promotion to brigadier general a few days later and in the queen's Blenheim bounty list, a welcome bonus of £273. Almost a year later, he personally led the successful charge at the Lines of Brabant, alongside Marlborough. William Cadogan would be present at every major English battle during this period – and survive, leaving us with the impression of a skilful soldier of physical and mental prowess.

WILLIAM WAS A DILIGENT AND INSIGHTFUL chief of intelligence, entrusted with the most secret of Marlborough's plans. One of his talents was to see the importance of this role in modern warfare – deception and feint to keep the enemy guessing, plus thorough reconnaissance – in the days when a messenger on horseback could outride an army on the march. On 23 May 1706, Brigadier General Cadogan and his advance party discovered the enemy's position in the fog by the Great Geete and sent a messenger galloping back to warn the Allies. It was the information Marlborough needed to bring their next battle forward to an immediate start at Ramillies. Following a feint, northwards on the right, the plan was to outflank troops to the south/left and make a classic full-tilt attack at the centre of enemy lines. Not all the commanders were told in advance, however, in order that the initial false attack should be fully convincing to the enemy. William's first ten messengers were sent away by General Orkney. Only when William himself rode over, to insist that he conveyed the duke's orders, was a withdrawal begun. William then re-joined the duke at the centre line for an enormous battle involving 25,000 cavaliers. The English out-thought and then out-fought the French.

More sieges followed and towns fell: Louvain, Brussels, Ghent and Antwerp, at the last of which William was handed the keys of the city by the French and Spanish regiments in surrender. William was promoted to major general.

> Over the next two years Cadogan organized an espionage network with such efficiency that few moves made by the French passed undetected. He took care to have trustworthy agents posted at the principal sea-ports, and the result was a flow of accurate information.[15]

At Menin the deep understanding between William and Marlborough was made explicitly clear. The duke dropped his glove during pre-battle reconnaissance and asked William to pick it up. Superior-status posturing? Not at all. As William guessed, this unusual step outside protocol (ordinarily, an equerry would have fetched the glove) was a secret signal. Back at camp, Marlborough told him that the gesture had marked the spot for the gun emplacement. William, who read him so well, replied that he had already given the order.

A second occurrence underlines just how indispensable he was to Marlborough. William was out foraging for supplies near the besieged city of Tournai when he became separated from his party and his usual surveillance antennae failed him:

I was thrust by the croud. I endeavoured to step into a Ditch on the right of the way we passed, with great difficulty I got out of it, and with greater good Fortune escaped falling into the Hussars' hands who first came up with me…it made us fall to the share of the French Carabiniers, who followed their Hussars and Dragoons from whom I met with Quarter and Civility, save their taking my watch and money…My Lord Duke has been so extremely kind as to propose exchanging the Marquis de Croissy for me, so I hope my prison will not be of very long continuance.[16]

Marlborough had indeed written post-haste to the French commandant. Prisoner-of-war William was exchanged in very short order. Reunited, the general and his chief of staff duly took the village of Ath on 2 October, bringing the fighting season for 1706 to a close, and William was sent to babysit the army of the southern Netherlands over the winter. His year was crowned with an award, the Prussian Order of Generosity (mostly about the huge diamond to be placed at its centre: 'I am told there is a thousand Ducats designed for me to buy a Jewel as soon as the affair of the Winter Quarters is fully regulated'[17]), and an appointment, as Lieutenant of the Tower of London. The latter put him at the helm of ordnance and in receipt of a sinecure. A bit of advance planning for life after the cessation of hostilities was underway.

WILLIAM'S FIRST CHILD, Sarah, was baptized at the Great Church, or St James's Church, in The Hague that September. In Amsterdam, engaged in pre-war summits and strategies, William had pursued a diplomatic mission of his own. His wife Margaretta Cecilia Munter (1675–1749) was the archetypal good catch: a wealthy heiress and, happily, an attractive young lady in her mid-twenties. Her father Willem Munter was Heer [Lord] van Zanen en Raaphorst and a councillor of the supreme court of Holland, at The Hague. After a two-year romance, William and Margaretta were married at the Walloon Church in The Hague, in April 1704.

Not much is made or known of Margaretta other than her role as a wife and mother. But in choosing her, William stepped outside the confines of nationalism, demonstrated his loyalty to the Anglo–Dutch alliance (and royal family) and gave us an insight into his international outlook and linguistic ability. A second daughter, Margaretta, was born on 21 February 1708.

WILLIAM WAS AS FLUENT IN GERMAN as he was in Dutch and French.[18] In early 1707 Marlborough sent him on diplomatic trips to Hanover and Vienna. As autumn drew in, he assisted Marlborough with the Anglo–Dutch regency formed to diffuse the power of the Austrian king put in charge of the formerly Spanish (but Dutch-speaking) Netherlands. Marlborough wrote to Lord Godolphin on 3 October:

> I have thought, as well as I can, how to leave the business of this country, at my return to England, and I think it must be to Cadogan; so that if the queen pleases I shall acquaint the States-General, and the council of state of this country, that in the absence of Mr. Stepney, he is charged with the care of her majesty's business.[19]

Quite what a diplomatic dance William was able to do is evidenced by this arrangement holding in the Netherlands until the end of the war. Later that year, Queen Anne made it official, appointing William 'Envoy

ABOVE Countess Cadogan (née Margaretta Munter), after Sir Godfrey Kneller, Bt., oil on canvas

Extraordinary to the States-General and…Plenipotentiary in negotiations we are entered into in concert with other Princes and States for what relates to the common interest,' and a salary recorded in her Warrant Book at a whopping £5 per day.[20]

William was now based at The Hague. His thoughts on life as a European statesman were drily outlined to his old friend Raby on 19 January 1708:

> I assure your Lordship that nothing like a hint about peace passed at our conference…I will give you in a few words the description of Brussels. Count Corneille is the Principal Trickster and Oxenstiern the Top Wit. My Lord Aylesbury a shining Beau, and his Lady a celebrated To[a]st, not a woman but puts on as much red as my Lady Falkland, as is as coquette as our former friend my lady S—n. They play deep and pay ill, and in short there is a tolerable deal of scandal but no f—ng. Tho to doe the women Justice tis not their fault.[21]

His more shadowy role as a spymaster was called upon when the pretender to the Crown – the son of the late Catholic King James II – was rumoured to be readying to set out from Dunkirk for Scotland in March 1708. William's confirmation of Jacobite forces massing by the port gave Marlborough a chance to pursue the French to the Firth of Forth, thwarting this Stuart attempt on the Crown.

William had developed a taste for espionage. In June 1709 he was one of two volunteers to undertake an intelligence-gathering mission near the River Deule. General Dopf set out with a cavalry escort. By contrast, 'it is said that [William], descending from his high position as Marlborough's Chief of Staff and Quartermaster General, traversed at the peril of his life, disguised as a labourer, a large section of Villars's front'.[22] We must wonder quite how such a physically distinctive man had passed unnoticed; though the popularly recounted tale of a smiliar feat undertaken dressed as a wine merchant suggests legendary abilites.[23] Intelligence on the enemy's position led to success at a second siege of Tournai, concluded on 5 September.

The Siege of Tournai – Marlborough attacks the town, bravely defended by de Surville – after fifty-six days it is forced to surrender, etching by Pass published London, 1709

TWO MORE MAJOR BATTLES to mention. At the Battle of Oudenarde, in July 1708, William rode in alongside the Hanoverian Elector's son George – future King George II of England – leading sixteen battalions of British infantry, eight squadrons of Hanoverian dragoons and thirty-two regimental guns. His brother Charles, by this point an officer in Cadogan's Horse, was also there. William was in the vanguard, ordering pontoons for the troops to cross the River Scheldt and drawing the enemy's first enthusiasm of fire, preparing the way for Marlborough to storm through to victory.

Then came Malplaquet on 11 September 1709, 'the most desperate and bloody attack and battle that had been fought in the memory of men,' according to an historian writing in 1747.[24] Funny how each successive war is thought to have been the worst before mankind outdoes itself once more. William's brother-in-law Brigadier General Sir Thomas Prendergast, 1st Baronet, was mortally wounded. Happily, his brother Charles once again fought alongside him unscathed. It was at Mons, as the French retreated, that William came unstuck: this time, it was not his horse but his own aide-de-camp who was killed in close proximity; William himself was gravely wounded, as Marlborough described to his wife:

>...poor Cadogan was wound'd in the neck...I was with him this morning when they drest his wound. As he is very fatt there greatest apprehension is growing feaverish. We must have patience for two or three dressings before the surjeans can give their judgement. I hope in God he will do well, for I can intierly depend upon him.[25]

The corpulent William recovered and was sent back to Brussels. Blenheim, Ramillies, Oudenarde, Malplaquet: Marlborough and his chief of staff were four for four.

All parties were getting sick of it. The Allies had suffered the loss or injury of some 25,000 men, and even those behind desks, such as William's old school contemporary Lord Brydges, wanted to prevent 'our danger of losing a person so valuable to his country on such sort of service...[we] hope it will prove a warning to you how you expose yourself on such like occasions again'.[26]

WILLIAM HAD A SIDELINE as a Whig MP, even while living in Brussels. At the election of 1710, he retained his seat despite a landslide victory by those who wanted an end to the war (Tories 320, Whigs 150, forty undecided). William, who had sat since May 1705, would be returned at five successive elections. Though he spent little time on the benches, he was adept at his role as the Duke of Marlborough's voice in the House of Commons. As war fatigue set in, and the Duchess of Marlborough fell from Queen Anne's good graces, William lost his diplomatic post in Brussels and was suddenly recalled to England. Tory knives were out. On 11 January 1712, as a parliamentary commission into financial irregularities in procurement neared its conclusion, the queen announced Marlborough's immediate dismissal to her council. Fiercely loyal to the man who had talent-spotted and promoted him, William wrote to him on 20 January:

>My concern and astonishment att the fatal news of Your Grace's being removed are as hard to be expressed as the terror and

> consternation it has struck all people with here…For these five and thirty years past, it was an established custom to present the General Commanding in Chief with a considerable annual gratification in proportion to the number of troops…
>
> I persuade myself 'tis unnecessary to repeat the assurances of my intention to follow Your Grace in all fortunes…[27]

Marlborough told him to stay put; he could continue as his eyes and ears. On paper, William's new boss was the Duke of Ormonde, but when Marlborough left England's shores, in December 1712, for self-imposed exile in Europe, it was to William that he transferred a £50,000 pot for safekeeping. William sold his colonelcy of the Cadogan Horse and wrote to the Lord Treasurer:

> The Duke of Marlborough's ill health and the inconvenience a winter's journey exposes him to and his being without any friend to accompany him, makes the requesting leave to wait on him an indispensable duty on me who, for so many years have been honoured with his confidence and friendship, and owe all I have in the world to his favour.[28]

William repaired to the Manor of Raaphorst. He also leased a much smaller estate nearby, De Drie Papagaaien (The Three Parrots). Leaving Margaretta and the girls at home, he then bounced between London, The Hague and Hanover – where he was a frequent visitor to the court. There, he and Marlborough cooked up a plan with the Elector George and his son, their brother-in-arms from Oudenarde, to ensure a Protestant succession in the ever-nearer event of the childless and gouty Queen Anne's death. It came on 1 August.

William attended the coronation of King George I on 20 October 1714 in a new role as Master of the Robes. He was swiftly reinstated to his previous positions as Lieutenant of the Ordnance at the Tower of London, and Envoy Extraordinary and Minister Plenipotentiary to the States-General of Holland; and he took a new colonelcy of the Coldstream Guards. With

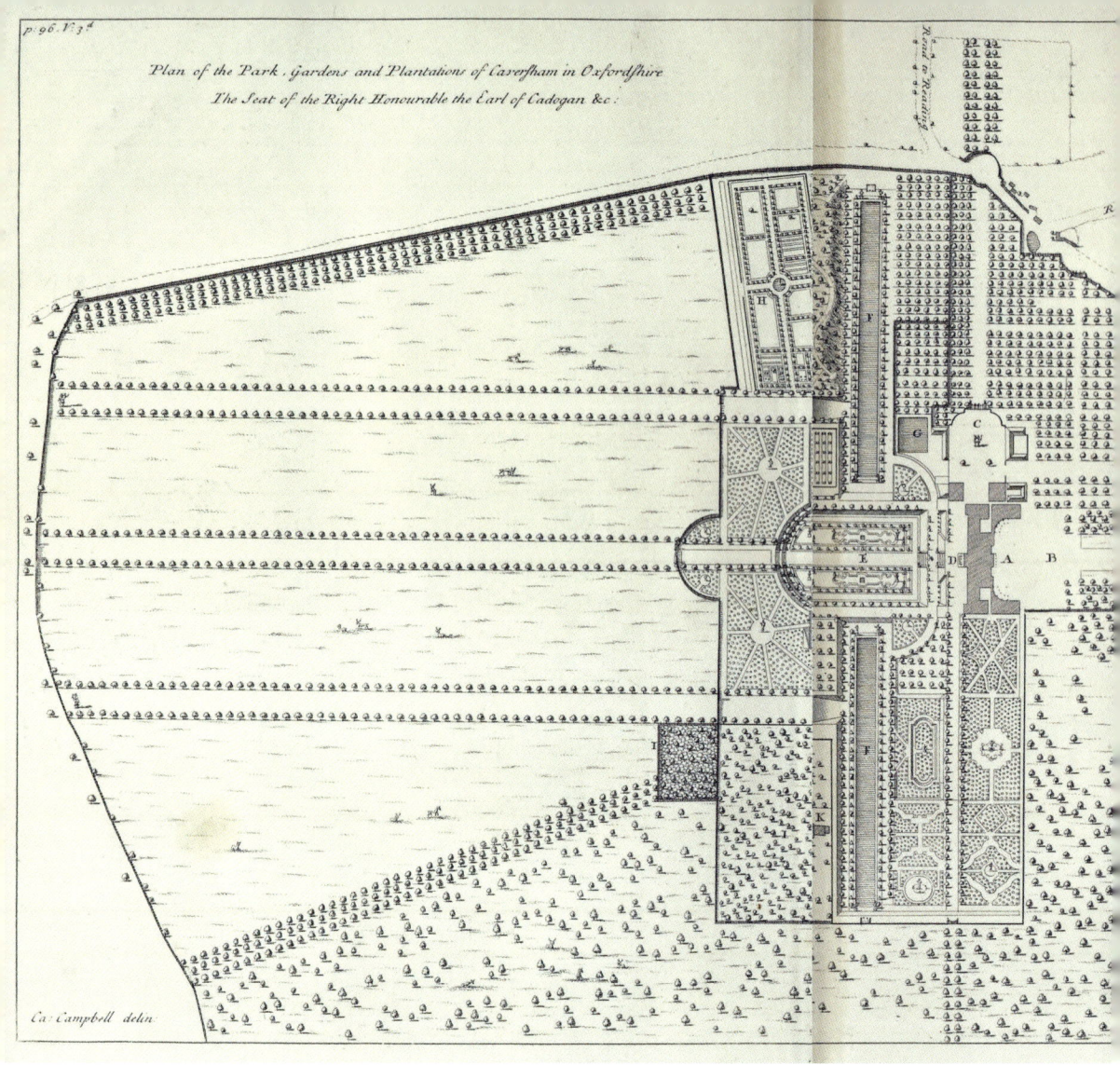

Plan of the Park, Gardens and Plantations of Caversham, Oxfordshire, the Seat of the Right Honourable the Earl of Cadogan &c., pages from Colen Campbell, Vitruvius Britannicus, *vol. 3, published 1725*

his star once again in the ascendant, William needed a fitting residence. The Manor of Oakley, in Aylesbury Vale, Buckinghamshire, purchased during a brief return to England in March 1707, when £9,450 bought the modest red-brick house opposite the church and 370 acres, was no longer grand enough.[29]

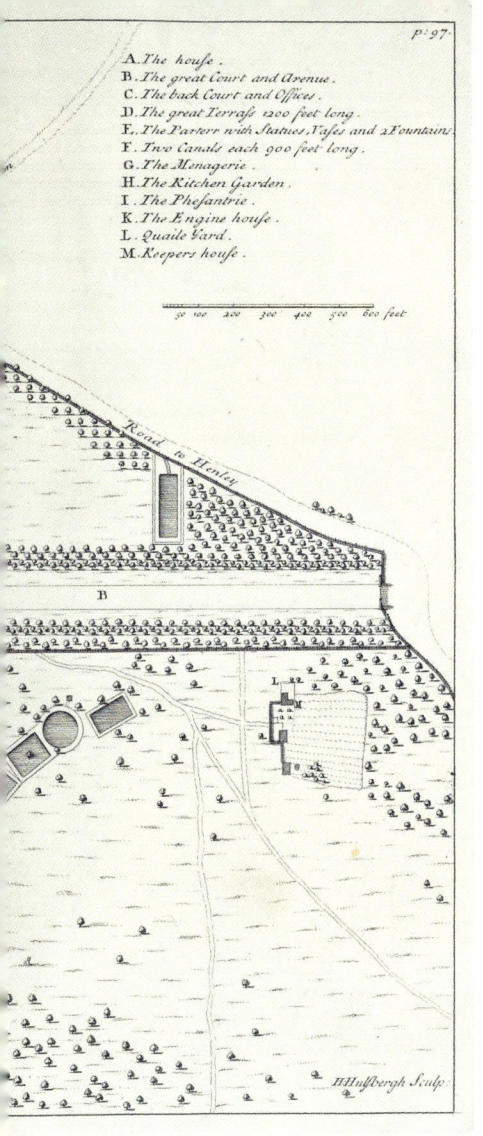

A. The house.
B. The great Court and Avenue.
C. The back Court and Offices.
D. The great Terrass 1200 feet long.
E. The Parterr with Statues, Vases and 2 Fountains.
F. Two Canals each 900 feet long.
G. The Menagerie.
H. The Kitchen Garden.
I. The Phesantrie.
K. The Engine house.
L. Quaile Yard.
M. Keepers house.

In July 1714 William leased the thousand-acre Caversham Estate from the Dowager Countess of Kildare, for £200 a year plus 'One Brace of Fat Bucks and One Brace of Fat Does' from the deer park.[30] Still close enough to Blenheim and his parliamentary constituency of New Woodstock, it was within striking distance of the courts at Windsor Castle and London. Four years later he bought the freehold.[31] There had been a succession of houses demolished and rebuilt at Caversham Park for at least five hundred years. William immediately set about making his own improvements. The third volume of compendious architectural survey *Vitruvius Britannicus* (1725), made a gushing report on this Georgian pile:

...the eye is entertained with most beautiful Prospects; particularly from the grand Terras, 1200 Feet long [a quarter of a mile], towards *Reading* and the *Thames*...The Parterre is nobly adorned with Fountains, Vases and Statues, particularly Four Originals in Statuary Marble, of King WILLIAM [III], King GEORGE [I], Duke of MARLBOROUGH, and Prince EUGENE, all so very like, that they are known at Sight;...Two great Canals 900 Feet long, with a Dorick Portico at each End. From the great Iron Gates, to the End of the Park Pale, are Four beautiful Lawns, divided by Three Walks of very lofty Trees, 2200 Feet long, and the whole Park is well Wooded, Watered, and plenty of Deer, a Pheasantry, Menagerie, and all manner of Conveniencies....[32]

William's new house proudly – somewhat ostentatiously – displayed his loyalties. But while 'His command of German and his knowledge of Hanover's politics made him a favourite of the King', the townspeople of Reading were less keen, viewing him as an outsider (William had not lost his Irish accent). At the 1714–15 election, when he put his brother up for the seat, crowds demonstrated under slogans of 'No Hanover, no Cadogan,' and 'No Foreign Government!'[33] Charles would take the constituency in 1716 but hold it only for six years.

On 21 June 1716 William was created Baron Cadogan of Reading, and the town's high steward, its occupants' sometime antipathy towards him notwithstanding. This was in part a reward for crushing the Jacobite rebels once more the previous winter – this time, decisively – in Scotland. William had maintained a discreet watching brief on his commander, the Duke of Argyll, whose sympathies as a Scotsman were at odds with his role as commander-in-chief of the king's three-thousand-strong forces north of the border. Time for more clandestine manoeuvres:

> I have writt the enclosed in French that if your Grace thinks proper it may be shown the King…The Postmaster of Edinburgh is a creature of the Duke of Argyles and opens all letters. When your Grace has therefore any thing in particular to write to me, it may be addressed to the Postmaster at Berwick…[34]

His multilingualism perhaps would have made any intercepted messages indecipherable to postmasters. Once again, William's abilities at keeping a healthy army on the march were put to good use, as the rebels were pushed northwards. The Old Pretender slipped away to France and his supporters scattered or surrendered. William was appointed to a Scottish Order, as Knight of the Most Ancient and Most Noble Order of the Thistle.

This first barony also recognized his crowning diplomatic achievement. William was instrumental in the signing of the Third Barrier Treaty (on 15 November 1715) between Great Britain, the United Provinces and the Holy Roman Emperor Charles VI (ruler of the Austrian Netherlands), which agreed defence against the French. This advancement may have been the start of some prodigious spending, which would come back to haunt the family.

On 17 March 1717 he was sworn into the Privy Council. He shuttled back and forth between London – where he had a house in newly built Hanover Square – and his young family at The Hague. On 8 May 1718 he was further ennobled:

> …we having great reason to be extremely satisfied with the services he has since done…we have thought fit to confer upon him a new degree of honour, and to create him Earl of Cadogan, in Denbighshire; Viscount of Caversham, in Oxfordshire; and Baron of Oakley, in Buckinghamshire.[35]

Intriguingly, the earldom had been, at William's request, linked to an obscure and possibly fantastical spot in Wales too far north of Rhwng Gwy a Hafren for any discernable ancestral links: 'the place I propose is called Cadogan near Wrexam on the borders of Wales.'[36] Maps of Denbighshire reveal only 'Plas Cadwgan', a late medieval house – 'plas' meaning large house, or palace, rather than place – by that date almost entirely rebuilt (and demolished in 1967). The 'of' was dropped fairly swiftly: the Cadogans became Earls Cadogan.

William embraced all the pomp. On 8 June 1718 he made a formal entry into The Hague as His Majesty's Ambassador. He stayed at the Mauritshuis for three days of toasts and dinners, and conducted a successful audience in French with the president of the States-General. Over the next couple of years, he worked on completion of the Quadruple Alliance and the Treaty of the Hague (1720), which finally forced Philip V of Spain to renounce his claims in Italy. William was as much a lynchpin in the diplomacy that followed the Wars of Succession as he had been in the field during battle.

'a person illustrious by his descent from the honourable and most ancient stock of the Britons, but much more illustrious by his virtues....In all his counsels and votes in the House of Commons, a sacred regard to the public good, and the true liberty of his country. In the exploits of war, an undaunted bravery and a greatness of soul have, upon every occasion shone forth in the brightest light...'

KING GEORGE I, PATENT TO WILLIAM CADOGAN'S ENNOBLEMENT

ABOVE Badge of the Scottish Order of the Thistle. William was appointed Knight of this Most Ancient and Most Noble Order in 1716. King George I ennobled him Baron Cadogan of Reading in 1716 and Baron Cadogan of Oakley, Viscount of Caversham and Earl Cadogan in 1718.

WILLIAM SECURED A BRILLIANT MATCH for his elder daughter, Lady Sarah. It has been suggested that it was a vast sum owing to William from a gambling debt that was the impetus for such an upwardly mobile manouevre.[37] Even with this offset, the sums were enormous: William promised a dowry of £20,000 and a further £60,000 to be paid within three years to secure a suitable property for the couple and their heirs. And there was a default clause regarding payment, which held him liable for an even larger amount: £100,000 (a figure today north of £20 million).[38] The groom-to-be was an illegitimate grandson and namesake of King Charles II, the only son and sole heir to Charles Lennox, 1st Duke of Richmond, 1st Duke of Lennox and duc d'Aubigny. On 4 December 1719 Lady Sarah Cadogan, aged thirteen, married the Earl of March, on the cusp of eighteen, at a church in The Hague. The bride was returned immediately to her parents and the groom departed with his tutor.

A rather lovely anecdote later retold by their great(x4)-grandson, then Earl of March (later the 8th Duke of Richmond), concerns their reacquaintance three years later. Somewhat dreading doing his marital duty 'with the poor little bride of whom he had nought but the distasteful recollections occasioned by the sordid circumstances of their union,' Lord March decided to have a last night of bachelordom at the theatre. There, he spotted 'a beauteous lady with whom he promptly fell over head and ears in love at first sight.'[39] She was, of course, his wife Lady March, the toast of the city. They sailed for England on the king's yacht and were installed at Goodwood, which he inherited the following year. The unusually happy marriage of Lady Sarah Cadogan and the 2nd Duke of Richmond would result in twelve children.

THE WHIFF OF FINANCIAL IRREGULARITY tainted William's later years. Old Queen Anne had received a formal complaint from the Deputies of Ghent about William skimming a proportion of taxes for his own pocket. In June 1717 he faced an indictment in the House of Commons, led by Sir Robert Walpole, for alleged fraud related to the transport of troops during the Scottish rebellion – bringing to mind the accusations against

Marlborough of 1712, and William's indignant retort that such behaviour was 'an established custom'. Responsible for billeting, supplies and even salaries of his men, William had seen fit to siphon off a little here and a little there since his days in Flanders. For example:

> In 1707 he borrowed money from his father-in-law…in order to buy up pistoles [gold coin], which he sold to the Army at a substantially higher rate. Brydges [his Old Westminster cohort] arranged for up to £14,000 to be provided well in advance of the time payments were due. The two profiteers thus reckoned to make as much as 25,000 guilders pure gain. Cadogan spent a good deal of time each winter buying gold and then selling it at a profit.[40]

He played the Netherlands' currency exchanges, using his growing financial acuity to build his fortune. Rather damningly, however, money was paid into his wife's account; and he and Brydges ran a book, betting on the outcome of military manoeuvres using William's insider information. Nonetheless, William's Whig friends saw the motion defeated.

William enjoyed risk during the heyday of London's clubland. At the gaming tables, he had secured his daughter Sarah's marriage, but he lost as big as he won, as his friend Lord Raby recounted: 'I should scold at you for loosing mony at play as I hear you have lately don[e], I thought you had shook off that passion…'[41] His profligate spending included ploughing a rumoured £130,000 into the redevelopment of Caversham. The books needed balancing. On 17 April 1719 the Dublin town house and his grandfather's estate in County Meath were sold to his cousin Lord Shelburne, for £4,355; two years later 473 acres of County Limerick and the castle at Adare went for £3,157.[42] The Cadogans were Irish landowners no more. In 1720 the South Sea Bubble burst, bringing the stock market crashing down with it. And then that £50,000 entrusted to him by Marlborough came back to bite him. Initially, William had invested the duke's running-away fund of 1712 in steady Dutch government funds, but he had soon been

The 2nd Duke and Duchess of Richmond, English school, oil on canvas. The second duchess was William's elder daughter, Lady Sarah Cadogan.

tempted by hot-ticket Austrian loans promising a much higher return. When these securities subsequently crashed in value, William found himself unable to return the much-reduced principal or offer any interest. All was well while the duke thrived, but after he was invalided by two strokes in 1716, his less-than-understanding wife began to poke about in his affairs. And following the death of William's old friend in June 1722, she brought a lawsuit against William – and won. In 1730 Sarah, Dowager Duchess of Marlborough, would come to own the Manor of Oakley as part of the posthumous tidying of the 1st Earl's affairs.

Thankfully, in 1723 William's newly duked son-in-law Charles gave him a three-year extension on settlement of the dowry. William was keen to show willing in the interim: 'I shall accept whatever bills you may have occasion to draw on me,' he wrote on 1 August 1724.[43] Not so much a blackguard or thief, perhaps, but a Cadogan with an eye for a flutter and a tendency to overextend. He wouldn't be the last.

THE PINNACLE OF WILLIAM'S military career came with the loss of his greatest friend. Regarded by the king as 'the best officer in England, and the most capable of commanding the army',[44] he had been its acting head for years during Marlborough's decline and in 1722 became its commander-in-chief. He had already accepted new roles as Master Surveyor of the Ordnance, Colonel of the 1st Foot Guards (the Grenadiers), and a commissioner of Chelsea Hospital. But he was not universally popular; an infamous poem pilloried him as 'Ungrateful to the ungrateful man he grew by, a big, bad, bold, blustering, bloody, blundering booby.'[45] A final Jacobite plot to wrest power from the Hanoverians began to brew. William took personal command of the king's safety, camping out with troops in Hyde Park for several months. When, crisis over, King George I left for Hanover, William was appointed one of the Lords Justice of the Realm.

Having survived battles, bullets, incarceration and official inquiry, his health was deteriorating through a surfeit of good living. In 1724 he quit London for Caversham, writing to the Duke of Richmond:

> ...yesterday I had a violent Feaverish fit which lasted a great while. Sir Hans Sloane ordered the Bark of which I have taken already no small quantity...I have still a pain in my head which makes the writing uneasy to me.[46]

The following year, matters took a turn for the worse, 'I have been extremely ill since the last operation, of the Stone Cholick...What retards the cure is a sharp Humour That falls upon the Wound...'.[47] Headaches, an operation, an infected wound, kidney stones...even cheering visits from his little granddaughter Caroline Lennox couldn't stave off the inevitable. William Cadogan, this bullish man of great appetites and abilities, bluff and bold, puffed his last on 17 July 1726, aged only fifty-four. 'The Earle [Cadogan] dyed in top dress, & kept on him to the last, his Great Wig, Imbroydered Coat, Brocad[e] vest, Ried topt Shoes, diamont Buckles etc.'[48] At his own request, he was buried privately, at night, in Henry VII's chapel in Westminster Abbey. Alexander Pope, who had satirized him mercilessly, wrote:

He certainly knew himself best at last, and knew best the little value of others, whose neglect of him, whom they so grossly followed and flattered in the former scene of his life, showed them as worthless as they could imagine him to be were he all that his worst enemies believed of him. For my own part, I am sorry for his death...[49]

His old friend from Trinity student days, Lord Raby, Earl of Strafford, provided a more fitting epitaph that encapsulates William's part in settling the world order for the next several decades:

I do believe the greatest part of Lord Marlborough's victories are owing to him [Cadogan], and even the Pensionary [Holland's Chancellor] said to me *si vous voulez avoir un duc de Marlbourough, un Cadogan est Necessiare*.[50]

He left two daughters and his wife Margaretta, who lived another twenty years, but there were no sons. Accordingly, his chapter draws to a close, his legacy to the Cadogan family – as a many-times-great-uncle to the present earl – a natural pride in his role in British national life. William had marshalled the transition from the Stuarts to the Hanoverians. As the Georgians settled in, the story of the Cadogans is taken up by William's brother Charles and his bride Elizabeth Sloane, daughter of William's physician; and we follow in Daniel Defoe's footsteps to 'Chelsey, a town of palaces.'[51]

ABOVE Sir Hans Sloane, attr. Jonathan Richardson, c.1720, oil on canvas

Abridged family tree

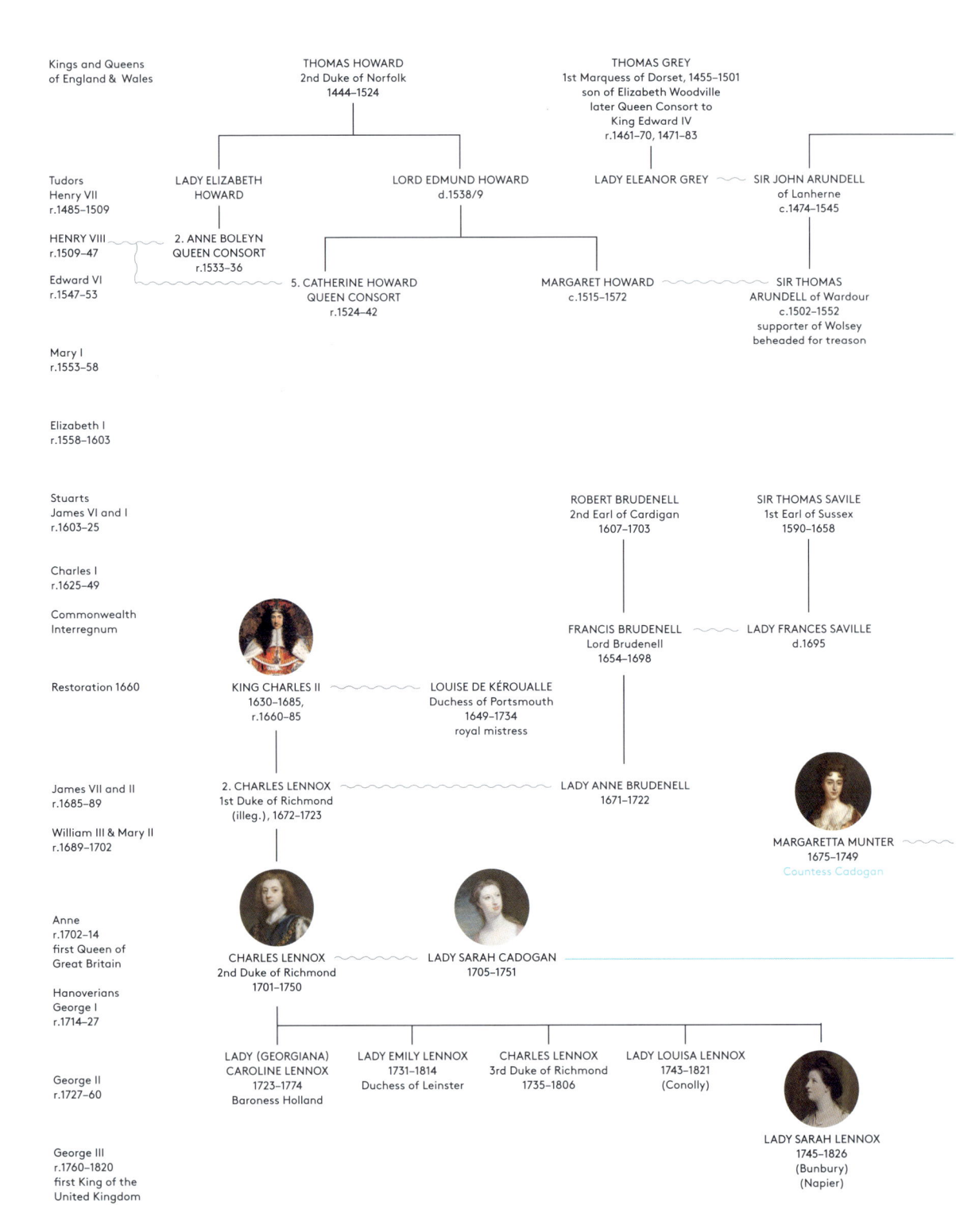

Kings and Queens of England & Wales

Tudors
Henry VII r.1485–1509
HENRY VIII r.1509–47
Edward VI r.1547–53
Mary I r.1553–58
Elizabeth I r.1558–1603

Stuarts
James VI and I r.1603–25
Charles I r.1625–49
Commonwealth Interregnum
Restoration 1660
James VII and II r.1685–89
William III & Mary II r.1689–1702
Anne r.1702–14, first Queen of Great Britain

Hanoverians
George I r.1714–27
George II r.1727–60
George III r.1760–1820, first King of the United Kingdom

THOMAS HOWARD, 2nd Duke of Norfolk, 1444–1524

THOMAS GREY, 1st Marquess of Dorset, 1455–1501, son of Elizabeth Woodville later Queen Consort to King Edward IV r.1461–70, 1471–83

LADY ELIZABETH HOWARD

LORD EDMUND HOWARD d.1538/9

LADY ELEANOR GREY

SIR JOHN ARUNDELL of Lanherne c.1474–1545

2. ANNE BOLEYN QUEEN CONSORT r.1533–36

5. CATHERINE HOWARD QUEEN CONSORT r.1524–42

MARGARET HOWARD c.1515–1572

SIR THOMAS ARUNDELL of Wardour c.1502–1552, supporter of Wolsey, beheaded for treason

ROBERT BRUDENELL, 2nd Earl of Cardigan, 1607–1703

SIR THOMAS SAVILE, 1st Earl of Sussex, 1590–1658

FRANCIS BRUDENELL, Lord Brudenell, 1654–1698

LADY FRANCES SAVILE d.1695

KING CHARLES II 1630–1685, r.1660–85

LOUISE DE KÉROUALLE, Duchess of Portsmouth, 1649–1734, royal mistress

LADY ANNE BRUDENELL 1671–1722

2. CHARLES LENNOX, 1st Duke of Richmond (illeg.), 1672–1723

MARGARETTA MUNTER 1675–1749, Countess Cadogan

CHARLES LENNOX, 2nd Duke of Richmond, 1701–1750

LADY SARAH CADOGAN 1705–1751

LADY (GEORGIANA) CAROLINE LENNOX 1723–1774, Baroness Holland

LADY EMILY LENNOX 1731–1814, Duchess of Leinster

CHARLES LENNOX, 3rd Duke of Richmond, 1735–1806

LADY LOUISA LENNOX 1743–1821 (Conolly)

LADY SARAH LENNOX 1745–1826 (Bunbury) (Napier)

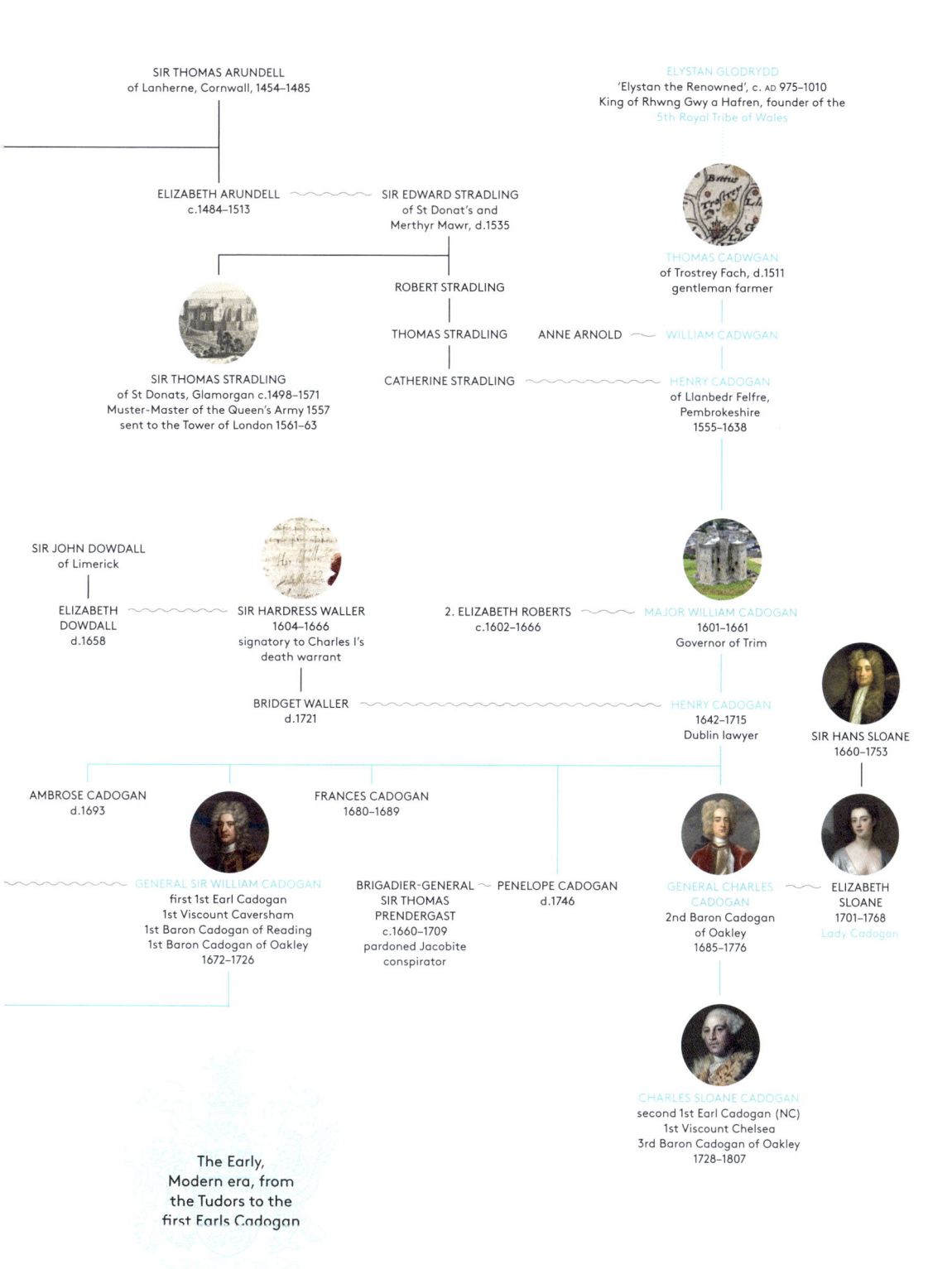

SIR THOMAS ARUNDELL
of Lanherne, Cornwall, 1454–1485

ELYSTAN GLODRYDD
'Elystan the Renowned', c. AD 975–1010
King of Rhwng Gwy a Hafren, founder of the
5th Royal Tribe of Wales

ELIZABETH ARUNDELL
c.1484–1513

SIR EDWARD STRADLING
of St Donat's and
Merthyr Mawr, d.1535

THOMAS CADWGAN
of Trostrey Fach, d.1511
gentleman farmer

ROBERT STRADLING

THOMAS STRADLING ── ANNE ARNOLD ~ **WILLIAM CADWGAN**

CATHERINE STRADLING ~ **HENRY CADOGAN**
of Llanbedr Felfre,
Pembrokeshire
1555–1638

SIR THOMAS STRADLING
of St Donats, Glamorgan c.1498–1571
Muster-Master of the Queen's Army 1557
sent to the Tower of London 1561–63

SIR JOHN DOWDALL
of Limerick

ELIZABETH DOWDALL
d.1658

SIR HARDRESS WALLER
1604–1666
signatory to Charles I's
death warrant

2. ELIZABETH ROBERTS
c.1602–1666
~ **MAJOR WILLIAM CADOGAN**
1601–1661
Governor of Trim

BRIDGET WALLER
d.1721
~ **HENRY CADOGAN**
1642–1715
Dublin lawyer

SIR HANS SLOANE
1660–1753

AMBROSE CADOGAN
d.1693

FRANCES CADOGAN
1680–1689

GENERAL SIR WILLIAM CADOGAN
first 1st Earl Cadogan
1st Viscount Caversham
1st Baron Cadogan of Reading
1st Baron Cadogan of Oakley
1672–1726

BRIGADIER-GENERAL SIR THOMAS PRENDERGAST
c.1660–1709
pardoned Jacobite
conspirator
~ **PENELOPE CADOGAN**
d.1746

GENERAL CHARLES CADOGAN
2nd Baron Cadogan
of Oakley
1685–1776
~ **ELIZABETH SLOANE**
1701–1768
Lady Cadogan

CHARLES SLOANE CADOGAN
second 1st Earl Cadogan (NC)
1st Viscount Chelsea
3rd Baron Cadogan of Oakley
1728–1807

The Early,
Modern era, from
the Tudors to the
first Earls Cadogan

Map of Chelsea (detail of four sheets), Richard Horwood, 1794, coloured engraving

THE GEORGIANS

CHAPTER 4

Custodians of Caversham & Chelsea

—

CHARLES, 2ND BARON CADOGAN OF OAKLEY (1685–1776),
HIS WIFE ELIZABETH SLOANE (1701–1768) AND THEIR SON
CHARLES SLOANE CADOGAN (1728–1807)

General Charles Cadogan, 2nd Baron Cadogan of Oakley, distinguished himself largely by his fortuitous marriage. As the younger brother of William, 1st Earl Cadogan, KT, PC, Viscount Caversham and 1st Baron Cadogan of Oakley and Reading, he was perhaps destined to fall under the shadow cast by his ambitious and capable sibling. Charles, like William, was a career soldier, and he saw action alongside his brother at Oudenarde and Malplaquet. At the close of the War of the Spanish Succession he was a lieutenant colonel in the 2nd Foot (Coldstream Guards); he purchased a colonelcy in the 4th Foot (the King's Own Regiment) in 1719.[1] In his thirties Charles embarked upon an unremarkable political career as a Whig MP, first for Reading (1716–22), the nearest parliamentary seat to Caversham Park, and then Newport (1722–26), on the Isle of Wight where William was Governor. The comprehensive *History of Parliament* records his decade in the Commons in one line: 'he acted in Parliament with his brother in support of Sunderland against Walpole.'[2] His success at by-elections in both seats and his early military promotion may be attributable to his brother's good standing. Diarist Thomas Hearne, writing in 1717,

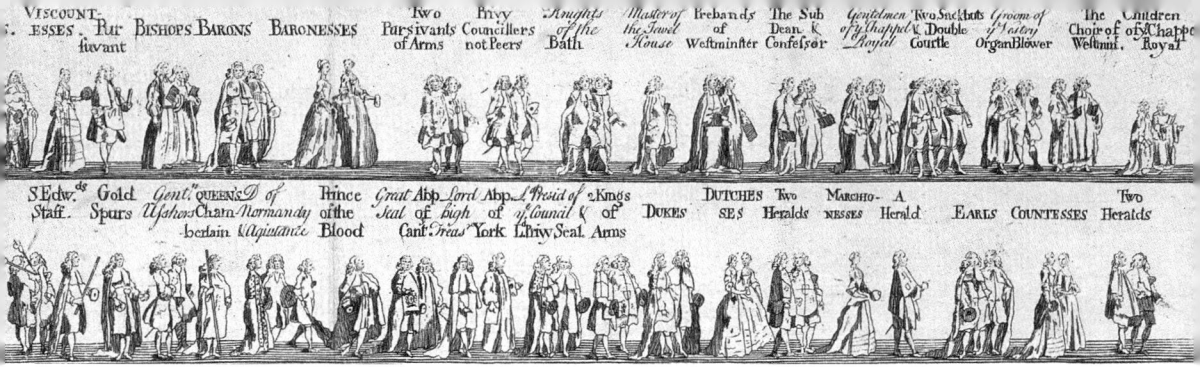

Coronation procession of King George II (detail), 1727, engraving. The year after Charles inherited his brother's title, becoming 2nd Baron Cadogan of Oakley, he attended the coronation of George II at Westminster Abbey. This contemporary engraving depicts the procession by rank (rows two and three of five shown). The crowd witnessed the première of *Zadok the Priest*, which was commissioned for the occasion from composer George Frederick Handel and has preceded the anointing of every British monarch since.

the year of Charles's wedding, was less than generous, describing him as 'a loose person, and of no great income'.[3]

He must have had something. How did he catch the eye of Elizabeth Sloane (1701–1768), the younger daughter of Sir Hans Sloane, a titan of the British Enlightenment? Perhaps his portrait provides a clue; perhaps where Hearne saw 'looseness' others saw charm. He was in good odour with the royal family. When William died in 1726, King George I saw fit to pass Charles the Barony of Oakley by special remainder (though not to extend it to either the viscountcy or earldom); a diplomatic trip to Vienna with his brother in 1720 had perhaps improved Charles's reputation in the interim.[4] A second Hanoverian king, George II (r.1727–60), ascended the throne the following year and it is 'extremely likely'[5] that Charles was among the massed nobility who attended the coronation at Westminster Abbey. His incremental climb up the staff ranks of the Army included an appointment in 1742 to the 2nd Troop of Horse Guards, which 'gave him the privilege of taking the court duty of gold stick'.[6] This brought him into direct and near-constant contact with the king: 'The Gold Stick in Waiting is considered responsible for the safety of the Royal Person: his duty is to see that a sufficient Guard is in attendance, and to be always near the Sovereign, especially on occasions of State.'[7] His presence at the coronation of George III (r.1760–1820), in 1761, was recorded by the College of Arms.[8] Charles finally reached the summit of his military career the same year, becoming 'the senior general in the army'.[9]

Charles Cadogan, 2nd Baron Cadogan of Oakley, studio of Michael Dahl, oil on canvas

Elizabeth Sloane, studio of Michael Dahl, oil on canvas

There were other strings to Charles's bow. His application to the king for the Governorship of Hull apparently fell on deaf ears,[10] but he was appointed to the role at Sheerness from 1749 to 1752 and then at Gravesend and Tilbury from 1752 until his death. Each of these posts was strategically important to a maritime nation. Additionally, Charles was elected a Fellow of the Royal Society, founded in London in 1660 by King Charles II to promote science and recognize excellence in the field.[11] He was a contemporary there of Sir Isaac Newton, who was the society's president from 1703 to 1727 (Newton received his knighthood in 1705, the first British scientist to receive honours). It was not all discoveries and inventions – there was a strong social element:

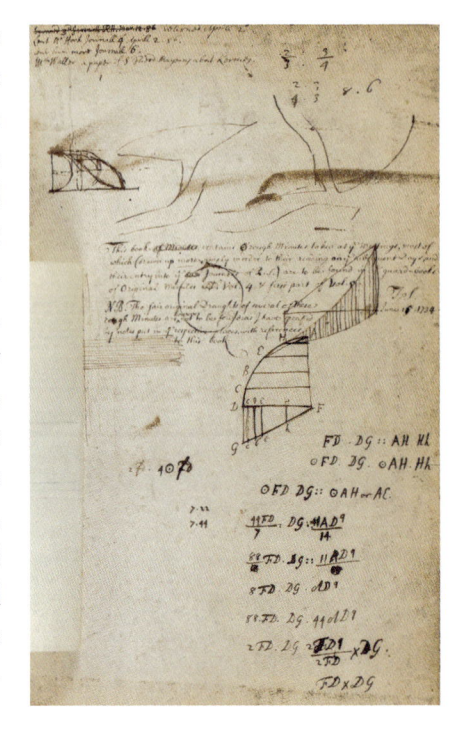

> The Fellows of the Royal Society, after the Fire [the Great Fire of London, 1666], held their anniversary dinner on November 30th, at the Crown tavern in Threadneedle Street; but for some cause, possibly more scientifically cooked viands, moved to the Pontack's Head; and in 1694, [John] Evelyn again records, 'We all dined at Pontack's as usual.' In 1731, a scarce tract, entitled 'The Metamorphoses of the Town', sufficiently attests the character of Pontack's as the resort at that period of extravagant epicures, and, in the bill of fare of 'a guinea ordinary,' figure 'a ragout of fatted snails,' and 'chickens not two hours from the shell.'[12]

ABOVE Draft minutes of the Royal Society, MS/575, 1684–86. A record of experiments, publications and natural curiosities sits alongside sketches and marginalia. The bulk was compiled by Sir Hans Sloane, who was Secretary 1693–1713 and President 1727–41. This page dates from Samuel Pepys's presidency.

Pontack's on Abchurch Lane, 'the celebrated French eating-house', was the venue for the Royal Society's dinners until 1746, and was frequented by luminaries from architect Sir Christopher Wren to satirist Jonathan Swift.[13] Following Sir Isaac Newton's term, the next president of the Royal Society was Sir Hans Sloane – owner of the Manor of Chelsea. It is not hard to imagine that the two men enjoyed a cross-generational friendship, cemented over well-lubricated dinners at Pontack's, no doubt further endearing Charles Cadogan to Sir Hans's daughter, Elizabeth. It was their marriage, on 25 July 1717 at the church of St George the Martyr, Holborn, that brought the Chelsea estate into the Cadogan family.

CHARLES'S INHERITANCE was a mixed blessing: William's death left huge debts to be settled. The Duke and Duchess of Richmond, already happily married for several years, finally ran out of patience and obtained a court order to ensure that her dowry of £60,000 was paid. Co-executors Charles, his cousin Lord Shelburne and fellow 'Old Westminster' Lord Carteret set about finding the money.

The lease on the house in Piccadilly was sold, together with its contents, in a public auction that took place over the course of a week. 'Three Dozen of Tea and other Napkins, and four Table Cloths'? Yours for £1,5s. After the lease itself at £105, the most expensive items were 'a State Coach, gilt and painted Panels and Sides, lin'd

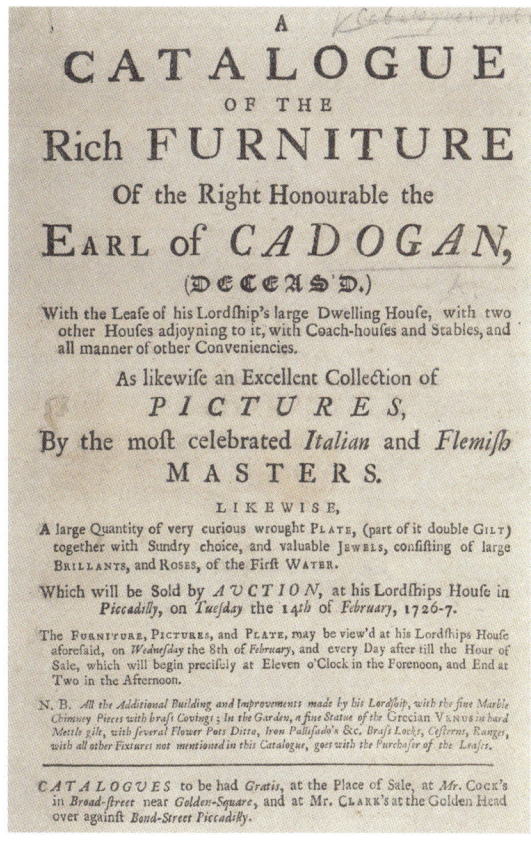

Catalogue of sale of the possessions of William, 1st Earl Cadogan, 1727. The catalogue uses the dual dating system showing both Julian (1726) and Gregorian (1727) calendars.

with crimson flower'd Velvet', at £52,10s. and a 'Green *Genoa* Velvet Bed, lin'd with a *French* silk and trim'd with rich lace', for £80. The 1st Earl Cadogan had amassed several large paintings by Rubens – including a *Bacchanal* noted as 'a capital Picture' – a Rembrandt, three Van Dycks, a Holbein, a Tintoretto and a Dürer. A separate sale was arranged for William's collection of jewels ('large brilliants'). Any sadness over selling off the family silver would have been softened by the knowledge that this was only one of several houses, and the Cadogans were perhaps sanguine about treasures that had only recently been acquired.

The new Lord Cadogan is recorded at his own London town house at 49 Albemarle Street in 1731. Next, for a period of twenty years, Charles and his wife Elizabeth lived at 17 Bruton Street (from 1742 to 1762). Two centuries later that house would be home to the Earl and Countess of Strathmore – maternal grandparents to Queen Elizabeth II, born there on 21 April 1926.[14] On leaving Bruton Street, Charles and Elizabeth made a final move, to 3 New Burlington Street. These are today's addresses; house numbering in London took time to take off from an idiosyncratic start at the turn of the eighteenth century and the system would not be standardized until the Metropolis Management Act (1855), 150 years later. Helpfully, some house names were retained, even in the capital city.

Chelsea House, also known in the latter part of Charles's life as Cadogan House, stood on the King's Road site now occupied by the Saatchi Gallery (the grand present building dates from the turn of the nineteenth century). Quite how it fitted in with the family's other property is unknown, as is the date of its construction. The benchmark *Victoria County History* describes its situation:

> The [area] of Gospelshot north and east of Garden Row up to King's Road…was the site of a mansion, stable and gardens, held with a parcel of leasehold meadow containing 6½ acres. The house was built by 1745, and by 1788 the leases belonged to Charles Lord Cadogan [3rd Baron]; the house was said to have been used by the Cadogan family in the 1770s.[15]

An exact survey of the cities of London and Westminster, the borough of Southwark, with the country near ten miles round (detail of four sheets), John Rocque, 1741–45, engraved by Richard Parr in 1746 and printed by W. Pratt, 1747. Chelsea is clearly marked in this survey created a decade before the manor passed through inheritance to Elizabeth, wife of Charles Cadogan, 2nd Baron Cadogan of Oakley.

Dating of the house here comes from Rocque's map of London (1741–45) and tells us only that it was already standing when, at that time, the Manor of Chelsea was owned by Charles's father-in-law.

YOUNG LADY CADOGAN evidently had a close relationship with her father. In a letter she wrote to him from Bath in 1738, addressed 'Dear Papa' and signed 'your Dutyfull and affectionate daughter', she describes taking the waters and mixing at the 'hot and crowding' Pump Rooms. Elizabeth's letter affirms the ongoing friendship the Cadogans enjoyed with the royal family.

> This place is very full, with very little good company, except what belongs to their Royal Highnesses. They are equally civil

The Duchess of York leaves 17 Bruton Street, home of her parents the Earl and Countess of Strathmore, where on 21 April 1926 she had given birth to her first child, the future Queen Elizabeth II (seen as a babe in arms). From *The Coronation Book of King George VI and Queen Elizabeth* (1937). The Georgian town house was home to Charles, 2nd Baron Cadogan, and his wife Elizabeth in the mid 18th century.

> to every body and play at cards in the publick rooms, without form and with their own family and attendants. The first night I appeared the Prince did me the honour to look for me and made abundance of fine speeches about Caussham [Caversham].[16]

'The Prince' is likely to have been Frederick, the Prince of Wales (1707–1751), father of George III. From Elizabeth's record of their conversation, we can surmise that Caversham had been graced by a royal visit. She also writes of fashionable curatives, a hot topic from her stay in Bath. Whether Elizabeth shared her father's interest, or her writing reveals a kind heart with her reader's ear in mind, she includes a fascinating vignette about contemporary medicine:

4. CUSTODIANS OF CAVERSHAM & CHELSEA

> His Highness told me he has sent for Cheney who ordered him to be blooded. He tasted his blood, then told him he was a glutton in eating tho' not in drinking, and many other things I have forgot; besides him there are 13 physicians settled here, 5 more accidental, in all 19 which Lord Chesterfield says is the reason the waters do no good, indeed the manner people drink them in, is ridiculous.[17]

This seems a healthy level of scepticism, informed perhaps by developments in scientific knowledge, not least at the Royal Society. Elizabeth is recorded elsewhere recommending an infusion of bark for the relief of fever – today we know that willow bark contains the same active ingredient as aspirin, salicin. She wrote to her Caversham neighbour:

> Lady Cadogan has known such wonderfull good effects from the enclosed Method of Infusing the Bark (so preferable to any Decoction) that she sends it to Mr Loveday wishing he would try this Prescription which has taken off many Feverish disorders that nothing else would relieve.[18]

The instructions were: infuse one ounce of Peruvian bark for forty-eight hours and add four teaspoons of brandy to the strained liquor; to be taken three times a day before meals.

ABOVE *Lady Cadogan (née Elizabeth Sloane)*, Sarah Stanley, 1725, bodycolour on card. This portrait by Elizabeth's sister shows the influence of court miniaturist Bernard Lens, from whom she probably had lessons. According to the inscription on the verso Elizabeth also painted, but sadly there is no record of her work.

The Early Eighteenth Century Pump Room, Henry Venn Lansdown, c.1855, watercolour

SIR HANS HAD BOUGHT THE MANOR OF CHELSEA from Charles Cheyne in 1712, when it included eleven houses, a selection of tenements and 166 acres. The estate was about three-quarters its size as recorded in the *Domesday Book*, when 'Cercehede', between the Rivers Thames and Bourne, comprised land for five ploughs and woodland for sixty pigs, worth in all £9 for Norman tax purposes. Parcels of land had been sold off prior to Sloane's acquisition, including the ground for the Royal Hospital; but he had added to his holding (a further ten acres) with the purchase of Beaufort House from the Duke of Beaufort in 1737. When he died in 1753, a venerable old man of ninety-two, Sir Hans bequeathed his estate to his daughters, in two moieties, or legal halves. Elizabeth and her older sister Sarah sold Henry VIII's manor house by the river almost immediately after their father's death and granted leases for six more houses on Cheyne Walk.[19] After that, for the next twenty years, under the gentle stewardship of Elizabeth – doubtless guided by her husband Charles, 2nd Baron – not much on the medieval site changed. A few houses were built to the west of Old Church Street, and the estate remained surrounded by fields.

Along with land holdings, at his death Sir Hans left a vast collection – 71,000 objects – of natural history specimens, books, coins and medals. These he bequeathed to King George II for the nation, in return for £20,000 to his heirs. An outstanding legacy of national importance, it formed part of the founding collections of both the British Museum and later the Natural History Museum. Charles, 2nd Baron, was a founding trustee of the British Museum, and Cadogan family members have been 'Sloane Trustee' there until very recent history. His observations on the museum's opening are a curious mixture of social awareness and the desire to run it like a gentlemen's club. His first suggestion was that hours of opening, restricted to May, June and July, should be further restricted to mornings only, as the museum would be staffed by volunteers with other jobs who would be unlikely to get more time off. The second was that rather than all visitors signing in and out, each trustee might have a stamp allowing entry to between one and five people under that trustee's name. The trustee would be the judge of the 'fitness of the persons he lends his own ticket to'.[20] The British Museum was established by Act of Parliament on 7 June 1753 and opened to the public – free to 'all studious and curious Persons' – on 15 January 1759, on the same site in Great Russell Street where it stands today. In the 1850s, Sir Richard Owen, a curator at the British Museum, convinced its board that a new building was needed to house its natural history collection, which was again running out of space. The Natural History Museum would open in South Kensington on 18 April 1881 in a building designed as 'a cathedral to nature'. Sir Hans's original specimen trays are preserved there amongst a collection now running to eighty million specimens.

These two major public institutions were not the only beneficiaries. Chelsea Physic Garden still enjoys lease conditions set by Sir Hans in 1721. Having studied there himself, he recognized its value as a seat of learning and offered it to the Society of Apothecaries at £5 a year in perpetuity. The only stipulation was that 'it be forever kept up and maintained as a physic garden' and that fifty plant specimens a year be delivered to the Royal Society until two thousand pressed and mounted species had been received.[21] They kept going at this rate until, by 1795, the total had reached 3,700.

THE GEORGIANS

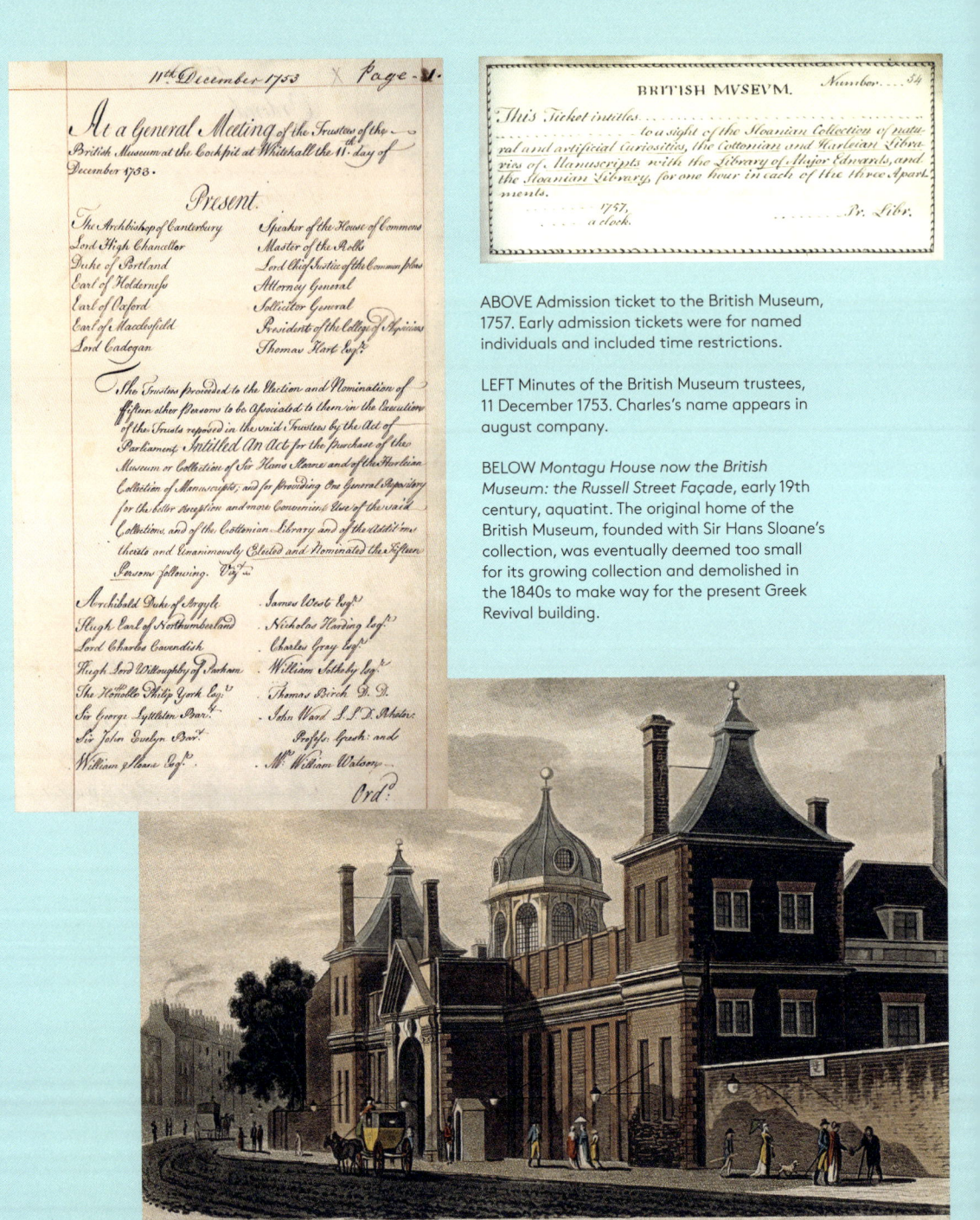

ABOVE Admission ticket to the British Museum, 1757. Early admission tickets were for named individuals and included time restrictions.

LEFT Minutes of the British Museum trustees, 11 December 1753. Charles's name appears in august company.

BELOW *Montagu House now the British Museum: the Russell Street Façade*, early 19th century, aquatint. The original home of the British Museum, founded with Sir Hans Sloane's collection, was eventually deemed too small for its growing collection and demolished in the 1840s to make way for the present Greek Revival building.

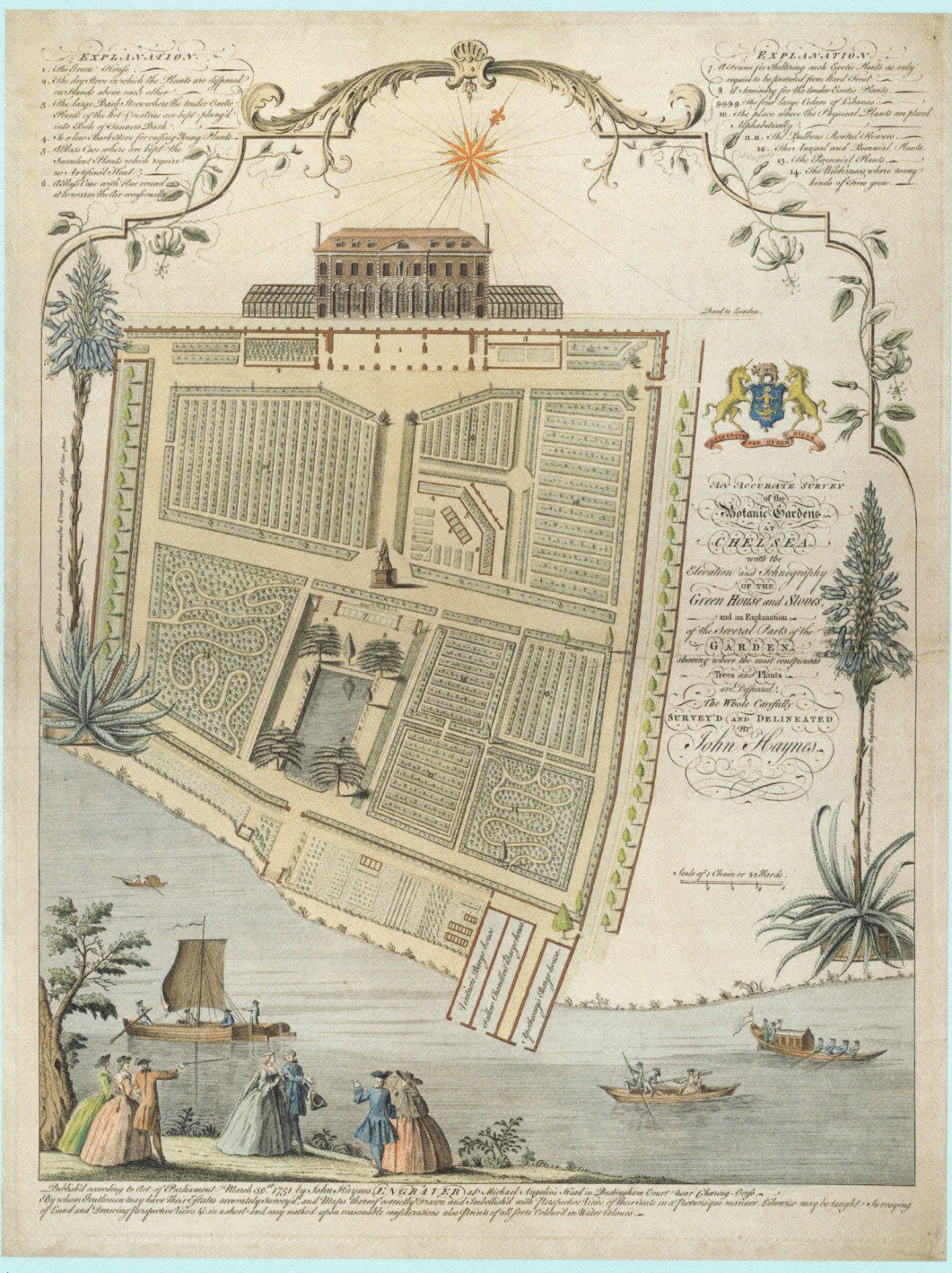

An accurate survey of the Botanic Gardens in Chelsea, John Haynes, 1751, engraving with watercolour

ABOVE *Map of the Estate and Manor of Chelsea in the County of Middlesex*, T. Richardson, Esq., London, 1769. The village of Chelsea is centred around Chelsea Old Church, the original river crossing over the Thames and the eastern border with Westminster at Blandel (Bloody) Bridge.

The Manor of Chelsea, 1753

	Diagonal & Cross Hatch	Sloane purchase from Cheyne 1712
	Straight Hatch	Sloane purchase from Beaufort 1737
	Cross Hatch only	Eventually the Sloane–Stanley Estate

RIGHT *The Manor of Chelsea, 1753*, Robert Pearman, 1986. Pearman's key overlays James Hamilton's *Map of Chelsea, Surveyed in the Year 1664*, continued to 1717 and published in London, 1810.

Not least, Sir Hans made a lasting contribution to the history of the Cadogan family and of Chelsea, via his legacy to his daughters. Elizabeth's will is the document that united the two:

> I give to my husband Charles Lord Cadogan the whole annual income of my half of the Chelsea Estate for his natural life subject to the two hundred pounds per annum settled by me (on Sir Hans Sloane's death) to make good my son Charles Sloane Cadogan's marriage settlement. I give unto my son Charles Sloane Cadogan (after Lord Cadogan's death) the income of my half of the Chelsea Estate for his natural life and after his death to his eldest son Charles Henry Cadogan and in case of his death without male issue to the next brother and in succession of seniority to all my son's children lawfully begotten.[22]

Elizabeth's younger grandchildren were given in trust a share of £3,130, to be divided equally. So began the centuries-old associations between Chelsea, the British Museum, the Natural History Museum, the Physic Garden and the Cadogan family. Elizabeth died in 1768.

CHARLES WAS FOCUSED on Caversham Park, their country home. He had secured its future when William died by buying it from his brother's estate (clearly, no longer a man 'of no great income'). The sweeping grandeur of William's vision was replaced by comfort and domesticity as Charles made the practical decision to reduce the size of the mansion to a family scale. A guidebook published in 1761 lists his priorities 'as less regarding the outward Glare of Magnificence than Use and Convenience'.[23] It was still remarkably beautiful and luxurious. The drawing room had a set of decorative wall-hangings by eminent Soho artisan Paul Saunders, including 'a pilgrimage to Mecca, the camels, horses, dogs amazingly well executed.'[24] Several examples of the pilgrimage survive, notably at Audley End, Petworth and Holkham Hall. Clearly, the Cadogans had the very latest in fashionable decor. And not everything was replaced in the redesign: the painting depicting William, 1st Earl Cadogan, as aide-de-camp to the Duke of Marlborough was now hung in the dining room. That was just the ground floor – there were twenty more rooms to enjoy on the first and second floors and the top floor housed a full retinue of staff. It must have had an air of permanence and stability. Ultimately, however, Caversham's days as a home to the Cadogan family would last only seventy years.

Charles wasn't entirely parsimonious when it came to the gardens, however, commissioning Lancelot 'Capability' Brown, to update the formal layout of parterres and canals. Brown was concurrently employed by the 4th Duke of Marlborough to landscape the grounds at Blenheim Palace, perhaps his most famous commission. Links between the two great families did not end with the deaths of the great military leaders of the Spanish War of Succession. Charles had lost the Manor of Oakley and other land in Buckinghamshire – a mansion house and some 373 acres of pasture – to the 1st Duke's widow, Sarah, Dowager Duchess of Marlborough, in 1730, and Churchills and Cadogans would be further entwined by more than one marriage in the years to come.

At Caversham, Brown created a lake, installed a walled kitchen garden and a dug a ha-ha; he also set out a winding approach to the lodge that lay south-east of the house, a trademark of his work. Part of his scheme included clearing thickets of bushes and trees that had surrounded the old gardens. According to the social diarist Mrs Lybbe Powys, of nearby Hardwick House, Oxfordshire, writing in 1776:

> Tho' we never have any friends at Hardwick that we don't take them to see Caversham Lodge, yet I've not here mentioned it, as I knew it was to undergo many alterations; those are nearly finished, and from always being a pleasing, 'tis now a very fine place, the situation beautiful, and these grounds laying out were the first performance of the since so celebrated Brown, who made a just tho' droll observation on the vast number of trees of an amazing growth all through the whole spot, 'that it was

impossible to see the trees for wood.' ...he has made it one of the finest parks imaginable...[25]

The house and gardens were quite the visitor attraction. Lady Mary Coke, another diarist and letter-writer, was equally impressed: 'Have you ever seen it? 'tis a very fine place, & the House a very good one; that is to say, the part of it they shew, which is only one floor. 'Tis finished & furnished with expence and taste.'[26] Cadogan family connections with the famous gardener would also be numerous. Between 1772 and 1774 he landscaped the 230-acre park at Paultons for Hans Stanley, Charles's nephew, while his son-in-law Henry Holland (who married Bridget Brown in 1773) worked on an ambitious proposal for the Cadogans' London estate. This would be the great legacy at the other end of Charles's long life.

'HANS TOWN' (NAMED IN HONOUR OF SIR HANS SLOANE) was laid out on eighty-nine acres of fields on the edge of London: the initial town planning that shaped the streets of Chelsea today. Negotiations had begun as early as 1770. Henry Holland's link with the man who had remodelled Caversham Park undoubtedly gave the Cadogans confidence in a designer who lacked formal training, in addition to his first commission, for the Whig hangout Brooks's Club in St James's Street. The seven-year negotiations over Hans Town span the final years of the elderly Charles, 2nd Baron, who reached his nineties, and the outbreak of the American War of Independence in 1775, in which two of his grandsons were sent to fight. While both these factors would have occupied the family's minds, perhaps the protracted process merely reflects the scale of such a visionary undertaking. It was a huge decision.

In 1776 the 2nd Baron died and his son Charles Sloane Cadogan (1728–1807), 3rd Baron Cadogan of Oakley, took the helm. The arrangement was finally agreed a year later, under an innovative system of ninety-nine-year leases that allowed architects to propose exciting new buildings while Cadogan would act as master planner and maintain a watchful eye.

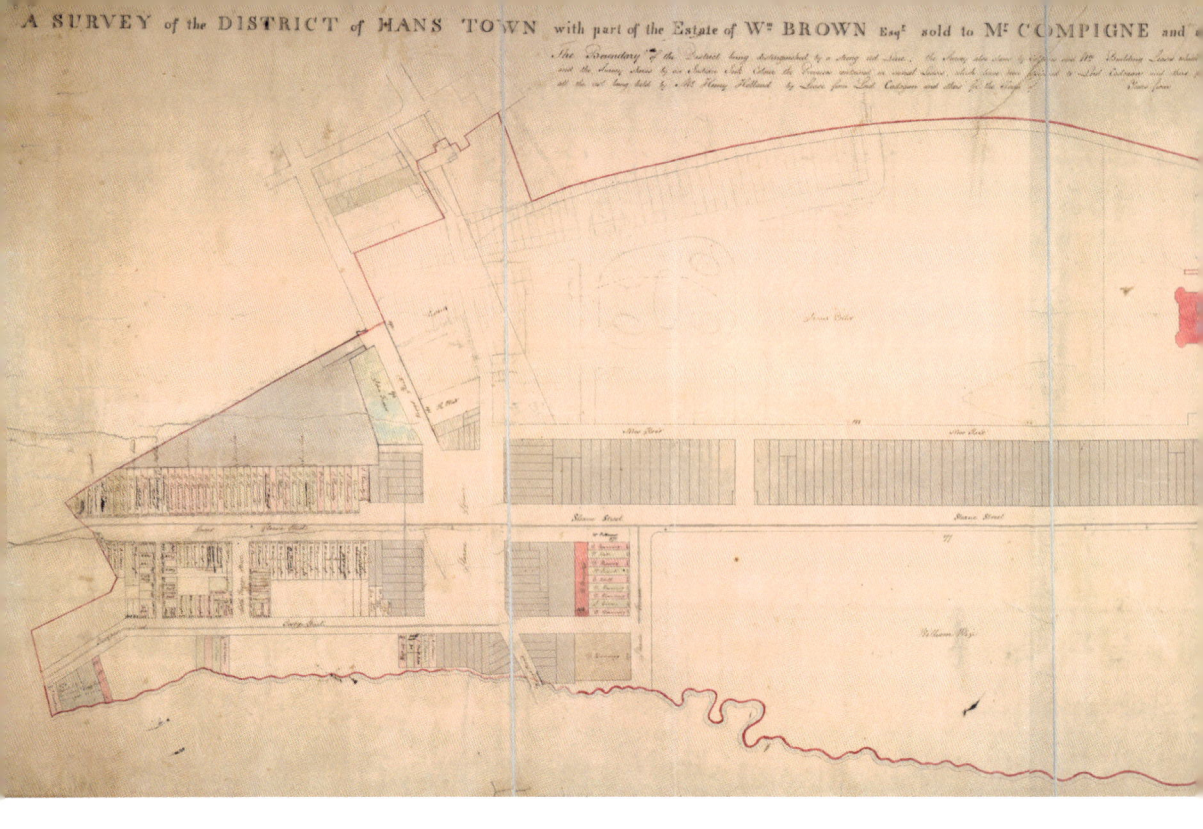

Work was carried out for the next two decades. Classic Georgian town houses – at the time, the very latest style: big windows, buildings two or three bays wide and three storeys tall (plus basement and attic) – lined the new boulevard Sloane Street, flowing into Hans Place, Hans Street and Hans Crescent in long, elegant terraces. Cadogan Place and Sloane Square took shape. The scheme gradually replaced the fields and market gardens between Knightsbridge to the north and Blacklands – what is now Turks' Row, behind the Saatchi Gallery – to the south with a new town catering to the emerging middle classes. Spacious houses were large enough for a family with a small staff, and for entertaining. The first were occupied by 1779 and Sloane Square was virtually complete within a year.

> Holland built a good many of the houses himself, but by 1780 such was the popular demand that he had had to sublet a number of plots to other developers, and within very few years Hans Town became one of the most fashionable areas in London.[27]

Henry Holland, John Opie, late eighteenth century, oil on canvas

Survey of the District of Hans Town (detail), 1770, pencil and ink on paper. Holland's original plan is a drawn survey, with the boundary of Hans Town outlined in red. Indian ink is used to indicate buildings on the Cadogan Estate, the rest of the buildings being held on a proposed lease from Cadogan. Gaps are left for completion with the number of years and price for the contract.

Hans Town was one of the first 'new towns' and became the model for many developments in central London during the construction boom of the late eighteenth and early nineteenth centuries (Camden Town, for example, was laid out in 1791).

Brown's gardens also passed into others' hands. Humphry Repton, an equally famous landscape gardener, worked on Cadogan Place. Fashions in garden design would come full circle: he reintroduced formal layouts including architectural terraces and flower beds, describing this scheme in his *Enquiry into the Changes of Taste in Landscape Gardening* (1806) as 'a new mode of treatment'.[28] By 1807 a plant demonstrator at Chelsea Physic Garden, William Curtis, had moved a nursery to Cadogan Place. Greenhouses filled with plants arranged by botanical classification covered its southern rectangle, which played host to concerts and lectures; in the

The Pavilion, Hans Place, Chelsea, London, Illustration from Thomas Faulkner, *An Historical and Topographical Description of Chelsea* (London, 1829), vol. 2

1820s the gardens were opened as a public promenade. While the greenhouses have now gone, today the gardens provide a much-needed green lung for local residents. Sadly, very few of Henry Holland's town houses survive untouched. Number 123 Sloane Street is the best example, sandwiched between more modern buildings.

Henry Holland built himself a rather grand mansion, Sloane Place, on the site south of Hans Place now occupied by Cadogan Square and the west end of Pont Street. It is remembered as 'the Pavilion', a sobriquet that nods to his commission, a decade later, to enlarge Brighton Pavilion for the Prince of Wales (future King George IV): his Chelsea house is seen as the advertisement that got him the job . Holland's 'General Plan' shows ample space for 'pig stys' and 'dung', together with a hen house, pigeon house, hot house and kitchen garden. Stabling, too, was essential, as horses still provided the main mode of transport, whether ridden or drawing carriages. His extensive gardens, occupying sixteen acres of the twenty-one-acre plot, were landscaped by his father-in-law (natch) and included a lake and an ice house – the very height of fashion – in the form of a ruined Gothic temple.

Improvements in lifestyle, such as this, reveal how the old class lines were blurring, as architectural historian Ellen Leslie observes:

> The eighteenth century saw a significant increase in the number of ice houses being constructed, mainly serving great manor houses and their estates…London of the 1700s experienced rapid growth including the construction of grand houses and villas, for new wealthy individuals. So it was during this period that what was once the preserve of royalty became accessible to the gentry and well-to-do.[29]

This was the Age of Reason, the full flourishing of the Enlightenment – equality, rationalism and progress were the watchwords. It was the age of Adam Smith's economic magnum opus *Wealth of Nations* (1776) and of Edward Gibbon's *History of the Decline and Fall of the Roman Empire* (1776–89). Old certainties were being called into question; old orders were being torn down. Across the pond, a new superpower was cutting the colonial apron strings. In France, Voltaire was arguing for the separation of Church and State, and for freedoms of speech and religion. While Henry Holland was building a folly by the sea for a decadent prince, over the Channel things were hotting up and an anti-monarchist revolution would soon break out. The Cadogans would again take to the world stage.

Back in Chelsea, Holland's timber-framed residence was demolished shortly after his death in 1806; its gardens were absorbed by later redevelopment. The site is commemorated in the name of Pavilion Road. Metal bollards at the corner of D'Oyley Street and Cadogan Place, and outside the Danish Embassy at 55 Sloane Street, mark the boundary of what was once Hans Town. The family had begun to shape Chelsea in a purposeful way that would safeguard its future: Charles and Elizabeth's only child had taken the helm and ushered in a new era. Perhaps this bold move encouraged him to act with courage in his family life. He had been a widower for over a decade; now with a title and a plan for the future, the time was ripe for him to find a new companion.

CHAPTER 5

Family Affairs

—

CHARLES SLOANE CADOGAN, 3RD BARON CADOGAN,
1ST VISCOUNT CHELSEA AND 1ST EARL CADOGAN
(NEW CREATION) (1728–1807)

The year 1777 has a double significance in the story of the Cadogan family. Charles Sloane Cadogan, a year after inheriting the barony, made two momentous decisions: as well as giving final approval to Henry Holland's proposal to lay out Hans Town in Chelsea, at forty-nine he decided to marry again. He was an active member of the House of Lords, with a town house in Whitehall and a country residence. In addition to the freehold of the Manor of Chelsea he held various juicy sinecures. He was a catch.

He had married his first wife, the Hon. Frances Bromley (1728–1768), daughter of Henry Bromley, 1st Baron Montfort, aged just nineteen, after Magdalen College, Oxford. This connection had led him directly into politics and a seat in the Commons for twenty years. Adopting Bromley family tradition, Charles Sloane Cadogan became the Whig MP for Cambridgeshire when he turned twenty-one. It also brought some turbulence.

Charles Sloane Cadogan, 3rd Baron Cadogan of Oakley and
1st Earl Cadogan of the New Creation (1728–1807),
Sir Joshua Reynolds, 1755, oil on canvas

OPPOSITE
The Hon. Mrs Cadogan
(née the Hon. Frances Bromley, 1728–1768),
Sir Joshua Reynolds, oil on canvas

Frances's father was a colourful figure. In 1741 he had reportedly bought his title for a sum settled with the Countess of Yarmouth, chief among the king's mistresses, under direction from Sir Robert Walpole.[1] At the end of 1754, he applied to the Prime Minister for some employment – the Governorship of Virginia, the fox hounds, or the first commissionership of trade – pressing for an immediate reply.

> 'I gave him the proper answers on every one', Newcastle wrote in his account of the interview, 'and asked him why he was so pressing…He was very reasonable but seemed dejected.' Next morning, 1 Jan. 1755, he sent for his lawyer, executed his will, inquired whether it would hold good even if he were to shoot himself, and on being told that it would went into the next room and blew his brains out. He left debts of £30,000, with an estate out of repair and in a very ruinous condition.[2]

Henry Bromley, 1st Baron Montfort of Horseheath and Whig MP, George Townshend, 1751/58, pen and ink. Frances's father was a member of one of the earliest cricket clubs, the London Cricket Club, and had a fondness for gambling.

Montfort had been keeping his financial difficulties – and an inveterate gambling habit – from those around him. 'His strange end surprised me a good deal, as he seemed as happy as a great taste for pleasure, and an ample fortune to gratify it could make him,' wrote Lady Hervey to a friend, a few days later.[3] Thomas Bromley, Frances's brother, became the 2nd Baron Montfort; having taken over the Cambridgeshire seat for a single year, he moved up to the House of Lords and returned it to Charles Sloane Cadogan.

Frances was undoubtedly unsettled both by her father's suicide and his perilous financial affairs. A year later, in 1756, her only daughter, Mary, died in infancy. The world at large was a place of uncertainty: a decade after the last Jacobite rebellion had been crushed at Culloden, the Seven Years' War pitted Great Britain and her Germanic allies against France and a coalition

5. FAMILY AFFAIRS

of Russia, Spain, Sweden and the remains of the Holy Roman Empire.[4] Worse was to come at home. Frances's mother-in-law Elizabeth died suddenly on 20 May 1768, 'being hurried away by a dropsy and asthma'.[5] The younger woman never recovered. Frances died on 25 May:

> I inquired of the Maid who shew'd us the House what occasion'd her death, & She told me it was intirely owing to the shock of Her Mother in law's death, that She was never well from that moment, & went quite distracted. At the end of four days She dyed raving mad. 'Tis the more particular as they never were thought to live in any friendship with each other, but then Ly Cadogan died extremely sudden, & perhaps She was present...[6]

Lady Mary Coke, who recorded this vivid description of Frances's last days while visiting a couple of months later, was a notorious gossip; her account of any strain between the two women may be mere repetition of rumour. She also noted that Frances left her husband richer by the interest on 'four score thousand' pounds for life – a fortune – entailed to their descendants.[7] Mr Loveday, who had received the benefit of Elizabeth's bark-infused brandy, recorded her death more prosaically: 'the apprehension of my lady's death caused hysterics; then, a delirium; she died, however, of a putrid fever.'[8] The two ladies of Caversham, Lady Cadogan (Elizabeth) and Mrs Charles Sloane Cadogan, were buried together in the family vault at St Peter's Church.

LEFT Flagon, St Peter's Church, Caversham, 1754. One of three pieces of communion silverware gifted by Lady Cadogan, it is still in use today. BELOW Inscription detail

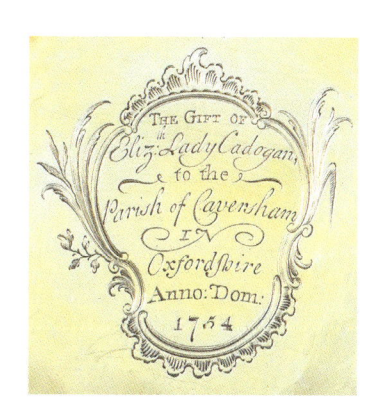

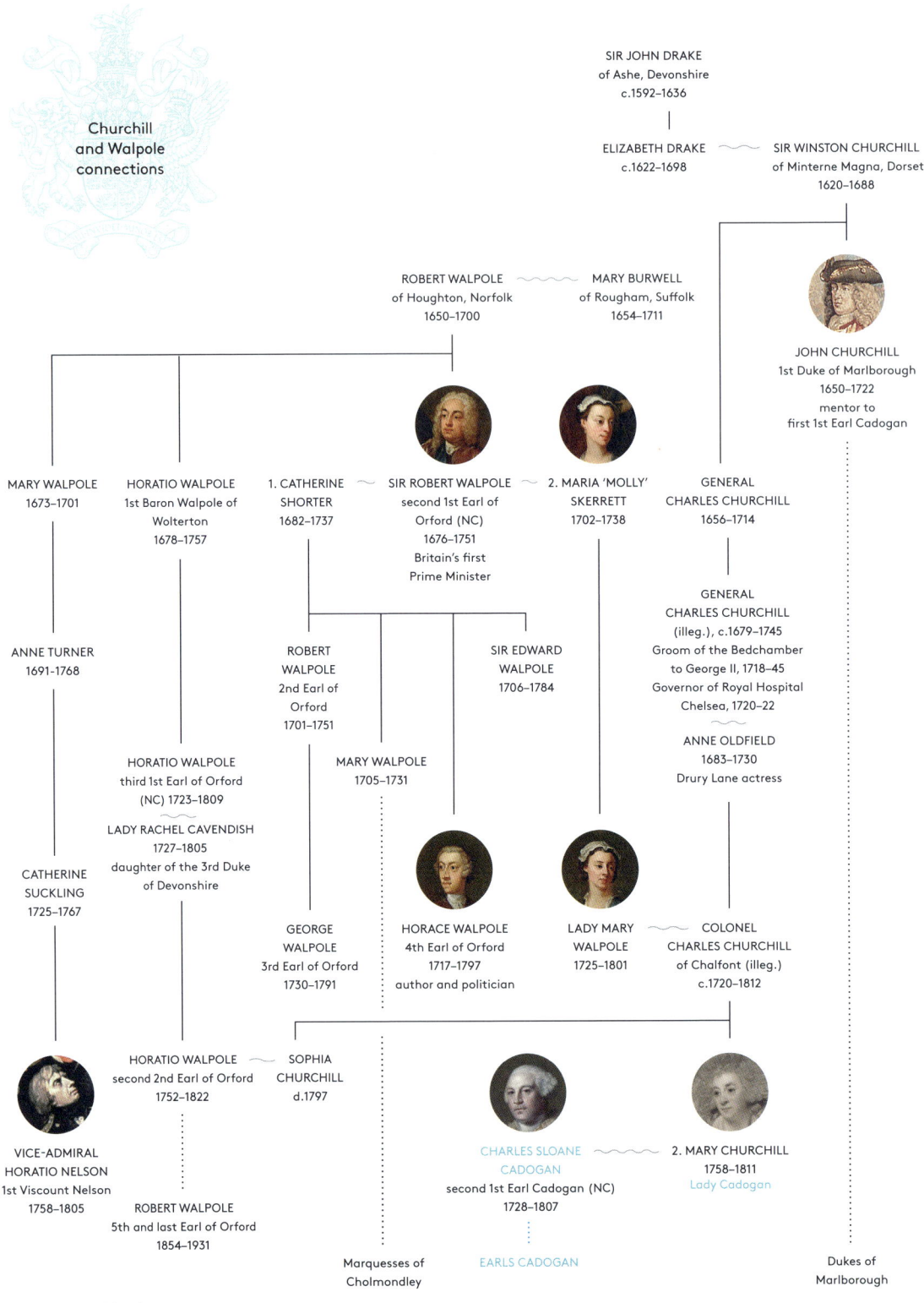

Churchill and Walpole connections

Abridged family tree

SIR JOHN DRAKE
of Ashe, Devonshire
c.1592–1636

ELIZABETH DRAKE ~ **SIR WINSTON CHURCHILL**
c.1622–1698 | of Minterne Magna, Dorset
1620–1688

ROBERT WALPOLE ~ **MARY BURWELL**
of Houghton, Norfolk | of Rougham, Suffolk
1650–1700 | 1654–1711

JOHN CHURCHILL
1st Duke of Marlborough
1650–1722
mentor to
first 1st Earl Cadogan

MARY WALPOLE
1673–1701

HORATIO WALPOLE
1st Baron Walpole of
Wolterton
1678–1757

1. CATHERINE SHORTER ~ **SIR ROBERT WALPOLE** ~ **2. MARIA 'MOLLY' SKERRETT**
1682–1737 | second 1st Earl of Orford (NC) 1676–1751 Britain's first Prime Minister | 1702–1738

GENERAL CHARLES CHURCHILL
1656–1714

ANNE TURNER
1691–1768

ROBERT WALPOLE
2nd Earl of Orford
1701–1751

SIR EDWARD WALPOLE
1706–1784

GENERAL CHARLES CHURCHILL
(illeg.), c.1679–1745
Groom of the Bedchamber
to George II, 1718–45
Governor of Royal Hospital
Chelsea, 1720–22

HORATIO WALPOLE
third 1st Earl of Orford
(NC) 1723–1809
~
LADY RACHEL CAVENDISH
1727–1805
daughter of the 3rd Duke
of Devonshire

MARY WALPOLE
1705–1731

ANNE OLDFIELD
1683–1730
Drury Lane actress

CATHERINE SUCKLING
1725–1767

GEORGE WALPOLE
3rd Earl of Orford
1730–1791

HORACE WALPOLE
4th Earl of Orford
1717–1797
author and politician

LADY MARY WALPOLE
1725–1801
~
COLONEL CHARLES CHURCHILL
of Chalfont (illeg.)
c.1720–1812

VICE-ADMIRAL HORATIO NELSON
1st Viscount Nelson
1758–1805

HORATIO WALPOLE ~ **SOPHIA CHURCHILL**
second 2nd Earl of Orford | d.1797
1752–1822

CHARLES SLOANE CADOGAN ~ **2. MARY CHURCHILL**
second 1st Earl Cadogan (NC) | 1758–1811
1728–1807 | Lady Cadogan

ROBERT WALPOLE
5th and last Earl of Orford
1854–1931

Marquesses of
Cholmondley

EARLS CADOGAN

Dukes of
Marlborough

Sir Robert Walpole with his Family and Friends, Charles Jervas and John Wootton, c.1738, oil on canvas. Sir Robert is in the centre with Maria Skerrett (seated); behind them stand Lady Cadogan's mother, Lady Mary Churchill (née Walpole), and Uncle Horace.

IN 1777 THE 3RD BARON CADOGAN of Oakley caught the eye of nineteen-year-old Mary Churchill (1758–1811), a bright spot of both French and English society. '*On la trouve jolie, et qu'elle ressemble en beau à notre Dauphine* [Marie Antoinette],' wrote society hostess Madame du Deffand. '*Elle a eu la meilleure education du monde; elle est attentive, obligeante, elle a de la gaîté, de la grâce.*'[9] The Marquise was writing to Horace Walpole, Whig MP, art historian, man of letters – and Mary's uncle. The bride brought not only her own personal charm to the match but connections to two prominent families.

Anyone who thinks their ancestors were prudes is in for a shock. While order of birth within marriage was a crucial determinant of inheritance and status, illegitimate children abounded, as did lovers and liaisons. Indeed, peerages have been created specifically to recognize such situations – though not in the case of the Cadogan family. The new Lady Cadogan held the curious distinction of descent from illegitimacy on both sides and on one side for two generations. Several members of the family shared names, so reference to a family tree becomes invaluable. Colonel Charles Churchill (c.1720–1812), her father, was born to forty-something General Charles Churchill (c.1679–1745) by his mistress Anne Oldfield (1683–1730), a leading actress with the theatre company at Drury Lane and perhaps the source of Mary's allure. 'Ample testimony is borne to Mrs. Oldfield's beauty, vivacity, and charm, and to the excellence of her acting.'[10] Anne inherited a considerable sum from the father of her first illegitimate child (both men were named Arthur Mainwairing), and at her own death was thus able to leave her younger son, Charles, a house in Grosvenor Street. In turn, Mary's paternal grandfather was himself illegitimate, son of his namesake General Charles Churchill (1656–1714) by a lady whose identity is unrecorded – too scandalous, perhaps! General Churchill senior was a legitimate younger son of the first Sir Winston Churchill, MP (1620–1688), and his wife Elizabeth Drake (of the same family as Sir Francis Drake), and brother to the 1st Duke of Marlborough. The Churchill connection might perhaps be more accurately described as a reconnection, given Marlborough's close ties with William, first 1st Earl Cadogan.

Astonishingly, the mother of the bride, Lady Mary Churchill (née Walpole, 1725–1801), was also an illegitimate child. Her father was Sir Robert Walpole (1676–1745), occupant of number 10 Downing Street from 1735. After his first wife died, in 1737, he waited a scant few months before marrying Lady Mary's mother Maria 'Molly' Skerrett (1702–1738), his mistress of many years. Installed by Walpole first at the Old Lodge, Richmond Park, she had also lived with him at his house on Paradise Row in Chelsea – somewhat improbably accessed through the stable yard of the Royal Hospital.[11] Molly was widely accepted in society as his consort while his first wife was alive, even received by Queen Caroline. Sadly, she died the year after becoming Lady Walpole, following a miscarriage, and was buried at the family seat, Houghton Hall in Norfolk.[12] When Sir Robert was created Earl of Orford, on his effective retirement from politics in 1742, he legitimized Lady Mary as his daughter with a patent of rank and precedence granted by King George II, so she married Colonel Charles Churchill as a genuine catch. The Churchills and Walpoles continued to intermingle: it is interesting to note that the new Lady Cadogan's sister, Sophia Churchill, married her second cousin Horatio Walpole, 2nd Earl of Orford (New Creation); also, that Mary Churchill's Walpole connection brought Horatio, Viscount Nelson (1758–1805), into the Cadogan family as a second cousin once removed.

WHAT OF THE SEVEN CHILDREN from Charles Sloane's first marriage? We know most about his eldest two boys, Charles Henry Sloane Cadogan, heir apparent, and William Bromley Cadogan the clergyman (to whose stories we will come), but the other five? Sadly, not a single portrait is known to survive. Two died as children (Mary, 1756, and Henry, 1761–74), but another three lived beyond their teens: Thomas, George and Edward. They were not present at their father's union with Mary Churchill because all were on active duty in the military – as mentioned, two of them were fighting in the American War of Independence (1775–83).

Edward, the youngest, had chosen the British Army and was a captain of the 49th Regiment of Foot. The regiment embarked for Newfoundland and, having arrived in Boston, fought in battles throughout 1776 and 1777. After sailing for the West Indies the following year, their final engagement during the revolutionary war took place that December at the Battle of St Lucia, a triumph for the British over the French Navy. Victorious in battle, Edward Cadogan (1758–1779) was defeated by yellow fever eight months before reaching his majority: the first of the three military brothers to die. It is likely he is buried in the former military cemetery at Praslin on St Lucia.[13] Today yellow fever is controlled by vaccination and insect repellent, and many can ward off its worst effects with good hydration

The arrival of an English officer at Indian docks, c.1820, print. George Cadogan fought in Madras with the British East India Company.

and a packet of paracetamol; but in the late eighteenth century there were few defences against an infection spread by mosquito bite. Its onset was sudden, developing from a headache, fever and vomiting to jaundice (the yellowing from where it gets its name), bleeding from the mouth, nose and eyes, organ failure, shock and death in a matter of days. Twenty years after Edward's death, in the year to April 1796, some 6,500 white troops out of 16,000 in the West Indies died of sickness, mostly victims of yellow fever.[14] That's forty per cent.

George, like Edward, was a soldier. The army he joined rivalled the British Army in size but was privately owned by the East India Company. Since incorporation by royal charter, under Queen Elizabeth I, the company's role had gradually changed from trade in commodities including spices, tea and silk to defence and control of territory as a political agent. This led to effective rule in India from the mid-eighteenth century, before the formal establishment of the British Raj. George sailed to India on the *Horsenden*, disembarking at Madras. There, he was felled accidentally by his own side, likely during the defeat of Colonel Baillie's division of the Madras Army.

George Cadogan (1754–1780) lost his life in his mid-twenties, killed by 'a random shot from our lines while he was reconnoitring'.[15]

Thomas had joined the Royal Navy. Aged eighteen he received an officer's commission, as acting second lieutenant, on 26 July 1770, and via HMS *Mercury*, *Ferret*, *Achilles*, *Diana* and *Antelope*, was promoted to his first command, on HMS *Porcupine*. In 1779 he captained HMS *Licorne* off Newfoundland, with Lieutenant Edward Pellew on board – Pellew would later feature prominently in the career of Thomas's half-brother, another George. Thomas was in his fifth month as captain of HMS *Glorieux*, captured from the French at the Battle of the Saintes, when she was caught in the Central Atlantic hurricane off the Grand Banks of Newfoundland on the night of 16/17 September 1782. It was a disaster. Together with the *Ville de Paris* (another lucrative prize from Saintes), HMS *Centaur* (herself previously French), British-built HMS *Ramillies* and a host of merchant craft, the fleet under the command of Admiral Thomas Graves foundered. The *Ville de Paris* and *Centaur* sank (just twelve men surviving from the latter); the *Ramillies* was damaged and later destroyed. The *Glorieux* was seen sailing without foremast, bowsprit or main top-mast;[16] Captain Thomas

A View of the Sea on the Morning after the Storm, with the distressed situation of the Centaur, Ville de Paris and the Glorieux as seen from the Lady Juliana…, Robert Dodd, engraving, after unknown artist, published by John Harris, Robert Sayer & John Bennett, 17 February 1783. An Atlantic hurricane cost many lives on the night of 16/17 September 1782, including Thomas Cadogan's.

Cadogan (1752–1782) went down with his ship at the age of thirty, all hands lost.[17] What tremendous bad luck it must have seemed to the boys' father, to lose all three military sons unmarried and apparently childless, and not one to enemy action.

THERE IS A CODA TO THOMAS'S STORY. A bundle of old papers found among Chelsea Physic Garden documents, and now stored in the Cadogan family's archive, provides the bare bones of what looks to modern eyes like a human tragedy. The first letter is from Thomas Cadogan himself, dated July 1782, addressed to 'Mr William Leith, at his boarding school, Little Chelsea, London'. Its contents show that his line might not have died with him:

> As I have not the pleasure of being personally known to you: I have requested of my friend Mr Morgan to recommend a young namesake and relation of mine to your care…As I have his welfare much at heart…and request your protection and care of this young gentleman's education till my arrival, and beg you will be so good to address Messrs Ommaney and Page [Navy Agents, 10] America Square, London, for any expenses incurred till I have the pleasure of seeing you.[18]

This letter was written only two months before his death; but to answer the questions it raises, we look back a decade, to September 1772, when Thomas arrived in Jamaica for four months on *Achilles*. There he moored in Port Royal, 'employed watering and stowing the hold', before his promotion to second lieutenant on *Diana*.[19] Five years later – the historic year his father approved the Hans Town plan and married his stepmother – Thomas was back in the Caribbean in March, taking command of the sloop *Porcupine*; and during 1781 he served again on the Jamaica station. His adventures during this time included being struck by lightning.[20] Correspondence from one Kingston-based Jane Frazer (or Fraiser, or Frasier; she uses all these spellings), 'a woman of mixed ancestry',[21] states clearly that he also fathered a son: Thomas 'Tom' or 'Tommy' Cadogan. Appealing to the family after

5. FAMILY AFFAIRS

One of Tom's letters to schoolmaster Mr William Leith, Esq, Paradise Row, Chelsea, sending love to 'all Chelsea Friends'

her lover's death, Jane wrote to his older brother, the Reverend William Bromley Cadogan, in 1783:

> It was always his intention to send our dear boy to your protection and I am to hope you will consider my unhappy situation and shew him your countenance for his support. 'Tis very natural to suppose Mr Leith will require payment [for] his existence which if you will order I shall be ever obliged…My whole dependence was on Capt Cadogan whose intention was to settle an annuity upon me and our child…I think it is my duty to address you instead of His Lordship and must [fall] on your Humanity for the support of [this] child not being in my power to provide for him as the Son of my Dear Capt Cadogan.[22]

William dutifully wrote to Mr Leith: there would be a delay in payment of school fees and Cadogan family support. Part of the reason given was that his father, Charles Sloane, was out of the country.

> ...I should have wrote to him however had not my eldest brother [Charles Henry] told me that he was apprized of the circumstance and meant to do something in it as soon as poor Captain Cadogan's affairs are settled, but there is at present a lawsuit about some prize money, which I believe hinders the settlement of them.[23]

Prize money was paid by the Admiralty for captured enemy ships and the large sums involved frequently led to legal disputes over the correct share. Thomas had enjoyed success almost immediately upon taking command of the *Licorne*. His scalps of 1779 included the privateer *Audacieuse* and the *General Sullivan*.[24] Acting in support of Captain William Waldegrave (commanding *La Prudente*), he also shared in the capture of the frigate *Capricieuse* on 5 July 1780.[25]

Nothing happened. Jane wrote twice to Tommy's schoolmaster the following year. 'I am under much concern until I hear of Capt Cadogan's family patronizing my child.' She waited a few months before sending her next letter: 'I propose writing Lord Cadogan and his son the clergyman by the next packet. The family having got such a large [sum] of fortune by the untimely death of the dear Father, may, I hope, be induced to take some notice of the son.' Jane Frazer is last heard asking the school to place her son in business.[26] Perhaps the Cadogans were wisely wary of letters from the other side of the world claiming dependency; who knows how many others they received.

Young Tommy, mercifully, had thrived in Chelsea and found in Mr Leith a substitute father figure. In February 1797 he set sail for the Cape of Good Hope on board the *Sir Edward Hughes*, writing back:

> My Father's family I now consider as nothing to me, therefore was induced to accept this under the pleasing and consolatory hope that a Gracious Providence had pointed it out for me... I am very sorry that the balance of my education is not discharged...I will do my utmost myself...to that desirable end.[27]

Panorama of Cape Town (detail), Lady Anne Barnard, c.1797–1802, watercolour

Tom would have to make his own way. The Cape was a disputed colony during the Napoleonic Wars, passing through Dutch, French and British hands, and Tom, classed as a 'free mustee' on his arrival in 1800,[28] soon found a position as a secretary in the Office for Prisoners of War. He wrote to Mr Leith, the 'country is delightful'; you 'hardly see a poor man'; the 'manner of living of the inhabitants is in great style'. He set up in the import/export business and soon met the sharp end when 'a combination of Dutch rascals (excuse the term)' refused to pay for goods they had ordered, 'to the amount of upwards of £5,000'.[29] Tom took his case to court and won back the full amount plus interest. From there he built on success – and his view of the Dutch mellowed. On 6 November 1808, Tom married Sophia Bergh at the Dutch Reform Church in Cape Town. They settled at 2 Keizergacht (now Darling Street) and had several children, of whom a son (also named Thomas Charles Cadogan, 1810–1896), and two daughters (Sophia and Jane) survived to adulthood. Tom died at fifty-two a 'well-known merchant', drowned at sea on the treacherous trade route from Table Bay to Port Elizabeth, on 7 October 1829.[30]

THE SADNESS OF BURYING three adult children – Edward, George and Thomas – in quick succession aside, during the early years of their marriage Charles Sloane and Mary 'lived affectionately and happily together'.[31] The nursery at Caversham was noisy again with a second family as his new wife

THE GEORGIANS

'My niece's match with Lord Cadogan, since she herself approves it, gives me great satisfaction. She is one of the best and most discreet young women in the world, and her husband, I am sure, is fortunate.'

HORACE WALPOLE, 1777

OPPOSITE
Lady Cadogan (née Mary Churchill, 1758–1811), John Dean after Sir Joshua Reynolds (1786), 1787, mezzotint

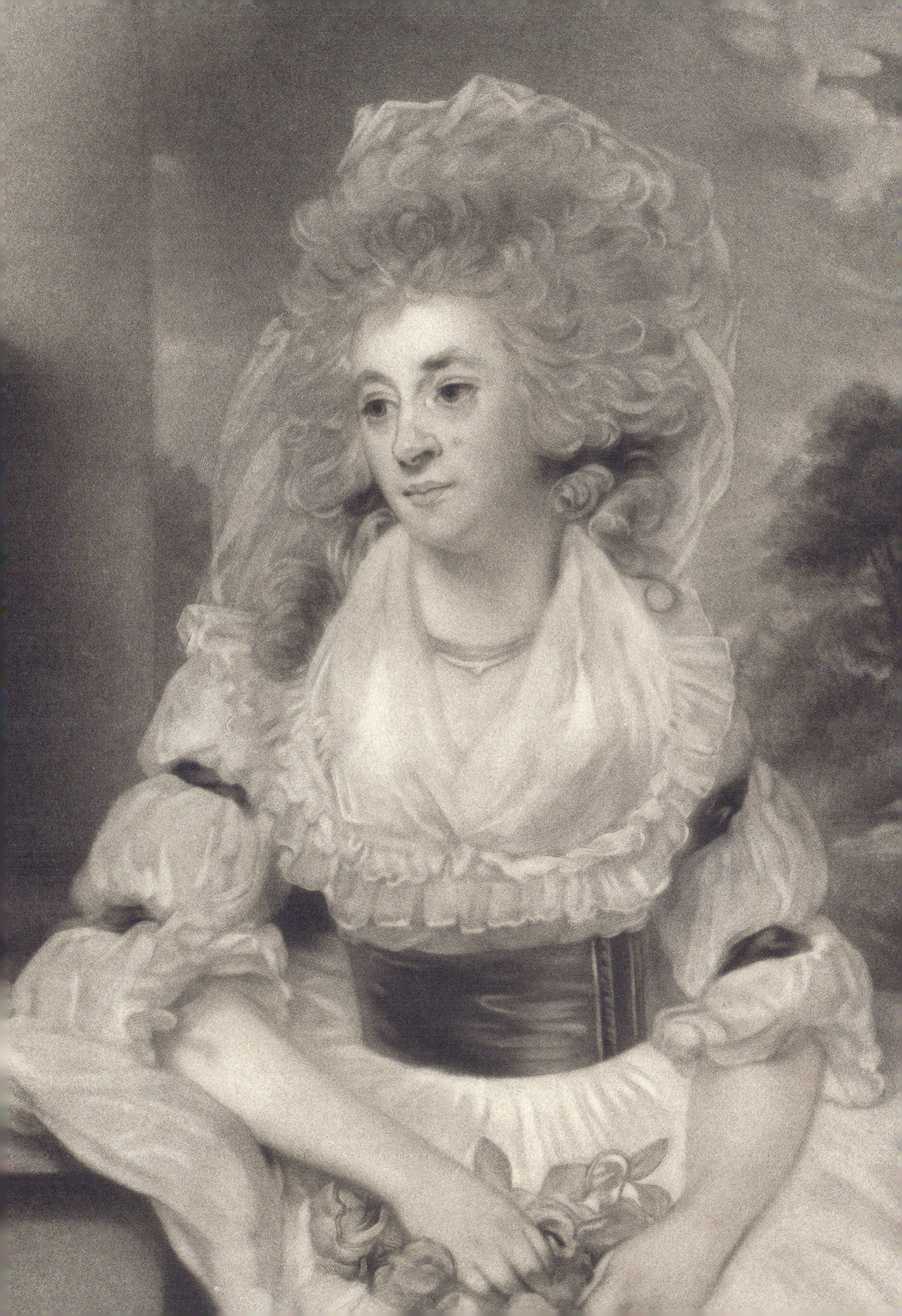

Downham Hall, Santon Downham, postcard. Downham was at risk of disappearing into the sands of Suffolk. Surprisingly little is known about such a large building and few photographs or plans survive; though records show that new tree plantations were soon established after it came into Cadogan hands in 1785. It is likely that Charles Sloane replaced or remodelled the previous house on the site to create this Georgian iteration.

bore him four babies: Emily (b.1778), Henry (b.1780), Charlotte (b.1781) and another George (b.1783). In 1777 Horace Walpole had written, 'My niece's match with Lord Cadogan, since she herself approves it, gives me great satisfaction. She is one of the best and most discreet young women in the world, and her husband, I am sure, is fortunate.'[32] Witnesses would later bear testimony to Mary's fidelity 'in the days of her beauty, in the days of her health...the breath of slander never tainted her character'.[33] But by 1785 the marriage was in trouble. Charles Sloane took drastic action and moved the family to Downham Hall, on the Suffolk–Norfolk border, selling Caversham to an illegitimate grandson of King George I, seemingly on a whim:

> In consequence of some unhappy connubial events…[Cadogan] sold land, house, furniture wine in the cellar, and, if we are to credit report, the very roast beef on the spit, to Major Marsac, for a sum of money one day before dinner.[34]

The sum of money has been estimated at £100,000.[35] The Cadogans' new home at Santon Downham held the pleasures of fishing and shooting, though it lacked the charm of Caversham. Diarist Mrs Lybbe Powys, writing in 1781, was less than complimentary this time:

> …near here is the new purchase of our Oxfordshire neighbour, Lord Cadogan, called Sandy Downham; indeed, nothing but sand is visible – no tree, or hardly a bush… But for his Lordship to sell so beautiful a spot as Caversham Park to purchase the above dreary wild spot is certainly beyond one's ideas.[36]

Even making the journey was treacherous, in the days of carriages and before the invention of tarmacked roads: 'for about thirteen miles, deep sand over the horses' hoofs', for which the solution was to mix the sand with chalk.[37] Charles Sloane was taking a literal approach in making it difficult for his wife to receive visitors.

Having made the move, from 1787 he also leased the Jacobean red-brick Merton Hall nearby in Norfolk. We might speculate that perhaps Mary lived in one house and he in the other. (Neither Merton nor Downham survives in a state the pair would recognize. Downham was demolished by the Forestry Commission in 1923; of Merton only the original gatehouse and later north-east wing of 1846 stand, the rest having been destroyed by fire in 1954.) Relations, if not improved, certainly continued along conjugal lines. A daughter named Sophia died in infancy in 1786. Later that year Mary sat for a portrait by Sir Joshua Reynolds, the first president of the Royal Academy of Art (founded by King George III in 1768), in which she appears wistful and preoccupied. Another daughter, Louisa, followed in 1787 and her youngest, Edward, was born in 1789.

Five years later, it was over. Charles Sloane sued his wife for 'criminal conversation' – adultery – with Reverend William Henry Cooper, eldest son of Sir Grey Cooper, their neighbour in Suffolk and fellow parliamentarian. Closer in age to Mary than her husband, Cooper was a teenager and she not yet thirty when the Cadogans arrived in the county (Charles Sloane was by then in his late sixties). By the time of the trial, Cooper was married with three young children; having left a brief career in the 3rd Foot Guards he was training for a life in the Church and had secured a position as a prebendary of Rochester Cathedral. The death of his father-in-law, insolvent, had left the young couple obliged to sell their house in Hanover Square and thus, at the start of their acquaintance, Charles Sloane had invited them to Upper Grosvenor Street, 'his house, which was perpetually open to them. He endeavoured by all means to console this family in their affliction, and held out the arm of friendship.'[38] Intimacy between the two families increased as the Cadogans divided their time between country pursuits at Downham and the delights of the London season.

The transcript of the trial, which took place before a jury in 1794, provides a glimpse of daily life in a large London house at the turn of the nineteenth century. Conducting an affair under the noses of a full retinue of staff required subterfuge to a level bordering on the comic. Detailed witness testimony from a housemaid reveals second staircases, spying and the invention of mundane errands to distract staff from their usual posts:

> There was in Lord Cadogan's house, what is called a well-staircase. A person could see from the top to the bottom of it... In the passage leading to her own room, there was an open place, from which she could look down on the stone staircase. There were then three men in the hall; one of the chairmen; Joseph Price, the under-butler, and James Chapman, her Ladyship's own footman; and these three persons were disposed of in this manner by Farley Bull—The chairman was sent out with a note to Lady Churchill; Chapman was sent down to the kitchen with a china dish and a chicken on it to warm; and Price was sent after

> Chapman to get some of the broth in which the chicken had been boiled. The coast being thus clear, Farley Bull immediately came down the stone stairs, and looking towards the passage, she said, Hem! Hem! twice, aloud. She was looking towards the other stairs, where, if any body had been coming, she must have seen them...the witness saw Mr. Cooper run down the stone stairs very quick...[39]

Mrs Farley Murray Bull, Mary's personal maidservant, did not appear in court to defend herself or her mistress, which stood neither in good stead. The prosecution emphasized the importance of Christian family values for the good of society against Reverend Cooper's apparent abandonment of these and his betrayal of Charles Sloane's generosity. Mary's guilt was portrayed as the result of 'some peculiar seduction.'[40] A conviction secured, the cuckolded husband was awarded £2,000 in damages, which Cooper was unable to pay. The lovers fled for the countryside. 'The pair were not hard to follow, since Mary cut an unusual figure, carrying a birdcage with two bullfinches in it, and they were soon tracked down to the Angel Inn in Abergavenny.'[41] Two years later, Charles Sloane was granted a 'Definite Sentence of Divorce', which he followed with a Private Act of Parliament (passed in 1797) that dissolved the marriage while crucially retaining the legitimacy of the children.[42] Divorce was still highly unusual – there were only 131 divorces in England in the entire eighteenth century – and was largely the preserve of the aristocracy and gentry.[43] It was certainly scandalous.

Mary abandoned England for the Churchill holiday home in Nancy, north-eastern France, where she died at the age of fifty-three. The Reverend Sir William Henry Cooper, who succeeded to the baronetcy following the death of Sir Grey in 1801, is recorded 'detained as a prisoner' (perhaps still for non-payment of the £2,000) in January 1812, when his brother Frederick was appointed executor to prove Mary's will in his absence. The will contained financial bequests to Cooper, her loyal servants and 'unto my beloved and much injured child Edward Cadogan in case he shall not be provided for by his father Lord Cadogan.'[44]

ON 27 DECEMBER 1800 Charles Sloane Cadogan, 3rd Baron Cadogan of Oakley, was elevated to 1st Earl Cadogan and Viscount Chelsea, in a new creation of the earldom.[45] (To recap: all but one of the peerages created for his Uncle William, 1672–1726, right-hand man to the Duke of Marlborough, had died with him.) And so, a second 1st Earl Cadogan gave the family another chance for the title in perpetuity, through direct 'heirs male of his body'. It was a reward for many years of service in public life: Charles Sloane had worked at the Palace of Westminster for half a century. He was noted by Lord Rockingham in 1766, as 'among the "Swiss", i.e. those prepared to serve any Administration,'[46] though for many years he displayed unswerving loyalty in one direction. His Commons voting record closely matched the interests of Prince Edward, the Duke of York (for whom he was Keeper of the Privy Purse, 1756–67), until the prince's death freed him to vote as he liked – '[h]enceforth he is never found voting against the Government.'[47] This pattern remained constant despite changes in

Pitt addressing the House of Commons, Karl Anton Hickel, 1793–95, oil on canvas.
Pitt the Younger was Britain's youngest ever Prime Minister, just twenty-four when appointed. Charles Sloane Cadogan's unwavering support for Pitt in the Lords saw him elevated to 1st Viscount Chelsea and (second) 1st Earl Cadogan.

successive governments during the last decade of his ministerial career, which saw three Prime Ministers: William Pitt the Elder (Whig, 1766–68); the 3rd Duke of Grafton (Whig, 1768–70); and finally Lord North (Tory, 1770–82). Sitting in the Lords was by no means the end of his involvement in politics; under the British parliamentary system the upper chamber has a vote that can block or approve bills from the Commons.

Politics drew from a very small and interconnected pool of aristocratic families, the majority of them related in some way. Data from a hundred years later shows little change:

> 82 percent of dukes were elected to the British House of Commons before inheriting their titles (or succeeded before the age of 21), 55 percent of earls, and 41 percent of baronets, while only 29 percent of heads of untitled families owning substantial landed estates gained a seat in the lower house.[48]

When the king appointed Lord Rockingham for a second term (Whig, 1782), the Prime Minister chose for the newly created post of Foreign Secretary the eloquent and charming Charles James Fox – Charles Sloane's second cousin. The next two Prime Ministers were also Charles Sloane's relations.[49] It was, quite simply, how the world worked.

The appointment of Rockingham was a reaction to the defeat of British troops at the Battle of Yorktown, Virginia, in 1781. Lord Cornwallis's surrender effectively signalled the end of the American War of Independence that had claimed two of Charles Sloane's sons, though peace negotiations rumbled on for two years afterwards. Arguments over the cost of the war and the growing power of the East India Company threatened to bring about a constitutional crisis as the Fox–North coalition government met opposition from the king. Adeptly, he replaced them in December 1783 with William Pitt the Younger. At the 1784 general election voters backed this audacious move at the polls, resulting in a golden period of political stability. Pitt remained in Downing Street for an astonishing seventeen unbroken years. A mutually beneficial relationship between Parliament and the Crown would be effective in warding off the revolutionary fever that had won the new United States of America its freedom. In France it would lead royalty to the guillotine and its people into expansionist wars under their new leader Napoleon Bonaparte.

Royal blood now flowed through the veins of several leaves on the extended Cadogan family tree. Charles Sloane's cousin Lady Sarah Cadogan (1705–1751) had married a grandson of King Charles II: the 2nd Duke of Richmond, whose father's title was one of many peerages created for a royal lovechild. In the mid-eighteenth century, their daughters Sarah, Caroline, Emily and Louisa (granddaughters of William, the first 1st Earl Cadogan) captivated society. Lady Sarah Lennox (1745–1826) had for a brief moment in 1761 looked likely to become the next queen, before politics steered the Prince of Wales to a foreign Protestant princess. Despite several scandals, Sarah remained a favourite with the king, the distant cousin who had fallen for her charms.[50]

Charles Sloane's proximity to the royal family brought him plum roles in which he could enjoy the pleasures of the outdoors, the dinner table and the coffers: in addition to Keeper of the Privy Purse, he was Surveyor of Kensington Garden (1764–69); appointments as Clerk of the Venison Warrant (1769–78) and Master of the Mint (1769–84) followed.[51] As a young man, he had known George II as his sovereign, but for the majority of Charles Sloane's adult life, George III sat on the throne.

King George III is the unlucky monarch best known for two misfortunes: madness and the loss of Britain's American colonies. There is far more to George. He was pivotal in forming the country's sense of self: the first of the Hanoverian kings whose native tongue was English. At his first State Opening of Parliament, in 1760, he had declaimed: 'Born and educated in this country, I glory in the name of Briton.'[52]

Forty years later, he oversaw the Acts of Union (1800) creating the United Kingdom of Great Britain and Ireland, formally effected on 1 January 1801. He made an arranged marriage – meeting his wife Princess Charlotte of Mecklenburg-Strelitz on their wedding day – in which he was reportedly faithful and happy, and which lasted over fifty years.

Lady Sarah Bunbury Sacrificing to the Graces, Joshua Reynolds, 1763–65, oil on canvas. Lady Sarah (née Lennox) is portrayed as a devotee of the attendants to Venus, the Roman goddess of love and beauty. Two years earlier the granddaughter of William, first 1st Earl Cadogan, had captured the heart of the Prince of Wales.

Charles Sloane had been in the upper house since 1776, the reliable voter for the status quo, providing unwavering support to the Pitt administration. He was doubtless near the top of the list in a final round of rewards before Pitt resigned over Irish Catholic emancipation seven weeks later.

The 1st Earl Cadogan (NC) and 1st Viscount Chelsea would enjoy his new titles for less than a decade. (By tradition, eldest sons are known by

THE GEORGIANS

LEFT *Children of the Royal Military Asylum, Chelsea*, J.C. Stadler after Charles Hamilton Smith, 1813, coloured etched aquatint. From the series 'Costumes of the Army of the British Empire, according to the last regulations', published by Colnaghi & Co., Cockspur Street, 1815.

FOOT *Royal Military Asylum for Children of Soldiers of the Regular Army*, Johann Andreas Ziegler, c.1801, watercolour. The building went up on the site of old Chelsea/Cadogan House.

BELOW Button from the children's uniforms

the lesser title.) He was increasingly infirm and preferred to stay at home at Downham Hall rather than risk the long carriage ride to London. More change was afoot in Chelsea, as Hans Town neared completion: the site of Chelsea/Cadogan House – leased to Sir Walter Farquhar, 1st Bt, from 1788 – was purchased by the government in 1801 for the erection of the Royal Military Asylum, a boarding school for the children of fallen soldiers.[53] Britain was entering a period of conflict that would last twenty years. 'Frederick, the "Grand Old" Duke of York of the nursery rhyme, and commander-in-chief of the British Army, had far more than "ten thousand men" to worry about, let alone their dependants.'[54] Life in Westminster showed no signs of slowing down either. After a break of three years, in 1804 William Pitt the Younger returned briefly to the office of Prime Minister, until his sudden death two years later at the age of forty-six. William Wilberforce, Pitt's close friend from university days, finally saw the result of years of tireless campaigning in the Abolition of Slavery Act, which passed on 25 March 1807.[55] The world was changing. Charles Sloane was a grandfather, two of his three daughters having married into the Wellesley family – now there's a tale to come. Charles Sloane Cadogan, 1st Earl Cadogan (NC), 1st Viscount Chelsea, 3rd Baron Cadogan of Oakley, died on 5 April 1807. He is buried at Santon Downham, in a new family vault he had built for the purpose.

As a revived earldom peeked over the brow of the nineteenth century, heir apparent Charles Henry was a bachelor approaching fifty in questionable health and unlikely to marry and continue the Cadogan line. Reverend William Bromley, the other of Frances's surviving sons, was married but had yet to become a father. Questions had been brewing for at least a decade. In October of 1789, William reported 'unpleasant accounts from abroad, respecting the health of my brother. He has been extremely ill for three months; and indeed there was a time, when all hopes of his recovery seemed to be over, but the last two letters have spoke more favourably of him.'[56] The following year, he wrote that his father was expecting Charles Henry to return home in July or August of 1790. By 1800, one brother would be declared a lunatic and the other would be dead.

CHAPTER 6

Evangelists & Educators

—

REVEREND WILLIAM BROMLEY CADOGAN (1751–1797)
AND HIS WIFE JANE (D.1827)

The Reverend William Bromley Cadogan was unusually enthusiastic about his vocation to the Church. Aware from a young age that his brother Charles Henry, two years older, was destined to inherit the family title, he was encouraged towards one of the few careers suited to his status. Life as a country parson was an agreeable choice, though the calling may not have been entirely William's. His mother, Frances, and his grandmother Elizabeth Sloane, 'both piously disposed', gave him religious instruction from infancy that had a marked effect. By the age of six he was heard to 'read the English Bible into French and the French Bible again into English'; as a child he knew Psalm 139 by heart.[1] His father took him to visit the Bishop of Bangor, whose wife commented on his precocious religiosity: 'Sir, your early and particular inclination for holy orders leads me to hope that yours is a real call of the Holy Ghost to take upon you this office.'[2]

After Westminster School, where he won several prizes and was captain of the school, William applied himself at Christ Church, Oxford. There he was 'considered as one of the first scholars in his college', obtaining a BA in 1773. Experiencing university as a test of his devotion, not just through the rigours of his degree but in the company of other inquiring minds, he 'sought a refuge…in the study of his Bible: many sleepless nights did he spend

Reverend William Bromley Cadogan, Charles Howard Hodges, 1784, engraving on paper, published by T. Towne, London

THE GEORGIANS

LEFT Chelsea Old Church in the 18th century

BELOW The Old Rectory, Chelsea, James Hedderley, c.1860–70. Reverend William Bromley Cadogan restored the house when he was appointed to the living at Chelsea in 1775. Charles Kingsley, father of the novelist of the same name, was a later resident.

on this account, and, as I am assured, often watered his couch with tears.'[3] What a delicate flower, one might think. But he was far from a pious, nerdy dullard. William got into such a heated discussion of Christian doctrine over dinner with a friend in college 'as to finish the debate by throwing the salt-cellar into the face of his opponent.'[4] This was an anecdote William himself later told a curate to illustrate his frustration at the limits of his knowledge, though perhaps also as a warning against the follies of youth and impetuous temper.

In 1775 a vacancy arose at Chelsea Old Church, where the parish was in the gift of the Cadogan family. No surprise, William got the job as his grandfather's chaplain. He spent a small fortune (£800) repairing his impressive quarters. Rambling houses were built to accommodate well-bred young men entering the Church, with book-lined libraries and a position at the centre of the village. No wonder 'The Old Rectory' is today one of the most desirable addresses in Britain; thousands are now in private hands. Chelsea Old Rectory still has one of the largest private gardens in London, at two acres (the average is less than one twentieth of an acre; Buckingham Palace has forty). William threw himself into his new role, visiting the sick and distributing food to the poor – though he had a tendency to insist they recite the Lord's Prayer first. A young man of twenty-four, he was a firebrand preacher of judgement to come. Chastising shopkeepers for opening on a Sunday, he remained fearless in the face of their death threats; early-morning bell-ringers were silenced by passages expounded from the Bible. Perhaps unsurprisingly, his proposal to rebuild and expand the church was rejected.

> At Chelsea...Mr. C. was not popular after the novelty of his coming as the son of Lord Cadogan ceased. The train of coaches that first attended his church soon drew off, and the parish in general did not choose to be disturbed.[5]

William had only recently taken up the living at St Giles's, Reading, a mile from the family seat at Caversham. He had been presented to St Giles's a full year before by no less than Earl Bathurst, Lord High Chancellor of Great

Britain, but there had been a short delay while they waited for William to be ordained into the priesthood. When the Chelsea living came up, it was first the Archbishop of Canterbury and then the sovereign who smoothed the way. On 23 May 1777 Frederick Cornwallis (Canterbury) used his powers to confer an MA – a 'Lambeth degree', a legacy from the Peter's Pence Act (1533), by which Henry VIII transferred degree-awarding powers from Papal Rome to the chief religious figure of the Church of England (the monarch being its head). Two days later, King George III conferred 'dispensation to hold benefices in plurality', creating William Bachelor of Divinity.[6]

At St Giles's William immediately caused ructions by dismissing his curate on the grounds of his being a Methodist. The Church of England in the eighteenth century was experiencing its own enlightenment from within: evangelical preachers, led by John Wesley (1703–1791), began to differ from mainstream Anglicanism in their emphasis on direct, transformational experience of the Holy Spirit and a personal relationship with God through the Gospel. They favoured simple worship and the inclusion of laity in church services, and lobbied for improvements in general living conditions. This rather democratic approach would eventually lead dissenters away to their own meeting houses and alternative church buildings, forming a new denomination in 1795. Such a splintering threatened to undermine the Church of England's position of power and, ultimately, that of the Crown – it was not just the Catholics in Ireland who concerned George III. Fat bishops with a lascivious eye for an actress, and elderly vicars fond of the bottle or the card-table had long been lampooned. In an age when everyone attended a Sunday service, from king to farm labourer, the Church's position was a matter that occupied many minds; and for some became a hotly contested theological debate. 'John Wesley heard of [William's] zeal, and sent him a set of his writings, but Cadogan responded by burning the books in his own kitchen.'[7]

The compiler of William's memoirs speculates that this early 'natural hauteur' was understandable as 'the son of a Nobleman then in office and court-favour'; that he felt 'the strongest conflicts between the dictates of his conscience, and the influence of his habits and circumstances.'[8] These would come to resolution in part through careful religious instruction by the 'sensible, polite, tender' widow of the previous vicar at Reading, who took him under her wing. She brought him into contact with the elderly Reverend William Romaine, Rector of St Ann Blackfriars and fellow bookish alumnus of Christ Church, Oxford.[9] Together these two influences would change the course of William's ministry. He declared at her funeral that Mrs Talbot was 'the best friend I ever had in my life, but…a Mother to me in love, in every good office, and in continual prayers for my person and ministry.'[10] He had lost his own mother as a teenager. When his father remarried a couple of years after the move to St Giles's, William had matured sufficiently to be a witness at the ceremony – the only one of Charles Sloane's children to attend – welcoming a stepmother his own age.

THE REVEREND WILLIAM BROMLEY CADOGAN LIVED A CHASTE EARLY LIFE, as befits a clergyman (and quite in contrast to his stepmother's lover). He reportedly fell in love with a beautiful and accomplished Roman Catholic lady, but as neither one could persuade the other to convert, they agreed to a lifelong friendship. In 1782 he married an Army widow, Mrs Jane Bradshaw (née Graham, d.1827). Chelsea resident Jane was well connected, as evidenced by the list of executors of her will, including the Marquess of Cholmondeley and the Duchess of Montrose. Theirs was a happy marriage and William's letters always addressed her as 'my dear life'.[11] William embarked upon a life of steadiness and remarkably uniform routine, dividing his time between his two parishes in Chelsea and Reading. 'What can we tell more of a man who trod so regularly his course of duty, that the path you found him in to-day, you might be sure of meeting him in to-morrow?'[12]

Poor Jane suffered from unspecific ill health. She travelled the country in search of respite, including in 1792 a six-week stay at Bristol taking the waters at Hotwells. Gentlemen and ladies mixed in the Pump Rooms, and a social whirl of engagements – dinners, balls, evenings at the theatre – sprang up to entertain visitors initially attracted by the health craze, who stayed for the opportunities to mingle. William's own grandmother, Elizabeth, had written to her father from Bath of playing cards with the Prince of Wales.

A View of the Hot Wells Bristol, T. Morris, 1805, etching

Devout Jane, whose husband described her as 'an help meet for me',[13] seems unlikely to have indulged in such worldly pursuits. Her general infirmity, whether real or imagined, had one concrete effect, in keeping her husband in England when he might have joined his brother travelling in Continental Europe. Charles Henry would be often sorely disappointed.

The pair – and particularly Jane – were concerned with loftier ideals. The year of their wedding, William was a founding trustee of a new charitable boarding school in Reading. Such schools for the poor were nothing new and trusteeships were commonly part of a vicar's parish duties. Britain's public schools, already several hundred years old, had sprung from a similar impulse: Eton College was established in 1440 by King Henry VI to provide free education to seventy poor boys. However, this was different: it was exclusively for girls. The impetus had sprung in 1777 from a charitable legacy left by local grandee and a suggestion for its use from an alderman; practicalities were picked up by a trio of local vicars. William joined the Reverend Charles Sturges, Vicar of St Mary's, and the Reverend Doctor Nicholls, Vicar of St Lawrence's.[14]

It was well funded by annual subscription; 'the Hon. Charles Cadogan', likely William's brother Charles Henry, and 'the Hon. Mrs Cadogan' appear in the minute books. South Sea shares were held for use in the school's support. On the opening page of the first minute book, beautiful copperplate handwriting sets out its mission:

> …in the year of our Lord 1782 a School was taken and opened or instituted for the maintenance and education of six poor girls belonging to the said three parishes in Reading aforesaid two chosen from each of the same parishes and a proper mistress and other assistants were provided to take care of teach and instruct such children in reading writing needlework and other necessary employment…[15]

Literacy was a key part of the curriculum. Each girl was furnished with a Bible and comprehension of religious texts was the prime motivator in their instruction. Considering the rich density of biblical language, however, such an education would have set these girls up to read whatever they liked once they left school. Today's Church of England primary schools – free and open to all members of the local parish – retain aspects of this ideal. After only two years, a motion was passed that pupils should also be taught basic accounting: 'It was likewise agreed that the Girls should continue in the School to the Age of Fifteen Years, and that for the last half year they should be instructed in Writing and Accompts [accounts].'[16]

For centuries, monasteries and nunneries had been seats of learning. In the Tudor–Stuart period, young ladies were occasionally lucky enough to receive the same education as their brothers, taught alongside them at home.[17] The plays of Aphra Behn (c.1640–1689) were on the London stage when William, 1st Earl Cadogan, was a Westminster schoolboy – but she was such a notable exception that King Charles II employed her as a spy. Literacy among the labouring classes had, since Caxton, been the preserve of a few Lollards reading their English-language Bibles in secret. Industrialization had begun to effect change, however, and by the time Reverend William and his wife were weighing into public education in the late eighteeenth century, the sheer availability of books and daily newspapers, and increasing urbanization, had seen numbers begin to rise across the population.[18]

The Berkshire town of Reading already had its Blue Coat School for boys, one of the earliest of sixty-odd charity schools, known as 'bluecoats', that had opened across Great Britain following the model of Christ's Hospital since its foundation in 1522.[19] The new girls' school up the road quite naturally became known as the 'Green Girls' School', owing to the hue of their uniforms. Pupils stitched clothing for inmates of the local prison, receiving tuppence from every sovereign earned (a little under one per cent) as a reward and encouragement. Competent girls were apprenticed to respectable housekeepers, as domestic servants or to learn a trade and good behaviour was rewarded with a half-guinea, on receipt of a written recommendation from the employer. Its fine reputation meant that by 1815 the school had expanded from six to twenty-one pupils.[20]

TALES OF WILLIAM'S LATER GOOD CHARACTER fill the memoirs published after his death – how he wrote off debts of tithes due from farmers in distress and also from a Quaker who refused to pay on principle. He fed the poor through the winter with thirty pounds of beef a week; catechized the local children; and was 'the large-hearted friend of all'.[21] His bearing, however, didn't change:

> He had early contracted a scowling sort of aspect which might have led a stranger to doubt of his being so amiable and benevolent as he really was: and spoke sometimes with a kind of bluntness, heightened by a rough and deep toned voice, which concealed...a humility which was sterling.[22]

6. EVANGELISTS & EDUCATORS

RIGHT Sampler by a pupil of the Green Girls' School. Harriet Burton, 1854, textile. Harriet's design includes two girls in their distinctive uniform of green dresses and white aprons.

BELOW RIGHT Ledger of the Green Girls' School. Minute Books, Book One, September 1797. The ledgers for 1788 include payment to one Mr Clarke 'for teaching three girls writing and accounts'; by 1797 he was 'Mr Clarke, Writing Master', paid £2. 12s. 0d.

BELOW *A Pupil of Green Girls' School, Reading*, Annie Margaret Bradley, 1898, oil on canvas

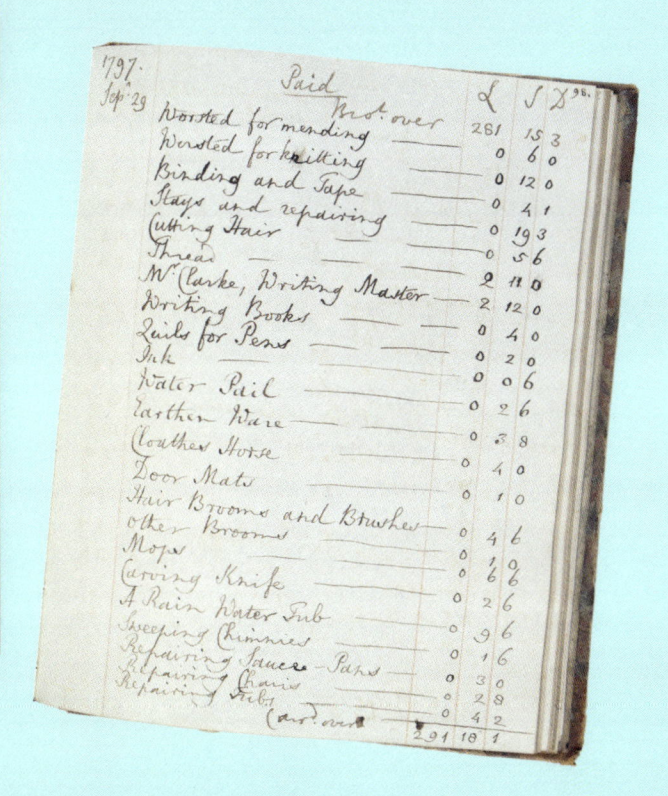

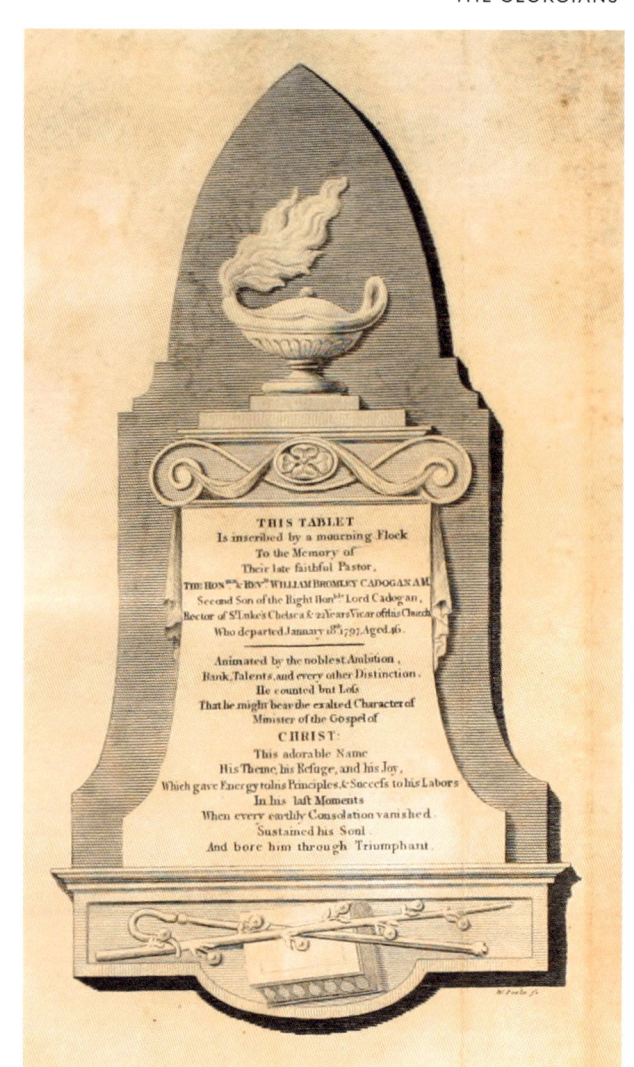

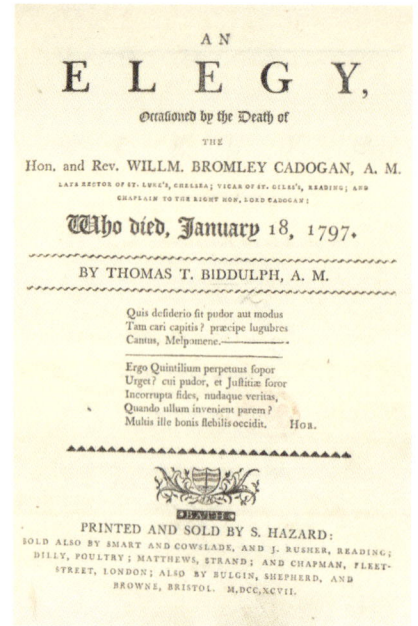

ABOVE Title page of *An Elegy*, 1797. Reverend William became a charismatic and popular preacher. Several volumes of his discourses, sermons and letters were published posthumously and he is remembered as a religious writer.

LEFT Monument in St Giles's Church, Reading, 1797, illustration from *An Elegy*. William's 'mourning flock' erected a memorial to 'their late faithful pastor' in his country parish church.

William never lost his zeal, either. Rather, it seems he experienced an epiphany through his friendship and instruction by the Calvinist Romaine, who regularly gave a Thursday evening lecture at Reading, and for whom William delivered a funeral sermon. A friend remarked, 'When Mr. Cadogan came first to St Giles's, he did not preach the gospel. The people waited six years, and the Lord brought him to the knowledge of himself.'[23] William had become a minister of such charisma and religious fervour that he succeeded in Reading where he had failed in Chelsea: in 1784 a gallery was added to the church of St Giles's to accommodate the swelling congregation and five years later even this was insufficient. He extemporized prayers and sermons, thundering away from the pulpit on the love of Christ and salvation for all. Asked to present a guest lecture at Nicholas Hawksmoor's Christ Church, Spitalfields, and:

> ...perceiving the extent of voice necessary to fill the largest Parish Church in London, crouded [sic] from end to end, he so exerted himself as to burst a vein which filled his mouth and throat with blood: but deeply impressed with his subject, and animated at seeing such a vast multitude hanging upon his lips, he determined, if possible, to sustain the continued inconvenience.[24]

His florid style was ridiculed by *The Gentleman's Magazine*, as 'nothing more nor less than the ranting effusions of methodistical orthodoxy'.[25] His popularity, however, is evident in the number of his sermons that were published, as well as a collection of hymns and psalms that was reprinted three times.[26] William died a week after his forty-sixth birthday, following a short illness apparently brought on by overwork. Memoirs were published by his friend and fellow clergyman Richard Cecil – the man who had invited him to speak at Spitalfields. Clearly, he left big shoes to fill. The congregation at Reading, where a memorial to him was erected, were said to burst into tears at the mention of his name for months afterwards.

WILLIAM'S INVOLVEMENT IN EDUCATION might well have been par for the course of duty. But Jane Cadogan took girls' education to heart. It is not known how old she was when she married, but she and William had no children and we might speculate that she directed her mothering instinct elsewhere. Jane founded another girls' school in Reading: the School of Industry. Details of her will, initially of 1802, amended in 1806, include a property in Friar Street:

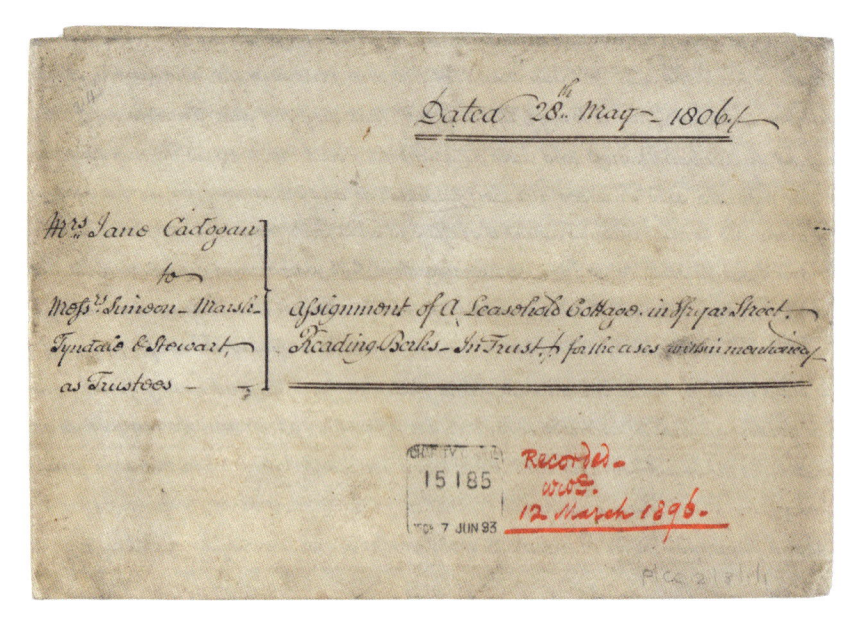

Jane Cadogan's Deeds of Trust, 1806. Jane left property to the School of Industry she founded. Girls from the poor families of Reading were taught to read in addition to the basics of housework and light industry.

> ...the said Jane Cadogan, being desirous of establishing a School for the education of poor Female children, has lately purchased the Leasehold Messuage Cottage or Tenement hereafter described and intended to be hereby assigned as a school-house for that purpose.[27]

The School of Industry was supported by the light industry of others. 'Many ladies in the town and neighbourhood employ their leisure hours making a variety of articles in fancy-work [ornamental embroidery, needlework, etc.], which are afterwards disposed of at fairs...the money arising from which is appropriated to the maintenance of the school.' In 1815 this type of fund-raising, a version of the familiar cake sale, changed the lives of thirty-four girls 'who are taught reading and plain-work, and are likewise clothed.'[28]

After Jane's death in 1827, the suitably ecclesiastical list of trustees chose to dispose of the Friar Street property. The school itself endured, appointing new trustees as late as 1889, but it did not last long into the twentieth century. The Elementary Education Act (1880) made schooling compulsory by law for all children between the ages of five and ten – although poorer parents often ignored this and of those who did attend, 300,000 worked outside school hours in 1901.[29] Better use of Jane's legacy was required, as a local history of 1923 notes:

> The Hon. Mrs. Cadogan's educational fund consists of £1,241 6s. 8d. consols with the official trustees, arising under deeds of gift 1844 and 1871. The annual dividends, amounting to £31 0s. 8d. yearly, are, under a scheme of 14 May 1897, applicable in helping girls in connexion with the Church of England.'[30]

The Green Girls' School met a similar fate in the march of progress: its doors were closed in 1921. Under a scheme instituted in 1929, the charity became a grant-awarding body; at the turn of the twenty-first century, the Green Girls' Foundation had funds of a quarter of a million pounds.[31] The broad vision executed by Reverend William and his wife Jane lives on in the foundation's activities, supporting higher education for disadvantaged girls in the Reading area.[32]

CHAPTER 7

Adventure & Affliction

—

CHARLES HENRY,
2ND EARL (1749–1832)

For much of his adult life, Charles Henry Sloane Cadogan, eldest son and last surviving child from Charles Sloane's first marriage, to Frances Bromley, was unwell. The cause has been subject to some speculation, while the effects are well recorded. To begin at the beginning: his early life was spent in the service of his country. He bought a commission into the 3rd Regiment of Foot Guards in 1762, barely into his teens; and he was a captain before coming of age at twenty-one. But, a decade later he appears on the Army list still at the rank of captain, albeit with a different regiment, the 61st Foot. Something had gone wrong: the eldest son of an aristocratic family might ordinarily have expected a rapid ascent to command or even staff ranks, not to be languishing as a junior officer after a career of sixteen years. This less-than-meteoric rise marks a pretty sorry military career. Charles Henry's name is missing from the Army list two years later, indicating that he must have sold out his commission.

His father had been Whig MP for Cambridgeshire since the year of his birth and, coupled with the family connections with the Montforts, by tradition Charles Henry would have stood for election when the time came. As the 1770s rolled on, the family considered their options. Charles Henry's grandfather was approaching his nineties and change would be upon them all soon enough.

Charles Henry, 2nd Earl Cadogan (1749–1832), Sir Joshua Reynolds, oil on canvas

> In 1770…Montfort thought of putting up Cadogan's eldest son, Captain Cadogan, for the county; and before the general election of 1774, [Charles Sloane] Cadogan, expecting soon to succeed to his father's peerage, would have liked to cede the seat at Cambridge to him, but in the end himself had to fight hard for it…'In the autumn of 1775', writes the Cambridge scholar, William Cole, '…his eldest son, my dear friend Captain Charles Cadogan being fallen ill of a malady of which there was no great prospect of his getting the better of [insanity], he declined all interest at Cambridge'.[1]

The insertion of 'insanity' is Sir Lewis Namier's, in his exhaustive *History of Parliament* (1964); whether it was seen as such as early as 1775 is unclear and even unlikely given the lucidity of his letters from years later. However, Charles Henry's 'malady' was evident enough to preclude his entry into politics. On the 2nd Baron's death in 1776, Charles Sloane, 3rd Baron Cadogan of Oakley, moved up to the House of Lords and the Cambridgeshire seat passed out of Cadogan hands.

With his health already in doubt, Charles Henry did well to stay in the Army as long as he did. Details of the next part of his life are hazy and he disappears for five years. He reappears on Saturday, 19 July 1783, embarking upon a Grand Tour, as was the fashion for young men – and occasionally, women – of privilege from the seventeenth to the nineteenth century.[2] Most of these prototypical British tourists set off soon after they reached their majority at twenty-one and spent a year or so in Continental Europe (a gap year, of sorts). Charles Henry, in his thirties, was gone for seven years.

The rather circuitous route of his tour suggests that it was largely spontaneous rather than formally planned. Piecing together an accurate map from his letters is almost impossible – he doubled-back, revisited favourite sites or people, and describes trips already made to one place from another. He followed invitations from one location to the next and stayed for a few weeks where he found good company. His hosts were uniformly fellow aristocrats and crowned heads. It seems he had rather a good time, making exhaustive lists of locales and antiquities he had visited and jotting little descriptions. Only twenty-nine of his letters survive in the family archive – all addressed to his brother Reverend William Bromley Cadogan – an infrequent correspondence averaging out to as few as once in three months.

Having disembarked at Ostend, he passed through Brussels, Spa, Nancy and Neuchâtel before sending back a missive from Guévaux to the effect that the Alps came off favourably when compared with Welsh mountains or the Highlands. From there, the list covers Lausanne—Geneva—Genoa —Leghorn—Turin. In early 1785, he arrived in Naples.

British Gentlemen in Rome, Katharine Read, c.1750, oil on canvas. The Grand Tour expanded the horizons of young aristocrats taking in art, antiquities and culture. Charles Henry, 2nd Earl Cadogan, took an extended tour from 1783 to 1790.

> I have been here near three months and independent of the curiosities the place and Country afford, have spent a most gay time. I have frequented nothing but balls, masquerades and operas…I have been three times at the top of Mount Vesuvius and have dined in the crater…Sir William Hamilton…has given me recommendations to all the principle people in Sicily and Malta.[3]

The Vesuvian dinner party was surely arranged by Hamilton. British Ambassador to the Kingdom of Naples, '[his] diplomatic duties seem to have occupied little of his time or thought', allowing him to concentrate on 'collecting art and living as agreeably as possible'.[4] Hamilton's entry in the *Oxford Dictionary of National Biography* includes a whole section on his interest in volcanoes; another details the infamous *ménage à trois* that developed in later life between himself, his second wife Emma and Horatio, Lord Nelson.

Reaching Malta, Hamilton's recommendation, was a punishing undertaking: 'I was dead sick, and had I not been so should have been greatly alarmed, as we were in a boat with six rowers called a Sparonara [speronaro],

Sir William Hamilton leading a tour to Vesuvius, Pietro Fabris, 1776, etching with gouache. On the left, Sir William Hamilton guides the Queen of Naples to the site. Charles Henry stayed with Sir William and dined in the crater of the volcano.

Sir William Hamilton and Lady Emma Hart, Joseph W. Reed, 1 December 1790, etching and engraving. From 'Histories of the Tête à Tête annexed...', *Town and Country Magazine*. Hamilton was a collector of antiquarian objects and the satirist imagines Hart as his Venus de Medici; the couple married the following year. As Lady Hamilton, Emma became Lord Nelson's mistress.

and had 80 miles across the canal [from Sicily]'.[5] Charles Henry was certainly intrepid. The route was notoriously treacherous, as described in a guide book of the 1780s:

> In order to elude the pursuit of the African pirates, and of the other Barbaresque vessels which infest these seas, the Sparonaras are constructed with peculiar attention to swiftness; they are built in the form of a boat, and are in general very small, and so flat and narrow as to be quite unable to bear a high sea, which necessarily obliges them to keep as near the shore as possible. These vessels are managed by rowers, who, in general, do not sit, but stand opposite to the prow, and push their oars in the same manner as the Venetian Gondoliers...The passage between these two islands is regarded as one of the most stormy and dangerous in the Mediterranean...[6]

The island proved to be 'most curious, and the knights most hospitable in every respect.' And so it goes on. Charles Henry saw the sights in Rome; he toured Cartagena—Gibraltar—Lisbon—Madrid—Barcelona; travelled up through the South of France to Lyon, around the smaller cantons of Switzerland and on to Schaffhausen; along the Danube past Munich to Vienna; up and down the Nile, Cairo via Damietta and down by Rosetta. He was in Constantinople between August and November 1785, making multiple 'jaunts in order to see every thing worth notice.'[7]

From there he pottered about the Mediterranean for a couple of years, taking in the sights of ancient civilizations, all the while making new friends, gadding about in Athens—Corinth—Smyrna—Palermo—Trapani—Agrigento—Cape Passaro—Syracuse and Catania. He took a boat out to see Stromboli, another active volcano, perhaps inspired by his host in Naples, on whom he dropped in again before pushing on to Ancona, Bologna and Venice. It wasn't only Western culture that interested him: Palmyra, Baalbek, Tyre, Sidon and Jaffa all figured on his route. Biblical names appear: Jerusalem—Nazareth—Damascus; he scribbled and jotted; Aleppo—Alexandria. His writing is not always complimentary to his host nations, though it does reveal a man genuinely concerned with the preservation of historic sites of interest.

> Every place in these parts has something belonging to it more or less interesting, though the barbarians who now inhabit the Country continue as they have done for ages to destroy every trace of antiquity remaining.[8]

He headed back to Constantinople before setting off in another direction, literally and culturally: the Germanic states. Starting in present-day Romania, he headed to Wallachia, Moldova and on to Cracow. Here he stayed for several months. Charles Henry first mentions an inflammation that had settled in his eye in the autumn of 1785; it crops up again in September of 1786. By the time he reached Cracow, in March 1787, it had worsened considerably:

The Bay of Naples from Posillipo, Pietro Fabris, c.1770, oil on canvas. Several well-known buildings are visible, including the Palazzo Donn'Anna on the left and the Castel Sant'Elmo on the hilltop, with Mount Vesuvius beyond. The small boat in the foreground is perhaps similar to that taken by Charles Henry over to Sicily in a dangerous crossing.

> I must undergo two months['] confinement at least. The cornea of my eye was ulcerated all round, and formed a hard spot over it like a skin, which I was obliged to have cut through in four different places with a lancet…I have I assure you found no Country I like so well as my own…But God forbid that you should ever pay so dear for any of your tours, as I have paid for mine in Turkey.[9]

His health concerns were centred at this time on new physical issues; interesting to note that he appears to lay the blame in Turkey. The bustling city of Istanbul, at the juncture between Europe and Asia, has long had a reputation as a liminal place of excess. Could it have been an infection he picked up on his travels? Or was it just a simple cataract?

> I now begin to be afraid of being nearly if not quite blind of one eye…I would go directly to Vienna, were it not for the excessive civilities I rec'd from the King…The King has given me the kindest invitations to his Capital, where I am also sure

of being capitally rec'd by him…I wish I could give you a better account of my eye; which I am sadly afraid I shall lose…Indeed I have acquired the acquaintance of the King of Poland, who is without dispute in every respect one of the first men in Europe, by it; though even this is a poor recompense.[10]

King Stanisław II August Poniatowski (r.1764–95) was the last king of an independent Poland. He had travelled on his own Grand Tour of Western Europe in his youth and doubtless found shared interests with Charles Henry. Stanisław was in Cracow after visiting his ex-lover Catherine II (Catherine the Great, Empress of Russia, r.1762–96), who by that time had already annexed part of his country, as had Prussia and Austria. Perhaps they discussed such affairs of the heart and state; the two men became close enough friends to touch on the recent suicide of Hans Stanley (1721–1780), grandson of Sir Hans Sloane, and Charles Henry's first cousin once removed. Hans was a politician, diplomat and Lord of the Admiralty under Pitt the Elder, who paid him 'the highest compliments imaginable'; in 1762 he was created privy counsellor. But Hans suffered poor mental health, or depression – 'he never laughed'. In January 1780, during a visit to Earl Spencer at Althrop, he 'cut his throat with a penknife in the woods, and died before assistance could be obtained.'[11] Charles Henry, whose own mental health would only worsen later, did indeed take up Stanisław's invitation to Warsaw, before travelling through Lower Crimea to Cracow, where he finally sought help from a famous oculist.

Frequently, Charles Henry asked his brother, Reverend William, to join him on the Continent. From Cracow, in February 1788: 'I'll abate now in my demands, and still hope for the pleasure of seeing you in June in Hanover.'[12] The following month, he provides detailed practical instructions for the proposed trip.[13] Jane's ill health prevented their plans from coming to fruition, though she has recovered whenever Charles Henry next enquires. He writes from Berlin of a visit to the rooms of Martin Luther clearly planned as an engaging diversion for his clergyman brother; a plan he stuck to so that William might enjoy the report vicariously.[14]

William's replies have been lost, but we can infer that they were friendly. Two years apart in age, the brothers were the eldest and last surviving of seven siblings. There is something rather sad about William's inability to make it out to see his older brother, and a heartbreaking, hopeful resilience to Charles Henry's ongoing requests.

The tour resumed. Minden—'Pyrmont Wells' (the spa town of Bad Pyrmont)—Harz Forest—Prague—Dresden—Berlin—Wittenberg—Hanover—Hamburg—Copenhagen—Lübeck—the Duchy of Mecklenburg—Frankfurt—Nuremberg—'Ratisbon' (now Regensburg)—Augsburg. It was business as usual. In Brunswick, in late 1788, he was 'hospitably rec'd by the Duke and Duchess, with whom I dine every day'. The same letter contains a cryptic reference to a potential marriage: 'If Miss Jennings is not snapt up by somebody before my return, perhaps I may open proposals to the Jury.'[15] She pops up again in a letter from Munich a couple of months later. 'My scheme for Miss Jennings is a timely one, but who knows what time with its wings may bring about?' He doesn't sound terribly enthusiastic. Had such a match come off, the course of history for the Cadogan family might have been forever altered. However, the elusive Miss Jennings disappears into the ether. Charles Henry's time in Germany ended with 'the young Princes at Gottingeby' and 'great hospitality from the Elector of Magence [Mainz] at Aschaffenburg'.[16]

In January 1789 William mentions to a parishioner receipt of 'a letter from my brother about a fortnight ago, he was then in Florence on his way to Rome, and was in very good health, but did not talk of returning to England.'[17] Charles Henry had decided to stay and enjoy himself. Rome and Turin got a second look that year, with mentions of antiquities, princes, doges, cardinals and ambassadors. From this point on, he writes in Latin, seemingly for his own amusement, with an invitation to his younger, cleverer brother to correct him wherever necessary. He describes his attendance at various religious ceremonies, though perhaps this was largely to interest his brother. By November something had changed; his health in doubt once more, his thoughts were turning to home. He wrote from Nîmes:

The Company of Undertakers. Et plurima mortis imago, William Hogarth, 1736, etching. A satirical coat of arms, bordered in black like a mourning card, carries the motto: 'And many other images of death'. The figures of the top row are caricatures of medical practitioners of the day. Below, massed ranks of quacks sniff disinfectant and inspect the contents of urinals.

OPPOSITE
Dr William Cadogan, physician (1711–1797), W. Dickinson, 1772, after R.E. Pine (1769), mezzotint. Dr William Cadogan's pioneering work on childhood inoculation saved many lives. An essay on his personal experience of gout ran to ten editions.

I'm advised to remain the winter in these parts, and on no account to think of Spain, all which I shall accurately observe. I'll not trouble you with a tedious account of my past illness: suffice it to say that by the Grace of the Almighty, I hope to have escaped, so as to pass a few more years comfortably in England, among my relations and friends.[18]

This sounds pretty serious; probably it wasn't just the eye. On New Year's Day 1790, his letter is full of hope: '...the beach at Montpellier is congenial to my health. Sometimes I walk, sometimes I ride; and by the grace of God, my strength grows daily.'[19] He returned to England later that year.

MODERN MEDICINE AS WE KNOW IT is a very recent phenomenon. Understanding of physical and mental illnesses, attitudes and treatments that seemed quite normal to our ancestors now seem positively cruel and barbaric. By the end of the eighteenth century, things were improving. In 1745 King George II had founded the London College of Surgeons, providing a university education for the profession and doing away with the 'barber-surgeons' who had combined operations and blood-letting with cutting hair. Chelsea Physic Garden was broadening knowledge of medicinal plants.

Another branch of the Cadogan family had produced Dr William Cadogan (1711–1797, Charles Henry's fourth cousin),[20] a celebrated paediatrician and writer whose work led to a significant reduction in the child mortality rate, which stood at over fifty per cent at the turn of the eighteenth century. Inoculation was an innovation steadily gaining acceptance and William had great success against smallpox.[21] John Rendle-Short, who wrote a detailed account of his life, vividly imagines its contrasts:

>...he knew the glitter of [David] Garrick's fashionable drawing-room, he conversed with Sir Joshua Reynolds and other notables, and, as night closed in and the giant chandelier was lighted with a hundred candles, he would dance with his daughter in the whirl of London society until the ball was ended. Then he would go out into the blackness of the unlit London night, the streets ankle deep in mud and filth; where a man seen walking in fine clothes was likely to be set upon by vagabonds or have mud slung at him. Ladies of the street with their low-cut bodices and seemingly immune to the cold would touch him on the shoulder, beggars would whine and, by the roadside or doorstep or dunghill, small bundles could be seen which cried and moved weakly when touched. These were the outcasts, the foundlings.[22]

In 1754 Dr William was appointed physician at the famous Foundling Hospital in London; it was the UK's first children's charity and also, surprisingly, its first public art gallery. His other medical obsession in later life was gout, on which he published a widely read essay addressing treatment of the fashionable disease, writing from first-hand experience.[23]

Despite such improvements, however, medical knowledge was still shrouded in mystery to all but the elite: doctors' theses were still written in Latin. The notorious quack Samuel Solomon made a vast fortune selling his 'Cordial Balm of Gilead' as a cure-all until the 1810s, when its primary ingredient was revealed to be half a pint of herb-steeped brandy. This is not entirely dissimilar to Elizabeth Cadogan's (née Sloane) recipe to cure a fever, though hers at least included an infusion of bark.

Developments in understanding mental health lagged even further behind. At the time Charles Henry returned from his travels, it was fashionable for young ladies and elegant gentlemen of his generation to suffer from 'the nerves' – a name given to hundreds of undiagnosed complaints symptomatic of a society ill at ease. Political tensions in Europe were a constant worry; war and revolution were in the air. The very success of the nation, as a centre of international trade, increasing in wealth and

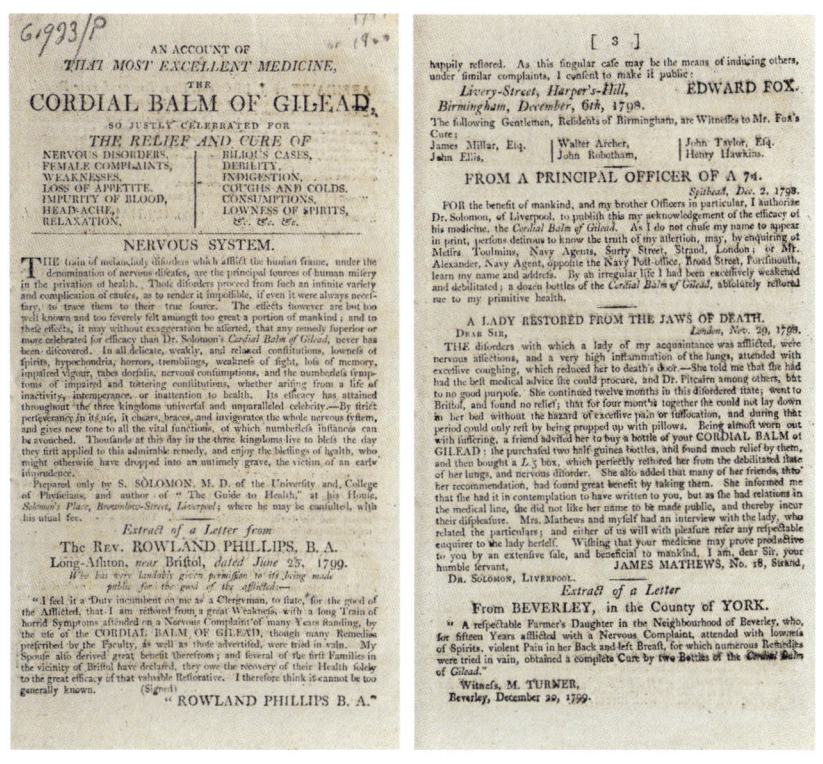

An account of that most excellent medicine, the Cordial Balm of Gilead, Samuel Solomon, 1799. In a notorious example of quackery, Solomon claimed 'relief and cure of nervous disorders, female complaints, weaknesses, loss of appetite, impurity of blood, head-ache, relaxation…'; even 'A Lady Restored from the Jaws of Death'.

luxury, was seen as corrupting to its moral fabric. Parallels were drawn with the fall of the Roman Empire.[24] Eyes looked across the English Channel to France and saw what had become of a decadent elite. Everyone was a hypochondriac on edge.

At some point in the 1790s, after his return home, Charles Henry's mental health deteriorated rapidly. He was lucky to have been born to an aristocratic family and thus afforded decent care and attention. He avoided the manacles, abuse and paying spectators (often well-to-do ladies) of an asylum, such as the infamous Hospital of St Mary of Bethlehem in London, whose nickname lives on in a word to describe 'a scene of mad confusion or uproar': bedlam.[25] Even so, a veil has been drawn across the details of his life that makes it difficult to discover much about the illness that plagued his later years. One clue is perhaps in heredity. His mother, Frances Bromley, 'dyed raving mad', due to shock at the loss of her mother-in-law; her own father, Charles's maternal grandfather Lord Montfort, had committed suicide. This suggests that depression, or at least a difficulty in dealing with unfortunate events and circumstances – with the birth of modern psychotherapy still over a hundred years off – might well have run in the Bromley family. It was not unusual, either. On his Great-Aunt Sarah's side, the unsmiling Hans Stanley had lost his father to suicide in 1734.

The King himself, George III, was thought to be suffering from a mental illness; it first showed itself in 1788, though he recovered quickly from this initial bout. Twentieth-century medical investigation suggests that he had in fact inherited a metabolic disorder, porphyria. While this diagnosis is not universally accepted, it opens the door to potential confusion between primarily physical versus primarily mental illness throughout the medical community at the time.

An alternative medical history for Charles Henry proposes to unite the two. Syphilis was rife throughout Europe in the eighteenth century, and

Royal Dipping, John Nixon, 1789, coloured engraving. 'Mad King George' – note his shaven head – took his family on holiday to Weymouth in July that year, having been told that seabathing would be good for his health. This print reflects the newfound affection of the public for their king: when he entered the water, a band began to play the national anthem.

Charles Henry, a young man away from home with the Army and later on the Grand Tour, would not have been unusual in encountering the disease. One element in particular points to this: that it has several distinct phases. Left untreated at initial infection and presentation as a chancre or sore, which appears to heal, its secondary phase includes a rash, fever, sore throat, muscle aches and fatigue – certainly enough to stall an active military career. Most tellingly, it can lie dormant for up to thirty years before appearing in new symptoms, including damage to the eyes.[26] Recent medical literature includes a description of a corneal ulcer – such as the one Charles Henry had lanced – as 'the presenting feature in a patient with syphilis'.[27]

Had Charles Henry become infected long before he made it to Turkey? Was the ulcer a syphilitic return? That in itself would be miserable enough, but in his later life, and in history, the emphasis has been on Charles Henry's mental illness. That too might be explained by this pernicious affliction. Neurosyphilis, a tertiary stage of the disease, can lead to altered behaviour, difficulty coordinating muscle movements, paralysis, sensory deficits and dementia. The scarcity of biographical information means that a diagnosis will remain forever an open question, but if even the king's physicians at the time had failed in proper understanding, it is quite possible that Charles Henry Sloane Cadogan merely lacked a good dose of penicillin and some topical steroids.[28]

Retinitis Syphilitica, Dr Pierce Mansfield, 1868, watercolour. This page from the medical and surgical journal of HMS *Racoon* is an early record of syphilis in the eye. Four views show different stages of treatment, as viewed through an ophthalmoscope.

BY THE TURN OF THE CENTURY, Charles Henry's ability to look after the family's interests and estates – let alone himself – looked increasingly shaky. The situation reached a crisis in December 1799. His father took action:

A Toast During the Dilettanti Society Dinner, Thatched House Tavern, St James's Street, J.H. le Keux after Thomas Hosmer Shepherd, 1841, steel engraving. The tavern was a meeting place for societies and clubs, as well as the location of Charles Henry's inquiry.

we cannot say if this was brought on by his increasing age and prospect of an earldom, or a sudden deterioration in Charles Henry's health. In what today seems a rather bizarre procedure, a writ *de lunatico inquirendo* was issued and a jury met at a pub in St James's Street, London (the Thatched House Tavern), where Charles Henry was found to be 'a lunatic [who] doth not enjoy lucid intervals'.[29] A committee board of four trustees was appointed to govern the affairs of the eldest son and heir to the 1st Earl Cadogan (NC) 'whereas I am very desirous that great attention should be paid to him...after my decease': a Walpole, a Churchill, a Sloane and a Somerset gentleman called William Dickenson.[30] We might surmise that Dickenson was the family lawyer. The other three were trusted friends of Charles Sloane, of his generation – and members of the extended family.

Only seven years later, Charles Henry became the 2nd Earl Cadogan – but it was these trustees who took charge. The lease on Merton Hall was not renewed; other leasehold properties and Cadogan houses were sold, according to his father's will, to provide annual allowances for his three younger half-brothers and sisters.[31] The focus was on London and the Cadogan family's estate in Chelsea grew. Charles Henry was bequeathed his grandmother Elizabeth Sloane's half of the Manor of Chelsea (which she had inherited in 1753 and in due course passed down as 'the Cadogan moiety'). It was the only landed property left by the 1st Earl to his eldest son. The rest of the freehold estates were devised to the trustees for the use and benefit in trust of his children by Mary Churchill. Charles Henry lived at Santon Downham, kept in trust for him as a residence.

The 2nd Earl Cadogan, poor 'insane' Charles Henry, lived a long life and died in 1832 at the age of eighty-three. His death was registered in Enfield, north London, in relative obscurity.[32] (Santon Downham had been sold.) He is buried at St Luke's Church in Chelsea with only the barest of details of his life recorded, according to his father's instructions:

> ...for my Eldest Son Lord Viscount Chelsea when he dies the inscriptions on such Monuments to be only the time of the birth and death of the party remembered and the years of their age and the same inscriptions to be put on the respective Coffin plate which Coffins...should be of remarkable strength and thickness.[33]

All seven children from the 1st Earl's first marriage had died without legitimate heirs. Meanwhile, upheavals across the Channel had taken another trio of brothers – Henry, George and Edward, from his second marriage – to war, this time with Revolutionary France.

ABOVE Hans Sloane-Stanley (1739–1827), Sir Francis Leggatt Chantrey, c.1817, pencil. This strong profile reveals a sculptor's eye: Chantrey undoubtedly used it to produce a bust. Second cousin Hans was one of Charles Henry's trustees. He changed his name to Sloane-Stanley on inheriting Paultons, the Stanley estate in Hampshire.

Sloane and Stanley connections

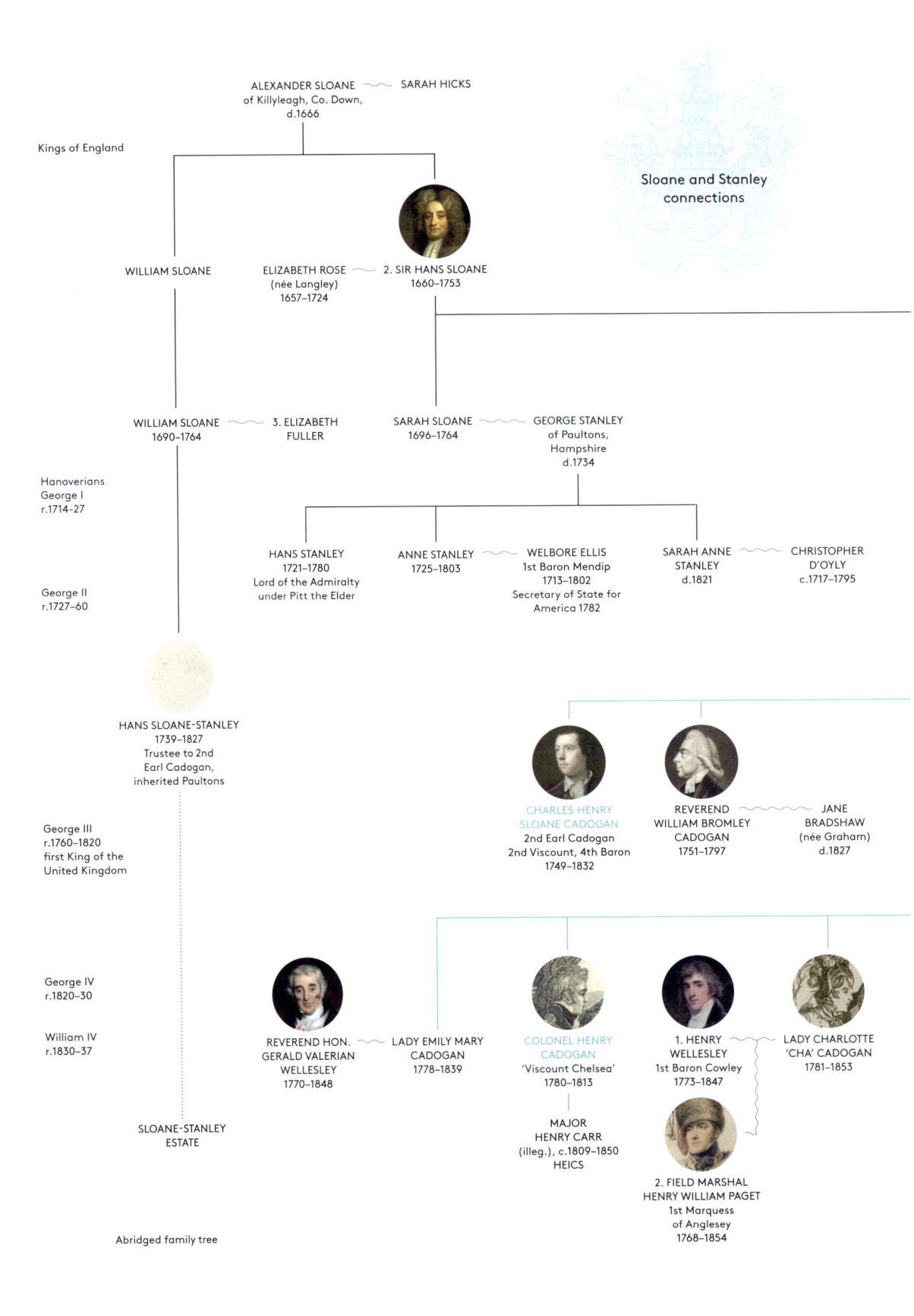

Kings of England

ALEXANDER SLOANE ～ SARAH HICKS
of Killyleagh, Co. Down,
d.1666

WILLIAM SLOANE

ELIZABETH ROSE ～ 2. SIR HANS SLOANE
(née Langley)   1660–1753
1657–1724

WILLIAM SLOANE ～ 3. ELIZABETH FULLER
1690–1764

SARAH SLOANE ～ GEORGE STANLEY
1696–1764   of Paultons,
                   Hampshire
                   d.1734

Hanoverians
George I
r.1714–27

George II
r.1727–60

HANS STANLEY
1721–1780
Lord of the Admiralty
under Pitt the Elder

ANNE STANLEY ～ WELBORE ELLIS
1725–1803   1st Baron Mendip
                 1713–1802
                 Secretary of State for
                 America 1782

SARAH ANNE ～ CHRISTOPHER
STANLEY   D'OYLY
d.1821   c.1717–1795

HANS SLOANE-STANLEY
1739–1827
Trustee to 2nd
Earl Cadogan,
inherited Paultons

George III
r.1760–1820
first King of the
United Kingdom

CHARLES HENRY
SLOANE CADOGAN
2nd Earl Cadogan
2nd Viscount, 4th Baron
1749–1832

REVEREND ～ JANE
WILLIAM BROMLEY   BRADSHAW
CADOGAN   (née Graham)
1751–1797   d.1827

George IV
r.1820–30

William IV
r.1830–37

REVEREND HON. ～ LADY EMILY MARY
GERALD VALERIAN   CADOGAN
WELLESLEY   1778–1839
1770–1848

COLONEL HENRY
CADOGAN
'Viscount Chelsea'
1780–1813

1. HENRY ～ LADY CHARLOTTE
WELLESLEY   'CHA' CADOGAN
1st Baron Cowley 1781–1853
1773–1847

MAJOR
HENRY CARR
(illeg.), c.1809–1850
HEICS

2. FIELD MARSHAL
HENRY WILLIAM PAGET
1st Marquess
of Anglesey
1768–1854

SLOANE-STANLEY
ESTATE

Abridged family tree

Children of the second 1st Earl Cadogan (NC)

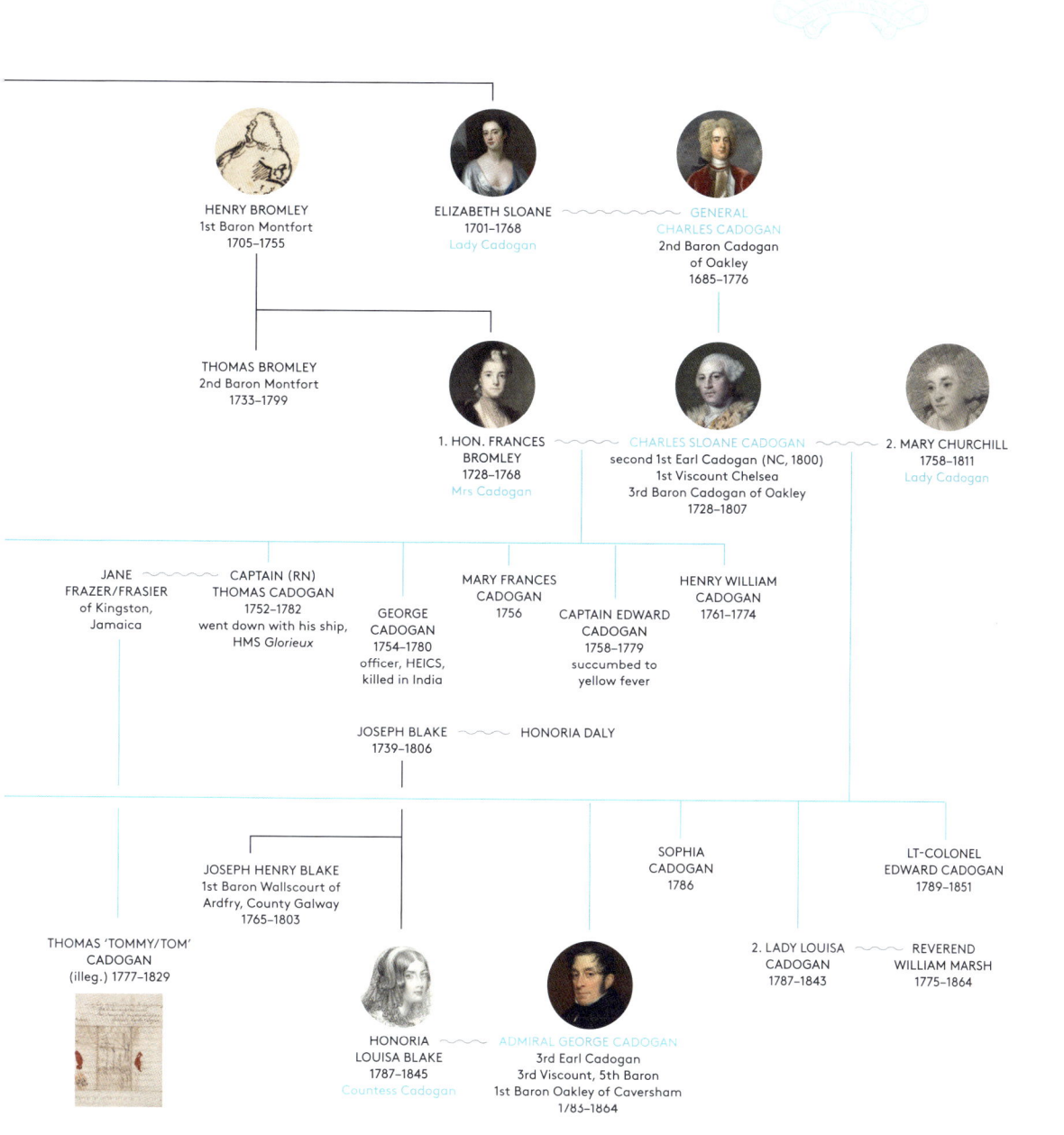

HENRY BROMLEY
1st Baron Montfort
1705–1755

ELIZABETH SLOANE
1701–1768
Lady Cadogan

GENERAL CHARLES CADOGAN
2nd Baron Cadogan of Oakley
1685–1776

THOMAS BROMLEY
2nd Baron Montfort
1733–1799

1. HON. FRANCES BROMLEY
1728–1768
Mrs Cadogan

CHARLES SLOANE CADOGAN
second 1st Earl Cadogan (NC, 1800)
1st Viscount Chelsea
3rd Baron Cadogan of Oakley
1728–1807

2. MARY CHURCHILL
1758–1811
Lady Cadogan

JANE FRAZER/FRASIER
of Kingston, Jamaica

CAPTAIN (RN) THOMAS CADOGAN
1752–1782
went down with his ship, HMS *Glorieux*

GEORGE CADOGAN
1754–1780
officer, HEICS, killed in India

MARY FRANCES CADOGAN
1756

CAPTAIN EDWARD CADOGAN
1758–1779
succumbed to yellow fever

HENRY WILLIAM CADOGAN
1761–1774

JOSEPH BLAKE
1739–1806

HONORIA DALY

THOMAS 'TOMMY/TOM' CADOGAN
(illeg.) 1777–1829

JOSEPH HENRY BLAKE
1st Baron Wallscourt of Ardfry, County Galway
1765–1803

SOPHIA CADOGAN
1786

LT-COLONEL EDWARD CADOGAN
1789–1851

2. LADY LOUISA CADOGAN
1787–1843

REVEREND WILLIAM MARSH
1775–1864

HONORIA LOUISA BLAKE
1787–1845
Countess Cadogan

ADMIRAL GEORGE CADOGAN
3rd Earl Cadogan
3rd Viscount, 5th Baron
1st Baron Oakley of Caversham
1783–1864

Wellington's Victory, or The Battle of Vittoria,
Op. 91, Ludwig van Beethoven, 1813

NAPOLEONIC WARS
& THE WELLINGTON
CONNECTION

CHAPTER 8

Made in the Royal Navy

—

CAPTAIN GEORGE CADOGAN

(1783–1864)

George Cadogan made an unusual career choice for an aristocratic boy. Perhaps he was inspired during days by the coast at the family's retreat at Lowestoft, and enjoyed messing about in boats. Perhaps tales of his famous third cousin Horatio Nelson put derring-do and life on the high seas at the top of his wish-list. Or perhaps his parents, recently separated, sent an unruly boy away to sea. No record exists to tell us, but wherever the first impulse came from, the decision that George would join the Royal Navy reveals an assumption on all sides that he was unlikely to inherit his father's peerage.

Perfect for a boy with an adventurous spirit, naval life was nonetheless a very dangerous option. If the battles didn't kill you, any one of several diseases readily contracted while in port might. If you survived such onslaughts from fellow man and microbe, the sea itself might see you done for – dashed upon the rocks or flung from the rigging in a high wind. In short, you might be blown up; you might froth at the mouth; you might drown. George would have been well aware of the fates of his older half-brothers, including Captain Thomas who had gone down with his ship, HMS *Glorieux*, the year before he was born. On the upside, with the Royal Navy a young man could see the world; capturing enemy ships was both exciting and financially rewarding; and men of the right temperament could expect

Destruction of the Droits de l'homme, Thomas Luny (1759–1837), oil on canvas. HMS *Amazon* (far right, with torn sails) and HMS *Indefatigable* (centre) fighting the French ship the *Droits de l'homme* in Audierne Bay, 13/14 January 1797. With just a year's experience at sea, thirteen-year-old George Cadogan, one of the youngest of his cohort, stuck to his station on the quarterdeck during *Indefatigable*'s most famous engagement.

rapid advancement. After a childhood of sandy toes under the watchful eye of a governess at Downham Hall, he spent a single year at Newcombe's School in Hackney, 'a fashionable school with a notable tradition of staging highly regarded dramatic productions...a popular choice for the sons of prominent Whigs.'[1] And then George Cadogan – eighth son of Charles Sloane Cadogan, his second by Mary Churchill – went away to sea at the tender age of twelve.

Boarding the frigate HMS *Indefatigable* on 15 December 1795, George took the rank of first-class volunteer: an officer in training, apprenticed to the captain. There were generally a few such 'young gentlemen' on each ship, swapping in and out of roles and tasks while they learned the ropes. George was joined on *Indefatigable* by Henry Hart, a relation of Sir Percival Hart Dyke; Richard Delves Broughton, youngest son of Sir Thomas, 6th Baronet; and several others from more humble backgrounds. On board, the boys' education would not be neglected. There was a schoolmaster in the form of a warrant officer who instructed them in writing, mathematics and navigation. From their fellow sailors they also learned the practical arts of seamanship: the boatswain taught knotting and splicing, and topmen imparted the intricacies of furling and unfurling the many sails. This latter daily task, known as exercising aloft, brought a frisson of danger – one slip of the foot could result in a fall of a hundred feet to death on the deck or in the sea below. George would be paid £6 a year until he passed his lieutenant's exam and took a commission.[2]

Indefatigable was in dock at Plymouth undergoing repairs when George came aboard. The year before, she had been modified to a 'razee' (from the French *rasé*: literally, razored), in an operation that sliced off the upper gun-deck. This dramatic weight-loss transformed her from a powerful, but heavy, third-rate ship of the line (battleship) into an extremely well-armed fifth-rate frigate. *Indefatigable* now had forty-four guns to a standard frigate's thirty-two and she was lighter than a warship: she could out-gun an enemy frigate and outrun a ship of the line. Her mission was to ferry men and munitions, while causing maximum disruption to enemy supply lines and taking prizes along the way: George's placement was an exciting prospect. It had been arranged for him by a family friend (another George), the 2nd Earl Spencer, who was First Lord of the Admiralty (the political head of the Royal Navy, no less). He wrote to the ship's captain:

> A son of Lord Cadogan a very old friend of mine is destined to the sea service…I have undertaken to recommend him to you. He is, I understand, between 12 and 13 years of age…I have told his father that he can be no better placed for this purpose than with you.[3]

The letter's recipient was Sir Edward Pellew, a salty Cornishman who had himself run away to sea at thirteen. His name, and that of his ship, will be familiar to readers of C.S. Forester's historical novels, first published in the 1930s: fictional naval hero Horatio Hornblower spent part of his career on

8. MADE IN THE ROYAL NAVY

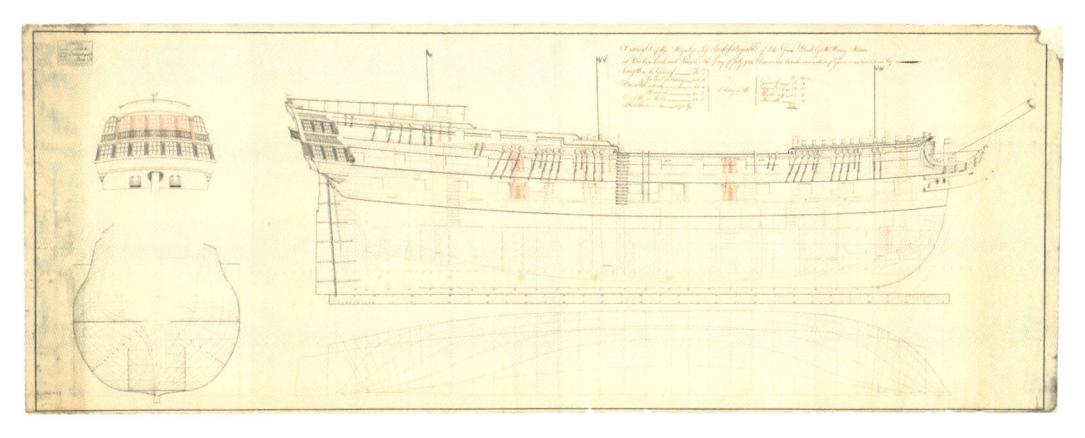

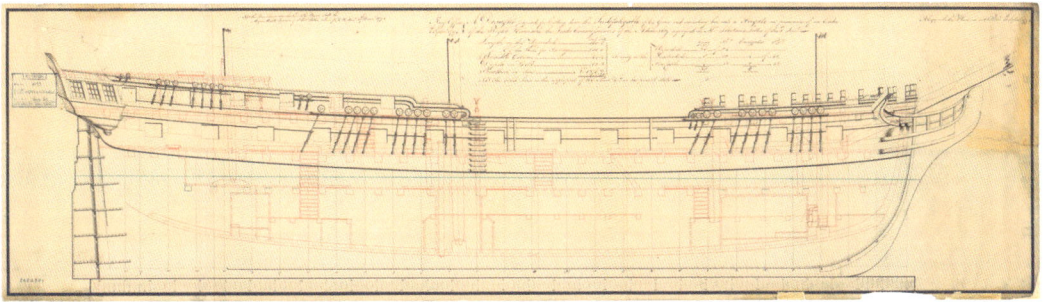

HMS *Indefatigable*, Portsmouth dockyard, ink on paper. TOP 1784. A scale plan (1:48) technical drawing shows the original third-rate ship as built and launched at Buckler's Hard by Henry Adams. ABOVE 1794. By the time George came aboard, this proposal to 'razee' the ship of the line by removing her upper deck had transformed her into a heavy frigate.

board *Indefatigable* under Pellew's command. It is in this role, as captain of that frigate, that the real-life Pellew is most famous. Over many years, the large, bluff but kindly sailor nurtured the young officers in his charge, advanced their interests as his own and 'gained the lasting love and devotion of his men.'[4] The system of patronage extended to all young volunteers who set their heart on life at sea, providing 'vertical links of mutual dependence and obligation'.[5] Those links ran up and down the chain of command. Early in his own career, Pellew had served as a second lieutenant under Thomas Cadogan on HMS *Licorne*, stationed at Newfoundland in 1779.

Following the foundation of the French Republic in September 1792, an army of a million men, the largest in the world, continued the expansionist policies of the *ancien régime*, conquering Belgium, the Rhineland, Savoy and the County of Nice. Dangerous revolutionary ideas had spread like wildfire on the Continent. In the British Isles, however, confidence was high that the constitutional monarchy could survive any whispers of *'liberté, égalité, fraternité'* in the ears of John Bull, whatever fashionable society and an anxiety-inducing press might propose to the contrary. Pitt the Younger was more concerned with protecting the balance of military and economic power – defending borders, colonies and trade routes – than with threats to the liberal order. Britain's prowess as a sea-going nation was about to be tested.

In October 1795 General Napoleon Bonaparte crushed a royalist revolt in Paris and the Royal Navy began preparing to defend British shores from attack by a new European superpower. King George III and his Prime Minister could call upon a corps who had recently seen battle during the American War of Independence, including Nelson and Admiral Lord Howe, the gouty commander-in-chief of the Channel Fleet. By contrast, the French had guillotined many of their senior naval officers. It was in this heightened atmosphere that Pellew took the helm of *Indefatigable* just as George embarked.

First, there was a dramatic incident at home. The ship was still in dock at the end of January, and Pellew sitting down to dinner, when news of a vessel in trouble at nearby Plymouth Hoe reached his ears – it was the *Dutton*, laden with troops returning home from the West Indies. Immediately, he dashed out to help; finding that no one could hear his instructions over the wind, or would accept payment to help:

> ...he gave an instance of the highest heroism: for he fixed the rope about himself and gave the signal to be drawn on board... He then became active in getting out the women and the sick... The soldiers were falling into disorder when Sir Edward went on board. I saw him beating one with the flat of his broadsword, in order to make him give up a bundle he had made up of plunder. They had but just time to save the men, before the ship was nearly under water...she is now in pieces.[6]

The Distressful Situation of the Dutton East Indiaman, John Jeffreys, 1 September 1796, aquatint and etching, from a drawing by Nicholas Pocock. George had recently embarked on HMS *Indefatigable*, still in dock, when the *Dutton* was wrecked. His captain, Edward Pellew, took charge of a risky rescue operation that made his name.

Such bravery was recognized with a title to add to the knighthood: he became Sir Edward Pellew, 1st Baronet of Treverry. Pellew had been the last to leave the ship. These actions of honourable self-sacrifice and outstanding leadership would have made quite an impression on young George.

INDEFATIGABLE FINALLY SET SAIL ON 9 MARCH 1796. Leading a squadron of four other frigates, a lugger and three chasse-marées, she headed for the Bay of Biscay. The British fleet was carrying arms, ammunition and supplies to the French resistance fighting against their government. While there, Pellew's men had immediate success in taking a prize: a French frigate, *Unité*. On the way back, after a chase of 168 miles, a second frigate, *Virginie*, surrendered to *Indefatigable* which 'for all the damage suffered... has but one man wounded'.[7] George had experienced his first battle at sea. Notably, Pellew and his wife invited the defeated Captain Bergeret to live with them at their home in Falmouth while he was a prisoner on parole, and the two men became lifelong friends.

Even as a boy, George was rewarded for these actions. When the Admiralty bought a captured enemy ship, the prize money was shared out among everyone who had taken part, from the admiral to the lowliest ordinary seaman. Prices for prizes ran down a scale from ships of the line to the smallest merchant craft. A seaworthy 32-gun frigate – such as *Unité* or *Virginie* – was worth over thirty-five years' salary to the captain, four to a lieutenant and perhaps eighteen months' wages to the ordinary seaman. Huge sums: a successful captain could build a fortune. (Remember, George's older half-brother Thomas had amassed enough prize money in his short life at sea for his estate to be tied up in legal wranglings after his death.) George himself, still in his early teens, was already supplementing his meagre salary.

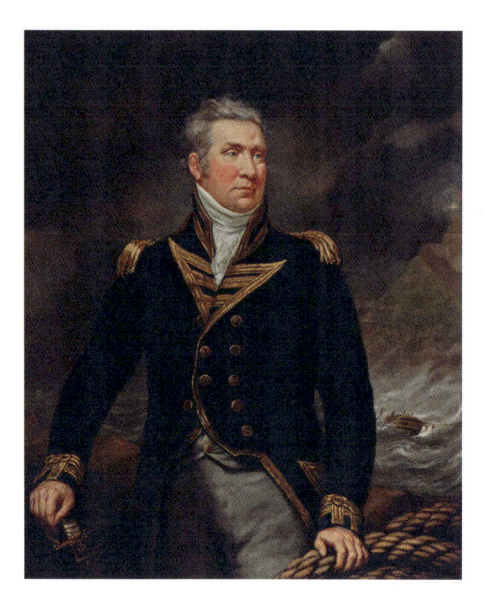

Sir Edward Pellew, 1st Viscount Exmouth, James Northcote, 1804, oil on canvas. Pellew's heroism in rescuing men from the *Dutton* is recorded in the background of this portrait.

The following year brought perhaps the most famous episode in *Indefatigable*'s history and cemented its iconic status in the French Revolutionary and Napoleonic Wars: engagement with *Droits de l'homme* on 13 January 1797. The Brest Fleet was returning home after a failed invasion attempt on the west coast of Ireland. Captain Pellew, at sea with two vessels (the other was a standard 36-gun frigate, HMS *Amazon*), spotted a French ship of the line near Ushant, in the English Channel, and correctly identified that in rough seas the heavy 74-gun vessel couldn't open its lower gun doors without risking flooding. This levelled the playing field, removing the danger to his smaller ships of being sunk by a broadside, and setting size against speed. It was the perfect opportunity to show what his pumped-up razee could do. He gave chase. The French ship tried to ram the British frigates; musket fire and shells flew for ten hours as *Droits de l'homme* tried to outrun its enemy. George, then four months shy of his fourteenth birthday, was in the thick of it on board *Indefatigable*.

> The sea was high, the people on the main deck were up to their middles in water; some guns broke their breechings four times over and some drew the ring bolts from the sides and many of them were repeatedly drawn immediately after loading; all our masts were much wounded; the main topmast completely unrigg'd and saved only by uncommon alacrity.[8]

Ships' logs and captains' accounts give us an extraordinary amount of detail. A sudden break in the clouds at 4.20 am revealed how close the three ships were to land, as moonlight picked out the white tips of the breaking waves: 'not an instant could be lost and every life depended on the prompt execution of my orders,' Pellew wrote to his bosses at the Admiralty.[9] Both the British ships took evasive action, but the larger French vessel was unable to turn in time and was dashed on the rocks, all lives lost. *Amazon* was grounded and her crew captured. Only *Indefatigable* got away, limping into Falmouth a few days later. It was a formative experience for those young men who were present, recognized as 'unique in the annals of naval warfare...[an] unparalleled act of seamanship'.[10] Pellew picked out George for a report back to Earl Spencer:

> Little Cadogan is a delightful boy, I think he promises to be everything the heart can wish. He is stationed on the quarter-deck, where I assure you my Lord, he was my friend. He stood the night out in his shirt and kept himself warm by his exertions. I can not say too much in his praise.[11]

When in 1847 the British government issued the Naval General Service Medal, the engagement of *Droits de l'homme* was one of the specific actions granted a named clasp. No prize money for George this time, but honour and glory.[12]

GEORGE MADE STEADY PROGRESS, building his wealth and reputation. Able seaman, midshipman, master's mate – the ratings changed throughout his teenage years, but his general duties were the same: muck in and learn from everyone around you, particularly the captain. When Pellew was promoted from *Indefatigable* to his first ship of the line, HMS *Impétueux*, in 1799, he was unwillingly parted from a loyal and well-drilled crew of four years' standing, but somehow he made it possible for George and a handful of his contemporaries to accompany him.

These were the war years of Quota Acts when violent methods of forced recruitment were sanctioned by law in order to maintain fighting numbers. The enduring myth in the popular imagination (formed in part from contemporary caricatures by Gillray, Rowlandson and others) has the impress service, the 'pressgangs', coming ashore to kidnap men from field, hearth and tavern, leaving wailing women and infants in their wake. In reality, they preferred to operate at sea, where they would find experienced sailors – who could not escape without risk of drowning. That's not to say they didn't look on land when necessary. 'The men pressed into service were usually sailors in the merchant fleets, but might just as often [have been] ordinary apprentices and labourers.'[13] Many crews set sail without a full complement of men and not everyone on board a fighting Navy ship was there voluntarily.

Floggings were common for minor offences. On board *Impétueux*, Pellew literally whipped his new – and reputedly malcontent – crew into shape. Perhaps inevitably, this led to a mutiny only two months into his command. Two or three hundred men had gathered on deck and were demanding a boat.

> ...the more I endeavoured to pacify them, and bring them to reason, the louder the noise became; many saying...'We will have a boat; d—, we'll take one.' This convinced me they were determined to go the greatest lengths, and was more than either my patience or my duty permitted me to bear. I only answered, 'You will, will you!' and flew into my cabin for my sword...[14]

A Splendid Record of British Bravery...displayed in the Six French Ships of the line captured the [Glorious] First of June 1794, as they appeared on their arrival in Portsmouth Harbour, R. Livesay, 1796, ink on paper. Inscribed below: 'Britannia thus, her dreadful thunder hurls/Rides o'er the waves sublime, and now,/Impending hangs o'er Gallia's humbled coast./She rules the circling deep, and awes the world.' The result of Britain's first naval engagement with France during the Revolutionary War, Admiral Lord Howe's prize *L'Amerique* (left, shown with French flag below the Union Jack) was taken into service by the Royal Navy, renamed first HMS *America* and later (1795) HMS *Impétueux*. George joined Pellew on board in 1799.

With the help of his officers – and, no doubt, with his 'young gentlemen' alongside – Pellew faced them down. The even-handed captain enclosed the men's letter of complaint with his own requesting a court martial for the mutineers. Three men were hanged at the yardarm. Four received a hundred lashes; one poor soul took double that. Prisoners were rowed 'all around the fleet' (from ship to ship), to the accompaniment of a slow drum beat, receiving the apportioned number in sight of each ship's crew. The episode would prove to be a valuable lesson for George; a few years later, he would face a mutiny among his own men.[15]

The Point of Honour, George Cruikshank, 1 July 1825, etching. Flogging was a frequent punishment in Nelson's Navy and both Pellew and his protégé George would find cause to mete it out. All hands are piped on deck to witness punishment. Officers gather to the left; a file of marines crowds the quarterdeck, ready to uphold order; the bosun stands ready with his cat-o'-nine-tails.

The journey to captain over the intervening years was eventful. George picked up experience along the Atlantic coast at Quiberon Bay and Ferrol. France was now under the control of 'first consul' Bonaparte, following a *coup d'état*, and her armies had increased French domination on land, occupying parts of Switzerland, the Papal States and Naples. Austria left the war; Nelson, newly promoted Vice-Admiral of the White, defeated the Danes at the Battle of Copenhagen and was rewarded with a viscountcy. In October 1801, news reached *Impétueux* that preliminaries to the Treaty of Amiens were underway and, conscious that peace would result in being 'paid off' (decommissioned), Pellew returned his ship to Falmouth on 1 November with plans to become an MP. Forsaking the sea himself, he was at pains to secure the careers of his charges. George boarded HMS *Narcissus* (lead ship of a new class of 32-gun frigates) as a midshipman a month later and sailed for Malta where, on 25 January 1802 – underage by a good fifteen months – he sat his lieutenant's exam. The panel recorded:

…his diligence and sobriety[;] he can splice, knot, reef a sail, work a ship in sailing, shift his Tides, keep a Reckoning of a ship's way by Plane Sailing and Mercator, observe by Sun or Star and find the Variation of the Compass…by certification, [he] appears to be more than Twenty Years of Age.[16]

He would have looked the part, in his smart blue and white uniform of frocked coat and breeches, cocked hat under his arm, a confident protégé of Sir Edward Pellew. Just a few days shy of the required six years' experience, he carried the necessary certificates of service – and practical knowledge – to satisfy the Navy Board. George was now a commissioned officer. In April Lieutenant Cadogan was appointed to 38-gun HMS *Leda*.

The short-lived Peace of Amiens ended when Britain declared war on France in May the following year; Bonaparte had apparently used the time to regroup and plan again for an invasion. There were scuffles in the Channel. Sir Edward Pellew MP couldn't resist getting back in on the action and joined Cornwallis's fleet, captaining HMS *Tonnant*. Admiral Lord Nelson left his *ménage à trois* with the volcano-fancying Hamiltons, and his infant daughter, to take the helm of HMS *Victory* as commander-in-chief in the Mediterranean. His nemesis Bonaparte, now Emperor Napoleon, 'placed a bust of Nelson on his dressing table as a reminder of the man who had caused him and France the most trouble during the preceding war.'[17] In 1804 Pellew abandoned his brief parliamentary career to take up the prestigious appointment of

No. 5 Midshipman, Thomas Rowlandson, 1799, hand-coloured etching. Royal Navy officers' uniforms were regulated from 1748; differences in rank were shown by the shape and colour of the lapels and cuffs. The young gentleman carries a sextant and schoolbook: midshipmen (identifiable by a white patch on their collars) were taught navigation, astronomy and trigonometry, as well as undertaking watches on deck. Following examination, promotion to lieutenant meant command of a battery of guns in action and dispatch on shore in charge of press gangs.

commander-in-chief of the East Indies station. He received another letter from Lord Spencer, suggesting that:

> ...if you could take George Cadogan out [with you], you will confer an obligation both on his father and on myself which would be sensibly acknowledged, and in pushing him forward, I think you know enough of him to be convinced that he would never discredit your patronage.[18]

Instead, George was sent to Port Royal in the West Indies. The day before his twenty-first birthday, he was given his first command: an 18-gun sloop-of-war, HMS *Cyane*. Lieutenant commander was a rank awarded by selection and marked him out as tipped for future promotion: he was now known by custom as 'captain', though achieving full 'post rank' (awarded with a ship of twenty guns or more and guaranteeing a steady climb up the senior appointments), would take a little longer. The Navy's role in the region was to protect British trading colonies and thereby hold up confidence at home.

GEORGE TOOK HIS FIRST PRIZE on 12 November 1804. Perhaps a little naïvely, the action gave him 'thorough satisfaction at the steady and determined conduct of all the officers and crew of the *Cyane*'[19] and a precocious confidence. No doubt the French ship's name gave him an additional glow of pride. He wrote back to his bosses at the Admiralty:

> I have the honour to inform you, that, on the 11th instant, at three a.m. off the Island of Mariegalante, after a short chase and running fight of thirty minutes, I had the good fortune to come up with and capture le *Buonaparté*, a very fine Privateer Brig, pierced for 22 guns, mounting 18 long French 8-pounders, and 150 men. I am happy to add that we have received no material damage in our masts or hull, and have only a few men hurt, occasioned by the explosion of a cartridge on the main deck.[20]

8. MADE IN THE ROYAL NAVY

A few months later, he took his second: a Spanish privateer, *Justica*, which had four guns and ninety-five men on board. However, his luck ran out in the spring of 1805 when he fell for a *ruse de guerre* enacted by the French ship *Hortense*. Captain Lameillerie wrote to his commander, Vice-Admiral Villeneuve:

> ...at five o'clock in the evening I saw a war ship that I judged to be the enemy from its reconnaissance signals, heading towards us under full sail. I waited for it and hoisted the English flag and he did the same immediately. I identified it as an English corvette and very shortly it was in cannon range to windward. Realising its mistake it altered course and took flight. I tacked and with a stormy gale blowing to the east chased it through the night. The enemy sailed as close to the wind as it could, tacking many times, and I followed each movement. At last, having tried by all means to escape, its cannons and some of its guns were thrown into the sea and it struck its flag without fighting. I asked its captain on board and he named himself as the Honourable George Cadogan...[21]

An oldie but a goodie: the false flag. George was clearly held in some esteem by the French, who noted 'Mr Cadogan, commander of the corvette, has caused much damage to commerce in this area during the past year.'[22] He was taken prisoner and held at Fort-de-France on Martinique for eight weeks. Accounts of his time there vary. George himself wrote to his commander-in-chief to complain that his captors' 'infamous conduct' would

RIGHT Sword, Thomas Aila, 18th century. 'I leave you a relic of my father...This is the sword of the Spanish Admiral which your grandfather took possession of after destroying his fleet numbering about eight to one...'. This note from George's daughter Lady Augusta to the 5th Earl Cadogan was found inside the sword's case.

'disgrace the most barbarous'.²³ Conversely, a mention of the 'liberal treatment of Capt Cadogan & the prisoners who fell into the hands of Admiral Villeneuve'²⁴ reached the ears of King George III via Charles Grey, First Lord of the Admiralty. It would secure the Frenchman's own release after he was captured by the British fleet at the most famous sea battle of the age. Skirmishes in the Channel came to a head at the Battle of Trafalgar, on 21 October 1805. Villeneuve, commanding the French fleet, struck his flag and surrendered to HMS *Conqueror* – captained by Sir Edward Pellew's brother, Israel. Nelson lost his life but secured a decisive victory against greater numbers of French and Spanish ships, establishing a golden age of British naval supremacy.

Life at sea was increasing its appeal. The Navy's historical reputation, famously encapsulated by Winston Churchill as rum, sodomy and the lash, tells only part of the story. Pre-sanitization, beer had long been drunk as an alternative to water, both on land and at sea. From the mid-seventeenth century sailors were given a half-pint of rum daily; then from 1740 for the next 230 years the tot was mixed with water at 4:1.[25] Finding the right amount of Dutch courage was undoubtedly part of the fighting fleet's success. Other improvements to rations and logistics had enabled George's squadron to stay at sea for eight months while blockading the French ports of L'Orient and Rochefort in 1801. Provisions could be sent out from Britain periodically: bread, pease, beef, port and lemon juice. The last of these spelled the end of scurvy, which had plagued sailors of centuries past. To paraphrase the eminent naval historian N.A.M. Rodger, if this life was so bad, how come the British won every major naval engagement for 150 years?

George was not at Trafalgar. After a routine court martial over the loss of *Cyane* (which fully exonerated him), and six months in England, he returned to Jamaica. Appointed post captain, he was given command of HMS *Ferret*, a brand-new sloop of war, on 22 March 1806. The muster list shows that her crew was assembled from a ragbag of 'seamen between cruises, newly pressed or recruited men, prisoners awaiting trial and some already convicted of offences'.[26] George soon had a discipline problem on his hands; mutiny erupted at midnight on 26 September. Several accounts have been published. George and his first lieutenant, Mr White, were disturbed from sleep by shouts and pounding of feet on deck. In the most exciting version 'George then appeared at the gunroom door, naked, with a pistol in one hand and a cutlass in the other.'[27] In another, while still in his nightshirt, he jumped up through a skylight and confronted a seaman with a cutlass who 'confessed it was his job to cut him down as he came up the ladder.'[28] Sadly, the captain's log has been lost, but the court martial record survives, including this testimony from Edward Jones, his would-be assassin:

> The Captain came up and asked what's the matter men, and told them to come forward and tell their grievance, as soon as they saw the Captain they all ran forward and laid down their arms again except myself...I told him the grievance of the Ship's company was ill usage by flogging and starting and that they were all of one mind and were to confine him to his own Cabin and give charge of the Vessel to Mr White and Mr Hannah to take her into Port Royal; the Captain stepped over to me between two of the guns and said now your life is in my hands, I asked him to take my life at once, he said he was more of a gentleman than to do the like of that, since the rest of your cowardly partners have gone away and left you, he then ordered me aft and confined me.[29]

The crew had blinked. Following Pellew's early example, George's courage in the face of mutiny had regained him control of his ship. Jones was one of the few spared; eleven men were hung at the yardarm. George wrote home to his father:

> My mind is really in so agitated and wretched a state...[they] have since tried all [the] unfortunate deluded wretches who are all doomed to suffer here tomorrow morning. I have not the words to express my feelings upon the occasion – and am only upheld by the conscious rectitude of the cause for which they suffer and of having done justice to my country, and having acquitted

myself, I trust, with personal credit. They are all thank God sensible of their guilt and in their last moments acknowledged their ingratitude to me and their treachery to their country…I am very low, & unwell…[30]

His father was sufficiently moved by George's plight – doubtless it awakened memories of the loss of Edward ('What I fear most for is his health in that cursed climate'[31]) – to forward the letter to Lord Spencer, who in turn sent it on to the new First Lord of the Admiralty, Thomas Grenville. Spencer asked Grenville to move George's commission to another frigate, '[t]hough from the tenor of this letter, I really would not be surprised to hear that he had died of the yellow fever which always seizes people when they are in low spirits.'[32] Things looked bleak, but it was another six months before George was invalided out, in June 1807. Sadly, he did not make it home in time to see his father before he died; his half-brother, poor 'insane' Charles Henry, was now the 2nd Earl Cadogan.

The Death of Nelson, 21st October 1805, Benjamin West, 1806, oil on canvas

After a couple of months' rest and recuperation, George was appointed commander of sixth-rate, 22-gun HMS *Crocodile* and on 15 December 1807 sailed for the Cape of Good Hope. Trouble flared again on George's new ship and there were two floggings a week. The ringleader, Midshipman William Badcock, was discharged in June the following year. When he fell ill and subsequently died, the accusations of cruel and excessive punishment levelled by Badcock's grandfather, playwright Richard Cumberland, brought George to another court martial:

> Witness after witness testified that [Badcock] was insolent, insubordinate and ungovernable, that he continually left the deck during his watch, was repeatedly contemptuous to the officer and, most tellingly, that he had been disrated by the ship's previous captain.[33]

George was cleared of all charges. These inquiries into treatment of his crew – on the *Ferret* and *Crocodile* – have conspired to paint George as 'a pitiless officer whose remorseless use of the lash made Pigot appear gentle'.[34] However, recent comparison between *Ferret*'s master's log and those of other ships in the area at that time 'shows that it was by no means excessive'.[35] The Admiralty certainly backed him. Following his acquittal, he was given progressively larger and more heavily armed fifth-rate frigates: in 1809 he took HMS *Pallas* (thirty-two guns) out to Walcheren; and in 1811 accepted command of the brand-new frigate HMS *Havannah* (thirty-six).

Under his old mentor Pellew, now commander-in-chief of the Mediterranean Fleet, George patrolled the coast of the 'Illyrian Provinces' annexed by Napoleon, which included parts of north-eastern Italy and present-day Croatia and Austria. This he did not only with minimal loss to his crew, but generously recognizing their contribution to the capture and destruction of enemy ships. In January 1813, he wrote to his superior: '...I must beg leave to call your attention to the great skill and gallantry with which this service was executed by the first lieutenant, William Hamley, the officers and men under his orders...'.[36] Details were published in the *Naval Chronicle* and picked up for wider readership by the *Gentleman's Magazine*:

Vice-admiral Sir Edw. Pellew has also transmitted a letter from the Hon. Captain Cadogan of his Majesty's ship the *Havannah*, to Rear-adm. Fremantle, giving an account of the destruction, on the 7th of February [1813], of an Enemy's convoy of twenty-five sail, four of them gun-boats, by the boats of the *Havannah*...A battery of seven guns was destroyed by the marines, and two of the vessels brought out, the rest scuttled and left full of water. The convoy came from Venice, and the vessels were laden with ordnance stores. This service was performed without the loss of a man.[37]

Twenty-five ships taken and not a man lost; so it continued for several months. George was to leave his sea-going career on a high.

His final action was on board *Havannah*, leading an Anglo-Austrian force to victory at the Siege of Zara (present-day Zadar in Croatia), at the end of November 1813. The French capitulated 'after sustaining a cannonade of thirteen days from the English batteries, consisting of 32-pound carronades, eight 18-pounders, and seven 12-pound long guns, as well as two howitzers worked by Austrians.'[38] Forwarding this description of George's, his fleet commander included a covering note to the Secretary of the Admiralty, John Wilson Croker:

A Scene on the Main Deck of a Line of Battle Ship in Harbour, Thomas Sutherland; J.B. East, 1 June 1820, hand-coloured aquatint. During the Napoleonic Wars sailors were rarely given shore leave in case they deserted, so they spent a lot of time on board and found ways to amuse themselves.

Critical situation of His Majesty's Ships off Toulon in the Winter of 1812, Capt. Pearce, watercolour. HMS *Curacoa* and *Havannah* standing in to reconnoitre the French Fleet in Toulon Harbour. Captain George, on the *Havannah*, captured an impressive fifty-eight armed vessels around the Ilyrian Provinces.

> The judgment, perseverance, and ability shewn by him, on every occasion, will not, I am persuaded, escape their Lordships' observation. Captain Cadogan, with the crews of a frigate and a sloop, has accomplished as much as required the services of the squadron united at Trieste.[39]

Quite the compliment: at the siege of Trieste a month earlier Fremantle had enjoyed nearly five times the firepower. Success at Zara proved to be the tipping point in the Adriatic Campaign.

So why did George leave the high seas at the peak of his glittering career? The answer is simple: family. Even before the death of their father, the private lives of the Cadogan boys had come under increasing scrutiny. When Charles Henry, 2nd Earl Cadogan, became the family's titular head in 1807, not one of them was married and the future of the title and estate was uncertain. What unfolded over the five years to Zara is a tale of births (both legitimate and not), an early death and a hopeful marriage. But first, the Cadogan sisters would be embroiled in scandal. In the last years of George III's reign, George found himself acting in defence of the realm at sea and – pistol in hand – defending the honour of the family name at home in London.

CHAPTER 9

Pistols at Dawn

—

SCANDALOUS LADY CHARLOTTE (1781–1853)

One bright spring morning in 1809 (30 May, a Tuesday), at 7 am, twenty-six-year-old naval captain George Cadogan, fresh off HMS *Crocodile*, marked out the agreed number of paces across Wimbledon Common, turned to face his opponent and fired a pistol. How he came to be there is, in part, a tale of three Henrys. The first is politician Henry Wellesley, youngest brother of Arthur, the future Duke of Wellington; the second is Colonel Henry Cadogan, George's older brother; and the third is Henry, Lord Paget, dashing cavalry officer, future Earl of Uxbridge and 1st Marquess of Anglesey. Why was George there? Well, as with so many duels, *cherchez la femme*. It is really her story.

Lady Charlotte Sloane Cadogan, universally known as Cha, had an unsettled early life as the third child of Charles Sloane Cadogan and his second wife, Mary Churchill. She was four when the family left Caversham Park, and she grew up in Suffolk at Downham. At home among the sandy wastes and the rabbits, she had plenty of company in the nursery: Emily (b.1778), Henry (b.1780) and George (b.1783) were playmates until the boys went off to school; little Louisa (b.1787) and Edward (b.1789) arrived after the move across county lines. Sadly, her seventh sibling, Sophia, died in infancy (1786).

For much of her childhood, Chelsea was a building site, as the plan approved by her father became a reality and streets were laid out in the configuration that survives to this day. It was not the only borough under construction; Georgian London was expanding rapidly. The young family's

The Elopement of Lady W— with Lord Paget, George Cruikshank, 1814, etching

home in town was rather peripatetic: they uprooted first from 14 St James's Square to 3 New Burlington Street (her grandparents' house), then to 21 Hanover Square and finally, in 1793, to 41 Upper Grosvenor Gardens. Shortly after this last move, her mother's affair was discovered, with the resultant ugly court case and parental separation. Such upsetting events doubtless left their emotional mark – Cha was just entering her teens, an impressionable age – and, rather unfairly, the whiff of scandal hung around Mary's girls by association. Lady Emily Mary Cadogan (1778–1839), the eldest, was eighteen when the divorce came through in 1796. Who would marry the daughters of a wayward wife?

Happily, everyone's prospects were improved by the new creation of the Cadogan earldom in 1800. Emily caught the eye of a young man from an Irish family whose star was also in the ascendant: the Wellesleys. Their late patriarch Garrett (or Garret) Wesley, a musical prodigy, had been elevated to the peerage in 1760 when he was created 1st Earl of Mornington. Five of his sons survived to adulthood.[1] Richard, 2nd Earl of Mornington from 1781, elevated to Marquess Wellesely in 1799, was busy expanding British colonial rule in the East as Governor-General of Bengal. It was Richard who encouraged his brothers to affect the addition of three letters to the family surname. Son number two had assumed a hyphenated surname, becoming William Wellesley-Pole, in recognition of a large inheritance from his godfather, who was also his great-uncle.[2] He was rich. The third brother, Major-General Arthur, was enjoying a successful military career that would later make him a household name. Emily set her cap at number four: the Reverend the Honourable Gerald Valerian Wellesley (1770–1848). As a clergyman he offered an appealing stability and respectability, and the two families shared a connection with Dublin. Emily and Gerald were married on 2 June 1802.

Gerald's mother Anne, the Dowager Countess of Mornington, was not amused. In addition to Emily's mother's adulterous nature, there was the stigma of insanity in the family: the girls' half-brother Charles Henry had been declared 'a lunatic' only a couple of years earlier. However, Emily found an ally in her French sister-in-law, Hyacinthe, who wrote to her husband Richard:

> For myself I have always found Lady Emily very friendly, frank and kindly and her *manners* very different from those of your devil [*diablesse*] of a mother and your fake and sulky sister. As for your mother…I compare her company to that of the Freemasons, where only those who are in on the secrets are admitted…[3]

The occasion for this letter was dramatic news of another tie binding the Cadogans and the Wellesleys: an imminent second wedding. Diplomat Henry Wellesley (1773–1847), the youngest of the five brothers, had recently returned from India where, after a period as Richard's private secretary, his brief appointment as Governor of Oude/Oudh (operating out of Lucknow in present-day Uttar Pradesh) had come to an ignominious end.

9. PISTOLS AT DAWN

Henry was turning thirty unemployed, under parliamentary inquiry and not in the best of health – a bit of a lost soul. Emily had presented him with a fresh purpose in the form of her little sister Cha. Hyacinthe's report gives a further insight into Wellesley family dynamics:

> You will be astonished, my love, to hear that Mr. Henry is to be married immediately to the sister of Lady Emily Wellesley, eldest daughter of Lord Cadogan, who is neither rich nor pretty. Poor Henry is so indolent, so lazy that I am sure that it is only the fact he met this young person in Mr. Gerald's house, where he was staying and where she was visiting her sister, that made him fall in love with her rather than her beauty or her virtue…Your mother and sister are furious about this marriage…They say Mr Henry was too eager to get married; that is true, but he was caught in the nets of two sisters who love him very much.[4]

After a whirlwind engagement lasting just a month, the couple raced ahead with their plans. Cha's wedding ceremony was conducted by her brother-in-law, the Reverend Gerald, on 20 September 1803 and celebrated 'at the home of her father Lord Cadogan; although no other member of the family was present.'[5] Brothers Henry and George were away fighting Napoleon; her mother was in France, having lost all contact with her children in the divorce. (Well into the nineteenth century, fathers were granted absolute control – sole custody – of their children, 'but also could, and usually did forbid any contact whatsoever with the mother.'[6]) The country venue was unusual for an aristocratic marriage (more usually held in London),

ABOVE Henry Wellesley (later Lord Cowley, 1773–1847), John Hoppner, oil on canvas

though perhaps an accommodation for her elderly father, travelling less and less in old age.

Lady Harriet Cavendish, a daughter of the Duke of Devonshire, would later refer to Henry Wellesley as 'quite a *Héro de Romance* in person and manner' and the marriage 'for love'.[7] It certainly wasn't for money. Cha brought only £5,000 from her father, as had Emily – modest sums for the daughters of an earl.[8] The Dowager Countess of Mornington, who evidently regarded her son Henry as a catch, begrudgingly accepted the inevitable: she had a second Cadogan daughter-in-law. She wrote to Richard, her eldest:

> It is impossible but [Cha] must love Henry and feel that she is in a situation infinitely beyond what she could expect, therefore I hope she will make it her study to render him happy, but I can see no charm of either person or manner, *mais il ne faut pas disputer les goûts*, and he must certainly be a better judge than I can possibly pretend to be of what constitutes his own happiness. Lady Emily, her sister...was determined that this match should take place from the moment she heard of Henry's arrival, and laid her plans accordingly. I can forgive Lady Charlotte, but for her I confess 'tis out of my power to get over the vexation and cruel disappointment she has occasioned me.[9]

Anne, the mother-in-law from hell, would live for another twenty-eight years. She died in 1831 at the age of eighty-nine, remembered in the annals of history as a severe and demanding

Anne Wellesley (née Hill), Countess of Mornington (1742–1831), Thomas Hodgetts, 1839, mezzotint, published by Welch & Gwynne, after Priscilla Anne Fane (née Wellesley-Pole, Anne's granddaughter). Anne is shown surrounded by portrait busts of her sons Richard, Arthur and Henry.

woman largely ignored by her children. Gerald Wellesley became Rector of Chelsea in 1805, and he and Emily started what would become a large family of three boys and four girls. Henry Wellesley was appointed a Lord of the Treasury in 1804 but resigned in order to look for a diplomatic post. There were moves to make him envoy to Spain; he asked Pitt for Governorship of the Cape; nothing came of either plan. In April 1807 he was elected as MP jointly for Eye in Suffolk and Athlone in Ireland, and again assigned to the Treasury. That same month the Cadogans lost their guiding paternal hand. Charlotte's attention wandered.

HENRY, LORD PAGET (1768–1854), strode into Cha's life at a musical party given by his father at Uxbridge House in early 1808. The Pagets and the Cadogans had been friends for years. Henry, the eldest son, was glamour personified: a dashing cavalry officer, heir to an earldom, he was known for his 'immensely high sartorial standard'.[10] He was also married, to the equally toothsome Lady Caroline Villiers, younger daughter of the Earl of Jersey – known, confusingly, as 'Car' – and the couple had eight children. Cha herself had given birth to her third child in January. She was twenty-six to Paget's forty. He 'fell desperately in love'.[11]

Before long an opportunity presented itself when Cha was advised to go horse-riding for the good of her health. Paget was well placed to loan her a suitable mount and play escort while her husband was kept busy at the Treasury, 'disliking his duties'.[12] He was too much for Cha to resist. Even thirty years later, the sight of Paget – 'so handsome' – on horseback had quite an effect, as Queen Victoria recorded in her diary: 'I met [Paget] in Hyde Park, and he rode with me the whole time; he rides so well, so gracefully, it is quite wonderful; and he rode a beautiful horse.'[13] Eyebrows were raised by Cha's trots *à deux*, and shot further skyward as her condition became apparent. Arthur Wellesley later wrote that 'the riding parties ceased; & about this time Mr Wellesley had perceived the extraordinary attention paid to Lady Charlotte by Lord Paget, & had in consequence remonstrated with her upon the subject.'[14] At the end of the summer parliamentary session of 1808, Henry Wellesley and his wife left town.

Hidden away across the River Thames in rural Putney, Charlotte gave birth to a son. She named him Gerald, perhaps in an effort to underline ties to her husband's family, and specifically to the man who had led her marriage vows. Allowing his wife to return to London in February 1809 – on the condition that she did not go riding – Henry told her that his confidence in her was unbounded, accepting her protestations that Paget was 'a common acquaintance…I believe he liked my society last year but I have no reason to believe that he thinks of me in any way that can be objectionable.'[15] Lady Caroline Paget had also been persuaded to stay in her marriage, though she was clearly unhappy.

Paget had been writing love letters to Cha throughout their separation. While she was in Putney, he had been away fighting in the Corunna Campaign. Back in town she met him for walks in Green Park, throwing caution to the wind and dismissing her footman chaperone (hardly discreet). After less than a month Henry Paget told his brother Charles, a naval officer, 'that his only hope in an éclat not taking place rested on no less than the death of Henry Wellesley.'[16] Cha's sickly husband was bedridden with a liver complaint, but declined to oblige this morbid fantasy.

Meanwhile, rumours had started up about Paget's wife, Car, and the 6th Duke of Argyll. Car denied it: 'She owned the greatest friendship and regard for him (two dangerous feelings to cherish) but no more…'.[17] Argyll and Paget were old friends from their days on the Grand Tour, having shared a house in Vienna in 1787; they may even have crossed paths at the end of that year with Charles Henry, now 2nd Earl Cadogan. And Argyll was no stranger to extramarital intrigue: until her recent demise he had been living with Car's sister,

ABOVE General Officer's sabretache worn by Lt.-Gen. Henry Paget, 2nd Earl of Uxbridge, as Colonel of the 7th (Queen's Own) Light Dragoons, English school, c.1815, red Morocco leather and gold embroidery OPPOSITE *Henry Paget, 1st Marquess of Anglesey*, Henry Edridge, 1808, pencil and watercolour. Dashing Henry proved irresistible to Cha.

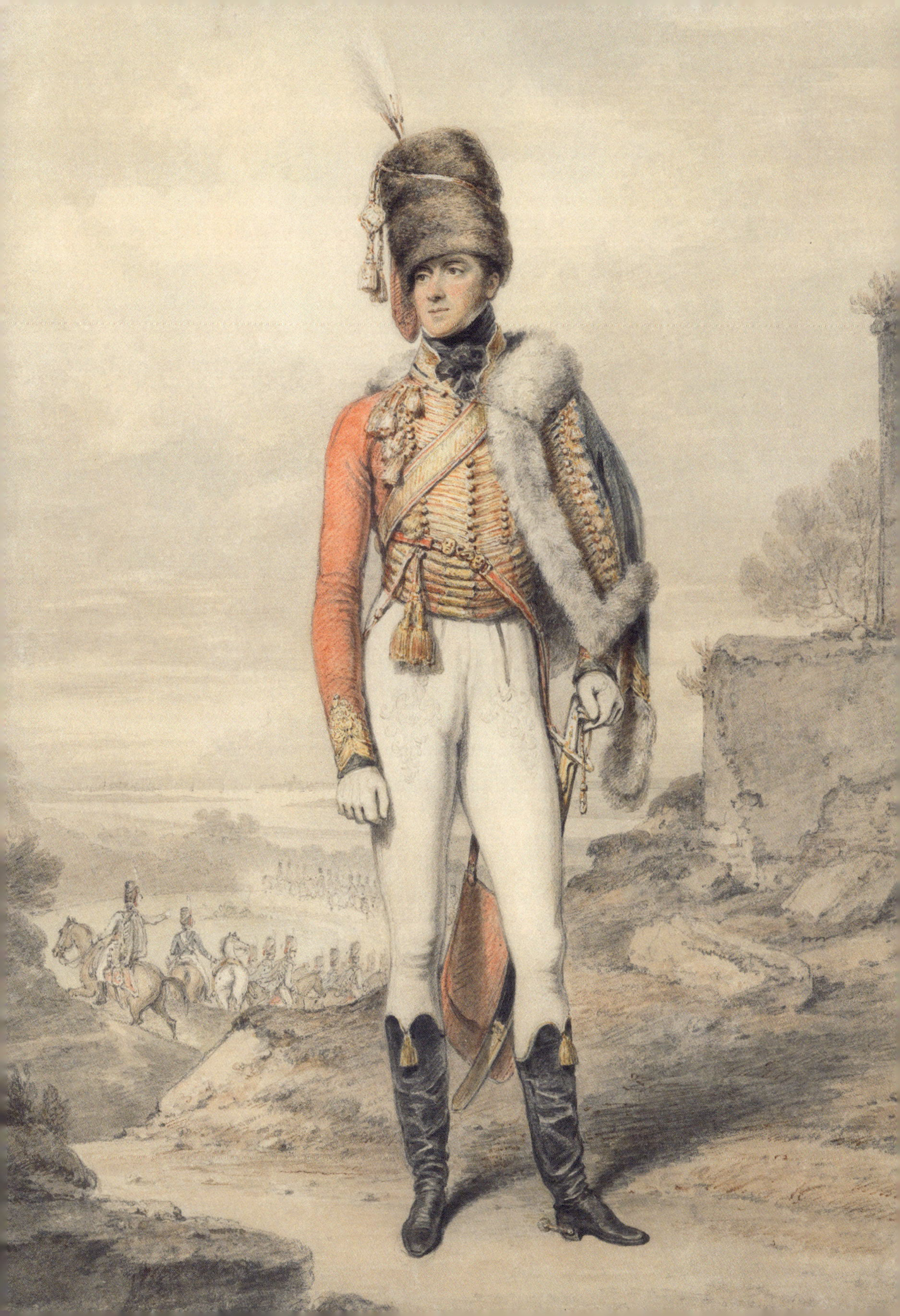

Lady Charlotte Russell (née Villiers). Paget seems to have welcomed news of his old friend and his wife becoming lovers; it gave him the courage he needed for a frank discussion. Charles Paget wrote to another brother that Henry seemed:

...to feel no doubt not only of a present attachment between her [Car] and Lorne [Agyll] but of a future either legal or illegal connection. The first he supposes in the event of his deserting Car and her gaining a Divorce and her subsequently becoming Duchess of Argyll, or secondly in his going on with the intercourse which now subsists between himself and Lady Charlotte Wellesley (without a blow up [pregnancy]) which would, as he says, justify her in the illegal process. This is the way, my dear fellow, he talks, and it is quite marvellous that on subjects so enormously dreadful he should be able to be so cool and deliberate.[18]

A View of Argyle [the Duke of Argyll], Richard Dighton, 1819, colour etching

The letter's recipient, diplomat Arthur Paget, had himself eloped just a year earlier, with the daughter of the Earl of Westmorland, Lady Augusta Fane (at the time, Boringdon). She was now Lady Augusta Paget, his wife and the mother of his child. Car's decision to call on audacious Augusta – risqué in itself, but accompanied by Argyll, and only shortly after Lady Charlotte Russell's death, positively devil-may-care – had 'already begun to gain some observation in the world'.[19] Arthur, presumably, would have provided a sympathetic ear. But what on earth was going on?

9. PISTOLS AT DAWN

Expectations from marriage were shifting. Among royalty and the nobility, it had often been a practical union of property and an assurance of aristocratic heredity, while extra-marital affairs of the heart and loins were rife; Car's own mother, Lady Jersey, had been a mistress of the Prince of Wales for six years, from 1793 to 1799. *The Female Jockey Club, or, A Sketch of the Manners of the Age* (1794) declared:

> It has never been held the virtue of nobility to cultivate domestic happiness; their minds are devoted to far more sublime pursuits... To confine sensibility to one *thing*, and that thing a husband, would very ill become a woman of spirit, sprung from an *ennobled* and most *loyal* family.[20]

The turn of the nineteenth century and the Regency period saw an explosion of literature examining morality within personal life. Jane Austen's novels famously positioned love within marriage as the pinnacle of happiness; *Pride and Prejudice*, which she drafted while staying at her brother's house at 64 Sloane Street, was published in 1813. Cha and Paget weighed up their own emotional fulfilment against facing social ruin. There was the additional threat of pillory in the newspapers: public morality, then as now, loved to be outraged by tales of what the butler saw. For Cha, Car, Argyll and two of the three Henrys (Paget and Wellesley), scandal seemed inevitable. The stage was set for March madness.

ON THE NIGHT OF SUNDAY, 5 March 1809, the tinderbox was lit by a locked door and a rustling of papers. Henry Wellesley had roused himself from his sickbed to visit his wife in her bedroom. Cha was so flustered when he arrived that his suspicions boiled over. He accused her of an 'improper correspondence' with Paget and such a row ensued that he 'shouted in his fury that she or he must quit the house the following day "for that he knew everything".[21] Cha did not need to be told twice: the following morning she hurried out to Green Park and hailed a cab. Henry Paget scribbled a brief note to his brother:

> My dear Arthur,
>
> At the very instant that your letter arrived, I received a message from a person in a Hackney Coach in Park Lane to come immediately.
>
> An Éclat took place last night and Lady Charlotte Wellesley, dreading a further discussion this morning, that event which we have long dreaded, has actually taken place. I pity you all. Pity us in return – we are in want of it.
>
> Adieu – Paget.[22]

The eloping lovers galloped off to the house of Paget's Dutch aide-de-camp, Baron Tuyll, who diplomatically booked himself into a hotel. Through the mundanity of a dressmaker's delivery, Wellesley discovered their whereabouts and the next morning the pair faced the first letter from Cha's cuckolded husband. Taking all the blame for the failure of her marriage, Cha penned a reply through an intermediary, in which she sounds utterly distraught. It is clear that both she and Paget expected nothing less than to be completely cut off from family, friends and society.

> Could you tell all the resistance that has been made to this most criminal most atrocious attachment, could you know what are my Sufferings at this Moment you would feel for me. Henry has not deserved this of me…he has ever been *kind to me to the greatest Degree*…About my dear dear children I must say one word. Do you think I dare hope ever by any remote or indirect means to hear sometimes of them? You know how much I love them…My dear little Henry and Charlotte, God bless you.[23]

Her third child, William, was a toddler who perhaps she thought would be unaware of developments. Less surprisingly, Gerald – a babe in arms – receives no mention either: Henry Wellesley had never really bought her story. The Wellesleys did not abandon him entirely, however. The 'miserable little Being' would be raised by Catherine 'Kitty' Pakenham, wife of

9. PISTOLS AT DAWN

The JERSEY Smuggler detected..., James Gillray, 24 May 1796, etching, published by H. Humphrey. The Prince of Wales's marriage to Caroline of Brunswick was financial and political, and he took up with his mistress again soon after: the Countess of Jersey, Henry Paget's mother-in-law.

Arthur, the future Duke of Wellington. She took pity on the 'wretched infant...rejected by every body'.[24]

Wednesday, two days after Cha's flight. Henry Wellesley made his best offer, pulling on his wife's heartstrings as a mother: 'for the sake of her welfare, and that of her children, he would consent to receive her again.' His conditions were that she never see Paget again – and that 'she must return instantly, for the next day would be too late.'[25] She refused him a second time and the flurry of letters continued. While the convention of letter-writing undoubtedly landed the lovers in hot water, it provides us today with vivid accounts of events and their impact. The Paget family's papers survive in great quantity and are a rich source – if a little one-sided in their point of view. Sadly, no record exists of what the Cadogans were saying among themselves.

Old Lord Uxbridge laid it on thick, making his appeal to Cha as 'an aged & perhaps dying Father', imploring her 'to restore my Son to his distracted Family'; he threatened to leave them penniless.[26] The Paget fraternity tried to talk Henry round, expressing their outrage privately to each other. 'Oh! That that nefarious damned Hellhound should have so entrapped that before noble fine creature,'[27] wrote Charles to Arthur. Lord Graves, Henry's brother-in-law, also chipped in:

> As for poor Paget I am afraid his case is desperate – he is still in Town with that *maudite sorcière*. Baron Tuyll gave some hope this morning so that we began to think better, but I have heard nothing more, which confirms my fears. The people in the streets talk of it – even the mob – & I am afraid every one sees Paget's conduct in the most unfavourable light.[28]

Henry wouldn't go back to the family home in Brook Street for fear of seeing his children, 'the inevitable consequence' of such torture being 'that he should return to his lodging and put an end to that existence which, as he said, would to God had been put an end to on one of the many occasions I [was offered] when in Spain.'[29] Decorum prevented Car from entering the lovers' hideaway on Mount Street and she was too distressed for a tête-à-tête in the park. Charles Paget arranged for a hackney coach to wait at the bottom of Upper Brook Street, where its enclosed carriage would keep the couple away from prying eyes. After forty minutes, Henry Paget opened the door and ran off. Charles found Car inside 'overwhelmed with violent grief and bathed in tears'.[30] Car decamped to a cottage outside London belonging to Lord Kinnaird. Cha and Paget went into hiding.

> London is full of impenetrable fog and horror at Lord Paget's elopement – he went off the day before yesterday with Lady Charlotte Wellesley. It is in every way shocking and unaccountable. ...I think him inexcusable and detestable. How the White Hart will ring with my aunt Spencer's comments upon this event...[31]

Lady Harriet Cavendish – and society at large – was fizzing and twittering with gossip. Some were damning. Lady Williams-Wynn wrote, 'What a misfortune to his family that he [Paget] did not find in Spain the Tomb of honour which they say he so eagerly sought.'[32] Better death than dishonour.

What happened next is a case of life imitating art. London was a rapidly growing city, with a population that expanded from 630,000 to two million in the Georgian era. Literacy was also increasing. The very first edition of *The Times* had been published in 1788 and, following the introduction of steam-driven roller presses, would soon be heading towards a readership of five thousand. Splashed over the newspapers, the story of scandalous Lady Charlotte briefly pushed the Duke of York, commander-in-chief of the Army, and his former mistress Mrs Clarke – who were embroiled in a cash-for-military-appointments scandal – off the front pages. Spurious reports of Paget's death at the hand of an avenging Henry Wellesley began to circulate. Wilder still, of Sir Arthur Wellesley having 'pursued the fugitives, overtaken them on the Oxford Road, and inflicted a dangerous abdominal wound upon the ravisher of his ailing brother's wife.'[33] There had been accounts of a fictitious duel; in order to avoid further embarrassment, an actual duel must now take place. In the event, it was not the Wellesleys but the Cadogans who stepped up.

HENRY CADOGAN (1780–1813) was the eldest of Mary Churchill's sons, the boy between sisters Emily and Cha (and the subject of the next chapter). He was co-signatory, with his brothers, of a letter to Cha threatening to call Paget out – meaning, to a duel – if she did not return home. Perhaps they hoped that fear of his death would force her hand; it did not. The Pagets understood the seriousness of the situation, describing the Cadogan brothers as 'most violent. They will have her or the most fatal consequences may be the result.'[34] The Cadogans' 'battle-keen' ancestors would have been proud.

The man in the street might settle a score with his fists; gentlemen engaged in ritualized armed combat. Judicial duels (trial by battle) were reported among Germanic tribes by Tacitus and Caesar; in England they lasted from the time of William the Conqueror until as late as 1819.

By contrast, duels of honour were a private matter. Seconds mediated and often tried to talk opponents out of it; if the duel went ahead they saw that the rules were observed and recorded the result. Pistols replaced swords as the weapon of choice in the mid-eighteenth century and between 1785 and 1845, a thousand duels with powder and ball were recorded, about one in five resulting in a fatality. In such cases, there was the added risk of prosecution for the victor, though many defendants were acquitted:

> Judges undoubtedly connived at jury leniency, to the considerable annoyance of enlightened opinion that opposed duelling…the law openly embraced a hot-blooded duel, the taking of the field, as part of its lesser species of homicide, chance medley manslaughter.[35]

Rarely, one side would withdraw, and rarer still the pair would liven things up with inventive deciders such as firing blunderbusses from hot-air balloons over Paris, or hurling billiard balls at each other (both French ideas). Alexander Pushkin was killed during his twenty-ninth encounter, in St Petersburg in 1837; British Prime Ministers including Pitt, Canning and the future Duke of Wellington faced down opponents. Duels were so common that they took place over the most trivial of matters – Lord Byron's great-uncle killed his cousin over the best way to hang game birds; the heir to the 6th Earl of Berkeley called out a critic over a bad book review. The only surprise in a duel arising over Cha and Paget is that it took so long.

On the night of 14 March 1809, Henry's second, Mr Sloane (probably William Sloane-Stanley, a distant cousin) put his surgeon on notice to be ready to attend the aftermath of a duel. The surgeon also served the Duke of Sussex, a progressive younger son of King George III, who thus got wind of the plan and 'that d—d meddling Duke threatened to give the information at Bow Street [police station] for apprehension of the Parties.'[36] Lord Graves persuaded Sussex not to meddle. Paget himself made it known that he would not accept a challenge, but that if Henry Wellesley or the Cadogans 'feel themselves aggrieved they may come to his lodgings and shoot him.'[37] A couple of days later, the lovers agreed to

Killing no Murder, or a New Ministerial way of Settling the affairs of the Nation!!, Isaac Cruikshank, September 1809, etching, published by John Johnston. Castlereagh (left), Foreign Secretary, fires a huge pistol at Canning, Secretary of War, who, wounded in his thigh, drops a smaller but five-barrelled pistol inscribed G.R. [George Rex].

a trial separation. The situation looked desperate, as Paget told his brother Charles, who related it in a letter to Arthur:

> ...it would be as much out of the question to control or vanquish their passions & affections for each other as it would be for him to attempt at the head of the 7th to overpower the united forces of Buonaparte; that one of two things therefore must take place after the month's separation, both or either of which they were prepared to adopt, the one being allowed to retire together & seclude themselves for ever from the sight of man; the only other alternative: self-destruction.[38]

Pretty dramatic. They held out for a week: by 23 March Cha and Paget were back together. Henry Cadogan was furious. This time, even the risk of arrest would not stop him. Death seemed to hold no fear either, despite his position as next in line to inherit the earldom; rather, given Charles Henry's mental state, Henry was already effectively the head of the family, and it fell to him to uphold the Cadogans' honour. A colonel in the 18th Foot, Henry possessed the confidence and bravery of a military man despite his opponent being a lieutenant-general, two ranks his superior:

> I hereby request you to name a time and place where I may meet you, to obtain satisfaction for the injury done myself and my whole family by your conduct to my sister. I have to add that the time must be as early as possible, and the place not in the immediate neighbourhood of London, as it is by concealment alone that I am able to evade the Police.[39]

Paget refused him. He thanked Henry for the 'extreme kindness you have already shewn your sister' – an offer to quit the Army and look after Cha and her children – but confessed that his life now belonged to her.

> She has lost the world upon my account, and the only atonement I can make is to devote myself, not to her happiness (which with her feeling mind is, under the circumstances, impossible) but to endeavour, by every means in my power to alleviate her suffering.[40]

Henry Cadogan threw his hands up in exasperation. He sent a copy of his own letter and Paget's reply to his second, asking Sloane to show them to anyone who wished to read them 'in order that what has passed may not be misrepresented'.[41] That, for Henry, was that. He departed for Portugal with his brother-in-law Sir Arthur Wellesley two weeks later.

George Cadogan, however, couldn't let it go. He threw down the gauntlet twice in May and, the second time, Paget picked it up. With the knowledge that Cha was sure of the protection of her brother Henry, should anything happen to him, perhaps his honour finally demanded that he accept the challenge. There was no going back: Paget had not contested the case of criminal conversation brought against him by Henry Wellesley, who was awarded £2,000 in damages. And so, at 7 am, 30 May, on Wimbledon Common, having separated by twelve paces, their seconds – Captain M'Kenzie, RN, for Cadogan and Lieutenant Colonel Hussey Vivian of the 7th Hussars for Paget – directed them to fire simultaneously:

> Captain Cadogan fired, Lord Paget's pistol flashed – this having been decided to go for a fire, a question arose whether Lord Paget had taken aim as intending to hit his antagonist. Both the seconds being clearly of opinion that such was not his intention (although the degree of obliquity he gave the direction of the pistol was such as to have been discovered only by particular observation), Captain M'Kenzie stated to Capt. Cadogan that as it appeared to be Lord Paget's intention not to fire at him, he could not admit of the affair proceeding any further.[42]

George had missed; Paget had missed deliberately. He wasn't ready to kill Cha's brother and add to her sorrows.

WHEN THE SMOKE FINALLY CLEARED, a new configuration would emerge. Curiously, Wellesley accepted Cha back on a temporary basis when Paget was sent away to Holland on military duty in July. On his return, Paget moved back in with Car, likely as a holding pattern while everyone waited for Wellesley's divorce to go through, which it did in February 1810. On 4 March, Cha gave birth to a daughter, Emily Paget – no attempt was made to attach the child to the Wellesleys this time. In April, Car asked Paget for a divorce of her own and he obliged by taking Cha to Scotland for a few weeks.

Scottish law (unlike English law) allowed a wife to obtain a divorce from a provably adulterous husband. However, an inconvenient subclause prevented remarriage with the other party and so a certain amount of subterfuge, beyond the expected pseudonyms (they chose 'Mr & Mrs Price') was required. The Countess of Bessborough (sister of the Duchess of Devonshire) gossiped that Cha had 'positively refus'd letting Ld. Paget domiciliate with any other woman'. The evidence given in court was that the lady who accompanied him '(like the Masque de fer of old) eat [sic], drank and slept in a black veil', thus enabling the hotel maids to declare they had no idea who shared Henry Paget's bed.[43] This fancy dress was seen through by everyone, who nonetheless played along. A second divorce was granted in October 1810.

Before the year was out, two remarriages had taken place: Car became the Duchess of Argyll and Cha the new Lady Paget. And they all lived happily ever after – even Henry Wellesley, who would go on to remarry and enjoy ennoblement. Paget's widowed mother found herself 'being disposed to bury in oblivion Present events'.[44] As early as March 1809, Lady Sarah Lyttelton (née Lady Sarah Spencer) had declared: 'Everybody was scandalized as they ought to be with the dreadful *esclandre* of Lord Paget and Lady Charlotte Wellesley; but everybody has almost forgotten it, as it happened a good ten days ago.'[45]

ABOVE *View of the Public Office Bow Street, with Sir John Fielding presiding, & a prisoner under examination*, Daniel Dodd, published by Alexander Hogg, London, 1795. The Duke of Sussex threatened to report Henry Cadogan, Henry Paget and their seconds for planning a duel over the honour of Lady Charlotte. The Bow Street Runners predated Robert Peel's Metropolitan Police force, founded twenty years after the duel took place.

9. PISTOLS AT DAWN

JUST WHAT WAS IT ABOUT CHA? Artist and diarist Joseph Farington recorded that 'She had been remarked for great levity of manner before she was married.'[46] Hyacinthe Wellesley described the Cadogan sisters as '*femmes qui sont* very high spirit and very *gai*'[47] and even Cha's first mother-in-law had described her as 'a good natured sort of person'.[48] The younger generation, happily, accepted their new mama with open arms. At the end of 1811, the Countess of Bessborough, who was still showing an interest, wrote:

> Ld. Paget's children are all in town…they talk with filial tenderness of Mama Argyll and Mama Paget: Vive la Liberté!…Without much beauty, without much cleverness, without any one particularly attractive quality that can be defin'd this same Ly. Paget [Cha] is the most fascinating of human beings to man or woman;…to see her you would imagine she was innocence itself – how strange![49]

For Cha it all turned out well; Emily, however, would revivify the fears of the Dowager Countess of Mornington less than a decade after the Wimbledon Common duel. And the spectre would rise a generation later, when young members of the Cadogan family would again fall in love with a Paget and a Wellesley. In the intervening years, the significance of the tumultuous personal lives of Cha, Car, three Henrys and Argyll would be felt not just by their families, but on the world stage. 'In 1809 there was an event that caused great scandal at the time, and affecting as it did the relations between the greatest military commander and the greatest cavalry leader of the day, had its effect upon history.'[50] Sir Arthur Wellesley, brother of Cha's first husband, would object to her second husband's presence on the same field.

ABOVE Charlotte Paget, Marchioness of Anglesey (née Cadogan, 1781–1853), Sir William Ross

Henry Cadogan (1780–1813)

CHAPTER 10

Wellington's Aide-de-Camp

—

COLONEL HENRY CADOGAN (1780–1813)

Colonel Henry Cadogan, career soldier and exasperated defender of his sister's honour, is the 3rd Earl who might have been. The eldest son from the 1st Earl Cadogan (NC)'s second family, he had risen swiftly through the ranks of the British Army and, since his father's death, Henry now enjoyed a healthy annuity of £700 a year.[1] War with the French meant there was plenty to keep a natural soldier busy. The Peninsular War had been raging since 1807, the war that gave us 'guerrilla warfare' (the Spanish word *guerrilla* means a 'little war'), a new style of fighting that involved a lot of back-and-forth over territory. Napoleon had occupied Portugal and, reneging on an agreement with his former ally, supplanted the Spanish king with his brother, Joseph Bonaparte. The British joined with the Portuguese to repel the French, acting to defend trade routes and preserve their status in the world order.

Henry set sail for Lisbon on 22 April 1809, in the company of his brother-in-law Lieutenant-General Sir Arthur Wellesley. A year earlier (shortly after joining his new regiment, the 71st Highlanders), he was at Wellesley's side as aide-de-camp on a vessel departing the Irish coast. Only a day out of Cork, the pair boarded Captain George Cadogan's HMS *Crocodile*, a fast cruiser, to complete the trip to Oporto. We can only guess what a fly on the poop-deck might have overheard in exchanges between brothers Henry and George, and the slightly older Wellesley, whose two younger brothers were still married to the eldest Cadogan girls. Emily and Cha were both pregnant for the fourth time: Emily by Gerald Wellesley, and Charlotte, wife of Henry Wellesley, by.... Their estranged mother was trying to keep her head down – and attached to her neck – in Revolutionary France. Trustees had been in charge of the Cadogan family's Chelsea estate for a year, Charles Henry (now the 2nd Earl) having been judged mentally incapacitated. A bright spot was little brother Edward's recent promotion to lieutenant.[2] Now, the three men aboard *Crocodile* must focus their minds on fighting Napoleon.

Two weeks later they arrived at Oporto. George then sailed them round the coast closer to Lisbon, where Wellesley met Admiral Sir Charles Cotton and took the decision to land at Mondego Bay. A British force of around 14,000 men under Wellesley's command came ashore in the first week of August 1808. His men, combined with those of his generals, defeated Junot's forces at Vimeiro on 21 August. Wellesley was recalled to London amid squabbling among the top brass about who should be commander-in-chief. Henry may well have accompanied him on the journey back; certainly, he was back in town and challenging his sister's lover to a duel a few months later. Following the fall of Madrid, Paget had returned to England in January a hero, albeit temporarily blinded by opthalmia. He had provided enough distraction in leading the defeat of the *Chasseurs à cheval* – 'perhaps the most brilliant exploit of the British cavalry during the whole six years of war' – to give the British Army a chance to retreat to the coast at Corunna and get away.[3]

By early 1809 Spain and Portugal were back under the tricolour. Returning to the fray that spring, with Henry at his side, Wellesley led a combined Anglo–Portuguese army in swiftly reclaiming Oporto, and once more driving the French out of Portugal. He wanted to push the *Grande Armée* back further and to that end sent Henry as emissary to the Spanish Captain-General, Don Gregorio García de la Cuesta, to arrange collaboration. On 30 May 1809, Wellesley wrote:

The Landing of the British Army at Mondego Bay, Henri L'Evêque, c.1808, watercolour, from the series 'Campaigns of the British Army in Portugal'

> I now send to your Excellency's head quarters two officers in my confidence, Lieutenant-Colonel Bourke of the quarter master general's department, and the Honourable Lieutenant-Colonel Cadogan, one of my aides de camp, in order to explain to your Excellency my sentiments, and ascertain those of your Excellency respecting the cooperation of the two armies under our command respectively, in an attack upon Marshal Victor, with a view to the destruction of his corps, if possible, or if not possible its removal from its threatening position on the frontier of Portugal and of Andalusia.[4]

This was an important role for Henry. Wellesley wrote to the Minister for War Robert Stewart, Viscount Castlereagh, the following day: 'I have sent Colonel Bourke and Colonel Cadogan to Cuesta to arrange a plan of co-operation in an attack upon Victor.'[5] Henry was suitably persuasive,

Elvas, Forts la Lippe and Lucie, with the surrounding country, Matthew Dubourg after Henry Smith, print, published by Edward Orme, London, 1813. The dedication below continues: 'distant glances of Badajos, Albuera, and the hills erased by the British Army under Field Marshal the Marquess of Wellington, on the march from Talavera, in the campaign of 1809.'

and he then waited with Cuesta at the fort of Miravete, Almaraz (a hundred miles south-west of Madrid), for Wellesley's arrival.

The battle took place at Talavera. The French attacked on the night of 27 July and fighting continued all through the next day. Henry was present, and we might imagine him at his commander's side throughout. Wellesley placed his confidence in his own men, fewer than half the number of fighting French. The victory was hard-won: 7,268 French dead to 5,365 British. 'Never was there such a Murderous Battle!' wrote Wellesley in the aftermath.[6] The British didn't have long to celebrate, however, as news of the Austrians' capitulation caused Napoleon to turn his attention west. Wellesley's troops were in no fit state to face a freshly populated French army. Regretfully, they abandoned Talavera, retreating with depleted and hungry troops, and marched towards Portugal.

Victory was victory, nonetheless – however short-lived – and Arthur was rewarded with elevation. His older brother William, of the extra barrel (Wellesley-Pole), advised him on choosing his title: 'After ransacking the Peerage and examining the map, I at last determined upon Viscount Wellington of Talavera and Baron Douro of Welleslie in Somerset.'[7] The name was 'exactly right'.[8] On 16 September 1809, Arthur Wellesley became Wellington, a name that would ring down through the ages, as well-known today as it was in his own lifetime.

ON THE VERY SAME DAY, George Cadogan was appointed captain of HMS *Pallas* and dispatched to the Low Countries. He was heading out to the same theatre of war as his Wimbledon Common opponent of six months before; this time they were on the same side. Henry Paget had already departed for Holland, commanding a central column of the Army in a huge joint-forces operation. On 30 July 1809 they landed at Walcheren, an island at the mouth of the River Scheldt: their mission to destroy enemy ships heading to and from French-held Antwerp and render the strategic port unusable. British troops took the island easily, but things went wrong soon after, when relations between Army and Navy commanders broke down.[9] This gave the enemy time to reinforce their last remaining position, at the port of Flushing, which survived a prolonged siege in August. Using natural geography to their advantage, the French opened the town's sluice gates to flood the low-lying countryside – and the British trenches. It was already a hot and humid summer, and Walcheren was the perfect breeding ground for mosquitoes. By the end of the month, the British force of 40,000 had become 24,000: modern medical knowledge concludes that 'Walcheren fever was likely a combination of malaria, typhus, and typhoid fever.'[10]

George was part of the evacuation, ferrying the dead and dying back across the North Sea, and – thankfully – he avoided contagion. The British finally withdrew at the close of the year, as Commodore Edward Owen reported back to his naval commander:

ABOVE *The burning down of the town hall in Flushing*, Friedrich Christoph Dietrich, etching on paper, published by J. Groenewould & Zoon, 1809. The town hall was destroyed during the bombing of the city by the British.

RIGHT *Map of the mouths of the Scheldt for the expedition to the island of Walcheren*, Ramboz and Monin, c.1830–38, etching/engraving on paper. From A. Hugo, *France militaire. Histoire des armées françaises de terre et de mer de 1792–1837* (Paris, 1833–38).

BELOW *Panoramic view of the Bombardment of Flushing during Walcheren's Expedition*, c.1809, watercolour drawing

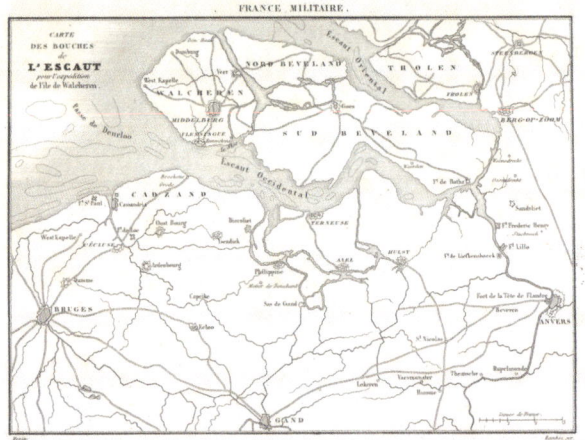

> The boats assembled, and embarked the rear-guard of the army, under the direction of the Hon. Captain Cadogan; whilst the few remaining guns of Veer and Armuyden points were rendered useless, and every other article of stores was taken off...In the Hon. Captain [George] Cadogan, of the *Pallas*, I found a most zealous second and supporter.[11]

Henry's regiment fared better than many – perhaps George had been passing on advice, brother to brother. 'The 71st escaped more lightly than other regiments, which was attributed to their taking a medicine of brandy and gunpowder recommended by the Navy.'[12] An explosive remedy. Henry Paget also survived, returning to London and his complicated love-life.

The debacle at Walcheren in combination with the humiliation of ceding Talavera brought simmering tensions in Parliament to boiling point. The government fell. In December, a new Tory administration saw Wellington's two older brothers rise to power: Richard Wellesley became Foreign Secretary; William Wellesley-Pole was appointed Irish Chief Secretary.

THE FOLLOWING YEAR HENRY RETURNED to active regimental duty – his time as a staff officer was over. In October 1810 he arrived at the Palace of Mafra, near Lisbon, ready to lead the 2nd division of 71st Highlanders in support of Wellington's men. Much of the early part of the year had passed in a waiting game; then, on 27 September, 'old nosey' had scored a resounding victory against Marshal Masséna at Busaco, 'yet another example of the British line over the French column, of Wellington's use of the reverse slopes, and of his employment of a strong skirmishing line to thwart the French *tirailleurs* [light infantry].'[13] A tactical withdrawal towards Lisbon followed,

Anecdote of the bravery of the Scotch piper of the 71st Highland Regiment, at the Battle of Vimiero, aquatint drawn by Manskirch, engraved by Clark and Dubourg, published 1816. A wounded piper continued to play to bolster his comrades' morale at the battle of 1808. The image shows how unsuited their uniforms were to the Portuguese climate.

where the British took up position behind a huge set of defensive earthworks known as the Lines of Torres Vedras. The construction of these parallel structures, straddling the peninsual from coast to riverside, was the strategic masterstroke of the campaign; somehow, the plan had been kept from the enemy. As military historian Major-General Sir C.W. Robinson remarked a century later, 'The secrecy…appears almost inexplicable. It says much for the activity of Wellington's posts, and the patriotism of the Portuguese.'[14]

Henry's regiment, the 71st – including youngest Cadogan brother Edward, newly commissioned as a captain[15] – was billeted around Lisbon, 'sickened every hour of the day with the smell of garlic and oil'.[16] A strange sight they must have made in the balmy Portuguese capital, dressed in their tartan kilts, bonnets and scarlet jackets. A week after their arrival, they marched north to Mafra, one of the 152 forts dotted along the Lines, where Henry was waiting. First sight of the enemy came the following day, 14 October, at Sobral de Monte Agraço:

10. WELLINGTON'S AIDE-DE-CAMP

ABOVE *Arthur Wellesley, 1st Duke of Wellington*, and RIGHT *Napoleon Bonaparte*, Thomas Heaphy, 1813, watercolour. Heaphy completed a series of thirty-two portraits of officers in southern France and Spain over a period of eighteen months during the Peninsular War. These astonishingly immediate sketches from life were studies for a group portrait *The Duke of Wellington in Consultation with his Officers previous to a General Engagement* (present whereabouts unknown). It was possibly at Wellington's invitation that the artist joined the cavalry staff to make these studies.

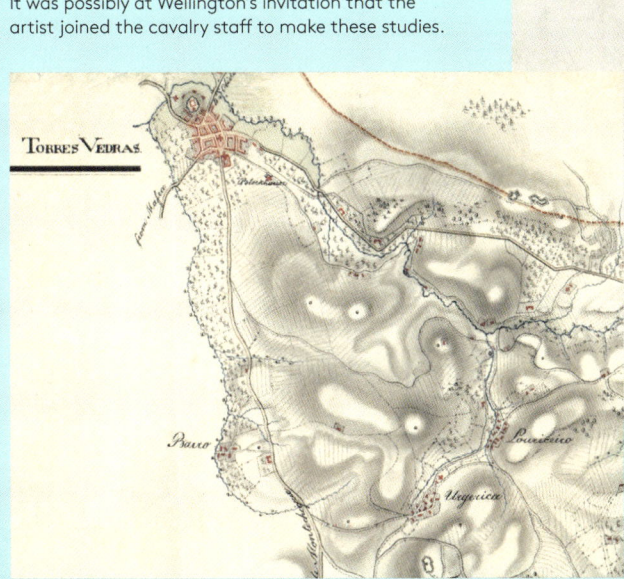

LEFT *Situation of a Part of the First Line of Defence of Lisbon* (detail), E. Preuss, pen and ink and watercolour, 1810. The road taken by Henry Cadogan and the 71st up from Mafra to Torres Vedras is marked top left on this map (section from Alhandra to Torres Vedras).

> Colonel Cadogan called to us, at the foot of the hill, 'My lads, this is the first affair I have ever been in with you; show me what you can do, now or never.' We gave a hurra and advanced up the hill, driving their advanced skirmishers before us, until about half way up, when we commenced a heavy fire and were as hotly received…We got behind a mud wall and kept our ground in spite of their utmost efforts.[17]

Brief moments of humour and humanity during that winter are described by a soldier of the 71st whose diary survives. The French got hold of a bullock, which dodged their butcher's knife and ran straight across to the British, who 'hurraed at them' and made a show of its slaughter before returning half the meat 'for godsake'. In a darker incident, a group stumbled across a half-empty tun and all drank heartily before discovering the corpse of a French soldier at its bottom. 'Sickness came upon me and, for a long time afterwards, I shuddered at the sight of red wine.'[18]

Eventually, the French abandoned their position. Henry's men advanced after them, witness to the horrors left by a retreating army, and regularly seeing action against the rear-guard commanded by Marshal Ney. Henry was a practical officer who understood that an army marches not only on its stomach, but on its feet: coming across a quantity of leather in an abandoned tannery, he ordered that each of his men should have a pair of new soles and heels. It is possible that Henry and other officers were already aping their commander's innovative style of footwear: the low-heeled leather riding boots he designed that became known as Wellingtons.[19]

ON 3 MAY 1811, the two sides met at Fuentes de Oñoro, twenty miles south-east of the blockaded fortress of Almeida on the Spanish border. Henry fired up his men for the charge: 'You have had nothing to eat for two days. There's biscuits and rum in that village. Come and get it!…At 'em, 71st! Charge 'em down the Gallowgate!'[20] British, Portuguese and German regiments faced the French together in gruesome close combat, often making use of their bayonets. After a day's fighting, a truce was called

A Wellington Boot – or the Head of the Armye, William Heath, October 1827, hand-coloured etching, published by Thomas McLean

so that both sides could collect their wounded. A French band played and the men kicked a football. The following day the narrow stone streets were again a hell of hand-to-hand fighting, vividly described by Lieutenant Grattan of the 88th regiment, which was sent in to finish the job:

> Every street, and every angle of a street, were the different theatres for the combatants; inch by inch was gained and lost in turn…towards mid-day the town presented a shocking sight: our Highlanders lay dead in heaps, while the other regiments, though less remarkable in dress, were scarcely so in the number of their slain; the French grenadiers, with their immense caps and gaudy plumes, [lay] in piles of twenty and thirty together – some dead, others wounded, with barely strength sufficient to move;

> ...impossible for them to crawl out of the range of dreadful fire of grape and round shot which the enemy poured into the town: great numbers perished in this way, and many were pressed to death in the streets.[21]

The 71st were cut down by two-thirds, to two hundred men; but they – and Colonel Henry Cadogan – prevailed. The 79th Highlanders suffered heavier losses; two of their divisions were wiped out and their commanding officer killed. It was a slim and Pyrrhic victory: Almeida itself was blown up by the French a few days later.[22]

Henry wrote to his brother-in-law with family concerns uppermost in his mind:

> There is no reflection however that gives me such pleasure as that this conduct has been instrumental in bringing George his ship and affecting by this means permanent good to another...
>
> I have received letters from Louisa and Charlotte, as well as many other people of late which have given me gratification. Considering how little was said by Lord Wellington about my conduct, it is deeply gratifying to think that others have done me complete justice.[23]

Henry was sure that his success had secured command of HMS *Havannah* for his brother George. In the same letter, the intimate links between the Cadogan, Wellesley and Paget families are made plain. Henry refers to the fallout from his sister's elopement, saying he will write to Charlotte 'very soon. All things will come right I think. The children will accept [the situation]. Lord Wellington seems to expect Lord P.[aget] in this country.' He was right about the children, and Henry's general optimism was understandable: Paget, a heroic and experienced general, was an obvious choice to lead the cavalry. However, neither Wellington nor Paget was comfortable with the idea of working together. William Wellesley-Pole's snide appraisal of the situation suggests he was still stung on his brother's behalf: 'If I know anything of Ld. Paget's character he will not stoop to waive his Rank to serve under you.'[24] Personal antipathy aside, the problem of rank was one that could be solved. In August, a letter from the new Secretary of State for War Lord Liverpool advised Wellington:

> You will perceive by the 'Gazette' of last Tuesday that you have been promoted to the rank of General in Spain and Portugal, and you may conclude from this circumstance that it is determined to send Lord Paget immediately to command the cavalry under you. I have not myself seen the Duke of York since he saw Lord Paget at the Prince's desire, but I understand from Torrens that Lord Paget declines service altogether under the present circumstances. As the cavalry has been so very considerably increased, I should not have felt myself, under your letter, warranted in opposing Lord Paget's appointment, though it is impossible not to feel some objections to it; but I thought it very desirable, to obviate eventual difficulties, that your promotion to local rank should not be deferred, and I therefore urged the adoption of this measure at all events, to which the Prince Regent and the Duke of York readily acceded.[25]

Prince Frederick, Duke of York, had been reappointed commander-in-chief of the Army following the cash-for-military-appointments inquiry; the Prince Regent had enjoyed a secret, illegal marriage to a twice-widowed Roman Catholic called Maria Fitzherbert, his mistress. British society was certainly no stranger to scandal. However, history has judged that it was the sexual and religious propriety of Britain's Spanish allies that prevented two of her greatest military leaders joining forces in the Peninsular War, as 'it might make a bad impression at Cádiz to invite so soon the seducer of Henry [Wellesley]'s wife.'[26] That Paget and Cha were now husband and wife would have made no odds to a country that still looked to Rome. A little family difficulty for the Cadogans thus played out on the world stage.

HENRY WAS A POPULAR COMMANDER. Receiving word of Wellington's victory at Salamanca in July 1812 – his friend and mentor the generalissimo – he secured a double allowance of rum for his men. 'Colonel Cadogan took the end of a horn, called *a tot*, and drank, "success to the British arms".'[27] Food and drink were often uppermost in the men's minds, foraged rather than supplied, and conditions in camp swung between feast and famine. At Alba de Tormes, one of Henry's men was so delighted to stumble across a piece of meat – near the field hospital – that he had cooked and eaten most of it before his comrades spotted its true nature. 'The others looked and knew it to be the forearm of a man. The hand was not at it; it was only the part from a little below the elbow and above the wrist. The man threw it away but never looked squeamish; he said it was very sweet and was never a bit worse.'[28] Hunger was a great leveller. Henry sought to punish a group of men for raiding a flourmill, but was forced to cede the moral high ground by the appearance of a chicken:

> ...he rode along the column looking for the millers, as we called them. At this moment a hen put her head out of his coat-pocket, and looked first to one side, and then to another. We began to laugh; we could not restrain ourselves. He looked amazed and furious at us, then around. At length the Major rode up to him, and requested him to kill the fowl outright, and put it into his pocket. The Colonel, in his turn, laughed, called his servant, and the millers were no more looked after.[29]

Henry relayed his own tale about a front-line chicken to Lady Shelley, who later became a confidante of Wellington. The passage reveals much about the friendship between the two men and their easy company:

> Colonel Cadogan tells me that before the Battle of Salamanca, when the French and English armies were in sight of each other, Lord Wellington, having made every arrangement, retired to his tent to take some rest and refreshment. He had given orders

Taking His Breakfast, from *The Military Adventures of Johnny Newcome*, Thomas Rowlandson, 1815, hand-coloured etching and aquatint, published by Patrick Martin & Co, 1815

to be called in the event of any movement by the enemy. The French kept up a cannonade, which bore so immediately upon Wellington's tent that his servants did not dare wait at table. While he was in the act of carving a chicken, an aide-de-camp came to tell Wellington that Marmont had made a movement to the left. Wellington sprang to his feet, ran out of the tent with the chicken on his fork, and exclaimed, 'Then we have them, by G–!' Colonel Cadogan also tells me that Wellington is now in winter quarters behind Ciudad Rodrigo, and amuses himself with hunting. In order to enjoy the sport in safety, videttes are stationed at intervals over a district of 10 miles. Wellington and his officers seldom have a good run, as the foxes are too fat, and are killed immediately or are run to ground among the rocks. Colonel Cadogan says that Lord Wellington is particularly gay and playful in conversation; enjoys fun and is always the first to promote amusement.[30]

They could afford to relax a little. Napoleon's attention turned east, consumed from June to December by his disastrous invasion of Russia. Tchaikovsky's famously exuberant *1812 Overture* (1880) commemorates the Tsar's victory in a bloody campaign that ended in the loss of nearly one million lives – many of the retreating French fell victim to the harsh winter. While Napoleon licked his wounds, Henry and the 71st were part of Wellington's huge Allied force amassing in readiness for a final push in the Peninsular War.

AS EARLY AS JULY 1811, shortly after Fuentes de Oñoro, Henry Cadogan was mourned and eulogized: reports of his death were greatly exaggerated, to misquote Mark Twain. He took it in good humour; a young man of thirty-one, he dreamed of a hero's end:

> I have always thought and still more and more do I think that the man who at anytime of life is carried off in the field of battle has lived long enough and died most gloriously...Certainly the greatest gratification in life is the thought that one may be remembered and regretted in such a death and from the false reports that were lately in circulation about me I have had a delightful proof that this would be my case.[31]

His remarks were sadly prescient: death would come for him at Vittoria, where battle lines were drawn on the morning of 21 June 1813. Massive numbers were involved: 72,000 Allies against 57,000 Frenchmen. Joseph Bonaparte's three lines faced four divisions, including Wellington at the centre and Henry on the right under General Sir Rowland Hill. During hand-to-hand fighting, in which the 71st lost fourteen officers and some 301 men, Henry fell from his horse, mortally wounded. Wellington wrote to his brother Gerald:

> I cannot express to you how much I feel for this loss, let alone on private grounds. He was an officer of the greatest zeal and promise and attached to his profession enthusiastically. After he

BATTLE OF VITTORIA, JUNE 21. 1813.

ABOVE 'The Heroic Death of Col. Cadogan, at the Battle of Vittoria', from *The History of the Present War in Spain and Portugal, from its commencement to the Battle of Vittoria...* by Theophilus Camden, published London, 1813

TOP *The Battle of Vittoria, 21 June 1813*, coloured aquatint by J.C. Stadler after William Heath, published by Thomas Tegg, 1 April 1818. The victory of General Sir Arthur Wellesley, Marquess of Wellington, at Vittoria brought about the final downfall of French rule in Spain.

RIGHT *The Death of Colonel Cadogan*, ballad, 1813

231

The Death of Colonel Cadogan
Of the 71st Regiment.

TUNE:— *The Flowers of the Forest.*

How lovely is Clydsdale in the dawn of the morning,
Where the river does meander along the gay vale,
Where the daisies and blue bells the hills are adorning,
The black bird is piping his notes in the dale.
But nae mair to me will those pleasures a-waken,
My brave gallant hero lies cold in the clay,
And now I must wander alone and forsaken
The sweet flowers of Clydsdale is all wed away.
At the sight of Vittoria by thousands surrounded,
Those band of brave warriors dealt death 'midst their foe,
Till a shriek of despair, pale bleeding and wounded,
They saw their brave chieftain, my Henry laid low,
O, bear me to yon height, he exclaimed we are victorious,
He smil'd at their flight, till his life ebb'd away.
Now ladies, if you'll hear me, Cadogan died glorious,
The flowers of Clydsdale bloomed sweetly that day.
I'll go to his grave, and I'll deck it with flowers
I'll brave all the dangers that dwells in the waves,
On the green sod that wraps him, I'll spend my night hours,
And wander all day, 'midst the tombs of the brave,
If the lasses of Spain, would on the mourner take pity,
They would weep as at eve with their lovers they stray,
And Vittoria's high mountains would re-echo the ditty,
The sweet flowers of Clydsdale is all wede away.

was mortally wounded and knew that he was dying he desired that he might be carried to a spot from which he could see the operations of the day and he did live to witness the total defeat of the enemy.

I can write no more on this distressing subject. Pray give my best love to Emily and believe me,

Ever Yours affectionately,

Wellington[32]

A surviving fellow officer of the 71st wrote to George with details of his brother's death. 'The enemy gave way, and we followed, animated by the gallant example of our leader, when a fatal shot deprived us of him, you of a brother, and the army of a hero.'[33] His soldiers had his body washed and properly prepared for burial, returning to lay him to rest on the field of battle. They fired a three-round salute over his grave.

Henry's death was mentioned in dispatches. Wellington wrote to the Prince Regent: 'In [Henry] his Majesty has lost an officer of great zeal and tried gallantry, who had already acquired the respect and regard of the whole profession, and of whom it might be expected, that if he had lived he would have rendered the most important services to his country.'[34] (He was less flattering about his own troops, who let the French escape into the Pyrenees, notoriously labelling them the scum of the earth.) Victory at Vittoria was the decisive battle that broke Napoleon's hold on Spain. Wellington was promoted to field marshal. Posthumously, Henry was also lauded, by leaders and public alike.

In July 1813, Viscount Castlereagh described to the House of Commons a plan 'paying the debt of national gratitude to some distinguished officers', including:

> ...the Hon. Colonel Henry Cadogan, who distinguished himself so greatly in the action of Fuentes d'Onore [*sic*], for which he was praised by the Marquis of Wellington. At the great victory of Vittoria, he had no wish after receiving his wound but to

see the conclusion of the British triumph, and to behold the termination of that splendid success of our gallant army.[35]

At St Paul's Cathedral, London, and Glasgow Cathedral; and at his home chapels of St Mary's, Santon Downham, and St Luke's, Chelsea, monuments to Henry can be seen to this day. A sketch of that at St Luke's appears as the frontispiece to the second volume of Faulkner's *History of Chelsea* (1829); a further tribute from one who served with Henry, that 'there never was a more agreeable companion or kinder friend' was published widely. Lady Shelley recorded in her diary that 'our first intimacy [hers with Wellington] began with mutual regret at the death of Colonel Cadogan, the man who first taught me to appreciate the Duke's exalted character.'[36] Henry and Vittoria captured the public imagination. Beethoven's *Battle Symphony* (Op. 91, 1813),

Monument to Henry Cadogan at St Paul's Cathedral, London

dedicated to the Prince Regent, has the alternative titles *Wellington's Victory, or the Battle of Vittoria*. Among its multi-strain melodies, the acute ear can pick out the well-known tune 'For He's a Jolly Good Fellow'. It might stand as a further epitaph to Colonel Henry Cadogan.[37]

To a family steeped in warrior ancestry, Henry stands out as a man they recognize. Nearly two hundred years later, a young Viscount Chelsea (later, 9th Earl Cadogan) took a battlefield tour in the region. The village stood unchanged since Henry's days and, with his fellow officers, Edward was able to locate his great(x5)-uncle's burial spot to within ten feet, and pay his respects. Just a week later, in an amazing coincidence, he was presented with an object that made a physical link to Henry – his telescope, still in its case. After a loan to The Royal Highland Fusiliers Museum (the Highland Fusiliers were formed from regiments including the 71st in 1959), it was officially handed back to the Cadogan family at a ceremony in Glasgow.

Wellington's Victory, or The Battle of Vittoria, 1813, Ludwig van Beethoven, title page of piano score with engraving, published by S.A. Steiner, Vienna

Telescope belonging to Colonel Henry Cadogan, by Matthew Berge (Late Ramsden), c.1800, mahogany and brass. Presented to his great(x5)-nephew, then Viscount Chelsea, in 2010, nearly 200 years after Henry's death, it is a rare surviving example of a telescope from this period complete with its case.

Colonel Henry Cadogan never married, although a single line in a letter composed by Wellington several years after his death suggests that there is more to his story. Writing to Lieutenant-General Sir Edward Barnes, commander-in-chief of the forces in the East Indies, he recommended 'Henry Carr, an officer in the service of the East India Company on the Bengal establishment. Carr is the son of the late Colonel Cadogan of the Seventy-First Regiment of Foot.'[38] Such valuable patronage was bestowed sparingly and implies a personal interest. Additionally, the record of Carr's application for cadetship seven years earlier includes this exchange:

> Q: What is the profession, situation, residence of your parents or nearest kin?
> A: My Guardian, Hon. Capt. [George] Cadogan RN, Downham Hall, Brandon, Suffolk.[39]

His marriage certificate – he married Miss Sophia Mainwaring in a ceremony at St Paul's Cathedral, no less – gives his father's details as: Henry Cadogan. That he was Henry's illegitimate child does not seem in doubt. His baptismal record at the Episcopal Chapel, Glasgow, on 4 December 1809, lists his parents as George and Maria Carr; Maria's role as birth or adoptive mother will likely remain a mystery. Major Henry Carr (*c.*1809–1850) made no impact on the succession to the Cadogan earldom, however; Colonel Henry Cadogan's death created a new heir apparent in his younger brother. It was time for George to leave the high seas.

CHAPTER 11

Greatness Thrust Upon Him
—
GEORGE, 3RD EARL (1783–1864)

On 21 June 1813, George Cadogan's world changed dramatically. After nearly twenty years in the Royal Navy, suddenly, at the age of thirty Charles Sloane's eleventh child found himself next in line to inherit the earldom. Trustees were looking after the 2nd Earl, who was in no fit state to marry or produce an heir. Happily – apparently not put off by the affairs, elopements, disguises and divorces of his sisters, and having survived a duel with the future head of the cavalry – George had married in April 1810. His bride was Honoria Louisa Blake (1787–1845), a girl from County Galway whose brother had been created Baron Wallscourt of Ardfry.[1] Happier still, shore leave had blessed them with three children in quick succession: Augusta (b.1811), Henry (b.1812) and Honoria (b.1813). George had lost five half-brothers before Colonel Henry fell at Vittoria; he was duty-bound to remove himself from the pitfalls of active service that had seen so many Cadogans of his generation shuffle off their mortal coil.

ABOVE *George Cadogan with his dog Fen (a gift from Sir Walter Scott)*, Sir Francis Grant, c.1830, oil on canvas
TOP George's new coat of arms, granted to him as Baron Oakley of Caversham

OPPOSITE Countess Cadogan (née Honoria Blake), Lady Augusta Cadogan, 1850, after unknown artist (1843), lithograph

The siege of Zara was to prove a fitting valediction; the 'crowning action' of his career.[2] As he stepped onto dry land at the very end of December 1813, preparations were already underway to recognize George's 'distinguished gallantry', under orders from the Austrian emperor:

> I wish…for Colonel Widmayer of the Liccaner Regiment and Second Lieutenant Krapfreiter of the Artillery together with the British Royal Navy Captain George Cadogan, who are all with General Tomassich in Dalmatia, to be awarded the Knight's Cross of this Order [of Maria Theresa] for outstanding distinction in the face of the enemy…Franz[3]

Francis II ('Franz') had founded the Austrian Empire in 1804, thereby ensuring he would maintain a titular level-pegging with Napoleon; two years later, defeat at Austerlitz had led to his abdication as the last Holy Roman Emperor, putting him on the back foot. He felt the outcome of each battle even more deeply following the personal humiliation of his daughter Marie-Louise's forced marriage to the French emperor in 1810. Zara was an opportunity to celebrate – loudly: George was invited to Vienna for a grand ceremony with military honours, conducted on 9 January 1814 in the presence of Austrian troops under Marshal Ferdinand, Duke of Württemberg, 'so that they may be reminded of your merits and inspired to glory with our brothers-in-arms from your Nation.'[4]

The British were not quite as swiftly efficient in their recognition, which came almost exactly twelve months later. As the year 1815 turned, Prince George, the Prince Regent, proclaimed he 'thought it fit' to order an expansion of the Most Honourable Military Order of the Bath:

> …to the end that those Officers who have had the opportunities of signalizing [sic] themselves by eminent services during the late war may share in the honours of the said Order, and that their names may be delivered down to remote posterity, accompanied by the marks of distinction which they have so nobly earned.[5]

The Battle of Waterloo (detail), Jan Willem Pieneman, 1824, oil on canvas. This huge painting (18 x 27 ft) is one of dozens created in the years after Waterloo, reflecting contemporary fascination with the battle. It was exhibited in a special temporary pavilion in Hyde Park for several months in 1825. Wellington (in black) hears that Prussian help is on its way; Uxbridge is beside him in the right foreground; the wounded Prince of Orange is taken away in the left foreground; in the distance Napoleon stands with his brother Jerome and orders his guards to attack. It is essentially a set of portraits of the officers present.

In the newly restructured Order of the Bath, George Cadogan was installed Companion, adding the letters CB to the KMT that Emperor Franz had placed after his name. Sir Arthur Wellesley, George's brother-in-law, had been elevated to Duke of Wellington and Marquess of Douro on 11 May the year before, adding to several victory titles bestowed by crowned European heads.[6]

Prince George's description of 'the late war' was a little premature. Boney had not quite given up: he escaped for one last hurrah, known as 'the Hundred Days'. This would culminate in Wellington's most famous engagement: the Battle of Waterloo. On 18 June 1815 the conflicts that had rattled and rolled across Europe for over twenty years were settled decisively, a few miles south of Brussels, by an Anglo-Dutch army of 68,000 under Wellington, supported by 45,000 Prussians under Blücher. Enough time had now passed for Cha's second husband Henry Paget, who had inherited the earldom of Uxbridge in 1812, to fight side-by-side with Wellington without risking anyone's sense of propriety. The Duke of York and the

Prince Regent had appointed Uxbridge (who had been out of a job since his 1809 elopement) to lead the cavalry. It was a popular choice, if not Wellington's. A captain of the 5th Hussars captured the feeling:

His Lordship is still the Lord Paget of 1808, the same fine and anxious spirit as ever…He is not only the cleverest cavalry officer in the British Empire, but unfortunately he is almost the only one with a cavalry genius.[7]

Uxbridge galloped up to Wellington during the final attack. Seconds later, a grape shot passed over the neck of the duke's horse and shattered the earl's knee. Their interaction in the field is almost comically sanguine:

In the popular version, Uxbridge exclaims 'By God, sir, I've lost my leg!' Wellington momentarily removes the telescope from his eye, considers the mangled limb, says 'By God, sir, so you have!' and resumes his scrutiny of the victorious field.[8]

The Anglesey leg, James Potts, 1830, lime-wood and leather

Napoleon's 72,000 troops were defeated and on 22 June he abdicated for the second time. Exile this time was to one of the world's most remote islands – St Helena in the South Atlantic. News of Uxbridge was carried to Cha, who immediately assumed the worst and 'fell into hysterics'; the letter from him describing his injury left her 'so wonderfully relieved that she bore the truth with great composure'.[9] The Prince Regent placed the royal yacht at her disposal and she rushed across the Channel, arriving at her husband's side on 25 June. She brought with her one of their many children – Clarence, just four years old.

The Napoleonic Wars were finally over. Between 1793 and 1815 Britain had lost nearly a quarter of a million men, of whom fewer than thirty thousand are estimated to have died from battle wounds.[10] The country would need years to recover from its economic effects (high taxation and unemployment were the alternatives to military service). But Britain had new heroes. Wellington was rewarded with a large fortune of £400,000 and an estate in Hampshire.[11] Previously the home of the political Pitt family, Stratfield Saye House was sold to the nation in order for it to be gifted to the talented general. It has been home to the Dukes of Wellington ever since. Lord Uxbridge's leg was amputated and buried under a commemorative plaque, in its own wooden coffin. His subsequent nickname 'One Leg' was the title for a commanding biography by his great-great-grandson. He was fitted with a state-of-the-art mobility aid: one of the earliest artificial limbs, articulated at the knee and toes. Back in London, the Prince Regent made him Marquess of Anglesey: Cha became a marchioness.

CADOGAN HEIR PRESUMPTIVE GEORGE was safely ensconced at Downham Hall with his wife of five years and their young family (a fourth child – another George, b.1814 – had arrived the year he returned home, providing a spare to his heir). His younger sister Louisa, nearing thirty, unmarried, was living with them and, as yet, showing no signs of leaving. The family settled into a comfortable existence on £1,500 a year.[12] It was now George's job to look after the family's London estate, still under trusteeship, and to provide a voice of military experience to his country.

Prince George was guided through his own Regency by Prime Minister Lord Liverpool. The king's ill health occasionally rallied, but mostly faltered. Liverpool wrote to Wellington:

> The accounts of the King are still very bad. His mind acquires no strength; and though his constitution is wonderfully strong, it is scarcely possible that it can resist for any length of time the attacks to which it has been lately exposed.[13]

Poor mad King George III, 'Farmer George', lived almost another decade. The Prince Regent, dubbed 'Prinny' by his subjects, was kept away from politics and pursued a life of indulged leisure that encouraged and enabled a flowering of the arts. He was particularly keen on refashioning royal residences, undertaking works at both Windsor Castle and Buckingham Palace. Most famously, he promoted the architect John Nash to Surveyor General and had the Royal Pavilion at Brighton, originally commissioned from the Cadogans' Chelsea collaborator Henry Holland, transformed into a mini-Mughal palace, complete with onion dome. Nash also stepped in to Holland's redesign of Carlton House. It was the settlement of escalating debts incurred on this project – doubling in the two years 1793–95, on Holland's watch – that had led to the prince's ill-fated marriage to Caroline of Brunswick. Perhaps that was why Prinny had him replaced. The prince loved to entertain, and Carlton House was the setting one warm July night in 1816 for a milestone in Cadogan family history.

The Hall, Carlton House, 1 April 1808, etching by Thomas Rowlandson after Auguste Charles Pugin's design. Hand-coloured aquatint by John Bluck published by Rudolph Ackermann in *A Microcosm of London*, plate 15.

Ties between the Cadogans and the Wellesleys were unravelling. The loss of George's older brother Colonel Henry had distanced the military connection with Wellington (though George himself had sailed him to Mondego Bay in 1808). Cha's divorce from Henry Wellesley was fading from public and private consciousness. So much so that her two husbands, past and present, were both invited to a grand dinner. In attendance were the Dukes of York and Wellington, and several cabinet ministers. Their host, the Prince Regent, had suffered an embarrassing memory lapse, recorded by a Wellesley brother:

> ...and said he was much distressed at Lord Anglesey and Henry [Wellesley] being in the room together; that he had never recollected it till he saw them, etc., etc., and he desired me to take an opportunity of explaining to Henry that the circumstances had arisen from mere misadventure. I told him that I was sure Henry was quite easy about the matter, and I informed his R[oyal].H[ighness]. that in a conversation I had lately had with Henry, he had observed that he now considered Lord Anglesey as the best friend he had ever had in his life.
>
> Castlereagh observed coolly that the meeting was a fortunate circumstance, for it would be impossible they should not very often meet, and therefore the sooner the thing was over the better; upon which [the] P[rince].R[egent]. observed that Castlereagh was the most impudent fellow existing, and so broke up the conversation. Henry did not seem at all annoyed at the meeting...[14]

Henry Wellesley was clearly over it – he had taken a new wife earlier that year, the eldest daughter of the Marquess of Salisbury. Separately, Cha's second husband had already shaken hands with his old friend the Duke of Argyll, now married to Anglesey's own ex-wife Caroline.[15] So far so civilized: life was moving on. Against this backdrop it was unfortunate that Emily's marriage to the Reverend Gerald Wellesley would soon find itself in trouble.

GERALD WELLESLEY WAS RECTOR OF CHELSEA from 1805 to 1832. While we don't know much about the mild-mannered man – Cadogan family historian Robert Pearman described him as 'impartial and conciliatory' – we know he was not idle. For over twenty years he was a chaplain of the Royal Household, appointed in 1799. At Chelsea he oversaw the building of a new parish church: St Luke's. Henry Holland's 1777 design for Hans Town had included a church on land that today forms the gardens in Cadogan Place, 'but this plan came to nought seemingly as a result of some unholy bickering between the local incumbents as to the likely effect upon their respective congregations.'[16] In 1818 Parliament passed the first of two Church Building Acts, voting to award grants for building work on new Anglican churches and to provide new endowments, capturing the mood of national thanksgiving following Wellington's victory at the Battle of Waterloo. Gerald's congregation was increasingly squashed in the hard, wooden pews at Chelsea Old Church. They made a successful application and on 12 October 1820 the foundation stone was laid at St Luke's Church on Sydney Street, just off the King's Road. St Luke's is one of the first of several hundred places of worship built under the scheme; other well-known 'Commissioners' churches' in London include All Souls, Langham Place (designed by John Nash), and Holy Trinity Brompton. James Savage's neo-Gothic design in Bath stone was consecrated on St Luke's Day, 18 October 1824. Only four years later, with congregations still swelling, a chapel of ease for St Luke's was deemed necessary and construction began on a second of Savage's designs. Completed in 1830, Holy Trinity, Upper Chelsea (as it was known), was popular enough to be given its own parish the following year.

Emily had more than done her duty and given Gerald seven children: four girls and three boys. But the famously high-spirited young girl (Cha's partner-in-crime) had sought love elsewhere – indeed, rather close to home. 'Lady Emily played ducks and drakes with her marriage...counting among her seducers the same Lord Paget who ran off with her sister.'[17] Signs of her discontent had been aired as early as 1803, to the perennially indiscreet Lady Harriet Cavendish, who wrote to a friend: '...when Mama mentioned

11. GREATNESS THRUST UPON HIM

ABOVE *The Honourable Gerald Valerian Wellesley (1770–1848), DD*, Richard Evans (1784–1871), oil on canvas. Gerald is shown as Prebendary of Durham Cathedral. He uprooted the family north, where they flourished.

FAR LEFT *St Luke's*, Chelsea, etching by S. Lacey after Thomas Hosmer Shepherd, published 1828 by Jones & Co., London. The new church was consecrated in 1824.

LEFT *Holy Trinity Church, Sloane Street*, c.1830, engraving, published in *The Gentleman's Magazine*

the beauty of the Wellesley family to her one morning…she stopped her by exclaiming, "Oh! as for Gerald's looks, I cannot boast much of them!".[18] Gerald, for his part, was no saint: 'In spite of his clergyman's collar, he too had a reputation with the ladies…the Prince of Wales told Hyacinthe that he considered Gerald "one of the greatest roués he had ever met".[19] Things came to a head.

> …through jealousy because Lady Emily would not give up Lord Wallscourt, a young Irish Peer, just of age, whom she had introduced into her house as a visitor to her daughter, but in fact for her own purposes, Lord Anglesey betrayed her to her husband, Dr [Gerald] Wellesley, showing her letters and securing from her proofs which he afterwards placed in the Doctor's hands…[20]

Lord Wallscourt was Joseph Henry Blake, 2nd Baron – nephew to George's wife Honoria. If there was an affair, it was brief: Joseph died in 1816, aged only twenty-one. Sadly for her husband, Emily's exit from the marriage effectively destroyed his career. The Duke of Wellington petitioned the Prime Minister for his brother's promotion to the Irish bishopric of Clyne, but found refusal hard punishment for having 'an adulterous wife and that in its operation it does punish, and in the case of my brother may punish, the innocent for the sins of the guilty'.[21] Instead, Gerald moved the family north in 1824, taking up a new position as Rector of Bishop Wearmouth, County Durham, and, in 1827, Canon of Durham Cathedral. Good news was to come from the move: two of his daughters would later marry sons of the local MP, Thomas Liddell, 1st Baron Ravensworth.

Emily's abandonment did little outward harm to her other children, despite the youngest, George, being only four at the time. Admiral Sir George Greville Wellesley, GCB, would hold the office of First Sea Lord between 1877 and 1879. His older brothers were also military. Captain Arthur joined the Rifle Brigade and died in his mid-twenties. Colonel William chose the 10th Foot, lived a long life and fathered twelve children; his descendants married into families including the Lords Fairfax of

Cameron and the Marquesses of Dufferin and Ava. A third daughter had a childless union with a man of the cloth. The only ripple was felt by Emily and Gerald's youngest daughter, Mary Sarah, who would find objections raised to her choice of suitor (about which more later). By the time Emily and Gerald separated, trouble was also afoot at Downham Hall.

In 1819 Honoria's name became linked to Henry FitzGerald de Ros (later 21st Baron de Ros), great-grandson of Sarah Cadogan and Charles, 2nd Duke of Richmond. The previous year, he had been caught *in flagrante delicto* with Lady Harriet Spencer and subsequently disowned their lovechild, earning him the nickname 'de Rot'. Lord de Ros was briefly an ineffectual MP, for Looe (1816–18) – 'no [Parliamentary] speech is known' – but is remembered chiefly for bringing (and losing) a trial for libel in 1837 at which he refuted accusations of cheating at cards.[22] Sadly for Honoria, her son Horace, who arrived the year after these rumours, did not survive infancy (b. and d.1820). Baby Frederick William (b.1821) was also the subject of lasting society gossip. 'I was told his real father was a very good-looking Italian Prince who visited London in the '20s of the last century,' wrote Lord Colebrook (whose wife was a Paget), in a note to Queen Mary of 1937.[23] The naval captain and his family left British shores for a while to weather the storm. A new reason for celebration came two years later with the marriage of George's younger brother Edward – Mary Churchill's 'beloved child', now a thirty-three-year-old major in the 8th West India Regiment – to Miss Ellen Donovan.

CHELSEA OCCUPIED GEORGE'S MIND. 'The Cadogan moiety' (half) of the Estate was still held in trust for George's half-brother Charles Henry, 2nd Earl Cadogan. The trustees – and well-meaning Gerald Wellesley – had run into trouble in 1809, unsuspectingly letting Chelsea Common for building leases to an underage developer, a situation ultimately resolved by Private Act of Parliament. George, since 1813 effectively head of the family, was now able to exert more control. One of his first decisions was to purchase Winchester House, the Stuart part of the old manor house Chelsea Place, from the bishopric of Winchester (its owners since 1664), adding its two-and-a-half acres to the manorial estate. Four years later King George IV gave his royal assent to an act enabling its demolition, along with a second for general developments.[24] The dilapidated old building was replaced by new houses at the southern end of Oakley Street and on the eastern side of Cheyne Walk. Construction began on Cadogan Street and the new Wellington Square, renamed Trafalgar Square (and under a new raft of trustees a century later, Chelsea Square).

In 1821, George inherited the other half of Sir Hans Sloane's Chelsea estate, 'the Stanley moiety', when the last surviving child of Sarah Stanley, his great aunt, died childless. Sarah Sloane (1696–1764, Elizabeth's older sister) had married George Stanley, a Hampshire landowner, and had three

Map of London, made from an actual survey in the years 1824, 1825 & 1826. Extended and comprising the various improvements to 1835, Christopher Greenwood and John Greenwood, published by E. Ruff & Co., London. Scale 1:7,920 or 8 inches to the mile. The survey was original to the Greenwoods and at a larger scale than Ordnance Survey maps of the time.

children, each of whom would be heir in turn. Hans left his estate to his eldest sister Anne; her marriage to Welbore Ellis, MP, Baron Mendip of Mendip, did not produce children. On Anne's death in 1803 it passed to Sarah, the youngest sibling. Sadly, her marriage to Christopher D'Oyly, MP, was also childless. When Sarah died in 1821, the Stanley estate was divided. Paultons, the Hampshire property from their father, with its gardens landscaped by Capability Brown, passed to his second cousin Hans Sloane, MP (1739–1827, one of Charles Henry's trustees, who added the name 'Stanley' to his surname, becoming Sloane-Stanley). Under a proviso in Hans Stanley's will regarding a lack of legitimate male heirs, Sarah Sloane's moiety of the Chelsea estate passed to her nephew Charles Sloane Cadogan, 1st Earl Cadogan NC, or his heirs. In turn, the 1st Earl's will bypassed the 2nd Earl (with the exception above), and thus in convoluted fashion the land was bequeathed to the eldest living son of Mary Churchill: George.

Chelsea was part of the London boom. In the first two decades of the nineteenth century, its population doubled; during the 1820s close on seventy per cent of farming families left the area or changed their occupation.[25] At the closing of the decade, Thomas Faulkner guessed at George's plans – and their meaning for the future of the area – in the second edition of his famous, if flawed, topographical history:

> It is intended to form a communication with Lord Grosvenor's new magnificent Square by means of a street to run parallel with the north-east corner of Cadogan Place. By this means Chelsea will obtain a direct connection with London, and henceforth it must be considered as part of the great Metropolis of the British Empire.[26]

The following year (1830) saw the previously private King's Road opened up to become a public highway. A cacophony of development all around led to the diversion of the River Westbourne underground into a series of pipes at Sloane Square. It had flowed from the Hampstead ponds down to the Thames, passable via 'Bloody' Blandel Bridge since the Middle Ages.

Downham Hall was sold to Lord William Powlett (later the 3rd Duke of Cleveland), and the family – George, Honoria, their two girls and ten-year-old Frederick (the older boys were away at school) – back from Paris, moved into a smart London town house in sight of the home of the Duke of Wellington, now Prime Minister.[27] (Wellington recorded his first Cabinet meeting as 'An extraordinary affair. I gave them their orders and they wanted to stay and discuss them.'[28]) His tenure introduced full emancipation of Catholics in Ireland; he appointed the man who twenty years previously had run off with his brother's wife as Lord Lieutenant of Ireland. Among the shifting sands, his estranged wife Kitty, Duchess of Wellington, died in April 1831, having raised Cha's son, Gerald, to his majority. Water had definitively passed under that bridge, too. A fly once again began to buzz in George's ointment: the rumour-mill started up again around Honoria's fidelity. Moving in the same circles was Sir James Graham, a notably tall and handsome Whig MP and future Home Secretary, known in his youth as a Brummell-esque dandy, and recently appointed First Lord of the Admiralty. Diarist Charles Greville remarked in 1830 that 'Mrs. Cadogan and Mrs. Fox had been the objects of his adoration.'[29]

On 26 June 1830, after a decade on the throne and a lifetime of good living, the morbidly obese and bed-bound king breathed his last. He was suffering from gout, dropsy and hardened arteries; he was nearly blind. His only legitimate child, Princess Charlotte, predeceased him in 1817, and so the crown passed to his sixty-four-year-old brother William. George would be back among like minds at the office.

KING WILLIAM IV (r.1830–37) – the 'sailor king' – appointed George his extra naval aide-de-camp and included him in the list of peerages created in honour of his coronation. On 10 September 1831, George became Baron Oakley of Caversham (a nod to the family's long-standing connections with both places), taking his seat in the House of Lords four days later. His new coat of arms depicted a lion rampant regardant and a black eagle 'navally crowned' and beribboned with the Knight's Cross of the Order of Maria Theresa, together with the Cadogan family shield. George commissioned a portrait befitting his new status, from the painter Sir Francis Grant, future president of the Royal Academy of Arts. He was Lord Oakley for just fifteen months. Two days before Christmas Day 1832, his older half-brother Charles Henry, 2nd Earl Cadogan, died in obscurity in north London.

George, the eldest surviving son of Charles, 1st Earl Cadogan NC, inherited the title – quite remarkably, for an eleventh child. Freshly minted as 3rd Earl Cadogan, he welcomed a raft of new responsibilities. The 'Cadogan moiety' was bequeathed to him, and the Chelsea estate was reunited under a single lord of the manor. In addition, he became an hereditary trustee of the British Museum (an honour bestowed on descendants of Sir Hans Sloane), and a Sloane family trustee. Early in 1833 he leased a splendid mansion house, 138 Piccadilly, overlooking Buckingham Palace and Green Park. He decided to retain close ties to the palace; he had a lot in common with the monarch, who found himself in turbulent waters.

As recently as 1828, William (then Duke of Clarence and Lord High Admiral) had tested royal prerogative. Following a difference of opinion with his council of officers (and indeed Parliament), he embarked from Plymouth with a squadron of ships and disappeared for ten days; it had not ended well. However painful, it was a timely reminder that he must always act constitutionally. Challenges to authority had been germinating in the popular consciousness since the Peterloo Massacre of 1819. Across the Channel, the July Revolution of 1830 had ousted one French king in favour of another more amenable to constitutional monarchy; there were mass protests in Germany. George, the trusted aide, had a ringside seat as Britain narrowly avoided revolution.

The Great Reform Act (1832) was passed in June. This swept away the old rotten boroughs, of which Old Sarum – a seat held 1796–97 by George's brother-in-law Richard Wellesley, 2nd Earl of Mornington, under Pitt the Younger – was famously emblematic. As Prime Minister, the Duke of Wellington had received this anonymous plea:

> ...if representatives were given to Manchester, Birmingham, etc., and the laughing stock of allowing two Members to represent

The Reformers' Attack on the Rotten Tree..., c. April 1831, hand-coloured etching, published by E. King, Chancery Lane. The tree's branches include Old Sarum, a seat previously held by relations of the Cadogans. In the background behind the reformers, the king, in admiral's uniform, stands on 'Constitution Hill'.

> the clump of trees and heap of stones at Old Sarum [ended], making one Member suffice for the virtuous borough of Gatton '*et omne hoc genus*', all clamour would cease...[30]

Now a new PM, the 2nd Earl Grey, took up the populist cause. There were riots on the streets of Bristol, Nottingham and Derby, and a run on the gold reserves of the Bank of England. The Cabinet resigned and was reinstated, threatening to force the bill through by the creation of as many new Whig peers as it took. The Lords backed down, having blocked the bill twice – many abstained – and the king gave his royal assent. For the first time, hundreds of thousands of British men in the new industrialized cities were enfranchised. Next came the Factory Act (1833), outlawing the employment of children under nine working in the 'dark Satanic Mills' of William Blake's vision, and restricting their hours.[31] The Slavery Abolition Act (also 1833) extended the measures of 1807 to include territory held by the East India Company, and therefore the entire British Empire. Some of the reforms remain controversial: the Poor Law Amendment Act (1834) forced the rural unemployed to look for work in cities or face the consequences of the new prison-like workhouses. It gave young writer Charles Dickens a new target for his outspoken social commentary. '*Oliver Twist* was originally conceived as a satire on the new poor law…which was perceived by Dickens as a monstrously unjust and inhumane piece of legislation.'[32]

By this time, Dickens was courting the daughter of George Hogarth, editor of *The Evening Chronicle* in which *Sketches by Boz* had appeared. He and Catherine Hogarth were married at St Luke's, Chelsea, on 2 April 1836, two days after publication of the first part of the *Pickwick Papers* that would make his name. The Reverend Gerald Wellesley had left St Luke's in 1832; the new rector was the Reverend Charles Kingsley, in post 1836–60. His son – also Charles Kingsley – authored the equally influential story of *The Water Babies* (1863), in which Tom the chimney sweep escapes a life of danger and hardship for aquatic adventure. Parliament responded with regulation, passing updated Chimney Sweepers' Acts (1864 and 1875), which changed the lives of many such children. In the popular imagination, Dickens and Kingsley, along with such towering figures as Isambard Kingdom Brunel and Charles Darwin, have come to embody nineteenth-century Britain and its new golden age.

William IV teapot, 1832, silver and ivory. An octagonal teapot with naturalistic Welsh dragon handle and spout, its central panel shows the quartered arms of Cadogan impaling Blake, representing George, 3rd Earl Cadogan, and his wife Honoria Blake. The handle on the lid is in the form of an earl's coronet. This teapot was presented to George the year he inherited the earldom.

FIRST, A CODA: George was quick to join the Nelson Memorial Committee, creating a London landmark that still stands as a reminder of his childhood hero, the naval demigod of the Napoleonic Wars. In the spring of 1838, over a glass or two at the Thatched House Tavern in St James's Street (where poor Charles Henry, 2nd Earl, had suffered the indignity of an inquiry into his sanity), Admiral Sir Pulteney Malcomb and Vice-Admiral Sir Thomas 'kiss me' Hardy proposed and passed a resolution to raise funds for a monument by public subscription. In less than a month, they had the support of the Cabinet members. An advert was prepared for the national press inviting designs 'from Architects, Artists or other persons' and offering prizes of £200, £150 and £100 to be given for first, second and third places.[33]

Forty models and 124 designs were submitted to a panel headed up by their Royal Highnesses the Dukes of Sussex and Cambridge; George and the original committee were joined by head of the Army Lord Hill, future PM Sir Robert Peel and – rather incongruously – the poet Lord Byron.[34] William Railton's design was chosen: a fluted column of Devon granite, atop four bas-relief panels cast in the bronze of captured guns, depicting the Battle of St Vincent, the Battle of the Nile, the Bombardment of Copenhagen and the death of Nelson.

Charles Barry, Britain's leading architect, who had recently won the public commission to lay out Trafalgar Square, told the government's select committee on 13 July

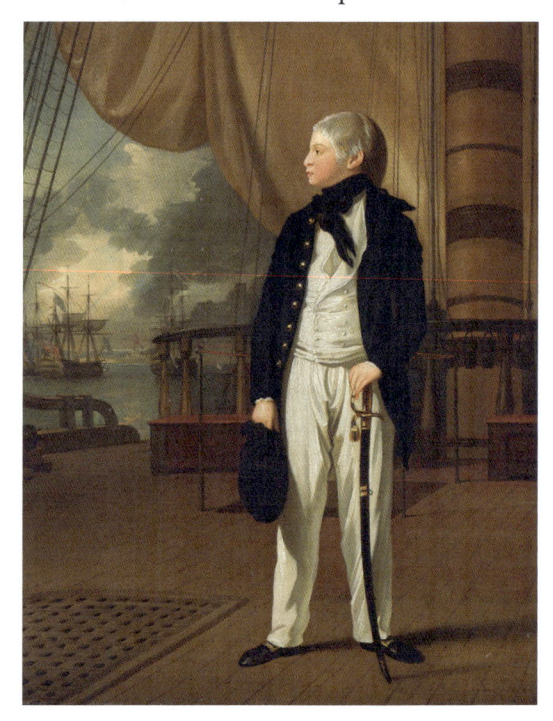

HRH Prince William Henry, serving as midshipman on board HMS Prince George, etching by Francesco Bartolozzi after Benjamin West, published 15 January 1782. The sailor king served under Nelson, to whom he remained a loyal friend for life.

Trafalgar Square, James Pollard, c.1838/39, oil on canvas. Charles Barry had recently laid out the square and objected to the proposed positioning of Nelson's Column.

1840 that: '...it will have an injurious effect upon the National Gallery, whilst the Gallery will form an unfavourable background for the column...I am of the opinion that the column will be improperly placed in Trafalgar Square.'[35] Had the government gone with Barry's proposals, one of London's most famous landmarks might have stood in St James's Square or at Oxford Circus. Despite his concerns and his close links with Parliament – construction had also recently begun on Barry's 1836 design for the new Palace of Westminster in collaboration with Augustus Pugin – the monument was placed in its originally intended position. Three years later, Edward Hodges Baily's statue of the great British sailor was raised aloft. Nelson's Column has dominated the public piazza ever since, standing 185 feet (56 metres) tall.

George was now in his fifties, and the world was changing. Within a few short years, the last English King of Hanover had succumbed to infirmity and a young, girlish monarch would usher in a new age, which saw Britain at the zenith of its power worldwide and a fresh generation of Cadogans at its heart.

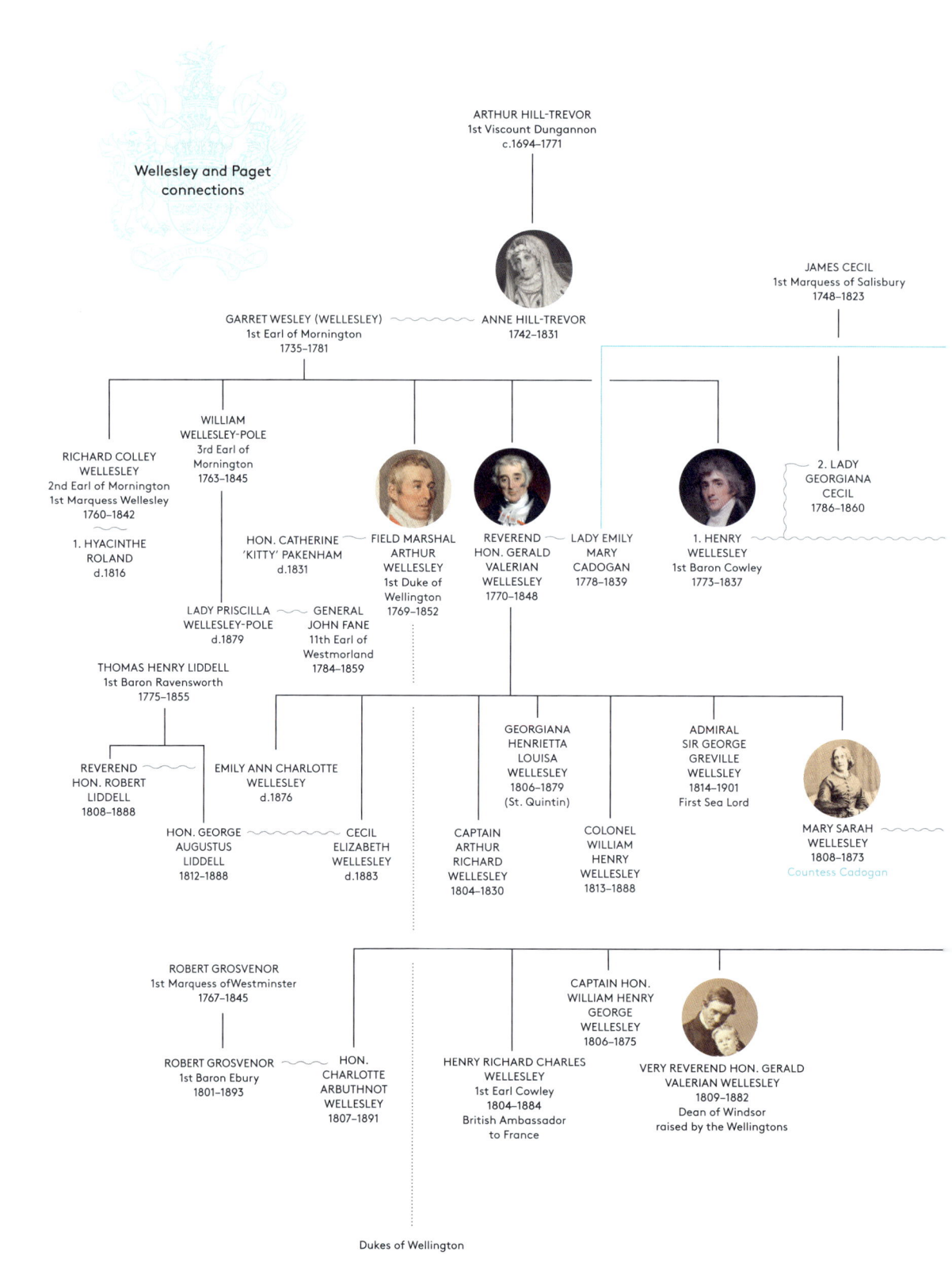

Wellesley and Paget connections

ARTHUR HILL-TREVOR
1st Viscount Dungannon
c.1694–1771

GARRET WESLEY (WELLESLEY) ∼ **ANNE HILL-TREVOR**
1st Earl of Mornington   1742–1831
1735–1781

JAMES CECIL
1st Marquess of Salisbury
1748–1823

RICHARD COLLEY WELLESLEY
2nd Earl of Mornington
1st Marquess Wellesley
1760–1842

1. **HYACINTHE ROLAND**
d.1816

WILLIAM WELLESLEY-POLE
3rd Earl of Mornington
1763–1845

HON. CATHERINE 'KITTY' PAKENHAM
d.1831

FIELD MARSHAL ARTHUR WELLESLEY
1st Duke of Wellington
1769–1852

REVEREND HON. GERALD VALERIAN WELLESLEY
1770–1848

LADY EMILY MARY CADOGAN
1778–1839

1. **HENRY WELLESLEY**
1st Baron Cowley
1773–1837

2. **LADY GEORGIANA CECIL**
1786–1860

LADY PRISCILLA WELLESLEY-POLE ∼ **GENERAL JOHN FANE**
d.1879   11th Earl of Westmorland
                                          1784–1859

THOMAS HENRY LIDDELL
1st Baron Ravensworth
1775–1855

REVEREND HON. ROBERT LIDDELL
1808–1888

EMILY ANN CHARLOTTE WELLESLEY
d.1876

GEORGIANA HENRIETTA LOUISA WELLESLEY
1806–1879
(St. Quintin)

ADMIRAL SIR GEORGE GREVILLE WELLSLEY
1814–1901
First Sea Lord

HON. GEORGE AUGUSTUS LIDDELL
1812–1888

CECIL ELIZABETH WELLESLEY
d.1883

CAPTAIN ARTHUR RICHARD WELLESLEY
1804–1830

COLONEL WILLIAM HENRY WELLESLEY
1813–1888

MARY SARAH WELLESLEY
1808–1873
Countess Cadogan

ROBERT GROSVENOR
1st Marquess of Westminster
1767–1845

CAPTAIN HON. WILLIAM HENRY GEORGE WELLESLEY
1806–1875

ROBERT GROSVENOR
1st Baron Ebury
1801–1893

HON. CHARLOTTE ARBUTHNOT WELLESLEY
1807–1891

HENRY RICHARD CHARLES WELLESLEY
1st Earl Cowley
1804–1884
British Ambassador to France

VERY REVEREND HON. GERALD VALERIAN WELLESLEY
1809–1882
Dean of Windsor
raised by the Wellingtons

Dukes of Wellington

Abridged family tree

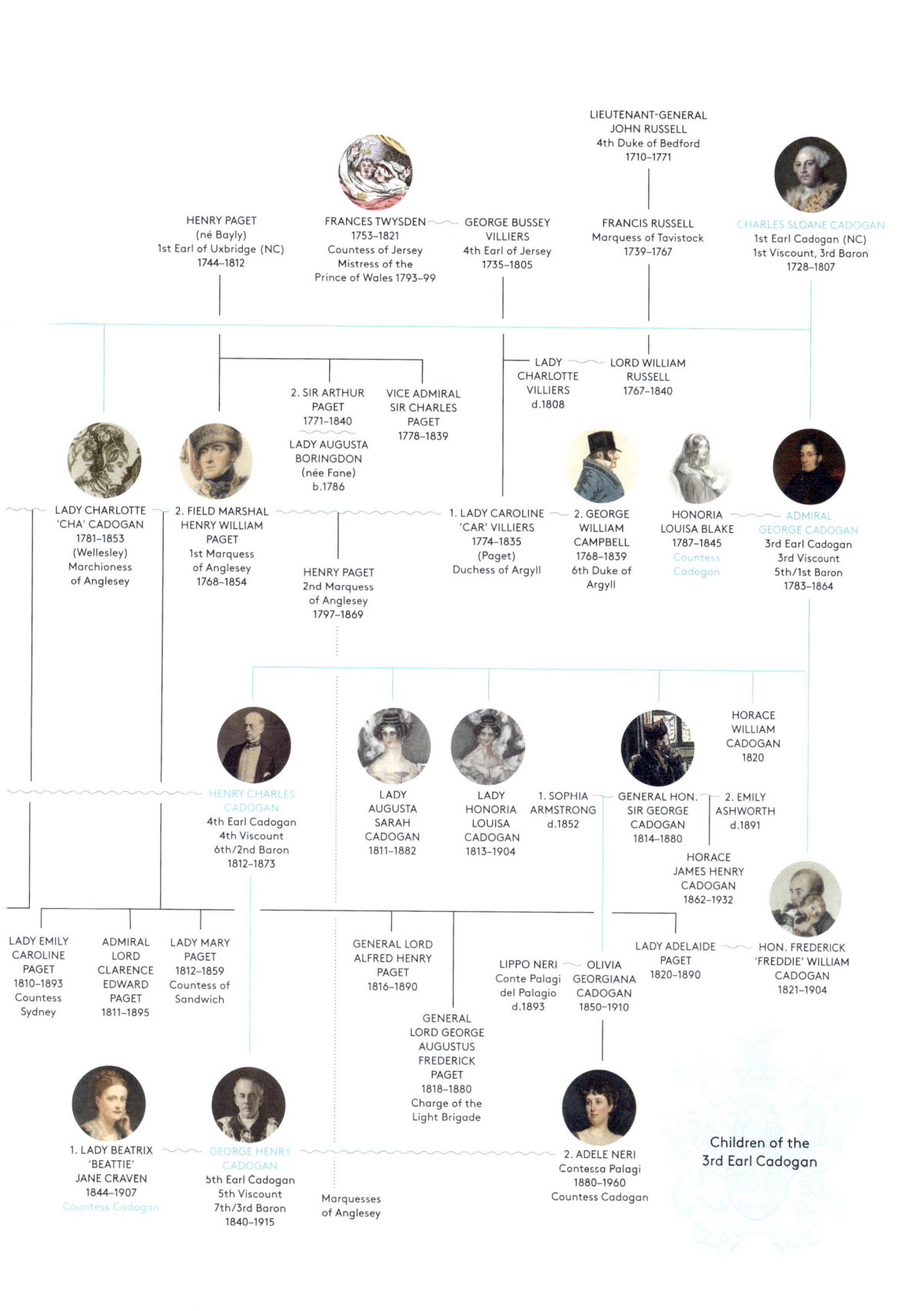

Children of the 3rd Earl Cadogan

LIEUTENANT-GENERAL JOHN RUSSELL
4th Duke of Bedford
1710–1771

HENRY PAGET (né Bayly)
1st Earl of Uxbridge (NC)
1744–1812

FRANCES TWYSDEN
1753–1821
Countess of Jersey
Mistress of the Prince of Wales 1793–99

GEORGE BUSSEY VILLIERS
4th Earl of Jersey
1735–1805

FRANCIS RUSSELL
Marquess of Tavistock
1739–1767

CHARLES SLOANE CADOGAN
1st Earl Cadogan (NC)
1st Viscount, 3rd Baron
1728–1807

2. SIR ARTHUR PAGET
1771–1840

VICE ADMIRAL SIR CHARLES PAGET
1778–1839

LADY AUGUSTA BORINGDON (née Fane)
b.1786

LADY CHARLOTTE VILLIERS
d.1808

LORD WILLIAM RUSSELL
1767–1840

LADY CHARLOTTE 'CHA' CADOGAN
1781–1853
(Wellesley)
Marchioness of Anglesey

2. FIELD MARSHAL HENRY WILLIAM PAGET
1st Marquess of Anglesey
1768–1854

1. LADY CAROLINE 'CAR' VILLIERS
1774–1835
(Paget)
Duchess of Argyll

2. GEORGE WILLIAM CAMPBELL
1768–1839
6th Duke of Argyll

HONORIA LOUISA BLAKE
1787–1845
Countess Cadogan

ADMIRAL GEORGE CADOGAN
3rd Earl Cadogan
3rd Viscount
5th/1st Baron
1783–1864

HENRY PAGET
2nd Marquess of Anglesey
1797–1869

HENRY CHARLES CADOGAN
4th Earl Cadogan
4th Viscount
6th/2nd Baron
1812–1873

LADY AUGUSTA SARAH CADOGAN
1811–1882

LADY HONORIA LOUISA CADOGAN
1813–1904

1. SOPHIA ARMSTRONG
d.1852

GENERAL HON. SIR GEORGE CADOGAN
1814–1880

2. EMILY ASHWORTH
d.1891

HORACE WILLIAM CADOGAN
1820

HORACE JAMES HENRY CADOGAN
1862–1932

LADY EMILY CAROLINE PAGET
1810–1893
Countess Sydney

ADMIRAL LORD CLARENCE EDWARD PAGET
1811–1895

LADY MARY PAGET
1812–1859
Countess of Sandwich

GENERAL LORD ALFRED HENRY PAGET
1816–1890

LIPPO NERI
Conte Palagi del Palagio
d.1893

OLIVIA GEORGIANA CADOGAN
1850–1910

LADY ADELAIDE PAGET
1820–1890

HON. FREDERICK 'FREDDIE' WILLIAM CADOGAN
1821–1904

GENERAL LORD GEORGE AUGUSTUS FREDERICK PAGET
1818–1880
Charge of the Light Brigade

1. LADY BEATRIX 'BEATTIE' JANE CRAVEN
1844–1907
Countess Cadogan

GEORGE HENRY CADOGAN
5th Earl Cadogan
5th Viscount
7th/3rd Baron
1840–1915

2. ADELE NERI
Contessa Palagi
1880–1960
Countess Cadogan

Marquesses of Anglesey

Mansions, Cadogan Square, William Young Architect, lithograph by Maurice B. Adams, published in Building News, 1876.

THE VICTORIANS

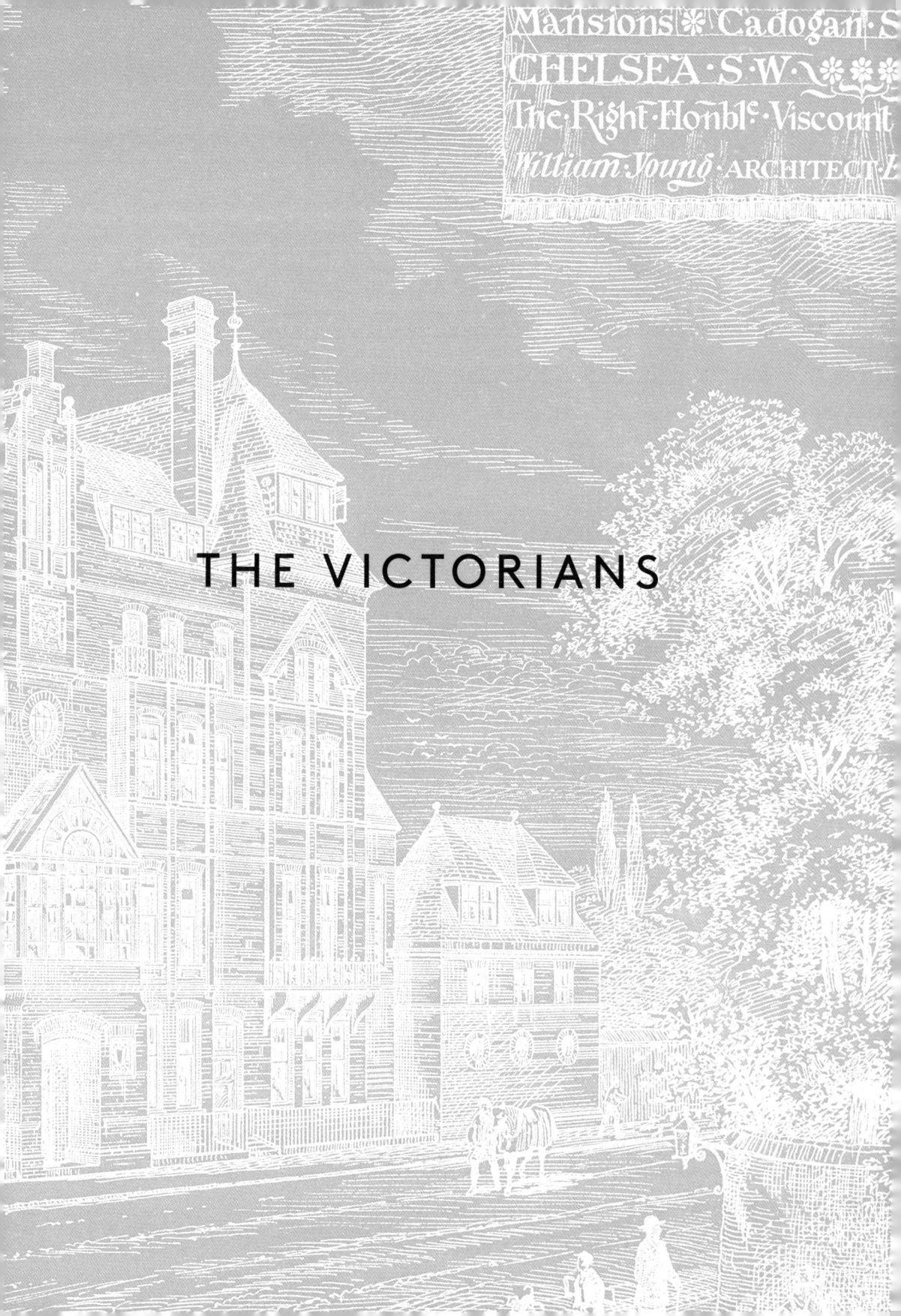

CHAPTER 12

Palaces, Parliament & Postings

—

HENRY, 4TH EARL (1812–1873)

Henry Charles Cadogan, George's eldest son, assumed the courtesy title Viscount Chelsea when his father inherited the earldom in 1832. His was a long apprenticeship; he would wait a further thirty years before his own all-too-brief tenure. A recent graduate of Oriel College, Oxford, Henry entered the diplomatic service and quickly found a position as an attaché in St Petersburg (1834–35), at the court of Tsar Nicholas I. It was undoubtedly prestigious – having pushed back Napoleon's forces in 1812, Russia had emerged as a European superpower, the world's third-largest empire – though Henry's role was limited:

> The family embassy of the early nineteenth century employed the services of unpaid attachés to perform the routine work of the chancery. These attachés have generally been described as young aristocrats completing, as it were, their education by using the European missions as a sort of European finishing school before they assumed their proper role either in London political life or County society....[1]

At the Russian imperial court, Henry attended soirées and dinners with a cast of titled characters: it was a glittering society. It was not without its critics though – literary legends Alexander Pushkin and Nikolai Gogol were both living and writing in St Petersburg during Henry's stay – and

Viscount Chelsea (later, 4th Earl Cadogan), Camille Silvy, March 1861, albumen print

Imperial Court Masquerade in the Anichkov Place, Nikolay Becker, 1837, watercolour, pen and ink on paper

the Tolstoy-esque round of princes, counts and generals he encountered were the social upper crust sitting atop a volcano of division. The serfs (of whom we must imagine Henry saw very little, if anything) endured feudal hardship unimaginable to an earl's son, raised in the largely temperate climate of a British parliamentary democracy.

Before he left for Russia, Henry had fallen in love. The object of his affection was his first cousin Mary Sarah Wellesley (1808–1873), Emily and Gerald's daughter, four years his senior. On his return, he asked for permission to marry her; the Cadogans were not amused. Henry's grandson Eddie would write 125 years later of 'opposition on the score of consanguinity',[2] but that seems a red herring given marriage between first cousins was neither unusual nor unlawful. A letter from his father, of 27 May 1835, to 'My dear Henry', withholding his blessing, makes for painful reading:

> It would only be deceiving you were I to hold forth a hope that I ever can give my consent to your marriage with Mary Wellesley. I cannot in justice to myself accept the responsibility you have offered me, and must leave you therefore Master of your own actions and arbiter of your future fate. From this moment I am determined to interfere no more....Believe me when I assure you that in requesting you will not reply to this letter I am actuated by kind and prudential notions alone. Our hearts and dispositions have naturally but few sympathies and, weakened as those now are by our relative positions, I dread lest anything which may fall from you should make impressions I have neither health [n]or nerve to encounter.
> I remain, Your affectionate father, Cadogan.
> I sent a copy of this to Mary Wellesley by this day's Post.[3]

It is sad to read that Henry and his father had 'naturally but few sympathies', but Eton and the Foreign Office would have provided a very different schooling from active service in the Royal Navy. Perhaps they were innately quite different in character too; Cadogan family historian Robert Pearman describes Henry as 'a pale, scholarly figure by comparison'.[4] A distressing stalemate took hold.

In Paris once more for the season, Henry's mother Honoria collared her brother-in-law Lord Anglesey, who reported to his wife, Henry's Aunt Cha:

> ...Ly Cadogan did not cease for half an hour to tell me of their miseries about a projected marriage. I tried to guess who the Parties were, & beat about the bush, but to no purpose. At length it came out that Ld Chelsea & Miss Wellesley were the Persons, & I was compelled to acknowledge that I had never heard one syllable of the matter, nor of the young Lady's former attachment to Lord Graves which she detailed to me. All of which ignorance or (as she probably thought) stupidity, seemed to fill her with amazement.[5]

Lord Graves was Anglesey's nephew; it was a very small world. Clearly having got nowhere with the baffled, ageing cavalry leader, Honoria looked to a friend of the young couple, the Marchioness of Londonderry. She wrote beseechingly, 'You are the only person who can do any good. Your influence over Henry is immense and I cannot therefore help appealing to you and entreating you to use it in persuading him to change his course with his Father for his own sake and for Mary's.'[6] Her opening position was to request a 'simple expression of repentance for the language he has used'. Loyal Lady Londonderry's reply, not surprisingly, offered sympathy but no help:

> My affection for Mary, my long knowledge of and my friendship for her makes me, I own, sanguine as to the ultimate happiness of the union, though I can perfectly understand objections that may be most natural and that the affection and anxiety of parents might point to a more ambitious choice for their oldest son…in my conversation with Lord Chelsea he appeared resigned to wait patiently if hopes were given of ultimate consent but your letters and his Father's breathed irrevocable opposition…[7]

The marchioness's letter encapsulates accepted social norms, especially in marriage, that today we might dismiss as snobbery: the belief that aristocrats should associate only with other aristocrats of equal status.

Lady Chelsea (née Mary Sarah Wellesley), Camille Silvy, February 1863, albumen print. The following year she became Countess Cadogan.

Henry was direct heir to an earldom and a considerable estate; Mary was the daughter of a clergyman, albeit a well-connected one. Honoria wrote to another brother-in-law, the Duke of Wellington, at that time Foreign Secretary. Apprised by her of the true nature of George's objections – nothing to do with status anxiety – his sage advice was not to visit the sins of the father (or in this case, the mother) on the child:

> It appears from your note of yesterday that I had been mistaken respecting Lord Cadogan's objection to the marriage. It is in fact to the conduct of the mother that the objection is…Setting aside for a moment the virtue of this objection to the daughter who was a child when separated from the mother and who never can have felt other than aggravated evil from the mother's conduct, it could never be expected from Gerald that he should be a consenting party to a sentence against his daughter upon such grounds and still less that I should be the person to endeavour to reconcile him to make an objection… I cannot be a party to an objection which is essentially unjust…[8]

George feared Mary might have inherited a genetic predisposition to stray, following in the footsteps of her mother Emily, her Aunt Cha and grandmother Mary Churchill (his own sisters and mother). Perhaps not unaware of the question marks over his own wife's fidelity, it seems he was wary of all wives. George's overprotective stance backfired: after a year of heated arguments, Henry defied his father and obtained a special marriage licence. Henry's completely unstuffy letter to Lady Londonderry a few days before the wedding underlines a generational difference between the two men:

> The veil is beyond beautiful. It has given general satisfaction and Mary is fully alive to its merits. I do so wish you could be here…to see her wear it. It is too hard upon you to have had all the bother and none of the fun…I hear that my people are more abusive than ever. I am fit to be tied especially as I am not allowed

to write a piece as I should wish telling them a bit of my mind… Many, many thanks for your kind wishes. I have nothing to give you in return except a great lump of cake which I hope you will receive on Thursday morning.[9]

The marriage took place at 6 pm on 13 July 1836, at Durham Cathedral, where Mary's father the Reverend Gerald was prebendary. Gerald – the only family member present – wrote to their ally Lady Londonderry, bursting with paternal pride: 'Any thing looking so lovely as Mary did I cannot describe to you…looking so fresh and beautiful as if she had been just created. She has been so happy lately….'[10] After an inauspicious start, theirs would be a lasting, loving match.

WHEN QUEEN VICTORIA ASCENDED THE THRONE ON 20 JUNE 1837, she retained George, 3rd Earl Cadogan, as naval aide-de-camp to the Crown. Almost exactly a year later, George and Countess Cadogan were commanded 'all excuses set apart'[11] to attend her coronation at Westminster Abbey. Sir George Hayter's painting, from sketches made in the church during the ceremony, is a window onto the opulence of the occasion. Lords and ladies dressed in their coronation robes of crimson silk-velvet (full capes and capelets ringed with rows of ermine, the number of which was determined by rank – George's gown had three rows befitting an earl, as worn again a century later by his great-great-grandson), stand against a background of draped red velvet and gold embroidery. Next to the queen as she accepted the sacrament were two Paget girls, Lady Caroline (Car's eldest daughter, now the Duchess of Richmond), and teenage Lady Adelaide (Cha's daughter, of whom more later).[12]

The mood was exuberant: the Duke of Wellington was applauded; the crowd of foreign dignitaries provided chatter and spectacle:

> The five-hour ceremony was made the more strenuous for the Queen by her 'remarkably maladroit' clergymen: the Archbishop of Canterbury misplaced the orb, the ruby coronation ring was

The Coronation of Queen Victoria in Westminster Abbey, 28 June 1838, Sir George Hayter, 1839, oil on canvas. Hayter depicts the moment immediately after the crown was placed on Victoria's head, to shouts of 'God Save the Queen!', after which the peers – including George, 3rd Earl Cadogan – donned their own coronets.

too small and had to be forced upon the royal finger and the Bishop of Bath and Wells missed two pages of the Order of Service – an omission that had to be made good by recalling the Queen from her retreat into St Edward's Chapel.[13]

Thankfully the seriousness of the event prevented its full descent into farce. A further moment of humour from the new queen's court is provided by Countess Cadogan, who – never one to shy away from involving men of high office in domestic matters – wrote to the Prime Minister the next day on a matter of national importance. Her new French gown was delayed at customs as the weekend began:

> My Dear Lord Melbourne
> I am sorry to have to bother you with my *toilette* concerns, but I am in a scrape out of which you can get me, I imagine. They bid me send the letter to a Lord of the Treasury so I suppose the first is the best. Little Graham '*croyant bien faire*' sent me a gown and cap with [the Duke of] Palmella's things by way of safety and expedition. The Custom House finding this with my name imagine it was an attempt at smuggling, which certainly never

entered my head – on this occasion at least. As you will see by the letter, I fully intended paying the duty as I constantly do for things they send me from Paris. I assure you I had no dishonest intention, neither had Pauline – so pray get me my gown or else how am I to go to the Palace on Monday?
Believe me most truly yours
H. Cadogan
The Duke de Palmella can bear witness for me that no smuggling was intended, by the fact of my name and address being on the case.[14]

Melbourne's aide at 10 Downing Street sent his apologies at finding it 'impossible to [help] without establishing a precedent...So many cases are likely to occur of either friends or servants passing their goods among the baggage of Ambassadors that it is necessary to be very rigid upon this point.'[15] Poor Honoria: a wardrobe full of clothes and simply nothing to wear?

GEORGE WAS STILL BUSY with plans on the reunified Chelsea estate, carrying out developments as and when opportunity arose. To the east of

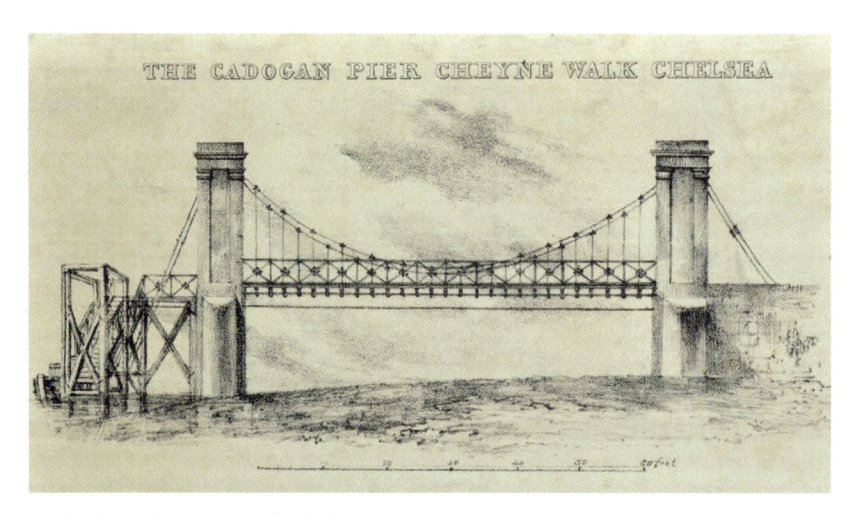

The Cadogan Pier Cheyne Walk, Chelsea, C. Warren, lithograph, published by Thomas Faulkner, Chelsea, 17 April 1841

Chelsea's waterfront with Cheyne Walk in the background and Chelsea Old Church in the distance, Thomas Hosmer Shepherd, early 1850s, watercolour

Queen Street (now Flood Street) he had Elizabeth Street (now Christchurch Street) and Caversham Street built in 1839. A second chapel of ease for Chelsea, Christ Church, paid for by the Hyndman Trust, provided a local place of worship for the working-class residents of the area who were employed as domestic servants in the large houses on Cheyne Walk and in Hans Town.[16] Edward Blore's church sat among the remaining medieval market gardens and nurseries around the King's Road, in what was still a green and pleasant area. In 1847, George purchased garden ground on the west side of Milman's Street from Gorges House, and Ashburnham Cottage.[17] He gave land opposite the church for new boys' and girls' schools, where his benefaction is commemorated in a plaque above the door of Christ Church Infant School, opened in 1850. The area around First, Hasker, Ovington and Walton Streets grew up.

Chelsea was well-placed to adapt to the boom in river transport during the Victorian age of steam – the Chelsea Steamboat Company, established in 1841, was one of several. 'Traffic peaked in the early 1840s, with intense competition between the companies: in 1844 eight steamboats travelled between London Bridge and Chelsea, four times an hour, and traffic was increasing.'[18] Cadogan Pier was built on Cheyne Walk, on George's instruction, to increase access to Chelsea's new housing. 'It was a landmark structure and was the prime river gateway for visitors to Chelsea.'[19] Bar rebuilding to make way for Albert Bridge, it has remained in place ever since. As the 1850s drew to a close, Chelsea Bridge opened, a direct link to the park at Battersea; and work began on the Embankment. Chelsea echoed to the sound of industrious building work.

There was happiness for George at home: his sister Lady Louisa finally moved out from under his roof in April 1840 to marry the Reverend William Marsh, vicar of St Mary's, Leamington. She was fifty-two; he was a decade her senior. Her husband had grown up in Reading, where one of George's older half-brothers had determined the course of Marsh's life: 'His intention was to enter the Army, but when he was eighteen the sudden death in his presence of a young man in a ballroom deeply shocked him, and under the influence of the Hon. and Revd William [Bromley] Cadogan he became an evangelical.' Curious indeed. Marsh was far calmer than the roaring Cadogan reverend – '[h]is conciliatory manners gained him friends among all denominations' – but equally uxorious.[20] Louisa became stepmother to five children from his first marriage.

ON 12 MAY 1840 Lady Chelsea presented Henry with a son and heir, judiciously named George Henry, born in Durham. A second son, Arthur Charles Lewin (1841–1918), arrived just as Henry embarked on a new career: six days after the birth, voting opened in a general election, at which he was returned as one of two MPs for Reading. He served under Sir Robert Peel's Conservative-Tory government alongside Lord Wellington (his wife's Uncle Arthur). A single whiff of irregularity cropped up in 1842, when the Reading constituency was included in an anti-corruption investigation by select committee. Detailing the sums of money spent during the election campaign by Henry (£2,000), his fellow Reading MP Mr Russell (£1,000) and their agents (£3,000),[21] its inconclusive findings record:

> Mr Russell, Lord Chelsea, and their agent, distinctly assert that no part was expended in direct bribery; though it is admitted by both sitting Members, that so large a sum could not all have been spent in legal and proper disbursements; and their agent, when asked as to this expenditure, and more especially whether beer-shops had been opened, declined to answer…Of the expenditure of this money nothing very accurate could be ascertained…[22]

Henry tendered his resignation, which was refused. The Honourable Member for Reading's young family grew, welcoming Charlotte Georgiana Mary (1843–1908) and Cecil James George (1846–1918).

There was a string of bereavements. Mary's mother, Lady Emily, was first, in December 1839. She had never reconciled to her children or to Gerald, who refused to divorce her; her body was returned to England from Boulogne and she was buried at St Luke's. The eldest of the Chelsea brood, Emily Frances, died in childhood (1838–1843); Henry's Aunt Louisa died the same year (Marsh married a third and final time). Then, his mother Honoria died while on a visit to the fashionable spa at Wiesbaden in September 1845. His parents had been married for thirty-five years; she is buried at St Luke's alongside Louisa. Two Wellesley brothers were next: Henry, Cha's first husband, now 1st Baron Cowley (d.1847), and Mary's father, the Reverend Gerald (d.1848). Henry lost his seat at the 1847 election, and during a five-year break from public duties produced a final son, Charles George Henry (1850–1901). The Chelseas acquired a large mansion house at 13 Cadogan Place (referred to in later estate minute books as 28 Lowndes Street), which became the new Chelsea House.

At the close of the decade Major Henry Carr, the illegitimate son of Colonel Henry Cadogan, whom George had sponsored, left a widow of only two years and no children. Edward Cadogan, the youngest of George's brothers, died in 1851, a twice-married lieutenant-colonel with clasps for Vimeira and Corunna on his General Service Medal.[23] In 1852, the Duke of Wellington died, having spent the last years of his life sharing his house with his mistress's widower. His funeral was an event of national mourning: he lay in state at the Royal Hospital Chelsea, before a procession to St Paul's witnessed in person by an estimated 1.5 million people.[24] There was an inescapable feeling of the changing of the guard: George, 3rd Earl, had outlived most of his generation and many of the next. He did not have to worry about continuity of the Cadogan line, however; this time, the path to succession was clear.

Henry got back in the parliamentary game in 1852, taking the Dover constituency with a very clean campaign. That was the last of his political luck: an attempt to switch to Middlesex at the next election was unsuccessful and he quit the Commons in 1857, having spent nearly twenty years on and off the benches. He returned to the diplomatic service. In March 1858 Lord Malmesbury, Foreign Secretary, recommended Henry for the position of First Secretary to the British Embassy in Paris. Viscount Chelsea received his royal commission from Queen Victoria at the end of the month and travelled across the Channel soon after. He received an annual salary of £1,000 plus a £400 clothing allowance to be spent on topper and tails (a vivid

RIGHT Henry's appointment as Secretary to the British Embassy, signed by Queen Victoria

BELOW Henry's luggage tag bearing the Foreign Office seal and signed by Lord Malmesbury, 1858

illustration of his largely social, public-facing duties). Fashion historians at the Victoria and Albert Museum tell us:

> Men wore matching coats, waistcoats and trousers, with hairstyles characterised by large mutton-chop side-burns and moustaches, after the style set by Prince Albert. Shirts had high upstanding collars and were tied at the neck with large bow-ties… The bowler hat was invented around 1850, but was generally seen as a working-class hat, while top-hats were favoured by the upper classes.[25]

Mrs Beeton's *Book of Household Management*, which first appeared in 1859 as a monthly part-work for the prosperous middle classes, suggests that a budget of £1,000 a year would employ a cook, upper housemaid, nursemaid, under housemaid and a manservant.[26] For an aristocrat, however, it was a meagre sum. Only a gentleman with a private income could afford a diplomatic occupation, would have understood its rules, or indeed would have been offered the position. However, this ran counter to the emerging Victorian ideal of the free market, in this case the labour market, and had not gone unchallenged. In 1853, Lord Clarendon had begun to formalize career progression within the diplomatic service, to factor in length of career and track record, and imposing a structural hierarchy.[27] Entry to the civil service by examination was not far off (introduced in 1870). Henry's appointment rubbed up against the nineteenth-century Foreign Office's attempts to modernize and professionalize its workings.

Henry was the first cousin of the British Ambassador to France, Henry, 1st Earl Cowley – Cha's son from her first marriage. Malmesbury justified his choice in a letter to Queen Victoria that plainly states the advantage of family ties. Cowley had requested help in the Chancery and at the Paris salons; Henry was 'qualified to help out on both these points for he was Cowley's relation and friend and anxious to transact business and is fond of good society.'[28] The two Henrys worked together closely, with Cadogan expected to fulfil a deputy's role, stepping into the ambassadorial shoes on occasion. This was no small beer. A posting to the British Embassy in Paris was one of the most prestigious in the world, tasked with representing one empire to another at the centre of what was considered civilized society. Napoleon III had made the transition from president to emperor only four years after the 1848 revolutions, a wave of unrest across Europe that toppled monarchies in France, Austria, Italy and Poland. His was an imperial court and Henry's main responsibility was to keep London apprised of information gathered at the dizzying whirl of balls, soirées, salons and informal dinners. The location was the palatial British Ambassador's residence, then, as now, a grand town house: the Hôtel de Charost, on the rue du Faubourg Saint-Honoré. Wellington had bought it from Napoleon's sister in 1814 (indeed, the duke's gold was largely responsible for financing Boney's comeback from Elba to Waterloo).

While in Paris, Henry kept a diary: the *Diplomatic Common Place Book*. Inside, its pages are inscribed in his beautiful copperplate handwriting. Notes at the back detail embassy life and his difficulties with Lord Cowley; at the front, are records of diplomatic dispatches – news and current affairs from around the world (their idiosyncratic chronology makes it likely these were written up later from notebooks). Life had certainly changed in the intervening years since his posting to St Petersburg, as communications

Henry's *Diplomatic Common Place Book*

had been revolutionized by the invention of the telegraphic system. Such cutting-edge technology caused as much fear as excitement – it was ever thus – and the year Henry was posted to Paris, as the first transatlantic cable was laid, the *New York Times* decried:

> Superficial, sudden, unsifted, too fast for the truth, must be all telegraphic intelligence. Does it not render the popular mind too fast for the truth? Ten days brings us the mails from Europe. What need is there for the scraps of news in ten minutes?[29]

Mail crossed the Atlantic several times a week, together with cargo and passengers; the Cunard Line ran a weekly steamer to Liverpool, from New York and Boston alternately.[30] Telegraphy was a leap ahead: transmission speed was a zippy one character every two minutes and five seconds. Queen Victoria's brief, congratulatory message to the US President took 17 hours and 40 minutes to arrive.[31]

Henry was fluent in French, the language of diplomacy since the mid-eighteenth century, when it replaced Latin. (Henry's diary records Count Walewski, French Minister of Foreign Affairs, saying that his government 'thinks French and English Consular Agents will always hold a higher position than others.'[32]) His interpretation of nuance in diplomatic language, however, led to an incident of note during his time in Paris. On 1 January 1859, the French emperor and his wife delivered their customary New Year greetings to assembled ambassadors. Greeting Count Joseph Alexander Hübner, Napoleon III said, 'I regret that our relations are not as friendly as I would wish, but please write to Vienna and say that my

ABOVE Cooke and Wheatstone five-needle telegraph, 1837. British pioneers had first used electromagnetism to point needles at letters of the alphabet on 25 July 1837. Technological advances in communication were a boon to Henry's job at the British Embassy in Paris.

Delegates at the Congress of Paris, Mayer Frères & Pierson, 25 February 1856. The front row, from left to right, seated: Baron Hübner, Ali Pasha, Lord Clarendon, Count Walewski, Count Orloff, Baron de Bourqueney and Lord Cowley (British Ambassador to Paris, Henry's boss).

personal feelings towards the Emperor are still unchanged.'[33] Baron Hübner – experienced on the world stage; a man who had attended the 1856 Paris Congress – gave these ambiguous pleasantries no further thought; but Henry inferred a hostile, bellicose meaning. 'Lord Chelsea…went straight from the Tuileries to the fashionable Union Club in Paris and reported that Louis Napoleon had addressed words to the Austrian Ambassador which meant war.'[34] His intuition sent shivers from political salons to the financial markets, as reported in *The Times* two days later:

> …corroboration regarding the menacing and impatient manner of the remark addressed by the Emperor Napoleon to the Austrian Minister at the usual levée on New Year's Day caused an instantaneous fall of three-eighths per cent. Accounts of a more serious decline on the Paris Bourse increased the adverse feeling, and the market closed heavily…[35]

The markets remained jittery: '…since the 1st of January quotations, not only of Consols but of all descriptions of securities, had been drooping [sic] through the effect of the shock of the warning given to M. Hübner….'[36]

Henry could have used more discretion, but he had not been wrong. In February Lord Cowley was sent to Vienna on a confidential mission to mediate talks between Austria and France, and Henry took over as chargé d'affaires. The crisis deepened. On 28 April, *The Times* reeled in shock:

> The news from Berlin of the French and Russian treaty…took the Stock Exchange this morning by complete surprise, and caused the markets to open in a state of panic…the general depreciation in the nominal value of the funded and share property of the country, even since yesterday, may be roughly estimated as equal at least to about 50 millions sterling.[37]

The following day, Austrian forces crossed the Ticino. By the summer an all-out war saw France, allied with Piedmont, redrawing the hazy borderlines of southern Europe, enabling Italy to take steps towards unification. At home, the government fell, and Henry was recalled from Paris. More change was afoot. The year 1859 saw publication of John Stuart Mill's *On Liberty*, stressing the need for active participation in a democracy; and Charles Darwin's *On the Origin of Species*, the founding text of evolutionary theory. Across the pond, from 1861 to 1865, the United States battled with itself during the American Civil War.

ON 15 SEPTEMBER 1864, the third most senior officer in the Royal Navy – Admiral of the Red – died at home in Piccadilly with his unmarried daughters, at the age of eighty-one. A hiatus from active service of twenty-seven years had proved no hurdle to promotion, as his name gradually crept up the Navy list through retirements and reorganization. His advisory position at the palace, along with service on prominent committees, doubtless did not hold him back. George was held in high regard, described by socialite the Countess of Blessington as

> …frank high-spirited and well bred – the very *beau idéal* of a son of the sea, possessing all the attributes of that generous race,

joined to all those said to be peculiar to the high-born and well educated.[38]

Henry stepped into his father's shoes, becoming 6th Baron Cadogan of Oakley, 2nd Baron Oakley of Caversham and 4th Earl Cadogan. There was some unsightly squabbling with his siblings (who feature next in our story) over their father's will. Sisters Augusta and Honoria felt the sharp end of 'this most painful state of things'[39] when Henry sent a strongly worded letter about the silver plate and the diamonds; they agreed that the Cosway miniatures and their carriage should go to the head of the family. Of the brothers, Freddie was provided for, but George the spare was cut out entirely, owing by his own account to '…[an] enormous perversion of fact that must have existed in my poor Father's mind…the fiction that I was a millionaire.' He told Henry that:

> Augusta…talked some time ago of seeing whether it was in her power to leave me or mine by will the small sum left by the will in her power. But [she] has lately informed me that there is no loophole for any disposition in my favour and that the after recommendation as to the loose money, points like the rest after my sisters indubitably to Frederick. I have therefore no interest whatever under my Father's will…[40]

Life moved on. Henry, already sitting in the House of Lords, was appointed Captain of the Yeomen of the Guard, becoming a privy counsellor in a ceremony at Osborne House on the Isle of Wight, alongside the 7th Duke of Marlborough. He served as an advisor to Queen Victoria under two Prime Ministers – Lord Derby and Benjamin Disraeli – seeing in the Second Reform Act (1867), which doubled the electorate. The following year Gladstone took the helm for the Liberals. Further reforms included the Education Act (1870), which established a board to build and manage primary schools: many of the resulting red-brick establishments stand among terraced streets across Britain today.

12. PALACES, PARLIAMENT & POSTINGS

The world was spinning faster and faster, more and more connected. Isambard Kingdom Brunel, who enjoyed a riverside Chelsea childhood at 98 Cheyne Walk, had criss-crossed the south-west with the Great Western Railway, begun in 1833; his daring Clifton Suspension Bridge in Bristol was finished posthumously in 1863. Development continued on the Cadogan Estate: south of the King's Road Redesdale, Redburn and Radnor Streets (now Radnor Walk), and Tedworth Square were built on former nursery land. In the south-western corner, freeholds of 44 ½ acres, including Cremorne and Ashburnham, were sold to developers in 1866. Chelsea was a hub of London life: Sloane Square Underground station opened on Christmas Eve, 1868. Sadly, Henry did not live to see Albert Bridge or Chelsea Embankment completed (in August 1873 and May 1874 respectively). He died of a combination of heartbreak and pneumonia on 8 June 1873, at his eldest son's house, Woodrising Hall in Norfolk, four months after his wife Mary, and the pair were buried together in the family vault at St Luke's.[41] Together they had witnessed the birth of a new era. The Victorians were not just politicians, reformers, town planners and engineers, however. Chelsea was gaining a reputation as a haven for artists; Henry's siblings – so different from their elder brother – had embraced their talents in the fashionable pastime of sketching and painting, recording their lives at home, in royal and court circles, and on the battlefield at first hand.

Chelsea Embankment Looking East, William Strudwick, c.1872. This early photograph shows the Chelsea Embankment during construction; paving slabs are stacked ready to be laid.

CHAPTER 13

Art & Europe

—

LADIES AUGUSTA (1811–1882) AND HONORIA (1813–1904),
AND GENERAL SIR GEORGE CADOGAN (1814–1880)

Ladies Augusta Sarah Cadogan (1811–1882) and Honoria Louisa Cadogan ('Hony', 1813–1904), spinster sisters of Henry, 4th Earl Cadogan, have an image problem that has long seen them consigned to a footnote. 'The typical amateur English watercolour painter is still often assumed to be a Victorian maiden aunt,' begins an article on Honoria in *Country Life*, published in 1992, '...travelling the British Isles and the Continent, painting churches, landscapes, watering places and the country houses of her extended kindred.'[1] Her sister must also contend with associations conjured by the Aunt Augustas of literature, falling somewhere between the formidable Wildean Lady Bracknell and the criminal eccentric of Graham Greene's *Travels with My Aunt*. Honoria quietly nursing their ageing father in the parental home, her increasing dottiness revealed in spidery handwriting; Augusta worrying to brother Freddie over who might inherit the opera glasses given to them by the duc d'Orléans[2] – it would be easy to make assumptions that the pair had led small lives with narrow horizons. But both ladies were intimately involved in royal life, travelled widely and had far more about them than a whiff of Miss Havisham and a collection of monogrammed paintboxes.

The young Cadogan ladies were taken to live in a cosmopolitan capital. Recording 'the recollections of my earliest youth, passed entirely in Paris, in close intimacy with many of the families representing the greatest names in French history,'[3] in her dotage Augusta was able to reel off a

...both ladies were intimately involved in royal life, travelled widely and had far more about them than a whiff of Miss Havisham and a collection of monogrammed paintboxes.

ABOVE *Lady Augusta Cadogan* and RIGHT *Lady Honoria Cadogan*, after Sir John Hayter, stipple and etching on chine collé by John Henry Robinson, 1849. Illustrations to Finden's *Female Aristocracy of the Court of Queen Victoria* (1849).

great list of fashionable and influential visitors, including Talleyrand, Beaupoil de Saint-Aulaire, Prosper de Barante, Chateaubriand...

>...Pozzo di Borgo; Lamartine, whose English wife bought him into British society; Mme. De Broglie, daughter of Mme. De Staël...Victor Hugo, then a very young man known only by his poems and *Notre Dame de Paris*...[4]

Such literate, engaging company can only have inspired the curiosity of adolescent minds. Augusta's memoir, published in two parts in *Macmillan's Magazine* (1877/78), invites us into the world of her youth and allows us a glimpse of the character it formed. Alongside simple *déjeuners en famille*, her memories include *gaufres*, *galettes* and *plaisirs* eaten in the Tuileries, where 'we exercised ourselves at the skipping-rope...double twirls in one leap being highly applauded by the critical audience of fly-caps [nannies]... and wooden-legged *Invalides*'[5] – veterans of the recent Napoleonic wars. The girls were witness to the dying breaths of a centuries-old way of life.

They crossed the Channel in 1823, only thirty years after the regicide and Reign of Terror; *Madame la Guillotine* and her thousands of aristocratic victims were still fresh in the collective memory. After Waterloo the monarchy had been restored in King Louis XVIII '*la desirée*', but it was an uneasy court: two competing branches of the French royal family emerged, wracked with 'anxiety for the throne which hung on the balance', as Augusta recalled:

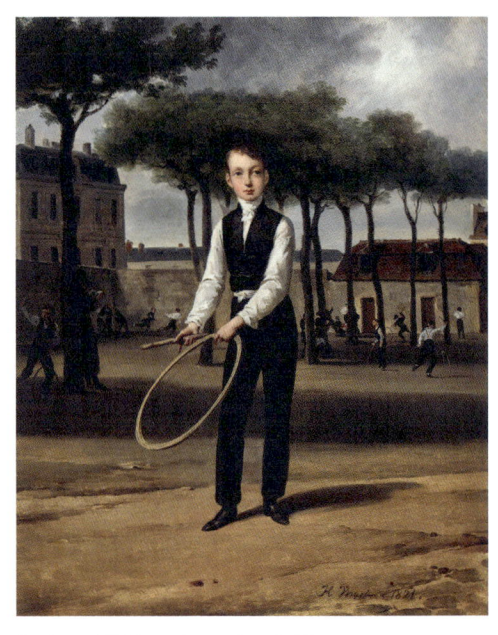

Ferdinand-Philippe-Louis, duc de Chartres, tenant un cerceau, Horace Vernet, 1821, oil on canvas. The eldest son of the duc d'Orléans, seen here aged eleven, was a year older than the eldest of the Cadogan girls, and a playmate of theirs in Paris. His father was crowned King of the French in 1830.

It happened in our case that amongst the noble émigrés returned from England my parents had some personal friends, and a family connection in the Faubourg St. Germain, and thus saw them in their own homes, a favour seldom accorded to strangers. We children continued playmates of our still older friends, the children of the Orléans family, which gave us a foot in both camps – for opposite camps they were…the gloomy Duchesse d'Angoulême, who had never forgiven the murder of her parents [Louis XVI and Marie Antoinette], naturally kept aloof from the duc d'Orléans…[6]

Support in the palatial *hôtels particuliers* was for the Bourbons; but autocratic rule by King Charles X from 1824 gave rise to the popular conception of the *ancien régime* as '*n'ayant rien appris, et rien oublié*' (having learned nothing, and forgotten nothing). The duc d'Orléans, by contrast, represented modernity: 'The liberal education which Louis-Philippe gave his sons, sending them to walk daily, satchel on back, to the Collège de France, to pursue their studies in common with boys of all classes, went counter to all their ideas.'[7]

Welcomed behind the large wooden gates of both town houses and châteaux, the girls absorbed the atmosphere and attitudes of the French nobility living in reduced circumstances; the fading evening *salon* culture, once ruled with *bienveillance* by *grandes dames*, surrounded by devoted younger relations and the sparkling conversation of guests. At the Château de Mouchy:

> The drawing-room treasures of laque, buhl, Sèvres, had been hidden and saved by faithful servants during the Revolution…. The furniture, which had been confiscated in [17]'93, was even in the best rooms replaced by common chairs, covered with white cotton, bound with red. But they were delighted with the cotton covers imported from England, notwithstanding the hostess's aversion for *La perfide Albion*. I heard her say to my mother,

'Voyez-vous? en fait d'Anglais je n'aime que vous et les Godfrey's salts' – just imported as a novelty.[8]

Somehow the Cadogans were exceptions to the general distrust of all things English. Sadly, the château, which had survived Revolution, would be demolished a century later, having suffered badly under occupation.[9]

Perhaps George sensed upheavals to come. The family left Paris on 30 May 1830, just two months before the July Revolution deposed Charles X and replaced him with a constitutional monarch, Louis-Philippe I, 'King of the French' – a king of the people, not the land – his ancestral coat of arms intertwined with the tricolour. They returned home to a sea change in the United Kingdom, marked by the death of King George IV.

Waltzing at Almacks, George Cruikshank, 1817/18. During the Regency, a voucher of entry to Almack's Assembly Rooms was one of the highest stamps of social approval. An exclusive club run by a coterie of ladies – among them Lady Jersey (caricatured dancing), the Princess Lieven and Lady Cowper – its weekly balls in mixed company were essential marriage markets.

THE FAMILY WAS NOW BASED IN LONDON: Freddie was sent to Westminster School and the girls were perfectly placed for their mother to set about husband-hunting. Lieutenant-Colonel Sir Henry Cooke – a 'shrewd observer and a lively satirist'[10] – sent a friend this gossipy round-up from the capital:

> Mrs Cadogan *fait des frais* [has gone to a lot of expense] to dispose of the girl. Lazarus arose blooming in comparison with her quick-silver countenance. The very atmosphere seems to render her a living barometer, but I despair of seeing her *set fair*....Raikes has returned among us, or rather the clubs and Crockford's, with increased quantum of shirt-frill and breast-button. I guess there

will be great demand for such goods. There is a great struggle to keep Almack's alive....[11]

Cooke's rather unkind comments were at least liberally distributed. It was June 1830: Augusta was nineteen and Honoria seventeen. The likely course of events is that they were presented as debutantes shortly after King William IV ascended the throne. Augusta's early watercolour dated the following year shows the pair in court dress: all in white, with ostrich feathers in their hair and the required train of at least three yards. Fledgling painting skills admitting – and Augusta did not flatter any of her subjects, who tend to resemble one another – they were, it must be said, no oil paintings.

Nearly a decade later, the *Queen's Gazette* records an afternoon visit to the palace. It was two months before the young queen's coronation; there are the Cadogan girls, approaching thirty, sandwiched between a Cholmondley and a Canning:

> 5 April [1838] – The Queen held her first Drawing Room this season at St. James's. Her Majesty arrived at two o'clock, attended by the Ladies and Gentlemen of her Household in Waiting, and escorted by a party of Life Guards...Soon after two o'clock the entire company were admitted to the Throne Room. The following is a list of the nobility and gentry who had the honour of being presented to Her Majesty:–[...]
> Cholmondley, Lady H......................March. Cholmondley
> Cadogan, Lady Augusta....................Countess Cadogan
> Cadogan, Lady Honoria....................Countess Cadogan
> Canning, Lady......................Marchioness Lansdowne[12]

During the long Drawing Room (presentation of ladies, the equivalent to a levee for gentlemen), their mother also presented Lady Maria West (née Walpole), a cousin by marriage; Lady Yarde-Buller, a forbear of the first wife of the 7th Earl Cadogan, was another sponsor. Having waited patiently in an antechamber, ladies were ushered before the royal presence to curtsy, give or receive a kiss – Augusta and Honoria received one each on the head as daughters of an earl – and then had to curtsy their way out of the room, never turning their faces from the monarch.[13] Did the sisters wear the same dresses as they had in 1830, perhaps with a small tweak to the lace or adjustments to the neckline and waistline? Repurposing white court dresses would become all the rage two years later, after Queen Victoria wore a dress of white Honiton lace to marry Prince Albert, beginning the English tradition of the white wedding.[14]

The Cadogan ladies were by then well-known at court. Queen Victoria's journals, an exhaustive, handwritten record of the minutiae of her days, are peppered with references to the girls' attendance. A typical entry from Kensington Palace, the week she turned sixteen, reads:

Honoria and Augusta Cadogan, Augusta Cadogan, 1831, watercolour. Keen amateur portraitist Augusta lacked any vanity.

> 29 May [1835]. I awoke at near 8 and got up at 9. At ½ past we breakfasted. At ½ past 10 we went out driving with Lehzen. At 12 came the Dean till 1. At 1 we lunched. At ½ past 3 came the Dean till ½ past 4. At 7 we dined. [18 names]. ...After dinner came [24 names...] the Earl and Countess of Cadogan and the Ladies Augusta and Honoria Cadogan, [12 names...] Lord and Lady Cowley and Miss Wellesley [12 names...]. Mme. de Praslin is the only daughter of Count Sebastiani. She has a fine face, but is very short and fat. A M. Begrez sang, very badly indeed; and a M. Sowinsky, a Pole, played on the piano very well indeed....I stayed up till ½ past 11.[15]

Honoria and Augusta crop up every couple of months for the next few years, at formal gatherings and intimate soirées, along with their parents. In 1837, Queen Victoria remarks about their mother, 'Lady Cadogan was looking very handsome.'[16] But their father George, 3rd Earl, who had discouraged Henry's marriage to Mary Wellesley a couple of years earlier, appears to have been equally unhelpful towards prospective suitors to his girls. The monarch and her Prime Minister indulged in a little gossip:

> 21 July 1838…Lord Melbourne…spoke of the Ladies Cadogan, not being married, which he said was their Father's fault, who prevented people's coming, and said they must either declare or cease coming: 'No man should interfere with those things' said Lord Melbourne…
>
> 7 November 1839…I then told Lord M. that I heard it was said Car Lennox was really to marry Horace Pitt; talked of her conduct towards him certainly having been very questionable; 'The Pagets think of nothing else but marrying,' said Lord M. I then said that Mary Sandwich & Adelaide Paget were so very different in that respect, & conducted themselves so well: Lord M. said they were very different to others, & had a great fear on account of the strange conduct of their own family…Talked of poor Augusta & Honoria being nice girls; Lord M. said he told them once: 'Remember your own family,' & that they had a great pull to get over that; '"Oh! We know that," they said.'[17]

Lady Caroline Gordon-Lennox was the granddaughter of the Marquess of Anglesey and his first wife, Car; Lady Adelaide Paget (1820–1890) and Lady Mary Sandwich (née Paget, 1812–1859), were the Cadogans' first cousins, daughters of the marquess by their Aunt Cha. The queen's diaries record that she often asked the girls to sing after dinner, and Adelaide carried the royal train during the coronation; clearly, they were favourites.[18]

Experienced, worldly Lord Melbourne had a long memory for the indiscretions of others, viz. Augusta and Honoria's aunts and grandmother, however, and a stubborn insistence on the legality of his own paternity. (The two attitudes were perhaps not unrelated.[19]) A generation older than the young queen, tall and good-looking, his opinion held court. Queen Victoria was clearly fond of the girls, however. In 1846, a year after the death of their mother and with Prince Albert now the queen's chief advisor, the palace found the elder of the two sisters a role: at thirty-five Augusta became lady-in-waiting to the Duchess of Cambridge, Queen Victoria's aunt. She joined the royal family at the Ascot races, at Chobham Camp, playing billiards – sketching all the while. Honoria, meanwhile, began twenty years as her father's dutiful family housekeeper and nursemaid at 138 Piccadilly, though she did make the occasional escape, even accompanying her sister on royal holidays.

ON 29 NOVEMBER 1851 FREDDIE CADOGAN – Augusta and Honoria's baby brother, now a barrister – married his first cousin Adelaide Paget; there were no objections from his father this time. Adelaide was also the

Interesting simplicity – Canadian revolt explained, John 'HB' Doyle, lithograph, printed by Alfred Ducôte and published by Thomas McLean, 2 March 1838. Queen Victoria's diary records her wide-ranging discussions with Prime Minister Lord Melbourne, which included the Cadogan ladies' prospects for marriage.

Queen Victoria, P. Albert & the Royal children, Augusta Cadogan, 1853, watercolour

apple of her mother's eye: 'I have directed that Adelaide may have my little personal property, composed of a few articles (not worth dividing) with a reserve of some Trinkets to the other Children…'.[20] The Very Reverend Gerald Valerian Wellesley, the bride's brother, officiated. Augusta sketched their wedding day at Uxbridge House and, a few years later, the couple as doting new parents. After Oriel College, Oxford, Freddie had been called to the bar at Inner Temple. Newly married, he decided to enter political life, standing unsuccessfully in 1852 and 1857 before claiming Cricklade, Wiltshire, for the Liberal Party in 1868, a seat he held for six years. He is mentioned in the memoirs of renowned diarist Charles Greville, in an entry from May 1860, bringing back a sensitive report from the court of the last monarch of France, Napoleon III:

> Frederick Cadogan came over from Paris the other day, and told Clarendon that Cowley was in very bad spirits about the aspect of foreign affairs, that all intimacy and confidence between the

ABOVE *The Library, Piccadilly*, Honoria Cadogan, watercolour

OPPOSITE *Fred.k Cadogan & Cha*, Augusta Cadogan, c.1854, watercolour. Charlotte Louisa Emily Cadogan (1853–1947) married the Reverend Henry Montagu Villiers, son of the Bishop of Durham, and had five children. She presented two volumes of Lady Augusta's watercolours to Queen Mary in 1937.

Emperor and him was at an end, and that it was more and more evident that His Majesty meant to follow his own devices, whatever they might be, without reference to anybody, or caring for the opposition or the assent of any other Powers.[21]

(This was only a year after his brother's own sensitive report from Paris; Lord Cowley remained at the British Embassy until his retirement in 1867.) Aside from his parliamentary career, and unofficial diplomacy, Frederick Cadogan, MP, was Deputy Lieutenant for Middlesex and served as a Justice of the Peace in both Middlesex and Westminster. Meanwhile, Adelaide became an author, writing books on parlour games and diversions, including plays she adapted from French and a blow-by-blow guide to German versions of the card game Patience.

The couple had three girls and a boy. Ethel Henrietta Maud Cadogan (1854–1930), their middle daughter, became a favourite at court, perhaps due to her willingness to join the queen and Princess Beatrice, the youngest royal daughter, in singing trios, *tableaux vivants* and plays. Queen Victoria's journals record Ethel – 'a very nice girl'[22] – staying at Balmoral, Windsor Castle and Osborne House. She served the queen for over twenty years, as extra maid-of-honour (1876–80), maid of honour (1880–97), and woman of the bedchamber (1898–1901). Her only brother, Henry George Gerald Cadogan (1859–1893), joined the diplomatic service. During his time as secretary of the legation at Tehran, he embarked upon a doomed love affair with Gertrude Bell, often described as the female Lawrence of Arabia. Her father disapproved, owing to Henry's impecuniosity, and their engagement was called off. Henry died a few months later, unmarried, at thirty-four.[23]

The Cadogan ladies occupied themselves with the usual charitable good works. Dog-lover Augusta was a regular donor to Battersea's Temporary

Writer, archaeologist and political mover Gertrude Bell alongside Winston and Clementine Churchill and T.E. Lawrence, Cairo, 1921, G.M. Georgoulas. Bell had a doomed love affair with Freddie and Adelaide's son Henry Cadogan, who she met while visiting her uncle Sir Frank Lascelles in Tehran, in 1892.

Home for Lost and Starving Dogs.[24] They followed medical developments, including nursing – their brother George met Florence Nightingale in the Crimea, more of which later – and, along with several other family members, they took a fashionable interest in homeopathy. Lord Anglesey had himself been treated by the founder of this branch of medicine, Samuel Hahnemann, and was vice-president of the first London Homeopathic Hospital, which opened in Golden Square in 1850. In April 1858 the 2nd Duke of Wellington presided over a public dinner given to provide the means for a new building in Great Ormond Street; a 'fancy bazaar' attended by Honoria and Augusta was held in June, at the Riding School of the Cavalry Barracks, Knightsbridge, that raised a substantial £1,800. The building was refurbished again in 2005 and reopened by the Prince of Wales (King Charles III) as the Royal Hospital for Integrated Medicine.

IT WAS ART, however, that had captured Augusta and Honoria's hearts. Augusta describes the elderly Princesse de Poix as 'looking like a Rembrandt stepped out of its frame'; her mind's eye vivdly recalled the *tableaux vivants* depicting Raphaelite and Titianesque goddesses at a party of 1823, put together by 'painters Gérard and Sir Thomas Lawrence', fifty years later. (Lawrence, at that time, was president of the Royal Academy and a favourite of King George IV.) Indeed, Augusta ascribes the process of memoir-writing an artistic allegory:

> These reminiscences of my early years have been developed by the light of reason and experience from the tenacious memory of childhood, as we see the photographic lens develop unsuspected objects in dark corners.[25]

Photography was the great artistic discovery of her lifetime. William Henry Fox Talbot stumbled across the first photographic images in 1834, four years after the girls arrived back in London. Louis Daguerre's 'daguerreotype' and Fox Talbot's 'calotype' were formally presented, respectively to the Académie des Sciences in Paris and the Royal Society in London, at the close of the decade. Fox Talbot's method was patented in 1841 and, with its capacity for mass reproduction, became the basis of photography until the digital age.[26]

Twenty-three photographic portraits of the Cadogan family by Camille Silvy – 'a pioneer of early photography and one of the greatest French photographers of the nineteenth century'[27] – are now in the collection of the National Portrait

Gerald Valerian Wellesley (1809–1882) and his son Victor, 1867, albumen print

Gallery (itself founded in 1856). The images are startling and immediate. Patriarch George, 3rd Earl, the naval officer who had battled Napoleon, stares out across centuries of history from the seat of his carriage. For his children, and the generations that followed, posing appears increasingly natural. Silvy's studio albums of the 1860s were conceived as an important historical record: members of the royal family including Prince Albert (the Prince Consort) and the Prince of Wales (future King Edward VII) appear alongside aristocratic families, influential politicians and clergy, and other notable persons of the age. Many of the images were turned into collectable *cartes-de-visite*, the roughly 3¾ x 2¼-inch calling cards then at the height of their decade in fashion. Queen Victoria kept a photograph of Cha's son Gerald Valerian Wellesley – the vicar who had married Freddie and Adelaide, who became her Dean of Windsor – and his son Victor, in her personal collection.

Augusta and Honoria stuck to painting. Augusta focused on portraiture, sketching vignettes of everyday life, albeit including crowned heads. Honoria, by contrast, is known for her landscapes. Both ladies captured scenes from distant shores in their travelling sketchbooks – the passion plays at Oberammergau, the Spanish steps in Rome (they were in Italy 1842–44) – and copied from the Italian Renaissance masters. In 1848 Honoria travelled to Aix-la-Chapelle and Brussels; the following year Boulogne; and there were also trips to Switzerland and, much later, in 1881, Antibes.

ABOVE *Lord Cadogan (en voiture)*, *Admiral Cadogan*, Camille Silvy, 1860, albumen print. George, 3rd Earl Cadogan, appears three times in the first chronological Day Book album; the National Portrait Gallery holds over 10,000 individual portraits from the Silvy studio.

13. ART & EUROPE

At home in London, the artistic community in Chelsea was blossoming. Joseph Mallord William Turner (after whom Mallord Street is named) and James Abbott McNeill Whistler (who drank at The Swan) were drawn to the area's picturesque houses and riverside views, and the light reflecting on the water. Dante Gabriel Rossetti, with his infamous menagerie of exotic animals, helped establish a bohemian community around Tite Street and Cheyne Walk; a Pre-Raphaelite influence duly crops up in the Cadogan ladies' sketchbooks. (In the twentieth century a distant relation, Frank Cadogan Cowper, RA, 1877–1958, 'the last Pre-Raphaelite', would become known for his portraits and historical illustrations.[28]) At the same time hundreds of inexpensive studios were popping up in the area around Manresa Road and Glebe Place. Opportunities for artistic exchange and influence abounded, and within her lifetime Honoria's style developed to merit exhibition with the Royal Society of British Artists. The *Country Life* review that described her as 'on the face of it…the perfect upper-class

Assemblée Nationale, Honoria Cadogan, watercolour

Victorian spinster of the cliché' went on to single out her talent from among exhibitors at the *World of Drawings and Watercolours* of 1992. A lifetime of amateur daubing had been well spent.

ANGLO-FRENCH ANTIPATHY was once again on the rise in the 1870s, aggravated by disputes over colonial territories in Africa. Though a conscious lament for a lost world, Augusta's memoirs are also a plea against the hasty judgements of xenophobia:

> I miss those gardens to almost every considerable house, their mossy walls...I miss even the horns practising *La Chasse du jeune Henri*...I miss the deep shades of the Parc Monçeau...There was a simplicity in it all, a repose in the life...
>
> In our judgment of other nations, should we not consider how little, through the difference of our habits and ideas, we can understand theirs and trace the inner history of their lives?... Should we not...balance the good with the evil of their character, and temper our conscious superiority with a doubt whether we might not in some respects take example from them?[29]

Without overstating the case, Augusta and her siblings were (within the constraints of their class and time), Francophiles, Europeans. Indeed, Augusta was the only one to have been born on English soil, at Downham: Henry and Honoria were delivered in Palermo, while their father was still a captain in the Royal Navy; George arrived in Vienna; and baby of the bunch Freddie was a native Parisian (though all were British subjects).[30]

The ladies moved out of their father's house and lived together in Clarges Street for a decade, before Augusta moved to 22 Queen Street with a skeleton staff (housekeeper, cook, housemaid and footman). In her late sixties she developed breast cancer, and underwent a mastectomy in 1880, pre-dating by just a few years the methods of Halsted and Mayer that would begin to save lives.[31] It metastasized to her lungs and she died on 28 November 1882. In the event, it was her nephew George who received the Orléans opera glasses, together with an extensive library. Honoria lived into her nineties, making return visits to Italy until the end. She just tiptoed into the new century, and died in 1904, the same year as their brother Freddie – by that time she was living under his roof, along with Ethel, at 48 Egerton Gardens. Honoria's name lives on in the auction rooms; perhaps a century after it was painted, one of her watercolours achieved its upper estimate at Christie's New York.[32] The royal connection also survives. Charlotte Villiers, the baby seen in Freddie's arms, gifted two large, red volumes of Augusta's watercolours to Queen Mary in 1937.

> I have just received your Majesty's kind and interesting letter, in answer to which I hasten to say that I am only too delighted and gratified to know that you will accept the books for yourself. It makes me so happy to realise that they give you pleasure – another instance of the marvellous royal memory.[33]

Following the 1992 *World of Watercolour* exhibition, in the hushed library at Windsor Castle, an authentication of works in the Royal Collection was completed by David Brichieri-Colombi, an Anglo-Italian descendant of the ladies' brother George, whose story we come to next.[34]

GENERAL THE HONOURABLE SIR GEORGE CADOGAN, KCB (1814–80), the middle brother, between bookends Henry, 4th Earl Cadogan, and lawyer Freddie, has a better-known life story: a career Army officer. He, like his sisters, was a competent watercolourist – arguably the most competent of the three. Drawing would have been on the curriculum both at Eton, as a suitable accomplishment for a gentleman, and during his military training, as a valuable skill in reconnaissance and mapmaking. The Royal Military Academy at Woolwich had employed a drawing master from at least the mid-eighteenth century, including one of the founder members of the Royal Academy of Arts, Paul Sandby (himself a noted watercolourist).[35] Art critic Huon Mallalieu wondered if he could detect the influence of George Bryant Campion, sometime master at Woolwich, in works by Honoria.[36]

Lord Stratford distributing the Order of the Bath at English Headquarters, 27 August 1855, George Cadogan, watercolour, ink and pencil. La Marmora, Pélissier and Simpson watch Lord Stratford, assisted by George Paget, invest Rear-Admiral Sir Edmund Lyons, followed by Major-General Sir Colin Campbell, Generals Scarlett, Eyre, Airey and Bentick.

George joined the Grenadier Guards as a teenage lieutenant in 1833, and by 1854 was a colonel. He served in the Crimean War (1853–56) and was present at all the major theatres of the Eastern campaign: Alma, Balaklava, Inkerman and the siege of Sevastopol. His eyewitness depictions of army life, paired with letters written home by a fellow officer, were published in 1979 as *Cadogan's Crimea*.[37]

George was British liaison officer to the Sardinian Expeditionary Corps. He had intimate access to the pomp and bunting, and the extravagant banquets that accompanied high-powered meetings of the most senior generals, as well as a boot-level view of the battlefields. Carrying a pocketbook and pencil, he made sketches marked 'from nature', sometimes working them up in colour during downtime when he returned to camp. The leaves pasted into his album, now sequestered at the National Army Museum in Chelsea, offer a window onto mid-nineteenth-century warfare and a leap into the mind of a sensitive artist with a dry-as-dust sense of humour. He pasted in an autograph from Field Marshal Joseph Radetzky – he of the march by Joseph Strauss (Op. 228) – with the note 'I stole his pocket handkerchief by accident but refused to give it back on purpose so he gave me the enclosed certificate to save me from a court martial.' His self-portraits in all manner of billets, quarters and lodging are given titles such as *The Home Office, Treasury and War Department*. George manages to look quite louche.

He had a gift for capturing personality and incident, both fine detail and the essence of a scene. Fulsome notes – in English, in French – of who, what and where, circle the outside of his compositions. Specifics of military uniform are carefully captured to ensure no dent in regimental or national pride (in some pictures, every man is wearing a different style of hat). But above all, George's images share a common humanity – the captured Tartar, the French Marshal Pélissier and British General Simpson, the distraught wife finding her husband's body on the battlefield – all are portraits of individuals, complete with complex inner lives.

Queen Victoria was a fan, writing in her journal after he dined at Buckingham Palace in March 1855, 'Col: Cadogan has been serving in the Crimea, & is going back immediately. He draws beautifully.'[38] He had been invalided out from Scutari. She appointed him commissioner to the Sardinian Army in the Crimea the following month. George's letter confirming the appointment, from the Duke of Cambridge at St James's Palace to 'my dear Cadogan,'[39] is also in the collection of the National Army Museum. The queen mentions looking at George's sketches again in July 1856, a couple of months after the Treaty of Paris had ended the war and a week before he joined her at Osborne House for a couple of days in the company of Army top brass:

> 5 August 1856...On coming home, saw Sir Wm Codrington, only returned a day or 2 ago from the Crimea, — quite unchanged, — simple & modest, as ever, — as unassuming as if he had never been Commander in Chief of such an Army. He was much pleased to hear of its being so admired...Vicky, Ld Clarendon,

(she only appeared afterwards, her luggage not having arrived) Sir Wm Codrington, Col: Pakenham & Col: Cadogan (come for 2 days) dined.[40]

The queen's interest in culture came to the fore under her husband's influence. Following the Great Exhibition of 1851, he was the driving force behind the idea to use funds raised from the visiting public to create permanent educational establishments. The Museum of Manufactures opened the following year, evolving into the South Kensington Museum (opened in 1857), with displays dedicated to the industrial and decorative arts, as well as a fledgling science collection. 'Albertopolis' was born, an area centred around Exhibition Road just north-west of the Cadogan Estate, that today is a mini-city of culture, including the Victoria and Albert Museum, the Science Museum, the Natural History Museum, the Royal College of Music and the Royal Albert Hall.

George continued to paint. At a certain point towards the end of the 1850s, the quality drops off – the images of the withdrawal perhaps reflecting a less vivid, visceral experience. Perhaps he was simply sick of it all: sick of sketching cholera, of burying the dead. The Crimean War, while a victory for Britain and her allies, is alive in the collective memory as an unnecessarily bloody campaign of blunders – epitomized by the decision to send sword-wielding cavalry to charge modern guns, as vividly described by Alfred, Lord Tennyson, in his poem 'The Charge of the Light Brigade' ('Half a league, half a league, Half a league onward/ All in the valley of Death/ Rode the six hundred'). Warfare was going through a massive cultural shift: men were still fighting in the uniforms of the Napoleonic era but with the tools of the Industrial Age: telegraphs, railways and explosive shells. The carnage of the Crimean War and its widespread reporting would have been unrecognizable to previous generations of battle-keen Cadogans.

At breakfast tables in London, Paris and St Petersburg, gentlemen pored over every success and failure. It was the first war to be documented in photojournalism. The resulting public outcry called for warfare to be pulled into the modern age – and not just the fighting forces but the

My Rooms, Sardinian Headquarters: the Home Office, Treasury and War Department, George Cadogan, watercolour. A second view of the same room is titled *The Hall of Audience and le 'Garde Meuble'*. Marginal notes read: 'It is intended to make General LaMamora endeavouring to get in an operation always attended with great difficulty – his spectacles getting entangled with my tapestry.'

auxiliary services providing supplies, communications and field hospitals. Enter Florence Nightingale.

> In October William Howard Russell sent dispatches to *The Times* in which he described the neglect of the wounded and the lack of nurses (*The Times*, 9, 12, 15, and 29 Oct 1854). Much of the public indignation fell on the head of Sidney Herbert, now secretary of state at war, who on 15 October wrote to Nightingale, asking her to take a party of nurses, at the government's expense, to Scutari. The letter crossed with one from Nightingale herself to Elizabeth Herbert offering to take a small private expedition, evidently the consolidation of an emerging plan.[41]

George produced two portraits of the 'Lady of the Lamp' in the Crimea, one of which she signed and dated. The *Dictionary of National Biography* records that 'Portraits are of particular importance in the life of a publicly well-known recluse. Nightingale generally refused to sit, and disliked being photographed.' George, we might imagine, possessed the charm to persuade her. In 1860, The Florence Nightingale Training School for Nurses opened at St Thomas's Hospital, London, funded by a testimonial fund collected for her following her war services, which helped to establish nursing as a respected profession.

After the war George was appointed military attaché at the British Embassy in Florence (then the capital of Italy). It was heaven for a man with an artistic eye – filled with Renaissance gems. Two final commands as colonel saw him leading the 106th Regiment of Foot (Bombay Light Infantry), from 1870 to 1874, before three years at the 71st (Highland) Regiment of Foot, following in the footsteps of his Uncle Henry, the hero of Vittoria, who died the year before his birth. Medals and honours were bestowed. George was decorated with chivalric orders by the royal families of Great Britain, Italy and the Ottoman Empire: Knight Commander of the Order of the Bath (1875), Commander (2nd Class) of the Order of Saints Maurice and Lazarus, and Knight (3rd Class) in the Order of the Medjidie. George was made a general in 1877.

ABOVE Florence Nightingale, George Cadogan, watercolour

RIGHT Colonel Lord George Augustus Frederick Paget, KCB (1818–1880), 4th Light Dragoons, on his horse. The son of Cha and Anglesey, George survived the Charge of the Light Brigade and married his first cousin Agnes Charlotte, daughter of Sir Arthur Paget, in 1854.

Three years later, he died at home in London from 'gout and internal complications' (albuminuria, a malfunction of the kidneys often related to diabetes and high blood pressure), at the comparatively young age of sixty-six.[42]

George was survived by his five children. His first wife, Sophia Armstrong, had died three weeks after the birth of their fourth daughter in 1852, and after only seven years of marriage. He wed again, after the Crimean War, in the summer of 1857 – both his brothers signed the register at St Peter's in Pimlico – and took his new bride to Italy. At no. 22 via Alfieri, Turin, the rather beautiful Emily Ashworth bore him a son, Horace James Henry (1862–1932), who returned to London to live with his widowed mother at 13 Park Place in 1881. Sir George's eldest girls both died unmarried – Mary (1847–82) in London and Honoria Frances (1849–1917), intriguingly, in India – and, as is so often the case, not much more is known about them.[43] But, brought up in Florence, the two younger girls married illustrious Italian nobility. Sophia Isabella Harriet (1852–1928) wed the Marchese Augusto Brichieri-Colombi and had four children (one of her descendants would authenticate the watercolour albums at Windsor Castle). Daughter number three, Olivia Georgiana (1850–1910), chose Lippo Neri, Conte Palagi Del Palagio. Their union would produce a son and two daughters. Sir George had seen his brother Henry inherit the earldom in 1864, and, towards the end of his life, he witnessed his nephew take the reins; he could not have predicted that his granddaughter Adele Palagi would provide happiness in the 5th Earl's final years. But before then, there was much work to be done, and George Henry, 5th Earl Cadogan – the archetypal Victorian of many talents – was the man to achieve it.

RIGHT Emily Cadogan (née Ashworth, 1834–1891), William Henry Mote, after John Hayter, c.1850s, hand-coloured stipple engraving

"Chelsea & the Colonies"

'Chelsea & the Colonies' (Statesmen, no. 361), Spy, chromolithograph. Published in Vanity Fair, 4 June 1881. 'He is the great proprietor of Chelsea, a politician of moderate talents and much industry, a lover of horses and horse-racing, a man of high honour and of insipid and courteous manner, a persevering speaker, and altogether a creditable gentleman.'

CHAPTER 14

Politics & Property

—

GEORGE HENRY, 5TH EARL (1840–1915),
CREATOR OF MODERN CHELSEA

George Henry Cadogan, 5th Earl Cadogan, KG, KP, PC, JP (1840–1915) is a towering figure in Cadogan family history. A career politician, he served in the Cabinets of Disraeli and Salisbury; a consummate courtier and diplomat, he was a schoolboy friend of the Prince of Wales and a trusted personal advisor to Queen Victoria, who appointed him Viceroy of Ireland. He was the first ever London County Council Member for Chelsea and its first mayor. His lasting legacy is visible in the very fabric of the area – in the tall, red-brick, gabled buildings that characterize much of Chelsea today. He was also a keen sportsman who loved the turf, and a knowledgeable farmer who was most at home at Culford, his country estate in Suffolk. George Henry enjoyed a life of privilege, but it was his personal attributes – a keen intelligence, applied with discretion and energy – and his Christian faith that shaped his life and achievements as 'altogether a creditable gentleman'.[1]

Following his father into politics, *The Times* reported this declaration of 7 September 1868:

> My political principles are Liberal–Conservative in support of all measures which may tend to the improvements, moral and physical, of my fellow countrymen and which are rendered indispensable by the spirit of progress of the age in which we live...[2]

During an address to the electorate a few days later, at Bury in Lancashire, he expanded on his principles as the defence of our country, its constitution and religion. His first foray to the ballot box was uncharacteristically unsuccessful. Viscount Chelsea was a difficult sell to a northern manufacturing town suspicious of an untried young aristocrat; the Lancashire Cotton Famine of 1861–65 was fresh in the electorate's mind. Happily, he had already found fulfilment in another quarter as a married man and father of a growing young family, roles that would sustain him throughout his life. Three years later, George Henry was ready for another stab at politics.

The Bath by-election of 1873, which he won with fifty-three per cent of the vote, was contested during the sobering rise of the temperance movement. Calls against the demon drink had, since the 1830s, become politicized, linked to the Chartists' demand for universal suffrage: if the working classes could prove themselves morally fit and clear-headed, they should not be denied the vote. Publicans, not surprisingly, protested. George Henry's aims of moral improvement were matched by his beliefs in a free-market economy. *The Western Times* (Devon) commented:

The Tree of Intemperance, Showing Diseases and Vices caused by Alcohol, Currier & Ives, c.1849, lithograph. The Permissive Prohibitory Liquor Bill so contentious during George Henry's successful election campaign was discussed over a decade of resolutions in Parliament but ultimately dropped.

> If not really a Publicans' victory, the struggle was conducted as if the pubs, as if their trade interest, were all in all in it; and Lord Chelsea, to give significance to the fact, said he should hasten up to town today to vote against the Permissive [Prohibitory Liquor] Bill the next day if the rules of the House would permit him.[3]

He gave a 'lengthy and clever address' of thanks to supporters in which he declared it 'his duty to give his support to any trade suffering from any specific attack or injured by a special enactment (loud cheers).'[4] The Bath by-election also came hot on the heels of the controversial Ballot Act (1872) that introduced the system of voting in secret that the British electorate takes for granted today. George Henry's comments on the matter were recorded:

> Although the ballot rendered it impossible to thank his friends individually for the assistance they had given towards his return, he could give a pretty shrewd guess in many cases respecting the support he had received...(cheers and laughter).[5]

The *Bath Chronicle* aptly described George Henry as possessing 'quiet humour, well-aimed sarcasm, [and a] rapid and complete grasp of a subject'.[6] Politics was, to some degree, a family affair: his successful electoral campaign was run by his younger brother Cecil; in Parliament he joined ageing Uncle Freddie in his last year as MP for Cricklade. His was to be one of the briefest Commons careers in British history. On 8 June, his father died, and George Henry was obliged to relinquish his seat in the lower house for a hereditary seat in the House of Lords.

At thirty-three, the 5th Earl Cadogan was evidently keen to do more than enjoy a postprandial nap on the red-leather benches. He made his first speech to the Lords on 19 March 1874 – one of 532 in total recorded by Hansard. His political aptitude was swiftly put to good use by Disraeli, who on 22 May 1875 moved him from the Colonial Office – where George Henry noted 'nothing going on of importance'[7] – to the War Office, as Under-Secretary for War, the first of many high-ranking appointments.

The wars in question were ongoing colonial tussles throughout Africa and the Indian subcontinent: Britain was an international superpower, with a growing empire. The East India Company, in whose service his Great-Uncle George had been shot by his own side a hundred years earlier, had transferred rule of India to the Crown in 1858. On 1 May 1876, Disraeli declared Queen Victoria Empress of India; her Indian subjects received the news at the first Delhi Durbar the following year.

Throughout his life, George Henry kept a diary. A kindred spirit to the queen in this respect, he noted daily errands, dining companions and locations, train times, attendance at church and the state of his health. He liked lists:

> In 1871, including days of coming and going, we spent 112 days at Woodrising, 59 abroad, 34 visiting. I spent 25 days at Bath, Ramsgate, St. Leonards and Brighton without Beattie. She had 15 days at Ashdown without me. The rest of the time we spent in London.[8]

In town, during the 1870s, he suffered a continual stream of coughs, colds and sore throats: late-nineteenth-century London was choked by smog from industry and domestic coal fires. The first parliamentary attempts to tackle air pollution had come twenty years earlier in the Smoke Nuisance Abatement (Metropolis) Bill (1853). During a week-long fog in December 1873, 'one of the thickest and most persistent of this century', close to a

The 5th Earl's diaries: one hard-backed and date-stamped volume per year

hundred cattle died of suffocation – 'exhibiting symptoms as if they had inhaled a noxious gas' – at the Royal Smithfield Club.[9] The *Medical Times and Gazette* was prompted to publish an article 'Killed by the Fog' detailing the injurious effect on human lungs – as well as numerous fatal accidents caused by an inability to see oncoming vehicles.[10] (The surprisingly speedy one-horse, two-wheeled hansom cab had largely replaced the hackney carriage and thousands crowded the city's streets, jostling for space with another new menace: trams.[11]) As medical knowledge advanced, a double round of legislation then prodded private landlords to make improvements to their buildings. The Public Health Act (1875) created a local authority responsible for sanitation in each metropolitan area and required all new buildings to include a running water supply; and the Artisans' and Labourers' Dwellings Improvement Act (also 1875) demanded the demolition of slum areas. A large number of leases on Cadogan land were falling in. It was an opportunity George Henry grabbed with both hands.

ALONG CHEYNE WALK, older riverside properties were rebuilt or improved piecemeal, taking advantage of the increased connectivity provided by Chelsea Embankment, finally completed in 1874. A transformation took place: a noisy, dirty site of industry became a fashionable address. Several large houses were commissioned, from architects Richard Norman Shaw, RIBA president Edward I'Anson and Edwin Godwin. C.F.A. Voysey, leading light of the Arts and Crafts Movement, remodelled the interior of no. 13, Garden Corner, built on the site of the Old Swan pub and now preserved with a Grade II* Listing. Cheyne Gardens was carved out from the large gardens set back from the river; and Tite Street, beloved of artists, sprang up in 1877.[12] Dan Cruickshank's *Built in Chelsea: Two Millennia of Architecture and Townscape* (2022) provides an in-depth guide to the intricacies of these designs, and many others on the Cadogan Estate.

The twenty-one-acre site occupied by Sloane Place ('the Pavilion') was looking particularly dismal. Hans Town, Henry Holland's Georgian joy, had fallen out of fashion, and the departure of prosperous families had led many leaseholders to subdivide buildings for multiple occupation.

Pont Street, Chelsea, Herbert Menzies Marshall, c.1905, colour lithograph. Illustration for *The Scenery of London*, described by G.E. Mitton (A&C Black, 1905).

Illegal subletting was rife, putting profit before the welfare of the tenants or the upkeep of material structures. George Henry agreed a plan to redevelop the site with houses of a similar quality to those in Lowndes Square (which, along with much of Bloomsbury and Pimlico, had been designed by the noted builder Thomas Cubitt). He had an idea to link Belgravia to the Brompton Road, via Pont Street and what is now Beauchamp Place. When the appointed builder disappeared into thin air, George Henry simply formed a new company to oversee the job. The Cadogan and Hans Place Estate Ltd (1875–90), headed by Colonel Sir W.T. Makins, MP, leased construction work to other companies, thus avoiding further exposure to the common occurrence of builders going bust. Makins favoured red brick.[13] Taking a pragmatic, long-term view, the Estate amassed a stockpile of the materials used in construction, ensuring that repairs and restoration would be in keeping for generations to come.

And so it was at George Henry's behest that the red-brick buildings with which Chelsea is synonymous went up. The exhaustive *Victoria County History* records:

The Queen Anne style seemed to be an appropriate response to a demand for a new urban style. The version developed here, with forms and motifs borrowed from 17th-century Flemish town houses, emphasized the individuality of each house, stressed vertical rather than horizontal lines, and replaced 'the hated sham of stucco with the honesty of brick'. In planning, too, the new development broke new ground: houses had deep and ingenious plans, and on the south side of Cadogan Square J.J. Stevenson adopted almost standard plans with varied frontages, a novel idea for speculative development. By adopting the new style the Cadogan Estate placed itself in the forefront of advanced taste…This startlingly different style eventually eliminated the use of the once ubiquitous Italianate, and its description by Sir Osbert Lancaster as 'Pont Street Dutch' made its association with the rebuilt Cadogan Estate even stronger.[14]

Cadogan Square was the jewel in the crown. Shaw designed nos 68 and 72 (Sussex House prep school, at no. 68, dubs its old boys 'Old Cadogans'). His hand is instantly recognizable from his more famous, later buildings: the original New Scotland Yard (1888–90) and its neighbour on Victoria Embankment, a pair of turreted red-and-white striped castles 'designed to repel riots',[15] that are now used as parliamentary offices. William Young, who George Henry commissioned to rebuild his London house (described in the next chapter), designed nos 54 to 60 (even) above Milner Street. Much of the rest of the square – nos 63 to 79 (odd) along the south side – and parts of Pont Street were completed by speculative developers who nevertheless retained the individualistic style, which was continued north-west along Hans Place and Lennox Gardens. The north and east sides were completed largely by Trollope and Sons, to the designs of George Robinson. To the south, another leafy garden square was overlaid on what had once been the gardens of Henry Holland's Pavilion: Cadogan Gardens, which runs into Draycott Place and its parallel Culford Gardens.

Nos 52 and 50 Cadogan Square (left to right), architect Sir Ernest George, 1886 and 1887 respectively. Cadogan Square represents the apogee of the Queen Anne style with which Chelsea – and the Cadogan Estate – has become associated.

The redevelopment continued: in 1887 George Henry came to an agreement with speculative builder William Willett, who constructed Lower Sloane Street, Sloane Gardens and Holbein Mews to the south of Sloane Square. The eponymous Willett Building on the square, by architect E.W. Mountford, was designed with two interior lightwells, innovative for their time, that appealed to the early advocate of daylight saving time. While much of the street layout remained, the architecture of Georgian Chelsea all but disappeared, though rare survivors include no. 123 Sloane Street (largely untouched), and no. 64, refaced in Portland and Blue Pennant stone by Fairfax Wade in 1897, as fashion turned again, this time towards Edwardian Baroque. George Henry's plan worked – the area was brought back to life, its cachet and population restored:

> The area rapidly assumed a character suitable to its position, poised between aristocratic Belgravia and artistic Chelsea. The first occupants varied between upper class and upper middle class, between rich and very rich, and between gently artistic and mildly philistine...The style's appearance in so well-heeled a neighbourhood was impressive evidence that it really had arrived, and probably did as much as anything else to release the flood of 'Queen Anne' that followed in the 1880s.[16]

Naturally, the widespread clearance of run-down property and its occupants led to some outspoken criticism, and in some quarters, the 5th Earl was condemned as a greedy landlord.[17] In 1887 the Anti-eviction League, through the mouthpiece of Lord William Compton, MP (himself a London landowner), presented George Henry with their concerns regarding the welfare of small tradesmen in Chelsea who would be displaced by developments. Compton received the same polite brush-off and refusal to be drawn as all such sticky-beaks:

> The special considerations to which you have drawn my attention are not new – and have weighed with me in the decisions to

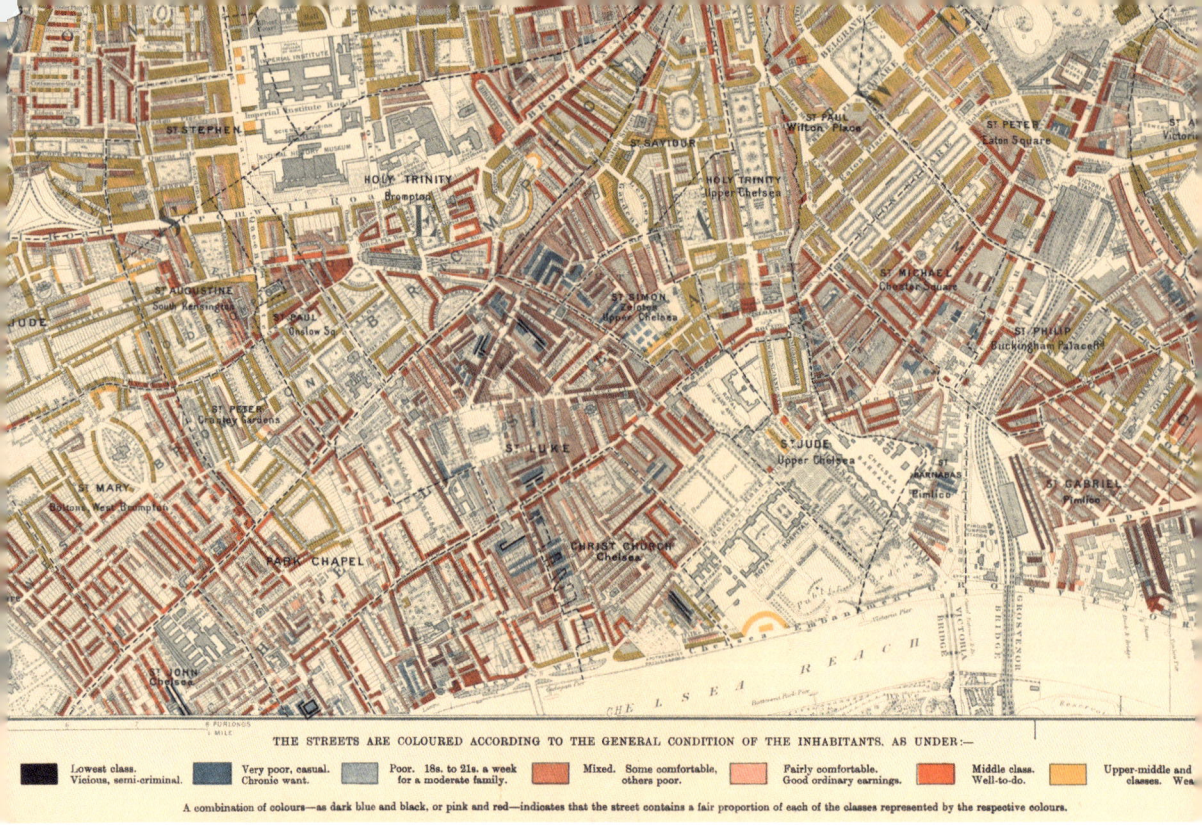

Poverty Map (detail), Charles Booth, 1898/9

which I have felt it is my duty to come during the past 3 years; and they have been my main justification for the very large sacrifices which I have thought it right to entail not only upon myself but on my successors…I do not ask to discuss the matter further with you, because I have always found that the intervention of a third party between myself and my tenants is liable to much misunderstanding…and generally to the defeat of the intentions, however disinterested, of the party who interferes…[18]

Letters to similar effect were written to Lady Wentworth, regarding the developments on Cheyne Walk and safeguarding church buildings, and to Canon Eyrton, who throughout 1889 repeatedly badgered him about 'house farming' (the practice of leaseholders letting to tenants direct, rather than his preferred method of subletting through families, which the clergyman felt maintained a decorous atmosphere).

14. POLITICS & PROPERTY

George Henry met his critics in the press head-on, however. In December 1889, he accepted an interview at Chelsea House with a reporter from the *Pall Mall Gazette*. 'I am prepared', he said, 'to take the whole responsibility for what has been done on my property.' Asked about the lack of provision for the poor who had been moved on, he responded:

> When I leased the estate to Mr Willett, he sublet it...an unconscionable delay took place in the erection of the houses for the poor...I may say that I insisted that these buildings should be built, and desired that they should be erected first of all.[19]

A further site, in North Street, had been sold and was no longer part of the Estate. George Henry, however, had given his tenants some protection, in the form of five- or seven-year leases, 'so that they might not be summarily turned out, so that that they might either continue to hold the houses during those years, or be bought out.' He estimated the cost to him of this decision alone at £25,000.

George Henry's genuine concern for the welfare of the people of the parish is also traceable through several gifts of property, often with attached covenants governing their use. He gifted plots to the local council for the fire station, the library and Chelsea Hospital for Women. The Vestry was also a beneficiary, granted the lease of Parochial Hall on Flood Street, although George Henry ensured that no rent was collected; now renamed Remembrance Hall, it is used by local schoolchildren and community groups. In 1889, he gave another parcel of land for Chelsea Town Hall. Built in 1906, today it is a London landmark at 165–81 King's Road, its steps frequently garlanded with confetti. (More prosaic council business moved to a new building for the combined Royal Borough of Kensington and Chelsea, in 1976.)

George Henry's philanthropy was part of a wave of beneficence among his peers. He made significant gifts to the new social housing trusts, including that set up by Sir Edward Cecil Guinness with Deeds of Trust on 3 February 1890. His letter of 20 March that year:

> I have the honour to make an offer to the Guinness Trustees of a site on my Chelsea estate, as a free gift for the purpose of providing Dwellings for the poorer Classes in that District. The site referred to occupies a central position in Chelsea and is rather more than an acre in extent. It forms part of the Garden of Blacklands House, Marlborough Road, and it has never yet been built upon. The soil is gravel, and the situation appears to be in every way suitable for purposes connected with your Trust. …and I shall be glad to hear that you are able to accept the offer which I have great pleasure in making…[20]

The reply from trustee the Rt. Hon. C.T. Ritchie, MP, came the very next day, remarking '…I have much pleasure in placing [your letter] before my colleagues tomorrow…I will write specially to *The Times* and the *D.T.* so that proper prominence be obtained.'[21] As Baroness Hanham, leader of the local council 1989–2000 remarked in 2015, the diversity of Chelsea remains one of its strengths:

> Chelsea's small, largely riverside, land base has meant that this public housing has rested side by side with the development of properties for more affluent residents…This juxtaposition, however, remains one of the charms of Chelsea. A truly mixed community where people who come there to live want to stay.[22]

In addition to the freehold, buying out the sitting tenant had cost George Henry £40,000. 'The property is freehold, but subject to an unexpired term of 14 years, held by Dr Sutherland; and this term I have purchased, in order to render the site immediately available for building operations.'[23]

GEORGE HENRY'S DIARIES REVEAL HIM to have been a regular churchgoer: every Sunday, sometimes twice, almost without fail. When in London, he typically attended local Chelsea churches Holy Trinity Sloane Street or St Saviour's, Walton Place, in the morning and Westminster Abbey or St Paul's

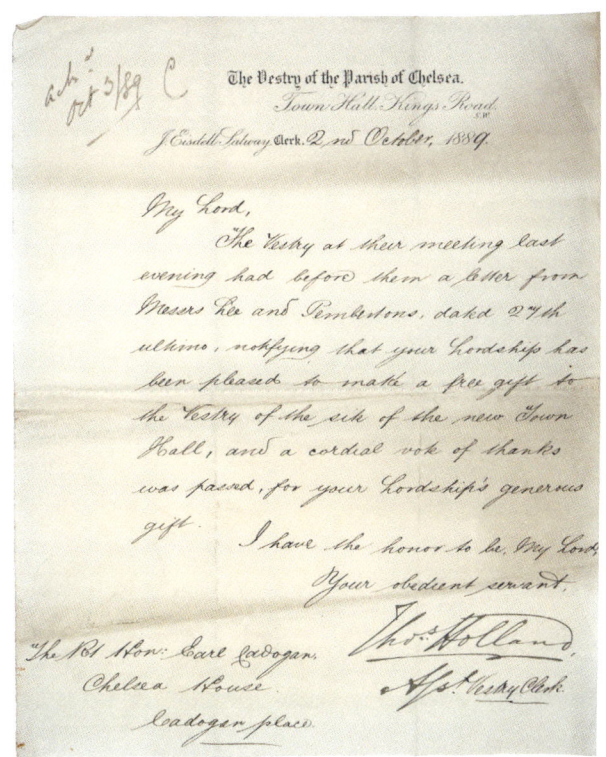

A letter from the vestry acknowledges the gift of the site for Chelsea Town Hall from the 5th Earl Cadogan in 1889. It has since become famous as the most stylish Register Office in London, its steps frequently strewn with wedding confetti.

Cathedral in the afternoon. At his behest Holy Trinity, the late addition to Hans Town of 1828–30, was demolished and completely reimagined. George Henry wasn't a saint, but as architectural historian Alan Powers has outlined, the thinking behind it was a win–win for churchgoers, the Estate and residents alike:

> The decision to rebuild was the 5th Earl's, who not only funded the rebuilding but gave additional land for a larger building. While this may have been altruistic, it was well known in London development that a good church attracted a better class of resident, and the new Holy Trinity, designed by John Dando Sedding, was something exceptional.[24]

Sedding was a cutting-edge choice in 1888. He had recently been Master of the Art Workers' Guild (1886–87), and was a prominent advocate of collaboration between painters, sculptors and architects, creating integrated designs.

Respect for craft and craftsmanship was on the rise: a new exhibition space for design – the Victoria and Albert Museum – opened in 1891, the year after Sedding's Holy Trinity was consecrated. The church's glories include sculptures by F.W. Pomeroy and an enormous east window with stained-glass designed by Edward Burne-Jones and made by Morris & Co. Sedding's own designs include the marble pulpit, the green-marble chancel wall and ironwork gates. Poet Sir John Betjeman later described it as 'the cathedral of the Arts and Crafts Movement',[25] an accolade borne out by its selection as a leading example of the style in *Churches 1870–1914* (2011) published by the Victorian Society.

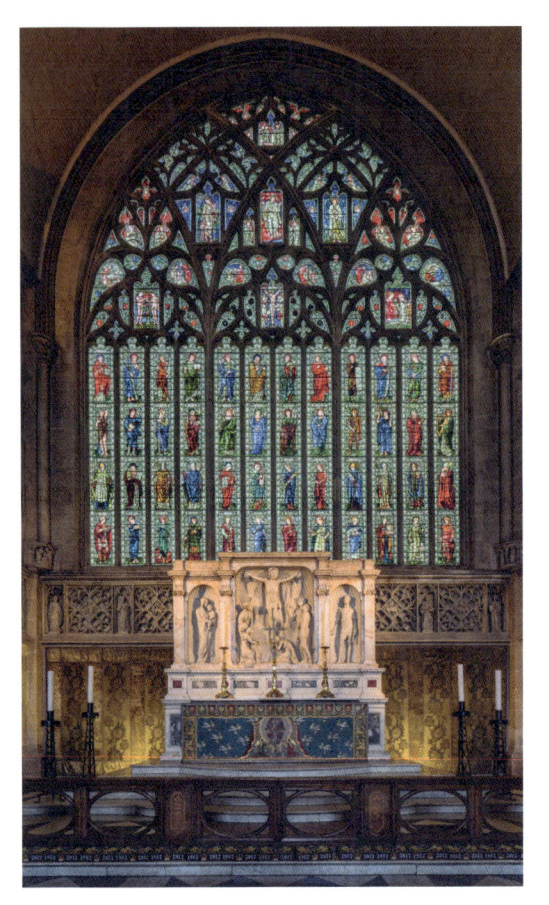

The east window designed by Edward Burne-Jones and made by Morris & Co., Holy Trinity Sloane Street

CHELSEA ACQUIRED MANY of today's familiar landmarks at this time. The rebuilt Court Theatre (1888), Peter Jones (1889) and the Royal Court Hotel (1894, now the Sloane Square Hotel), appeared, the theatre swiftly becoming famous for its George Bernard Shaw seasons. Sloane Square itself was opened up to the public, at George Henry's behest, 'for the benefit of the surrounding neighbourhood'.[26] Halfway along Sloane Street, the Cadogan Hotel (1887) was adopted as a hang-out by aristocrats, artists and even royalty. During its construction, the hotel incorporated a neighbouring building that was the London pad of Lillie Langtry, actress and lover of the future king of England, Edward VII – a personal friend of George Henry's. Further notoriety followed in 1895, the year *An Ideal Husband* and *The Importance of Being Earnest* were first staged, when the hotel was the scene of Oscar Wilde's arrest for gross indecency. Wilde, then resident at no. 34 Tite Street – interior-decorated at his request by E.W. Godwin and J.A.M. Whistler – was convicted and sent to Reading Gaol, where he served two years of hard labour. It was the beginning of the end for one of Victorian Chelsea's most colourful characters. The hotel itself reopened after a complete refit in 2019, as the Belmond Cadogan Hotel, reviewed by the *Daily Telegraph* as combining 'the glossiness of Knightsbridge with the artistic vibe of Chelsea'.[27]

That artistic vibe was underscored at Carlyle Mansions, erected in 1886 and named after Scottish writer Thomas Carlyle (aka the Sage of Chelsea), founder of the London Library, the largest independent lending library in the world. The house at 24 Cheyne Row where he and his wife Jane welcomed the most prominent literary and philosophical figures of the Victorian age – 'absolutely central to the intellectual history of Great Britain in the nineteenth century'[28] – is preserved in aspic by the National Trust. Residents at Carlyle Mansions including Henry James, T.S. Eliot, W. Somerset Maugham and Ian Fleming have since earned the building the punning nickname 'Writers' Block'. Further mansion blocks were erected at no. 1 Sloane Gardens (1889) and Cadogan Mansions on Sloane Square (1895). In 1889 *The Builder* commented:

> So great a change has been made here that no one who visited the district four or five years ago would know it. Narrow streets of squalid houses have given place to wide avenues of mansions.[29]

Purpose-built for artists, the Rossetti Studios building on Flood Street was constructed in 1894 by Edward Holland (no relation of Henry), who created each individual live/work space with north-facing windows, which let in clear natural light. In December 2014, the Cadogan Estate reacquired Rossetti Studios to preserve their heritage and ensure their ongoing occupation by working artists. Like so many of Chelsea's architectural gems, the building is listed by Historic England:

> Rarity: survival of working studios, in an area where these were once common, with rare surviving features including unusual slit doors for access for canvases, galleries for storing canvasses, living accommodation, changing rooms... [30]

Chelsea was changing; running the Estate was becoming more demanding. George Henry called in the professionals. With one eye on a succession plan, at fifty he settled his estate: the incumbent earl would be held as tenant for life of property run by the Cadogan Estate Office, established in 1890.[31]

GEORGE HENRY'S POLITICAL CAREER continued apace. He was appointed to the Privy Council in 1885 and Lord Privy Seal the following year (1886–92). In addition to a daily journal, he kept reams and reams of correspondence, a window onto his busy working life: everything from the social concerns of that one very persistent clergyman and offers to paint a picture (retrospectively) of his wedding day, to affairs of state. From the Admiral of the Fleet, 11 January 1887:

> Pray, read the campaign, remembering that the figures are not mine, but those of the optimist Lord Brassey...A British statesman or Admiral, pretending to tactical knowledge, ought to be thoroughly dissatisfied with the above comparison. Dire calamity must befall Great Britain, etc., etc., should a French war occur.[32]

An enclosure of minutiae details 'French, Italian & English Armour-Plated Vessels with armour over 15 inches and breech-loading guns over 43 tons.' The volume and detail of information is mind-boggling. George Henry's papers also include poems and meditations plus, thankfully, evidence of the old dry humour under the deluge of paper, in cuttings of political jokes. Back on serious matters, two further letters of 1887 stand out, the first from Lord Salisbury, the Prime Minister:

Sloane Square, S.W., Christina Broom, c.1905, glass plate photograph. Looking west towards the King's Road, Chelsea, the old Peter Jones building (1889) is visible behind three girls waiting to cross the road. Traffic includes a horse-drawn carriage and double-decker buses.

> I have received the Queen's permission to ask you to join the Cabinet. With the difficult functions you will have to deal with, it will be an advantage to you to take part in the Councils – as well as an advantage to us.[33]

Salisbury clearly got on with George Henry, his distant relation; the year before, he had offered to share his office space: 'If you will only take up your quarters with me, 10 Downing St.'[34] The second is a congratulatory note to 'my dear George' from 'Albert Edward', the Prince of Wales:

> ...your letter received this evening announcing that Lord Salisbury had asked you to join the Cabinet has given me the greatest pleasure. Most sincerely do I congratulate you on what must be the zenith of a man's ambition if he cares about politics, and now I feel sure you will care more than ever for politics and the affairs of state.[35]

His Cabinet appointment came three weeks after perhaps his most important speech to the House of Lords. On 31 March 1887 George Henry introduced the government's proposals for the latest in a line of bills addressing the Irish land question. A political hot potato since the Great Famine of 1845–49 – which had seen mass evictions, a million deaths and a million emigrations, leading to a population decrease of twenty-five per cent – the issue had become pressing with further economic depression and a population increasingly inclined to violence. George Henry involved himself intimately in these matters, just as he did in Chelsea.

The bill of 1887 looked back to Gladstone's Land Act (1870), proposing further revisions to amendments of 1881 and 1885. It established a grace period of six months for tenants handed eviction judgements; and for those tenants who became temporarily insolvent through no fault of their own, it gave local Irish county court judges discretion to grant 'a reasonable stay of execution; and for as long a period as the Judge shall determine the tenant shall not be removed from possession of his holding.'[36] Tenants and leaseholders were given rights to fair rent; and middlemen could reduce their own payments if their tenants did so by appeal. George Henry was at pains to point out that the bill respected property law without infringing the rights of landlords. Rather, it introduced new benefits for them in the form of exemption from payment of rates in cases where either they received no rent from their tenant, or 'a system of intimidation prevents the landlord from letting his land.' Indeed, he said, 'It is drawn up, as we believe, in a spirit of fairness and a spirit of justice.'[37] *The Spectator* declared his 'a speech which makes us wish his Lordship intervened more frequently in debate. It was a model of lucidity.'[38] A further Act of 1891 set up a multi-million-pound loan fund to enable tenants to buy the land they farmed.

The Cadogan family's ancient links to Ireland were further strengthened with George Henry's appointment as Lord Lieutenant and Governor-General of Ireland 1895–1902. Salisbury, back in office, requested George

OPPOSITE TOP George Henry's letters patent under the Great Seal appointing him Keeper of the Privy Seal, 1886, and correspondence regarding his and his father Henry's appointment to the Privy Council OPPOSITE BELOW His son Eddie recalled, 'Most of his time seemed to be spent at his writing table...of meticulous habit, he was a very deliberate worker....He was always a willing slave to routine. Each year was planned on the lines of its predecessor.'

Victoria by the
To all to whom these presents
Know ye
And further Know ye
Keeper of Our Privy Seal
Warrant under the Queen's Sign Manual
Muir Mackenzie
AT THE COURT AT OSBORNE HOUSE,
ISLE OF WIGHT.
PRESENT.
EXCELLENT MAJESTY
My Lord,
The Right Hon[ble]
The Earl Cadogan

Henry for the post. He replied: 'I feel it is my duty to accept. My own inclinations would lead me to prefer the Paris Embassy...I will undertake the Lord Lieutenancy with a seat in the Cabinet which you have done me the honour to offer me.'[39] The Paris Embassy had been his father's posting; his slight hesitancy over Ireland was justified. Only thirteen years earlier, Lord Frederick Cavendish had been assassinated shortly after arriving in Dublin on his first day in office as Chief Secretary for Ireland (his under-secretary Thomas Burke was also killed). However, George Henry had an unswerving sense of duty and, already a trusted confidant of Queen Victoria, he was a very suitable choice for Viceregent.

The family sailed into Kingstown Harbour to the accompaniment of a gun salute before processing in state up to Dublin Castle. His son Eddie, then fifteen, recalled, 'from that moment life was to be one of pageantry, but it was a pageantry not too persistent to

RIGHT Broadside poster encouraging tenant farmers to support the Irish National Land League movement, 1881

BELOW 'Battering Ram: Back with Them, Away with Them', Robert French, 1887/8, print from glass negative. In 1887 George Henry introduced a bill that aimed to reduce such evictions by half.

be irksome, and quite sufficiently realistic to be glamorous.'[40] George Henry again took up the cause for the Irish tenant, arguing for more favourable purchase terms during discussions of the latest Land Act (1896). He wrote confidently of the situation to Queen Victoria, in the customary third person:

> The Lord Lieutenant of Ireland presents his humble duty to Your Majesty...Lord Cadogan is happy to report that in all the Districts [sic] visited by him he found marked evidences of prosperity and contentment, and an improved state of feeling amongst all classes of the population...Your Majesty will be pleased to hear that the harvest in Ireland is estimated to prove a good one...there are many indications to show that the Irish people are generally weary of political strife.[41]

In 1900 the elderly monarch decided to pay an unprecedented three-week state visit, a clear demonstration of her affection for the Cadogans. George Henry had arranged a right royal reception, which delighted the queen. She wrote in her diaries:

> 4 April 1900...We landed at Victoria Wharf at ½ p.11, being received by Ld & Ly Cadogan...At Trinity College the Students sang 'God Save the Queen' and shouted themselves hoarse. The cheers & often almost screams were quite deafening. Even the Nationalists in front of City Hall seemed to forget their politics & cheered & waved their hats. It was really a wonderful reception I got & most gratifying...
>
> 26 April 1900...I left the Vice Regal Lodge with regret, having spent a very pleasant time there...they wished us goodbye, also the Cadogans, who do everything admirably & have been most civil & kind...I felt quite sorry that all was over...though I own I am very tired & long for rest & quiet...Even when I used to go round the ground in my pony chair & the people outside caught sight of me, they would at once cheer & sing 'God Save the Queen.'[42]

State Entry of His Excellency the Lord Lieutenant and Governor-General of Ireland (5th Earl Cadogan) into Dublin, 1895

George Henry stayed on as Viceroy until August 1902. Retirement had been looming for his old ally Lord Salisbury and he felt the time was right to do the same. He received heartful letters from the Duke and Duchess of Connaught, who had worked closely with him in Ireland. Bertie wrote from the royal yacht that he was 'sincerely sorry to think you are now about to retire into private life and that he shall thus be deprived of your useful assistance in the government of the country.'[43]

GEORGE HENRY'S ATTACHMENT TO CHELSEA never wavered. In 1895 he had been elected Member for Chelsea at the newly formed London County Council. It was a position he forfeited only to take up his post in Ireland. While still in Dublin, in 1900 he was elected Chelsea's first mayor (his grandson would be its last). Back in England, despite no longer being in charge of the day-to-day running of the family's Chelsea estate, he continued

14. POLITICS & PROPERTY

to take a great interest in its affairs. In 1905, Cadogan sold 1.6 acres east of Beaufort Street – at half the market value – on which the council built the Thomas More Estate; and gifted the local authority a further half-acre on Manor Street. 'The site was given free of cost by Lord Cadogan, subject to certain conditions, one of which was that the tenancy of the dwellings should be restricted to those whose total income did not exceed 25s. a week.'[44] The face of Chelsea continued to change into the new century.

So much for the politics and property of the 5th Earl: his public life. There is more to the story of George Henry. He and his wife Beattie were also society hosts who entertained royalty with dinners at Chelsea House and on country shoots; a loyal, lifelong friend, he reputedly paid off the gambling debts of the Prince of Wales; and despite his own strong moral compass, he was the father of several wayward children. These stories deserve chapters of their own.

Queen Victoria driving her famous white donkey in the grounds of the Viceregal Lodge, Phoenix Park, Dublin, 16 April 1900. 'Taken at Her Majesty's command.' In a letter dated 25 April, she writes 'to express her sincerest thanks to him Lord & Lady Cadogan for all their kindness & the trouble they have taken during one's pleasant visit to Ireland & her ___[?] some of the undeniable humour in which they discharged these duties. The Queen will send pictures as a personal remembrance but of herself.'

CHAPTER 15

Court & Countryside

—

GEORGE HENRY, 5TH EARL, AND THE CROWN

By the time George Henry took his first steps into politics, he was already celebrating three years of happy marriage to Lady Beatrix 'Beattie' Jane Craven (1844–1907). Over four decades she would prove to be 'her husband's right hand; they were a singularly devoted couple'.[1] It was an aristocratic match. Beattie's father was William Craven, 2nd Earl of Craven; her mother, Lady Emily Mary Grimston, was the daughter of the 1st Earl of Verulam. Naturally, all the Grimston girls had married earls: Beattie's aunts brought the Cadogans connections to the Villiers family (Earls of Clarendon), the Pleydell-Bouveries (Radnor) and Alexanders (Caledon). Her sisters made similarly starry marriages, to the Egertons (Earls of Wilton), Coventrys (Coventry) and Brudenell-Bruces (Marquesses of Ailesbury). Only the youngest Craven girl, Lady Emily, married a commoner – but he was the son of the Belgian Prime Minister Sylvain Van de Weyer. George Henry married Beattie on 16 May 1865 at Coombe Abbey in Warwickshire, an imposing twelfth-century

Countess Cadogan (née Beatrix 'Beattie' Jane Craven, 1844–1907)

monastery that had been the Craven family's country house since 1622. The groom, Viscount Chelsea (since the previous September), had just turned twenty-five; his bride was twenty-one. Beattie was not just the right girl at the right time from the right family. She was the love of his life.

George Henry had been set a powerful example of a successful love match by his own parents (Henry, 4th Earl, and Mary Wellesley) who had overcome disapproval to secure their personal happiness. Henry would brook no such interference in his son's choice:

> I shall write in a few days to Craven and give him the formal information of your 'ways & means', which I conclude you have already done unofficially...I can truly say that there is nothing in my power I would not gladly do to contribute to your comfort and happiness.
> God help you, my dearest boy, love from your affectionate Father, Cadogan.
> I have seen the 4 diamonds – they are very handsome. They & Beattie will mutually hit it off...[2]

Another important and lifelong relationship had already been established: while at Eton, George Henry had made friends with the future king. In 1857, he was one of four schoolboys hand-picked to accompany Albert Edward – 'Bertie' – on a walking tour of Germany. George Henry was embedded in the politics and power of the age, even as a child. In November of the same year, he was invited to a party at Windsor Castle. Queen Victoria recorded in her diary:

> 9 November 1857...Our dear Bertie's 16th birthday...All was festive, & I put on a new dress...After dinner the other 2 Boys & 3 Girls, Mrs Grey, Mary Barrington, Mrs Wellesley & her youngest sister, the Van de Weyers, Hoods, & daughter, Mary Biddulph & Bertie's 3 companions, Wood, Cadogan & Gladstone, joined us, & there was a little dance...[3]

Studio portrait of a walking tour group to Königswinter, Shafgans, July 1857, photograph with overpainting. Behind George Henry (seated, front left) stands William H. Gladstone, eldest son of the four-times British Prime Minister, who followed his father into Parliament as a Liberal MP. The Prince of Wales stands in the centre, in a dark bow tie. Flanking him are: (left) the Hon. Frederick Stanley, future Earl of Derby and Governor-General of Canada, who married George Henry's first cousin Lady Constance Villiers; and (right) Charles Lindley Wood, later Viscount Halifax.

Note that the guests included Wellesleys and Van de Weyers: quite the Cadogan family gathering. George Henry left Eton (Oppidan Wall and Field XIs, 1858), with a commendation, in a note written to his father: 'He will leave with a good character and a good opinion of all who have had anything to do with him…'.[4] He then went up to Christ Church, Oxford. The Prince of Wales was also sent to Oxford, briefly, and had private lectures at Frewin Hall, now part of Brasenose College, with a handful of other students, among whom were his three companions of old, Gladstone, Wood – and George Henry.

15. COURT & COUNTRYSIDE

ON THE LANCASHIRE HUSTINGS in September 1868, he stood a proud father of two, having welcomed his second son, Henry Arthur – known as 'Haggy' – three months earlier. George Henry and Beattie went in for nicknames in a big way. Their firstborn, a toddler named Albert Edward George Henry (b.1866), after the Prince of Wales, was known as 'Georgie'. Then, after Haggy, in swift succession came Gerald Oakley (b.1869, 'Jerry'), Emily Julia (b.1871, 'Tiny'), and Lewin Edward (b.1872, who seems to have been spared the diminutive). The following year was too busy for a baby: 1873 was the year George Henry won the Bath seat before inheriting the earldom, forfeiting the House of Commons and moving up to the Lords.

Having set about the complete remodelling of Chelsea, he decided that the family home could also do with an upgrade. Together with his younger siblings Arthur, Charlotte, Cecil and Charles, he had grown up in the house on the corner of Cadogan Place and Lowndes Street. Within a few months of his father's death, George Henry again commissioned William Young, who transformed it into a much grander residence befitting his status and ambition. Chelsea House was now an imposing six-storey mansion of twenty-one rooms, attended by a uniformed staff of thirty.

ABOVE Young parents George Henry and Beattie

LEFT Exterior of Chelsea House, Cadogan Place, 1887

The library at Chelsea House, decorated in clasically Victorian style: familiar portraits hang on walls decorated with Cordova leather, embossed and picked out with gold, cream, white and red. '[S]umptuous magnificence and gold-gleaming splendour meet the eye at every turn; but the prevailing impression is that it is a place full of slumberous peace, too infinitely reposeful to be categori[z]ed.' 'Celebrities at Home,' *The World*, 18 June 1912

Post-war Prime Minister and Chelsea resident Harold Macmillan recalled his child's-eye-view of the house as:

> a kind of baronial castle, only outmatched in importance by Buckingham Palace...On the steps outside there could generally be seen as we passed a splendid figure, with powdered hair or wig, blue coat, red velvet waistcoat, blue velvet knee-breeches, white or yellow stockings and silver buckled shoes. This person, who commanded our deepest respect, we firmly believed to be Earl Cadogan himself, proudly surveying his tenants and his household.[5]

George Henry and Beattie kept the nursery and schoolroom busy. Sophie Beatrix Mary (b.1874), was the sixth and last of the early brood.

15. COURT & COUNTRYSIDE

There were two weddings in the summer of that year. George Henry's sister Charlotte, in her mid-thirties, married an older clergyman. The Reverend Maynard W. Currie was Rector at Hingham in Norfolk, near the country house George Henry had taken for several years, Woodrising Hall. The couple would enjoy thirteen years of wedlock but no children. Charles, a decade George Henry's junior, was in Gothenburg to wed Henriette Wilhelmina Montgomery, the inspiration for an abundant line of cousins, starting with three boys. But first, tragedy struck the Cadogans.

In July 1878, Georgie, eleven-year-old Viscount Chelsea, fell desperately ill. Queen Victoria sent telegrams from Osborne House daily, asking after him. He died on 2 August, having succumbed to pneumonia and peritonitis. After the Victorian fashion, 'Georgie's relics' were shut up in the family archive and his parents fell into grief. Beattie was already pregnant with the first of a final round of boys: William George Sydney (b.1879, 'Willie'), who was soon joined by Edward Cecil

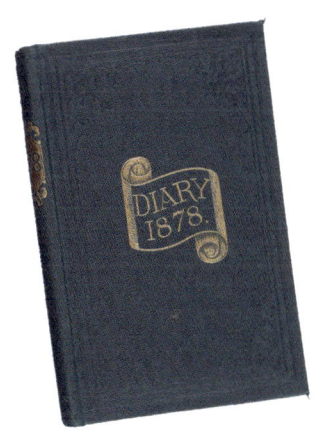

ABOVE AND RIGHT George Henry's diary entries at Georgie's death: 'We laid our darling in his grave...'

TOP Georgie, Viscount Chelsea

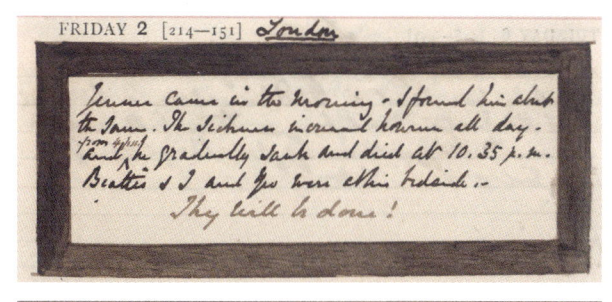

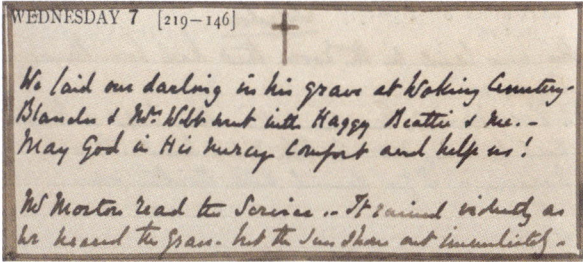

George (b.1880, 'Eddie') and Alexander George Montagu (b.1884, 'Alec'). Tellingly, Eddie would later write in his memoir *Before the Deluge* (1961), 'Lapse of time failed to heal the wound of this bereavement inflicted upon my Father and Mother.' Willie, Eddie and Alec would be forever a trio.

George Henry was a Victorian father of the old school. He and Beattie instilled habit and discipline in their children, though not entirely without mercy: 'They rose early, took breakfast in the nursery and then went to their mother, who would read from the Bible and make a commentary, enriched by a pronounced sense of humour.'[6] George Henry, ever with an eye on duty, diverted what scant time he had left after conducting affairs of state and taking care of Chelsea to indulging his children.

Queen Victoria summed him up in a diary entry from Windsor, where he was fast becoming a regular guest:

> 28 June 1877…A beautiful & very warm evening. — The Grenadier Band played very well, & we sat out till nearly 11, listening to it. — Ld Cadogan was a former playfellow of Bertie's, & is Under Sec[retar]y for War, a nice, quiet, sensible & gentlemanlike person.[7]

Over the course of a lifetime, the childhood playfellows would weather differences in lifestyle and temperament, in an enduring friendship. A typical note, written in middle age, and in parts indecipherable, reads:

> Xmas Day 1883, Sandringham
> My dear George, Many thanks for your 2 kind letters. We are so pleased to hear that you & Lady Cadogan [like] our little Xmas offerings – & we beg you both to accept our very best wishes for the present season & for next year…I am so sorry you have been so bothered _____[?] that stupid account at the Turf Club. Mr <Stech> must be the greatest ass possible as I should _____[?] have _____[?] the _____[?] of your £45 to _____[?] if <Stech> had not written to <F. Shaollys> – that you had not paid in case _____[?] answered his letters. How he tells I was paid at once!

He was got rid of – & I told him the opinion of the members of the club. Ever yours very sincerely, Albert Edward[8]

Filling in the blanks, we might infer that George Henry was also in the habit of paying off Bertie's debts.

Their wives, Alexandra and Beattie, whose families had known each other since childhood, exchanged sheaves of paper in which no small detail of their lives was omitted. Beattie was a prolific correspondent. Mary Adelaide, Duchess of Teck and mother of the future Queen Mary, congratulated Beattie on her 'dear child's successful debut' – from the date, most likely Tiny – commenting on her prettiness and beautiful complexion. Princess Charlotte of Saxe-Meiningen wrote of 'how often my thoughts fly back to you all'. Princess Victoria, the Prince of Wales's daughter, described her grandfather's lumbago.[9]

Chelsea House occupied a central position in the whirl of the annual London season, with the family in residence from May to July. The Cadogans were regular theatre-goers and George Henry took his own box at Covent Garden from 1889. He frequently dined at the Carlton Club, and he and Beattie attended an endless carousel of private balls and concerts.

It reached its apogee on 22 June 1887. Queen Victoria, preparing for a state ball at Buckingham Palace to celebrate her Golden Jubilee, asked George Henry to entertain her guests at a dinner. Chelsea House was filled with palms and exotics; the 70-ft ballroom on the first floor was transformed into a banqueting hall for the occasion. The superlatively

Sandringham game card, 28 November–1 December 1882. George Henry and Bertie often hosted each other on shoots. On this four-day royal shoot, George Henry was one of nine guns that took an exceptionally high bag offered to satisfy the sporting Prince of Wales.

impressive royal guest list was headed by the Prince and Princess of Wales and their daughters Princesses Louise and Victoria, welcoming the King of Denmark, King of Greece and King of the Belgians; the Crown Prince of Austria; the Crown Prince and Princess of Portugal; the Crown Prince of Sweden; the Grand Duke and Duchess Serge of Russia; the Duke of Aosta; Prince and Princess William of Prussia; the Infantes Antonio & Eulalie; and the Hereditary Prince and Princess of Saxe-Meiningen. Neither the grand Victorian mansion nor many of these ancient monarchies would survive long into the next century. Meanwhile, the Cadogans' relationship with the British royal family continued to deepen and George Henry's diaries for 1889 record a long stay at Balmoral in September.

FOR ALL ITS GLORIES, CHELSEA HOUSE did not satisfy the family's needs for fresh air, sports and active entertaining: George Henry's diaries note tennis, walking, shooting, riding, ice-skating and cricket. He began to look for a new country house. The Prince of Wales tried unsuccessfully to persuade him to rent up the road from Sandringham, in Norfolk:

I am sorry to hear that you think the house at Castle Rising would be too small to accommodate you all...selfishly speaking, I was most anxious to recommend it to you as we should have been so pleased to have had you both as neighbours.[10]

George Henry was invited to buy Caversham, the home of his ancestor William, the first 1st Earl, which had been sold out of the family almost exactly a century earlier by the second 1st Earl (NC), Charles Sloane Cadogan. In George Henry's hand across the top of the owner's letter is scrawled, 'I visited Cavasham [sic] Oct 19/86 but found it impossible to make an offer for it. C.'[11] The reason is not noted, but the house bore little resemblance to the Cadogan mansion, having been entirely rebuilt in the Italian Baroque style in the 1850s, after the previous Georgian building was destroyed by fire. (It would be commandeered during World War II, and for seventy-five years was home to the BBC Monitoring Station.) His eyes lighted on Babraham Hall, in Cambridgeshire, which he leased from the Adeane family while his search continued.

In early 1889, George Henry found what he was looking for: Culford Hall near Bury St Edmunds in Suffolk, a grand porticoed mansion house with four hundred acres of parkland set out by Humphrey Repton and 11,000 acres of sporting land. William Young was again engaged as his architect, enlarging the 1st Marquess of Cornwallis's 1790s house – remodelled

Culford Hall, Suffolk

after his defeat at Yorktown – to truly palatial proportions: fifty-one bedrooms, fifteen bathrooms, eleven receptions rooms and staff accommodation. In March, Beattie wrote to her son Willie, at Eton, that Babraham 'looked very sad, all our furniture had gone out of the house & there was a decidedly forlorn look about the same as Culford looked choked up with all our furniture stacked up in the middle of the hall.'[12]

Putting down roots in Suffolk would prove a hugely positive decision, not just for George Henry and the Cadogans but for the wider community. 'He enlarged and improved the farmland despite the agricultural depression of the period.'[13] In October 1889 he invited everyone for dinner – 'about four hundred availed themselves of his lordship's hospitality' – and gave a unifying speech:

> He desired them to look upon him not so much as a landlord but as a neighbour and a friend, and as one of themselves. (Applause.) There were people whose business seemed to be to try and divide communities – to divide one class from another; but he hoped that in Culford that sort of feeling would be discouraged. (Loud applause.)[14]

He was profiled by *Country Life* as a benevolent gentleman farmer. 'The Jerseys are cared for as if they are human beings…These cow houses have evidently been built with the intention of securing the greatest comfort for the animals.'[15] His prize-winning cattle had recorded pedigrees, just like racehorses. Pride of the herd, Golden Streak, was 'by Strawberry out of Sunbeam: grandam was Moonbeam by Prince Louis and her great grandam was Rising Moon.' He also bred Suffolk sheep. In a second article, the magazine declared 'Lord Cadogan has already taken his place as one of the foremost flock-masters of his time.'[16]

George Henry planted huge numbers of trees: in 1906 he was increasing the woodland by thirty-five acres per annum, for the purpose of breeding and rearing game. By 1913 2,500 acres of the 13,000-acre estate was woodland and the nursery was caring for 70,000 Scots Pine seedlings.[17]

15. COURT & COUNTRYSIDE

Culford was run as a self-sufficient estate with its own shops and skilled craftsmen – carpenters, mechanics, wheelwrights – who made furniture and carried out building works. An electrical plant on site generated all the necessary power for over a thousand lightbulbs, installed in 1903; indeed, Culford had all mod cons. 'In preparation for the royal visit of King Edward VII…the 5th Earl Cadogan installed a new bathroom, affectionately known today as the King's Loo.'[18] Given his early adoption of new technologies, it is likely Culford already had a telephone system. It was a forward-thinking, sustainable community, with an enlightened landlord.

SPORTS WERE TO BE TAKEN SERIOUSLY. In 1873 George Henry had accepted a term as president of Marylebone Cricket Club, which he described as 'the woolsack of cricket'.[19] These were the glory days of the MCC – already approaching its centenary – captained by the legendary W.G. Grace, who played for England 1880–99. All George Henry's boys were keen cricketers. Beattie, for her part, led a daily family ride out to Hyde Park from the Chelsea House stables, passing on her love of horses.

George Henry was mad for the turf. He registered his colours in 1879 and immediately scored a string of wins with Mazurka. At the Astley Stakes at Lewes, on 6 August 1880, *The Times* reported 'a sensation such as we have not seen for years—a dead heat between three for first place, and a dead heat between two for the fourth place; indeed, we believe nothing similar would be found if the *Calendar* was searched from its commencement.'[20] The following year, Mazurka beat

W.G. Grace, Archibald Stuart-Wortley, 1890, oil on canvas

No. 443, December 22, 1909] SPORTING AND COUNTRY HOUSE SUPPLEMENT. THE TATLER

SPORTING AND COUNTRY HOUSE SUPPLEMENT

THE LATE LADY LURGAN ON HER FAVOURITE HUNTER

The death of Lady Lurgan, elder daughter of Lord Cadogan, at Westbury Manor, Brackley, Northants, last week, where she had been staying for some time with her sister, Lady Sophie Scott, will be regretted by a very large circle of friends, to whom she was generally known as "Tiny." Her ladyship, who was thirty-eight years of age, was married to Lord Lurgan in 1893, and she leaves one son aged seven years. She was a keen follower of the hounds, and as the photograph shows one of the few women who look really well on a horse, but gave up towards the end of last season owing to ill-health. Our photograph was taken at her last appearance in the hunting field, when she was out with the Whaddon Chase. Great sympathy is felt with her popular husband and her father, whose great and irreparable loss of his wife and his eldest son took place quite recently

125

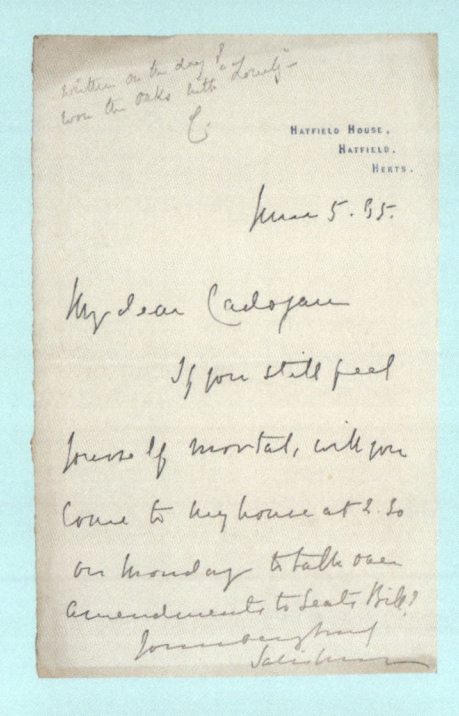

Written on the day I won the Oaks with "Lonely"

HATFIELD HOUSE,
HATFIELD,
HERTS.

June 5. 95.

My dear Cadogan

If you still feel yourself mortal, will you come to my house at 2.30 on Monday to talk over Amendments to Scots Bill?

Yours very truly
Salisbury

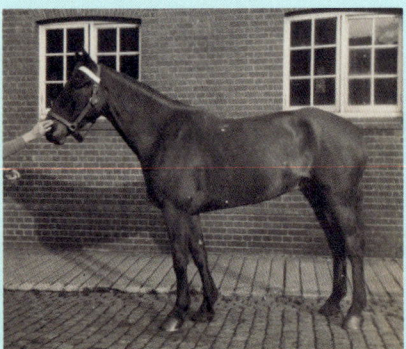

CLOCKWISE FROM TOP Congratulations from the Prime Minister the day Lonely won the Oaks; two winners from a fat album of equine portraits so familiar they are unlabelled; the 5th Earl's daughters were both excellent riders.

odds of 7:1 to take the Coronation Stakes at Ascot; she ran in the Stewards' Cup at Goodwood and 'won easily by a length.'[21] During racing season, George Henry and Beattie would stay for several days – in a cottage at Newmarket, or as guests of the Richmonds for festival week at Goodwood – alongside the Prince and Princess of Wales and the society figures who dominated the sport at the end of the nineteenth century. Indeed, trainer George Lambton (himself the son of the 2nd Earl of Durham) later remarked that Lady Cadogan 'knew as much and more about a horse than most men.'[22] Lord Cadogan's successes were outlined in a 1912 profile piece in *The World*'s curiously titled series 'Celebrities at Home':

> Lonely, a charming mare by Hermit, who won the Oaks in 1885, was his only classic winner, but Goldfield was so close to victory in the Two Thousand Guineas of 1882 that Lord Falmouth, the owner of Galliard, who actually caught the judge's eye first, turned round to Lord Cadogan in the stand and congratulated him on his success…but the best horse, in his owner's estimation, that ever carried the Eton blue was Prisoner, who [won] the Markeaton Stakes at Derby, the Doncaster Cup, the Royal Stakes at Epsom, and a Triennial at Ascot…[23]

His emotional involvement was common-enough knowledge for the Prime Minister to tease in 1885, '…if you still feel mortal, will you come to my house at 2.30 on Monday to talk over amendments to Seats Bill?', over which the 5th Earl has pencilled 'Written on the day I won the Oaks with Lonely'.[24] He was elected to the Jockey Club in 1882, during a period of typically nineteenth-century professionalization. Horse-racing had been rife with corruption, epitomised by the Epsom Derby of 1844, won by a ringer running alongside two doped animals and a jockey who pulled his horse up short. The subsequent punishment of the miscreants 'established the Jockey Club as the upholder of turf morality and the distributor of discipline'[25] – George Henry was among kindred spirits and joined Lord Randolph Churchill, Lord Hartington and the Marquis of Londonderry in combining these duties with a ministerial post. The models of training, breeding and racing set down are still observed today around the world. About this time, Queen Victoria began to consult him in matters equestrian. Correspondence survives between George Henry and her Master of the Horse, the 6th Duke of Portland, in which he relates her decisions over the administration of Plate Money to the 'direct encouragement of breeding'.[26] In 1885 George Henry penned an article for *The Fortnightly Review* entitled 'The State of the Turf'. The thrust of his essay was to call for the eradication of betting:

> ...whatever may be the evils and malpractices which disgrace the turf, and whatever reform they may assume, it is impossible to ignore the fact that all the scandals and all the dishonesty which so seriously discredit it are traceable to one cause, namely the excessive and ever-increasing amount of betting, which causes so much misery and ruin to the thousands who now indulge in it.[27]

Five years after penning this tirade, George Henry would find himself bailing out the future 6th Earl Cadogan, who had come a cropper not at the races but at the card table.

IN 1891, GEORGE HENRY became mixed up in the infamous 'royal baccarat scandal'. Discretion and loyalty to the Crown, two of his strong suits, forbade him from keeping a record of his role: he returned his sovereign's correspondence for safekeeping – 'Lord Cadogan with his humble duty to Your Majesty begs to return the letters which he has had the honour to receive for perusal.' – and, unusually for such a meticulous man, kept no copies of his own.[28] The Prince of Wales's libertine lifestyle had strayed into very public view, much to his now-reclusive mother's distress. She wrote from Balmoral:

> The Queen writes a few hurried lines to repeat to Lord Cadogan how much she hopes he will tell the Prince of Wales how

distressed, how humiliated she has felt at his being dragged into a court of justice with people who are unworthy of his acquaintance…But the effect of the whole examination – the fact of his playing at all at such gaming is very bad, not because he is himself conscious of ever being wrong, but because it enables bad people [to say] 'Why the Prince of Wales does it' – and the harm all this does the country is incalculable…Parents heart broken and every sort of misery brought upon respectable people by this wretched gambling…It makes her very, very unhappy.[29]

The heir to the throne was put on the stand in a public court of law, called as a witness in a case of illegal gambling, broken codes of honour and accusations of slander.[30]

The playboy prince had attended a small house party at Tranby Croft, in East Riding, Yorkshire, as a guest of shipping magnate Arthur Wilson. Among the party was Lieutenant-Colonel Sir William Gordon-Cumming, a Scottish baronet who 'gloried in the sobriquet of the most arrogant man in London'.[31] At the card table during their stay, younger players, less accustomed to the ways of courtiers, thought they saw Gordon-Cumming cheating – changing his stake after the cards had been dealt.[32] The gravity of the offence was doubly deepened by the high reputational stakes: first, gambling at baccarat (a game of pure chance) was illegal, and second, the heir to the throne was playing as banker, using his own crested set of counters. Natural recourse would be to haul a cheat before the law; but how to do so without staining the prince? Confronted,

The Baccarat Case: Sketches in Court, Arthur Wilson, cover of *The Penny Illustrated Paper*, 6 June 1891. The Prince of Wales was called as a witness during the trial; George Henry was asked by Queen Victoria to intervene.

Gordon-Cumming agreed to sign a document stating that he would never again play cards, in return for a code of silence. Word got out, however. In his anger, and with his engagement to an American Dollar Princess threatened, the accused filed a writ for slander against his hosts. Bertie, who was called by the plaintiff, became deeply unpopular.

Queen Victoria appealed to George Henry for help. In number-coded telegrams they discussed the wisdom of Bertie making a statement to the House of Commons. The earl was firmly against such a move, advising it would be seen as the defensive action of a guilty party. George Henry's alternative suggestion was that henceforth none of the heir's friends should allow him to the baccarat table. A neat diplomatic solution: the Prince of Wales switched his game of choice to bridge; the Prime Minister wrote to George Henry of the monarch's 'full approbation referring to the service you had done her in more than one recent conjunction in which her family was deeply concerned.'[33] A long-held Cadogan family fable has it that George Henry quietly settled Bertie's debts; given George Henry's sense of duty, his discretion and his fabulous wealth it is likely that this contains a germ of unprovable truth. Queen Victoria invested him Knight in the Order of the Garter the following month.

FOUR YEARS LATER, when he became Viceregent in Ireland, the whole family was a hit. George Henry had previously taken up Irish tenants' rights, but Beattie in particular was popular, as remarked upon by *The Ladies' Field*: 'Lady Cadogan's reign at Dublin Castle was perhaps the most brilliant social epoch the Irish capital has even known and she never lost sympathetic touch with the poor workers of Ireland.'[34] A 'Court Circular' of 1897 records:

> Earl Cadogan remains for the present in Dublin. Prince Edward of Saxe-Weimar, Princess Henry of Pless, M. de Soveral, the Duke and Duchess of Abercorn and Lady Alexandra Hamilton, the Marquis and Marchioness of Dufferin and Ava, the Countess of Erne and Lady Evelyn Chrichton, the Earl of Coventry, the Countess of Mayo,

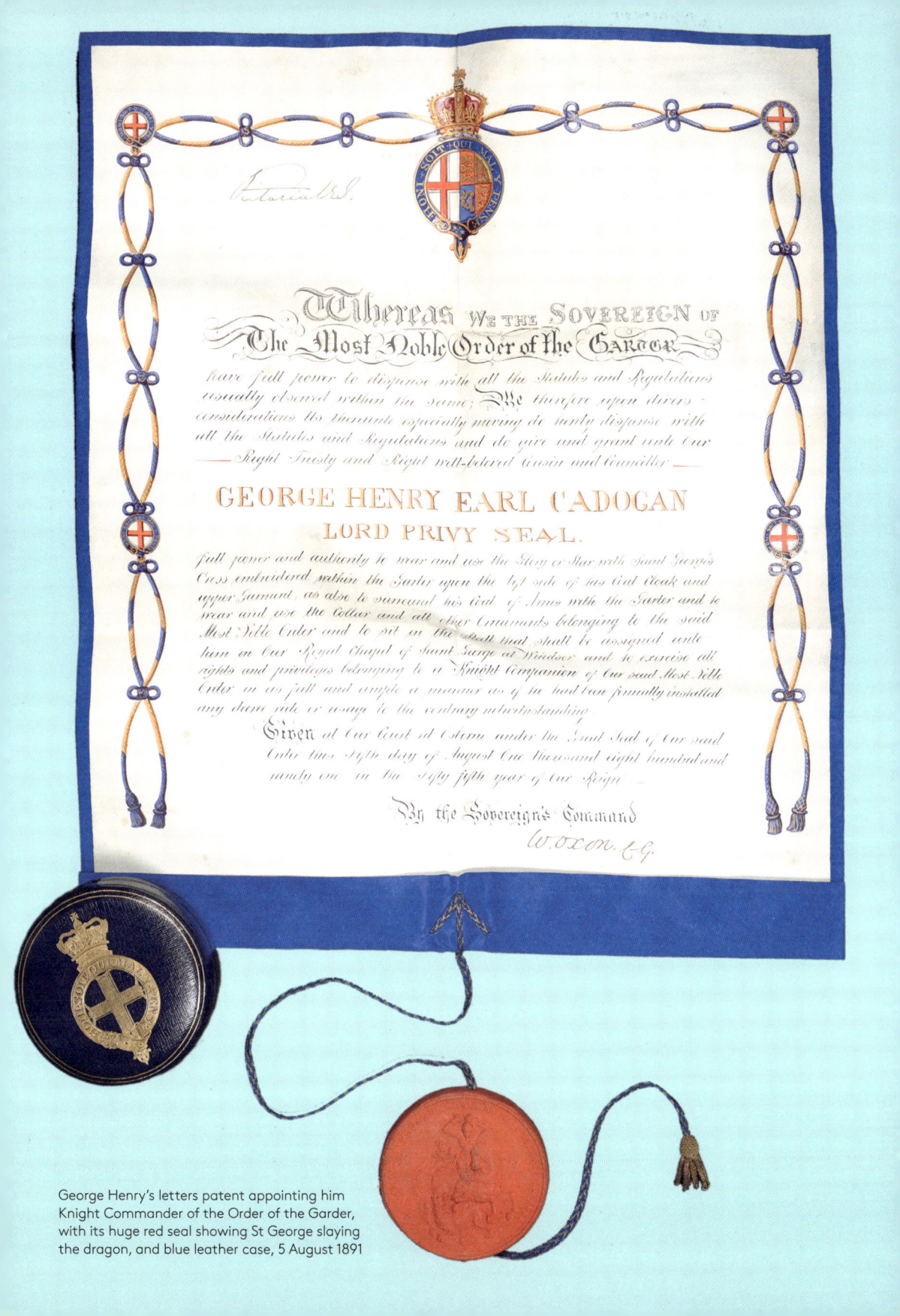

George Henry's letters patent appointing him Knight Commander of the Order of the Garder, with its huge red seal showing St George slaying the dragon, and blue leather case, 5 August 1891

the Earl of Enniskillen and Lady Kathleen Cole, Mr Gerald and Lady Betty Balfour, Lord and Lady Langford, Lord and Lady Lurgan, the Hon. Norah Dawnay, Sir Donald Mackenzie Wallace, and Colonel Saunderson, M.P., have left the Viceregal Lodge.[35]

The Cadogans had returned to the birthplace of their ancestor William, the first 1st Earl, in quite some style.

ONLY ONE RIPPLE seems to have disturbed the Dublin millpond. In April 1899 George Henry found himself hastening to avoid bringing high office into disrepute through the behaviour of one of his own children: his worst nightmare. He drafted a letter to the Prime Minister:

> A terrible sorrow has unexpectedly fallen upon us. Scandal and gossip in England will have done the worst, and spared me the task of troubling you with a narration of what we have suffered. I only write to ask you to accept my resignation of the Ld-Lieutenancy and to lay it before Her Majesty. It is, I know, essential that those who have been instructed with the task of representing Her Majesty in any sphere should both in themselves and their families be *sans* reproach and scandals.[36]

Nearly a century after Lady Charlotte swapped her Henrys, her great-great-niece Lady Sophie had left her husband and run off with a married man.

Three years earlier, at the age of twenty-two, youngest Cadogan daughter Sophie had enjoyed a society wedding to Sir Samuel 'Sammy' Scott, 6th Bt (1873–1943), at Holy Trinity Sloane Street. A glittering reception was held at Chelsea House, reported in *The Times*:

> The wedding presents were exhibited in the ballroom. The Prince and Princess of Wales presented the bride with a diamond aigrette set with two large turquoises; the Princesses Victoria and Maud gave her a gold bonnet-pin encrusted with diamonds

'His Excellency Earl Cadogan, K.G., Lord Lieutenant of Ireland, and his family at the Viceregal Lodge, Phoenix Park, Dublin,' *The Illustrated London News*, 7 September 1895. Standing (l–r): Willie, Haggy, George Henry and Beattie, Lewin; seated (l–r): Sophie, Alec and Eddie. There were always dogs.

and a large turquoise; the Duke and Duchess of York's gift was a gold parasol-handle set round with turquoises and diamonds... The gems given by the bridegroom to the bride comprised a superb diamond tiara, and a broad diamond collar formed of seven rows of stones, another collar of diamonds and sapphires, a magnificent ruby bracelet.[37]

But poor Sophie 'became afflicted in 1899 with melancholia, the result of a severe illness, following the premature birth of a child' who did not survive.[38] A few weeks later, a distraught Sammy wrote to his father-in-law, George Henry, at 1 am on the morning of Monday, 17 April, 'All I know is that she has left me...I know how fond you are of her and I fancy you know how I worshipped her.' The following day:

Garden party in honour of the Duke of York's visit at the Viceregal Lodge, Dublin, Chancellor, 18 August 1897. The duke was by then second in line to the British throne, his elder brother having died in 1892. He succeeded his father in 1910 as King George V. It was one of two visits paid to George Henry during his viceroyalty: the second was in 1899.

> ...on Good Friday Sophie told me that she cared only for [Algernon] Burnaby, but this was after having been on rather better terms with me for some time...Every blame is on me, I foolishly trusted a man I thought a friend of oldish standing. I was blind and trusted Sophie too much especially as we were on bad terms. I have put on a detective...but have heard nothing.[39]

Sophie had simply disappeared; Burnaby had threatened to shoot himself if she left him. Her older sister Tiny wrote to their mother:

> This morning we heard through the detective that Burnaby was expected at his own place Baggrave [Hall, Leicestershire] today, but we have not heard if he has gone there...we haven't had a line or a sign of any sort or kind from her, and she still has only her despatch box and a little travelling bag with her...they have found out that whilst she was in Ireland he was staying with his wife and mother-in-law, and he left the same day as she did with a small bag and without his servants.
> If only we can find her, Sammy is ready to take her back.[40]

ABOVE Sir Samuel Scott, 6th Bt. (1873–1943). Sammy had an old head on young shoulders, having inherited his father's title and eponymous bank at the age of nine. A lieutenant in the Royal Horse Guards (Blues), he resigned his commission a few months after his marriage to Sophie and in February 1898 was elected Unionist MP for Maylebone West.

Lady Sophie Scott (née Cadogan 1874–1937), Keturah Collings, 1907, pencil on paper. 'Lady Sophie may be briefly described as of that rare type of beauty which combines the most exquisitely fair complexion and clearly cut features with the dark, brilliant eyes and soft brown hair of a brunette. Whether in the mazes of a waltz, or ardent cyclist that she is, on the "bike", whether walking in the stately viceregal procession, or mounted on her favourite hunter, her grace of movement is singularly apparent.' The Sketch, 8 April 1896

Tiny ran into a maid collecting Sophie's dog, clothes, books and music, and interrogated her. 'Henstridge reported [Sophie] looking very ill, mentally much worried, and not seeming in the least happy…'.[41] Tiny (Lady Emily Lurgan) and their eldest brother Haggy (Viscount Chelsea) set off for Baggrave the next day.

> Chelsea waited some way off on the road and I sent the carriage away – After ringing for a long time a woman opened the door, and when I asked for Sophie, tried to shut it in my face, but I asked her to go and ask Lady Sophie if she would see Lady Lurgan for 5 minutes, and the moment she heard my name she let me in. I found Sophie in a small smoking room alone – She looked very bad, and broke down…[42]

The letters flew throughout May and June. Sammy took himself off to sea, but continued correspondence from his yacht. After a couple of months, divorce and lawyers were mentioned, though Sammy promised 'to wait to the last moment'.[43] George Henry proposed a period of reflection in New Zealand for Sophie. However, after further deputations from the family, Sophie was finally persuaded to leave her lover and his empty threats. She laid low in the country while the rumours blew over in London.

Sammy welcomed her back and George Henry was dissuaded from falling on his professional sword. A contrite Sophie, staying at Bexhill with Haggy, wrote to her father, 'I must thank you most awfully for your goodness to me, I couldn't thank you properly myself, but it was a bad time for me.'[44] She rejoined her husband 'with every intention of doing her best to make him a good wife in the future' and the pair shipped off to Ceylon (Sri Lanka).[45] The trip would be cut short, for reasons we will come to later, though ultimately the marriage would not. All might have been forgiven and forgotten, had not the scorned Mrs Burnaby (née the Hon. Sybil Cholmondley) fallen in love. Sophie made newspaper headlines around the world. In December 1901 the *Chicago Tribune* reported:

15. COURT & COUNTRYSIDE

Much sympathy will be felt for Sir Samuel Scott…by the unfortunate revival of the scandal concerning his wife, Lady Sophie, daughter of Lord Cadogan, the Viceroy of Ireland…Apparently the Hon. Mrs Burnaby, sister of Lord Delamere, is anxious to marry, and for this purpose to secure a dissolution of her marriage to Algernon Burnaby. So, in spite of all the influence that could be brought to bear by the King, the royal family, and by the most powerful leaders of London society, she proceeded to sue her husband for a divorce, naming Lady Sophie as co-respondent…

I may add that Algernon Burnaby is ostracised by every one… and by orders of the late Queen he was quietly dismissed from the army…'[46]

Queen Victoria had evidently been sympathetic. Although Sophie was prevented by protocol – and the monarch's position as head of the Church of England – from reappearing at court, she was still received in private. (The Burnabys divorced.) Away from prying eyes, Sophie had a longed-for son, Henry Edward Scott (b. and d.1902, a cruelly short life). The couple had no more children.

Backed by Bertie and Lord Salisbury, George Henry kept his position as Lord Lieutenant of Ireland until August 1902, when even the *Daily Express*, previously highly critical, expressed 'the regret with which we view his departure from these shores'.[47] However, the Cadogans had not left for good. Since 1893 Tiny had been happily married to William 'Billy' Brownlow, 3rd Baron Lurgan, an Anglo-Irish aristocrat (Brownlow House, 25 miles south-west of Belfast in Northern Ireland, is today owned by the Orange Order). Following a London season, Billy resumed his position as State Steward under the new

RIGHT 'Billy' [William Brownlow, 3rd Baron Lurgan], (*Statesmen*, no. 585), Spy, chromolithograph. Published in *Vanity Fair*, 9 January 1892

Viceroy, the 2nd Earl of Dudley. The pair would have a bumpier ride than George Henry, with political demands for Irish independence on the rise. Incidentally, Jerry, who stayed on as ADC, was there on 23 September to welcome the procession into Dublin.

IN JANUARY 1901, QUEEN VICTORIA – the last of the Hanoverians the first 1st Earl Cadogan had helped bring to power – died during the 64th year of her reign. George Henry had received telegrams with updates on her health several times a day and was invited to the funeral at St George's Chapel, Windsor. She was laid to rest holding a plaster cast of Prince Albert's hand and a lock of John Brown's hair. Bertie became Britain's new king: Edward VII, of the House Saxe-Coburg-Gotha.

> His Majesty deeply appreciates such expressions of sympathy from one whom he has known so long and the King feels that the recent visit of Her late Majesty to Ireland must necessarily bring back many memories to you. I am desired to say that His Majesty still hopes it may be possible for himself and the Queen to visit Ireland in the course of this year – and he mentioned the same to Lord Salisbury who entirely acquiesced. The King especially wished me to add that should his visit take place this year he sincerely hopes that you and Lady Cadogan may still be occupying the same place.[48]

In early 1902 George Henry hosted Bertie's nephew, Prince Henry of Prussia, in Ireland: 'Edward R. to Lord Lieutenant. Delighted you have had the opportunity of seeing the German fleet and am glad to think that he is your guest.'[49] Europe was united by these familial ties; Kaiser Wilhelm of Germany had rushed to Victoria's deathbed from Berlin. Under the warm and hazy sun of Edward's reign, Europe would be lulled into a brief period of peaceful slumber. Royal house parties at Chelsea and Culford continued, attended by foreign dignitaries and diplomats. George Henry remained a man of 'quiet tact and good judgment'.[50]

Beattie and George Henry in contemplative poses of later life. The 5th Earl Cadogan wears his ceremonial robes and decorations of the Order of the Garter.

Modesty prevented him from accepting further honours and elevation. He wrote to the new Prime Minister:

> My dear Arthur, I have some difficulty in answering the hypothetical question which you have put to me. In November 1900 Lord Salisbury wrote to inform me of her late Majesty's proposal to mark her entire satisfaction with my conduct of affairs by conferring upon me a Marquisate, to which I replied that neither Lady Cadogan nor I had any ambitions in that direction and that I trusted that I should not be guilty of disrespect if I humbly asked to be allowed to decline this Honour. I am yours sincerely, Cadogan[51]

Change came all too quickly. A decade hence, a new king would sit on the throne at the outbreak of war; George Henry would have a new Countess Cadogan and a new heir apparent. Haggy's sadly abbreviated story was destined to be outshone by those of his daughters.

Abridged family tree

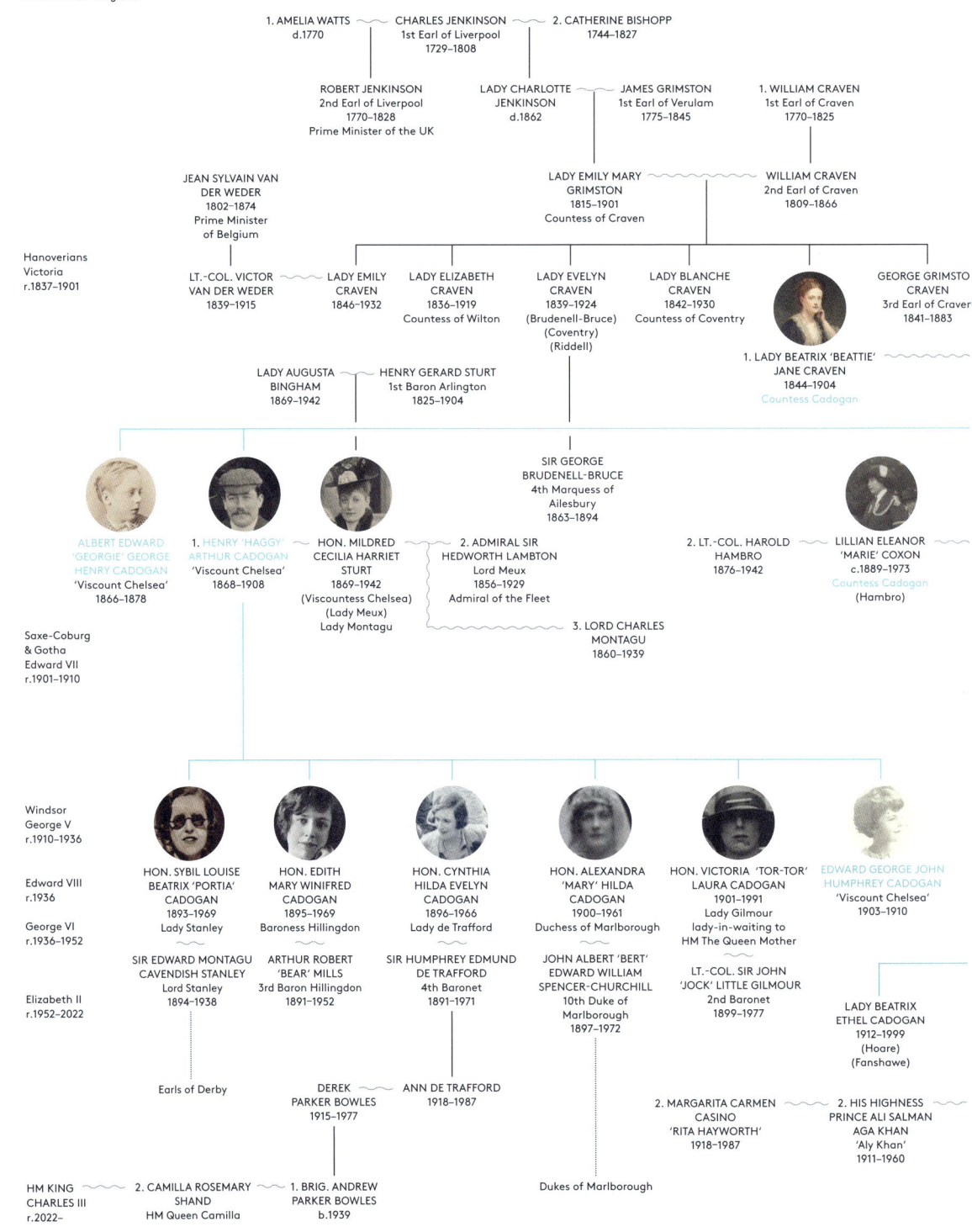

Kings & Queens of the United Kingdom

Hanoverians
Victoria r.1837–1901

Saxe-Coburg & Gotha
Edward VII r.1901–1910

Windsor
George V r.1910–1936
Edward VIII r.1936
George VI r.1936–1952
Elizabeth II r.1952–2022

---

1. AMELIA WATTS d.1770 ~ CHARLES JENKINSON 1st Earl of Liverpool 1729–1808 ~ 2. CATHERINE BISHOPP 1744–1827

ROBERT JENKINSON 2nd Earl of Liverpool 1770–1828 Prime Minister of the UK

LADY CHARLOTTE JENKINSON d.1862 ~ JAMES GRIMSTON 1st Earl of Verulam 1775–1845

1. WILLIAM CRAVEN 1st Earl of Craven 1770–1825

LADY EMILY MARY GRIMSTON 1815–1901 Countess of Craven ~ WILLIAM CRAVEN 2nd Earl of Craven 1809–1866

JEAN SYLVAIN VAN DER WEDER 1802–1874 Prime Minister of Belgium

LT.-COL. VICTOR VAN DER WEDER 1839–1915 ~ LADY EMILY CRAVEN 1846–1932

LADY ELIZABETH CRAVEN 1836–1919 Countess of Wilton

LADY EVELYN CRAVEN 1839–1924 (Brudenell-Bruce) (Coventry) (Riddell)

LADY BLANCHE CRAVEN 1842–1930 Countess of Coventry

GEORGE GRIMSTON CRAVEN 3rd Earl of Craven 1841–1883

1. LADY BEATRIX 'BEATTIE' JANE CRAVEN 1844–1904 Countess Cadogan

LADY AUGUSTA BINGHAM 1869–1942 ~ HENRY GERARD STURT 1st Baron Arlington 1825–1904

SIR GEORGE BRUDENELL-BRUCE 4th Marquess of Ailesbury 1863–1894

ALBERT EDWARD 'GEORGIE' GEORGE HENRY CADOGAN 'Viscount Chelsea' 1866–1878

1. HENRY 'HAGGY' ARTHUR CADOGAN 'Viscount Chelsea' 1868–1908 ~ HON. MILDRED CECILIA HARRIET STURT 1869–1942 (Viscountess Chelsea) (Lady Meux) Lady Montagu ~ 2. ADMIRAL SIR HEDWORTH LAMBTON Lord Meux 1856–1929 Admiral of the Fleet

3. LORD CHARLES MONTAGU 1860–1939

2. LT.-COL. HAROLD HAMBRO 1876–1942 ~ LILLIAN ELEANOR 'MARIE' COXON c.1889–1973 Countess Cadogan (Hambro)

HON. SYBIL LOUISE BEATRIX 'PORTIA' CADOGAN 1893–1969 Lady Stanley

HON. EDITH MARY WINIFRED CADOGAN 1895–1969 Baroness Hillingdon

HON. CYNTHIA HILDA EVELYN CADOGAN 1896–1966 Lady de Trafford

HON. ALEXANDRA 'MARY' HILDA CADOGAN 1900–1961 Duchess of Marlborough

HON. VICTORIA 'TOR-TOR' LAURA CADOGAN 1901–1991 Lady Gilmour lady-in-waiting to HM The Queen Mother

EDWARD GEORGE JOHN HUMPHREY CADOGAN 'Viscount Chelsea' 1903–1910

SIR EDWARD MONTAGU CAVENDISH STANLEY Lord Stanley 1894–1938

ARTHUR ROBERT 'BEAR' MILLS 3rd Baron Hillingdon 1891–1952

SIR HUMPHREY EDMUND DE TRAFFORD 4th Baronet 1891–1971

JOHN ALBERT 'BERT' EDWARD WILLIAM SPENCER-CHURCHILL 10th Duke of Marlborough 1897–1972

LT.-COL. SIR JOHN 'JOCK' LITTLE GILMOUR 2nd Baronet 1899–1977

LADY BEATRIX ETHEL CADOGAN 1912–1999 (Hoare) (Fanshawe)

Earls of Derby

DEREK PARKER BOWLES 1915–1977 ~ ANN DE TRAFFORD 1918–1987

2. MARGARITA CARMEN CASINO 'RITA HAYWORTH' 1918–1987 ~ 2. HIS HIGHNESS PRINCE ALI SALMAN AGA KHAN 'Aly Khan' 1911–1960

HM KING CHARLES III r.2022– ~ 2. CAMILLA ROSEMARY SHAND HM Queen Camilla ~ 1. BRIG. ANDREW PARKER BOWLES b.1939

Dukes of Marlborough

Children of the 4th & 5th Earls Cadogan onwards

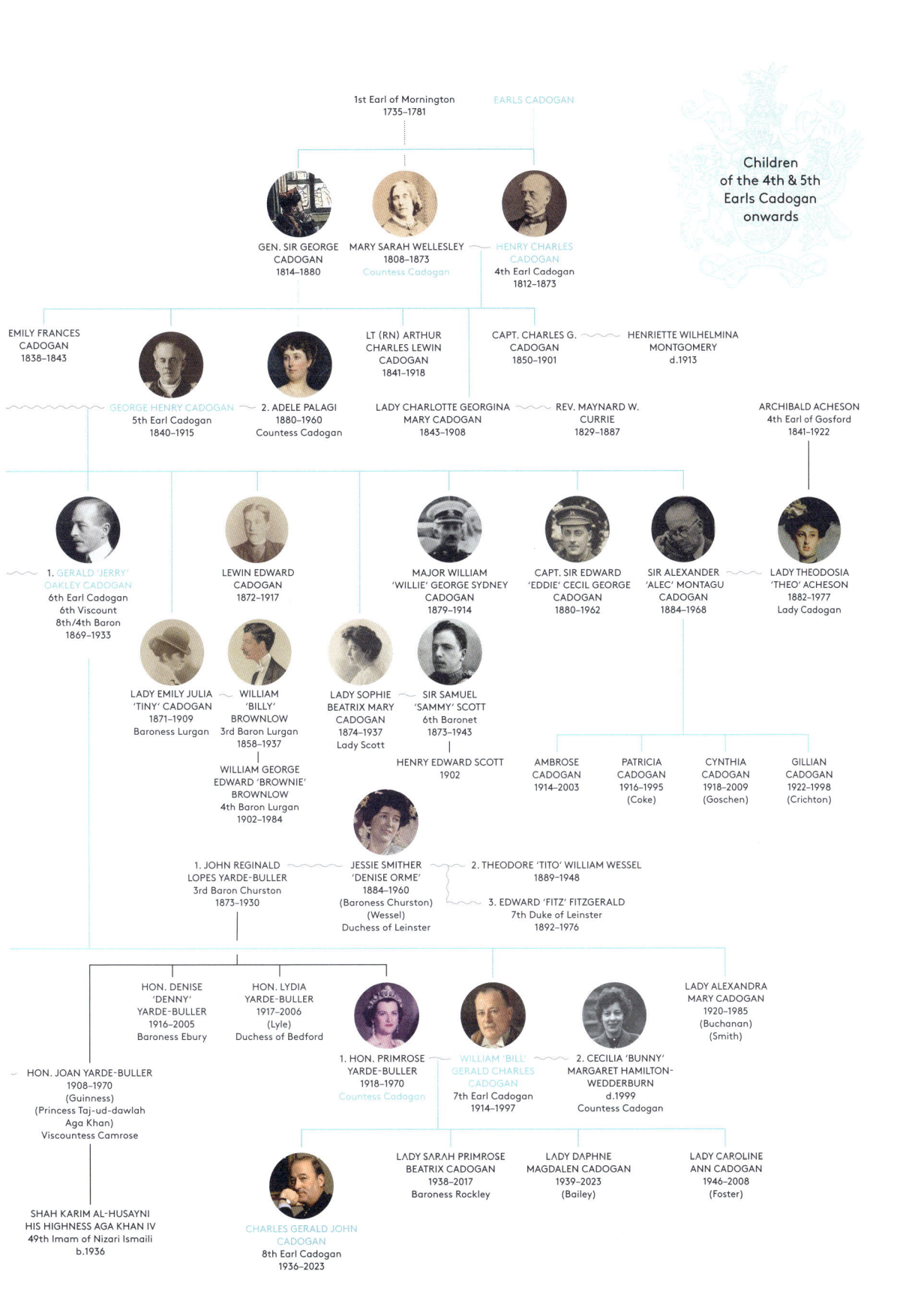

1st Earl of Mornington 1735–1781 — EARLS CADOGAN

- **GEN. SIR GEORGE CADOGAN** 1814–1880
- **MARY SARAH WELLESLEY** 1808–1873 (Countess Cadogan)
- **HENRY CHARLES CADOGAN** 4th Earl Cadogan 1812–1873

Children:

- **EMILY FRANCES CADOGAN** 1838–1843
- **GEORGE HENRY CADOGAN** 5th Earl Cadogan 1840–1915
  - 2. **ADELE PALAGI** 1880–1960 Countess Cadogan
- **LT (RN) ARTHUR CHARLES LEWIN CADOGAN** 1841–1918
- **CAPT. CHARLES G. CADOGAN** 1850–1901 — **HENRIETTE WILHELMINA MONTGOMERY** d.1913
- **LADY CHARLOTTE GEORGINA MARY CADOGAN** 1843–1908 — **REV. MAYNARD W. CURRIE** 1829–1887
- **ARCHIBALD ACHESON** 4th Earl of Gosford 1841–1922

Next generation:

- 1. **GERALD 'JERRY' OAKLEY CADOGAN** 6th Earl Cadogan, 6th Viscount, 8th/4th Baron 1869–1933
- **LEWIN EDWARD CADOGAN** 1872–1917
- **MAJOR WILLIAM 'WILLIE' GEORGE SYDNEY CADOGAN** 1879–1914
- **CAPT. SIR EDWARD 'EDDIE' CECIL GEORGE CADOGAN** 1880–1962
- **SIR ALEXANDER 'ALEC' MONTAGU CADOGAN** 1884–1968
- **LADY THEODOSIA 'THEO' ACHESON** 1882–1977 Lady Cadogan

- **LADY EMILY JULIA 'TINY' CADOGAN** 1871–1909 Baroness Lurgan — **WILLIAM 'BILLY' BROWNLOW** 3rd Baron Lurgan 1858–1937
  - **WILLIAM GEORGE EDWARD 'BROWNIE' BROWNLOW** 4th Baron Lurgan 1902–1984
- **LADY SOPHIE BEATRIX MARY CADOGAN** 1874–1937 Lady Scott — **SIR SAMUEL 'SAMMY' SCOTT** 6th Baronet 1873–1943
  - **HENRY EDWARD SCOTT** 1902

Children of Sir Alexander:
- **AMBROSE CADOGAN** 1914–2003
- **PATRICIA CADOGAN** 1916–1995 (Coke)
- **CYNTHIA CADOGAN** 1918–2009 (Goschen)
- **GILLIAN CADOGAN** 1922–1998 (Crichton)

- 1. **JOHN REGINALD LOPES YARDE-BULLER** 3rd Baron Churston 1873–1930
- **JESSIE SMITHER 'DENISE ORME'** 1884–1960 (Baroness Churston) (Wessel) Duchess of Leinster
- 2. **THEODORE 'TITO' WILLIAM WESSEL** 1889–1948
- 3. **EDWARD 'FITZ' FITZGERALD** 7th Duke of Leinster 1892–1976

- **HON. JOAN YARDE-BULLER** 1908–1970 (Guinness) (Princess Taj-ud-dawlah Aga Khan) Viscountess Camrose
- **HON. DENISE 'DENNY' YARDE-BULLER** 1916–2005 Baroness Ebury
- **HON. LYDIA YARDE-BULLER** 1917–2006 (Lyle) Duchess of Bedford
- 1. **HON. PRIMROSE YARDE-BULLER** 1918–1970 Countess Cadogan
- **WILLIAM 'BILL' GERALD CHARLES CADOGAN** 7th Earl Cadogan 1914–1997
- 2. **CECILIA 'BUNNY' MARGARET HAMILTON-WEDDERBURN** d.1999 Countess Cadogan
- **LADY ALEXANDRA MARY CADOGAN** 1920–1985 (Buchanan) (Smith)

- **SHAH KARIM AL-HUSAYNI HIS HIGHNESS AGA KHAN IV** 49th Imam of Nizari Ismaili b.1936

- **CHARLES GERALD JOHN CADOGAN** 8th Earl Cadogan 1936–2023
- **LADY SARAH PRIMROSE BEATRIX CADOGAN** 1938–2017 Baroness Rockley
- **LADY DAPHNE MAGDALEN CADOGAN** 1939–2023 (Bailey)
- **LADY CAROLINE ANN CADOGAN** 1946–2008 (Foster)

Officers of the Royal Wiltshire Yeomanry (detail), H.J. Jarman, Bury St Edmunds, c.1943. Major William Cadogan, 7th Earl Cadogan, MC, is seated third from left.

THE TWENTIETH CENTURY

CHAPTER 16

Society & Succession

—

HENRY 'HAGGY' CADOGAN (1868–1908)
AND THE 'CADOGAN SQUARE'

For the Cadogans, the brief reign of Edward VII, life-long friend of the 5th Earl, was a *decennium horribilis*. Entering his sixties, George Henry faced first the deaths of his brother Charles in 1901 and infant grandson Henry (Sophie and Sammy's son), in 1902, before saying goodbye to the last of his father's generation, elderly Aunt Honoria and her brother Uncle Freddie, in 1904. Worse was to follow. During Christmas 1906 at Culford, Beattie fell ill with influenza. Daily updates – a good night; very weak; not so well – were printed in *The Times*'s Court Circular. After rallying briefly, Beattie succumbed on 9 February 1907. Her children had no time to make it to Culford for last goodbyes. George Henry received a letter from the king the next day:

The Archbishop of Canterbury Anointing the King, Frank Dadd, published in *The Graphic*, coronation number, 13 August 1902. The 5th Earl was one of the four Knights of the Garter selected to hold the pall during the anointing, the most sacred part of the ceremony.

'Their Majesties' Visit to Culford Hall – The Royal House Party', *Madam*, 24 December 1904. The Cadogans chartered a special train, and crowds cheered its arrival as a band played the national anthem; four hundred tenants lined the drive waving Union flags. Alongside King Edward VII and Queen Alexandra, Earl and Countess Cadogan, the group included Haggy and his wife (Lord and Lady Chelsea), and, lurking at the fringes of the image, Jerry (standing second from right in baker boy cap).

We have known each other for over 50 years! And that must [pass] as an excuse for intruding on your great grief. I cannot describe to you with what horror I read in *The Observer* this morning that dear, kind, Lady Cadogan had passed away...Such a charming person...she will be missed and regretted by not only her relations but her large circle of friends – amongst whom I wish to be included...[1]

The head of the Royal Household wrote from Buckingham Palace, 'Here they are in despair...The Queen could hardly speak on her way to Chapel.'[2] At Bury St Edmunds, flags on churches and public institutions were lowered to half-mast; hundreds of obituaries appeared worldwide. The influential *Lady's Pictorial* mourned her as 'a lady who never made an enemy'.[3] The key to Beattie's charm perhaps lay in her 'practical common-sense dealings...a most refreshing dislike of humbug and cant, and also a joyous sense of the ironies and absurdities of life.'[4] To the end she was a keen golfer and gardener; annual trips to the Duke of Richmond's Gordon Castle, on the Spey, developed her skills as an angler; and from Killiechonate, a lodge in the shadow of Ben Nevis, she mountaineered. In town, the *Chelsea Mail* opined:

'no appeal was ever made in vain to her ladyship to help any good cause in a practical way or by her personal influence. For over 30 years she has been the first lady of Chelsea.'[5] Plunged into grief, George Henry shut up her bedroom at Chelsea House exactly as she had left it.

The Estate, and its inheritance, were now uppermost in the 5th Earl's mind. Money troubles had plagued the older Cadogan boys for years; his hapless heir apparent 'had managed to involve himself in all sorts of unsavoury scandals', amassing debt the *Washington Post* would estimate at 'something like a quarter of a million dollars'.[6]

HENRY ARTHUR CADOGAN ('HAGGY', 1868–1908) had become Viscount Chelsea at the age of ten. His early promise is summed up in his father's papers by a sheaf of congratulatory notes on the 1887 Eton vs Harrow match at Lords:

> I think that where one's boy makes 72 not out in his first match at Lords, his father ought to be acclaimed and I congratulate you sincerely and without any hesitation, for I should not like to apprise that you are not prouder of Chelsea's performance than of having brought the Irish Land Bill yourself through the Lords.[7]

After Eton, Haggy spent a couple of years at Trinity College, Cambridge, during which he sat Parts I and II of his Prelims – but was disqualified from progressing to a degree by his placement in 'fourth class'.[8] Rooms in the Great Court and non-rowing membership of the Third Trinity Boat Club had doubtless trumped any interest in academia.

In 1889, as Haggy approached his majority, George Henry and his advisor Lord March discussed the Cadogan succession plan. With admirable perspicacity, March wrote:

> I have also suggested that provision should be made in the event of Chelsea's death in your lifetime – Pemberton [of Lee & Pembertons Solicitors] may think that a remote contingency and not necessary to be taken into account, but it might very

16. SOCIETY & SUCCESSION

Eton v. Harrow at Lords, Albert Chevalier Tayler, 1886, oil on canvas

> possibly happen (one has to be cold blooded in consideration of these things)...[9]

The young viscount was gazetted to the 3rd Volunteer Battalion of the Royal Fusiliers and quickly promoted to captain. This first career was, however, a brief one: in June 1893, his father received this letter, marked 'private', from a senior officer:

> Your son is reported to me as absent without leave from his militia, and though he has been written to no answer has been sent. I shall be forced to act as laid down in the regulations but I never bring any officer's name before the Adjutant General until I have given him every chance. It is for this reason I write this note to you, and I hope you understand I am only acting with the wish to save your son's name, Lord Chelsea, being brought before H R Highness, Commander-in-Chief.[10]

The Army was not mentioned again. A stint as Private Secretary to First Lord of the Treasury Arthur Balfour – who would go on to become Prime Minister – was followed by two terms as Conservative MP for Bury St Edmunds (1892–1900). During those eight years, Hansard records 'Contributions by year, 0 in total'. In May 1900, Edward W. Lake, a 'steely, independent, highly competent' character who ran the local Greene King brewery and was elected mayor of the town six times,[11] took it upon himself to write to George Henry:

> He has absolutely neglected his Constituents by not answering letters and by not taking any interest in the place and I am sure it would be wise for him not to stand again...I do not think he really cares about Parliamentary life. It is a great pity as with a little trouble he might have held this seat as long as he liked.[12]

Haggy was full of apologies. 'I have with one exception (which occurred when Mildred was ill) done everything I was asked to do...I cannot say how sorry I am, as I know it will be a blow to you.'[13] At thirty-two, he found himself three careers down, unemployed and struggling to match his allowance of £5,000 a year with both a rapacious spending habit and a fondness for gambling.

His wife, the Hon. Mildred Cecilia Harriet Sturt (1869–1942), was equally profligate. Haggy's union with the daughter of Henry Gerald Sturt, 1st Baron Alington of Crichel, MP for Dorset, and Lady Augusta Bingham (daughter of the 3rd Earl Lucan and granddaughter of the 6th Earl Cardigan), at Holy Trinity Sloane Street on 30 April 1892, had been celebrated with great fanfare:

> At the invitation of the Earl and Countess of Cadogan [sic], upwards of 2,000 of the poor of Chelsea, including 1,000 poor children, were entertained at the Crystal Palace yesterday in honour of the wedding of their son, Viscount Chelsea...the visitors at once joined in the various amusements provided

Beattie and George Henry, Haggy and Mildred (holding a baby), with an older lady, possibly Beattie's mother Countess Craven

for them in the grounds. These included swings, gymnasiums, Ascott's steam roundabouts, and the large boat on the lake. At a quarter past twelve the bugle sounded, and the company assembled on the terrace for dinner.[14]

Haggy had made promises from Castle Rising to his father: 'I really don't know how to write and thank you for your great kindness and generosity to me, but by living quietly and on our own income and doing nothing extravagant.'[15] He was certainly full of good intentions.

Perhaps it was Mildred who saw her father-in-law's early largesse as an invitation to rely on a blank Cadogan cheque; she would not be the first or last wife to believe that one's lifestyle must live up to one's title. An undated and heavily reworked draft in George Henry's hand, headlined 'Suggestion', to Lord March (acting as unofficial trustee), proposed an extension of

Haggy's allowance by £2,000 a year. There were two conditions: that it be used to settle his debts and that he provide a written promise 'that Ld Chelsea will not borrow any further money from money-lenders without Lord March's consent.'[16]

As Christmas 1907 approached, George Henry had had enough. He sent a terse letter to Mildred, probably the closest to fury the mild-mannered man ever came:

> ...as to 'who is chiefly responsible for Chelsea's difficulties' the answer is simply you and he...I have a pretty good idea of the money Lurgan, and to a lesser degree, Jerry, 'stood in', but let me assure you that those sums are as drops in the ocean compared to what I as Chelsea's own father have had to pay for the extravagance of your two lives...I am to pay another £9,000 a year for the rest of my life, so I am now saddled with over £23,000 a year for Chelsea.[17]

These were huge sums, even to a rich man. Astonishingly, Mildred replied: 'I must ask you to be so kind as not to write to me or speak to [me] about these money troubles of Chelsea's which have made me feel very ill, as my health will not stand it.'[18] The 7th Duke of Richmond (by now elevated from Lord March), did his best to reassure his old friend:

> I had a letter from Sammy Scott yesterday disclosing the lamentable financial trouble that Chelsea has got into again...He tells me you have asked him to act for you and of course I will do anything I can to help you. I can't see where the end of it all is to be, no sooner is he got out of one scrape than he goes headforemost into another one.[19]

Haggy only just made it to forty, taken by cancer on 2 July 1908. Thankfully, for Mildred, *deus* would appear *ex machina*.

The Chelseas had been living at an estate cottage, Temple House, in the grounds of stately Hertfordshire home Theobalds Park. Their landlady was

16. SOCIETY & SUCCESSION

COUNTRY LIFE

VOL. XXI.—No. 539. [REGISTERED AT THE G.P.O. AS A NEWSPAPER.] SATURDAY, MAY 4th, 1907. [PRICE SIXPENCE. BY POST, 6½d.]

MISS ALICE HUGHES. 52, Gower Street.
VISCOUNTESS CHELSEA AND HER CHILDREN.

'Viscountess Chelsea and Her Children', *Country Life*, cover, 4 May 1907. Mildred is pictured with (left to right): Edith (standing), Edward, Tor-Tor (on her lap), Alexandra, Cynthia and Portia (standing).

banjo-playing eccentric Lady Valerie 'Val' Meux, 'a voluptuous beauty… [who] seems to have met [Sir] Henry Meux [3rd Bt] at the Casino de Venise in Holborn, where she was possibly engaged as a hostess.'[20] She left her vast estate in 1910 to naval hero Vice-Admiral Sir Hedworth Lambton (1856–1929) on condition that he changed his surname to hers (which he did). Whether or not Mildred knew of this arrangement in advance, doubtless his inheritance ended her – and some of George Henry's – financial woes: she had married him that April.

FIVE-YEAR-OLD EDWARD George John Humphrey Cadogan (b.1903) was now Viscount Chelsea. At the age of thirty-four, Mildred had provided Haggy with a male heir, their sixth child following a bevy of daughters. After the third girl, and with Mildred glowing again in 1900, Lewin – second in line to inherit the earldom, behind Jerry, should the Chelsea line be entirely female – had written to his father asking 'whether Mildred has had her baby and if it is a boy' (it wasn't).[21] Three years and a fifth and final girl later, Edward's birth seemed to secure the succession. Six weeks after his mother remarried, however, this longed-for little boy suddenly fell ill with appendicitis, on Saturday 29 May 1910. Since his young Uncle Georgie's death in 1878, treatments for infection had advanced. King Edward VII's acute appendicitis had delayed, but not cancelled, the coronation of 1902 after successful intervention; the late king's surgeon was called for and operated immediately, but to no avail. The boy died on Thursday, 2 June, at just seven years old.

'Death of the Young Viscount Chelsea', *Daily Mirror*, 3 June 1910. Edward was buried at Culford with his father.

George Henry had buried three heirs; a new Viscount Chelsea was thrust into the limelight. 'Had there been the slightest premonition of what was in store for the child [Edward], old Lord Cadogan would assuredly never have permitted his son Gerald to suffer the stigma of being gazetted as insolvent, with no assets…'.[22] We will come back to Jerry. For George Henry, meanwhile, the losses and difficulties had begun to seem relentless.

In November 1908 his sister Charlotte had died. At the end of 1909 his eldest daughter, Emily (Tiny), lost her protracted battle with breast cancer having developed secondary growths in the lung – just like her artistic Great-Aunt Augusta – at the age of only thirty-eight. *The Morning Post* described her 'fearless courage under all circumstances' and saluted her skill as a horsewoman riding to Lord Rothschild's hounds, and with the Pytchley and Grafton Packs.[23] She left a son, named William George Edward Brownlow after his father, whom he would succeed as 4th Baron Lurgan ('Brownie', 1902–1984). Tiny died at Westbury Manor, the home of her sister Sophie.

These events, compounded by the death of his old friend Bertie on 6 May and the closing of the Edwardian era, 'caused Lord Cadogan, always a rather reticent and serious-looking man, to withdraw from politics, from the turf, and from society, and to render him still more grave and silent than before.'[24] He was required less in town: the role of the House of Lords was beginning to contract, and would be marked officially by the Parliament Act (1911) that established primacy of the Commons. The family was deeply concerned. Eddie wrote to Willie: 'he must have a complete rest. That is his only chance. He is going, I hope, to the Riviera in about a fortnight.'[25]

THE RIVIERA DID HIM GOOD. A year later, on 12 January 1911, seventy-year-old George Henry took everybody – perhaps even himself – by surprise, by getting married again – in Italy. His bride was Adele Palagi (1880–1960), the charming daughter of an Italian count descended from the Medici. She was also his first cousin, once removed: granddaughter of his great-uncle the painter, General Sir George Cadogan. Overcoming a forty-year age gap and her devout Roman Catholic faith, they had fallen in love. He wrote to Willie, 'I can only say that she makes me as happy as possible and I think everybody seems devoted to her.'[26] The press hoped that 'Chelsea House will perhaps be once more a centre of brilliant hospitality',[27] despite Adele's very different character from Beattie's. In May, *The Bystander* reported: 'The new Lady Cadogan...is alleged to own views of a somewhat pedantically aristocratic nature on the subject of entertaining.'[28] More importantly, however, the children were persuaded:

> She made him an ideal wife throughout the short term of wedded happiness. Her never failing tact, kindness and unselfishness won all our hearts and she became, both as wife and afterwards as widow, the rallying point for many years in our family.[29]

She became Countess Cadogan in time to attend the June coronation of a new king: George V (r.1910–36). George Henry was again one of four aristocratic bearers of the canopy over the monarch's head; Mildred's husband Hedworth Meux was involved as Keeper of the Crown Jewels. Captured in an early, silent British Pathé newsreel, the event is both ancient, befeathered pomp and tantalizing modernity.[30]

On 6 March 1915, George Henry died of 'carcinoma of the liver and exhaustion' at the age of seventy-four. He was eulogized as a great sportsman and successful Governor of Ireland, but he would be principally remembered as 'The Landlord Who Changed the Face of Chelsea', as *The Star*'s headline proclaimed.[31] He was laid to rest in the family vault at Culford Church, next to Beattie. The committal prayer was read by the Rector of Chelsea, who described him as: 'beloved Lord of the Manor...He felt the responsibility of his position and wealth deeply, and earnestly endeavoured to fulfil his duty to the utmost of his ability.'[32]

ABOVE Countess Cadogan (née Adele Palagi, 1880–1960)

Adele, now Dowager Countess Cadogan, was obliged to leave Chelsea House, though as Alec observed, 'I need hardly say that doesn't impair her cheeriness of good sense, and I expect she will settle down and be much happier in her own house.'[33] She wrote to Eddie:

> I think it will be very nice when all the dear little touches of your father will be in…you do not know what a blessing it has been for me to remain at Chelsea House so long, and I am so grateful to you all for it…[34]

Her unstinting devotion to the Catholic Church would reach even into the afterlife. At her death in 1960 she left her entire estate, including private papers and Cadogan family jewellery, to its titular head in England and Wales, the Archbishop of Westminster.[35] (The ultimate intended beneficiary was her place of worship, the Church of the Immaculate Conception, known as 'Farm Street'.) Over forty years at 26 Chesham Place she had remained otherwise on good terms with the children, even taking her step-grandchildren under her wing. The social baton passed to a glamorous new generation.

THE 'CADOGAN SQUARE' – AS HAGGY'S DAUGHTERS Portia, Edith, Cynthia and Mary were dubbed – were the most eligible young debutantes in London during the 1910s. Sybil Louise Beatrix Cadogan ('Portia', 1893–1969), was a honeymoon baby; the Princess Royal was her godmother. There followed Edith Mary Winifred (1895–1952) and Cynthia Hilda Evelyn (1896–1966): that made three. Number four was Alexandra Mary Hilda ('Mary', 1900–1961), named after her godmother, the queen. Well-connected and exuberant, they were ideally suited to the life that was mapped out for them. Alec wrote to Eddie in 1916:

> They've [Mildred and Hedworth] got into their new house in London…The girls have a large sitting room of their own, which appears to be a rendezvous daily of all the young men in London and all members of the Royal Family under 25. Luckily, it's got a

polished floor, and I understand that after tea the furniture and carpets disappear and [there is] dancing on with energy till dinner![36]

The four sisters epitomized an innocent, leisured life never quite recaptured after the Great War (though the Bright Young Things of the 1920s gave it a good shot – Portia attended a 1927 fancy dress party dressed as a red pillar box). A huge number of their generation would face a previously unthinkable future as spinsters; but as granddaughters of an earl, members of the Square were assured husbands.

Edith was snapped up in her first season: engaged in 1915 and married in August 1916. Her beau was the Hon. Arthur Robert Mills MP ('Bear', later 3rd Baron Hillingdon), from a wealthy and philanthropic banking family. He was said to be a collector, but not a reader, of books:

> …I have lived in a state of whirlwind rush between July 10th and August 8th…our engagement was a fiendish rush…dressmakers and lawyers! – punctuated with parties (rather dreadful!!) to meet new relations…Adele has been a perfect brick to us.[37]

The couple would go on to have five children; she named her eldest son Charles Hedworth Mills in a nod to her stepfather, 'the Admiral'. Edith – perhaps the most intellectual of the girls – began to take an interest in ethics and politics, to the surprise of some family members. In February 1916 she was invited to 'an odd party' by the Bishop of Winchester. 'Can you see Edith at a religious meeting?' wrote Cynthia, her junior by a year. 'Of course it will turn out a terrific rag and it's really rather profane.'[38] It seems she had misjudged her more serious sister. Edith, who was already accustomed to taking dictation from her mother on business matters, wrote to Uncle Eddie:

> Of course the definitions of religion and luxury made terrific debates…Mummy and I went to hear Mr Asquith make his statement in the House. It was frightfully interesting though I

16. SOCIETY & SUCCESSION

don't think he spoke very well. We were in the Sergeant-at-Arms Gallery, which I like much better than the Ladies Gallery.[39]

It was not her first visit to Parliament. Eddie wrote to his older brother Willie that he had enjoyed a surprise visit from teenage Portia, Edith and Cynthia at the House in 1910; he put them in Mrs Lowther's private gallery and 'they got so excited I think the police thought them militant suffragettes!'[40] The suffragettes may have been on a pause during the war, but the Representation of the People Act (1918) that followed it began the unstoppable change, initially granting the vote only to property-owning ladies over thirty. Edith would have to wait a further ten years to exercise her right to Equal Enfranchisement. She became a prominent political figure as chairman of the Central Women's Advisory Committee of the Conservative Party in 1935, and was appointed DBE in 1939.

ABOVE Angel/Herald mascot, logo of the Women's Social and Political Union (WSPU), c.1905, Sylvia Pankhurst. Sylvia lived at 45 Park Walk, Chelsea, and later at 120 Cheyne Walk.

LEFT Emmeline Pankhurst giving speech from a balcony in Glebe Place, Chelsea, 21 February 1914

Cynthia – who, regarded as the best-looking of the sisters, sometimes jokingly signed herself 'Cinders' – married dutiful war-hero Captain Humphrey Edmund de Trafford (later Sir Humphrey, 4th Bt, MC), on 2 October 1917, in a Roman Catholic ceremony at Brompton Oratory. The couple shared a love of horses and set about establishing a successful stud farm at their family home, Newsells Park in Hertfordshire. As young married ladies, the Square were often spotted together at the races. In October 1923, sensational diarist Henry 'Chips' Channon, 'the Pepys of the interwar years'[41] recorded:

> All the usual Newmarket habitués, all the *haute noblesse* of horsedom... [are] best exemplified by the Cadogan sisters. They appear every day nattily dressed in blue mackintoshes and regularly lose from being too knowledgeable.[42]

The de Traffords had several flat-racing winners – Humphrey's best year was perhaps 1959, in which Alcide took the King George Stakes and Parthia the Epsom Derby. He was senior steward of the Jockey Club twice, either side of World War II. Cynthia was a stalwart of Hertfordshire society. In 1930 *The Tatler*, which pictured her at home with her four daughters, reported that 'Lady de Trafford, who hunts and goes racing with enthusiasm, has a very attractive appearance and wears the nicest clothes.'[43] Her eldest daughter, Ann, married a Parker Bowles; her second daughter, Mary, married a Bowes-Lyon, cousin of Queen Elizabeth the Queen Mother.

'Who's Who in Herts', *The Tatler*, 1930. Cynthia's daughters are pictured at Newsells Park.

16. SOCIETY & SUCCESSION

PORTIA, THE ELDEST OF THE SQUARE, was a vivacious flirt who loved parties and was once talked of as a future Queen of England. As a granddaughter of the 5th Earl Cadogan, confidante to the Crown, she was eminently suitable. On 7 April 1914 Buckingham Palace announced that she had been given a position at court, as a maid of honour to Queen Mary. 'London is a wonderful place for stories,' she wrote. 'They must originate from Friary Court [at St James's Palace] where all the Ladies work. It is therefore rightly named: "The School for Scandal"!!'[44] By Christmas 1915, she was a firm friend of the young royals, enjoying trips to the zoo and taking tea: '…one evening "Mummy and I" took Prince Albert and Prince __ to the gaiety having had dinner at Chelsea House first. Prince Albert is most awfully nice, but not as nice as the little Prince of Wales!'[45] Portia had caught the eye of not one but two future kings, first- and second-in-line to the throne and very close to her in age. The new year saw rounds of parties and dinners with the brothers, chaperoned by Lady Keppel, or the Dowager Countess Cadogan (Adele). Alec wrote to Eddie of their niece:

'Nicknames of Notables: What their friends call them: Portia', *The Bystander*, Wednesday, 16 October 1935

> Portia has stayed in London – wild horses wouldn't drag her from it. She lives at theatres – matinées in the afternoon and evening performances after dinner, mostly with the Prince of Wales [Edward VIII] when he's on leave, with Prince Albert [George VI] if he isn't. The natural result is that she's going white as a sheet and as thin as a match![46]

In the spring of 1916 there were tea dances given by the Devonshires, the Salisburys and the Spencers, at which the foxtrot was all the rage. Portia became the focus of the Prince of Wales in '[h]is first attempt...at a serious affair'.[47] During a stay at Windsor Castle that August she began to feel the pressure as she was drawn closer to the bosom of the royal family:

> I came down alone in a motor with the King, Queen and Princess Mary!!...The meals are a bit trying as all told we are only ten... Being so few [guests] one gets next to the K. every other night which is somewhat exhausting!!...
> We have been having great weekend parties at Coworth [Park, house of the Earls of Derby]. A fortnight ago Victoria [Stanley] gave one of her own there...needless to say it was a very wild one. Uncle Alec and Theo were there. Uncle Alec went quite mad. Half the party were paddling in the fountain at 2.45 on Sunday night (or rather Monday morning) and the other half were throwing Lady Derby's best cushions into the fountain.[48]

With admirable self-knowledge, Portia backed away from the stiff formality of a royal role to a life in which she – later described as 'the funniest woman in London'[49] – could relax and be herself. On 17 July 1917 she married the fabulously rich and popular the Rt. Hon Sir Edward Montagu Cavendish Stanley, Lord Stanley, heir to the Derby earldom, at the Guards' Chapel. He was an Oxford friend of the Prince of Wales; King George V, Queen Mary and Queen Alexandra all signed the register. Her husband was the baby of the House of Commons, elected at the age of twenty-two; he progressed to deputy chairman of the Conservative Party (1927–29), Privy Council member and – briefly – member of the Cabinet before his premature death in 1938. Unlike her sister Edith, however, Portia never seems to have taken much interest in politics.

Certain members of the royal family never quite forgave her. Portia's other sometime beau Prince Albert, Duke of York, had married the Hon. Elizabeth Bowes-Lyon the year before. A tension developed between the prince's friends from his bachelor days and his young wife. '[The duchess] said the people who never left them in peace she found she could not make friends with:...Portia [Stanley], whom she says hates her...Cynthia de T.[rafford], Philip Sassoon, the old crowd...they take her friendship as a right.'[50] Portia struggled to shake a reputation for arrogance; she may have also inspired a watchful jealousy. For a time, she fell out with the mercurial Prince of Wales, who confessed he had been in her 'clutches'.[51] Having found the love of his life, however, he welcomed Portia back into the fold. At a summer party given by Emerald Cunard, during 'David's' brief reign as King Edward VIII (r. 1936), Channon lists: 'Wallis Simpson, demure, thin, simply dressed but with a new parure of rubies (a gift from the K.[ing]), Philip Sassoon and others...Diana, a vision, Sheila and Portia Stanley both sat talking to Wallis...'.[52] Portia and Wallis spent the evening of the State Opening of Parliament at the Channons', attending a 'brilliant dinner of fifteen'. And following the abdication crisis, the Stanleys were invited to dine at Buckingham Palace as early as March 1937; Prince Albert had become King George VI (r.1936–52) and evidently still enjoyed her company. The Stanleys' home at 43 Belgrave Square became a fixture on the social scene, 'now called "the 43" in imitation of the ill-famed nightclub'.[53]

Her husband's early death seems to have taken a toll on Portia, and her fondness for a tipple became more pronounced. But she still held considerable sway. The *Evening Standard* caught up with the Square the following year, in 1939: 'Lady Stanley is a remarkable looking woman with good features, tall, well-groomed, making altogether an attractive figure...long in advice and sometimes short in temper. She is a master of epigrams and a mistress of wit.'[54] Widowed in her mid-forties, Portia did not remarry. When her father-in-law died in 1948, his title went to her son John, 18th Earl of Derby.

MARY, THE YOUNGEST of the Cadogan Square, made perhaps the starriest match, intertwining the family tree once more with the Churchills': her groom was John Spencer-Churchill, Marquess of Blandford ('Bert', future 10th Duke of Marlborough). They were both exceptionally tall and both keen golfers; he was a good shot and gardener, while she was a first-rate

The Tatler

Vol. LXV. No. 848.
London, September 26, 1917
Price Sevenpence.

THE HON. CYNTHIA CADOGAN

'The girls have a large sitting room of their own, which appears to be a rendezvous daily of all the young men in London and all members of the Royal Family under 25.'

ALEC TO EDDIE, MARCH 1916

LEFT Cynthia's engagement to Humphrey de Trafford, on the front cover of *The Tatler*
BELOW A spread on Edith's wedding to Bear Mills

MILLS-CADOGAN—WHICH WAS THE MOST IMPORTANT
Royalty Attends the Pretty Ceremony between Representatives o

THE HON. CYNTHIA CADOGAN AND THE HON. ALEC CADOGAN

The Hon. Cynthia Cadogan is the younger sister of the bride and one of the daughters of the late Lord Chelsea. Lady Meux, who remarried, was before her first marriage Lady Mildred Sturt, a daughter of Lord Alington. The Hon. Alec Cadogan is the youngest brother of the present Lord Cadogan.

SIR JOHN AND LADY LISTER-KAYE

Sir John Lister-Kaye is the third baronet in the revived title, though the original one dates back to Charles I. He succeeded his grandfather in 1871. Sir John Lister-Kaye was formerly in the Blues, and married in 1881 Natica, the daughter of Señor Antonio Yznaga del Valle of Ravenswood, Louisiana, U.S.A., and of Cuba

LORD STANLEY (LEFT) AND
Lord Stanley, who is Lord Derby's heir
dier Guards, acted as best man at th
Hon. Arthur Mills and the Hon. Edith Ca
Knightsbridge, on the 8th. Lord Stanley
the present war

RIGHT Mary's wedding to Bert Spencer-Churchill, Lafayette, 17 February 1920

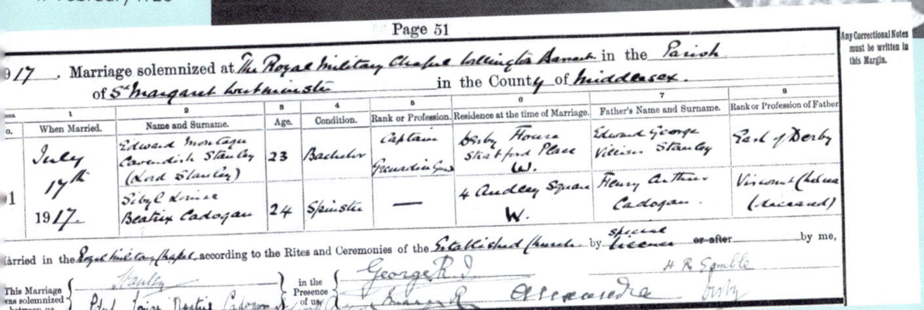

LEFT Portia's marriage register signed by King George V, Queen Mary and Queen Alexandra

BELOW Her engagement to Edward Stanley covered in *The Sketch*

DAILY SKETCH.

ENGAGEMENT OF LORD DERBY'S HEIR.

THE BRIDE AND BRIDEGROOM

The Hon. Arthur Mills, who was married to the Hon. Edith Cadogan on the 8th, is the only son of Lord and Lady Hillingdon, and is a lieutenant in the West Kent Yeomanry. The Hon. Edith Cadogan is the second daughter of Lady Meux and the late Lord Chelsea.

society bridge player. Their wedding at St Mary's Westminster, in the grounds of Westminster Abbey, on 17 February 1920, was international headline news, described by the *New York Times*:

> The wedding was the most important social event of the kind since the marriage of Princess Patricia of Connaught [granddaughter of Queen Victoria]...a year ago...The gifts were many and costly. They included a diamond brooch from King George [V] and Queen Mary, a diamond pendant from Dowager Queen Alexandra and presents from other members of the royal family.[55]

Mary had married an Anglo-American; her mother-in-law, née Consuelo Vanderbilt, came from one of the richest and most prominent New York families. The Vanderbilt dowry (rumoured to be about US$ 10 million) had been poured into Blenheim Palace – still one of the largest houses in England – which consumed vast fortunes in its upkeep (US$ 370,000 a year in 1895, the year of Consuelo's marriage), and the arrangement had been entirely pragmatic.[56] Bert cut an eccentric figure for a love match, as the Churchills' biographer recounts:

The 9th Duke and Duchess of Marlborough and their two sons, John Singer Sargent, 1905, oil on canvas

> He was often described as having stepped from the pages of a P.G. Wodehouse novel. Essentially the product of an Edwardian upbringing, he dressed, acted and spoke accordingly, often adding 'What, what?' to the end of his sentences. Unlike his father, however, he made a very stable marriage, and the palace was filled during his stewardship of it with laughter and children playing.[57]

The famously acerbic writer Auberon Waugh went a step further, describing him as 'one of the most richly absurd characters the English aristocracy ever produced.'[58] Mary could be described as long-suffering. 'Bert bullied his well-meaning Duchess, and was openly unfaithful to her.'[59]

During World War II Blenheim was turned over to Malvern School – the family retreated to the east wing – and the duchess became a senior officer in the Auxiliary Territorial Service. 'A large lady with a pronounced military bearing,'[60] she was nicknamed 'the general' by her husband.[61] She produced five children, including a late-in-life second son, Charles, who was afforded all the pomp owing to a ducal baby.

> ...despite the fact that the Battle of Britain was occurring in the skies of southern Britain, [Mary] was determined this latest child should have a traditional christening at Blenheim.
> One of the guests, Diana Cooper, wrote in her diary of 'champagne and tenantry on the lawns and nannies and cousins and healths drunk, all to the deafening accompaniment of aeroplanes skirmishing, diving, looping and spinning' in the sky above.[62]

Winston Churchill liked Mary, who played bezique with him when he came to visit his cousin at Christmas. At her request, he became godfather to her son John ('Sunny'), 11th Duke of Marlborough.

After the war, a financial rescue plan was once again required. Bert was determined to do things differently and Blenheim opened to the public in 1950. The Marlboroughs welcomed an eclectic bunch, including – at Mary's invitation – a Christian Dior catwalk, in 1954. Consuelo's memoirs

Mary and her husband sit either side of Princess Margaret at the Blenheim Dior show, 1954

record: 'How rewarding are my memories of Blenheim in my son's time. His life [there], with Mary and his children, was all that I wished mine could have been.'[63] Their descendants live at Blenheim to this day.

THE FIFTH SISTER WAS NEVER PART OF THEIR CLUB. The unworldly Victoria Laura ('Tor-Tor', 1901–1991) was quite different in both looks and outlook from the Square. She was also the sole beneficiary of 'the Admiral's' will. It seems likely that her mother had made a head-start on her second marriage and that Tor-Tor was not a Cadogan at all, but a Lambton/Meux.[64] Her seven-year marriage (1922–29) to stockbroker Lt-Col. Sir John 'Jock' Little Gilmour, 2nd Bt, produced two children. Her son Ian Hedworth John Little Gilmour was editor of the *The Spectator* (1954–59) and Conservative Defence Minister (1971–74). Tor-Tor became lady-in-waiting to Portia's nemesis, the young Duchess of York. A loyal companion to the last, she watched *Dynasty* with the Queen Mother into their nineties, deafness notwithstanding. Tor-Tor's death in 1991 marked the passing of a bygone era.

The young Cadogan Square were the apotheosis of aristocratic glamour. In 1939, the *Evening Standard* pronounced:

> the most powerful social family between the twenties and thirties was the family of Cadogan. In many respects, the Cadogan family provides us with the most remarkable story in our social annals.[65]

Portia's breathless deb's dispatches, detailing suitors and dances, had made their way to her Uncle Eddie on the front lines during World War I; it is hard to imagine a greater contrast in setting between two sides of correspondence. Jerry by that time had left the fighting behind. For Willie, the career soldier, it would end in tragedy.

Official party during the royal tour of the Duke and Duchess of York to New Zealand, March 1927, silver gelatin print. Tor-Tor stands behind the duke.

CHAPTER 17

Brothers in Arms

—

CAPTAIN GERALD (1869–1933), MAJORS WILLIAM (1879–1914)
AND SIR EDWARD CADOGAN (1880–1960)

Major William George Sydney Cadogan MVO ('Willie', 1879–1914), fifth son of the 5th Earl, was everybody's favourite. At Eton, where 'hard work was systematically discouraged',[1] he, like his older brothers, excelled at sports, particularly cricket, at which he played for the school's 1st XI. He had arrived 'a small, pale, demure-looking boy'[2] but settled in easily, later sharing a room with his younger brothers in jovial confusion. Godolphin House was now run by young poet and essayist A.C. Benson, who added the well-known words of 'Land of Hope and Glory' to Elgar's *Coronation Ode* (1902). As Benson later recalled:

> [Willie] became popular at once, he stuck to business, and he threw himself with untiring energy into his games. At the end of his time he was in the Eleven and Pop...He was always good-natured, kind and sociable. He had a way of making his intentions felt without saying much about them. He could always be entirely trusted, and depended upon to do the right, sound, kindly and sensible thing...he was exactly, in temperament and character, what one would most desire that a boy should be.[3]

RIGHT William Cadogan, c.1893, Benson's Boys' Album, Eton College

The 10th Royal Hussars after repulsing attack by Boers at Colesburg, South Africa, 4 January 1900, Works and Sun Sculpture Studios, 1900, stereoscopic photograph. *South African War through the Stereoscope*, pt 1, vol. 1 (Underwood & Underwood, 1900)

At seventeen he joined the 4th (Eton College) Volunteer Battalion of the Oxfordshire Light Infantry, and, after Sandhurst, on 22 February 1899 – not a month past twenty – marched straight from the playing fields of Eton into the 10th Royal Hussars (Prince of Wales's Own). Willie left England's shores in November and was swiftly promoted to lieutenant, on the first day of the new century, having had his first taste of battle at Colesburg, South Africa, halfway around the world.

The Attack on Cronje's Force at Vedute Drift near Paardeberg, Godfrey Douglas Giles, 1900, oil on canvas

THE SECOND BOER WAR (1899–1902), one of the last armed follies of the British Empire, also brought older members of the Cadogan cohort to the fight. Third son Gerald ('Jerry'), whose relationship with the British Army had been a little bumpy – two false starts, in the 3rd Battalion of the Royal Fusiliers (City of London Regiment) and the 1st Life Guards, punctuated by sojourns in Cambridge and Dublin – surfaced on active duty as a captain in the 3rd Battalion of the Suffolk.[4] He sailed out in February 1900, on the SS *Canada*. Almost immediately on landing, he joined Willie in action at the Battle of Paardeberg, a crucial victory for the British. Settling into service life, Jerry reported home to his mother:

> I had the honour of holding the *kopje* [hill] the first night after we occupied it with the whole of my company. It is not a very pleasant task as one has to be up nearly the whole night, and to be ready at four in the morning in case of attack...we generally have a hand in all the fun that is going on...[5]

17. BROTHERS IN ARMS

With two of her boys together halfway across the world, Beattie had perhaps charged level-headed Willie with keeping a weather eye on his wayward older sibling. He sent her a letter of reassurance:

> I have been over to lunch with Jerry, and he came over and lunched here yesterday. I also met him at dinner yesterday with his old regiment!...Jerry looks awfully fit and well, and seems to like being out here very much.[6]

A brother-in-law soon joined them in uniform. Sophie and her forgiving husband had set sail for Ceylon (Sri Lanka) on their second honeymoon in 1899. When world events intervened, they made a diversion. Both Jerry and Willie found themselves on the *Golden Eagle* during an outbreak of typhoid fever:

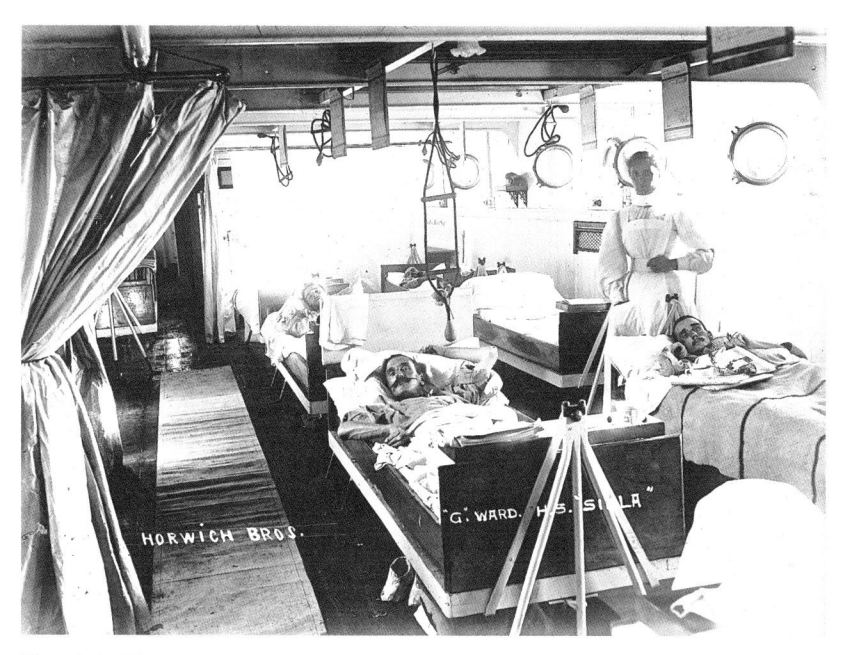

Wounded soldiers on G Ward, HMHS *Simla*, Horwich Bros, c.1902. Sammy Scott lent his yacht *Golden Eagle* to be used similarly as a hospital ship.

It was too splendid finding Sophie and her yacht down here on my arrival yesterday. The authorities were very good to me and did not give me the slightest bother about my living on the yacht, in fact the Chief Staff Officer told me that it was the best place I could possibly go to...Willie, I am sorry to say, leaves us today. He is looking wonderfully better but I am afraid he had a rather bad time of the fever...[7]

All-round good egg Sammy presented his yacht to the government for use as a hospital ship and rejoined the Army, as a volunteer in the Imperial Yeomanry.[8] (He had previously resigned his commission as a lieutenant in the Royal Horse Guards [Blue] the year he married.) His generosity was rewarded with a mention in dispatches.

Sophie seems to have acted as social glue among the siblings. She had written to her mother about a planned rendezvous with another young Cadogan floating around the southern hemisphere – the outlier, who did not suit a uniform. 'You might tell Lewin to find out <u>exactly</u> when his ship is due at Colombo, and either send me a wire or a note to the Poste Restante there.'[9]

LEWIN EDWARD CADOGAN (1872–1919), the often-overlooked brother between Jerry and Willie, had been shipped off in disgrace. His health had been in question since at least the mid 1890s, when he wrote to Willie, 'the doctor said that I was not well enough to go on working and that I must stop at once for at least a month.'[10] Three years under 'Sir Horace' in private banking, 'plodding along every day and all day for the miserable pay of £90 a year', led him to conclude 'I cannot be a Bank Clerk all my life.'[11] Instead, he became a blotchy alcoholic with a gout-ridden leg, and an indolent gambler. From on board the Dampfer *Friedrich der Grosse* (on the

ABOVE A young Lewin Cadogan, from a series of portraits in a family album post run to Australasia), at the end of 1899, he wrote to 'Darling Mother' of cricket games – 'the ship was rolling a bit and it seemed impossible to stand steady to bat' – and, rather petulantly, of his disappointment: 'I was very hurt at not having one line from Eddie or Alec to say goodbye.'[12] On dry land, he took a deep breath and wrote home to 'Dearest Father' from the Wellington Club on 7 March 1900:

> ...I will try and do my best and improve myself to the best of my ability. One cannot 'take off one's dirty clothes' all in a second, but time will show what I can do and it will be the happiest moment of my life if I can prove to you that, even though successes may not be mine, yet I have tried and can give you proof of the effort.[13]

Sadly, even connections with the Governor-General of New Zealand and her future Prime Minister – 'Lord Ranfurly gave me an introduction to a Mr. Coates', from the same letter – were wasted on him. Lewin's new leaf was beginning to shake in the wind: 'I made you a promise that I would not gamble on the way out here, or after, but I must plead guilty to playing a game of piquet with a friend of mine...I did not win or lose much and that could hardly be called gambling.'[14] There were family discussions about getting Lewin over to South Africa, though even Jerry doubted the wisdom of such a plan: 'If he would only work I have not the slightest doubt he would make a very good thing of it; if he does not intend to do that it is the last place in the world he ought to come.'[15]

Lewin resolved to try his luck in Tasmania, arriving via the SS *Westralia* in early July 1901. He wrote from the none-too-salubrious Heathorn's Family Hotel, Hobart, which advertised itself as 'within a stone's throw of the terminus of the Main Line railway':[16]

> I arrived here about a fortnight ago...you could only take this place to be what it really is, namely the survival of the first Colonial convict establishment. There are very few people in the town, and it is the quietest and most deserted looking place

HEATHORN'S HOTEL, HOBART, TASMANIA (F. GOLDING, Proprietress).
Close to Railway Station, Wharves, Theatre, Domain and Trams.
TENNIS AND CROQUET LAWNS.   MOTOR GARAGE.

Heathorn's Hotel, Hobart, 1909

> I ever was in…I have already had a coat and stick stolen from me in the hotel…Please give my love to all at home, and father, try not to be too hard on me.[17]

Poor Lewin. Despite several trips home, with renewed hopes on all sides, he never really settled. 'Lewin has started off for Ceylon. History repeats itself absolutely with him. I do think he will be better in a warmer climate than here and I do not think he is in a good state of health, but I hope there will be no troubles and that he will at all costs live a decent life, but what a wasted one!'[18]

MEANWHILE, WILLIE, under Lord Roberts, and Jerry, in command of Wiltshire Company under De Lisle, saw almost constant actions that spring: at Poplar Grove and Driefontein, Houtnek (Thoba Mountain), the Vet and Zand Rivers. Once the Boers had been pushed back from Pretoria, the British expected to come straight home; it didn't quite work out that way.

The conflict's grim reputation stems from two counter-guerrilla ideas from Lord Kitchener (Roberts' successor): the infantry's scorched-earth policy and the introduction of concentration camps for Boer families. But there were positive developments. Winston Churchill, then a war correspondent, commented in *Ian Hamilton's March* (1900):

> There is no doubt that our Infantry have profited by the lessons of this war. The widely extended lines of skirmishers moving forward, almost invisible against the brown grass of the plain, and taking advantage of every scrap of cover, presented no target to the Boer fire.[19]

The dangers of the modern long-sighted rifle – and its user, the sniper – had been especially evident to British soldiers of the First Boer War twenty years earlier, whose white-leather straps over a red-jacketed chest provided convenient crosshairs. Men of the Second Boer War wore the camouflage of khakis and pith helmets. The great technological innovations of the Crimean War were now a core component of the Army's strategy: telegrams, telephones, hot air balloons, searchlights powered by mobile generators and steam railways. Both Willie and Jerry oversaw 'musketry' training (the language had yet to catch up); Jerry as a squadron commander, and Willie commanding a section of mounted infantry.

Willie was on operations until the end of May 1902. He received the first of his honours with a Queen's Medal with four clasps and the King's Medal with two. Jerry was appointed a special service officer in the new South African Constabulary (SAC); his first task was to take charge of hundreds of police horses landing at Port Elizabeth. He then spent the summer of 1901 in a dynamite factory in the Transvaal, which he bore with Tiggerish good humour. 'It seems a

General Kelly-Kenny's Infantry creeping on the Boers at Dreifontein – on the march to Bloemfontein

really charming place, we are situated high up overlooking a lovely valley with big woods all round.'[20] Engagement with the Boers was limited to occasional skirmishes, allowing time for field sports:

> We shot about 30 to 40 head, mostly guinea fowl and hares and one or two quail and one buck…I think Major Wilberforce and I were about the only people who hit anything at all, which does not say too much for the rest. The German Consul hit me, but only very slightly, and I am sure that is the only thing he hit all day.[21]

After the war, Jerry returned home to England via Sydney and San Francisco. Willie's regiment was sent to India and he was promoted to captain. Naturally, he found time to play in a first-class cricket match – the 1904 Annual Bombay Presidency Match (Europeans vs Parsees, Europeans comprehensively thrashed) – when not dispatching his official duties ('we had quite an exciting time of it in Pindi during the disturbances…'[22]). His military record is marked '1904; distinguished.'[23]

THE LONGSTANDING RELATIONSHIP between the Cadogan family and the royal family was strengthened by Willie's appointment as honorary aide-de-camp to George, Prince of Wales, during his 1905/6 Indian tour. 'I was most anxious that it should be given to you, but, as you know, you told us you preferred my not asking for anything of the sort for you – so I have been careful not to say a word. It is very pleasant to think that your selection is entirely owing to your own merits,' wrote his father.[24] Rewarded by investiture in the Royal Victorian Order (MVO), given for personal service to the Crown, he also received the Cross of Honour of the Order of the Crown of Würtemberg. Willie, 'always popular with officers and men alike',[25] rose to major. In December 1911 King George V and Queen Mary were back in India for a week of celebrations surrounding their proclamation as Emperor and Empress, the 3rd Delhi Durbar. It was an expression of Empire at its apogee – a state procession, a review of fifty thousand troops, a garden party, fabulous jewels – and Willie was at the monarch's side throughout.

King George V and Queen Mary at the Red Fort during the Delhi Durbar, December 1911

On 13 September 1912 he was appointed equerry to the new young Prince of Wales, a pre-Portia Prince Edward, and the following month accompanied him up to Oxford, becoming a permanent resident during termtime. The *Oxford Magazine* recalled: 'He was almost daily in Magdalen College...he was constantly to be seen wherever field sports and games attract. An Eton man, he was, if not a scholar, well read.'[26] Willie spent the last of the pre-war years among the dreaming spires. In August 1914 he was back in London with Eddie, who noted on Tuesday 3: 'Returning to Chelsea House I found Willie in great fettle – as all soldiers should be at the outbreak of war...[he] has been going round to White's Club listening to the elderly *habitués* there talking big...'[27] The following day, Britain declared war. Willie, with full permission from the king, rejoined the 10th Hussars. His regiment was deployed to the Western Front as part of the British Expeditionary Force. The BEF would suffer over ninety thousand casualties before Christmas.[28]

WILLIE WAS KILLED IN ACTION on 12 November 1914, at Ypres. He had written to his father just days earlier, 'we have been fighting day and night for about 3 weeks now…I have lost so many friends during the last week or so. That is the worst part of the show.'[29] That final letter was delivered in the same envelope as the following notice from his commanding officer:

> I cannot tell you how grieved I am to inform you of poor Willie's death, which occurred yesterday morning shortly after ten. He was sitting in a dug out beside a haystack…and a piece of shell must have come practically vertically down striking him high up on the left thigh, severing the femoral artery. He just called 'find for the doctor' and became unconscious at once. He died in less than three minutes. It is so dreadfully sad and has cast a swoon over the whole Regiment: we were all so fond of him…[30]

The Prince of Wales and Major the Hon William G.S. Cadogan together in Germany, 1913

Only the day before, Willie had been hit in the head by a splinter of shell and sent back to camp to rest. He had insisted on returning to his squadron the next morning, declaring that he felt all right as he reported for duty with a bandaged head.

Willie's name was mentioned in dispatches for 'gallant and distinguished service in the Field'.[31] Billy Lurgan wrote to his father-in-law, 'my dear Cadogan':

> Why all the best ones are taken it is hard to understand. He was one of those who could ill be spared by his family or friends or by the country either. Jonny Ward tells me that the Prince

> of Wales is heartbroken & everybody at Buckingham Palace miserable at his loss...[32]

Letters of condolence came from Kensington Palace and St James's Palace, from the wider royal family and the Lord Chamberlain.

The Prince of Wales had lost a true friend. His frequent, chatty letters to Willie describe shooting successes at Balmoral, Christmas at Sandringham – 'I am certainly more than pleased that Xmas is over, for as you say I do not in the least appreciate the plum pudding, paté de foie gras, etc. and am rather tired of writing 50 letters a day' – and hint at plans for hijinks – 'my brother and I are leaving here on the 20th and shall sleep the night in London before he rejoins his ship and return to Oxford, the next day. So perhaps you would meet us there and [we] can have a good night!!'[33] Just a week into the war, the prince had written chummily from Warley Barracks in Essex:

> I am very happy to have joined up and am at last taking part in all this...I am so sorry for having caused so much trouble by grumbling and grousing these 1st awful days, but I couldn't stick remaining silent. I am more than grateful to you for all you did in getting me here; I did not deserve it at all.[34]

The heir to the throne was not allowed to fight, though he did visit the Front – where his itinerary was amended to include paying his respects at Willie's grave in Ypres cemetery.

The blow at home was enormous. His parents' pride in him is most clearly expressed in a letter George Henry wrote after his wife's death: 'She was devoted to you and so proud of you and so loved the good qualities and works by which you always made us so happy.'[35] He was equally admired by his brothers. Lewin wrote a note of comfort to Eddie: 'Perhaps he died the death he would have <u>chosen</u> himself...I have the most vivid and loving recollections.'[36] At least Willie was spared the horrors of prolonged trench warfare.

ABOVE 'The King, the Prince of Wales, and Prince Albert devoted yesterday to visiting a series of places made memorable in the continuous fighting around Ypres...[they] visited two cemeteries, in one of which were the graves of Lord Charles Nairn and Major Cadogan,' *The Times*, (9)10 December 1918. Lt Ernest Brooks, 8 December

THE EXTENDED CADOGAN FAMILY served alongside their countrymen in an all-encompassing war that swallowed a generation. Every one of Freddie and Adelaide Cadogan's grandsons fought. Their daughter Margaret lost her only son, 2nd Lt Edward Bagot, aged just nineteen, at the Battle of the Somme, that five-month grind of attrition. Younger daughter Charlotte Villiers was luckier, her four sons all survived: Major Paul was awarded DSO in 1917 and Captain (RN) Gerald OBE in 1919; Sir Francis and Major Oliver were both inspired to join the new Royal Flying Corps, which would become the Royal Air Force on 1 April 1918. This was incredibly daring, given that the Wright brothers had achieved the first powered, manned flight only a decade earlier. Oliver was mentioned in dispatches, admitted *Chevalier, Ordre national de la Légion d'honneur*, awarded the *Croix de Guerre*, and, in 1918, DSO.

RIGHT Cap badge, Royal Flying Corps (RFC), 1912

17. BROTHERS IN ARMS

At the end of 1914, King George V created a new decoration, the Military Cross, for exemplary gallantry during land operations. Two of the Cadogan Square's husbands were recipients: Portia's husband, Edward (also awarded the *Croce di Guerra*), serving in the Grenadiers, and Cynthia's husband, Humphrey, in the Coldstream Guards. Edith's husband Bear became heir to the barony of Hillingdon when his older brother Charles was killed in action in 1915; Mary's husband, Bert, was a lieutenant in the 1st Life Guards; Tor-Tor's husband, John, won the *Croix de Guerre Belgian*. Among Willie and Eddie's first cousins, John Cadogan was a lieutenant in the Scots Guards; his brother Commander (RN) Francis Cadogan took part in the Anzac landing and Dover patrol, and fought in the Black and Caspian Seas.

In the popular imagination it was, and perhaps remains, the regular Tommies going 'over the top' who suffered mind-bendingly enormous losses; after the first few months all but wiped out a million volunteers, the Military Conscription Act (1916) put all men aged eighteen to forty-one in uniform. That so many Cadogan family members survived might speak of their position of privilege among the officer class. Their many awards for bravery, however, show that they were in the thick of it. Indeed, the family's attitude is summed up by Eddie, who turned down an offer of relative safety in a staff position. 'I refused without any hesitation because I considered it such a rotten thing to do to leave your regiment when you go out on active service for the first time. I think everybody ought to try the front line if they can.'[37]

MAJOR THE HON. SIR EDWARD CECIL GEORGE CADOGAN, KBE, CB, JP, DL ('Eddie', 1880–1962) was thirty-three at the outbreak of war. He volunteered for active service as a captain in the 1st Suffolk Yeomanry. After almost a year of 'terribly tedious' training at Woodbridge – escaping for weekends with schoolfriend Walter Guinness and his wife Lady Evelyn Guinness, at nearby Sutton – on 24 September 1915 the regiment sailed from Liverpool. Eddie found Sammy Scott, Bear Mills and many friends among the six thousand troops on board. As they passed the coast of North Africa, the reality of their mission sank in:

'Officers of Suffolk Yeomanry, August 1914 at the outbreak of war.' Eddie's caption includes the note 'self', underneath his figure second from right.

> I heard a shot from one of our guns and shouts of 'Submarine!' Then the alarm system sounded; a series of short hoots, which froze the marrow in one's bones. We all went to our stations and donned our lifebelts…the *Olympic* began to keel over at a terrible angle so much so that I began to wonder whether we had been hit and that what I thought was our gun might have been a torpedo. But as a matter of fact what had happened was the Captain was trying to turn the boat round on a sixpence.[38]

Eddie spent his first night at Anzac Cove huddled up on the beach with Walter Guinness, under cliffs that rang with rifle fire. Having left the relative comfort of the *Olympic* (bringing a half-bottle of champagne with him), Eddie would now survive on rations of bully beef, boiled water, rice, biscuits and apricot jam – always apricot. Within weeks the men were dodging lice, dysentery and typhoid fever, and the young captain was inoculated against cholera.

Eddie passed the time compiling a diary. He took many photographs of Army life, and, in the tradition of his great-uncle George in the Crimea,

17. BROTHERS IN ARMS

he also sketched. These entries, with his later notes, were published posthumously in collected form as *Under Fire in the Dardanelles* (2006). His sense of humour prevailed even in a 'very bad dug-out' (Tuesday, 19 October 1915):

> I manage somehow and after an apology of a supper crawl into my rabbit hole, light a talk lamp and read [Dickens's] *Pickwick* – the only book I have brought with me. Nobody seems to have got any literature at all on this peninsula and as parcels seem to mis-fire the prospects for the library are not cheerful.

He drew comparisons with London society life: 'My shift is from 11pm to 1am…difficult and sleepy work…like a chaperone trying to keep awake at a ball!' It was an apposite joke from a bombing officer keeping a watchful eye on the enemy's position. When a sniper hit his periscope, he elected to stay at the Front despite shrapnel injuries to the face and hands. There were occasional glints in the gloomy monotony: an excellent tea given by Tony Rothschild and Leonard Avery; news of any kind; but danger was ever-present. Tuesday, 16 November 1915:

The Gallipoli Campaign, April 1915 – January 1916. RMS *Olympic*, sister ship of RMS *Titanic*, arriving at Mudros Harbour, with Eddie and the others on board. Following the great ocean-liner disaster of 1912, *Olympic* had been retrofitted with several safety upgrades: more lifeboats, a longer double skin, and its watertight bulkheads raised from deck E to deck B.

A German aeroplane flew over our dump. As usual shrapnel was sent up after it. A piece of it fell down into our valley and killed Water Guinness's servant, a man called Day, tearing his head and shoulder open…he was a good fellow and used to do a great deal for us at Woodbridge where he was Walter G's chauffer. He was engaged to be married, poor fellow.

On 14 December 1915, after nearly sixty days under continuous fire, Eddie's regiment was evacuated. It saved his life: during the withdrawal he felt 'agonizing pains in my legs'; four days earlier he had noticed, 'Am getting a curious sort of affection [*sic*] of the skin on my fingers which look as if they are rotting'. Safely on-board ship he found 'a horrible red, plush sofa which seemed the height of luxury to me' and collapsed with a fever. He took his first bath in months: 'I received a shock. I was a skeleton and bright yellow from the jaundice!'

ABOVE LEFT 'Our front line trench' and ABOVE RIGHT 'Trench periscope', Edward Cadogan, 1915. Eddie took photographs throughout the Dardanelles campaign.

17. BROTHERS IN ARMS

After three weeks at the Red Cross Convalescent Hospital in Alexandria, he enjoyed four days in Cairo at number 8 Zamalek, Gezireh, a residence of the diplomatic service. A sense of normality – for a Cadogan – returned in the form of a shooting party with the High Commissioner and dinners at hotel restaurants in Alexandria, hanging out with Frank Goldsmith. There followed several camps used as staging posts for supplies, including over six months at Dabaa, 'the pleasantest months of the war...It was extraordinarily healthy: we rode most of the day and bathed.' There were concerts, golf, tennis and tug-o'-war; and tourist trips to the Temple of Philae and Karnak Temple in Luxor.

On Easter Day 1917 they were on the move again, headed for Palestine, in an oppressive climate: dust storms and sudden rains that filled the air with mosquitos. 'We wore drill with shorts, a kit which gets clammy in the daytime heat and freezing at night.' Nonetheless, the men were in better spirits:

> On the 4th June we mustered all the Old Etonians we could find in the brigade. We contrived a quite luxurious supper on a kind of plateau behind the trenches, which was, in fact, well under fire...I remember particularly a lobster salad, which was indeed a luxury in those days. We decided to send a telegram to the Headmaster which somebody translated into Latin. I can recollect only three words of it '*Apud portas Gazae* [at the gates of Gaza]'!

Eddie saw out the rest of the war in the Intelligence Corps, working with the Arab Bureau. He watched the Turks' attempt to recapture Jerusalem from the Mount of Olives, and describes the road to Damascus in November as 'a lovely route reminding me somewhat of the Corniche Road in the French Riviera'. (You can take the chap out of Chelsea, but not Chelsea out of the chap.) While at Damascus, Eddie had 'the honour and privilege of having a personal interview with King Feisal [Faisal] the First' of Syria (he would later become King of Iraq), following capture of the city in September by his Arab Army.

Despite everything, he had had a good war; Eddie was mentioned in dispatches. For him, the armistice was a complete anticlimax. Injured during the recall, he had an operation on his leg and was stretchered back to Blighty. 'I was proud to have been in uniform from the day the war broke out until it ended.'

EDDIE RETURNED TO THE HOUSE OF COMMONS, where he had been Secretary to the Speaker since 1911. He held his post until James Lowther retired in 1921; that same year Eddie was created Companion of the Most Honourable Order of the Bath (CB). Having plotted his career path as a schoolboy – destination Parliament via Balliol College, Oxford, and the Bar – he was duly elected MP for Reading (a Cadogan family tradition), the following year. He held the seat briefly before switching to the Middlesex (London) constituency of Finchley, from 1924 until 1935. Eddie's eloquent contributions to the House were many and varied – anaesthetics for horses during gelding; provision of children's playgrounds – a career total of 432: he applied himself.

Eddie's dedication to improving young lives was evident in his active engagement, from its earliest beginnings in 1909, with the Boys' Club Movement, ultimately as chairman. He purchased a derelict 170-acre farm in the Chiltern Hills – The Warren Farm, Aston Hill, Lewknor – to provide an annual summer camp and weekends away for East-End boys. Perhaps informed by his time as a barrister, he was particularly interested in keeping boys out of borstals at a time when the school leaving age was just fourteen. An early speech to Parliament, of 1925, outlined: 'To put the argument on its lowest level, surely youth in good employment is a better investment for the State than the prison, the workhouse, or the dole.'[39] In 1937, Eddie was awarded the King George VI Coronation Medal as chairman of the Juvenile Organizations Committee.

ABOVE A portrait of Eddie labelelled 'Eton Boy'

The Speaker of the House of Commons, the Rt. Hon. James Lowther, MP, and his state coach, accompanied by the Sergeant-At-Arms and the Speaker's secretary (Eddie, right), going to the coronation of King George V, 22 June 1911

He was a progressive Conservative. The Home Secretary appointed him chairman of a new Corporal Punishment Committee to investigate judicial use in the penal systems of Great Britain.[40] The Cadogan Report (1938) made a unanimous case for abolition; its recommendations were finally brought into law in section 2 of the Criminal Justice Act (1948).[41] His experience in international diplomacy saw him appointed to the seven-member Indian Statutory Commission (1927–30). The resulting Simon Report recommended the gradual establishment of representative government. Consequences of the commission would affect the lives of millions. The Government of India Act (1935) – passage of which saw Eddie go toe-to-toe with Winston Churchill in the House – would form the basis of the Indian Constitution.[42] (Eddie later recalled frequent lunches at Blenheim as a student, during one of which Winston, 'always full of superabundant energy', returned 'covered with mud. He had been enthusiastically and energetically excavating some Roman remains.'[43])

Eddie was knighted in 1939. He returned briefly to life as a backbench MP, but by the time of his re-election in 1940, as one of two MPs for Bolton, Lancashire, war had again broken out. Now in his sixties, he served with the RAF Volunteer Reserve.[44] He lost his parliamentary seat in the post-war Labour landslide.

In later life, urbane Eddie became a mildly comic figure. Having enjoyed a head of lustrous black hair in his youth, his vanity demanded he retain the illusion into old age. Securing a thick bootlace in the back collar-stud hole in his shirt, he would draw it tightly over his crown and fix the other end between his teeth, before painting his bald pate with boot polish – removing the lace to reveal a perfect parting. As children, Charles, 8th Earl Cadogan, and his sister Lady Sarah trained their yellow parrot to interrogate 'Uncle Eddie' on sight with, 'Is it a wig? Is it a wig?'[45] Such fond family memories round out the seriousness of his life as a dedicated public servant and a man of faith. He died on 13 September 1962, at home at Beaumont House, Marylebone, aged eighty-one.

YOUNGER SONS HAD ALWAYS found their marriage prospects among the limited pool of the aristocracy further constrained by the lack of grand title, estate or fortune. But once the eldest had secured a match, to be relieved of such obligations could be freeing. Willie confided to Eddie:

> I have always said that matrimony is a contagious or rather an infectious disease…I really was beginning to think that I might have some day to do a little bit in that line myself, if none of the others did, but I was never enthusiastic about it, not being of a domestic temperament, and now I think I can consider myself absolutely free to live the life of a wanderer![46]

Eddie himself was a confirmed bachelor. 'I contemplated marriage. In the end, however, I came to the conclusion that the match would have been unsuitable.'[47]

Lewin, second in the Cadogan line from 1910, came close. His marriage to Canadian Miss Mary Beresford Windham was announced in *The Times* as 'provisionally arranged' for 17 May 1911. A week before the event was to take place, it was 'unavoidably postponed', and then never mentioned again, despite its erroneous publication in the international press. The official reason given was 'owing to the illness of the Hon. Lewin Cadogan'.[48]

Eddie at home in his study. He coloured-in his greying eyebrows freehand.

Private correspondence tells a different story. On 25 April, Eddie confided to Willie, '...Lewin for the last 7 or 8 days has left his young lady in the lurch [and] has not written to her...She has appealed to me to find him....' Their father wrote:

> He appears to be leading his old life at Brighton – but as far as we know he has behaved disgracefully to the young lady to whom he was engaged. I had to make all the settlements and no end of trouble but I have not heard a word from him about what he is doing. So one can only leave him to his own devices.[49]

Lewin died unmarried back in Hobart, on 12 August 1917, and is buried at Queenborough Cemetery, Sandy Bay.

The last of the brothers, Alec, would enjoy a long and happy marriage. He would also find professional success, rising to the top of the Foreign Office and accompanying world leaders to peace conferences following both World Wars. Before we come to his story, we pick up the thread of Jerry's – his marriage, his money and why his mother might have been so concerned.

CHAPTER 18

The Sporting Life

—

GERALD, 6TH EARL (1869–1933)

On 6 March 1915, at the age of forty-two, Lieutenant-Colonel Gerald Oakley Cadogan ('Jerry'), succeeded as 6th Earl Cadogan. He had already led a life of several distinct acts when, in the summer of 1910, his world was turned upside down by his nephew's death. On 25 January 1911, *The Sketch* published the news that Jerry's bachelor days were now numbered. 'Following hard on the announcement of [5th] Earl Cadogan's marriage to the Countess Adele Palagi comes the engagement of his Lordship's eldest surviving son, Viscount Chelsea, to Miss Marie Coxon....Miss Coxon, who is about twenty-one...made her début in Society about three years ago.' She was exactly half his age. The *Bystander* described her as 'well known in London and Dublin Society as a lady of decided beauty, versatile talent, and vivacious disposition.'[1]

Lilian Eleanor Marie Coxon ('Marie' or, occasionally, 'Yum', c.1889–1973), was not from aristocratic stock. Little is known about her father George Coxon, who lived at Craigleith, Cheltenham. Her mother – also Lilian (née Piercy) – was one of six daughters of a Denbighshire industrialist

Gerald Oakely Cadogan, 6th Earl Cadogan

OPPOSITE Countess Cadogan (née Marie Coxon), photographed by Lallie Charles for *The Sketch*, 17 March 1915

and member of the Institution of Civil Engineers. *Hearth and Home* reported breathlessly, 'The Piercy sisters were all much admired in their girlhood, and went about a great deal in foreign as well as English Society.'[2] Marie was well-suited to Jerry, sharing his interest in all things equine and reassuringly familiar links with both Wales and Italy (her grandfather owned mines in Sardinia). Jerry married his young bride on 7 June 1911. Only six guests were invited to the quiet ceremony at Christ Church, Down Street, in Mayfair. Reports in over a hundred newspapers were limited to descriptions of the bride's outfit – a cream satin dress and a hat trimmed with white roses – and the name of the best man, Captain Claude Raul Champion de Crespigny of the Grenadier Guards. Forgoing a reception, the bride and groom headed straight home to 7 Park Lane. George Henry wrote to Willie in India:

> You will have heard all about Gerald. I hear good accounts of his wife – but we have not met her yet – the Bankruptcy proceedings makes it really impossible, but we have exchanged friendly letters – and I have settled to give him an allowance of £4,000 a year which at all events for the present is, I think sufficient.[3]

A big society wedding might well have been deemed inappropriate given the groom's recent financial embarrassments.

THE FIRST WHISPERS OF JERRY'S DIFFICULTIES had appeared almost twenty years earlier. A discreet exit from the Royal Fusiliers had been arranged in 1892; a telegram notifying his father of his safe return after five days AWOL from Camberley provides a clue though not a smoking gun.[4] Eighteen months later, George Henry wrote in his diary: 'I had to go to London about Gerald's affairs. Colonel Byng came to see me and it was settled that Gerald was to leave the Life Guards at once.'[5] Two for two. It would be too easy to write young Jerry off as a playboy; it is likely to have been the Cadogan family name that had got him into trouble in the first place. The 5th Earl – 'one of the richest London landlords' as the popular press would have it[6] – enjoyed a lavish lifestyle. But his children seem to have been largely ignorant of financial realities. Creditors mistakenly assumed the existence of a comfortable allowance, extending generous lines of credit, far more than a naïve young man could afford to repay, but which a gambler – for Jerry it was almost certainly cards, the fashionable choice of the young soldier – was never going to refuse. His older brother Haggy had fallen victim to a similar fate, and been removed from the Royal Fusiliers four months earlier. Something had to be done.

The 5th Earl Cadogan drew up a document that would allow for future debts to be paid while protecting the Cadogan fortune. On 21 December 1893, Jerry signed away his rights to the Estate in the unlikely occurrence of a series of unfortunate events. He would never have guessed that these would come to pass:

> ...by way of sale to the Earl by the said Gerald Oakley Cadogan of his Estate for life of and in the Cadogan Family Estates therein mentioned in remainder expectant upon the decease of the Earl and also expectant upon the decease of The Honourable Henry Arthur Cadogan [Haggy] the eldest Son of the Earl and commonly called 'Lord Viscount Chelsea' and the failure of his male issue....[7]

After what reads like a comprehensive scolding, in January 1894 Jerry was dispatched to the other side of the world in disgrace.

Rehabilitation was not long in coming. A supplemental indenture 'in consideration of the natural love which the Earl bears to the said Gerald Oakley Cadogan and for divers[e] other good considerations him hereunto moving' was filed, dated 18 June the same year. George Henry, 'desirous of making a provision for the said Gerald Oakley Cadogan and his Wife and issue (if any)', created a complex legal agreement: a 'Conversion of Reversionary Life Estate' in which he conveyed Jerry's potential future inheritance to trustees.[8] Should Jerry become 6th Earl Cadogan, running of the Estate would pass to the Earl of March (the Hon. Charles Gordon-Lennox, later 7th Duke of Richmond), a distant cousin, and Sir Frederick

William Johnstone, 8th Baronet. The trustees would provide him with an income for life, but he would have no control over Chelsea or Culford. In effect, Jerry would be tenant-in-possession '...until some other event shall happen whereby such life estate or some part thereof would if belonging absolutely to him become vested in or charged in favour of some other person or persons....' No betting the family mansion at the card table; and should the spectre of bankruptcy appear, the purse strings would be pulled tightly closed. It was tough love.

Jerry's appointment as aide-de-camp to his father in Ireland and his active service during the Second Boer War gave him chances to prove himself, and he was determined not to disappoint. His nonchalant letters belie a pride in his work. '...I think I may say that it is a very credible job, at least the authorities are pleased, which is the great thing.'[9] Once he was back among old friends in London, however, it was easy to fall back into bad habits. Chinese whispers among the siblings had long been commonplace. Eddie recounted to Willie:

> Apropos of Jerry I met an awful bounder not long ago who accosted me with the remark: 'I think I know about you; you live over the Gaiety.' I hastened to assure him that it was a case of mistaken identity...It did not however require any mental gymnastics to guess at the explanation of my acquaintance's mistake. It also helped explain the £9,800...[10]

Alec gossiped from Culford in January 1910 that 'Jerry is behaving as he does in the ante-room at White's'; another of his letters, from Chelsea House, includes a report of heated discussions between Jerry and their father:

> they are fighting it out somewhere...Tonight we dine *en famille*, & I have brought a mail shirt to wear under the ordinary linen one. I hear there is to be no hitting below the waist & firearms are forbidden; however, I dare say we shall have quite a good rough & tumble...[11]

18. THE SPORTING LIFE

When, that same summer, Jerry became the new Viscount Chelsea, the accompanying spotlight threw his old problem into sharp relief. His father confided (to Willie again):

> I have had a very severe business with all the changes and Jerry's affairs – I have had to buy him out of his Bankruptcy ([£]14,000) but on condition that he pays a large sum to you his younger brothers & sisters at my death. In the meantime I have been terribly worried & have had to borrow money for immediate necessities. I must say Jerry is behaving very well in all ways now....[12]

The 5th Earl tried to understand. In the same letter he mentions his own recent bad luck at the races, 'so wonderfully bad' (though minor in comparison) that it had been reported in the papers. Jerry's younger brothers, however, were exasperated. Willie replied: 'I am so sorry that you have again had this trouble about Jerry. I cannot understand him.... I can see only one hope for him and that is that he should marry a really strong determined woman.'[13]

Happily, the marriage between Jerry and Marie was a success. They had three children, beginning in May with the arrival of Beatrix Lilian Ethel (1912–1999), followed by William Gerald Charles (1914–1997) and, after a short gap during which Jerry became the 6th Earl, Alexandra Mary (1920–1985). There were no longer Cadogans at Chelsea House. After Adele moved out,

A page from White's infamous *Betting Book*. Cadogans have been members of London's oldest gentlemen's club (founded in 1693), since the 2nd Baron joined.

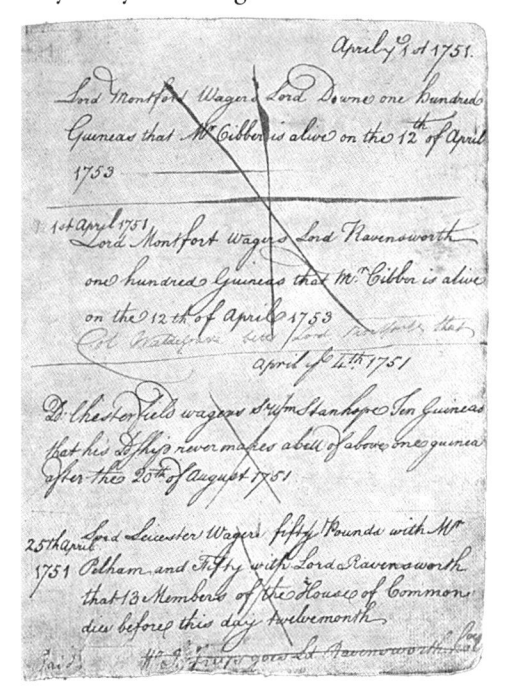

'Yum, who I believe to be in London, is going to install herself there for a bit ...with a view finally to settling whether it will be let or not.'[14] Later in 1916, the mansion was occupied by sometime owner of the White Star Line Sir Owen Philipps, KCMG (he sold the lease back to the Cadogan Estate in 1930).[15] Jerry and Marie favoured Grosvenor Street, living first at number 33 and, from 1928, across the road at number 48, their final London address.

A countryman at heart, a naturalist and birdwatcher, Jerry spent the majority of his time with his young family at Culford Hall, running the Suffolk estate, enjoying sports and the great outdoors. He wrote to Eddie: 'Nothing much going on here and times are very dull; but personally I have an awful lot of work to do and don't find time lying very heavily on my hands. I haven't slept a night in London for six months, thank God!'[16] Under his father, Culford had played host to royal house parties, and Jerry continued the tradition of the sociable shoot. *The Tatler* gave a generous spread to 'Lord and Lady Cadogan at Culford Hall: Their Beautiful Seat, Famous for its Coverts, in Suffolk' in September 1916.

THE CADOGAN ESTATE IN CHELSEA was duly placed in the hands of trustees, who acted on recommendations from agent Mr Cave, made under the presumption of what the late Lord Cadogan would have done. A period of adjustment led to some late payment of bills (not least to the Estate's auditors), and a brief stall in charitable donations. It was a long list: Chelsea Conservative & Unionist Association, Chelsea Hospital for Women, Chelsea Health Society, Victoria Hospital for Children, the Surgical Aid Society, Property Protection Society and, in addition to St Luke's, there was support for St Simon's, St Saviour's and Christchurch. The 5th Earl's will left £10,000 apiece to the younger boys and half that to Lewin; Tiny's husband, Lord Lurgan, was released from outstanding debt.[17]

Britain had been at war since August 1914 and business as usual began to fade into memory. Duke of York Square was the headquarters of the London Irish Rifles. Many commercial buildings had been given over to war work – the Flood Street Studios, for example, were used by the Red Cross Society as a hospital (and privately, the grand old ladies of Chelsea

Jerry at home at Culford Hall with his son and eldest daughter, c.1920

opened their doors to provide auxiliary hospitals, including fourteen beds at Lady Mountgarret's house, 18 Cadogan Gardens, which was to become the Cadogan Estate's office for many years). Barely any new leaseholders came forward. In 1916 the Chelsea Club quit 147–53 Fulham Road, its home since 1838 – one of several long-standing tenants who surrendered a lease rather than renewing it. Others simply disappeared, such as the fishmonger at 132 King's Road, Mr Faulkner, who turned in his key and walked away. The trustees had to decide how best to secure the future of the Estate and prevent Chelsea becoming a ghost town. They agreed to reduced rents on a case-by-case basis, some held over until the end of the war and others slashed by fifty per cent. Not all requests were granted. Mr Hayford, a gentleman's outfitter at 202–205 Sloane Street, asked to pay only 37.5 per cent of the £200 rental value when his lease came up for renewal in 1917 (he had been paying £25 per annum since 1886). After examining the outfitter's books, trustee Charles Gordon-Lennox found this 'quite inadequate'.

After the war, lifestyle changes forced businesses to adapt or die. Mr Bax, a tailor at 101 Sloane Street, who had been five quarters behind with the rent in 1916, reported to the Estate in 1921 that 'the demand for liveries, formerly quite an important branch of this business, has practically ceased.' Gordon-Lennox declared that 'no pressure was to be applied for the arrears at present.' This strategy of retention paid off and by midsummer the following year only two tenants on the Estate were in arrears. An explosion in car-ownership can be traced in the number of garages and dealerships that opened, often in what had been stables. In 1921 Wolseley Motors leased land behind the Town Hall and an enterprising Mr Knowles took 164 King's Road in addition to the forecourts of 7–11 (odd) Jubilee Place.[18]

Department stores in Chelsea were a retail success story. Sloane Square stalwart Peter Jones was thriving: in 1918 owner John Lewis approached the Estate asking to buy the leasehold of numbers 4 to 20 (even) King's Road and premises behind Symons Street, in total roughly thirty units; the draper already occupied the shops fronting 23–26 Sloane Square. It was agreed that 'If there is to be any sale, it would seem to be much better that the whole of the island site is to be sold.' A lease on the 'island' bordered by Sloane Square, Symons Street, Cadogan Gardens and the King's Road was duly transferred for £60,000.[19] At the opposite end of Sloane Street, Estate records for 1920 show a price of £31,000 agreed for the sale of numbers 206–12 'on 21 March last' (1919) to Harvey Nichols, which was expanding the site it had occupied since 1831. Business in Chelsea, and the Cadogan Estate, began to recover.

Chelsea had long drawn an artistic and fashionable crowd; by the time of the 1921 census, the area had the highest concentration of (male) artists in London. In 1924, the trustees agreed to lease refurbished buildings to the Chenil Gallery, which had been on the King's Road since 1905.

> The trustees of the Cadogan Estate, realizing that such an institution must form the nucleus of an immense development of the district, both socially and commercially, have made some remarkable concessions which will enable a series of buildings

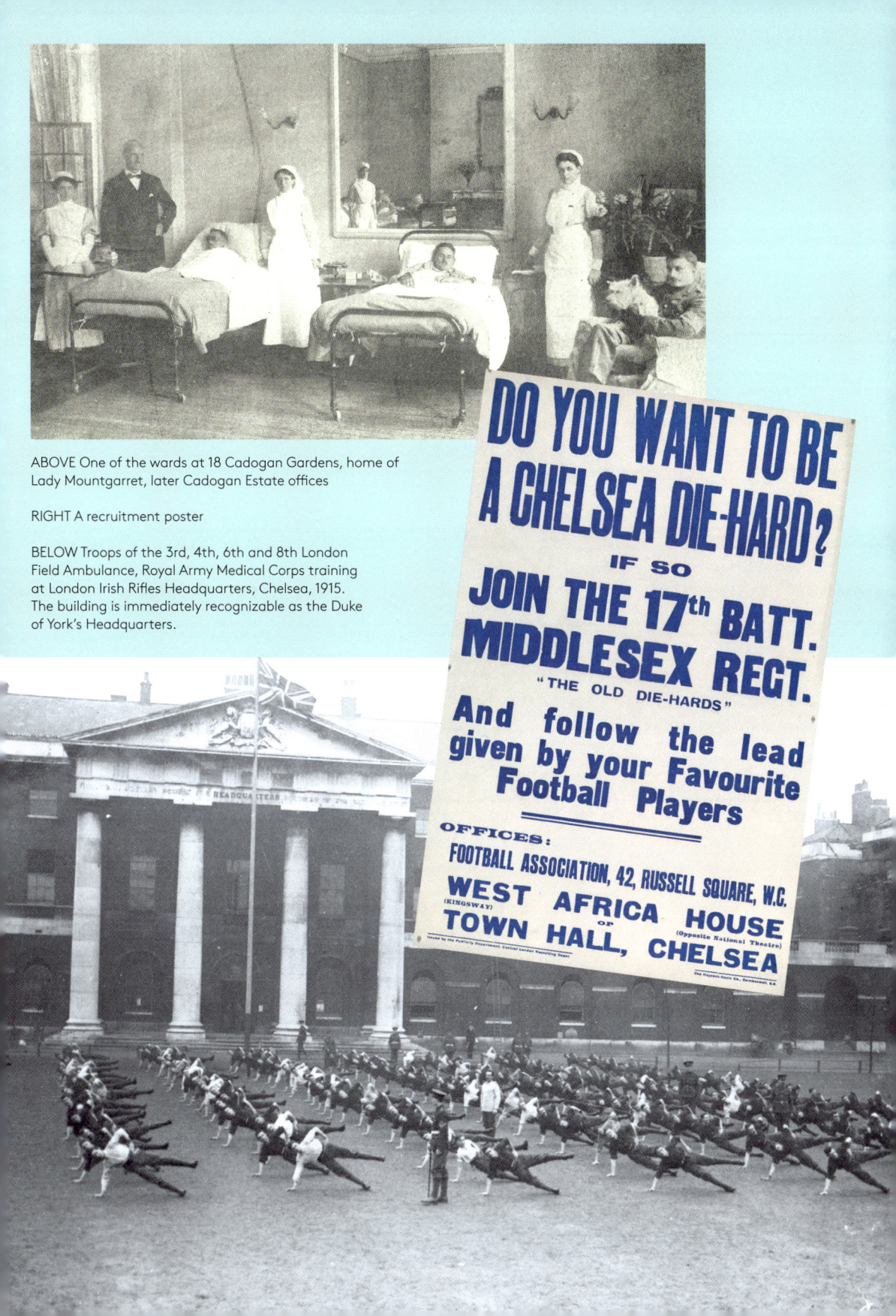

ABOVE One of the wards at 18 Cadogan Gardens, home of Lady Mountgarret, later Cadogan Estate offices

RIGHT A recruitment poster

BELOW Troops of the 3rd, 4th, 6th and 8th London Field Ambulance, Royal Army Medical Corps training at London Irish Rifles Headquarters, Chelsea, 1915. The building is immediately recognizable as the Duke of York's Headquarters.

DO YOU WANT TO BE A CHELSEA DIE-HARD?
IF SO
JOIN THE 17th BATT. MIDDLESEX REGT.
"THE OLD DIE-HARDS"
And follow the lead given by your Favourite Football Players

OFFICES:
FOOTBALL ASSOCIATION, 42, RUSSELL SQUARE, W.C.
WEST AFRICA HOUSE (KINGSWAY) or (Opposite National Theatre)
TOWN HALL, CHELSEA

Augustus John, RA, lays the foundation stone of the New Chenil Studios and Galleries, King's Road, Chelsea, 25 October 1924

>to be erected exceeding a total area of 13,000 sq feet.
>The terms on which the property is being leased will make it possible to the promoters of this well thought scheme to exhibit and to sell the works of young artists of London…[20]

The gallery reopened in 1925 with an exhibition of sculpture organized by the Chelsea Arts Club, based around the corner at 143 Old Church Street.

IN 1922, JERRY WAS OFFERED AN IMPORTANT ROLE in the sporting life of the nation at a time when health and fitness were becoming a matter of patriotic duty. In 1918 Prime Minister Lloyd George had lamented the million-or-so men rejected from military service as unfit. 'You cannot maintain an A 1 Empire with a C 3 nation.'[21] Voluntary organizations including the People's League of Health, the Sunlight League, and the New Health Society sprang up; the new Ministry of Health was founded in 1919. The British Olympic Association (BOA), founded following Great Britain's participation in the 1896 'Games of the I Olympiad' in Athens, was picking up speed.

> In November 1922 [BOA secretary Reginald] Kentish was the prime mover behind what he later described as a 'great meeting at the Army and Navy Club of men of commanding influence in sport and in society, which unanimously resolved to support the Olympic Gamers.' ... Shortly after the meeting, the post of Chairman was taken on by the sixth Earl of Cadogan [sic]...' ... As the 1924 *Official Report* noted, from the time of his appointment through to the Paris Games, Cadogan as Chairman tirelessly travelled the country meeting with NGBs and drumming up support for the Olympic cause; 'no man', the report claimed, 'could have thrown himself more heart and soul into his work.'[22]

The post of chairman was all-encompassing and very public – the position Lord Coe held during the London 2012 Olympics – Jerry was frontman and figurehead, a driving force. Picture Jerry in his fifties touring Britain garnering enthusiasm for and investment in sport, a passionate advocate for something he truly believed in. The 6th Earl had, at last, found his calling.

Controversy presented itself at the 1924 Olympics in Paris. The London newspapers seized upon sensationalist tales of animosity between the Americans and their hosts, the French. Jerry adamantly refuted these stories, aware that British participation at future Olympiads was threatened and continuing his hate–hate relationship with the newspapers: 'Cadogan went so far as to attack the "small", "misinformed" sections of the press that he claimed exaggerated every difficulty.... "there is no intention whatsoever" of withdrawing.'[23] Famously, the 1924 Games also brought a private moral dilemma into the public realm. Great Britain had two excellent sprinters in Harold Abrahams and Eric Liddell, both expected to run in the hundred-metre dash. However, heats were scheduled for a Sunday, the Christian Sabbath, and Liddell – a devout son of Scottish missionaries of the Wee

Free Church – refused to run. Jerry was intimately involved in behind-the-scenes discussions. His grandson Charles, 8th Earl Cadogan, told the story with immediacy: 'George V, who became unofficially involved, asked the 6th Earl to persuade Liddell personally. "Quite frankly, I don't hold out much hope," said Jerry, to which his sovereign retorted, "Tell him that the King and the nation want him to run!"'[24] The Oscar-winning film *Chariots of Fire* (1981) reimagines this scene to dramatic effect, at Jerry's expense: Patrick Magee portrays him as a villainous old duffer who snaps, 'In my day it was King first and God after!' (Jerry's son believed that his father would have understood Liddell's religious convictions and was reportedly angered by the film's inaccuracy.) A neat solution was found: Abrahams, of Polish and Welsh Jewish descent and thus free from such constraints, went on to win the race for Team GB in a time of 10.6 seconds. The pair both ran in the four hundred metres, scheduled for a weekday, which was won by Liddell – who broke Olympic and world records.

While Jerry's introduction to sports administration reveals his and its clubability – that invitation from Kentish was followed by initiation into the newly formed Athlon (Athletics London) Masonic Lodge (no. 4674), in 1925[25] – access to sports facilities was undergoing a process of democratization. Eddie was busy helping to found the National Playing Fields Association, and Jerry was equally on-message:

In February 1925 Cadogan led a wide-ranging discussion about future policy...Members agreed at the end of debate that the BOA's objectives, including the promotion of improved facilities 'in order that all classes may be encouraged to engage in sport for sport's sake' and efforts to 'educate public opinion about the importance of physical recreation in improving the nation's health and developing good citizenship.'[26]

It was not just talk, either. The official history of Chelsea Football Club records that during the 1920s, 'Club president Lord Cadogan regularly opened his estate at Culford Hall for their recreation.'[27]

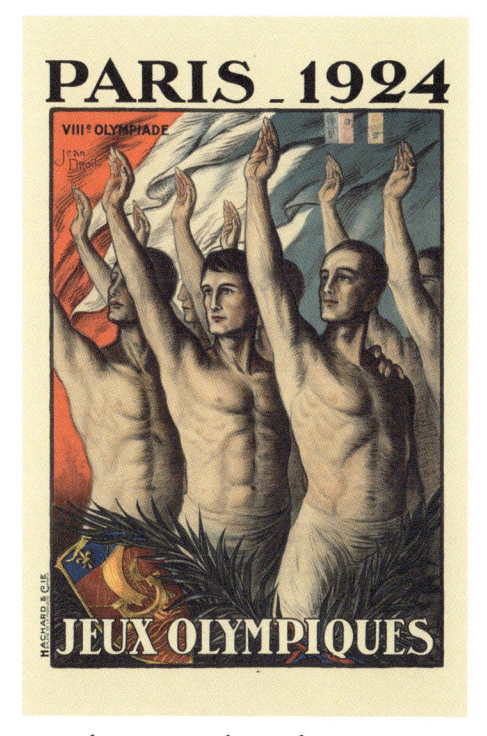

'The Pensioners' – a nickname referring to the veterans housed nearby at the Royal Hospital, long emblematic of the area – were a Second-Division team put together one evening in March 1905, in a room above the Rising Sun pub at 477 Fulham Road. For the first few seasons, players wore the horse-racing colours of the club's inaugural president, like jockeys; Weatherbys Ltd, central administrator of British horse racing, records that the pale blue has been registered to the Cadogan family since at least the 1890s. By the time Jerry became 6th Earl, the club had changed its colours to royal blue. However, the team has since renewed its visual links to the family, revisiting the paler shirts as a 'historic livery'[28] and referencing their renowned early Welsh ancestor in the club badge.

OPPOSITE *Liddel* [sic]: *Recordman du monde*, 2 July 1924, signed photograph kept by Jerry's son ABOVE Olympic Games poster, Jean Droit, 1924
ABOVE RIGHT Olympic gold winner's medal, André Rivaud, 1924, gilt silver

Elystan's lion rampant regardant appears in blue (holding a crozier) on the badge of Chelsea Football Club, since this featured (in gold) on the coat of arms of the old London Metropolitan Borough of Chelsea, alluding to the Cadogans' Lordship of the Manor of Chelsea. Thus, the lion of Elystan Glodrydd (in blue) has become one of the most famous, well recognized global brands in the 21st century![29]

With sad irony, Jerry's own ill health forced him to resign from the BOA in the autumn of 1926. (The timing also took him out of the spotlight shortly before details of his latest financial scrape were to emerge.) For four years he had played his part as a champion of a new ideal. In the aftermath of the Great War, the Olympics had acquired a special significance as a further indication by the participating nations of their intention never again to find themselves engaged in mutual destruction, but to work peacefully together: sport as metaphor. Indeed, to some, the Olympic Games took on an overtly pacifist meaning. At the end of the 1920s, diplomat Philip Noel-Baker wrote that the BOA had 'brought British opinion to bear upon the development of amateur sport throughout the world'.[30]

JERRY'S WIFE MARIE took up the family baton for wholesome outdoorsiness. She became a leading light in the Girl Guides Association, appointed County Commissioner of Suffolk. Foundation of the Guides is a story of sisters doing it for themselves. 'In 1909, a group of girls appeared at a Boy Scout Rally in the UK declaring themselves to be Girl Scouts. Lord Robert

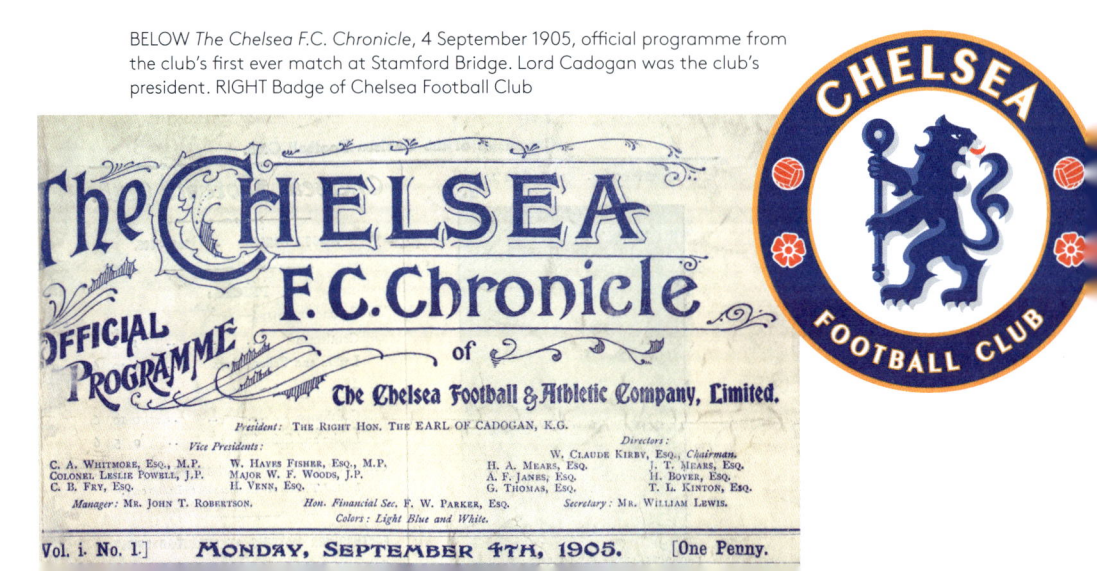

BELOW *The Chelsea F.C. Chronicle*, 4 September 1905, official programme from the club's first ever match at Stamford Bridge. Lord Cadogan was the club's president. RIGHT Badge of Chelsea Football Club

'Princess Mary on the Platform', July 1926. Countess Cadogan, County Commissioner of the Girl Guides, stands to the princess's left at the front of the stage.

Baden-Powell, the founder of Boy Scouts, decided that there should be a Movement for girls.'[31] Baden-Powell had been Jerry's commanding officer in the South African Constabulary during the Boer War, and a connection formed between the two families.

Modelled on military units, like their male counterparts, the Girl Guides wore uniforms, practised parades and drills, and swore allegiance to the Crown (then as now), along with adherence to various moral duties including honesty, sobriety and helpfulness. Physical health and strength were emphasized, but UK Guides Association founder (Baden-Powell's sister) Agnes outlined in *The Handbook for Girl Guides: Or How Girls Can Help Build the Empire* (1912) that:

> 'none of us like women who ape men'. At the same time, girls should also be 'Be Strong' and 'Handy' in preparation for their 'greatest duty in life', namely teaching their children to be 'good,

hardworking, honourable, and useful citizens for our great British Empire.'[32]

On 3 July 1926, Jerry and Marie played host to several thousand Guides who attended a rally and inspection by the association's president:

> Princess Mary yesterday afternoon visited Culford Park…where over 6,000 Girl Guides and Brownies from Suffolk, Norfolk, Essex and Cambridgeshire engaged in a march past. Her Royal Highness, who was a guest of the Earl and Countess Cadogan, was received by Lady Baden-Powell, the Chief Guide.[33]

It was front-page news in the local and national press.[34] It was a good show, but all was not well: Jerry's financial acumen had not improved. On 17 December 1926, an article in the *Daily Mail* reported:

> A meeting of the creditors of Earl Cadogan, against whom a receiving order was made on Tuesday, is to be held in London next Wednesday week…It was stated at Lord Cadogan's house at Grosvenor Street last night that he had gone to the United States, and at his country seat at Bury St. Edmunds that he left about a week ago on a sea trip.[35]

Had Jerry really done another bunk? He had a wife and young family to consider; he was an affectionate and loving father; plus his name appears on passenger lists of steamships criss-crossing the globe throughout his adulthood – his absence could have been unfortunate timing. Besides, Jerry was not the only one with money worries.

THE DIVERSE POPULATION OF CHELSEA was not immune from the stagnation of the UK economy. It was largely the upper classes who had been invited to the exuberant party that was the Roaring Twenties, of jazz music, motor cars, radio, television and 'talkies'. The poorest, still recovering from the war and long before the safety-net of state support, were the hardest hit – the trustees' minute books include long lists of Cadogan properties that required updating, making a dearth of affordable housing scarcer still. Addresses in College Place and the King's Road feature heavily, plus a smattering in Sloane Street and elsewhere. Cadogan Square, mostly flats, was to be kept as an area of private residences, following the wishes of the late 5th Earl. Rents began to rise slowly.

In July 1925 the Chelsea Housing Association was formed as a pressure group to lobby the local council to provide new, well-maintained housing for the poor in addition to clearing unsanitary slums. Their president was Lady Bertha Dawkins, lady-in-waiting to Queen Mary: the ladies of the chatterati were drawn to such causes. As the decade drew to a close, a second Labour government was elected. Britain was waking up to the major hangover of the Great Depression.

> In 1929 the Association again criticized the borough council for not taking advantage of state assistance under the Housing Acts to provide housing; not one of more than seven thousand people living in overcrowded conditions had been rehoused by the council, and their delay in building new houses had put pressure on tenants throughout the borough. At the same time 966 notices had been served on the Cadogan syndicate in connection with its property in the central area, and the Association felt there was a need for permanent reconstruction there and a private Act to deal with it.[36]

The trustees running the Cadogan Estate were under pressure. Financier, newspaper and shipping magnate Sir John Ellerman, a self-made millionaire, provided one solution. Throughout the 1920s the secretive Yorkshireman had set about acquiring property in London: part of the Covent Garden estate from the Duke of Bedford in 1920; twenty-one acres in Marylebone from Lord Howard de Walden in 1925. In 1929 he added a portion of Chelsea to his portfolio, purchasing fourteen acres of land owned by The Cadogan and Hans Place Estate (no. 3), though still in mortgage to the

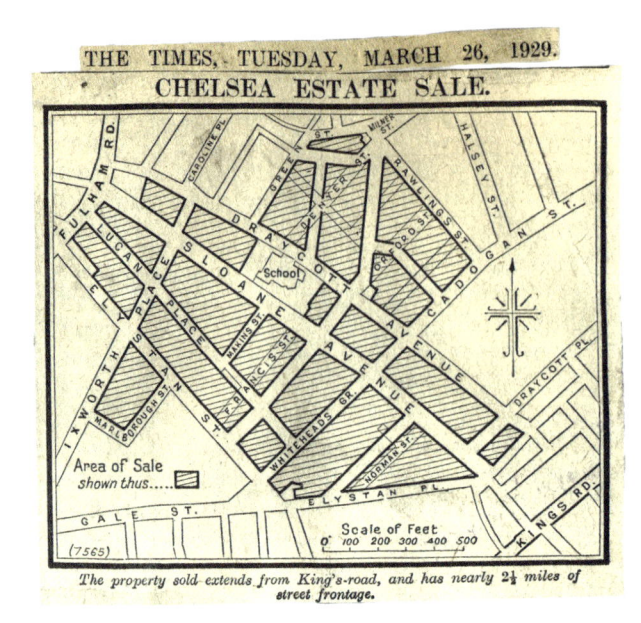

'Chelsea Estate Sale', *The Times*, 26 March 1929. A map shows approximately fourteen acres sold to Ellerman by the Cadogan and Hans Place Estate (no. 3).

Cadogan Trust. It was a dilapidated site comprising the greater part of old Chelsea Common. *The Times* declared it:

> The most important transaction in London real estate that has been announced for a long while....[T]he existing houses, which represent the earlier type of the development of portions of the district, will necessarily have to be cleared away...to-day the class of house mainly found on the property now sold does not conform to the demands of the modern householder. Of course, too, sites can be utilized to greater advantage for blocks of flats than for individual dwellings in such central situations as Chelsea.[37]

The area east of Draycott Avenue was a densely populated, working-class neighbourhood scheduled for clearance and demolition. Eviction notices were served to two hundred tenants and there were demonstrations by those who refused to move until they were rehomed. This caught the attention of the National Unemployed Workers' Union, which 'appointed Mr. Thomas Bradbury, organizer for the Fulham and Chelsea districts, to look after the interests of the tenants.'[38] It caused a sensation. On 22 September 1930, the *Evening News* reported:

> Hundreds of men armed with sticks and staves are guarding a group of streets in Chelsea today…They have called themselves the army of defence…'The landlords mean to clear the whole area. You could be next.'[39]

Many were ex-servicemen; they wore smart red ties, which gave the impression of a uniformed militia. The *Star* declared, 'A portion of Chelsea has been turned into an armed camp.'[40] Bradbury organized an alarm system of whistles, bells and clappers that would sound to alert the mob to the presence of bailiffs; and he could call for reinforcements using telephones and dispatch riders. The newly formed Chelsea Tenants' Defence League reckoned on evictions affecting nearly a thousand residents. Women served tea, buns and cigarettes to the pickets; they lined windowsills with broken glass. An attempt was made to calm the situation:

> An official said: 'People are not being pitched into the street right and left. Some five families have had to go so far. They were not put out by us but by the order of the County Court judge. Every family was shown the utmost consideration so far as we were concerned. Some of the folks have been in the houses for months and months without paying any rent…I am not aware that luxury flats are going to be built on the site of this tumble-down property. A mountain has been made out of almost nothing at all.'[41]

The following day, the *Daily Express* dubbed it 'The Chelsea Eviction War' and printed a quote that showed Cadogan was still involved, though the paper erroneously ascribed ownership of land that was under new management:

'Chelsea Evictions', *Daily Express*, 18 September 1930

> An official of the Cadogan Trust, which owns the property, declared last night that there was no wish or desire on the part of the owners to cause hardship. 'Every effort is being made to find suitable accommodation for these people,' he said. 'No evictions are contemplated, so far as I know, either this week, next week, or next month, in fact.'[42]

Sadly, the worst fears of a handful of families were realized as they found themselves in the workhouse: events that cast a long shadow at the Cadogan Estate, which clearly felt a moral responsibility. Ellerman constructed a few 'superior town houses', but the majority of new buildings he put up were indeed blocks of flats.[43]

The trustees ploughed on with improvements, embarking on a major redevelopment of Chelsea Square (as the area's early nineteenth-century Trafalgar Square was renamed), and its central garden of 2.5 acres, which had been sublet to a lawn tennis club. Demolition of existing buildings that could not be altered to suit modern needs began in 1932. Architects Darcy Braddell and Humphry Deane designed red-brick, three-storey houses with garages, with a mews to the north of the square and more substantial houses on the south; neo-Regency villas in white stucco at numbers 40 and 41, completed in 1930 and 1934, were designed by Oliver Hill.[44] There were rumblings in Chelsea's artistic community. The *Evening News* reported on 4 June 1931, 'Chelsea will soon be no place for artists. It is getting horribly up to date. It is being fitted with every modern convenience. Wherever you go in the search for flats or studios you will find a bathroom.'[45] The proposed building of a second Fulham power station had them up in arms decrying the effect of noxious fumes on their colours and the quality of light. The Royal Court Theatre on Sloane Square was struggling and in 1932 wrote to the trustees with a proposal to surrender their lease; their mortgagees wanted to erect shops and flats. 'The applicants state...it would appear that Sloane Square is no longer considered a suitable position for a theatre.'[46] A temporary alternative was found in the building's use as a cinema.[47]

Warning signs of renewed difficulty had begun to show up in commercial leases, which now plunged into freefall. Behind the Town Hall, Wolseley Motors had gone into liquidation in 1926. Rent appeals started up again. In 1932 a list of casualties included Miss Marjorie Matthews, scholastic agent, going bust in the basement of 130 Sloane Street; on the King's Road the Patent Steam Building Co. closed number 179; Messrs Harding & Sons, bootmakers at 185, and Messrs Cohen & Sons, antique furniture dealers at 187–89, left three adjacent properties empty. Chelsea Conservative Club, which had taken on a lease only the year before, quit 191–93 King's Road.[48] The 1930s would be rough. Into this already charged atmosphere came news that would shake the Estate and the family once again.

GERALD, 6TH EARL CADOGAN, died on 4 October 1933. He was sixty-four; his widow Marie would live into her mid-eighties (she married their Suffolk neighbour Lieutenant-Colonel Harold Hambro in 1941). Their eldest, Beatrix, was married to Henry Hoare, a scion of the banking family, with an infant son, also Henry (b.1931). Alexandra was a young girl entering her teens. William, always known as Bill, was nineteen and had just left Eton. But first, to Alec.

CHAPTER 19

Riding the Whirlwind

—

SIR ALEXANDER
CADOGAN (1884–1968)

Of all the 5th Earl's children, it was the youngest, Alexander ('Alec'), who most obviously inherited both his intellectual capabilities and sense of *noblesse oblige*. While Eddie championed the nation's youth, Alec was at the coalface of international relations, war and peace at stake. His ability to digest huge volumes of information – 'I saw copies of the telegrams, which I read hurriedly (I read hundreds a day)'[1] – within sheaves of government papers, and form a considered opinion, saw him rise to become a trusted advisor at the Foreign Office and later at the United Nations. Alec was also an unlikely practical joker and caricaturist, the archetypal baby of the bunch, though these instincts were later visible only as flashes – a waggish Pop waistcoat – under a stylishly sober exterior: 'his infrequent remarks are like sips of an iced vintage champagne – so cool and dry that you can hardly taste them unless you are a connoisseur.'[2]

Alec enjoyed a charmed youth at Chelsea House and Culford. He wrote home from the short-lived Mortimer's vicarage prep school in Berkshire, at the age of nine: 'Eddie and I have made our room look very nice. I like being here much better than being in London. I like some of the boys very much.'[3] Haggy wrote to him with the sports news; Sophie had him to stay on the yacht during leave. Alec was a popular boy, whose dry humour was already emerging. An Eton contemporary 'later recalled the pleasure with which the back row [of the class] awaited the next cartoon or caricature

Alec, Willie, Sophie and Eddie (left to right), in the garden at Culford, 1893

to be handed down from Cadogan further in front.'[4] Returning after short leave during Michaelmas half 1901, Alec wrote home:

> Dear Father
> Thank you so much for your letter. I think you will be glad to hear that I have got into 'Pop'! I am the first case of a person getting in without colours that there has been for some time, which I hope makes it all the more satisfactory...I am so glad to hear you caught another fish the day I left you; mine made very good eating...
> Goodbye for the present
> From your loving son, Alec[5]

Membership, then as now, was an indicator of social success. George Henry, a rather serious man, had expressed some concerns to the boys' housemaster. The response gives an insight into Alec's developing persona:

> Dear Lord Cadogan
> I write to thank you for your letters. I am interested to learn that

> Alec's tastes incline towards diplomacy or to the Bar. I think he has qualifications for it but unless his present attitude towards work alters considerably, I do not think he would do much at the Bar, which is predominantly a laborious profession...He is often grave, but I don't think that this necessarily means that he is out of spirits...
> Very sincerely yours,
> Arthur Benson[6]

He crowned his school career as president of the Eton Society, editor of the *Eton College Chronicle* and captain of the Oppidans. A place at Oxford duly secured – 'his brother [Eddie] is such a nice fellow that we should be very glad to have another chick out of the same nest', wrote his tutor to Benson[7] – life at Balliol continued in much the same vein. A leading light of the Annandale Society, he had a penchant for sending a waterfall of crockery cascading down staircases; his cricket team, the Erratics, travelled to friendlies against local villages by brake (an enormous horse-drawn carriage).

Alec had a natural authority and wit. Sir Lawrence Jones, 5th Bt, his contemporary at both Eton and Balliol, described him in retrospect 'with hair beautifully brushed, and the air even then of a Permanent Under-Secretary for Foreign Affairs'.[8] We've all met a twenty-year-old like that; Alec, who later added a cigarette holder, was a particularly elegant example at a slim five-foot-ten. He graduated from Balliol in 1906 with a second-class degree in history, and set the Diplomatic Service firmly in his sights. After two years of study, he was rewarded with top marks in the competitive examinations of October 1908.

ALEC'S FIRST POSTING was as an attaché to the embassy at Constantinople (Istanbul), in January 1909. Eighteen months later he was awarded an allowance for knowledge of Turkish and was promoted to Third Secretary. Still in his mid-twenties, he had not yet shaken off his undergraduate sense of humour. Fellow Balliol man Harold Nicolson, already chastely courting Vita Sackville-West, joined Alec at the embassy in January 1912, recounting in his semi-fictionalised comic memoir *Some People* (1927):

19. RIDING THE WHIRLWIND

...most of our spare time was to be spent in planning escapades for [the head of chancery's] entertainment. Gerald Tyrwhitt had started the pastime, and in the hands of Alec Cadogan it had been pushed to a fine art.[9]

Nicolson describes a practical joke in which official red despatch boxes were primed with sprung cardboard folders, bent back on themselves, which on unlocking would 'leap gaily three or four feet into the air':

> The effect was increased if one inserted on the top little boxes of nibs, or paper-clips, or, best of all, a tin of tooth-powder. We would in the early morning prepare one or two of these destructive engines, and attach a label marked 'Chancery: urgent.'[10]

The full joy lay not in the suspense – would the box explode or not? – but in their boss's attempts to disguise his increasingly ginger approach. Eventually, his reluctance to deal with official boxes meant the game was discontinued in the interests of public service. It was replaced by others, until a colleague suggested they had gone too far. 'Cadogan and I were disconcerted by this accusation of bullying, and from that moment Titty was no longer teased. He was acutely pained by this neglect.'[11]

Alec's second posting, in April 1913, was to Vienna: historic jewel of the Austro-Hungarian Empire, at the centre of Europe both geographically and diplomatically, and a hub of spies. Indeed, in the 1930s, Thomas Kendrick, head of the British Passport Office (read MI6 – 'virtually the same organization at the time'[12]), would run a network from the city that

ABOVE Constantinople, 1912: Alec (far left), Gerald Tyrwhitt and their victim 'Titty' (third and second left, respectively)

included Kim Philby. It is improbable that such a posting, for a man of Alec's intelligence, would not have included some small role within an earlier network. By June 1914, he had learned enough (and matured enough) to have been placed temporarily in charge of the embassy when the telegram came through from the consul at Sarajevo reporting the murder of the heir presumptive, Archduke Franz Ferdinand. Alec was recalled from enemy territory: the time for games was over. World War I seems to have removed any outward sign of Alec's early bounce. The sharp shock of Willie's death at Ypres foreshadowed the loss of huge numbers of his school and college cohort. His dedication to work became more pronounced; Alec's star was rising at the Foreign Office, where he was regarded as first among equals.

THERE WAS A BRIGHT SPOT on the home front: on Saturday, 3 August 1912, Alec had married Lady Theodosia Louisa Augusta Acheson ('Theo', 1882–1977), and they were extremely happy. The youngest daughter of the 4th Earl of Gosford (Gosford Castle in County Antrim, Ireland, not the fictitious Gosford Park of the eponymous 2001 film) had the blue blood of the Tudors running through her veins. A direct descendant of King Henry VII (through her maternal grandfather, the 7th Duke of Manchester), and thus to Owen Tudor, Theo also shared a common Welsh ancestry with the Cadogans. She was a strong character, who took the lead in family matters, though she never meddled in politics. Finding happiness with Alec at the age of thirty, Theo wrote to Eddie:

> I loved all you said about Alec. I am most awfully happy in a way that I did not think possible in this contrary world; at present Alec seems to do everything for me, but I do hope that I shall always be able to make him happy too.[13]

The wedding took place at noon at St George's Hanover Square; Alec's boss, the British ambassador at Constantinople, signed the register. The reception was given at Derby House (Theo's older sister had married the earl's youngest brother; Alec's niece Portia – one of his bridesmaids – later married his eldest

The Acheson Sisters, John Singer Sargent, 1902, oil on canvas. Lady Theodosia is shown at right. The portrait hangs at Chatsworth, home of the Dukes of Devonshire (Theo's step-grandmother, the duchess, often chaperoned her).

son); and the king and queen, and ageing Queen Alexandra, were among those who presented gifts of fabulous jewels. So far so Cadogan. The first of their four children, Ambrose (1914–2003), was born in the spring before they left Vienna, and 'roared like a tiger'.[14] Three girls followed: Patricia ('Trish', 1916–1995), Cynthia (1918–2009) and Gillian (1922–1998).

ALEC SERVED AT THE VERSAILLES PEACE CONFERENCE (alongside his old colleague Nicolson), before in 1923 being selected to head up the League of Nations section at the Foreign Office. His job was to analyse any documents that might come before the league, assessing what reactions these might provoke, before providing a brief to ministers. It brought him the first of several close friendships with successive Prime Ministers:

> All this meant frequent and prolonged absences from home, for it was the high noontide of the League's authority and Sir Austen Chamberlain and his successors…attended frequently at Geneva. Cadogan made himself indispensable to them. He knew the business thoroughly, proffered advice with modesty and brevity and was often consulted by other delegations, and by the permanent Secretariat, who trusted him completely.[15]

LEFT Alec (circled) stands two rows behind Lord Parmoor (head of the British delegation) and Ramsay MacDonald (twice Prime Minister)

BELOW The huge number of delegates. League of Nations, Geneva, F. Jullien, September 1924

Alec (circled) watches as Prime Minister Stanely Baldwin ratifies the Locarno Pact (1925) in the Foreign Office's grandest reception rooms, still known today as the Locarno Suite. Around the table are the Marquess di Medici and Briand, Austen Chamberlain and Lord Peel.

Chamberlain's belief in 'tea party diplomacy' – meeting in small groups to negotiate, often in relaxed hotel surroundings – matched Alec's shrewd preference for the immediacy of face-to-face discussion over the exchange of official memoranda 'of which the first draft has probably been prepared by a subordinate anxious to score a point.'[16] The Locarno Pact (1925) agreed peace in Europe, and the following year Alec was appointed Companion in the Most Distinguished Order of Saint Michael and Saint George. Their optimistic motto, '*auspicium melioris aevi*' (augury of a better age), was fitting both to the man and the times.

At the World Disarmament Conference (1932), he was Secretary-General to the British delegation. Major-General A.C. Temperley, who headed up the British War Office team, provides perhaps the most complete description of professional Alec:

> Riding the whirlwind, magnificently capable and imperturbable, was Mr Alexander Cadogan…He knew everything, was never in a hurry, never ruffled however irritating the caller might be, and he possessed an uncanny judgment of the right course to adopt in a given situation. He did not usually offer advice, but the man who consulted him and rejected it was taking a serious responsibility…[17]

Alec worked closely with dashing Under-Secretary for Foreign Affairs Anthony Eden on the 'MacDonald Plan' that followed in March 1933. MacDonald told the Commons that 'the figures were produced by two or three of the most admirable servants that a Government has ever had looking after its interests in an international Conference.'[18] The plan's reception, against the background of the Great Depression, was mixed: Winston Churchill in particular voiced concern that the plan would focus minds back on the mechanics of war, when economics should be their most pressing concern. The two were of course entirely intertwined: in Germany, where one in three working-age adults was unemployed, Hitler had been elected Chancellor that January. The Geneva Conference stalled; Alec confessed in his diary to a 'dull day…how sick I am of this job.'[19] He was glad to accept a post as Minister to the Legation in Peking (Beijing).

Alec, Theo and the girls sailed in early 1934. Looking back in her nineties, Theo remembered this posting as a 'particularly happy time' during which Alec created 'the first herbaceous border in China', and she was presented beautiful silks by the wife of Chiang Kai-shek.[20] Alec's job was to offer muted British support against the aggression of the Japanese Empire, while attempting to retain good relations with the latter. It was a highwire act, as he wrote to Eden, 'It is rather like the situation in Europe in the decade before the [1914–18] War…Everyone knew that it *must* come: no one could tell *when*…it will be Japan who will pull the trigger.'[21] He had been

ABOVE Alec and his daughter Cynthia with Nationalist Chinese leader Chiang Kai-shek and his wife, photographed by Theo, Peking, 1936 OPPOSITE French Foreign Minister Aristide Briande at the Lugano Peace Conference, Alexander Cadogan, 1928, pencil on paper. Alec's sketches and caricatures provided light relief during rounds of peace conferences.

subtly schooled at his father's side – almost by osmosis – to take the long view, one of continuity and custodianship; his sober intelligence made him perfectly suited to the job of preserving Great Britain's long-term interests. He was promoted to Ambassador. Then, in 1936, Eden (now Foreign Secretary) recalled him to London to take up the position of Senior Deputy Under-Secretary at the FO, a position far more powerful than its mealy-mouthed title suggests. Alec's astuteness became apparent once more when the Second Sino-Japanese War erupted the following year.

In the lead-up to World War II, Alec's instinct for restraint and belief in the power of open diplomacy was balanced by his pragmatism: peace, but not at all costs. Again, he called it early, 27 April 1937: 'If everyone in Germany is mad, and if all are bent on our destruction, disaster *must* come... If our rearmament is backward, we must have time. We must *do* something.' Alec was promoted to Permanent Under-Secretary for Foreign Affairs on 1 January 1938, serving as chief civil servant to Viscount Halifax, then Foreign Secretary. Neville Chamberlain was Prime Minister, leading with a policy of appeasement. Alec would play a significant role in Britain's change of tack.

An MI5 mole at the Germany Embassy discovered secret meetings between Fritz Hesse, head of the Dienststelle Ribbentrop, and Chamberlain's press relations officer, George Steward – an attempt to bypass official channels. In August 2011, the National Archives opened a secret file – discovered in a safe at the Permanent Under-Secretary's office in 1985 – marked 'Negotiations with Hess[e] 1938' that includes Alec's thoughts on the affair. *The International History Review* summarized its importance:

> Sir Vernon Kell, the Head of MI5, called Cadogan at the Foreign Office on 28 November to let the Permanent Undersecretary know of Steward's activity...Cadogan agonized about whether or not to tell Viscount Halifax...afraid that Halifax was 'getting rather fed up' and the incident might lead him to resign. He typed up a memorandum himself as a means to weigh up the pros and cons of telling Halifax and made no copies. The document laid undiscovered for forty-seven years...Cadogan's soul-searching memorandum foretold the increasing disillusionment with Chamberlain's policy within Britain's foreign-policy-making elite, the search in the Foreign Office and the Cabinet to find better alternatives, and Halifax's increasingly important role, influenced by advice from Cadogan and Foreign Office officials, in leading foreign policy debates in the Cabinet in 1939.[22]

Alec's deciders were 'the patent fact that Tiger-riding at this particular moment is appallingly dangerous'; and secondly, '"*suppressio veri*" is a dangerous thing to do.' Number one: he believed Chamberlain was on the wrong course; number two, he must not suppress the truth. Remarking on his predecessor, Lord Ricketts (Permanent Secretary to the FCO 2006–10), writes: 'He gave Halifax "a piece of my mind". This evidently shook Halifax who, after a sleepless night, turned against Chamberlain's approach and began to work for a harder-edged strategy. Cadogan had achieved what Vansittart never could: real influence on policy.'[23]

Alec was rewarded in the January 1939 New Year's Honours, commenting to his diary with typically crisp humour:

GCMG announced this morning, so am beginning to get flood of telegrams and letters, which adds to one's work…Eddie has got KBE – a tardy recognition of his devoted work – and Edith Hillingdon [their Square niece] is a Dame! So the family have done well, and when they retire they can set up a co-operative ironmongery store.[24]

Alec was the embodiment of the self-possessed, unflappable mandarin, and indeed its apogee, as head of the Foreign Office. Eden, reinstalled as Foreign Secretary at the end of 1940, later reminisced, 'As Permanent Under-Secretary and therefore my principal official advisor Cadogan was at all times wise and thorough.'[25]

His habit of keeping a diary crystallized in the 1930s to become a daily after-dinner ritual; just like his father. Unlike George Henry's, Alec's entries are amusingly frank, peppered with exclamation marks and comedic shorthand for titans of the world stage: Gousev, the Russian Ambassador to London 1943–46, is 'Frogface'; Sir Hughe Knatchbull-Hugesson, Ambassador to Turkey, 'Snatch;' Osmund Cleverly, Principal Private Secretary to Chamberlain, 'Nit-Wit-in-Chief'. The pages also include commentary on the flowers blooming in London's parks (including Buckingham Palace Gardens, after Lord Halifax was given a key), and trips to the National Gallery (thumbs up for Rembrandt, down for Jacob Epstein). Seemingly, he always imagined a wider readership, acknowledging early on, 'I can't remember all of the details…And perhaps that may make this Diary more readable.'[26] In 1971 a selection

Alec and Halifax take a walking meeting in St James's Park, 9 September 1938

from the war years, edited by historian David Dilks, was published by Faber, together with letters to Theo – which read almost as a continuation – in a volume running to nearly nine hundred pages.

WORLD LEADERS FOUND ALEC was invariably in the room at inter-Allied conferences, the trusted advisor at the shoulder of the great man, and he travelled frequently and widely. In Rome, in January 1939, the delegation was received in some style, put up in the beautiful Villa Madama, designed by Raphael; talks were held at the Palazzo Venezia, where Mussolini had set up his office and from where he had given his speech declaring the Italian Empire in 1936. Alec, having grown up at Cadogan House and Culford Hall, took the grandeur of both company and setting in his stride: 'Banquet at Palazzo Venezia at 9…Musso[lini] and Ciano took us round the museum later.'[27]

In London, he moved between the Palace and Downing Street within the hour. Six days after the declaration of war:

> 9 September 1939. 6 [pm] Buck House to see the King. Called in about 6.10 and stayed till 6.50. He rather depressed – and a little *défaitiste* – result, I think, of a talk with Joe K[ennedy, US Ambassador to the UK] who sees everything from the angle of his own investments. Back to No. 10 at 7 to see H.J.W. [Horace Wilson, head of the civil service] who showed me Press announcement of a '3-year war'. Asked how I thought that would go down.[28]

He was an important conduit in matters of national security. At a lunch party on 10 July 1940, he noted that King George VI was 'amused at C's report of the quisling activities of [his] brother.'[29] C was the head of MI6; the brother was the exiled Duke of Windsor, whose friendships and outspokenness looked increasingly dangerous, first as the source of leaks and, after the fall of France, as a potential rival. Alec had been briefed three days prior on an intelligence report out of Prague: 'Germans expect assistance from Duke and Duchess of Windsor, the latter desiring at any price to become Queen.'³⁰ Following the couple's successful removal to The Bahamas, Alec's royal chats returned to familiar ground: 'Talk with the King about de Gaulle – who didn't impress him much – and partridges, which appear to be good.'³¹ In the next round of honours, he was promoted Knight Commander of the Bath (KCB).

Alec is perhaps most widely remembered as a fearless wartime advisor to Winston Churchill, who invited him to Cabinet meetings early on in his premiership. In August 1941, he accompanied Churchill aboard HMS *Prince of Wales* to meet Roosevelt, drafting the Atlantic Charter, the founding document of the post-war rules-based order, while off the coast of Newfoundland. Arriving in Cairo, on Monday, 3 August 1942: 'PM lay on his bed in his underwear and held forth to us. He seemed none the worse for the journey.' They flew on to Moscow to draft a joint communiqué with Stalin. Following a nineteen-course Kremlin banquet, at which Stalin and Molotov led a round of interminable toasts in praise of Russia's war efforts, Churchill went off the deep end back at the dacha. It was Alec who persuaded him that they must stay:

'I had never', records [Churchill's doctor, Charles] Wilson, an eye-witness, 'seen anyone talk to the P.M. like this.' At last Churchill said: 'Well, you have been in the Foreign Office all this time. Do as you think. But I want it recorded that I thought it would be disastrous.'

Draft of the Atlantic Charter, August 1941, worked up by Alec onboard HMS *Prince of Wales*, with Churchill's handwritten comments. It inspired the United Nations Charter signed by fifty countries at San Francisco on 26 June 1945.

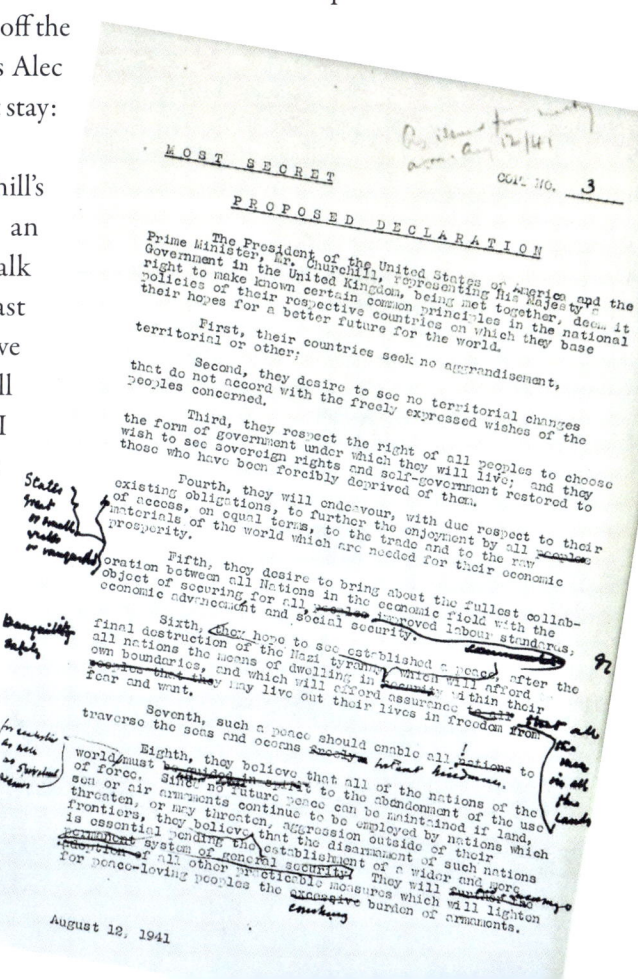

Yalta Conference, February 1945. Seated: Churchill, Roosevelt, Stalin. Standing behind them (left to right): British Foreign Secretary Anthony Eden MP, US Secretary of State Edward Stettinius, British Permanent Under-Secretary of State for Foreign Affairs Alexander Cadogan, Soviet Commissar for Foreign Affairs Vyacheslav Molotov, and American Ambassador in Moscow Averell Harriman.

Authorised again to take his own line, Cadogan said he could not do that if the prime minister thought it would be disastrous. There was a silence. Churchill rose to go to bed. Cadogan got up, said 'Good night,' and left for his hotel. It was now 3 a.m. By 10.30 the next morning, when Cadogan returned to the dacha, Churchill had repented.[32]

In Washington DC in August 1944, Alec chaired the British delegation in talks at the Dumbarton Oaks Conference. He was also at Yalta and Potsdam, the following year, at Churchill's side through negotiations with Stalin and Roosevelt – the Big Three – that would establish the terms of peace and establishment of democracy in European occupied territories following Germany's surrender. Just like his ancestor William, the first 1st Earl, Alec was a straight-talking right-hand man to a great wartime leader: a Cadogan and a Churchill once again serving the nation side-by-side.

OPPOSITE Dumbarton Oaks, 1944: Virginia picnic

OF HIS FAULTS, ALEC was not a great delegator. This left him with a huge workload: he was chief administrator of a large civil service department, the least enjoyable part of his role. 'He abhorred long-winded official reports and once, as Permanent Under-Secretary, threatened to take stenographers away from diplomats unless they turned in shorter notes.'[33] Office hours and contingency arrangements also came under Alec's remit. Churchill's new War Rooms gave the PM a placc of safety from which to operate. Monday, 9 September 1940: 'Went over to basement with H., Grey and Jones. Sent round circular saying people must try to get home by Black-out.'[34]

At the start of the Blitz, Alec recorded the number of planes out and back, and British successes relative to German. He describes the bombing of Buckingham Palace and of the Foreign Office itself. On 19 September, Theo's widowed mother, Lady Gosford, was forced to leave her London flat in Portman Square when it was bombed. As was quite natural for a dowager countess, she moved into Claridge's. A month later, Theo took the decision to evacuate the family from 18 Sloane Gardens to the Carlton Hotel, which stood on Haymarket. Alec was not pleased.

> 21 October 1940. In present circs. of our squalid existence in a hotel, I can't keep up this diary. I don't remember what happened this day. There was a Cabinet at No. 10 at 5 – PM away and nothing v. interesting. We dined with the H's [Halifaxes] at the Dorchester to meet Philip Lothian [British Ambassador to the US]…We dined on the 6th Floor, to an accompaniment of 4.5"

guns, which knock the glasses off the table, tear your eyebrows out and snap your braces. Poor Dorothy evidently completely rattled, but H's deafness, I suppose, stands him in good stead.[35]

This vignette is an aristocratic embodiment of oft-cited 'Blitz spirit'; they dined through stiff upper lips. Ten days later, Alec moved the family to a suite on the second floor, 'which might make life seemingly human again'. A window was blown out on 13 November; by 23 November the family had transferred to Lansdowne House. 'Rooms are cheap and seem very nice. There must be a snag somewhere – service I suspect and, obviously, a band at dinner.' (Dinner, he later noted, was indeed 'Barbarous.') Alec was, perhaps, something of a snob – forgivably, given his upbringing. *The Times* reported closure of the Carlton's residential section for good later that month, after 160 rooms were damaged;[36] the Savoy had also been badly hit. In December it was the turn of the BBC and House of Commons. Chelsea was also taking a pasting, and the Cadogan Estate's managers found themselves walking around bomb damage daily. Alec still had to dress for the office: 'Bought some shirts (my laundry having been bombed!).'[37]

Thankfully, for Alec, there was a country bolthole. In July 1939 the family had bought High Corner – renamed Thatched Cottage, in Northiam, Sussex.[38] There, Alec dug the kitchen garden, tended the chickens, and temporarily avoided the mountains of paperwork that inevitably began to follow him. In May 1944 he once again took up sketching. Even while travelling on missions of international import, his spirits were lifted by beauty. While in Washington DC attending Churchill in his September 1943 meetings with President Eisenhower, he wrote to Theo about the 'Mellon gallery' (National Gallery):

> I can't begin to describe it: it's one of the most lovely buildings I have ever seen. Seldom more than half a dozen pictures in any one room, hung to the best effect on the most beautiful panelling – unbelievable Rembrandts, Van Dycks, Italian primitives, Goyas, el Grecos...[39]

'Members of the Security Council: Sir Alexander Cadogan', cutting from personal papers now held at the Churchill Archives Centre, marked New York 1948

Alec found himself back in the US after the war, appointed Permanent Representative to the United Nations in 1946: the 'wider and permanent system of international security' proposed in the Atlantic Charter. He and Theo arrived in New York on 18 March, on the SS *Queen Mary*, packed with diplomatic officials (they would crisscross the Atlantic several times). Eddie, the last surviving sibling, came out to visit. After four years, approaching seventy, Alec retired from the Foreign Office, in June 1950. They settled in London at no. 2 Westminster Gardens, Marsham Street: 'After years of travelling it is where we finally made our home. So I want to stay here until the end of my days,'[40] Theo later said.

On 1 January 1951, in the penultimate set of New Year's Honours awarded by King George VI, Alec became the first civil servant to be given the Order of Merit (OM), the highest of the merit orders, given at the sovereign's sole discretion. He had already been admitted to the Privy Council; his old Oxford College, Balliol, had elected him a fellow. Alec, however, was not a man to rest on his laurels.

IN 1952 ALEC WAS APPOINTED CHAIRMAN of the board of governors of the BBC by his old friend Winston Churchill. Perhaps the idea had been germinating for a while – a decade earlier, he had noted (Monday, 17 March 1941): 'PM storming about idiocies of BBC – which *are* idiocies. The place *must* be properly controlled.' He was referring to radio; wartime restrictions had placed the single television transmission station at Alexandra Palace (broadcasting to only twenty thousand television sets in 1939) into blackout.[41] For five years during the 1950s, Alec presided over a media overhaul that would establish a new normal:

> The Coronation of Queen Elizabeth II, broadcast live on 2 June 1953, was the event that did more than any other to make television a mainstream medium. More than 20 million people watched the service on television, outnumbering the radio audience for the first time. The BBC knew the event would be popular…but could not foresee that it would mark the coming of age of television, as well as the modernisation of the monarchy.[42]

Such a watershed moment had been calmly orchestrated behind the scenes: Alec had welcomed the young queen and prince consort on an official visit to Broadcasting House three months earlier. (He and Theo were commanded to attend the event itself in person.) Relationships established during his diplomatic years continued, albeit from a different angle. His longstanding friendship with Eden, now Prime Minister, and perceived support for military action in Egypt during the Suez Canal Crisis of 1956 led to hot water over the corporation's impartiality.[43] His loyalty, however, was always to his country first, over policy or politician. When anti-communist MP Sir Waldron Smithers paid him a visit in 1954, he dismissed the man's

Queen Elizabeth II during the coronation ceremony at Westminster Abbey, John Cura, 2 June 1953, tele-snap (photograph taken directly from a television screen). The groundbreaking broadcast was made during Alec's chairmanship of the BBC's board of governors.

dark, McCarthyist mutterings about infiltration and traitors at the BBC on a lack of evidence and – intriguingly, once more – 'I assured him that we worked closely with MI5.'[44]

Alec spent his final decade indulging in his hobbies: oil-painting, gardening and golf. 'Mr Cadogan gained a reputation for keeping his temper, except on the golf course, where he shot in the low 80s.'[45] He died at eighty-three, on 9 July 1968, at home in Westminster Gardens. Among the obituaries published worldwide were numerous wry anecdotes, including this gem:

> Companions described his transatlantic airline flight when the door next to his seat blew off. Immaculate in striped trousers, black coat, furled umbrella between his knees, Cadogan turned up his collar and said softly: 'Drafty in here.'[46]

The ultimate insider, discreet and omnipresent, Alec was 'the very model of a British diplomat – imperturbable, immaculate, inscrutable'.[47] Theo survived him by a decade in the large flat hung with his paintings, where she died on 16 October 1977. They are buried in St Mary's churchyard, Culford. Alec had been one of the architects of the post-war international order; the peace he had envisioned and then managed was fought for by his young nephew Bill, under whose auspices Chelsea would be changed forever.

CHAPTER 20

Military Man & Modernizer

—

WILLIAM, 7TH EARL (1914–1997)

The Rt. Hon. Lt.-Col. William Gerald Charles Cadogan, 7th Earl Cadogan, 9th Baron Cadogan of Oakley and 5th Baron Oakley of Caversham, MC, DL ('Bill'), is a figure of such recent history that his name can bring a smile not just to family members, but to longstanding residents of Chelsea and beyond. Pink gin in hand, tapping out the bowl of his pipe on an enormous snake ring, Bill was the embodiment of a generation that witnessed and drove huge change across a century: the world into which he was born was, quite simply, not the same when he left it. His early life between the wars at Culford, where he was given his own patch of land – roughly a thousand acres – which he used for shooting, was uniquely aristocratic; he had his own gun and keeper and, naturally, he became a fantastic shot. Eton schooldays were brightened by letters from his adoring father Jerry, filled with exotic adventures to entertain his 'darling old boy' – meeting Howard Carter to look at Tutankhamun's tomb in 1927 or watching a snake-charmer reciting the Koran. In 1932 Bill enrolled at Sandhurst, and it was there that his charmed childhood ended when he succeeded to the earldom the following autumn.

Bill inherited as a minor: the age of English adulthood would not be lowered to eighteen until the Family Reform Act (1969). A kind of regency came into effect. Sammy Scott, in his sixties and a decade into retirement from his career as a Conservative MP, took a paternal interest in his

William, 7th Earl Cadogan, Mayor of Chelsea, Sam Morse-Brown, 1964, oil on canvas

wife's young godson. He was doubly well placed to do so, having acted on behalf of Bill's grandfather and as named executor of Jerry's will ('limited to settled land'). Probate was settled at a surprisingly healthy £2 million.[1] Inevitably, the second of life's certainties – death and taxes – came hot on the heels of the first, to punitive effect. The top rate of Estate Tax had increased from eight per cent in 1894, at its introduction, to forty per cent in 1925, and was still climbing.[2] The Cadogans' dues – at fifty per cent – were heavily compounded by the gap of only eighteen years between the demise of the 5th and 6th Earls. *The Bystander* had commented in 1931:

> ...the politicians have got the country into such a position that there is practically no chance for any great estate to survive financially the death of two consecutive heads of the family. It might be possible if there were a couple of very long minorities…In fifty years' time who can say with any assurance if a single one of the great houses will still be in private hands?[3]

There was no cash, only assets – some of which would have to be liquidated. Time for Bill to make his first big call as 7th Earl Cadogan.

Culford Hall, his childhood home, was broken up into lots and sold. George Henry's arboreal vision was preserved by the Forestry Commission (Forestry England), which purchased thousands of acres now forming part of the King's Forest. The manor house was bought together

ABOVE Bill as a young Viscount Chelsea, with his father at Culford, 1920s

with a further 480 acres, becoming Culford School, where Queen Mary's mulberry tree still stands in the grounds. In this, the Cadogans were not alone: countless other grand houses were disposed of during the 1920s and 1930s. (Coombe Abbey was sold by the Cravens and became a hotel.) Above those voices urging him to keep his comital country retreat, Bill had trusted Sammy Scott's alone advising him to prioritize and preserve the Estate in Chelsea.

Change was coming to town, too. On 24 January 1935, a month before his twenty-first birthday, Bill received this letter from Sammy:

> You will have appreciated at all our Trustees' meetings how difficult it is to own an estate like yours…I speak of many years' experience. Appoint a good man as agent to deal with the tenants and collect rents as this is not an easy task as accounts may very easily get into a big muddle. …
>
> Forgive this very long letter which is the last I shall write to you as your Trustee. You know you can always come to me for any help or advice as I have told you. I say this all the more as though I have not seen very much of you I am really fond of you.[4]

Chelsea House, where Bill's grandparents had frequently entertained royalty, was demolished and replaced by a smart block of flats. Designed in 1934 by Thomas Tait, architect of the old *Daily Telegraph* offices at 135–41 Fleet Street, the building's semi-circular Art Deco façade rounds the corner atop a row of service shops at the north-eastern tip of Cadogan Place. Many of Sloane Street's dilapidated Henry Holland houses were replaced with one-bedroom mansion flats. But as the Great Slump continued, these necessary overhauls were not universally popular. 'In 1936 the [Chelsea] Society complained about the number of vast blocks of flats built the previous year, hoping that no more would be built….'[5] There were those who lamented the lack of 'ordinary' house building. At nos 64 and 66 Old Church Street, private single dwellings were reimagined by 'starchitects' Erich Mendelsohn and Walter Gropius as the height of modernist luxury,

Chelsea House flats, Cadogan Place, architect Thomas Tait, 1935

Gropius's white-rendered façade reminiscent of a 1930s ocean liner. The newly rounded aesthetic also showed up on Sloane Square, in the pioneering glass-and-steel curve of Peter Jones, designed by William Crabtree in 1936. These developments were filled with optimism; things were also looking up for the Estate.

A HANDSOME YOUNG ARMY OFFICER, the 7th Earl Cadogan was a catch. *The Times* Court Circular reports him dining in town with a long list of grand families with eligible daughters. Bill, however, had made his decision. He was secretly engaged to the Honourable Primrose Lilian Yarde-Buller (1918–1970). She wrote to him in November 1935:

> I was delighted to get your letter…I love you so much it scares me – what you say about my age is perfectly true; but you see I've been the youngest of four sisters, but I have always been equal in anything they did, the result is that I am much older than my age and do know my own mind. If I went through forty seasons I know I should not find anyone who could make me care more or happier than you, so you see anyhow my season

is not going to help me much. I know you are being sweet and giving me a chance in case I should change: I won't change ever darling and would like you to think this over. Couldn't we come to something definite on my 17th birthday, then when you were away hunting and I in London dancing I should be happy knowing that I was yours....[6]

Primrose wrote twice a day. Her mother, sensing a girl who knew her mind, gave 'full permission to get married whenever we like after May.'[7] On 11 June 1936, the ceremony took place at Holy Trinity Sloane Street. Primrose was given away by her brother Richard, 4th Baron Churston (her father had died in 1930). She was seventeen; he was just twenty-two. A society wedding it was, but, unusually for the Cadogans, not attended by royalty: Primrose had not yet been presented at court.

Primrose had a glamorous, slightly racy family. Her father Johnnie Yarde-Buller ('Yardie') had been aide-de-camp to Lord Curzon in India and, later, to the Duke of Connaught. He was also possessed of 'an unbelievable charm. It is said of him that he could have enticed a bird off a tree had it worn skirts.'[8] His wife was ex-Gaiety Girl Jessie Smither, known by her stage name of Denise Orme. At her evening soirées she would lead sing-alongs from the piano and encourage dancing; she was also an incorrigible storyteller. According to her unpublished memoirs, she had performed for Edward Elgar and Hubert Parry; the family

ABOVE *The Tatler*, Wednesday 3 June 1936. Bill and Primrose out dancing the week before their wedding. LEFT Miss Denise Orme (Bill's future mother-in-law), *The Play Pictorial*, cover, 1906

remembers tales of tuition by Rachmaninov and duets with Menuhin. By the time of Bill and Primrose's wedding, her second marriage (to Danish millionaire and diplomat Theodore 'Tito' Wessel) had also run its course; she had set her sights on Edward FitzGerald, 7th Duke of Leinster ('Fitz'). Every morning, Primrose recounted, her mother would apply individual false eyelashes pulled from a sable-hair paintbrush; one day, caught under a cloudburst, '…all her eyelashes will go for six, and if there is anything she hates it is that – I swear if Fitz sees her with none he'll die – he believes they are real, poor man.'[9] Primrose liked to say that her mother had always wanted to die a duchess; Fitz would indeed become Denise's third and final husband. Her four daughters all made society matches.

Early letters between Bill and his wife reveal the passion of their romance and their shared sense of humour. The newlyweds were blessed with three children in swift succession, of which Charles Gerald John, 8th Earl Cadogan (1937–2023), was the first. Seven weeks earlier, Bill had transferred from the Coldstream Guards to the Royal Wiltshire Yeomanry (Prince of Wales's Own Hussars), as a reservist. This would allow him time to take a more active role at home and on the Estate. Sarah Primrose Beatrix (1938–2017) arrived the following year. In June 1939, with Primrose pregnant again, the young 7th Earl watched an air-raid rehearsal from the roof of Peter Jones. By the time Daphne came along (1939–2023), Britain was at war.

A page from the family's press cuttings book of 1938

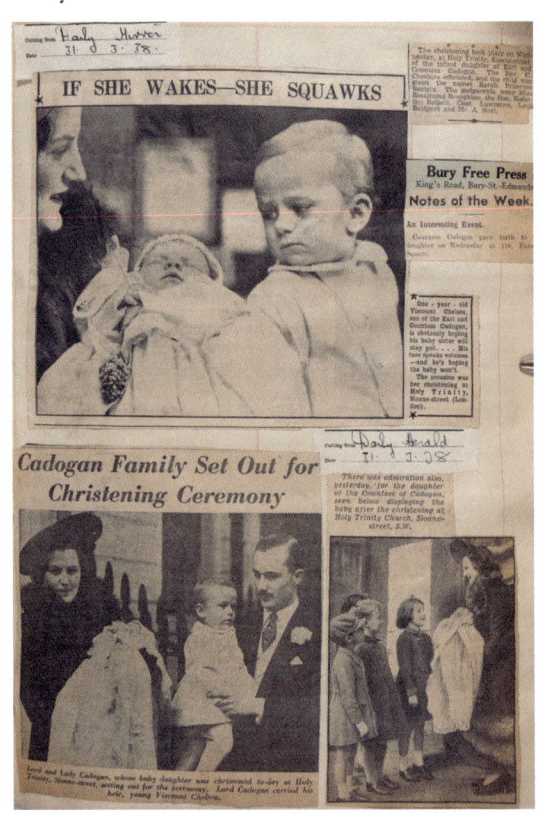

Bill (circled) with his regiment, which was deployed to the Middle East

THE EARLY YEARS of Bill's war are not much recorded. The Royal Wiltshire saw action in Iraq and Iran, and took part in the successful campaign against French Vichy forces in Syria. His brother-in-law Prince Aly Khan, who was married to Primrose's eldest sister Joan, stumbled across him in Egypt:

> [Aly] made his way to Egypt and at El Mansura, where he found an elite outfit of British yeomanry camped at an old Roman aqueduct, he simply walked in and asked to join them. Among the officers were some old friends including Lord Weymouth and the Earl of [*sic*] Cadogan.[10]

The two men's friendship had been cemented by a shared a love of racing. Bill had revived Cadogan blue racing colours with his first horse, Khushi, a gift from Aly in 1937; the following year, he bought Banuddin from the Aga Khan. Aly became a valuable member of British military intelligence in Cairo, making propaganda broadcasts to Muslim audiences on behalf of the Allies and recruiting agents. For a time, Primrose came to stay with Aly and her sister (who had taken the name Princess Taj-ud-dawlah Aga Khan) in Gezira. Primrose would write later, 'Give my love to dear Wey[mouth], I often remember our drives down the Tel Aviv Road…and our dinner in Jerusalem with a magnum of champagne….'[11] Reality intruded on this illusory safe haven when Rommel's German Army made its first assault in North Africa: the Siege of Tobruk, over the border in neighbouring Libya, began in April 1941. Primrose joined the exodus from Egypt, heading to South Africa.

Again, there was heroism and tragedy in the extended Cadogan family. That summer, two young men were lost at sea – missing in action – while on missions for the Special Operations Executive (SOE), the secret ministry of ungentlemanly warfare, in the Middle East. Bill's second cousin Captain Christopher 'Kit' Michael Cadogan had arranged delivery of 'toys' to agents in Syria planning an attack on Aleppo aerodrome; he was on board the SS *Resah* when it was torpedoed and was last seen on a raft with a Turkish commando. Kit's brother-in-law Major Sir Anthony Palmer set off from Haifa leading twenty-three Palmach commandos on Operation Boatswain, a mission to sabotage Tripoli's oil refineries; their boat never arrived. Both men left pregnant widows. After the war Dame Henriette Palmer became lady-in-waiting to Princess Elizabeth, and was at her side when she learned of her father King George VI's death.

While all this was happening, the Royal Wiltshire underwent a revolution. Battlefield horsepower of the four-legged kind was consigned decisively to history by delivery of the four-wheeled, first motorized and then armoured. By December, its men were in tanks.

BILL WAS DECORATED WITH THE MILITARY CROSS for his actions at the Second Battle of El Alamein (23 October to 11 November 1942). He was part of Operation Supercharge, spearheading Lieutenant General Montgomery's breakthrough attack, ordered on the night of 1/2 November. His citation describes how, despite sustaining injury himself: 'This officer throughout showed complete disregard for his own safety and was an inspiration and tonic to those around him by his actions, calmness and qualities of leadership.' He never spoke of it. El Alamein, a brutal battle of attrition at close quarters, was a notable victory for the Allies. It established Monty as a household name and boosted morale at home, but it came at huge personal cost to the young men who had won it, both those who survived, including Bill, and those who did not. Primrose's sister Lydia lost her first husband, Captain Ian Archibald de Hoghton Lyle ('Archie') of the Black Watch (Royal Highlanders) 7th Battalion, in the opening hours of the three-week engagement.

Bill saw further actions, in Italy in 1944. His tanks set out from Alexandria Harbour in April, arriving at Bari, on the east coast, at the end of the month. 'A tank when you get to know it acquires a sort of "soul" of its own very much like a horse and it is true to say that the crews become genuinely fond of their own tanks,' he wrote later, in a dark-purple notebook labelled *Journal of Italy*. The regiment moved up right behind Cassino on 22 May and prepared to drive north, cross-country. Ceprano–Torrice–Rome–Panicale–Pescia–Magnano: after two months pushing on at a 'hot pace', the first phase of fighting ended and the regiment took a few days' rest. Bill assessed the country ahead, ridge after ridge, rising higher and higher, recording that: 'with determination and the ubiquitous bulldozer, and Indian sappers, there are very few places a Sherman cannot get to.' Descriptions of engagements are minimal, with rare exceptions that encapsulate the horror and savagery of war:

> By now it was just first light and on rounding a spur the company [of Ghurkas] found a whole German Bn moving up a gully starting to launch an attack. Screaming their battle cry and grinning with lust for blood they drew their kukris and rushed down upon the Germans. For a moment the enemy stood frozen with horror, then turned and fled. They were too late. The Ghurkas rushed upon them chopping off heads, arms and legs right left and centre. In a matter of minutes the whole action was over and the German Bn were legging it back where they had come leaving 70 mutilated bodies behind them.[12]

20TH CENTURY

A mine explodes close to a British artillery tractor as it advances through enemy minefields at El Alamein, 1942

Bill in the desert

'This officer throughout showed complete disregard for his own safety and was an inspiration and tonic to those around him by his actions, calmness and qualities of leadership.'

The Women's Land Army at Culford Camp

Princess Elizabeth (future Queen Elizabeth II) examining the engine of an Austin 10 'Tilly' light utility truck, 1945. Primrose also became a driver during the war.

20. MILITARY MAN & MODERNIZER

ABOVE The 7th Earl's decorations (left to right): the Military Cross; 1939 to 1945 Star; Africa Star with 8th Army clasp; Italy Star; Defence Medal; War Medal; Her Majesty The Queen's Coronation Medal 1953 and BELOW his Military Cross citation

Bill, by contrast, was shooting with a rifle from the top of his tank. As Edward, 9th Earl Cadogan, recalls, 'He never mentioned taking German tanks out, he mentioned them taking him out – "being brewed up" – but the main thing really was to try to survive.'[13] In August, repatriation orders came through. Bill and his regiment were sent to Villa Guillichini, north of Arezzo, to decompress for three weeks; they bathed in Lake Trasimeno and contemplated the return home. It was hardly long enough. A Military Cross also went to Portia's eldest son, Major Edward Stanley of the Grenadier Guards, that year.[14]

AS THE WAR PROGRESSED, CHELSEA, the village on the river – so easy to spot from the sky – began to take direct hits. On the morning of Wednesday, 13 November 1940, daylight revealed that Sloane Square station had been blown up with huge loss of life. Casualties were taken to the Royal Court Hotel (now the Sloane Square Hotel), where 'The Manager, Mr Wilde, gave everyone a stiff drink.'[15] Chelsea Old Church was almost demolished by an aircraft-dropped landmine on 'The Wednesday' of 16 April 1941. (Only the Thomas More chapel survived, around which the church would be reconstructed after the war.) Chelsea suffered again in 1944 and 1945 with the advent of V-1 and V-2 flying bombs that turned her newer blocks of flats into high-density casualty lists. At World's End, eighty-six were killed in Guinness Trust flats erected on the site given by the 5th Earl; at the corner of Sloane Court East and Turks Row a plaque today commemorates seventy-four American military personnel and three civilians who lost their lives in a single blow to their billet. The Royal Hospital Chelsea took a direct hit from a V-2 rocket in January 1945. Upper Cadogan Place and Cadogan Square were requisitioned by the Air Ministry for tethering barrage balloons, and then air raid shelters. Carlyle Square was given over to allotments for growing food.

Amidst the clamour and uncertainty, there were voices of calm on the Cadogan Estate. Bill had taken great care to put the right people in place. Managers Robbie Robertson and Arthur Steward walked the streets daily, from the offices at 120A Sloane Street, to examine bomb damage and assess

Air raid damage at Sloane Square Underground station, District Line, November 1940. High-angle view showing the damage caused to the arched roof of the station; the pile of rubble on the extreme right marks the site of the station building. A number of rescue workers can be seen in the shot.

the suitability of repairs – which they sometimes carried out themselves with whatever was to hand, Heath Robinson-style. Robbie also did his best to manage the community. Under these extenuating circumstances:

> ...tenants often decided that they couldn't continue to rent from the Estate any longer. It was quite usual for them to come by the Estate office and simply leave the keys of their property.[16]

When buildings were being reduced to rubble, this was hardly surprising, though it led to great financial strain for the trustees to wrestle. The government's compensation scheme under the War Damage Act (1941) was labyrinthine, if not ungenerous – at its winding-up in 1964, it had awarded over £1.3 million (set against £0.2 million collected in taxes from property owners for the purpose)[17] – and the Estate would take many years to recover. Chelsea, however, had come off relatively unscathed in comparison with the East End.

With Bill fighting abroad, the family moved to the safety of the countryside. Many grand country houses and estates had been requisitioned; Culford Camp, Bury St Edmunds, was filled with Land Girls. Arriving back in the winter of 1941, Primrose took the children to her mother's house, Beech Hill Farm in Sussex. She joined the Auxiliary Territorial Service (ATS) and – to the amusement of her family – became a driver, providing artillery units with 'tea and wads' from her NAAFI van. She wrote to Bill during the spring of 1942:

> I got down here in time to put the children to bed – they were madly excited to see me…blew bubbles in the bath for ages and then came prayers. I, for some unknown reason, got the giggles when Sarah started…She gave me a startled look and then roared too – Nanny was most disapproving but I simply couldn't help it. Charles, is, of course always naughty when he says them – he either <is> frightfully loudly or terribly fast. Daphne's effort is like listening to the Arabs – No word is fully pronounced and her voice goes either as high as it can or as deep …Daphne for some reason smells of onions. Nanny and I can't trace what it is. She probably had a go at the dogs' dinners – she eats anything – and was found some months ago on the floor, having finished half a pot of floor polish. All she said was 'Nice tomato' – I can't tell you how pretty she is….[18]

Sussex's proximity to London began to look dangerous as the Doodlebug bombs fell; the children hid under a billiard table when the planes went over. Lydia had gone up to Glendelvine, the Lyle estate on the River Tay near Dunkeld, setting up camp in Wester Gourdie, the old dower house, with her older sister Denise ('Denny'). Primrose now also headed north. In Scotland, the children had ready playmates in a rolling crowd of under-tens: Charles, Sarah and Daphne Cadogan; cousins John and Nicole ('Minty') Yarde-Buller, and Lorna and Gavin Lyle. This jolly company was sometimes joined by the Duke and Duchess of Bedford and their sons Robin and

Rudy; there was also a French family of six living in the kitchen, brought over by the maid Rachelle.

The 8th Earl recalled two occasions on which his mother received the dreaded motorcycle message that her husband was missing, presumed dead; both times these proved to have been despatched in error. Lorna Alexander, née Lyle, remembers the grave reality for her own mother, Lydia, and the support of family:

> Mummy was looking out of the window when the postman came round and she knew it was for her. You know it must have been terrible, terrible… [But] I think family for them was enormous. It was so close and the sisters, they were like that [crossed fingers]… they used to giggle and tease each other…[19]

Her brother, Sir Gavin Archibald Lyle, 3rd Bt., born on 13 October 1941, would never know his father; their widowed mother later married John Russell, 13th Duke of Bedford ('Ian'), in 1947, and moved into Woburn Abbey. This otherwise happy period in Scotland – the children climbing trees, buying green lemonade – left a lasting impression on the Cadogan family: when a neighbouring estate, Snaigow, came up for sale, Bill snapped it up.

BILL RETURNED TO HIS FAMILY FOREVER CHANGED by what he had experienced at the front. The war had also taken a formative figure from his life: Sammy Scott died on 21 February 1943. In the twenty-first century, the Ministry of Defence provides specialist mental health services to soldiers suffering from combat stress, adjustment disorder and PTSD; published figures for 2019/20 show that one in eight personnel sought help.[20] In 1940s Britain, however, many veterans simply muddled through. Bill began his war memoir of Italy. It would be fifty years later, as a grandfather, that he began to open up to Edward (then Viscount Chelsea), returning from service in the First Gulf War. Hauntingly, 'you never get the smell [of blood] out of your nostrils.' There was also a story of hope and humanity. The tanks were rolling past a woman giving birth at the side of the road;

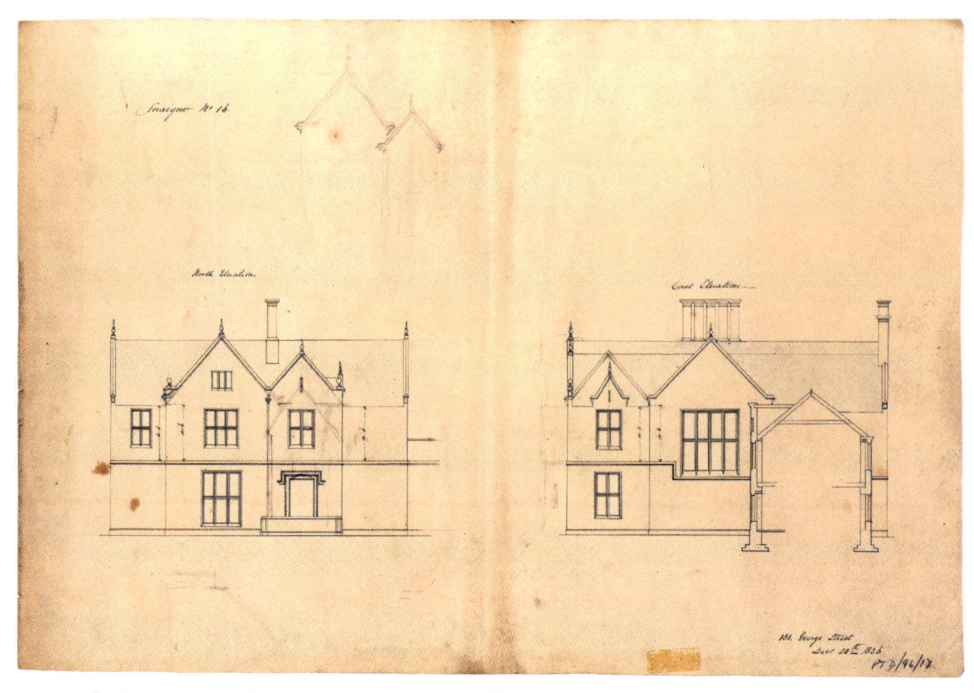

Snaigow, north and east elevations, architect William Burn, 18 December 1826

Bill, being a no-nonsense countryman, got out and got on with delivering the baby. He retired from the Army as an honorary lieutenant-colonel in 1946, when the Territorials were demobbed.

Bill retreated to Snaigow, burying himself in the Scottish Highlands. His children remember him rising early for breakfast, donning corduroy trousers, scruffy Harris tweed jacket and flat cap, and heading out to sit on a tractor and work the land – a routine he followed doggedly. On Sundays they would join him pulling up docks. Sometimes heavy artillery was called for: 'Having done a lot of blowing up in the Army, he loved blowing up tree stumps,' his son Charles, 8th Earl, remembered. A third sister, Caroline Ann ('Cazzy', 1946–2008), was the last of the siblings. Sadly, Bill's marriage did not survive. Primrose, like her mother, was an attractive lady with a love of life; she had married exceptionally young and struggled to endure the long separation of war – the divorce would be decreed in 1960. That same year, the vast, crumbling house – all leaky roofs and long, damp corridors – was demolished and replaced:

After the Second World War, the hold of neo-Georgian on surviving instances of country-house design was complete but the post-war shortage of building materials (particularly reserved from luxury work) caused a delay in activity...Basil Hughes took centre place in 1960 with a new house at Snaigow.[21]

Today the Snaigow Estate, where Bill is fondly remembered, comprises 2,800 acres of arable, beef, forestry and sporting land, with a renowned pheasant shoot.

Bill's contribution to Masonic life grew. Having first been initiated on 21 May 1935, he became Master of Cadogan Lodge (no. 162) in 1949, First Principal of Cadogan Chapter (no. 162) in 1956 and Master of Royal Alpha Lodge (no. 16) in 1961. Details of Cadogan Lodge's early history (originally Black Fryers Bridge Lodge, constituted in 1767), have been lost, but the name-change to Cadogan came in 1836. In 1839, 'the April meeting was held at the Manor House, King's Road, Chelsea, with three members present and no reason available for the change of venue. In May, however, the proprietor of the Manor House was initiated...'.[22] At that date George, 3rd Earl Cadogan, was living at 138 Piccadilly; the Lodge, however, bears the family motto –'*qui invidet minor est*' (he who envies is inferior) – so we are left to guess at the beginnings of family membership until 1926, when Jerry's is the first name to appear. Bill's commitment took him to Grand Rank. On 2 March 1960, his appointment as Right Worshipful Deputy Grand Master of the United Grand Lodge of England (UGLE), and Second Grand Principal, was 'received with loud and prolonged applause'.[23] Annually reappointed until 1969, at Lord Scarborough's death he became Pro Grand Master to HRH the Duke of Kent, and Pro First Grand Principal – positions he then held for thirteen years.

Bill gradually re-immersed himself in public life. He served on Chelsea Borough Council from 1954 to 1959. In 1964 he was elected Mayor of Chelsea, as his grandfather had been, the two men bookending the history of this office as its first and last holders: the following year saw the creation of the Royal Borough of Kensington and Chelsea. A sense of an ending was also present in Bill's tenure as the last family trustee at the British Museum. On 10 July 1963 the British Museum Act (1963) abolished hereditary posts that had been held for over two hundred years, replacing them with appointments by the Crown and Parliament.[24]

There were also new beginnings. His son Charles (then Viscount Chelsea), came of age in 1958, and the time had come to revisit arrangements on the Estate, after two decades of careful management. The entail set up by the 5th Earl was duly broken and in 1961 Cadogan Estates Ltd was created as majority shareholder of the family's Chelsea landholdings. The 7th Earl and his heir retained a small share in personal ownership: death duties would not threaten Chelsea again. Bill opened a new chapter in his private life, with marriage to Cecilia Margaret Hamilton-Wedderburn ('Bunny', d.1999). Poor Bunny was subjected to mild teasing because she couldn't say her r's: Bill gave her two spaniels named Rory and Rumpelstiltskin. The couple travelled extensively on Masonic missions across the globe. In November 1961, Bill installed the Nawab of Rampur as the first Grand Master of India, and stayed at His Highness's residence at New Delhi:

> One of the points that impressed me most about the Grand Lodge of India is its universality, for they had no less than five different Volumes of the Sacred Law lying open on the altar for use by the Grand Officers in taking their Obligations, demonstrating that Masonry in India is open to all races and religions.[25]

There were trips to Iceland (1963); the West Indies (1966); Zambia, Kenya and Uganda (1967); the Far East (1968); and South Africa (1978). They were often away for months at a time.

ABOVE The 7th Earl and his soon-to-be second Countess, 7 January 1961

CHELSEA WAS AT THE HEART OF THE SWINGING SIXTIES. Hanging out at The Pheasantry, and 'Going down the King's Road' were fashionable pursuits in themselves. The Chelsea Drugstore, which opened in 1968, became a cultural landmark, appearing in Stanley Kubrick's *A Clockwork Orange* (as the 'Musik Bootick'), and the Rolling Stones's *You Can't Always Get What You Want*. The Beatles opened a Chelsea branch of Apple Tailoring. Chelsea Football Club had passed Bill the role of president in 1934; now Charles too was to be found at Stamford Bridge, at a time when the stands were populated by film stars, popstars, and even Henry Kissinger. 'Few clubs have managed to exude glamour as Chelsea did between 1967 and 1972' records the club's official history.[26]

The decade that saw a man on the moon also saw a giant leap forward on the Estate. It began with architecture. The five-star Carlton Tower Hotel (Carlton Tower Jumeirah), on the corner of Cadogan Place and Sloane Street, went up in 1961, the tallest hotel in London. An acre at the corner of Cheyne Walk and Oakley Street, once the site of Winchester House, was sold freehold; at 127–135 Sloane Street, the Georgian plot pattern was replaced by Liscartan and Granville Houses. Lionel Brett (future president of RIBA, Lord Esher) was commissioned as architect–planner on the Estate. His proposal to redevelop the whole of Sloane Street along modernist lines would have seen it looking more like the Barbican, with raised walkways at the top and bottom ends of Cadogan Place and a vast European-style piazza. This idea proved unpopular locally, however, and, more importantly, Bill didn't like it. Brett's firm completed two projects: Fordie House, at no. 82 (1964), and the Sekers Building, at nos 190–92 Sloane Street (1965), 'a distinguished and well-detailed post-war office commercial building designed in a wholly contemporary idiom with respect for context'.[27] (Bill, according to the architect, was 'horribly shocked' by its appearance.[28]) A second proposal for comprehensive development made in 1965, this time of nine-and-a-half acres at the western edge of the Estate, failed at appeal. Further improvements were instead made piecemeal. Town houses were built in Astell Street and Cale Street; a recognizably 1960s design by George West of Harrison West transformed nos 1–6 Sloane Square (on the corner of Sedding Street), projecting the first floor over the street on concrete pillars. Arne Jacobsen's bold 1969 design for the Royal Danish Embassy at no. 55 Sloane Street successfully blended the new – a painted-metal exterior of glazed, cantilevered boxes – with a respect for history – its storeys echoing the number and width of those in surrounding mansion blocks to the front and mews houses to the back.

Two major pieces of legislation had a significant impact on landowners. The Leasehold Reform Act (1967) opened the door to holders of certain long residential leases acquiring the freehold of their property (further enshrined as a right in 1993).[29] Secondly, the Civic Amenities Act (1967) marked a widespread shift in social attitudes to Britain's built landscape, in its creation of the first Conservation Areas, 'having a definite architectural quality or historic interest to merit designation.'[30] Many individual buildings were protected by listings. These changes produced a rethink that has come to shape the policy of London's great estates ever since. The Cadogan Estate turned its attention to diversified use, refurbishment and active management. Reacquisition and reinvestment (particularly of money from forced freehold sales, the unexpected silver lining), would direct development of whole areas while retaining the essential character of streets and buildings: a new kind of grand scheme.

The next thirty years – the 1970s, 80s and 90s – saw this curatorial approach develop and deepen. Bill's guiding principle – and his achievement – was to hand over the Estate in better shape than he had inherited it. Run-down houses on the north side of Tedworth Square were replaced by flats whose brown brick and projecting oriel bay windows echoed the forms of local artists' studios constructed a hundred years earlier. On the

ABOVE Danish Embassy, Sloane Street. The 7th Earl Cadogan laid one of three foundation stones on 9 June 1975 alongside Queen Margrethe II and Ambassador Erling Kristiansen. OPPOSITE Bill with familiar pipe, photographed by John Bignell

south side of Pont Street, an upgrade saw the most visible changes at the rear of buildings evacuated by the Danish Embassy, the façades of the red-brick houses largely intact, a memory of the 5th Earl Cadogan's vision preserved. Living, breathing, Chelsea evolved, as the punks moved into the King's Road, followed by the Sloane Rangers. As the turn of the twenty-first century approached, Chelsea was on the cusp of its latest reimagining.

BILL'S MIND WAS ACTIVE TO THE LAST. Well beyond retirement age he retained responsibility for the livings at Holy Trinity and St Luke's, joint patronage of Chelsea Old Church and more than a passing interest in the Chelsea Estate. He was chairman of the London Advisory Board of the Salvation Army. Past Master of both the V.W.H. (Cricklade) Hunt and the Grafton, he was a steward of the Jockey Club from 1957. Having retired as Pro Grand Master in 1982, he remained an active member at the Lodges, 'a highly valued elder statesman', and chairman of a committee that coordinated the work of the Masonic charitable institutions.[31] Indeed, it was discreetly generous Bill who in 1966 founded the family's grant-awarding trust, today known as The Cadogan Charity.

It was not all work: he was a beloved grandfather of eleven. His heir, Charles, had three children: Anna-Karina, Edward and William. Lady Sarah and James Hugh Cecil, 3rd Baron Rockley, had Caroline, Anthony (4th Baron) and Camilla. Lady Daphne ('Dippy') had Alexander, Kevin and Leonie with her husband David Bailey (not the photographer). And Lady Caroline ('Cazzy') and Euan Foster had two boys, Guy and Hugo. After a long and fulfilling life, Bill, 7th Earl Cadogan, straight-talking military man and modernizer, died at Snaigow on 5 July 1997.

Afterword

—

EDWARD, 9TH EARL CADOGAN

Continuing a long-standing family tradition, when my father, Charles, became the 8th Earl upon my grandfather's death, I inherited the title of Viscount Chelsea. In our family, this title transition means more than just a name change; it also carries the responsibility of learning how to manage Chelsea and run one of London's 'Great Estates'.

Although I initially felt reluctant to leave behind a life of adventure and action, my twelve-year career in the RAF Regiment ended as I dedicated myself to understanding the workings of the Chelsea estate. I spent fifteen years as an apprentice at the Cadogan Estate office, which provided me with a comprehensive education and a unique vantage point from which to witness the positive impact that my father, grandfather and those before them had on shaping the evolution of this neighbourhood. Their accomplishments inspired me and fuelled my ambition for the future.

I share my father and grandfather's love for the outdoors and Scotland's wilds. However, nothing beats the culture and community of Chelsea. London is one of the best cities globally, and Chelsea is the epitome of the London experience; it's an incredible place to be. The Cadogan family has always maintained its primary home here, where we spend much of our time. Being a custodian of, and connecting with, this extraordinary neighbourhood is a privilege central to our identity.

The spirit of excitement, challenge and exploration still runs through my veins. I've been incredibly fortunate to maintain a parallel career in the military while juggling between property and the Army. By joining the Territorial Army (51st Highland, 7th Battalion The Royal Regiment of Scotland) in 2002, following in the footsteps of my ancestor, Colonel Henry Cadogan, who was also a Highlander, I found I could sustain my military career. I went on to become the Commanding Officer of 7 SCOTS in 2010, handing over command two years later when my responsibilities in London called again.

In 2012, I was entrusted with the chairmanship of Cadogan, which was a great honour. The occasion was marked with a grand handover celebration in the Great Hall of the Natural History Museum, where my father was a trustee. He held court and delivered one of his famous speeches. Dippy the Diplodocus oversaw the proceedings, while over a thousand distinguished guests from Chelsea and beyond were in attendance.

Inspired by my father's bold developments for the community, such as the creation of Cadogan Hall, I wanted to continue his legacy. To date, one of the major projects of my tenure, with my team led by Hugh Seaborn, has been the re-creation of Pavilion Road, which has won several awards for architecture, sustainability and community. At the heart of our approach is consultation with those who live in, work in and visit Chelsea. We aim to create places for people to enjoy. Pavilion Road was previously a service road running parallel to elegant Sloane Street. It was vastly contrasting in character and slightly run-down. It comprised Victorian stables, coach houses and garages – some lived-in and others used for storage.

We asked people what they would like to see here, and, based on their responses, we transformed it into a 'village heart'. It is now a picturesque pedestrianised mews with artisan boutiques such as a 'butcher, baker, candlestick maker', restaurants and independent stores. The place has a friendly, vibrant atmosphere where people greet strangers with a 'good morning'. It is rare for London to have such a warm and welcoming environment, which is why I love to pick up a coffee here first thing in the morning.

One of my favourite spots in Chelsea is shaded by two ancient mulberry trees in Cadogan Place Gardens. Their sprawling branches are now supported on crutches, but they bear witness to a time at the beginning of the eighteenth century when another part of Chelsea was home to one of the earliest attempts to produce silk in the UK. Over two thousand mulberries, on whose leaves the silkworm feeds, were planted here to render England independent of importing Italian raw silk, on which huge duties were imposed.

Looking at things from the perspective of the lifespan of trees is a valuable exercise. Mindful of the proverb, 'Blessed is he who plants trees under whose shade he will never sit,' thoughts are conjured up about my ancestors' approach to managing the estate for the good of future generations, as well as the significant events and changes that have taken place over the past three centuries.

Three hundred years ago, an epidemic of bubonic plague ravaged southern France, causing great fear in England. Today, this event is unremembered. Will the COVID-19 pandemic that caused life to come to a standstill in 2020 be similarly wiped from our collective consciousness? Whatever, it has shaped a great deal of what has happened over the past few years, from strengthening community feeling in Chelsea as everyone pulled together and supported each other in the face of adversity to the delay of numerous endeavours. At the same time, the world stood still in lockdown.

It was crucial for me and my family that we were part of the support during the pandemic and into the recovery stages. We provided financial assistance to the most vulnerable businesses, contributing to the survival of many that might otherwise have failed, as well as the local community, including support for the NHS and key workers, and local charities who were able to reach those most in need. The most gratifying aspect was witnessing Chelsea's remarkable resilience and rapid recovery, outpacing other areas of London. This achievement stands as a testament to the exceptional spirit of our community.

History serves as a valuable tool. In the words of Winston Churchill, 'The longer you can look back, the farther you can look forward.'

Looking ahead, the main themes of my stewardship, which I want to promote and develop, are sustainability and preserving nature in our towns. Our initiatives so far have included continuing to support the many gardens and green spaces in Chelsea, encouraging rewilding and establishing 'pocket forests' to promote the growth of pollinators and biodiversity. We have begun transforming Sloane Street into a beautiful tree-lined boulevard with more greenery and broader pavements, creating an improved environment for pedestrians and traffic while simultaneously and sensitively renewing and adapting some historic Victorian and Edwardian buildings. We strive to reduce waste and recycle whenever possible, and have pledged to achieve carbon neutrality by 2030.

In addition to environmental concerns, the physical and mental well-being of the community is of the utmost importance. People seek a sense of identity, connection and emotional resonance with the places where they live, work, shop and socialise. Chelsea boasts a unique character and a rich heritage rooted in creativity, from the bohemians and artists of the nineteenth century to the King's Road's 'Swinging 60s' and the many international fashion and design brands that currently call it home. The saying, 'The world always seems brighter when you've just made something that wasn't there before' speaks for itself. We are eager to evolve and celebrate this remarkable artistic legacy and vibrancy during its next chapter, well into the twenty-first century and beyond.

NOTES

1: PRINCES OF FFERLYS & MONMOUTHSHIRE FARMERS

1. *Brut y Tywysogion* (The Chronicle of the Princes) is a translation of a lost Latin work, the *Cronica Principium Wallie*. The *Cronica*, in turn, was based on the *annales* that were kept by churches and monasteries. Entries run from AD 682 to 1332.
2. The *Brut RBH* gives first mention of Elystan as the great-grandfather of Euron ferch Hoedlyw ap Cadwgawn ap Elstan, the mother of Maredudd (d.1129) ap Cadwgon ap Bleddyn. Alternative spellings include Elstan, derived from the Anglo-Saxon Athelstan. Burke's, vol. 2 (1847), p. 887, records his birth as in the second year of the reign of King Athelstan, AD 927 or AD 933; P.C. Bartrum has revised this date to c. AD 975. See Bartrum, *Welsh Genealogies* and *WCD*, p. 247. Welsh titles of the time are descriptive rather than bestowed.
3. Plato, *Laws*, 1, 637c–637e. He also described their drunkenness.
4. Wales had a population estimated at under 250,000 in AD 1200. Emma Mason, 'Portrait of Britain AD 1200', *History Today*, vol. 50, no. 5 (May 2000)
5. Iorwerth Hirflawdd is first mentioned in *De Situ Brecheniauc*, where he is referred to as: 'Gereuerth, King of Powys, whence are named the Iorwerthian'. Bartrum, *WCD*, p. 390
6. Bartrum, *WCD*, p. 108
7. Ashe, *Kings and Queens*, p. 80
8. See Bartrum, *WCD*, pp. 338–42; *Historia Brittonum*
9. In the twelfth century Geoffrey of Monmouth popularized him as Vertigernus in his classic Arthurian romance. Arthur may well have been a Roman too. See Jenkins, *Short History*, p. 14
10. Ashe, *Kings and Queens*, p. 223
11. Hines, 'From Anleifr to Havelok', p. 199
12. BL Harleian 2253; Bodleian Laud, Misc., 108; Cambridge MS Gg. 427.2
13. Ashe, *Kings and Queens*, p. 110
14, 15. Bartrum *WCD*, p. 152, quoting *Historia Brittonum* § 62; Bartrum *WCD*
16. Both wives are charted in Dwnn, *Heraldic Visitations*, vol. 1, p. 139 & vol. 2, p. 152. There are four further mentions of Gwenllian in Dwnn vol. 1, pp. 271, 288, 313 & 332. His editor notes the difficulty. Burke's, vol. 2 (1847), p. 887, favoured Gwladys; Bartrum mentions only Gwenllian.
17. Place of burial recorded in the BL Harleian MS 1973, f. 11; date of death added as a note by the editor to Dwynn, *Heraldic Visitations* (1846).
18. See Bartrum, *WCD*, p. 247
19. Other ladies linked to Cadwgan are Margaret, daughter of Brochwel ap Aiddan, and the unnamed daughter of Rhun ap Cynan. Philip Beddows, 'Family in Context', unpublished MS. Beddows, a distant relation of the Cadogan family, undertook invaluable research on the early history to coincide with the millennial anniversary of Elystan's Glodrydd's death, in 2010.
20. Philip Beddows, 'Monuments and Heritage', unpublished MS
21. *See, for example*, Lord, *Medieval Vision*, p. 19
22. Rev. William Warrington, *The History of Wales* (J. Johnson, 1788), p. 139, quoting the *Flores Historiarum* (AD 1400)
23. *Brut RBH*. Remfry in *Native Welsh Dynasties*, p. 16, confirms Cadwgan ab Elystan and not Cadwgan ap Bleddyn.
24. *The British Numismatic Journal and Proceedings of the British Numismatic Society* (1911), p. 85
25, 26. *The Domesday Book* I, ff. 179b, quoted in Remfry, p. 18; ff. 183b, 186b (Penguin trans. pp. 506, 713)
27, 28. *Brut RBH*; Gwgan was raising one of Hywel's sons, as was the custom, which doubled the treachery.
29. Ralph de Mortimer (fl. c.1080–after 1155)
30. https://mortimerhistorysociety.org.uk/the-mortimers/mortimer-castles/cymaron-castle/
31. *Brut RBH*
32, 33. Stephenson, *Medieval Wales*, p. 102, quoting pp. 53–54; p. 68, quoting p. 63 of Thomas Jones's 1952 translation of the Peniarth MS 20 Version of the *Brut*, regarded by the NLW as 'fuller and more correct'
34. Both the *Brut y Tywysogion* and the later *O Oes Gwrtheyrn Gwrtheneu* (From the Age of Vortigern the Thin, a fourteenth-century text) – describe various border engagements at this time; the 'Battle of Crogen' emerges in the eighteenth century.
35. Stephenson, *Medieval Wales*, pp. 68, 142
36. *DWB*
37, 38. 'Journey through Hereford and Radnor', Giraldus Cambrensis, *The Itinerary of Archbishop Baldwin Through Wales*, Book I (Oxford, Mississippi, 1997)
39. Stephenson, *Medieval Wales*, p. 115. Stephenson refers to Paul Remfry, *A Political History of Abbey Cwmhir* (SCS Publishing, 1994), pp. 8–12; Huw Price (ed.), *Acts of the Welsh Rulers, 1120–1283* (University of Wales Press, 2005), no. 114 & note; B.G. Charles, 'An Early Charter of the Abbey of Cwmhir', *Transactions of the Radnorshire Society*, no. 40 (1970): 68–74.
40. *Brut Penn.*, pp. 91–92
41. Chrimes, *Henry VII*, pp. 41–43, et al.
42. *ODNB*. doi: 10.1093/ref:odnb/27797

2: OPPORTUNITY IN IRELAND

1. Translation of his epitaph on the monument in Christ Church Cathedral, Dublin. Rev. John Finlayson, *Inscriptions on the monuments…* (Hodges, Foster, & Figgis, 1878), p. 96
2. Henry VIII's Act of Union with Wales (1536)
3. M. Perceval-Maxwell, *The Scottish Migration to Ulster in the Reign of James I* (London, 1973), p. 313, quoted in Alison James, 'The English Atlantic World: A View from London', *Pennsylvania History: A Journal of Mid-Atlantic Studies*, vol. 64 (Summer 1997): 46–72
4. HoP *Commons 1604–1629*; Clarendon, *History of the Rebellion* ed. W.D. Macray, i. 342
5. Alice Stopford Green, 'Rule of the English Parliament, 1640–1750', in *Irish Nationality* (1911), n.p.
6. *Ormonde MSS*, old ser., 2.16
7. 'Sir Phelim Roe O'Neill, XLVIII. May the 14th, 1642…' By T.A. and P.G. (London, 1642), in Gilbert (ed.), *Contemporary History of Affairs in Ireland 1641–1652*, appendix, p. 427

8. 'Deposition by Reverend George Creichtonn, Vicar of Lurgan, in the county of Cavan', 15 April 1643. Ibid., appendix p. 538
9. Ormonde to Owen O'Neill, 11 August 1646. Carte Papers xviii, p. 127. Ibid., appendix p. 695
10. Captain Cadogan to Ormonde, 12 September 1646. Carte Papers xviii pp. 265–68. Ibid., appendix pp. 705–6
11. *Ormonde MSS*, old ser., 2.24–5. '*Poltron*, in Faulconry, is a Name given to a Bird of Prey, when the Nails and Talons of his Hind-Toes are cut off, wherein his chief Force and Armour lay; in order to intimidate him, and prevent his flying at great Game.'
12. J.R. MacCormack, 'The Irish Adventurers', *Irish Historical Studies*, vol. 10 (1957): 31
13. Karl S. Bottigheimer, 'English Money and Irish Land: The "Adventurers" in the Cromwellian Settlement of Ireland', *Journal of British Studies*, vol. 7, no. 1 (1967): 27
14. Pearman, *Cadogan Estate*, p. 37. Four shillings in 1642 would translate very roughly to less than £50 in 2020. BoE
15. Prendergast, *Cromwellian Settlement*, p. 94. Bottigheimer, 'English Money and Irish Land': 12–13
16. Pepys, *Diaries*, 3 April 1665
17. Baron Thomas Babbington Macaulay, *History of England*, vol. 1, ch 3 (1848), quoting figures from Lyson's *Environs of London*. See also Walter Thornbury, *Old and New London: A Narrative of its History, its People and its Places* (Cassell, Petter & Galpin, 1873), p. 51
18. Pepys, *Diaries*, 9 April 1666
19. Lybbe Powys, *Diaries* (1762), p. 105
20. *Court of Claims, Submissions and Evidence 1663*, ed. Geraldine Tallon (Irish Manuscripts Commission, 2006), p. 355, no. 904
21, 22. T.C. Barnard, 'Lawyers and the Law in Later Seventeenth-Century Ireland', *Irish Historical Studies*, vol. 28, no. 111 (1993): 256–282; 260
23. Colm Lennon, 'Dublin, Part II: 1610 to 1756', *Irish Historic Towns Atlas*, no. 19 (Royal Irish Academy, 2008)
24. Pearman, *Cadogan Estate*, p. 39
25. Translation of inscription at Christ Church Cathedral, Dublin. Finlayson, *Inscriptions*, op. cit., p. 97
26. ODNB. doi: 10.1093/ref:odnb/22715

3: MARLBOROUGH'S RIGHT-HAND MAN, MULTILINGUAL SPY

1, 2. Watson, *Shadow*, p. 220; p. 3
3. Gordon Manley, '1684: The Coldest Winter in the English Instrumental Record', *Weather*, vol. 66, no. 5 (2011): 133-136
4. Chelsea Pensioners. https://www.chelsea-pensioners.co.uk/governance
5. Their correspondence is in the British Library: Strafford Papers (BL22,196).
6. William's pay was 10s. per day. Cited in Pearman, *First Earl Cadogan*, p. 31. Bonus equivalent to over £40,000 in 2020. BoE
7. Dr Gregori Galofré-Vilà et al., 'Highs and Lows of an Englishman's Average Height Over 2,000 Years', working paper, University of Oxford. https://www.ox.ac.uk/news/2017-04-18-highs-and-lows-englishmans-average-height-over-2000-years-0
8. Cadogan to Raby, 20 September 1703. Strafford Papers, Sloane 3392
9. 'A scarlet caterpillar, upon which all eyes were at once fixed, began to crawl steadfastly day by day across the map of Europe, dragging the whole war with it.' Churchill, *Marlborough*, vol. 2, p. 324
10. Major John Blackadder, *Diary (1700–1728)*, ed. A. Crichton (London, 1824), pp. 129–30
11. Captain Richard Pope, HMC, Cowper, III, quoted in Watson, *Marlborough's Shadow*, p. 32
12. Dr Hare's Journal, cited by Churchill, *Marlborough*, vol. 2, p. 291
13. Colonel Jean Martin de la Colonie, Horsley (ed.), *Chronicles of an Old Campaigner*, p. 135
14. Legge-Pomeroy, *Regimental History*, p. 104
15. Patricia Dickinson, 'Lieutenant General William Cadogan's Intelligence Service: part 1', *The Army Quarterly* (January 1979): 161
16. Cadogan to Raby, BL Add MS 22196, op cit. f. 33. William was exchanged not for the Marquis but for Lieutenant-General Pallavinci.
17. Cadogan to Raby, BL Add MS 22196, op cit. f. 45
18. Thompson, *Whigs & Hunters*, p. 100
19. Marlborough to Lord Godolphin, Helchin, 3 October 1707. Coxe, *Memoirs*, vol. 2, p. 164
20. 'Warrant Books: September 1709, 1-5', in *Calendar of Treasury Books, Volume 23, 1709*, ed. William A. Shaw (London, 1949), pp. 327–47. BHO
21. Cadogan to Raby, 19 January 1708. BL Add MS 22196, 129V. M38832
22. Churchill, *Marlborough*, vol. 6, p. 106
23. As told to Lord Cadogan, battlefield tour to Blenheim, 2004
24. Brig.-Gen. Richard Kane, *Campaigns of King William and Queen Anne (1747)*, NAM 355 541. Watson, *Shadow*, p. 145
25. Marlborough to his wife Sarah. Churchill, *Marlborough*, vol. 6, p. 181
26. Brydges quoted in Pearman, *First Earl*, p. 67
27. Cadogan to Marlborough, 20 January 1712, quoted in Pearman, *First Earl*, p. 75
28. Cadogan to Robert Harley, Earl of Oxford, quoted in Pearman, *First Earl*, p. 78
29. PRO C/54/498
30. Lease with County Library, Royal County of Berkshire D/Ex 258/12
31. County Library, Royal County of Berkshire D/Ex 258/14
32. Campbell, 'Caversham', in *Vitruvius Britannicus*, p. 290
33. Thompson, *Whigs & Hunters*, p. 101
34. Cadogan to Marlborough, Edinburgh, 19 December 1715. Blenheim Collection B2–26
35. See Collins' *Peerage* (1812), pp. 415–17
36. Cadogan to Marlborough, 23 February 1716. BL
37. Watson, *Shadow*, p. 216
38. Goodwood MSS (West Sussex Record Office), 97
39. Earl of March, *A Duke and His Friends* (Hutchinson, 1911), p. 64
40. Watson, *Shadow*, p. 109, from letters Cadogan to Brydges, 12 & 28 November 1707
41. Raby to Cadogan, 1 November 1707. BL Add MS 22196, op. cit. ff. 99–100
42. Registry of Deeds, Dublin 23–334–13596 & 36–191–21992
43. Cadogan to Charles Lennox, 1 August 1724. Goodwood MSS. 106/539

NOTES

44 Cited in Thompson, *Whigs & Hunters*, p. 202
45 Bishop Atterbury, attr. *ODNB*. doi: 10.1093/ref:odnb/4310
46, 47 Cadogan to Charles Lennox, 1 August 1724. Goodwood MSS 106, f. 8; 14 September 1725. Goodwood MSS 106, f. 38
48 Anon. to the Lord Advocate, London, 23 July 1726. Duncan Warrand (ed.), *More Culloden Papers*, vol. 3 (Inverness, 1923–1930), p. 8
49 Pope to Hugh Bethel, 9 August 1726. *The Works of Alexander Pope*, vol. 9, *Correspondence* vol. 4, ed. Rt. Hon. John Wilson Croker et al. (John Murray, 1868), p. 149
50 Raby to Lord Chancellor Harley, 1713
51 Daniel Defoe, *A Tour Thro' the Whole Island of Great Britain*, vol. 2 (London, 1724; reprinted Dent/E.P. Dutton, 1928), p. 11

4: CUSTODIANS OF CAVERSHAM & CHELSEA

1, 2 'Ensign, Col. Heyman Rooke's Ft. 1704, cornet 5 Drag. Gds. 1708, lt. 1709, capt. 1712; Capt. and lt.-col. 2 [Coldstream] Ft. Gds. 1715; col. 4 Ft. 1719–34...' (the list continues, see note 9). HoP *Commons 1715–1754*
3 Hearne, vol. 6 (1902), p. 75
4 Charles Cadogan to Sir Hans Sloane, 19 and 30 March 1720, Sloane MSS 4045, ff. 300, 312. HoP *Commons 1715–1754*
5 R.C. Yorke, Archivist, College of Arms, to Robert Pearman, 5 March 1996
6 Cannon, *Record of the Fourth* (1839), p. 147
7 Cannon, *Record of the Life Guards* (1837), p. 169
8 R.C. Yorke, Archivist, College of Arms, to Robert Pearman, 5 March 1996
9 (for the start of this list, see note 1) '...col. 6 Drags. 1734–43; brig.-gen. 1735; maj.-gen. 1739; col. 2 tp. Life Gds. 1743-d.; lt.-gen. 1745; gov. Sheerness 1749–52, Gravesend and Tilbury 1752-d.; gen. 1761.' HoP *Commons 1715–1754*
10 Charles Cadogan to Sir Robert Walpole, Prime Minister, 13 May 1738. Cholmondley (Houghton) Papers Ch(H) Corresp. 2763. Cambridge University Library

11 Royal Society Council Minutes copy in corresp. Mary Sampson, Archivist, The Royal Society, to Robert Pearman, 22 November 1995
12 Guildhall, *Catalogue of London Traders*, p. 9
13 Cunningham, *Hand-Book of London*, pp. 402–403
14 The house has been demolished but two plaques on the new building at the site mark the event.
15 'Settlement and building: From 1680 to 1865, South-East Chelsea and the Royal Hospital', in VCH *Chelsea*, pp. 41–47
16, 17 Elizabeth Cadogan, Bath, to Sir Hans Sloane, 28 October 1738
18 Lady Cadogan to John Loveday, [April 1756], quoted in Markham, *Loveday*, p. 405
19 Chelsea Place (built in 1535/36) was sold for £302. John Julius Norwich, 'The Cadogan Estate: A History', in C&C, p. 21
20 Charles Cadogan's observations to the trustees of the British Museum, 12 December 1756. BM
21 Copy, by Lee & Pemberton's, 'Release by Sir Hans Sloane, Bart, to Society of Apothecarys of the Physic Garden, London', 20 February 1721
22 Last Will and Testament of Elizabeth Lady Cadogan (née Sloane), 5 February 1757
23 Guidebook published in 1761, quoted in G. L-W Mackenzie, 'Twelve Lordships Since the Conquest: Caversham Park, a Retrospect', Berkshire County Library, unpublished MS
24 Helen Wyld, 'Tapestry in 18th-Century Britain', *The Furniture History Society Newsletter*, no. 186 (May 2012): 4. *See also* W.G. Thomson (ed.), *A History of Tapestry* (Hodder & Stoughton, 1930), p. 490, quoted in 'Appendix 1: The Soho Tapestry Makers', in *Survey of London*, vols 33 & 34, pp. 515–20
25 Lybbe Powys, *Diaries*, pp. 161–62
26 *Letters and Journals of Lady Mary Coke*, vol. 2 (1970), p. 313
27 John Julius Norwich, 'The Cadogan Estate', in C&C, p. 28
28 Humphry Repton, *An Enquiry into the Changes of Taste in Landscape Gardening* (1806), p. 59, quoted in Brent Elliot, 'A Horticultural Heritage', in C&C, p. 91

29 Ellen Leslie, 'The Ice House Uncovered', *Country Life*, 4 October 2010

5: FAMILY AFFAIRS

1 *HMC Egmont Diary*, i. 72-73, 215, 371; iii. 165, 259-60; *CJ*, xxi. 689, quoted in HoP *Commons 1715–1754*
2 Walpole to Bentley, 9 January 1755; Add. 5808, f. 223; Newcastle to Hardwicke, 2 January 1755, Add. 35414, f. 258; Lewis Namier, *The Structure of Politics at the Accession of George III* (Springer, 1957), p. 450 n. 3, all quoted in HoP *Commons 1715–1754*
3 Lady Hervey to Lady Mary Montagu, 7 January 1755. Cokayne, *Complete Peerage*, 2nd edn, vol. 9 (1936), p. 133
4 'The Economist Explains: Why the First World War Wasn't Really', *The Economist*, 2 July 2014
5 Loveday, *Diaries*, 20 May 1768
6, 7 *Letters and Journals of Lady Mary Coke*, vol. 2 (1970), p. 313
8 Loveday, *Diaries*, 25 May 1768
9 'One finds her pretty, and that in her beauty she resembles our *Dauphine*...She has had the best education in the world; she is attentive, obliging; she has gaiety and grace.' (author's translation) Madame du Deffand to Horace Walpole, 15 February and 2 April 1771. Walpole, *Correspondence with Madame du Deffand...*, pp. 27, 56
10 *ODNB* (archive edn). doi: 10.1093/odnb/9780192683120.013.20677
11 Godfrey, 'Paradise Row, south side: Walpole House', in *Survey of London*, vol. 2, pp. 3–7
12 Maria Skerrett's correspondence with letter-writer Lady Mary Wortley Montagu survives. *See* Grundy, *Montagu*, pp. 249–50
13 Pearman, *Cadogans at War*, p. 15 & p. 189 n. 9
14 Mark A. Smith, 'Andrew Brown's "Earnest Endeavor": The "Federal Gazette"'s Role in Philadelphia's Yellow Fever Epidemic of 1793', *The Pennsylvania Magazine of History and Biography*, vol. 120, no. 4 (October 1996): 321–42, http://www.jstor.org/stable/20093070
15 Cecil, 'Memoirs', p. xi. This has become the accepted, perhaps more palatable, version of

George's demise. Sir Henry Oakes's *An Authentic Narrative of the Treatment of the English, Who Were Taken Prisoners on the Reduction of Bednore, by Tippoo Saib…* (London, 1785), vol. 4, pp. 26–27, gives a different date and a grimmer story, that he was banged on the head while being carried, injured. V.C.P. Hodson's *Index of Officers of the Bengal Army, 1758–1834* (NAM) does not list George's name. His passage on the *Horsenden*, however, is confirmed.

16 'Historical Chronicle', *The Gentleman's Magazine*, vol. 52 (London, 1782): 500

17 Winfield, *British Warships*, p. 88. In all, 3,500 lives were lost that night.

18 Captain Thomas Cadogan, Jamaica, to Mr William Leith, 18 July 1782

19 NMM, Log ADM/L/A/8, HMS ACHILLES

20 https://morethannelson.com/officer/hon-thomas-cadogan/

21 Jackie Loos, 'Swift journey by sea to PE turns into a deadly one', *Cape Argus*, 12 March 2015

22 Jane Frazer, Kingston, Jamaica, to William Bromley Cadogan, 28 June 1783

23 William Bromley Cadogan, Reading, to Mr Leith, 5 August 1783

24 These he took on 31 May and 19 June 1779. https://morethannelson.com/officer/hon-thomas-cadogan/

25 William Laird Clowes, *The Royal Navy: A History from the Earliest Times to the Present* (Sampson Low, Marston & Co., 1897–1903)

26 Jane Frazer, Jamaica, to Mr Leith, 14 April 1784; 29 March 1785

27 Thomas 'Tom' Cadogan, on board the *Sir Edward Hughes*, to Mr Leith, 18 February 1797

28 Loos, 'Swift journey', op. cit.

29 Thomas 'Tom' Cadogan, Cape of Good Hope, to Mr Leith, 10 October 1800

30 Loos, 'Swift journey', op. cit.

31, 33 Erskine et al., *Trial of Lady Cadogan*, p. 26; p. 3

32 Horace Walpole, Strawberry Hill, to the Countess of Ossory, 8 August 1777, in *Letters*, p. 282

34 *Biographical Index to the House of Lords* (1808)

35 G. L-W Mackenzie, 'Twelve Lordships Since the Conquest: Caversham Park, a Retrospect', Berkshire County Library, unpublished MS, quoted in Pearman, *Cadogans at War*, p. 190 n. 13

36, 37 Lybbe Powys, *Diaries*, pp. 213–14. Note Caversham was in the county of Oxfordshire at the time.

38, 39, 40 Erskine et al., *Trial of Lady Cadogan*, p. 6; pp. 31–32, p. 4

41 'Cadogan v Cadogan', in Stone, *Broken Lives*, p. 277

42 37 Geo. III c. 58. https://www.legislation.gov.uk/changes/chron-tables/private/21

43 Wolfram, 'Divorce in England 1700–1857', pp. 157, 163

44 PRO, PROB 11/1529

45 For clarity the second 1st Earl is often signalled as such with 'NC' for new creation.

46, 47 HoP *Commons, 1754–1790*

48 Percentages for the year 1883. Wasson, *Aristocracy*, p. 18

49 The 2nd Earl of Shelburne (Whig, 1782–83), Rockingham's successor, shared a great-grandfather with Charles Sloane Cadogan in Sir Hardress Waller. The Duke of Portland (Tory, 1783), shared his Aunt Margaret, the late Lady Bentinck, younger daughter of the first 1st Earl Cadogan and wife of Portland's uncle.

50 George III and Lady Sarah Lennox shared a common ancestor in James VI and I (r.1567, 1603–1625).

51 The role of Surveyor of Kensington Gardens increased to £1,000 a year in 1767; by 1774, Master of the Mint brought in £30,000. Walpole, *George III*, vol. 2, pp. 300–301

52 *The Oxford Dictionary of Quotations*, ed. Elizabeth Knowles, 7th edn (OUP, 2009)

53 'Settlement and building: From 1680 to 1865, South-East Chelsea and the Royal Hospital', in VCH *Chelsea*, pp. 41–47, citing Middlesex Land Registry 1789/3/78–79; 6 Geo. IV, c. 16 (Private)

54 Perrett, *Cadogan: The Heart of Chelsea*, p. 79

55 Wilberforce was a tenant of the Cadogan Estate, resident at 44 Cadogan Place

56 William Bromley Cadogan, Reading, to Mrs Deane, 16 October 1789. 'Letters', in *Discourses*, p. 371

6: EVANGELISTS & EDUCATORS

1, 2, 3, 4, 5 Cecil, 'Memoirs', p. xii; pp. xiii–xiv; p. xvi; p. xvii; p. xxiv

6 Tiff Kirby, Assistant Archivist, Lambeth Palace Library, to the author, 4 November 2019

7 *ODNB*. doi: 10.1093/ref:odnb/46765

8 Cecil, 'Memoirs', p. xl

9 Romaine was a sometime Professor of Astronomy. *See, for example*, J.C. Ryle, 'William Romaine and His Ministry', in *Five Christian Leaders of the Eighteenth Century* (Banner of Truth Trust, 1960), pp. 60–86.

10 Cadogan, *Upon the death of Mrs. Talbot*, p. 6

11 *ODNB*, op. cit.

12 Cecil, 'Memoirs', p. x

13 William Bromley Cadogan to the Rev. John Halward, Chelsea, 20 January 1782. Cadogan, *Discourses*, p. 332

14 Man, *History of Reading*, p. 208

15, 16 Green Girls' Charity School Minute Books, Book One, 1782; 10 December 1784. Berkshire Record Office D/QR13/2/1

17 See Norma McMullen, 'The Education of English Gentlewomen 1540–1640', *History of Education*, vol. 6, no. 2 (1977): 87–101

18 Steven Cowan, *The Growth of Public Literacy in Eighteenth Century England* (University College London, 2012) URI: https://discovery.ucl.ac.uk/id/eprint/10019999

19 'Records of Christ's Hospital and Bluecoat Schools', LMA, Information Leaflet no. 29

20 Man, *History of Reading*, p. 212

21, 22, 24 Cecil, 'Memoirs', p. ci; p. cxiii; p. xcvii

23 Cooke, *Five Letters*, p. iii

25 *The Gentleman's Magazine*, vol. 63, no. 1 (1793): 246

26 Cadogan, *Psalms and Hymns…* (A.M. Smart and T. Cowslade, 1785; reprinted 1787, 1793, 1803)

27 BRO D/P98 3/9/14

28 Man, *History of Reading*, p. 212

29 UK Parliament. The first of these Acts was passed in 1870, but it was that of 1880 that made education compulsory by law.

30 Ditchfield and Page, 'The Borough of Reading: Charities', pp. 378–84

31 Green Girls' Foundation (registered charity no. 309149). BRO D/QR/13/7–8
32 Green Girls' Foundation, year ending Dec 2017, income £14.7K, spending £8K. Charity Commission

7: ADVENTURE & AFFLICTION

1 HoP *Commons 1754–1790*
2 *See, for example*, Brian Dolan, *Ladies of the Grand Tour* (Harper Collins, 2001)
3 Charles Henry Cadogan, Naples, Italy, to William Bromley Cadogan, 5 March 1785
4 *ODNB*. doi: 10.1093/ref:odnb/12142
5 Charles Henry Cadogan, Naples, to William Bromley Cadogan, 26 May 1785
6 Anon., *The Present State of Sicily and Malta*, extract from *Mr Brydone, Mr Swinburne and other Modern Travellers* (G. Kearsley, 1788), pp. 196–97
7, 8, 9, 10 Charles Henry Cadogan to William Bromley Cadogan, Constantinople, 25 August 1785; Alexandria, 15 March 1786; Cracow, 10 March 1787; Cracow, 11 July 1787
11 *ODNB*. doi: 10.1093/ref:odnb/26270
12, 13, 14, 15, 16 Charles Henry Cadogan to William Bromley Cadogan, Cracow, 20 February 1788; Vienna, 29 March 1788; Berlin, 19 May 1788; Brunswick, 27 August 1788; Munich, 19 October 1788; ibid.
17 William Bromley Cadogan to Mrs Deane, Reading, 30 January 1789. 'Letters', in *Discourses*, p. 368
18, 19 Charles Henry Cadogan, to William Bromley Cadogan, Nîmes, 1 November 1789; Montpellier, 1 January 1790
20 Dr William Cadogan (1711–1797) lived roughly contemporaneously with Charles Sloane Cadogan, 3rd Baron Oakely (1728–1807), later 1st Earl Cadogan (NC).
21, 22 Rendle-Short, 'William Cadogan', pp. 288–309; p. 288. *See also* William Cadogan's *An Essay upon Nursing and the Management of Children* (1748).
23 Dr William Cadogan, *A dissertation on the gout and all chronic diseases jointly considered as proceeding from the same causes. What these causes are and a rational and natural method of care proposed...* (J. Dodsley, 1771). It ran to ten editions in two years. Rendle-Short, 'William Cadogan', p. 300
24 Dr Thomas Trotter warned that Rome 'became a prey to barbarous hordes; who undebauched by refined pleasures, found the enervated Romans an easy conquest. Let Great Britain look to this example.' Thomas Trotter, *A View of the Nervous Temperament* (2nd edn, 1807), quoted in Wilson, *Decency & Disorder*, p. 33.
25 *See* Jonathan Andrews et al., *The History of Bethlem* (Routledge, 1997).
26 *See, for example*: Sarah Young, 'Ocular Syphilis Outbreak: The Inflammatory Eye Disease That Can Make You Go Blind is On the Rise', *The Independent*, 31 October 2017
27, 28 According to studies in recent medicine. 'The patient was then started on systemic penicillin, as well as topical steroids. The response to the treatment was good and the ulcer began to heal.' A.P. Vignesh, R. Srinivasa and S. Vijitha, 'Ocular syphilis masquerading as bilateral peripheral ulcerative keratitis', *Taiwan Journal of Ophthalmology*, vol. 6, no. 4 (2016): 204–205. Published online by US National Library of Medicine, National Institute of Health, doi: 10.1016/j.tjo.2016.06.002
29 'The Hon Charles Henry Cadogan, of Upper Grosvenor Street, Middlesex: commission and inquisition of lunacy, into his state of mind and his property', 10 December 1799, PRO C 211/5 C129
30 Will and Testament of Charles Sloane Cadogan, 1st Earl (NC), 4 April 1801
31 Henry and George, both over twenty-one, received annual allowances of £700 and £400 respectively; Edward £100 until he reached his majority, when this would increase to £400. Their sisters Emily and Charlotte had received marriage settlements of £5,000 each, and Louisa received the interest from a matching sum until she might marry. Pearman, *Cadogans at War*, p. 91
32 *Pigot's Directory* (1826). 'Unfortunately, this entry does not give an address.' Graham Dalling, Local History Officer, London Borough of Enfield, to Robert Pearman, 24 November 1995
33 NA PROB 11/1460/273

8: MADE IN THE ROYAL NAVY

1 Noel-Smith and Campbell, *Hornblower's Historical Shipmates*, p. 81
2 Compare George's wage with that of Mr Clarke, the writing master at the Green Girls' School in Reading, paid £2. 12s. 0d. George's equivalent would be £556 in 2022. BoE.
3 Spencer to Pellew, 25 September 1795. NMM, Caird Library: Papers of Lord Exmouth, Edward Pellew, Box 22, MSS/92/027. Evan Nepean, Secretary to the Board of Admiralty, was at the time the occupant of Lord Cadogan's house in Whitehall.
4 A 'large volume of moving condolence letters sent to the family on Pellew's death, from men who had served with him since boyhood' is cited by Noel-Smith and Campell, in *Hornblower's Historical Shipmates*, p. 2
5 Rodger, *Wooden World*, p. 275
6 Unattributed letter dated 18 February 1796, in Parkinson, *Edward Pellew*, p. 133. The wreck still lies in Plymouth Sound.
7 Captain Jacques Bergeret of *Virginie*, to his fleet Admiral, in Parkinson, *Edward Pellew*, pp. 147–49, quoted in Pearman, *Cadogans at War*, p. 45. Pearman includes more of Bergeret's letter, which gives a detailed account of the battle.
8, 9, 10 Pellew to Evan Nepean, 17 January 1979. Debrett (ed.), *State Papers*, vol. 6, pp. 12–13; ibid.; p. 4
11 Pellew to Spencer, 17 January 1797, NMM, Caird Library: Papers of Lord Exmouth, Edward Pellew, Box 22, MSS/92/027
12 George collected three clasps in total: *Virginie* and *Droits de l'homme* from *Indefatigable*; and from his time as master's mate on *Impétueux*, 29 August Boat Service 1800, for 'cutting out the *Guêpe*.' PRO/ADM 171/8
13 UK Parliament. https://www.parliament.uk/about/living-heritage/transformingsociety/

private-lives/yourcountry/overview/pressgangs-/
14 Pellew to Rear-Admiral Sir Charles Cotton, 8 June 1799. Osler, *Life of Exmouth*, p. 405
15 'There is no indication whether Cadogan witnessed the captain defending his quarterdeck from the mutineers; he was certainly aboard the ship at the time, though unlike his fellow *Indefatigable* midshipman, Henry Hart, he did not testify at the subsequent court martial'. Noel-Smith and Campbell, *Hornblower's Historical Shipmates*, p. 83
16 PRO Kew ADM 6/100. The examination took place on board the sixty-four-gun *Monmouth*, at anchor in Valetta Harbour, Malta.
17 RMG. https://www.rmg.co.uk/discover/explore/nelson-and-napoleon
18 Pellew of Canonteign Collection, Devon Records Office, Spencer to Pellew, 22 May 1804. Noel-Smith and Campbell, *Hornblower's Historical Shipmates*, p. 83
19, 20 George Cadogan, His Majesty's Sloop *Cyane*, off Antigua, to Commodore Sir Samuel Hood, KB, 12 November 1804. *Naval Chronicle* vol. 13 (Jan-June 1805): 146–47
21, 22 Archives de France, Marine BB 4 230/232, ff. 195/6 and 129. Translated by Robert Pearman in *Cadogans at War*, p. 80; p. 81
23 ADM 12/117, Digest 79: 31, Cadogan to Cochrane, 8 July 1805
24 Charles Grey (later 2nd Earl Grey), First Lord of the Admiralty, to King George III, 22 March 1806. A letter from George III in reply, Windsor Castle, 23 March 1806, reads: 'The King does not object to Mr Grey's proposal that Admiral Villeneuve and a limited number of the officers immediately attached to him may be permitted to return to France'. *Later Correspondence of George III*, ed. Aspinall, vol. 4, p. 412
25 Black Tot Day (1970) marked the end of a daily alcoholic measure for sailors. *See* Pack, *Nelson's Blood* and Rodger, *Command of the Ocean*, vol. 2
26 ADM 37/1605–1606, Muster Table of His Majesty's Sloop the *Ferret*, 1805–1806

27 Pearman, *Cadogans at War*, p. 85
28 Campbell, 'George Cadogan: The Ferret Mutiny, 26 September 1806', in *Indefatigable 1797*. Campbell lists five differing accounts, including Robert Pearman's.
29 ADM 1/5373, Ferret Court Martial, 1806. Campbell, *Indefatigable 1797*
30, 31, 32 Huntington Library, ST6 Correspondence Box 137(29), Cadogan to Earl Cadogan, 13 October 1806; (28), Earl Cadogan to Spencer, 27 November 1806; (73), Spencer to Grenville, 29 November 1806
33 ADM 1/5395, Cumberland Memorial in Cadogan Court Martial, 1809
34 James, *Mutiny*, p. 71. Hugh Pigot was an infamously cruel captain of HMS *Hermione*.
35 Noel-Smith and Campbell made the comparison in *Hornblower's Historical Shipmates*. Their notes refer to J.D. Bryn, Jr., *Crime and Punishment in the Royal Navy: Discipline on the Leeward Island Station 1784–1812* (Scolar Press, 1989), Appendix B, pp. 211–20.
36 George Cadogan, HMS *Havannah*, Adriatic, to Captain Rowley, HMS *Eagle*, 10 January 1813. *Naval Chronicle*, vol. 30 (July–Dec 1813): 76. Similar letters appear in the same volume from 27 March (pp. 238–39) and 29 June (pp. 435–36).
37 *Naval Chronicle*, vol. 30 (July–Dec 1813): 82; 'Interesting Intelligence from the London Gazettes', *The Gentleman's Magazine*, vol. 83, part 2 (July–Dec 1813): 279
38 George Cadogan, [HMS *Havannah*, before Zara], to Rear-Admiral Fremantle, 6 December 1813. *Naval Chronicle*, vol. 31 (1814): 76
39 Rear-Admiral Fremantle, HMS *Milford*, Trieste, to John Wilson Croker, December 1813. Ibid.

9: PISTOLS AT DAWN
1 There were two further brothers who did not survive childhood: Arthur (1762–1768) and Francis (1765). Birth order given is for surviving sons at the time of Emily's marriage.
2 '[H]is ever-obliging cousin Sir Chichester Fortescue, Ulster King of Arms...allow[ed] him to impale the de Lacy Lion Rampant in his escutcheon.' Longford, *Wellington*, p. 39
3, 4 Lady Wellesley to Lord Wellesley, Brighton, 22 August 1803; ibid.; 25 September 1803. *Diary and Correspondence of Henry Wellesley*, pp. 13, 14 (in French, translation by the author of this book). Emily wrote to Hyacinthe, who reported back to her husband.
5 Pearman, *Cadogans at War*, p. 74
6 Stone, *Broken Lives*, p. 14
7 Lady Harriet Cavendish to the Marquis of Hartington, 8 March 1809. Leveson-Gower (ed.), *Hary-O*, pp. 307–11
8 About half a million pounds in today's money. BoE. Compare this with the £60,000 dowry from the first 1st Earl Cadogan to his daughter the 2nd Duchess of Richmond.
9 Lady Mornington to her son Richard Wellesley, 3 February 1804. *Diary and Correspondence of Henry Wellesley*, pp. 14–15
10 Leveson-Gower (ed.), *Hary-O*, pp. 307–11; Anglesey, *One Leg*, p. 62. (Paget family letters quoted from *One Leg* unless otherwise noted.)
11 Anglesey, *One Leg*, p. 89
12 HoP *Commons 1790–1820*
13 QVJ (Lord Escher's typescripts). Buckingham Palace, 9 July 1838, vol. 6, p. 126; Buckingham Palace, 24 April 1839, vol. 10, p. 107
14 Sir C. Webster (ed.), *Some Letters of the Duke of Wellington to his brother, William Wellesley-Pole*, RHS, *Camden Miscellany, XVIII*, 1948, nos 22 and 23. Pearman, *Cadogans at War*, pp. 101–104
15 Anglesey in *One Leg* (1961) noted this letter as from the Plas Newydd Papers, in his possession, with no further details. He gave the family seat to the National Trust in 1976.
16 Henry Lord Paget to Charles Paget, 3 March 1809
17, 18, 19 Charles Paget to Arthur Paget, n.d. [1809]. The heir to the Duke of Argyll is given the courtesy title Marquess of Lorne and Kintyre. George was heir from 1770 to 1806, so Charles Paget is using the title by which he would have known George as a young man.
20 Charles Piggott, *The Female Jockey*

Club, or, A Sketch of the Manners of the Age (D.I. Eaton, 1794), pp. 246–47
21 Anglesey, *One Leg*, p. 93
22 Henry Lord Paget to Arthur Paget, 6 March 1809
23 Lady Charlotte Wellesley to Charles Arbuthnot, 7 March 1809
24 Wellington MSS, *Duchess's Journal*, 12 August 1809 and 29 January 1811, in the possession of the Duke of Wellington, quoted in Longford, *Wellington*, p. 136
25 Henry Wellesley to Lady Charlotte Wellesley, 8 March 1809
26 Lord Uxbridge, Uxbridge House, to Lady Charlotte Wellesley, 8 March 1809
27 Charles Paget to Arthur Paget, 9 March 1809
28, 29, 30 Quoted in Anglesey, *One Leg*, p. 97; p. 98; p. 99
31 Lady Harriet Cavendish to the Marquis of Hartington, 8 March 1809. Leveson-Gower (ed.), *Hary-O*, pp. 307–308. Her 'aunt Spencer' might be either the Countess of Bessborough or Lavinia Spencer, Countess Spencer (née Bingham).
32 Lady Williams Wynn (Charlotte Grenville), Brook Street, to Henry Williams Wynn, 14 March 1809. *Correspondence of Charlotte Grenville*, pp. 145. Her father George Grenville was PM 1763–65.
33 Anglesey, *One Leg*, p. 99. He paraphrases *The Times*, 11 March 1809.
34 Lord Eniskillin (Paget's brother-in-law) to Arthur Paget, n.d. [1809]
35 Jeremy Horder, 'The Duel and the English Law of Homicide', *Oxford Journal of Legal Studies*, vol. 12, issue 3 (Autumn 1992): 427. doi: 10.1093/ojls/12.3.419
36, 37, 38 Charles Paget to Arthur Paget, 14 March 1809; ibid.; 16 March 1809
39 Henry Cadogan, Cook's Hotel, Dover Street, to Henry Paget, 28 March 1809
40 Henry Paget to Henry Cadogan, 30 March 1809
41 Henry Cadogan to Mr Sloane, made public 16 May 1809
42 A statement was issued the following day, signed by the two seconds and printed in *The Morning Chronicle*, 31 May 1809. Clarke, *The Countess*, p. 305
43 Lady Bessborough to Lord Granville Leveson Gower, 9 September 1810. *Granville: Private Correspondence*, p. 366
44 Lord Graves to Arthur Paget, June 1811
45 Lady Lyttelton, Holywell, to the Hon. Robert Spencer (her brother), 20 March 1809. *Correspondence of Sarah Spencer*, p. 63
46 Joseph Farington, 26 May 1809. *Farington Diary*, p. 175
47 Hyacinthe, Brighton, to Richard Wellesley, 22 August 1803. *Diary and Correspondence of Henry Wellesley*, p. 13. Text given in the original languages.
48 Lady Mornington to her son Richard Wellesley, 3 February 1804. *Diary and Correspondence of Henry Wellesley*, pp. 14–15
49 Lady Bessborough to Lord Granville Leveson Gower, 9 September 1810. *Granville: Private Correspondence*, p. 366
50 A.F. Freemantle, *England in the Nineteenth Century*, vol. 2, 1806–1810 (Allen & Unwin, 1930), p. 416

10: WELLINGTON'S AIDE-DE-CAMP

1 Ensign 18th Royal Irish Ft. 1797, lt. 1798; captain 2nd (Coldstream) Gds 1799; major 53rd Ft 1804; lt.-col. 18th Ft. 1805; lt-col. 71st Ft. 1808. Annuity would be over £50,000 in today's money (2018). BoE
2 Ensign 20th Ft. 1806; lt. 26 Feb 1808. NAM Archive 83 (1370)
3 Oman, *History of the Peninsular War*, vol. 1, p. 536
4, 5, Duke of Wellington's Papers, MS61/WP1/263/48; MS61/WP1/263/60
6 Brett-James, *Wellington at War*, p. 159
7 Raglan MSS, no. 93, 22 August 1809, from W. Wellesley-Pole. Paget, *Wellington's Peninsular War*, p. 26
8 Arthur Wellesley to William Wellesley-Pole, n.d., quoted in Wellesley, *Wellington*, p. 180
9 Lord Chatham, brother of William Pitt, led the Army; Rear-Admiral Sir Richard Strachan the Navy.
10 See John Lynch, 'The Lessons of Walcheren Fever, 1809', *Military Medicine*, vol. 174, no. 3 (March 2009): 315–319. Also Martin R. Howard, 'Walcheren 1809: A Medical Catastrophe', *BMJ: British Medical Journal*, vol. 319, no. 7225 (18–25 Dec 1999), 1642–45. https://www.jstor.org/stable/25186694
11 Commodore Edward Owen, HMS *Clyde*, off the North Foreland, to Sir Richard Strachan, 28 December 1809. *Naval Chronicle*, vol. 23 (reissue, 2010), p.83
12 Hibbert (ed.), *A Soldier of the Seventy-First*, p. 47, n.3. Henry Cadogan was a staff officer at the time and consequently not present at Walcheren.
13 Annual celebrations at Busaco mark this victory with a parade in the uniforms of 1810. The Portuguese played a distinguished part in the battle. Paget, *Wellington's Peninsular War*, p. 109
14 Robinson, *Wellington's Campaigns*, p. 242
15 Capt. 20th Ft 4 January 1810; transferred to 71st Ft 23 August 1810. NAM Archive 83 (1370)
16, 17, 18 Hibbert (ed.), *A Soldier of the Seventy-First*, pp. 49; 51; 55 & 56. The acknowledgement page of the 1976 US edition suggests the author was 'a certain Thomas Howell'.
19 The *OED* gives first usage as: '1813, Morning Chron. 17 Nov., A young man...of a genteel appearance, although shabbily dressed in a blue coat, white waistcoat, military pantaloons, and Wellington half-boots.'
20 A street in Glasgow. Oatts, *Proud Heritage*, pp. 23, 24
21 Hibbert (ed.), *A Soldier of the Seventy-First*, p. 62
22 See Longford, *Wellington*, pp. 166–69; Hibbert (ed.), *A Soldier of the Seventy-First*, p. 63
23 Henry Cadogan, Camp near Elvas, to Gerald Wellesley, 2 July 1811. PA GB-061/CAD 14
24 William Wellesley-Pole to Wellington, 16 June 1811, Raglan MSS. no. 114. Longford, *Wellington*, p. 172
25 The Earl of Liverpool, London, to Wellington, 8 August 1811. Wellington, *Supplementary Despatches*, p. 196
26 Longford, *Wellington*, pp. 171–72
27, 28, 29 Hibbert (ed.), *A Soldier of the Seventy-First*, pp. 73; 74; 74–75
30 Shelley, *Diary*, p. 46

NOTES

31 Henry Cadogan to Gerald Wellesley, Camp near Elvas, 2 July 1811. PA GB-061/CAD 14
32 Wellington to Reverend Gerald Wellesley, 24 June 1813. PA GB-061/CAD 20
33 Lieutenant Alexander Duff to George Cadogan, 30 June 1813. PA GB-061/CAD 21
34 Wellington's dispatches of 22 and 24 June, received 3 July and reprinted in *The Gentleman's Magazine*, vol. 83, part 2 (1813): 72
35 *The Gentleman's Magazine*, vol. 83, part 2 (1813): 267–68. Castlereagh was Foreign Minister.
36 *See, for example*, Clarke, *An Impartial History*, p. 674; Shelley, *Diary*, p. 102
37 Beethoven in fact used it as the signature tune for the French; the English had 'God Save the King!'
38 Duke of Wellington's Papers, MS61/WP1/1232/2
39 *Index of Applicants for East India Company Cadetship 1775–1860*, India Office Records, year 1824–25

11: GREATNESS THRUST UPON HIM

1 'Hon'ble. Geo. Cadogan, capt., R.N., of St. George's, Hanover Sq.' married Honoria Louisa Blake at Hampton Court Palace, by special licence, on 4 Apr 1810.
2 Obituary, *The Illustrated London News*, 24 September 1864, no. 1279. vol XLV (collected edn, Elm House, 1864), p. 322
3 Emperor Francis II, Freiburg, to Prince Metternich, 26 December 1813. Österreichisches Staatsarchiv – Kriegsarchiv, Wien
4 Ferdinand, Duke of Württemberg, Vienna, to George Cadogan, 8 January 1814. PA GB: 061/CAD 27
5 'Whitehall, 2 January 1815', *The London Gazette*, No. 16972, 4 January 1815, pp. 17–20
6 Count of Vimeiro, Duke of Ciudad Rodrigo, Marquess of Torres Vedras, and Duke of Vittoria; later also Prince of Waterloo from both the Netherlands and Belgium.
7 Captain Jones of the 15th Hussars, journal entry 5 June 1815, in H.C. Wylly, *XVth (the King's) Hussars, 1759–1913* (Caxton, 1914), p. 230
8 Anglesey, *One Leg*, p. 149
9 Diary of Baron Stockmar, quoted in Anglesey, *One Leg*, p. 366
10 W.B. Hodge, 'On the mortality arising from military operations', *Quarterly Journal of the Statistical Society*, vol. 19 (Sept 1856): 219–71
11, 12 Approximately £35 million; and £130,000, in today's money. BoE
13 Liverpool to Wellington, London, 8 August 1811. Wellington, *Supplementary Despatches*, p. 196
14 William Wellesley-Pole, Saville Row, to Bagot, 5 July 1816 (marked 'received 19 September'). Bagot (ed.), *George Canning*, p. 30
15 They shook at a levée at Carlton House. Argyll to A. Paget, 22 June 1811, in Lord Hylton (ed.), *The Paget Brothers, 1790–1840* (John Murray, 1918), p. 195
16 Pearman, *Cadogan Estate*, p. 79
17 Butler, *Eldest Brother*, p. 430
18 Lady Harriet Cavendish to a friend in Paris, Leveson-Gower (ed.), *Hary-O*, p. 42
19 Jane Wellesley, *Wellington*, p. 233
20 Butler, *Eldest Brother*, p. 532, quoted in Jane Wellesley, *Wellington*, with the attribution: 'wrote a member of the family later'.
21 Autograph draft of a memorandum, Duke of Wellington, London, to Robert Banks Jenkinson, 2nd Earl of Liverpool (Prime Minister), 1 September 1826. Duke of Wellington's Papers, MS61/WP1/861/26
22 HoP *Commons 1790–1820*
23 Notes from letters of Lord Colebrook to Queen Mary, Royal Archives
24 Chelsea Common: 53 Geo. III Cap. 190; grant of building leases: 6 Geo. IV Cap. 16; Winchester House: 6 Geo. IV Cap. 17
25 In 1821 there were 275 families engaged in agriculture; in 1831 there were eighty-seven. Pearman, *Cadogan Estate*, p. 82
26 Faulkner, *Chelsea and its Environs*, pp. 352–53
27 George and Honoria moved into 16 Park Lane – just up the road from Apsley House.
28 UK Government. https://www.gov.uk/government/history/past-prime-ministers/arthur-wellesley-1st-duke-of-wellington
29 Greville Papers, vol. 2, 1830, p. 88
30 Anon. to the Duke of Wellington, 1830, Duke of Wellington's Papers, MS61/WP1/1159/3. Old Sarum Constituency, HoP *Commons 1820–1832*
31 The famous phrase comes from William Blake's poem 'And did those feet in ancient time...' (1804), best known set to Hubert Parry's music as the hymn *Jerusalem* (1916).
32 *ODNB*. doi: 10.1093/ref:odnb/7599
33 PRO WORKS 6.119, Nelson Memorial Committee Minute Book 1838–447
34 'Report from the Select Committee on Trafalgar Square Together with the Minutes of Evidence Taken Before them and Appendix', in *Parliamentary Papers 1780–1849*, vol. 12, part 9: session 16 January – 11 August 1840, no. 548 (House of Commons, 1840), pp. 32–33. Ten further dukes, three marquesses (including Anglesey), thirteen earls including George and Earl Spencer; and a raft of admirals and vice-admirals were on the board.
35 Ibid., p. 11

12: PALACES, PARLIAMENT & POSTINGS

1 Ray Jones, 'The Social Structure of the Diplomatic Service, 1815–1914', *Histoire Sociale*, no. 14 (1981): 50–66
2 Cadogan, *Before the Deluge*, p. 3
3 3rd Earl Cadogan to Viscount Chelsea, 27 May 1835. The Londonderry Collection at Durham County Council Archive, D/Lo/C549
4 Pearman, *Cadogan Estate*, p. 89
5 Marquess of Anglesey to Marchioness of Anglesey, n.d. [1835]
6 Countess Cadogan to Marchioness of Londonderry, Hôtel Meurice, Paris, n.d. [1835]
7 Marchioness of Londonderry to Countess Cadogan, January 1836
8 Duke of Wellington to Countess Cadogan, 21 May 1836. PA GB-061 CAD/41
9 Viscount Chelsea, Durham, to Marchioness of Londonderry, 9 July 1836. The Londonderry Collection, at Durham County Council Archive, D/Lo/C549
10 Rev. Gerald Wellesley, Durham, to Marchioness of Londonderry, 13 July 1836. Ibid.
11 Norfolk 'By Her Majesty's Command' to 3rd Earl Cadogan, Court of St James's, 9 May 1838. PA GB-061 CAD/45

12. Their names appear in the engraving *Key to Mr Leslie's picture of Queen Victoria receiving the Holy Sacrament at her Coronation*, by Sir Francis Graham Moon, 1st Bt, after Charles Robert Leslie, 1839. National Portrait Gallery, Reference Collection, NPG D33660
13. Pearman, *Cadogans at War*, p. 164, quoting Raymond Hudson, 'Vivat Victoria', *The Lady*, 21–27 June 1988
14. Countess Cadogan to Lord Melbourne, 29 June 1838. Royal Archives, Windsor, Box 21/3
15. W. Couper to Countess Cadogan, 10 Downing Street, 29 June 1838. Royal Archives, Windsor, Box 21/3
16. 'Miss Catherine Elizabeth Hyndman's Bounty to the Church of England (now known as Hyndman's Trustees) [was] set up for a variety of ecclesiastical purposes including the purchase and acquisition of advowsons thus giving the right to appoint to parishes. The Declaration Document is dated 6 December 1836.' http://www.simeons.org.uk/hyndmans-trust-history
17. 'Chelsea Manor', in VCH *Chelsea*, pp. 108–115
18. 'The Parish of Chelsea: Communications', in VCH *Chelsea*, pp. 2–13
19. https://www.cadoganpier.com/history/
20. *ODNB*. doi: 10.1093/ref:odnb/18116
21. These sums were in the same ballpark as those spent by other campaigning politicians.
22. *The Spectator*, vol. 15, no. 735, 30 July 1842 (collected edn, F.C. Westley/Joseph Clayton, 1842), p. 728
23. Lt.-Col. 8th West India Regiment, 10 January 1837; transferred to British East India Regiment. Edward Cadogan's second marriage, on 4 April 1849, was to Jeanne-Marie-Zoé Dupierris, at his home in Tarbes, Hautes-Pyrénées. She was paid a widow's pension. NA WO/42/C2
24. The population of the UK in 1851 is estimated at 27,368,800. ONS
25. VAM. http://www.vam.ac.uk/content/articles/h/history-of-fashion-1840-1900/
26. The collected book form was first published by her husband in 1861. *The Book of Household Management*, ed. Mrs I. Beeton (S.O. Beeton, 1861), p. 86
27. See Jones, *British Diplomatic Service*; Bourne, *The American Historical Review*, vol. 90, issue 1 (February 1985): 136–37, doi: 10.1086/ahr/90.1.136-a; Steiner, 'The Old Foreign Office' in *Opinion publique*, pp. 177–95
28. Jones, *The British Diplomatic Service*, p. 27
29. *New York Times*, 19 August 1858, quoted in Adrienne LaFrance, 'In 1858, People Said the Telegraph Was "Too Fast for the Truth": Sound familiar?', *The Atlantic* (Boston, Mass.), 28 July 2014
30. The official name of the government-subsidized company was The British and North American Royal Mail Steamship Company. 'Enterprise and Prosperity of the Transatlantic Steamship Companies', *New York Times*, 7 June 1865
31. Duncan Geere, 'How the First Cable was Laid Across the Atlantic', *Wired*, 18 January 2011
32. Viscount Chelsea, *Diplomatic Common Place Book*, 7 July 1856
33. Ridley, *Napoleon III*, p. 444, quoting Count Alexander Graf von Hübner, *Neuf ans de souvenirs d'un Ambassadeur d'Autriche à Paris sous le second empire 1851–1859*, (Plon-Nourrit, Paris, 1905), p. 244
34. Ridley, *Napoleon III*, p. 444
35. 'Money-Market and City Intelligence', *The Times*, 3 January 1859. See also subsequent coverage, 4, 5, 6, 7, 8 January 1859
36. Evans, *History of the Commercial Crisis 1857–58*, p. 149
37. 'Money-Market and City Intelligence', *The Times*, 28 April 1859. Over £6.3 billion in today's money. BoE
38. Marguerite Gardiner, *The Idler in France* (Paris, 1841), p. 252, quoted in Noel-Smith and Campbell, *Hornblower's Historical Shipmates*, p. 89
39. Lady Honoria Cadogan to 4th Earl Cadogan, n.d. [1864]. The sisters were paying ground rent to the Cadogan Estate at this point.
40. Viscount Chelsea to 4th Earl Cadogan, n.d. [1864]
41. In 1969 the Cadogan coffins were removed to a communal area in the crypt to make space. The crest remains on the old crypt door.

13: ART & EUROPE

1. Huon Mallalieu, 'Around the Watercolour Fair: Huon Mallalieu Focuses on One Artist', *Country Life*, 16 January 1992
2. 'My dear George, I am by Augusta's wish writing to you, _____[?] to some items of her personal property, formerly my father's, which she wishes you to accept: a pair of enamel opera glasses given to my mother [Honoria Blake] by the duc d'Orléans...'. Frederick Cadogan to 5th Earl Cadogan, 30 October 1882
3, 4, 5, 6, 7 Lady Augusta Cadogan, 'La Grande Dame de l'Ancien Régime', *Macmillan's Magazine*, vol. 36 (May–Oct 1877): 494–504; 'Part II', *Macmillan's*, vol. 37 (November 1877–April 1878): 389–97. Quoted passages from vol. 36, p. 494; vol. 37, p. 396–97; vol. 36, p. 497; vol. 36, p. 495; ibid.; vol. 37, p. 391.
8. 'Treacherous England'; 'Do you see? In fact, of the English I like only you and Godfrey's salts.' (translation by the author). Cadogan, *Macmillan's*, vol. 37, p. 391
9. Sophie Derrot, 'La renaissance du château de Mouchy (1855–1866)', *Livraisons d'histoire de l'architecture*, vol. 29 (2015): 115–23, doi: 10.4000/lha.472
10. *The Times*, 4 Feb.; 13 Mar.; *The Gentleman's Magazine* (1837), i. 656-7; Fitzgerald, ii. 254; PROB 11/1876/265, quoted in HoP *Commons 1820–1832*
11. Lieutenant-Colonel Sir Henry Cooke to Lord Fitzgerald, 16 June 1838, quoted in Percy Hetherington Fitzgerald, *The Life and Times of William IV: Including a view of socifal life and manners during his reign*, vol. I (Tinsley Brothers, 1884), p. 211–12. Duke of Wellington's papers, MS61/WP1/1120/1
12. 'Queen's Gazette', 5 April 1838, *Court Magazine and belle assemblée [afterw.] and monthly critic and the Lady's magazine and museum (United Series)*, vol. XII, no. v (May 1838), collected edn

(Leighton and Murphy, 1838), pp. 472–75

13 'Presentation at Court', *Modern Etiquette in Public and Private* (revised edn, Frederick Warne & Co., 1887), pp. 34–36

14 'The Victoria Connection', VAM. https://www.vam.ac.uk/articles/the-victoria-connection

15, 16, 17, 18 QVJ (Lord Escher's typescripts). Kensington Palace, 29 May 1835, vol. 1, pp. 12–17; Kensington Palace, 11 March 1837, vol. 3, p. 58–59; Buckingham Palace, 21 July 1838, vol. 6, p. 183 & Windsor Castle, 7 November 1839, vol. 13, pp. 27–28; *see, for example,* Windsor Castle, 13 June 1838, vol. 6, p. 26

19 'His mother was Elizabeth Lamb, née Milbanke…but owing to the desuetude of her marriage his true father was widely held to be anyone but Lord Melbourne; contemporary suspicion rested on the fabulous aesthete Lord Egremont.' ODNB. doi: 10.1093/ref:odnb/15920

20 Marchioness of Anglesey to Marquess of Anglesey, 1 January 1850, The Plas Newydd Papers. Anglesey, *One Leg*, p. 334

21 Greville Papers, 17 May 1860, vol. 8., p. 36

22 QVJ (Princess Beatrice's copies). Balmoral, 12 November 1874, vol. 63, p. 284

23 The story was retold by Werner Herzog in the biopic *Queen of the Desert* (2015), starring Nicole Kidman as Bell, with James Franco as Henry Cadogan.

24 Battersea Dogs' and Cats' Home Archive. Claire Horton, Chief Executive of Battersea Dogs' and Cats' Home, to 8th Earl Cadogan, 29 January 2019

25 Cadogan, *Macmillan's*, vol. 37, pp. 396, 397

26 British Patent 8842 (1841)

27 National Portrait Gallery. https://www.npg.org.uk/index.php?id=5754

28 Frank was the grandson of the Reverend Edward Cadogan (1833–1890). His line is descended from Cadwgan William Cadwgan (1565–1647), eldest son of William ap Cadwgan (1508–1594), an ancestor he shares with physician Dr William Cadogan (1711–1797).

The Earls Cadogan descend from the second son, Henry (1575–1635).

29 Cadogan, *Macmillan's*, vol. 37, pp. 391, 392–93

30 Norfolk Record Office; LMA

31 *See, for example, International Journal of Surgical Oncology*, 5 June 2011. doi: 10.1155/2011/980158

32 Lady Honoria Cadogan, *The Great Hall of a Gothic Country House*, n.d., watercolour over pencil and gouache on paper. Lot 5, sale 8045, 19th Century Paintings, Christie's New York, East, 24 October 1997

33 Mrs Charlotte Villiers to Queen Mary, 18 March 1937. Royal Archives, Windsor Castle

34 David Brichieri-Colombi, great-great-grandson of Colonel Sir George Cadogan, 'received an invitation from Lady Millar at Windsor Castle to authenticate watercolours by Honoria Cadogan in the Royal Collection.' Letter to Kira Charatan

35 Paul Sandby, RA, was appointed chief drawing master in 1768. ODNB. doi: 10.1093/ref:odnb/24613

36 Mallalieu, 'Around the Watercolour Fair,' 16 January 1992

37 Lt.-Col. Somerset J. Gough Calthorpe, *Cadogan's Crimea: Illustrated by General the Hon. Sir George Cadogan K.C.B.* (abridged and illustrated edn, Hamish Hamilton, 1979)

38 QVJ (Princess Beatrice's copies). Buckingham Palace, 24 March 1855, vol. 39, p. 177. *Also* 'We dined alone with Vicky & afterwards looked at sketches by Col. Cadogan.' Osborne House, 29 July 1856, vol. 42, p. 67

39 Duke of Cambridge, St James's Palace, to Colonel George Cadogan, 3 April 1855. NAM

40 QVJ (Princess Beatrice's copies). Osborne House, 5 August 1856, vol. 42, pp. 84–85

41 ODNB. doi: 10.1093/ref:odnb/35241

42 NA WO 42/3

43 NA PPR 1882; PPR 1917; PPR 1932

14: POLITICS & PROPERTY

1 'Chelsea & The Colonies: 5th Earl Cadogan', *Statesmen*, no. 361, *Vanity Fair* (1881)

2 'Election Intelligence: Bury (Lancashire)', *The Times*, 7 September 1868, p. 5

3 Editorial, *The Western Times* (Devon), 8 May 1873, p. 2

4, 5 'New Member for Bath', *Frome Times*, 21 May 1873, p. 3

6 'Our New Member', *Bath Chronicle and Weekly Gazette*, 15 May 1873, p. 8

7, 8 5th Earl Cadogan, *Diaries*, 8 February 1875; 20 February 1872

9 Rollo Russell, *London Fogs* (Edward Stanford, 1880), p. 2 and Georg Hartwig, *The Aerial World: A Popular Account of the Phenomena and Life of the Atmosphere* (Longmans, Green, 1874), p. 139, quoted in Corton, *London Fog*, pp. 87, 88

10 'Killed by the Fog', *Medical Times and Gazette: A Journal of Medical Science, Literature, Criticism and News*, 13 December 1873. Corton, *London Fog*, pp. 79–80

11 The Tramways Act (1870) saw the construction of several new routes criss-crossing London.

12 Shaw designed nos 8, 9–11, 15, 17 and 18.

13 See Weinreb and Hibbert, *London Encyclopedia*, p. 118

14 'Settlement and Building: From 1865 to 1900', in VCH *Chelsea*, pp. 66–67

15 https://www.parliament.uk/about/living-heritage/building/northern-estate/normanshaw-parliament-st1/

16 Mark Girouard, *Sweetness and Light: The Queen Anne Movement, 1860–1900* (Clarendon Press, 1977), p. 93, quoted in Paul Velvet, '60 Cadogan Square – Heritage Report', July 2019. RBKC

17 *See, for example*, 'The Chelsea Evictions', *West London Observer*, 14 December 1889, which reports a crowded local meeting led by the local MP, Mr Whitmore.

18 5th Earl Cadogan, Office of the Privy Council, 10 Downing Street, to Lord William Compton, n.d. [in reply to Compton's of 19 February 1887]

19 'The Reported Evictions in Chelsea: An Interview with Earl Cadogan', *Pall Mall Gazette*, 17 December 1889, p. 6

20 5th Earl Cadogan, Chelsea House, to Guinness Trust, 20 March 1890

21 C. Ritchie, House of Commons, to 5th Earl Cadogan, 21 March 1890

22 Baroness Hanham CBE, foreword

NOTES

to Gillian Best, *From Hovel to Penthouse: A History of Social Housing in Chelsea* (Chelsea Society, 2015), p. iii

23 5th Earl Cadogan, Chelsea House, to Guinness Trust, 20 March 1890. Cost equivalent to £5 million in 2018. BoE
24 Alan Powers, 'Architecture of the Estate', in C&C, p. 149
25 'The phrase seems to have been coined by John Betjeman in Betjeman (ed.), *Collins Guide to English Parish Churches* (Collins, 1958), p. 255'. Crawford, 'Arts & Crafts Churches', in A. Saint and T. Sladen (eds), *Churches 1870–1914*, p. 78 fn. 12. *See also* Alec Hamilton, 'The Lure of the Arts & Crafts Church', *Ecclesiology Today*, 46 (July 2012): 3–22
26 Lee & Pembertons, 44 Lincoln's Inn Fields, to G.R. Strachan, Esq., 17 January 1889
27 Fiona Duncan, *Telegraph Review*
28 A.N. Wilson, 'The Legacy of Thomas Carlyle: A Conversation Between Simon Heffer, Ian Hislop and A.N. Wilson', National Trust, 23 March 2017, 3'30"
29 *The Builder*, 9 January 1889, p. 50
30 NHLE: Rossetti Studios
31 Cadogan Estate Office, Agenda & Minute Book 22, pp. 1, 66
32 Thomas Symonds, Admiral of the Fleet, to 5th Earl Cadogan, 11 January 1887
33, 34 Marquess of Salisbury to 5th Earl Cadogan, 18 April 1887; 5 June 1886
35 Prince of Wales to 5th Earl Cadogan, 18 April 1887
36, 37 Hansard. Bill to amend the Land Law (Ireland) Act, 1881, and the Purchase of Land (Ireland) Act, 1885; and for other purposes connected therewith— Presented (The Lord Privy Seal). First Reading 31 March 1887.
38 'News of the Week', *The Spectator*, no. 3,066, 2 April 1887, p. 3
39 5th Earl Cadogan, to Marquess of Salisbury, 27 June 1895
40 Cadogan, *Before the Deluge*, p. 52
41 5th Earl Cadogan, Amhuinnsuidhe Castle, North Harris, to Queen Victoria, 5 October 1896
42 QVJ (Princess Beatrice's copies). Vice Regal Lodge, Phoenix Park, 4 April 1900, vol. 110, pp. 125–29; Royal Yacht *Victoria & Albert*, 26 April 1900, vol. 110, pp. 153–54
43 King Edward VII, Royal Yacht *Victoria & Albert*, Cowes, to 5th Earl Cadogan, 16 July 1902
44 *The Times*, 3 February 1909, p. 10

15: COURT & COUNTRYSIDE

1 'The Late Countess Cadogan', *Lady's Pictorial*, 16 February 1907
2 4th Earl Cadogan to Viscount Chelsea, n.d. [1865]
3 QVJ (Princess Beatrice's copies). Windsor Castle, 9 November 1857, vol. 44, pp. 90–91
4 Reverend Russell Day, Eton College, to 4th Earl Cadogan, 11 December 1858
5 Rt. Hon. H. Macmillan, *Winds of Change 1914–1939* (Macmillan, 1966), p. 30
6 Dilks (ed.), *Diaries*, p. 2
7 QVJ (Princess Beatrice's copies). Windsor Castle, 28 June 1877, vol. 67, pp. 179–80
8 Prince of Wales, Sandringham, to 5th Earl Cadogan, 25 December 1883
9 Duchess of Teck to Countess Cadogan, 3 March 1889; Charlotte, Hereditary Princess of Saxe-Meiningen, to Countess Cadogan, 24 October 1883; Princess Victoria to Countess Cadogan, 1 January 1904
10 Prince of Wales to 5th Earl Cadogan, n.d. [1883]
11 F. Crawshay to 5th Earl Cadogan, 6 October 1886
12 Countess Cadogan, Chelsea House, to William Cadogan, 18 March 1889
13 Alan Powers, 'Architecture of the Estate', in C&C, p. 139
14 'Lord Cadogan and His Tenantry', *St James's Gazette*, Monday, 7 October 1889, p. 8
15, 16 'Lord Cadogan's Jerseys', *Country Life*, vol. 19, no. 473, 27 January 1906; 'Lord Cadogan's Sheep', *Country Life*, vol. 19, no. 475, 10 February 1906
17 Ibid. *See also* 'Notes on the Woods of Culford Hall', *Country Life*, vol. 33, no. 860, 28 June 1913.
18 https://www.culford.co.uk/about-us/culford-history. No mention of the telephone, but Alexander Graham Bell's patent had been awarded in 1876.
19 Mike Marqusee, *Anyone But England: Cricket, Race and Class* (Bloomsbury, 2016), n.p.
20, 21 'Racing Intelligence', *The Times*, 8 August 1880; 28 July 1881
22 George Lambton, *Men and Horses I Have Known* (1924; revised edn, Allen & Co, 1986), p. 53
23 'The Right Hon. The Earl Cadogan, K.G., P.C., LL.D., at Chelsea House: Celebrities at Home, no. 1667', *The World*, 18 June 1912, p. 926
24 Marquess of Salisbury, Hatfield House, to 5th Earl Cadogan, 5 March 1885
25 Rebecca Louise Cassidy, *Horse People: Thoroughbred Culture in Lexington and Newmarket* (Baltimore, MD: John Hopkins University Press, 2010), n.p.
26 5th Earl Cadogan, to Lord Portland, 7 August 1887.
27 5th Earl Cadogan, 'The State of the Turf. The Present State of Horse-Racing and the General Features of Its Present Management and Rules and Regulations', *The Fortnightly Review*, vol. 43 (London, Jan–June 1885): 112
28 5th Earl Cadogan to Queen Victoria. Royal Archives, RC/64
29 Queen Victoria, Balmoral Castle, to 5th Earl Cadogan, 6 June 1891. Royal Archives, RC/66
30 Baccarat was declared illegal by the High Court in 1885. See Dixon, *From Prohibition to Regulation*
31 *ODNB*. doi: 10.1093/ref:odnb/39392
32 *See* Ridley, *Bertie*, pp. 280–91
33 Marquess of Salisbury to 5th Earl Cadogan, 21 July 1891
34 Obituary of Countess Cadogan, *The Ladies' Field*, 16 February 1907. The castle was used during the winter for official entertaining.
35 'Court Circular', *The Times*, 31 August 1897, p. 7
36 5th Earl Cadogan to Marquess of Salisbury, 24 April 1899
37 'Marriage of Sir Samuel Scott and Lady Sophie Cadogan', Court Circular, *The Times*, 30 June 1896, p. 10
38 Frederick Cunliffe-Owen, 'Letter of the Marquise de Fontenoy' [pseudonymous column], *Chicago Tribune*, 5 December 1901, p. 16
39 Sir Samuel Scott, 6th Bt., 7 Grosvenor Square, to 5th Earl

Cadogan, Monday and Tuesday [17 & 18 April 1899]
40, 41, 42 Lady Emily Lurgan, 21 Lowndes Street, to Countess Cadogan, Wednesday [19 April 1899]; Sunday [23 April 1899]; ibid.
43 'Please do not for a moment think that I am the least altered towards her. I shall wait to the last moment, as the only thing I wish and desire is for her to come back to me.' Sir Samuel Scott, S.Y. *Normania*, to 5th Earl Cadogan, 3 June 1899
44 Lady Sophie Scott, Glen Severn, Wilton Road, Bexhill-on-Sea, to 5th Earl Cadogan, n.d. [June/July 1899]
45 Lord Lurgan, Runnymede, to 5th Earl Cadogan, n.d. [June/July 1889]
46 Cunliffe-Owen, 'Letter of the Marquise de Fontenoy', op. cit.
47 *Daily Express* quoted in 'Ireland: Departure of Lord Cadogan', *The Times*, 13 August 1902, p. 5
48 Sidney Grosvenor, equerry in waiting, Osborne House, to 5th Earl Cadogan, 31 January 1901
49 King Edward VII, Windsor Castle, to 5th Earl Cadogan, telegram, 17 May 1902
50 Cadogan, *Before the Deluge*, p. 7
51 5th Earl Cadogan to Prime Minister Arthur Balfour, 25 July 1902

16: SOCIETY & SUCCESSION
1 King Edward VII, Buckingham Palace, to 5th Earl Cadogan, 10 February 1907
2 Horace Farquhar, later 1st Earl Farquhar, Buckingham Palace, to 5th Earl Cadogan, 13 January 1907
3 'The Late Countess Cadogan', *Lady's Pictorial*, 16 February 1907
4 Eulogy by C.A. Whitmore at the Chelsea Benevolent Society, reproduced in the *West Middlesex Advertiser*, 13 February 1907
5 *Chelsea Mail*, 15 February 1907
6 Marquise de Fontenoy [Frederick Cunliffe-Owen], 'Bankrupt Becomes Heir to Earldom', *The Washington Post*, 10 June 1910, p. 6
7 <Sequer> to 5th Earl Cadogan, 12 July 1887
8 Diana Chardin, Librarian, Trinity College, Cambridge, to Kira Charatan, 2002
9 [7th Duke of Richmond and Gordon], Molecomb, Chichester, to 5th Earl Cadogan, 27 January 1889
10 <M.G.> to 5th Earl Cadogan, [10 or 18] June 1893
11 *ODNB*. doi: 10.1093/ref:odnb/50414
12 Edward N. Lake, Westgate House, Bury St Edmunds, to 5th Earl Cadogan, 30 May 1900
13 Viscount Chelsea, 31 Green Street, Park Lane, to 5th Earl Cadogan, June 1900
14 'Lord Chelsea's Wedding Fête', *Daily Chronicle*, 13 August 1892
15 Viscount Chelsea, Castle Rising, King's Lynn, Norfolk, to 5th Earl Cadogan, Thursday [summer 1892?]
16 5th Earl Cadogan, draft note to [7th Duke of Richmond and Gordon], n.d. [pre-1903]
17 5th Earl Cadogan to Viscountess Chelsea, 1 December 1907 [Copy]
18 Viscountess Chelsea, 48 Bryanston Square, London, to 5th Earl Cadogan, 5 December 1907
19 7th Duke of Richmond, Goodwood, Chichester, to 5th Earl Cadogan, 24 January [1908]
20 *ODNB*. doi: 10.1093/ref:odnb/97889
21 Lewin Cadogan, Wellington Club, Wellington, New Zealand, to 5th Earl Cadogan, 7 March 1900
22 *The Washington Post*, 10 June 1910, op. cit.
23 *The Morning Post*, n.d.
24 *The Washington Post*, 10 June 1910, op. cit.
25 Edward Cadogan to William Cadogan, 1 February 1910
26 5th Earl Cadogan, Culford Hall, to William Cadogan, n.d. [January 1912]
27 *Ladies' Pictorial*, 21 January 1911
28 *The Bystander*, 12 May 1911
29 Cadogan, *Before the Deluge*, p. 185
30 'Coronation of George VI' (1911), British Pathé, film IDs: 1800.01, 1800.10, 1804.01, 1804.02, 2870.08.
31 *The Star*, 6 March 1915
32 'Letter from the Rector', Chelsea Rectory, 31 March 1915
33 Alexander Cadogan, 8 Gloucester Square, to Edward Cadogan, 30 January 1916
34 Adele, Dowager Countess Cadogan, Chelsea House, to Edward Cadogan, 8 July 1916
35 PPR *England & Wales, National Probate Calendar (Index of Wills and Administrations), 1858–1955*, 1960 p. 4. Estate of £56,845 0s 4d equal to approximately £1.3 million in 2020. BoE.
36 Alexander Cadogan, 8 Gloucester Square, to Edward Cadogan, 19 March 1916
37 Lady Edith Cadogan, Lairg Lodge, to Edward Cadogan, 25 August 1915
38 Lady Cynthia Cadogan, Crichel, Wimborne, to Edward Cadogan, 21 February 1916
39 Lady Edith Cadogan, Theobolds Cross, Waltham Cross, to Edward Cadogan, 3 May 1916
40 Edward Cadogan, Chelsea House, to William Cadogan, 15 November [1910]
41 Rachel Cooke, 'Gossip, sex and social climbing: the uncensored Chips Channon Diaries', *The Guardian*, 28 February 2021
42 Channon, *Diaries*, 17 October 1923
43 'Who's Who in Herts', *The Tatler*, no. 5833 (July 1930): 203
44, 45 Lady Sibyl Cadogan, Admiralty House, Portsmouth, to Edward Cadogan, 25 November 1915; 26 December 1915
46 Alexander Cadogan, 8 Gloucester Square, to Edward Cadogan, 6 February 1916
47 Roger Powell, *Royal Sex: The Scandalous Love Lives of the British Royal Family* (Amberley, 2010)
48 Lady Sibyl Cadogan, Windsor Castle, to Edward Cadogan, 20 August 1916
49 Channon, *Diaries*, 27 January 1937
50 Lady Helen Hardinge, *Diary*, 7 July 1924, Lady Murray papers, quoted in Vickers, *Queen Mother*, p. 77
51 Godfrey (ed.), *Letters from a Prince*, p. 194
52, 53 Channon, *Diaries*, 2 July 1936; 27 January 1937
54 'The Remarkable Cadogan Family', *Evening Standard*, 20 May 1939
55 'King and Queen at Blandford Nuptial', *The New York Times*, 18 February 1920, p. 11
56 Lovell, *Churchills*, p. 133. The figure would be in the hundreds of millions of today. BoE
57 Ibid., p. 481
58 Obit. 11th Duke of Marlborough, quote in reference to his father. *Daily Telegraph*, 16 October 2014
59, 60 Pearson, *Private Lives*, p. 214
61 Spencer-Churchill, *Blenheim*, p. 202
62 Pearson, *Private Lives*, p. 260

63 Consuelo Balsan, *The Glitter and the Gold* (Heinemann, 1953), p. 236
64 *See, for example*, Sir John Colville, *Those Lambtons!* (Hodder & Stoughton, 1988); Vickers, *Queen Mother*, p. 78
65 'The Remarkable Cadogan Family', *Evening Standard*, 20 May 1939

17: BROTHERS IN ARMS

1   Frederick Pethick-Lawrence, *Fate Has Been Kind* (Hutchinson, 1943). Baron Pethick-Lawrence (1871–1961) was a near-contemporary of Jerry's at Eton.
2, 3 A.C. Benson, 'In Memoriam: Major the Hon. William G.S. Cadogan', *Eton Magazine*, Michaelmas 1914
4   Fusiliers, 1888; 2 lt., 1st Life Gds. 1892
5   Gerald Cadogan, Kareekloof, to Countess Cadogan, 4 April 1900
6   William Cadogan, Bloem Spruit Camp, Bloemfontein, to Countess Cadogan, 14 April 1900
7   Gerald Cadogan, RFS *Golden Eagle*, to 5th Earl Cadogan, 6 June 1900
8   Frederick Cunliffe-Owen, 'Letter of the Marquise de Fontenoy' [pseudonymous column], *Chicago Tribune*, 5 December 1901, p. 16
9   Sophie Cadogan, Hotel Bristol, Paris, to Countess Cadogan, n.d.
10 Lewin Cadogan, Culford Hall, to William Cadogan [1890s]
11 Lewin Cadogan to 5th Earl Cadogan, 8 October 1895
12 Lewin Cadogan, *Dampfer Friedrich Der Grosse*, to Countess Cadogan, 20 November 1899
13, 14 Lewin Cadogan, Wellington Club, Wellington, New Zealand, to 5th Earl Cadogan, 7 March 1900; 8 March 1900
15 Gerald Cadogan, South African Constabulary Recruiting Office, to 5th Earl Cadogan, 16 December 1900
16 'Heathorn's Family Hotel, Hobart', *Launceston Examiner*, Tasmania (Exhibition Supplement), 26 November 1891, p. 4
17 Lewin Cadogan, Heathorns Hotel, Liverpool Street, Hobart, Tasmania, to 5th Earl Cadogan, 19 July 1901
18 5th Earl Cadogan, Culford, to William Cadogan, n.d. [1907/8]
19 Churchill, *Hamilton's March*, pp. 391–92
20, 21 Gerald Cadogan, South African Constabulary, Dynamite Factory, Zuurfontein, to Countess Cadogan, 3 April 1901; n.d. [May 1901]
22 William Cadogan, Lower Topa, Marone Hill, to 5th Earl Cadogan, 23 May 1907
23 PRO WO 76/544
24 5th Earl Cadogan, Kiliechonate, Spean Bridge, to William Cadogan, 7 September 1905
25, 26 Obituary, 'Major the Honourable William Cadogan, M.V.O.', *Oxford Magazine*, 20 November 1914
27 Cadogan, *Under Fire*, pp. 12–13
28 NAM. https://www.nam.ac.uk/explore/1914-mons-christmas
29 William Cadogan, 'On active service', to 5th Earl Cadogan, 4 November 1914
30 Eustace Therman, 'On active service', to 5th Earl Cadogan, 13 November 1914
31 *London Gazette*, 17 February 1915, p. 1653
32 Lord Lurgan, 21 Lowndes Square, to 5th Earl Cadogan, 12 November 1914
33 Prince of Wales, York Cottage, Sandringham, to William Cadogan, 29 December 1913; 5 January 1914
34 Prince of Wales, Warley Barracks, Brentford, Essex, to William Cadogan, 12 August 1914
35 5th Earl Cadogan, Culford, to William Cadogan, 14 February 1907
36 Lewin Cadogan, Minallo, Pine Street, West Hobart, to Edward Cadogan, 24 November 1914
37, 38 Edward Cadogan's diaries, 15 October 1915; 1 October 1915. Cadogan, *Under Fire*, pp. 47; 35
39 Hansard. 'Unemployment Insurance.' HC Deb 09 March 1925 vol. 181 cc965-1089. 99
40 'Obituary: Sir Edward Cadogan – politician and soldier', *The Guardian*, 14 September 1962, p. 2
41 Hansard. 'Corporal Punishment (Committee).' HC Deb 06 May 1937 vol. 323 c1224. Prisoners waited another twenty years for their reprieve from the birch, brought into law in the Criminal Justice Act (1967). https://www.legislation.gov.uk/ukpga/1967/80
42 Hansard. 'Government of India Bill.' HC Deb 05 June 1935 vol. 302 cc1885-2015
43 Cadogan, *Before the Deluge*, p. 95
44 'Obituary', *The Guardian*, 14 September 1962, op. cit.
45 As told to the author by the Hon. Camilla Mountain, September 2018
46 Cadogan, *Before the Deluge*, p. 158
47 William Cadogan, Rawalpindi, to Edward Cadogan, 9 February 1911
48 'May Weddings', *The Times*, 1 May 1911
49 5th Earl Cadogan, Culford, to William Cadogan, n.d. [1912]

18: THE SPORTING LIFE

1   *The Bystander*, 1 February 1911
2   *Hearth and Home*, 2 February 1911
3   5th Earl Cadogan, Culford, to William Cadogan, n.d. [1911]
4   Notification of Gerald's safe return, telegram dated 28 January 1892, Diaries of 5th Earl Cadogan, 1884–94
5   Diaries of 5th Earl Cadogan, 20 October 1893
6   *Daily Mail*, 17 December 1926
7, 8 'The Right Honourable George Henry Earl Cadogan, KG, to The Earl of March and Another, Conveyance of Reversionary Life Estate of the Honourable G.O. Cadogan', 18 June 1894
9   Gerald Cadogan, South African Constabulary, Knoppieslgaate, to Countess Cadogan, 18 September 1901
10 Edward Cadogan, Chelsea House, to William Cadogan, n.d. [1909/10]
11 Alexander Cadogan, Culford, to William Cadogan, 13 January 1910; Chelsea House, n.d.
12 5th Earl Cadogan, Hotel Excelsior, Aix-les-Bains, to William Cadogan, 2 August 1910
13 William Cadogan, Rawalpindi, to 5th Earl Cadogan, 9 March 1911
14 Alexander Cadogan, 8 Gloucester Square, to Edward Cadogan, 27 February 1916
15 Cadogan Estate Agendas and Minute Books, 1916 and 1930
16 6th Earl Cadogan, Culford, to Edward Cadogan, 8 January 1916
17 It took a while to see the full amount. Alec wrote to Eddie from the Foreign Office on 30 March 1916, 'The Trustees have paid us each the remaining £2,500 due to us from the £5,000 taken on account of Jerry's debts.'
18 Cadogan Estate Agendas and Minute Books, 1915–21

19 Cadogan Estate Agendas and Minute Books, 1918
20 *The Queen*, February 1924
21 David Lloyd George, *The Times*, 13 September 1918, pp. 7–8
22, 23 Jeffreys, *British Olympic Association*, p. 53, quoting Fairlie, *Official Report of Olympiad 1924*, p. 74; p. 56 quoting 64, 94
24 8th Earl Cadogan, 4 December 2018
25 The 6th Earl later joined Old Etonian Lodge (no. 4500) and Cadogan Lodge (no. 162).
26 Jeffreys, *British Olympic Association*, p. 57, quoting Harold Abrahams (ed.), *British Olympic Association Official Report of the IXth Olympiad 1928* (BOA, 1929)
27 Rick Glanville, *Chelsea Football Club: The Official History in Pictures* (Headline, 2006), p. 58
28 Change kits 1986–89 and Third Stadium kit 2023/24. Chelsea FC. www.chelseafc.com
29 Philip Beddows, 'Heraldry Connected with Elystan Glodrydd', unpublished MS
30 Philip Noel-Baker, *Man of Sport, Man of Peace. Collected Speeches and Essays of Philip Noel-Baker, Olympic Statesman 1889–1992*, ed. Don Anthony (Sports Editions, 1991), pp. 40–41, quoted in Jeffreys, *British Olympic Association*, p. 60
31 World Association of Girl Guides and Girl Scouts. https://www.wagggs.org/en/about-us/our-history/
32 Agnes Baden-Powell, *The Handbook for Girl Guides: Or How Girls Can Help Build the Empire* (London, 1912), quoted in Zweiniger-Bargielowska, *Managing the Body*, p. 135
33 Clipping from *The News of the World*. 'The Girl Guides Suffolk: A Press Cutting Book of the Great Rally, 3 July 1926', Cadogan Archive
34 '6000 Girl Guides parade for Princess Mary', *Daily Mirror*, 5 July 1926. 'Eastern Counties Girl Guides: Princess Mary Reviews Wonderful Rally at Culford', *East Anglian Daily Times*, Monday 5 July 1926. 'The Girl Guides Suffolk', op.cit.
35 'Earl Cadogan: Receiving Order Against Him', *Daily Mail*, 17 December 1926
36 *The Times*, 18 February 1929
37 'Sale of Chelsea Estate: Redevelopment of 14 Acres', *The Times*, 26 March 1929
38 'Spies and Men With Sticks: Chelsea Tenants Prepare Against Evictions', *The Star*, 22 September 1930
39 *Evening News*, 22 September 1930
40, 41 'Spies and Men With Sticks', op. cit.
42, 43 'The Chelsea Eviction War', *Daily Express*, 23 September 1930
44 'Settlement and building: Twentieth century, up to the second world war', VCH *Chelsea*, pp. 79–90
45 *Evening News*, 4 June 1931
46 Cadogan Estate Agendas and Minute Books, 1932
47 'Social history: Social and cultural activities', in VCH *Chelsea*, pp. 166–176
48 Cadogan Estate Agendas and Minute Books, 1916 & 1930

19: RIDING THE WHIRLWIND

1 Cadogan, *Diaries*, 20 June 1939, GBR/0014/ACAD 1/8
2 'Sir Alexander Cadogan, Calm Diplomat', *The Daily Telegraph*, 10 July 1968, p. 18
3 Alexander Cadogan to 5th Earl Cadogan, 29 April 1894
4 A.F. Schofield, Librarian of Cambridge University 1923–49, quoted in *ODNB*. doi: 10.1093/ref:odnb/32234
5 Alexander Cadogan, Eton College, Windsor, to 5th Earl Cadogan, 22 September 1901
6 A.C. Benson, Eton College, Windsor, to 5th Earl Cadogan, 21 September 1901
7 J.L. Strachan-Davidson, Balliol College, Oxford, to A.C. Benson, 9 November 1902
8 L.E. Jones, *An Edwardian Youth* (Macmillan, 1956), pp. 49, 64
9, 10, 11 Nicolson, *Some People*, pp. 136; p. 137; 139
12 Richard Norton-Taylor, 'Spymaster – The Secret Life of Kendrick by Helen Fry – review', *The Guardian*, 10 February 2015
13 Lady Theodosia Acheson, 22 Mansfield Street, London, to Edward Cadogan, n.d. [1911]
14 Alexander Cadogan, Vienna IV, Theresianumgasse II, to 5th Earl Cadogan, 20 March 1914
15, 16 Dilks (ed.), *Diaries*, p. 4; p. 5
17 General Temperley, *The Whispering Gallery of Europe* (Collins, 1938), p. 108
18 Hansard. 'European Situation', HC Deb 23 March 1933 vol. 276 cc511-626
19 Dilks (ed.), *Diaries*, p. 8
20 Brenda Parry, 'Widow of Foreign Office Chief Has to Sell Treasures', *Daily Telegraph*, 12 March 1977, p. 17
21 Alexander Cadogan to Antony Eden, 30 April 1935. Papers of Sir Alexander Cadogan, courtesy of Lady Theodosia Cadogan, Dilks (ed.), *Diaries*, p. 10
22 G. Bruce Strang, 'Sir Alexander Cadogan and the Steward-Hesse Affair: Assessments of British Cabinet Politics and Future British Policy, 1938', *The International History Review*, vol. 43, no. 3 (2021): 657–676 doi: 10.1080/07075332.2020.1777455
23 Sir Peter Ricketts, 'Sir Alexander Cadogan – Churchill's indispensable man', Engelsberg Ideas, 23 March 2022. https://engelsbergideas.com/portraits/sir-alexander-cadogan-churchills-indispensable-man/
24 Cadogan, *Diaries*, 2 January 1939, GBR/0014/ACAD 1/8
25 Avon, *The Reckoning*, p. 285
26, 27, 28 Cadogan, *Diaries*, 20 June 1939; 11 January 1939; 9 September 1939, GBR/0014/ACAD 1/8
29 Cadogan, *Diaries*, 10 July 1940, GBR/0014/ACAD 1/9. Interesting to note, this passage is omitted from the Dilks *Diaries*, which were published within the duke's lifetime.
30 Report from Informant in Close Touch with [former Foreign Minister] Neurath's Entourage, 7 July 1940, RA GVI/C/042A/202 and FO 1093/23, NA, quoted in Lownie, *Traitor King*, p. 119
31 Cadogan, *Diaries*, 4 September 1940, GBR/0014/ACAD 1/9
32 Dilks (ed.), *Diaries*, pp. 472–73, including quote of Wilson from Lord Moran, *Winston Churchill: the Struggle for Survival* (1966), p. 78
33 Associated Press, 'Sir Alexander Cadogan, Churchill Aide, Diplomat' [obituary], *The Boston Globe*, 10 July 1968, p. 39
34 Cadogan, *Diaries*, 9 September 1940, GBR/0014/ACAD 1/9

35 Cadogan, *Diaries*, 21 October 1940, GBR/0014/ACAD 1/9
36 'London Hotels Hit', *The Times*, 29 November 1940, p. 2
37 Cadogan, *Diaries*, 20 Jan 1941, GBR/0014/ACAD 1/10
38 NHLE 1216892
39 Alexander Cadogan to Lady Theodosia Cadogan, 4 September 1943
40 *Daily Telegraph*, 12 March 1977, op. cit.
41 Communications Committee, 'First Report: The British Film and Television Industries', vol. 1 (House of Lords, 2010), HL Paper 37-I. A.D. Bain, 'The Growth of Television Ownership in the United Kingdom', *International Economic Review*, vol. 3, no. 2 (May 1962): 146. doi: 10.2307/2525421
42 BBC. https://www.bbc.com/historyofthebbc/anniversaries/june/coronation-of-queen-elizabeth-ii. The royal household cites even more impressive figures: '27 million people in the UK (out of the 36 million population) watched the ceremony on television and 11 million listened on the radio.' https://www.royal.uk/50-facts-about-queens-coronation-0
43 See Tony Shaw, 'Cadogan's Last Fling: Sir Alexander Cadogan, Chairman of the Board of Governors of the BBC', in *Whitehall and the Suez Crisis*, eds Anthony Gorst and Saul Keelly (Frank Cass, 2000), pp. 126–45
44 Cadogan, *Diaries*, GBR/0014/ACAD 1/25
45 Obituary, *Boston Globe*, op. cit.
46 United Press, 'Alexander Cadogan Dies, Unexcitable Civil Servant', *Transcript-Telegram* (Holyoke, Mass.), 10 July 1968, p. 32
47 Tribune Wire Services, 'Cadogan, Ace Diplomat for Britain, Dies', *Chicago Tribune*, 10 July 1968, p. 30

20: MILITARY MAN & MODERNIZER

1 PPR *England & Wales*, *National Probate Calendar (Index of Wills and Administrations), 1858-1995*, p. 580. Typed calculations headed 'Estimated Duties Payable', show £1.15 million, dated 21 November 1936, Cadogan Archive
2 Hansard (1894). Lesley Hoskins et al., 'The Death Duties in Britain 1859–1930', *History of Wealth* (working paper, Cambridge, 2014); Marie M. Fletcher, 'Death and Taxes: Estate Duty – a neglected factor in changes to British business structure after World War Two', *Business History* (22 March 2021). doi: 10.1080/00076791.2021.1892642
3 'The Passing Hour', *The Bystander*, 23 December 1931, p. 579
4 Sir Samuel Scott, 78 Mount Street, to 7th Earl Cadogan, 24 January 1935
5 'Settlement and building: Twentieth century, up to the second world war', in VCH *Chelsea*, pp. 79–90 noting *The Times*, 12 May 1936
6, 7 Primrose Yarde-Buller, Pear Tree Cottage, 11 Meliva Place, St John's Wood, to 7th Earl Cadogan, 21 November 1935
8 Denise Orme, *Cinderella with Variations*, unpublished MS, courtesy Lorna Alexander
9 Countess Cadogan, Lillingstone Lovell Manor, Buckingham, to 7th Earl Cadogan, 10 October 1939
10 Lovell, *Riviera Set*, p. 219
11 Countess Cadogan, Beech Hill Farm, Rushlake Green, to 7th Earl Cadogan, 18 March 1942.
12 7th Earl Cadogan, *Journal of Italy*, unpublished MS
13 As told to the author, 20 November 2018
14 *London Gazette*, Thursday, 15 June 1944. He was by then 3rd Baron Stanley of Preston, 5th Baron and 12th Baronet Stanley of Bickerstaff, co. Lancaster, succeeding his grandfather as 18th Earl of Derby in February 1948.
15, 16 John Simpson, 'Chelsea in Two World Wars', in C&C, p. 52; p. 53
17 Hansard. 'War Damage Bill', HC Deb 12 February 1964, vol. 689 cc431-48
18 Countess Cadogan, Beech Hill Farm, Rushlake Green, to 7th Earl Cadogan, 18 April 1942
19 Lorna Alexander to the author, London, 11 March 2019
20 UK Government. 'UK Armed Forces Mental Health: Annual Summary and Trends Over Time, 2007/8 –2019/20', MoD, 18 June 2020. https://assets.publishing.service.gov.uk/government/uploads/system/uploads/attachment_data/file/892426/20200618_Annual_Report_19-20_O.pdf
21 *Oxford Companion to Scottish History*, ed. Michael Lynch (Oxford, 2007), p. 327
22 H.O. Ellis, *Cadogan Lodge no. 162: Historical Notes*, p. 21
23 UGLE. *Proceedings of Grand Lodge of England*, vol. 28, 1960–1964, pp. 11–13
24 BM. https://www.britishmuseum.org/sites/default/files/2019-10/British-Museum-Act-1963.pdf
25 UGLE. 'Report of the Deputy Grand Master, R.W. Bro. Rt. Hon. The Earl Cadogan, MC, DL, on the Masonic Mission to India in November 1961', *Proceedings of Grand Lodge of England*, vol. 28, 1960–1964, p. 156
26 Rick Glanvill, *Chelsea Football Club: The Official History in Pictures* (Headline, 2006) p. 162
27 RBKC Planning. https://www.rbkc.gov.uk/planning/listedbuildings/listeddetails.asp?ID=448909
28 Lionel Gordon Baliol Brett, 4th Viscount Esher, *National Life Story Collection: Architects' Lives*. BL C467/14 (7 of 13)
29 UK Government. https://www.legislation.gov.uk/ukpga/1967/88/contents; https://www.legislation.gov.uk/ukpga/1993/28
30 https://historicengland.org.uk/advice/planning/conservation-areas/
31 UGLE. 7th Earl Cadogan's entry at Freemasons' Hall

SELECT RESOURCES & BIBLIOGRAPHY

With thanks to Lord Cadogan for generous access to the family's private archives.

ACAD: Alexander Cadogan Papers at the Churchill Archives Centre, Cambridge. https://archives.chu.cam.ac.uk/collections/research-guides/acad/
BHO: British History Online. http://www.british-history.ac.uk
BL: British Library. https://www.bl.uk
BM: British Museum. http://www.britishmuseum.org
BoE: Bank of England Inflation Calculator. https://www.bankofengland.co.uk/monetary-policy/inflation/inflation-calculator
CCEd: Clergy of the Church of England Database. http://theclergydatabase.org.uk
EH: English Heritage. https://www.english-heritage.org.uk
Hansard. https://hansard.parliament.uk; https://api.parliament.uk/historic-hansard/
HoP: History of Parliament. http://www.historyofparliamentonline.org/
LMA: London Metropolitan Archives. https://www.cityoflondon.gov.uk/things-to-do/history-and-heritage/london-metropolitan-archives
NA: National Archives of the UK. https://www.nationalarchives.gov.uk
NAL: National Archives Legislation. https://www.legislation.gov.uk/
NAM: National Army Museum. https://www.nam.ac.uk/
NHLE: National Heritage List for England. https://historicengland.org.uk/listing/the-list/
NHM: Natural History Museum. http://www.nhm.ac.uk
NMM: National Maritime Museum Collections. http://collections.rmg.co.uk
NMRC: National Monuments Record of Wales. https://coflein.gov.uk
ONS: Office for National Statistics. https://www.ons.gov.uk
PA: Parliamentary Archives. https://archives.parliament.uk/
PPR: Principal Probate Registry.
RBA: Royal Berkshire Archives. https://www.royalberkshirearchives.org.uk
RCAHMW: Royal Commission on the Ancient and Historical Monuments of Wales. https://rcahmw.gov.uk
RCT: Royal Collection Trust. https://www.rct.uk/
RMG: Royal Museums Greenwich. https://www.rmg.co.uk/
UGLE: United Grand Lodge of England. https://www.ugle.org.uk/freemasons-hall/museum-freemasonry
UK Government. https://www.gov.uk/government/history/
WO: War Office. Officers' Birth Certificates, Wills and Personal Papers. https://discovery.nationalarchives.gov.uk/browse/r/h/C259
WP: Duke of Wellington's Papers, University of Southampton. https://www.southampton.ac.uk/archives/cataloguedatabases/well/index.page

Anglesey, George Charles Henry Victor Paget, Marquess of, *One Leg: Life and Letters of Henry William Paget, K.G., First Marquess of Anglesey, 1768–1854* (Jonathan Cape, 1961; reprint edn Leo Cooper, 1996)
Anon., *A Catalogue of the Rich Furniture of the Right Honourable the Earl of Cadogan (deceas'd.) With the Lease of his Lordship's large dwelling house,... Which will be sold by auction... on Tuesday the 14th of February, 1726–7 [sic]* (1727)
Ashe, Geoffrey, *Kings and Queens of Early Britain* (Academy Chicago, 1990)
Bagot, J. (ed.), *George Canning and His Friends*, vol. 2 (John Murray/E.P. Dutton, 1909)
Barnard, T.C., 'Lawyers and the Law in Later Seventeenth-Century Ireland', *Irish Historical Studies*, vol. 28, no. 111 (1993): 256–282, https://www.jstor.org/stable/30007492
Bartrum, *WCD*: Bartrum, P.C., *A Welsh Classical Dictionary: People in History and Legend up to about 1000* (National Library of Wales, 1993)
— *Welsh Genealogies AD 300–1400*, 8 vols (University of Wales, 1974)
Bottigheimer, K., 'English Money and Irish Land: The "Adventurers" in the Cromwellian Settlement of Ireland', *Journal of British Studies*, vol. 7, no. 1 (1967): 12–27, www.jstor.org/stable/175378

Bourne, Kenneth, 'Review of Raymond A. Jones, *The British Diplomatic Service, 1815–1914*', *The American Historical Review*, vol. 90, issue 1 (February 1985): 136–37, doi: 10.1086/ahr/90.1.136-a
Brett-James, Antony, *Wellington at War 1794–1815. A Selection of His Wartime Letters* (MacMillan, 1961)
Brut Penn.: *Brut y Tywysogion, Peniarth MS 20 Version*, trans. and ed. Thomas Jones (University of Wales, 1952)
Brut RBH: *Brut y Tywysogyon, Red Book of Hergest Version*, trans. and ed. Thomas Jones (University of Wales, 1955)
Bryan, George, *Chelsea in the Olden & Present Times* (Bryan, 1869)
Burke, John B., *A General and Heraldic Dictionary of the Peerage and Baronetage of the British Empire* (5th edn, Henry Colburn, 1838)
— *A Genealogical and Heraldic Dictionary of the Landed Gentry, a Companion to the Baronetage and Peerage*, 3 vols (Henry Colburn, 1843–49)
Burke's: *Burke's Peerage, Baronetage and Knightage*, ed. Charles Mosley (107th edn, Burke's 2003), https://www.burkespeerage.com
Butler, Iris, *The Eldest Brother: The Marquess Wellesley, the Duke of Wellington's Eldest Brother* (Hodder & Stoughton, 1973)
C&C: *Cadogan & Chelsea: The Making of a Modern Estate*, ed. Anjali Bulley (Unicorn/Cadogan, 2017)
Cadogan, Lady Adelaide, *Illustrated Games of Patience* (Sampson Low, Marston, Searle and Rivington, 1887)
Cadogan, Lady Augusta, 'La Grande Dame de l'Ancien Régime', *Macmillan's Magazine*, vol. 36 (May–Oct 1877): 494–504; 'Part II', *Macmillan's Magazine*, vol. 37 (November 1877–April 1878): 389–97
Cadogan, Hon. Sir Edward, KBE, CB, *Before the Deluge: Memories and Reflections 1880–1914* (John Murray, 1961)
— *The Roots of Evil: Being a Treatise on the Methods of Dealing with Crime and the Criminal During the Eighteenth and Nineteenth Centuries in Relation to Those of a More Enlightened Age* (John Murray, 1937)

SELECT RESOURCES & BIBLIOGRAPHY

— *Under Fire in the Dardanelles*, see Charatan, Kira and Camilla Cecil (eds)

Cadogan, Reverend William Bromley, *A funeral sermon, occasioned by the death of the Rev. W. Romaine... Preached at St Anne's, Black-Friars, on Sunday Morning, August 9, 1795* (G. Thompson, 1795)

— *Discourses of the Honourable and Reverend William Bromley Cadogan...with Memoirs of his Life*, ed. Rev. Richard Cecil (F. & C. Rivington, 1798)

— *Psalms and Hymns Collected by William Bromley Cadogan, M.A ...* (A.M. Smart and T. Cowslade, 1785; reprinted 1787, 1793, 1803)

— *The Love of Christ...a sermon preached in the parish church of St. Giles, in Reading, On Sunday, December the 4th, 1785. Upon the death of Mrs. Talbot, Relict of the Rev. William Talbot, late Vicar of the said Church* (A.M. Smart and T. Cowslade, 1785)

Cadogan, Dr William, *A dissertation on the gout and all chronic diseases jointly considered as proceeding from the same causes. What these causes are and a rational and natural method of care proposed...* (J. Dodsley, 1771)

Calthorpe, Lt. Col. Somerset J. Gough, *Cadogan's Crimea*, illustrated by General the Hon. Sir George Cadogan, KCB (Hamish Hamilton, 1979, abridged and illustrated edn)

Campbell, Colen, 'Caversham (Anno 1723)', in *Vitruvius Britannicus: The Classic of Eighteenth-Century British Architecture* (Dover Publications, 2006)

Campbell, Lorna, *Indefatigable 1797*. https://indefatigable1797.wordpress.com/about/

Cannon, Richard, *Historical Records of the British Army, Comprising the History of Every Regiment in His Majesty's Service*, 63 vols (Adjutant General's Office, Horse Guards, et al., 1837–83); particularly: *Historical Record of the Life Guards* (1837); *Historical Record of the Fourth, or the King's Own, Regiment of Foot* (Longman, Orme & Co., 1839)

Cecil, Reverend Richard, 'Memoirs of the Hon. and Rev. W. B. Cadogan', in Reverend William Bromley Cadogan, *Discourses*

Channon, Chips, *Henry 'Chips' Channon: The Diaries 1918–1938*, vol. 1, ed. Simon Heffer (Random House, 2021)

Charatan, Kira and Camilla Cecil (eds), *Under Fire in the Dardanelles: The Great War Diaries & Photographs of Major Edward Cadogan* (Pen & Sword, 2006)

Churchill, Winston S., *Ian Hamilton's March* (Longmans, Green & Co., 1900)

— *Marlborough: His Life and Times*, book 1 (Sphere, 1967); vol. 2 (George G. Harrap, 1934); vol. 6 (Scribner, 1938)

Chrimes, S.B., *Henry VII* (Yale University Press, 1999)

Clarke, Hewson, *An impartial history of the naval, military and political events in Europe from the commencement of the French revolution to the...conclusion of a general peace*, vol. 3 (Brightly & Childs, 1815)

Clarke, Tim, *The Countess: The Scandalous Life of Frances Villiers, Countess of Jersey* (Amberley, 2016)

Cokayne, George E. et al., *The Complete Peerage*, 14 vols (2nd edn, St Catherine's Press, 1936)

— *The Complete Baronetage* (W. Pollard & Co., 1900–1906); vol. 2 (1902)

Coke, Lady Mary, *Letters and Journals of Lady Mary Coke 1756–74*, ed. J.A. Home, vol. 2 (David Douglas, 1889–96; reprinted Kingsmead 1970)

Collins, Arthur, *The Peerage of England*, vol. 7 (1786; 4th edn, H. Woodfall et al., 1812)

Cooke, John, *Five Letters to a Friend, Occasioned by the Death of the Rev. William Bromley Cadogan* (London, 1797)

Corton, Christine L., *London Fog: the Biography* (Harvard University Press, 2015)

Cowan, Steven, 'The Growth of Public Literacy in Eighteenth Century England', unpublished PhD thesis, University College London (2012)

Coxe, William, *Memoirs of the Duke of Marlborough: With His Original Correspondence*, 3 vols (H.G. Bohn, 1847–48)

Crawford, Alan, 'Arts & Crafts Churches', in A. Saint and T. Sladen (eds), *Churches 1870–1914: Studies in Victorian Architecture and Design*, vol. 3 (Victorian Society, 2011)

Croot, Patricia E.C. (ed.), *A History of the County of Middlesex: Volume 12, Chelsea* (Victoria County History, 2004), see VCH Chelsea

Cunningham, Peter, *Hand-Book of London. Past and Present*, rev. edn (John Murray, 1850)

Debrett, John (ed.), *A Collection of State Papers, Relative to the War Against France, Now Carrying-on by Great Britain and the Several Other European Powers*, vol. 6 (J. Debrett, 1798)

Debrett's. https://debretts.com

Derrot, Sophie, 'La renaissance du château de Mouchy (1855–1866)', *Livraisons d'histoire de l'architecture*, vol. 29 (2015): 115–23, doi: 10.4000/lha.472

Dickinson, Patricia, 'Lieutenant General William Cadogan's Intelligence Service: part 1', *The Army Quarterly* (January 1979): 161

Dilks, David (ed.), *The Diaries of Sir Alexander Cadogan, OM 1938–1945* (Faber & Faber, 2010)

Ditchfield, P.H., and William Page (eds), 'The Borough of Reading: Charities', in *A History of the County of Berkshire: Volume 3* (London, 1923), pp. 378–84

Dixon, David, *From Prohibition to Regulation: Bookmaking, Anti-Gambling, and the Law* (Oxford: Clarendon Press, 1991)

Dunn, Samuel (ed.), *General Index to the Journals of the House of Commons [1774–1800]* (reprint edn, Hansard & Sons, 1827)

DWB: Dictionary of Welsh Biography down to 1940, eds John E. Lloyd and R.T. Jenkins (National Library of Wales, 1959); see also https://biography.wales

Dwnn, Lewys, *Heraldic Visitations of Wales and Part of the Marches, Between the Years 1586 and 1613, Under the Authority of Clarencieux and Norroy, Two Kings at Arms*, ed. Sir Samuel Rush Meyrick, 2 vols (W. Rees for the Welsh MSS Society, 1846)

Erskine, The Hon. Thomas, *Mr Baldwin and Mr Law, The Trial at Large of The Right Honourable Lady*

SELECT RESOURCES & BIBLIOGRAPHY

Cadogan for Adultery with The Rev. Mr. Cooper (J. Ridgway, 1794)

Evans, D. Morier, *The History of the Commercial Crisis 1857–58, and the Stock Exchange Panic of 1859* (Groombridge and Sons, 1859)

Farington, Joseph, *The Farington Diary*, ed. James Greig, vol. 5 (Hutchinson & Co., 1922–28)

Faulkner, Thomas, *An Historical and Topographical Description of Chelsea and Its Environs* (J. Tilling, 1810) [frequently inaccurate]

Fox-Davies, Arthur Charles, *A Complete Guide to Heraldry* (T.C. & E.C. Jack, 1909)

Fry, Helen, *Spymaster: the Man Who Saved MI6* (Yale University Press, 2021)

Gentleman's Magazine and Historical Chronicle, The, vols. 6–152 (E. Cave et al., 1736–1833)

George III, King, *Later Correspondence of George III: Volume Four, 1802–1807*, ed. A. Aspinall, (Cambridge University Press, 1968)

Gilbert, John T. (ed.), *Contemporary History of Affairs in Ireland 1641–1652*, vol. 1, part 2 (Irish Archaeological and Celtic Society, 1879)

Godfrey, Rupert (ed.), *Letters from a Prince: Edward, Prince of Wales, to Mrs Freda Dudley Ward, March 1918 – January 1921* (Little, Brown, 1998; Warner, 1999)

Granvill, Rick, *Chelsea Football Club: The Official History in Pictures* (Headline, 2006)

Granville, 1st Earl, *Lord Granville Leveson Gower (First Earl Granville): Private Correspondence, 1781 to 1821*, vol. 2, ed. Castalia, Countess Granville (John Murray, 1916)

Grattan, William ['Grattan of the 88th'], *Adventures with the Connaught Rangers, from 1808 to 1814*, vol. 1 (Henry Colburn, 1847)

Green, Alice Stopford, 'Rule of the English Parliament, 1640–1750', in *Irish Nationality* (Henry Holt/Williams & Norgate, 1911), pp. 158–91

Grenville, Charlotte, *The Correspondence of Charlotte Grenville, Lady Williams Wynn... 1795–1832*, ed. Rachel Leighton (John Murray, 1920)

Greville Papers. Greville, Charles Cavendish Fulke, *The Greville Memoirs: Journal of the Reigns of King George IV, King William IV and Queen Victoria*, 8 vols, ed. Lytton Strachey (1874–87; new edn ed. Henry Reeve, 1903–1905, reprinted Cambridge University Press, 2011)

Grundy, Isobel, *Lady Mary Wortley Montagu: Comet of the Enlightenment* (Oxford University Press, 2001)

Guildhall Library: H.B.H. Beaufoy and J.H. Burn, *A Descriptive Catalogue of London Traders, Tavern, and Coffee-House Tokens Current in the Seventeenth Century* (Corporation of the City of London, 1853)

Hamilton, Alec, 'The Lure of the Arts & Crafts Church', *Ecclesiology Today*, issue 46 (July 2012): 3–22

Hamilton, C.I., 'Sir James Graham, the Baltic Campaign and War-Planning at the Admiralty in 1854', *The Historical Journal*, vol. 19, no. 1 (March 1976): 89–112, https://www.jstor.org/stable/2638356

Hearne, Thomas, *Remarks and Collections of Thomas Hearne*, ed. C.E. Doble et al., vol. 6 (Oxford Historical Society, 1902)

Hibbert, Christopher (ed.), *A Soldier of the Seventy-First: The Journal of a Soldier of the Highland Light Infantry 1806–1815* (Leo Cooper, 1975; reprint edn Squadron/Signal, 1976)

Hines, John, 'From Anleifr to Havelock: The English and the Irish Sea', in *Celtic–Norse Relationships in the Irish Sea in the Middle Ages 800–1200*, pp. 187–214, doi: 10.1163/9789004255128_012

Holmes, Richard, *Marlborough: Britain's Greatest General* (Harper Perennial, 2009)

HoP Commons. *The History of Parliament: the House of Commons 1604–1629*, eds John P. Ferris and Andrew Thrush (Cambridge University Press, 2010); *1660–1690*, ed. Basil Duke Henning (Boydell & Brewer, 1983); *1690–1715*, eds Eveline Cruickshanks, Stuart Handley, David W. Hayton (Boydell & Brewer, 2002); *1715–1754*, ed. Romney Sedgwick (Boydell & Brewer, 1970); *1754–1790*, ed. Sir Lewis Namier and John Brooke (Secker & Warburg, 1985); *1790–1820*, ed. R. Thorne (Boydell & Brewer, 1986); *1820–1832*, ed. David Fisher (Cambridge University Press, 2009)

Horder, Jeremy, 'The Duel and the English Law of Homicide', *Oxford Journal of Legal Studies*, vol. 12, issue 3 (Autumn 1992): 419–30, doi: 10.1093/ojls/12.3.419

Howard, Martin R., 'Walcheren 1809: A Medical Catastrophe', *BMJ: British Medical Journal*, vol. 319, no. 7225 (18–25 Dec 1999): 1642–45, https://www.jstor.org/stable/25186694

James, Lawrence, *Mutiny: in the British and Commonwealth Forces, 1791–1956* (Buchan & Enright, 1987)

Jeffreys, Kevin, *The British Olympic Association: A History* (Springer, 2014)

Jenkins, Simon, *A Short History of England: The Complete Story of Our Nation in a Single Volume* (Profile Books, 2012)

Jones, Ray, 'The Social Structure of the Diplomatic Service, 1815–1914', *Histoire Sociale/Social History*, vol. 14, no. 27 (1981): 49–66

Katz, Catherine G., *The Daughters of Yalta: the Churchills, Roosevelts and Harrimans* (William Collins, 2020)

Landale, James, *Duel: A True Story of Death and Honour* (Canongate, 2005)

Legge-Pomeroy, Major the Hon. Ralph, *The Regimental History of the 5th Dragoon Guards, 1685–1922* (William Blackwood, 1924)

Lennon, Colm, 'Dublin, Part II: 1610 to 1756', *Irish Historic Towns Atlas*, no. 19 (Royal Irish Academy, 2008), https://www.ria.ie/irish-historic-towns-atlas-online-dublin-part-ii-1610-1756

Leveson-Gower, Sir George (ed.), *Hary-O, The Letters of Lady Harriet Cavendish 1796–1809* (John Murray, 1940)

Literary Gazette and Journal of Belles Lettres, Arts, Sciences, &c., ed. Henry Colburn (London, 1838)

Loeber, Rolf et al., 'Journal of a Tour to Dublin and the Counties of Dublin and Meath in 1699', *Analecta Hibernica*, no. 43 (2012): 47–67, www.jstor.org/stable/23317179

Lofmark, Carl, *A History of the Red Dragon*, ed. G.A. Wells, Welsh Heritage Series no. 4 (Gwasg Carreg Gwalch, 1995)

SELECT RESOURCES & BIBLIOGRAPHY

London Gazette, The, https://www.thegazette.co.uk

Longford, Elizabeth, *Wellington* (Weidenfeld & Nicholson 1969 & 1972; abridged edn 1992; reissued Abacus, 2012)

Lord, Peter, *Medieval Vision: The Visual Culture of Wales* (University of Wales, 2003)

Lovell, Mary S., *The Churchills: A Family at the Heart of History – from the Duke of Marlborough to Winston Churchill* (2nd edn, Little, Brown, 2012)

Lownie, Andrew, *Traitor King: The Scandalous Exile of the Duke and Duchess of Windsor* (Blink, 2021)

Lybbe Powys, Mrs Philip, *Passages from the Diaries of Mrs Philip Lybbe Powys of Hardwick, Oxon., A.D. 1756 to 1808*, ed. Emily J. Climenson (Longmans, Green & Co., 1899)

Lynch, John, 'The Lessons of Walcheren Fever, 1809', *Military Medicine*, vol. 174, no. 3 (March 2009): 315–319, doi: 10.7205/MILMED-D-01-7708

Macaulay, Baron Thomas Babbington, *History of England*, vol. 1 (Porter & Coates, 1848)

MacCormack, J.R., 'The Irish Adventurers and the English Civil War', *Irish Historical Studies*, vol. 10, no. 37 (1957): 21–58, doi: 10.1017/S002112140001614X

Man, John, *The History and Antiquities, Ancient and Modern, of the Borough of Reading, In the County of Berks* (Snare & Man, 1816); *A Supplement with Corrections and Additions by the Author* (1816)

Manley, Gordon, '1684: The Coldest Winter in the English Instrumental Record', *Weather*, vol. 66, no. 5 (2011): 133-136, doi: 10.1002/wea.789

Markham, Sarah, *John Loveday of Caversham (1711–1789): The Life and Tours of an Eighteenth-Century Onlooker* (M. Russell, 1984)

Marshall, John, *Royal Naval Biography …an Account of all the Naval Actions* [1760– publication], vol. 1 (Longman et al., 1823)

Mason, Emma, 'Portrait of Britain AD 1200', *History Today*, vol. 50, no. 5 (May 2000)

McMullen, Norma, 'The Education of English Gentlewomen 1540–1640', *History of Education*, vol. 6, no. 2 (1977): 87–101, doi: 10.1080/0046760770060201

Naval Chronicle, The, 40 vols (Bunney & Gold/Joyce Gold, London, January 1799 to December 1818); particularly: vol. 23, January–July 1810; vol. 30, June–December 1813; vol. 31, January–June 1814. Clarke, James Stanier and John McArthur (eds); *The Naval Chronicle* (reissue, Cambridge University Press, 2010)

Nevill, Ralph, *Floreat Etona: Anecdotes and Memories of Eton College* (Macmillan, 1911)

Nichols, Frederick Doveton, and Ralph E. Griswold, *Thomas Jefferson, Landscape Architect* (University of Virginia Press, 1981)

Nicolson, Harold, *The Harold Nicolson Diaries 1907–1964*, ed. Nigel Nicolson (Weidenfeld & Nicolson, 2004)

— *Some People* (Constable & Co., 1927)

Noel-Smith, Heather, and Lorna M. Campbell, *Hornblower's Historical Shipmates: the Young Gentlemen of Pellew's Indefatigable* (The Boydell Press, 2016)

Oatts, Lt Col. L.B., *Proud Heritage: The Story of the Highland Light Infantry, 1777–1959* (Thomas Nelson, 1952)

ODNB: *Oxford Dictionary of National Biography*, http://www.oxforddnb.com

Oman, Sir Charles William Chadwick, KBE, *A History of the Peninsular War,* 7 vols (Clarendon/Oxford University Press, 1902–1930)

Osler, Edward, *The Life of Admiral Viscount Exmouth* (Smith, Elder & Co., 1835)

Pack, A.J., *Nelson's Blood: The Story of Naval Rum* (Naval Institute Press, 1996)

Paget, Julian, *Wellington's Peninsular War: Battles and Battlefields* (Pen & Sword, 2005)

Parkinson, C. Northcote, *Edward Pellew, Viscount Exmouth, Admiral of the Red* (Methuen, 1934)

Pearman, Robert, *The Cadogan Estate: The History of a Landed Family* (Haggerston Press, 1986)

— *The Cadogans at War 1783–1864: The Third Earl Cadogan and His Family* (Haggerston Press, 1990)

— *The First Earl Cadogan 1672–1726* (Haggerston Press, 1988)

Pearson, John, *The Private Lives of Winston Churchill* (A&C Black, 2011)

Pepys, Samuel, *Diaries*, https://www.pepysdiary.com

Perrett, Tamsin, *Cadogan: the Heart of Chelsea* (Cadogan, 2016)

Piggott, Charles, *The Female Jockey Club, or A Sketch of the Manners of the Age* (D.I. Eaton, 1794)

Pinfold, John, 'Horse Racing and the Upper Classes in the Nineteenth Century', *Sport in History*, vol. 28, no. 3 (2008): 414-430, doi: 10.1080/17460260802315496

Pope, Dudley, *Life in Nelson's Navy* (Unwin Hyman, 1987)

PPR: Principal Probate Registry; *Calendar of the Grants of Probate and Letters of Administration made in the Probate Registries of the High Court….; England & Wales, National Probate Calendar (Index of Wills and Administrations), 1858–1995*

Prendergast, John Patrick, *The Cromwellian Settlement of Ireland* (2nd edn, McGlashan & Gill, 1875)

'Queen's Gazette, The', *The Court Magazine and Monthly Critic, and Lady's Magazine and Museum*, ed. Dobbs, vol. 12 (1838)

QVJ: *Queen Victoria's Journals*, www.queenvictoriasjournals.org

Remfry, Paul Martin, *The Native Dynasties of Rhwng Gwy a Hafren, 1066 to 1282*, MA Diss. (University College of Wales, Aberystwyth, 1989; Castle Studies Research & Publishing, 2010)

Rendle-Short, John, 'William Cadogan, Eighteenth-Century Physician', *Medical History*, vol. 4, no. 4 (October 1960): 288-309, doi: 10.1017/S0025727300025631

Ridley, Jane, *Bertie: A Life of Edward VII* (Chatto & Windus, 2012)

Ridley, Jasper, *Napoleon III and Eugénie* (Constable, 1979)

Robinson, Maj.-Gen. Sir C.W., *Wellington's Campaigns, Peninsula–Waterloo, 1808–1815: Also Moore's Campaign of Coruña, for Military Students* (Hugh Rees, 1907; rev. edn, Friedland Books, 2017)

Rodger, N.A.M., *The Command of the Ocean: A Naval History of Britain, 1649–1815*, vol. 2 (W.W. Norton, 2005)

— *The Wooden World: An Anatomy of the Georgian Navy* (Fontana Press, 1988)

Saumarez Smith, Otto, *Boom Cities: Architect Planners and the Politics of Radical Urban Renewal in 1960s Britain* (Oxford University Press, 2019)

Shelley, Lady Frances, *The Diary of Frances, Lady Shelley, 1787–1817*, ed. Richard Edgcumbe, 2 vols (John Murray, Charles Scribner, 1912)

Spencer, Charles, *Killers of the King: The Men Who Dared to Execute Charles I* (Bloomsbury, 2015)

Spencer, Sarah, *Correspondence of Sarah Spencer, Lady Lyttelton, 1787–1870*, ed. the Hon. Mrs Hugh Wyndham (John Murray, 1912)

Spencer-Churchill, Henrietta, *Blenheim and the Churchill Family* (Cico Books, 2005)

Stearn, William T., 'The Chelsea Physic Garden 1673–1973: Three Centuries of Triumph in Crises; A Tercentenary Address', *Garden History*, vol. 3, no. 2 (1975): 68–73, doi: 10.2307/1586380

Steiner, Zara, 'The Old Foreign Office: from a Secretariat Office to a Department of State', in *Opinion publique et politique extérieure en Europe. I. 1870–1915. Actes du Colloque de Rome* (13–16 février 1980), collected edn (École Française de Rome, 1981), pp. 177–95

Stephenson, David, *Medieval Wales c.1050 to 1332: Centuries of Ambiguity* (University of Wales Press, 2019)

Stone, Lawrence, *Broken Lives: Separation and Divorce in England 1660–1857* (Oxford University Press, 1993)

Survey of London (London County Council): vols 2, 4 & 7, Chelsea, parts I–III, ed. Walter H. Godfrey (1909, 1913, 1921); vol. 13, St Margaret, Westminster, part II: Whitehall I, ed. Montagu H. Cox and Philip Norman (1930); vols 29 & 30, St James Westminster, part I, ed. F.H.W. Sheppard (1960); vols 33 & 34, St Anne Soho, ed. F.H.W. Sheppard (1966)

Tallon, Geraldine (ed.), *Court of Claims, Submissions and Evidence 1663* (Irish Manuscripts Commission, 2006)

Thompson, E.P., *Whigs & Hunters* (Allen Lane, 1975; reprint edn Penguin, 1990)

Thornbury, Walter, *Old and New London: A Narrative of its History, its People and its Places* (Cassell, Petter & Galpin, 1873)

Turvey, Roger K., *The Welsh Princes* (Routledge, 2014)

VCH Chelsea: *A History of the County of Middlesex: Volume 12, Chelsea*, ed. Patricia E.C. Croot (Victoria County History, 2004)

Vickers, Hugo, *Elizabeth the Queen Mother* (Random House, 2013)

Walker, Paul F., *History of Armour 1100–1700* (Crowood, 2013)

Walpole, Horace, *Correspondence* (The Lewis Walpole Library, Yale, 2011). http://images.library.yale.edu/hwcorrespondence/

— *Correspondence with Madame du Deffand and Mademoiselle Sanadon* (Oxford University Press, 1939)

— *Letters Addressed to the Countess of Ossory, from the Year 1769 to 1797*, ed. R. Vernon Smith (2nd edn, Richard Bentley, 1848)

— *Memoirs of the Reign of King George III*, vol. 2 (Richard Bentley, 1845)

Warrand, Dunan (ed.), *More Culloden papers*, vol. 3 (R. Carruthers, 1923–1930)

Warrington, Reverend William, *The History of Wales* (J. Johnson, 1788)

Wasson, Ellis, *Aristocracy and the Modern World* (Palgrave Macmillan, 2006)

Watson, J.N.P., *Marlborough's Shadow: The Life of the First Earl Cadogan* (Leo Cooper, Pen & Sword, 2003)

Weinreb, Ben, and Christopher Hibbert, *The London Encyclopaedia*, eds John and Julia Keay (Macmillan, 1983; rev. 3rd edn, 2011)

Wellesley, Henry, *The Diary and Correspondence of Henry Wellesley, First Lord Cowley, 1790–1846*, ed. Col. the Hon. F.A. Wellesley (Hutchinson, 1930)

Wellesley, Jane, *Wellington: A Journey Through My Family* (2nd edn, Weidenfeld & Nicolson, 2015)

Wellington, Duke of (ed.), *Supplementary Despatches, Correspondence, and Memoranda of Field Marshal Arthur Duke of Wellington, K.G.*, 11 vols (John Murray, 1858–64); vol. 4

Wilson, Ben, *Decency & Disorder: The Age of Cant 1789–1837* (Faber & Faber, 2007)

Winfield, Rif, *British Warships in the Age of Sail 1714–1792* (Seaforth, 2007)

— and Stephen S. Roberts, *French Warships in the Age of Sail 1626–1786* (Pen & Sword, 2017)

Wing, William, *Caversham Park and Manor. Caversham Retold: A Journey into the Past* (Reading, 1930)

— 'Lecture on "Old Caversham"', 12 November 1894, reprinted from the *Reading Mercury and Berks County Paper*, Reading Library 4670572

Wolfram, Sybil, 'Divorce in England 1700–1857', *Oxford Journal of Legal Studies*, vol. 5, no. 2 (Summer, 1985): 155–86, doi: 10.1093/ojls/5.2.155

Woodfall, G., *Acts and Votes of Parliament Relating to the British Museum: with the Statutes and Rules Thereof, and the Succession of Trustees and Officers* (British Museum, 1824)

Wyld, Helen, 'Tapestry in 18th-Century Britain: Based on the Paper Given at the 2011 Annual Lecture', *The Furniture History Society Newsletter*, no. 186 (May 2012): 1–6

Yates, Sarah, and Peter Murray, *Great Estates: How London's Landowners Shape the City* (NLA – London's Centre for the Built Environment, 2013)

Yorke, Philip, *The Royal Tribes of Wales* (John Painter, 1799)

Zurrida, Stefano, Fabio Bassi et al., 'The Changing Face of Mastectomy (from Mutilation to Aid to Breast Reconstruction)', *International Journal of Surgical Oncology*, vol. 2011, article ID 980158 (2011), doi: 10.1155/2011/980158

Zweiniger-Bargielowska, Ina, *Managing the Body: Beauty, Health, and Fitness in Britain 1880–1939* (Oxford University Press, 2011)

ACKNOWLEDGEMENTS

My thanks, first and foremost, go to Lord Cadogan, for his commitment to this project, his enthusiastic personal involvement and the blessing of the late Lord Cadogan. My deep gratitude extends to the family for sharing their archives and memories, and for so generously entrusting me with the freedom to write as I found. To those who find themselves and close relations within the pages of this book, I hope I have done you justice. Please forgive any omissions arising from the practicalities of space in the telling of your family's long and illustrious history.

Huge thanks to Hugh Seaborn, who initiated the project, and to Kira Charatan of Cadogan Estates Ltd, who first asked me to write this book and who never stopped believing during its evolution. Thank you for all the wheels spun and balls juggled; thank you for your patience. I will forever be grateful to Pauline Hubner and Karin Fremer, who lived this project with me and whose expertise is evident in the images and design; it was a lot of hard work and a lot of fun. Thank you to Charlie Smith Design for the final push over the line; Ramona Lamport for a fresh pair of eyes; Lucy Duckworth, Ian Strathcarron and the team at Unicorn for producing this book so beautifully.

To Camilla Mountain, my unwavering support, sounding-board, sanity-checker, tireless fellow researcher and editor; my friend – thank you. I'm sorry the endnotes are not shorter. I can hear your voice in my head.

I owe a debt to those who have gone before me, especially Robert Pearman, whose research into the Cadogan family took place in a pre-Internet age of typed letters of enquiry, and whose meticulously documented findings provided a springboard for new investigations: hats off! To Philip Beddows, whose impressive knowledge of the early Welsh family made my research less daunting. Thank you to all those archivists and historians who lent their time and expertise – Dave Walker, now retired from the Kensington Central Library, his successor Sophia Hall, and Isabel Hernandez; Dr James Lloyd, Dr Lynsey Darby and Dr Dominic Ingram at the College of Arms; Carly Collier, late of the Royal Collection Trust, and the keepers at the Museum of Freemasonry. There were many others. For sharing their memories, particular thanks to Lorna Alexander and the Very Reverend Derek Watson.

I'd like to thank the friends who opened their homes as writing sanctuaries; everyone who enabled the life of this writer through practical assistance, especially the Morley family. Hugo, I adore you.

Thank you, finally, to Lord Moore, whose foreword sums up what we all want to say – to Charles, late 8th Earl Cadogan, we wish you could have held this finished book in your hands as planned. I like to think it would have tickled you.

PICTURE CREDITS

a = above; b = below; c = centre; l = left; r = right

10–11 By permission of Llyfrgell Genedlaethol Cymru/The National Library of Wales; 13 Map artwork by Chris Diamond; 15 Photo © The Trustees of the British Museum; 16 Photo © Crown copyright: RCAHMW; 17 Photo © Lambeth Palace Library/Bridgeman Images; 18 By permission of Llyfrgell Genedlaethol Cymru/The National Library of Wales; 20 Photo © Robin Owain; 22 Private Collection; 23 Photo courtesy City of Bayeux; 25 Photo © Crown copyright: RCAHMW; 26 Photo © Robert Owain. Courtesy St Mary's Church, New Radnor; 27a Mary Evans Picture Library; 27b Photo © Illustrated London News Ltd/Mary Evans; 29 From the British Library archive/Bridgeman Images; 30 Getty Research Institute, Los Angeles; 31 By permission of Llyfrgell Genedlaethol Cymru/The National Library of Wales; 36–37 Rijksmuseum, Amsterdam; 38 Alamy Stock Photo; 39 Yale Center for British Art, New Haven; Paul Mellon Collection, acc. B1977.14.17890; 40 From the British Library archive/Bridgeman Images; 42 Map artwork by Chris Diamond; 44 The National Archives, ref. KB27/1681/2; 45a From the British Library archive/Bridgeman Images; 45bl Private Collection. Photo © Peter Willi/Bridgeman Images; 45br By permission of the Master and Fellows of St John's College, Cambridge; 47 Ben Ryan Photography/Alamy Stock Photo; 49 Plate from *Parallelum Olivae nec non Olivarii... Protectoris* (1656), by Louis de Gand; 50 Photo © London Metropolitan Archives/Bridgeman Images; 51 Photo Tristan Hutchinson, courtesy Christ Church Cathedral, Dublin; 52 Photo Royal Collection Trust/© His Majesty King Charles III, 2024/Bridgeman Images; 53 Royal Borough of Kensington & Chelsea Local Studies & Archives; 55 From the British Library archive/Bridgeman Images; 56 Parliamentary Archives, London, HL/PO/JO/10/1/297A; 59 Courtesy of Cadogan; 60 Yale Center for British Art, New Haven; Paul Mellon Collection, acc. B1976.7.113; 61 Photo © National

PICTURE CREDITS

Maritime Museum, Greenwich, London; 63 Photo © Image: Crown Copyright, UK Government Art Collection; 64–65 Rijksmuseum, Amsterdam; 67 Photo Blenheim Palace, Oxfordshire/Bridgeman Images; 71 Courtesy of Cadogan; 73 Grosvenor Prints/Mary Evans Picture Library; 76–77 Getty Research Institute, Los Angeles; 80 Photo © National Museums Scotland/Bridgeman Images; 83 Photo The Trustees of the Goodwood Collection/Bridgeman Images; 85, 88–89 Courtesy of Cadogan; 91 Photo Heritage Images/Diomedia; 92, 93 Courtesy of Cadogan; 94 Photo © The Royal Society; 95 From the British Library archive/Bridgeman Images; 97 David Rumsey Map Collection, www.davidrumsey.com; 98 Photo © Illustrated London News Ltd/Mary Evans; 99 Photo © The Trustees of the British Museum; 100 Photo © Victoria Art Gallery, Bath/Bridgeman Images; 102al, 102ar Photos © The Trustees of the British Museum; 102b, 103 Wellcome Collection, London; 104a Courtesy of Cadogan; 104b Robert Pearman. Courtesy of Cadogan; 108–109 From the British Library archive/Bridgeman Images; 109 Private Collection/Bridgeman Images; 110 Image © London Metropolitan Archives (City of London); 112, 113 Courtesy of Cadogan; 114 Photo © National Portrait Gallery, London; 115l, 115r Courtesy St Peter's Church, Caversham; 117 Houghton Hall, Kings Lynn, Norfolk. Photo Pete Huggins; 120 Photo Mary Evans Picture Library; 121 Photo © The Trustees of the British Museum; 123 Courtesy of Cadogan; 125 Private Collection; 127 Yale Center for British Art; New Haven; Paul Mellon Collection, acc. B1977.14.9829; 128 Private Collection; 132 Photo © National Portrait Gallery, London; 135 Art Institute of Chicago, Mr. and Mrs. W. W. Kimball Collection, ref. 1922.4468; 136al The New York Public Library Digital Collections; 136ar, 136b Courtesy of Cadogan; 139 Rijksmuseum, Amsterdam. Purchased with the support of the F.G. Waller-Fonds; 140a Yale Center for British Art, New Haven; Paul Mellon Collection, acc. B1977.14.15684; 140b Royal Borough of Kensington & Chelsea Local Studies & Archives; 144 From the British Library archive/Bridgeman Images;

147a, 147bl Photos © Reading Museum (Reading Borough Council). All rights reserved; 147br Photo Berkshire Record Office; 148l From *Discourses of the Honourable and Reverend William Bromley Cadogan...* London, 1798; 148r From the British Library archive/Bridgeman Images; 150a, 150b Photos Berkshire Record Office; 153 Courtesy of Cadogan; 155 Yale Center for British Art, New Haven; Paul Mellon Collection, acc. B1981.25.272; 156 Wellcome Collection, London; 157 Courtesy of The Lewis Walpole Library, Yale University, New Haven; 159 Photo © Compton Verney/Bridgeman Images; 162, 163, 165l, 165r Wellcome Collection, London; 166 Photo © Historic Royal Palaces/Claire Collins/Bridgeman Images; 167 The National Archives, ref. ADM 139/101; 168 Florilegius/Alamy Stock Photo; 169 Photo © National Portrait Gallery, London; 172–173 Staatsbibliothek, Berlin; 175 Photo © Falmouth Art Gallery/Bridgeman Images; 177a, 177b, 179 Photos © National Maritime Museum, Greenwich, London; 180 Photo © National Portrait Gallery, London; 183 Photo © National Maritime Museum, Greenwich, London; 184 Photo © The Trustees of the British Museum; 185 Photo © National Maritime Museum, Greenwich, London; 187 Courtesy of Cadogan; 190 Photo © National Museums Liverpool/Bridgeman Images; 192, 193 Photos © National Maritime Museum, Greenwich, London; 195 Photo © The Trustees of the British Museum; 197 Photo © Stratfield Saye Preservation Trust; 198 Yale Center for British Art, New Haven; Paul Mellon Collection, acc. B1977.14.10305; 200 Photo © National Army Museum/Bridgeman Images; 201, 202 Photos © National Portrait Gallery, London; 205 Courtesy of The Lewis Walpole Library, Yale University, New Haven; 209 Photo © The Trustees of the British Museum; 212 Wellcome Collection, London; 214 Courtesy of Cadogan; 217 Courtesy of the Council of the National Army Museum, London; 218 Photo © The Trustees of the British Museum; 220a, 220c Rijksmuseum, Amsterdam; 220–221 Photo © National Maritime Museum, Greenwich, London; 222 Courtesy of the Council of the National

Army Museum, London; 223al, 223r Photos © National Portrait Gallery, London; 223b Library of Congress, Washington D. C., Geography and Map Division; 225 Courtesy of The Lewis Walpole Library, Yale University, New Haven; 229 Metropolitan Museum of Art, New York; The Elisha Whittelsey Collection, The Elisha Whittelsey Fund, 1959 (acc. 59.533.1623(5)); 231a Courtesy of the Council of the National Army Museum, London; 231bl British Library, London; 231br National Library of Scotland, Edinburgh, CC-BY-NC-SA; 233 Royal Commission on Historical Monuments 234 Photo Staatsbibliothek, Berlin/Bridgeman Images; 235 Courtesy of Cadogan; 236 Photo © National Portrait Gallery, London; 237al College of Arms MS Grants, vol. 38, p. 279. Reproduced by permission of the Kings, Heralds and Pursuivants of Arms; 237 Courtesy of Cadogan; 239 Rijksmuseum, Amsterdam; 240 Photo © National Trust Images/Andreas von Einsiedel/Bridgeman Images; 242 Metropolitan Museum of Art, New York; The Elisha Whittelsey Collection, The Elisha Whittelsey Fund, 1959 (acc. 59.533.2109); 245a Courtesy of University College, Durham Castle, Durham University, Acc. 18.704; 245bl Getty Research Institute, Los Angeles; 245br Image © London Metropolitan Archives (City of London); 248 David Rumsey Map Collection, www.davidrumsey.com; 252 Photo © The Trustees of the British Museum; 253 Courtesy of Cadogan; 254 Photo Sotheby's, London. Courtesy French & Company, New York; 255 Denver Art Museum, Gift of the Berger Collection Educational Turst, 2018.18. Photo courtesy Denver Art Museum; 258–259 Image © London Metropolitan Archives (City of London); 261 Courtesy of Cadogan; 262 Album/Alamy Stock Photo; 264 Courtesy of Cadogan; 267 Photo Royal Collection Trust/© His Majesty King Charles III, 2024/Bridgeman Images; 268 Image © London Metropolitan Archives (City of London); 269 Royal Borough of Kensington & Chelsea Local Studies & Archives; 272l, 272r, 274 Courtesy of Cadogan; 275 Photo © Science Museum Group; 276 Photo Royal Collection Trust/© His Majesty King

493

PICTURE CREDITS

Charles III, 2024/Bridgeman Images; 279 Photo Museum of London; 281a, 281b Photo © The Trustees of the British Museum; 282 Chateaux de Versailles et de Trianon, Versailles, France. Photo Christophe Fouin/RMN-Grand Palais/Dist. Photo SCALA, Florence; 284 Photo © The Trustees of the British Museum; 286 Photo Royal Collection Trust/© His Majesty King Charles III, 2024/Bridgeman Images; 288 From the British Library archive/Bridgeman Images; 289 Photo Royal Collection Trust/© His Majesty King Charles III, 2024/Bridgeman Images; 290 The Canon Gallery, Chichester, West Sussex/Bridgeman Images; 291 Photo Royal Collection Trust/© His Majesty King Charles III, 2024/Bridgeman Images; 292 Gertrude Bell Archive, Newcastle University Library (ref. GB/PERS/F/003); 293 Photo Royal Collection Trust/© His Majesty King Charles III, 2024/Bridgeman Images; 294 Photo © National Portrait Gallery, London; 295 The Canon Gallery, Chichester, West Sussex/Bridgeman Images; 298, 301, 302a Courtesy of the Council of the National Army Museum, London; 302b Photo Roger Fenton, 1855. Library of Congress, Manuscript Division, Fenton Crimean War Photographs (LC-USZC4-9139); 303 Photo Mary Evans Picture Library; 304 Yale Center for British Art, New Haven; Gift of Michael H. LeWitt, Peter A. LeWitt, and Erwin Strasmick, acc. B1979.14.626; 306 Wellcome Collection, London; 308 Courtesy of Cadogan; 310 Private Collection/© Look and Learn/Bridgeman Images; 312 Photo Martin Charles/RIBA Collections; 314 Courtesy LSE Library, London; 317 Courtesy of Cadogan; 318 Photo © David Iliff; 321 Photo Museum of London; 322al, 322ar, 322b Courtesy of Cadogan; 324ar Courtesy of the National Library of Ireland (EPH E124); 324b Courtesy of the National Library of Ireland (L_ROY_01771); 326 Photo Balean/TopFoto; 327, 328 Courtesy of Cadogan; 330 Photo Royal Collection Trust/© His Majesty King Charles III, 2024/Bridgeman Images; 331a, 331b, 332, 333a, 333bl, 333br, 335, 336, 337 Courtesy of Cadogan; 339 Photo © Marylebone Cricket Club/Bridgeman Images; 340al Photo © Illustrated London News Ltd/Mary Evans; 340ar, 340cr, 340br, 340bl Courtesy of Cadogan; 343 Mary Evans Picture Library; 345 Courtesy of Cadogan; 347 Photo © Illustrated London News Ltd/Mary Evans; 348 Photo Royal Collection Trust/© His Majesty King Charles III, 2024/Bridgeman Images; 349al Photo © Illustrated London News Ltd/Mary Evans; 349r Courtesy of Cadogan; 351 Photo © National Portrait Gallery, London; 353l, 353r, 356–357 Courtesy of Cadogan; 358 Photo © Illustrated London News Ltd/Mary Evans; 359 Courtesy of Cadogan; 361 Photo © Marylebone Cricket Club/Bridgeman Images; 363 Courtesy of Cadogan; 365 Country Life, Saturday 4 May 1907. Courtesy Future Publishing Ltd; 366 Royal Borough of Kensington & Chelsea Local Studies & Archives; 368 Courtesy of Cadogan; 371l Photo Alfred Groß/Ullstein Bild via Getty Images; 371r The Women's Library, LSE Library, London; 372 Photo © Illustrated London News Ltd/Mary Evans; 373 Courtesy of Cadogan; 376a Photo © Yevonde Portrait Archive/ILN/Mary Evans Picture Library; 376–377 Photo © Illustrated London News Ltd/Mary Evans; 377a Image © Victoria and Albert Museum, London; 377c Courtesy City of Westminster Archives; 377br Photo © John Frost Newspapers/Mary Evans Picture Library; 378 Blenheim Palace, Oxfordshire. Photo Bridgeman Images; 380 Photo Keystone-France/Gamma-Rapho via Getty Images; 381 Alexander Turnbull Library, Wellington, New Zealand, PAColl-8602-36; 382 Reproduced by permission of the Provost and Fellows of Eton College; 383, 384 Courtesy of the Council of the National Army Museum, London; 386 Courtesy of Cadogan; 389 Rijksmuseum, Amsterdam; 391 Photo Royal Collection Trust/© His Majesty King Charles III, 2024/Bridgeman Images; 392 PA Images/Alamy Stock Photo; 394a Imperial War Museum, London. Photo © IWM Q 3432; 394b Courtesy of the Council of the National Army Museum, London; 396 Courtesy of Cadogan; 397 Imperial War Museum, London. Photo © IWM Q 13632; 398l, 398r, 400 Courtesy of Cadogan; 401 The Print Collector/Heritage Images/Diomedia; 403 Courtesy of Cadogan; 404 Royal Borough of Kensington & Chelsea Local Studies & Archives; 405 Courtesy of Cadogan; 409 Photo © Illustrated London News Ltd/Mary Evans; 411 Courtesy of Cadogan; 413a Royal Borough of Kensington & Chelsea Local Studies & Archives; 413c Imperial War Museum, London. Photo © IWM Art.IWM PST 0968; 413b Imperial War Museum, London. Photo © IWM Q 53928; 414 Photo Topfoto; 416 Courtesy of Cadogan; 417a 'Ville olympiade Jeux Olympiques', Olympic games, Paris, 1924. Poster designed by Jean Droit. © Comité International Olympique (CIO); 417b Winner's gold medal, Olympic Games, Paris, 1924. Designed by André Rivaud. © Comité International Olympique (CIO); 418l From the British Library archive/Bridgeman Images; 418r Peter Probst/Alamy Stock Photo; 419 Courtesy of Cadogan; 422 Royal Borough of Kensington & Chelsea Local Studies & Archives; 424 Photo S. R. Gaiger/Topical Press Agency/Getty Images; 427 Courtesy of Cadogan; 429 Churchill Archives Centre, the Papers of Alexander Cadogan, ACAD 2/1; 431 The Devonshire Collections, Chatsworth. Reproduced by permission of Chatsworth Settlement Trustees/Bridgeman Images; 432l, 432b, 433, 434 Churchill Archives Centre, the Papers of Alexander Cadogan, ACAD 2/1; 435 Churchill Archives Centre, the Papers of Alexander Cadogan, ACAD 2/3; 437 Churchill Archives Centre, the Papers of Alexander Cadogan, ACAD 2/5; 439 Photo © Foreign, Commonwealth and Development Office; 440 Imperial War Museum, London. Photo © IWM TR 2828; 441 Churchill Archives Centre, the Papers of Alexander Cadogan, ACAD 2/6; 443 Churchill Archives Centre, the Papers of Alexander Cadogan, ACAD 2/4; 445 Photo © Science Museum Group; 447, 448 Courtesy of Cadogan; 450 RIBA Collections; 451a Courtesy of Cadogan; 451b Mary Evans Picture Library; 452, 453 Courtesy of Cadogan; 456al Courtesy of the Council of the National Army Museum, London; 456ar Courtesy of Cadogan; 456bl Imperial War Museum, London. Photo © IWM TR 914; 456br Courtesy of the Council of the National Army Museum, London; 457a Courtesy of Cadogan; 457b The National Archives, ref. WO 373/23/468; 459 Photo © TfL from the London

Transport Museum collection; 462 Photo © Courtesy of HES (William Burn Collection); 464 Photo Topfoto; 466 Arcaid Images/Alamy Stock Photo; 467 Photo John Bignell. Royal Borough of Kensington & Chelsea Local Studies & Archives

INDEX

Italic numbers indicate illustrations, the captions may appear on other pages. All dates are AD. Places and buildings are in Chelsea unless stated otherwise. Subjects with their own chapter are listed with chapter number (page range); family tree; and main portrait; followed by additional references.

Abrahams, Harold 415–16
Acheson, Lady 'Theo' see Cadogan, Lady Theodosia Louisa Augusta 'Theo' (née Acheson, 1882–1977)
Achilles, HMS 120, *122*
Albert, Duke of York see George VI, King
Albert, Prince (consort to Queen Victoria) 273, 286, 288, *289*, 294, 300
Albert Edward 'Bertie', Prince of Wales see Edward VII, King
Alexander, Lorna (née Lyle) 460, *461*
Aly Khan, Prince 355, 453–54
American War of Independence (1775–83) 107, 119, 133, 134, 178
Anglesey, 1st Marquess of see Paget, Field Marshal Henry William
Anglesey, Charlotte, Marchioness of see Cadogan, Lady Charlotte 'Cha' Sloane (1781–1853)
Anne, Queen 62, 63, 71–72, 74, 75, 81
Argyll, George Campbell, 6th Duke of 200, 202, *202*, 212, 243, 257
Argyll, Caroline Campbell (née Villiers), Duchess of see Paget, Lady Caroline 'Car'
artists
 in Chelsea 279, 295, 309, 318, 319, 412, 414, 425, 466
 galleries 96, 108, 148, 164, 255, 293–94, 412, 414, *414*, 437, 442
 studios 295, 319–20, 410, 425, 466
 see also paintings by Cadogan family members
Ashworth, Emily see Cadogan, Emily (née Ashworth, 1834–1891)
Atlantic Charter (1941) 439, *439*, 443
Augustus Frederick, Prince, Duke of Sussex 208, 212, 254
Auxiliary Territorial Service (ATS) 379, 460

Babraham Hall, Cambridgeshire 337, 338
Baccarat Case, the 342–44, *343*
Baden-Powell, Olave St Clair (née Soames) *419*, 420
Baden-Powell, Robert, Lord 418–19

Balfour, Arthur, 1st Earl 353, 362
Bath, Somerset 97–99, *100*, 143, 308
 by-election (1873) 306–7, 331
Battle of
 El Alamein 454–55, *456*
 Blenheim 36–37, *64–65*, 67, 68, 74
 Bosworth 29, 30
 the Boyne 62
 Catraeth (Catterick) 19
 Crogen 25, *25*
 Fuentes de Oñoro 224–26, 230, 232
 Malplaquet 73–74, 90
 Oudenarde 73, 74, 75, 90
 Paardeberg 384, *384*
 Ramillies 68–69, 74
 Schellenberg 66–67
 St Lucia 119
 Talavera 218, *218*, 221
 Trafalgar 188, *190*
 Vittoria 230–34, *231*, *234*, 236, 302
 Waterloo 239–40, *239*, 244, 274, 282
Bedford, John 'Ian' Robert Russell, 13th Duke of 355, 460–61
Bedford, Lydia Russell, Duchess of see Lyle, Lydia (née Yarde-Buller)
Bell, Gertrude 291, *292*
Blake, Honoria Louisa see Cadogan, Honoria Louisa, Countess (née Blake, 1787–1845)
Blake, Joseph Henry, 2nd Baron Wallscourt 171, 246
Blenheim Palace, Oxfordshire 77, 106, 378, 379–80, 401
Bonaparte, Napoleon 134, 178, 185, 191, 197, 215, 216, 218, *223*, 230, 232, 238, *239*, 240, 260, 274, 294
Bowes-Lyon, Elizabeth see Elizabeth, Queen (consort of George VI)
Boys' Club Movement 400
Bradshaw, Jane see Cadogan, Jane (née Graham, m. Bradshaw, d.1827)
Brett, Lionel (Lord Esher, architect) 465
Brichieri-Colombi, Marchese Augusto 303
Brichieri-Colombi, David 297, 303
Brichieri-Colombi, Sophia Isabella Harriet (née Cadogan, 1852–1928) 303
British Army
 1st Suffolk Yeomanry (Duke of York's Own Loyal Hussars) 395, *396*, 398
 10th Royal Hussars (Prince of Wales's Own) 383, *383*, 391, 392
 51st (Highland), 7th Battalion The Royal Regiment of Scotland 468
 71st (Highland) Regiment of Foot 215, 221, 222, *222*, 224–26, 230, 232, 234, 235, 302

495

INDEX

Black Watch (Royal Highlanders), 7th Battalion 455
Cadogan's Horse (6th Horse) 63, 68, 73
Coldstream Guards 75, 90 (2nd Foot Guards); 395, 452
Grenadier Guards 84 (1st Foot Guards); 298, 395, 406, 458
Ghurkas 455
Household Cavalry 91 (2nd Troop of Horse); 384, 395, 406
King's Own 90 (4th Foot Guards)
Royal Horse Guards (Blues) 349, 386
Royal Wiltshire Yeomanry (Prince of Wales's Own Hussars) 452, *453*, 455, 458
Scots Guards (3rd Foot) 130, 152
Suffolk Yeomanry, 3rd Battalion 384
British Broadcasting Corporation (BBC) 337, 442, 444–45
British Museum 101, 102, *102*, 105, 251, 464
British Museum Acts (1753, 1969) 101, 464
British Olympic Association (BOA) 415, 417, 418
Bromley, Hon. Frances see Cadogan, Frances (née Bromley, 1728–1768)
Bromley, Henry, 1st Baron Montfort 112, 114, *114*, 166, 171
Bromley, Thomas, 2nd Baron Montfort 114, 171
Brown, Lancelot 'Capability' 106–7, 110, 249
Brunel, Isambard Kingdom 253, 279
Brut y Tywysogion 12, 22, 23–24, 24–25, 472 n.1
Bruton Street, London 96, *98*
Brydges, James, 1st Duke of Chandos 60, 74, 82
Burnaby, Algernon 348, 350-51

Cadogan, Lady Adelaide (née Paget, 1820–1890) 257, 266, *267*, 287, 288–89, 291, 394
Cadogan, Adele, Countess (née Neri, Contessa Palagi, 1880–1960, wife of 5th Earl) 257, 303, 355, 367–68, 368, 369, 370, 373, 404, 409
Cadogan, Albert Edward George Henry 'Georgie' (1866–1878), Viscount Chelsea 331, 333, *333*, 354
Cadogan, Alexander George Montagu 'Alec' (1884–1968)
Ch 19 (426–45); 355; *443*
on the 'Cadogan Square' 369–70
on Gerald Oakley 'Jerry' 408
and Sybil 'Portia' 373, 374
portraits and photographs 347, 427, *429*, *432*–*33*, *435*, *437*, *440*, *441*, *443*
Cadogan, Hon. Alexandra Mary Hilda 'Mary' (1900–1961) see Spencer-Churchill, Alexandra Mary Hilda 'Mary'; 'Cadogan Square'
Cadogan, Lady Alexandra Mary (1920–1985) 355, 409, 425
Cadogan, Ambrose (1914–2003) 355, 432
Cadogan, Lt (RN) Arthur Charles Lewin (1841–1918) 270, 355
Cadogan, Lady Augusta Sarah (1811–1882) Ch 13 (280–92); 257; *281*
paintings and lithograph *236*, *286*, *289*, *291*, *294*
letter with Spanish sword 187
Cadogan, Beatrix 'Beattie' Jane, Countess (née Craven, 1844–1907, wife of 5th Earl) 257, 328, *328*, 331, *331*, 332, 333–34, 339, *340*, 341, 347, 354–55, 358–60, 363
Cadogan, Lady Beatrix Lilian Ethel (1912–1999) 354, 409, *411*, 425
Cadogan, 'Bill' (1914–1997) see Cadogan, William Gerald Charles 'Bill', 7th Earl
Cadogan, Bridget (née Waller, d.1721) 54, 56–57, 87
Cadogan, Cecilia Margaret 'Bunny', Countess (née Hamilton-Wedderburn, d.1999, wife of 7th Earl) 355, 464, *464*
Cadogan, Charles (1685–1776), 2nd Baron Ch 4 (90–107); 87, 171; 92
Cadogan, Charles (1936–2023), 8th Earl 7, 9, 355, 402, 416, 452, *452*, 461, 462, 464, 468, 469
Cadogan, Captain Charles George Henry (1850–1901) 271, 333, 355
Cadogan, Charles Henry Sloane (1749–1832), 2nd Earl Ch 7 (152–69); *170*; *153*; 105, 137
Cadogan, Charles Sloane (1728–1807), 3rd Baron, later 1st Earl (NC) Ch 4 (107–11), Ch 5 (112–37); 87, 116, 171, 257; *113*
Cadogan, Lady Charlotte Georgina Mary (1843–1908) see Currie, Lady Charlotte (née Cadogan)
Cadogan, Lady Charlotte 'Cha' Sloane (1781–1853, m. Wellesley, m. Paget) Ch 9 (194–213), *195*, *213*; 170, 216, 226, 241, 257
Cadogan, Lady Charlotte Louisa Emily (1853–1947) see Villiers, Lady Charlotte Louisa Emily (née Cadogan)
Cadogan, Captain Christopher 'Kit' Michael (1917–1941) 454
Cadogan, Hon. Cynthia Hilda Evelyn (1896–1966) see De Trafford, Cynthia Hilda Evelyn, Lady (née Cadogan); 'Cadogan Square'
Cadogan, Lady Daphne Magdalen (1939–2023, m. Bailey) 355, 452, 460, 467
Cadogan, Hon. Edith Mary Winifred (1895–1969) see Hillingdon, Edith Mary Winifred, Lady (née Cadogan); 'Cadogan Square'
Cadogan, Captain Edward (1758–1779) 119, 171
Cadogan, Lieutenant-Colonel Edward (1789–1851) 171, 216, 222, 247, 271–72
Cadogan, Edward (1966–), 9th Earl 234, 235, 461, Afterword 468–71
Cadogan, Major Sir Edward Cecil George 'Eddie' (1880–1962) Ch 17 (395–403); 355; 396
and the 'Cadogan Square' 370–71
on death of Georgie 334
on George Henry, 5th Earl 322
on life in Ireland 324–25
portraits and photographs 347, *400*–*401*, *403*, *427*
on proposed marriage of Henry Cadogan and Mary Wellesley 262
on William 'Willie' Cadogan 391
Cadogan, Edward George John Humphrey (1903–1910) Viscount Chelsea 354, 365–66, 366
Cadogan, Elizabeth, Lady (née Sloane, 1701–1768) 87, 91, 93, 95, 96, 97–99, *99*, 100, 105, 115, *115*, 138, 143, 164, 169, 171
Cadogan, Lady Emily Julia 'Tiny' (1871–1909) see Lurgan, Emily Julia 'Tiny', Lady (née Cadogan)
Cadogan, Lady Emily Mary (1778–1839) see Wellesley, Lady Emily (née Cadogan)
Cadogan, Emily (née Ashworth, 1834–1891) 257, 303, *303*
Cadogan, Ethel Henrietta Maud (1854–1930) 291
Cadogan, Frances (née Bromley, 1728–1768) 112, *112*, 114–15, 137, 138, 152, 166, 171
Cadogan, Commander (RN) Francis (1885–1970) 395
Cadogan, Frederick 'Freddie' William (1821–1904) 247, 250, 257, 278, 280, 284, 288–89, 291, *291*, 292, 296, 297, 307, 358

INDEX

Cadogan, George (1754–1780) 120–21, 171
Cadogan, Admiral George (1783–1864), 3rd Earl Ch 8 (174–93), Ch 11 (236–55); 171, 257; *237*
  character 277–78
  Chelsea and 247–49, *248*, 268–70
  coronation of Queen Victoria 266–67, *267*
  daughters' prospects 287
  duel 210–11
  Napoleonic Wars (1803–1815) 215–16, 219, 221, 226
  portraits and photographs *237*, *294*, 294
  on proposed marriage of Henry Cadogan and Mary Wellesley 263, 265
Cadogan, General Sir George (1814–1880) Ch 13 (297–303); 257, 355; *301*
  paintings 297, 298–99, *298*, 300, *301*, *302*
Cadogan, George Henry (1840–1915), 5th Earl Ch 14 (304–327), Ch 15 (328–353); 257, 355; *353*
  and Beattie 358–60
  birth 270
  Edward VII and 329, *330*, 334–35, 342–44, 352, 358–59
  and Gerald Oakley 'Jerry' 407–8, 409
  and Henry Arthur 'Haggy' 360–64
  on Lewin 403
  portraits, caricatures and photographs *304*, *323*, *330–31*, *347*, *353*, *363*
  will 410
  on William 'Willie' Cadogan 393
Cadogan, Gerald Oakley 'Jerry' (1862–1933), 6th Earl Ch 17 (384–86, 88–90), Ch 18 (404–25); 355; *405*
  in Ireland 352
  portraits and photographs *359*, *405*, *411*
Cadogan, Henriette Alice (1914–2005, m. Palmer, m. Abel Smith) 454
Cadogan, Henriette Wilhelmina (née Montgomery, d.1913) 333, 355
Cadogan, Henry (1642–1715) ch 2, 54, 56–57; 87
Cadogan, Colonel Henry (1780–1813) Ch 10 (214–35); 170; *214*, *468*
  duel, offer of 207, 210
Cadogan, Henry Arthur 'Haggy' (1868–1908), Viscount Chelsea Ch 16 (360–64, 366); 354; *363*
  in Ireland 347
  and Sophie 350, 366

Cadogan, Henry Charles (1812–1873), 4th Earl Ch 12 (260–79); 257, 270, 355; *261*
  Mary Wellesley and 262–66
Cadogan, Henry George Gerald (1859–1893) 291
Cadogan, Honoria Louisa, Countess (née Blake, 1787–1845, wife of 3rd Earl) 171, 236, *236*, 247, 250, *253*, 257, 263, 264, 265, 267–68, 271
Cadogan, Lady Honoria Louisa 'Hony' (1813–1904) Ch 13 (280–297); 257; *281*, *286*
  family 236, 250, 278, 358
  paintings 280, *290*, 294, 295–96, *295*, *297*
Cadogan, Horace James Henry (1862–1932) 257, 303
Cadogan, Jane (née Graham, m. Bradshaw, d.1827) 143–45, 149–51, *150*, 170
Cadogan, John Cecil (1883–1970) 395
Cadogan, Lewin Edward (1872–1919) 331, *347*, 355, 366, 386–88, *386*, 393, 402–3, 410
Cadogan, Lilian Eleanor Marie 'Marie/Yum', Countess (née Coxon, c.1889–1973, wife of 6th Earl) 354, 404, *404*, 406, 409–10, 418–20, *419*, 425
Cadogan, Lady Louisa (1787–1843) see Marsh, Lady Louisa (née Cadogan)
Cadogan, Margaretta Cecilia, Countess (née Munter, 1675–1749, wife of 1st Earl) 70–71, *71*, 85, 86
Cadogan, 'Marie' see Cadogan, Lilian Eleanor Marie 'Marie/Yum', Countess (née Coxon, c.1889–1973)
Cadogan, 'Mary' (1900–1961) see Spencer-Churchill, Alexandra Mary Hilda 'Mary', Duchess of Marlborough (née Cadogan); 'Cadogan Square'
Cadogan, Mary, Lady (née Churchill, 1758–1811) 116, 117–19, 125–31, *127*, 169, 171, 207, 247, 265
Cadogan, Mary Sarah, Countess (née Wellesley, 1808–1873, wife of 4th Earl) 256, 262–66, *264*, 279, 287, 329, 355
Cadogan, Olivia Georgiana (1850–1910) see Neri, Olivia Georgiana (née Cadogan)
Cadogan, Penelope (d.1746) see Prendergast, Penelope (née Cadogan)

Cadogan, Hon. 'Portia' (1893–1969) see Stanley, Sybil Louise Beatrix 'Portia', Lady (née Cadogan)
Cadogan, Primrose Lilian, Countess (née Yarde-Buller, 1918–1970, wife of 7th Earl) 285, 355, 450–52, *451*, *452*, 453–54, 460, 461, 462
Cadogan, Lady Sarah (1705–1751) see Lennox, Sarah, Duchess of Richmond (née Cadogan)
Cadogan, Lady Sarah Primrose Beatrix (1938–2017), Baroness Rockley 355, 402, 452, *452*, 460, 467
Cadogan, Sophia Isabella Harriet (1852–1928) see Brichieri-Colombi, Sophia Isabella Harriet (née Cadogan)
Cadogan, Sopie (née Armstrong, d.1852) 257, 303
Cadogan, Lady Sophie Beatrix Mary (1874–1937) see Scott, Lady Sophie Beatrix Mary (née Cadogan)
Cadogan, Hon. Sybil Louise Beatrix 'Portia' (1893–1969) see Stanley, Sybil Louise Beatrix 'Portia', Lady (née Cadogan)
Cadogan, Lady Theodosia Louisa Augusta 'Theo' (née Acheson, 1882–1977) 355, 374, 430, *431*, 434, 435, 438, 441, 442, 443, 444, 445
Cadogan, Captain (RN) Thomas (1752–1782) 119, 121–25, 171, 174, 177, 180
Cadogan, Thomas 'Tom/Tommy' (c.1777–1829) 122–25, *123*, 171
Cadogan, Thomas Charles (1810–1896) 125
Cadogan, 'Tiny' (1871–1909) see Lurgan, Emily Julia 'Tiny', Lady (née Cadogan)
Cadogan, Hon. Victoria Laura 'Tor Tor' (1901–1991) see Gilmour, Victoria Laura 'Tor Tor', Lady (née Cadogan)
Cadogan, Major William (1601–1661) Ch 2 (38–53), 87; *42*, *51*
Cadogan, General Sir William (1672–1726), first 1st Earl Ch 3 (58–85); 87; *59*
  posthumous 95–96, *95*
  and John Churchill (1st Duke of Marlborough) 58–85, 116
Cadogan, Dr William (1711–1797) 163–64, *163*
Cadogan, Reverend William Bromley (1751–1797) Ch 6 (138–49); *139*; 170
  and Charles Henry, 2nd Earl 137, 155, 159–60, 161, 163
  and Thomas 'Tom/Tommy' 123–24
  and Reverend William Marsh 270

INDEX

Cadogan, Major William George Sydney 'Willie' (1879-1914) Ch 17 (382-86, 388-94); 355; *392*,
   and Alexander 'Alec' *427*, 430
   on Gerald Oakley 'Jerry' 409
   portraits and photographs *347, 382, 392, 427*
Cadogan, William Gerald Charles 'Bill' (1914-1997), 7th Earl Ch 20 (446-67); 355; *447*; *467*
   early years *411*, 425, 446, *448*
   family 355, 451-52, *452*, 467
   Military Cross 454-55, *457*
   portraits and photographs 356-57, *453, 456, 457, 458*
Cadogan Charity, The 467
Cadogan earldom (peerage)
   First Creation (1718) 79-80
   New Creation (NC, 1800) 132, 475 n. 45
Cadogan Estate 108-9, 279, 309, 310-311, 319-20, 410-12, 421-25, *422*, 458-59, 465, 466
Cadogan Estates Ltd 464
Cadogan Gardens 311, 410-11, 412, *413*
Cadogan Hotel 318-19
Cadogan House, King's Road *see* Chelsea House/Cadogan House
Cadogan Pier, Cheyne Walk 268, 270
Cadogan Place 108, 109-10, 111, 244, 249, 271, 331, *331*, 449, *450*, 458, 465, 469 *see also* Chelsea House, Cadogan Place
Cadogan Square 110, 258-59, 311, *312*, 421, 458
'Cadogan Square' (Portia, Edith, Cynthia and Mary) Ch 16 (369-81); 354; *365*, 376-77,
   husbands during World War I 395
Cadogan's Horse 63, 68, 73
Cadwaladr ap Cadwallon (d. AD 664) 29, 30, 33
Cadwallon ap Madog (d.1179), Prince of Maelienydd 25-26, 34, 35
Cadwgan/Cadwgon ab Elystan Glodrydd, Lord of Radnor 12, *13*, 20-21, *20*, 25, 32, 34
Caldey Stone, Caldey Island, Pembrokeshire 21
Cambridge, Duke of, Prince George 299
Cambridge, Duchess of, Princess Augusta of Hesse-Kassel 288
Cambridge, parliamentary seat 112, 114, 152, 154
Cambridge University 41, 360, 384
Cape Colony, South Africa 125, *125*, 199
Cape of Good Hope 191, 124
Carlton Club 335

Carlton Hotel, London 441-42
Carlton House, London 242, *242*
Carlton Tower Hotel (Carlton Tower Jumeirah) 465
Carlyle, Thomas 319
Carlyle Mansions, Chelsea 319
Carlyle Square, Chelsea 458
Carr, Major Henry (HEICS), (c.1809-1850) 170, 235, 271
Casnar/Kasnat/Casanauth Wledig ('the Ruler', fl. c.500) 15, 16, 32
Castle Cymaron/Cwm Aran, Radnorshire 24-25, 28, 34
Castlereagh, Robert Stewart, Viscount (later, 2nd Marquess of Londonderry) 209, 217, 232-33, 243
Cavendish, Lady Harriet 'Harry-O' 198, 206-7, 244, 246
Caversham, Baron Oakley of (1831) *237*, 250
Caversham, Viscount of (1718) 79, 80, 90
Caversham Park, Oxfordshire (now Berkshire) 53, 58, 76-77, *77*, 82, 84, 87, 90, 98, 99, 105-7, 115, 125, 128-29, 141, 194, 337
Caversham Street 269
Cecil, James, 1st Marquess of Salisbury 243, 256
Celts 12, 14, 20-21, *20*, 25, 40
Chamberlain, Sir Austen 432-33, *433*
Chamberlain, Neville 435-36, *437*
Channon, Henry 'Chips' 372, 375
Chariots of Fire (1981) 416
Charles I, King 41, 43-44, *44*, 54, 56
Charles II, King 51-52, *52*, 81, 86, 94, 134, 146
Charles III, King 27, 354
Charles X, King of France 251, 283, 284
Chelsea, history
   Tudor 31
   seventeenth century 52, 53
   under Charles, 2nd Baron 96-97, 97, 100
   under Charles, 1st Earl (NC) 88-89, 101, 104, 105, 107-11, 108-9, *110*, 136, 137
   under Charles, 2nd Earl 169
   under George, 3rd Earl 244, *245*, 247-49, *248*, 251, 268-69, *268-69*, 270
   under Henry, 4th Earl 279
   under George Henry, 5th Earl 309-11, *312*, 313-20, *321*, 331, 326-27
   during World War I 410-11, *413*
   interwar period 412, 414, *414*, 420-25, *422*, *424*, 449-50, *450*
   during World War II 458-59, *459*
   under William, 7th Earl 465-67

Chelsea, Manor of 31, 95, 97, *97*, 100, *104*, 169, 251; (Lordship of) 368, 418
Chelsea, Mildred (née Sturt, 1869-1942), Viscountess 354, 362-64, *363*, 365, 366, 368, 369, 380
Chelsea, Viscount (1800) 132
   as a courtesy title 135, 137, 170, 260, 354, 367, 468
Chelsea Common 88-89, 97, *104*, 247, *248*, 314, 422, *422*
Chelsea Embankment 270, 279, *279*, 309
Chelsea Football Club 417-18, *418*, 465
Chelsea House, Cadogan Place 271, 315, 327, 331-32, *331*, 335-36, 339, 346-47, 360, 368, 369, 373, 391, 408, 409-10, 426, 438, 449, *450*
Chelsea House/Cadogan House, King's Road 96-97, 137
Chelsea Old Church *104*, 140, *141*, 244, 269, 458, 467
Chelsea Old Rectory 140, *141*
Chelsea Old Town Hall 315, *317*, 412, 425
Chelsea Physic Garden 53, 101, *103*, 109, 163
Chelsea Place 30, 31, 100, 247-48
Chelsea Square 248, 424
   see also Trafalgar Square, Chelsea; Waterloo Square, Chelsea
Chenil Gallery, King's Road 412, 414, *414*
Cheyne, Charles 100
Cheyne Gardens 301
Cheyne Row 319
Cheyne Walk 30, 100, 248, *268*, 269, *269*, 270, 279, *279*, 295, 309, 314, 371, 465
Chiang Kai-shek, 434, *435*
China 434-35
Christ Church, Chelsea 269
Churchill, General Charles (1656-1714) 116, 118
Churchill, General Charles (c.1679-1745) 116, 118
Churchill, Colonel Charles (c.1720-1812) 116, 118, 119
Churchill, John, 1st Duke of Marlborough 58, 62, 63, 66-67, *67*, 68-70, 71, 73-75, 82-83, 106, 116, 118
Churchill, Mary (1758-1811) *see* Cadogan, Mary, Lady (née Churchill)
Churchill, Lady Mary (née Walpole, 1725-801) 116, *117*, 118, 119
Churchill, Sarah, Duchess of Marlborough 73, 74, 83, 106
Churchill, Sophia *see* Walpole, Sophia (née Churchill)

INDEX

Churchill, Sir Winston (1620–1688) 116, 118
Churchill, Sir Winston (1874–1965) 188, 292, 379, 389, 401, 434, 439–40, *439*, *440*, 444, 470
Churchill family 116, 118–19, 168
Churston, John Reginald Lopes Yarde-Buller, 'Johnnie/Yardie', 3rd Baron (1873–1930) 355, 341
Civil War see English Civil War
coat of arms 13, *237*, 250, *253*, 418
Colesburg, South Africa 383, *383*
Commonwealth interregnum 49–51
Compton, William, 5th Marquess of Northampton 313
Constantinople see Istanbul
Cooke, Lieutenant-Colonel Sir Henry 284–85
Coombe Abbey, Warwickshire 328–29, 449
Cooper, Reverend Sir William Henry, Bt 130–31
Cornwallis, Charles, 1st Marquess 133, 137
Cornwallis, Admiral Sir William 185
County Meath, Ireland 42, 47, *47*, 49, 50–51, 53, 57, 82
Cowley, Henry Wellesley, 1st Earl see Wellesley, Henry, 1st Earl Cowley
Cowper, Frank Cadogan, RA 295
Coxon, Lilian Eleanor Marie (c.1889–1973) see Cadogan, Lilian Eleanor Marie 'Marie' (née Coxon), Countess
Cracow, Poland 158–60
Craven, Lady Beatrix 'Beattie' Jane (1844–1907) see Cadogan, Beatrix 'Beattie' Jane, Countess (née Craven)
cricket 114, 336, 339, *339*, 360, *361*, 382, 387, 390, 428
Crimean War (1853–56) 298, *298*, 299, 300–302, *301*
Crocodile, HMS 191, 194, 215–16
Cromwellian Settlement of Ireland 42, 49–51
Cuhelyn ab Ifor, Lord of Buellt 14, 32
Culford Camp, Suffolk *456*, 460
Culford Gardens, Chelsea 411
Culford Hall and Park, Suffolk 305, 337–39, *337*, 352, 358, *359*, 366, 368, 408, 410, *411*, 417, *419*, 420, 426, *427*, 438, 445, 446, 448–49, *448*
Culford School 449
Cunedda Wledig (King Kenneth, c. AD 386–460) 18–19, 33
Currie, Lady Charlotte (née Cadogan) 271, 331, 333, 355

Currie, Reverend Maynard W. 333, 355
Cwgan Stone, Llanrhaeadr-ym-Mochnant, Powys 13, 20–21, *20*
Cyane, HMS 185, 186
Cymaron Castle, Radnorshire 24, 25, 28, 34

Damascus, Syria 399
Danish Embassy, Sloane Street 111, 466, *466*, 467
Dardanelles Campaign 396–98, *398*
de Ros, Henry FitzGerald 'de Rot', 21st Baron 247
De Trafford, Cynthia Hilda Evelyn, Lady (née Cadogan, 1896–1966) 354, 365, 369, 370, 371, 372, 375, *376* see also 'Cadogan Square'
De Trafford, Sir Humphrey Edmund, 4th Bt. 354, 372, 395
Deffand, Madame du 117
Delhi Durbars 308, 390, *391*
Derby, Edward John 'John' Stanley, 18th Earl of 375, 458
Diana, HMS 121, 122
Dickens, Charles 253, 397
Dior, Christian 379, *380*
diplomatic service 71–72, 75, 78–79, 217, 260, 262, 272–77, *272*, *274*, *276*, 302, 399, 401, 428–30
see also Foreign Office; League of Nations; United Nations (UN)
Domesday Book 23, 100
Downham Hall, Suffolk 128, *128*, 129, 130, 194, 235, 250
D'Oyly, Christopher 170, 249
D'Oyley Street 111
Droits de l'homme (French ship) 175, 180–81
Dublin, Leinster 41, *42*, 43, 44, 46, 48–49, 51, 54, *55*, 61, 62, 82, 87, 196–97, 324–25, 326, *326*, *327*, 344, 346, *347* 348, 352, 384, 404
see also Christ Church Cathedral; Trinity College; Viceregal Lodge
duels 194, 207–8, *209*, 210–11
Duke of York Square 9, 108, 410 see also Royal Military Asylum
Dumbarton Oaks Conference (1944) 440, *441*
Dutton (HEIC merchant ship) 178–79, *179*, *180*

East India Company, Hon. (HEIC) 120–21, 133, 170, 171, 235, 253, 308
see also *Dutton* (HEIC merchant ship)
Ebury, Denise 'Denny' Grosvenor (née Yarde-Buller, 1916–2005), Baroness 355, 460

Eden, Anthony 434, 435, 437, *440*, 444
Edward the Confessor, King 21, 35
Edward I, King 28, 35
Edward VII, King 'Bertie' 329, *330*, 321, 326, 329, 334–35, 342–44, *343*, 336–37, 352, 358, *358*–59, 366, 382
Edward VIII, King (Duke of Windsor), 27, 373, 374, 375, 391, 392, 393, *394*, 438–39
Edward, Duke of York and Albany (1739–1769) 132
Egypt 158, 292, 399, 439, 444, 453–54
Einion Clud, Prince of Elfael (d.1177) 25–26, *25*, 34, 35
Einion o'r Porth (d.1191), Prince of Elfael 26, *26*, 27, 28, 34
Eisenhower, Dwight D. 442
Elizabeth, Queen (consort of George VI) 98, 372, 374–75, 380–81, *381*
Elizabeth II, Queen 27, 96, *98*, 444, *445*, 454, 456
Ellerman, Sir John, 1st Bt. 421–22, 424
Ellis, Welbore, 1st Baron Mendip 170, 249
elopements *195*, 202, 203–7, 226, 240, 346–49, 350
Elystan Glodrydd ('the Renowned', c. AD 975–1010) 12–16, *13*, 19–21, 27, 29, 31, 32, 34, 40, 87, 418, 472 n.2
Elystan Place; Elystan Street 12
English Civil War 43–45, 48–49, 53, 56
ennoblements
  Baron Cadogan of Oakley, Buckinghamshire (1718) 79, 80
  Baron Cadogan of Reading (1716) 78, 80
  Baron Oakley of Caversham (1831) *237*, 250
  Earl Cadogan (1718, 1800 NC) 79–80, 132
  Viscount of Caversham (1718) 79, 80, 90
  Viscount Chelsea (1800) 132
  see also family trees
espionage 48, 58, 68–69, *69*, 72, 429–30, 435–36, 438, 444–45, 453
Eton College, Berkshire
  Benson, A.C. (housemaster) 382, 427–28
  Cadogans at 263, 297, 329–30, 338, 360, 382–83, *382*, 391, *400*, 425, 426–28, 446
  cricket 360, *361*
  foundation of 144
  Fourth of June 399

Faisal I, King of Iraq 399
family trees 32–33, 34–35, 86–87, 116, 170–71, 256–57, 354–55

499

INDEX

Ferret, HMS 121, 188–90, 191
First World War *see* World War I (1914–18)
Flood Street (Queen Street) 269, 296, 315, 319, 410
Flushing, Holland 219, *220–21*
football club *see* Chelsea football club
Foreign Office 263, 272, 432–37, *432, 433, 435, 437*
Fox Talbot, William Henry 293
France 78, 114–15, 131, 158, 163
   see also Olympic Games (1924); Paris; named conflicts
Francis II (Franz), Emperor of Austria 238, 239
Franco–Austrian War (1859) 277
Frazer (Fraiser, Frasier), Jane 122–23, 124, 170
Frederick, Duke of York 137, 227
Frederick, Prince of Wales 98, 99
Freemasonry 416, 463, 464, 467
French Revolutionary Wars (1792–02) *175*, 177–81, *183*, 184–85
   see also Napoleonic Wars (1803–15)

Gallipoli Campaign 395–98, *397, 398*
gambling 82, 83, 114, 334–35, 342–44, *343*, 387, 406–7
   see also Baccarat Case
Gascoyne-Cecil, Robert *see* Salisbury, Robert Gascoyne-Cecil, 3rd Marquess of
George I, King 75, *77*, 78, 80, 84, 91, 128
George II, King 73, 91, *91*, 101, 116, 119, 134, 163
George III, King 91, 129, 134, 142, 166, *166*, 178, 188, 241
George IV, King 246, 250
   as Prince Regent 134, 227, 232, 238, 239, 240, 241–42, 243
George V, King 27, 348, 368, 390, 374, *377, 391*, 394, 395, *401*, 410, 416
George VI, King (Prince Albert, Duke of York) 98, 373, 374, 375, *381*, 394, 438–39, 443, 454
Germany 65, 161, 329, 330, 392
   see also World War II (1939–1945)
Gilmour, Ian Hedworth John Little 380
Gilmour, Sir John 'Jock' Little 354, 380, 395
Gilmour, Victoria Laura 'Tor Tor', Lady (née Cadogan, 1901–1999) 354, 365, 380–81, *381*
Girl Guides 418–20, *419*
Gladstone, William Henry 329, 330, *330*
Glendelvine, Perthshire 460–61
Glorieux, HMS 121, *121*, 171, 174
Golden Eagle (yacht) 350, 385–86, 426

Gordon-Cumming, Lieutenant-Colonel Sir William 343–44, *343*
Gordon-Lennox, Lady Caroline Amelia 'Car' (m. Ponsonby, 1819–1890) 287
Gordon-Lennox, Caroline, Duchess of Richmond (née Paget, 1796–1874) 266
Gordon-Lennox, Charles, 7th Duke of Richmond 360–61, 363–64, 407–8, 411, 412
Gordon-Lennox, Charles Henry, 8th Duke of Richmond 81
Graham, Sir James 250
Grand Tours 154–58, *155*, 161, 200
Graves, Thomas, 2nd Baron 206
Green Girls' Foundation 151
Green Girls' School, Reading 144–46, *147*, 151
Grosvenor Street 118, 130, 410, 420
Guinness, Walter, 1st Baron Moyne 395, 396
Gwrtheyrn Gwrtheneu ('the Thin', fl. c.425–50), King Vortigern of the Britons 15, 16, *17*, 32

Hague, The, Netherlands 70, 72, 75, 79, 81, 82
Halifax, Edward Wood, Viscount (later Earl of) 435–36, *437*
Hamilton, Sir William 156, *156–57*
Hamilton-Wedderburn, Cecilia Margaret 'Bunny' *see* Cadogan, Cecilia Margaret, Countess (née Hamilton-Wedderburn, wife of 7th Earl)
Hans Town 107–11, *108–9*, 112, 244, 309–10, 137, 269
Hans Crescent; Hans Place; Hans Street, Chelsea 208
Havannah, HMS 191–93, *193*, 226
Henry I to Henry III, Kings 24–28
Henry VII, King 29–31
Henry VIII, King 31, 40
Hesse, Fritz 435–36
Hillingdon, Arthur Robert Mills 'Bear', 3rd Baron 354, 370, *376*, 395
Hillingdon, Edith Mary Winifred, Lady (née Cadogan, 1895–1969) 354, 365, 369–71, *376*, 437
   see also 'Cadogan Square'
Holland, Henry 107, 108, *108–10*, 109, 110, 111, 242, 449
Holy Trinity Sloane Street 244, *245*, 316–18, *318*, 346, 362, 451, 467
horse-racing (the turf) 305, 334, 338, 339, *340*, 341–42, 367, 372, 417, 453
Houghton Hall, Norfolk 119
Hübner, Joseph Alexander, Count 275–76

hunting 28, 57, 229, 349, 372, 451, 467
Hywel Dda ('the Good', c. AD 880–950) 16–18, *18*, 19, 23, 29, 33, 34

Impétueux, HMS 182–83, *183*, 184
Indefatigable, HMS 175–77, *175, 177*, 178, 179, 180–81, 182
India 120–21, *120*, 171, 196, 303, 308, 390, *391*, 401, 451, 464
Intelligence Corps 399
Iorwerth Hirflawdd ('of the Long Struggle', b. c.770) 14–15, 32, 35
Ireland Chs 2, 14, 15; 41–51, 324–26
   Act of Settlement (1662) 42, 53
   Adventurers' Act (1642) 49–51
   Battle of the Boyne 62
   Cadogan property 39, 42, 49–51, 53, 54, 57, 82
   George Henry, 5th Earl and 322, 324–26, *326*, 348, 351
   Henry Cadogan (1642–1715) and 54, 56–57
   Irish Rebellion (1641) 41, 44, 46
   Land Law (Ireland) Acts (1887, 1896) 322, 324, 325
   Victoria, Queen, visit of 325, *327*
   Major William Cadogan (1601–1661) and 41, *42*, 43, 44, 46–51, *51*
Istanbul (Constantinople), Turkey 158, 159, 425, 428–29, *429*, 430, 437
Italy 15, 156, *156*, 161, 191, 277, 294, 297, 302, 303, 367, 406, 438, 455, *457*, 458, 461
   see also Rome; Naples

Jacobean era 38–41
Jacobites 57, 72, 78, 84, 87
Jamaica 122, 170, 186, 188–90
James VI and I, King 39
James VII and II, King 60, 61, 62, 72
Jockey Club 341, 372, 467
John, King 28, 35
Johnstone, Sir Frederick William, 8th Bt. 407–8

Kendrick, Thomas 429–30
King's Road, Chelsea 52, 96, 249, 269, 315, *321*, 379, 411, 412, *414*, 420–21, 425, .463, 465, 467, 471
   see also Chelsea House/Cadogan House; Chelsea Old Town Hall; Chenil Gallery; Duke of York Square
Kingsley, Charles 253
Kennedy, Joseph 'Joe' P. 438

landscaping *see* Brown, Capability; Repton, Humphrey
Lawrence, T.E. (of Arabia) 291, *292*
League of Nations 432–33, *432*

INDEX

Lennox, Charles, 2nd Duke of Richmond 81, 83, *83*, 84 86, 95, 134, 247
Lennox, Lady Georgiana Caroline 'Caroline' (1723–1774, m. Fox) 84, 86
Lennox, Lady Sarah (1745–1826) 86, 134, *135*
Lennox, Sarah, Duchess of Richmond (née Cadogan, 1705–1751) 70, 81, *83*, 84, 86, 134, 247
Licorne, HMS 121, 124, 177
Liddell, Eric 415–16, *416*
Liddell, Thomas *see* Ravensworth, Thomas, 1st Baron
Limburg, Belgium, siege of 63–64
Lisbon, Portugal 158, 215, 216, 221–22, *223*
Llewelyn ap Cadwgan ('Llewillen Rex', d.1099) 22, *22*, 34
Llywellyn Fawr (Llywellyn the Great, 1173–1240), Ruler of All Wales 28, 34, 35
Locarno Pact (1925) 433, *433*
Londonderry, Frances Vane, Marchioness of 264, 265–66
Londonderry, Robert Stewart, 2nd Marquess of *see* Castlereagh, Robert Stewart, Viscount
Louis-Philippe I, King of France 283, 284
Lowndes Street *see* Chelsea House, Cadogan Place
Lurgan, Emily Julia 'Tiny', Lady (née Cadogan, 1871–1909) 346, 335, 348, 350, 351, 355, 367
Lurgan, William 'Billy' Brownlow, 3rd Baron 346, 351–52, *351*, 355, 364, 392–93
Lurgan, William George Edward 'Brownie' Brownlow, 4th Baron 355, 367
Lyle, Sir Gavin Archibald, 3rd Bt 461
Lyle, Captain Ian Archibald de Hoghton 'Archie' 455
Lyle, Lorna *see* Alexander, Lorna (née Lyle)
Lyle, Lydia (née Yarde-Buller, later Russell, Duchess of Bedford, 1917–2006) 355, 455, 460, 461

Mabinogion, The 16
MacDonald, Ramsay *432*, 434
Macmillan, Harold 332
Macsen Wledig *see* Magnus Maximus
Madog ab Idnerth (d.1140), King of Rhwng Gwy a Hafren 24, 25, 34, 35
Madog ap Maelgwyn (d.1212), Prince of Maelienydd 28, 34
Maelgwyn ap Cadwallon (d.1197), Prince of Maelienydd 26, 34

Magnus Maximus, Emperor (Macsen Wledig, d. AD 388) 15, *15*, 16, 32
Malmesbury, James Harris, 3rd Earl of 272, *272*, 273
Malta 156–58, 184–85
March, Lord *see* Lennox, Charles, 2nd Duke of Richmond; Gordon-Lennox, Charles, 7th Duke of Richmond
Margaret, Princess 380
Marlborough, Dukes of *see* Churchill; Spencer-Churchill
Marsh, Lady Louisa (née Cadogan, 1787–1843) 129, 171, 194, 226, 241, 270, 271
Marsh, Reverend William 171, 270, 271
Mary of Teck, Queen (consort of King George V) 27, 247,290, 297, 335, 374, 377, 378, 390, *391*
Mary, Princess Royal 374, *419*, 420
Marylebone Cricket Club (MCC) 339
Mediterranean Fleet 185, 191–92
Melbourne, William Lamb, 2nd Viscount 267–68, 287–88, *288*
Merfyn Frych (Mervyn the Freckled, d. AD 844) 18, 30, 33
Merton Hall, Norfolk 129, 168
Meux, Vice-Admiral Sir Hedworth (né Lambton) 354, 366, 368, 369
Meux, Lady Valerie 'Val' 364, 366
MI5 435–36, 444–45
MI6 429, 438
Military Cross (MC) 372, 395, 454–55, *457*, 458
Mortimer/de Mortimer family, marcher lords of Wigmore 24–26, 28, 29, 34–35
Munter, Margaretta Cecilia *see* Cadogan, Margaretta Cecilia, Countess
museums 101, 105, 300
see also British Museum; Natural History Museum

Naples, Italy 156, *156*, 158, *159*
Napoleon I, Emperor *see* Bonaparte, Napoleon
Napoleon III, Emperor 274, 275–76, 289
Napoleonic Wars (1803-15) 125, 134, 185, 188, 191–93, *193*, 215–19, *220*, 221, 235, 239–41
see also French Revolutionary Wars (1792–1802); Peninsular War (1807–14)
Narcissus, HMS 184
Natural History Museum 101, 105, 300 469
Nelson, Vice-Admiral Horatio Nelson, 1st Viscount 116, 119, 156, 157, 174, 178, 184, 185, 188, *190*, 254
Nelson's Column 254–55

Neri, Lippo, Conte Palagi Del Palagio 257, 303, 367
Neri, Olivia Georgiana (née Cadogan) 257, 303

New Burlington Street, London 96, 195
New Zealand 350, *381*, 387
Newcastle, Thomas Pelham-Holles, 1st Duke of 114
Newfoundland, Canada 119, 121, 177, 439
Newsells Park, Hertfordshire 372, *372*
Nicolson, Harold 428 29, *432*
Nightingale, Florence 301–2, *302*
Nine Years' War (Ireland, 1593–1603) 41
Nine Years' War (1688–97) 62
Norfolk *see* Houghton Hall; Merton Hall; Sandringham; Woodrising Hall

Oakley, Baron, of Caversham (1831) 171, *237*, 250
Oakley, Buckinghamshire, Baron Cadogan of (1718) 79, 80, 87
Oakley, Manor of 76, 83, 106
Oakley Street, Chelsea 248, 465
Old Church Street, Chelsea 100, 414, 449
Oldfield, Anne 116, 118
Olympic, RMS 396, 397
Olympic Games (Paris, 1924) 414–16, *416*, *417*
'Orme, Denise' *see* Yarde-Buller, Jessie (née Smither, 1884–1960), Baroness Churston
Ormonde, James Butler, 1st Duke of 48
Ormonde, James Butler, 2nd Duke of 75
Owain Glyndŵr 29, 35
Oxford University 27, 112, 138, 141, 143, 260, 289, 330, 374, 391, 393, 400, 428, 444

Padarn Beisrudd (Paternus of the Red Cloak, fl. AD 300) 19, 33
Paget, Lady Adelaide (1820–1890) *see* Cadogan, Lady Adelaide
Paget, Sir Arthur 202, 203–4, 206, 209, 304
Paget, Lady Augusta (née Fane, previously Lady Boringdon) 202, 257
Paget, Lady Caroline 'Car' (née Villiers, later Duchess of Argyll) 199, 200, 202, 206, 211, 212, 243, 257, 287
Paget, Vice-Admiral Charles 200, 202, 206, 209
Paget, Charlotte, Marchioness of Anglesey *see* Cadogan, Lady Charlotte 'Cha' Sloane (1781–1853)
Paget, Lady Emily Caroline (1810–1893) 211, 257

501

INDEX

Paget, George Augustus Frederick 257, *302*
Paget, Henry (né Bayly), 1st Earl of Uxbridge 199, 206, 257
Paget, Field Marshal Henry William, 1st Marquess of Anglesey, 2nd Earl of Uxbridge 243, 170, 257
  duel with George Cadogan 210–11
  and Lady Emily Wellesley (née Cadogan) 244, 246
  and Lady 'Cha' Wellesley (née Cadogan) *195*, 199–200, *200–201*, 202, 203–4, 206–7, 208–12
  Napoleonic Wars (1803–1815) 216, 219, 221, 226–27, 239–40
  on proposed marriage of Henry Cadogan and Mary Wellesley 263
Paget, Lady Mary (1812–1859, m. Earl of Sandwich) 257, 287
Paget family 257
paintings by Cadogan family members
  Lady Honoria Louisa 'Hony' *290*, 294, 295–96, *295*
  Lady Augusta Sarah *286*, *289*, *291*, 294
  General Sir George *297*, 298–99, *298*, 300, *301*–2
Palagi, Adele *see* Cadogan, Adele, Countess
Pallas, HMS 191, 219, 221
Palmer, Major Sir Anthony Frederick Mark, 4th Bt 454
Palmer, Dame Henriette Alice (née Cadogan, later Abel Smith, 1914–2005) 454
Paris, France 272, 273–74, 275–77, 280, 282–84, 289, 296, 263, 324, 415–16
Paultons, Hampshire 107, 169, 170, 249
Pavilion, The (Sloane Place), Hans Place 110, *110*, 111, 309–10
Pavilion Road 111, 469
Pellew, Edward, 1st Viscount Exmouth 121, 176–77, 178–79, 180–81, *180*, 182–83, 184, 185–86, 191–92
Peninsular War (1807–14) 215–18, *217–18*, 221–22, *222–23*, 224–30, *231*, 232
Pepys, Samuel 51–52, *53*
Piccadilly, London 58, 95, 251, 277, *288*, 290, 463
Pillar of Eliseg, Denbighshire *13*, 15, *16*, 33
Pitt, William, the Elder 133, 160, 170
Pitt, William, the Younger *132*, 133–34, 135, 137, 178, 199, 208, 251
political careers
  Charles, 2nd Baron 90, 94
  Charles Sloane, 1st Earl (NC) 112, 114, 132–35

Edward Cecil 'Eddie' 400–401
Frederick 'Freddie' 289, 291
George Henry, 5th Earl *304*, 305–8, 320–22, *323*, 324–26
Henry Arthur 'Haggy' 362
Henry Charles, 4th Earl 270–71, 272
William, 1st Earl 74
Maj. William Cadogan 44, 49
Pont Street 110, 310, *310*, 311, 467
Pont Street Dutch 311
Pontack's Head, Abchurch Lane, London 94–95
Pope, Alexander 84–85
Porcupine, HMS 121, 122
Portugal *see* Peninsular War (1807–1814)
Prendergast, Penelope, Lady (née Cadogan, d.1746) 57, 87
Prendergast, Sir Thomas, 1st Bt 57, 73, 87
Prince of Wales *see* Edward VII; Edward VIII; Frederick, Prince of Wales; George IV as Regent; Wales (investitures)
Prince of Wales, HMS, (53) 439

Queen Anne style 310–11, *312*

Raaphorst, Manor of, Wassenaar, The Hague 70, 75
Raby, Lord *see* Wentworth, Thomas, 1st Earl of Strafford (1672–1739)
Ravensworth, Thomas Liddell, 1st Baron 246, 256
Reading, Berkshire 78, 80, 87, 90, 141–42, 144–46, *147*, 148–49, 149–51, *150*
Reading, Baron Cadogan of (1716) 78, 80
Regency period 170, 203, 241–42, 256–57, *284*
  see also George IV as Prince Regent
regicide 21–22, 44, 56, *56*, 57
Repton, Humphry 109, 337
Rhodri Mawr (Roderick the Great, c. AD 820–878) 18, 33, 34
Rhys ap Gruffudd (The Lord Rhys, d.1197) 25, 26, 34
Richmond, Dukes of *see* Lennox; Gordon-Lennox
rivers *see* Thames, River; Westbourne, River; *see also* Chelsea Embankment
Robertson, Robbie 458–59
Rockingham, Charles Watson-Wentworth, 2nd Marquess of 132, 133
Rome, Italy 16, *155*, 158, 161, 294, 438, 455
Roosevelt, Franklin D. 439, 440, *440*

Rossetti Studios 319–20
  see also artists' studios
Royal Air Force 401, 468
Royal Flying Corps 394, *394*
Royal Hospital Chelsea 60, 84, 100, 116, 118, 272, 417, 458
Royal Military Asylum (Duke of York Square) 96, *136*, 137
Royal Navy 121, 122–23, *122*, 124, Ch 8 (174–93), 219, 221, 254, 277, 394, 395
  French Revolutionary Wars (1792–1802) 175, 184–85, *183*
  Napoleonic Wars (1803–15) 185, 188, 191–93, *193*, 215–16, *217*, 219–21, *220*
Royal Society, London 94–95, *94*, 99, 101, 293
Russell, John 'Ian' Robert, 13th Duke of Bedford 460–61
Russia 160, 230, 260, 262, *262*

Salisbury, James Cecil, 1st Marquess of 243, 256
Salisbury, Robert Gascoyne-Cecil, 3rd Marquess of 305, 320–21, 322, 324, 326, *340*, 341, 351, 352, 353
Sandringham, Norfolk 334, *335*, 336–37, *336*, 393
Sandwich, Mary Montagu (née Paget, 1812–1859), Countess of 257, 287
Santon Downham, Suffolk 128, *129*, 137, 169, 233
  see also Downham Hall, Suffolk; St Mary's, Santon Downham
schools 144–46, *147*, 149–51, *150*, 175, 269 *see also* Culford School; Eton College; Sussex House School; Westminster School
Scotland 39, *45*, 72, 78, 211–12, 460–61
  Glendelvine, Perthshire 460–61
  Gordon Castle, Moray 359
  Snaigow, Perthshire 461, *462–63*, *462*, 467
Scott, Sir Samuel 'Sammy', 6th Bt. 346–51, *349*, 355, 364, 385–86, 395, 446, 448, 449, 461
Scott, Lady Sophie Beatrix Mary (née Cadogan, 1874–1937) 332, 346–51, *347*, *349*, 355, 358, 367, 385–86, 425, *427*
Second Boer War (1899–1902) 383–86, *383*, *384*, *385*, 388–90, *389*
Second World War *see* World War II
Shelley, Frances, Lady 228–29, 233
shooting 129, 336, *336*, 375, 390, 393, 399, 410, 446, 463
Silvy, Camille 261, 264, 293–94, *294*
Simpson, Wallis, Duchess of Windsor 375, 438–39

502

INDEX

Skerrett, Maria 'Molly' see Walpole, Maria, Lady (née Skerrett)
Sloane, Elizabeth (1701–1768) see Cadogan, Elizabeth, Lady (née Sloane)
Sloane, Sir Hans, 1st Bt 84, 85, *85*, 87, 91, 94, 95, 100, 101, 102, *104*, 105, 107, 160, 170, 248, 251
Sloane, Sarah (1696–1764) see Stanley, Sarah (née Sloane)
Sloane family 168, 170, 251
Sloane Place 'The Pavilion' 110, *110*, 309–10
Sloane Square 108, *108*, 249, 313, 318, 319, *321*, 412, 425, 450, 465–66
Sloane Square Underground station 279, 458, 459
Sloane Street 88–89, 108, *108*, 110, 111, 313, 318, 411, 412, 421, 425, 458, 465, 466, *466*, 470
Sloane-Stanley, Hans (1739–1827) *169*, 170, 249
Sloane-Stanley, William 208
Snaigow, Perthshire 461, 462–63, *462*, 467
South Africa see Cape Colony; Cape Town; Colesburg; Second Boer War (1899–1902)
Spain see Peninsular War (1807–1814)
Special Operations Executive (SOE) 454
Spencer, George, 2nd Earl 176, 181, 186, 190
Spencer-Churchill, Alexandra Mary Hilda 'Mary', Duchess of Marlborough (née Cadogan, 1900–1961) 354, 365, 369–70, 375, *377*, 378–80, 379, 380 see also 'Cadogan Square'
Spencer-Churchill, Consuelo, Duchess of Marlborough (née Vanderbilt) 378, *378*, 379–80
Spencer-Churchill, John Albert Edward William 'Bert', 10th Duke of Marlborough 354, 375, *377*, 378–79, *378*, 380, 395
St Donat's Castle, Vale of Glamorgan 38, *38*, 87
St Giles's Church, Reading 141–42, 148–49, *148*
St Luke's Church, Chelsea 169, 233, 244, *245*, 253, 271, 467
St Mary's Church, Culford 366, 368, 445
St Mary's Church, Santon Downham 233
St Paul's Cathedral, London 233, *233*, 235, 272, 316–17
St Peter's Church, Caversham 115, *115*

St Petersburg, Russia 260, 262, *262*
Stanisław II August Poniatowski, King of Poland (r.1764–95) 159–60
Stanley, Anne (m. Ellis) 170, 249
Stanley, Sir Edward Montagu Cavendish 354, 374, *377*, 395
Stanley, George of Paultons, Hampshire 166, 170, 248–49
Stanley, Hans (1721–1780) 107, 160, 166, 170, 249
Stanley, Edward John 'John', 18th Earl of Derby 375, 458
Stanley, Sarah (née Sloane, 1696–1764) 99, 170, 248–49
Stanley, Sarah Anne (m. D'Oyly, d.1821) 170, 248, 249
Stanley, Sybil Louise Beatrix 'Portia', Lady (née Cadogan, 1893–1969) 354, 365, 369–70, 373–75, *373*, *377*, 381, 395, 430, 458
see also 'Cadogan Square'
Stanley family 170, 248–249, 330, 374
Steward, Arthur 458–59
Stradling family 31, 38, 87
Strafford, 1st Earl of see Wentworth, Thomas, 1st Earl of Strafford (NC)
Sturt, Hon. Mildred Cecilia Harriet see Cadogan, Mildred (née Sturt), Viscountess
Suffolk 116, 128, 130, 194, 235, 305, 337–39, 410, 425
constituency of Eye 199
Girl Guides 419, 420
Woodbridge 395, 398
see also Culford Hall and Park; Downham Hall; St Mary's, Santon Downham
suffragettes 371, *371*
Sussex House School, Cadogan Square 311
Sydney, Emily Caroline Townshend, Countess (née Paget, 1810–1893) 211, 257
Syria 399, 453, 454

Tasmania 387–88, *388*, 403
Thames, River 31, 60, *60*, 77, *104*, 200, 249, *269*, 270, *279*, 309
see also Chelsea Embankment
Thatched House Tavern, St James's Street 168, *168*, 254
Theobalds Park, Hertfordshire 364, 366
Tite Street, Chelsea 309, 319
Tournai, Belgium, sieges of 69–70, 72, 73
Trafalgar Square, Chelsea 248, 424
Trelystan, Powys 20
Trim Castle, County Meath 47, *47*, 49, 51, 87

Trinity College, Dublin 54, 61, 85, 325
Trostrey, Monmouthshire 31, *31*, 87
Turkey 159, see also Gallipoli; Istanbul
Tyrwhitt, Gerald (14th Baron Berners) 429, *429*

Ulster Plantation (Jacobean) 41, *42*, 44
United Nations (UN) 426, 439, 443, *443*
United States of America 40–41, 133 34, 170, 277, 420, 442–43
American War of Independence 107, 119, 133–34, 178
New York 275, 378, 443, *443*
Washington DC 440, *441*, 442
see also named politicians
Uxbridge, Henry Paget (né Bayly), 1st Earl (NC) 199, 206, 257
Uxbridge, Henry Paget, 2nd Earl see Paget, Field Marshal Henry William, 1st Marquess of Anglesey

Valle Crucis pillar see Pillar of Eliseg
Vanderbilt, Consuelo see Spencer-Churchill, Consuelo
Versailles Peace Conference 432
Vesuvius, Mount 156, *156*
Vicerregal Lodge, Phoenix Park, Dublin 325, *327*, 346, *347*, 348
Victoria, Queen 325, *327*, 329, 266–67, *267*, 287, 300, 335–36, 342–43
on Augusta and Honoria Cadogan 285–88, *288–89*
on Ethel Cadogan 291
on Sir George Cadogan (1814–1880) 299–300
on George Henry, 5th Earl 334
and Gerald Valerian Wellesley 294
on Henry Paget 199
Vienna, Austria 71, 91, 158, 159, 200, 238, 296, 429–30
Ville de Paris (French ship) 121, *121*
Villeneuve, Admiral Pierre-Charles 187, 188
Villiers, Lady Charlotte Louisa Emily 290, *291*, 297
Villiers, Frances, Countess of Jersey 203, *205*, 257
Villiers family 394
Vortigern, King of the Britons (fl. 425–50) see Gwrtheyrn Gwrtheneu
Votadini tribe 19

Walcheren campaign (1809) 191, 219–21
Wales Ch 1 (12–35); 40, 79, 87, 155
ancestry 253, 406, 417, 430
dragon of *17*, 29, 30, 33, *253*

INDEX

family trees 32–33, 34–35
medieval map of 13
see also named locations
Waller, Bridget (1638–1721) *see* Cadogan, Bridget (née Waller)
Waller, Sir Hardress 54, 56, *56*, 87
Wallscourt, Joseph Henry Blake, 2nd Baron 171, 246
Walpole, Horace, 4th Earl of Orford 116, 117, *117*, 126, 128
Walpole, Horatio, 2nd Earl of Orford (NC) 116, 119
Walpole, Maria 'Molly', Lady (née Skerrett) 116, *117*, 118–19
Walpole, Lady Mary *see* Churchill, Lady Mary (née Walpole)
Walpole, Sir Robert (later, 1st Earl of Orford NC, 1676–1751) 81, 90, 114, 116, *117*, 118–19
Walpole, Sophia (née Churchill) 116, 119
Walpole family 116, 117–19, *117*, 168, 285
War of the Spanish Succession (1701–14) 58, 62–74
Wellesley, Anne (née Hill-Trevor), Countess of Mornington 196, 198–99, *198*, 213, 256
Wellesley, Field Marshal Arthur, 1st Duke of Wellington 194, 196, *198*, *223*, *225*, 241, 256, 168, 246, 266, 270, 272, 274, 292,
on Lady Cha and Paget 199, 207, 226–27, 239
and Colonel Henry Cadogan 210, 215–18, *216*, 226, 228–29, 230, 232, 233, 235, 239, 243
and Reverend Gerald Valerian Wellesley 204–5, 250
and brother Reverend Gerald Valerian Wellesley 246
Peninsular War (1807–1814) 215–19, 221–22, *223*, *225*, 227, 228–30
on proposed marriage of Henry Cadogan and Mary Wellesley 265
Waterloo, Battle of 239–40, *239*, 274
Wellesley, Lady Charlotte (née Cadogan, 1781–1853, later Paget) *see* Cadogan, Lady Charlotte 'Cha' Sloane (m. Wellesley, m. Paget)
Wellesley, Lady Emily Mary (née Cadogan, 1778–1839) 195, 196, 198, 199, 244, 246, 256, 265, 271
Wellesley, Admiral Sir George Greville 246, 256
Wellesley, Lady Georgiana, Baroness Cowley (née Cecil) 256, 286
Wellesley, Reverend Hon. Gerald Valerian (1770–1848, husband of Lady Emily Cadogan) 170, 196, 197, 199, 216, 230, 244, *245*, 246–7, 253, 256, 265, 271
Prebendary of Durham Cathedral *245*, 246, 266
Rector of Chelsea 199, 244, 253
Wellesley, Very Reverend Hon. Gerald Valerian (1809–1882), Dean of Windsor 200, 204–5, 250, 256, 289, 293, 294
Wellesley, Henry, 1st Baron Cowley (1773–1847) 194, 170, 196–99, *197*, *198*, 199–200, 203–5, 207, 208, 211, 212, 216, 227, 243, 256, 271, 286
Wellesley, Henry, 1st Earl Cowley (1804–1884) 256, 273, *276*, 277
Wellesley, Hyacinthe-Gabrielle (née Roland), Marchioness, and Countess of Mornington 196, 197, 213, 246, 256
Wellesley, Mary Sarah (1808–1873) *see* Cadogan, Mary Sarah, Countess (née Wellesley)
Wellesley, Richard Colley, 1st Marquess, and 2nd Earl of Mornington 196, 198, *198*, 221, 251, 256
Wellesley, Victor 293, 294
Wellesley family 137, 195–96, 256
Wellesley-Pole, William 196, 219, 221, 226–27, 256
Wellington, Duke of *see* Wellesley, Arthur, 1st Duke of Wellington
Wentworth, Thomas, 1st Earl of Strafford (1593–1641) 41, 43–44, *45*
Wentworth, Thomas, 1st Earl of Strafford NC, 3rd Baron Raby (1672–1739) 61–62, *63*, 63, 66, 72, 82, 85
Wesley, John 142
West, Lady Maria (née Walpole) 285
West Indies 119, 120, 185–90, 439
see also Jamaica; Martinique
Westbourne, River 52, 249
Westminster School, London
Cadogans at 58, 60, 138, 145, 284
connections 82, 95
Whistler, James Abbott McNeill 295, 391
White's Club 9, 391, 408, *409*
Wilde, Oscar 280, 318–19
Willett, William 313, 315
Williams I and II, Kings 22, 23
William III, King 61, *61*, 62
William IV, King 250, 251, 252, 253, *254*
Williams-Wynn, Charlotte, Lady 207
Winchester House, Chelsea 247–48, 465
Windsor, Duchess of *see* Simpson, Wallis
Windsor, Duke of *see* Edward VIII, King
Windsor Castle, Berkshire 77, 242, 291, 297, 303, 329, 334, 374
Wood, Charles Lindley, 2nd Viscount Halifax 329, 330, *330*
Woodrising Hall, Norfolk 279, 308, 333
World War I (1914–18) 370, 391–400, *394*, 396–98, 410–12, *413*, 418, 430
World War II 336, 379, 435–36, 438–42, *439–41*, 452–55, *453*, *456–57*, 458–61
Blitz 441–42
bombing of London 442, 460
damage to Chelsea 458, *459*

Y Gododdin 19, 33
Yarde-Buller, Denise *see* Ebury, Denise Grosvenor, Baroness
Yarde-Buller, Jessie (née Smither, stage name 'Denise Orme'), Baroness Churston (later, Duchess of Leinster, 1884–1960) 355, 451–52, *451*
Yarde-Buller, John Reginald Lopes 'Johnnie/Yardie' (1873–1930), 3rd Baron Churston 355, 451
Yarde-Buller, John Francis (1934–2023), 5th Baron Churston 460
Yarde-Buller, Hon. Lydia (1917–2006) *see* Lyle, Lydia
Yarde-Buller, Hon. Nicole 'Minty' (b.1936) 460
Yarde-Buller, Hon. Primrose Lilian (1918–1970) *see* Cadogan, Primrose Lilian, Countess
York, Albert, Duke of *see* George VI, King
York, Elizabeth, Duchess of *see* Elizabeth, Queen (consort of George VI)
Young, William 258–59, 311–32, 331, *331*, 337–38
Ypres, Belgium 391–93, *394*

Zadar (Zara), Croatia, siege of 192–93, 238

IMPORTANT INTEGRATION FORMULAS

$$\int x^n dx = \frac{x^{n+1}}{n+1} + c, \quad n \neq -1$$

$$\int k \cdot f(x) dx = k \cdot \int f(x) dx$$

$$\int e^x dx = e^x + c$$

$$\int x^{-1} dx = \int \frac{1}{x} dx = \ln|x| + c$$

$$\int (f(x) + g(x)) dx = \int f(x) dx + \int g(x) dx$$

$$\int (f(x) - g(x)) dx = \int f(x) dx - \int g(x) dx$$

$$\int (f(x))^n \cdot f'(x) dx = \frac{(f(x))^{n+1}}{n+1} + c, \quad n \neq -1$$

$$\int (f(x))^{-1} \cdot f'(x) dx = \int \frac{f'(x)}{f(x)} dx = \ln|f(x)| + c$$

$$\int e^{f(x)} \cdot f'(x) dx = e^{f(x)} + c$$

Substitution

$$\int f(x) dx = \int f(g(u)) \cdot g'(u) du$$

Integration by Parts

$$\int uv' dx = uv - \int vu' dx$$

Rectangle Rule

$$\int_a^b f(x) dx \approx \frac{b-a}{n} (f(x_1^*) + f(x_2^*) + \cdots + f(x_n^*)), \text{ where } x_i^* \text{ is the midpoint of the } i\text{th subinterval } [x_{i-1}, x_i]$$

Trapezoid Rule

$$\int_a^b f(x) dx \approx \frac{b-a}{2n} (f(x_0) + 2f(x_1) + 2f(x_2) + \cdots + 2f(x_{n-1}) + f(x_n)),$$
where the ith subinterval is $[x_{i-1}, x_i]$

Simpson's Rule

$$\int_a^b f(x) dx \approx \frac{b-a}{3n} (f(x_0) + 4f(x_1) + 2f(x_2) + 4f(x_3) + \cdots + 2f(x_{n-2}) + 4f(x_{n-1}) + f(x_n)), \text{ where the } i\text{th subinterval is } [x_{i-1}, x_i]$$

BRIEF CALCULUS WITH APPLICATIONS

BRIEF CALCULUS WITH APPLICATIONS

**CHRIS VANCIL
CLIFF SWAUGER**

University of Kentucky

HARPER & ROW, PUBLISHERS, New York
Grand Rapids, Philadelphia, St. Louis, San Francisco,
London, Singapore, Sydney, Tokyo

Sponsoring Editor: Peter Coveney
Project Editor: Steven Pisano
Art Direction: Kathie Vaccaro
Text Design: Caliber Design Planning, Inc.
Cover Coordinator: Mary Archondes
Cover Design: Circa 86
Cover: László Moholy-Nagy, "Yellow Circle," 1921. Oil wash on canvas,
    $53\frac{1}{8} \times 45\frac{1}{4}''$. Collection, The Museum of Modern Art, New York. The Riklis
    Collection of McCrory Corporation (fractional gift). Photograph © 1989
    The Museum of Modern Art, New York.
Text Art: RDL Artset, Ltd.
Production: Linda Murray

Brief Calculus with Applications
Copyright © 1990 by Harper & Row, Publishers, Inc.

All rights reserved. Printed in the United States of America. No part of this book may be used or reproduced in any manner whatsoever without written permission, except in the case of brief quotations embodied in critical articles and reviews. For information address Harper & Row, Publishers, Inc., 10 East 53rd Street, New York, NY 10022-5299.

Library of Congress Cataloging-in-Publication Data

Vancil, Chris N.
    Brief calculus with applications / Chris Vancil, Cliff Swauger.
        p.   cm.
    ISBN 0-06-046766-5
    1. Calculus.   I. Swauger, Cliff.   II. Title.
QA303.V36   1990
515—dc20   89-19898
                                                                           CIP

89 90 91 92   9 8 7 6 5 4 3 2 1

To Cathy and "The Boy"—C.V.
To Jan and "The 3 K's"—C.S.

CONTENTS

CHAPTER 1 GRAPHS AND FUNCTIONS 1

1.1 Equations in Two Variables and Their Graphs 2
1.2 Lines 8
1.3 Functions 20
1.4 Graphs of Functions 31
1.5 Logarithms 42
1.6 Exponential and Logarithmic Functions 52
1.7 Other Functions 58
    Chapter 1 Review 62

CHAPTER 2 LIMITS AND TANGENT LINES 69

2.1 Limits 69
2.2 Continuity 80
2.3 Tangent Lines 93
2.4 Slopes of Tangent Lines 99
    Chapter 2 Review 105

CHAPTER 3 THE DERIVATIVE 111

3.1 Definition of the Derivative 112
3.2 Basic Differentiation Formulas 123
3.3 Rates of Change 132
3.4 The Chain Rule 141
3.5 The Product and Quotient Rules 152
    Chapter 3 Review 161

CHAPTER 4 ADDITIONAL TOPICS ON THE DERIVATIVE 165

4.1 Higher-Order Derivatives   166
4.2 Implicit Differentiation   170
4.3 Related Rates   177
Chapter 4 Review   188

CHAPTER 5 APPLICATIONS OF THE DERIVATIVE 191

5.1 Increasing and Decreasing Functions   192
5.2 Extreme Points   201
5.3 Concavity and the Second Derivative Test   210
5.4 Inflection Points   223
5.5 Curve Sketching   229
5.6 Absolute Extreme Points   240
5.7 Maximum–Minimum Problems   247
5.8 Business Applications   262
Chapter 5 Review   270

CHAPTER 6 INTEGRATION 277

6.1 Antiderivatives   278
6.2 Indefinite Integrals Continued   288
6.3 The Definite Integral   294
6.4 Area   302
6.5 The Definite Integral as the Limit of a Sum   313
Chapter 6 Review   323

CHAPTER 7 ADDITIONAL TOPICS IN INTEGRATION 327

7.1 Substitution   328
7.2 Integration by Parts   335
7.3 Integration Using Tables   341
7.4 Approximate Integration   346
7.5 Laws of Growth and Decay   352
Chapter 7 Review   360

CHAPTER 8 MULTIVARIABLE CALCULUS 363

8.1 Functions of Two Variables   364
8.2 Partial Derivatives   371
8.3 Extreme Points   378
8.4 Lagrange Multipliers   386
8.5 Double Integrals   395
Chapter 8 Review   401

PREFACE

This book is designed to present the fundamentals of calculus to students in the management, life, social, and physical sciences. It is suitable for either a one-semester or two-quarter course. Its only prerequisite is two years of high-school algebra or a course in intermediate algebra.

APPROACH

Our objective has been a text that students will understand and instructors will find easy to use. Four years of class-testing versions of this text have helped us achieve that aim. They have shown us how to develop topics in a progression that students and teachers will find natural. Our approach is geometric and intuitive; although skills play an important role in the text, and applications to a wide variety of fields appear frequently, there is a significant emphasis on concepts.

We have been precise throughout, and important theorems are always proved or justified. Yet students should find the writing style friendly and informal. And we use figures extensively to illustrate, justify, and test the concepts.

Our approach can mean leaving out some necessary condition of a theorem. In Theorem 5.1 on page 194, for example, the hypothesis should really state that the function is differentiable on an open interval containing a, an interior point. But all of the functions in the text to which we apply the theorem satisfy that condition. So we have been brief and simple to decrease the odds that students will miss the forest for the trees. Our goal was to ensure that students have more than a reasonable chance of understanding and applying the mathematics.

ORGANIZATION OF THE TEXT

Our experience indicates that the organization of a text can make it easier to use for both students and instructors. We have given considerable attention to achieving a clear, natural topic sequence.

Chapter 1 contains the topics from college algebra that are needed for the successful study of calculus. It places heavy emphasis on graphs, which are central to the entire text. This chapter requires students to write equations involving specified variables and to write one quantity as a function of another. These skills are the foundation of related rates and maximum–minimum problems, which appear later. Exponential and logarithmic functions are introduced in Chapter 1, rather than in an isolated chapter later as in other texts, so that they can be included wherever appropriate. They are preceded by coverage of exponential and logarithmic equations, because these equations may be used to find the x-intercepts of the functions.

Chapter 2 focuses on the important concepts of limit, continuity, and the tangent line. The chapter relies heavily on graphs so that students understand these basic concepts, which other texts at this level often slight.

Chapter 3 begins by discussing the derivative, relying on the discussion of tangent lines in Chapter 2. The emphasis is on its interpretation as an instantaneous rate of change. The rest of the chapter is devoted to formulas for differentiation. We present the chain rule before the product and quotient rules; this approach increases the power of the latter and provides a convenient proof of the quotient rule.

Chapter 4 is arranged for maximum flexibility. Only the first section, on higher-order derivatives, is required later in the text. The rest of the chapter, which covers implicit differentiation and related rates, may be omitted or covered at any time.

Chapter 5 centers on two important applications of the derivative: curve sketching and maximum–minimum problems. The chapter emphasizes concepts as well as analytic skills and makes considerable use of graphs. Extra attention is given to determining whether a relative extreme point is absolute, an important detail omitted in many other texts.

Chapter 6 begins the discussion of integration. It defines the definite integral as the net change in an antiderivative, not as the limit of a Riemann sum. We believe that this makes more sense to students—who, of course, later see the connection between the two. All theorems concerning integrals are then tied to the corresponding theorems for derivatives in Chapter 3.

Chapter 7 covers topics related to integration. Included is an important application, the laws of growth and decay.

Chapter 8 briefly introduces the calculus of several variables. It draws heavily on the student's understanding of the calculus of one variable, noting parallels wherever possible.

PEDAGOGICAL AIDS

Numerous examples, exercises, and problems in each chapter reinforce student comprehension:

- Exercises—with answers—integrated into the narrative allow students to test their understanding. The exercises, which are always similar to preceding examples, may also be used as additional classroom illustrations.
- Sections then conclude with problems, carefully written to provide practice in skills, concepts, and applications. Most of the time, problems are matching pairs, and answers to the odd-numbered ones (excluding proofs) appear in a separate section at the end of the text.
- Further review problems span the chapter, beginning with true–false questions. Answers to the entire chapter review also appear at the end of the book.

Other pedagogical aids help bring out important concepts and skills:

- Figures play a major role in the text, as well as in the problem sets.
- Important results are always clearly set off.
- Students needing a quick review of intermediate algebra will benefit from the Topics for Review at the end of the text.

ANCILLARIES

The following ancillaries are available free to adopters:

- An *Instructor's Solutions Manual*, by the authors, provides instructors with answers to all even-numbered problems and step-by-step solutions to all proofs.
- *CalcTest*, an algorithm-based, computerized test generator, offers instructors a set of core questions for class testing. It allows selection of a large number of numerical variations on approximately 80 standard questions taken from the text.
- A *Test Bank*, based on CalcTest, shows hard copy of two versions of the questions for each chapter, along with student answer sheets and solutions.

ACKNOWLEDGMENTS. A special thanks goes to James Beidleman and Raymond Cox, who taught from preliminary versions and provided both encouragement and suggestions. In addition, Raymond Cox also provided some of the applications. We also thank Tom Moss, who checked answers to all the problems.

We wish to thank the following individuals who reviewed the manuscript and offered helpful suggestions:

 Fred Brauer, *University of Wisconsin*
 Richard A. Brualdi, *University of Wisconsin*
 Nicholas De Lillo, *Manhattan College*
 Bruce Edwards, *University of Florida*
 Garret Etgen, *University of Houston*
 Joe Evans, *Middle Tennessee State University*
 Howard Frisinger, *Colorado State University*
 Karl Gentry, *University of North Carolina, Greensboro*
 Charles Groetsch, *University of Cincinnati*
 Boyd Henry, *The College of Idaho*
 John Hogan, *Marshall University*
 J. R. Ingraham, *The Citadel*
 Herbert Kasube, *Bradley University*
 Ronnie Khuri, *University of Florida*
 Norman Lee, *Ball State University*
 Stanley Lukawecki, *Clemson University*
 Thomas Lupton, *University of North Carolina, Wilmington*
 Russell Maik, *Wichita State University*
 Brenda Marshall, *Parkland College*
 Philip Montgomery, *University of Kansas*
 Donald Passman, *University of Wisconsin*
 Glen Pfeiffer, *University of New Mexico*
 Holly B. Puterbaugh, *University of Vermont*
 J. Doug Richey, *Henderson County Junior College*
 Stephen Rodi, *Austin Community College*
 Charles Votaw, *Fort Hays State University*

Finally, we wish to thank the staff at Harper & Row for its enthusiastic support and professional assistance; Brian Moses, who typed the manuscript; our families, who provided much-needed encouragement and release time from domestic chores; and the numerous students who used the preliminary versions. Their comments, suggestions, and support are sincerely appreciated.

CHRIS VANCIL
CLIFF SWAUGER

CHAPTER 1

GRAPHS AND FUNCTIONS

CHAPTER OUTLINE
1.1 Equations in Two Variables and Their Graphs
1.2 Lines
1.3 Functions
1.4 Graphs of Functions
1.5 Logarithms
1.6 Exponential and Logarithmic Functions
1.7 Other Functions

This chapter deals with some introductory ideas that are needed for a successful study of calculus. The first two sections focus on equations in two variables and their graphs. Section 1.3 follows, covering one of the most important topics in mathematics—the concept of functions. The remainder of the chapter introduces many graphs that are used throughout the text.

1.1 EQUATIONS IN TWO VARIABLES AND THEIR GRAPHS

In many applications of calculus, problems are stated in words, and one must produce a correct equation before proceeding to a solution. In the first part of this section we concentrate on writing the equation only.

In these problems we are told which algebraic symbols represent some of the unknown quantities. Upon finding a statement of equality, we may wish to introduce some additional variables. Then, using the symbols, we translate the statement of equality into an equation. If the statement is correctly translated, we should be able to identify what each term (or group of terms) represents in the problem. Writing the statement of equality in English before attempting to write the equation helps produce a correct equation. Finally, if necessary, we must substitute for any of the extra variables that we introduced.

It is essential that you *understand the problem*. Read the problem as many times as necessary to comprehend the information given. Draw a picture if helpful. If you introduce a variable not specified in the problem, define it. If the variable represents a measurable quantity, such as distance, length, or time, identify the units of measurement.

EXAMPLE 1

Ship A is steaming north at 10 miles per hour (mph), and ship B is steaming east at 15 mph. At 2:00 ship B is 5 miles due east of ship A. Let d represent the distance (in miles) between ships, and let t represent the elapsed time (in hours) since 2:00. Write an equation involving d and t only.

■ SOLUTION

We have the situation shown in Figure 1.1. We have let

x = distance traveled by B since 2:00 (in miles),

y = distance traveled by A since 2:00 (in miles).

Note that a right triangle has been formed. The lengths of the two legs are y and $x + 5$, and the hypotenuse is d. By the Pythagorean theorem,

$$d^2 = y^2 + (x + 5)^2.$$

We have an equation that contains d but not t. To eliminate x and y we use the fact that

$$\text{distance} = \text{rate} \times \text{time}.$$

Since ship A is moving 10 mph we have

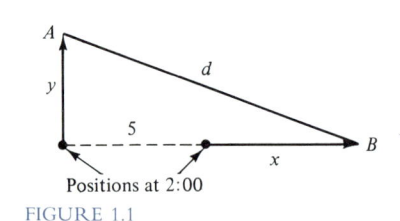

$$y = 10t.$$

Positions at 2:00
FIGURE 1.1

TOPICS FOR REVIEW 407

SELECTED PROOFS 437

ANSWERS TO SELECTED PROBLEMS 441

INDEX 469

Because ship B is traveling at 15 mph,
$$x = 15t.$$
Substituting for x and y thus gives the desired equation:
$$\begin{aligned}d^2 &= (10t)^2 + (15t + 5)^2 \\ &= 100t^2 + 225t^2 + 150t + 25 \\ &= 325t^2 + 150t + 25.\end{aligned}$$

EXERCISE

A certain baserunner runs at a top speed of 32 feet/second. The opposing catcher can throw the ball at a speed of 130 feet/second. The runner attempts to steal third base. The catcher (who is 90 feet from third base) throws the ball toward the third baseman when the runner is 30 feet from third base. Let d represent the distance (in feet) between the ball and the runner, and let t represent elapsed time (in seconds) after the catcher's throw. Write an equation involving d and t only.

■ ANSWER
$$d^2 = (30 - 32t)^2 + (90 - 130t)^2 = 9000 - 25{,}320t + 17{,}924t^2$$

We shall now consider equations in the variables x and y only. Examples include
$$2x - y = x + y - 3, \quad y = x^2, \quad \text{and} \quad x^2 + y^2 = 9.$$

The symbolism (a,b) is used to designate an **ordered pair**, a pair of real numbers a and b where the order is important. Thus $(1,2)$, $(5,-3)$, and $(2,1)$ are examples of ordered pairs. And because the order is significant, $(1,2)$ is different from $(2,1)$.

When $a < b$, the notation (a,b) also denotes the open interval from a to b. (See Appendix A.1 for a discussion of intervals.) But within the context of a particular problem, it will be apparent whether the symbolism refers to the open interval or to the ordered pair.

A **solution** of an equation in x and y is an ordered pair (a,b) which makes the equation true when x is replaced by a and y is replaced by b. Hence $(2,1)$ is a solution of $2x + y = 5$, but $(1,2)$ is not.

Given an equation in x and y, we use its solutions to give us a "picture." To do so we must first consider two perpendicular number lines intersecting at their origins. Such a system, as in Figure 1.2, is called a **Cartesian coordinate system.** By convention the number lines are vertical and horizontal with the positive directions up and right. It is useful to have

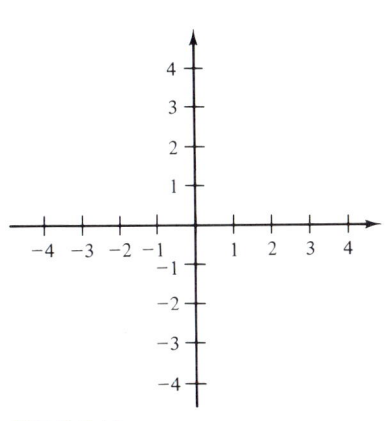

FIGURE 1.2

GRAPHS AND FUNCTIONS

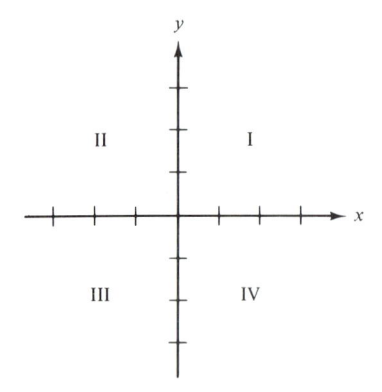

FIGURE 1.3

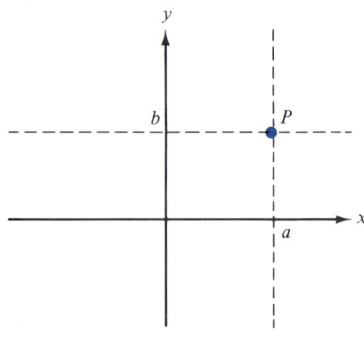

FIGURE 1.4

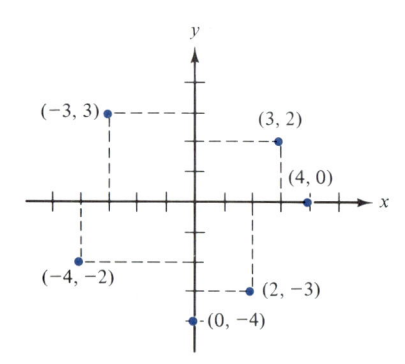

FIGURE 1.5

the unit lengths of each line the same, but this is not always practical or convenient.

In this system each number line is called an **axis.** The horizontal line is called the *x*-axis, and the vertical line is called the *y*-axis. The point of intersection is called the **origin.** The plane determined by such a system is called the **Cartesian** or **coordinate plane** or the **xy-plane.** The two axes divide the plane into four distinct regions called **quadrants,** numbered I through IV, as indicated in Figure 1.3. The points on the axes are not part of any quadrant.

With this system each point in the plane is associated with a unique ordered pair, and each ordered pair corresponds uniquely to a point in the plane. Given a point *P*, the ordered pair associated with it can be found as follows. Construct the line passing through *P* perpendicular to the *x*-axis. The *x*-axis coordinate of the point of intersection of the *x*-axis with the constructed line is the first entry of the ordered pair that corresponds to *P*. Construct the line passing through *P* perpendicular to the *y*-axis. The *y*-axis coordinate of the point of intersection of the *y*-axis with the constructed line is the second entry of the ordered pair corresponding to *P*. In Figure 1.4 we see that the point *P* is associated with (a,b).

Note that every point on the *x*-axis is associated with an ordered pair of the form $(a,0)$ for some *a*, and every point on the *y*-axis is associated with an ordered pair of the form $(0,b)$ for some *b*. The ordered pair corresponding to the origin is $(0,0)$. Some points and associated ordered pairs are indicated in Figure 1.5.

Whenever the axis coordinates do not appear, as in Figure 1.5, we assume that the distance between consecutive hash marks is one unit. If the axes are not labeled, we assume that the horizontal axis is the *x*-axis and that the vertical axis is the *y*-axis.

Because of the one-to-one relationship that exists between points in the plane and ordered pairs, we frequently interchange the terms. And when we refer to the point $P(a,b)$, we mean that the point is labeled *P* and its corresponding ordered pair is (a,b). Furthermore, we call the first entry of an ordered pair the **x-coordinate** and the second entry the **y-coordinate.**

The **graph of an equation** in *x* and *y* is the set of points in the *xy*-plane which are solutions of the equation. Most equations have infinitely many solutions; hence the graph cannot be constructed by plotting them all. We plot a few solutions and connect them with a curve that follows the general trend of the plotted points.

EXAMPLE 2

Graph $y = x + 1$.

■ *SOLUTION*

We begin by constructing a table that lists some of the infinitely many solutions of this equation. We choose some values for *x* and find the cor-

1.1 EQUATIONS IN TWO VARIABLES AND THEIR GRAPHS 5

responding values for y. For example, when $x = -3$, $y = -3 + 1 = -2$. When $x = -2$, $y = -2 + 1 = -1$, and so on. We get the following table:

x	-3	-2	-1	0	1	2	3
y	-2	-1	0	1	2	3	4

This table is simply another way of representing the ordered pairs. Each column refers to an ordered pair, with the entry in the top row being the x-coordinate and the entry in the bottom row being the y-coordinate. The graph of these ordered pairs is shown in Figure 1.6.

Since the solution set is infinite, and these solutions appear to lie along a straight line, we suspect that the graph of $y = x + 1$ is the line determined by these points. See Figure 1.7.

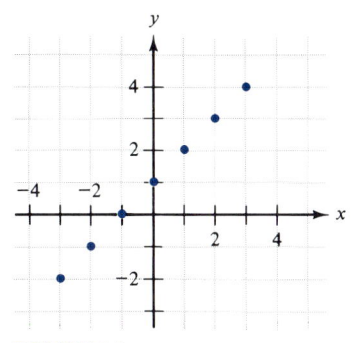

FIGURE 1.6

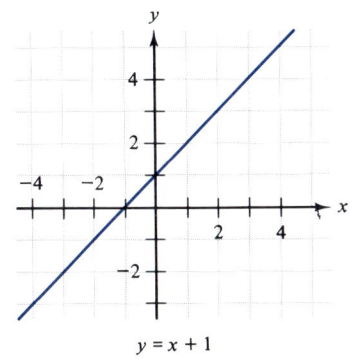

FIGURE 1.7
$y = x + 1$

When graphing equations by finding arbitrary solutions, how can we be certain that we have plotted representative points? And how can we be sure that we have connected them properly to give us an accurate sketch? The fact is that we cannot unless we have a general idea of what the graph looks like before we begin. In Sections 1.2, 1.4, and 1.6, we obtain a general idea of the graph by examining the equation. Later, in Section 5.5, we use calculus techniques to sketch the graph. Meanwhile, suggested values for plotting points are included with the problems.

EXAMPLE 3

Graph $x = y^2$.

■ SOLUTION

We construct a table that lists some of the solutions by selecting some values for y and finding the corresponding values for x. We get the following:

x	4	1	0	1	4
y	-2	-1	0	1	2

The graph of these ordered pairs is shown in Figure 1.8. Although these points do not lie along a straight line, we can still make a guess about the graph. See Figure 1.9.

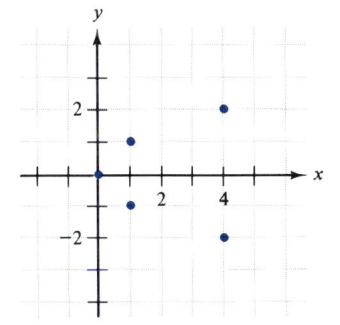

FIGURE 1.8

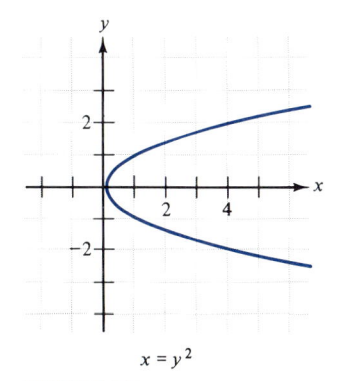

FIGURE 1.9
$x = y^2$

GRAPHS AND FUNCTIONS

EXERCISE

Graph the given equation after plotting solutions with the given values:
(a) $y = -x + 1$, x-values: $-2, -1, 0, 1$, and 2.
(b) $x = -y^2$; y-values: $-2, -1, 0, 1$, and 2. [Recall that $-y^2 = -(y^2)$.]

■ ANSWER
See Figure 1.10.

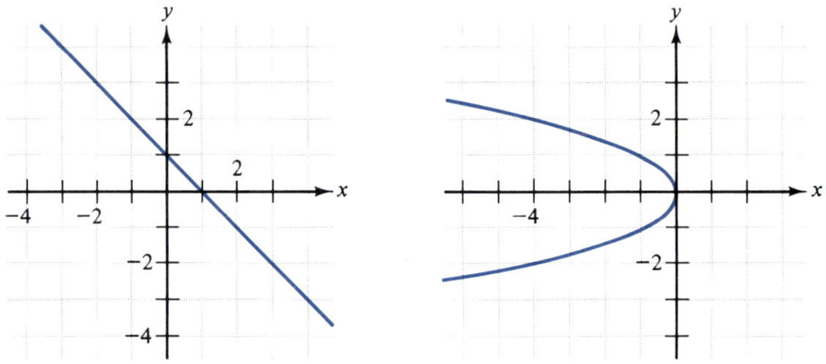

(a) $y = -x + 1$ (b) $x = -y^2$

FIGURE 1.10

PROBLEM SET 1.1

In Problems 1 and 2, plot the following points using a coordinate system.

1. $(1,3), (-2,-4), (0,-2), (1.5,-3), (-\frac{5}{2},0), (-1,2)$
2. $(0,3), (2,2), (-3,-1), (\frac{1}{2},-\frac{5}{2}), (5,0), (-4,1)$

In Problems 3 and 4, list the ordered pair that corresponds to each of the points in the following plane.

3.

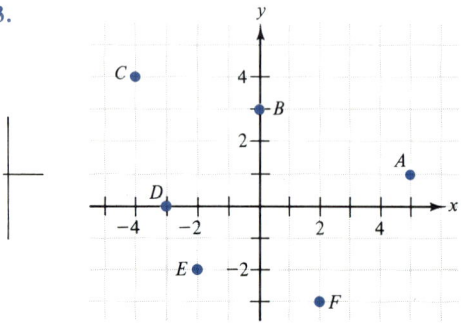

4.

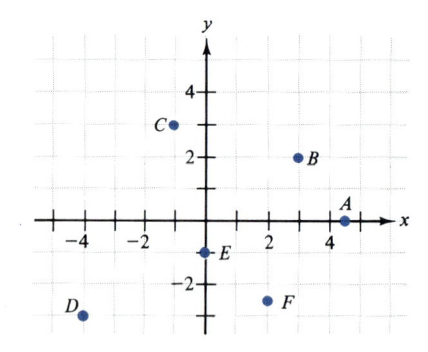

5. If $x > 0$ and $y < 0$, then the point $P(x, -y)$ is in which quadrant?

6. If $x < 0$ and $y > 0$, then the point $P(-x, -y)$ is in which quadrant?

In Problems 7–10, find each missing coordinate so that the ordered pair is a solution of the given equation.

7. $xy = 1$: **(a)** $(3,?)$, **(b)** $(-\frac{1}{4},?)$, **(c)** $(?,\pi)$, **(d)** $(?,-0.1)$
8. $\sqrt{x} = 1 + y$: **(a)** $(4,?)$ **(b)** $(\frac{4}{25},?)$, **(c)** $(?,2)$, **(d)** $(?,-\frac{9}{10})$
9. $y = 4^x$: **(a)** $(3,?)$, **(b)** $(\frac{5}{2},?)$ **(c)** $(?,\frac{1}{16})$, **(d)** $(?,1)$
10. $y = x^3 + 1$: **(a)** $(-1,?)$, **(b)** $(\sqrt[3]{7},?)$, **(c)** $(?,28)$, **(d)** $(?,-7)$

In Problems 11–22, sketch the graph of each equation after plotting points with the given values.

11. $y = 2x$; x-values: $-2, -1, 0, 1,$ and 2
12. $y = -\frac{1}{2}x$; x-values: $-4, -2, 0, 2,$ and 4
13. $y = -x - 2$; x-values: $-3, -2, -1, 0,$ and 1
14. $y - 1 = 3x$; x-values: $-1, -\frac{1}{3}, 0, \frac{1}{3},$ and 1
15. $x = -2 + 2y$; y-values: $-1, 0, 1, 2,$ and 3
16. $x = \frac{1}{4} - \frac{1}{2}y$; y-values: $-\frac{7}{2}, -\frac{3}{2}, 0, \frac{1}{2},$ and $\frac{5}{2}$
17. $y = x^2$; x-values: $-2, -1, 0, 1,$ and 2
18. $y = x^3$; x-values: $-2, -1, 0, 1,$ and 2
19. $y = (x - 1)^2$; x-values: $-1, 0, 1, 2,$ and 3
20. $y = (x - 1)^3$; x-values: $-1, 0, 1, 2,$ and 3
21. $y = x^2 - 1$; x-values: $-2, -1, 0, 1,$ and 2
22. $y = x^3 - 1$; x-values: $-2, -1, 0, 1,$ and 2

23. Let V represent the volume of a sphere and let A represent the surface area. Write an equation involving V and A only.
24. Let V represent the volume of a cube and let A represent the surface area. Write an equation involving V and A only.
25. In a rectangle 8 feet wide and 10 feet high, a line is drawn from the lower right-hand corner to a point on the opposite side, which is x feet below the upper left-hand corner (see figure below). Let A represent the area of that portion of the rectangle that is above the line. Write an equation involving A and x only.

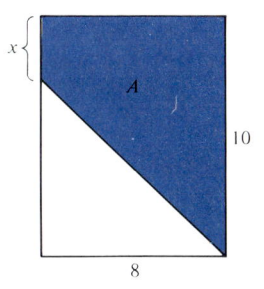

26. In a square whose side measures 15 feet, a line is drawn from the lower right-hand corner to a point on the opposite side, which is x feet below the upper left-hand corner. Another line is drawn from the lower left-hand corner to a point on the opposite side which is $(x/3) + 5$ feet above the lower right-hand corner (see figure below). Let A represent the area of the shaded region. Write an equation involving A and x only.

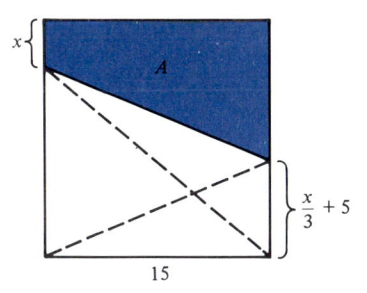

27. To film an action sequence for a movie it is decided to have a moving camera proceed at 60 mph due north on a straight road toward an intersection. It will be photographing a speeding car that is moving due west from the intersection at 80 mph. When the filming begins the camera is $\frac{1}{4}$ mile south of the intersection and the car is at the intersection. Let d represent the distance (in miles) between the camera and the car, and let t represent the elapsed time (in hours) since filming began. Write an equation involving d and t only.

28. At 1:00 a jogger crosses an intersection heading due north at 6 mph. An hour later a second jogger passes the same intersection heading due east at 8 mph. Let d represent the distance (in miles) between joggers, and let t represent the elapsed time (in hours) since 2:00. Write an equation involving d and t only.

29. Sand poured on the ground at a constant rate forms a conical pile whose height is one-third the radius of the base. Let V represent the volume of the sand and h represent the height. Write an equation involving V and h only.

30. At a railroad depot, the grain hoppers are conical, 8 feet high, and 8 feet in diameter at the top. A full hopper is opened and dispenses grain into a box car. Let V represent the volume of the grain in the hopper and let h represent the height. Write an equation involving V and h only.

1.2 LINES

An equation in variables x and y is called **linear** in x and y provided that it can be expressed in the form

$$Ax + By + C = 0,$$

where A, B, and C are constants, with A and B not both zero. Some examples of linear equations are

$$x + y + 2 = 0, \quad y = 2x - 1, \quad y = -2, \quad \text{and} \quad x = 5.$$

On the other hand,

$$y = x^2, \quad x^2 + y^2 = 4, \quad \text{and} \quad y + \sqrt{x} = 0$$

are *not* linear.

As the name suggests, the graph of a linear equation is a straight line. We use this fact in the first example.

EXAMPLE 1

Graph $2x - 3y + 6 = 0$.

■ SOLUTION

Because a line is determined by any two points, it suffices to find any two solutions. When $x = 1$, $y = \frac{8}{3}$, and when $x = 2$, $y = \frac{10}{3}$. Thus $(1, \frac{8}{3})$ and $(2, \frac{10}{3})$ are solutions. The graph is shown in Figure 1.11.

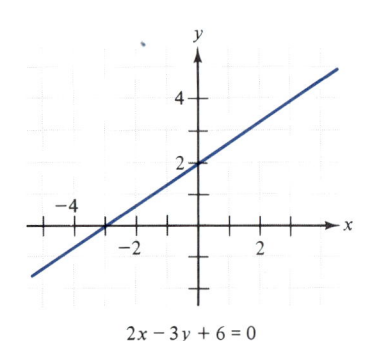

$2x - 3y + 6 = 0$

FIGURE 1.11

The *y*-coordinate of a point of intersection of a graph with the *y*-axis is called a **y-intercept**. Graphically, *y*-intercepts are the values on the *y*-axis where the graph crosses. Algebraically, they are the values of *y* when $x = 0$. Similarly, the *x*-coordinate of a point of intersection of a graph with the *x*-axis is called an **x-intercept**. Graphically, *x*-intercepts are the values on the *x*-axis where the graph crosses. Algebraically, they are the values of *x* when $y = 0$. As seen in Example 2, locating the intercepts provides a quick means of determining the graph of a linear equation.

EXAMPLE 2

Graph $3x + 2y - 6 = 0$.

■ SOLUTION

We locate the intercepts. When $x = 0$, $y = 3$, and when $y = 0$, $x = 2$. Noting that the *y*-intercept is 3 and that the *x*-intercept is 2, we get the graph in Figure 1.12.

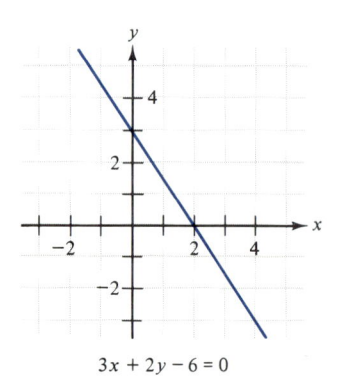

$3x + 2y - 6 = 0$

FIGURE 1.12

1.2 LINES

EXAMPLE 3

Graph $x = -1$.

■ SOLUTION

To determine the graph it suffices to find two solutions, like $(-1,0)$ and $(-1,2)$. The graph is shown in Figure 1.13.

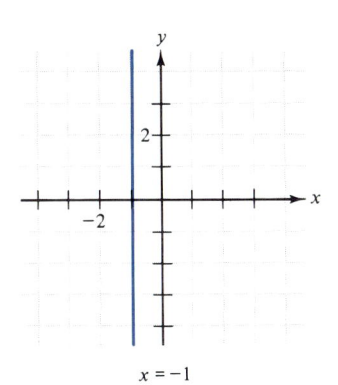

FIGURE 1.13

Perhaps some clarification is needed about the equation $x = -1$. Is it really an equation in x and y since it doesn't contain the variable y? The answer is "yes." Because we are working with equations in two variables, we are thinking of this equation as

$$x + 0y = -1.$$

Viewing the equation $x = -1$ in two variables, instead of one, significantly alters the solutions and the graph. When considered an equation in two variables, the solutions consist of all ordered pairs whose first coordinate is -1. The graph is a vertical line (perpendicular to the x-axis). If the equation were viewed as an equation in a single variable, the solution would be the single real number -1. Its graph would be a single point on a number line. Thus when working with equations in two variables, we are working in the plane. Solutions are ordered pairs, even if one of the variables doesn't appear in the equation.

Similarly, an equation such as $y = 2$ is thought of as

$$0x + y = 2.$$

Its graph is the horizontal line (perpendicular to the y-axis) with y-intercept 2.

EXERCISE

Graph the following equations: (a) $2x + y - 4 = 0$, (b) $x + 2 = 0$, and (c) $y = 1$.

■ ANSWER
See Figure 1.14.

Before considering the problem of finding the equation of a given line, we need some definitions. Let $\mathscr{L}$ be a nonvertical line, and let $P_1(x_1,y_1)$ and $P_2(x_2,y_2)$ be two distinct points on $\mathscr{L}$. The **slope** of $\mathscr{L}$, usually denoted

GRAPHS AND FUNCTIONS

(a) $2x + y - 4 = 0$

(b) $x + 2 = 0$

(c) $y = 1$

FIGURE 1.14

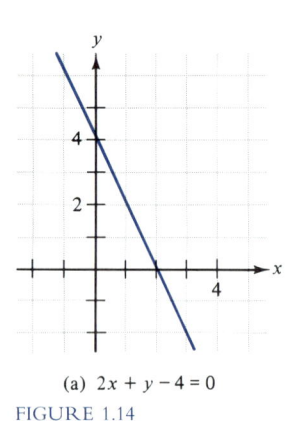

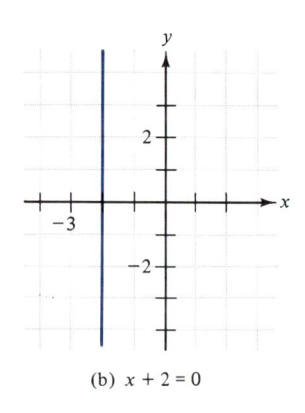

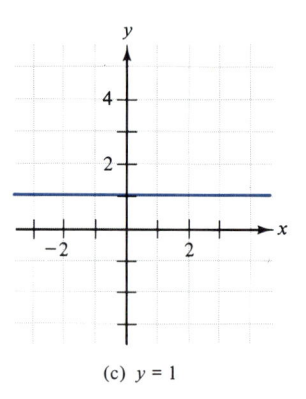

by m, is the ratio

$$m = \frac{y_2 - y_1}{x_2 - x_1}. \tag{1-1}$$

This ratio is sometimes written as $\Delta y/\Delta x$ (Greek letter delta), where Δy and Δx represent change in y and change in x, respectively.

EXAMPLE 4

Determine the slope of the line passing through $(2,3)$ and $(-1,5)$.

■ SOLUTION

We divide the difference in y-coordinates by the difference in x-coordinates, with the subtraction occurring in the same order. We get

$$m = \frac{5 - 3}{-1 - 2} = -\frac{2}{3}.$$

EXERCISE

Determine the slope of the line passing through $(-1,2)$ and $(3,4)$.

■ ANSWER

$\frac{1}{2}$

FIGURE 1.15

The slope of a given line is independent of the points chosen; that is, we get the same ratio value regardless of which two points on the line are used. To see this, consider four points on the line: $P_1(x_1,y_1)$, $P_2(x_2,y_2)$, $P_3(x_3,y_3)$, and $P_4(x_4,y_4)$. Let Q be the point with ordered pair (x_2,y_1) and let R be the point with ordered pair (x_4,y_3). See Figure 1.15.

Triangles P_1QP_2 and P_3RP_4 are similar because corresponding angles are equal. Because corresponding sides of similar triangles are proportional,

$$\frac{P_2Q}{P_1Q} = \frac{P_4R}{P_3R}.$$

Upon calculating these distances, we have

$$\frac{y_2 - y_1}{x_2 - x_1} = \frac{y_4 - y_3}{x_4 - x_3}.$$

Thus we get the same ratio value whether we use P_1 and P_2 or P_3 and P_4. Consequently, any two distinct points may be used to determine the slope. Furthermore, since

$$\frac{y_2 - y_1}{x_2 - x_1} = \frac{y_1 - y_2}{x_1 - x_2},$$

the order in which the points are taken is immaterial. Note, however, that the order of subtraction in the numerator and denominator must agree.

Note that the definition of slope applies to nonvertical lines only. For a vertical line, Equation (1-1) gives us a zero in the denominator. Hence slope is not defined for vertical lines, and we say that such lines have slope undefined.

Slope is a measure of the change in y relative to the change in x. To say that the slope of a line is $\frac{3}{2}$ means that, moving along the line, y increases 3 units as x increases 2 units. [Or, since $\frac{3}{2} = (-3)/(-2)$, y decreases 3 units as x decreases 2.] A line with slope $-\frac{3}{5}$ has the property that y decreases 3 units as x increases 5 (or y increases 3 as x decreases 5). As the x-values increase, a line with positive slope rises, while one with negative slope falls. A line with zero slope is one in which the y-values don't change; that is, the y-values are constant. Hence a line with zero slope is horizontal.

EXAMPLE 5

Graph the line that passes through (1,2) and has slope $-\frac{3}{4}$.

■ SOLUTION

To graph the line we need to locate two of its points. We already have (1,2), and the slope gives us another. Because y decreases 3 as x increases 4, the point $(5,-1)$, three units below and four units to the right of (1,2), is on the line. We get the graph shown in Figure 1.16.

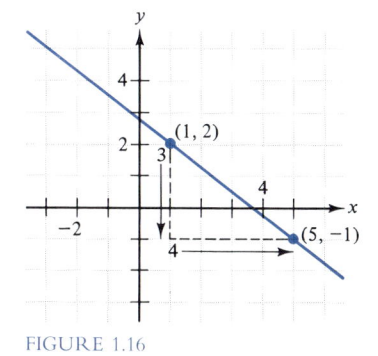

FIGURE 1.16

EXERCISE

Graph the line that passes through $(-2,1)$ and has slope $-\frac{2}{3}$.

■ ANSWER
See Figure 1.17.

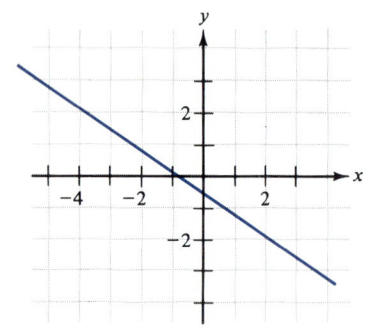

FIGURE 1.17

Given a linear equation, we can find the y-intercept by substituting 0 for x and solving for y. And we can find the slope of the line by finding two solutions and applying the definition of slope. However, as the next theorem indicates, there is another technique for finding the slope and y-intercept.

THEOREM 1.1

Let $\mathscr{L}$ be a line whose equation is $y = ax + b$, where a and b are constants.* Then the slope of $\mathscr{L}$ is a, and the y-intercept is b.

Proof When $x = 0$, $y = b$, so the y-intercept is b. To determine slope we need one additional point on the line. When $x = 1$, $y = a + b$. Hence two points are $(0,b)$ and $(1, a + b)$. The slope is thus

$$m = \frac{(a+b) - b}{1 - 0} = a.$$

Because $m = a$, the given equation may be written

$$y = mx + b.$$

This form is called the **slope–intercept form** of a linear equation.

This theorem gives us an alternative method of finding the slope and y-intercept. If the equation is solved for y in terms of x, then the coefficient of x is the slope, and the constant term is the y-intercept.

EXAMPLE 6

Determine the slope and y-intercept of $5x - 2y + 6 = 0$.

■ SOLUTION
First we put this equation in slope–intercept form. Solving for y we get

$$-2y = -5x - 6$$
$$y = \tfrac{5}{2}x + 3.$$

Thus the slope is $\frac{5}{2}$, and the y-intercept is 3.

---

* The equation is linear because it is equivalent to $ax - y + b = 0$.

1.2 LINES

EXERCISE

Determine the slope and *y*-intercept for (a) $y = -3x + 5$ and (b) $-2x + 7y - 3 = 0$.

■ *ANSWER*
(a) Slope is -3; *y*-intercept is 5. (b) Slope is $\frac{2}{7}$; *y*-intercept is $\frac{3}{7}$.

We now turn our attention to the problem of finding the equation of a line given specific information. As you expect, the equation will be linear. Since we can graph a line if we know the slope and *y*-intercept, it is reasonable to expect that we can find its equation. This is proved in the next theorem, which is the converse of Theorem 1.1.

THEOREM 1.2 The equation of a line with slope m and *y*-intercept b is

$$y = mx + b.$$

Proof Let $\mathscr{L}$ be the line with slope m and *y*-intercept b, and let (x,y) represent each point in the plane. Then (x,y) is on $\mathscr{L}$ if and only if $(x,y) = (0,b)$ or the slope of the line connecting (x,y) and $(0,b)$ is m; that is, $(y - b)/x = m$. Therefore (x,y) is on $\mathscr{L}$ if and only if $y = mx + b$.

EXAMPLE 7

Determine the equation of the line with slope -2 and *y*-intercept $-\frac{3}{2}$.

■ *SOLUTION*
By Theorem 1.2, we get

$$y = -2x - \frac{3}{2}.$$

EXERCISE

Determine the equation of the line with slope 3 and *y*-intercept -2.

■ *ANSWER*
$y = 3x - 2$

We can graph a line if we know one point on the line and the slope. Accordingly, we can find the equation of such a line.

THEOREM 1.3 The equation of the line passing through (x_1, y_1) with slope m is

$$y - y_1 = m(x - x_1). \tag{1-2}$$

Proof Let $\mathscr{L}$ be the line passing through (x_1, y_1) with slope m, and let (x, y) represent each point in the plane. Then (x, y) is on $\mathscr{L}$ if only if $(x, y) = (x_1, y_1)$ or the slope of the line connecting (x, y) and (x_1, y_1) is m; that is, $(y - y_1)/(x - x_1) = m$. Therefore (x, y) is on $\mathscr{L}$ if and only if $y - y_1 = m(x - x_1)$.

Equation (1-2) is called the **point–slope form** of the equation of a line. The slope–intercept form, however, is perhaps a more useful format for a linear equation. Hence, although our initial equations in Example 8 are in point–slope form, we put the final result in slope–intercept form.

EXAMPLE 8

Determine the equation (in slope–intercept form) of the described lines: (a) passing through $(-1, 3)$ with slope $\frac{2}{3}$ and (b) passing through $(2, -1)$ and $(-3, 2)$.

■ SOLUTION
(a) By Theorem 1.3, the equation of the line in point–slope form is

$$y - 3 = \tfrac{2}{3}(x - (-1)).$$

Putting this equation in slope–intercept form, we get

$$y = \tfrac{2}{3}x + \tfrac{11}{3}.$$

(b) We can determine the equation of a line if we know the slope and one point on the line. Although we aren't given the slope here, we can use the two points to calculate it. We have

$$m = \frac{-1 - 2}{2 - (-3)} = -\frac{3}{5}.$$

Now we use the slope and one of the points to write the equation in point–slope form. Using $(2, -1)$, we get

$$y + 1 = -\tfrac{3}{5}(x - 2). \tag{1-3}$$

In slope–intercept form this equation is

$$y = -\tfrac{3}{5}x + \tfrac{1}{5}. \tag{1-4}$$

1.2 LINES

To get Equation (1-3) in Example 8(b), we used the point $(2, -1)$. Had we used $(-3, 2)$ instead, we would have obtained

$$y - 2 = -\tfrac{3}{5}(x + 3).$$

But this equation is equivalent to Equation (1-3). This can easily be seen by writing this equation in slope–intercept form. We get

$$y = -\tfrac{3}{5}x + \tfrac{1}{5},$$

which is Equation (1-4).

EXERCISE

Determine the equation (in slope–intercept form) of the described lines: (a) passing through $(-4, -6)$ with slope $\tfrac{1}{4}$ and (b) passing through $(-2, 3)$ and $(4, 1)$.

■ ANSWER
(a) $y = \tfrac{1}{4}x - 5$;   (b) $y = -\tfrac{1}{3}x + \tfrac{7}{3}$

FIGURE 1.18

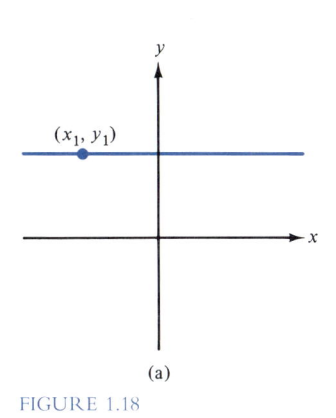

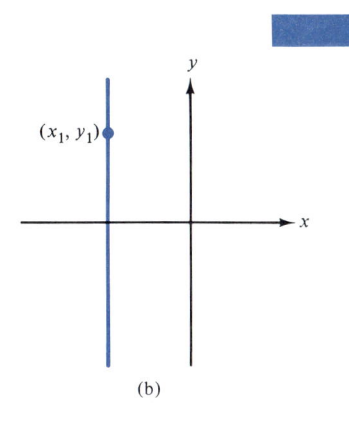

What is the equation of the horizontal line passing through (x_1, y_1)? [See Figure 1.18(a).] Because its slope is 0 and its y-intercept is y_1, its equation is $y = 0x + y_1$; that is, $y = y_1$. (This seems reasonable since the y-coordinates of the points on a horizontal line are all the same.) Of course, since a vertical line has slope undefined, its equation does not have a slope–intercept form. But because every point on a vertical line has the same x-coordinate [see Figure 1.18(b)], the equation of the vertical line passing through (x_1, y_1) is $x = x_1$.

For a specified product, the number of units sold (the **demand**) varies according to the price. The lower the price, the greater the demand. The equation that relates the demand and the price is called the **demand equation**. In graphing a demand equation it is customary to label the vertical axis as price, while the horizontal axis is labeled demand. A linear demand equation is graphed in Figure 1.19.

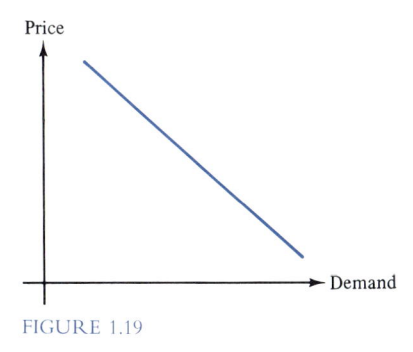

FIGURE 1.19

Note that the slope is negative. As the price becomes lower, the demand becomes greater.

EXAMPLE 9

Records at a high school indicate that when the ticket price for a basketball game is $4, an average of 2000 tickets are sold, and when the price is $3.50, an average of 2500 are sold. Determine the demand equation, assuming it is linear, and determine the price required to sell 3200 tickets.

■ *SOLUTION*

Let
$$p = \text{price (in dollars)},$$
$$x = \text{demand}.$$

We are told that when $p = 4$, $x = 2000$, and when $p = 3.50$, $x = 2500$. With a linear demand equation, we have the graph illustrated in Figure 1.20.

To determine the equation of this line we must first find its slope. We get

$$m = \frac{4 - 3.50}{2000 - 2500} = \frac{0.50}{-500} = -0.001.$$

To get the equation we use either point. With (2000,4) we have

$$p - 4 = -0.001(x - 2000).$$

Solving for p gives

$$p = -0.001x + 6.$$

To determine the price required to sell 3200 tickets, we note that when $x = 3200$,

$$p = -0.001(3200) + 6 = 2.80.$$

The price required is $2.80.

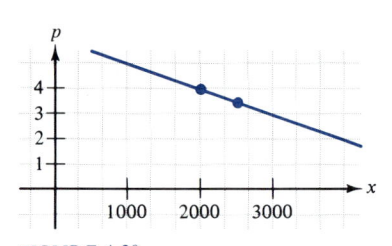

FIGURE 1.20

EXERCISE

Records at a high school indicate that when the ticket price for a football game is $6, an average of 5000 tickets are sold, and when the price is $5.50, an average of 6000 are sold. Determine the demand equation, assuming it is linear, and determine the price required to sell 7500 tickets.

■ *ANSWER*
$p = -0.0005x + 8.5$; $4.75

1.2 LINES

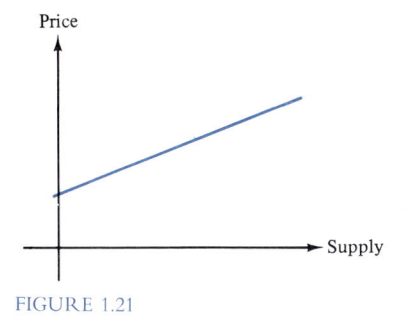

For a specified product, the number of units made available (the **supply**) also varies according to the price. The higher the price, the greater the supply. The equation that relates the supply and the price is called the **supply equation**. A linear supply equation is graphed in Figure 1.21.

FIGURE 1.21

EXAMPLE 10

When the price is $500, a manufacturer makes 6000 televisions available for market. If the price increases $50, there are 2000 more televisions available. Determine the supply equation, assuming it is linear, and determine the price required to supply 12,000 televisions.

■ SOLUTION
Let

$$p = \text{price (in dollars)},$$

$$x = \text{supply}.$$

We are told that when $p = 500$, $x = 6000$, and when $p = 550$, $x = 8000$. With a linear supply equation we have the graph in Figure 1.22.

To determine the equation of this line we first find its slope:

$$m = \frac{550 - 500}{8000 - 6000} = \frac{50}{2000} = 0.025.$$

Using the point (6000, 500) we have

$$p - 500 = 0.025(x - 6000).$$

Solving for p gives

$$p = 0.025x + 350.$$

To determine the price required to supply 12,000 units, we note that when $x = 12,000$,

$$p = 0.025(12,000) + 350 = 650.$$

The price required is $650.

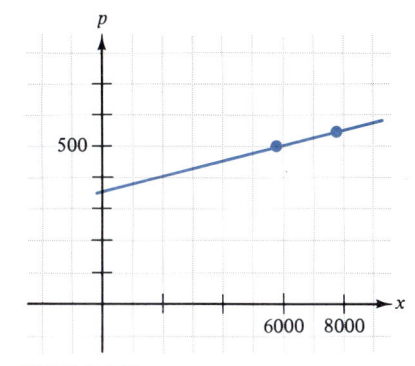

FIGURE 1.22

EXERCISE

When the price is $50, a manufacturer makes 4000 radios available for market. If the price increases $10, there are 500 more available. Determine the supply equation, assuming it is linear, and determine the price required to supply 6000.

■ ANSWER
$p = 0.02x - 30$; $90

PROBLEM SET 1.2

In Problems 1–8, graph the equation.
1. $x - 2y - 3 = 0$
2. $3x + y - 3 = 0$
3. $5x + 3y - 15 = 0$
4. $-2x + \pi y - 2\pi = 0$
5. $x - 3 = 0$
6. $x = -\frac{5}{2}$
7. $2y + 3 = 0$
8. $3y - 9 = 0$

In Problems 9–18, determine the slope of the line passing through the given points.
9. $(1,2), (5,4)$
10. $(3,4), (-2,-2)$
11. $(-7,2), (4,-3)$
12. $(-1,\frac{1}{3}), (\frac{2}{3},-4)$
13. $(0,0), (\pi/6, 3\pi/2)$
14. $(\sqrt{27}, \sqrt{3}), (0,0)$
15. $(2\sqrt{2}, -3\sqrt{3}), (-3\sqrt{2}, 2\sqrt{3})$
16. $(\sqrt[3]{\frac{1}{2}}, 2\sqrt[3]{4}), (-3\sqrt[3]{\frac{1}{2}}, -2\sqrt[3]{4})$
17. $(3,-6), (7,-6)$
18. $(2, 7^{1/2}), (2, 5^{2/3})$

In Problems 19–22, graph the line described.
19. Passing through $(1,-1)$ with slope $-\frac{1}{2}$
20. Passing through $(-2,-1)$ with slope $\frac{2}{5}$
21. With y-intercept 3 and slope 0
22. With y-intercept 0 and slope $-\frac{5}{3}$

23. We have the following table of possible slopes:

    Undefined, $-3, -2, -1, -\frac{1}{4}, 0, \frac{1}{4}, 1, 2, 4$

    Match each line with its correct slope from the table above.

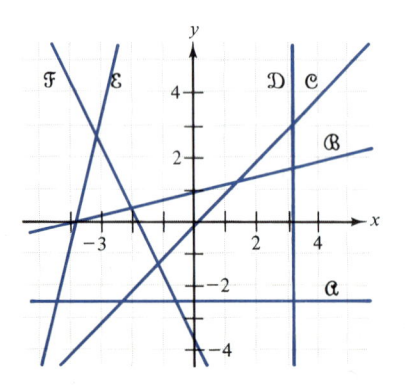

24. Which of the four lines has the greatest slope and which has the least?

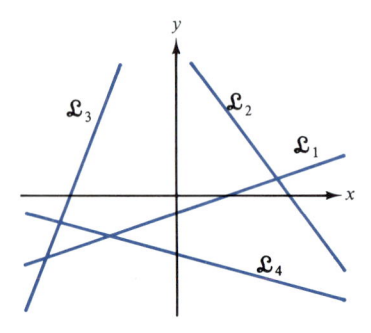

In Problems 25–34, determine the slope and y-intercept.
25. $y = 6x - 7$
26. $y = -3x + 1$
27. $3x + 8y - 16 = 0$
28. $-4x + 7y + 21 = 0$
29. $4 + 2(y + 2) = 0$
30. $-3x - \pi = 0$
31. $\dfrac{2 - 5x}{-3} = \dfrac{2 + 5y}{4}$
32. $\dfrac{1 + \sqrt[3]{2}\, x}{\sqrt{2}} = \dfrac{1 - \sqrt{2}\, y}{\sqrt[3]{4}}$
33. $2x - 3(y - 1) = -7$
34. $1 + \frac{1}{2}(6 - 2x) = -(5 - 2y)$

In Problems 35–44, determine the equation (in slope–intercept form if possible) of the line described.
35. Slope -5 and y-intercept $\sqrt{2}$
36. Slope 6 and y-intercept $-\frac{1}{4}$
37. x-intercept -6 and y-intercept 4
38. x-intercept $-\pi/4$ and y-intercept $-3\pi/2$
39. Passing through $(-1,-7)$ with slope $\frac{3}{2}$
40. Passing through $(-\frac{1}{3}, \frac{2}{3})$ with slope $-\frac{1}{2}$
41. Passing through $(-\sqrt[3]{5}, 3)$ and $(\sqrt[3]{4}, 3)$
42. Passing through $(\frac{1}{16}, -1)$ and $(\frac{1}{16}, 1)$
43. Passing through $(0.8, 0.6)$ and $(0.4, -0.2)$
44. Passing through $(1, -1)$ and $(-3, 2)$

Two lines with slopes m_1 and m_2 are parallel if and only if $m_1 = m_2$ and are perpendicular if and only if $m_1 m_2 = -1$. The midpoint of the line segment joining the points (x_1, y_1) and (x_2, y_2) is

$$\left(\frac{x_1 + x_2}{2}, \frac{y_1 + y_2}{2} \right).$$

This information is needed in Problems 45–54.

45. Determine the equation of the line with x-intercept 3 and parallel to the line with x- and y-intercepts 6 and −4, respectively.
46. Determine the equation of the line passing through (−1,−2) and parallel to the line passing through (−1,7) and (4,7).
47. Determine the equation of the line passing through (−1,4) and perpendicular to the line $3x - y + 5 = 0$.
48. Determine the equation of the line that is the perpendicular bisector of the segment joining points (7,4) and (−1,−2).
49. If the line through (a,5) and (4,3) is perpendicular to the line $2y = 6x + 1$, find a.
50. If the line through (a,2) and (−1,4) is parallel to the line $y = 4x$, find a.
51. Determine the equation of the line perpendicular to the line $3x - 5y - 15 = 0$ at the midpoint of the segment cut from this line by the axes.
52. Determine the constants m, b, and m_1 so that the lines $y = mx + b$ and $y = m_1 x - 16$ will be perpendicular and intersect at the point (6,2).

In Problems 53 and 54, let $\mathscr{L}_1$, $\mathscr{L}_2$, $\mathscr{L}_3$, and $\mathscr{L}_4$ be the lines indicated in the following coordinate system. (Note: $\mathscr{L}_1$ is perpendicular to $\mathscr{L}_4$, $\mathscr{L}_2$ is parallel to the y-axis, and $\mathscr{L}_3$ is parallel to the x-axis.)

53. (a) What is the equation of $\mathscr{L}_2$?
    (b) What is the equation of $\mathscr{L}_3$?
    (c) What is the equation of $\mathscr{L}_4$?

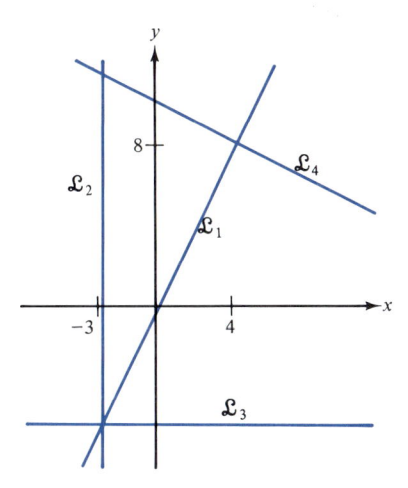

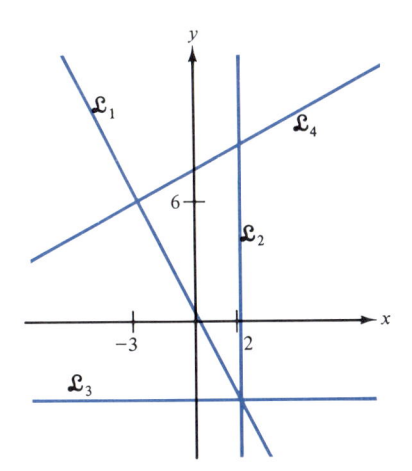

54. (a) What is the equation of $\mathscr{L}_2$?
    (b) What is the equation of $\mathscr{L}_3$?
    (c) What is the equation of $\mathscr{L}_4$?

55. The construction cost of a new house is $75 per square foot. Let C represent cost and x square feet.
    (a) Find an equation that expresses the relationship between C and x.
    (b) Determine the construction cost of a house with 1536 square feet.
    (c) The construction cost of a house is $174,375. Determine the square footage of the house.

56. In a particular state, the annual license for all motorized boats is $5.00 plus $0.50 per foot.
    (a) Express the relationship between the annual license L (in dollars) and the length x (in feet) of the boat.
    (b) How much is the license for a 26-foot boat?
    (c) If the license for a boat is $23.50, determine the length of the boat.

57. For out-of-state travel, a faculty member is reimbursed the following daily rates: $20.00 for subsistence, $55.00 for lodging, and $0.18 per mile for transportation expenses. Let R equal the total daily reimbursement and x equal the total daily mileage.
    (a) Find an equation that expresses the relationship between R and x.
    (b) Determine the total reimbursement if a faculty member is gone for 3 days and travels 145 miles the first day, 12 miles the second day, and 163 miles the third day.

58. If a wager of $2.00 is placed on a horse to win, then the approximate payoff for a win is

$$y = 2.00 + x(2.00)$$

where, if the odds are a to b, then $x = a/b$. (a and b are integers, and a/b is reduced to the lowest terms.)

For example, if the odds are 3 to 2, then $x = \frac{3}{2}$ and $y = 2.00 + \frac{3}{2}(2.00) = 5.00$.
  (a) Determine the approximate payoff for a win if the odds are 8 to 5.
  (b) Determine the odds if the payoff for a win is $3.20.
  (c) Determine the odds if the payoff for a win is $11.00.

59. A radio station announces charges for advertising time of $820 for a 15-second commercial and $1150 for a 30-second commercial. Assume the relationship between cost and duration is linear.
  (a) Write an equation for the cost C of a commercial that is t seconds long.
  (b) How much will it cost for a 105-second commercial?
  (c) What is the duration of a commercial if it costs $3460?

60. A manufacturer of a certain item determines that it costs $1700 to produce 5 items and $3800 to produce 12 items. Assume that production cost is linear.
  (a) Write an equation for the cost C of producing x items.
  (b) How much will it cost to produce 20 items?
  (c) If the production cost is $13,100, how many items are produced?

61. Records at a travel agency indicate that when the round-trip plane fare to Washington, DC from Cincinnati, Ohio is $408, an average of 132 tickets are sold per week, and when the price is $268, an average of 192 tickets are sold. Determine the demand equation, assuming it is linear, and determine the price required to sell 225 tickets per week.

62. A motel manager determines that when the price for a double room is $85 per night, an average of 65 rooms are occupied, and when the price is $70, an average of 90 rooms are occupied. Determine the demand equation, assuming it is linear, and determine the number of rooms occupied if the rate is $61.

63. When the price is $15, an auto supply manufacturer makes 2800 heavy-duty radial tuned shocks available for market. If the price is increased $6, there are 400 more available. Determine the supply equation, assuming it is linear, and determine the price required to supply 4200.

64. When the price is $750, a manufacturer makes 5200 refrigerators available for market. If the price increases to $1075, there are 5200 more available. Determine the supply equation, assuming it is linear, and determine the price required to supply 8800.

1.3 FUNCTIONS

In everyday language we sometimes relate two quantities. For example, we may say that the amount of sales tax paid on an item depends on its selling price; or the monthly charge for electricity depends on the amount used; or the cost of mailing a letter depends on its weight; or the volume of a sphere depends on its radius.

If two quantities X and Y are related such that each permissible value of X yields a *unique* value of Y, we say that **quantity Y is a function of quantity X**. Because this type of relationship exists for the quantities described in the preceding paragraph, we may say that the amount of sales tax paid on an item is a function of its selling price; or the monthly charge for electricity is a function of the amount used; and so on.

In most applications of calculus it is necessary to express relevant quantities in a functional relationship. Such a relationship then serves as a mathematical model of the situation.

To illustrate, let's consider a long rectangular sheet of metal 10 inches wide which is to be bent into a rain gutter by turning up the sides at right angles. Suppose we wish to express the cross-sectional area as a function of the height.

1.3 FUNCTIONS

The cross-sectional area is found by multiplying its dimensions; that is,

$$\text{cross-sectional area} = \text{width} \times \text{height}. \quad (1\text{-}5)$$

We must define the following variables:

A = cross-sectional area (in square inches),

w = width (in inches),

h = height (in inches).

See Figure 1.23. With these variables we are able to translate statement (1-5) into an algebraic equation:

$$A = wh. \quad (1\text{-}6)$$

In order to write A as a function of h, we must now substitute for w. So we search for information that will connect the variables w and h. Because the piece of metal is 10 inches wide,

$$2h + w = 10.$$

Solving this equation for w yields

$$w = 10 - 2h.$$

Returning to Equation (1-6) and replacing w with $10 - 2h$, we get

$$A = (10 - 2h)h = 10h - 2h^2.$$

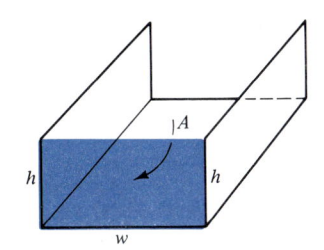

FIGURE 1.23

EXAMPLE 1

A box with an open top and a square base has a capacity of 32 cubic feet. The cost of the material for the bottom is 3¢ per square foot, and the cost of the side material is 2¢ per square foot. Write the cost of the box as a function of the length of the base.

■ SOLUTION

The cost of the box equals the cost of the sides plus the cost of the bottom. To get these costs we must know the surface areas. So let

C = cost of box (in cents),

x = length of square base (in feet),

h = height of box (in feet).

See Figure 1.24. The area of the bottom is x^2, so its cost is $3x^2$. The area of each side is xh, so the cost of four sides is

$$2(4xh) = 8xh.$$

Consequently, the total cost may be written

$$C = 3x^2 + 8xh. \quad (1\text{-}7)$$

In order to express C as a function of x, we must substitute for h. We need a connection between x and h. Because the volume is 32 cubic feet,

$$x^2 h = 32.$$

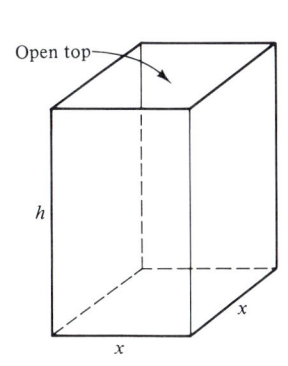

FIGURE 1.24

Solving for h gives
$$h = \frac{32}{x^2}.$$
Replacing h with this expression in Equation (1-7) gives
$$C = 3x^2 + 8x \cdot \frac{32}{x^2} = 3x^2 + \frac{256}{x}.$$

EXERCISE

A can with an open top and circular base has a volume of 32 cubic inches. The cost of the side material is $\frac{1}{2}$¢ per square inch, and the cost of the bottom material is $\frac{3}{4}$¢ per square inch. Write the cost of the can as a function of the radius.

■ ANSWER

$$C = \frac{3}{4}\pi r^2 + \frac{32}{r}$$

An equation in x and y is a statement of the relationship between two variables. If the relationship is such that for each permissible value of x, there corresponds a unique value of y that makes the equation true, then we say that **y is a function of x.** Examples include
$$x + y = 3, \quad y = |x|, \quad \text{and} \quad x = y^3.$$
Once we select a value for x, the value for y is uniquely determined. We have but one choice for y to make the equation true. In this regard, x is referred to as the **independent variable,** and y is called the **dependent variable.**

On the other hand, we don't have this property in any of the following:
$$x^2 + y^2 = 9, \quad x = |y|, \quad \text{and} \quad x = y^2.$$
In the first, for instance, when $x = 0$, we have $y = 3$ or $y = -3$. The y-value is not uniquely determined. In the second, when $x = 1$, $y = 1$ or $y = -1$. In the third, when $x = 4$, $y = 2$ or $y = -2$. The values for y are not uniquely determined. Thus, for each of these last three equations, y is *not* a function of x.

EXERCISE

Determine whether y is a function of x for (a) $x^2 + y^2 = 4$; (b) $|x| = |y|$; and (c) $y = x^3$.

■ ANSWER
(a) No; (b) no; (c) yes

1.3 FUNCTIONS

We can determine whether y is a function of x by looking at the graph of an equation. In fact, y is a function of x if and only if no vertical line intersects the graph of the equation in more than one point. Indeed, if there exists a vertical line that intersects the graph in two or more points, there will be two or more y-values that correspond to the same x-value. Such a situation indicates that y is *not* a function of x.

EXERCISE

Determine whether y is a function of x for the graphs in Figure 1.25.

■ ANSWER
(a) Yes; (b) no; (c) no; (d) yes; (e) no; (f) yes

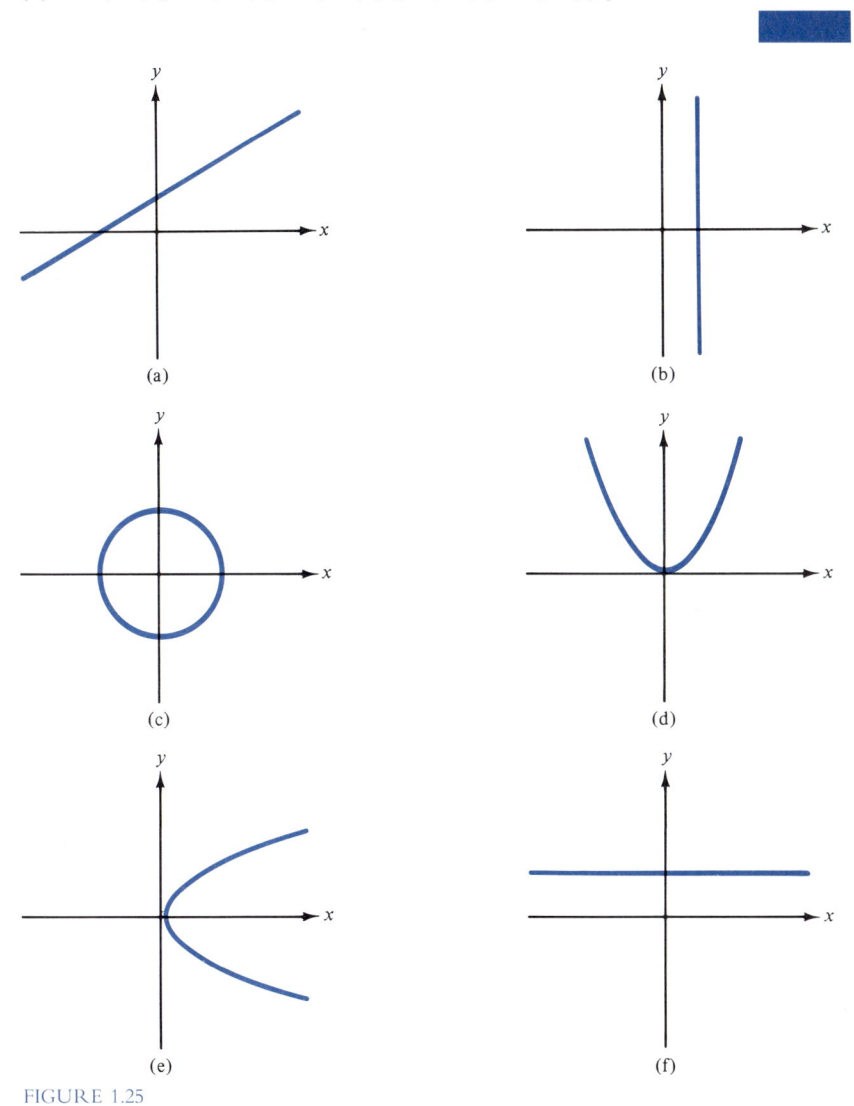

FIGURE 1.25

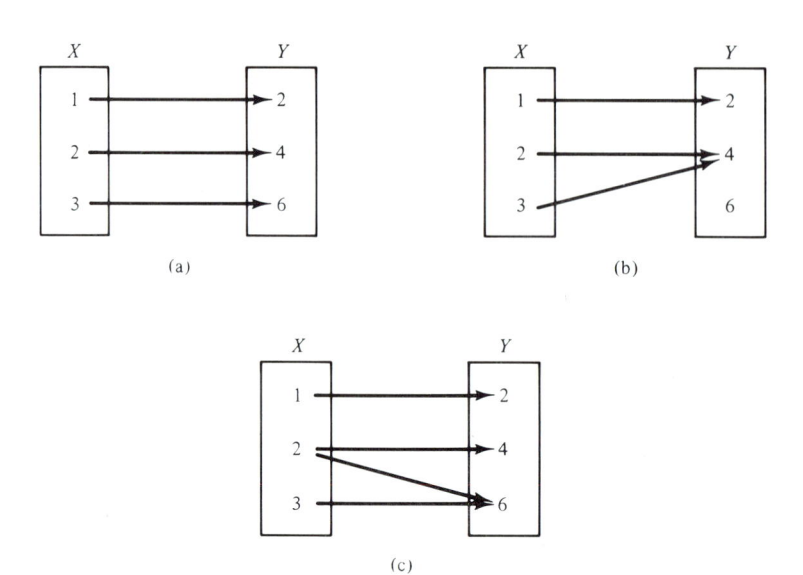

FIGURE 1.26

The preceding discussion leads us to a formal definition of the term "function." Let X and Y be nonempty sets. A **function** from X to Y is a correspondence that associates each element of X with a unique element of Y.

The two correspondences depicted in Figure 1.26(a) and (b) are both functions. Each element of X is associated with one and only one element of Y. But the correspondence shown in Figure 1.26(c) is not a function. There is an element of X (namely, 2) that is associated with two different elements of Y.

Let f be a function from X to Y. If $a \in X$ is associated with $b \in Y$, then we say that b is the **value of f at a**. We denote this value by $f(a)$, read "f at a," and call a, the element in parentheses, the **argument**. So if f denotes the function in Figure 1.25(b), then

$$f(1) = 2, \quad f(2) = 4, \quad \text{and} \quad f(3) = 4.$$

The set X is called the **domain** of the function, and the set of values of f, $\{f(a) \mid a \in X\}$, is called the **range** of f. Referring to the function of Figure 1.26(b) again, the domain is $\{1,2,3\}$ and the range is $\{2,4\}$.

FIGURE 1.27

EXERCISE

Let f be the function defined in Figure 1.27. Determine each of the following: (a) $f(0)$, (b) $f(3)$, (c) $f(1)$, (d) domain, and (e) range.

■ ANSWER
(a) $f(0) = 5$; (b) $f(3) = 1$; (c) f isn't defined at 1; (d) $\{0, -1, 3\}$; (e) $\{1, 5\}$

1.3 FUNCTIONS

Functions are usually defined by writing a **formula of definition.** For example, suppose that we want to associate each real number with its square. Let x be a variable with domain R (set of real numbers). Hence x is to be associated with x^2. This correspondence is a function. Let's call it f. Thus the value of f at x is x^2. In mathematical terms we state that

$$f(x) = x^2. \qquad (1\text{-}8)$$

Equation (1-8) is the formula of definition of f. Because the variable x represents each real number, Equation (1-8) says that the value of f at each real number is its square. Thus the function is defined.

To find $f(-2)$, the value of the function at -2, we use the formula of definition and substitute -2 for x. We have

$$f(-2) = (-2)^2 = 4.$$

When a function is defined with a formula, the domain of the function is the domain of the variable. And although the variable chosen is frequently x, it does not have to be. For the previous function our formula of definition could have been

$$f(t) = t^2 \quad \text{or} \quad f(u) = u^2.$$

Each formula describes the same correspondence.

EXAMPLE 2

Let x be a variable with domain R, and let f be defined by $f(x) = 2x + 1$. Determine each of the following: (a) $f(3)$, (b) $f(-2)$, (c) $f(a)$, (d) $f(x + h)$, (e) $f(x) + f(h)$, (f) $f(x) + h$, and (g) $f(f(0))$.

■ SOLUTION

(a) To calculate $f(3)$, we simply use the formula of definition and replace x by 3. Thus

$$f(3) = 2 \cdot 3 + 1 = 7.$$

The solutions for the rest are obtained similarly.

(b) $f(-2) = 2(-2) + 1 = -3$.
(c) $f(a) = 2a + 1$.
(d) To find $f(x + h)$ we do the same. That is, for each x in the formula we substitute the argument $x + h$. Hence

$$f(x + h) = 2(x + h) + 1 = 2x + 2h + 1.$$

(e) $f(x) + f(h) = 2x + 1 + 2h + 1 = 2x + 2h + 2$.
(f) $f(x) + h = 2x + 1 + h$.

(g) We may work from inside out or vice versa. From inside out we get

$$f(f(0)) = f(2 \cdot 0 + 1) = f(1) = 2 \cdot 1 + 1 = 3.$$

The same result is obtained working outside in. We have

$$f(f(0)) = 2 \cdot f(0) + 1 = 2(2 \cdot 0 + 1) + 1 = 2 + 1 = 3.$$

Note that for the function of Example 2, $f(x + h) \neq f(x) + f(h)$ and $f(x + h) \neq f(x) + h$.

EXERCISE

Let x be a variable with domain R, and let f be defined by $f(x) = 3x - 2$. Determine each of the following: (a) $f(-3)$, (b) $f(1)$, (c) $f(a)$, (d) $f(x + h)$, (e) $f(x) + f(h)$, (f) $f(x) + h$, and (g) $f(f(0))$.

■ ANSWER
(a) -11; (b) 1; (c) $3a - 2$; (d) $3x + 3h - 2$; (e) $3x + 3h - 4$; (f) $3x - 2 + h$; (g) -8

When the domain of a function is not explicitly specified, it is assumed to be the set of all real numbers whose functional values are defined and real. Thus if $h(x) = 1/x$, the domain of h is $R - \{0\}$ since $1/x$ is not defined if x is zero. And if $g(x) = \sqrt{x}$, then the domain of g is $[0, \infty)$ because $\sqrt{x}$ is not real if x is negative. (See Appendix A.1 for a discussion of intervals.)

EXERCISE

Determine the domain of each of the following functions: (a) $f(x) = 1/(x + 2)$ and (b) $g(x) = \sqrt{x - 1}$.

■ ANSWER
(a) $R - \{-2\}$; (b) $[1, \infty)$

In some cases the domain must be specified. For example, suppose that we want to associate each *positive* number with its square. We could

write
$$g(x) = x^2, \quad x > 0,$$

where the specification "$x > 0$" tells us that x represents positive numbers only. That is, the domain of g is $(0,\infty)$. So $g(-2)$, for instance, doesn't exist because g isn't defined at -2. The formula may be applied only to those elements in the domain. And although a domain may be any set, all the single-variable functions considered in this text (with a few exceptions) have domains that are intervals or unions of intervals.

In conclusion, note that, given an equation in x and y such that y is a function of x, we say that the equation defines a function f because $y = f(x)$ for some function f. The formula of definition for f may be found by solving the equation for y in terms of x. For example, let f be the function defined by

$$2x + 3y = 5.$$

If we want to write the formula of definition for f, we solve the equation for y in terms of x. Here we get

$$y = -\tfrac{2}{3}x + \tfrac{5}{3}.$$

The right-hand side of the equation is the right-hand side of our formula if we use the variable x. Thus

$$f(x) = -\tfrac{2}{3}x + \tfrac{5}{3}.$$

EXERCISE

For each of the following, y is a function of x. Let f be the function defined and determine $f(x)$. (a) $3x + y = 2$. (b) $x^2 - 2y + 3x = 5$. (c) $(y - 2)/3 = x^2$.

■ ANSWER
(a) $f(x) = 2 - 3x$. (b) $f(x) = (x^2 + 3x - 5)/2$. (c) $f(x) = 3x^2 + 2$

PROBLEM SET 1.3

In Problems 1 and 2, determine whether y is a function of x.

1. (a) $2x - y = 0$ (b) $y = |-x|$ (c) $y^2 - x^2 = 9$
(d) $y^2 - x = 9$ (e) $y = 2^x$ (f) $y = \sqrt[3]{x}$

2. (a) $x + \sqrt{2}\,y = 1$ (b) $x^2 = 1 - y^2$
(c) $xy = 1$ (d) $x = |y^2|$
(e) $y = \sqrt{x}$ (f) $y - 1 = 0 \cdot x$

GRAPHS AND FUNCTIONS

In Problems 3 and 4, determine whether y is a function of x.

3.

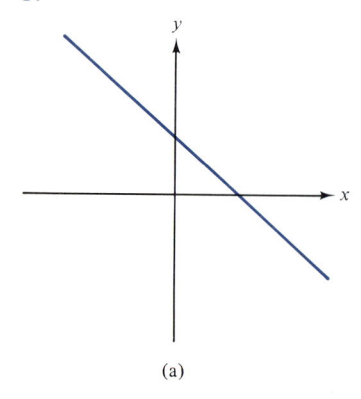

(a) 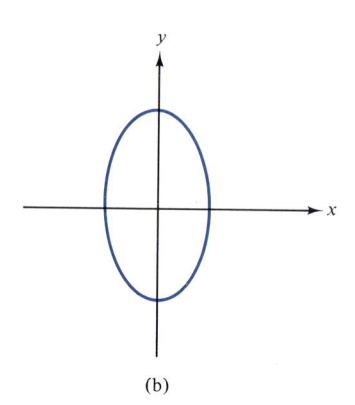　(b) 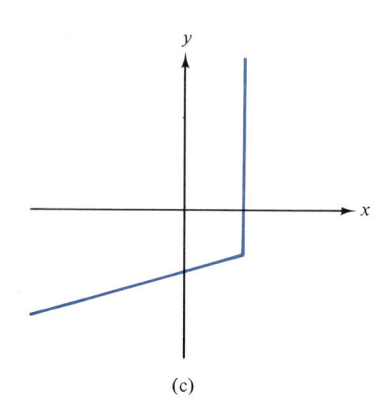　(c)

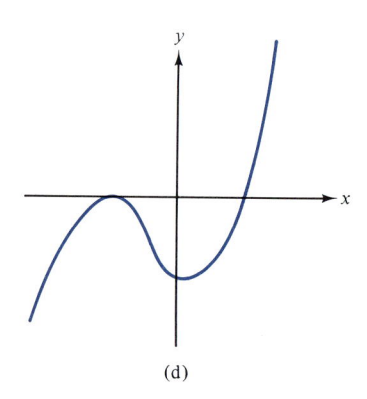

(d) 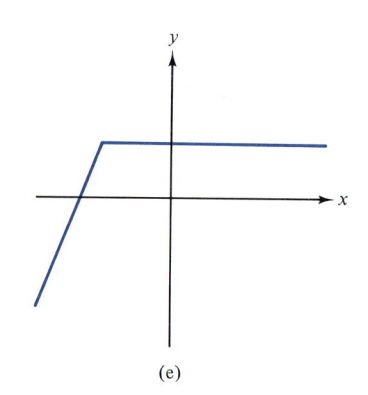　(e) 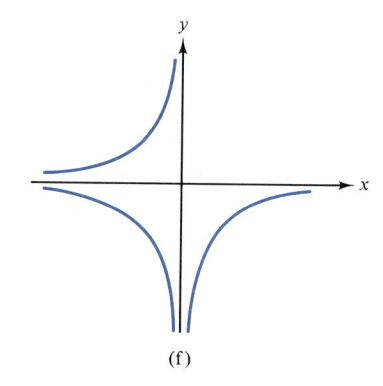　(f)

4.

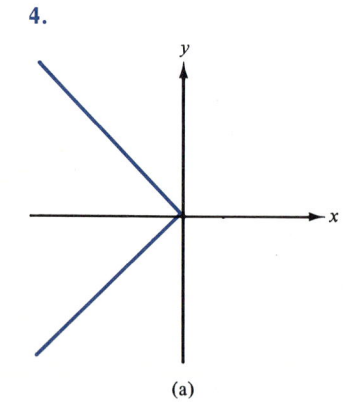

(a) 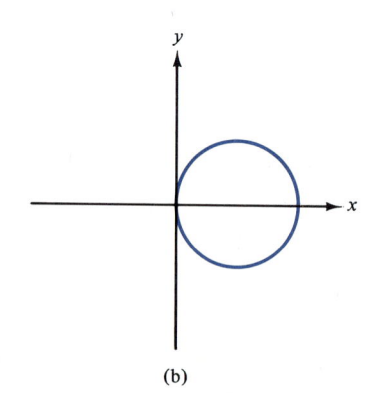　(b) 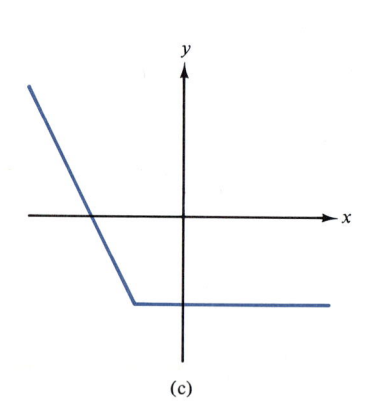　(c)

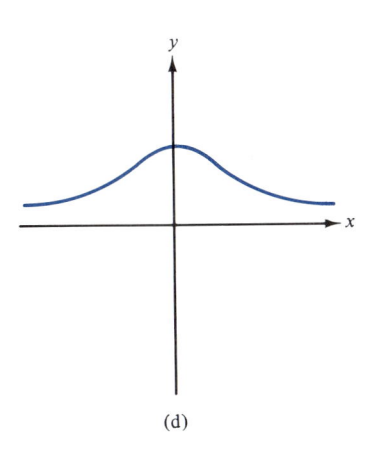

(d) 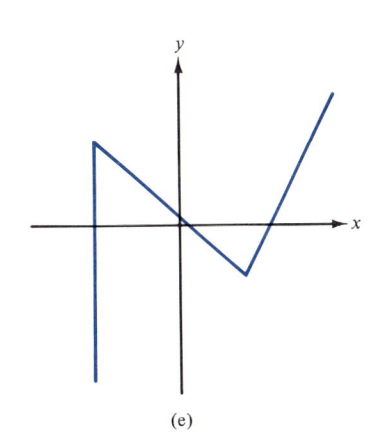   (e) 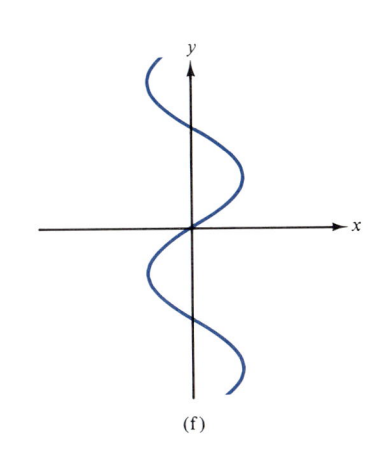   (f)

In Problems 5 and 6, determine whether the correspondences are functions. For those that are, state the domain and range.

5.

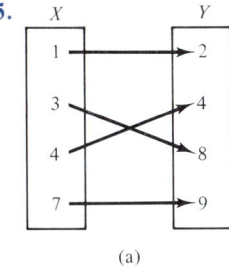

(a) 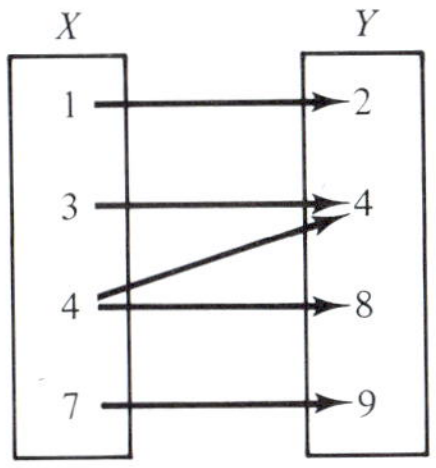   (b)

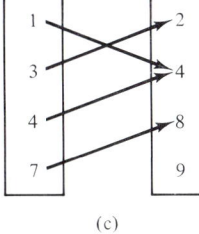

(c) 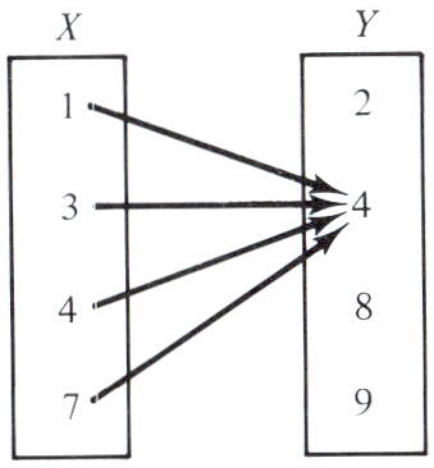   (d)

6.

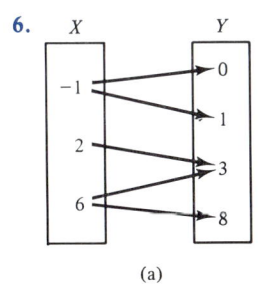

(a) 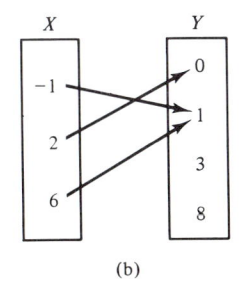   (b)

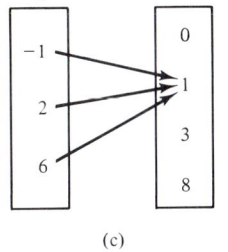

(c) 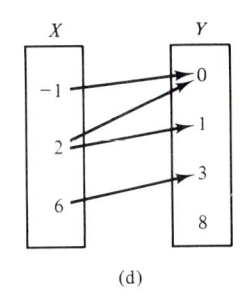   (d)

7. Let f be the function defined below.

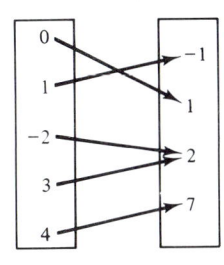

Determine each of the following: **(a)** $f(0)$, **(b)** $f(-2)$, **(c)** $f(1) + 3$, **(d)** $f(1 + 3)$, **(e)** $f(1) + f(3)$, **(f)** $f(3 - 2)$, **(g)** $f(f(0))$, **(h)** domain, **(i)** range, and **(j)** a, if $f(a) = 1$.

8. Let f be the function defined below.

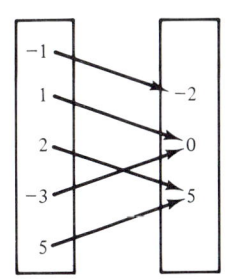

Determine each of the following: (a) $f(1)$, (b) $f(2)$, (c) $f(5) - 2$, (d) $f(2 - 1)$, (e) $f(2) - f(1)$, (f) $f(1 + 1)$, (g) $f(f(2))$, (h) domain, (i) range, and (j) a, if $f(a) = -2$.

In Problems 9–18, let x be a variable with domain R. For the function f defined, determine each of the following.

9. $f(x) = x - 3$: (a) $f(0)$, (b) $f(4)$, (c) $f(a)$, (d) $f(x + 2)$, (e) $f(x) + f(2)$, (f) $f(x) + 2$
10. $f(x) = -2x + 1$: (a) $f(2)$, (b) $f(-\frac{1}{2})$, (c) $f(\pi)$, (d) $f(x + 1)$, (e) $f(x) + f(1)$, (f) $f(x) + 1$
11. $f(x) = x^2 + x$: (a) $f(0)$, (b) $f(-3)$, (c) $f(1/a)$, (d) $f(x + h) - f(x)$, (e) $f(x^2)$
12. $f(x) = 5 - x^2$: (a) $f(-1)$, (b) $f(\sqrt{2})$, (c) $f(-x)$, (d) $f(2 + h) - f(2)$, (e) $f(f(0))$
13. $f(x) = \sqrt{2} + 1$: (a) $f(0)$, (b) $f(1)$, (c) $f(x^2)$, (d) $f(\sqrt{2})$, (e) $f(a + h) - f(a)$
14. $f(x) = 1/\pi$: (a) $f(1/\pi)$, (b) $f(3.14)$, (c) $f(\sqrt{x})$, (d) $f(1/x)$, (e) $f(f(1))$
15. $f(x) = 1/(x^2 + 1)$: (a) $f(2)$, (b) $f(-\frac{1}{3})$, (c) $f(1/t)$, (d) $f(x - 5)$, (e) $f(3^{3/2})$
16. $f(x) = -2/(1 + 2x^2)$: (a) $f(-1)$, (b) $f(1/\sqrt{6})$, (c) $f(1/t^2)$, (d) $f(x - 1)$, (e) $f(8^{-1/2})$
17. $f(x) = |x - 2|$: (a) $f(0)$, (b) $f(2)$, (c) $f(\sqrt{3})$, (d) $f(-|-1|)$, (e) $f(f(2^{-1}))$
18. $f(x) = |1 - x|$: (a) $f(-1)$, (b) $f(\pi/3)$, (c) $f(5) - f(-3)$, (d) $f(|-2| - |4|)$, (e) $f(|-2|) - f(|4|)$

In Problems 19–28, determine the domain of each function.

19. $f(x) = 5$
20. $f(x) = 1/(\pi - 1)$
21. $f(x) = 2/(x - 2)$
22. $f(x) = -1/(x + 4)$
23. $f(x) = \dfrac{5x^2}{(x^2 - 4)(x^2 + 1)}$
24. $f(x) = \dfrac{x + 9}{x^3 - 9x}$
25. $f(x) = \sqrt{x + 4}$
26. $f(x) = \dfrac{1}{x\sqrt{x + 3}}$
27. $f(x) = \sqrt{x^2 + 25}$
28. $f(x) = \sqrt{|x|}$

In Problems 29–32, y is a function of x. Let f be the function defined and determine $f(x)$.

29. $4x - y = -3$
30. $3x + 2(y - 1) = 6$
31. $\dfrac{y - 1}{2} = \dfrac{x^2}{5}$
32. $2(y - 4) + x = x(x + 1)$

33. If $f(x) = x^2 + 1$, show that $f(a + 3) - f(a - 3) - 12a = 0$.
34. If $f(x) = x - 2$, show that $(x + 3)f(x) - (x + 2)f(x + 1) + 4 = 0$.

35. The area of a square is x^2 and the perimeter is $4x$, where x represents the length of a side. Express the area A as a function of the perimeter P.
36. Consider a square whose side has length a and whose diagonal has length l. Express the area of the square as a function of the length of its diagonal.
37. A rectangular field of area 15,000 square feet is to be enclosed by a fence and then divided into two lots by a fence parallel to one of the sides. Write the total length of the fence as a function of the length of the inner fence.
38. A rectangular plot of ground has an area of 1300 square feet. It is to be enclosed by a fence and then divided into four smaller rectangles with three fences parallel to the width of the plot. Each interior fence costs $3.00 per foot and the other fence costs $7.00 per foot. Write the cost of the fence as a function of the length of the plot of ground.
39. A closed rectangular box, with a square base, has a volume of 6000 cubic centimeters. Write the surface area of the box as a function of the length of the base.
40. A closed rectangular box, with a square base, has a surface area of 78 square feet. The cost of the material for the top is 4¢ per square foot, the cost of the bottom material is 6¢ per square foot, and the cost of the side material is 3¢ per square foot. Write the cost of the box as a function of the length of the base.
41. An outdoor track consists of a rectangular region with a semicircular region adjoined at each end. The perimeter of the track is 440 yards. Write the area of the rectangular region of the track as a function of the radius of the semicircular region.
42. A Norman window (a rectangular piece of glass topped by a semicircular sheet of glass) has a perimeter of 40 feet. Write the area of the window as a function of the radius of the semicircle.

A function f is said to be an even function if $f(x) = f(-x)$ and odd if $f(-x) = -f(x)$. This information is needed in Problems 43–48. In Problems 43–48, determine whether each function is even, odd, or neither.

43. $f(x) = x^2 - 3$
44. $f(x) = 5 - x^{-1}$
45. $f(x) = x^3$
46. $f(x) = \begin{cases} -1 & \text{when } x > 0 \\ 0 & \text{when } x = 0 \\ 1 & \text{when } x < 0 \end{cases}$
47. $f(x) = |x|$
48. $f(x) = \dfrac{1}{|x^3|}$

1.4 GRAPHS OF FUNCTIONS

The **graph of a function** f whose domain and range are subsets of R is the set of all points $(x, f(x))$ in the xy-plane such that x is in the domain of f. Hence $f(a)$ is the y-coordinate of the point on the graph of f whose x-coordinate is a. Also note that, with x restricted to this domain, the graph of f is exactly the same as the graph of the equation $y = f(x)$, in which y is a function of x. Thus no vertical line intersects the graph of a function in more than one point. Further, given the graph, the domain is the projection of the graph onto the x-axis, and the range is the projection of the graph onto the y-axis.

We'll begin our study of graphs by examining a broad class of functions called polynomials. A function f whose formula of definition may be expressed in the form

$$f(x) = a_n x^n + a_{n-1} x^{n-1} + \cdots + a_1 x + a_0,$$

where n is a nonnegative integer and $a_n, a_{n-1}, \ldots, a_1, a_0$ are constants with $a_n \neq 0$, is called a **polynomial function of degree n.** The term $a_n x^n$ is called the **leading term,** and the constant a_n is referred to as the **leading coefficient.** For example, f and g, defined by

$$f(x) = -2x^4 + 4x^3 - 5 \quad \text{and} \quad g(x) = x^2 - 2x + 3 + 7x^3$$

are polynomials of degrees 4 and 3, respectively. The leading terms are $-2x^4$ and $7x^3$, respectively, and the leading coefficients are -2 and 7. On the other hand,

$$h(x) = \sqrt{x} \quad \text{and} \quad r(x) = \frac{2}{x-3}$$

are *not* polynomial functions.

Polynomial functions of degree 0, defined by

$$f(x) = a,$$

where $a \neq 0$, and the special function $f(x) = 0$, are called **constant functions.** The graph of a constant function is a horizontal line.

A polynomial function of degree 1, defined by

$$f(x) = ax + b,$$

where $a \neq 0$, is called a **linear function.** Its graph is the line with slope a and y-intercept b.

A polynomial function of degree 2, defined by

$$f(x) = ax^2 + bx + c,$$

where $a \neq 0$, is called a **quadratic function.** Its graph is a U-shaped figure (if $a > 0$) or a ∩-shaped figure (if $a < 0$) called a **parabola.**

GRAPHS AND FUNCTIONS

The simplest of quadratic functions is defined by
$$f(x) = x^2.$$

To sketch its graph we select some x-values and determine corresponding values of the function. We get the following table:

x	-3	-2	-1	0	1	2	3
$f(x)$	9	4	1	0	1	4	9

Plotting these points and connecting them with a curve that follows their general trend, we get the graph in Figure 1.28.

The lowest point of a parabola (when it opens upward) or the highest point (when it opens downward) is called the **vertex**. The vertical line passing through the vertex is called the **axis**. For the parabola in Figure 1.28, the vertex is (0,0), and the y-axis is the axis of the parabola.

Note that if the plane were folded along the axis of a parabola, the two halves would coincide exactly. In this sense a parabola is said to be **symmetric** about its axis.

The vertex of the parabola defined by
$$y = f(x) = ax^2 + bx + c,$$
occurs at $x = -b/(2a)$. We may see this by rewriting the equation:

$$y = a\left(x^2 + \frac{b}{a}x\right) + c$$

$$y = a\left(x^2 + \frac{b}{a}x + \frac{b^2}{4a^2}\right) + c - a \cdot \frac{b^2}{4a^2}$$

$$y = a\left(x + \frac{b}{2a}\right)^2 + c - \frac{b^2}{4a}.$$

If $a > 0$, the vertex is the lowest point. This occurs when y equals its smallest value. Since the second and third terms of

$$a\left(x + \frac{b}{2a}\right)^2 + c - \frac{b^2}{4a}$$

are constant, the smallest y-value depends on

$$a\left(x + \frac{b}{2a}\right)^2.$$

Since this term is nonnegative, the smallest value occurs when

$$\left(x + \frac{b}{2a}\right)^2 = 0.$$

$f(x) = x^2$

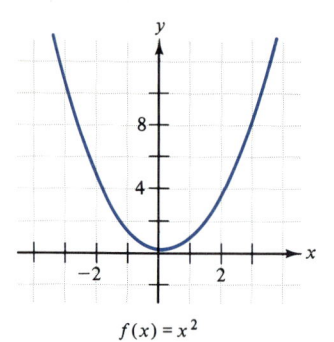

FIGURE 1.28

1.4 GRAPHS OF FUNCTIONS

Solving for x gives

$$x + \frac{b}{2a} = 0$$

$$x = \frac{-b}{2a}.$$

Similarly, if $a < 0$, the vertex is the highest point. This happens when y equals its largest value, which, again, is at $x = -b/(2a)$.

EXAMPLE 1

Sketch the graph of $f(x) = -x^2 + 2x + 3$.

■ SOLUTION
The vertex occurs at

$$x = \frac{-b}{2a} = \frac{-2}{2(-1)} = 1.$$

Now we select additional x-values on each side of the vertex and determine the corresponding values of the function. We get the following table:

x	−2	−1	0	1	2	3	4
$f(x)$	−5	0	3	4	3	0	−5

Plotting these points gives the graph in Figure 1.29.

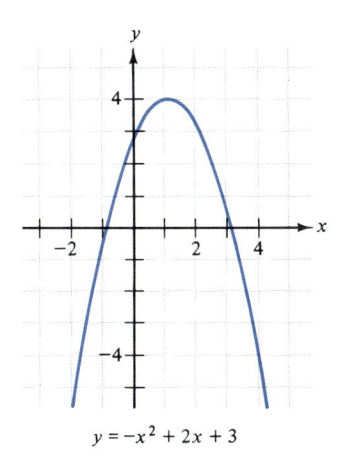

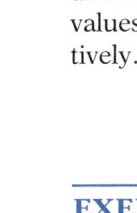

$y = -x^2 + 2x + 3$
FIGURE 1.29

In Example 1 note that not all the $f(x)$-values have to be computed directly. Because the parabola is symmetric about $x = 1$, its axis, the $f(x)$-values when $x = 2, 3, 4$ must be the same as when $x = 0, -1, -2$, respectively. (Note the symmetry of the table.)

EXERCISE

Sketch the graph of $f(x) = 3x^2 - 6x + 1$.

■ ANSWER
See Figure 1.30.

$f(x) = 3x^2 - 6x + 1$
FIGURE 1.30

The graphs of polynomial functions of degrees greater than 2 can be quite complex. We develop some techniques in Section 5.5 to deal with

(a) $y = x^3$

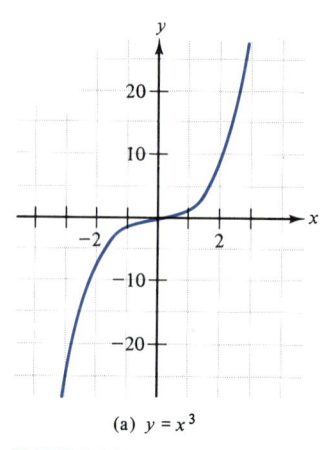

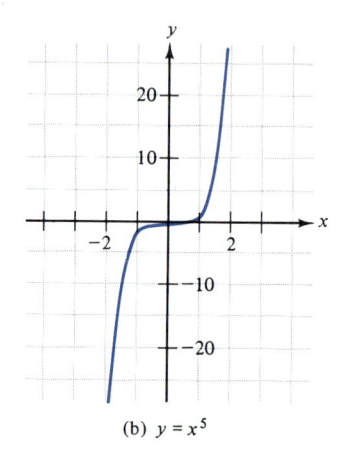

(b) $y = x^5$

FIGURE 1.31

them. Until then, we restrict our attention to elementary polynomial functions and their transformations. We begin with the graphs of $y = x^3$ and $y = x^5$, shown in Figure 1.31.

The basic shape of these two graphs is shared by the graphs of $y = x^7$, $y = x^9$, and so on. Each contains the points $(1,1)$, $(-1,-1)$, and $(0,0)$. Each is almost flat about the origin [on the interval $(-1,1)$] and steep elsewhere [on $(-\infty, -1)$ and on $(1, \infty)$]. So the graphs of $y = x^{2n+1}$, where n is a positive integer, are similar. The principal difference is that the greater the exponent, the greater this flatness and steepness.

Now let's consider the graphs of $y = x^2$ and $y = x^4$, shown in Figure 1.32. The basic shape of these two graphs is also shared by the graphs of $y = x^6$, $y = x^8$, and so on. (However, only $y = x^2$ is a parabola.) Each contains the points $(1, 1)$, $(-1, 1)$, and $(0, 0)$. Each is almost flat about the origin [on the interval $(-1, 1)$] and steep elsewhere [on $(-\infty, -1)$ and on $(1, \infty)$]. So the graphs of $y = x^{2n}$, where n is a positive integer, are similar. The principal difference is that the greater the exponent, the greater this flatness and steepness.

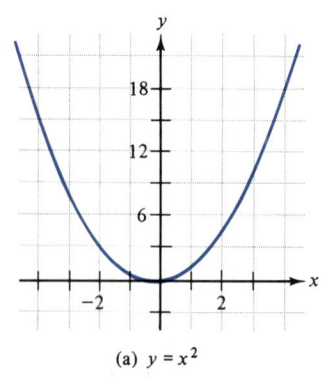

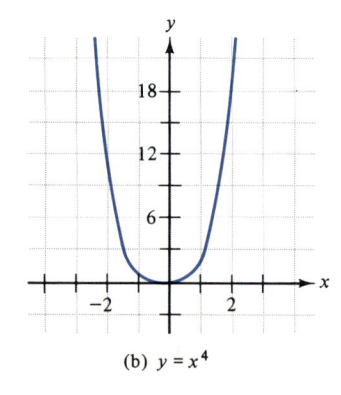

(a) $y = x^2$

(b) $y = x^4$

FIGURE 1.32

1.4 GRAPHS OF FUNCTIONS

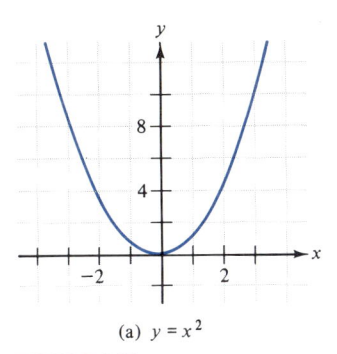

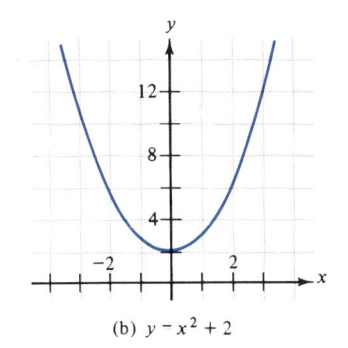

(a) $y = x^2$

(b) $y = x^2 + 2$

FIGURE 1.33

Some functions have graphs whose shapes are the same as those of elementary polynomial functions but whose locations in the xy-plane are different. Such graphs are *transformations* of elementary graphs. We will examine three types of transformations: vertical shifts, horizontal shifts, and reflection about the x-axis.

Let c be a positive constant. Then the graph of $y = f(x) + c$ is the graph of $y = f(x)$ shifted up c units. So, as seen in Figure 1.33, the graph of $y = x^2 + 2$ is simply the parabola $y = x^2$ shifted up two units.

Similarly, if c is a positive constant, then the graph of $y = f(x) - c$ is the graph of $y = f(x)$ shifted down c units. The graphs of $y = x^3$ and $y = x^3 - 1$ are shown in Figure 1.34.

Let c be a positive constant. Then the graph of $y = f(x - c)$ is the graph of $y = f(x)$ shifted to the right c units. So the graph of $y = (x - 1)^2$, as noted in Figure 1.35, is the parabola $y = x^2$ shifted to the right one unit.

In a similar fashion, if c is a positive constant, then the graph of $y = f(x + c)$ is the graph of $y = f(x)$ shifted to the left c units. The graphs of $y = x^3$ and $y = (x + 1)^3$ are seen in Figure 1.36.

Of course, as seen in Example 2, the graph may be the result of both a horizontal and a vertical shift.

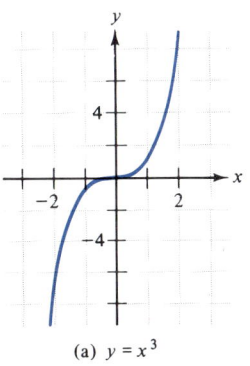

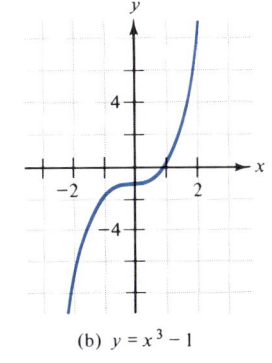

(a) $y = x^3$

(b) $y = x^3 - 1$

FIGURE 1.34

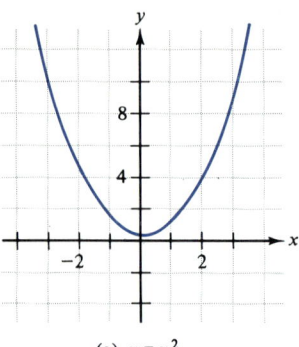

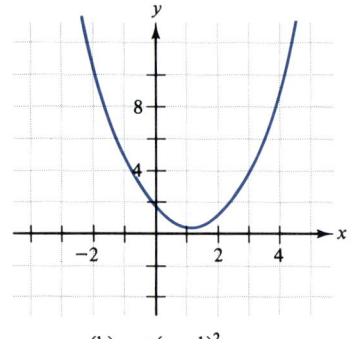

(a) $y = x^2$

(b) $y = (x - 1)^2$

FIGURE 1.35

(a) $y = x^3$

(b) $y = (x + 1)^3$

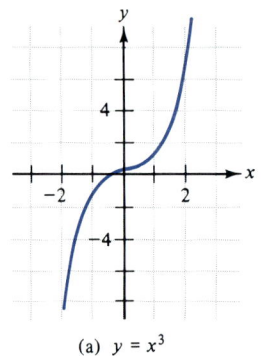

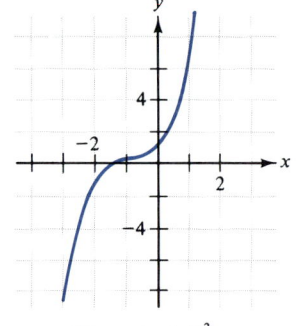

FIGURE 1.36

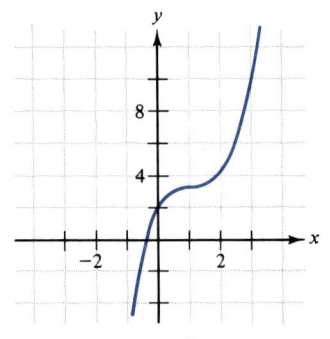

$y = (x - 1)^3 + 3$
FIGURE 1.37

EXAMPLE 2

Sketch the graph of $y = (x - 1)^3 + 3$.

■ SOLUTION
The graph is a transformation of $y = x^3$. It is this basic graph shifted to the right one unit and up three units as shown in Figure 1.37.

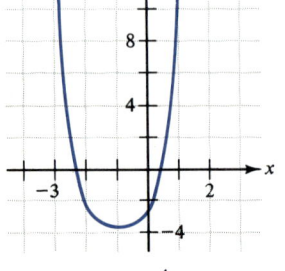

EXERCISE

Sketch the graph of $y = (x + 1)^4 - 4$.

■ ANSWER
See Figure 1.38.

$y = (x + 1)^4 - 4$
FIGURE 1.38

The graph of $y = -f(x)$ is a reflection of the graph of $y = f(x)$ about the x-axis. This means that for each point P on the graph of $y = f(x)$, the point Q, which has the property that $\overline{PQ}$ is perpendicular to and bisected

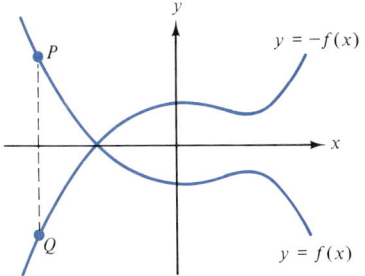

1.4 GRAPHS OF FUNCTIONS 37

by the x-axis, is on the graph of $y = -f(x)$. This relationship is pictured in Figure 1.39. In other words, if the plane were folded along the x-axis, the two graphs would coincide exactly.

Thus the graph of $y = -x^3$, shown in Figure 1.40, is simply a reflection of the graph of $y = x^3$ about the x-axis.

A summary of the effects on the graph of $y = f(x)$, where c is a positive constant, follows:

$y =$	Effect
$f(x) + c$	Shift up c units
$f(x) - c$	Shift down c units
$f(x - c)$	Shift right c units
$f(x + c)$	Shift left c units
$-f(x)$	Reflection about the x-axis

Reflection about the x-axis
FIGURE 1.39

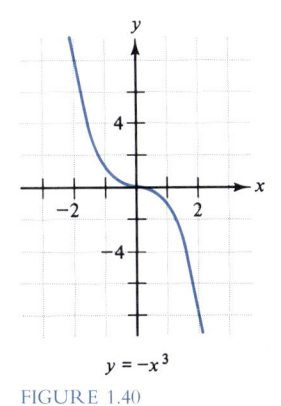

$y = -x^3$
FIGURE 1.40

Let's examine the graph of $y = -(x - 3)^2 + 5$, noting how each of the constants affects the graph of the elementary polynomial $y = x^2$. The graph of $y = (x - 3)^2$ is a shift of the basic parabola to the right three units. The graph of $y = -(x - 3)^2$ gives a reflection about the x-axis. And $y = -(x - 3)^2 + 5$ shifts the parabola up five units. These transformations appear in Figure 1.41.

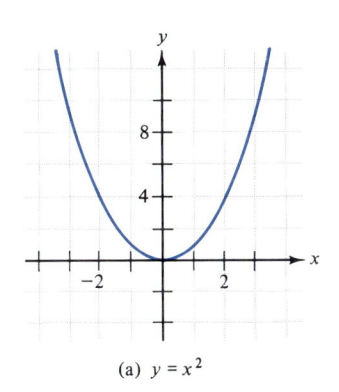

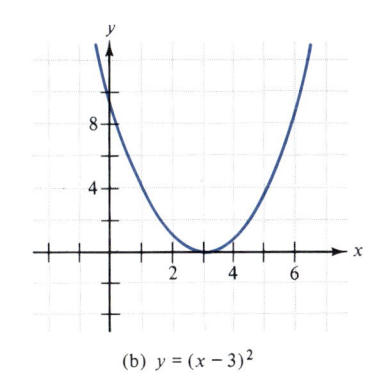

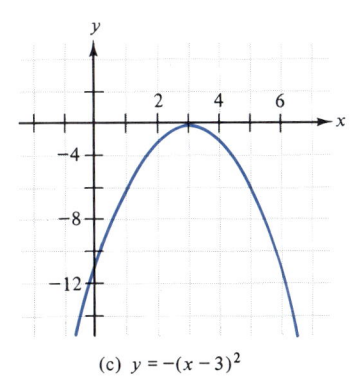

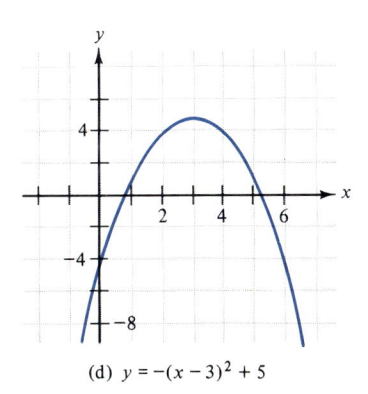

(a) $y = x^2$

(b) $y = (x - 3)^2$

(c) $y = -(x - 3)^2$

(d) $y = -(x - 3)^2 + 5$

FIGURE 1.41

38 GRAPHS AND FUNCTIONS

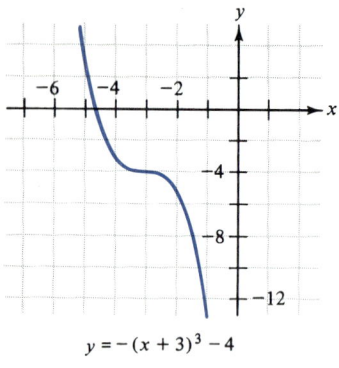

EXERCISE

Sketch the graph of $y = -(x + 3)^3 - 4$.

■ ANSWER
See Figure 1.42.

FIGURE 1.42 $y = -(x+3)^3 - 4$

A function f whose formula of definition may be expressed in the form

$$f(x) = \frac{P(x)}{Q(x)},$$

where P and Q are polynomial functions, is called a **rational function.** Thus a rational function is the quotient of two polynomials. For example, f and g, defined by

$$f(x) = \frac{2x + 1}{x - 5} \quad \text{and} \quad g(x) = \frac{1}{x^2 - 4},$$

are rational functions. [All polynomial functions are rational functions also, with $Q(x) = 1$.] Because a rational function is not defined at values that make the denominator zero, the domain of f is $R - \{5\}$, that is, $(-\infty, 5) \cup (5, \infty)$, and the domain of g is $R - \{2, -2\}$, that is, $(-\infty, -2) \cup (-2, 2) \cup (2, \infty)$.

The graphs of rational functions can be quite complex. Until we get to Section 5.5, we restrict our attention to elementary rational functions and their transformations. We begin with the graphs of $y = 1/x$ and $y = 1/x^3$, shown in Figure 1.43.

Note that even though neither function is defined at 0, we can choose values of x as close to 0 as we please. As x gets closer to 0 from the positive side, y increases without bound (i.e., y is eventually greater than each positive number). And as x gets closer to 0 from the negative side, y decreases without bound (i.e., y is eventually less than each negative number). Hence, as x approaches 0, the graph approaches, but does not

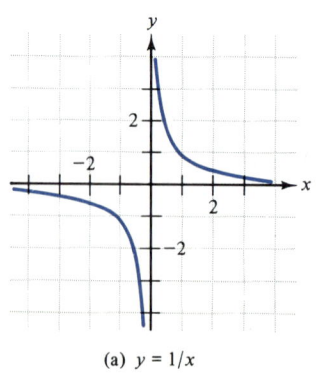

(a) $y = 1/x$ (b) $y = 1/x^3$

FIGURE 1.43

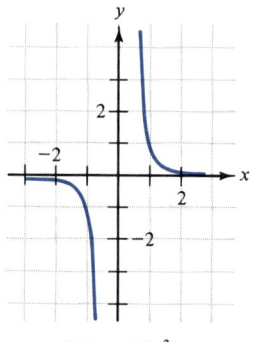

1.4 GRAPHS OF FUNCTIONS

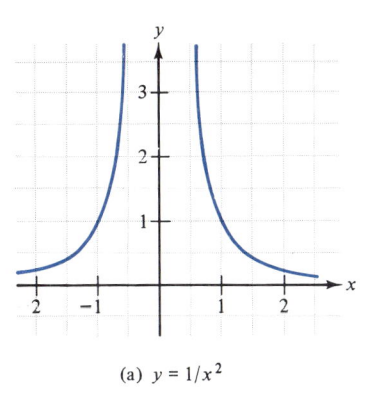

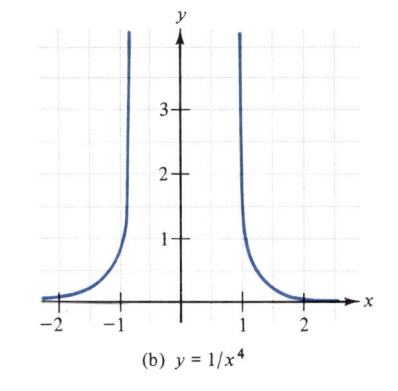

(a) $y = 1/x^2$

(b) $y = 1/x^4$

FIGURE 1.44

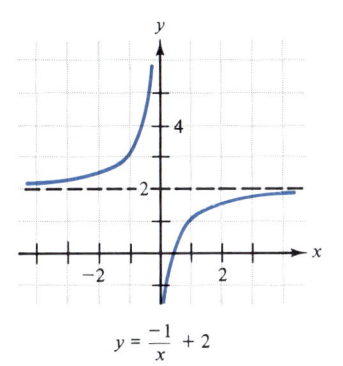

$y = \dfrac{-1}{x} + 2$

FIGURE 1.45

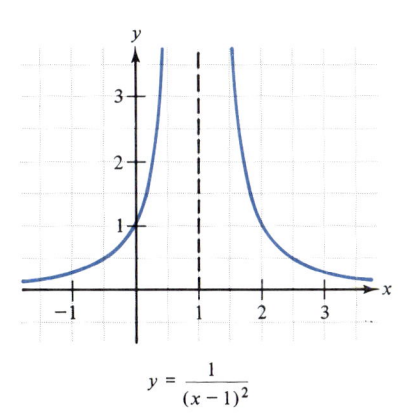

$y = \dfrac{1}{(x-1)^2}$

FIGURE 1.46

intersect, the line $x = 0$ (the y-axis). A line with the property that the distance from a point P to the line approaches zero as P moves away from the origin along some part of the graph is called an **asymptote**. In Figure 1.43 the y-axis is a *vertical* asymptote.

Also note that as x increases without bound, y gets closer to 0. And y also gets closer to 0 as x decreases without bound. Hence the graph approaches the line $y = 0$ (the x-axis). Thus the x-axis is a *horizontal* asymptote in Figure 1.43.

The basic shape of these two graphs is shared by the graphs of $y = 1/x^5$, $y = 1/x^7$, and so on. Each has two pieces, called *branches*, in the first and third quadrants. Each contains the points $(1,1)$ and $(-1,-1)$. Each has a vertical asymptote of $x = 0$, and each has a horizontal asymptote of $y = 0$. Each is steep about the origin [on $(-1,0)$ and on $(0,1)$] and almost flat elsewhere [on $(-\infty,-1)$ and on $(1,\infty)$]. So the graphs of $y = 1/x^{2n-1}$, where n is a positive integer, are similar. The principal difference is that the greater the exponent, the greater this flatness and steepness.

Let's now consider the graphs of $y = 1/x^2$ and $y = 1/x^4$, shown in Figure 1.44. The basic shape of these two graphs is shared by the graphs of $y = 1/x^6$, $y = 1/x^8$, and so on. Each has two branches, in the first and second quadrants. Each contains the points $(1,1)$ and $(-1,1)$. Each has a vertical asymptote of $x = 0$ and a horizontal asymptote of $y = 0$. Each is steep about the origin [on $(-1,0)$ and on $(0,1)$] and almost flat elsewhere [on $(-\infty,-1)$ and on $(1,\infty)$]. So the graphs of $y = 1/x^{2n}$, where n is a positive integer, are similar. The principal difference is that the greater the exponent, the greater this flatness and steepness.

Of course, these elementary rational functions can undergo the same types of transformation as the elementary polynomial functions. For example, the graph of $y = (-1/x) + 2$, shown in Figure 1.45, is simply the graph of $y = 1/x$ reflected about the x-axis and then moved up two units, with the horizontal asymptote being $y = 2$. Note that when an asymptote is a line other than the x- or y-axis, it is indicated by dashes.

The graph of $y = 1/(x - 1)^2$ (Figure 1.46) is the graph of $y = 1/x^2$ shifted to the right one unit, with the vertical asymptote being $x = 1$.

EXAMPLE 3

Sketch the graph of $y = \dfrac{-1}{(x+2)^3} - 3$.

■ SOLUTION

This graph (Figure 1.47) is a transformation of $y = 1/x^3$. It is this basic graph shifted to the left two units, then reflected about the x-axis, then shifted down three units.

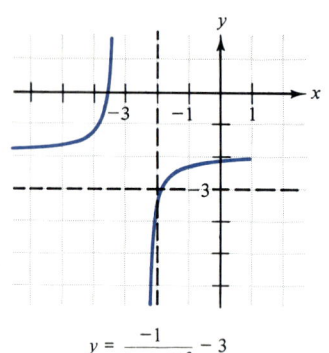

$y = \dfrac{-1}{(x+2)^3} - 3$

FIGURE 1.47

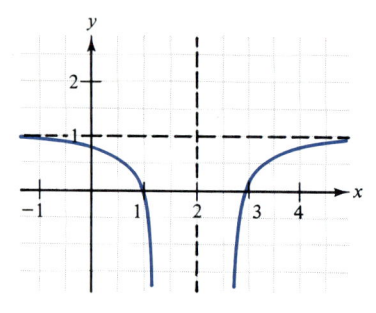

EXERCISE

Sketch the graph of $y = \dfrac{-1}{(x-2)^2} + 1$.

■ ANSWER
See Figure 1.48.

$y = \dfrac{-1}{(x-2)^2} + 1$

FIGURE 1.48

PROBLEM SET 1.4

1. Let f be the function with the following graph.

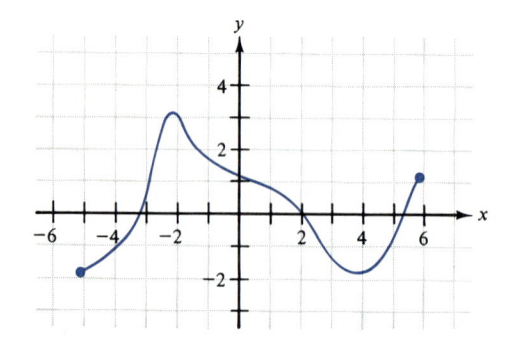

   (a) What is the range of f?
   (b) What is the domain of f?
   (c) $f(0) = ?$
   (d) $f(-2) = ?$
   (e) $f(2+4) = ?$
   (f) $f(-5) + f(6) = ?$
   (g) $f(f(4)) = ?$
   (h) If $f(a) = 0$, then $a = ?$
   (i) If $f(f(b)) = 3$, then $b = ?$

2. Let f be the function with the following graph.
   (a) What is the domain of f?
   (b) What is the range of f?
   (c) $f(2) = ?$
   (d) $f(-5) = ?$
   (e) $f(3-3) = ?$
   (f) $f(-7) - f(-1) = ?$
   (g) $f(f(6)) = ?$
   (h) If $f(a) = -3$, then $a = ?$
   (i) If $f(f(b)) = 0$, then $b = ?$

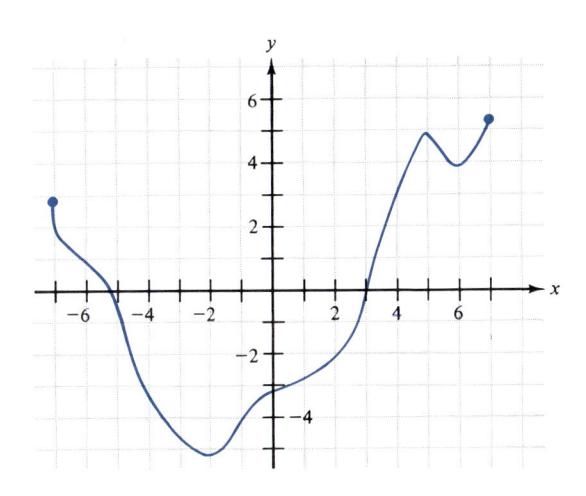

In Problems 3–16, sketch the graph of the polynomial.

3. $y = x^2 - 4x$
4. $y = -x^2 - 2x$
5. $y = -4x^2 - 4x + 3$
6. $y = x^2 - 4x + 5$
7. $y = x^2 - \frac{1}{2}$
8. $y = x^3 + 1$
9. $y = (x - 2)^3$
10. $y = (x + 3)^2$
11. $y = 1 - x^4$
12. $y = -2 - x^3$
13. $y = (x + 2)^2 - 2$
14. $y = (x - \frac{3}{2})^3 + \frac{3}{2}$
15. $y = 3 - (x - 1)^3$
16. $y = -(x - \pi)^2 - 1$

In Problems 17–24, sketch the graph of the rational function.

17. $y = \dfrac{1}{x} - 1$
18. $y = \dfrac{1}{x^2} + 2$
19. $y = \dfrac{1}{x + 2} + 2$
20. $y = \dfrac{1}{(x - \frac{1}{2})^3} - 1$
21. $y = \dfrac{-1}{(3 - x)^2} + 2$
22. $y = \dfrac{-1}{(1 - x)^3}$
23. $y = \dfrac{x - 2}{2x}$
24. $y = \dfrac{-x^2 - 1}{x^2}$

In Problems 25–30, choose the equation that best describes the given graph.

25. (a) $y = x^3 - 2$
    (b) $y = (x - 2)^3$
    (c) $y = (x + 2)^5$
    (d) $y = -(x + 2)^3$
    (e) $y = (x + 2)^2$

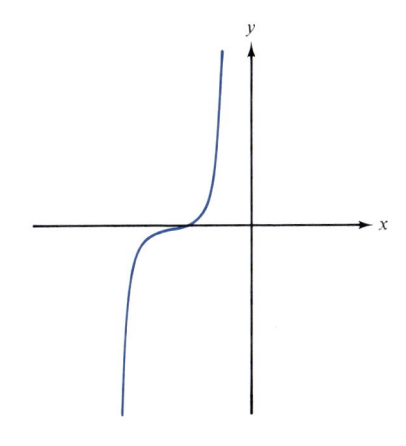

26. (a) $y = -(x^2 + \sqrt{3})$
    (b) $y = -(x + \sqrt{3})^2$
    (c) $y = x^4 + \sqrt{3}$
    (d) $y = (-x)^2 + \sqrt{3}$
    (e) $y = -x^2 + \sqrt{3}$

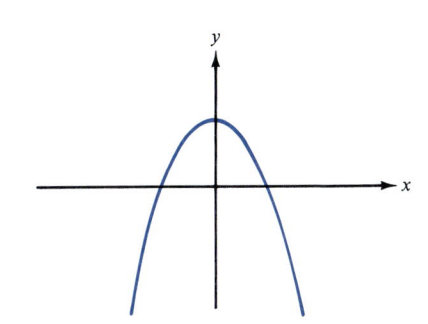

27. (a) $y = (x + 1)^2 - 5$
    (b) $y = (x - 1)^2 - 5$
    (c) $y = (1 - x)^2 + 5$
    (d) $y = (x - 1)^3 - 5$
    (e) $y = 5 - (x - 1)^4$

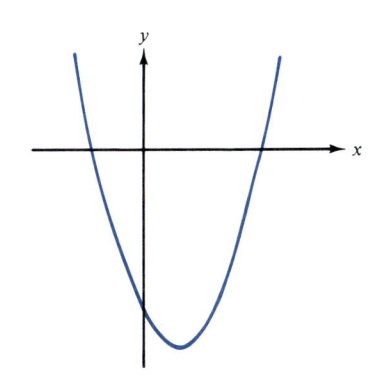

28. (a) $y = (x + 4)^3 + 2$
(b) $y = 2 - (x - 4)^5$
(c) $y = -(x - 4)^3 - 2$
(d) $y = (-x - 4)^3 + 2$
(e) $y = -(x + 4)^2 + 2$

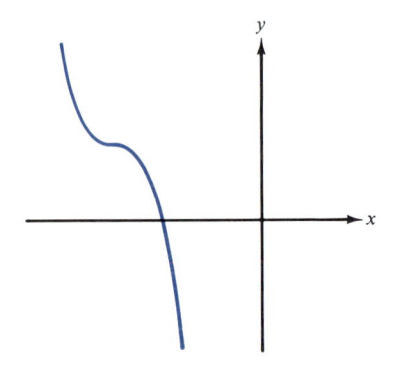

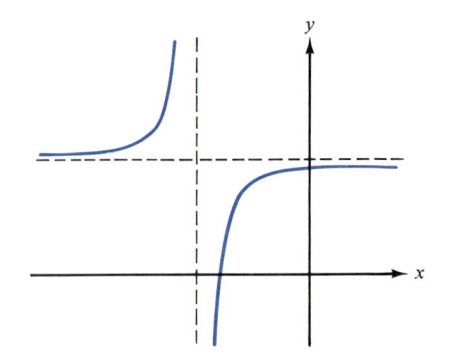

29. (a) $y = \dfrac{-1}{(x - 3)} + 3$
(b) $y = \dfrac{1}{(x + 3)^3} + 3$
(c) $y = \dfrac{-1}{(x + 3)^3} - 3$
(d) $y = \dfrac{-1}{(x + 3)^3} + 3$
(e) $y = \dfrac{1}{(x - 3)} + 3$

30. (a) $y = \dfrac{1}{(x + 2)^4} - 1$
(b) $y = \dfrac{-1}{(2 - x)^2} - 1$
(c) $y = \dfrac{1}{(x - 2)^2} - 1$
(d) $y = \dfrac{1}{(x - 2)^3} - 1$
(e) $y = \dfrac{1}{(x + 2)^2} - 1$

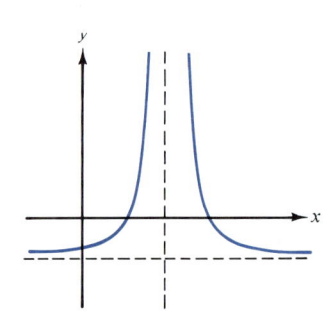

1.5 LOGARITHMS

Let $b > 0$, $b \neq 1$, and let k be any positive number. Then there exists a unique number j such that $b^j = k$. This number j is called the **logarithm to the base b of k.** Denoted by $\log_b k$, it is that number which when used as an exponent to b gives k. (See Appendix A.2 for a review of exponents.) For example,

$$\log_{10} 100 = 2 \quad \text{because } 10^2 = 100,$$
$$\log_2 8 = 3 \quad \text{because } 2^3 = 8,$$
$$\log_{10} \tfrac{1}{10} = -1 \quad \text{because } 10^{-1} = \tfrac{1}{10},$$
$$\log_{1/2} 4 = -2 \quad \text{because } (\tfrac{1}{2})^{-2} = 4.$$

1.5 LOGARITHMS

By definition then the equation
$$\log_b k = j$$
means that
$$b^j = k.$$

It is important to realize that these two equations mean the same thing, as we frequently convert one to the other. Note that we may take the logarithm of a positive number only. It is not possible to take the logarithm of a negative number or of zero because b^j is always positive since $b > 0$.

EXERCISE

Convert each equation containing a logarithm into an equivalent equation containing an exponent, or vice versa: (a) $\log_5 125 = 3$; (b) $\log_3 \frac{1}{9} = -2$; (c) $3^4 = 81$; and (d) $4^2 = 16$.

■ ANSWER
(a) $5^3 = 125$; (b) $3^{-2} = \frac{1}{9}$; (c) $\log_3 81 = 4$; (d) $\log_4 16 = 2$

EXERCISE

Find the following numbers: (a) $\log_3 9$, (b) $\log_{10} \frac{1}{100}$, (c) $\log_{1/4} 4$, and (d) $\log_\pi 1$.

■ ANSWER
(a) 2; (b) -2; (c) -1; (d) 0

Logarithms to the base 10 are called **common logarithms.** As a matter of convenience, $\log_{10} x$ is written simply as $\log x$. Thus $\log \frac{1}{100} = -2$.

Another frequently used logarithmic base is e, an irrational number approximately equal to 2.71828. (It is defined in the next chapter.) Although this appears to be an unusual base, it naturally arises in many scientific applications, such as bacteria growth and radioactive decay. Logarithms to the base e are called **natural logarithms,** and $\log_e x$ is usually written $\ln x$. It is easy to find the common logarithm of a number that can readily be expressed as a power of 10. But how do we calculate log 3? And how do we find ln 5? To approximate such values, we use a calculator.

EXERCISE

Approximate the following to the nearest thousandth: (a) log 3 and (b) ln 5.

■ ANSWER
(a) 0.477; (b) 1.609

From the definition we see that for all positive numbers x,
$$b^{\log_b x} = x.$$
This is because $\log_b x$, that number which when used as an exponent to b gives x, is being used as an exponent to b. So the result must be x. And for all real numbers t,
$$\log_b b^t = t.$$
This result also follows directly from the definition.

Hence we see that
$$10^{\log x} = x \quad \text{and} \quad \log 10^t = t,$$
$$e^{\ln x} = x \quad \text{and} \quad \ln e^t = t.$$
For example, $10^{\log 2} = 2$ and $\ln e^{-3} = -3$.

EXAMPLE 1

Simplify the following: (a) $5^{-2\log_5 k}$ and (b) $\log_3 9^y$.

■ SOLUTION

(a) Using the definition and rules for exponents, we get
$$5^{-2\log_5 k} = (5^{\log_5 k})^{-2} = k^{-2} = \frac{1}{k^2}.$$

(b) Again using the definition and rules for exponents, we get
$$\log_3 9^y = \log_3 (3^2)^y = \log_3 3^{2y} = 2y.$$

EXERCISE

Simplify the following: (a) $2^{3\log_2 x}$ and (b) $\log_5 125^k$.

■ ANSWER
(a) x^3; (b) $3k$

We now examine some important properties of logarithms, sometimes referred to as **laws of logarithms.**

Let $b > 0$, $b \neq 1$. Then for all $u > 0$ and all $v > 0$:

(i) $\log_b(uv) = \log_b u + \log_b v$.

(ii) $\log_b\left(\dfrac{u}{v}\right) = \log_b u - \log_b v$.

(iii) $\log_b u^k = k \log_b u$ for all real numbers k.

1.5 LOGARITHMS

These properties follow directly from the laws of exponents. Let $m = \log_b u$ and $n = \log_b v$. From the definition of logarithm we have

$$u = b^m \quad \text{and} \quad v = b^n.$$

Using the laws of exponents it follows that

$$uv = b^m \cdot b^n = b^{m+n}.$$

Using the definition of logarithm and then substituting, we get

$$\log_b(uv) = \log_b b^{m+n} = m + n = \log_b u + \log_b v.$$

The proofs of (ii) and (iii) are similar.

This theorem says that the logarithm of a product is the sum of the logarithms, the logarithm of a quotient is the logarithm of the numerator minus the logarithm of the denominator, and the logarithm of a positive number raised to a power is the power times the logarithm of the number. Applications are found in Examples 2 and 3.

EXAMPLE 2

Express $\log(x\sqrt{y}/z^2)$ in terms of $\log x$, $\log y$, and $\log z$.

■ *SOLUTION*

Since the logarithm of a quotient is the difference of the logarithms, the given expression may be written

$$\log(x\sqrt{y}) - \log z^2.$$

Because the logarithm of a product is the sum of the logarithms, the first term can be rewritten. The previous expression becomes

$$\log x + \log \sqrt{y} - \log z^2.$$

The last two terms may be rewritten because the logarithm of a number raised to a power is the power times the logarithm of the number. (Note that $\sqrt{y} = y^{1/2}$.) Thus we finally get

$$\log x + \tfrac{1}{2} \log y - 2 \log z.$$

EXAMPLE 3

Express $\log x - \log y + 2 \log z$ as a single logarithm.

■ *SOLUTION*

By using the second property of logarithms, we may combine the first two terms and write the given expression as

$$\log \frac{x}{y} + 2 \log z.$$

Using the third property, we may rewrite the last term. The preceding expression becomes

$$\log \frac{x}{y} + \log z^2.$$

And finally, using the first property we get

$$\log \frac{xz^2}{y}.$$

EXERCISE

(a) Express $\log(x^2 y / \sqrt[3]{z})$ in terms of $\log x$, $\log y$, and $\log z$. (b) Express $\frac{1}{2} \log x - 2 \log y + \log z$ as a single logarithm.

■ ANSWER

(a) $2 \log x + \log y - \frac{1}{3} \log z$; (b) $\log \dfrac{z\sqrt{x}}{y^2}$

Logarithms may be used to solve exponential equations. An **exponential equation** is one in which the variable appears in one or more exponents. For example,

$$3^x = 2 \quad \text{and} \quad e^{3x} = 12$$

are exponential equations. As illustrated in Examples 4, 5, and 6, this type of equation can be solved by taking the logarithm of each side.

EXAMPLE 4

Determine the solutions of $2^x = 5$.

■ SOLUTION

By taking the natural logarithm of each side, we get the equivalent equation

$$\ln 2^x = \ln 5.$$

After using the laws of logarithms to rewrite the left side, we have

$$x \ln 2 = \ln 5. \tag{1-9}$$

Equation (1-9) is a linear equation in x and may be solved accordingly.

1.5 LOGARITHMS

Dividing both sides by the coefficient of x, we get

$$x = \frac{\ln 5}{\ln 2} \quad (\approx 2.322).$$

Since the domain of x is R, the solution is $\ln 5/\ln 2$ (≈ 2.322).

Note that in Example 4 we could have used the logarithm to a base other than e. For instance, we could have used the common logarithm and written the solution as $\log 5/\log 2$. But the natural logarithm appears more frequently in calculus than the common logarithm, so we generally use the natural logarithm.

EXAMPLE 5

Determine the solutions of $e^{2x} = 15$.

■ SOLUTION

By taking the natural logarithm of each side, we get

$$\ln e^{2x} = \ln 15,$$

which is equivalent to each of the following:

$$2x = \ln 15$$

$$x = \frac{\ln 15}{2} \quad (\approx 1.354).$$

Since the domain is R, the solution is $(\ln 15)/2$ (≈ 1.354).

EXERCISE

Determine the solutions to the following: (a) $5^x = 12$ and (b) $e^{-3x} = 20$.

■ ANSWER

(a) $\dfrac{\ln 12}{\ln 5}$ (≈ 1.544); (b) $\dfrac{-\ln 20}{3}$ (≈ -0.9986)

If money is compounded n times per year at an annual interest rate of r (in decimal form), then $A(t)$, the amount of money after t years, is given by

$$A(t) = P\left(1 + \frac{r}{n}\right)^{nt}, \qquad (1\text{-}10)$$

where P is the original principal invested. This equation is needed in Example 6.

EXAMPLE 6

How long (to the nearest tenth of a year) will it take $1000 to grow to $2500 if interest is compounded quarterly at 8%?

■ SOLUTION
Since $P = 1000$, $r = 0.08$, and $n = 4$, Equation (1-10) becomes

$$A(t) = 1000\left(1 + \frac{0.08}{4}\right)^{4t} = 1000(1.02)^{4t}.$$

We wish to know the value of t that makes $A(t) = 2500$. So we substitute 2500 for $A(t)$ and then solve for t. We get

$$2500 = 1000(1.02)^{4t}$$
$$2.5 = (1.02)^{4t}$$
$$\ln 2.5 = \ln(1.02)^{4t}$$
$$\ln 2.5 = 4t \ln 1.02$$
$$t = \frac{\ln 2.5}{4 \ln 1.02} \approx 11.6.$$

It will take approximately 11.6 years.

EXERCISE

How long (to the nearest tenth of a year) will it take $1000 to grow to $3000 if interest is compounded semiannually at 9%?

■ ANSWER
12.5 years

An equation in which the variable appears in one or more logarithms is called a **logarithmic equation.** For example,

$$\log x = 7 \quad \text{and} \quad \ln 5x = 1 + \ln 3x$$

are logarithmic equations. The principal idea in solving such equations is to get the given equation equivalent to one of the form

$$\log(p_x) = c \quad \text{or} \quad \ln(p_x) = c, \qquad (1\text{-}11)$$

1.5 LOGARITHMS

where p_x is an algebraic expression in x and c is a constant. Then, from the definition of logarithm, we have

$$p_x = 10^c \quad \text{or} \quad p_x = e^c,$$

which will be a linear or quadratic equation. This method is illustrated in Examples 7 and 8.

EXAMPLE 7

Determine the solutions to the following: (a) $4 + \log x = 5 + 2 \log x$ and (b) $5 + \ln x = 3 + 4 \ln x$.

■ *SOLUTION*
(a) Our first goal is to write this equation like the first part of statement (1-11). To this end we have the following:

$$\log x - 2 \log x = 5 - 4$$
$$-\log x = 1$$
$$\log x = -1. \tag{1-12}$$

Using the definition of logarithm, we see that Equation (1-12) is equivalent to

$$x = 10^{-1} = \tfrac{1}{10}.$$

Since the domain of x is $(0,\infty)$, the solution is $\tfrac{1}{10}$.

(b) Our first goal is to write this equation like the second part of statement (1-11). The given equation is equivalent to each of the following:

$$-4 \ln x + \ln x = 3 - 5$$
$$-3 \ln x = -2$$
$$\ln x = \tfrac{2}{3}.$$

From the definition of logarithm we get

$$x = e^{2/3} \quad (\approx 1.948).$$

Since the domain is $(0,\infty)$, the solution is $e^{2/3}$ (≈ 1.948).

EXERCISE

Determine the solutions to the following: (a) $5 + \log x = 4 + 3 \log x$ and (b) $3 \ln x + 5 = \ln x + 2$.

■ *ANSWER*
(a) $\sqrt{10}$ (≈ 3.162); (b) $e^{-3/2}$ (≈ 0.2231)

GRAPHS AND FUNCTIONS

In the next example we must use laws of logarithms to get the equation in the proper form.

EXAMPLE 8

Determine the solutions to the following: (a) $\ln(x + 1) = 2 + \ln x$ and (b) $\ln x = 3 - \ln(x + 1)$.

■ SOLUTION
(a) First we want to get the given equation in the form ln (expression) equals a constant. We get

$$\ln(x + 1) - \ln x = 2.$$

By the second law of logarithms we get

$$\ln \frac{x + 1}{x} = 2.$$

Thus we have

$$\frac{x + 1}{x} = e^2.$$

Solving the preceding linear equation gives

$$x + 1 = e^2 x$$
$$x - e^2 x = -1$$
$$x(1 - e^2) = -1$$
$$x = \frac{-1}{1 - e^2} \quad (\approx 0.1565).$$

Since this number is in the domain, the solution is $-1/(1 - e^2)$ (≈ 0.1565).
(b) The given equation is equivalent to

$$\ln x + \ln(x + 1) = 3.$$

By the first law of logarithms this is

$$\ln(x(x + 1)) = 3$$
$$\ln(x^2 + x) = 3$$
$$x^2 + x = e^3$$
$$x^2 + x - e^3 = 0.$$

By the quadratic formula,

$$x = \frac{-1 \pm \sqrt{1 + 4e^3}}{2}.$$

Approximating, we get

$$x \approx 4.009 \quad \text{or} \quad x \approx -5.009.$$

1.5 LOGARITHMS

Since -5.009 is not in the domain, the solution is
$$\frac{-1 + \sqrt{1 + 4e^3}}{2} \quad (\approx 4.009).$$

EXERCISE

Determine the solutions to the following: (a) $\ln x = 3 + \ln(x-2)$ and (b) $\ln(x-2) = 5 - \ln x$.

■ ANSWER
(a) $-2e^3/(1-e^3)$ (≈ 2.105); (b) $1 + \sqrt{1 + e^5}$ (≈ 13.22)

PROBLEM SET 1.5

In Problems 1–6, convert each equation into an equivalent equation containing an exponent.

1. $\log_4 64 = 3$
2. $\log_2 \frac{1}{16} = -4$
3. $\log_{1/3} 9 = -2$
4. $\log_{1/2} \frac{1}{4} = 2$
5. $\log_4 2 = \frac{1}{2}$
6. $\log_8 4 = \frac{2}{3}$

In Problems 7–12, convert each equation into an equivalent equation containing a logarithm.

7. $10^{-1} = \frac{1}{10}$
8. $3^2 = 9$
9. $(\frac{1}{3})^3 = \frac{1}{27}$
10. $(\frac{1}{2})^{-2} = 4$
11. $16^{-1/2} = \frac{1}{4}$
12. $8^{-2/3} = \frac{1}{4}$

In Problems 13–22, find the number.

13. $\log 100$
14. $\log_2 32$
15. $\log_3 \frac{1}{3}$
16. $\log_{1/4} 64$
17. $\log_9 3$
18. $\log_{16} \frac{1}{8}$
19. $\ln e^2$
20. $\ln(1/e^3)$
21. $\ln \sqrt{e}$
22. $\ln \sqrt[3]{e^2}$

In Problems 23–28, approximate each to the nearest thousandth.

23. $\log 20$
24. $\log 0.5$
25. $\ln 0.5$
26. $\ln 10$
27. $\ln \sqrt{2}$
28. $\ln \sqrt[3]{15}$

In Problems 29–34, simplify.

29. $6^{2 \log_6 k}$
30. $5^{-\log_5 k}$
31. $\log 10^x$
32. $\log_9 \sqrt[k]{9}$
33. $3^{\log_9 x}$
34. $\log_8 4^x$

In Problems 35–38, write each expression as a sum, a difference, or a multiple of logarithms.

35. $\log \dfrac{xy}{\sqrt{z}}$
36. $\log \dfrac{x^2}{yz}$
37. $\ln \dfrac{\sqrt{xy}}{z^2}$
38. $\ln \sqrt{\dfrac{xy}{z}}$

In Problems 39–42, write each expression as a single logarithm.

39. $\log x - \log y + \frac{1}{2} \log z$
40. $2 \log x + \log y - \log z$
41. $-2 \ln x + \frac{1}{2} \ln y - \ln z$
42. $\ln x + 3 \ln y - \frac{1}{3} \ln z$

43. If $\log 2 = a$ and $\log 3 = b$, compute the following (in terms of a and/or b).
    (a) $\log \frac{2}{3}$
    (b) $\log 27$
    (c) $\log 36$
    (d) $\log \sqrt[3]{8}$
    (e) $\log(16/81)^7$

44. If $\ln 5 = p$ and $\ln 7 = q$, compute the following (in terms of p and/or q).
    (a) $\ln 35$
    (b) $\ln 625$
    (c) $\ln(5/49)$
    (d) $\ln \sqrt[3]{49}$
    (e) $\ln(125/7)^{-6}$

In Problems 45–60, find the solutions.

45. $6^x = 14$
46. $5^x = 18$
47. $8^{2x} = 73$
48. $3^{4x} = 12$
49. $5^{-x} = 2$
50. $8^{-2x} = 21$
51. $9^x = \frac{1}{3}$
52. $8^{2x} = 16$
53. $e^{-x} = 7$
54. $e^{-3x} = 11$
55. $e^{2x+3} = 15$
56. $e^{2-x} = \frac{1}{2}$
57. $7e^{5x} = 28$
58. $5e^{7x} = 15$
59. $2e^{2x-3} = 25$
60. $3e^{5-2x} = 20$

61. How long (to the nearest tenth of a year) will it take $500 to grow to $800 if interest is compounded quarterly at 10%?

62. How long (to the nearest tenth of a year) will it take $2000 to grow to $5000 if interest is compounded semiannually at 12%?

In Problems 63–76, find the solutions.

63. $\log 2x = -1$
64. $\log 3x = 2$
65. $\log x + \log x^2 = 3$
66. $\log x^3 - \log x = 2$
67. $\log(2x - 17) = 2 - \log x$
68. $\log(3 - 9x) = 1 + \log(x^2 - x)$
69. $\ln 3x = 2$
70. $\ln 2x = -1$
71. $6 - \ln x = 3 + \ln x$
72. $5 + 2 \ln x = -1 - \ln x$
73. $\ln x + \ln(x/4) = 3$
74. $\ln(x + 1) = 2 + \ln(2x - 3)$
75. $\ln(2x + 5) + \ln x = 2$
76. $\ln(2 - x) + \ln(1 - x) = 3$
77. The pH of a liquid is defined as pH $= -\log[H^+]$, where $[H^+]$ is the concentration of hydrogen ions in the solution. Determine the pH of the following:
    (a) sea water, $[H^+] = 10^{-8.2}$
    (b) milk of magnesia, $[H^+] = 10^{-10.5}$
    (c) vinegar, $[H^+] = 10^{-2.25}$
    (d) phosphoric acid, $[H^+] = 3 \cdot 10^{-2}$
    Find the hydrogen ion concentration for liquids with the following pH values:
    (e) pure water, pH $= 7$
    (f) hydrochloric acid, pH $= 3$
    (g) ammonia, pH $= 8.2$

1.6 EXPONENTIAL AND LOGARITHMIC FUNCTIONS

Let $b > 0$, with $b \neq 1$, and define a function f with domain R by

$$f(x) = b^x.$$

A function whose formula of definition may be written in this form is called the **exponential function with base b.** For example, if f is the exponential function with base 5, then

$$f(x) = 5^x, \quad f(2) = 25, \quad f(-1) = \tfrac{1}{5}, \quad \text{and} \quad f(\tfrac{1}{2}) = \sqrt{5}.$$

Note that the base of an exponential function cannot be 1. Because $1^x = 1$ for all x, the function defined by $f(x) = 1^x$ is simply a constant function. Since such a function differs significantly from $f(x) = b^x$, where $b \neq 1$, we *require* $b \neq 1$.

Note the difference between the exponential function $y = 2^x$ and the polynomial function $y = x^2$. With the exponential function the base is constant and the exponent varies. This is just the opposite of the polynomial, where the base varies and the exponent is constant. And as we shall see in Example 1, the graph of $y = 2^x$ looks nothing like the parabola $y = x^2$.

EXAMPLE 1

Sketch the graph of $y = 2^x$ (the exponential function with base 2).

■ SOLUTION
Using integral x-values between -3 and 3, we get the following table:

x	-3	-2	-1	0	1	2	3
y	$\tfrac{1}{8}$	$\tfrac{1}{4}$	$\tfrac{1}{2}$	1	2	4	8

1.6 EXPONENTIAL AND LOGARITHMIC FUNCTIONS

After plotting these points and connecting them with a curve that follows their general trend, we get the graph in Figure 1.49.

There are a couple of important facts to be noted about the exponential function just graphed. First, it passes through (0,1). Second, the x-axis is a horizontal asymptote. These two observations can be made about the graphs of all elementary exponential functions: that is, regardless of the base, the graph of an elementary exponential function passes through (0,1) and has the x-axis as a horizontal asymptote.

$y = 2^x$

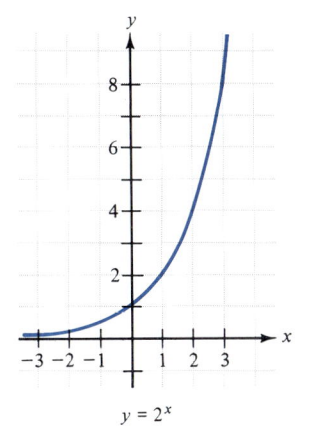

FIGURE 1.49

EXERCISE

Sketch the graph of $y = 3^x$.

■ ANSWER
See Figure 1.50.

Another frequently occurring base is e, the base for natural logarithms. The number e is approximately equal to 2.71828. When mathematicians say *the* exponential function, they are referring to the exponential function with base e.

To sketch the graph of

$$y = e^x$$

we select integral x-values between -2 and 2. Let's approximate the corresponding y-values to the nearest tenth by using our calculators. We get the following table:

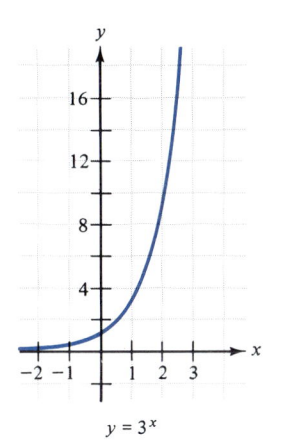

$y = 3^x$

FIGURE 1.50

x	-2	-1	0	1	2
y	0.1	0.4	1.0	2.7	7.4

After plotting these points, we get the graph shown in Figure 1.51.

EXAMPLE 2

Sketch the graph of $y = -2 + e^{x-1}$.

■ SOLUTION
The graph is a transformation of $f(x) = e^x$. Since

$$e^{x-1} = f(x - 1),$$

$y = e^x$

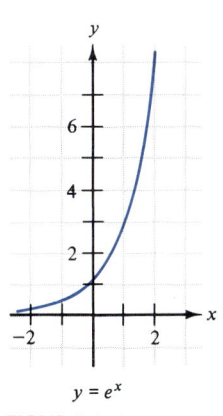

FIGURE 1.51

$y = e^{x-1}$ is the basic graph shifted right one unit. Hence
$$y = -2 + e^{x-1}$$
is the basic graph shifted right one unit and down two units, as shown in Figure 1.52.

Note that the line $y = -2$ is the horizontal asymptote. And if we need to be accurate about the y-intercept, we approximate $-2 + e^{-1}$ with our calculators, getting -1.6 to the nearest tenth. Approximating the x-intercept requires solving an exponential equation:
$$0 = -2 + e^{x-1}$$
$$e^{x-1} = 2$$
$$x - 1 = \ln 2$$
$$x = 1 + \ln 2 \approx 1.7.$$

$y = -2 + e^{x-1}$

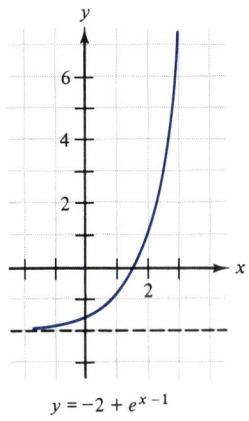

FIGURE 1.52

EXERCISE

Sketch the graph of $y = -2 + e^{x+2}$.

■ ANSWER
See Figure 1.53.

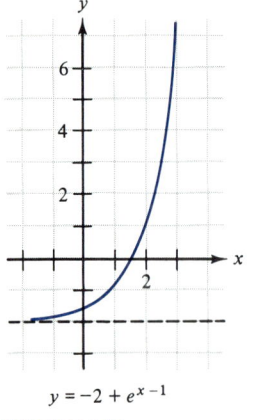

$y = -2 + e^{x+2}$

FIGURE 1.53

Let $b > 0$, with $b \neq 1$, and define a function f with domain $(0, \infty)$ by
$$f(x) = \log_b x.$$
A function whose formula of definition may be written in this form is called the **logarithmic function with base b**. For example, if f is the logarithmic function with base 5, then
$$f(x) = \log_5 x, \quad f(25) = 2, \quad f(\tfrac{1}{5}) = -1, \quad \text{and} \quad f(\sqrt{5}) = \tfrac{1}{2}.$$
Note that the logarithmic functions are defined for positive numbers only since we cannot take the logarithm of a negative number or zero.

EXAMPLE 3

Sketch the graph of $y = \log_2 x$ (the logarithmic function with base 2).

■ SOLUTION
We select x-values that are powers of 2 so that the y-values may be easily computed. We get the following table:

x	$\tfrac{1}{8}$	$\tfrac{1}{4}$	$\tfrac{1}{2}$	1	2	4	8
y	-3	-2	-1	0	1	2	3

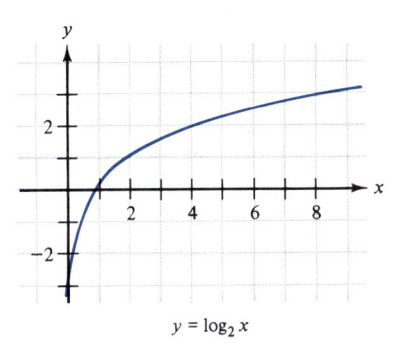

1.6 EXPONENTIAL AND LOGARITHMIC FUNCTIONS

Plotting these points and connecting them with a curve that follows their general trend, we get the graph in Figure 1.54.

FIGURE 1.54
$y = \log_2 x$

There are a couple of important facts to be noted about the logarithmic function just graphed. First, it passes through (1,0). Second, the y-axis is a vertical asymptote. These observations can be made about the graphs of all elementary logarithmic functions: that is, regardless of the base, the graph of an elementary logarithmic function passes through (1,0) and has the y-axis as a vertical asymptote.

In Example 3, we chose "convenient" values of x for the table. We selected values of x that could easily be expressed as powers of 2. What if we wanted our graph to be more accurate, however, and we wanted to plot the point whose x-coordinate is 6. How do we determine

$$\log_2 6?$$

Since our calculators don't have a logarithmic button for base 2, we use one of the following **change of base formulas:**

$$\log_b x = \frac{\log x}{\log b} \quad \text{or} \quad \log_b x = \frac{\ln x}{\ln b}.$$

Since our calculators are equipped with both common and natural logarithm buttons, it doesn't matter which we use. Estimating then, we have

$$\log_2 6 = \frac{\log 6}{\log 2} \approx 2.585.$$

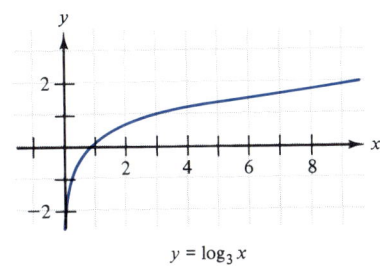

EXERCISE

Sketch the graph of $y = \log_3 x$.

■ ANSWER
See Figure 1.55.

FIGURE 1.55
$y = \log_3 x$

Let's now sketch the natural logarithmic function

$$y = \ln x,$$

the logarithmic function with base e. We select some values for x and approximate values for y to the nearest tenth. We get the following table:

x	0.5	1	2	4	6	8	10
y	-0.7	0	0.7	1.4	1.8	2.1	2.3

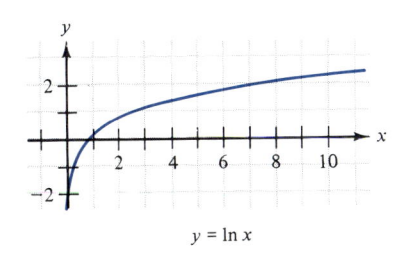

After plotting these points, we get the graph shown in Figure 1.56.

FIGURE 1.56
$y = \ln x$

GRAPHS AND FUNCTIONS

Note that for the natural logarithmic function, ln x is positive when $x > 1$, negative when $x < 1$, and zero when $x = 1$.

EXAMPLE 4

Sketch the graph of $y = -1 + \ln(x + 2)$.

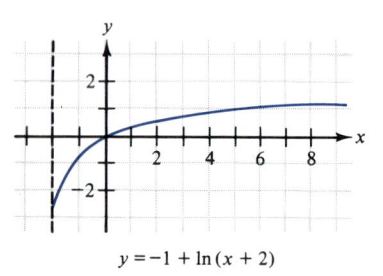

■ SOLUTION

The graph is a transformation of $y = \ln x$. It is this basic graph shifted to the left two units and down one unit, as shown in Figure 1.57.

FIGURE 1.57
$y = -1 + \ln(x + 2)$

Note that the line $x = -2$ is the vertical asymptote. And if we need to be accurate about the y-intercept, we approximate $-1 + \ln 2$ and get -0.3. Approximating the x-intercept requires solving a logarithmic equation:

$$0 = -1 + \ln(x + 2)$$
$$\ln(x + 2) = 1$$
$$x + 2 = e$$
$$x = e - 2 \approx 0.7.$$

EXERCISE

Sketch the graph of $y = -2 + \ln(x + 1)$.

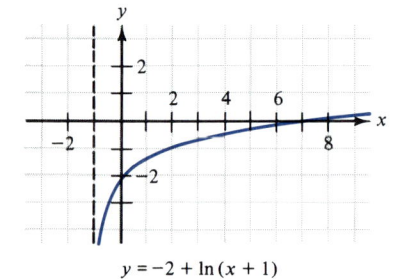

■ ANSWER

See Figure 1.58.

FIGURE 1.58
$y = -2 + \ln(x + 1)$

Before leaving this section, let's note the relationship between the exponential function with base e and the natural logarithm function. Given an equation in x and y, its **inverse** is the equation obtained by switching the variables. So $y = x^2$ is the inverse of $x = y^2$. Similarly,

$$y = e^x$$

is the inverse of

$$x = e^y. \qquad (1\text{-}13)$$

But Equation (1-13) is equivalent to

$$y = \ln x.$$

Hence the exponential function with base e is the inverse of the natural logarithm function. This is why $\boxed{\text{INV}}$ $\boxed{\ln x}$ is equivalent to $\boxed{e^x}$ on a calculator.

PROBLEM SET 1.6

In Problems 1–30, sketch the graph.

1. $y = 4^x$
2. $y = 5^x$
3. $y = (\frac{1}{2})^x$
4. $y = (\frac{1}{3})^x$
5. $y = 3^{1-x}$
6. $y = 3^{1+x}$
7. $y = -1/2^{-(x+2)}$
8. $y = -1/2^{-(2-x)}$
9. $y = e^{-x}$
10. $y = -e^{-x}$
11. $y = e^x - e$
12. $y = e^x - e^{-1}$
13. $y = -e^{x-1}$
14. $y = e^{x-0.5}$
15. $y = -3 + e^{x-2}$
16. $y = 4 - e^{1-x}$
17. $y = \log_4 x$
18. $y = \log_5 x$
19. $y = \log_{1/2} x$
20. $y = \log_{1/3} x$
21. $y = \log_2(x - 1)$
22. $y = \log_2(x + 1)$
23. $y = -1 + \ln x$
24. $y = 1 - \ln x$
25. $y = -\ln(-x)$
26. $y = \ln(-x)$
27. $y = \ln \dfrac{1}{x-1}$
28. $y = 2 \ln \sqrt{x - 2}$
29. $y = -1 + \ln(x + \frac{1}{2})$
30. $y = 1 - \ln(x - 1)$

In Problems 31–34, determine the x- and y-intercepts.

31. $y = e^{3x+1} - 5$
32. $y = e^{2x-1} - 8$
33. $y = \ln\left(\dfrac{x+4}{x+2}\right) - 3$
34. $y = \ln\left(\dfrac{2x+1}{x+3}\right) - 1$

In Problems 35–38, choose the equation that best describes each given graph.

35. (a) $y = \ln x$
    (b) $y = e^x - 1$
    (c) $y = (\ln x) - 1$
    (d) $y = \ln(x + 1)$
    (e) $y = \ln(x - 1)$

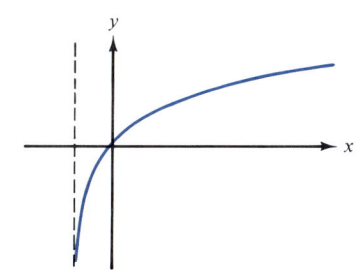

36. (a) $y = -2^x$
    (b) $y = -2^{-x}$
    (c) $y = -2 + \log_2 x$
    (d) $y = \log_2(x - 2)$
    (e) $y = 2^{-x}$

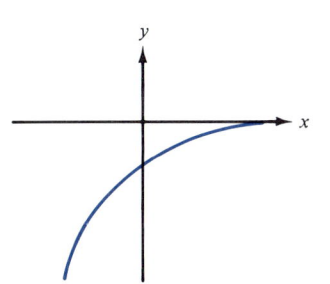

37. (a) $y = e^{x-2}$
    (b) $y = \dfrac{1}{e^x} - 2$
    (c) $y = -2 - \ln x$
    (d) $y = e^{-x-2}$
    (e) $y = 1/e^{x-2}$

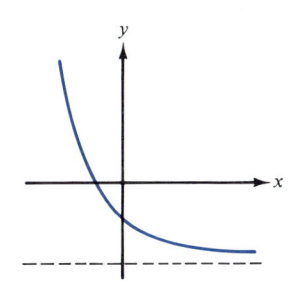

38. (a) $y = e^{-x}$
    (b) $y = \ln x$
    (c) $y = -e^x$
    (d) $y = 1 + \ln x$
    (e) $y = \ln \dfrac{1}{x}$

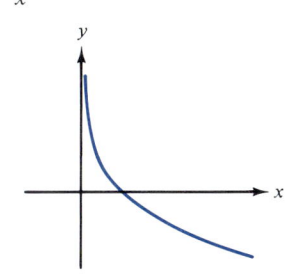

39. Prove the general change-of-base formula,
$$\log_b x = \dfrac{\log_a x}{\log_a b}.$$

1.7 OTHER FUNCTIONS

Some functions are "almost" polynomial, rational, exponential, or logarithmic. That is, their formulas are familiar, but the domain is different. For example, consider the function f defined by

$$f(x) = x^2, \quad x \neq 2.$$

The domain of this function is $R - \{2\}$. This function agrees with the polynomial function $y = x^2$ except that f is not defined at $x = 2$. Thus the graph of f is the graph of $y = x^2$ with the point (2,4) removed. See Figure 1.59. The nonsolid dot at (2,4) indicates that this point is *not* part of the graph.

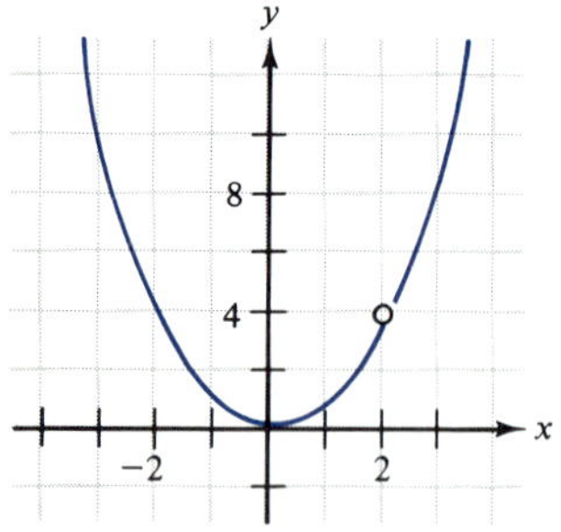

As another example consider the function g defined by

$$g(x) = \frac{1}{x}, \quad x > 0.$$

The domain of this function is $(0,\infty)$. This function agrees with the rational function $y = 1/x$ except that g is not defined on $(-\infty,0)$. Thus the graph of g is that part of the graph of $y = 1/x$ for which $x > 0$, that is, that part to the right of the y-axis. See Figure 1.60.

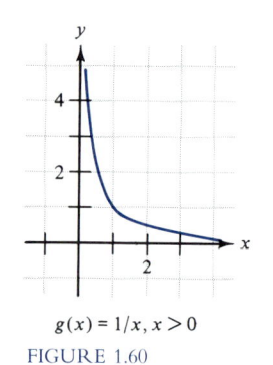

$f(x) = x^2, x \neq 2$
FIGURE 1.59

$g(x) = 1/x, x > 0$
FIGURE 1.60

EXERCISE

Graph the following functions: (a) $f(x) = x^3$, $x \neq 1$; and (b) $g(x) = 1/x^2$, $x < 0$.

■ ANSWER
See Figure 1.61.

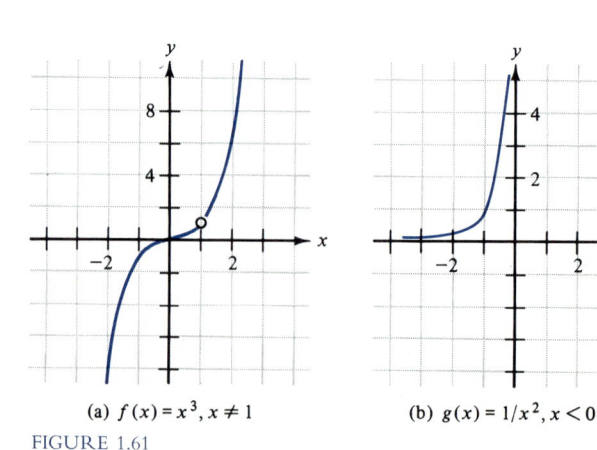

(a) $f(x) = x^3, x \neq 1$ (b) $g(x) = 1/x^2, x < 0$
FIGURE 1.61

1.7 OTHER FUNCTIONS

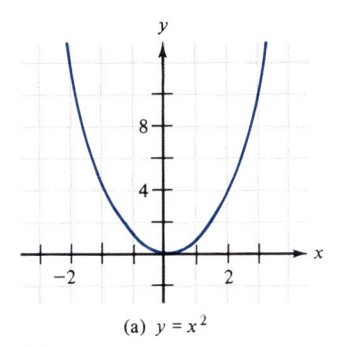

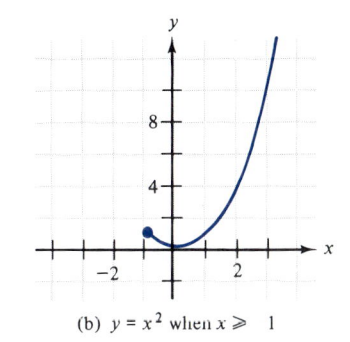

(a) $y = x^2$
(b) $y = x^2$ when $x \geq 1$

FIGURE 1.62

For some functions it is necessary to split the formula of definition. For example, we may encounter a function f defined by

$$f(x) = \begin{cases} x^2 & \text{when } x \geq -1 \\ x + 3 & \text{when } x < -1. \end{cases}$$

The domain of this function is R. To find the value of the function at any number in $[-1, \infty)$, we use the formula $f(x) = x^2$. To find the value of the function at any number in $(-\infty, -1)$, we use the formula $f(x) = x + 3$. Thus we have

$$f(-3) = 0, \quad f(2) = 4, \quad f(-1) = 1, \quad \text{and} \quad f(-2) = 1.$$

We may graph f by first graphing $y = x^2$, as in Figure 1.62(a). The graph of f coincides with this parabola *when $x \geq -1$*. Hence the graph of f at and to the right of the point $(-1, 1)$ (when $x \geq -1$) is that of Figure 1.62(b).

Next we graph $y = x + 3$, seen in Figure 1.63(a). The graph of f coincides with this line *when $x < -1$*. Thus the graph of f to the left of the point $(-1, 2)$ (when $x < -1$) is shown in Figure 1.63(b).

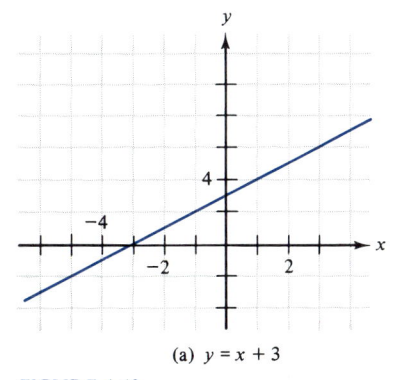

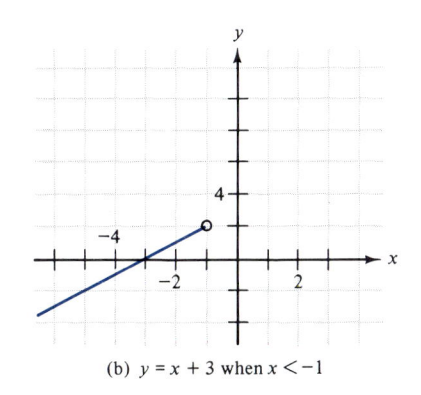

(a) $y = x + 3$
(b) $y = x + 3$ when $x < -1$

FIGURE 1.63

GRAPHS AND FUNCTIONS

Putting together the two pieces, in Figures 1.62(b) and 1.63(b), we get the graph of f. See Figure 1.64.

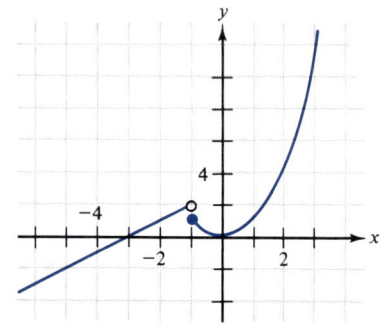

FIGURE 1.64

EXAMPLE 1

Graph f, where

$$f(x) = \begin{cases} e^x & \text{when } x > 0 \\ x^3 & \text{when } x < 0. \end{cases}$$

■ SOLUTION

The graph of $y = e^x$, when $x > 0$, is that part of the exponential function $y = e^x$ to the right of the y-axis. See Figure 1.65. To this we add that part of the polynomial function $y = x^3$ to the left of the point $(0,0)$ (when $x < 0$). See Figure 1.66.

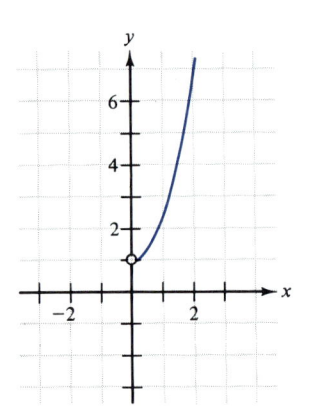

FIGURE 1.65

EXERCISE

Graph the following functions:

(a) $f(x) = \begin{cases} x^2 & \text{when } x \geq -2 \\ x + 4 & \text{when } x < -2. \end{cases}$ (b) $f(x) = \begin{cases} -e^x & \text{when } x > 0 \\ x^2 & \text{when } x < 0. \end{cases}$

■ ANSWER

See Figure 1.67.

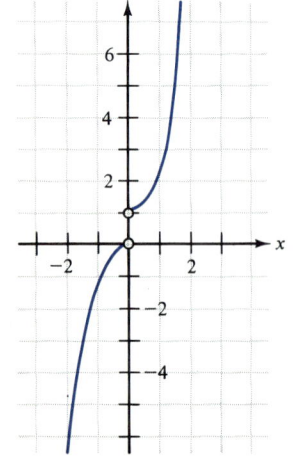

FIGURE 1.66

(a)

(b)

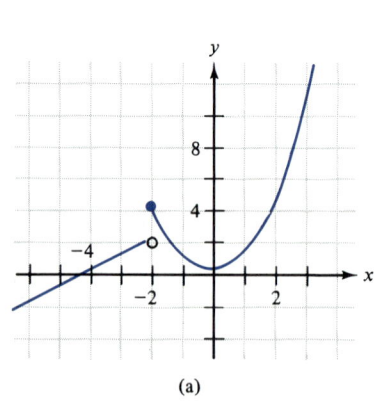

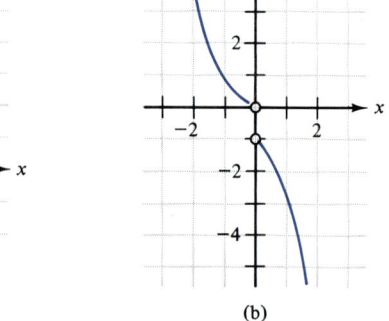

FIGURE 1.67

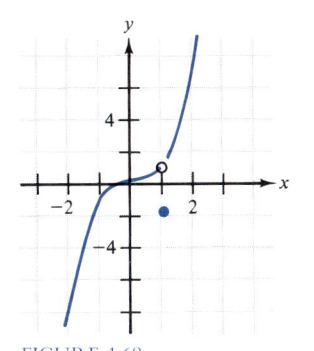

1.7 OTHER FUNCTIONS 61

FIGURE 1.68

EXAMPLE 2
Graph f, where
$$f(x) = \begin{cases} x^3 & \text{when } x \neq 1 \\ -2 & \text{when } x = 1. \end{cases}$$

■ SOLUTION
The graph of f coincides with the graph of $y = x^3$ except when $x = 1$. Hence the graph looks like $y = x^3$ with one point moved. See Figure 1.68.

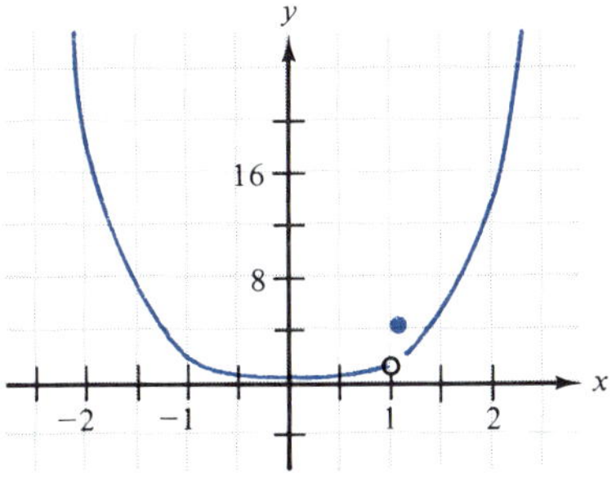

FIGURE 1.69

EXERCISE
Graph f, where
$$f(x) = \begin{cases} x^4 & \text{when } x \neq 1 \\ 4 & \text{when } x = 1. \end{cases}$$

■ ANSWER
See Figure 1.69.

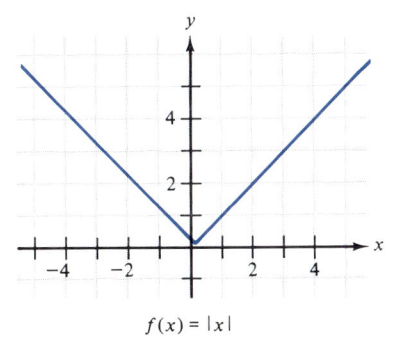

$f(x) = |x|$
FIGURE 1.70

Before leaving this chapter, let's examine two special functions that may be written with a split formula of definition. The first, the **absolute value function,** defined by $f(x) = |x|$, may be written

$$f(x) = |x| = \begin{cases} x & \text{when } x \geq 0 \\ -x & \text{when } x < 0. \end{cases}$$

Graphing the line $y = x$ for $x \geq 0$, and adding the graph of $y = -x$ for $x < 0$, we get the graph in Figure 1.70.

The second function uses the symbol $[x]$, which denotes the largest integer less than or equal to x. For example, $[2.5] = 2$, $[-\frac{3}{2}] = -2$, $[5] = 5$, $[\sqrt{2}] = 1$, and so on. The function defined by $f(x) = [x]$ is called the **greatest integer function.** Its formula of definition may be written

$$f(x) = [x] = \begin{cases} \vdots \\ -2 & \text{when } -2 \leq x < -1 \\ -1 & \text{when } -1 \leq x < 0 \\ 0 & \text{when } 0 \leq x < 1 \\ 1 & \text{when } 1 \leq x < 2 \\ 2 & \text{when } 2 \leq x < 3 \\ \vdots \end{cases}$$

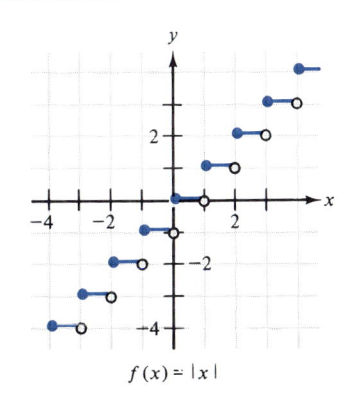

$f(x) = [x]$
FIGURE 1.71

Its graph is shown in Figure 1.71.

PROBLEM SET 1.7

In Problems 1–44, graph the function.

1. $f(x) = (x - 1)^2$, $x \neq -1$
2. $f(x) = 1 - x^3$, $x \neq -1$
3. $f(x) = e^{\ln x^2}$
4. $f(x) = e^{\ln x^4 - \ln x^3}$
5. $f(x) = \dfrac{-1}{x + 2}$, $x < -2$
6. $f(x) = \dfrac{1}{(x-1)^2} - 1$, $x > 1$
7. $f(x) = 2x + 1$, $x > -3$ and $x \neq 2$
8. $f(x) = -x - 2$, $x < 2$ and $x \neq -3$
9. $y = 2^x$, $x \geq -2$ and $x \neq 1$
10. $y = 2^{-x}$, $x \leq 2$ and $x \neq -1$
11. $f(x) = (1 - x)^3$, $-1 \leq x \leq 3$, $x \neq -\frac{1}{2}$, and $x \neq 2$
12. $f(x) = 4 - x^2$, $-3 \leq x \leq 3$, $x \neq 1$, and $x \neq -1$
13. $f(x) = \begin{cases} x + 1 & \text{when } x \geq 0 \\ -x & \text{when } x < 0 \end{cases}$
14. $f(x) = \begin{cases} 2x & \text{when } x > 1 \\ x - 1 & \text{when } x \leq 1 \end{cases}$
15. $f(x) = \begin{cases} x^2 & \text{when } x < 1 \\ 1 & \text{when } x \geq 1 \end{cases}$
16. $f(x) = \begin{cases} 1 - x^2 & \text{when } x \geq -1 \\ 0 & \text{when } x < -1 \end{cases}$
17. $f(x) = \begin{cases} (x - 1)^3 & \text{when } x \geq 0 \\ x^2 - 4 & \text{when } x < 0 \end{cases}$
18. $f(x) = \begin{cases} -(x - 2)^2 & \text{when } x \geq 2 \\ 3 - x^3 & \text{when } x < 2 \end{cases}$
19. $f(x) = \begin{cases} 1/(x + 1) & \text{when } x > -1 \\ -(x + 1)^3 & \text{when } x < -1 \end{cases}$
20. $f(x) = \begin{cases} (-1/x^2) + 1 & \text{when } x < 0 \\ (-x)^2 + 1 & \text{when } x \geq 0 \end{cases}$
21. $f(x) = \begin{cases} e^{x+1} & \text{when } x \leq 0 \\ \ln(x + 1) - 1 & \text{when } x > 0 \end{cases}$
22. $f(x) = \begin{cases} -\ln(x - 1) & \text{when } x \geq 2 \\ e^{-x+2} + 1 & \text{when } x < 2 \end{cases}$
23. $f(x) = \begin{cases} 2 & \text{when } x < -1 \\ (-x)^3 & \text{when } -1 \leq x \leq 1 \\ -2 & \text{when } x > 1 \end{cases}$
24. $f(x) = \begin{cases} 2x + 6 & \text{when } x \leq -2 \\ x^2 - 2 & \text{when } -2 < x < 2 \\ -2x + 6 & \text{when } x \geq 2 \end{cases}$
25. $f(x) = \begin{cases} (x + 1)^2 & \text{when } x \neq 2 \\ 1 & \text{when } x = 2 \end{cases}$
26. $f(x) = \begin{cases} x^3 + 2 & \text{when } x \neq -1 \\ -2 & \text{when } x = -1 \end{cases}$
27. $f(x) = \begin{cases} 1 + x^2 & \text{when } x \neq -2, -1, 1, 2 \\ -1 & \text{when } x = -2, -1, 1, 2 \end{cases}$
28. $f(x) = \begin{cases} 4 - x^2 & \text{when } x \neq -3, -1, 1, 3 \\ 2 & \text{when } x = -3, -1, 1, 3 \end{cases}$
29. $f(x) = \begin{cases} -x + 2 & \text{when } x \leq 2, \text{ and } x \neq -3, -1, 1 \\ x + 4 & \text{when } x = -3, -1, 1 \end{cases}$
30. $f(x) = \begin{cases} |x| & \text{when } x > -4, \text{ and } \\ & x \neq -3, -2, -1, 1, 2, 3 \\ -|x| & \text{when } x = -3, -2, 2, 3 \end{cases}$
31. $f(x) = |x + 2|$
32. $f(x) = |x - 3|$
33. $f(x) = |x - 1| + 1$
34. $f(x) = |x + 3| - 2$
35. $f(x) = |-e^x|$
36. $f(x) = |-e^{-x}|$
37. $f(x) = \dfrac{|x|}{x}(x - 3)$
38. $f(x) = \dfrac{|x + 1|}{x + 1}(x + 2)$
39. $f(x) = -[x]$
40. $f(x) = [x] + 2$
41. $f(x) = [x + 1]$
42. $f(x) = [x - 2]$
43. $f(x) = [x] - x$
44. $f(x) = [x] + x$
45. Suppose that in a population of microscopic organisms each organism divides to form two organisms every 5 seconds, and at time $t = 0$, two organisms are present. Sketch a graph showing the number, N, of organisms present when t ranges from 0 to 20 seconds.

CHAPTER 1 REVIEW

1. Determine whether each of the following is true or false.
   (a) If $x < 0$, then the point $(-x, x^2)$ is in the second quadrant.
   (b) If $f(x) = x + (1/x)$, then $f(f(1)) = f(\frac{1}{2})$.
   (c) The slope of the line passing through the points $(-4, 3)$ and $(2, -5)$ is $-\frac{4}{3}$.
   (d) The y-intercept of the line $2y = x + 10$ is 10.

(e) $|x| = -|-x|$
(f) $f(x) = x^3 - 4x^2 + x^{1/2} + 6$ is an example of a polynomial function.
(g) The domain of the function $f(x) = \sqrt{-x}$ is $(-\infty, 0]$.
(h) The equation of the vertical line passing through $(\pi, -\pi)$ is $y = -\pi$.
(i) The vertex of the parabola $y = 4x^2 + 8x$ is $(-1, -4)$.
(j) The x-intercept of $y = e^x - 3$ is $\ln 3$.
(k) The range of the function graphed below is $[-3, 3]$.

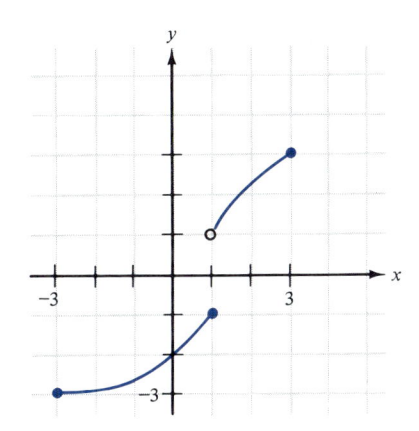

(l) $\ln e^8 = e^{\ln 8}$
(m) $5^{\log_2 5 16} = 4$
(n) $e^{5 + \ln x} = e^5 + x$
(o) $2 \ln 2 - \ln 6^2 + \ln 9 = 0$
(p) The graph below shows that y is a function of x.

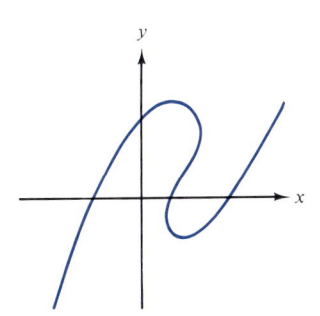

(q) If $f(x) = x + |x + 1|$, then $2 \cdot f(0) - 3 = f(-1)$.
(r) The equation of the line passing through the origin with slope 0 is $y = 0$.
(s) If $f(x) = x^2$, then $f(3 + 4) = f(3) + f(4)$.

(t) Line $\mathscr{L}$ below has negative slope.

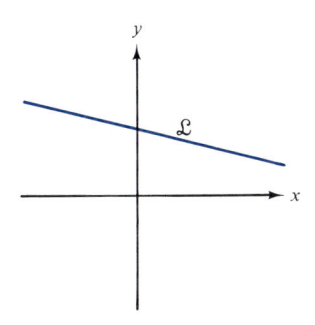

(u) If f is the function-defined below, then the range of f is $\{3, 7\}$ and the domain of f is $\{1, 2, 4\}$.

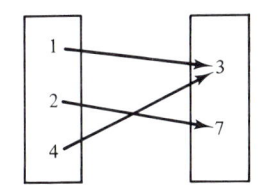

(v) The range of the function $f(x) = (x - 7)^2 - 5$ is $[7, \infty)$.
(w) $[|-\frac{1}{2}|] - |[-\frac{1}{2}]| = -1$
(x) $f(x) = 1/(x - 3)(x^2 - 5)$ is an example of a rational function.
(y) If $g(x) = \begin{cases} \sqrt{130 - x^2} & \text{when } 0 \leq x \leq \sqrt{130} \\ |12 - 2x| & \text{when } x > \sqrt{130} \end{cases}$, then $g(\frac{23}{2}) - g(3) = 0$.
(z) The point $((151)^{-1/2} - (1984)^{-1/3}, \pi^{2.7} - (2.7)^\pi)$ is in quadrant I.
(aa) The slope of a linear demand equation is negative.
(bb) If line l passes through the origin and has slope m, then the point $(1, m)$ lies on l.
(cc) If $f(x) = (x^2 - 4)/(x + 2)$ and $g(x) = x - 2$, then $f(x) = g(x)$ for all x.
(dd) If $f(x) = -3x$, then $f(a + h) = -3 \cdot f(a + h)$.
(ee) If $f(x) = 3^x$, then $f(6 + 9) = f(6) \cdot f(9)$.
(ff) The domain of the function $f(x) = \sqrt{\ln x}$ is the set of all positive numbers.
(gg) If $f(x) = \ln x$, then $f(2 + 5) = f(2) + f(5)$.
(hh) The graph of $y = \log(x - 1)$ has the line $x = 1$ as a vertical asymptote.
(ii) $|e^{-x}| = e^{-x}$ for all x.
(jj) If $f(x) = 2^{-x}$, then the range of f is the set of all nonnegative numbers.

GRAPHS AND FUNCTIONS

In Problems 2–6, determine the equation (in slope-intercept form if possible) of each line described.

2. Slope $\frac{2}{3}$ and y-intercept $-\ln 2$
3. Slope -3 and x-intercept 7
4. x-intercept $\sqrt{2} - 1$ and y-intercept $-\sqrt{2}$
5. Passing through $(10, -3)$ with slope $-\frac{1}{5}$
6. Passing through $(2, -5)$ and $(-4, 4)$

7. Let $f(x) = (x^2 + 1)/x$ and find **(a)** $f(-3)$, **(b)** $f(1/a^2)$, **(c)** $f(3 + h)$, **(d)** $1/f(1/x)$, **(e)** $(f(x) - f(4))/(x - 4)$, and **(f)** $f(f(1))$.

8. Let $f(x) = 1/\sqrt{x}$ and find **(a)** $f(1/4e^2)$, **(b)** $f(\sqrt{5})$, **(c)** $\sqrt{f(256)}$, **(d)** $f(9 + 16)$, **(e)** $f(13) \cdot f(1/468)$, and **(f)** $f(f(\pi^4))$.

In Problems 9–16, determine the domain of each function f.

9. $f(x) = \pi^3$
10. $f(x) = \sqrt{|5 - x|}$
11. $f(x) = \dfrac{3x + 6}{x^2 + x - 12}$
12. $f(x) = \dfrac{x + 2}{x^2 - 1}$
13. $f(x) = \sqrt{5 - x}$
14. $f(x) = \dfrac{3}{(x + 1)\sqrt{x + 3}}$
15. $f(x) = \dfrac{1}{e^x} - \sqrt{-\ln 0.5}$
16. $f(x) = \sqrt{e - 1} + \ln(x + e)$

In Problems 17–24, graph each function and then use the graph to determine the range.

17. $y = \dfrac{1}{1 - \sqrt{2}}$
18. $y = x^3 - 3$
19. $y = |x| + 1$
20. $y = \dfrac{1}{x^2} - 3$
21. $y = 5 - (x - 1)^2$
22. $y = 2x^2 - 8x - 3$
23. $y = e^x - 2$
24. $y = 2 + \ln x$

In Problems 25–28, use the graph of each function to determine the range.

25.

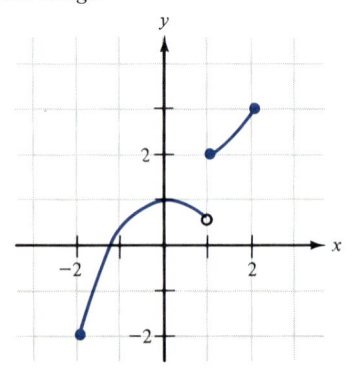

26.

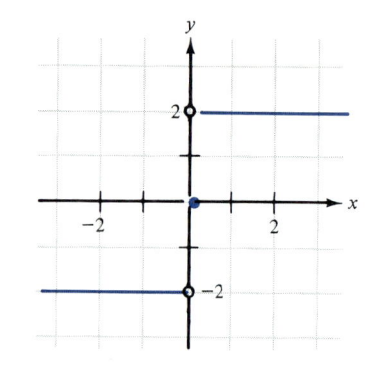

27.

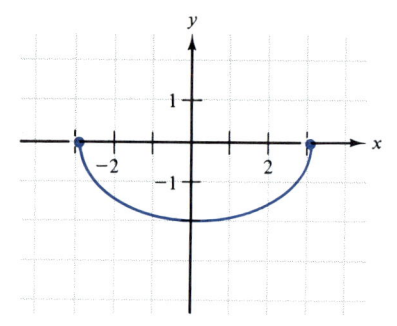

28.

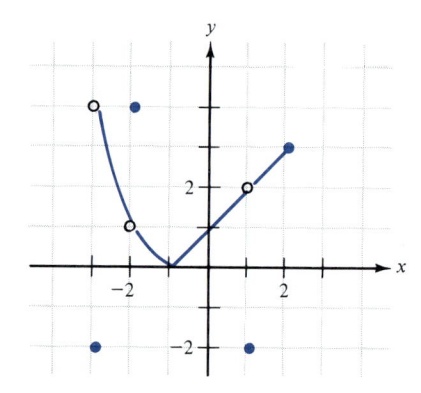

In Problems 29–46, graph each function.

29. $f(x) = x^2 + 2x - 15$
30. $f(x) = (x - 3)^3 + 1$
31. $f(x) = -(x + 3)^2 - 2$
32. $f(x) = \dfrac{-1}{(x + 1)} - 2$
33. $f(x) = \dfrac{3x^2 + 1}{x^2}$
34. $y = 2^{|x|} - 1$
35. $y = e^{x - e^{-1}}$
36. $y = 3 \ln \sqrt[3]{x + 1}$
37. $y = \ln e^{x^3}$
38. $f(x) = |x - 2| - 3$
39. $f(x) = \dfrac{x}{|x|}$
40. $f(x) = [|x|]$
41. $f(x) = |x + 1|, \ x \neq -2$
42. $f(x) = \dfrac{-1}{x - \pi}, \ x > \pi$

43. $f(x) = \begin{cases} -1/x & \text{when } x > 0 \text{ and } x \neq \frac{1}{2}, 1, 2, 3, 4 \\ 1/x & \text{when } x = \frac{1}{2}, 1, 2, 3, 4 \end{cases}$

44. $f(x) = \begin{cases} x & \text{when } 0 \leq x \leq 1 \\ 2 - x & \text{when } 1 < x \leq 2 \end{cases}$

45. $f(x) = \begin{cases} x & \text{when } x \neq 1, 2, 4 \\ -1 & \text{when } x = 1, 2, 4 \end{cases}$

46. $f(x) = \begin{cases} -x & \text{when } -2 \leq x \leq 0 \\ 1 - (x-1)^2 & \text{when } 0 < x \leq 2 \\ (1/x) + 1 & \text{when } 2 < x \leq 5 \end{cases}$

47. Let f be the function with the following graph:

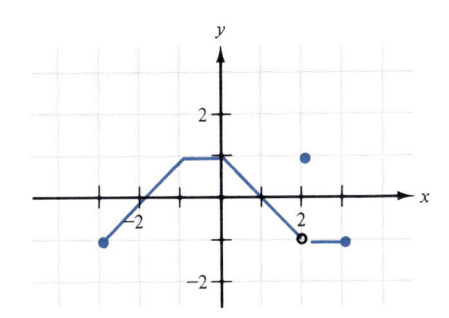

(a) What is the domain of f?
(b) What is the range of f?
(c) $f(-1) = ?$
(d) $f(0 + 3) = ?$
(e) $f(f(2)) = ?$
(f) If $f(x) = 0$, then $x = ?$
Graph the following:
(g) $y = -f(x)$
(h) $y = f(x) + 1$
(i) $y = f(x - 2)$
(j) $y = |f(x)|$
(k) $y = f(|x|)$
(l) $y = 2 - f(x + 3)$

48. Let $f(x) = \{x\}$, where $\{x\}$ denotes the distance from x to the nearest integer. For example, $f(3) = 0$, $f(1.5) = 0.5$, $f(-2.3) = 0.3$, $f(10.9) = 0.1$, and so on. Sketch the graph of $y = f(x)$.

49. Match each graph with the most appropriate equation.
(A) $y = 1 - (x + 1)^3$
(B) $y = \ln e^x$
(C) $y = -x^2 + 2x$
(D) $y = \dfrac{x^2}{x - 2}$
(E) $y = 1 - e^x$
(F) $x + e = 0$
(G) $y = x^4 + 2$
(H) $y = \begin{cases} -1/x & \text{when } x < 0 \\ 2 & \text{when } x > 0 \end{cases}$
(I) $y = \begin{cases} x - 1 & \text{when } x \geq 1 \\ -x + 1 & \text{when } x < 1 \end{cases}$
(J) $y = -x^2 + 1$
(K) $y = (x + 2)^{-1}$
(L) $y = -3$
(M) $x + 2y + 2 = 0$
(N) $y = -(x - 1)^3$
(O) $y = \begin{cases} -1/x^2 & \text{when } x < 0 \\ \frac{3}{2} & \text{when } x > 0 \end{cases}$
(P) $y = (x + 2)^2$
(Q) $y = |x + 1|$
(R) $y = e^{\ln x}$
(S) $y = 1 + \log_{1/2} x$
(T) $y = x - 1$

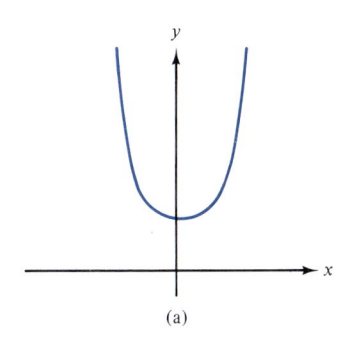

(a)

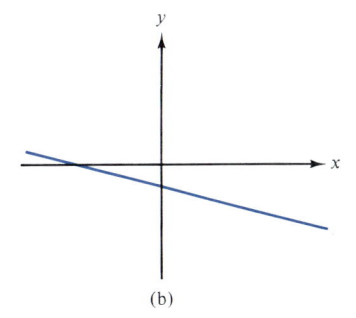

(b)

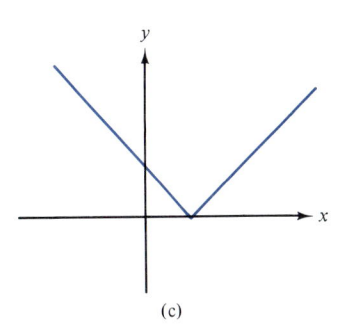

(c)

(d)

(h)

(e)

(i)

(f)

(j)

(g)

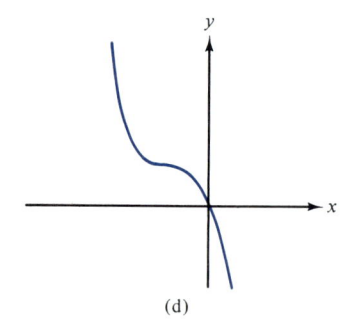

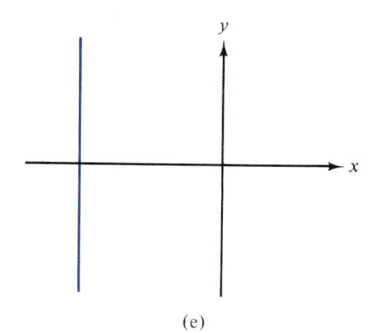

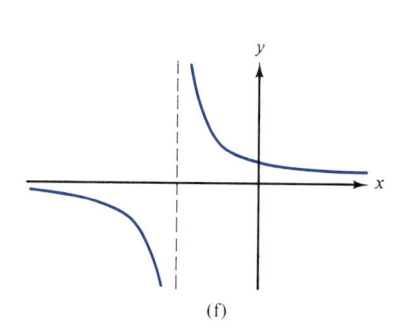

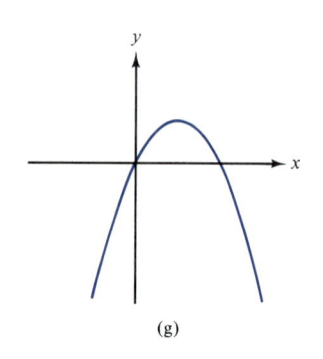

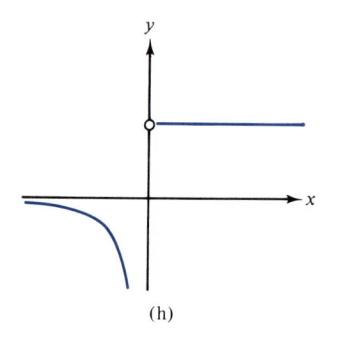

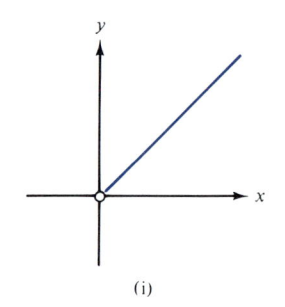

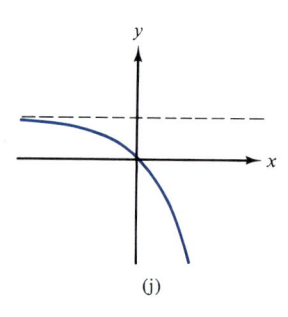

50. Convert the equation $16^{3/4} = 8$ into an equivalent logarithmic equation.

51. Convert the equation $\log_8 \frac{1}{32} = -\frac{5}{3}$ into an equivalent exponential equation.

52. Write $\log(x^2 \sqrt{y}/z^3)$ in terms of log x, log y and log z.

53. Write $\ln x - \frac{1}{3} \ln y + 2 \ln z$ as a single logarithm.

In Problems 54–67, find the solutions.

54. $5^x = 20$
55. $5^{-x^2} = \frac{1}{20}$
56. $e^{2x-1} = 15$
57. $e^{-x} = 10$
58. $e^{x^2} = 5$
59. $5e^{x-1} = 28$
60. $\log 5x = 2$
61. $\log x = 1 + \log x^3$

62. $\log(x + 21) = 2 - \log x$ **63.** $\ln 5x = -1$
64. $\ln x - \ln(2/x) = -2$ **65.** $\ln 2x - \ln x^2 = 5$
66. $\ln(-x) + \ln(-x/4) = 2$ **67.** $2 \ln x = 2 + \ln(x - 1)$

68. Income is related to education and experience. The average annual income of those people with zero years of education and experience is $5000. Studies have shown that an increase of one year of education or experience corresponds to a $1200 increase in annual income.
  (a) Determine an equation that expresses the correspondence between the annual income, I, and the number of years of education or experience, x.
  (b) Determine the average annual income that would correspond to a total of 17 years of education and experience.
  (c) How many years of education or experience would correspond to an average annual income of $42,200?

69. Life insurance counselors advise that family breadwinners should have life insurance and other death benefits totaling at least six times their annual salaries.
  (a) Find an equation that expresses the relationship between minimum life insurance, I, and annual salary, x.
  (b) Determine the minimum life insurance that a breadwinner should have if annual salary is $37,000.

70. The relationship between the Fahrenheit measurement, F, and the Celsius measurement, C, of temperature is linear. Water freezes at 32°F and 0°C and boils at 212°F and 100°C.
  (a) Express a relationship between the temperature in degrees Fahrenheit and the temperature in degrees Celsius.
  (b) Complete the following table.

°F	°C
?	10
−4	?
?	32
98.6	?

71. It costs $6.50 to transport 1 pound of merchandise 100 miles and $38.75 to transport 1 pound 850 miles. Assuming that the relationship between the cost of transportation and milage is linear, determine the cost to transport 1 pound of merchandise 550 miles.

72. On an electric range the temperature of a burner is related to the wattage of electricity supplied. If the rheostat is at setting 1, then 200 watts are supplied and the resulting temperature is 125°F. If the rheostat is at setting 5, then 1000 watts are supplied and the resulting temperature is 625°F. Assuming that the relation between wattage and temperature is linear, what wattage is required to achieve a temperature of 690°F?

73. If in Problem 72 the settings on the rheostat dial are linearly related to the supplied wattage, what rheostat setting is required to achieve a burner temperature of 437.5°F?

74. Using Problems 72 and 73, write an equation that relates the rheostat setting S with the burner temperature T and involves no other variables.

75. Water is leaking at a constant rate from a conical tank 10 feet high and 4 feet in radius at the top. Let V represent the volume of the water, and let r represent the radius of the surface of the water. Write an equation involving V and r only.

76. At noon, car A is 100 miles due west of Lexington and is headed toward Lexington at 60 mph and car B is 40 miles due north of Lexington and is headed away from Lexington at 50 mph. Let d represent the distance (in miles) between cars, and let t represent the elapsed time (in hours) since noon. Write an equation involving d and t only.

77. A tire distributor determines that when the price for a radial tire is $65, an average of 12,000 tires are marketed, and when the price is $56, an average of 18,000 are marketed. Determine the demand equation, assuming it is linear, and determine the price required to market 21,000 tires.

78. When the price is $1600, a manufacturer makes 2800 personal computers available for market. If the price increases $350, there are 1750 more available. Determine the supply equation, assuming it is linear, and determine the price required to supply 6700.

79. A farmer wishes to fence a rectangular field bordering a straight stream with 1000 yards of fencing material. The farmer will not fence the side bordering the stream. Write the area of the field as a function of the length of the side opposite the stream.

80. A printed page has 3-inch margins at the top and bottom and 2-inch margins on the sides. The area of the printed portion is 150 square inches. Write the area of the entire page as a function of the width of the paper.

81. A rectangular garden of area 75 square feet is to be surrounded on three sides by a brick wall costing $10 per foot and on one side by a fence costing $5 per foot. Write the total cost of the wall and fence as a function of the length of the fence.

82. A right triangular plot of ground has sides whose lengths are 300 and 400 meters. A rectangular building whose base is x meters wide and y meters long is to be built on the plot indicated in the following figure. Write the area of the base of the building as a function of x.

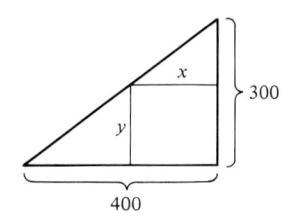

CHAPTER 2

LIMITS AND TANGENT LINES

CHAPTER OUTLINE
2.1 Limits
2.2 Continuity
2.3 Tangent Lines
2.4 Slopes of Tangent Lines

The foundation of calculus is the concept of an instantaneous rate of change. This idea is developed in this chapter against the background of graphs of functions. It takes form in the topics of tangent lines and the computations of their slopes, the subjects of the last two sections. To understand these topics we need to consider the idea of a limit and the important property of continuity.

2.1 LIMITS

In this section we study a concept that is fundamental to the ideas of calculus. We begin by considering

$$g(x) = \begin{cases} x^2 & \text{when } x \neq 2 \\ 3 & \text{when } x = 2 \end{cases}$$

and asking the question: What can be said about the values of $g(x)$ as x assumes values closer and closer to, but not equal to, 2? Refer to the following table.

Approach from Negative Side		Approach from Positive Side	
x	$g(x)$	x	$g(x)$
1	1	3	9
1.5	2.25	2.5	6.25
1.9	3.61	2.1	4.41
1.99	3.9601	2.01	4.0401
1.999	3.996001	2.001	4.004001

It appears that as x approaches 2, $g(x)$ gets closer and closer to 4. This is also apparent from the graph of g. See Figure 2.1. When x is near 2, $g(x)$ is near 4. In fact, we may get $g(x)$ as close to 4 as we want by getting x close enough to 2. This relationship is expressed through the following definition: Let f be a function defined at each point of some open interval containing a, except possibly a itself. Then we say that the **limit** of $f(x)$ as x approaches a is L, where L is a real number, and write

$$\lim_{x \to a} f(x) = L,$$

provided that $f(x)$ is arbitrarily close to L for all x sufficiently close to, but not equal to, a. That is, $f(x)$ is as near to L as we wish whenever x is near, but not equal to, a. Hence, returning to the function g, we write

$$\lim_{x \to 2} g(x) = 4.$$

The value of the function at the number being approached by x, called the **limit point**, does not determine the limit. The value may, or may not, equal the limit. We are concerned with what happens to $g(x)$ as x approaches, but does not equal, 2. In fact, the function does not even have to be defined at the limit point! Consider the function defined by

$$h(x) = x^2, \quad x \neq 2.$$

What is

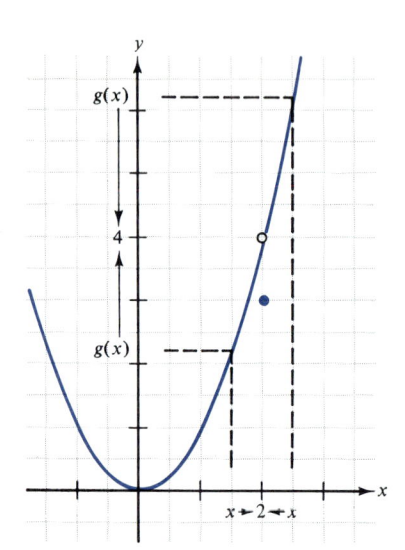

$$\lim_{x \to 2} h(x)?$$

FIGURE 2.1

2.1 LIMITS   **71**

The function h is identical to g except when $x = 2$. But since the value of the function at $x = 2$ does not determine the limit, the table for g at the beginning of the section can also serve for h. And with respect to the graph shown in Figure 2.2, the same thing is happening. As x gets closer and closer (but not equal) to 2, $h(x)$ gets closer and closer to 4. So

$$\lim_{x \to 2} h(x) = 4.$$

Finally, consider $f(x) = x^2$. What is

$$\lim_{x \to 2} f(x)?$$

Referring to the graph of f in Figure 2.3, we see that as x gets closer and closer to 2, $f(x)$ gets closer and closer to 4. Hence we write

$$\lim_{x \to 2} f(x) = 4 \quad \text{or} \quad \lim_{x \to 2} x^2 = 4.$$

When $x = 2$, it so happens that $f(x) = 4$. But, as we have already noted, this has nothing to do with *determining* the limit. We are concerned with what happens to $f(x)$ as x approaches, *but does not equal*, 2.

The limit doesn't always exist. Consider the function defined by

$$f(x) = \begin{cases} x^2 & \text{when } x \geq 0 \\ -x + 1 & \text{when } x < 0. \end{cases}$$

Let's try to determine $\lim_{x \to 0} f(x)$ by examining the graph shown in Figure 2.4.

From the graph we see that as x approaches 0 from the positive side, $f(x)$ approaches 0. But as x approaches 0 from the negative side, $f(x)$ approaches 1. See Figure 2.5. We therefore conclude that there is no limit. This is because the limit, if it exists, must be a *single* real number. The function must approach this single real number as x approaches a from both the positive and negative sides. Hence, for this function, we say

$$\lim_{x \to 0} f(x) \text{ does not exist.}$$

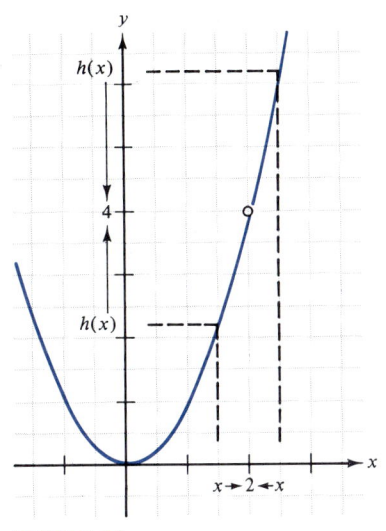

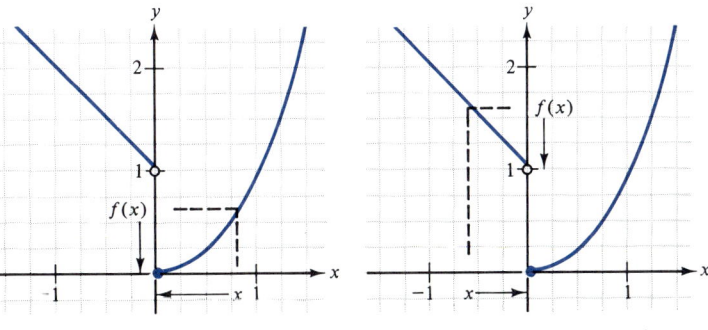

FIGURE 2.2

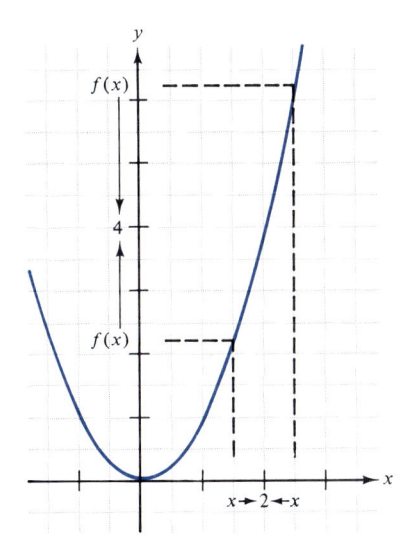

FIGURE 2.3

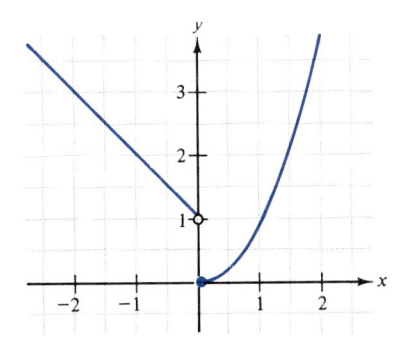

FIGURE 2.4

(a) Approach from positive side

(b) Approach from negative side

FIGURE 2.5

LIMITS AND TANGENT LINES

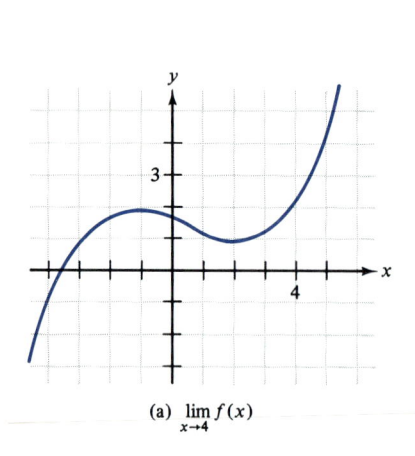

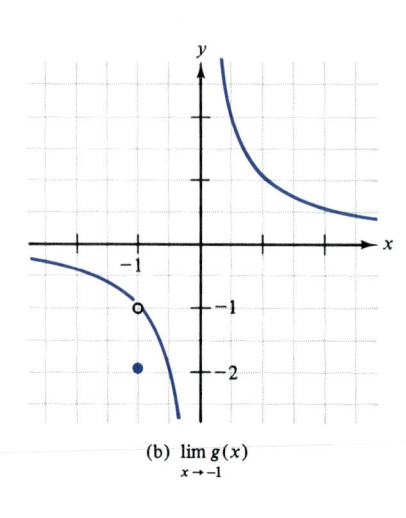

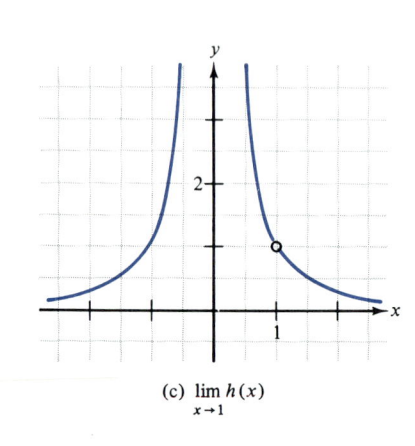

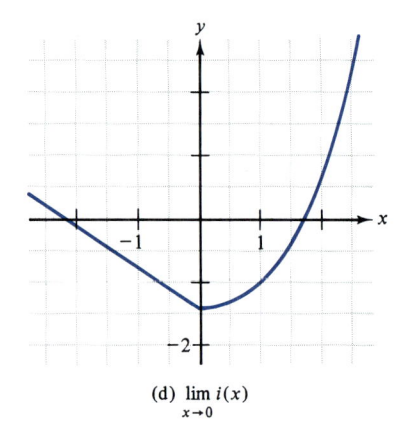

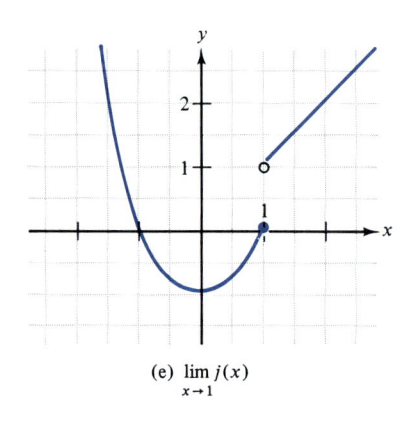

(a) $\lim_{x \to 4} f(x)$

(b) $\lim_{x \to -1} g(x)$

(c) $\lim_{x \to 1} h(x)$

(d) $\lim_{x \to 0} i(x)$

(e) $\lim_{x \to 1} j(x)$

FIGURE 2.6

$f(x) = (1 + x)^{1/x}$

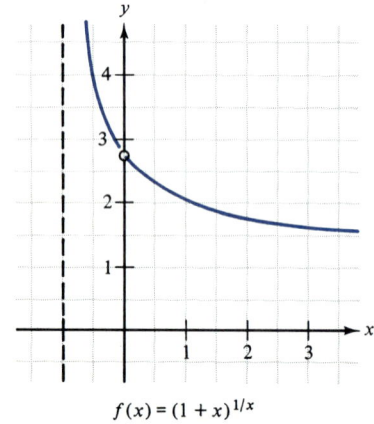

FIGURE 2.7

EXERCISE

Determine the limit (if it exists) for each function graphed in Figure 2.6; otherwise, specify "does not exist."

■ ANSWER
(a) $\lim_{x \to 4} f(x) = 2$. (b) $\lim_{x \to -1} g(x) = -1$. (c) $\lim_{x \to 1} h(x) = 1$.
(d) $\lim_{x \to 0} i(x) = -\frac{3}{2}$. (e) $\lim_{x \to 1} j(x)$ does not exist.

In Chapter 1 we introduced the irrational number e, which is approximately 2.71828. This irrational number is the limit of

$$f(x) = (1 + x)^{1/x}$$

as x approaches 0. The graph of this function is presented in Figure 2.7.

2.1 LIMITS

We see that $\lim_{x \to 0} f(x)$ exists and equals some number between 2 and 3. This number is called e. Therefore, by definition,

$$e = \lim_{x \to 0} (1 + x)^{1/x}.$$

Note that each time we have determined a limit, we have considered the behavior of $f(x)$ as x approaches the limit point from both sides: the positive side and the negative side. In the illustration with

$$f(x) = \begin{cases} x^2 & \text{when } x \geq 0 \\ -x + 1 & \text{when } x < 0, \end{cases}$$

whose graph is presented in Figure 2.4, we noted that as x approaches 0 from the positive side, $f(x)$ approaches 0. This is a **one-sided limit.** We write

$$\lim_{x \to 0^+} f(x) = 0.$$

The superscript + on 0 indicates that we are approaching from the positive side only. That is, $x \to 0$ and $x > 0$. We noted that as x approaches 0 from the negative side, $f(x)$ approaches 1. This one-sided limit is written

$$\lim_{x \to 0^-} f(x) = 1.$$

The superscript − on 0 indicates that we are approaching from the negative side only. That is, $x \to 0$ and $x < 0$. Because we got different results, we concluded that

$$\lim_{x \to 0} f(x) \text{ does not exist.}$$

Indeed, in order for the general limit to exist, both of the one-sided limits must exist and must be equal.

EXAMPLE 1

Determine $\lim_{x \to 1^+} f(x)$, $\lim_{x \to 1^-} f(x)$, and $\lim_{x \to 1} f(x)$ (if the limit exists), given the graph of f (Figure 2.8); otherwise, specify "does not exist."

■ SOLUTION
(a) As x approaches 1 from the positive side, $f(x)$ approaches 1. Thus

$$\lim_{x \to 1^+} f(x) = 1.$$

As x approaches 1 from the negative side, $f(x)$ approaches -1. So

$$\lim_{x \to 1^-} f(x) = -1.$$

Because the positive-side and negative-side limits are not equal,

$$\lim_{x \to 1} f(x) \text{ does not exist.}$$

74 LIMITS AND TANGENT LINES

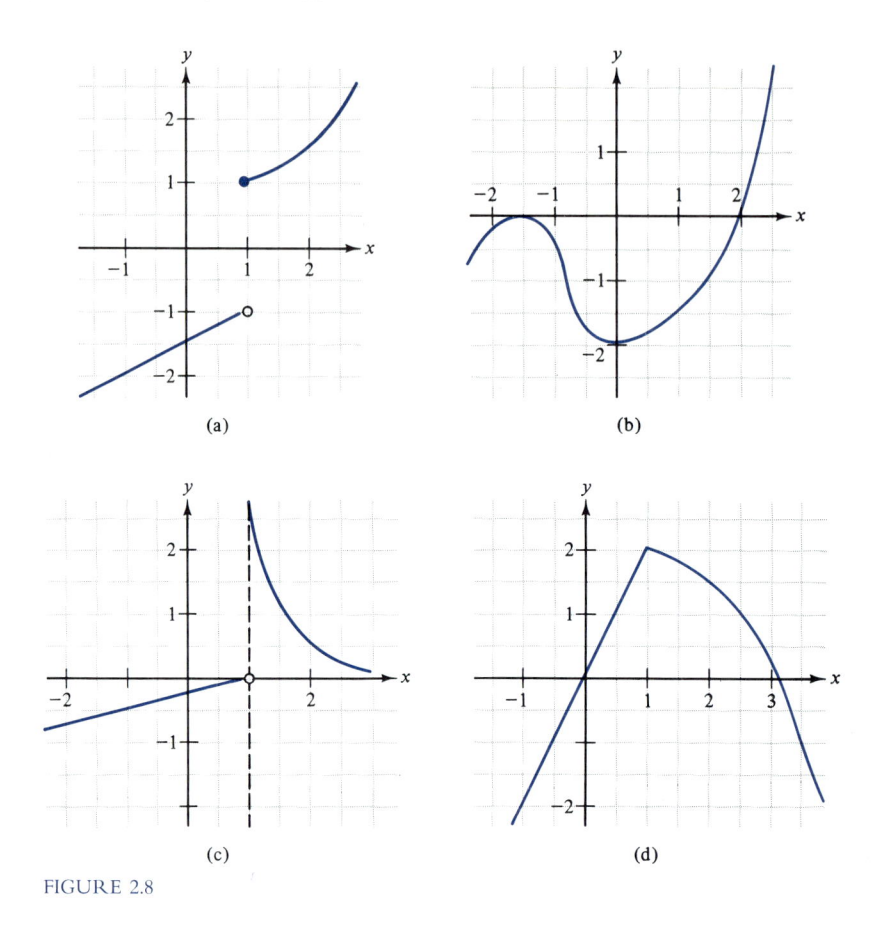

FIGURE 2.8

(b) As x approaches 1 from the positive side, $f(x)$ gets closer to $-\frac{3}{2}$. Hence
$$\lim_{x \to 1^+} f(x) = -\frac{3}{2}.$$
As x approaches 1 from the negative side, $f(x)$ gets closer to $-\frac{3}{2}$. So
$$\lim_{x \to 1^-} f(x) = -\frac{3}{2}.$$
Because these one-sided limits agree,
$$\lim_{x \to 1} f(x) = -\frac{3}{2}.$$

(c) As x approaches 1 from the positive side, $f(x)$ increases without bound. Thus
$$\lim_{x \to 1^+} f(x) \text{ does not exist.}$$
As x approaches 1 from the negative side, $f(x)$ approaches 0. Thus
$$\lim_{x \to 1^-} f(x) = 0.$$

2.1 LIMITS

Because the positive-side limit does not exist,
$$\lim_{x \to 1} f(x) \text{ does not exist.}$$

(d) As x approaches 1 from the positive side, $f(x)$ approaches 2. Thus
$$\lim_{x \to 1^+} f(x) = 2.$$

And as x approaches 1 from the negative side, $f(x)$ approaches 2. So
$$\lim_{x \to 1^-} f(x) = 2.$$

Because these limits are equal,
$$\lim_{x \to 1} f(x) = 2.$$

EXERCISE

Determine $\lim_{x \to -1^+} f(x)$, $\lim_{x \to -1^-} f(x)$, and $\lim_{x \to -1} f(x)$ (if the limit exists), given the graph of f (Figure 2.9); otherwise, specify "does not exist."

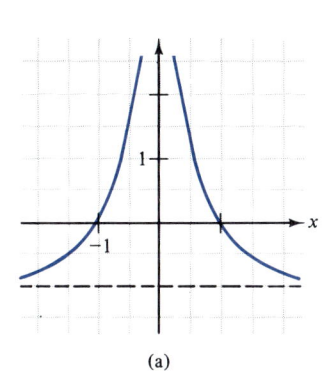

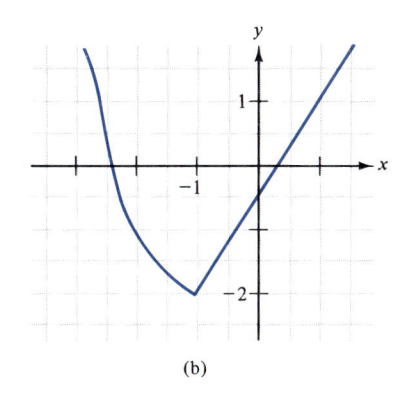

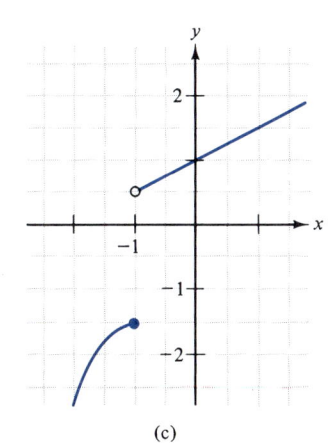

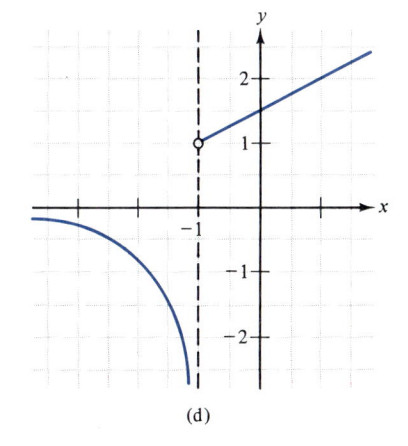

FIGURE 2.9

■ ANSWER
(a) $\lim_{x \to -1^+} f(x) = 0$; $\lim_{x \to -1^-} f(x) = 0$; $\lim_{x \to -1} f(x) = 0$.
(b) $\lim_{x \to -1^+} f(x) = -2$; $\lim_{x \to -1^-} f(x) = -2$; $\lim_{x \to -1} f(x) = -2$.
(c) $\lim_{x \to -1^+} f(x) = \frac{1}{2}$; $\lim_{x \to -1^-} f(x) = -\frac{3}{2}$; $\lim_{x \to -1} f(x)$ does not exist.
(d) $\lim_{x \to -1^+} f(x) = 1$; $\lim_{x \to -1^-} f(x)$ does not exist; $\lim_{x \to -1} f(x)$ does not exist.

With one-sided limits the definition of limit may be extended to include limit points that are endpoints of the domain. (An endpoint of the domain is an endpoint of one of the intervals making up the domain.) For example, consider $f(x) = x^3$, $x \geq 0$, whose graph is presented in Figure 2.10.

Because x represents nonnegative numbers only, x cannot approach 0 from the negative side. Hence it makes no sense to discuss

$$\lim_{x \to 0^-} f(x).$$

However, 0 may be approached from the positive side. Indeed,

$$\lim_{x \to 0^+} f(x) = 0.$$

When the limit point may be approached from one side only, the general limit is defined to be the one-sided limit. Thus

$$\lim_{x \to 0} f(x) = 0.$$

So in determining the general limit, we must usually approach the limit point from both sides. But if it is possible to approach from one side only, this one-sided limit is also the general limit.

$f(x) = x^3, x \geq 0$
FIGURE 2.10

EXERCISE

Determine $\lim_{x \to 1} f(x)$ for the function f graphed in Figure 2.11.

■ ANSWER
$\lim_{x \to 1} f(x) = 2$

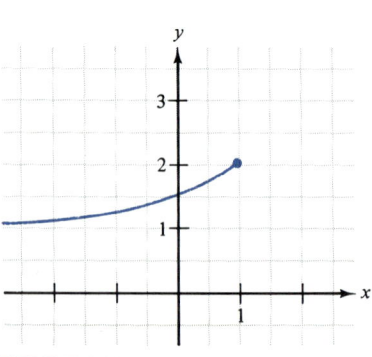

FIGURE 2.11

PROBLEM SET 2.1

In Problems 1–12, determine the limit (if it exists) for each function graphed; otherwise, specify "does not exist."

1. $\lim\limits_{x \to 3} f(x)$

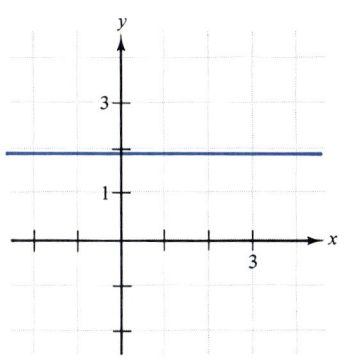

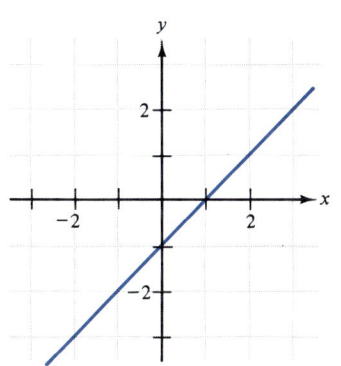

2. $\lim\limits_{x \to 0} f(x)$

3. $\lim\limits_{x \to -1} f(x)$

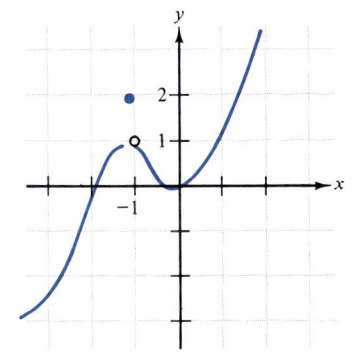

4. $\lim\limits_{x \to 2} f(x)$

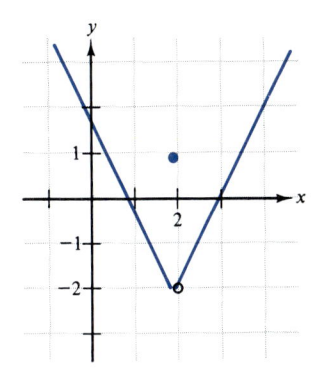

5. $\lim\limits_{x \to 4} f(x)$

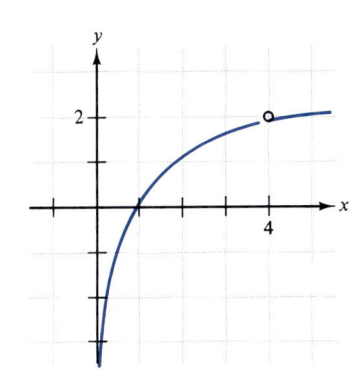

6. $\lim\limits_{x \to -2} f(x)$

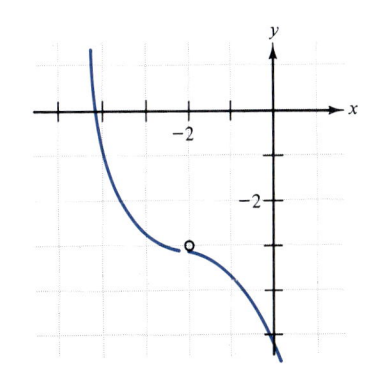

7. $\lim\limits_{x \to 0} f(x)$

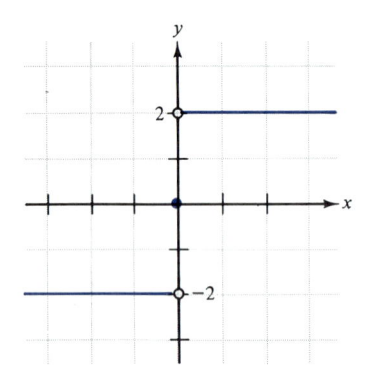

8. $\lim\limits_{x \to -1} f(x)$

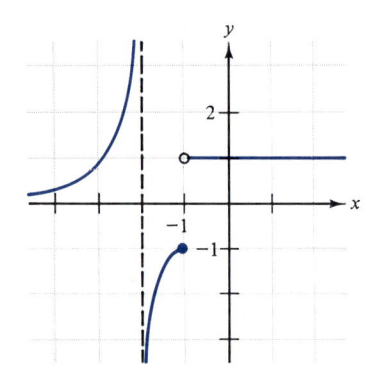

9. $\lim\limits_{x \to 3} f(x)$

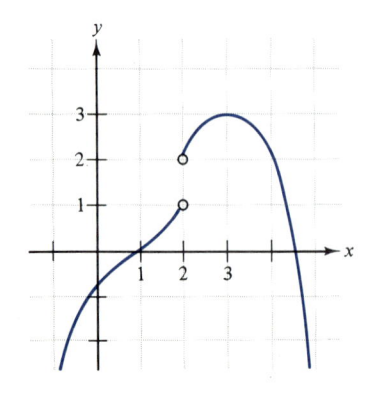

10. $\lim\limits_{x \to 1} f(x)$

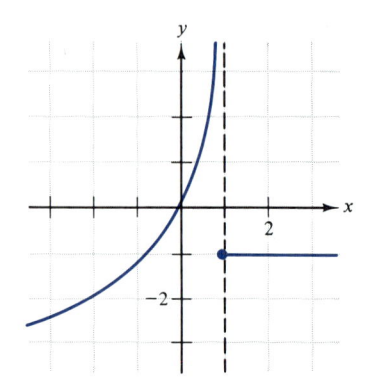

11. $\lim\limits_{x \to -2} f(x)$

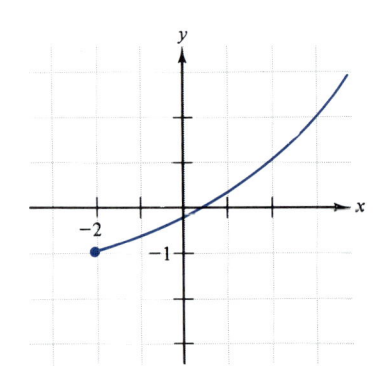

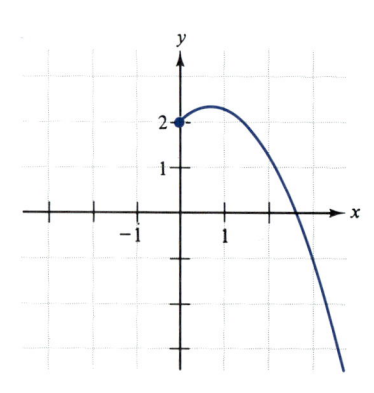

12. $\lim\limits_{x \to 0} f(x)$

In Problems 13–16, determine $\lim_{x \to 2^+} f(x)$, $\lim_{x \to 2^-} f(x)$, and $\lim_{x \to 2} f(x)$ (if the limit exists), given the graph of f; otherwise, specify "does not exist."

13.

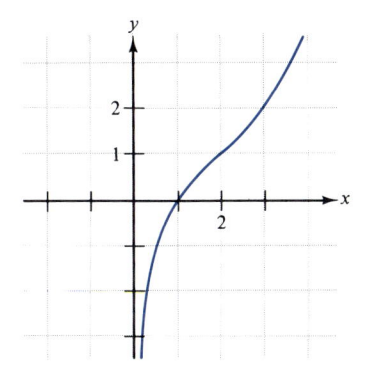

14.

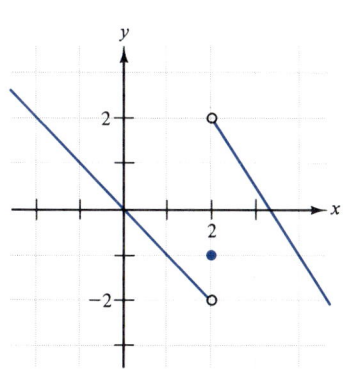

15.

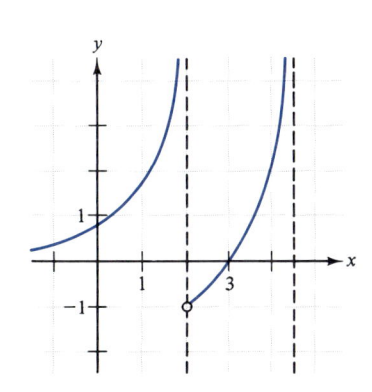

16.

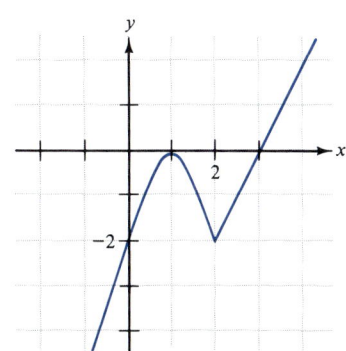

In Problems 17–26, graph the function f and determine each limit (if it exists); otherwise, specify "does not exist."

17. $f(x) = x^2 - 1$: $\lim_{x \to -1^+} f(x)$, $\lim_{x \to -1^-} f(x)$, $\lim_{x \to -1} f(x)$, $\lim_{x \to 0} f(x)$

18. $f(x) = \dfrac{2x}{x}$: $\lim_{x \to 0^+} f(x)$, $\lim_{x \to 0^-} f(x)$, $\lim_{x \to 0} f(x)$, $\lim_{x \to \pi} f(x)$

19. $f(x) = \begin{cases} (x^2/x) + 1 & \text{when } x \neq 0 \\ -1 & \text{when } x = 0 \end{cases}$: $\lim_{x \to 0^+} f(x)$, $\lim_{x \to 0^-} f(x)$, $\lim_{x \to 0} f(x)$, $\lim_{x \to 2} f(x)$

20. $f(x) = \begin{cases} x - 1 & \text{when } x \geq 1 \\ -x & \text{when } x < 1 \end{cases}$: $\lim_{x \to 1^+} f(x)$, $\lim_{x \to 1^-} f(x)$, $\lim_{x \to 1} f(x)$, $\lim_{x \to 10} f(x)$, $\lim_{x \to -\sqrt{2}} f(x)$

21. $f(x) = \begin{cases} 1/(x+2) & \text{when } x > -2 \\ -1 & \text{when } x \leq -2 \end{cases}$: $\lim_{x \to -2^+} f(x)$, $\lim_{x \to -2^-} f(x)$, $\lim_{x \to -2} f(x)$, $\lim_{x \to -7} f(x)$, $\lim_{x \to 1} f(x)$

22. $f(x) = \begin{cases} 1/(x-3)^2 & \text{if } x \neq 3 \\ 0 & \text{if } x = 3 \end{cases}$: $\lim_{x \to 3^+} f(x)$, $\lim_{x \to 3^-} f(x)$, $\lim_{x \to 3} f(x)$, $\lim_{x \to 4} f(x)$, $\lim_{x \to 0} f(x)$

23. $f(x) = \begin{cases} x & \text{when } -1 \leq x \leq 2 \\ 4 - x & \text{when } 2 \leq x \leq 4 \end{cases}$: $\lim_{x \to -1} f(x)$, $\lim_{x \to 2} f(x)$, $\lim_{x \to 4} f(x)$

24. $f(x) = |x| - 2$, $-3 \leq x \leq 2$ and $x \neq 1$: $\lim_{x \to -3} f(x)$, $\lim_{x \to 1} f(x)$, $\lim_{x \to 2} f(x)$

25. $f(x) = e^x - 2$, $-\ln 6 \leq x \leq \ln 6$ and $x \neq \ln 3$: $\lim_{x \to -\ln 6} f(x)$, $\lim_{x \to 0} f(x)$, $\lim_{x \to \ln 2} f(x)$, $\lim_{x \to \ln 3} f(x)$, $\lim_{x \to \ln 6} f(x)$

26. $f(x) = \begin{cases} \ln(x+1) & \text{when } 0 \leq x \leq e - 1 \\ x/(e-1) & \text{when } e - 1 < x \leq 2e - 2 \end{cases}$: $\lim_{x \to 0} f(x)$, $\lim_{x \to 1} f(x)$, $\lim_{x \to e-1} f(x)$, $\lim_{x \to 2e-2} f(x)$

27. For each part below, draw a graph of a function f satisfying the conditions.
    (a) $\lim_{x \to 1} f(x) = 3$ and $f(1) = 2$
    (b) $\lim_{x \to -1^-} f(x) = -2$, $\lim_{x \to -1^+} f(x) = 1$, and $f(-1) = 2$
    (c) $\lim_{x \to 3} f(x)$ exists, and $f(3)$ does not exist
    (d) $\lim_{x \to 0^-} f(x)$ does not exist, $\lim_{x \to 0^+} f(x) = 0$, and $f(0)$ does not exist
    (e) $\lim_{x \to 2} f(x) = f(2)$ and $f(2) = -2$

2.2 CONTINUITY

Let's return to the function $f(x) = x^2$. In Section 2.1 we determined that

$$\lim_{x \to 2} f(x) = 4.$$

It so happens that $f(2) = 4$; that is, the limit equals the value of the function at the limit point. We know that this doesn't have to happen. Indeed, the limit is *not determined* by the value of the function at the limit point. But this function f possesses an important property called continuity.

Let f be a function defined at each point of some open interval containing a. We say that f is **continuous at $x = a$** provided that

$$\lim_{x \to a} f(x) = f(a).$$

Otherwise we say that f is *discontinuous* at $x = a$.

Thus the function $f(x) = x^2$ is continuous at $x = 2$ because

$$\lim_{x \to 2} f(x) = f(2).$$

EXAMPLE 1

Given the graphs in Figure 2.12, determine whether each function f is continuous or discontinuous at $x = 2$.

■ SOLUTION

(a) Since $\lim_{x \to 2} f(x) = 1$ and $f(2) = 1$, we have $\lim_{x \to 2} f(x) = f(2)$. So this function is continuous at $x = 2$.

(b) We see that $\lim_{x \to 2} f(x) = 2$ but $f(2) = 1$. The limit is not equal to the value of the function at the limit point. Thus the function is discontinuous at $x = 2$.

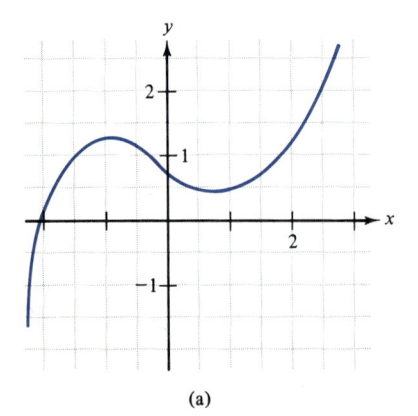

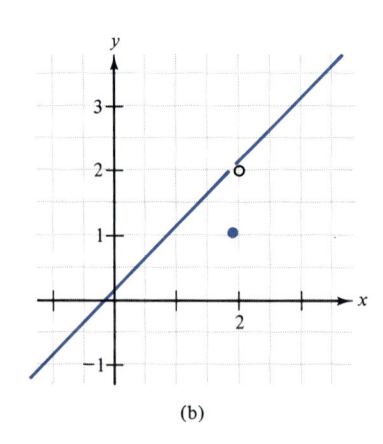

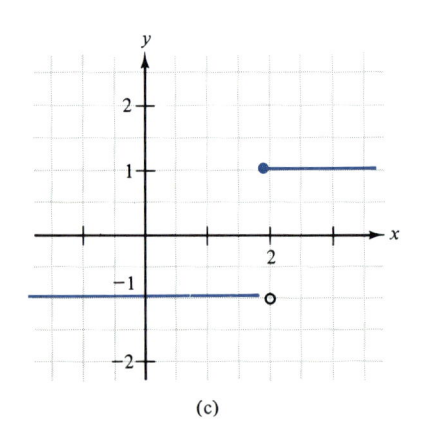

FIGURE 2.12

2.2 CONTINUITY

(c) We see that $\lim_{x \to 2} f(x)$ does not exist because $\lim_{x \to 2^+} f(x) = 1$ and $\lim_{x \to 2^-} f(x) = -1$. Since the limit doesn't exist, it cannot equal $f(2)$. Hence this function is discontinuous at $x = 2$.

EXERCISE

Given the graphs in Figure 2.13, determine whether each function f is continuous or discontinuous at $x = -3$.

■ *ANSWER*

(a) Continuous at $x = -3$. (b) Discontinuous at $x = -3$ because $\lim_{x \to -3} f(x)$ does not exist. (c) Discontinuous at $x = -3$ because $\lim_{x \to -3} f(x) = 1$ but $f(-3) = -2$.

A few observations need to be made. First, the concept of continuity has not been defined for points outside the domain. Hence, in this text,

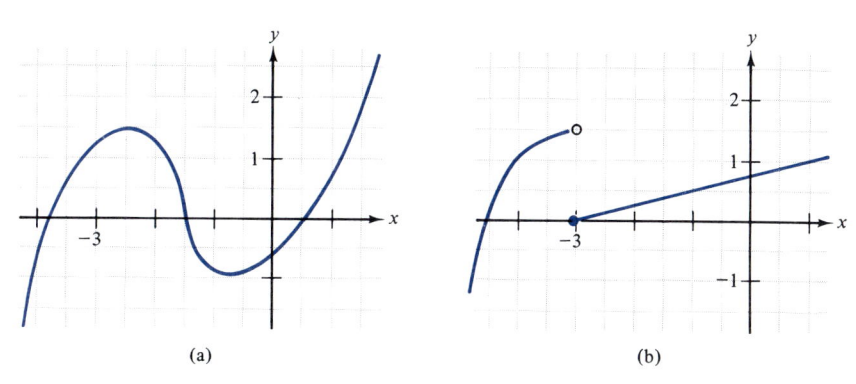

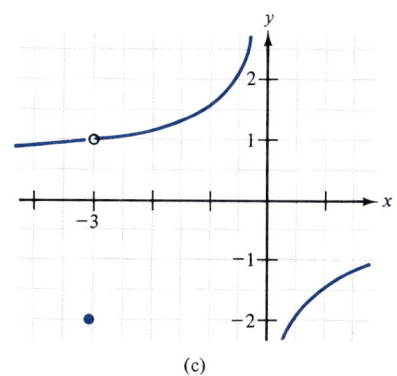

FIGURE 2.13

LIMITS AND TANGENT LINES

(a)

(b)

(c)

FIGURE 2.14

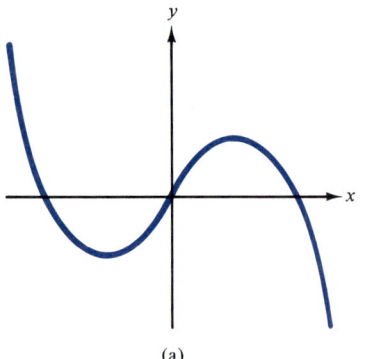

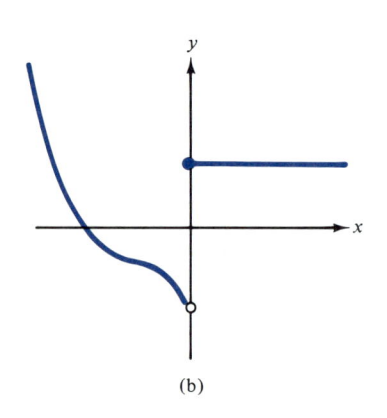

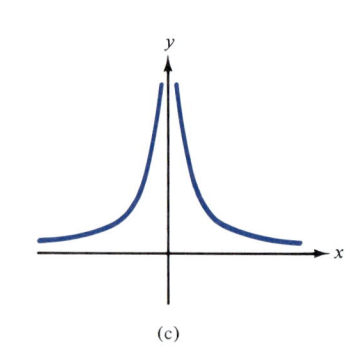

it doesn't make sense to discuss the continuity or discontinuity of $f(x) = 1/x$ at $x = 0$ or of $f(x) = \sqrt{x}$ at $x = -2$ because the function isn't defined there.* Second, a discontinuity can occur for one of two reasons: either the limit doesn't exist, as in Example 1(c), or it exists but doesn't equal the value of the function at the limit point, as in Example 1(b). Third, if a function is discontinuous at $x = a$, there is a "jump" or "break" in the graph at $x = a$. Indeed, this occurred in Example 1(b) and (c).

Let f be a function defined on an interval or union of intervals. We say that f is **continuous** provided that it is continuous at each point of its domain.† Graphically, a function is continuous provided that the only breaks in the graph occur where the function is not defined.

EXAMPLE 2

Determine whether each function graphed in Figure 2.14 is continuous or discontinuous.

■ *SOLUTION*

(a) Since there are no breaks in the graph, the function is continuous.

(b) There is a break in the graph at $x = 0$, and the function is defined at $x = 0$. Hence the function is discontinuous.

(c) There is a break in the graph at $x = 0$, but the function is not defined here. So the only break in the graph occurs where the function is not defined. Thus the function is continuous.

---

* In most texts at this level, the definition of continuity at $x = a$ is applied to all real numbers. Consequently, according to such texts, a function is discontinuous at any point outside its domain.
† If a text applies its definition of continuity at $x = a$ to all real numbers, its definition of continuity differs from ours. When we say that f is continuous, we mean continuous *on its domain*.

2.2 CONTINUITY

(a)

(b)

(c)

FIGURE 2.15

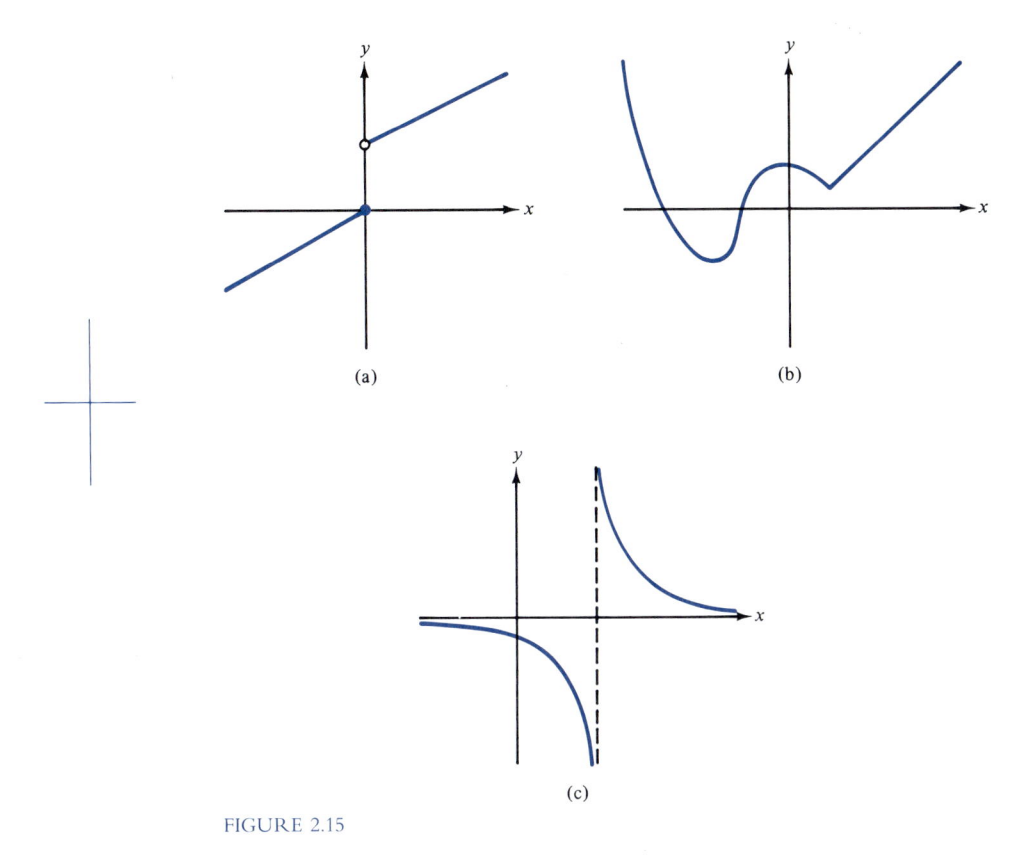

EXERCISE

Determine whether each function graphed in Figure 2.15 is continuous or discontinuous.

■ *ANSWER*
(a) Discontinuous; (b) continuous; (c) continuous

We now return to the subject of limits. In Section 2.1 we determined limits by examining the graph. Now we want to do it by using the function's formula of definition. If we know that a function is continuous, we may find the limit by substituting the limit point for the variable in the formula of definition. If the function is defined by $f(x) = mx + b$, we immediately see from its graph in Figure 2.16 that f is continuous. Hence linear and constant functions are continuous. The continuity of other functions is more difficult to establish and is based on the following properties of limits.

LIMITS AND TANGENT LINES

Linear function, $m \neq 0$

Constant function, $m = 0$

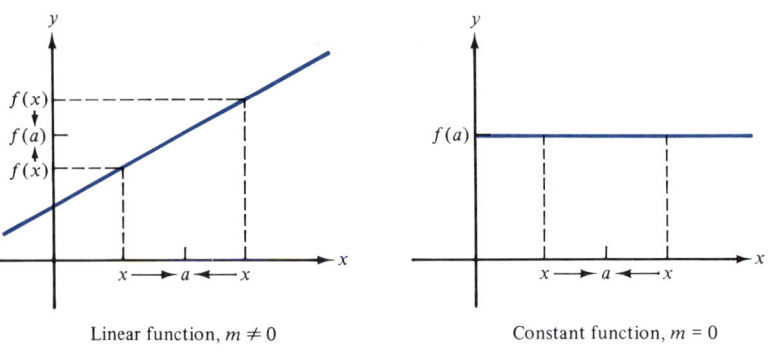

FIGURE 2.16

If $\lim_{x \to a} f(x)$ and $\lim_{x \to a} g(x)$ both exist, then

(i) $\lim_{x \to a} (k \cdot f(x)) = k \cdot \lim_{x \to a} f(x)$, where k is any constant.

(ii) $\lim_{x \to a} (f(x) + g(x)) = \lim_{x \to a} f(x) + \lim_{x \to a} g(x)$.

(iii) $\lim_{x \to a} (f(x) - g(x)) = \lim_{x \to a} f(x) - \lim_{x \to a} g(x)$.

(iv) $\lim_{x \to a} (f(x) \cdot g(x)) = \lim_{x \to a} f(x) \cdot \lim_{x \to a} g(x)$.

(v) $\lim_{x \to a} \dfrac{f(x)}{g(x)} = \dfrac{\lim_{x \to a} f(x)}{\lim_{x \to a} g(x)}$, provided $\lim_{x \to a} g(x) \neq 0$.

Part (i) states that the limit of a constant times a function is just the constant times the limit of the function. It means that a constant may be "factored out" when taking a limit.

Parts (ii) and (iii) say that the limit of a sum or difference is, respectively, the sum or difference of the limits. And even though the statements are made for only two functions, they are true for any number of functions. Parts (iv) and (v) state that the limit of a product or quotient is, respectively, the product or quotient of the limits. Of course, the limit in the denominator cannot equal zero.

This brings us to three important theorems concerning continuous functions.

THEOREM 2.1   All polynomial functions are continuous.

Thus, given a polynomial function P, we have

$$\lim_{x \to a} P(x) = P(a).$$

The limit is simply the value of the function at the limit point. We may compute the limit by substituting the limit point into the formula of

definition. For example, suppose
$$f(x) = x^2 + 3x + 2,$$
and we're trying to determine
$$\lim_{x \to 1} f(x).$$
We don't have to examine the graph. Because the function is a polynomial, we get
$$\lim_{x \to 1} f(x) = f(1) = 6.$$

THEOREM 2.2 All rational functions are continuous.

Thus, given a rational function R and a point a in its domain,
$$\lim_{x \to a} R(x) = R(a).$$
Again, the limit is simply the value of the function at the limit point. (We consider what happens when a isn't in the domain in a moment.) Thus, if we're trying to determine
$$\lim_{x \to 3} \frac{x-2}{x^2},$$
we just substitute because we have a rational function. We get
$$\lim_{x \to 3} \frac{x-2}{x^2} = \frac{3-2}{3^2} = \frac{1}{9}.$$

As noted in the next theorem, exponential and logarithmic functions also behave nicely.

THEOREM 2.3 All exponential functions and all logarithmic functions are continuous.

Thus
$$\lim_{x \to -2} e^x = e^{-2} = \frac{1}{e^2} \quad \text{and} \quad \lim_{x \to 5} \ln x = \ln 5.$$

EXERCISE

Compute the limits:

(a) $\lim_{x \to 1} (x^2 - 5x + 1)$, (b) $\lim_{x \to 0} \frac{x^2 - 1}{2x + 5}$,

(c) $\lim_{x \to -1} e^x$, (d) $\lim_{x \to 4} \ln x$.

■ ANSWER
(a) -3; (b) $-\frac{1}{5}$; (c) $1/e$; (d) $\ln 4$

Various combinations of continuous functions are also continuous. Given two functions f and g with domains D_f and D_g, they may be combined as a sum, a difference, or a product with a domain of $D_f \cap D_g$. And they may be combined as a quotient f/g for all $x \in D_f \cap D_g$ such that $g(x) \neq 0$. Such a combination of continuous functions yields new continuous functions, a result that comes directly from properties of limits.

THEOREM 2.4 Let f and g be functions. If f and g are continuous (on their domains), then each of the following is continuous (on its domain).

(i) $f + g$.
(ii) $f - g$.
(iii) fg.
(iv) f/g.

This theorem says that the sum, difference, product, and quotient of continuous functions are continuous. Hence, by this theorem, functions like

$$f(x) = x^2 + e^x, \quad g(x) = x \ln x, \quad \text{and} \quad h(x) = \frac{x^2}{e^x}$$

are continuous.

Furthermore, if n is any real number and if f is continuous, then the function defined by

$$g(x) = (f(x))^n$$

is also continuous. A function of this form is called a **power function.** So if the expression being raised to the power is polynomial, rational, exponential, or logarithmic, we know that the power function is continuous. For example,

$$g(x) = (3x^2 - 5)^{1/2} = \sqrt{3x^2 - 5}$$

is a continuous power function.

If f is continuous, then functions defined by

$$g(x) = e^{f(x)} \quad \text{or} \quad h(x) = \ln(f(x))$$

are also continuous. So if the argument of an exponential or logarithmic function is polynomial or rational, the function is continuous.

2.2 CONTINUITY

EXERCISE

Compute the limits: (a) $\lim_{x \to -2} \sqrt{3x^2 - 5}$, (b) $\lim_{x \to -1} e^{x^2}$, and (c) $\lim_{x \to 2} \ln(x^3 - 1)$.

■ ANSWER

(a) $\sqrt{7}$;   (b) e;   (c) $\ln 7$

Before proceeding let's emphasize that, as noted in Section 2.1, the limit is not *determined* by the value of the function at the limit point. The limit is determined by the values of the function *near, but not equal to,* the limit point. The fact that we may compute the limit as we have for these functions is a consequence of the fact that *these functions are continuous.*

Now consider

$$\lim_{x \to 2} \frac{x^2 - 4}{x - 2}.$$

Although the function

$$f(x) = \frac{x^2 - 4}{x - 2}$$

is rational and thus continuous, we cannot substitute 2 for x here because the function is not defined at $x = 2$. Indeed, if we try to compute $f(2)$, we get a zero in the denominator (and a zero in the numerator). Some algebraic manipulation is required first. Note that

$$\frac{x^2 - 4}{x - 2} = \frac{(x+2)(x-2)}{x - 2} = x + 2.$$

Thus

$$\lim_{x \to 2} \frac{x^2 - 4}{x - 2} = \lim_{x \to 2} (x + 2).$$

If we substitute 2 for x now, we get 4. So

$$\lim_{x \to 2} \frac{x^2 - 4}{x - 2} = \lim_{x \to 2} (x + 2) = 4.$$

Of course, the original function still isn't defined at $x = 2$. So how can we find $f(2)$? We can't. And we haven't. We used a slightly different function:

$$g(x) = x + 2.$$

This function *is* defined at $x = 2$, but it differs from

$$f(x) = \frac{x^2 - 4}{x - 2}$$

(a) $f(x) = \dfrac{x^2 - 4}{x - 2}$ (b) $g(x) = x + 2$

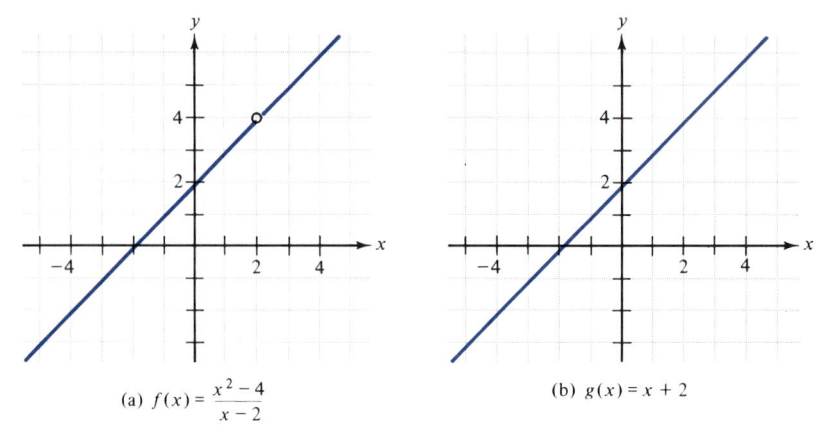

FIGURE 2.17

at one value only: $x = 2$, where f isn't defined. See Figure 2.17. But because the limit is determined by values of the function *near, but not equal to,* the limit point, the fact that these two functions differ at $x = 2$ (g is defined here, but f is not) is of no consequence. Because they agree at all other values, they will have equal limits.

EXAMPLE 3

Compute the limits:

$$\text{(a) } \lim_{x \to 1} \frac{x^2 + 2x - 3}{x - 1} \quad \text{and} \quad \text{(b) } \lim_{x \to 0} \frac{2x^2 + x}{x}.$$

■ SOLUTION

(a) We cannot simply substitute 1 for x because we get 0 in the denominator. (The function isn't defined at $x = 1$.) But we may factor the numerator first. We have

$$\lim_{x \to 1} \frac{x^2 + 2x - 3}{x - 1} = \lim_{x \to 1} \frac{(x - 1)(x + 3)}{x - 1}$$
$$= \lim_{x \to 1} (x + 3)$$
$$= 4.$$

(b) We cannot substitute 0 for x because we get 0 in the denominator. We must factor the numerator first. We get

$$\lim_{x \to 0} \frac{2x^2 + x}{x} = \lim_{x \to 0} \frac{x(2x + 1)}{x}$$
$$= \lim_{x \to 0} (2x + 1)$$
$$= 1.$$

2.2 CONTINUITY

EXERCISE

Compute the limits:

(a) $\lim_{x \to 3} \dfrac{x^2 - 9}{x - 3}$, (b) $\lim_{x \to -2} \dfrac{2x^2 + 3x - 2}{x + 2}$, and (c) $\lim_{x \to 0} \dfrac{3x^2 - 2x}{x}$.

■ ANSWER
(a) 6; (b) -5; (c) -2

EXAMPLE 4

Compute
$$\lim_{h \to 0} \frac{(x + h)^2 + (x + h) - (x^2 + x)}{h}.$$

■ SOLUTION

Although x may be a variable, for purposes of computing this limit it is treated as a constant. This is because it is the variable h that is approaching 0. Consequently, the expression
$$\frac{(x + h)^2 + (x + h) - (x^2 + x)}{h}$$
is a rational function of h. But we cannot simply substitute 0 for h because we get 0 in the denominator. Some algebraic manipulation is required first.

$$\lim_{h \to 0} \frac{(x + h)^2 + (x + h) - (x^2 + x)}{h} = \lim_{h \to 0} \frac{x^2 + 2xh + h^2 + x + h - x^2 - x}{h}$$
$$= \lim_{h \to 0} \frac{2xh + h^2 + h}{h}$$
$$= \lim_{h \to 0} (2x + h + 1)$$
$$= 2x + 1.$$

This last step is made by substituting 0 for the variable h.

EXERCISE

Compute
$$\lim_{h \to 0} \frac{(x + h)^2 - 2(x + h) - (x^2 - 2x)}{h}.$$

■ ANSWER
$2x - 2$

PROBLEM SET 2.2

In Problems 1–6, determine whether each function graphed is continuous or discontinuous at $x = -2$.

1.

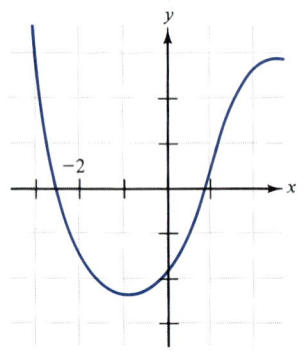

2.

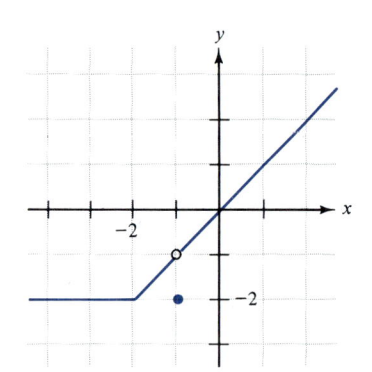

3.

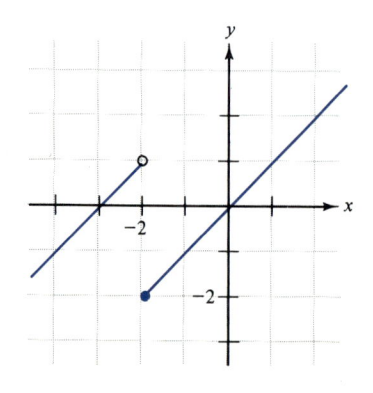

4.

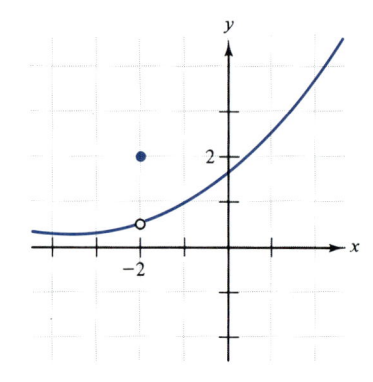

5.

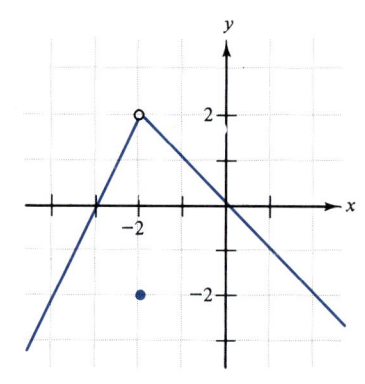

6.

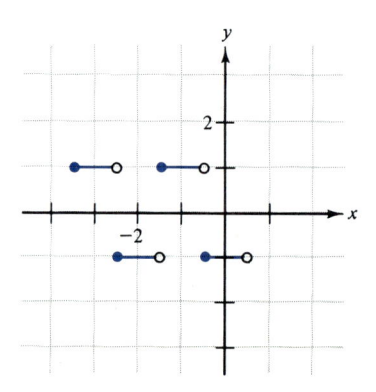

In Problems 7–14, sketch the graph of each function and determine whether it is continuous or discontinuous at $x = 3$.

7. $f(x) = \begin{cases} x + 1 & \text{when } x \neq 3 \\ 2 & \text{when } x = 3 \end{cases}$

8. $f(x) = \begin{cases} 1/(x-3) & \text{when } x \neq 3 \\ -1 & \text{when } x = 3 \end{cases}$

9. $f(x) = \begin{cases} 4 & \text{when } x \neq 1, 2, 4 \\ 2 & \text{when } x = 1, 2, 4 \end{cases}$

10. $f(x) = \begin{cases} -x + 4 & \text{when } x \leq 3 \\ 2x - 5 & \text{when } x > 3 \end{cases}$

11. $f(x) = \begin{cases} x^2 & \text{when } x < 3 \\ 6 & \text{when } x \geq 3 \end{cases}$

12. $f(x) = \begin{cases} |x - 3| - 1 & \text{when } x \neq 3 \\ -1 & \text{when } x = 3 \end{cases}$

13. $f(x) = \begin{cases} e^{2-x} & \text{when } x \leq 3 \\ \frac{1}{2}x - 1 & \text{when } x > 3 \end{cases}$

14. $f(x) = \begin{cases} 1 + \ln x & \text{when } 0 < x < 3 \\ \frac{1}{3}x + \ln 3 & \text{when } x \geq 3 \end{cases}$

15. Sketch the graph of a function that is continuous everywhere except at $x = 1, 2,$ and 3.

16. Sketch the graph of a function with domain $[-2\pi, 2\pi]$ that is discontinuous at $x = -\pi$, $x = 0$, and $x = \pi$, and continuous at all other points in the domain.

In Problems 17–22, determine whether each function graphed is continuous or discontinuous.

17.

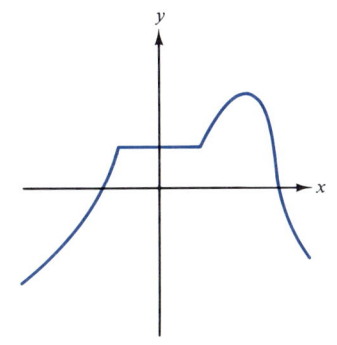

18.

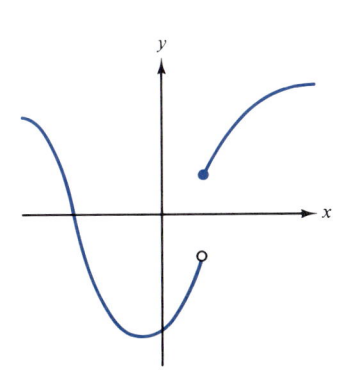

19.

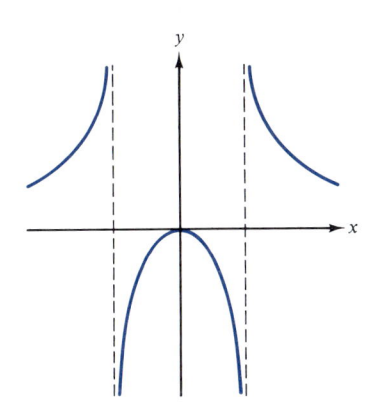

20.

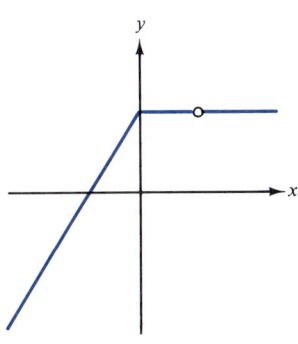

21.

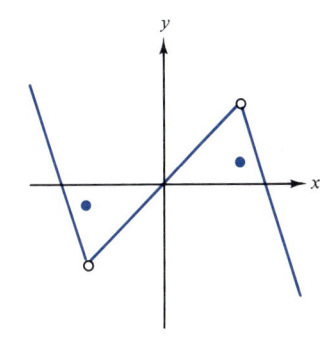

22.

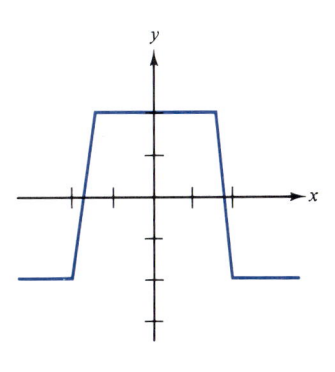

In Problems 23–68, compute the limit.

23. $\lim\limits_{x \to 1} 5$

24. $\lim\limits_{x \to 6} 6^2$

25. $\lim\limits_{t \to -3} 2t$

26. $\lim\limits_{x \to -1} (5 - x)$

27. $\lim\limits_{h \to 5} (h^2 - h - 10)$

28. $\lim\limits_{x \to -2} (3x^2 - 2x - 7)$

29. $\lim\limits_{x \to e} (3x + e)$

30. $\lim\limits_{x \to \ln 2} (4x - \ln 2)$

31. $\lim\limits_{x \to 2} (x^3 + x^2 + x + 1)$

32. $\lim\limits_{x \to -1} (-x^5 + x^3 - x)$

33. $\lim\limits_{t \to 0} \dfrac{t^2 + 2}{3t - 4}$

34. $\lim\limits_{x \to -3} \dfrac{2}{x^2 + 9}$

35. $\lim\limits_{x \to -4} \dfrac{x^2 + 3x - 4}{4 - x}$

36. $\lim\limits_{x \to 0} \dfrac{2 - x + x^3}{1 - x - x^2}$

37. $\lim\limits_{x \to -3} e^x$

38. $\lim\limits_{x \to 6} \ln x$

39. $\lim\limits_{x \to 3} \ln(2x - 5)$

40. $\lim\limits_{x \to -2} e^{x^2 - 4}$

41. $\lim\limits_{x \to 4} \sqrt{e^{3x-2}}$

42. $\lim\limits_{x \to 2} \sqrt[3]{\ln(x^2 + 1)}$

43. $\lim\limits_{x \to 2} \dfrac{x^2 - 4}{x - 2(x + 2)}$

44. $\lim\limits_{h \to 0} \dfrac{h^3 + h}{h^2 + h}$

45. $\lim\limits_{x \to 4} \dfrac{2x^2 - 8x}{x - 4}$

46. $\lim\limits_{x \to -2} \dfrac{x^2 - 3x - 10}{x + 2}$

47. $\lim\limits_{x \to 3} \dfrac{7x - 21}{x^2 - 9}$

48. $\lim\limits_{h \to 0} \dfrac{3h^2 - 2xh}{h}$

49. $\lim\limits_{t \to a} \dfrac{t^2 - a^2}{t - a}$

50. $\lim\limits_{x \to 2} \dfrac{x^4 - 16}{2 - x}$

51. $\lim\limits_{x \to 4} \dfrac{\sqrt{x} - 2}{2x - 8}$

52. $\lim\limits_{x \to 5} \dfrac{x - 5}{\sqrt{x} - \sqrt{5}}$

53. $\lim\limits_{x \to 2^+} \dfrac{x|x - 2|}{x - 2}$

54. $\lim\limits_{x \to 3^-} \dfrac{x - 3}{|x - 3|}$

55. $\lim\limits_{x \to 2} \dfrac{\dfrac{1}{x^3} - \dfrac{1}{8}}{x - 2}$

56. $\lim\limits_{t \to b^2} \dfrac{\dfrac{t}{b^2} - \dfrac{b^4}{t^2}}{t - b^2}$

57. $\lim\limits_{h \to 0} \dfrac{(2 + h)^2 + 5(2 + h) - (2^2 + 5 \cdot 2)}{h}$

58. $\lim\limits_{h \to 0} \dfrac{(4 + h)^2 - 3(4 + h) - (4^2 - 3 \cdot 4)}{h}$

59. $\lim\limits_{h \to 0} \dfrac{2(x + h)^2 - (x + h) - (2x^2 - x)}{h}$

60. $\lim\limits_{h \to 0} \dfrac{3(x + h)^2 - 4(x + h) - (3x^2 - 4x)}{h}$

61. $\lim\limits_{h \to 0} \dfrac{\dfrac{1}{-4 + h} - \dfrac{1}{-4}}{h}$

62. $\lim\limits_{h \to 0} \dfrac{\dfrac{-2}{3 + h} - \dfrac{-2}{3}}{h}$

63. $\lim\limits_{h \to 0} \dfrac{-3(a + h)^2 + 2(a + h) - 1 - (-3a^2 + 2a - 1)}{h}$

64. $\lim\limits_{h \to 0} \dfrac{-4(a + h)^2 - (a + h) + 5 - (-4a^2 - a + 5)}{h}$

65. $\lim\limits_{h \to 0} \dfrac{\dfrac{1}{3 + x + h} - \dfrac{1}{3 + x}}{h}$

66. $\lim\limits_{h \to 0} \dfrac{\dfrac{1}{1 - 2(x + h)} - \dfrac{1}{1 - 2x}}{h}$

67. $\lim\limits_{h \to 0} \dfrac{\dfrac{a + h}{1 + (a + h)^2} - \dfrac{a}{1 + a^2}}{h}$

68. $\lim\limits_{h \to 0} \dfrac{\dfrac{a + h}{2 - (a + h)^2} - \dfrac{a}{2 - a^2}}{h}$

In Problems 69–72, approximate each limit to the nearest ten thousandth by completing the accompanying tables.

69. $\lim\limits_{x \to 0} (1 - x)^{1/x}$

x	$(1 - x)^{1/x}$	x	$(1 - x)^{1/x}$
0.1		-0.1	
0.01		-0.01	
0.001		-0.001	
0.0001		-0.0001	

70. $\lim\limits_{x \to 2^+} (x - 2)^{x - 2}$

x	$(x - 2)^{x - 2}$
2.1	
2.01	
2.001	
2.0001	
2.00001	

71. $\lim\limits_{x \to 5} \dfrac{\sqrt{x-1} - \sqrt{9-x}}{x-5}$

72. $\lim\limits_{x \to 0} \dfrac{2^x - 3^x}{x}$

x	$\dfrac{\sqrt{x-1} - \sqrt{9-x}}{x-5}$
4.9	
4.99	
4.999	

x	$\dfrac{\sqrt{x-1} - \sqrt{9-x}}{x-5}$
5.1	
5.01	
5.001	

x	$\dfrac{2^x - 3^x}{x}$
0.1	
0.01	
0.001	
0.0001	
0.00001	

x	$\dfrac{2^x - 3^x}{x}$
−0.1	
−0.01	
−0.001	
−0.0001	
−0.00001	

2.3 TANGENT LINES

Generally speaking, we say that a tangent line to a curve at a point is the line that "best approximates" the curve at that point. In Figure 2.18, the line $\mathscr{L}$ is tangent to $y = f(x)$ at the point P.

What properties characterize the tangent line? With respect to a circle, a line is tangent provided that it intersects at one point only. But such a definition does not work here. There are many lines that intersect at P only which aren't tangent. See Figure 2.19. We define the tangent line by using **secants,** lines that intersect in two or more points. In Figure 2.20, we see two such secants PQ.

Let's allow the point Q to move along the curve toward P, as indicated in Figure 2.21. What happens to the secants PQ as Q gets closer and closer to, but not equal to, P? (If Q reaches P, we would have no secant line PQ.) They become better and better approximations to the tangent line $\mathscr{L}$. This motivates the following definition: Let f be a function defined at each point of some open interval containing a. Let $P = (a, f(a))$ and let Q represent each other point on the graph $y = f(x)$. If f is continuous at $x = a$ and if the secant lines PQ get closer and closer to a unique line $\mathscr{L}$ as Q approaches P (from both directions), then $\mathscr{L}$ is called the **tangent line at P.** Otherwise, we say that there is no tangent at P.

Thus to sketch a tangent line at a point P, we must consider the secants PQ as Q approaches P. If these secants approach a "limit line" from the

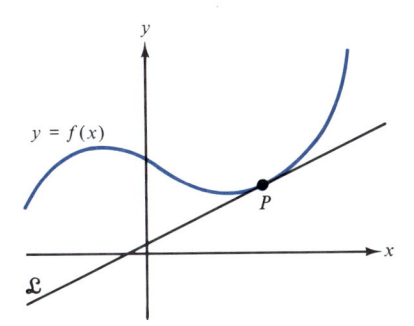

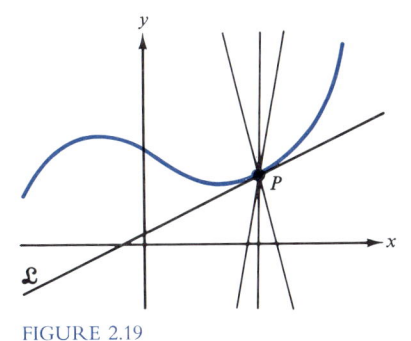

FIGURE 2.18

FIGURE 2.19

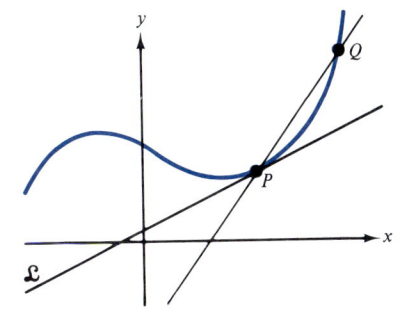

FIGURE 2.20

FIGURE 2.21

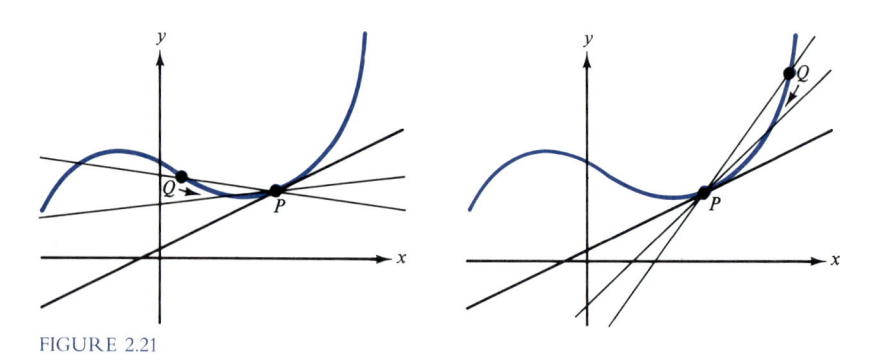

positive side and the same limit line from the negative side, then this limit line is the tangent at *P*. This procedure is illustrated in Example 1.

EXAMPLE 1

In Figure 2.22, sketch the tangent line at *P* (if it exists); otherwise, specify "no tangent."

■ SOLUTION

(a) From the positive side, the secants appear to approach the line $\mathscr{L}_1$ shown in Figure 2.23(a). From the negative side, the secants appear to

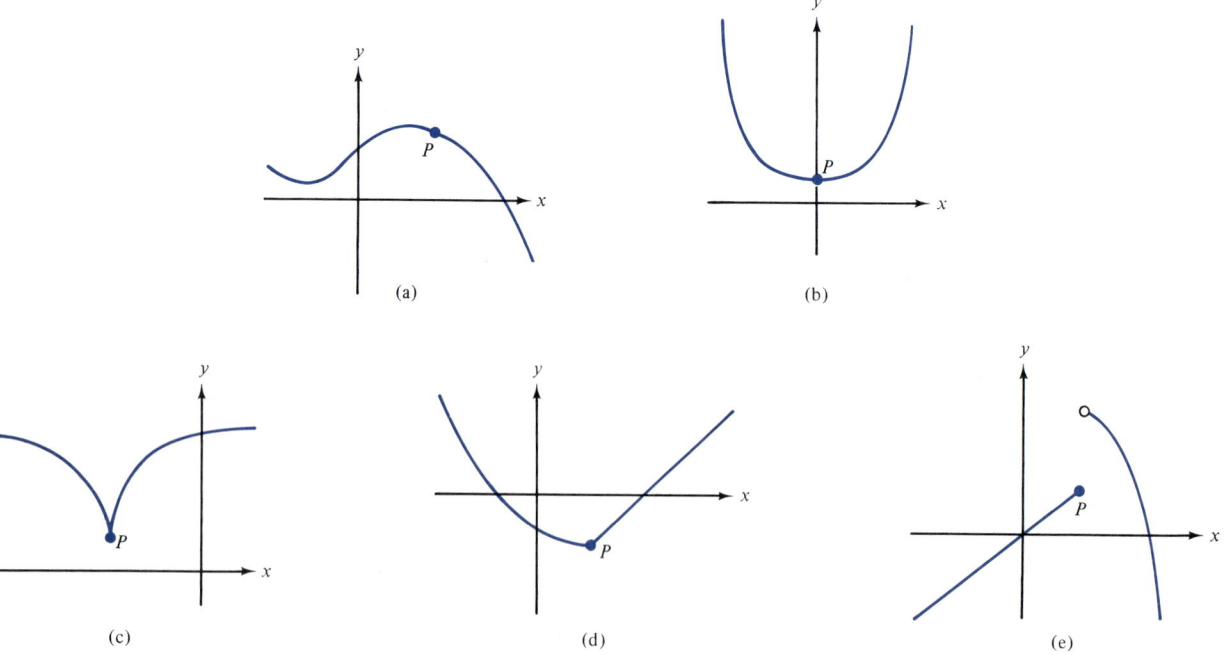

FIGURE 2.22

2.3 TANGENT LINES

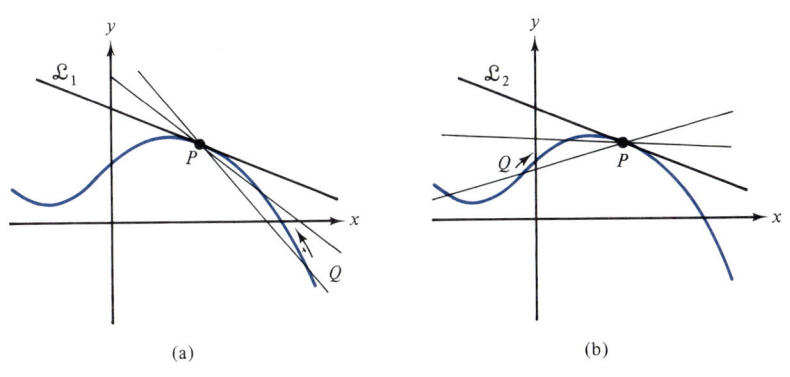

FIGURE 2.23

(a)　(b)

approach the line $\mathscr{L}_2$ shown in Figure 2.23(b). Because these two lines are identical, the tangent line is $\mathscr{L}_1$ (which is the same as $\mathscr{L}_2$).

(b) From both the positive and negative sides, the secants appear to approach the horizontal line through P. Thus the line through P with slope 0 is the tangent line. See Figure 2.24.

(c) From both the positive and negative sides, the secants appear to approach the vertical line through P, shown in Figure 2.25.

(d) From the positive side each secant is the line that coincides with the part of the graph to the right of P. Hence the line $\mathscr{L}_1$, shown in Figure 2.26(a), is the candidate for the tangent line. But from the negative side, the secants appear to approach the horizontal line through P. Hence the line $\mathscr{L}_2$, shown in Figure 2.26(b), is the candidate for the tangent line. The tangent line, if it exists, must be approached by the secants from *both* directions. Because $\mathscr{L}_1$ and $\mathscr{L}_2$ are not the same, there is no tangent line at P.

(e) Because the function is discontinuous at P, there is no tangent line.

From part (d) of the preceding example we may generalize that if P is at a "corner" of the graph, then there will be no tangent at P.

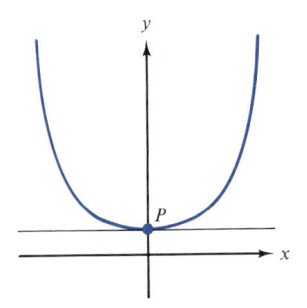

FIGURE 2.24

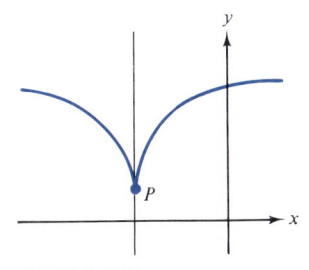

FIGURE 2.25

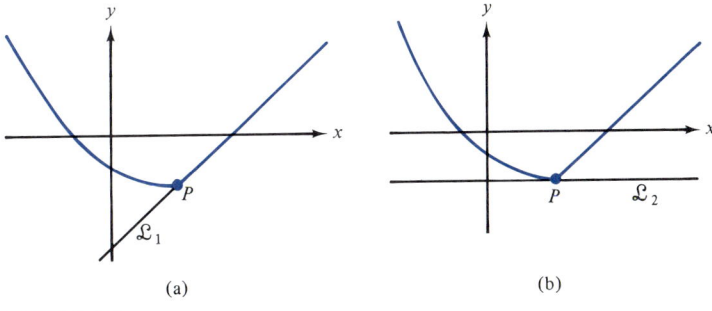

FIGURE 2.26

(a)　(b)

96   LIMITS AND TANGENT LINES

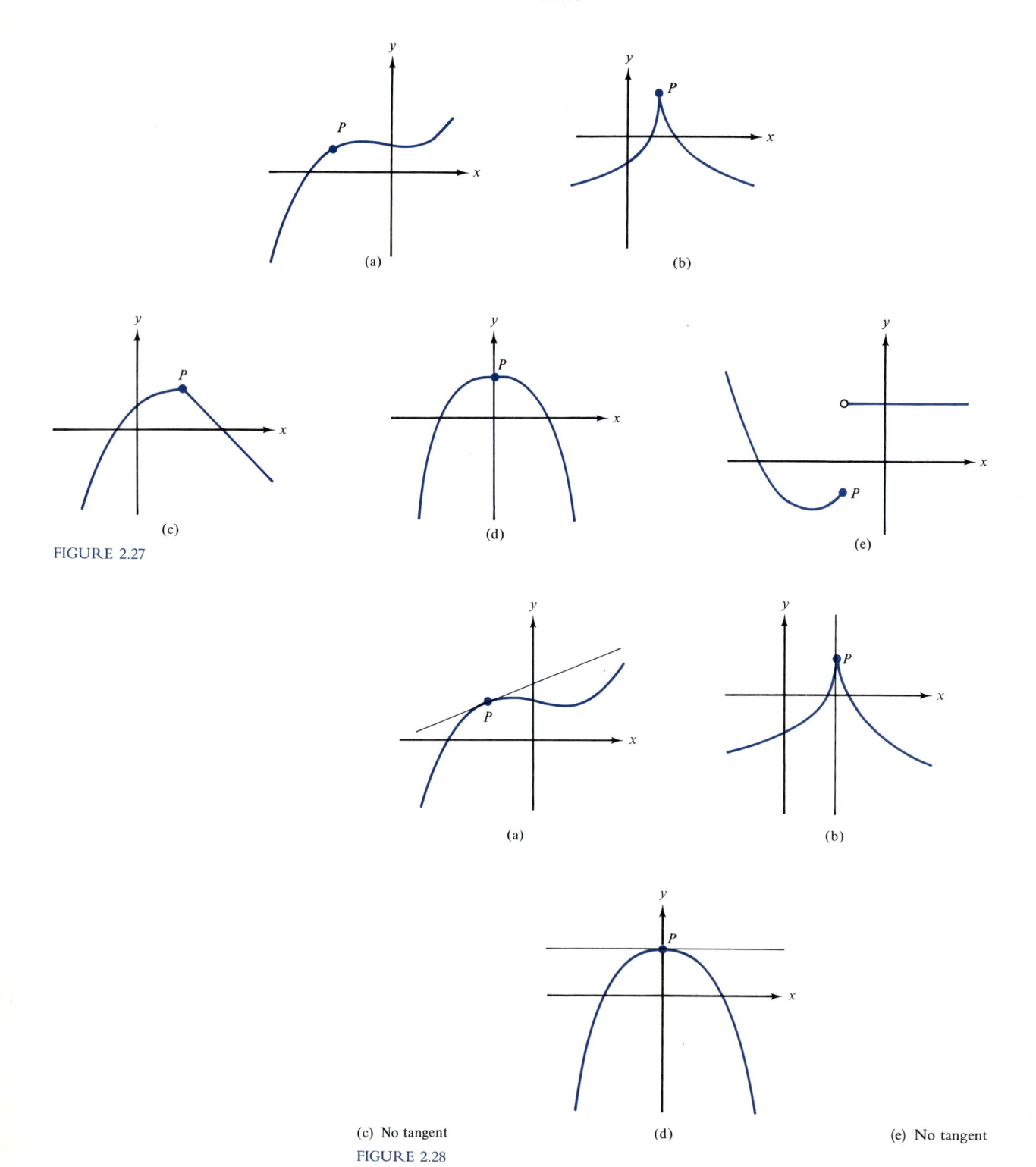

(a)

(b)

(c)

(d)

(e)

FIGURE 2.27

(a)

(b)

(c) No tangent

(d)

(e) No tangent

FIGURE 2.28

2.3 TANGENT LINES

FIGURE 2.29

EXERCISE

In Figure 2.27, sketch the tangent line at P (if it exists); otherwise, specify "no tangent."

■ *ANSWER*
See Figure 2.28.

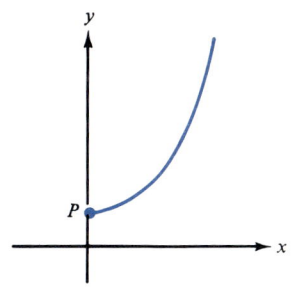

In a manner similar to the extension of the definition of limit, the definition of tangent may be extended to include endpoints of the domain. Consider the function graphed in Figure 2.29.

Because P is located at a left endpoint of the domain, Q cannot approach P from the negative side. Hence it makes no sense to analyze such secant lines PQ. However, P may be approached by Q from the positive side. Indeed, such secants PQ approach the horizontal line through P. So when the point P may be approached by Q from one side only, the tangent is defined to be this "one-sided" tangent. Thus the tangent line at P in Figure 2.29 is the horizontal line through P.

So in determining the tangent, we must usually let Q approach P from both sides. But if it is possible to approach from one side only, this one-sided tangent is the tangent.

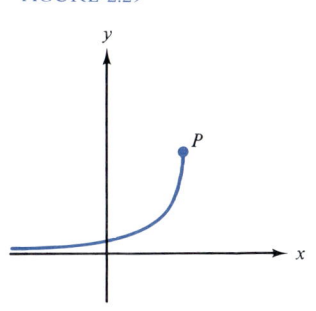

FIGURE 2.30

EXERCISE

In Figure 2.30, sketch the tangent line at P.

■ *ANSWER*
See Figure 2.31.

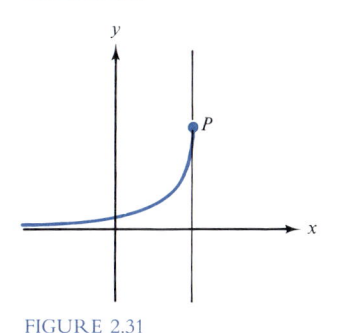

FIGURE 2.31

PROBLEM SET 2.3

In Problems 1–14, sketch the tangent line at P (if it exists); otherwise, specify "does not exist."

1.

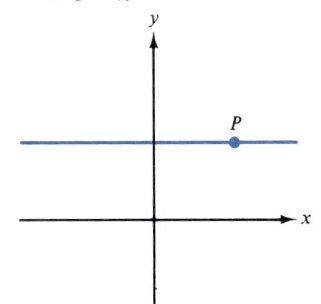

2.

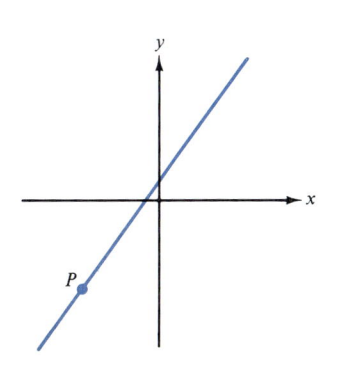

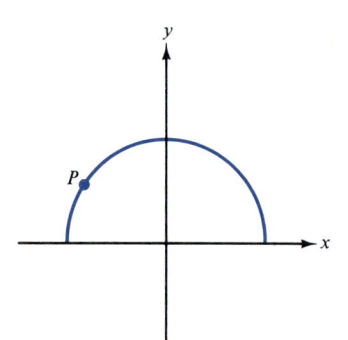

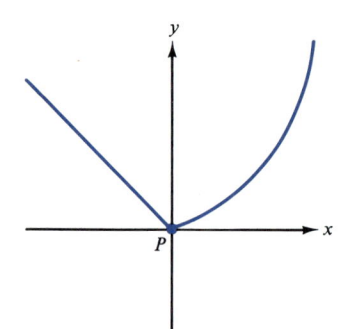

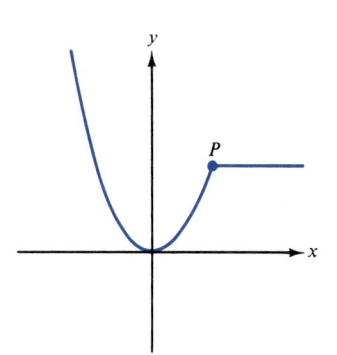

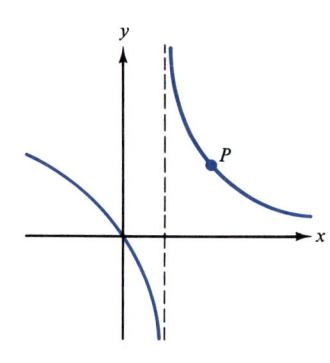

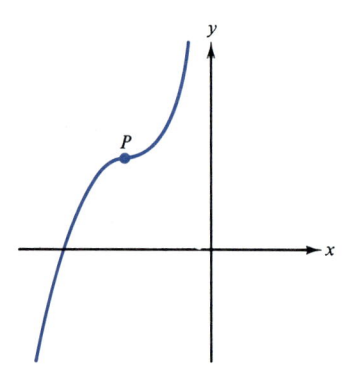

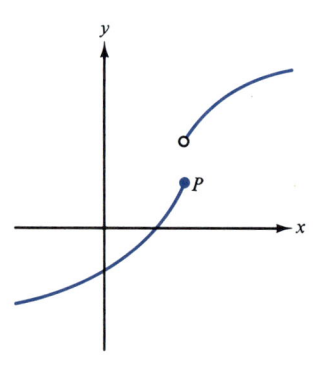

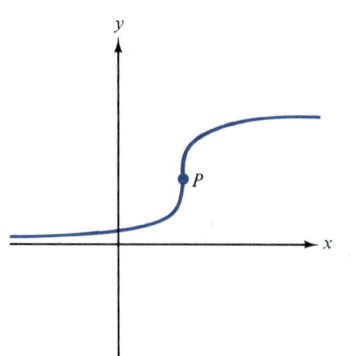

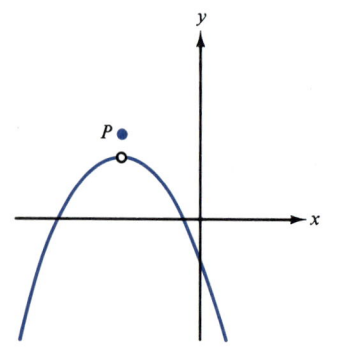

3.

4.

5.

6.

7.

8.

9.

10.

11.

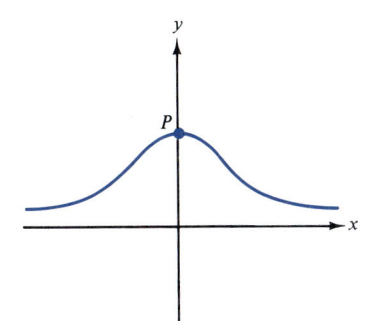

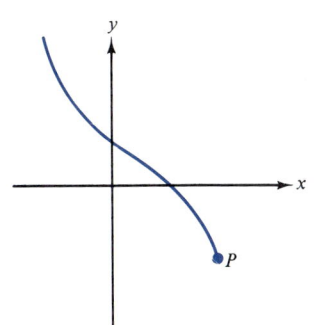

12.

13.

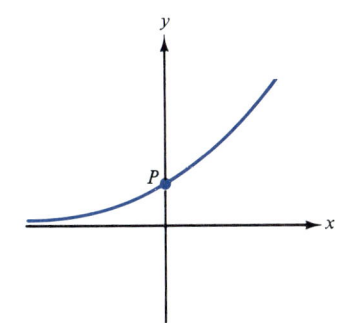

14.

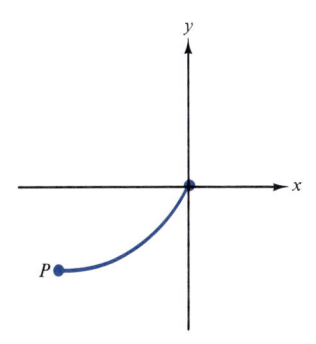

2.4 SLOPES OF TANGENT LINES

In this section we learn how to compute the slope of a tangent line. We begin by considering the same curve that appears at the beginning of the last section. See Figure 2.32.

Since the secants approach the tangent as Q approaches P, the slopes of the secants must approach the slope of the tangent. In fact, since the

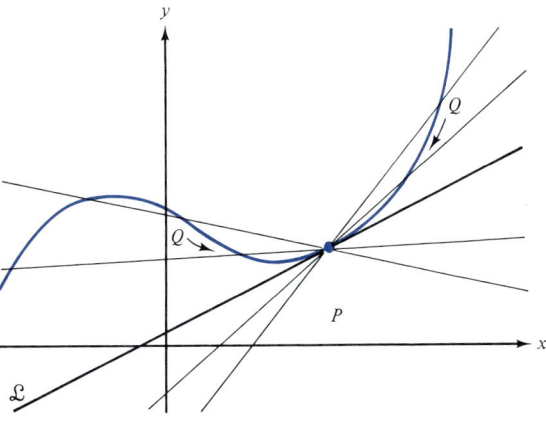

FIGURE 2.32

tangent line is the "limit line" of the secants, the slope of the tangent will be the limit of the slopes of the secants as Q approaches P!

Let $y = f(x)$ be the equation of the curve, let $P = (a,f(a))$, where a is a constant, and let Q be represented by $(t,f(t))$, where t is a variable. The slope of a secant PQ, which is the line through $(a,f(a))$ and $(t,f(t))$, is given by

$$\frac{f(t) - f(a)}{t - a}.$$

Q approaches P if and only if t approaches a. Thus the slope of the tangent line at $(a,f(a))$ is

$$\lim_{t \to a} \frac{f(t) - f(a)}{t - a}. \tag{2-1}$$

Let's put this concept to work by determining the slope of the tangent to the curve $f(x) = x^2 + 1$ at the point (2,5). Figure 2.33 leads us to anticipate a positive slope greater than 1. We must compute

$$\lim_{t \to a} \frac{f(t) - f(a)}{t - a},$$

where $a = 2$ and $f(a) = 5$. We get

$$\lim_{t \to 2} \frac{f(t) - f(2)}{t - 2} = \lim_{t \to 2} \frac{t^2 + 1 - 5}{t - 2}$$

$$= \lim_{t \to 2} \frac{t^2 - 4}{t - 2}$$

$$= \lim_{t \to 2} \frac{(t - 2)(t + 2)}{t - 2}$$

$$= \lim_{t \to 2} (t + 2)$$

$$= 4.$$

FIGURE 2.33

Hence the slope of the tangent line at (2,5) is 4.

There is an alternative form for the slope of the tangent line, which is, in general, easier algebraically. It arises by representing the point Q by $(a + h, f(a + h))$, where h is a variable, instead of by $(t, f(t))$. In this form the slope of a secant PQ, the line through $(a,f(a))$ and $(a + h, f(a + h))$, is

$$\frac{f(a + h) - f(a)}{a + h - a} = \frac{f(a + h) - f(a)}{h}.$$

Q approaches P if and only if h approaches 0. Thus the slope of the tangent line at $(a,f(a))$ is

$$\lim_{h \to 0} \frac{f(a + h) - f(a)}{h}. \tag{2-2}$$

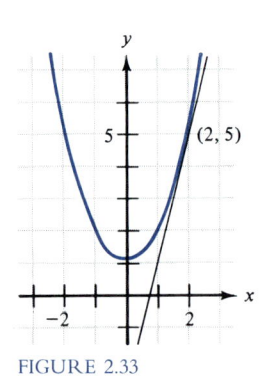

2.4 SLOPES OF TANGENT LINES

This limit is equivalent to the one in (2-1), but it is generally easier to use. Let's return to the illustration and use the limit of (2-2). The slope of the tangent to $f(x) = x^2 + 1$ at $(2,5)$ is

$$\lim_{h \to 0} \frac{f(2+h) - f(2)}{h} = \lim_{h \to 0} \frac{(2+h)^2 + 1 - 5}{h}$$

$$= \lim_{h \to 0} \frac{4 + 4h + h^2 - 4}{h}$$

$$= \lim_{h \to 0} \frac{4h + h^2}{h}$$

$$= \lim_{h \to 0} \frac{h(4+h)}{h}$$

$$= \lim_{h \to 0} (4 + h)$$

$$= 4.$$

EXAMPLE 1

Determine the slope of the tangent to $f(x) = 2 - x^2$ at $(-1, 1)$.

■ *SOLUTION*

We must compute

$$\lim_{h \to 0} \frac{f(a+h) - f(a)}{h},$$

where $a = -1$. We get

$$\lim_{h \to 0} \frac{f(-1+h) - f(-1)}{h} = \lim_{h \to 0} \frac{2 - (-1+h)^2 - 1}{h}$$

$$= \lim_{h \to 0} \frac{2 - (1 - 2h + h^2) - 1}{h}$$

$$= \lim_{h \to 0} \frac{2 - 1 + 2h - h^2 - 1}{h}$$

$$= \lim_{h \to 0} \frac{2h - h^2}{h}$$

$$= \lim_{h \to 0} (2 - h)$$

$$= 2.$$

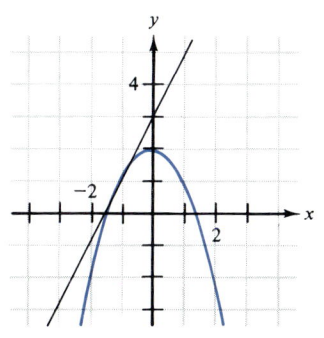

FIGURE 2.34

Thus the slope of the tangent at $(-1, 1)$ is 2. See Figure 2.34.

EXERCISE

Determine the slope of the tangent to $f(x) = -1 - x^2$ at $(3, -10)$.

■ ANSWER

-6

EXAMPLE 2

Determine the slope of the tangent to $f(x) = 1/x$ at $x = -2$.

■ SOLUTION

This example is asking us to determine the slope of the tangent at the point $(-2, f(-2))$. (The fact that we haven't been given the y-coordinate of the point is not bothersome because we have the formula for the function.) We get

$$\lim_{h \to 0} \frac{f(-2+h) - f(-2)}{h} = \lim_{h \to 0} \frac{\frac{1}{-2+h} - \frac{1}{-2}}{h}$$

$$= \lim_{h \to 0} \frac{\frac{1}{-2+h} + \frac{1}{2}}{h}$$

$$= \lim_{h \to 0} \frac{\frac{2 - 2 + h}{2(-2+h)}}{h}$$

$$= \lim_{h \to 0} \frac{h}{2(-2+h)} \cdot \frac{1}{h}$$

$$= \lim_{h \to 0} \frac{1}{2(-2+h)}$$

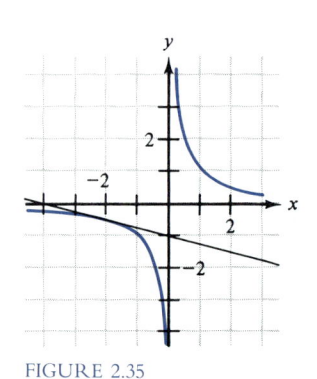

$$= -\tfrac{1}{4}.$$

Hence the slope of the tangent line at $x = -2$ is $-\tfrac{1}{4}$. See Figure 2.35.

FIGURE 2.35

EXERCISE

Determine the slope of the tangent to $f(x) = -1/x$ at $x = 3$.

■ ANSWER

$\tfrac{1}{9}$

2.4 SLOPES OF TANGENT LINES

EXAMPLE 3

Determine the equation of the tangent to $f(x) = x^2$ at $x = -2$.

■ SOLUTION

In order to determine the equation of the tangent line we must have a point on the line and must know the slope. Since the x-coordinate at the point of tangency is -2, the corresponding y-coordinate is $f(-2) = 4$. Thus $(-2, 4)$ is the point. To determine the slope, we compute a limit. We get

$$\lim_{h \to 0} \frac{f(-2 + h) - f(-2)}{h} = \lim_{h \to 0} \frac{(-2 + h)^2 - 4}{h}$$

$$= \lim_{h \to 0} \frac{4 - 4h + h^2 - 4}{h}$$

$$= \lim_{h \to 0} \frac{-4h + h^2}{h}$$

$$= \lim_{h \to 0} (-4 + h)$$

$$= -4.$$

So the tangent line has slope -4 and passes through $(-2, 4)$. Its equation is

$$y - 4 = -4(x + 2)$$

$$y - 4 = -4x - 8$$

$$y = -4x - 4.$$

EXERCISE

Determine the equation of the tangent to $f(x) = x^2$ at $x = 3$.

■ ANSWER
$y = 6x - 9$

Let P be a point on a curve at which there is a nonvertical tangent. Then the **slope of the curve** at P is simply the slope of the tangent line at P. Thus, if $y = f(x)$ and $P = (a, f(a))$, then the slope of the curve at P is

$$\lim_{h \to 0} \frac{f(a + h) - f(a)}{h},$$

EXAMPLE 4

Determine the slope of the curve $f(x) = x^2 + x - 1$ at $x = 2$.

■ SOLUTION

We have

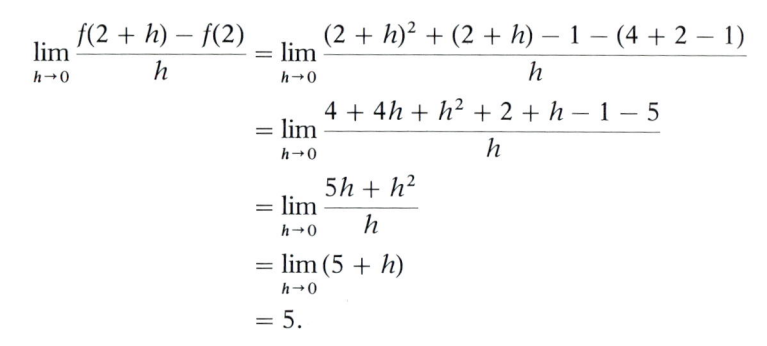

$$\lim_{h \to 0} \frac{f(2+h) - f(2)}{h} = \lim_{h \to 0} \frac{(2+h)^2 + (2+h) - 1 - (4 + 2 - 1)}{h}$$

$$= \lim_{h \to 0} \frac{4 + 4h + h^2 + 2 + h - 1 - 5}{h}$$

$$= \lim_{h \to 0} \frac{5h + h^2}{h}$$

$$= \lim_{h \to 0} (5 + h)$$

$$= 5.$$

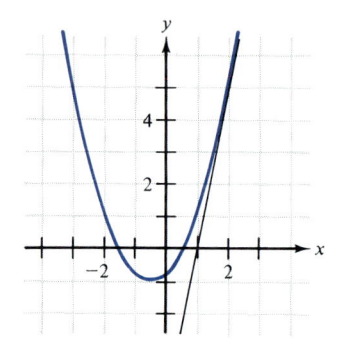

FIGURE 2.36

The slope of the curve at $x = 2$ is 5. See Figure 2.36.

EXERCISE

Determine the slope of the curve $f(x) = x^2 - x - 1$ at $x = 2$.

■ ANSWER

3

PROBLEM SET 2.4

In Problems 1–12, determine the slope of the tangent line to each function at the specified location.

1. $f(x) = 2x + 3$, $(1,5)$
2. $f(x) = 6 - x$, $(0,6)$
3. $f(x) = 3x^2 - \ln 2$, $(-1, 3 - \ln 2)$
4. $f(x) = x^2 + 6x$, $(-3, -9)$
5. $f(x) = (x + 1)^2$, $(2,9)$
6. $f(x) = (3x - 1)(x + 1)$, $(1,4)$
7. $f(x) = \dfrac{1}{1+x}$, $x = 0$
8. $f(x) = \dfrac{e + x}{x}$, $x = e$
9. $f(x) = 3x^{-2}$, $x = -2$
10. $f(x) = \dfrac{2x}{x - 1}$, $x = -1$
11. $f(x) = \sqrt{x}$, $x = 4$
    (*Hint:* Rationalize the numerator.)
12. $f(x) = x - \sqrt{x}$, $x = 1$

In Problems 13–18, determine the equation of the tangent to each function at the indicated x-coordinate.

13. $f(x) = 3$, $x = 5$
14. $f(x) = x - 2$, $x = 0$
15. $f(x) = 5e^2 - x^2$, $x = -2e$
16. $f(x) = 2x^2 - x$, $x = \frac{1}{4}$
17. $f(x) = x^3 - 3x^2 + 5$, $x = 0$
18. $f(x) = -3/x$, $x = -3$

In Problems 19–22, determine the slope of each curve at the indicated point.

19. $f(x) = -3 - x^2$, $(-1, -4)$
20. $f(x) = 5 - x^2$, $(-e^2, 5 - e^4)$
21. $f(x) = x^2 - x - 12$, $(4, 0)$
22. $f(x) = 3x^2 - 2x + 1$, $(1, 2)$
23. Show that the slope of a parabola $y = ax^2 + bx + c$ at its vertex is 0

CHAPTER 2 REVIEW

1. Determine whether each of the following is true or false.
  (a) $\lim_{x \to a}(mx + b) = ma + b$
  (b) $\lim_{x \to 0} 5 = 0$
  (c) A polynomial function is continuous at every real number.
  (d) For the function f, graphed below, $\lim_{x \to -2} f(x) = 5$.

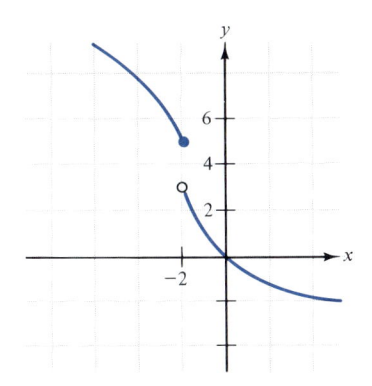

  (e) If $f(x) = \begin{cases} x^2 & \text{when } x \neq 2 \\ 6 & \text{when } x = 2 \end{cases}$, then f is continuous at $x = 2$.
  (f) If $\lim_{x \to a^+} f(x) = \lim_{x \to a^-} f(x)$, then $\lim_{x \to a} f(x)$ exists.
  (g) If a is any real number, then $\lim_{x \to a} a = a$.
  (h) The graph below has no tangent line at P.

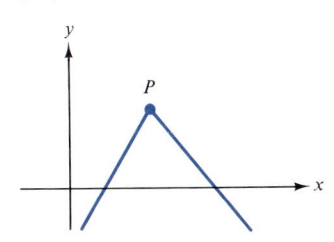

  (i) $\lim_{x \to 4} (2 - \sqrt{x})/(x - 4)$ does not exist.
  (j) The equation of the tangent to the parabola $y = (x - a)^2$ at its vertex is $y = 0$.
  (k) If $f(x) = x^2$, $x \neq \sqrt{3}$, then $\lim_{x \to \sqrt{3}} f(x) = 3$.
  (l) For the function g, graphed below, $\lim_{x \to 3} g(x) = 1$.

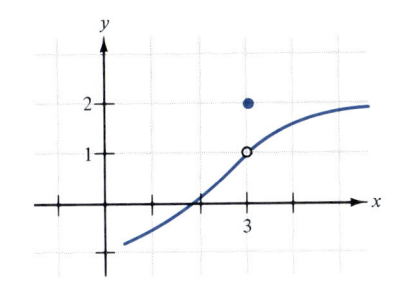

  (m) The tangent line at a point P cannot intersect the graph at more than one point.
  (n) The slope of the tangent line to the graph of $f(x) = x^2$ at $(3, 9)$ is
  $$\lim_{h \to 0} \frac{f(3 + h) - f(9)}{h}.$$
  (o) The function
  $$f(x) = \begin{cases} (x^2 - 1)/(x - 1) & \text{when } x \neq 1 \\ 1 & \text{when } x = 1 \end{cases}$$
  is continuous at $x = 1$.
  (p) If f is discontinuous at $x = 3$ and $\lim_{x \to 3} f(x) = 7$, then $f(3) \neq 7$.
  (q) The equation of the tangent line to $f(x) = 2x$ at $(-3, -6)$ is $y = 2x$.
  (r) If f is discontinuous at $x = a$, then there is no tangent line at $(a, f(a))$.
  (s) All rational functions are continuous.

(t) The graph below has a horizontal tangent at (2,0).

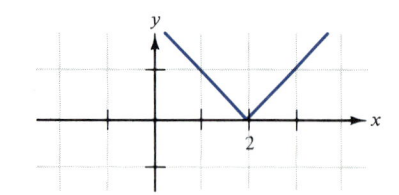

(u) The slope of the secant line through $(a,f(a))$ and $(t,f(t))$ is $(f(a) - f(t))/(a - t)$.

(v) The slope of the curve $f(x) = x^{40}$ at $x = 4$ is
$$\lim_{h \to 0} \frac{(4 + h)^{40} - (4)^{40}}{h},$$
provided that this limit exists.

(w) $\lim_{x \to -1} (x + 1)/(x^2 + 1)$ does not exist.

(x) If $f(x) = \begin{cases} x^2 & \text{when } x \leq 2 \\ x + 2.1 & \text{when } x > 2 \end{cases}$, then $\lim_{x \to 2} f(x) = 4$.

(y) If $f(x)$ and $g(x)$ are both continuous at $x = 2$, then $f(2) - g(2) = 0$.

(z) $\lim_{x \to 3} [x]$ does not exist

(aa) If f is continuous, then $y = e^{f(x)}$ is continuous.

2. Consider the following statements:
   (a) $\lim_{x \to 2^-} f(x)$ exists
   (b) $f(2)$ exists
   (c) $\lim_{x \to 2} f(x)$ exists
   (d) f has a tangent line at $x = 2$
   (e) f is continuous at $x = 2$

   (I) For each of the following graphs, determine which of the preceding statements are true and which are false.

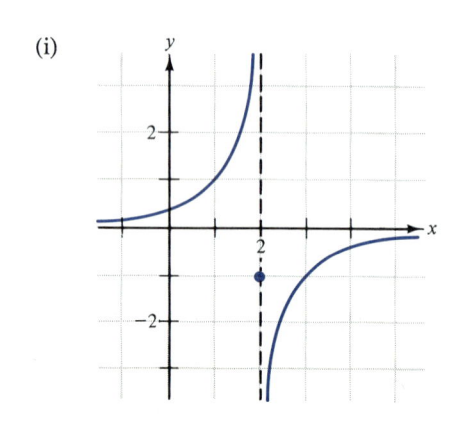

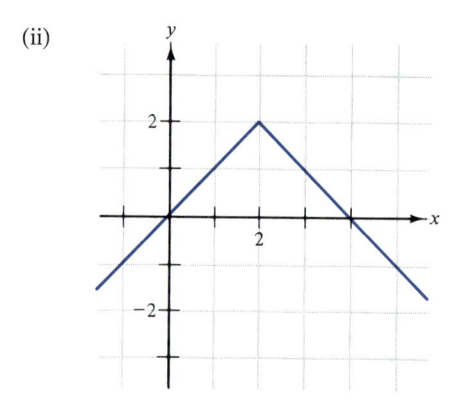

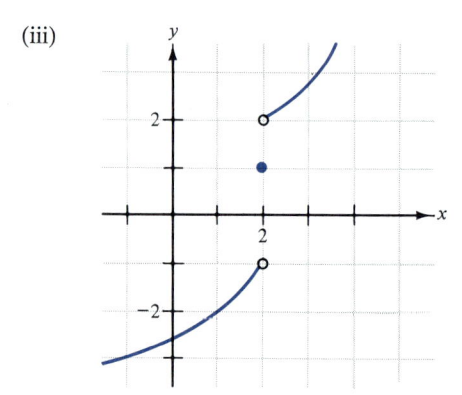

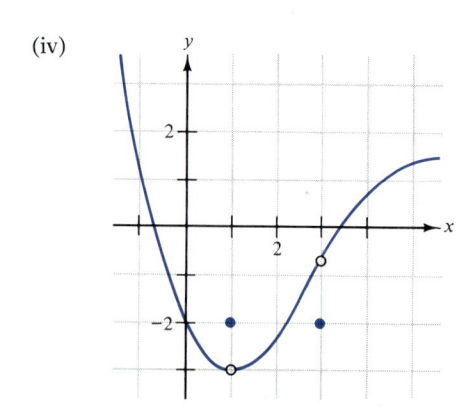

   (i)

   (ii)

   (iii)

   (iv)

   (II) For each of the following functions, determine which of the preceding statements are true and which are false.

   (i) $f(x) = \begin{cases} 3 & \text{when } x < 2 \\ x^2 & \text{when } x \geq 2 \end{cases}$.

(ii) $f(x) = \begin{cases} x^3 & \text{when } x \leq 2 \\ -x + 10 & \text{when } x > 2 \end{cases}$

(iii) $f(x) = \begin{cases} (6x - 12)/(4 - 2x) & \text{when } x \neq 2 \\ -3 & \text{when } x = 2 \end{cases}$

(iv) $f(x) = \begin{cases} 1/(x - 2)^2 & \text{when } x \neq 2 \\ 0 & \text{when } x = 2 \end{cases}$

3. Use the graph of f below to answer the following questions.

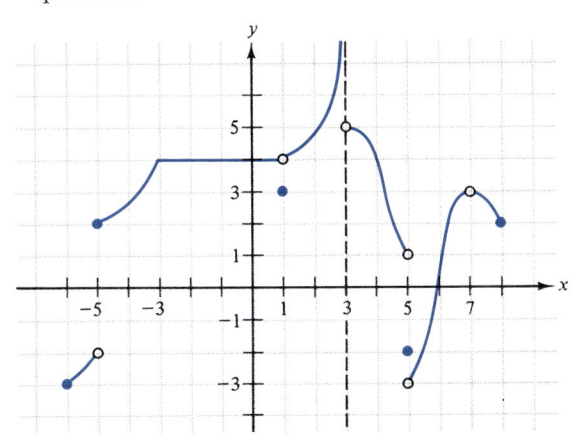

Determine the following:

(a) $\lim_{x \to -5^-} f(x)$ (b) $\lim_{x \to -5^+} f(x)$
(c) $f(-5)$ (d) $\lim_{x \to -3^-} f(x)$
(e) $\lim_{x \to -3^+} f(x)$ (f) $\lim_{x \to 1} f(x)$
(g) $\lim_{x \to 3^+} f(x)$ (h) $\lim_{x \to 3^-} f(x)$
(i) $\lim_{x \to 5} f(x)$ (j) $\lim_{x \to 6} f(x)$
(k) $\lim_{x \to 7} f(x)$ (l) $\lim_{x \to 8} f(x)$

Determine whether each of the following is true or false.

(m) f is discontinuous at $x = -5$
(n) f is continuous at $x = 0$
(o) f is continuous at $x = 1$
(p) f is discontinuous at $x = 5$
(q) f has a tangent line at $(0,4)$
(r) $\lim_{x \to 7^-} f(x) + \lim_{x \to 5^+} f(x) + f(1) = 3$
(s) f has a tangent line at $(-3, 4)$
(t) f has a tangent line at $(4, 3)$
(u) The slope of the tangent line to f at $(6, 0)$ is positive.
(v) The slope of the tangent line to f at $(-1, 4)$ is 0.
(w) The equation of the tangent line to f at $(-2, 4)$ is $x = 4$.

In Problems 4–22, compute the limits.

4. $\lim_{x \to -4} (\frac{1}{2}x^2 - 2x - 8)$

5. $\lim_{x \to \sqrt{2}} (x^6 - x^4 - x^2 - 2)$

6. $\lim_{x \to \ln 2} \dfrac{x - \ln 2}{3x}$

7. $\lim_{x \to -1} \dfrac{x^2 - 1}{x - 1}$

8. $\lim_{x \to \ln 3} e^{2x}$

9. $\lim_{x \to e^3 - 1} \ln(x + 1)$

10. $\lim_{x \to -3} \dfrac{x + 3}{x^3 - 9x}$

11. $\lim_{x \to -2} \dfrac{-x^2 - 2x}{x^2 + 5x + 6}$

12. $\lim_{x \to 4} \dfrac{3x - 12}{x^2 - 16}$

13. $\lim_{t \to a} \dfrac{at - a^2}{t^2 - a^2}$

14. $\lim_{x \to 0} \dfrac{(4 + x)^3 - 64}{x}$

15. $\lim_{x \to 0} \dfrac{e^{2x} - 1}{e^x - 1}$

16. $\lim_{x \to 0} \dfrac{1 - \sqrt{1 - x^2}}{x^2}$

17. $\lim_{x \to e^-} \sqrt{e - x}$

18. $\lim_{x \to 1^-} \dfrac{x^3 - 1}{|x - 1|}$

19. $\lim_{x \to 3} \left(\dfrac{3x}{x - 3} - \dfrac{9}{x - 3} \right)$

20. $\lim_{h \to 0} \dfrac{4(-1 + h)^2 - 3(-1 + h) - (4(-1)^2 - 3(-1))}{h}$

21. $\lim_{h \to 0} \dfrac{\dfrac{1}{(x + h)^2} - \dfrac{1}{x^2}}{h}$

22. $\lim_{h \to 0} \dfrac{-(a + h)^2 - (a + h) - 1 - (-a^2 - a - 1)}{h}$

23. If $f(x) = 2x^2 - 3$ compute $\lim_{h \to 0} \dfrac{f(3 + h) - f(3 - h)}{2h}$

24. Show that
$$\lim_{x \to 0} \dfrac{|x| - x}{x}$$
does not exist by computing
$$\lim_{x \to 0^+} \dfrac{|x| - x}{x} \quad \text{and} \quad \lim_{x \to 0^-} \dfrac{|x| - x}{x}.$$

In Problems 25–28, graph the function f and determine the limits (if they exist); otherwise, specify "does not exist."

25. $f(x) = \begin{cases} x & \text{when } x \neq 5 \\ 1 & \text{when } x = 5 \end{cases}$, $\lim_{x \to 5^-} f(x)$, $\lim_{x \to 5^+} f(x)$, $\lim_{x \to 5} f(x)$

26. $f(x) = \begin{cases} x^2 + 1 & \text{when } x \leq 0 \\ x + 1 & \text{when } x > 0 \end{cases}$, $\lim_{x \to 0^-} f(x)$, $\lim_{x \to 0^+} f(x)$, $\lim_{x \to 0} f(x)$

27. $f(x) = \begin{cases} 3 & \text{when } x < 2 \\ x^2 & \text{when } x \geq 2 \end{cases}$, $\lim_{x \to 2^+} f(x)$, $\lim_{x \to 2^-} f(x)$, $\lim_{x \to 2} f(x)$

28. $f(x) = \begin{cases} e^x - 1 & \text{when } x \leq 1 \\ 1 + \ln x & \text{when } x > 1 \end{cases}$, $\lim_{x \to 1^+} f(x)$, $\lim_{x \to 1^-} f(x)$, $\lim_{x \to 1} f(x)$

29. Determine a so that the function

$$f(x) = \begin{cases} \dfrac{x^2 + 2x - 15}{x + 5} & \text{when } x \neq -5 \\ a & \text{when } x = -5 \end{cases}$$

is continuous at $x = -5$.

30. Approximate $\lim_{x \to 1} x^{1/(1-x)}$ to the nearest hundred thousandth by completing the following tables.

x	$x^{1/(1-x)}$
0.9	
0.99	
0.999	
0.9999	
0.99999	
0.999999	

x	$x^{1/(1-x)}$
1.1	
1.01	
1.001	
1.0001	
1.00001	
1.000001	

In Problems 31–34, determine whether the function graphed is continuous or discontinuous.

31.

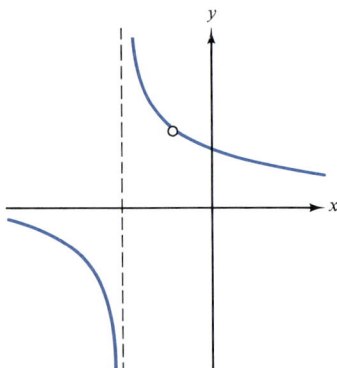

32.

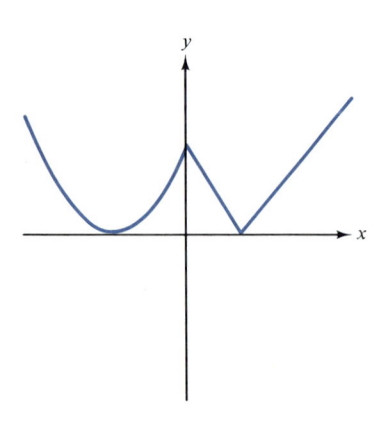

33.

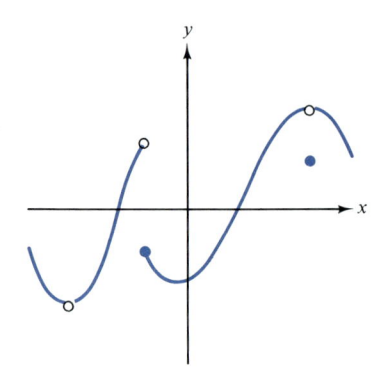

34.

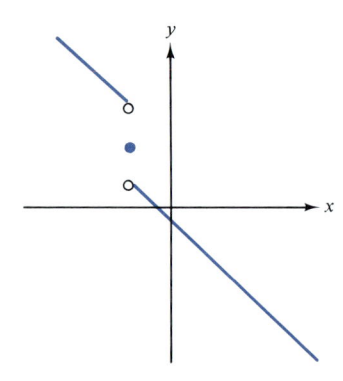

In Problems 35–38, sketch the tangent line (if it exists) at each P; otherwise, specify "does not exist."

35.

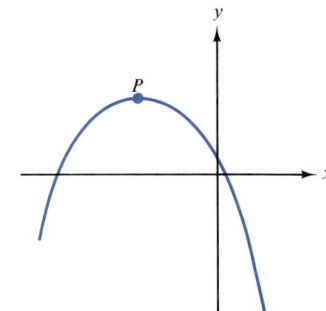

36.

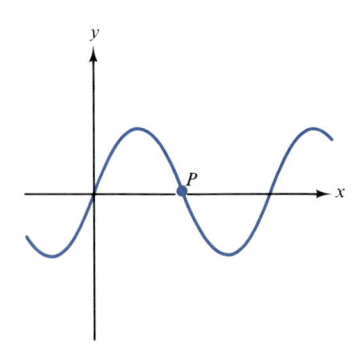

37.

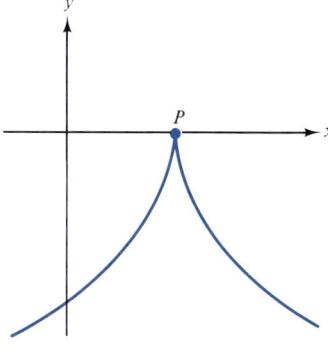

38.

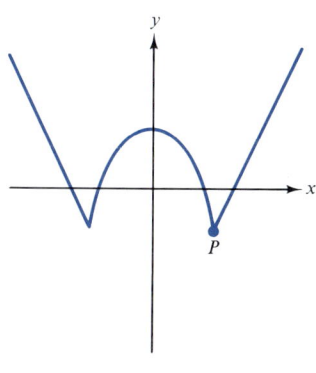

39. Sketch a graph of a function f having all of the following properties:
  (a) $\lim_{x \to 1^-} f(x)$ does not exist but $f(1)$ exists.
  (b) $\lim_{x \to 2} f(x)$ exists, but $f(2)$ does not exist.
  (c) $\lim_{x \to 3} f(x)$ exists and $f(3)$ exists, but f is not continuous at $x = 3$.

40. Sketch the graph of a function f having all of the following properties.
  (a) f is continuous everywhere except at $x = -2$ and 2.
  (b) f has a tangent line everywhere except at $x = -2$, 2, and 4.

In Problems 41–45, determine the slope of the tangent and the equation of the tangent to each function at the specified location.

41. $f(x) = 2x^2 - x$, $(-2, 10)$
42. $f(x) = 7e^2 - 5x^2$, $(e, 2e^2)$
43. $f(x) = x^2 + 6x + 9$, $x = -3$
44. $f(x) = x + (9/x)$, $x = 3$
45. $f(x) = \sqrt[3]{x}$, $x = 1$ (*Hint:* Rationalize the numerator.)

CHAPTER 3

THE DERIVATIVE

CHAPTER OUTLINE
3.1 Definition of the Derivative
3.2 Basic Differentiation Formulas
3.3 Rates of Change
3.4 The Chain Rule
3.5 The Product and Quotient Rules

This chapter begins with the derivative, which is the mathematical tool used to determine instantaneous rates of change. Then theorems are introduced that enable us to compute derivatives of elementary functions and particular combinations of elementary functions. The techniques are put to use in a section of applications. In the last two sections we significantly expand the types of functions we can differentiate.

3.1 DEFINITION OF THE DERIVATIVE

In Section 2.4 we learned how to compute the slope of a curve $y = f(x)$ at a specified point $(a, f(a))$. Thus, if asked to determine the slope of the curve $f(x) = x^2$ at $x = 1$, at $x = -2$ and at $x = 5$, we may do so by calculating three limits:

$$\lim_{h \to 0} \frac{f(1 + h) - f(1)}{h},$$

$$\lim_{h \to 0} \frac{f(-2 + h) - f(-2)}{h},$$

and

$$\lim_{h \to 0} \frac{f(5 + h) - f(5)}{h}.$$

But instead of computing three different limits, let's determine the slope of the curve at an arbitrary point $(x, f(x))$ and then substitute the appropriate x-values. We have

$$\begin{aligned}
\lim_{h \to 0} \frac{f(x + h) - f(x)}{h} &= \lim_{h \to 0} \frac{(x + h)^2 - x^2}{h} \\
&= \lim_{h \to 0} \frac{x^2 + 2xh + h^2 - x^2}{h} \\
&= \lim_{h \to 0} \frac{2xh + h^2}{h} \\
&= \lim_{h \to 0} \frac{h(2x + h)}{h} \\
&= \lim_{h \to 0} (2x + h) \\
&= 2x.
\end{aligned}$$

We now have a formula for the slope of $f(x) = x^2$ at an arbitrary point. When $x = 1$, $2x = 2$, and the slope of the curve at $x = 1$ is 2. When $x = -2$, $2x = -4$, and the slope of the curve at $x = -2$ is -4. Similarly, the formula tells us that the slope of the curve at $x = 5$ is 10. This formula ($2x$) is called the *derivative* and is now precisely defined.

Given a curve $y = f(x)$, let E be the set of all x such that the graph has a nonvertical tangent at $(x, f(x))$. Thus E is a subset of the domain of f. It contains the x-coordinates of those points at which the curve has a slope. Let's consider a new function that associates each element of E with the slope of the curve at the corresponding point. This new function, *derived*

3.1 DEFINITION OF THE DERIVATIVE

from f, is called the **derivative of f** and is denoted f'. Thus

$$f'(x) = \lim_{h \to 0} \frac{f(x+h) - f(x)}{h}.$$

And $f'(a)$ is the slope of the curve at $(a, f(a))$.

Returning to the curve $f(x) = x^2$, we see that

$$f'(x) = 2x.$$

And the slope of the curve at $x = 1$ is

$$f'(1) = 2(1) = 2.$$

EXAMPLE 1

Determine $f'(x)$ if $f(x) = 2x^2 + 3x - 1$, and then find the slope of the curve at $x = -2$.

■ SOLUTION

We apply the definition and compute the limit:

$$\begin{aligned}
f'(x) &= \lim_{h \to 0} \frac{f(x+h) - f(x)}{h} \\
&= \lim_{h \to 0} \frac{2(x+h)^2 + 3(x+h) - 1 - (2x^2 + 3x - 1)}{h} \\
&= \lim_{h \to 0} \frac{2x^2 + 4xh + 2h^2 + 3x + 3h - 1 - 2x^2 - 3x + 1}{h} \\
&= \lim_{h \to 0} \frac{4xh + 2h^2 + 3h}{h} \\
&= \lim_{h \to 0} \frac{h(4x + 2h + 3)}{h} \\
&= \lim_{h \to 0} (4x + 2h + 3) \\
&= 4x + 3.
\end{aligned}$$

To determine the slope of the curve at $x = -2$, we evaluate the derivative here. We get

$$f'(-2) = 4(-2) + 3 = -5.$$

EXERCISE

Determine $f'(x)$ if $f(x) = 2x^2 - 2x + 3$, and then find the slope of the curve at $x = -1$.

■ ANSWER

$f'(x) = 4x - 2;\ -6$

THE DERIVATIVE

EXAMPLE 2

Let $f(x) = x^2 - x$. Determine $f'(x)$ and the equation of the tangent line at $x = -1$.

■ SOLUTION
To determine the derivative we compute the limit:

$$f'(x) = \lim_{h \to 0} \frac{f(x+h) - f(x)}{h}$$

$$= \lim_{h \to 0} \frac{(x+h)^2 - (x+h) - (x^2 - x)}{h}$$

$$= \lim_{h \to 0} \frac{x^2 + 2xh + h^2 - x - h - x^2 + x}{h}$$

$$= \lim_{h \to 0} \frac{h(2x + h - 1)}{h}$$

$$= \lim_{h \to 0} (2x + h - 1)$$

$$= 2x - 1.$$

To determine the equation of the tangent line we must know its slope and have a point on the line. The slope at $x = -1$ is

$$f'(-1) = 2(-1) - 1 = -3.$$

Concerning the point at $x = -1$, we need the y-coordinate. This is obtained by using the *original* function:

$$f(-1) = (-1)^2 - (-1) = 2.$$

So the desired point is $(-1, 2)$. The equation of the line through this point with slope -3 is

$$y - 2 = -3(x + 1).$$

In slope–intercept form the equation for the tangent line is

$$y = -3x - 1.$$

EXERCISE

Let $f(x) = 2x^2 + x$. Determine $f'(x)$ and the equation of the tangent line at $x = -1$.

■ ANSWER
$f'(x) = 4x + 1$; $y = -3x - 2$

To **differentiate** a function means to determine its derivative. And we say that a function f is **differentiable at $x = a$** provided that its derivative

3.1 DEFINITION OF THE DERIVATIVE

f' is defined at $x = a$. Analytically, this means that

$$\lim_{h \to 0} \frac{f(a+h) - f(a)}{h}$$

exists. Geometrically, it means that the curve $y = f(x)$ has a nonvertical tangent at $x = a$. A function is called **differentiable** provided that it is differentiable at each point of its domain.

Consider the absolute value function $f(x) = |x|$. Analytically,

$$\lim_{h \to 0} \frac{f(a+h) - f(a)}{h}$$

exists for all $a \neq 0$. Indeed, for $a > 0$,

$$\lim_{h \to 0} \frac{f(a+h) - f(a)}{h} = \lim_{h \to 0} \frac{|a+h| - |a|}{h}.$$

For small h, $a + h$ is positive. Hence

$$\lim_{h \to 0} \frac{f(a+h) - f(a)}{h} = \lim_{h \to 0} \frac{a + h - a}{h}$$

$$= \lim_{h \to 0} \frac{h}{h}$$

$$= 1.$$

Similarly, for $a < 0$,

$$\lim_{h \to 0} \frac{f(a+h) - f(a)}{h} = -1.$$

Thus this function is differentiable at all such x-values. But for $a = 0$,

$$\lim_{h \to 0} \frac{f(a+h) - f(a)}{h}$$

does not exist. We see that

$$\lim_{h \to 0^+} \frac{f(0+h) - f(0)}{h} = \lim_{h \to 0^+} \frac{|h|}{h} = \lim_{h \to 0^+} \frac{h}{h} = 1,$$

whereas

$$\lim_{h \to 0^-} \frac{f(0+h) - f(0)}{h} = \lim_{h \to 0^-} \frac{|h|}{h} = \lim_{h \to 0^-} \frac{-h}{h} = -1.$$

Consequently,

$$\lim_{h \to 0} \frac{f(0+h) - f(0)}{h}$$

does not exist. So the function is not differentiable at $x = 0$.

Geometrically, we see this in the graph shown in Figure 3.1. The graph has a nonvertical tangent at all $x \neq 0$. But there is no tangent at $x = 0$. (The graph has a "corner" at $x = 0$.)

$f(x) = |x|$

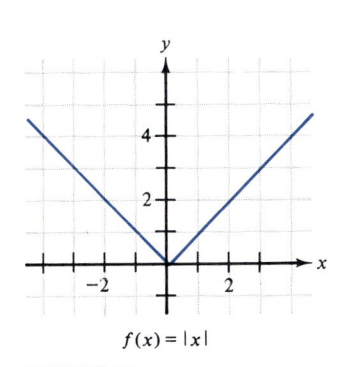

FIGURE 3.1

FIGURE 3.2

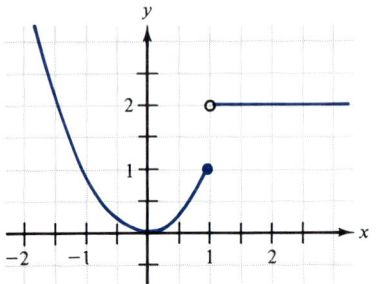

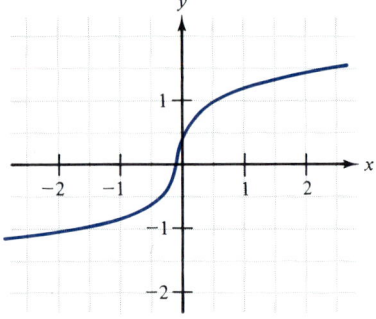

FIGURE 3.3

In Figure 3.2 we see the graph of a function that is not differentiable at $x = 1$ because it has no tangent there. Indeed, this function is discontinuous at $x = 1$.

We previously noted that if a function is discontinuous at $x = a$, then there is no tangent there. Thus, if a function is differentiable at $x = a$, it is continuous at $x = a$. But the converse isn't true. That is, continuity doesn't imply differentiability. The absolute value function is continuous at $x = 0$ but isn't differentiable there.

Let's consider one more graph. In Figure 3.3 we see the graph of a function that has a tangent at $x = 0$, but it's vertical. Consequently, this function is not differentiable at $x = 0$.

In this section we have already seen that, given the formula of definition for f, we may determine $f'(x)$. This in turn may be used to determine the slope of the graph of f at a specified point. To emphasize the connection between f and f', let's suppose that we don't have the formula for f or f' but have the graphs instead. To compute the slope of the graph of f at $x = a$ we find $f'(a)$ from the graph of f'.

EXAMPLE 3

Use the graph of f' [Figure 3.4(b)] to determine the slope of the graph of f [Figure 3.4(a)] at the specified location: (a) $x = 0$, (b) $x = 1$, (c) $(3,2)$, and (d) $x = -1$.

■ SOLUTION

(a) From Figure 3.4(a) we see that the graph appears to have a horizontal tangent at $x = 0$. That is, the slope at $x = 0$ appears to be 0. From Figure 3.4(b) we see that this is indeed the case because

$$f'(0) = 0.$$

(b) The graph of f tells us that f is not continuous at $x = 1$. (There's a break there.) Hence there is no tangent and no slope at $x = 1$. This is confirmed by the fact that f' is not defined at $x = 1$.

(c) The slope at $(3,2)$ is the slope at $x = 3$. Since

$$f'(3) = \tfrac{1}{2},$$

we see that the slope of $y = f(x)$ at $(3,2)$ is $\tfrac{1}{2}$.

(a) Graph of f (b) Graph of f'

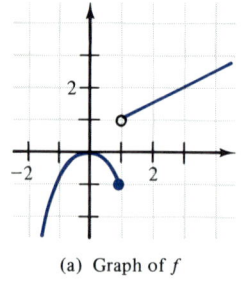

FIGURE 3.4

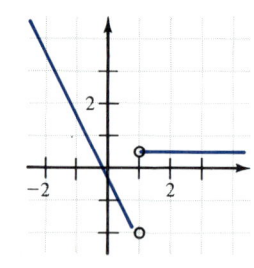

3.1 DEFINITION OF THE DERIVATIVE

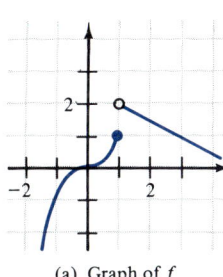

(a) Graph of f

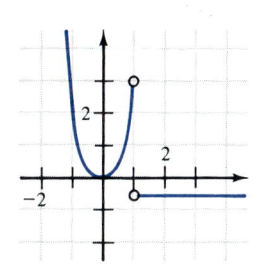

(b) Graph of f'

FIGURE 3.5

(d) About all we can determine from the graph of f is that the curve has a positive slope at $x = -1$. But the graph of the derivative shows that
$$f'(-1) = 2.$$
Hence the slope of $y = f(x)$ at $x = -1$ is 2.

EXERCISE

Use the graph of f' [Figure 3.5(b)] to determine the slope of the graph of f [Figure 3.5(a)] at the specified location: (a) $x = 0$, (b) $x = 1$, (c) $(3,1)$, and (d) $x = -1$.

■ *ANSWER*
(a) 0; (b) no slope; (c) $-\frac{1}{2}$; (d) 3

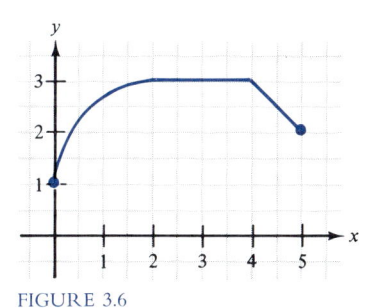

FIGURE 3.6

EXAMPLE 4

Sketch the graph of f' given the graph of f in Figure 3.6.

■ *SOLUTION*
To sketch the derivative we must examine the slope of the curve. At $x = 0$ there is a vertical tangent. So f' isn't defined at $x = 0$. At $x = 2$ the slope is 0. Between 0 and 2, the slope of the curve is decreasing. The closer we get to $x = 0$ the greater the slope. It appears that there is a vertical asymptote for the derivative at $x = 0$. Thus

$f'(0)$ doesn't exist, but there is a vertical asymptote at $x = 0$;

$f'(x)$ is decreasing as x approaches 2 from the negative side;

$f'(2) = 0$.

There is no tangent at $x = 4$, so f' isn't defined there. For values between $x = 2$ and $x = 4$, the slope is 0. Thus

$$f'(x) = 0 \quad \text{for } x \in (2,4);$$
$$f'(4) \text{ doesn't exist.}$$

118   THE DERIVATIVE

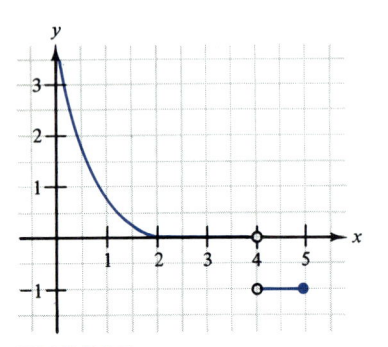

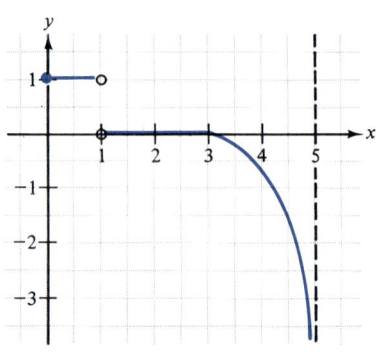

FIGURE 3.7

FIGURE 3.8

FIGURE 3.9

The slope is -1 between $x = 4$ and $x = 5$. So
$$f'(x) = -1 \quad \text{for } x \in (4,5].$$
Putting together the information on f' gives the graph in Figure 3.7.

EXERCISE

Sketch the graph of f' given the graph of f in Figure 3.8.

■ ANSWER
See Figure 3.9.

PROBLEM SET 3.1

In Problems 1–20, determine each $f'(x)$.

1. $f(x) = x^2 - 2$
2. $f(x) = 2x^2 + 1$
3. $f(x) = 3x + \dfrac{3}{e}$
4. $f(x) = \dfrac{1}{\ln 5} - 4x$
5. $f(x) = -8$
6. $f(x) = \sqrt{2} - 1$
7. $f(x) = (x + 3)(2x - 3)$
8. $f(x) = (3x + 2)(x - 1)$
9. $f(x) = x^3 + x$
10. $f(x) = x^2 - x^3$
11. $f(x) = \dfrac{1}{x}$
12. $f(x) = \dfrac{2}{x}$
13. $f(x) = \dfrac{1}{x - 3}$
14. $f(x) = \dfrac{3}{x + 3}$
15. $f(x) = \dfrac{x + 1}{x - 1}$
16. $f(x) = \dfrac{x^2}{x + 4}$
17. $f(x) = \dfrac{x - 2}{x^2}$
18. $f(x) = \dfrac{3x}{1 - x^2}$
19. $f(x) = \sqrt{x - 3}$
20. $f(x) = \sqrt[3]{x}$

In Problems 21–28, determine $f'(x)$ and the equation of the tangent line to the given function at the indicated location.

21. $f(x) = \dfrac{ex^2}{2}$, $x = -2$
22. $f(x) = \dfrac{-4x^2}{\ln 4}$, $x = \dfrac{1}{2}$
23. $f(x) = 2x + 1$, $x = \sqrt{2}$
24. $f(x) = 6 - 3x$, $x = 5$
25. $f(x) = x^2 - 6x + 9$, $y = 0$
26. $f(x) = x^3 - 1$, $y = 26$
27. $f(x) = (x - 2)/x^2$, $x = -2$ (Hint: Use the result from Problem 17.)
28. $f(x) = 3x/(1 - x^2)$, $x = 0$ (Hint: Use the result from Problem 18.)

In Problems 29–32, determine whether each function graphed is differentiable or not differentiable at $x = 2$.

29.

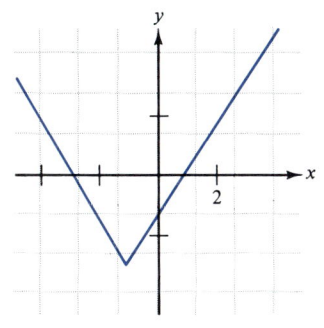

30.

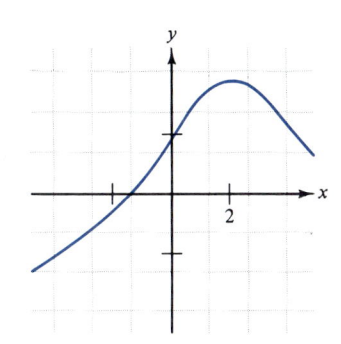

31.

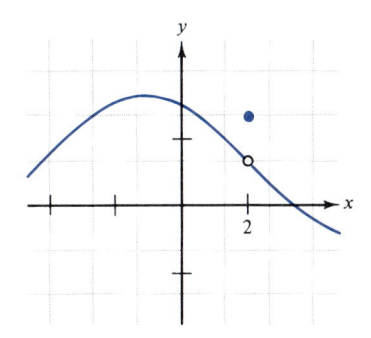

32.

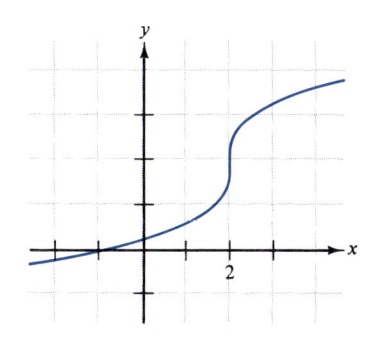

In Problems 33–36, determine whether each function graphed is differentiable or not differentiable.

33.

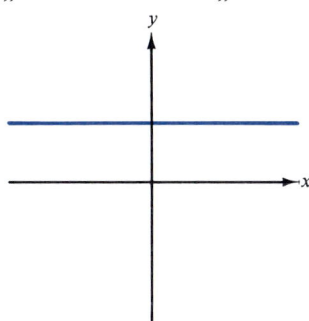

34.

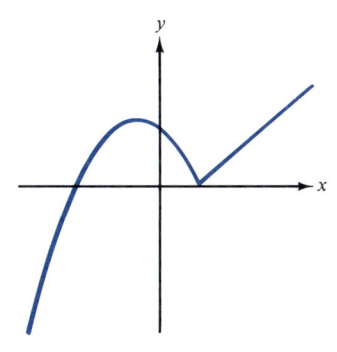

35.

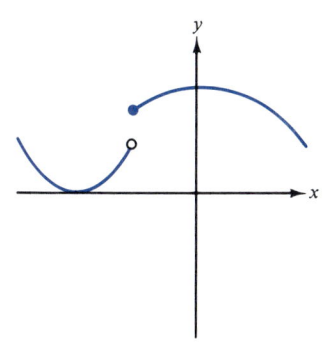

36.

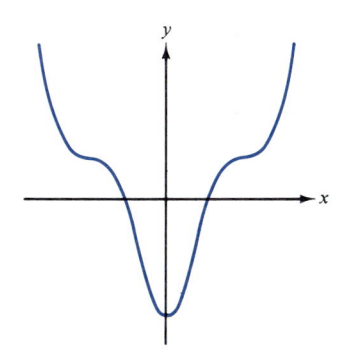

In Problems 37–42, use the graph of f' to determine the slope of the graph of y = f(x) at the specified location.

37. (a) $x = -\frac{1}{2}$; (b) $x = 0$; (c) $x = 2$; (d) $(4, 2)$

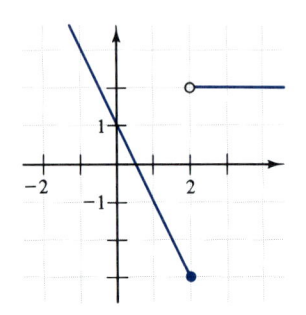

Graph of f

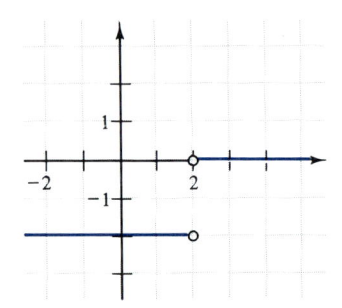

Graph of f'

38. (a) $x = -\frac{11}{3}$; (b) $x = -1$; (c) $x = 0$; (d) $(3, -3)$

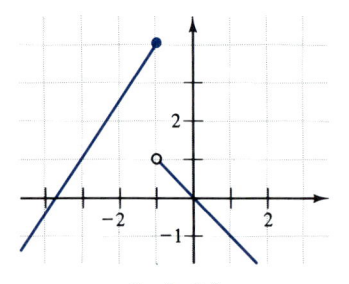

Graph of f

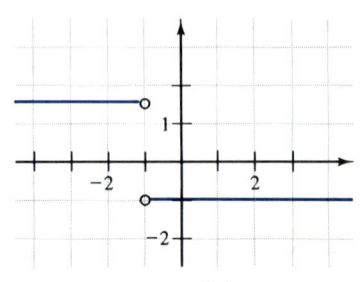

Graph of f'

39. (a) $(-2, 0)$; (b) $x = -1$; (c) $(1, 0)$; (d) $x = 2$

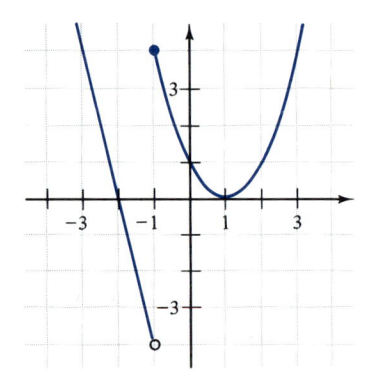

Graph of f

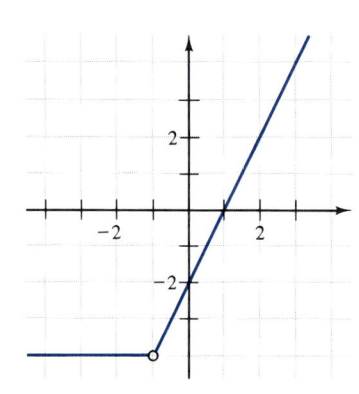

Graph of f'

40. (a) $(0, 1)$; (b) $(1, 0)$; (c) $x = 2$; (d) $x = \sqrt{6}$

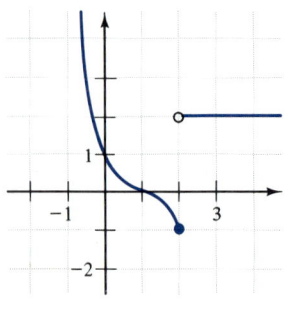

Graph of f

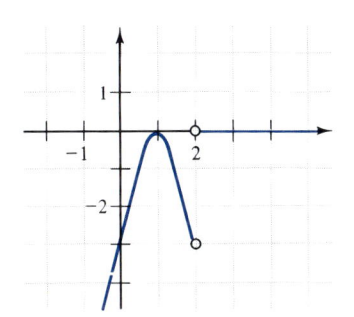

3.1 DEFINITION OF THE DERIVATIVE

Graph of f'

41. (a) $x = \frac{1}{3}$; (b) $(\frac{1}{2}, 1)$; (c) $x = 1$; (d) $(\frac{3}{2}, -1)$.

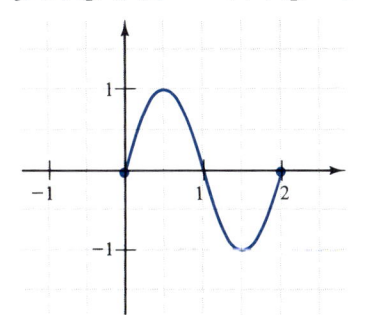

Graph of f'

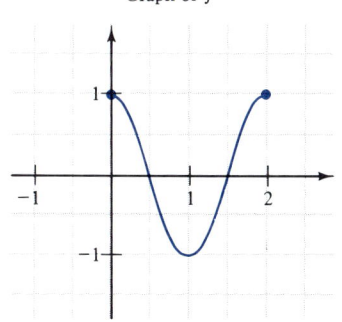

Graph of f

Graph of f'

42. (a) $x = -\frac{3}{2}$; (b) $x = -\frac{7}{6}$; (c) $(-1, -1)$; (d) $(-\frac{1}{2}, 0)$.

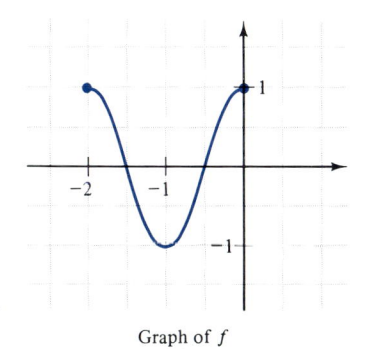

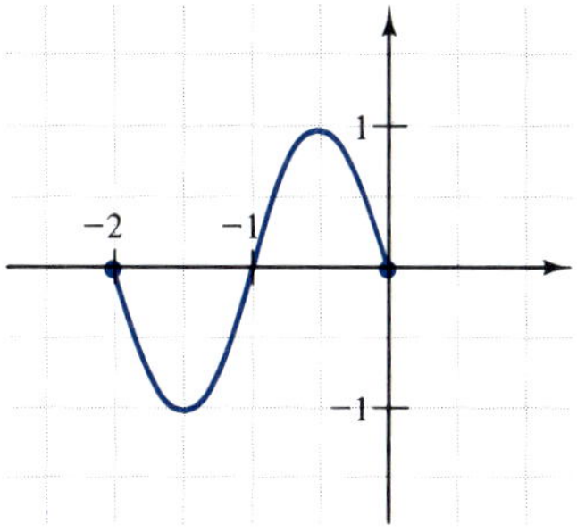

Graph of f

In Problems 43–48, sketch the graph of f' given the graph of f.

43.

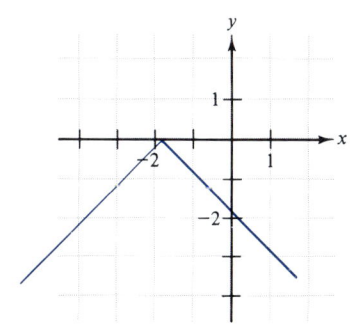

44.

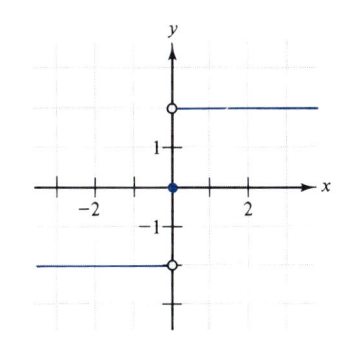

45.

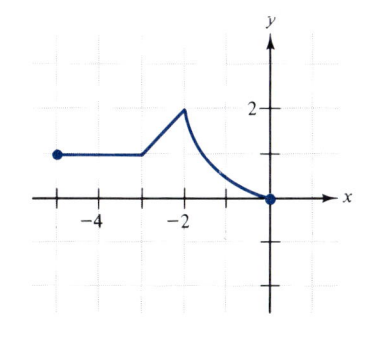

46.

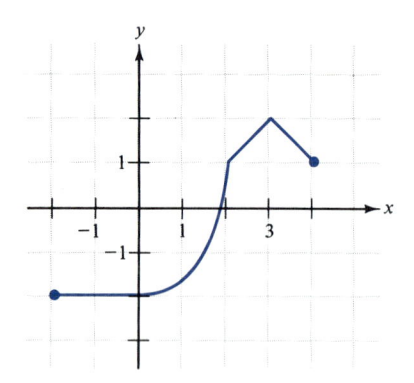

47.

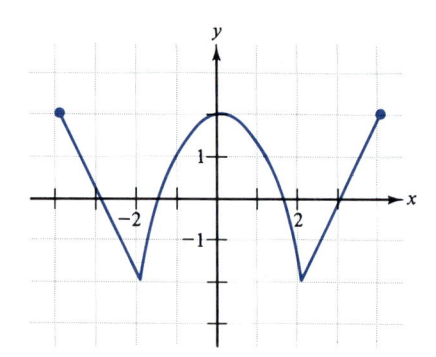

48.

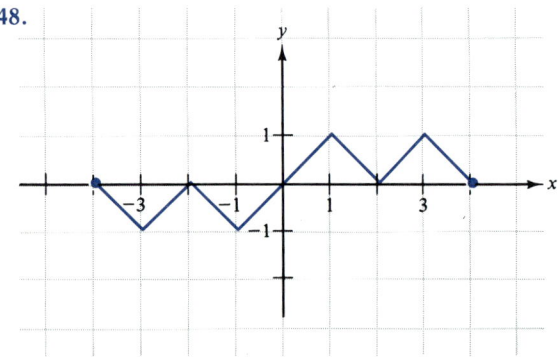

In Problems 49–52, sketch the graph of f and then sketch the graph of f'.

49. $f(x) = \begin{cases} 2x + 1 & \text{when } x \geq 0 \\ -x - 1 & \text{when } x < 0 \end{cases}$

50. $f(x) = \begin{cases} x^2 & \text{when } x \leq 0 \\ x & \text{when } x > 0 \end{cases}$

51. $f(x) = \begin{cases} 1/x & \text{when } x > 0 \\ -1 & \text{when } x \leq 0 \end{cases}$

52. $f(x) = \begin{cases} |x| & \text{when } x \leq 0 \\ [x] & \text{when } x > 0 \end{cases}$

53. Let f be the function with the following graph:

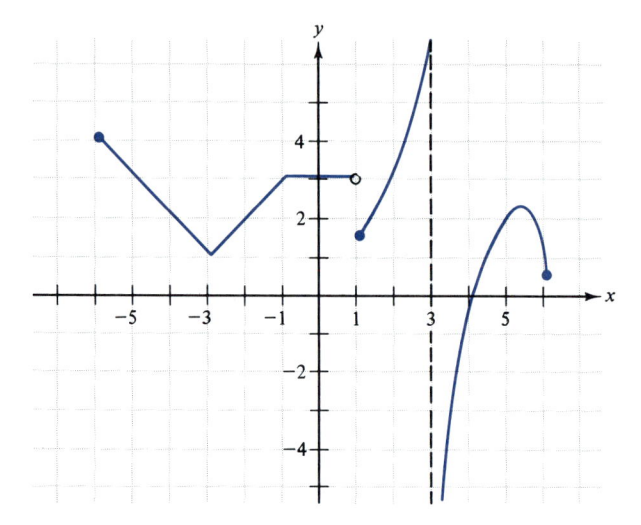

At the indicated x-value, determine whether f is differentiable and whether it is continuous.
(a) $x = -4$
(b) $x = -3$
(c) $x = -1$
(d) $x = 0$
(e) $x = 1$
(f) $x = 2$
(g) $x = 4$
(h) $x = 5$

54. Below is the graph of the function $g'(x)$.

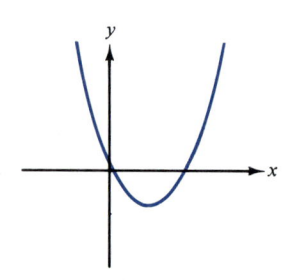

Which one of the five following graphs most closely resembles the graph of $g(x)$?

(a)   (b)   (c)   (d)   (e)

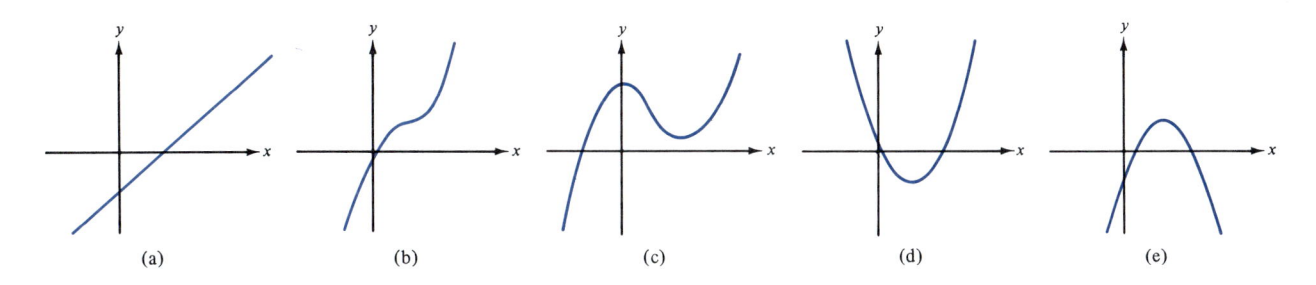

3.2 BASIC DIFFERENTIATION FORMULAS

In this section we encounter some elementary theorems concerning the computation of derivatives. By learning the theorems we may avoid determining derivatives by using limits.

THEOREM 3.1   If $f(x) = k$, where k is a constant, then $f'(x) = 0$.

Proof   We have

$$f'(x) = \lim_{h \to 0} \frac{f(x+h) - f(x)}{h}$$
$$= \lim_{h \to 0} \frac{k - k}{h}$$
$$= \lim_{h \to 0} 0$$
$$= 0.$$

This theorem says that the derivative of a constant is zero. Geometrically, this is easy to see. The graph of $f(x) = k$ is a horizontal line. The tangent at any point is simply the line itself, which has slope zero.

THEOREM 3.2
Simple Power Rule   If $f(x) = x^n$, where n is a constant, then $f'(x) = nx^{n-1}$.

According to this theorem, in differentiating $f(x) = x^n$, a simple power function, the exponent becomes the coefficient in the derivative, and then the exponent is reduced by one. Let's see this applied in Example 1.

EXAMPLE 1

Differentiate (a) $f(x) = x^{10}$; (b) $f(x) = \sqrt[4]{x^3}$; (c) $f(x) = 1/x^3$; and (d) $f(x) = x$.

■ SOLUTION

(a) By Theorem 3.2 we have

$$f'(x) = 10x^{10-1} = 10x^9.$$

(b) We first rewrite the formula of definition for the function. Using exponential notation instead of radical, we have

$$f(x) = x^{3/4}.$$

Thus, by the simple power rule,

$$f'(x) = \frac{3}{4} x^{-1/4} = \frac{3}{4x^{1/4}} = \frac{3}{4\sqrt[4]{x}}.$$

(c) Here we begin by putting the formula in the appropriate form:

$$f(x) = x^{-3}.$$

By Theorem 3.2 we get

$$f'(x) = -3x^{-4} = \frac{-3}{x^4}.$$

(d) We get

$$f'(x) = 1 \cdot x^0 = 1.$$

EXERCISE

Differentiate (a) $f(x) = x^{20}$; (b) $f(x) = \sqrt[3]{x^2}$; and (c) $f(x) = 1/x^5$.

■ ANSWER

(a) $f'(x) = 20x^{19}$; (b) $f'(x) = 2/(3\sqrt[3]{x})$; (c) $f'(x) = -5/x^6$

Before proceeding, let's take a moment to introduce an additional notation. If the given function is defined by an equation in two variables instead of by a formula of definition, then we attach a prime to the dependent variable to denote the derivative. For example, if $y = x^2$, we write $y' = 2x$. This notation is used when the functional notation is absent. So if we begin with $y = $ ____, we denote the derivative by y'. When we begin with $f(x) = $ ____, the derivative is denoted by $f'(x)$.

THEOREM 3.3 If $y = k \cdot f(x)$, where k is a constant, then $y' = k \cdot f'(x)$.

3.2 BASIC DIFFERENTIATION FORMULAS

This theorem says that the derivative of a constant times a function is the constant times the derivative of the function. It means that a constant factor may be "factored out" when taking a derivative. The proof is straightforward and is left as a problem.

EXAMPLE 2

Differentiate (a) $y = -5x^3$; (b) $y = 2/x$; and (c) $y = 7x$.

■ SOLUTION
(a) According to Theorem 3.3, the derivative of -5 times x^3 is -5 times the derivative of x^3. Thus we get

$$y' = -5(3x^2) = -15x^2.$$

(b) First we rewrite the equation as

$$y = 2x^{-1}.$$

The derivative is 2 times the derivative of x^{-1}. We get

$$y' = 2(-1 \cdot x^{-2}) = \frac{-2}{x^2}.$$

(c) We get

$$y' = 7 \cdot 1 = 7.$$

EXERCISE

Differentiate (a) $y = 2x^6$; (b) $y = 3/x^2$; and (c) $y = -6x$.

■ ANSWER
(a) $y' = 12x^5$; (b) $y' = -6/x^3$; (c) $y' = -6$

Example 2 suggests that Theorems 3.2 and 3.3 may be combined to extend the simple power rule.

THEOREM 3.4 If $f(x) = kx^n$, where k and n are constants, then $f'(x) = nkx^{n-1}$.

In order to differentiate kx^n, we multiply the exponent by the coefficient to get the coefficient in the derivative, and then we reduce the exponent by one. In essence, this is what we did in Example 2. The proof is straight forward and is left as a problem.

EXAMPLE 3

Differentiate (a) $f(x) = 5x^6$; (b) $y = x^5/4$; and (c) $y = \sqrt{x}/3$.

■ SOLUTION
(a) By Theorem 3.4, we multiply the exponent by the coefficient and then reduce the exponent by one. We get

$$f'(x) = 6 \cdot 5x^{6-1} = 30x^5.$$

(b) First we note that

$$y = \tfrac{1}{4}x^5.$$

By the extended simple power rule we get

$$y' = \tfrac{5}{4}x^4.$$

(c) Rewriting first we have

$$y = \tfrac{1}{3}x^{1/2}.$$

Thus

$$y' = \tfrac{1}{6}x^{-1/2} = \frac{1}{6x^{1/2}} = \frac{1}{6\sqrt{x}}.$$

EXERCISE

Differentiate (a) $f(x) = 4x^3$; (b) $y = x^4/5$; and (c) $y = \sqrt{x}/4$.

■ ANSWER
(a) $f'(x) = 12x^2$; (b) $y' = 4x^3/5$; (c) $y' = 1/(8\sqrt{x})$

THEOREM 3.5 If $f(x) = e^x$, then $f'(x) = e^x$.

The exponential function with base e is an unusual function. Its derivative is itself. This means that the slope of the curve at a specified point is the y-coordinate of the point (since $y' = y$).

Note that the simple power rule cannot be applied. That is, the derivative of e^x is *not* xe^{x-1}. This is because the simple power rule is to be used when we have a variable raised to a constant power, *not* when we have a constant raised to a variable power.

THEOREM 3.6 If $f(x) = \ln x$, then $f'(x) = 1/x$.

See the appendix for a proof of these two theorems.

EXAMPLE 4

Differentiate (a) $y = -3e^x$ and (b) $y = (\ln x)/2$.

■ SOLUTION

(a) The derivative of -3 times e^x is -3 times the derivative of e^x. Thus
$$y' = -3e^x.$$

(b) The derivative is $\frac{1}{2}$ times the derivative of $\ln x$. Hence
$$y' = \frac{1}{2}\left(\frac{1}{x}\right) = \frac{1}{2x}.$$

In Example 4(a) we see another function that equals its derivative. There are others, but all are of the form
$$y = ke^x$$
for some constant k. Indeed, since the derivative is k times the derivative of e^x, we see that
$$y' = ke^x.$$

EXERCISE

Differentiate (a) $y = 2e^x$ and (b) $y = (-\ln x)/3$.

■ ANSWER
(a) $y' = 2e^x$; (b) $y' = -1/(3x)$

Theorem 3.6 addresses the natural logarithmic function only, but we may differentiate logarithmic functions with other bases as well. If
$$y = \log_b x,$$
then by the change of base formula
$$y = \frac{\ln x}{\ln b} = \frac{1}{\ln b} \cdot \ln x.$$
Since the derivative is the constant $1/\ln b$ times the derivative of $\ln x$, we get
$$y' = \frac{1}{\ln b} \cdot \frac{1}{x}.$$

128 THE DERIVATIVE

Hence, of all the logarithmic functions, the natural logarithm is the one with the simplest derivative (since ln e = 1).

How do we determine the derivative of a sum of two functions or the derivative of a difference of two functions? The next two theorems tell us that it's as easy as we might hope.

THEOREM 3.7 If $y = f(x) + g(x)$, then $y' = f'(x) + g'(x)$.

Proof We have

$$y' = \lim_{h \to 0} \frac{f(x+h) + g(x+h) - (f(x) + g(x))}{h}$$

$$= \lim_{h \to 0} \frac{f(x+h) - f(x) + g(x+h) - g(x)}{h}$$

$$= \lim_{h \to 0} \left(\frac{f(x+h) - f(x)}{h} + \frac{g(x+h) - g(x)}{h} \right).$$

By properties of limits, the limit of a sum is the sum of the limits. Thus

$$y' = \lim_{h \to 0} \frac{f(x+h) - f(x)}{h} + \lim_{h \to 0} \frac{g(x+h) - g(x)}{h}$$

$$= f'(x) + g'(x).$$

THEOREM 3.8 If $y = f(x) - g(x)$, then $y' = f'(x) - g'(x)$.

So we see that the derivative of a sum is the sum of the derivatives. Also, the derivative of a difference is the difference of the derivatives. Even though the theorems are stated for the sum and difference of only *two* functions, they are nonetheless true for the sum and difference of any number of functions.

EXAMPLE 5

Differentiate (a) $y = x^2 + 10x$; (b) $f(x) = x^5 - 2/x^3 + 3x - 1$; and (c) $y = x^3 + e^x - 2 \ln x$.

■ SOLUTION
(a) Differentiating each term and adding, we get

$$y' = 2x + 10.$$

(b) Let's first rewrite $f(x)$:

$$f(x) = x^5 - 2x^{-3} + 3x - 1.$$

3.2 BASIC DIFFERENTIATION FORMULAS

Now we get

$$f'(x) = 5x^4 + 6x^{-4} + 3 = 5x^4 + \frac{6}{x^4} + 3.$$

(c) Differentiating each term yields

$$y' = 3x^2 + e^x - \frac{2}{x}.$$

EXERCISE

Differentiate (a) $y = x^3 - 5x$; (b) $f(x) = x^4 - 3/x^2 - x + 5$; and (c) $y = 2x^2 - e^x + 3 \ln x$.

■ ANSWER

(a) $y' = 3x^2 - 5$; (b) $f'(x) = 4x^3 + \frac{6}{x^3} - 1$; (c) $y' = 4x - e^x + \frac{3}{x}$

EXAMPLE 6

Find the slope of the graph of $f(x) = x^3$ at $x = -1$, at $x = 0$, and at $x = 1$.

■ SOLUTION

Since the derivative is the formula for the slope, we differentiate. We get

$$f'(x) = 3x^2.$$

To find the slopes at $x = -1$, at $x = 0$, and at $x = 1$, we use the formula for the derivative.

$$f'(-1) = 3(-1)^2 = 3;$$
$$f'(0) = 3 \cdot 0^2 = 0;$$
$$f'(1) = 3(1)^2 = 3.$$

Thus, at $x = -1$ and at $x = 1$, the slope is 3, at $x = 0$, the slope is 0.

EXERCISE

Find the slope of the graph of $f(x) = x^4$ at $x = -1$, at $x = 0$, and at $x = 2$.

■ ANSWER

The slope is -4 at $x = -1$, 0 at $x = 0$, and 32 at $x = 2$.

EXAMPLE 7

Determine the points on the graph of $y = 2x^3 - 3x^2 - 12x + 5$ at which the tangent line is horizontal.

■ *SOLUTION*

The tangent line is horizontal at any point at which the slope of the curve is 0. Since the derivative is the formula for the slope of the curve, we must find where it equals 0. Differentiating, we have

$$y' = 6x^2 - 6x - 12.$$

Now we set y' equal to 0 and solve for x:

$$6x^2 - 6x - 12 = 0$$
$$x^2 - x - 2 = 0$$
$$(x - 2)(x + 1) = 0$$
$$x = 2 \quad \text{or} \quad x = -1.$$

Thus the horizontal tangents occur at $x = 2$ and at $x = -1$. Because we must determine the points, not simply their x-coordinates, we must use the original function to calculate the corresponding y-coordinates. We see that

$$\text{when } x = 2, \quad y = 16 - 12 - 24 + 5 = -15;$$

and

$$\text{when } x = -1, \quad y = -2 - 3 + 12 + 5 = 12.$$

Thus the desired points are $(2, -15)$ and $(-1, 12)$. ∎

At this point it is convenient to introduce another notation. The value of y when $x = a$ may be denoted

$$y\Big|_{x=a}.$$

Thus, in the preceding example, we could have written

$$y\Big|_{x=2} = -15$$

instead of

$$\text{when } x = 2, \quad y = -15.$$

EXERCISE

Determine the points on the graph of $y = x^3 + 3x^2 - 9x + 5$ at which the tangent line is horizontal.

■ ANSWER
$(-3, 32)$ and $(1, 0)$

PROBLEM SET 3.2

In Problems 1–42, differentiate.

1. $f(x) = 7$
2. $f(x) = -\frac{1}{10}$
3. $f(x) = x^{13}$
4. $f(x) = x^{50}$
5. $f(x) = x^{\pi - 1}$
6. $f(x) = x^{\sqrt{2} + 1}$
7. $f(x) = x^{\ln 6}$
8. $f(x) = x^{-\ln 7}$
9. $f(x) = \frac{1}{x^4}$
10. $f(x) = \frac{1}{x^7}$
11. $f(x) = \sqrt[3]{x^5}$
12. $y = \sqrt{x^7}$
13. $f(x) = \sqrt[4]{\frac{1}{x^9}}$
14. $f(x) = \left(\frac{1}{x^5}\right)^{5.3}$
15. $f(x) = \sqrt{9x^9}$
16. $f(x) = (2x^2)^4$
17. $f(x) = \frac{11x}{5} + x \ln 3$
18. $y = \frac{-x}{3} + x \ln 5$
19. $f(x) = \frac{x^3}{3}$
20. $f(x) = \frac{x^{-2}}{-2}$
21. $y = \frac{e}{x^e}$
22. $y = ex^e$
23. $f(x) = \frac{3}{5x^{5/3}} + e^x$
24. $f(x) = \frac{1}{2x^2} + \ln x$
25. $y = 5e^x$
26. $y = \frac{-e^x}{4}$
27. $y = \frac{\ln x}{e}$
28. $y = -7 \ln x$
29. $y = \frac{-3}{(3x^3)^3} + \sqrt{3} x^{\sqrt{3}}$
30. $y = \frac{-1}{(2x^4)^4} - \pi x^{\pi^2}$
31. $y = 10x^{10} - x^{-10} - \frac{1}{10x^{10}} + 10^{-1}$
32. $y = \frac{x^6}{6} + \frac{6}{x^6} + \frac{1}{6x^6} + 6^6$
33. $y = 5ex^5 - 5e^x - 5e \ln x + 5e$
34. $y = \frac{x^6}{6e} - 6e^x + \frac{\ln x}{6e} - 6e$
35. $y = \ln \sqrt{x} + ex^3 - e^3$
36. $y = \ln x^3 - \frac{x^4}{e} + \ln \sqrt{5}$
37. $y = (2x + 3)^2$
38. $y = (x - 2)(3x + 1)$
39. $y = x - x^2(x^3 - 1)$
40. $f(x) = 2x^2 - x^4(5x - \frac{1}{2})$
41. $f(x) = \frac{x + \sqrt{5x^5}}{x}$
42. $y = \frac{x^2 + 1}{\sqrt{x}}$

In Problems 43–50, find the slope of the graph of each function at the specified x-coordinates.

43. $f(x) = 4 - 5x$, $x = -5$, $x = 0$, and $x = 9$
44. $f(x) = (4 + \sqrt{3})^2$, $x = -3$, $x = -2$, and $x = 4$
45. $f(x) = x^3 + 2x^2$, $x = -2$, $x = 0$, and $x = \sqrt{3}$
46. $f(x) = -2x^3 - 3x$, $x = -\frac{1}{2}$, $x = 1$, and $x = \sqrt{5}$
47. $f(x) = (1/x^2) - x - 6$, $x = \sqrt[3]{-9}$, $x = -\frac{1}{3}$, and $x = 1$
48. $f(x) = x^{2/3} - 5$, $x = -8$, $x = \frac{1}{27}$, and $x = \pi^3$
49. $f(x) = 3 \ln x - (1/x)$, $x = \frac{1}{3}$, $x = 1$, and $x = 3$
50. $f(x) = \frac{e^x}{2} + x^2$, $x = -1$, $x = 0$, and $x = \ln 4$

51. Determine the equation of the tangent line to $f(x) = x^3 - 4x + 1$ at $x = 1$.
52. Determine the equation of the tangent line to $f(x) = x^3 - 2x^2 + 5x - 10$ at $x = 1$.
53. Determine the point on the graph of $y = e^x - 7x$ at which the tangent line is horizontal.
54. Determine the point on the graph of $y = (x + 1)/x^2$ at which the tangent line is horizontal.
55. Determine the points on the graph of $y = x^3$ at which the slope of the tangent line is 12.
56. Determine the points on the graph of $y = 3 \ln x + (x^2/2)$ at which the slope of the tangent line is 4.
57. Prove that if $y = k \cdot f(x)$, where k is a constant, then $y' = k \cdot f'(x)$.
58. If $f(x) = x^3$, determine $f'(f(x))$ and $f(f'(x))$.
59. Prove that if $y = f(x) - g(x)$, then $y' = f'(x) - g'(x)$.

3.3 RATES OF CHANGE

Suppose that we are taking a car trip and that we have a trip odometer. Let s represent the trip odometer reading (which will be the distance traveled, in miles, from the starting point), and let t represent elapsed time, in hours, since beginning the trip. Note that s is a function of t. For each time t, there is a unique distance s that corresponds to it. So $s = f(t)$ for some function f. Let's suppose that

$$s = f(t) = 8t^2 + 4t, \quad 0 \leq t \leq 3.$$

The graph of this function is shown in Figure 3.10.

What is our average speed from $t = 1$ to $t = 2.5$? After 2.5 hours we have traveled

$$f(2.5) = 8(2.5)^2 + 4(2.5) = 60 \text{ miles.}$$

After 1 hour we have traveled

$$f(1) = 8(1)^2 + 4(1) = 12 \text{ miles.}$$

Hence our average speed during this period is

$$\frac{f(2.5) - f(1)}{2.5 - 1} = \frac{60 - 12}{1.5} = 32 \text{ mph.}$$

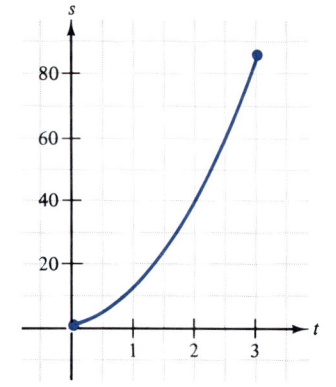

FIGURE 3.10

Note that the speed is given in miles per hour because the distance is measured in miles and the time is measured in hours. Also note that, in terms of the graph, this speed is simply the slope of a secant. (The slope is greater than it looks because of different unit distances on the axes.) See Figure 3.11.

The *instantaneous* speed when $t = 2$ is the speedometer reading at that very moment. How can we get this by using the function? Well, we could *approximate* by calculating the average speed from $t = 1.9$ to $t = 2$. We get

$$\frac{f(2) - f(1.9)}{2 - 1.9} = \frac{40 - 36.48}{0.1} = 35.2 \text{ mph.}$$

We could approximate from the other side as well. The average speed from $t = 2$ to $t = 2.05$ is

$$\frac{f(2.05) - f(2)}{2.05 - 2} = \frac{41.82 - 40}{0.05} = 36.4 \text{ mph.}$$

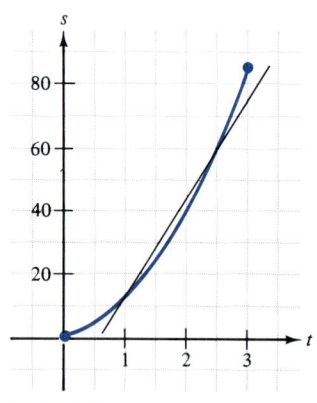

FIGURE 3.11

Note that the two approximations just made are of the type

$$\frac{f(2 + h) - f(2)}{h},$$

where $h = -0.1$ and $h = 0.05$. Our approximations will become better as h gets closer to 0. But in each approximation, note that we are calcu-

3.3 RATES OF CHANGE

lating an *average* speed. How can we get the *instantaneous* speed? We take the limit as h approaches 0. So the instantaneous speed at $t = 2$ is

$$\lim_{h \to 0} \frac{f(2 + h) - f(2)}{h}.$$

Of course, this is simply $f'(2)$, the value of the derivative at $t = 2$. Since

$$f'(t) = 16t + 4,$$
$$f'(2) = 32 + 4 = 36,$$

the instantaneous speed at $t = 2$ is 36 mph. Note that, in terms of the graph, this is simply the slope of the tangent line at $t = 2$. See Figure 3.12.

In the preceding illustration, the function $s = f(t) = 8t^2 + 4t$ is an example of a **position function**, a function that describes an object's position in terms of elapsed time. In the first example we encounter the concepts of velocity and acceleration. **Velocity** is a change in position with respect to a change in time. The formula for instantaneous velocity is obtained by differentiating the position function. **Acceleration** is a change in velocity with respect to a change in time. The formula for instantaneous acceleration is obtained by differentiating the velocity function.

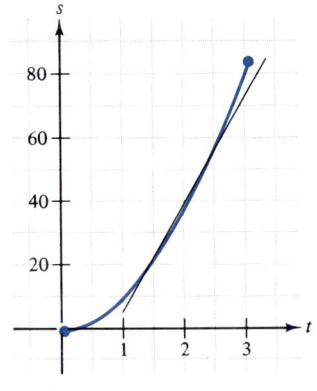

FIGURE 3.12

EXAMPLE 1

Suppose that the distance s (in feet) traveled by a sports car starting from rest is given by

$$s = 20t^{3/2}, \quad 0 \le t \le 10,$$

where t represents elapsed time in seconds. (a) How far has the car traveled when $t = 4$? (b) What is the velocity when $t = 4$? (c) What is the acceleration when $t = 4$?

■ SOLUTION

(a) To find the distance traveled we use the position function. We get

$$s\Big|_{t=4} = 20 \cdot 4^{3/2} = 20 \cdot 2^3 = 160.$$

Thus the car has traveled 160 feet.

(b) To determine the formula for velocity we differentiate the position function. We get

$$v = s' = 30t^{1/2}.$$

So

$$v\Big|_{t=4} = 30 \cdot 4^{1/2} = 60.$$

Because the distance is measured in feet and the time in seconds, our result is 60 feet/second.

(c) To determine the formula for acceleration we differentiate the velocity function. We have

$$a = v' = 15t^{-1/2} = \frac{15}{t^{1/2}} = \frac{15}{\sqrt{t}}.$$

Thus

$$a\Big|_{t=4} = \frac{15}{\sqrt{4}} = \frac{15}{2} = 7.5.$$

Since the velocity is measured in feet/second and the time in seconds, our answer is 7.5 feet/second/second, which may be written 7.5 feet/second^2.

EXERCISE

Suppose that the distance s (in feet) traveled by a sports car starting from rest is given by

$$s = 15t^{5/3}, \quad 0 \leq t \leq 10,$$

where t represents elapsed time in seconds. (a) How far has the car traveled when $t = 8$? (b) What is the velocity when $t = 8$? (c) What is the acceleration when $t = 8$?

■ ANSWER
(a) 480 feet; (b) 100 feet/second; (c) $8\frac{1}{3}$ feet/second^2

EXAMPLE 2

Suppose that an object is thrown upward and its distance s (in feet) above the ground after t seconds is given by

$$s = -16t^2 + 48t + 64.$$

(a) What is the maximum height attained? (b) With what velocity does the object strike the ground?

■ SOLUTION
(a) To determine the maximum height, we must first determine *when* the object reaches its maximum. We note that at its maximum height the velocity will be zero. Thus we must determine when the velocity will be zero. We do this by setting v equal to 0 and solving for t. Since

$$v = s' = -32t + 48,$$

we have

$$-32t + 48 = 0$$

$$t = 1.5.$$

3.3 RATES OF CHANGE

So the maximum height occurs in 1.5 seconds. Thus

$$s\big|_{t=1.5} = -16(1.5)^2 + 48(1.5) + 64 = 100.$$

The maximum height is 100 feet.

(b) To determine the velocity with which the object strikes the ground, we must first determine *when* it hits the ground. This occurs when s equals 0. We have

$$-16t^2 + 48t + 64 = 0$$
$$t^2 - 3t - 4 = 0$$
$$(t-4)(t+1) = 0$$
$$t = 4 \quad \text{or} \quad t = -1.$$

Since t represents elapsed time and cannot be negative, the object hits the ground when $t = 4$. Thus

$$v\big|_{t=4} = -32(4) + 48 = -80.$$

So the object strikes the ground with a velocity of -80 feet/second.

Note that the object in Example 2 strikes the ground with a negative velocity. This is because the object is moving *downward* at this time. It is moving downward at a speed of 80 feet/second. So velocity is a more general term than speed. Velocity indicates direction as well as magnitude. Speed is in fact the absolute value of the velocity. Of course, whenever the velocity is positive, speed and velocity are equal.

EXERCISE

Suppose that an object is thrown upward and its distance s (in feet) above the ground after t seconds is given by

$$s = -16t^2 + 80t + 96.$$

(a) What is the maximum height attained? (b) With what velocity does the object strike the ground?

■ *ANSWER*
(a) 196 feet; (b) -112 feet/second

Thus the derivative gives us a formula for the instantaneous rate of change. Indeed, if $Q = f(x)$, then $Q' = f'(x)$ is the formula for the instantaneous rate of change in Q with respect to x. At $x = a$, this instantaneous rate of change is $f'(a)$.

FIGURE 3.13

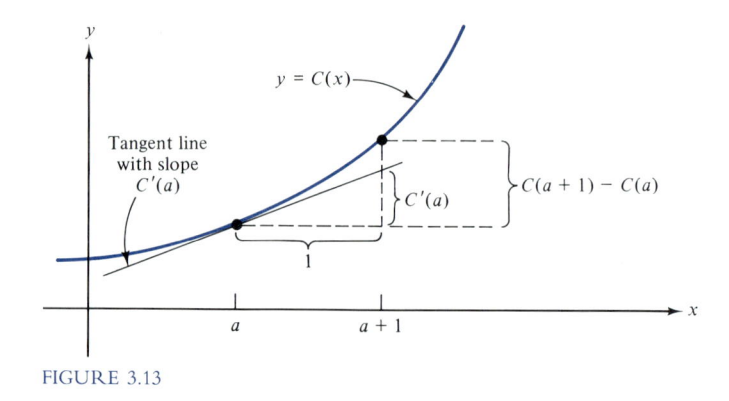

The derivative is used extensively in economics. To examine its use we must first define three important functions: The total cost of producing and marketing x units of a product is called the **cost function,** denoted $C(x)$. The total amount received from the sale of x units of the product is called the **revenue function,** denoted $R(x)$. And the total profit from the sale of x units is called the **profit function,** denoted $P(x)$. These functions are related as follows:

$$P(x) = R(x) - C(x).$$

They are frequently defined at nonnegative integer values only: $x = 0, 1, 2,$ and so on. However, for simplicity of analysis, economists assume that they are defined for all $x \geq 0$.

The **marginal cost function** is the rate of change in cost with respect to the output (number of units produced and marketed). Consequently, the marginal cost function is the derivative of the cost function. The marginal cost at a specified value then becomes an approximation of the additional cost required to produce one more unit. See Figure 3.13. The cost of producing one additional item, if the output is $x = a$, is $C(a + 1) - C(a)$. But this is close to $C'(a)$, the marginal cost at $x = a$. Similarly, the concepts of **marginal revenue** and **marginal profit** are defined.

EXAMPLE 3

A manufacturer of bicycles finds that the weekly cost (in dollars) of producing and marketing x bicycles is given by

$$C(x) = 0.02x^2 + 100x + 2000.$$

(a) Find the marginal cost when production is 30 units. (b) Show that this marginal cost is approximately the extra cost required to increase production from 30 to 31 units.

■ SOLUTION

(a) The marginal cost function is obtained by differentiating the cost function. We have

$$C'(x) = 0.04x + 100.$$

3.3 RATES OF CHANGE

Thus
$$C'(30) = 0.04(30) + 100 = 101.20.$$

So the marginal cost when $x = 30$ is $101.20.

(b) The cost of producing 30 units is given by
$$C(30) = 0.02(30)^2 + 100(30) + 2000 = \$5018.$$

And the cost for 31 units is
$$C(31) = 0.02(31)^2 + 100(31) + 2000 = \$5119.22.$$

The difference between these two is the cost required to increase production from 30 to 31. So
$$C(31) - C(30) = \$5119.22 - \$5018 = \$101.22.$$

This amount is but 2¢ different from the marginal cost when $x = 30$.

EXERCISE

A manufacturer of desks finds that the weekly cost (in dollars) of producing and marketing x desks is given by
$$C(x) = 0.05x^2 + 200x + 1000.$$

(a) Find the marginal cost when production is 40 units. (b) Show that this marginal cost is approximately the extra cost required to increase production from 40 to 41 units.

■ ANSWER
(a) $204; (b) extra cost is $204.05

Before proceeding, we need to introduce an additional notation for the derivative. It is needed because a given variable may be expressed as two or more different functions, depending on which independent variable is used. For example, suppose that a spherical balloon is being inflated. Its volume V is a function of its radius r. In particular,
$$V = \tfrac{4}{3}\pi r^3. \tag{3-1}$$

But the volume is also a function of the time elapsed since inflation began. For example, we might have
$$V = 36\pi t^{3/2}. \tag{3-2}$$

If we wish to find the change in volume with respect to the radius, we would differentiate the function defined in (3-1). If we wish to find the change in volume with respect to the time, we would differentiate the function defined in (3-2). But the notation V' would be ambiguous. It might mean either derivative. In order to clarify this we introduce a notation for the derivative which includes the independent variable in addition to the dependent one. When we are differentiating the function defined in (3-1), where V is a function of r, the notation is

$$\frac{dV}{dr}, \text{ the derivative of } V \text{ with respect to } r.$$

When we are differentiating the function defined in (3-2), where V is a function of t, the notation is

$$\frac{dV}{dt}, \text{ the derivative of } V \text{ with respect to } t.$$

Thus

$$\frac{dV}{dr} = 4\pi r^2,$$

$$\frac{dV}{dt} = 54\pi t^{1/2},$$

and any confusion is avoided. [Of course, if $y = f(x)$, then dy/dx is the same as y' or $f'(x)$. It is the slope of the curve, the instantaneous change in y with respect to x.] Furthermore, this notation emphasizes that the derivative is a rate of change in one variable with respect to another and helps establish the proper units for the rate of change.

EXAMPLE 4

The area A of a circle is given by

$$A = \pi r^2,$$

where r represents the radius. What is the rate of change in the area with respect to the radius when the radius is 3 feet?

■ SOLUTION

To find the instantaneous change in the area with respect to the radius, we compute the derivative of A with respect to r. We get

$$\frac{dA}{dr} = 2\pi r.$$

Evaluating, we have

$$\left.\frac{dA}{dr}\right|_{r=3} = 2\pi(3) = 6\pi \quad (\approx 18.85).$$

Hence the area is increasing 6π square feet/foot. That is, when $r = 3$, the area is increasing at a rate of 6π square feet per 1 foot increase in the radius.

EXERCISE

The surface area of a sphere is given by

$$S = 4\pi r^2,$$

where r represents the radius. What is the rate of change in the surface area with respect to the radius when the radius is 3 feet?

■ ANSWER
24π (≈ 75.40) square feet/foot

EXAMPLE 5

In a certain store, the percent of the price list learned after t hours is given by

$$P = 40t - 4t^2, \qquad 0 \leq t \leq 5.$$

How fast is P changing when $t = 3$?

■ SOLUTION
To find this instantaneous rate of change we must compute the derivative of P with respect to t. We get

$$\frac{dP}{dt} = 40 - 8t.$$

Evaluating, we get

$$\left.\frac{dP}{dt}\right|_{t=3} = 40 - 8(3) = 16.$$

The percent learned is increasing 16 percentage points per hour.

EXERCISE

In a certain store, the percent of the list of available inventory learned after t hours is given by

$$P = 25t - \frac{25}{16}t^2, \qquad 0 \leq t \leq 8.$$

How fast is P changing when $t = 4$?

■ ANSWER
Increasing 12.5 percentage points/hr.

PROBLEM SET 3.3

1. If $y = t^4 + t^3 - t$, find the rate of change of y with respect to t when $t = 1$.

2. If $g(x) = 2x^3 - x^2$, find the rate of change of $g(x)$ with respect to x when $x = 2$.

3. A particle moves along a straight line so that after t seconds, its distance (in centimeters) from a fixed point is $s = t^3 - \frac{15}{2}t^2 + 12t + 2$.
   (a) Determine the time when the velocity is 0.
   (b) Determine the acceleration when the velocity is 12 centimeters/second^2.

4. The distance s (in feet) traveled by a train starting from rest is given by $s = 5t^2 - (t^3/3)$, $0 \leq t \leq 10$, where t represents elapsed time in seconds.
   (a) How far has the train traveled when $t = 6$?
   (b) What is the velocity when the acceleration is 0?

5. A projectile is fired into the air from the top of a building. Its distance s (in feet) from the ground after t seconds is $s = -16t^2 + 160t + 176$.
   (a) What is the velocity when $t = 3$?
   (b) What is the acceleration when $t = 3$?
   (c) When does the projectile reach its maximum height?
   (d) What is the maximum height?
   (e) When does the projectile hit the ground?
   (f) With what velocity does the projectile hit the ground?

6. A ball is dropped from the roof of a building 256 feet high. Its distance s (in feet) from the ground is $s = -16t^2 + 256$, where t is in seconds.
   (a) What is the velocity of the ball when $t = 2$?
   (b) How fast will the ball be traveling when it hits the ground?

7. A particle moves along a straight line according to the formula $s(t) = t^3 - 2t^2 - t - 5$. Determine the values of t for which the particle's acceleration is equal to its velocity.

8. The distance s (in feet) traveled by a sports car starting from rest is given by $s = 28t^{3/2}$, $0 \leq t \leq 10$, where t represents elapsed time in seconds. Determine the value of t for which the car's velocity is equal to its acceleration.

9. A manufacturer of computers finds that the daily cost (in dollars) of producing and marketing x computers is given by $C(x) = 0.7x^2 + 50x + 3000$.
   (a) Find the marginal cost when $x = 20$.
   (b) Show that this marginal cost is approximately the extra cost required to increase production from 20 to 21 units.
   (c) Determine the number of computers produced and marketed when the marginal cost is $101.80.

10. The total revenue R (in dollars) for a certain item is $R(x) = 560x - 0.04x^2$, where x is the number of items produced and sold.
    (a) Find the marginal revenue when $x = 2500$.
    (b) Show that this marginal revenue is approximately the additional revenue if production is increased from 2500 to 2501 items.

11. A retailer determines that his monthly cost is $C(x) = 0.01x^2 + 20x + 400$ and his monthly revenue is $R(x) = 60x$.
    (a) Find the marginal cost, marginal revenue, and marginal profit.
    (b) Find the value of x so that the marginal cost is equal to the marginal revenue.

12. A firm estimates that its profit function is $P(x) = x^3 - 27x^2 + 243x$. Determine the value of x for which the marginal profit is zero.

13. The volume V (in cubic centimeters) of a right circular cone is $V = \frac{1}{3}\pi r^2 h$, where r is the radius of the base (in centimeters), and h is the height (in centimeters). If $h = 15$ centimeters, determine the average rate of change of V with respect to r as r changes from
    (a) 3 to 3.3
    (b) 3 to 3.1
    (c) 3 to 3.01
    (d) 3 to 3.001
    (e) Determine the instantaneous rate of change of V with respect to r when $r = 3$.

14. The volume V (in cubic feet) of a cube is $V = x^3$, where x is the length of a side (in feet). Determine the average rate of change (to the nearest hundredth) of V with respect to x as x changes from
    (a) 4.8 to 5
    (b) 4.9 to 5
    (c) 4.99 to 5
    (d) 4.999 to 5
    (e) Determine the instantaneous rate of change of V with respect to x when $x = 5$.

15. A population of ants has an initial size of 200 and grows according to the formula $N(t) = 200 + 5t^2$, where t is measured in days.

(a) Find the average rate of growth from $t = 3$ to $t = 7$.
(b) Find the instantaneous rate of change when $t = 7$.

16. The size of a bacteria population is given by $Q(t) = 50t^3 + 4000$, where t is in hours.
    (a) Find the average growth rate from $t = 1$ to $t = 3$.
    (b) Find the rate of change when $t = 3$.

17. Show that the rate of change of the area of a circle with respect to its radius is equal to the circumference of the circle.

18. Show that the rate of change of the volume of a sphere with respect to its radius is equal to the surface area of the sphere.

19. Water is being poured into a large container. After t minutes there are $g(t) = 2t^{1/2}$ gallons in the container. At what rate is the water flowing into the container when $t = 9$?

20. The surface area A (in square centimeters) of a cube is $A = 6x^2$, where x represents the length of a side (in centimeters). What is the rate of change in the area with respect to a side when $x = 5$?

21. The infiltration I (in inches) of water into soil is a function of time t (in hours) and defined by $I = A + Bt^{-1/2}$, where A and B are constants. Determine the rate of change of I with respect to t when $t = 4$.

22. The weight W (in pounds) of an animal is a function of age t (in years) and can be approximated by $W = at^{2/3}$, where a is a constant. Determine the rate of change of W with respect to t when $t = 8$.

23. Stefan's law states that $R = KT^4$, where R is the rate of emission of radiant energy per unit area, T is the Kelvin temperature of the surface, and K is a constant. Determine the rate of change of R with respect to T when $T = 200$.

24. Experimentally it has been determined that the specific heat H of ethyl alcohol is approximately

$$H(t) = (5.4)10^{-6}t^2 + (2.86)10^{-3}t + (5.07)10^{-1},$$

where t ranges between 0 and 60 degrees Celsius. Find the rate of change of H with respect to t when $t = 30$.

25. Given that the demand curve for a certain item is a straight line, show that the marginal revenue curve is also a straight line whose slope is twice that of the demand curve.

3.4 THE CHAIN RULE

Suppose that y is a function of u, and u is a function of x. Then y may be written as a function of x by substituting for u. Indeed, if $y = f(u)$ and $u = g(x)$, then $y = f(g(x))$. For example, suppose that

$$y = f(u) = u^3$$

and

$$u = g(x) = x^2 + 1.$$

Then

$$y = f(g(x)) = f(x^2 + 1) = (x^2 + 1)^3. \tag{3-3}$$

If we wish to differentiate y when expressed as a function of x, we could expand the right side of Equation (3-3). We get

$$y = (x^2 + 1)^3 = (x^2 + 1)(x^4 + 2x^2 + 1)$$
$$= x^6 + 3x^4 + 3x^2 + 1.$$

Hence

$$\frac{dy}{dx} = 6x^5 + 12x^3 + 6x.$$

In this illustration, we have determined dy/dx after expanding the right side of Equation (3-3). But what will we do if $y = u^{10}$ or $y = u^{3/4}$, when expansion is difficult or impossible.

Suppose $y = f(u)$ and $u = g(x)$ are differentiable functions and we wish to find dy/dx for the function $y = f(g(x))$. Since dy/du is the instantaneous rate of change in y with respect to u,

$$y \text{ is changing } \frac{dy}{du} \text{ times as fast as } u.$$

Similarly,

$$u \text{ is changing } \frac{du}{dx} \text{ times as fast as } x.$$

Thus to determine how fast y is changing with respect to x, we multiply dy/du by du/dx. Hence it seems reasonable that

$$\frac{dy}{dx} = \frac{dy}{du} \cdot \frac{du}{dx}.$$

This result is formalized in the following theorem.

THEOREM 3.9 If $y = f(u)$ and $u = g(x)$, then

$$\frac{dy}{dx} = \frac{dy}{du} \cdot \frac{du}{dx},$$

or equivalently, with functional notation,

$$\frac{dy}{dx} = f'(g(x)) \cdot g'(x).$$

Let's apply the chain rule to the first illustration, where

$$y = f(u) = u^3$$

and

$$u = g(x) = x^2 + 1.$$

We get

$$\frac{dy}{dx} = \frac{dy}{du} \cdot \frac{du}{dx}$$
$$= 3u^2 \cdot 2x$$
$$= 3(x^2 + 1)^2 2x$$
$$= 6x(x^2 + 1)^2.$$

3.4 THE CHAIN RULE

To compare with our previous result, let's expand. We get

$$\frac{dy}{dx} = 6x(x^4 + 2x^2 + 1)$$
$$= 6x^5 + 12x^3 + 6x,$$

the same result.

EXAMPLE 1

Determine dy/dx (a) if $y = u^{10}$ and $u = x^2 + 1$ and (b) if $y = u^{3/4}$ and $u = x^2 + 1$.

■ SOLUTION

(a) By the chain rule,

$$\frac{dy}{dx} = \frac{dy}{du} \cdot \frac{du}{dx}$$
$$= 10u^9 \cdot 2x$$
$$= 20x(x^2 + 1)^9.$$

(b) By the chain rule,

$$\frac{dy}{dx} = \frac{dy}{du} \cdot \frac{du}{dx}$$
$$= \tfrac{3}{4} u^{-1/4} \cdot 2x$$
$$= \frac{3x}{2\sqrt[4]{u}}$$
$$= \frac{3x}{2\sqrt[4]{x^2 + 1}}.$$

EXERCISE

Determine dy/dx (a) if $y = u^{20}$ and $u = x^3 - 1$ and (b) if $y = u^{2/3}$ and $u = x^3 - 1$.

■ ANSWER

(a) $60x^2(x^3 - 1)^{19}$; (b) $2x^2/\sqrt[3]{x^3 - 1}$

EXAMPLE 2

Suppose that a spherical balloon is being inflated. Its volume V is a function of its radius. In particular,

$$V = \tfrac{4}{3}\pi r^3.$$

Its radius is a function of the time elapsed since inflation began. Suppose that the radius is increasing 2 inches/second. How fast is the volume increasing when the radius is 3 inches?

■ SOLUTION

We are being asked to determine the change in volume with respect to time when $r = 3$. If we let t represent elapsed time in seconds, then, by the chain rule,

$$\frac{dV}{dt} = \frac{dV}{dr} \cdot \frac{dr}{dt}$$

$$= 4\pi r^2 \cdot \frac{dr}{dt}.$$

Because the change in radius with respect to time is 2 inches/second,

$$\frac{dr}{dt} = 2.$$

Thus

$$\frac{dV}{dt} = 4\pi r^2 \cdot 2$$

$$= 8\pi r^2.$$

So

$$\left.\frac{dV}{dt}\right|_{r=3} = 8\pi \cdot 9 = 72\pi \quad (\approx 226.2).$$

The volume is increasing 72π cubic inches/second.

EXERCISE

Suppose that a spherical balloon is being inflated. Its volume V is a function of its radius. In particular,

$$V = \tfrac{4}{3}\pi r^3.$$

If the radius is increasing 3 inches/second, how fast is the volume increasing when $r = 5$?

■ ANSWER

300π (≈ 942.5) cubic inches/second

3.4 THE CHAIN RULE

A principal application of the chain rule is the following theorem. It provides us with a means of differentiating general power functions.

THEOREM 3.10
General Power Rule

If $y = (f(x))^n$, where n is a constant, then
$$y' = n(f(x))^{n-1} \cdot f'(x).$$

Proof Let $u = f(x)$. Then
$$y = u^n.$$
By the chain rule,
$$\frac{dy}{dx} = \frac{dy}{du} \cdot \frac{du}{dx}$$
$$= nu^{n-1} \cdot f'(x)$$
$$= n(f(x))^{n-1} \cdot f'(x).$$

This theorem is a generalization of the simple power rule, which states that the derivative of $y = x^n$ is $y' = nx^{n-1}$. Like the simple power rule, it states that the exponent becomes the coefficient in the derivative, and then the exponent is reduced by one. But, with general power functions, we must go one step further and multiply by the derivative of the function being raised to the power. See Examples 3 through 5.

EXAMPLE 3

Determine y' for (a) $y = (x^2 - 1)^{50}$; (b) $y = 1/(\ln x)^3$; and (c) $y = \sqrt{x^2 + 1}$.

■ SOLUTION

(a) By the general power rule we get

$$y' = \overset{\text{Former exponent}}{50}(x^2 - 1)^{\overset{\text{Exponent reduced by 1}}{49}} \cdot \underset{\text{Derivative of function in parentheses}}{2x} = 100x(x^2 - 1)^{49}.$$

(b) First we rewrite y in the form
$$y = (\ln x)^{-3}.$$
Using the general power rule we get
$$y' = -3(\ln x)^{-4} \cdot \frac{1}{x}$$
$$= \frac{-3}{x(\ln x)^4}.$$

(c) Replacing the radical notation by exponential notation gives
$$y = (x^2 + 1)^{1/2}.$$

By the general power rule then,
$$y' = \tfrac{1}{2}(x^2 + 1)^{-1/2} \cdot 2x$$
$$= \frac{x}{\sqrt{x^2 + 1}}.$$

EXERCISE

Determine y' for (a) $y = (x^3 - 1)^{20}$; (b) $y = 1/(\ln x)^2$; and (c) $y = \sqrt{x^2 - x}$.

■ ANSWER

(a) $y' = 60x^2(x^3 - 1)^{19}$; (b) $y' = \dfrac{-2}{x(\ln x)^3}$; (c) $y' = \dfrac{2x - 1}{2\sqrt{x^2 - x}}$

EXAMPLE 4

Determine y' if $y = 10(x^2 + x)^{20}$.

■ SOLUTION

Since the derivative of a constant times a function is the constant times the derivative of the function, y' is 10 times the derivative of $(x^2 + x)^{20}$. Hence
$$y' = 10 \cdot 20(x^2 + x)^{19}(2x + 1)$$
$$= 200(x^2 + x)^{19}(2x + 1).$$

Example 4 suggests an extended general power rule. If
$$y = k(f(x))^n,$$
where k and n are constants, then
$$y' = nk(f(x))^{n-1} \cdot f'(x).$$

EXERCISE

Determine y' if $y = 5(x^3 - x)^6$.

■ ANSWER

$y' = 30(x^3 - x)^5(3x^2 - 1)$

THEOREM 3.11

If $y = e^{g(x)}$, then $y' = e^{g(x)} \cdot g'(x)$.

Proof This theorem is a direct result of the chain rule. Letting
$$u = g(x),$$
we have
$$y = e^u.$$
Thus
$$\frac{dy}{dx} = \frac{dy}{du} \cdot \frac{du}{dx}$$
$$= e^u \cdot \frac{du}{dx}$$
$$= e^{g(x)} \cdot g'(x).$$

EXAMPLE 5

Differentiate (a) $y = e^{x^2}$ and (b) $y = e^{x^3 - x}$.

■ SOLUTION
(a) By Theorem 3.11 we have
$$y' = e^{x^2} \cdot 2x$$
$$= 2xe^{x^2}.$$

(b) We get
$$y' = e^{x^3 - x} \cdot (3x^2 - 1).$$

EXERCISE

Differentiate (a) $y = e^{x^3}$ and (b) $y = e^{x - x^2}$.

■ ANSWER
(a) $y' = 3x^2 e^{x^3}$; (b) $y' = (1 - 2x)e^{x - x^2}$

Theorem 3.11 may be used to differentiate exponential functions with bases other than e. If
$$y = b^x,$$
then we may write
$$y = (e^{\ln b})^x = e^{(\ln b)x}.$$

By Theorem 3.11,
$$y' = e^{(\ln b)x} \cdot \ln b = b^x \cdot \ln b.$$

Therefore, of all the exponential functions, the one with base e has the simplest derivative (since $\ln e = 1$).

THEOREM 3.12 If $y = \ln(g(x))$, then
$$y' = \frac{1}{g(x)} \cdot g'(x) = \frac{g'(x)}{g(x)}.$$

Proof   This theorem is proved by using the chain rule. Letting
$$u = g(x),$$
we have
$$y = \ln u.$$
By the chain rule,
$$\frac{dy}{dx} = \frac{dy}{du} \cdot \frac{du}{dx}$$
$$= \frac{1}{u} \cdot \frac{du}{dx}$$
$$= \frac{1}{g(x)} \cdot g'(x) = \frac{g'(x)}{g(x)}.$$

EXAMPLE 6

Differentiate $y = \ln(x^3 - 1)$.

■ SOLUTION
Using Theorem 3.12 we get
$$y' = \frac{1}{x^3 - 1} \cdot 3x^2 = \frac{3x^2}{x^3 - 1}.$$

EXERCISE

Differentiate $y = \ln(x^2 + 5)$.

■ ANSWER
$y' = 2x/(x^2 + 5)$

3.4 THE CHAIN RULE

Although the natural logarithm function is defined for positive numbers only, the special function
$$f(x) = \ln|x|$$
is defined for all real numbers except zero. To compute its derivative we may first write the function with a split formula of definition:
$$f(x) = \begin{cases} \ln x & \text{when } x > 0 \\ \ln(-x) & \text{when } x < 0. \end{cases}$$

Thus
$$f'(x) = \begin{cases} \dfrac{1}{x} & \text{when } x > 0 \\ \dfrac{1}{-x}(-1) & \text{when } x < 0 \end{cases}$$
$$= \frac{1}{x},$$
which is the same formula obtained for the derivative of the natural logarithm function.

In a similar fashion, if
$$y = \ln|g(x)|,$$
then
$$y' = \frac{1}{g(x)} \cdot g'(x) = \frac{g'(x)}{g(x)}.$$

EXAMPLE 7

Differentiate $y = \ln|2x - 1|$.

■ SOLUTION

We get
$$y' = \frac{1}{2x - 1} \cdot 2$$
$$= \frac{2}{2x - 1}.$$

EXERCISE

Differentiate $y = \ln|3x^2 - 5|$.

■ ANSWER
$y' = 6x/(3x^2 - 5)$

The Richter scale is used to measure the intensity of an earthquake. The Richter number R is defined by

$$R = \log_{10} A,$$

where A is the amplitude of the shock wave recorded on a seismograph at a distance of 100 kilometers from the earthquake's epicenter. This information is needed in the following example and exercise.

EXAMPLE 8

Use the Richter number equation to determine how R is changing when $A = 23{,}000$ if A is increasing at the rate of 3000 per second.

■ SOLUTION

We are being asked to find the change in R with respect to time when $A = 23{,}000$. If we let t represent time in seconds, then, by the chain rule,

$$\frac{dR}{dt} = \frac{dR}{dA} \cdot \frac{dA}{dt}.$$

Let's first rewrite the Richter number equation by using the change of base formula. We get

$$R = \frac{\ln A}{\ln 10}.$$

Therefore,

$$\frac{dR}{dt} = \frac{1}{\ln 10} \cdot \frac{1}{A} \cdot \frac{dA}{dt}.$$

Since A is increasing 3000 per second,

$$\frac{dA}{dt} = 3000.$$

Hence,

$$\frac{dR}{dt} = \frac{3000}{A \ln 10}.$$

When $A = 23{,}000$ this gives

$$\frac{dR}{dt} = \frac{3000}{23{,}000 \ln 10} \approx 0.0566.$$

The Richter number is increasing approximately 0.0566 per second.

EXERCISE

Use the Richter number equation to determine how R is changing (to the nearest ten thousandth) when $A = 25{,}000$ if A is increasing at the rate of 2000 per second.

■ ANSWER
Increasing 0.0347/sec.

PROBLEM SET 3.4

In Problems 1–12, determine dy/dx

1. $y = u^3$ and $u = x^2 + x$
2. $y = u^4$ and $u = x^3 - x$
3. $y = u^4 - u^2$ and $u = \pi^2$
4. $y = u^7 - u^6$ and $u = 2^{1/2}$
5. $y = 1/u^3$ and $u = x - 3$
6. $y = u^{-2}$ and $u = 5x - 6$
7. $y = u^2 - u$ and $u = \ln x$
8. $y = \dfrac{u^2}{8} - \dfrac{u}{4}$ and $u = 4 \ln x$
9. $y = u^9 + u^5$ and $u = 1 + 2\sqrt{x}$
10. $y = u^4 - u$ and $u = 1 + (1/x)$
11. $y = \sqrt{u}$ and $u = e^x$
12. $y = \sqrt[3]{u}$ and $u = 3 + 3e^x$
13. If $y = f(u)$ and $u = g(x)$, use the chain rule to determine $g'(x)$ if

$$\frac{dy}{dx} = \frac{3}{1 + x^2} \quad \text{and} \quad f'(g(x)) = \frac{6\sqrt{x}}{1 + x^2}.$$

14. If $y = f(u)$ and $u = g(x)$, use the chain rule to determine dy/dx at $x = 2$ if

$$f'(3) = 5, \quad f'(2) = 4, \quad g'(2) = 7, \quad g(2) = 3.$$

In Problems 15–46, determine y'.

15. $y = (x^3 + x^2)^{15}$
16. $y = (x^4 - 1)^{10}$
17. $y = (1 + 4e^x)^{7/4}$
18. $y = (2 + 3 \ln x)^{5/3}$
19. $y = \dfrac{1}{2x + 1}$
20. $y = \dfrac{1}{x^2 + 5}$
21. $y = 3\sqrt[3]{x^6 + 8}$
22. $y = \sqrt{4x^4 + 4x + 4}$
23. $y = \dfrac{1}{\left(\dfrac{x^2}{2} - x^{-2}\right)^5}$
24. $y = \dfrac{\pi}{6}\left(\dfrac{x}{\pi} + 6\right)^6$
25. $y = e^{4x} + e^{-x}$
26. $y = e^{5x} - e^{-2x}$
27. $y = e^{x^4 + x^2 + e}$
28. $y = e^{3x^3 - x + 1}$
29. $y = 3e^{(x^3/3) - (x^2/2)}$
30. $y = \tfrac{1}{4}e^{2x^2 - 2x^{-2}}$
31. $y = e^{e^x + x^e}$
32. $y = e^{e^x + \ln x}$
33. $y = (e^{3x} + e^{-4x})^5$
34. $y = (e^{x^4} + e^{x^5})^{10}$
35. $y = \ln(2x) + x \ln 2$
36. $y = \ln(-5x) - x \ln 5$
37. $y = \ln(4x - 7) + \ln \sqrt[3]{2}$
38. $y = \ln(5 - 7x) - \ln \sqrt{5}$
39. $y = \ln x^3 + (\ln x)^3$
40. $y = \ln \sqrt{x} + \sqrt{\ln x}$
41. $y = \ln(\ln x)$
42. $y = (\ln(\ln x))^7$
43. $y = \ln(e^{9x} - e^{-9x})$
44. $y = \ln(e^{-x} + x^{-e})$
45. $y = 3 \ln|2x^5 - x|$
46. $y = \dfrac{\ln|3x^7 - 3|}{3}$

47. Determine $f'(-1)$ if $f(x) = (3x^3 - x + 1)^{30}$.
48. Determine $f'(2)$ if $f(x) = \sqrt{3x^2 + 4} + 5$.

In Problems 49–52, simplify each y by using the properties of logarithms and then find y'.

49. $y = \ln \dfrac{(x + 2)\sqrt{x - 3}}{x + 5}$
50. $y = \ln \dfrac{x^{2/3}(x + 4)^{5/2}}{(x^3 - 1)^{1/3}}$
51. $y = \ln \sqrt[3]{(2x^3 - 5)\sqrt{x^6 + 9}}$
52. $y = \ln \sqrt{\dfrac{x^2(2x + 1)}{4x - 7}}$

53. Determine the equation of the tangent line to $f(x) = \ln(x^2 + 1)$ at $x = 2$.
54. Determine the equation of the tangent line to $f(x) = e^{2x}$ at $x = 4$.
55. A cube is expanding in such a way that its edge, x (in inches), is a function of time and related by $x = 4t$, where t is in seconds. How fast is the volume increasing when $t = 2$?

56. A point (x,y) is moving along a curve $y = f(x)$ so that the coordinates x and y are functions of time. At the instant when the slope of the curve is $\frac{2}{5}$, the rate of change of the x-coordinate with respect to time is 3 feet/second. Determine the rate of change of the y-coordinate with respect to t at this instant.

57. The daily cost (in dollars) of producing x watches is $C(x) = 0.01x^2 + 20x + 300$. The manufacturer has determined that $x = t^2 + 25t$ watches can be produced in t hours, where $0 \leq t \leq 8$. Find the rate of change of the cost with respect to time when $t = 3$.

58. A circular metal plate expands when heated so that the rate of change of the radius with respect to time is 0.02 inch/second. How fast is the area increasing when the radius is 3 inches?

59. A spherical snowball is melting at the rate of 1 feet^3/hour. How fast is the surface area decreasing when the radius of the snowball is $\frac{1}{2}$ foot? (*Hint:* Surface area of a sphere of radius r is equal to $4\pi r^2$.)

60. An object moves along a straight line so that after t minutes its distance s (in feet) from a fixed point is
$$s = 15t + \frac{12}{t+3} - 3.$$
What is the velocity of the object when $t = 3$?

61. The distance s (in feet) of a certain object from a fixed point is given by
$$s = 30t + \frac{64}{(t+2)^2},$$
where t is time in minutes. Determine the velocity of the object when $t = 2$.

62. The **hyperbolic sine of x,** denoted by $\sinh x$, is defined by
$$\sinh x = \frac{e^x - e^{-x}}{2}$$
and the **hyperbolic cosine of x,** denoted by $\cosh x$, is defined by
$$\cosh x = \frac{e^x + e^{-x}}{2}.$$

(a) Show that $(\cosh x)^2 - (\sinh x)^2 = 1$.
(b) Show that $f(x) = \sinh x$ is an odd function [i.e., $f(-x) = -f(x)$] and that $f(x) = \cosh x$ is an even function [i.e., $f(-x) = f(x)$].
(c) Show that if $f(x) = \sinh x$, then $f'(x) = \cosh x$ and if $g(x) = \cosh x$, then $g'(x) = \sinh x$.

63. The **Gompertz growth function,** $G(t)$, is used in biology to estimate the size of a population at time t and is defined by $G(t) = ae^{-be^{-ct}}$, where a, b, and c are positive constants. Determine $G'(t)$.

64. The **logistic distribution** is used in population growth models and is defined by $f(x) = (1 + e^{-(ax+b)})^{-1}$, where a and b are constants and $a > 0$. Determine $f'(x)$.

65. The **inverse hyperbolic sine function,** denoted by $\sinh^{-1}$, is given by $\sinh^{-1} x = \ln(x + \sqrt{x^2 + 1})$. Show that if $f(x) = \sinh^{-1} x$, then $f'(x) = 1/\sqrt{x^2 + 1}$.

66. The training division of a large manufacturing firm has determined that a new worker's output Q (in hundreds), after t days on the job is approximately
$$Q = 25(1 - e^{-1.2t}).$$
What is the rate at which Q is increasing (to the nearest unit per day) when $t = 5$?

67. In a manual dexterity test the number of pieces, P, that a person can position correctly in a 1-minute test increases through practice according to the formula
$$P = \ln(t^4 + 1000),$$
where t is the subject's practice time (in minutes). Find the rate of increase of P (to the nearest tenth), when $t = 20$.

3.5 THE PRODUCT AND QUOTIENT RULES

Suppose we need to differentiate
$$y = (x^2 + 1)(x^3 - 1). \tag{3-4}$$

We may do so by writing the product as a sum. Upon expanding the right side of Equation (3-4) we have
$$y = x^5 - x^2 + x^3 - 1.$$

3.5 THE PRODUCT AND QUOTIENT RULES

Thus
$$y' = 5x^4 - 2x + 3x^2. \tag{3-5}$$

Although this method works well in this case, how do we handle
$$y = xe^x?$$

We must learn how to differentiate a product.

The first question that arises is: "Is the derivative of a product the product of the derivatives?" That is, if
$$y = f(x) \cdot g(x),$$
does
$$y' = f'(x) \cdot g'(x)?$$

Unfortunately, the answer is no. We may see this by considering the function defined in Equation (3-4). If we let $f(x) = x^2 + 1$ and $g(x) = x^3 - 1$, then
$$f'(x) \cdot g'(x) = 2x \cdot 3x^2 = 6x^3.$$

But this is clearly not the derivative we obtained in Equation (3-5). So the derivative of a product is *not* the product of the derivatives.

THEOREM 3.13
Product Rule

If $y = f(x) \cdot g(x)$, then
$$y' = f(x) \cdot g'(x) + g(x) \cdot f'(x).$$

This theorem says that the derivative of a product is the first function times the derivative of the second plus the second function times the derivative of the first. For a proof, see Appendix.

Let's return to the introductory function, defined in Equation (3-4), apply the product rule, and compare with Equation (3-5). We have
$$y = (x^2 + 1)(x^3 - 1).$$
Thus
$$y' = \underset{\text{Second}}{\underbrace{(x^2 + 1)}} \cdot \overset{\text{Derivative of second}}{\overbrace{3x^2}} + (x^3 - 1) \cdot \underset{\text{Derivative of first}}{\underbrace{2x}}.$$

(First; Second; Derivative of second; Derivative of first)

Simplifying we have
$$y' = 3x^4 + 3x^2 + 2x^4 - 2x$$
$$= 5x^4 + 3x^2 - 2x,$$

which is the result previously obtained in Equation (3-5).

Let's use the product rule to differentiate
$$y = xe^x.$$

We get

$$y' = \underset{\text{Second}}{\underset{\uparrow}{x}} \cdot \underset{\text{Derivative of } e^x}{e^x} + \underset{\text{First}}{\underset{\downarrow}{e^x}} \cdot \underset{\text{Derivative of } x}{1}$$

$$= e^x(x+1).$$

EXAMPLE 1

Determine y' for (a) $y = x \ln x$; (b) $y = 2x(x^2 + 1)^5$; and (c) $y = (x^2 + 1)^5(x^3 - 1)^3$.

■ SOLUTION

(a) Applying the product rule we have

$$y' = x \cdot \frac{1}{x} + (\ln x) \cdot 1$$

$$= 1 + \ln x.$$

(b) This function may be viewed as the product of two functions: the first being $2x$ and the second being the power function $(x^2 + 1)^5$. By the product rule then,

$$y' = 2x \cdot 5(x^2 + 1)^4 \cdot 2x + (x^2 + 1)^5 \cdot 2$$
$$= 2(x^2 + 1)^4(10x^2 + x^2 + 1)$$
$$= 2(x^2 + 1)^4(11x^2 + 1).$$

(c) This function may be viewed as the product of two power functions. By the product rule we get

$$y' = (x^2 + 1)^5 \cdot 3(x^3 - 1)^2 \cdot 3x^2 + (x^3 - 1)^3 \cdot 5(x^2 + 1)^4 \cdot 2x$$
$$= x(x^2 + 1)^4(x^3 - 1)^2[9x(x^2 + 1) + 10(x^3 - 1)]$$
$$= x(x^2 + 1)^4(x^3 - 1)^2(9x^3 + 9x + 10x^3 - 10)$$
$$= x(x^2 + 1)^4(x^3 - 1)^2(19x^3 + 9x - 10).$$

EXERCISE

Determine y' for (a) $y = x^2 e^x$; (b) $y = x^2 \ln x$; (c) $y = -5x(x^2 - 1)^{10}$; and (d) $y = (3x - 1)^5(2x^2 + 1)^6$.

■ ANSWER

(a) $y' = x^2 e^x + e^x \cdot 2x = xe^x(x + 2)$
(b) $y' = x^2 \cdot 1/x + (\ln x)2x = x(1 + 2 \ln x)$
(c) $y' = -5x \cdot 10(x^2 - 1)^9(2x) + (x^2 - 1)^{10}(-5)$
$ = -5(x^2 - 1)^9(21x^2 - 1)$

(d) $y' = (3x - 1)^5 \cdot 6(2x^2 + 1)^5(4x) + (2x^2 + 1)^6 \cdot 5(3x - 1)^4(3)$
$= 3(3x - 1)^4(2x^2 + 1)^5(34x^2 - 8x + 5)$

Let's use the derivative to illustrate a business principle: if the demand curve has a negative slope at $x = c$, then the marginal revenue is less than the price $x = c$. We may see this by letting

$$p = f(x)$$

be the demand curve. So the revenue function is

$$R(x) = p \cdot x = x \cdot f(x).$$

Hence the marginal revenue is

$$R'(x) = x \cdot f'(x) + f(x).$$

At $x = c$ we get

$$R'(c) = c \cdot f'(c) + f(c).$$

Since the demand curve has negative slope at $x = c$,

$$f'(c) < 0 \quad \text{and} \quad c \cdot f'(x) < 0.$$

Thus,

$$R'(c) = c \cdot f'(c) + f(c) < 0 + f(c) = f(c).$$

The marginal revenue is less than the price.

EXERCISE

For most businesses, the average labor cost per hour, A, is a function of the total number of hours of labor required, L. That is, $A = f(L)$ for some function f. Show that if the graph of $A = f(L)$ has positive slope at $L = c$, then the marginal *total* labor cost is greater than the average labor cost at $L = c$.

Suppose we must differentiate

$$y = \frac{x^2 - 1}{x}. \tag{3-6}$$

We may do so by writing the quotient as a difference. We get

$$y = \frac{x^2}{x} - \frac{1}{x} = x - x^{-1}.$$

Thus

$$y' = 1 + x^{-2} = 1 + \frac{1}{x^2} = \frac{x^2 + 1}{x^2}. \tag{3-7}$$

Although this method works for this function, what would we do if the numerator and denominator were reversed? That is, how would we differentiate

$$y = \frac{x}{x^2 - 1}?$$

We must learn how to differentiate a quotient.

We begin by asking: "Is the derivative of a quotient the quotient of the derivatives?" That is, if

$$y = \frac{f(x)}{g(x)},$$

does

$$y' = \frac{f'(x)}{g'(x)}?$$

Unfortunately, the answer is no. This may be seen by considering the function defined in Equation (3-6). If we let $f(x) = x^2 - 1$ and $g(x) = x$, then

$$\frac{f'(x)}{g'(x)} = \frac{2x}{1} = 2x,$$

which is certainly not the derivative we obtained in Equation (3-7). So the derivative of a quotient is *not* the quotient of the derivatives.

THEOREM 3.14
Quotient Rule

If $y = f(x)/g(x)$, then

$$y' = \frac{g(x) \cdot f'(x) - f(x) \cdot g'(x)}{(g(x))^2}.$$

Proof This theorem may be established by using the product rule. We first write

$$y = \frac{f(x)}{g(x)} = f(x) \cdot (g(x))^{-1}.$$

By the product rule,

$$y' = f(x) \cdot (-1)(g(x))^{-2} \cdot g'(x) + (g(x))^{-1} \cdot f'(x)$$

$$= \frac{-f(x)g'(x)}{(g(x))^2} + \frac{f'(x)}{g(x)}$$

$$= \frac{-f(x)g'(x)}{(g(x))^2} + \frac{g(x)f'(x)}{(g(x))^2}$$

$$= \frac{g(x)f'(x) - f(x)g'(x)}{(g(x))^2}.$$

3.5 THE PRODUCT AND QUOTIENT RULES

This theorem says that the derivative of a quotient is the denominator times the derivative of the numerator minus the numerator times the derivative of the denominator, all divided by the denominator squared.

Let's return to the function defined in Equation (3-6), apply the quotient rule, and compare with Equation (3-7). We get

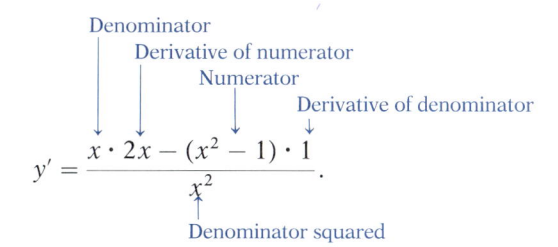

$$y' = \frac{\overset{\text{Denominator}}{x} \cdot \overset{\text{Derivative of numerator}}{2x} - \overset{\text{Numerator}}{(x^2-1)} \cdot \overset{\text{Derivative of denominator}}{1}}{\underset{\text{Denominator squared}}{x^2}}.$$

Simplifying we get

$$y' = \frac{2x^2 - x^2 + 1}{x^2} = \frac{x^2 + 1}{x^2},$$

which agrees with our previous result in Equation (3-7).

Let's use the quotient rule to differentiate

$$y = \frac{x}{x^2 - 1}.$$

We get

$$y' = \frac{\overset{\text{Denominator}}{(x^2-1)} \cdot \overset{\text{Derivative of numerator}}{1} - \overset{\text{Numerator}}{x} \cdot \overset{\text{Derivative of denominator}}{2x}}{\underset{\text{Denominator squared}}{(x^2-1)^2}}$$

$$= \frac{x^2 - 1 - 2x^2}{(x^2 - 1)^2}$$

$$= \frac{-1 - x^2}{(x^2 - 1)^2}.$$

EXAMPLE 2

Determine y' for

(a) $y = \dfrac{x^3 + 5}{x^2 + 1}$; (b) $y = \dfrac{1 + x^2}{e^x}$; and (c) $y = \dfrac{\sqrt{x}}{x - 1}$.

■ SOLUTION

(a) By the quotient rule we have

$$y' = \frac{(x^2 + 1) \cdot 3x^2 - (x^3 + 5) \cdot 2x}{(x^2 + 1)^2}$$

$$= \frac{3x^4 + 3x^2 - 2x^4 - 10x}{(x^2 + 1)^2}$$

$$= \frac{x^4 + 3x^2 - 10x}{(x^2 + 1)^2}.$$

(b) Using the quotient rule gives

$$y' = \frac{e^x \cdot 2x - (1 + x^2)e^x}{(e^x)^2}$$

$$= \frac{e^x(2x - 1 - x^2)}{e^{2x}}$$

$$= \frac{2x - 1 - x^2}{e^x}.$$

(c) Rewriting y with exponential notation in the numerator gives

$$y = \frac{x^{1/2}}{x - 1}.$$

By the quotient rule we have

$$y' = \frac{(x - 1) \cdot \frac{1}{2}x^{-1/2} - x^{1/2} \cdot 1}{(x - 1)^2}.$$

To simplify the numerator we need to eliminate the fraction $\frac{1}{2}$ and the negative exponent to $x^{-1/2}$. This may be accomplished by multiplying by $2x^{1/2}$. Of course, we must multiply the denominator by this quantity as well. We get

$$y' = \frac{(x - 1) \cdot \frac{1}{2}x^{-1/2} - x^{1/2} \cdot 1}{(x - 1)^2} \cdot \frac{2x^{1/2}}{2x^{1/2}}$$

$$= \frac{x - 1 - 2x}{2x^{1/2}(x - 1)^2} = \frac{-1 - x}{2\sqrt{x}(x - 1)^2}.$$

EXERCISE

Determine y' for

(a) $y = \dfrac{x}{x^3 + 1}$; (b) $y = \dfrac{x^5 + 1}{x^2 - 1}$; (c) $y = \dfrac{1 + x^3}{e^x}$; and (d) $y = \dfrac{\sqrt{x}}{2x + 1}$.

3.5 THE PRODUCT AND QUOTIENT RULES

■ ANSWER

(a) $y' = \dfrac{(x^3 + 1) \cdot 1 - x \cdot 3x^2}{(x^3 + 1)^2} = \dfrac{1 - 2x^3}{(x^3 + 1)^2}$

(b) $y' = \dfrac{(x^2 - 1)5x^4 - (x^5 + 1)2x}{(x^2 - 1)^2} = \dfrac{3x^6 - 5x^4 - 2x}{(x^2 - 1)^2}$

(c) $y' = \dfrac{e^x \cdot 3x^2 - (1 + x^3)e^x}{e^{2x}} = \dfrac{3x^2 - 1 - x^3}{e^x}$

(d) $y' = \dfrac{(2x + 1) \cdot \frac{1}{2}x^{-1/2} - x^{1/2} \cdot 2}{(2x + 1)^2} = \dfrac{1 - 2x}{2\sqrt{x}\,(2x + 1)^2}$

■

When differentiating products and quotients, bear in mind that it may be easier to rewrite the function and avoid the rule. For example, given

$$y = \sqrt{x}(2x + 3),$$

if you prefer to multiply this out to get

$$y = 2x^{3/2} + 3x^{1/2}$$

and then differentiate, as opposed to using the product rule, then do so. If the numerator or denominator of a quotient is a constant you can bypass the quotient rule. For example,

$$y = \dfrac{x^3 - x^2 + 3}{3}$$

may be written as

$$y = \tfrac{1}{3}x^3 - \tfrac{1}{3}x^2 + 1.$$

and

$$y = \dfrac{-5}{(x + 1)^3}$$

may be written as the power function

$$y = -5(x + 1)^{-3}.$$

PROBLEM SET 3.5

In Problems 1–26, differentiate using the product rule.

1. $y = (3x + 1)(2x - 6)$
2. $y = (5x + 3)(-x + 1)$
3. $y = x^3(x - 1)$
4. $y = x^4(2 - x^2)$
5. $y = e^x \ln x$
6. $y = e^{-x} \ln x$
7. $y = 3x(x + 1)^3$
8. $y = -2x(x - 5)^5$
9. $y = x^2 \ln|2x|$
10. $y = x \ln|7x|$
11. $y = (x + 1)^4(x - 3)^2$
12. $y = (x - 2)^3(x - 3)^7$
13. $y = x^2 e^{1/x}$
14. $y = x^3 e^{3x}$

15. $y = (x^2 - 1)^2(x^4 + 1)^4$
16. $y = (3x^2 + x)^3(x^4 - \pi)^3$
17. $y = e^x(e^x + 1)^7$
18. $y = e^x(e^x - 1)^8$
19. $y = \sqrt{2x - 7}(x^2 - 7)^3$
20. $y = \left(\dfrac{x^4}{4} - x\right)^4 \sqrt[4]{4x + 4}$
21. $y = (x^3 + 1)^3 \left(\dfrac{x}{3} - 1\right)^{-3}$
22. $y = (4 - 3x)^7(1 - x^{-2})^{-2}$
23. $y = \ln(x^2 \ln x^2)$
24. $y = \ln(x^e e^x)$
25. $y = (x + 1)(x - 2)^8(x + 3)^7$
26. $y = (x + 5)(x - 4)^6(2x + 1)^5$

In Problems 27–50, differentiate using the quotient rule.

27. $y = \dfrac{2}{2 + x^2 + x^4}$
28. $y = \dfrac{1}{x - x^3}$
29. $y = \dfrac{x}{\ln x}$
30. $y = \dfrac{x^2}{\ln x}$
31. $y = \dfrac{x^2 - 1}{x + 1}$
32. $y = \dfrac{6x^2 - 5x - 6}{3x + 2}$
33. $y = \dfrac{x + 1}{x - 1}$
34. $y = \dfrac{3x - 1}{x - 1}$
35. $y = \dfrac{x^2}{e^{x+1}}$
36. $y = \dfrac{x^3}{e^{3x+1}}$
37. $y = \dfrac{x + \pi}{x^4 - \pi x}$
38. $y = \dfrac{1 + x^5}{1 - x^5}$
39. $y = \dfrac{e^x}{(e^x - e)^4}$
40. $y = \dfrac{e^x}{(e^x + e)^5}$
41. $y = \dfrac{x}{(x^5 + 1)^5}$
42. $y = \dfrac{3x^2}{(x^3 + 2)^2}$
43. $y = \dfrac{2\sqrt{x}}{3 + x}$
44. $y = \dfrac{x^{1/3}}{1 + x^{1/3}}$
45. $y = \dfrac{e^{2x} + e}{e^{2x} - e}$
46. $y = \dfrac{e^x + ex}{e^x - ex}$
47. $y = \dfrac{x^4 - 1}{2x^2 + x}$
48. $y = \dfrac{x^3 - x}{x^3 + x}$
49. $y = \ln\left(\dfrac{e^x}{e^x + 1}\right)$
50. $y = \ln\left(\dfrac{e^{-x} - 1}{e^{-x}}\right)$

In Problems 51 and 52, differentiate.

51. $y = \dfrac{xe^x}{\ln x}$
52. $y = \dfrac{e^x}{x \ln x}$

53. If $f(x) = (3x + 1)\sqrt{2x + 1}$, then find $f'(4)$.
54. If $f(x) = \dfrac{x^2 + x + 1}{(x + 1)^3}$, then find $f'(-3)$.
55. Determine the equation of the tangent line to the graph of $y = (x^2 + 1)/(x - 1)$ at $x = 2$.
56. Determine the equation of the tangent line to the graph of $y = x\sqrt{8 - x^2}$ at $x = 2$.
57. Determine the points on the graph of $f(x) = (\ln x)^2/x$ at which the tangent line is horizontal.
58. Determine the points on the graph of the function $f(x) = (x - 1)^5(x - 2)^9 + 7x$ at which the tangent line has slope 7.
59. The lateral surface area A of a right circular cone of height 10 inches and radius r is given by $A = \pi r \sqrt{r^2 + 100}$. What is the rate of change in the surface area with respect to the radius when the radius is $\sqrt{44}$ inches?
60. The total surface area T of a right circular cone of height 4 feet and radius r is given by $T = \pi r(r + \sqrt{r^2 + 16})$. What is the rate of change in the surface area with respect to the radius when the radius is 3 feet?

The normal line to the graph of a differentiable function at a point (x,y) is defined as the line through (x,y) which is perpendicular to the tangent line. Two lines with slopes m_1 and m_2 are perpendicular if and only if $m_1 m_2 = -1$. This information is needed in Problems 61 and 62.

61. Determine the equation of the normal line to the graph of $y = x/(x^3 + 2)^3$ at the point $(-1, -1)$.
62. Determine the equation of the normal line to the graph of $y = (x - 3)^2 (x^2 + 1)^3$ at the y-intercept.
63. Show that if $f(x) = x^4$ and $g(x) = (4 - x)^{-4}$, then $f \cdot g' + g \cdot f' = f' \cdot g'$ (i.e., for these particular functions, the derivative of the product is equal to the product of the derivatives).
64. If $f(x) = xe^x$ and $g(x) = e^{\frac{1}{2}x^2 + x}$, show that the derivative of the product is equal to the product of the derivatives; that is, $f \cdot g' + g \cdot f' = f' \cdot g'$.
65. A particle moves along a straight line so that after t seconds its distance (in feet) from a fixed point is $s = 10t + te^{-t}$. What is the velocity when $t = 2$?
66. Show that if $y = (x - c)^n(x - k)^m$, where c, k, n, and m are constants, then
$$y' = (x - c)^{n-1}(x - k)^{m-1}((n + m)x - (mc + nk)).$$

CHAPTER 3 REVIEW

1. Determine whether each of the following is true or false.
   (a) If $f(x) = 5$, then the equation of the tangent line at $x = -7$ is $y = 5$.
   (b) If k is a nonzero constant and $y = e^x/k$, then $y' = y$.
   (c) If the profit from producing x units is $P(x) = (x^2 + 2)^3$, then the marginal profit is $3(x^2 + 2)^2$.
   (d) From the graph below it follows that
   $$\lim_{h \to 0} \frac{f(2+h) - f(2)}{h} < 0.$$

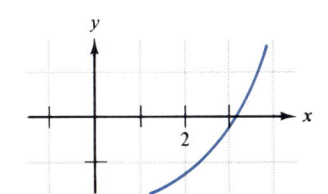

   (e) If $f(x) = x^{10,000}$, then $f'(-1) = -10,000$.
   (f) If $f(x)$ is discontinuous at $x = b$, then $f(x)$ is not differentiable at $x = b$.
   (g) The function $f(x) = |x - 1|$ is differentiable at $x = 0$.
   (h) If $f(x) = x^3$, then
   $$f'(x) = \lim_{h \to 0} \frac{(x+h)^3 + x^3}{h}.$$
   (i) If $f(x) = x^2 + 1$, then $f'(f(1)) = f(f'(\sqrt{3}/2))$.
   (j) Use the graph of the function below for the following seven statements.

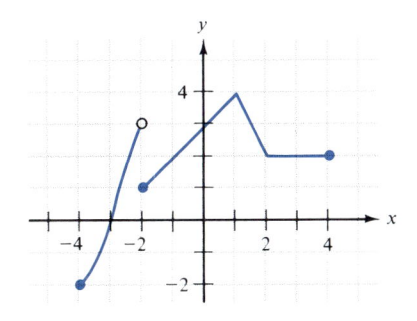

   (1) f is not differentiable at $x = -2$.
   (2) f is continuous at $x = f(-2)$.
   (3) f is differentiable at $x = 1$.
   (4) $f'(f(0)) = 0$.
   (5) f is discontinuous at $x = f(f(-3))$.
   (6) $f'(-1) = 0$.
   (7) $f'(\sqrt{2}) + f'(\pi) < 0$.
   (k) If k is any positive constant, $f(x) = \ln(kx)$, and $g(x) = \ln x$, then $f'(x) = g'(x)$.
   (l) The slope of the graph of
   $$f(x) = (3x)^3 + \frac{1}{(2x)^2}$$
   at $x = \frac{1}{3}$ is $-\frac{9}{2}$.
   (m) If $y = (x^2 + 1)(x - 1)^{-1/3}$, then $y' = (x^2 + 1) - \frac{1}{3}(x - 1)^{-4/3} + (x - 1)^{-1/3}(2x)$.
   (n) If $y = f(x) - g(x) - h(x)$, then $y' = f'(x) - g'(x) - h'(x)$.
   (o) If $f(x) = (x + 4)^2$ and $g(x) = x^2 + 4^2$, then $f'(x) = g'(x)$.
   (p) If $s = (t^4 + t)^3$, then $ds/dt = 3(t^4 + t)^2 4t^3 + 1$.
   (q) If $y = x^3 - x^{-1}$, then $y' = 3x^2 - x^{-2}$.
   (r) If $y = 2|x|$ and $x < 0$, then $y' = -2$.
   (s) If $y = x^3 + 12x^2 + 48x + 65$, then the tangent line is horizontal at $(-4, 1)$.
   (t) The distance s that a particle travels is given by $s = t^3 + 3t^2 - 9t$. When the acceleration is 18, the velocity is 5.
   (u) The function
   $$f(x) = \begin{cases} 2x & \text{when } x \geq 0 \\ -2x & \text{when } x < 0 \end{cases}$$
   is continuous but not differentiable at $x = 0$.
   (v) The slope of $y = e^x$ at $(1, e)$ is e.
   (w) Velocity is equal to the absolute value of the speed.
   (x) If the average speed during a car trip is 50 mph, then at least once during the trip the speedometer reading must be 50 mph.
   (y) Let f be a differentiable function with the following graph.

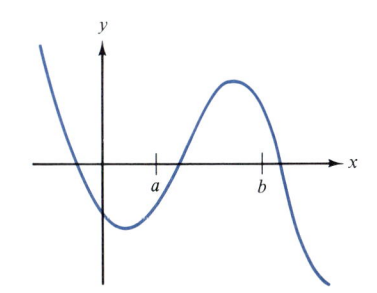

If $p = \lim_{h \to 0} \dfrac{f(a+h) - f(a)}{h}$ and

$q = \lim_{h \to 0} \dfrac{f(b+h) - f(b)}{h}$, then $p < q$.

(z) If f is the function with the graph presented below, then $f'(-1) + f(0) + f'(2) + f'(4) = 3$.

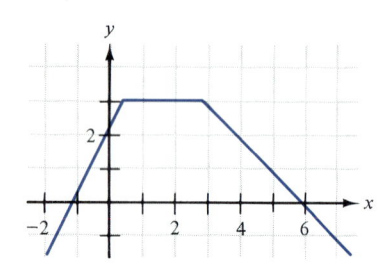

(aa) If $y = u^5$ and $u = e^x + 1$, then $dy/dx = 5(e^x + 1)^4$.

(bb) If $y = \ln|x|$, then $y' = 1/|x|$.

(cc) The graph of f' is presented below. It shows that the graph of f has a horizontal tangent at $x = 2$.

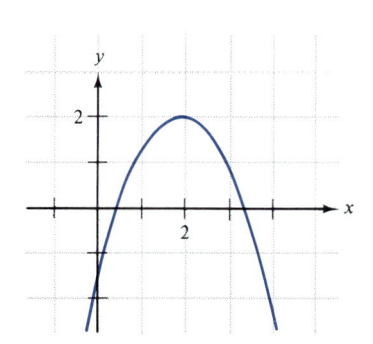

(dd) If $y = e^{\ln x} + \ln e^x$, then $y' = 2$.

In Problems 2–7, determine $f'(x)$ by using the definition of the derivative, that is,

$$f'(x) = \lim_{h \to 0} \dfrac{f(x+h) - f(x)}{h}$$

2. $f(x) = 4x^2 - x - \ln 3$
3. $f(x) = -5x^2 + 2x - \ln 2$
4. $f(x) = \dfrac{x}{x - 3}$
5. $f(x) = \dfrac{4x - 3}{x - 2}$
6. $f(x) = \dfrac{x^3 + 1}{x}$
7. $f(x) = \dfrac{x}{x^2 + 2}$

In Problems 8 and 9, determine $f'(2)$ by using the definition of the derivative. Then determine the equation of the tangent line at $x = 2$.

8. $f(x) = (2x + 1)(1 - 3x)$
9. $f(x) = \dfrac{1}{x - 2.5}$

In Problems 10–33, determine dy/dx.

10. $y = \left(\dfrac{1}{\sqrt[3]{x}}\right)^9$
11. $y = \dfrac{x^5}{5} - \dfrac{5}{x^5} + 5x$
12. $y = x^{-2} - \sqrt[4]{x} + \dfrac{1}{3^2}$
13. $y = \dfrac{x^e}{e} - \dfrac{e^x}{e} + e^e$
14. $y = (2x - 1)(x - 3)$
15. $y = \dfrac{x^6 - x^3 - \sqrt{x} + 1}{x}$
16. $y = u^2 - u$, $u = 5x - 2$
17. $y = 2/u$, $u = x^3 + x$
18. $y = 2e^{1 + \frac{1}{2}x} - e^{1 - x^2}$
19. $y = \ln|1 + ex|$
20. $y = (3x^3 - x)^7 + (10x)^{1/5}$
21. $y = (2x^4 - 6)^5 - \left(\dfrac{x}{\sqrt{3} + 1}\right)^{\sqrt{3} + 1}$
22. $y = (x^2 + 1)^3 (x^2 - 1)^4$
23. $y = (x^3 + x)^2 (x^3 - x)^5$
24. $y = x(x^2 + 1)^{-5}$
25. $y = x^4 e^{x^4}$
26. $y = \dfrac{\ln(x^2 - 1)}{x^2 - 1}$
27. $y = \dfrac{x^4 + x^2}{x^4 - x^2}$
28. $y = \dfrac{x^4 + 4}{1 - x^3}$
29. $y = \left(\dfrac{x + 2}{x - 4}\right)^4$
30. $y = \left(\dfrac{x^2 - 1}{x + 1}\right)^2$
31. $y = (\ln(\ln x))^9$
32. $y = \dfrac{e^{2x} - 1}{e^x(e^x - 1)}$
33. $y = \sqrt{1 + \sqrt{x}}$

34. Use the graph of f' to determine the slope of the graph of $y = f(x)$ at the specified location: **(a)** $x = -\pi$; **(b)** $x = -2$; **(c)** $(0, 1)$; and **(d)** $x = 3$.

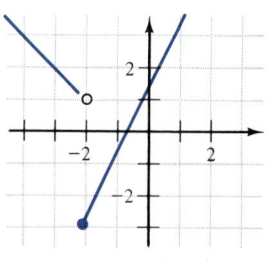

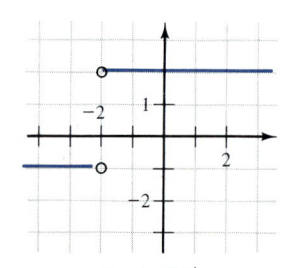

Graph of f

Graph of f'

In Problems 35 and 36 sketch the graph of f' given the graph of f.

CHAPTER 3 REVIEW

35.

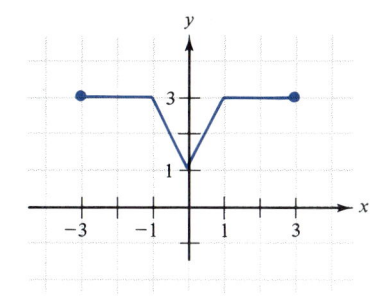

36.

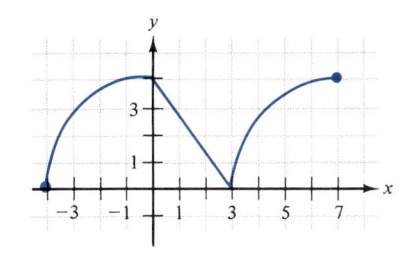

37. Evaluate

$$\lim_{h \to 0} \frac{f(3+h) - f(3)}{h},$$

where f is a function with derivative $f'(x) = (x^2 - 8)^{15}(x + 7)$.

38. Evaluate

$$\lim_{h \to 0} \frac{(2+h)^6 - 2^6}{h}.$$

39. If $y = t^2 - 3t + 1$, determine the value of t for which the rate of change of y with respect to t is 10.

40. Determine the points on the graph of $y = x/(x^2 + 1)^2$ at which the tangent line is horizontal.

41. Determine the equation of the tangent line to $f(x) = x^2 e^{-x}$ at $x = 1$.

42. Determine the points on the graph of $f(x) = (4x - 3)/(x - 2)$ at which the tangent line has slope -5.

43. Let $f(x) = x^4$.
  (a) Determine $f'(x^2)$.
  (b) Determine $g'(x)$, where $g(x) = f(x^2)$.

44. An object is dropped into a deep well and the distance s (in feet) of the object below ground level after t seconds is given by

$$s = 16t^2.$$

If the object hits bottom 3 seconds after the drop, (a) how deep is the well, and (b) with what speed does the object hit the bottom?

45. The distance s (in feet) traveled by a speedboat starting from rest is given by $s = 10t(1 + 2t)^{1/2}$, where t represents elapsed time in seconds.
  (a) How far has the boat traveled when $t = 4$?
  (b) What is the velocity when $t = 4$?
  (c) What is the acceleration when $t = 4$?

46. A used calculus book is thrown upward and its distance s (in feet) above the ground after t seconds is given by

$$s = -16t^2 + 48t.$$

  (a) What is the distance when $t = 2$?
  (b) What is the velocity when $t = 2$?
  (c) What is the acceleration when $t = 2$?
  (d) What is the maximum height attained?
  (e) With what velocity does the book strike the ground?

47. The distance s that a particle travels is given by $s(t) = 2t^2 + 4t + 9$. Determine the distance the particle will travel between the times when velocity is 20 and when velocity is 40.

48. Determine the constants a, b, and c so that the parabolas $y = x^2 + ax + b$ and $y = -x^2 + cx$ will have the same tangent line at the point (2,4).

49. The **average cost**, AC, of one unit is defined to be the total cost divided by the number of units produced; that is, $AC = C(x)/x$. Determine the first and second derivatives of the average cost.

50. A manufacturer of wet suits finds that the cost (in dollars) of manufacturing x wet suits is $C(x) = 0.03x^2 + 90x + 1700$.
  (a) Find the marginal cost when production is 55 units.
  (b) Show that this marginal cost is approximately the extra cost required to increase production from 55 to 56 units.

51. The volume V of the frustum of a cone (see figure below) is

$$V = \frac{\pi h}{3}(r_1^2 + r_1 \cdot r_2 + r_2^2).$$

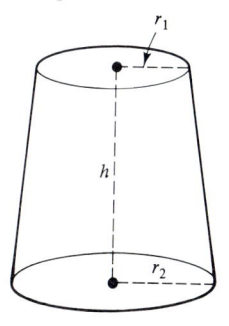

(a) Determine the rate of change of V with respect to h, if r_1 and r_2 remain constant.
(b) Determine the rate of change of V with respect to r_1, if r_2 and h remain constant.

52. The surface area A (in square centimeters) of a right circular cone of radius r and height h is $A = \pi r \sqrt{r^2 + h^2}$. If $h = 5$ centimeters, determine the average rate of change (to the nearest hundredth) of A with respect to r as r changes from
(a) 1.8 to 2
(b) 1.9 to 2
(c) 1.99 to 2
(d) 1.999 to 2
(e) Determine the instantaneous rate of change of V with respect to r when $r = 2$.

53. Sketch the graph of a function f that satisfies all of the following properties:
(a) Domain is $(-4, \infty)$.
(b) $f(0) = 3$.
(c) f is continuous for all $x \in (-4, \infty)$ except for $x = 6$.
(d) f is differentiable for all $x \in (-4, \infty)$ except for $x = 2, 4,$ and 6.

54. Let f and g be differentiable functions with $f(0) = 3$, $f'(0) = 4$, $f(2) = 2$, $f'(2) = 1$, $g(0) = 2$, and $g'(0) = -1$. If $y = f(g(x))/g(x)$, compute $y'|_{x=0}$.

55. Let x be the length of the edge of a cube, A the surface area, and V the volume. If the cube is expanding so that x, A, and V are functions of time t, show that

$$\frac{dV}{dt} = \frac{x}{4} \frac{dA}{dt}.$$

CHAPTER 4

ADDITIONAL TOPICS ON THE DERIVATIVE

CHAPTER OUTLINE
4.1 HIGHER-ORDER DERIVATIVES
4.2 IMPLICIT DIFFERENTIATION
4.3 RELATED RATES

This chapter covers a variety of topics. It begins by noting that we may differentiate a derivative. The next section shows how to find the derivative when there is no explicit formula. The chapter concludes with applications of the material of the second section.

4.1 HIGHER-ORDER DERIVATIVES

In Section 3.3 we learned that acceleration is the derivative of the velocity, and velocity is the derivative of a position function. Thus acceleration is the derivative of the derivative of a position function. Consequently, acceleration is called the *second derivative* of a position function.

Given a function, its **second derivative** is the derivative of the derivative. The notation to be used for the second derivative should be consistent with that of the first derivative, as indicated in the following table:

First derivative notation:	$f'(x)$	y'	$\dfrac{dy}{dx}$
Second derivative notation:	$f''(x)$	y''	$\dfrac{d^2y}{dx^2}.$

EXAMPLE 1

Determine the second derivative of

(a) $f(x) = 2x^4 - x^3 + 3x^2 - 5$,
(b) $y = (x^2 + 1)^{10}$,
(c) $y = \dfrac{2x - 1}{x + 1}$.

■ SOLUTION
(a) We begin by computing the first derivative:

$$f'(x) = 8x^3 - 3x^2 + 6x.$$

Differentiating once more gives the second derivative:

$$f''(x) = 24x^2 - 6x + 6.$$

(b) Using the general power rule to get the first derivative we have

$$y' = 10(x^2 + 1)^9 \cdot 2x = 20x(x^2 + 1)^9.$$

To determine the second derivative we use the product rule:

$$\begin{aligned}y'' &= 20x \cdot 9(x^2 + 1)^8 \cdot 2x + (x^2 + 1)^9 \cdot 20\\ &= 20(x^2 + 1)^8(18x^2 + x^2 + 1)\\ &= 20(x^2 + 1)^8(19x^2 + 1).\end{aligned}$$

4.1 HIGHER-ORDER DERIVATIVES

(c) By the quotient rule we have

$$\frac{dy}{dx} = \frac{(x+1) \cdot 2 - (2x-1) \cdot 1}{(x+1)^2}$$

$$= \frac{2x + 2 - 2x + 1}{(x+1)^2}$$

$$= \frac{3}{(x+1)^2} = 3(x+1)^{-2}.$$

We've written this as a power function to avoid the quotient rule. Differentiating once again we get

$$\frac{d^2y}{dx^2} = -6(x+1)^{-3} \cdot 1 = \frac{-6}{(x+1)^3}.$$

EXERCISE

Determine the second derivative of

(a) $f(x) = x^5 - 2x^4 + x^2 - 7$,
(b) $y = (1 - x^2)^6$,
(c) $y = \dfrac{1 - 2x}{x - 1}$.

■ ANSWER
(a) $f''(x) = 20x^3 - 24x^2 + 2$; (b) $y'' = -12(1 - x^2)^4(1 - 11x^2)$;
(c) $d^2y/dx^2 = -2/(x - 1)^3$

EXAMPLE 2

Determine the rate of change of the slope with respect to x at (2,1) for the graph of $y = x^3 - 2x^2 + x - 1$.

■ SOLUTION
We must find the instantaneous rate of change of the slope with respect to x at $x = 2$. The formula for slope is the first derivative:

$$\frac{dy}{dx} = 3x^2 - 4x + 1.$$

Differentiating once more we get the rate of change of dy/dx (the slope) with respect to x. We have

$$\frac{d^2y}{dx^2} = 6x - 4.$$

Hence
$$\left.\frac{d^2y}{dx^2}\right|_{x=2} = 12 - 4 = 8.$$

The slope is increasing 8 times as fast as x at (2,1).

Note that the first derivative gives us the slope, which is the instantaneous change in y with respect to x. The second derivative gives us the instantaneous *change in the slope* with respect to x.

EXERCISE

Determine the rate of change of the slope with respect to x at $(2, -4)$ for the graph of $y = -2x^3 + 2x^2 + 3x - 2$.

■ ANSWER
-20

Although we shall have little occasion to use anything beyond the second derivative, there are third derivatives, fourth derivatives, fifth derivatives, and so on. In general, the **nth derivative,** where $n > 1$, is the derivative of the $(n-1)$st derivative.

The prime notation is used for the third derivative, but it becomes cumbersome thereafter. So, in addition to d^4y/dx^4, the fourth derivative is denoted $f^{(4)}(x)$ or $y^{(4)}(x)$. The parentheses are used to distinguish the four from an exponent.

EXAMPLE 3

Determine the fourth derivative of $y = e^{2x}$.

■ SOLUTION
The first derivative is
$$y' = e^{2x} \cdot 2 = 2e^{2x}.$$

Differentiating again we get
$$y'' = 2e^{2x} \cdot 2 = 4e^{2x}.$$

Differentiation once more yields
$$y''' = 4e^{2x} \cdot 2 = 8e^{2x}.$$

Finally,
$$y^{(4)} = 8e^{2x} \cdot 2 = 16e^{2x}.$$

EXERCISE

Determine the fourth derivative of $y = e^{3x}$.

■ ANSWER

$81e^{3x}$

PROBLEM SET 4.1

In Problems 1–24, determine the second derivative.

1. $y = 3x^2 - 6x + 1$
2. $y = -2x^2 + 3x + 5$
3. $y = 4x^4 - ex^e + \dfrac{x^2}{2} - 7e^3$
4. $y = \dfrac{x^5}{5} - 2x^4 + \dfrac{x^e}{e} - (\ln 5)^4$
5. $y = \dfrac{1}{x^3} - \dfrac{2}{x^2} + \dfrac{1}{2x}$
6. $y = 9x^{1/3} + \dfrac{1}{3x^{1/2}} + \sqrt[4]{\pi}$
7. $y = \dfrac{1}{e^{6x}} - ex$
8. $y = \dfrac{-1}{e^{8x}} + e^2 x$
9. $y = \ln(4x^5)$
10. $y = \ln(6x^7)$
11. $y = (6x - 5)^9$
12. $y = \dfrac{1}{(3 - 5x)^7}$
13. $y = \dfrac{1}{(x^3 - 7)^6}$
14. $y = (5 - x^4)^5$
15. $y = x^2 \ln x$
16. $y = x^3 \ln x$
17. $y = \sqrt{x^2 + 4}$
18. $y = \sqrt[3]{x^3 + 8}$
19. $y = \dfrac{3x - 1}{3x + 1}$
20. $y = \dfrac{1 - 4x}{1 + 5x}$
21. $y = \dfrac{x}{1 + x^3}$
22. $y = \dfrac{x}{2 + x^2}$
23. $y = \ln(xe^{-x})$
24. $y = \ln(1 - e^x)$

In Problems 25–28, determine the rate of change of the slope with respect to x at the indicated point on the graph of each given function.

25. $y = \dfrac{1}{x - 1}, \ (3, \tfrac{1}{2})$
26. $y = x^4 - 3x^3 - 5x^2 - x + 10, \ (-1, 10)$
27. $y = e^x + e^{-x}, \ (0, 2)$
28. $y = \ln \dfrac{x}{2} + \ln \dfrac{x}{3}, \ (6, \ln 6)$
29. Determine $f''(8)$ if $f(x) = x^{2/3} + (1/x^{1/3})$.
30. Determine $f''(2)$ if $f(x) = 1/(x - 1)^5$.
31. If $Q = r^{-1} + r^{1/4}$, find d^2Q/dr^2.
32. If $V = (3t - 8)^6 + 4t^2 - 7$, find $(d^3V/dt^3)|_{t=3}$.
33. Determine the fourth derivative of $y = (3x - 7)^6$.
34. Determine the fourth derivative of $y = (2 - 3x)^7$.
35. Determine the fifth derivative of $y = (x + 1)\ln(x + 1)$.
36. Determine the fifth derivative of $y = xe^x$.
37. If $f(x) = \dfrac{5x - 3}{x + 2}$, then show that

$$4 \cdot f'(0) + 8 \cdot f''(0) + 16 \cdot f'''(0) = 65.$$

38. If $f(x) = (x + 1)^6$, then show that

$$f^{(8)}(2) + f^{(6)}(2) - f(2) + 9 = 0.$$

In Problems 39 and 40, determine the values of k so that $y = e^{kx}$ is a solution of the given equation.

39. $y'' - 2y' - 15y = 0$
40. $y''' + 2y'' - 8y' = 0$
41. If $f(x)$ is a polynomial of degree 2, that is, $f(x) = ax^2 + bx + c$, and $f(1) = 5$, $f'(-1) = -2$, $f''(2) = 6$, then determine $f(-3)$.
42. Find a formula for $f^{(n)}(x)$, where n is any positive integer if $f(x) = 1/(x - 2)$.
43. If the cost of producing x units of a certain commodity is given by $C(x) = 0.05x^2 + 30x + 2500$, determine the rate of change of the marginal cost with respect to the number of units produced.
44. Show that if $y = f(x) \cdot g(x)$, where f and g are twice-differentiable functions, then $y'' = f(x) \cdot g''(x) + 2f'(x) \cdot g'(x) + g(x) \cdot f''(x)$.
45. Certain types of population growth can be best approximated by a Von Bertalanffy growth curve of the form $y = a(1 - (1/c)e^{-kx})^3$, where a and k are positive constants and $c > 1$. Show that

$$\dfrac{d^2y}{dx^2} = \dfrac{3ak^2}{c} e^{-kx} \left(1 - \dfrac{1}{c} e^{-kx}\right)\left(\dfrac{3}{c} e^{-kx} - 1\right).$$

4.2 IMPLICIT DIFFERENTIATION

Suppose that we wish to find the slope of the graph of

$$5x + 2 + y = x^2$$

at $(2, -8)$. In this equation y is a function of x. Indeed, we may solve for y in terms of x. We have

$$y = x^2 - 5x - 2.$$

Thus

$$\frac{dy}{dx} = 2x - 5,$$

$$\left.\frac{dy}{dx}\right|_{x=2} = -1.$$

So the slope of the curve at $(2, -8)$ is -1.

Now suppose that we wish to find the slope of the graph of

$$x^2 + y^2 = 25$$

at $(3,4)$. In this equation y is *not* a function of x. For each permissible value of x, there does *not* correspond a unique value of y. This is easily seen from its graph, which is a circle of radius 5, centered at the origin. See Figure 4.1.

Because y is not a function of x, the equation cannot be solved for y in terms of x. We cannot write $y = f(x)$ for some function f. We can write

$$y = \pm\sqrt{25 - x^2},$$

but this is really shorthand notation for

$$y = \sqrt{25 - x^2} \quad \text{or} \quad y = -\sqrt{25 - x^2},$$

which are two different functions. But note that the graph of $y = \sqrt{25 - x^2}$ is the upper semicircle and contains the point $(3,4)$. See Figure 4.2. Thus we may differentiate

$$y = (25 - x^2)^{1/2}.$$

We get

$$\frac{dy}{dx} = \tfrac{1}{2}(25 - x^2)^{-1/2}(-2x)$$

$$= \frac{-x}{\sqrt{25 - x^2}},$$

$$\left.\frac{dy}{dx}\right|_{x=3} = \frac{-3}{\sqrt{25 - 9}} = -\frac{3}{4}.$$

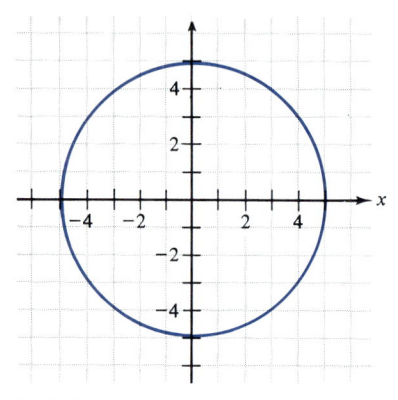

FIGURE 4.1

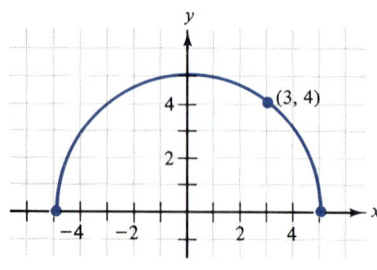

FIGURE 4.2

4.2 IMPLICIT DIFFERENTIATION

The desired slope is $-\frac{3}{4}$. Thus, even though the original equation, $x^2 + y^2 = 25$, does not define y as a function of x, we were able to find a function $y = \sqrt{25 - x^2}$, whose graph, a semicircle, coincides with the graph of the original equation, a circle, and contains the desired point, (3,4). We then proceeded to differentiate as usual.

Let's consider another problem. Suppose that we wish to find the slope of the graph of

$$y^4 + x = x^3 y^5 + 7$$

at $(-2,1)$. As with the circle, y is not a function of x. So we cannot solve for y in terms of x. But can we do what we did in the preceding illustration? Can we find a function f such that the graph of $y = f(x)$ coincides with the graph of

$$y^4 + x = x^3 y^5 + 7$$

and contains the point $(-2,1)$? It seems reasonable that such a function exists, but how do we find it? The interesting thing is, we don't have to find it. We just need to recognize that it exists. This alone enables us to differentiate it!

If $y = f(x)$ coincides with the graph of

$$y^4 + x = x^3 y^5 + 7,$$

then

$$(f(x))^4 + x = x^3 (f(x))^5 + 7,$$

for all x in the domain of f. Now let's differentiate both sides with respect to x. We get

$$4 \cdot (f(x))^3 \cdot f'(x) + 1 = x^3 \cdot 5(f(x))^4 \cdot f'(x) + (f(x))^5 \cdot 3x^2.$$

In alternate notation this is

$$4y^3 \cdot \frac{dy}{dx} + 1 = x^3 \cdot 5y^4 \cdot \frac{dy}{dx} + y^5 \cdot 3x^2.$$

Solving this equation for dy/dx gives

$$4y^3 \frac{dy}{dx} - 5x^3 y^4 \frac{dy}{dx} = 3x^2 y^5 - 1$$

$$\frac{dy}{dx}(4y^3 - 5x^3 y^4) = 3x^2 y^5 - 1$$

$$\frac{dy}{dx} = \frac{3x^2 y^5 - 1}{4y^3 - 5x^3 y^4}.$$

So we have differentiated the function without having its formula of definition! However, unlike previous derivatives, which are in terms of a single variable, this derivative is in terms of two variables. But that's okay.

It simply means that to compute the slope at $(-2,1)$, we must use both coordinates. When $x = -2$ and $y = 1$,

$$\frac{dy}{dx} = \frac{3(-2)^2(1)^5 - 1}{4(1)^3 - 5(-2)^3(1)^4} = \frac{12 - 1}{4 + 40} = \frac{11}{44} = \frac{1}{4}.$$

The slope at $(-2,1)$ is $\frac{1}{4}$.

This technique, where we differentiate a function without having an explicit formula for it, is called **implicit differentiation.** We find dy/dx without having a formula for y in terms of x.

Implicit differentiation could have also been used in our second illustration, the circle problem. Indeed, we don't have to determine the equation of the upper semicircle. All we need to do is recognize that there is *some* function $y = f(x)$ that satisfies

$$x^2 + y^2 = 25$$

and contains the point $(3,4)$. Then differentiation of both sides with respect to x yields

$$2x + 2y \cdot \frac{dy}{dx} = 0. \tag{4-1}$$

This technique is straightforward as long as we realize that y is a function of x and that we are differentiating *with respect to x*. This is extremely important as it significantly alters the results. If we differentiate y^2 *with respect to y* we get $2y$. But if y is a function of x and we differentiate *with respect to x*, we get

$$2y \cdot \frac{dy}{dx}.$$

This is because y^2 is a general power function of x. It is of the form

$$(f(x))^2,$$

so its derivative is

$$2(f(x)) \cdot f'(x).$$

Returning to Equation (4-1), we solve for dy/dx:

$$2x + 2y \cdot \frac{dy}{dx} = 0$$

$$\frac{dy}{dx} = \frac{-x}{y}.$$

Therefore, at $(3,4)$, the slope is $-\frac{3}{4}$. One advantage of implicit differentiation is that we may easily compute the slope at any point on the circle. The formula obtained in this fashion is valid for all points at which there is a slope, not just those of the upper semicircle. For example, the slope at $(-4,-3)$ is $-\frac{4}{3}$.

4.2 IMPLICIT DIFFERENTIATION

EXAMPLE 1

Determine dy/dx if $x^2 + xy - y^2 = 3$.

■ SOLUTION

Since y is not a function of x, we must differentiate implicitly. The derivative of x^2 is certainly $2x$, but what about the derivative of xy? Since we are treating y as a function of x, the term xy is a product of two functions. Thus, by the product rule, its derivative is

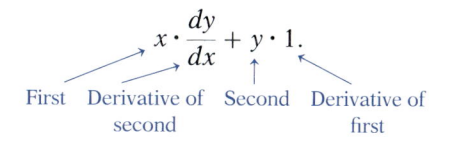

$$x \cdot \frac{dy}{dx} + y \cdot 1.$$

First — Derivative of second Second — Derivative of first

And what about the derivative of $-y^2$? Since we are assuming that y is a function of x, $-y^2$ is a general power function. Thus, by the power rule, its derivative is

$$-2y \cdot \frac{dy}{dx}.$$

Of course, the derivative of 3 is zero. So the derivative with respect to x of the original equation is

$$2x + x \cdot \frac{dy}{dx} + y \cdot 1 - 2y \cdot \frac{dy}{dx} = 0.$$

Solving for dy/dx, we get

$$x \frac{dy}{dx} - 2y \frac{dy}{dx} = -2x - y$$

$$\frac{dy}{dx}(x - 2y) = -2x - y$$

$$\frac{dy}{dx} = \frac{-2x - y}{x - 2y} = \frac{2x + y}{2y - x}.$$

EXERCISE

Determine dy/dx if $x^3 - xy + y^3 = 5$.

■ ANSWER

$$\frac{y - 3x^2}{3y^2 - x}$$

EXAMPLE 2

Determine the slope of the curve $x^3 + y^2 = xy$ at $(-2, -4)$.

■ SOLUTION

First, we must compute dy/dx, and we must do so implicitly. We have

$$3x^2 + 2y\frac{dy}{dx} = x\frac{dy}{dx} + y \cdot 1$$

$$2y\frac{dy}{dx} - x\frac{dy}{dx} = y - 3x^2$$

$$\frac{dy}{dx}(2y - x) = y - 3x^2$$

$$\frac{dy}{dx} = \frac{y - 3x^2}{2y - x}.$$

When $x = -2$ and $y = -4$, we get

$$\frac{dy}{dx} = \frac{-4 - 3(4)}{-8 + 2} = \frac{-16}{-6} = \frac{8}{3}.$$

The slope is $\frac{8}{3}$.

EXERCISE

Determine the slope of the curve $x^2 - xy = 2y^2$ at $(2,1)$.

■ ANSWER

$\frac{1}{2}$

EXAMPLE 3

Determine d^2y/dx^2 in terms of x and y if $x^2 + y^2 = 5$.

■ SOLUTION

First, we compute dy/dx implicitly. We get

$$2x + 2y\frac{dy}{dx} = 0$$

$$2y\frac{dy}{dx} = -2x$$

$$\frac{dy}{dx} = \frac{-x}{y}.$$

4.2 IMPLICIT DIFFERENTIATION

Now we differentiate again implicitly. We get

$$\frac{d^2y}{dx^2} = \frac{y(-1) + x\dfrac{dy}{dx}}{y^2}.$$

To put this result in terms of x and y only, we substitute for dy/dx. We have

$$\frac{d^2y}{dx^2} = \frac{-y + x\left(\dfrac{-x}{y}\right)}{y^2}$$

$$= \frac{-y^2 - x^2}{y^3}$$

$$= \frac{-(x^2 + y^2)}{y^3}$$

$$= \frac{-5}{y^3},$$

where the last substitution is made using the original equation.

EXERCISE

Determine d^2y/dx^2 in terms of x and y if $x^2 - y^2 = 3$.

■ ANSWER

$3/y^3$

Implicit differentiation is also used in differentiating something like

$$y = x^x.$$

The simple power rule cannot be applied because the exponent is a *variable, not a constant*. The problem is tackled with a method called **logarithmic differentiation**—a technique that includes implicit differentiation. Logarithmic differentiation is generally used when we have a variable quantity raised to a variable power. See Example 4.

EXAMPLE 4

Determine y' if $y = x^x$. (4-2)

■ SOLUTION

We begin by taking the logarithm of each side of this equation. We have

$$\ln y = \ln x^x.$$

The next step is to use laws of logarithms to simplify the right side. We get

$$\ln y = x \ln x. \tag{4-3}$$

Now we differentiate both sides of Equation (4-3) *with respect to x*. Since y is not written explicitly in terms of x, this is, of course, implicit differentiation, and we are treating y as a function of x. Hence $\ln y$ is of the form $\ln(g(x))$ for some function g. Thus differentiation of $\ln y$ with respect to x gives $g'(x)/g(x) = y'/y$. So we get

$$\frac{y'}{y} = x \cdot \frac{1}{x} + (\ln x) \cdot 1$$
$$= 1 + \ln x.$$

Solving for y', which is what we're trying to find, we get

$$y' = y(1 + \ln x).$$

Upon substituting for y, using the original equation, (4-2), we have

$$y' = x^x(1 + \ln x).$$

EXERCISE

Determine y' if $y = x^{x^2}$.

■ ANSWER
$x^{x^2}(x + 2x \ln x)$

PROBLEM SET 4.2

In Problems 1–22, determine dy/dx.

1. $\dfrac{x^2}{36} - \dfrac{y^2}{64} = 1$
2. $\dfrac{x^2}{4} + \dfrac{y^2}{9} = 1$
3. $\sqrt{x} + \sqrt{y} = \sqrt{5}$
4. $\sqrt[3]{y} - \sqrt[3]{x} = \sqrt[3]{3}$
5. $\ln(4x) + \ln(4y^2) = \ln e$
6. $\ln(3x^3) - \ln(2y^4) = \ln 6$
7. $e^{3x} + e^{3y} = 3x + 1$
8. $2e^{-4x} - 4e^{-2y} = 4x^2$
9. $x^4 + y^4 = x + y$
10. $x^3 - y^3 = 3x - y$
11. $\ln y + y^3 = x^2$
12. $\ln \dfrac{1}{y} - y^2 = x$
13. $2x^4 - xy + y^3 = 3$
14. $3y^2 + xy - x^5 = \pi^2$
15. $x \ln y + y \ln x = 4$
16. $x \ln x - y \ln y = 1$
17. $y = \tfrac{4}{7}(x - y)^{7/4}$
18. $y = \tfrac{3}{5}(y^2 - x)^{5/3}$
19. $x^3 + 2x^2y^2 + xy - 7 = 0$
20. $2x^5 - 3x^3y^3 + x^2y + 1 = 0$
21. $\dfrac{\ln y}{e^x} - x = 2$
22. $\dfrac{\ln x^3}{e^y} = x^3$

In Problems 23–30, determine the slope of each curve at the indicated point.

23. $\dfrac{1}{x^2} + \dfrac{1}{y^2} = 8$, $(\tfrac{1}{2}, -\tfrac{1}{2})$
24. $\dfrac{1}{x^3} - \dfrac{1}{y^3} = \dfrac{-9}{8}$, $(-1, 2)$
25. $21x = 21y + 7y^3 + 3y^7 - 11$, $(-2, -1)$

26. $12x - 15 = 12y - 6y^2 + 4y^3 - 3y^4 + 2y^6$, (2,1)
27. $xe^y = 1$, $(1/e, 1)$
28. $x^2 e^{y^2} = 1$, $(1/e, \sqrt{2})$
29. $8xy = (x^3 + y^3)^3$, (1,1)
30. $16x^2 y^2 = (x^4 + y^4)^4$, $(-1, -1)$

In Problems 31–34, determine the equation of the tangent to each curve at the indicated point.

31. $(x-3)^2 + (y+2)^2 = 25$, (6,2)
32. $\dfrac{(x-1)^2}{45} + \dfrac{(y-2)^2}{20} = 1$, (4,6)
33. $y = \dfrac{x-y}{x+y}$, $(0, -1)$
34. $y = \dfrac{x^2 - y}{x^2 + y}$, $(1, \sqrt{2} - 1)$

In Problems 35–38, determine d^2y/dx^2.

35. $x^2 - 3y^2 = 4$
36. $x^3 + y^3 = 1$
37. $\ln(3x) - \ln(3y^2) = 3$
38. $x^3 e^{y^3} = 1$

In Problems 39 and 40, determine d^3y/dx^3.

39. $y^3 + y = x$
40. $y + e^y = x$

In Problems 41–46, use logarithmic differentiation to find y'.

41. $y = x^{3x}$
42. $y = (2x)^x$
43. $y = (\ln x)^x$
44. $y = x^{\ln x}$
45. $y = x^{e^x}$
46. $y = (e^x)^{e^x}$

In Problems 47 and 48, determine dy/dx.

47. $e^{e^y} = x$
48. $x^x y^y = 1$

In Problems 49 and 50, show that the curves intersect at right angles at the origin. (Hint: Two nonvertical lines are perpendicular if and only if the slope of each is the negative reciprocal of the slope of the other.)

49. $4y - 3x + y^2 - x^2 y = 0$, $3y + 4x - x^3 + xy^2 = 0$
50. $7y + 5x - y^4 + xy = 0$, $5y - 7x + x^5 - x^3 y^3 = 0$

51. Suppose that a manufacturer's cost function C satisfies the equation $x^2 C^3 - C^4 = 100$. Determine the marginal cost.

52. The demand equation for a certain product is given by $p^3 + xp + 3x = 50$. Determine dp/dx.

53. The number of ions I in a solution at time t satisfies $(A + I)/(A - I) = e^{2At}$ where A is a constant. Determine dI/dt and show that dI/dt is never 0.

4.3 RELATED RATES

Suppose that $x = f(t)$ and $y = g(t)$ for some functions f and g, and that x and y are related as follows:

$$x^2 + xy = y^3.$$

Can we find the relationship between the rates dx/dt and dy/dt? Indeed we can, by using implicit differentiation. Substituting for x and y, we have

$$(f(t))^2 + f(t) \cdot g(t) = (g(t))^3.$$

Differentiating both sides with respect to t we get

$$2(f(t)) \cdot f'(t) + f(t) \cdot g'(t) + g(t) \cdot f'(t) = 3(g(t))^2 \cdot g'(t).$$

In alternate notation this is

$$2x \frac{dx}{dt} + x \frac{dy}{dt} + y \frac{dx}{dt} = 3y^2 \frac{dy}{dt}.$$

Thus we have the relationship between the rates dx/dt and dy/dt.

This technique is straightforward as long as we realize that x and y are functions of t and that we are differentiating *with respect to t*. This realization is extremely important as it significantly alters the result. Indeed, if we differentiate x^2 *with respect to x* we get $2x$. But if x is a function of t and we differentiate *with respect to t*, we get

$$2x\frac{dx}{dt}.$$

This is because x^2 is a general power function of t. It is of the form

$$(f(t))^2,$$

so its derivative is

$$2(f(t)) \cdot f'(t).$$

EXAMPLE 1

Suppose a point is moving along the curve $x^2 + 3y^2 = 13$. Find dy/dt when the point is at (1,2) if $dx/dt = 2$ here.

■ SOLUTION

Both x and y are functions of t such that

$$x^2 + 3y^2 = 13.$$

Differentiation of both sides with respect to t gives

$$2x\frac{dx}{dt} + 6y\frac{dy}{dt} = 0.$$

Solving for dy/dt gives

$$6y\frac{dy}{dt} = -2x\frac{dx}{dt}$$

$$\frac{dy}{dt} = -\frac{x\frac{dx}{dt}}{3y}.$$

When $x = 1$ and $y = 2$, $dx/dt = 2$, so

$$\frac{dy}{dt} = -\frac{1 \cdot 2}{3 \cdot 2} = -\frac{1}{3}.$$

EXERCISE

Suppose a point is moving along the curve $2x^2 + y^2 = 6$. Find dy/dt when the point is at (1,2) if $dx/dt = -2$ here.

■ ANSWER

2

EXAMPLE 2

The equivalent resistance R (in ohms) of two resistances R_1 and R_2 connected in parallel is given by

$$\frac{1}{R} = \frac{1}{R_1} + \frac{1}{R_2}. \qquad (4\text{-}4)$$

If R_1 is increasing at a rate of 1.0 ohm/second and R_2 is decreasing at a rate of 0.5 ohm/second, how is the equivalent resistance changing (in ohms/second, to the nearest ten thousandth) when $R_1 = 2$ and $R_2 = 2.5$?

■ SOLUTION
We are being asked to find

$$\frac{dR}{dt},$$

and we are told that

$$\frac{dR_1}{dt} = 1 \quad \text{and} \quad \frac{dR_2}{dt} = -0.5.$$

Since Equation (4-4) contains the variables R, R_1, and R_2, we may differentiate implicitly with respect to t. Rewriting Equation (4-4) first gives

$$R^{-1} = R_1^{-1} + R_2^{-1}.$$

Differentiation of both sides with respect to t gives

$$-R^{-2}\frac{dR}{dt} = -R_1^{-2}\frac{dR_1}{dt} - R_2^{-2}\frac{dR_2}{dt}.$$

Solving for dR/dt gives

$$\frac{dR}{dt} = \frac{\dfrac{1}{R_1^2} \cdot \dfrac{dR_1}{dt} + \dfrac{1}{R_2^2} \cdot \dfrac{dR_2}{dt}}{\dfrac{1}{R^2}}$$

$$= \frac{\dfrac{1}{R_1^2} - \dfrac{0.5}{R_2^2}}{\dfrac{1}{R^2}}$$

when we substitute for dR_1/dt and dR_2/dt. When $R_1 = 2$ and $R_2 = 2.5$, note that Equation (4-4) gives

$$\frac{1}{R} = \frac{1}{2} + \frac{1}{2.5} = 0.9.$$

Thus

$$\frac{dR}{dt} = \frac{\frac{1}{2^2} - \frac{0.5}{(2.5)^2}}{(0.9)^2}$$

$$= \frac{0.25 - 0.08}{0.81} \approx 0.2099.$$

The equivalent resistance is increasing at a rate of approximately 0.2099 ohm/second.

EXERCISE

The equivalent resistance R (in ohms) of two resistances R_1 and R_2 connected in parallel is given by

$$\frac{1}{R} = \frac{1}{R_1} + \frac{1}{R_2}.$$

If R_1 is increasing at a rate of 1.5 ohms/second, and R_2 is decreasing at a rate of 1.0 ohm/second, how is the equivalent resistance changing (in ohms/second, to the nearest ten thousandth) when $R_1 = 2$ and $R_2 = 4$?

■ ANSWER
Increasing ≈ 0.5556 ohm/second.

Physiologists have determined that an accurate estimate of a person's total body surface area A (in square meters) may be obtained by using

$$A = 0.202\, W^{0.425} H^{0.725}, \tag{4-5}$$

where W is the person's weight in kilograms and H is the person's height in meters. This information is needed in the following example and exercise.

EXAMPLE 3

Suppose a man who weighs 100 kilograms and is 2 meters tall is gaining weight at the rate of 0.05 kilogram per day. If his height is not changing, how fast is his surface area changing (in square meters per day, to the nearest ten thousandth)?

■ SOLUTION
Using the variables defined for Equation (4-5), we see that we are being asked to find

$$\frac{dA}{dt},$$

and we are told that
$$\frac{dW}{dt} = 0.05 \quad \text{and} \quad \frac{dH}{dt} = 0.$$

Using Equation (4-5) and differentiating implicitly with respect to t, we get

$$\frac{dA}{dt} = 0.202\left(W^{0.425} \cdot 0.725 H^{-0.275} \cdot \frac{dH}{dt} + H^{0.725} \cdot 0.425 W^{-0.575} \cdot \frac{dW}{dt}\right).$$

Substitution yields

$$\frac{dA}{dt} = 0.202(100^{0.425} \cdot 0.725 \cdot 2^{-0.275} \cdot 0 + 2^{0.725} \cdot 0.425 \cdot 100^{-0.575} \cdot 0.05)$$

$$= \frac{(0.202)(2^{0.725})(0.425)(0.05)}{100^{0.575}} \approx 0.0005.$$

The man's body surface area is increasing 0.0005 square meters/day.

EXERCISE

Suppose a boy who weighs 50 kilograms and is 1.5 meters tall is growing at the rate of 0.025 meter per month. If his weight is not changing, how fast is his surface area changing (in square meters per month, to the nearest ten thousandth)?

■ ANSWER
Increasing 0.0173 m²/month.

In the first three examples the variables were already defined and we were given an equation that related the dependent variables. In many related rate problems, however, we must define the variables and come up with the equation ourselves. Consider the following problem. If the base of a triangle is increasing at a rate of 2 inches/minute, and the altitude is decreasing at a rate of 3 inches/minute, how is the area changing when the base is 5 inches and the altitude is 6 inches?

First, let's determine what rate we are looking for: a change in the area *with respect to time*. And what rates do we have: a change in the base length with respect to time and a change in the altitude with respect to time. So let

$$A = \text{area (in square inches)},$$
$$b = \text{base (in inches)},$$
$$h = \text{altitude (in inches)},$$
$$t = \text{time (in minutes)}.$$

Hence, in terms of our variables, the rate we are looking for is
$$\frac{dA}{dt}.$$

And the rates we have are
$$\frac{db}{dt} = 2 \quad \text{(it's increasing)},$$

$$\frac{dh}{dt} = -3 \quad \text{(it's decreasing)}.$$

What we need is an equation that relates the dependent variables A, b, and h. The formula for the area of a triangle gives us this:
$$A = \tfrac{1}{2}bh.$$

Since each of these variables is a function of t, we may differentiate both sides with respect to t. We get
$$\frac{dA}{dt} = \frac{1}{2}\left(b \cdot \frac{dh}{dt} + h \cdot \frac{db}{dt}\right).$$
$$= \frac{1}{2}(-3b + 2h).$$

When $b = 5$ and $h = 6$, we get
$$\frac{dA}{dt} = \tfrac{1}{2}(-3(5) + 2(6)) = -\tfrac{3}{2}.$$

So the area is decreasing 1.5 square inches/minute.

Thus, in solving a related rates problem, we progress according to the following steps:

1. Determine what rate we are looking for and what rates we have.
2. Define the necessary variables and draw a picture if appropriate.
3. Translate the rates identified in step 1 into derivatives.
4. Find an equation that relates the dependent variables.
5. Differentiate both sides of the equation with respect to time.
6. Solve for the desired derivative and substitute known numerical values.
7. Answer the question.

Let's try this in Examples 4 through 6.

EXAMPLE 4

Suppose a child is flying a kite that is 200 feet above the ground. With 300 feet of string out, a gust of wind suddenly blows the kite horizontally. If the kite string unreeled at 10 feet/second, what was the speed of the wind (in feet/second, to the nearest hundredth)?

■ SOLUTION

We are looking for the wind speed, which is a change in the horizontal distance with respect to time, and we are told how fast the string is unreeling. See Figure 4.3.

Note that we are letting

$$x = \text{horizontal distance to kite (in feet)},$$
$$y = \text{length of string out (in feet)},$$
$$t = \text{time (in seconds)}.$$

We are being asked to find

$$\frac{dx}{dt},$$

and we have

$$\frac{dy}{dt} = 10.$$

So we must find an equation connecting x and y. Since we have a right triangle, by the Pythagorean theorem,

$$y^2 = x^2 + 200^2. \tag{4-6}$$

Differentiating both sides with respect to t we get

$$2y\frac{dy}{dt} = 2x\frac{dx}{dt}.$$

Solving for dx/dt, we have

$$\frac{dx}{dt} = \frac{y\dfrac{dy}{dt}}{x}.$$

We must determine the value when $y = 300$. Note that, by using Equation (4-6),

$$300^2 = x^2 + 200^2$$
$$x^2 = 300^2 - 200^2 = 50{,}000$$
$$x = \sqrt{50{,}000}.$$

Thus, substituting for y, x, and dy/dt, we get

$$\frac{dx}{dt} = \frac{300(10)}{\sqrt{50{,}000}} \approx 13.42.$$

The wind speed was approximately 13.42 feet/second (about 9 mph).

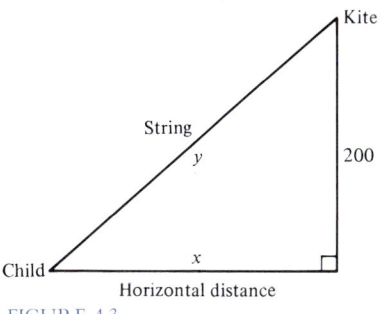

FIGURE 4.3

EXERCISE

Suppose a child is flying a kite that is 150 feet above the ground. With 200 feet of string out, a gust of wind suddenly blows it horizontally. If the kite string unreeled at 12 feet/second, what was the speed of the wind (in feet/second, to the nearest hundredth)?

■ *ANSWER*
18.14 feet/second

Let's note that Example 4 may also be solved by using the chain rule. If we solve Equation (4-6) for x, we get

$$x = \sqrt{y^2 - 200^2} = (y^2 - 200^2)^{1/2}.$$

So

$$\frac{dx}{dt} = \frac{dx}{dy} \cdot \frac{dy}{dt}$$
$$= \tfrac{1}{2}(y^2 - 200^2)^{-1/2} \cdot 2y \cdot 10$$
$$= \frac{10y}{\sqrt{y^2 - 200^2}}.$$

When $y = 300$,

$$\frac{dx}{dt} = \frac{10(300)}{\sqrt{300^2 - 200^2}} \approx 13.42.$$

EXAMPLE 5

Suppose a 6-foot man is walking away from a streetlamp that is 30 feet tall. How fast is the end of his shadow moving when he is 10 feet from the streetlamp if he is walking at a rate of 2 feet/second?

■ *SOLUTION*
We are trying to find the rate of change of the distance from streetlamp to the top of the shadow with respect to time, and we are given the rate of change of the distance from streetlamp to the man with respect to time. See Figure 4.4.

Note that we are letting

x = distance from streetlamp to man (in feet),

y = distance from streetlamp to top of shadow (in feet),

t = time (in seconds).

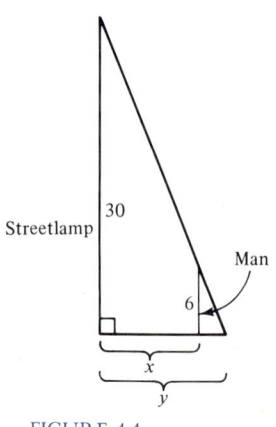

FIGURE 4.4

4.3 RELATED RATES

So we are trying to find
$$\frac{dy}{dt},$$
and we are given
$$\frac{dx}{dt} = 2.$$

So we must find an equation that relates x and y. The triangle formed by the two ends of the streetlamp and the top of the shadow is similar to the one formed by the man's head, his feet, and the top of the shadow. Because corresponding sides are proportional,
$$\frac{y}{30} = \frac{y-x}{6}.$$

If we wish, we may solve this equation for y. We get
$$30y - 30x = 6y$$
$$24y = 30x$$
$$y = \frac{5x}{4}.$$

Differentiating with respect to t, we get
$$\frac{dy}{dt} = \frac{5}{4} \cdot \frac{dx}{dt}.$$

Since $dx/dt = 2$,
$$\frac{dy}{dt} = \frac{5(2)}{4} = \frac{5}{2}.$$

The top of the shadow is moving at a rate of 2.5 feet/second. (Note that this rate doesn't depend on the man's distance from the streetlamp.)

EXAMPLE 6

Suppose that ship A is sailing due north of a tiny island, and ship B is sailing due east. If ship A is traveling at 10 mph and ship B at 12 mph, how fast is the distance between the two ships increasing when ship A is 5 miles north of the island and ship B is 8 miles east?

■ SOLUTION

We are trying to find the rate of change of the distance between the two ships, and we are given the rate of change of the distance from each ship to the island. See Figure 4.5.

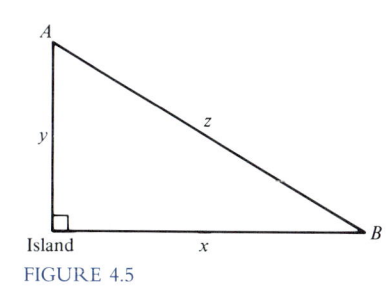

FIGURE 4.5

Note that we are letting

$$x = B\text{'s distance from island (in miles)},$$
$$y = A\text{'s distance from island (in miles)},$$
$$z = \text{distance from } A \text{ to } B \text{ (in miles)},$$
$$t = \text{time (in hours)}.$$

We must find
$$\frac{dz}{dt},$$
and we are given
$$\frac{dy}{dt} = 10 \quad \text{and} \quad \frac{dx}{dt} = 12.$$

So we must find an equation involving x, y, and z. By the Pythagorean theorem,
$$z^2 = x^2 + y^2.$$

Differentiating everything with respect to t we get
$$2z\frac{dz}{dt} = 2x\frac{dx}{dt} + 2y\frac{dy}{dt}.$$

Thus
$$\frac{dz}{dt} = \frac{x\frac{dx}{dt} + y\frac{dy}{dt}}{z}$$
$$= \frac{12x + 10y}{z}.$$

When $x = 8$ and $y = 5$, $z = \sqrt{64 + 25} = \sqrt{89}$, so
$$\frac{dz}{dt} = \frac{8(12) + 5(10)}{\sqrt{89}} = \frac{146}{\sqrt{89}} \quad (\approx 15.48).$$

The distance between the two is increasing approximately 15.48 mph.

EXERCISE

(a) Suppose a 6-foot man is walking away from a streetlamp that is 20 feet tall. How fast is the top of his shadow moving when he is 15 feet from the streetlamp if he is walking at a rate of 3 feet/second?

(b) Suppose that ship A is sailing due north of a tiny island, and ship B is sailing due east. If ship A is traveling at 15 mph and ship B at 18 mph, how fast is the distance between the two increasing when ship A is 8 miles north of the island and ship B is 10 miles east?

■ ANSWER
(a) $4\frac{2}{7}$ feet/second;   (b) $150/\sqrt{41}$ (≈ 23.43) mph

PROBLEM SET 4.3

1. Suppose a point is moving along the curve $x^3 + 2y^3 = 10$. Find dy/dt when the point is at $(2,1)$ if $dx/dt = 3$ here.

2. Suppose a point is moving along the curve $3x^3 - y^3 = 24$. Find dy/dt when the point is at $(-1,-3)$ if $dx/dt = 1$ here.

3. Helium gas is escaping from a spherical balloon at the rate of 20π feet^3/second. How fast is the radius decreasing when the radius is 10 feet?

4. A spherical ball of ice melts uniformly at the rate of 12π centimeters^3/minute. At what rate is the radius decreasing when the radius is 6 centimeters?

5. The area of a circular disk drive platter is increasing at the rate of 0.0065π inch^2/second. How fast is the radius increasing when the area is 6.25π inches^2?

6. A circular plate in a furnace is expanding so that its radius is changing at the rate of 0.02 centimeter/second. How fast is the circumference increasing when the radius is 5 centimeters?

7. At 1:00 a jogger crosses an intersection heading due north at 6 mph. An hour later a second jogger passes the same intersection heading due east at 8 mph. How fast is the distance between them increasing when the second jogger has been jogging for 1.5 hours since passing the intersection?

8. If a car is headed east toward Lexington at the rate of 60 mph and a motorcycle is headed directly north away from Lexington at the rate of 40 mph, how fast is the distance between the two changing when both are 20 miles from Lexington?

9. A boy, 5 feet tall, is walking away from a lamp pole that is 15 feet tall. The light on the top of the pole casts a shadow of the boy. If the boy is walking at the rate of 3 feet/second, how fast is the tip of the boy's shadow moving when the boy is 11 feet from the base of the pole?

10. A girl flies a kite at a height of 300 feet, and the wind is carrying the kite horizontally away from the girl at a rate of 25 feet/second. How fast must the girl let out the string when the kite is 500 feet away from her?

11. A pulley is at the top of a 3-foot pole, which is at the end of a dock that is 4 feet above the water. A canoe is being pulled in by a rope that is passing over the pulley at the rate of 3 feet/second. The rope is attached to the bow of the canoe, which is 2 feet above the water. How fast is the canoe approaching the dock when it is 12 feet from the dock?

12. A 17-foot ladder is leaning against a vertical wall. The ground is level but slippery and the foot of the ladder begins sliding directly away from the wall and soon reaches a constant rate of 5 feet/second. How fast is the top of the ladder sliding down the wall when the bottom of the ladder is 8 feet from the wall?

13. A baseball diamond is 90 feet square. A ball is bunted along the third-base line and travels at a constant rate of 9 feet/second. How fast is its distance from first base increasing when it is halfway to third base?

14. A base runner at first base, with a 7-foot lead off, attempts to steal second. If the runner is moving at a constant rate of 30 feet/second, how fast is the distance between the runner and home plate increasing when the runner is 10 feet from second base?

15. At a railroad depot, the grain hoppers are conical, 8 feet high, and 8 feet in diameter at the top. A full hopper is opened and dispenses grain into a box car at the rate of 2 feet^3/second. How fast is the depth of grain decreasing when the grain level is 3 feet from the top?

16. A trough is 14 feet long. Its ends are in the form of inverted isosceles triangles with altitudes and bases of 3 feet. Water is flowing into the trough at the rate of 2 feet^3/minute. How fast is the water level rising when the water is 1 foot deep?

17. An ellipse with equation

$$\frac{(x-3)^2}{4} + \frac{y^2}{16} = 1$$

has been drawn on a large piece of graph paper and attached to a wall. A projected point of light is being moved along a portion of the ellipse in such a way that its vertical component of velocity, dy/dt, is constantly 2 inches/second. Determine the horizontal component of velocity, dx/dt, when the light is at the point $(4, 2\sqrt{3})$.

18. As in Problem 17, a projected point of light is being moved along a portion of the hyperbola with equation $x^2 - 2x - y^2 - 2 = 0$. If its horizontal component of velocity is -3 centimeters/second, determine the vertical component of velocity when the light is at the point $(3, 1)$.

19. In testing a new lens, a TV camera is zooming in on an equilateral triangle. In the process the area of the triangle's image is increasing at the rate of 3 centimeters^2/second. How fast is the length of the image of a side increasing when the area is $25\sqrt{3}$ centimeters^2?

20. In a certain manufacturing process it is necessary to dissolve a large cube of salt in water. Assuming that during the dissolution process it retains its cubical shape but the surface area is decreasing at the rate of 12 inches^2/second, how fast is the volume decreasing when the surface area is 96 inches^2?

21. If the volume of a cylinder is decreasing at the rate of 125π centimeters^3/minute and the height is increasing at the rate of 3 centimeters/minute, how is the radius changing when the volume is 250π centimeters^3 and the height is 10 centimeters?

22. If the radius of a cylinder (with top) is increasing at the rate of 4 inches/minute and the height is decreasing at the rate of 5 inches/minute, how is the surface area changing when the radius is 9 inches and the height is 13 inches?

23. A pendulum's period, T, is a function of its length, l, and is given by

$$T = \pi\sqrt{\frac{l}{96}}.$$

A swinging wrecking ball is being hauled in at the rate of 0.3 meter/second. Determine the rate of change of the period when the chain is 24 meters long.

CHAPTER 4 REVIEW

1. Determine whether each of the following is true or false.
   (a) If $y = -5x^3$, then $x^3 y''' + x^2 y'' - 3xy' - 3y = 0$.
   (b) If $y = e^{-x}$, then $y''' = -y'$.
   (c) If $f(x) = -\pi/x$, then $f''(x) = (1/\pi^2)(f(x))^3$.
   (d) The nth derivative of $y = e^{ax}$ is $a^n e^{ax}$.
   (e) If $f(x) = e^{3x}$, then $f'''(0) = 27$.
   (f) If $f(x) = \ln(7x)$, then $f''(1) = -\frac{1}{7}$.
   (g) If $f(x) = xe^x$, then $f''(2) = 4e^2$.
   (h) If $f(x) = x^5$, then $f^{(n)}(x) = 0$ for $n \geq 6$.
   (i) If $y = \ln(ax^n)$ and $y_1 = \ln(ax)$, then

$$\frac{d^2 y}{dx^2} - n\frac{d^2 y_1}{dx^2} = 0.$$

   (j) Acceleration is the second derivative of a position function.
   (k) If $y^k = x^k$, where k is a constant, then $dy/dx = x^{k-1}/y^{k-1}$.
   (l) If $xy + y^3 = x$, then $y' = 1/(1 + 3y^2)$.
   (m) The slope of the graph of $x^2 + y^2 = 40$ at $(6, 2)$ is -3.
   (n) If $y = x^{1/\ln x}$, then $y' = 0$.
   (o) If $y = x^2$ and $dx/dt = 5$, then when $x = 3$, $dy/dt = 15$.
   (p) For the graph of $y = ex^3 + e^x$, the rate of change of the slope with respect to x at $(1, 2e)$ is $4e$.

In Problems 2–12, determine the second derivative.

2. $y = 2x^6 - x^{1/2}$
3. $y = \dfrac{3}{x^5} + \dfrac{1}{\sqrt[3]{x}}$
4. $y = e^{3x} + e^3$
5. $y = \ln(4x) - \ln 4$
6. $y = (1 + e^x)^{10}$
7. $y = \dfrac{x-3}{x+3}$
8. $y = e^{e^x}$
9. $y = \ln(\ln x)$
10. $y = \ln(ex^e)$
11. $y = e^x \ln x$
12. $y = xe^{x^4}$

In Problems 13–24, determine dy/dx.

13. $x^{2/3} + y^{2/3} = \pi^{2/3}$
14. $\sqrt{\dfrac{x}{y}} + \sqrt{\dfrac{y}{x}} = 1$
15. $x^4 + 4x^2 y^2 + y^4 = 4$
16. $e^x - e^y = e^{x-y}$
17. $e^{-5y} = x^5 - 10x$
18. $\ln(1 + y^3) = x + e^{\ln \pi}$

19. $x \ln y = e^x$
20. $\ln(xy) = e^x + e^y$
21. $y = \sqrt{x^x}$
22. $y = (3/x)^{5x}$
23. $y = (e^x)^{\ln x}$
24. $y = (\ln x)^{x^2}$

In Problems 25–28, determine d^2y/dx^2

25. $x^{1/2} + y^{1/2} = e^{1/2}$
26. $y^7 + y^3 = x$
27. $xe^{y^2} = 1$
28. $x^2 + 4xy + y^2 = 1$

29. Determine the fifth derivative of
$$y = (4x - 1)^{-1} + \pi^{-5}.$$

30. Determine the fourth derivative of
$$y = \frac{x^3}{1-x}.$$

31. Determine the third derivative of
$$y + \ln y = x.$$

32. If $f(x) = x \ln(7x)$, show that
$$x^3 f'''(x) + xf''(x) + xf'(x) - f(x) = 1.$$

33. Suppose a point is moving along the curve $x^2 - xy^3 = 6$. Find dy/dt when the point is at $(3, -1)$ if $dx/dt = -3$ here.

34. At noon, a car starts from Lexington traveling west at 55 mph. At 1 p.m., another car starts from Lexington and travels south at 45 mph. If both cars continue at the same speed and in the same direction, how fast is the distance between the two increasing at 2 p.m.?

35. A point moves along the parabola $y = (x^2/4) + 9$ in such a way that its x-coordinate increases uniformly at the rate of 3 inches/second. At what point on the parabola do the x and y coordinates increase at the same rate?

36. Water is leaking through a hole in the vertex of a conical reservoir at the rate of 40π feet^3/minute. If the reservoir is 30 feet deep and 40 feet across the top, how fast is the depth of the water decreasing when the reservoir is $\frac{1}{27}$ full?

37. If the height of a cylinder (with top) is increasing at the rate of 10 centimeters/second, and the radius is decreasing at the rate of 7 centimeters/second, how is the volume changing when the height is 20 centimeters and the radius is 15 centimeters?

CHAPTER 5

APPLICATIONS OF THE DERIVATIVE

CHAPTER OUTLINE
5.1 Increasing and Decreasing Functions
5.2 Extreme Points
5.3 Concavity and the Second Derivative Test
5.4 Inflection Points
5.5 Curve Sketching
5.6 Absolute Extreme Points
5.7 Maximum–Minimum Problems
5.8 Business Applications

This chapter is a study of important applications of the derivative. The first part of the chapter shows how the derivative is used to find the maximum and minimum values of a function. In Section 5.5 we see how the derivative is used as a tool in curve sketching. The chapter concludes with practical applications involving the optimization of various quantities.

5.1 INCREASING AND DECREASING FUNCTIONS

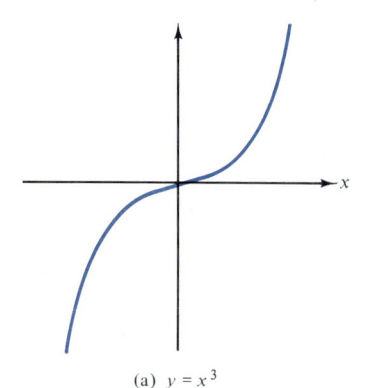

Consider the two functions graphed in Figure 5.1. As we move from left to right, the graph in Figure 5.1(a) rises, while the graph in 5.1(b) falls. This forms the basis of the concepts of increasing and decreasing.

Let f be a function defined on an interval I. We say that f is **increasing on I** provided that for all $x_1, x_2 \in I$ such that $x_1 < x_2$, we have $f(x_1) < f(x_2)$. For example, the function $f(x) = x^2$ is increasing on $(0, \infty)$ because if x_1 and x_2 are positive with $x_1 < x_2$, then $x_1^2 < x_2^2$. See Figure 5.2.

Geometrically, this definition means that the graph rises from left to right on the interval. Thus, given any two points on the graph on this interval, the point on the left is lower than the point on the right.

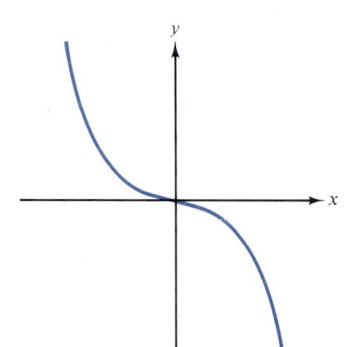

We say that a function f is **decreasing on an interval I** provided that for all $x_1, x_2 \in I$ such that $x_1 < x_2$, we have $f(x_1) > f(x_2)$. Geometrically, this means that the graph falls from left to right on this interval. Thus, given any two points, the point on the left will be higher than the point on the right. From Figure 5.2 we see that $f(x) = x^2$ is decreasing on $(-\infty, 0)$.

EXAMPLE 1

Given the graph in Figure 5.3, determine the open intervals on which the function is increasing and on which it is decreasing.

■ SOLUTION

We simply need to observe where the graph is rising and where it is falling. Since the graph is rising to the left of 1 and between 2 and 4, the function is increasing on $(-\infty, 1)$ and on $(2, 4)$. Because the graph is falling between 1 and 2 and to the right of 4, the function is decreasing on $(1, 2)$ and on $(4, \infty)$.

(a) $y = x^3$

(b) $y = -x^3$

FIGURE 5.1

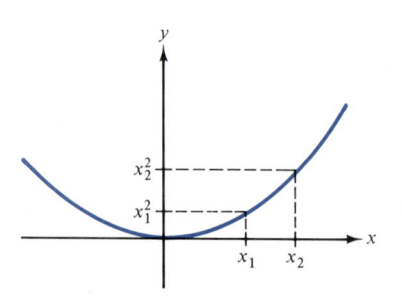

FIGURE 5.2

FIGURE 5.3

5.1 INCREASING AND DECREASING FUNCTIONS   193

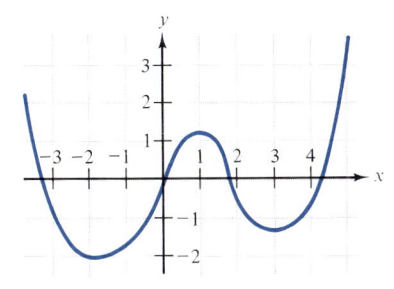

FIGURE 5.4

EXERCISE

Given the graph in Figure 5.4, determine the open intervals on which the function is increasing and on which it is decreasing.

■ *ANSWER*

Increasing on $(-2,1)$ and on $(3,\infty)$; decreasing on $(-\infty,-2)$ and on $(1,3)$.

Let f be a function with domain D, and let a be an interior point of the domain (which means a is an interior point of one of the intervals making up the domain). Then f is said to be **increasing at $x = a$** provided that there is an open interval I containing a such that f is increasing on I. To illustrate, consider the function graphed in Figure 5.5. This function is increasing at $x = 2$ because there is an open interval I containing 2 on which f is increasing. [Consider $I = (1,3)$, for instance.]

The definition of **decreasing at $x = a$** is analogous to that of increasing at $x = a$. The function graphed in Figure 5.5 is decreasing at $x = 5$.

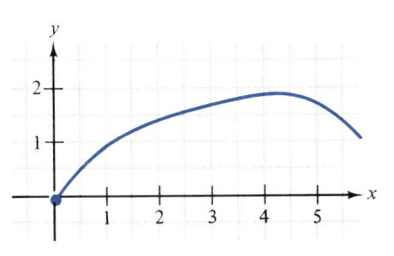

FIGURE 5.5

EXAMPLE 2

For $x = 1, 2, 3,$ and 4, determine whether the function graphed in Figure 5.6 is increasing, decreasing, or neither.

■ *SOLUTION*

The function is increasing at $x = 1$ because we can find an open interval like $(\frac{1}{2}, \frac{5}{4})$ on which the function is increasing. The function is decreasing at $x = 2$, but at $x = 3$ the function is neither increasing nor decreasing. We cannot find an open interval containing 3 on which the function is increasing or one on which the function is decreasing. For any open interval containing 3, the graph is decreasing to the left of 3 and increasing to the right of 3. At $x = 4$, the function is increasing.

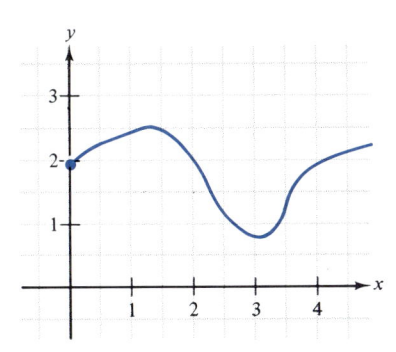

FIGURE 5.6

EXERCISE

For $x = 1, 2, 3,$ and 4, determine whether the function graphed in Figure 5.7 is increasing, decreasing, or neither.

■ *ANSWER*

Neither increasing nor decreasing at $x = 1$; decreasing at $x = 2$ and at $x = 3$; increasing at $x = 4$.

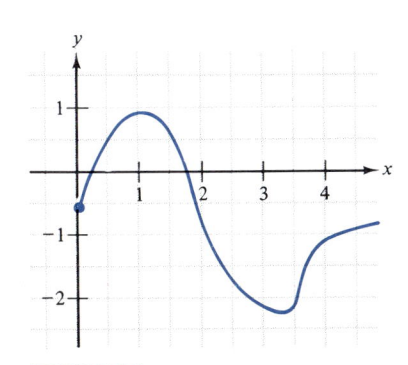

FIGURE 5.7

APPLICATIONS OF THE DERIVATIVE

The tangent is the linear approximation of a curve at a point, So if a graph has a tangent at $x = a$ with a positive slope, then the graph is rising at $x = a$. If the tangent at $x = a$ has a negative slope, then the graph is falling at $x = a$. Thus we may examine the slope of the tangent at $x = a$ to determine whether the function is increasing or decreasing.

EXAMPLE 3

For $x = 1, 2, 3$, and 4, determine whether the function graphed in Figure 5.8 is increasing, decreasing, or neither.

■ SOLUTION

The tangent line at $x = 1$ has a negative slope, so the function is decreasing at $x = 1$. At $x = 2$, the tangent is horizontal. In such a case we must resort to the definition and open intervals. For any open interval containing 2, we find the graph falling on the left and rising on the right. Therefore the function is neither increasing nor decreasing at $x = 2$. At $x = 3$ the tangent has a positive slope. So the function is increasing at $x = 3$. At $x = 4$ we find a horizontal tangent, so we look at open intervals. Because the function is increasing on $(3\frac{1}{2}, 4\frac{1}{2})$, the function is increasing at $x = 4$.

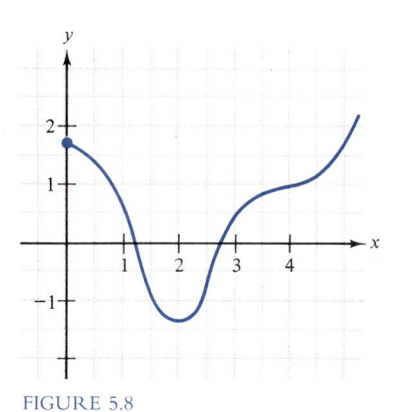

FIGURE 5.8

EXERCISE

For $x = 1, 2, 3$, and 4, determine whether the function graphed in Figure 5.9 is increasing, decreasing, or neither.

■ ANSWER

Increasing at $x = 1$; neither increasing nor decreasing at $x = 2$; decreasing at $x = 3$ and at $x = 4$.

We noted that if a graph has a tangent at $x = a$ with a positive slope, the function is increasing at $x = a$. If the tangent has a negative slope, then the function is decreasing. Since we may determine the slope of the tangent with the first derivative, the sign of the derivative tells us whether the function is increasing or decreasing.

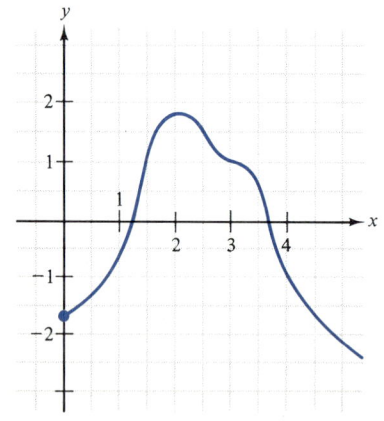

FIGURE 5.9

**THEOREM 5.1
First Derivative Rule**

Let f be a function, and let a be an interior point of its domain.

(i) If $f'(a) > 0$, then f is increasing at $x = a$.
(ii) If $f'(a) < 0$, then f is decreasing at $x = a$.

5.1 INCREASING AND DECREASING FUNCTIONS

In the absence of a graph, this theorem gives us a convenient means of determining whether the function is increasing or decreasing at a point. We merely determine the sign of its first derivative there.

EXAMPLE 4

For $x = -5$, 0, and 5, determine whether the function $f(x) = 2x^3 + 3x^2 - 30x + 16$ is increasing or decreasing.

■ SOLUTION

We use the first derivative rule. Differentiation gives

$$f'(x) = 6x^2 + 6x - 30 = 6(x^2 + x - 5).$$

Thus

$f'(-5) = 6(25 - 5 - 5) > 0 \Rightarrow f$ is increasing at $x = -5$;

$f'(0) = 6(-5) < 0 \Rightarrow f$ is decreasing at $x = 0$;

$f'(5) = 6(25 + 5 - 5) > 0 \Rightarrow f$ is increasing at $x = 5$.

EXERCISE

For $x = -4$, 0, and 2, determine whether the function $f(x) = -4x^3 + 15x^2 + 18x - 20$ is increasing or decreasing.

■ ANSWER

f is decreasing at $x = -4$; f is increasing at $x = 0$ and at $x = 2$.

Note that the first derivative rule doesn't tell us about the behavior of the function when $f'(a) = 0$. The function may be increasing, decreasing, or neither. Consider $f(x) = x^3$, $g(x) = -x^3$, and $h(x) = x^2$. All three of these functions have a derivative of zero at $x = 0$, but f is increasing at $x = 0$, g is decreasing at $x = 0$, and h is neither increasing nor decreasing at $x = 0$. See Figure 5.10.

So $f'(a) = 0$ doesn't tell us about the behavior of f with respect to increasing/decreasing at $x = a$. The function may be doing either or neither.

Before leaving this section, let's note an application. For a particular psychological test, if a subject is allowed to work for 1 hour, then the reliability of the test is r, where $0 < r < 1$. If the subject is allowed to work longer, t hours, where $t > 1$, then the reliability becomes

$$R = \frac{tr}{1 + (t - 1)r}.$$

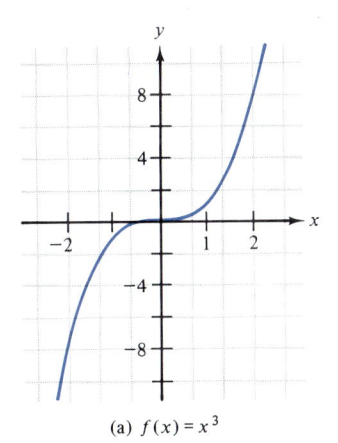

(a) $f(x) = x^3$

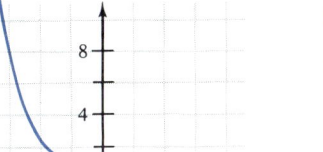

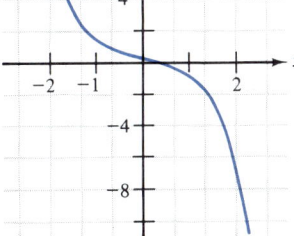

(b) $g(x) = -x^3$

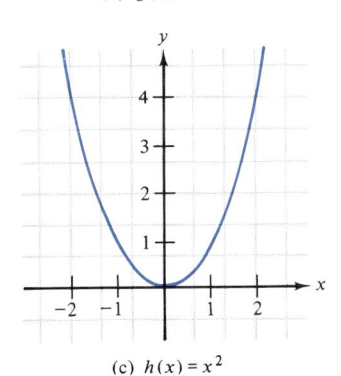

(c) $h(x) = x^2$

FIGURE 5.10

We would expect the reliability to increase as t increases. That is, we would expect R to be increasing for any $t > 1$. We can show that this is the case by using the derivative. We get

$$\frac{dR}{dt} = \frac{(1 + (t-1)r) \cdot r - tr \cdot r}{(1 + (t-1)r)^2}$$

$$= \frac{r + r^2 t - r^2 - r^2 t}{(1 + (t-1)r)^2}$$

$$= \frac{r(1-r)}{(1 + (t-1)r)^2}.$$

The denominator is always positive. As for the numerator, since $0 < r < 1$, both r and $1 - r$ are positive. Hence their product is positive. So the derivative is positive for any $t > 1$. By the first derivative rule, the reliability function is increasing for any $t > 1$.

EXERCISE

In studying the reaction time of nerves, it is found that if the strength of stimuli, s, is sufficiently strong, then the intensity of excitation, E, is given by

$$E = a \ln \frac{s}{b + cs},$$

where a, b, and c are positive constants. Show that E is increasing for any $s > 0$.

PROBLEM SET 5.1

In Problems 1–8, given each graph, determine the open intervals on which the function is increasing and on which it is decreasing.

1.

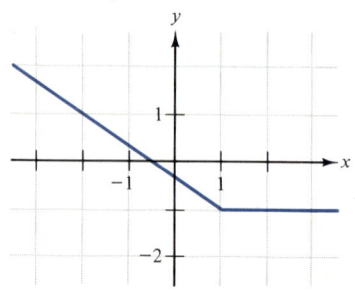

2.

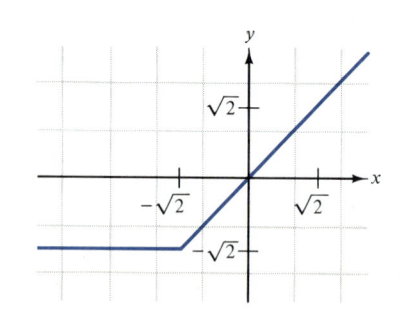

5.1 INCREASING AND DECREASING FUNCTIONS

3.

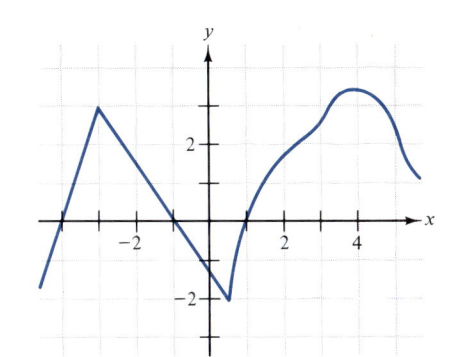

4.

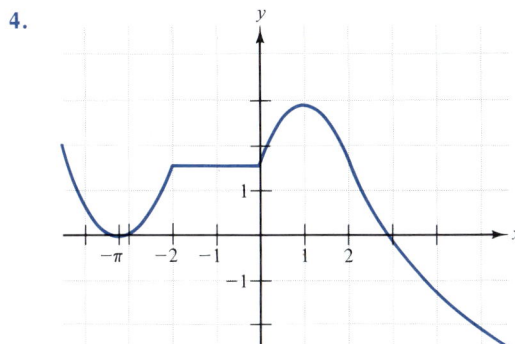

5.

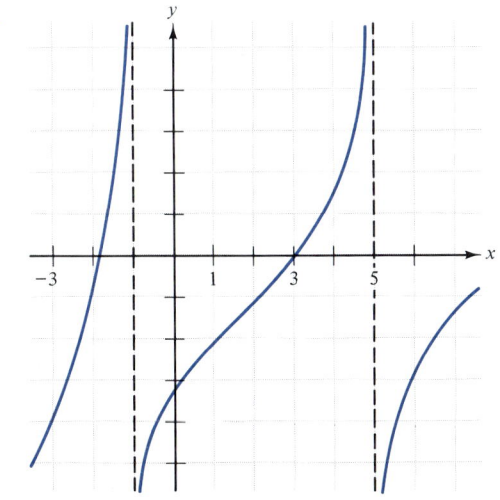

6.

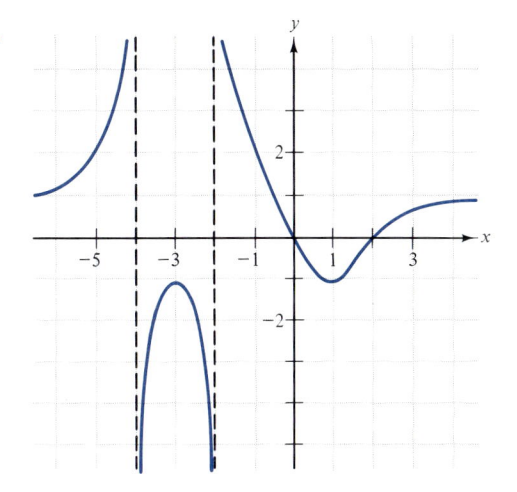

7.

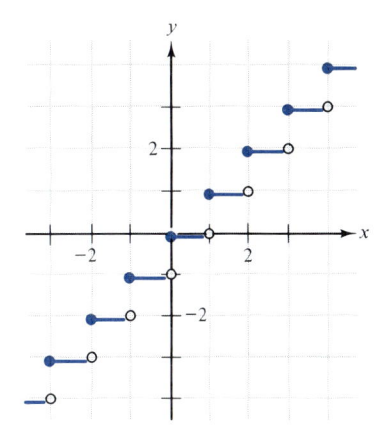

8.

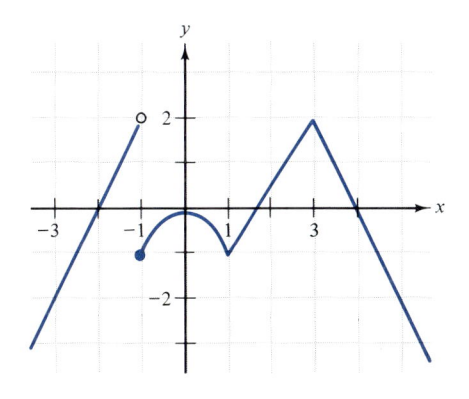

In Problems 9–16, for $x = -2, -1, 0, 1, 2,$ and 3, determine whether each function graphed is increasing, decreasing, or neither.

9.

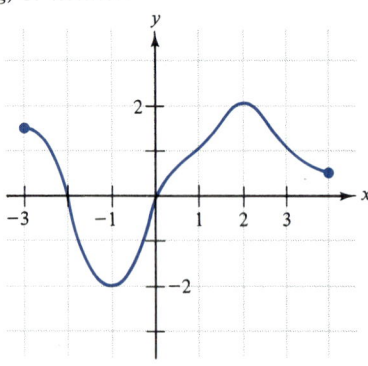

10.

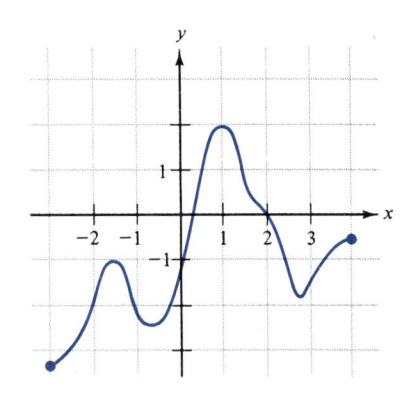

11.

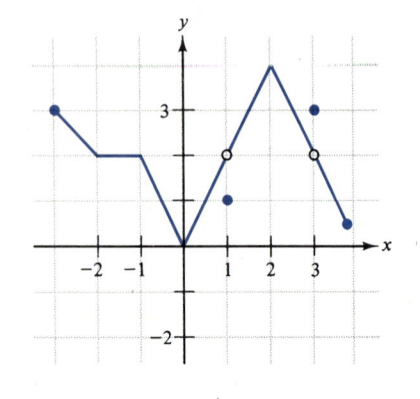

12.

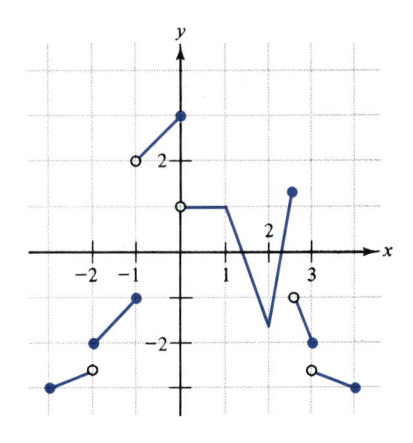

13.

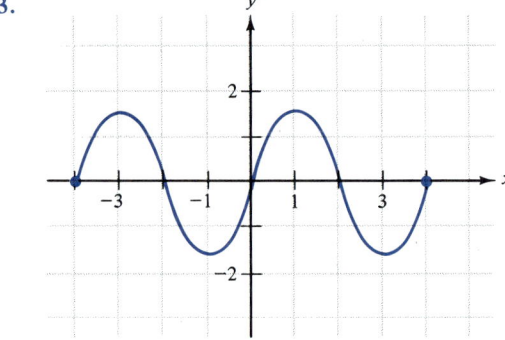

14.

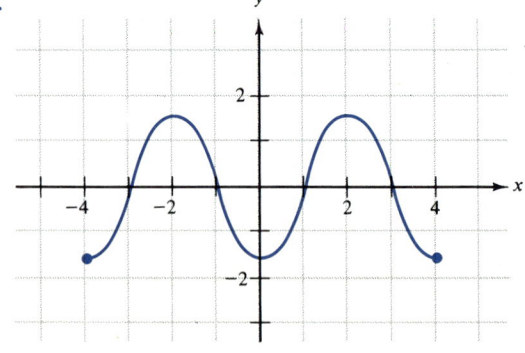

5.1 INCREASING AND DECREASING FUNCTIONS

15.

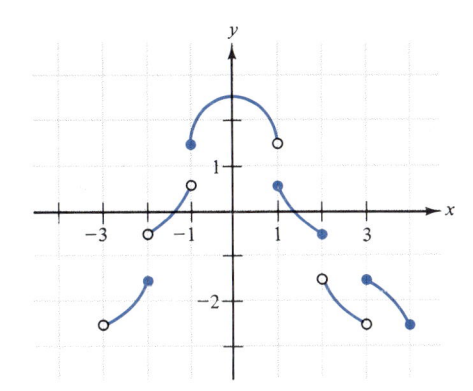

16.

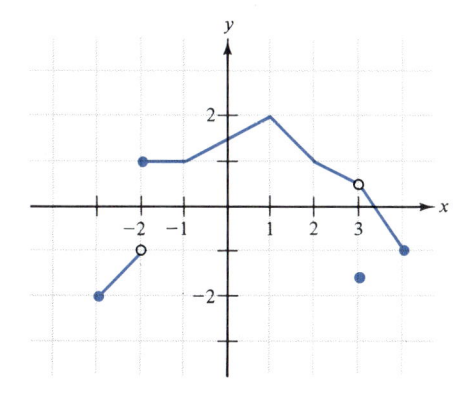

In Problems 17–32, use the first derivative rule to determine whether each function is increasing or decreasing at the indicated points.

17. $f(x) = 2x^3 + 3x^2 - 36x + 24$, $x = -4$, 1.99, and 5
18. $f(x) = x^3 - 6x^2 + 9x + 10$, $x = -7$, 0, and 1.01
19. $f(x) = \frac{8}{3}x^3 - 8x^2 - 2x + 10$, $x = -5$, -0.1, and $\sqrt{4.5}$
20. $f(x) = -\frac{4}{3}x^3 - x^2 + 3x - 5$, $x = -\sqrt{1.34}$, $\frac{1}{2}$, and π
21. $f(x) = -4x^5 + 5x^4 + 17$, $x = -6$, -1, and $\frac{9}{10}$
22. $f(x) = \frac{1}{16}x^4 - \frac{3}{2}x^2 + 10$, $x = -\frac{7}{2}$, 1, and 4
23. $y = e^{3x} - x^3$, $x = -2$, 0, and $\ln 2$
24. $y = x^2 e^{-x}$, $x = -1$, 1, and 3
25. $f(x) = \dfrac{4x + 7}{x - 3}$, $x = -\sqrt[3]{11}$, 0, and 10
26. $f(x) = \dfrac{3x - 5}{x + 4}$, $x = -12$, -4.01, and $\sqrt{\pi}$
27. $y = (1 + \ln x)/x$, $x = e^{-1}$, $\frac{1}{2}$, and 2
28. $y = x^2 - 18 \ln x$, $x = e$, π, and $2e$
29. $f(x) = (x + 3)^9 (x + 4)^7$, $x = -6$, $-\sqrt{11}$, and 1
30. $f(x) = (x - 1)^5 (x - 2)^6$, $x = -2$, 0, and $\pi/2$
31. $f(x) = \left(\dfrac{x^3}{3} - 9x\right)^4$, $x = -5.2$, -1, and 5
32. $f(x) = (x^2 - 4)^7 - (x^2 - 4)^6$, $x = -2.2$, 1, and $\sqrt[3]{10.7}$

In Problems 33–38, use the graph of f' to determine the open intervals on which f is increasing and on which f is decreasing.

33.

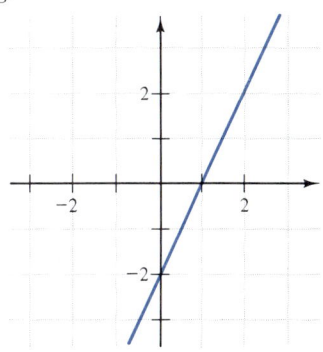

Graph of f'

34.

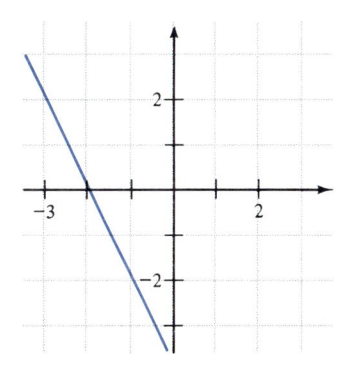

Graph of f'

35.

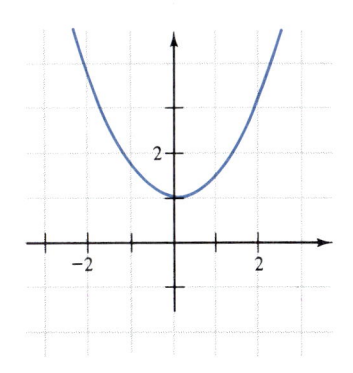

Graph of f'

36.

Graph of f'

37.

Graph of f'

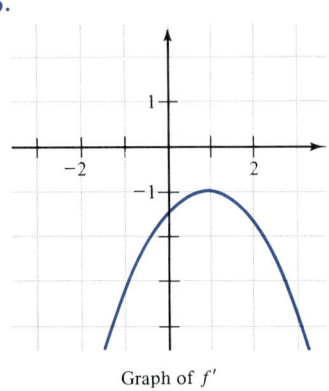

38.

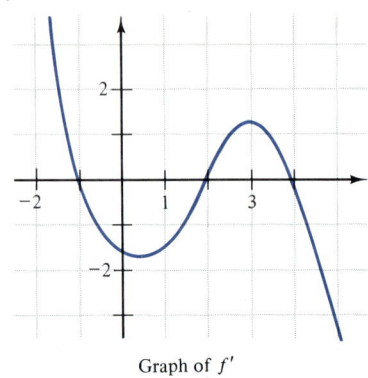

Graph of f'

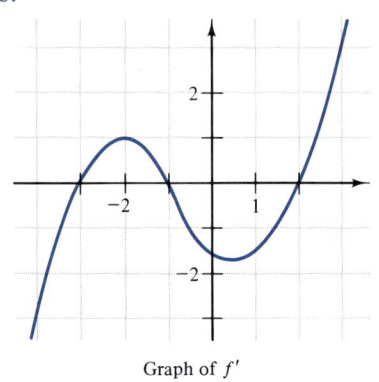

39. Determine which of the functions graphed below are increasing for all elements of the domain.

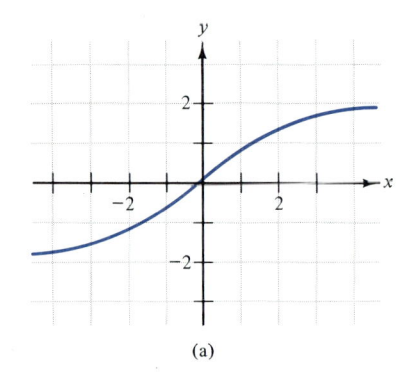

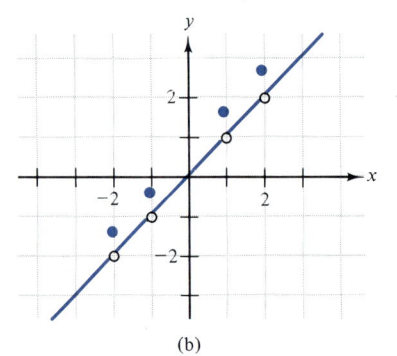

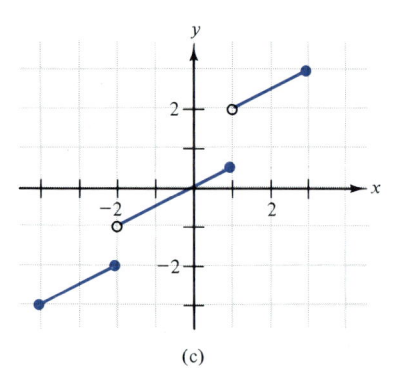

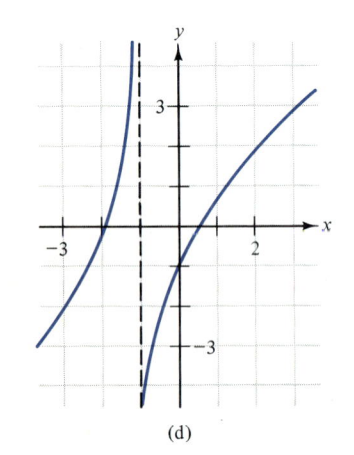

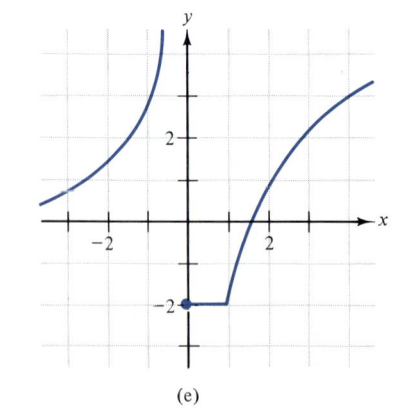

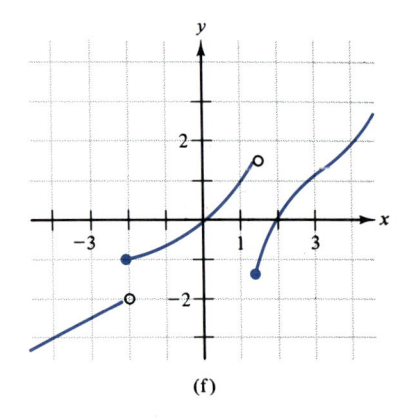

(a)

(b)

(c)

(d)

(e)

(f)

5.2 EXTREME POINTS

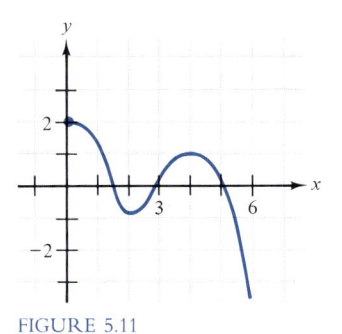

We shall soon be encountering problems in which we are asked to maximize or minimize a quantity. For example, we may need to maximize a profit or minimize a cost. We may need to maximize the area of a pasture with a given amount of fencing or minimize the amount of material needed for a container of specified volume. To do this we must study the theory of extreme points.

Let f be a function with domain D, and let $c \in D$. Then we say that f has a **relative maximum at $x = c$** provided that there is an open interval I containing c such that for all x in the interval $I \cap D$, $f(c) \geq f(x)$.

If c is an interior point of the domain, then there must be an open interval containing c such that $f(c) \geq f(x)$ for all x in the interval. If c is an endpoint, there must be a half-open interval containing c such that $f(c) \geq f(x)$. For example, consider the function f graphed in Figure 5.11.

There is a relative maximum at $x = 4$ because there is an open interval I in the domain which contains 4 and on which $f(4) \geq f(x)$ for all $x \in I$ [like $I = (3,5)$, for instance]. There is also a relative maximum at $x = 0$ because there is a half-open interval J in the domain which contains 0 and on which $f(0) \geq f(x)$ for all $x \in J$ (like $J = [0, 1)$, for instance).

In geometric terms then, to say that f has a relative maximum at $x = c$ means that *locally*, $(c, f(c))$ is the highest point on the graph. In Figure 5.11 we note that $(4,1)$ is not the highest point on the entire graph. But *locally* it is the highest point.

If f has a relative maximum at $x = c$, then the corresponding value $f(c)$ is called a **relative maximum,** and the corresponding point $(c, f(c))$ is called a **relative maximum point.**

Analogous definitions are made for **relative minimum at $x = c$, relative minimum,** and **relative minimum point.** Referring again to Figure 5.11, we see that f has a relative minimum at $x = 2$. The relative minimum is -1, and $(2, -1)$ is the relative minimum point.

The relative maximum points and relative minimum points form the **relative extreme points.** Thus the following exercise is asking us to find the relative maximum points and relative minimum points.

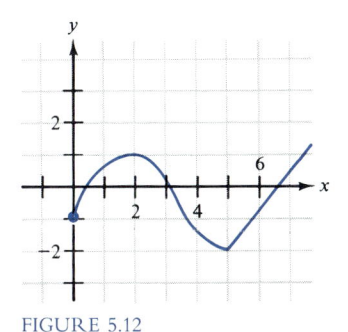

FIGURE 5.11

EXERCISE

Determine all relative extreme points of the function graphed in Figure 5.12.

■ ANSWER
Relative maximum point, $(2,1)$; relative minimum points, $(0, -1)$ and $(5, -2)$.

FIGURE 5.12

Determining extreme points in the absence of a graph is a bit more difficult. To do so we need the following definition: A number c in the domain of a function f is called a **critical value** provided that

(i) c is an endpoint of the domain of f, or
(ii) f' is not defined at $x = c$, or
(iii) $f'(c) = 0$.

(At endpoint of the domain is an endpoint of one of the intervals making up the domain.)

What's the connection between critical values and extreme points? Well, suppose a number c in the domain is *not* a critical value. Then c is an interior point of the domain, f' is defined at $x = c$, and $f'(c) \neq 0$. If $f'(c) > 0$, then f is increasing at $x = c$. If $f'(c) < 0$, then f is decreasing at $x = c$. In either case, $(c, f(c))$ is not an extreme point. Thus the extreme points must be located at critical values, as noted in the following theorem.

THEOREM 5.2 Let f be a function. If f has a relative maximum or minimum at $x = c$, then c is a critical value.

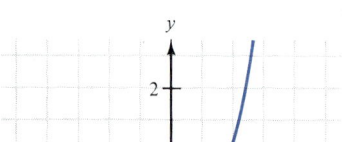

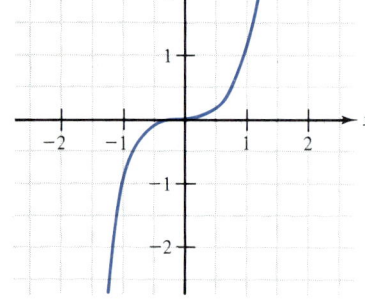

This theorem will facilitate our search for extreme points. It tells us that we may confine our analysis to critical values only. That is, Theorem 5.2 says that critical values give us *candidates* for extreme points. They give us *possible* extreme points. But they are the only values we need consider.

This is not to say that each critical value will give rise to a relative maximum or minimum. Indeed, for $f(x) = x^3$, we see that $x = 0$ is a critical value [since $f'(0) = 0$], but there is no relative maximum or minimum there. See Figure 5.13.

The endpoint of the domain of f is an easy critical value to locate. To determine the others, we differentiate f. Then we find where $f'(x)$ equals zero or fails to exist. For example, consider

$$f(x) = x^{4/3} + 4x^{1/3}.$$

$f(x) = x^3$

FIGURE 5.13

Differentiation yields

$$f'(x) = \frac{4}{3}x^{1/3} + \frac{4}{3}x^{-2/3}$$

$$= \frac{4x^{1/3}}{3} + \frac{4}{3x^{2/3}}.$$

To find out where $f'(x)$ equals zero, we set it to zero and solve for x. We get

$$\frac{4x^{1/3}}{3} + \frac{4}{3x^{2/3}} = 0$$

$$4x + 4 = 0$$

$$4x = -4$$

$$x = -1.$$

5.2 · EXTREME POINTS

Since -1 is in the domain of f, it is a critical value.

Now we note that $f'(x)$ fails to exist at $x = 0$ because $x = 0$ gives a zero in the denominator $3x^{2/3}$. Since $x = 0$ is in the domain of f, it is also a critical value.

But once we determine the critical values, how do we know whether we have a relative maximum or minimum there? The next theorem tells us.

THEOREM 5.3
First Derivative Test

Let f be a continuous function, and let c be a critical value in the interior of the domain. Choose interior points x_1 and x_2 such that $x_1 < c < x_2$, $[x_1, x_2]$ is in the domain of f, and c is the only critical value in $[x_1, x_2]$.

(i) If f is increasing at $x = x_1$ and decreasing at $x = x_2$, then f has a relative maximum at $x = c$.
(ii) If f is decreasing at $x = x_1$ and increasing at $x = x_2$, then f has a relative minimum at $x = c$.
(iii) If f is increasing at both $x = x_1$ and $x = x_2$, or if f is decreasing at both $x = x_1$ and $x = x_2$, then f has neither a relative maximum nor a relative minimum at $x = c$.

The geometric illustration of this theorem is seen in Figure 5.14.

This theorem says that for a given critical value in the interior we must choose a point to the left and a point to the right subject to two conditions: the two points and all points in between must be in the domain; and except for the critical value we are testing, neither point nor any in between is a critical value. Having selected the points, we check to see whether the function is increasing or decreasing at our choices. This is easily done by determining the sign of the first derivative there (thus the name "first derivative test"). Let's illustrate with a few examples.

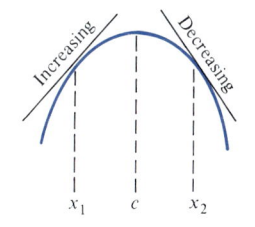

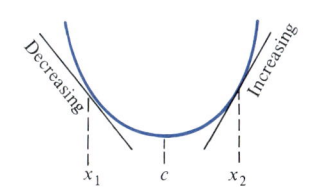

(a) Relative maximum

(b) Relative minimum

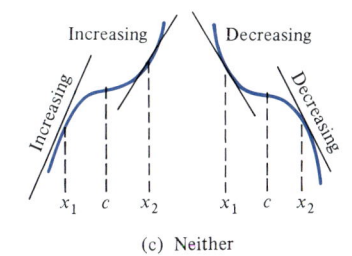

(c) Neither

FIGURE 5.14

EXAMPLE 1

Determine all relative extreme points of the following:

(a) $f(x) = \dfrac{x - 3}{e^x}$ and (b) $f(x) = x^3 + 5x^2 - 8x + 2$.

■ SOLUTION

(a) Our first task is to find the critical values. To this end we must differentiate:

$$f'(x) = \frac{e^x \cdot 1 - (x - 3)e^x}{e^{2x}}$$

$$= \frac{e^x(1 - x + 3)}{e^{2x}}$$

$$= \frac{4 - x}{e^x}.$$

Since the domain has no endpoints, the critical values are those in the domain for which $f'(x) = 0$ or at which f' is not defined. Since this derivative is defined for all real numbers (e^x is never zero), we need only consider $f'(x) = 0$. This occurs when the numerator equals zero, so

$$x = 4$$

is the only critical value.

To test $x = 4$, let's choose $x_1 = 0$ and $x_2 = 5$. Note that $[0, 5]$ is in the domain of f, and the only critical value in $[0,5]$ is the one we are testing.

$$f'(0) = \frac{4}{1} > 0 \quad \Rightarrow f \text{ is increasing;}$$

$$f'(5) = \frac{-1}{e^5} < 0 \quad \Rightarrow f \text{ is decreasing.}$$

Because f is increasing on the left and decreasing on the right, f has a relative maximum at $x = 4$. To determine the corresponding point we note that

$$f(4) = \frac{4-3}{e^4} = \frac{1}{e^4}.$$

So $(4, 1/e^4)$ is a relative maximum point.

(b) We first find the critical values. Differentiation yields

$$f'(x) = 3x^2 + 10x - 8.$$

Since the domain has no endpoints, and the derivative is defined for all real numbers, we need only consider $f'(x) = 0$. We get

$$3x^2 + 10x - 8 = 0$$

$$(3x - 2)(x + 4) = 0$$

$$x = \tfrac{2}{3} \quad \text{or} \quad x = -4.$$

Hence the two critical values are $\tfrac{2}{3}$ and -4.

To test $x = -4$, let's choose $x_1 = -5$ and $x_2 = 0$. Note that $[-5,0]$ is in the domain, and the only critical value in $[-5,0]$ is the one we are testing.

$$f'(-5) = 75 - 50 - 8 > 0 \quad \Rightarrow f \text{ is increasing;}$$

$$f'(0) = -8 < 0 \quad \Rightarrow f \text{ is decreasing.}$$

Because f is increasing on the left and decreasing on the right, f has a relative maximum at $x = -4$. To determine the corresponding point we note that

$$f(-4) = (-4)^3 + 5(-4)^2 - 8(-4) + 2 = 50.$$

Thus $(-4, 50)$ is a relative maximum point.

To test $x = \frac{2}{3}$, let's choose $x_1 = 0$ and $x_2 = 1$. We have

$$f'(0) = -8 < 0 \Rightarrow f \text{ is decreasing;}$$

$$f'(1) = 5 > 0 \Rightarrow f \text{ is increasing.}$$

Since the function is decreasing on the left and increasing on the right, f has a relative minimum at $x = \frac{2}{3}$. Because $f(\frac{2}{3}) = -\frac{22}{27}$, the relative minimum point is $(\frac{2}{3}, -\frac{22}{27})$.

EXERCISE

Determine all relative extreme points the following:

(a) $f(x) = \dfrac{2-x}{e^x}$ and (b) $f(x) = 4x^3 - 3x^2 - 18x + 15$.

■ ANSWER

(a) Point $(3, -1/e^3)$ is a relative minimum point. (b) Point $(-1, 26)$ is a relative maximum point; $(\frac{3}{2}, -\frac{21}{4})$ is a relative minimum point.

EXAMPLE 2

Determine all relative extreme points of $y = (x+1)^{1/3} - 2$.

■ SOLUTION

Differentiating we have

$$y' = \tfrac{1}{3}(x+1)^{-2/3} = \dfrac{1}{3\sqrt[3]{(x+1)^2}}.$$

There are no endpoints to consider because the domain is R. Also, y' is never zero because the numerator is a constant 1. However, y' is not defined at $x = -1$. Since -1 is in the domain of the original function, it is a critical value.

To test $x = -1$ let's choose $x_1 = -2$ and $x_2 = 0$.

$$y'\Big|_{x=-2} = \tfrac{1}{3} > 0 \Rightarrow y \text{ is increasing;}$$

$$y'\Big|_{x=0} = \tfrac{1}{3} > 0 \Rightarrow y \text{ is increasing.}$$

Because y is increasing on both the left and the right of $x = -1$, there is neither a relative maximum nor a relative minimum at $x = -1$. Since $x = -1$ is the only critical value, there are no relative extreme points for this function.

EXAMPLE 3

Determine all relative extreme points of $y = x + (4/x)$.

■ **SOLUTION**
Since $y = x + 4x^{-1}$, we get

$$y' = 1 - 4x^{-2} = 1 - \frac{4}{x^2}.$$

The derivative isn't defined at $x = 0$. But because 0 isn't in the domain of the original function (y isn't defined at 0), $x = 0$ is not a critical value. Thus any critical values will arise from setting $y' = 0$. We get

$$1 - \frac{4}{x^2} = 0$$

$$x^2 - 4 = 0$$

$$x^2 = 4$$

$$x = \pm 2.$$

So the only critical values are $x = -2$ and $x = 2$.

To test $x = -2$, let's choose $x_1 = -3$ and $x_2 = -1$. (Note that it would be incorrect to select $x_2 \geq 0$ because $[-3, x_2]$ wouldn't be contained in the domain.) We have

$$y'\big|_{x=-3} = 1 - \tfrac{4}{9} > 0 \quad \Rightarrow y \text{ is increasing;}$$

$$y'\big|_{x=-1} = 1 - 4 < 0 \quad \Rightarrow y \text{ is decreasing.}$$

Thus the function has a relative maximum at $x = -2$. Since $y = -4$ when $x = -2$, $(-2, -4)$ is a relative maximum point.

To test $x = 2$, let's choose $x_1 = 1$ and $x_2 = 3$. We get

$$y'\big|_{x=1} = 1 - 4 < 0 \quad \Rightarrow y \text{ is decreasing;}$$

$$y'\big|_{x=3} = 1 - \tfrac{4}{9} > 0 \quad \Rightarrow y \text{ is increasing.}$$

Thus the function has a relative minimum at $x = 2$. The relative minimum point is $(2, 4)$.

Note that for the function in Example 3, the relative maximum, -4, is *less* than the relative minimum, 4. This clearly illustrates that the concept of relative extreme points is local is nature.

5.2 EXTREME POINTS

EXERCISE

Determine all relative extreme points of (a) $y = 2 - (x - 1)^{1/3}$ and (b) $y = (18/x) + 2x$.

■ *ANSWER*
(a) No extreme points. (b) Point $(-3, -12)$ is a relative maximum point; $(3, 12)$ is a relative minimum point.

The first derivative test (Theorem 5.3) concerns critical values that are in the *interior* of the domain. What if the domain has an endpoint? Well, if the function is continuous, then it *must* have a relative maximum or minimum at that endpoint. In Example 4 we see how an abbreviated version of the first derivative test may be used to test an endpoint.

EXAMPLE 4

Determine all relative extreme points of $f(x) = 4x^3 - 15x^2 - 18x + 5$, $x \geq 0$.

■ *SOLUTION*
Differentiating we get
$$f'(x) = 12x^2 - 30x - 18.$$

Setting $f'(x) = 0$ and solving for x, we have
$$12x^2 - 30x - 18 = 0$$
$$2x^2 - 5x - 3 = 0$$
$$(2x + 1)(x - 3) = 0$$
$$x = -\tfrac{1}{2} \quad \text{or} \quad x = 3.$$

We may ignore $x = -\tfrac{1}{2}$ because it isn't in the domain. So the only critical values are $x = 3$ and the endpoint $x = 0$. To test $x = 3$ let's choose $x_1 = 2$ and $x_2 = 4$. We have
$$f'(2) = 12 \cdot 4 - 30 \cdot 2 - 18 < 0 \quad \Rightarrow f \text{ is decreasing;}$$
$$f'(4) = 12 \cdot 16 - 30 \cdot 4 - 18 > 0 \quad \Rightarrow f \text{ is increasing.}$$

Thus f has a relative minimum at $x = 3$. Since $f(3) = -76$, $(3, -76)$ is a relative minimum point. To test $x = 0$ we use an abbreviated first derivative test because we can select a value on one side only. Let's choose $x_2 = 2$. Note that $[0, 2]$ is contained in the domain, and 0 is the only critical value of $[0, 2]$. We have already noted that
$$f'(2) < 0 \quad \Rightarrow f \text{ is decreasing.}$$

Since it's decreasing on the right (and there's nothing on the left), f has a relative maximum at $x = 0$, and $(0,5)$ is a relative maximum point.

EXERCISE

Determine all relative extreme points of $f(x) = 4x^3 - 3x^2 - 36x + 10$, $x \geq 0$.

■ ANSWER

Point $(0,10)$ is a relative maximum point; $(2, -42)$ is a relative minimum point.

Before leaving this section, let's consider an application. The strength R of the human body's reaction to a dose D of certain drugs may be written

$$R = D^2\left(\frac{K}{2} - \frac{D}{3}\right),$$

where K is a positive constant. Let's find the dosage that gives the greatest reaction. That is, let's find the value of D that maximizes R. Differentiating, we get

$$\frac{dR}{dD} = D^2\left(\frac{-1}{3}\right) + \left(\frac{K}{2} - \frac{D}{3}\right)(2D)$$

$$= \frac{-D^2}{3} + KD - \frac{2D^2}{3}$$

$$= KD - D^2.$$

Setting this to zero gives

$$KD - D^2 = 0$$

$$D(K - D) = 0$$

$$D = 0 \quad \text{or} \quad D = K.$$

Since the dosage must be positive, the only critical value is $D = K$. We'll test it with the first derivative test by choosing $D_1 = K/2$ and $D_2 = 2K$. We get

$$\left.\frac{dR}{dD}\right|_{D=K/2} = K \cdot \frac{K}{2} - \left(\frac{K}{2}\right)^2 = \frac{K^2}{4} > 0 \quad \Rightarrow \quad R \text{ is increasing;}$$

$$\left.\frac{dR}{dD}\right|_{D=2K} = K \cdot 2K - (2K)^2 = -2K^2 < 0 \quad \Rightarrow \quad R \text{ is decreasing;}$$

Hence, the maximum reaction is at a dosage of K.

PROBLEM SET 5.2

In Problems 1–6, determine the relative extreme points of each function graphed.

1.

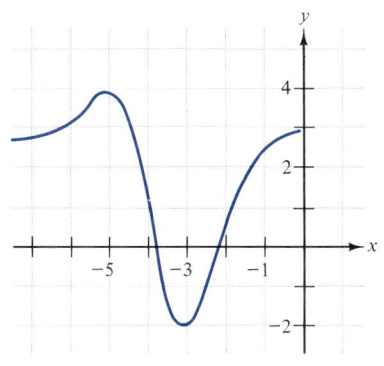

2.

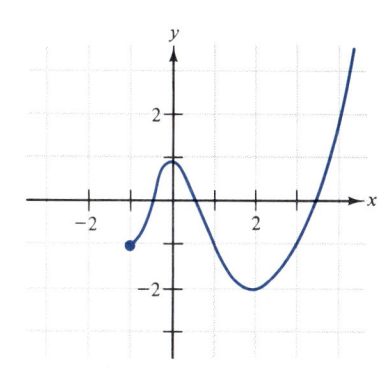

3.

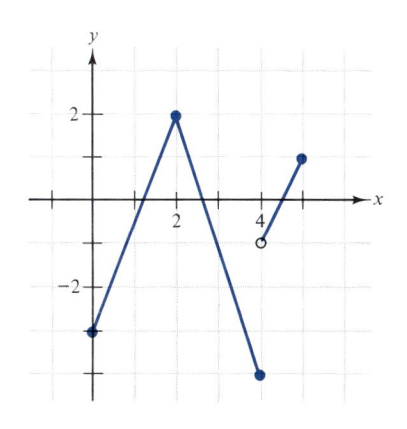

4.

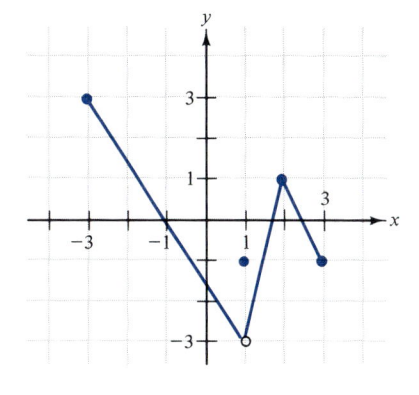

5.

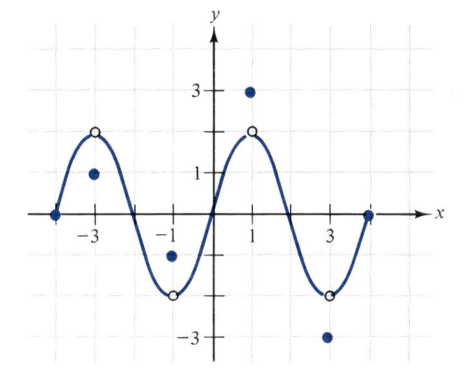

6.

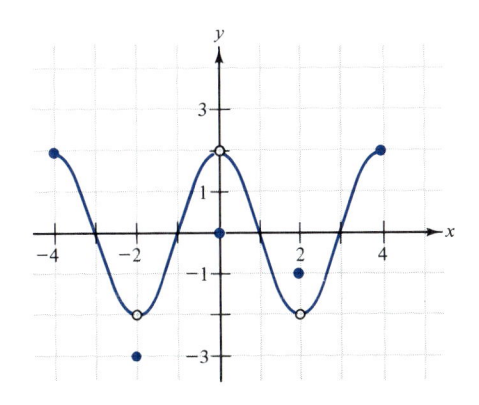

In Problems 7–32, determine all relative extreme points.

7. $f(x) = -x^2 + 6x + 3$
8. $f(x) = 2x^2 + 8x - 1$
9. $y = 3x - e^x$
10. $y = \frac{1}{2}e^{2x} - \frac{x}{e^3}$
11. $y = x^3 + 3x^2 - 9x - 7$
12. $y = x^3 - 3x^2 - 5$
13. $y = \frac{1}{2}x^2 - 6\ln(x-1)$
14. $y = (8\ln x) - x^2$
15. $f(x) = (x-2)^{1/5} + 3$
16. $f(x) = (x-5)^{2/3} - 1$
17. $y = \frac{x^4}{4} - 3x^2 + 1$
18. $y = \frac{x^5}{5} - 3x^3$
19. $f(x) = \frac{-x^2 + 6x - 5}{2x - 1}$
20. $y = \frac{x^2 - x + 5}{x + 4}$
21. $y = (\frac{8}{3} - x)/e^{-3x}$
22. $y = (x - \frac{3}{2})/e^{-2x}$
23. $f(x) = 1/(x-3)(x-4)$
24. $f(x) = -1/(2x+1)(4x+1)$
25. $f(x) = \sqrt{x}(x-3)$
26. $f(x) = \frac{1}{5}x^{5/3} - 2x^{2/3}$
27. $f(x) = x^3 + x^2 - 21x - 25, \ x \le 0$
28. $f(x) = x^3 + 6x^2 + 9x + \pi, \ x \ge 0$
29. $y = xe^{x/2}, \ x \le 1$
30. $y = xe^{-3x}, \ x \ge -1$
31. $f(x) = 1/(x + x^3), \ -5 \le x < 0$
32. $f(x) = \frac{54}{x^3} + 2x, \ 2 \le x \le 6$

33. A pharmacokinetic model for drug concentration C at time t is given by $C = Kte^{-Rt}$, where K and R are positive constants. Determine the time when the concentration reaches a maximum.

5.3 CONCAVITY AND THE SECOND DERIVATIVE TEST

Consider the two functions graphed in Figure 5.15. As we move from left to right, the tangents in Figure 5.15(a) turn counterclockwise, while the tangents in Figure 5.15(b) turn clockwise. This forms the basis of the concepts on concavity.

Let f be a function defined and differentiable on an interval I. We say that the graph of f is **concave up on I** provided that f' is increasing on I. For example, the graph of the function $f(x) = x^3$ is concave up on $(0, \infty)$ because $f'(x) = 3x^2$ is increasing on $(0, \infty)$.

Geometrically, this definition means that the tangent lines are turning counterclockwise. Therefore, given any two points on the graph on this

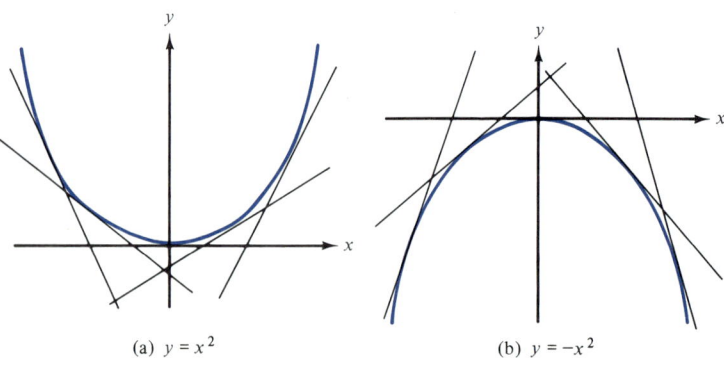

(a) $y = x^2$ (b) $y = -x^2$

FIGURE 5.15

5.3 CONCAVITY AND THE SECOND DERIVATIVE TEST

interval, the slope of the tangent at the left point is less than the slope of the tangent at the right point. This gives us a ∪-shaped graph.

We say that the graph of a function of f is **concave down on an interval I** provided that f' is decreasing on I. Geometrically, this means that the tangent lines are turning clockwise on this interval. Therefore, given any two points, the slope of the tangent at the left point is greater than the slope of the tangent at the right point. This gives us a ∩-shaped graph.

Note that the concavity of the graph of a function is independent of the function's increasing or decreasing. In Figure 5.15(a) the graph is concave up, but the function is decreasing on $(-\infty, 0)$ and increasing on $(0, \infty)$. In Figure 5.15(b) the graph is concave down, but the function is increasing on $(-\infty, 0)$ and decreasing on $(0, \infty)$. So information about concavity doesn't tell us whether a function is increasing or decreasing.

EXAMPLE 1

Given the graph in Figure 5.16, determine the open intervals on which the graph is concave up and on which it is concave down.

■ SOLUTION

We need to observe the shape of the graph. A shape of the type ∪ indicates concave up, while ∩ indicates concave down. We see that the graph is concave down on $(-\infty, -1)$ and on $(3, \infty)$. On $(-1, 3)$ the graph is concave up.

FIGURE 5.16

EXERCISE

Given the graph in Figure 5.17, determine the open intervals on which the graph is concave up and on which it is concave down.

■ ANSWER

Concave up on $(-\infty, -1)$ and on $(1, \infty)$; concave down on $(-1, 1)$.

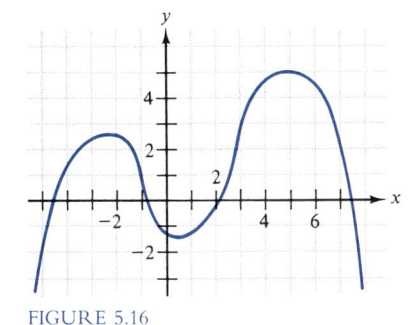

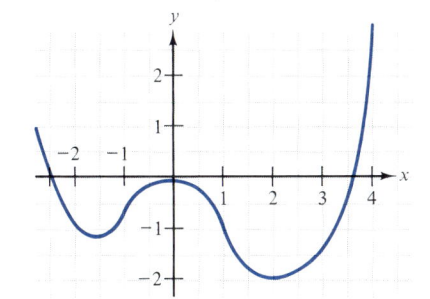

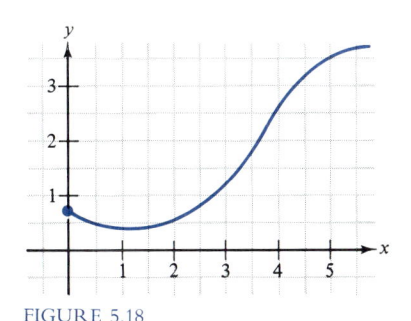

FIGURE 5.17

Let f be a function with domain D, and let a be an interior point of the domain. Then the graph of f is said to be **concave up at $x = a$** provided that there is an open interval I containing a such that the graph is concave up on I. To illustrate, consider the function graphed in Figure 5.18. This graph is concave up at $x = 2$ because there is an open interval I containing 2 on which the graph is concave up. [Consider $I = (1, 3)$, for instance.]

The definition of **concave down at $x = a$** is analogous to that of concave up at $x = a$. The graph in Figure 5.18 is concave down at $x = 5$.

FIGURE 5.18

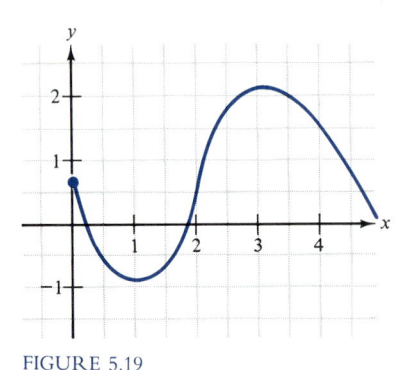

EXAMPLE 2

For $x = 1, 2, 3$, and 4, determine whether the graph in Figure 5.19 is concave up, concave down, or neither.

■ SOLUTION

The graph is concave up at $x = 1$ because we can find an open interval, like $(\frac{1}{2}, \frac{5}{4})$, on which the graph is concave up. The graph is neither concave up nor concave down at $x = 2$. We cannot find an open interval containing 2 on which the graph is concave up or one on which the graph is concave down. For any open interval containing 2, the graph is concave up to the left of 2 and concave down to the right of 2. At $x = 3$ and at $x = 4$, the graph is concave down.

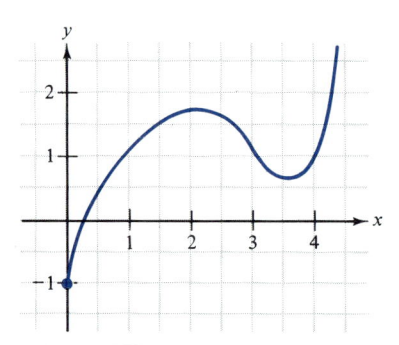

FIGURE 5.19

EXERCISE

For $x = 1, 2, 3$, and 4, determine whether the graph in Figure 5.20 is concave up, concave down, or neither.

■ ANSWER

Concave down at $x = 1$ and at $x = 2$; neither concave up nor concave down at $x = 3$; concave up at $x = 4$.

FIGURE 5.20

There is a relationship between concavity and the position of the tangent line with respect to the graph. If, locally, the tangent line at $x = a$ lies below the graph, then the graph is concave up at $x = a$. If, locally, the tangent line lies above the graph, the graph is concave down.

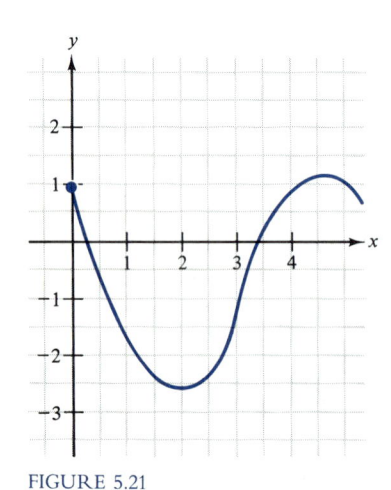

EXAMPLE 3

For $x = 1, 2, 3$, and 4, determine whether the graph in Figure 5.21 is concave up, concave down, or neither.

■ SOLUTION

At $x = 1$ and at $x = 2$, the tangent line lies below the graph. So the graph is concave up at $x = 1$ and at $x = 2$. At $x = 3$ the tangent line crosses the graph. So let's go to the definition and open intervals. For any open interval containing 3, we find the graph concave up on the left and concave down on the right. Hence the graph is neither concave up nor concave down here. The tangent line lies above the graph at $x = 4$. Thus the graph is concave down at $x = 4$.

FIGURE 5.21

5.3 CONCAVITY AND THE SECOND DERIVATIVE TEST   213

EXERCISE

For $x = 1, 2, 3,$ and 4, determine whether the graph in Figure 5.22 is concave up, concave down, or neither.

■ ANSWER
Concave up at $x = 1$; neither concave up nor concave down at $x = 2$; concave down at $x = 3$ and at $x = 4$.

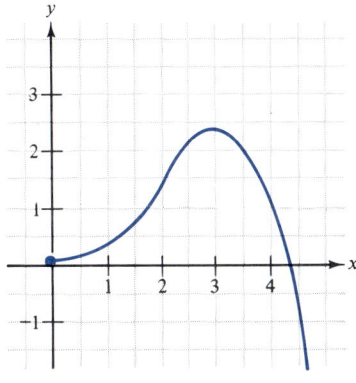

FIGURE 5.22

The first derivative gives us information regarding whether a function is increasing or decreasing. In a similar way, the second derivative tells us about concavity. If the second derivative is positive, then the first derivative is increasing. That is, the slopes are increasing, and this means that the graph is concave up. If the second derivative is negative, then the first derivative is decreasing. This means that the slopes are decreasing, and the graph is concave down. These results are summarized in the following theorem.

THEOREM 5.4
Second Derivative Rule

Let f be a function, and let a be an interior point of its domain.

(i) If $f''(a) > 0$, then the graph of f is concave up at $x = a$.
(ii) If $f''(a) < 0$, then the graph of f is concave down at $x = a$.

In the absence of a graph, this theorem gives us a convenient means of determining whether the graph is concave up or concave down at a point. We merely determine the sign of the function's second derivative there.

EXAMPLE 4

For $x = -5, 0,$ and 5, determine whether the graph of $f(x) = x^3 + 4x^2 - 9x + 8$ is concave up or concave down.

■ SOLUTION
We use the second derivative rule. Differentiation gives

$$f'(x) = 3x^2 + 8x - 9,$$
$$f''(x) = 6x + 8.$$

APPLICATIONS OF THE DERIVATIVE

Then

$f''(-5) = -30 + 8 < 0 \Rightarrow$ graph is concave down at $x = -5$;

$f''(0) = 8 > 0 \Rightarrow$ graph is concave up at $x = 0$;

$f''(5) = 30 + 8 > 0 \Rightarrow$ graph is concave up at $x = 5$.

EXERCISE

For $x = -4$, 0, and 3, determine whether the graph of $f(x) = x^3 - 5x^2 + 12x - 6$ is concave up or concave down.

■ ANSWER
Concave down at $x = -4$ and at $x = 0$; concave up at $x = 3$.

Note that the second derivative rule doesn't tell us about the behavior of the graph when $f''(a) = 0$. The graph may be concave up, concave down, or neither. Consider $f(x) = x^4$, $g(x) = -x^4$, and $h(x) = x^3$. All three of these functions have a second derivative of zero at $x = 0$, but the graph of f is concave up at $x = 0$, the graph of g is concave down at $x = 0$, and the graph of h is neither concave up nor down at $x = 0$. See Figure 5.23.

So $f''(a) = 0$ doesn't tell us about the behavior with respect to concave up/concave down at $x = a$. The graph may be doing either or neither.

Let's see how the second derivative may be used to find extreme points. If a graph has a horizontal tangent at a point, then the point isn't necessarily an extreme point. [The curve in Figure 5.23(c) has a horizontal tangent at (0,0), which is no extreme point.] But if the graph is also concave up or concave down, then the point will be extreme. This is the essence of the next theorem.

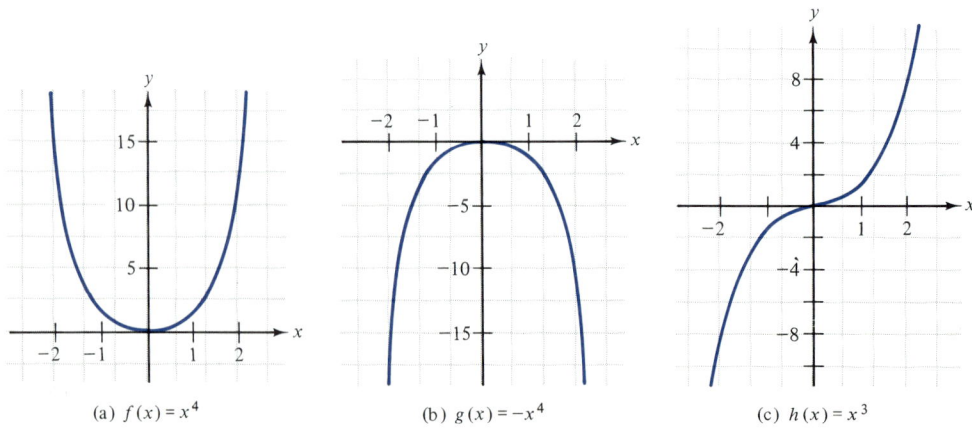

(a) $f(x) = x^4$ (b) $g(x) = -x^4$ (c) $h(x) = x^3$

FIGURE 5.23

THEOREM 5.5
Second Derivative Test

Let f be a continuous function, and let c be in the interior of the domain such that $f'(c) = 0$.

(i) If the graph of f is concave up at $x = c$, then f has a relative minimum at $x = c$.
(ii) If the graph of f is concave down at $x = c$, then f has a relative maximum at $x = c$.

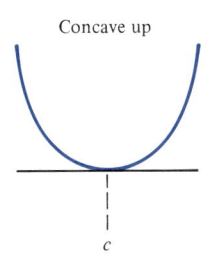

Concave up

(a) Relative minimum

Concave down

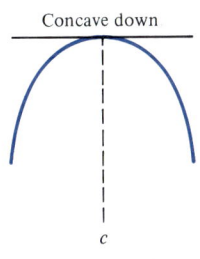

(b) Relative maximum

FIGURE 5.24

The geometric illustration of this theorem is seen in Figure 5.24.

This theorem says that for a given critical value in the interior which makes the first derivative equal zero, we check to see whether the graph is concave up or concave down there. Of course, this is done by determining the sign of the second derivative. (That's why the theorem is called the "second derivative test.")

When computation of the second derivative is easy, this test is easier than the first derivative test. However, note that it may be used only on those critical values that make the first derivative zero. For other critical values we *must* use the first derivative test. (If the first derivative isn't defined at a point, then the second derivative will not be defined there either.) Therefore the use of Theorem 5.5 is limited. Nonetheless, it is sometimes very convenient. Let's consider a couple of examples.

EXAMPLE 5

Determine all relative extreme points of $f(x) = \frac{1}{3}x^3 - 4x$.

■ SOLUTION

As always, we must first find the critical values. Differentiation gives

$$f'(x) = x^2 - 4.$$

Since there are no endpoints and since this derivative is defined for all real numbers, we need only consider $f'(x) = 0$. We get

$$x^2 - 4 = 0$$
$$x^2 = 4$$
$$x = \pm 2.$$

So the only critical values are $x = 2$ and $x = -2$. The second derivative is

$$f''(x) = 2x.$$

Using the second derivative test,

$$f''(-2) = -4 < 0 \implies \text{graph is concave down.}$$

So f has a relative maximum at $x = -2$. Since $f(-2) = \frac{16}{3}$, $(-2, \frac{16}{3})$ is a relative maximum point. Testing $x = 2$, we have

$$f''(2) = 4 > 0 \quad \Rightarrow f \text{ is concave up.}$$

Thus f has a relative minimum at $x = 2$. Because $f(2) = -\frac{16}{3}$, $(2, -\frac{16}{3})$ is a relative minimum point.

EXAMPLE 6

Determine all relative extreme points of $y = 2x^3 + 3x^2 - 36x + 10$, $x \geq 0$.

■ SOLUTION
Differentiating we get

$$y' = 6x^2 + 6x - 36.$$

Setting $y' = 0$ and solving for x, we have

$$6x^2 + 6x - 36 = 0$$
$$x^2 + x - 6 = 0$$
$$(x + 3)(x - 2) = 0$$
$$x = -3 \quad \text{or} \quad x = 2.$$

We may ignore $x = -3$ since it isn't in the domain. To test $x = 2$ let's use the second derivative test. We get

$$y'' = 12x + 6,$$

$$y''\big|_{x=2} = 24 + 6 > 0 \quad \Rightarrow \text{ graph is concave up.}$$

Thus the function has a relative minimum at $x = 2$. Since $y = -34$ when $x = 2$, $(2, -34)$ is a relative minimum point. The only remaining critical value to check is the endpoint $x = 0$. Since the second derivative test is for interior points only, we check it with an abbreviated first derivative test. Selecting $x_2 = 1$ we note that

$$y'\big|_{x=1} = 6 + 6 - 36 < 0 \quad \Rightarrow y \text{ is decreasing.}$$

Since the function is decreasing on the right (and there's nothing on the left), there is a relative maximum at $x = 0$, and $(0, 10)$ is a relative maximum point.

EXAMPLE 7

Determine all relative extreme points of $y = (x - 2)^4 + 5$.

SOLUTION
To find the critical values we differentiate:
$$y' = 4(x-2)^3.$$
The only critical value is one that makes $y' = 0$. It is $x = 2$. Testing, we have
$$y'' = 12(x-2)^2,$$
$$y''\big|_{x=2} = 12(2-2)^2 = 0.$$
Because the second derivative is zero at $x = 2$, the second derivative test is inconclusive. So we try the first derivative test. Choosing $x_1 = 0$ and $x_2 = 3$, we get
$$y'\big|_{x=0} = -32 < 0 \Rightarrow y \text{ is decreasing,}$$
$$y'\big|_{x=3} = 4 > 0 \Rightarrow y \text{ is increasing.}$$
Since the function is decreasing on the left and increasing on the right, we have a relative minimum at $x = 2$. Because $y = 5$ when $x = 2$, $(2,5)$ is the relative minimum point.

This last example illuminates the fact that the second derivative test is inconclusive when the second derivative is zero at a test value. (The graph may be concave up, concave down, or neither.) We must resort to the first derivative test in such cases.

EXERCISE

Determine all relative extreme points of (a) $f(x) = \frac{1}{3}x^3 - 9x$; (b) $y = 4x^3 - 15x^2 - 72x + 60$, $x \geq 0$; and (c) $y = (x+3)^4 - 5$.

ANSWER
(a) Point $(3, -18)$ is a relative minimum point; $(-3, 18)$ is a relative maximum point. (b) Point $(0, 60)$ is a relative maximum point; $(4, -212)$ is a relative minimum point. (c) Point $(-3, -5)$ is a relative minimum point.

Let's return to the equation considered at the very end of the preceding section. Recall that the strength R of the human body's reaction to a dose D of certain drugs may be written
$$R = D^2\left(\frac{K}{2} - \frac{D}{3}\right),$$

where K is a positive constant. It is important to know at what dosage a small change in D gives the greatest change in R. That is, at what dosage is the rate of change in R with respect to D maximal? This is a problem in maximizing dR/dD. We first note that

$$\frac{dR}{dD} = D^2\left(\frac{-1}{3}\right) + \left(\frac{K}{2} - \frac{D}{3}\right)(2D)$$

$$= \frac{-D^2}{3} + KD - \frac{2D^2}{3}$$

$$= KD - D^2.$$

This is what we must maximize. Differentiating, we get

$$\frac{d^2R}{dD^2} = K - 2D.$$

Hence the critical value is

$$D = \frac{K}{2}.$$

To test this we note that

$$\frac{d^3R}{dD^3} = -2 < 0 \;\Rightarrow\; \text{graph of } \frac{dR}{dD} \text{ is concave down.}$$

By the second derivative test (since d^3R/dD^3 is the second derivative of dR/dD), there is a maximum at $D = K/2$.

PROBLEM SET 5.3

In Problems 1–8, determine the open intervals on which the graph of the function is concave up and on which it is concave down.

1.

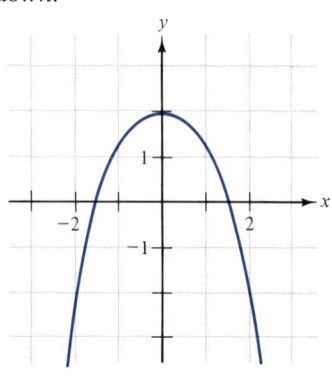

2.

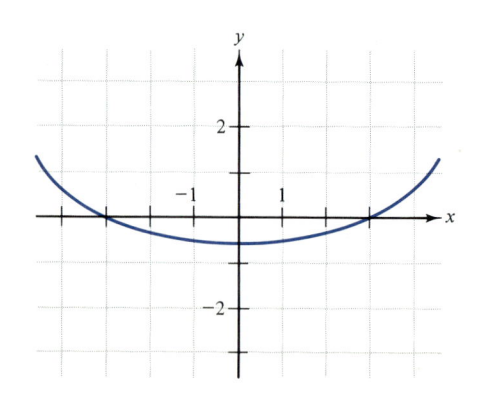

3.
4.
5.
6.
7.
8.

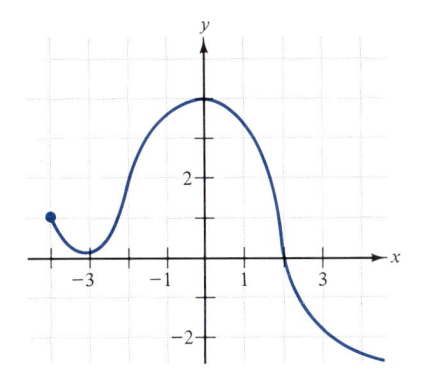

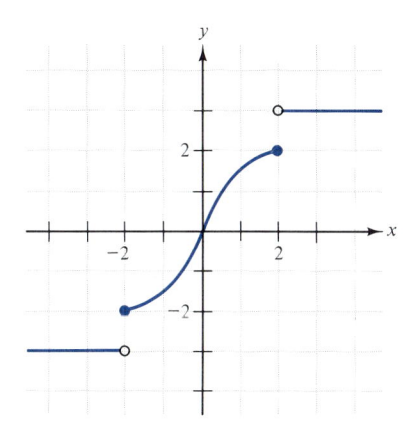

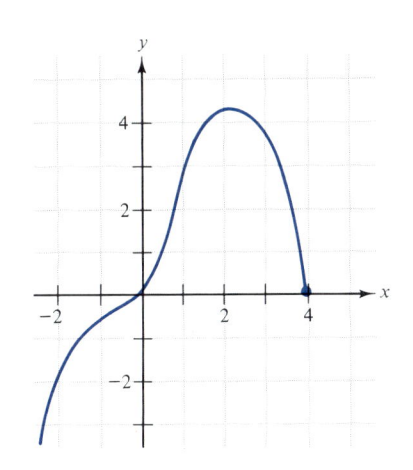

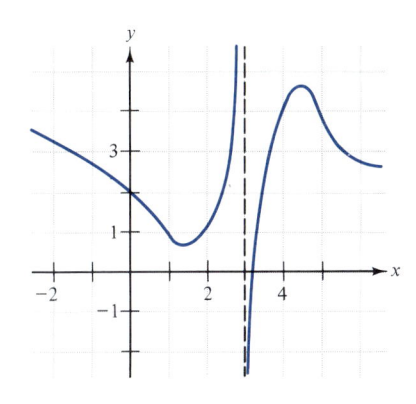

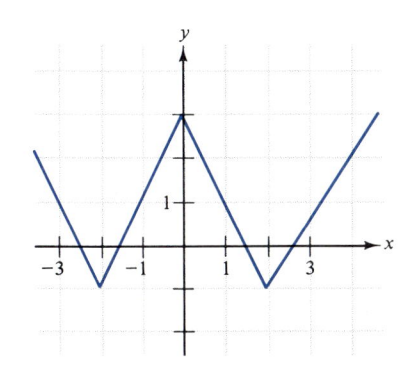

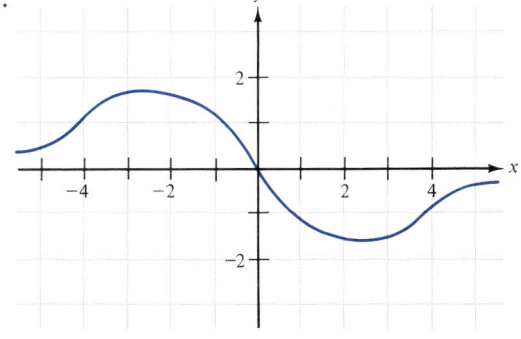

220 APPLICATIONS OF THE DERIVATIVE

In Problems 9–12, use the graph of f' to determine the open intervals on which the graph of f is concave up and on which it is concave down.

9.

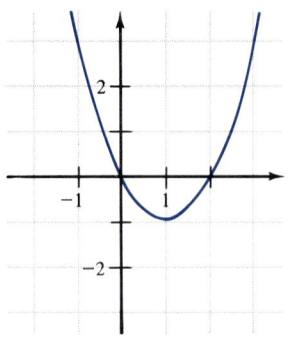

Graph of f'

10.

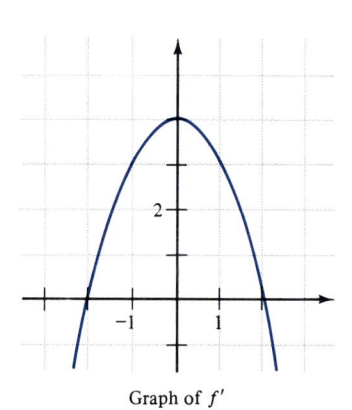

Graph of f'

11.

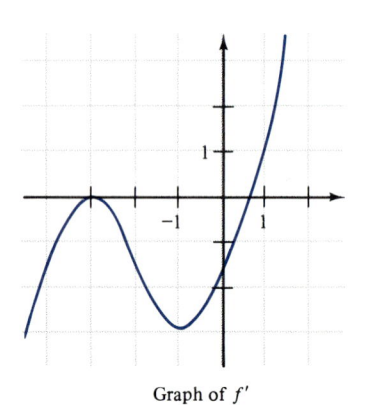

Graph of f'

12.

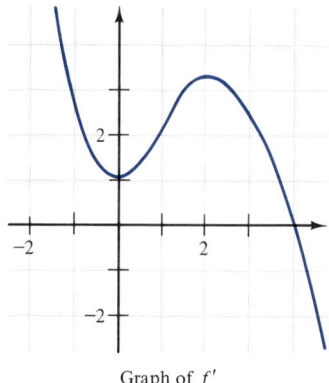

Graph of f'

In Problems 13–20, for $x = -2, -1, 0, 1, 2,$ and 3, determine whether each graph is concave up, concave down, or neither.

13.

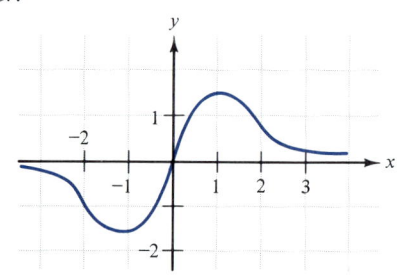

14.

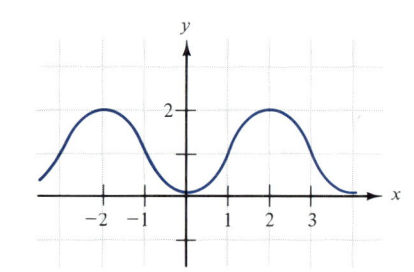

15.

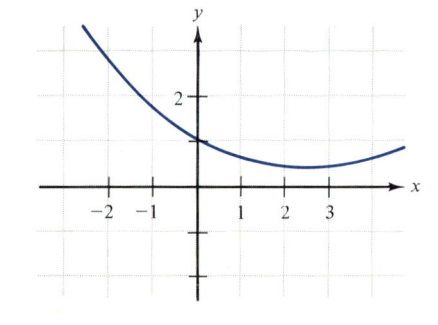

16.

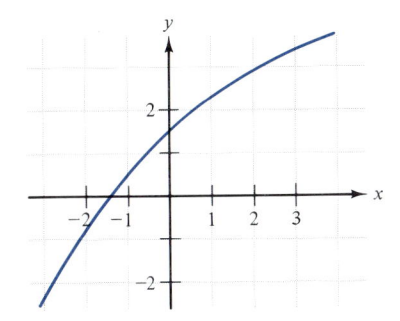

17.

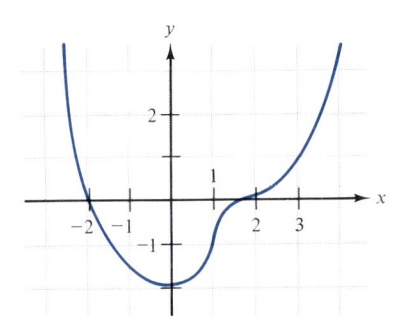

18.

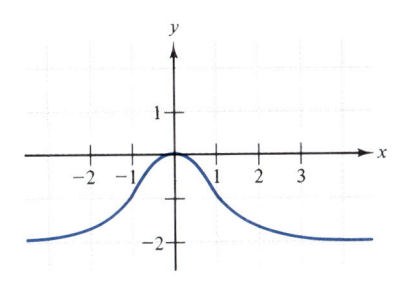

19.

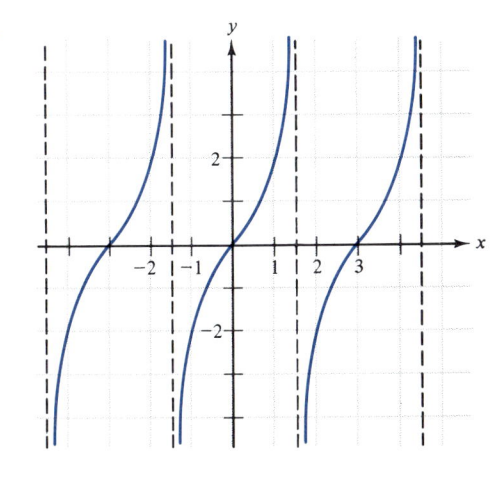

20.

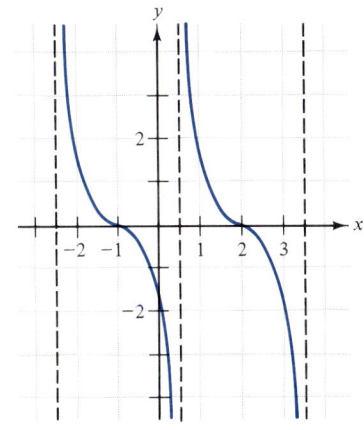

In Problems 21–32, use the second derivative rule to determine whether the graph of each function is concave up or concave down at the indicated points.

21. $f(x) = 5 + 3x - 2x^2$, $x = -4$, 0, and 5
22. $f(x) = -\sqrt{x}$, $x = 1$, $\sqrt[3]{3.8}$, and 25
23. $f(x) = \ln\left(\dfrac{5}{x}\right) - \dfrac{x^3}{3}$, $x = \frac{1}{2}, \frac{4}{5}$, and 1
24. $f(x) = \dfrac{x^4}{4} - e^{-3x}$, $x = 0, \frac{1}{3}$, and 1
25. $f(x) = \frac{8}{3}x^3 - 8x^2 + 5x - 1$, $x = -2$, 0, and 17
26. $y = x^4 - 4x^3 + 7x - \sqrt{2}$, $x = -\pi, \frac{3}{2}$, and $\sqrt{4.001}$
27. $y = 3 + (2x - 1)^6$, $x = -10$, 0, and 100
28. $y = \dfrac{2x - 1}{2x + 1}$, $x = -3, -0.51$, and 0
29. $y = xe^{-x}$, $x = -1$, $e - 1$, and $\ln 8$
30. $y = x^2 \ln x$, $x = \frac{1}{10}$, $1/e$, and $\ln 2$
31. $y = (x - 5)^5(x + 1)$, $x = -5$, $\sqrt{3} + \pi$, and 6
32. $y = x^2 + \dfrac{1}{x^2}$, $x = -1, -\frac{1}{100}$, and $\sqrt[4]{6}$

In Problems 33–36, use the graph of f'' to determine the open intervals on which the graph of f is concave up and on which it is concave down.

33.

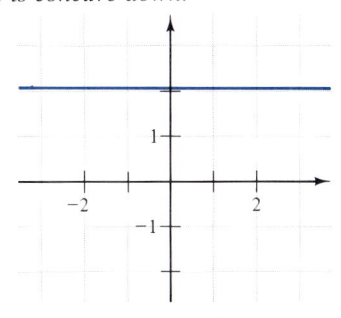

Graph of f''

34.

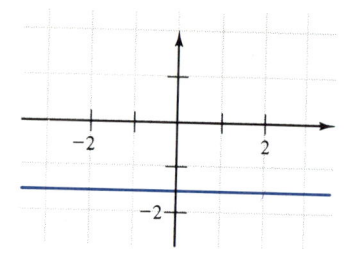

Graph of f''

35.

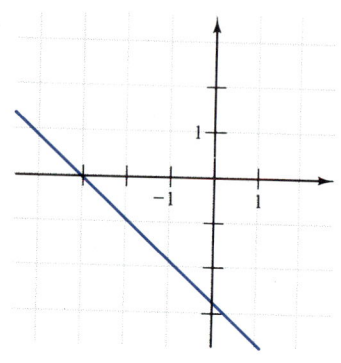

Graph of f''

36.

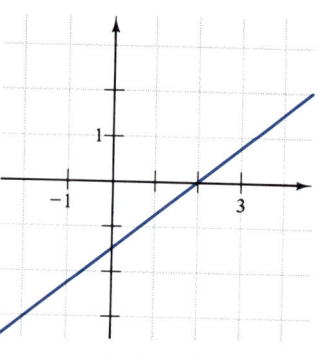

Graph of f''

In Problems 37–44, use the second derivative test to determine all relative extreme points of f.

37. $f(x) = (x-2)(x+4)$
38. $f(x) = x^3 - 3x^2 - 2$
39. $f(x) = -x^3 + 3x + 4$
40. $f(x) = x^4 - 2x^2 + \sqrt{3}$
41. $f(x) = x^2 + \dfrac{16}{x^2}$
42. $f(x) = x^2/(x^2 - 1)$
43. $y = -x\ln(2x)$
44. $y = x - e^{x+1}$

In Problems 45–52, determine all relative extreme points.

45. $y = 2 + 5x - x^5$, $x \le 0$
46. $y = x^4 - 18x^2$, $x \ge -2$
47. $y = -e^x - e^{-x}$, $x \le 2$
48. $y = e^x - 2x$, $x \ge -3$
49. $y = (x-2)^3 + 2$
50. $y = (x+1)^6 - 6$
51. $y = \tfrac{4}{3}x^3 - 2x^2 - 3x$, $-3 \le x \le 3$
52. $y = \tfrac{1}{3}x^3 + \tfrac{7}{2}x^2 + 12x + 15$, $0 \le x < 5$

53. Suppose the function f has the following properties: $f(3) = 7$, $f'(3) = 0$, and $f''(3) = -2$. What can be said about the graph of f at $x = 3$?

54. Suppose the function f has the following properties: $f(-2) = 0$, $f'(-2) = 0$, and $f''(-2) = 2$. What can be said about the graph of f at $x = -2$?

55. Show that the graph of the quadratic function $f(x) = ax^2 + bx + c$, $a \ne 0$, is concave up if $a > 0$ and concave down if $a < 0$.

56. Determine whether the following statement is true or false: If the graph of the function f is concave up on $[a,b]$, then

$$\frac{f(a) + f(b)}{2} > f\left(\frac{a+b}{2}\right).$$

57. Indicate which of the graphs below best corresponds to the graph of $3xy + y^2 = 7$ near the point $(2,1)$.

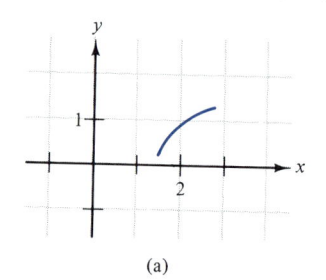

(a) 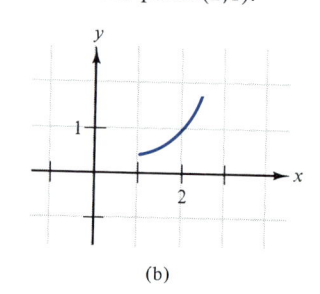 (b) 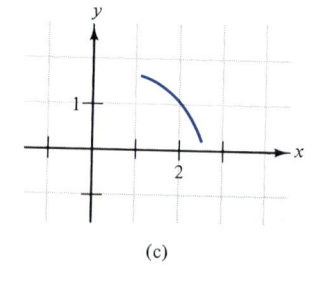 (c) 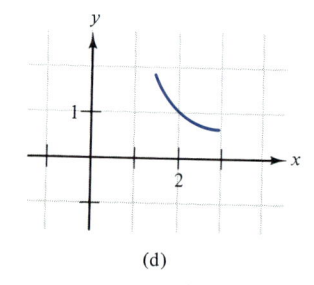 (d)

58. A pharmacokinetic model for drug concentration C at time t is given by $C = Kte^{-Rt}$, where K and R are positive constants. Use the second derivative test to determine the time when the concentration reaches a maximum.

5.4 INFLECTION POINTS

Consider the graph in Figure 5.25. The tangent line at $x = 2$ crosses the graph. The graph is neither concave up nor concave down at $x = 2$. The curve is concave down to the left of $x = 2$ and concave up to the right. Such points have a special designation. We say that $(c, f(c))$ is an **inflection point** provided that the graph has a tangent there and that there exists an open interval (a, b), containing c, such that the concavity on (a, c) differs from the concavity on (c, b). In other words, an inflection point is a point where the concavity changes. The tangent line at an inflection point will cross the graph.

Consider the function f graphed in Figure 5.26. The point $(-1, 2)$ is an inflection point because there is an open interval containing -1, like $(-2, 0)$, such that f is concave up on $(-2, -1)$ and concave down on $(-1, 0)$. That is, at $(-1, 2)$, the graph changes from concave up to concave down. The tangent at $(-1, 2)$ crosses the graph.

FIGURE 5.25

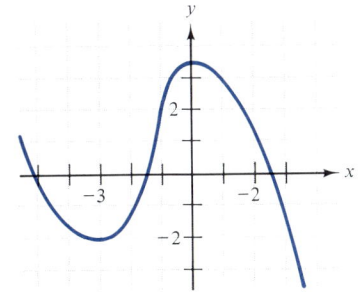

FIGURE 5.26

EXERCISE

Determine the inflection point of the function graphed in Figure 5.27.

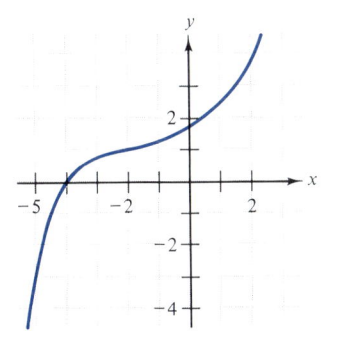

■ ANSWER
$(-2, 1)$

FIGURE 5.27

The curve of Figure 5.25 is concave down on $(-\infty, 2)$, so f' is decreasing. That is, the *slopes* are decreasing. On $(2, \infty)$ the graph is concave up, so f' is increasing. That is, the *slopes* are increasing. If the slopes are decreasing to the left of $x = 2$ and increasing to the right of $x = 2$, they must reach a minimum at $x = 2$. Thus the minimum slope is the slope of the tangent at $(2, 3)$. In general, the slopes have relative maximums or relative minimums at inflection points.

The graph in Figure 5.28 depicts the number of units painted by a factory worker t hours after beginning work. What is the significance of the inflection point?

The change in units painted with respect to time is a measure of the worker's efficiency. Thus the slope represents the instantaneous efficiency. Because the curve is concave up for $t < 5$, the worker's efficiency was increasing during the first 5 hours. Since the curve is concave down for $t > 5$, the worker's efficiency was decreasing during the last 3 hours. Consequently, at the inflection point, the worker's efficiency reached a maximum.

FIGURE 5.28

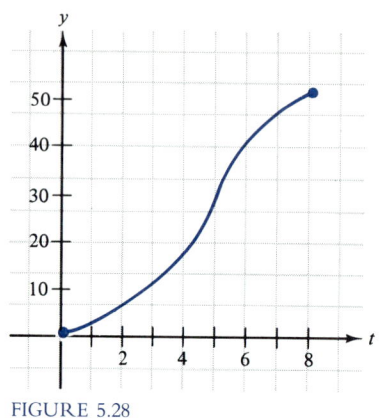

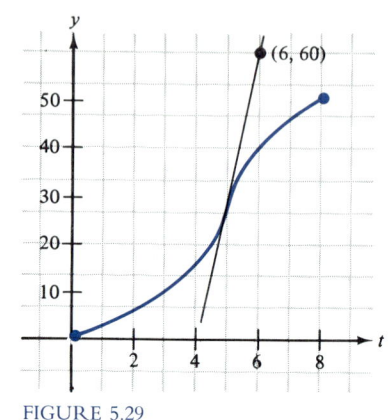

FIGURE 5.29

What was this maximum efficiency? It is the slope of the tangent line at the inflection point. Let's sketch the tangent and locate another point. See Figure 5.29. The slope is

$$m = \frac{60 - 30}{6 - 5} = 30.$$

The maximum efficiency was 30 units/hour.

Note that when a graph has different unit distances on its axes, the slope is not what it *appears* to be. The slope of the tangent in Figure 5.27 looks to be about 4 or 5. But the computation reveals otherwise.

Determining inflection points in the absence of a graph is a bit more difficult. But suppose that c is in the interior of the domain of f. If $f''(c) > 0$, then the graph is concave up. If $f''(c) < 0$, then the graph is concave down. In either case, $(c, f(c))$ is not an inflection point. This leads to Theorem 5.6.

THEOREM 5.6 Let f be a function, and let c be an interior point of the domain. If $(c, f(c))$ is an inflection point, then $f''(c) = 0$ or f'' is not defined at $x = c$.

This theorem says that those elements of the domain at which the second derivative is zero or at which the second derivative is not defined are the x-coordinates of *possible* inflection points. Such values are the only ones to consider. To determine whether an inflection point does indeed exist, we employ the next theorem. This theorem is analogous to the first derivative test, which is used to test critical values when looking for relative extreme points.

THEOREM 5.7
Inflection Point Test

Let f be a continuous function, and let c be an element of the domain such that $f''(c) = 0$ or $f''(c)$ does not exist. Choose interior points x_1 and x_2 such that $x_1 < c < x_2$, $[x_1, x_2]$ is in the domain of f, and the only possible inflection on $[x_1, x_2]$ is at $x = c$.

(i) If the concavities at $x = x_1$ and at $x = x_2$ differ, then f has an inflection point at $x = c$.
(ii) If the concavities at $x = x_1$ and at $x = x_2$ are the same, then f does not have an inflection point at $x = c$.

This theorem says that, given a value c for which $f''(c) = 0$ or $f''(c)$ doesn't exist, we must choose a point to the left and a point to the right subject to two conditions: the two points and all points in between must be in the domain; and except for the value we are testing, there is no possible inflection at either point or any in between. Having selected the points, we check the concavity at our choices. Of course, this is easily done by determining the sign of the second derivative there. Let's illustrate with an example.

EXAMPLE 1

Determine all inflection points of (a) $f(x) = x^3 - 3x^2 + 5$ and (b) $f(x) = x^2 \ln x$.

■ SOLUTION
(a) Our first task is to differentiate. We have
$$f'(x) = 3x^2 - 6x,$$
$$f''(x) = 6x - 6.$$

The second derivative is defined for all elements in the domain, and it equals zero when $x = 1$. So there is a possible inflection point at $x = 1$. To test this point let's choose $x_1 = 0$ and $x_2 = 2$. Note that $[0,2]$ is in the domain, and the only possible inflection on $[0,2]$ is at the value we are testing. We have

$$f''(0) = -6 < 0 \implies \text{graph is concave down;}$$
$$f''(2) = 6 > 0 \implies \text{graph is concave up.}$$

Because the concavities differ, there is an inflection point at $x = 1$. Since $f(1) = 3$, the inflection point is $(1,3)$.
(b) Differentiation yields
$$f'(x) = x^2 \cdot \frac{1}{x} + (\ln x) \cdot 2x = x + 2x \ln x,$$

$$f''(x) = 1 + 2x \cdot \frac{1}{x} + (\ln x) \cdot 2 = 3 + 2 \ln x.$$

The second derivative is defined for all elements in the domain. To find where it equals zero involves solving a logarithmic equation:
$$3 + 2 \ln x = 0$$
$$\ln x = \frac{-3}{2}$$
$$x = e^{-3/2} \quad (\approx 0.2231).$$

To test let's choose $x_1 = 0.1$ and $x_2 = 1$. We have
$$f''(0.1) = 3 + 2 \ln 0.1 < 0 \quad \Rightarrow \text{ graph is concave down;}$$
$$f''(1) = 3 + 2 \ln 1 > 0 \quad \Rightarrow \text{ graph is concave up.}$$

Thus there is an inflection point at $x = e^{-3/2}$. Since $f(e^{-3/2}) = -3/(2e^3)$, the inflection point is $(e^{-3/2}, -3/(2e^3))$.

Note that the process of finding inflection points with the inflection point test is analogous to that of finding extreme points with the first derivative test. The only differences are that there are no endpoints to consider, and we use the second derivative instead of the first.

EXERCISE

Determine all inflection points of (a) $f(x) = -x^3 - 6x^2 + 3x - 1$ and (b) $f(x) = x^3 \ln x$.

■ ANSWER

(a) $(-2, -23)$; (b) $\left(e^{-5/6}, \dfrac{-5}{6e^{5/2}} \right)$

In studies of epidemics, one function considered is the one that gives the number of infected individuals at time t. An inflection point on this graph indicates that the epidemic has reached its most virulent stage. This information is needed in the following example and exercise.

EXAMPLE 2

Suppose that the number of individuals infected by a particular disease at time t is
$$I(t) = 500t + 900t^2 - 100t^3,$$
where t is in months. What is the number of infected individuals when the disease reaches its most virulent stage?

5.4 INFLECTION POINTS

■ SOLUTION
We must locate the inflection point. Differentiation gives
$$I'(t) = 500 + 1800t - 300t^2$$
$$I''(t) = 1800 - 600t.$$

The second derivative equals zero when $t = 3$. To test let's choose $t_1 = 2$ and $t_2 = 4$. We get

$$I''(2) = 1800 - 1200 > 0 \Rightarrow \text{graph is concave up;}$$
$$I''(4) = 1800 - 2400 < 0 \Rightarrow \text{graph is concave down.}$$

Hence, there is an inflection point at $t = 3$. Since

$$I(3) = 500(3) + 900(9) - 100(27) = 6900,$$

there are 6900 infected individuals when the epidemic reaches its most virulent stage.

EXERCISE

Suppose that the number of individuals infected by a particular disease at time t is

$$I(t) = 100t + 750t^2 - 50t^3,$$

where t is in months. What is the number of infected individuals when the disease reaches its most virulent stage?

■ ANSWER
13,000

PROBLEM SET 5.4

In Problems 1–10, determine the inflection points of the function graphed.

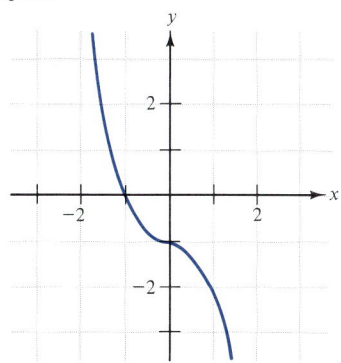

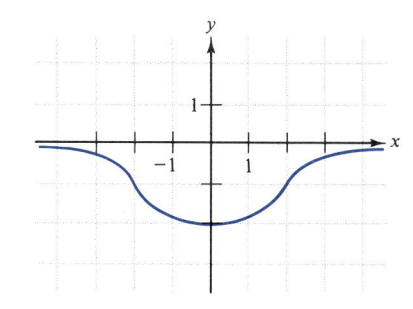

1.

2.

3.
4.
5.
6.
7.
8.
9.

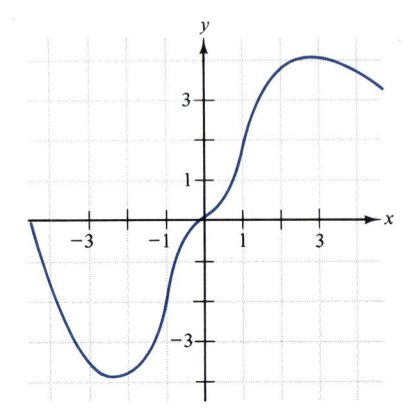

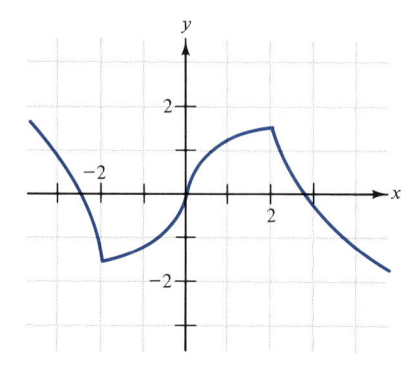

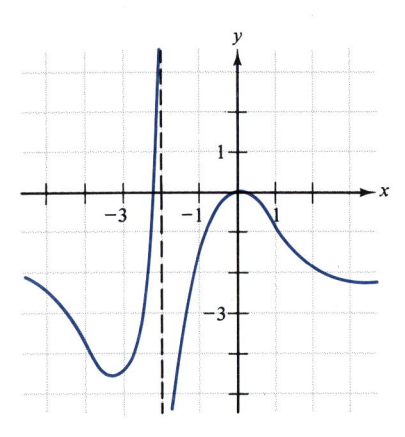

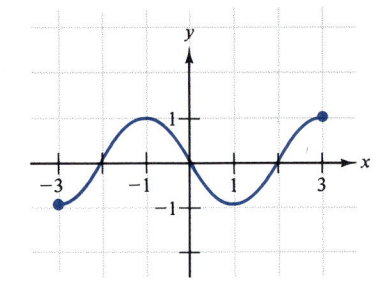

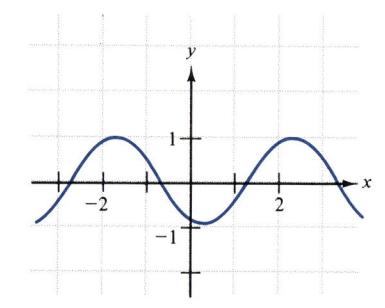

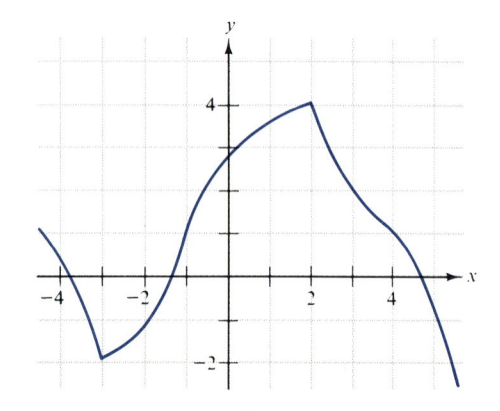

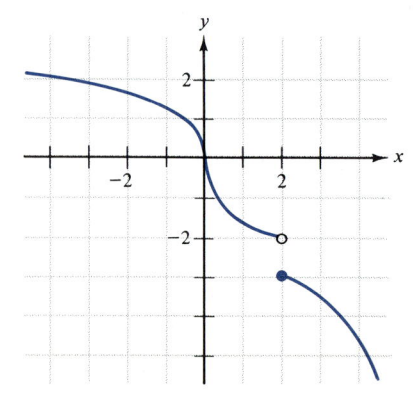

10.

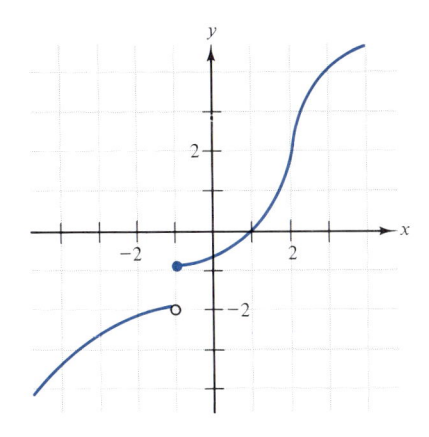

In Problems 11–26, determine all inflection points of the given function.

11. $f(x) = 6x^2 - 11x - 10$
12. $f(x) = \frac{1}{6}x^3 - x^2 + \frac{4}{3}x$
13. $y = 2x^3 - 12x^2 + 25$
14. $y = x^4 - 2x^3 + 3x - 1$
15. $y = x^4 - 6x^2$
16. $y = (x - 5)^{1/3}$
17. $y = 5 + (x + 3)^7$
18. $f(x) = \sqrt{x}(x - 3)$
19. $f(x) = \frac{3}{2}x^5 - \frac{5}{3}x^3$
20. $f(x) = 6x/(x^2 + 3)$
21. $y = e^{-1/x}$
22. $y = e^{-1/x^2}$

23. $y = \dfrac{\ln(1/x)}{x}$
24. $y = \sqrt{x}\,\ln x$
25. $y = xe^{x/3}$
26. $y = xe^{-x/2}$

27. Determine a and b so that $y = x^3 + ax^2 + bx + 1$ has an inflection point at (2, 3).

28. Determine the equation of the tangent line to $y = (2x + 6)^3$ at the inflection point.

29. Determine the x-coordinates of all inflection points of the function f, given that
$$f''(x) = (x + 3)(x - 2)^2(5 - x)^3.$$

30. Show that the graph of every cubic polynomial $f(x) = ax^3 + bx^2 + cx + d\,(a \neq 0)$ has one and only one inflection point.

31. Show that (2, 4) is not an inflection point of the graph of $f(x) = \frac{1}{12}x^4 - \frac{2}{3}x^3 + 2x^2$, even though $f''(2) = 0$.

32. In competitive ski jumping the height from the end of the ramp at which the skiers begin their run is adjusted so that no skier will land beyond the inflection point of the hill. Suppose that a hill can be approximated by the graph of
$$y = \dfrac{12{,}000{,}000 + x^2}{120{,}000 + x^2}, \quad 0 \le x \le 500.$$

Determine the inflection point.

5.5 CURVE SKETCHING

The behavior of a function is perhaps most easily understood by examining its graph. We learned to graph some elementary functions in Chapter 1, and in this section, we utilize some of the calculus tools to graph a wider variety of functions.

But first, we need to talk about asymptotes. Recall that the graphs of elementary rational functions and their transformations have vertical and horizontal asymptotes. For example, the graph of

$$f(x) = \dfrac{1}{x - 2} + 1,$$

a shift of $y = 1/x$ to the right 2 units and up 1 unit, is shown in Figure 5.30. It has a vertical asymptote of $x = 2$ and a horizontal asymptote of $y = 1$.

The line $x = 2$ is a vertical asymptote of this function because as x approaches 2 from the positive side, $f(x)$ increases without bound. It is also a vertical asymptote because as x approaches 2 from the negative side, $f(x)$ decreases without bound. This illustrates the concept of **infinite limits.**

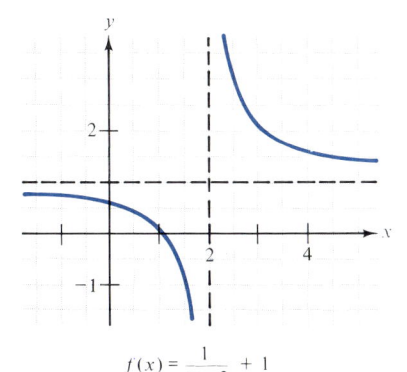

FIGURE 5.30

APPLICATIONS OF THE DERIVATIVE

Let f be a function defined on an open interval $(a, a + h)$ for some positive number h. Then we say that the limit of $f(x)$ as x approaches a from the right is infinity, and we write

$$\lim_{x \to a^+} f(x) = \infty,$$

provided that $f(x)$ is arbitrarily large for all x sufficiently close to a on the positive side. We say that the limit is negative infinity, and we write

$$\lim_{x \to a^+} f(x) = -\infty,$$

provided that $f(x)$ is arbitrarily large negative for all x sufficiently close to a on the positive side.

Similar definitions are made for

$$\lim_{x \to a^-} f(x) = \infty \quad \text{and} \quad \lim_{x \to a^-} f(x) = -\infty.$$

Thus, for the function being considered,

$$f(x) = \frac{1}{x - 2} + 1,$$

the vertical asymptote is $x = 2$ because

$$\lim_{x \to 2^+} f(x) = \infty \quad \text{and} \quad \lim_{x \to 2^-} f(x) = -\infty.$$

It is not difficult to see why this is so. As x approaches 2 from the positive side, the denominator of $1/(x - 2)$ is positive and approaches 0. Because the numerator is 1, the fraction is positive and increases without bound. Adding 1 to such a fraction has no significant effect, so

$$\lim_{x \to 2^+} \left(\frac{1}{x - 2} + 1 \right) = \infty.$$

As x approaches 2 from the negative side, the denominator of $1/(x - 2)$ approaches 0 again but is negative. Hence the fraction is negative and decreases without bound. Again, adding 1 has no significant effect, so

$$\lim_{x \to 2^-} \left(\frac{1}{x - 2} + 1 \right) = -\infty.$$

Such infinite limits indicate a vertical asymptote and are the basis of the following theorem.

THEOREM 5.8 Let f be a rational function defined by

$$f(x) = \frac{P(x)}{Q(x)},$$

and let a be a constant. If $Q(a) = 0$ and $P(a) \neq 0$, then the line $x = a$ is a vertical asymptote of the graph of f.

5.5 CURVE SKETCHING

Theorem 5.8 then tells us that we can determine the vertical asymptotes of a rational function by finding the values that make the denominator, but not the numerator, equal zero.

EXAMPLE 1

Determine the vertical asymptotes of

$$f(x) = \frac{x^2 - 2x - 3}{(2x - 1)(x + 2)}.$$

■ SOLUTION

Since $\frac{1}{2}$ and -2 make the denominator equal zero, they are candidates. Once we verify that they do not make the numerator zero,

$$(x^2 - 2x - 3)\Big|_{x=1/2} = \tfrac{1}{4} - 1 - 3 \neq 0,$$

$$(x^2 - 2x - 3)\Big|_{x=-2} = 4 + 4 - 3 \neq 0,$$

we conclude that the vertical asymptotes are

$$x = \tfrac{1}{2} \quad \text{and} \quad x = -2.$$

EXERCISE

Determine the vertical asymptotes of

$$f(x) = \frac{2x^2 + 3x - 2}{(x - 3)(3x + 2)}.$$

■ ANSWER
$x = 3$ and $x = -\tfrac{2}{3}$

We now direct our attention to the problem of finding the horizontal asymptotes. We noted that the line $y = 1$ is a horizontal asymptote of

$$f(x) = \frac{1}{x - 2} + 1.$$

This is because as x increases without bound, the $f(x)$-values get closer and closer to 1. Also, as x decreases without bound, the $f(x)$-values approach 1. This brings us to the concept of **limits at infinity**.

Let f be a function defined on (a, ∞) for some a. Then we say that the limit of $f(x)$ as x approaches infinity is L, where L is a real number, and write

$$\lim_{x \to \infty} f(x) = L,$$

provided that $f(x)$ is arbitrarily close to L for all x sufficiently large. A similar definition is made for the limit of $f(x)$ as x approaches negative infinity.

Thus, for the function being considered,

$$f(x) = \frac{1}{x-2} + 1,$$

the horizontal asymptote is $y = 1$ because

$$\lim_{x \to \infty} f(x) = 1 \quad \text{and} \quad \lim_{x \to -\infty} f(x) = 1.$$

It is not difficult to see why this is so. As x increases without bound, and as x decreases without bound, the denominator of the fraction $1/(x-2)$ gets large positive or large negative. In either case, since the numerator is a constant 1, the fraction approaches 0. Hence the sum

$$\frac{1}{x-2} + 1$$

approaches 1.

Therefore, in general, to determine the horizontal asymptotes, we need to examine the limits at infinity. Let's illustrate further by finding the horizontal asymptotes of the graph of the rational function

$$f(x) = \frac{x^2 - 2x - 3}{2x^2 + 3x - 2}.$$

As x increases without bound, both the numerator and the denominator increase without bound. Thus we're uncertain about the behavior of $f(x)$. Let's divide the numerator and the denominator by x^2. We get

$$f(x) = \frac{1 - \dfrac{2}{x} - \dfrac{3}{x^2}}{2 + \dfrac{3}{x} - \dfrac{2}{x^2}}.$$

As x increases without bound, the fractions $2/x$, $3/x^2$, $3/x$, and $2/x^2$ all approach zero. So the numerator approaches 1, and the denominator approaches 2. Thus

$$\lim_{x \to \infty} f(x) = \tfrac{1}{2}.$$

With a similar analysis we find that

$$\lim_{x \to -\infty} f(x) = \tfrac{1}{2}.$$

Thus the line $y = \tfrac{1}{2}$ is a horizontal asymptote.

Because the technique used in the preceding illustration may be applied to any rational function, we merely need to examine the ratio of the leading terms when looking for horizontal asymptotes. The analysis is the basis of the following theorem.

5.5 CURVE SKETCHING

THEOREM 5.9 For a rational function, we have the following conditions:

(i) If the degree of the numerator is less than the degree of the denominator, then the line $y = 0$ is a horizontal asymptote.
(ii) If the degree of the numerator is greater than the degree of the denominator, then there is no horizontal asymptote.
(iii) If the degree of the numerator is equal to the degree of the denominator, then the horizontal asymptote is the horizontal line whose y-intercept is the ratio of the leading coefficients.

EXAMPLE 2

Determine the horizontal asymptote (if any) of the following:

(a) $y = \dfrac{x^2}{x^2(x-1)}$; (b) $y = \dfrac{x^2 + x - 3}{(2x+1)(3x-2)}$; and (c) $y = \dfrac{x^2}{x-1}$.

■ SOLUTION
(a) The degree of the numerator is 2 while the degree of the denominator is 3. By Theorem 5.9(i), the horizontal asymptote is $y = 0$.

(b) The degree of both numerator and denominator is 2. So we look at the ratio of leading coefficients. Since the leading coefficient of the numerator is 1, and the leading coefficient of the denominator is 6, the horizontal asymptote is $y = \frac{1}{6}$.

(c) Since the degree of the numerator is greater than the degree of the denominator, there is no horizontal asymptote.

EXERCISE

Determine the horizontal asymptote (if any) of the following:

(a) $y = \dfrac{x}{(x-1)(2x+1)}$; (b) $y = \dfrac{(x-1)(3x+2)}{2x^2 + 3x + 1}$; and

(c) $y = \dfrac{x^2(x-1)}{(2x-3)(x-2)}$.

■ ANSWER
(a) $y = 0$; (b) $y = \frac{3}{2}$; (c) none

Let's now sketch the rational function

$$f(x) = \frac{x^2}{x-1}.$$

We first note that both the y-intercept and the x-intercept are 0. Furthermore, there is a vertical asymptote of $x = 1$, but there is no horizontal asymptote.

Next, we want to determine the x-values in the domain of f at which $f'(x)$ or $f''(x)$ are either zero or undefined. Of course, these are the values at which we have possible extrema or possible inflection points. We have

$$f'(x) = \frac{(x-1)2x - x^2 \cdot 1}{(x-1)^2}$$

$$= \frac{2x^2 - 2x - x^2}{(x-1)^2}$$

$$= \frac{x^2 - 2x}{(x-1)^2}.$$

Setting this to zero gives

$$x^2 - 2x = 0$$

$$x(x-2) = 0$$

$$x = 0 \quad \text{or} \quad x = 2.$$

Differentiating again we get

$$f''(x) = \frac{(x-1)^2(2x-2) - (x^2 - 2x) \cdot 2(x-1)}{(x-1)^4}$$

$$= \frac{2(x-1)(x^2 - 2x + 1 - x^2 + 2x)}{(x-1)^4}$$

$$= \frac{2}{(x-1)^3}.$$

So $f''(x)$ never equals zero. Both $f'(x)$ and $f''(x)$ fail to exist at $x = 1$. But $x = 1$ is not a critical value because 1 is not in the domain of f.

The values of $x = 0$ and $x = 2$ divide the domain $(-\infty, 1) \cup (1, \infty)$ into several intervals. On each of these intervals we determine whether the function is increasing or decreasing and whether the graph is concave up or concave down. We do this by selecting a value in the interval and determining the sign of the derivatives. For example, in the interval $(-\infty, 0)$ we might select $x = -1$ and note that

$$f'(-1) = \frac{1+2}{4} > 0,$$

$$f''(-1) = \frac{2}{-8} < 0.$$

Thus the function is increasing and is concave down on $(-\infty, 0)$.

We check the other intervals and summarize the results in the following table.

5.5 CURVE SKETCHING

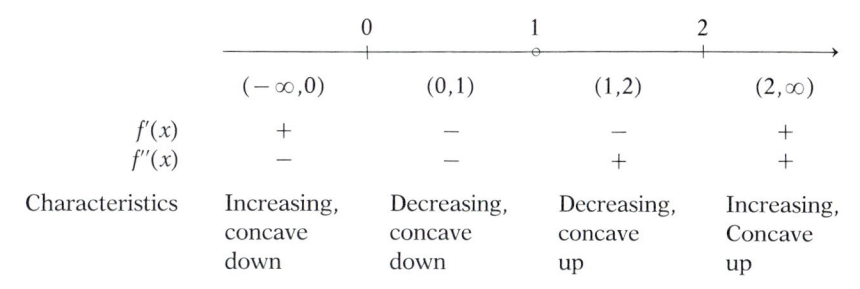

	$(-\infty,0)$	$(0,1)$	$(1,2)$	$(2,\infty)$
$f'(x)$	+	−	−	+
$f''(x)$	−	−	+	+
Characteristics	Increasing, concave down	Decreasing, concave down	Decreasing, concave up	Increasing, Concave up

What about the values 0 and 2? From the table we see that we have a relative maximum at $x = 0$ (because the function is increasing on the left and decreasing on the right) and a relative minimum at $x = 2$ (because the function is decreasing on the left and increasing on the right). Since

$$f(0) = 0 \quad \text{and} \quad f(2) = 4,$$

(0,0) is a relative maximum point and (2,4) is a relative minimum point. From the table we see that there is no inflection point. (Although the graph is concave up to the right of $x = 1$ and concave down to the left, there is no inflection point at $x = 1$ because the function isn't defined there.)

Plotting these points and using all the previous information, we obtain the graph in Figure 5.31.

Summarizing, we go through the following steps in sketching the graph:

1. Determine basic information: the *y*-intercept, the *x*-intercept(s) (if easy), and the asymptotes of rational functions (if any).
2. Determine the *x*-values of the domain at which $f'(x)$ or $f''(x)$ is either zero or undefined.
3. For each interval determined by the *x*-values of the preceding step, determine whether the function is increasing or decreasing and whether the graph is concave up or down.
4. Determine the relative extrema and inflection points.

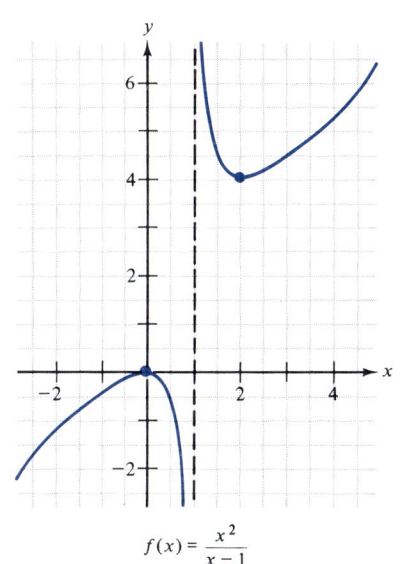

$f(x) = \dfrac{x^2}{x-1}$

FIGURE 5.31

EXAMPLE 3

Sketch the graph of $f(x) = -x^3 + 3x^2 + 9x + 2$.

■ SOLUTION

The *y*-intercept is 2, but the *x*-intercepts are difficult to find. So we proceed to step 2. The first derivative is

$$f'(x) = -3x^2 + 6x + 9.$$

Setting this to zero yields

$$-3x^2 + 6x + 9 = 0$$
$$x^2 - 2x - 3 = 0$$
$$(x - 3)(x + 1) = 0$$
$$x = 3 \quad \text{or} \quad x = -1.$$

Differentiating again we get
$$f''(x) = -6x + 6.$$

Setting this to zero gives us
$$-6x + 6 = 0$$
$$-6x = -6$$
$$x = 1.$$

Using $x = -1$, 1, and 3 to construct the table, we have the following:

	$(-\infty, -1)$	$(-1, 1)$	$(1, 3)$	$(3, \infty)$
$f'(x)$	−	+	+	−
$f''(x)$	+	+	−	−
Characteristics	Decreasing, concave up	Increasing, concave up	Increasing, concave down	Decreasing, concave down

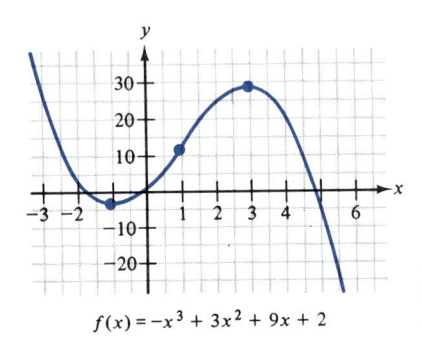

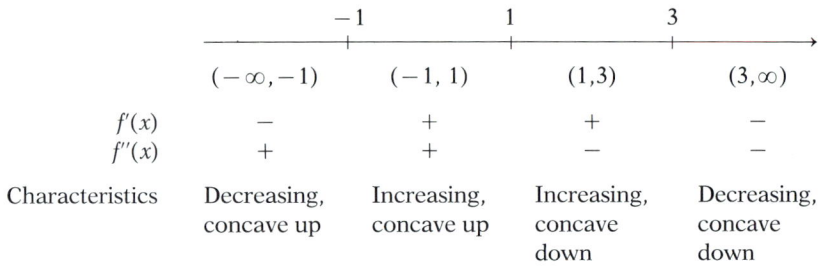

We have a relative minimum at $x = -1$ and a relative maximum at $x = 3$. Since $f(-1) = -3$ and $f(3) = 29$, $(-1, -3)$ and $(3, 29)$ are the respective minimum and maximum points. Also, we have an inflection point at $x = 1$. Since $f(1) = 13$, it is $(1, 13)$. This information provides the graph displayed in Figure 5.32.

$f(x) = -x^3 + 3x^2 + 9x + 2$

FIGURE 5.32

EXAMPLE 4

Sketch the graph of $f(x) = x^4 - \frac{11}{3}x^3 - \frac{3}{2}x^2 + 5$, $x \geq 0$.

■ SOLUTION

The y-intercept (which is also the value of the function at the endpoint of its domain) is 5. The first derivative is
$$f'(x) = 4x^3 - 11x^2 - 3x.$$

Setting this to zero gives
$$4x^3 - 11x^2 - 3x = 0$$
$$x(4x^2 - 11x - 3) = 0$$
$$x(4x + 1)(x - 3) = 0$$
$$x = 0 \quad \text{or} \quad x = -\tfrac{1}{4} \quad \text{or} \quad x = 3.$$

Of course, we ignore $x = -\frac{1}{4}$ because it isn't in the domain.

5.5 CURVE SKETCHING

The second derivative is

$$f''(x) = 12x^2 - 22x - 3.$$

Setting this to zero gives

$$12x^2 - 22x - 3 = 0$$

$$x = \frac{22 \pm \sqrt{(-22)^2 - 4(12)(-3)}}{2(12)}$$

$$= \frac{22 \pm \sqrt{628}}{24}$$

$$\approx \frac{22 \pm 25.059928}{24}$$

$$x \approx 2.0 \quad \text{or} \quad x \approx -0.1.$$

The negative value may be ignored since it isn't in the domain. Using 0, 2.0, and 3, we obtain the following table:

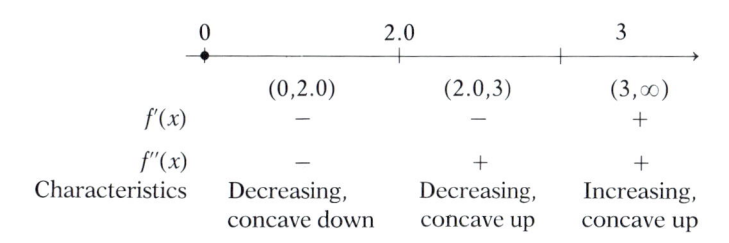

	(0, 2.0)	(2.0, 3)	(3, ∞)
$f'(x)$	−	−	+
$f''(x)$	−	+	+
Characteristics	Decreasing, concave down	Decreasing, concave up	Increasing, concave up

We see that the function has a relative maximum at $x = 0$ (an endpoint) and a relative minimum at $x = 3$. Also, there is an inflection point at $x \approx 2.0$. Upon computing the corresponding values of the function and using the previous information, we get the graph in Figure 5.33.

$f(x) = x^4 - \frac{11}{3}x^3 - \frac{3}{2}x^2 + 5, \; x \geq 0$

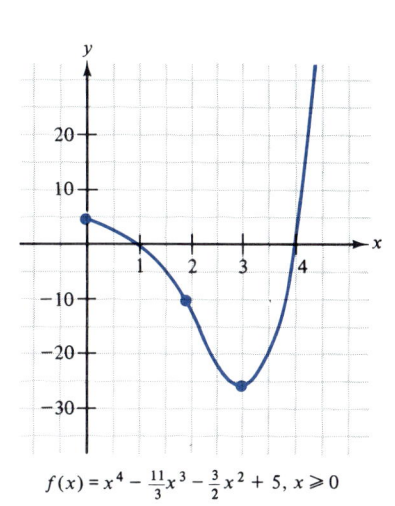

FIGURE 5.33

EXAMPLE 5

Sketch the graph of $f(x) = xe^x$.

■ **SOLUTION**

The y-intercept is 0. Since e^x is never zero, the only x-intercept is 0. The first derivative is

$$f'(x) = xe^x + e^x = e^x(x + 1).$$

Setting this to zero gives $x = -1$. The second derivative is

$$f''(x) = e^x + (x + 1)e^x = e^x(x + 2).$$

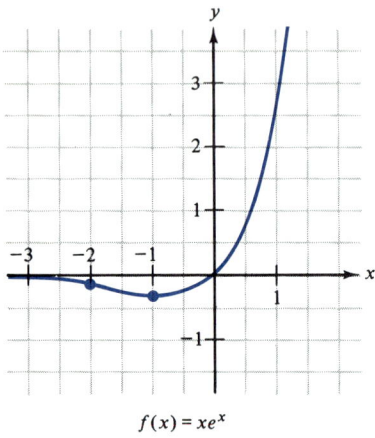

This equals zero at $x = -2$. Hence we get the following table:

	$(-\infty, -2)$	$(-2, -1)$	$(-1, \infty)$
$f'(x)$	−	−	+
$f''(x)$	−	+	+
Characteristics	Decreasing, concave down	Decreasing, concave up	Increasing, concave up

We have a relative minimum at $x = -1$. The relative minimum point is $(-1, -1/e) \approx (-1, -0.4)$. There is an inflection point at $x = -2$. It is $(-2, -2/e^2) \approx (-2, -0.3)$. This gives the graph of Figure 5.34.

FIGURE 5.34 $f(x) = xe^x$

EXERCISE

Sketch the graphs of the following:

(a) $f(x) = \dfrac{x^2}{x+2}$; (b) $f(x) = x^3 - 3x + 2$;

(c) $f(x) = \dfrac{x^4}{2} - \dfrac{5x^3}{3} - 6x^2 + 27$, $x \geq 0$; and (d) $f(x) = xe^{-x}$.

■ ANSWER
See Figure 5.35.

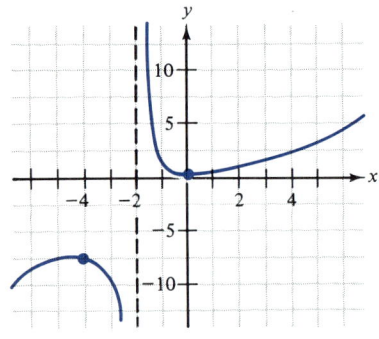

(a) $f(x) = \dfrac{x^2}{x+2}$

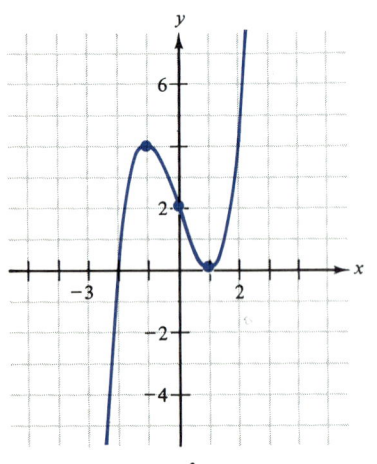

(b) $f(x) = x^3 - 3x + 2$

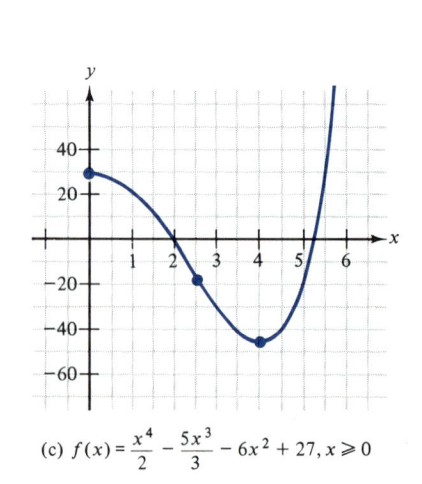

(c) $f(x) = \dfrac{x^4}{2} - \dfrac{5x^3}{3} - 6x^2 + 27$, $x \geq 0$

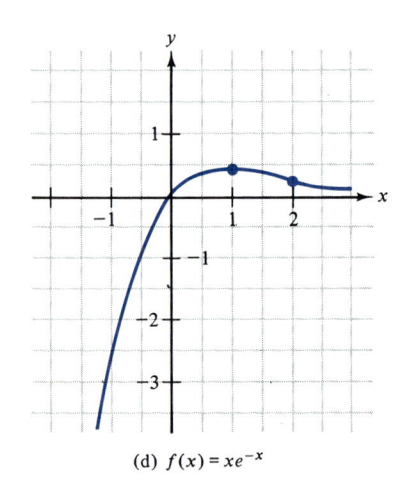

(d) $f(x) = xe^{-x}$

FIGURE 5.35

PROBLEM SET 5.5

In Problems 1–10, determine the vertical asymptotes.

1. $y = \dfrac{x}{x+4}$
2. $y = \dfrac{x}{x-5}$
3. $y = \dfrac{e^x}{e^x - 7}$
4. $y = \dfrac{\ln x}{2 + \ln x}$
5. $y = \dfrac{x^2}{x^3 - 4x}$
6. $y = \dfrac{x-1}{x^3 - x}$
7. $y = \dfrac{3x^2 - 10x + 3}{(x+3)(4x - \ln 3)}$
8. $y = \dfrac{4x^2 - 3x - 7}{(2x + \pi)(x - e)}$
9. $y = \dfrac{x^3 - 5x^2 - 6x}{\sqrt{2}(x+1)}$
10. $y = \dfrac{x^4 - 49x^2}{x(x+7)}$

In Problems 11–18, determine the horizontal asymptote (if any).

11. $y = \dfrac{x^3}{(x+2)(x-3)}$
12. $y = \dfrac{3x^5 - 1}{x^2(x-7)}$
13. $y = \dfrac{x^4 - 3}{x(x^2+1)^2}$
14. $y = \dfrac{3x^3 + 2x^2}{x^3(x^2 - 5)}$
15. $y = \dfrac{(x+1)(x-2)}{(2x-8)(x+5)}$
16. $y = \dfrac{(4x-1)(3x+2)}{(2x+5)(1-3x)}$
17. $y = \dfrac{(x+2)(x^2+1)(x^2-1)}{(\sqrt{2}x - 1)^2(\sqrt[3]{5}x + 1)^3}$
18. $y = \dfrac{(x^2+4)^3(x-3)^4 - 7x^9}{9x^{11}}$

In Problems 19 and 20, determine the vertical and horizontal asymptotes.

19. $y = \dfrac{x^3 + x^2 - x}{x(6x^2 - x - 12)}$
20. $y = \dfrac{6x^2 - x^2(x+3)}{x^3 + 2x^2 - 9x - 18}$

21. Construct a rational function that has vertical asymptotes of $x = -1$ and $x = 3$, and a horizontal asymptote of $y = 2$.

22. Construct a rational function that has vertical asymptotes of $x = -2$, $x = 1$, and $x = 4$, and a horizontal asymptote of $y = -3$.

In Problems 23–50, sketch the graph.

23. $y = \dfrac{x^2 + 1}{x}$
24. $y = \dfrac{x^2}{x+1}$
25. $y = \dfrac{e^x}{x+1}$
26. $y = \dfrac{e^x}{x}$
27. $y = \dfrac{x}{(x+1)^2}$
28. $y = \dfrac{2x}{x^2 + 4}$
29. $y = \dfrac{1}{1+x^2}$
30. $y = \dfrac{1}{1+x^3}$
31. $y = x^2 + \dfrac{1}{x^2}$
32. $y = x^2 + \dfrac{2}{x}$
33. $y = \dfrac{1 - x^2}{x^2 - 9}$
34. $y = \dfrac{x^2 - 4}{x^2 - 1}$
35. $y = x^3 - 3x^2 + 5$
36. $y = x^3 + 3x^2 - 3$
37. $y = x^3 - 6x^2 + 9x - 2$
38. $y = \dfrac{x^3}{3} - x^2 - 3x + 5$
39. $y = \dfrac{-x^3}{3} + x$
40. $y = -x^3 + 12x$
41. $y = -3x^4 + 4x^3$
42. $y = \dfrac{x^4}{4} - x^3$
43. $y = \ln(4 - x^2)$
44. $y = -\ln(9 - x^2)$
45. $y = x^2 e^x$
46. $y = x^2 e^{-x}$
47. $y = x \ln x$
48. $y = \dfrac{\ln x}{x}$
49. $y = xe^{-x^2}$
50. $y = e^{-x^2/2}$

51. Choose the equation that best describes the given graph.

(a) $y = \dfrac{3x^2(x-2)}{(x+3)(x-5)}$
(b) $y = \dfrac{3x(x-2)}{(x-3)(x+5)}$
(c) $y = \dfrac{3x(x-2)}{(x+3)(x-5)}$
(d) $y = \dfrac{3x(x-2)^2}{(x+3)(x-5)}$
(e) $y = \dfrac{3x(x-2)}{(x+3)(x-5)^2}$

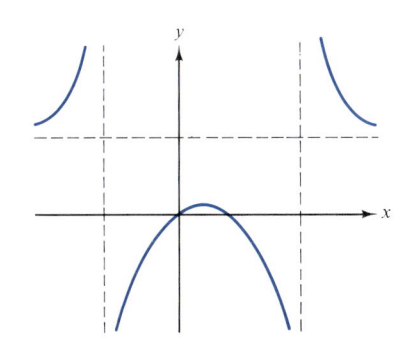

5.6 ABSOLUTE EXTREME POINTS

In Section 5.2 we focused on *relative* extreme points. Such points are *locally* the highest or lowest points. In Figure 5.36 we see that (2,3) and (5,6) are relative maximum points, and (3,1) is a relative minimum point.

Of the two relative maximum points, (5,6) is the highest point on the interval $(0, \infty)$. But there is no lowest point on $(0, \infty)$. In this section we're interested in finding such *absolute* highest points and lowest points on an interval. We need the following definitions.

Let f be a function defined on an interval I, and let $c \in I$. Then we say that f has an **absolute maximum on I at $x = c$** provided that $f(c) \geq f(x)$ for all $x \in I$. Geometrically, this means that on the interval I, $(c, f(c))$ is the highest point.

If f has an absolute maximum on I at $x = c$, then the corresponding value $f(c)$ is called the **absolute maximum on I,** and the point $(c, f(c))$ is called an **absolute maximum point on I.**

So in Figure 5.36 we see that the function has an absolute maximum on $(0, \infty)$ at $x = 5$. The absolute maximum is 6, and (5,6) is the absolute maximum point.

Analogous definitions are made for **absolute minimum on I at $x = c$, absolute minimum on I,** and **absolute minimum point on I.** Referring again to Figure 5.36 we find that there is no absolute minimum point on $(0, \infty)$. But on the interval (2,4), the point (3,1) is an absolute minimum point. See Figure 5.37.

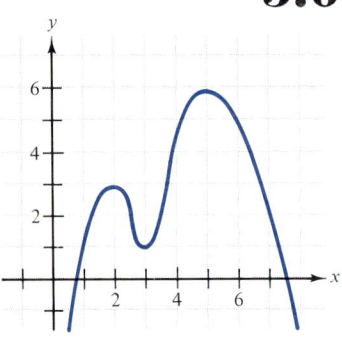

FIGURE 5.36

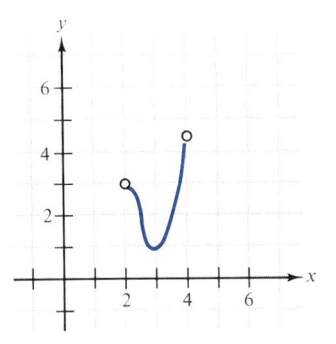

FIGURE 5.37

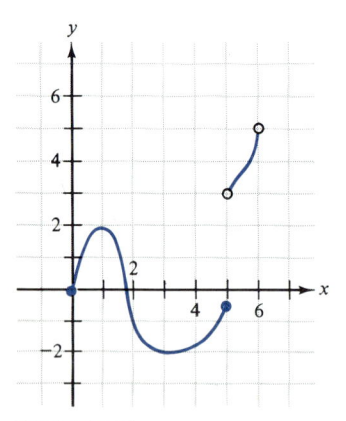

FIGURE 5.38

EXERCISE

Determine the absolute extreme points of the function graphed in Figure 5.38 on the the specified interval: (a) [0,5], (b) [0,6), and (c) (5,6).

■ *ANSWER*
(a) Absolute minimum point is $(3, -2)$; absolute maximum point is (1,2).
(b) Absolute minimum point is $(3, -2)$; no absolute maximum point.
(c) No absolute extreme points.

To determine the absolute extreme points on an interval we must find the relative extreme points. But this isn't enough. As we have seen, the relative extremes may not be absolute. To determine whether a relative is also absolute, let's consider the following question: How can we graph a function on an open interval (a,b) such that a relative maximum point $(c, f(c))$ is *not* absolute? One thing we could do would be to insert a relative minimum point. Its graph might appear like that in Figure 5.39. There is a relative maximum at $x = c$, but it isn't absolute.

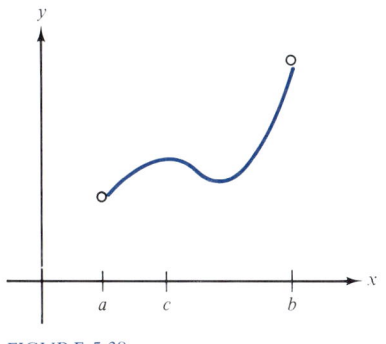

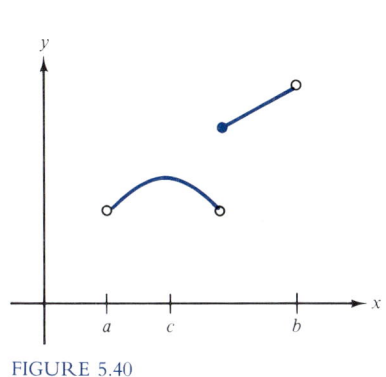

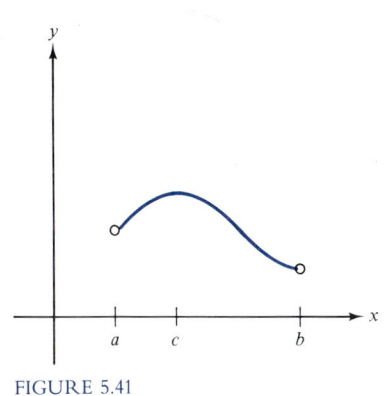

FIGURE 5.39

FIGURE 5.40

FIGURE 5.41

If the function must have no relative minimums, however, we must insert a point of discontinuity. The graph might appear like that of Figure 5.40. Again, there is a relative maximum at $x = c$, but it isn't absolute.

What if the function must have no relative minimums and must be continuous? Then there is no way to prevent the relative maximum from also being absolute. See Figure 5.41. This forms the basis of the next theorem.

THEOREM 5.10 Let f be a continuous function defined on an interval I, and let $c \in I$.

(i) If f has a relative maximum at $x = c$ and there is no relative minimum at an interior point, then f has an absolute maximum on I at $x = c$.
(ii) If f has a relative minimum at $x = c$ and there is no relative maximum at an interior point, then f has an absolute minimum on I at $x = c$.

Let's see how this theorem is used.

EXAMPLE 1

Determine the absolute extreme points of $f(x) = x^3 - 3x^2 - 2$ on $(1, 4)$.

■ SOLUTION

We proceed to determine the relative extreme points. We have

$$f'(x) = 3x^2 - 6x.$$

To find the critical values we set $f'(x) = 0$. We have

$$3x^2 - 6x = 0$$

$$3x(x - 2) = 0$$

$$x = 0 \quad \text{or} \quad x = 2.$$

Of course, 0 isn't in the interval so it needn't be considered. To test the critical value $x = 2$, let's use the second derivative test.

$$f''(x) = 6x - 6,$$

$$f''(2) = 12 - 6 > 0 \quad \Rightarrow \text{ graph is concave up.}$$

Thus f has a relative minimum at $x = 2$. Because f is continuous (it's a polynomial function), and there are no relative maximums on $(1,4)$, f has an absolute minimum at $x = 2$. Since $f(2) = -6$, the absolute minimum point is $(2, -6)$, which is the only extreme point on the interval.

EXERCISE

Determine the absolute extreme points of $f(x) = 2x^3 + 5x^2 - 4x + 7$ on $(-4, -1)$.

■ ANSWER
Absolute maximum point is $(-2, 19)$; no absolute minimum point.

EXAMPLE 2

Determine the absolute maximum point of $y = x^2 e^x$ on $(-\infty, -1]$.

■ SOLUTION
Differentiation gives

$$y' = x^2 e^x + e^x \cdot 2x = xe^x(x + 2).$$

The critical values are 0, -2, and the endpoint -1, but 0 isn't in the interval. To test $x = -2$, let's use the first derivative test. Choosing $x_1 = -5$ and $x_2 = -\frac{3}{2}$ we get

$$y'\Big|_{x=-5} = -5e^{-5}(-3) > 0 \quad \Rightarrow y \text{ is increasing;}$$

$$y'\Big|_{x=-\frac{3}{2}} = -\frac{3}{2}e^{-3/2}(\frac{1}{2}) < 0 \quad \Rightarrow y \text{ is decreasing.}$$

Therefore y has a relative maximum at $x = -2$. Since the function is continuous, and there are no relative minimums in the interior, $(-\infty, -1)$, it is also absolute. Because $y = 4/e^2$ when $x = -2$, $(-2, 4/e^2)$ is the absolute maximum point on $(-\infty, -1]$.

EXERCISE

Determine the absolute minimum point of $y = x^3 e^x$ on $(-\infty, -1]$.

■ *ANSWER*
$(-3, -27/e^3)$

EXAMPLE 3

Determine the absolute maximum point of $f(x) = x^3 + x^2 - x + 1$ on $[-2, 0]$.

■ *SOLUTION*
Differentiating we get

$$f'(x) = 3x^2 + 2x - 1.$$

We first find the critical values in the interior:

$$3x^2 + 2x - 1 = 0$$
$$(3x - 1)(x + 1) = 0$$
$$x = \tfrac{1}{3} \quad \text{or} \quad x = -1.$$

The only critical value in the interior is $x = -1$. Let's use the second derivative test:

$$f''(x) = 6x + 2,$$
$$f''(-1) = -6 + 2 < 0 \quad \Rightarrow \quad \text{graph is concave down.}$$

Thus f has a relative maximum at $x = -1$. Because there are no relative minimums in the interior, it is absolute. Since $f(-1) = 2$, $(-1, 2)$ is the absolute maximum point on $[-2, 0]$.

EXERCISE

Determine the absolute minimum point of $f(x) = 4x^3 - 9x^2 - 12x + 10$ on $[0, 3]$.

■ *ANSWER*
$(2, -18)$

In general, a continuous function doesn't have to have an absolute maximum or absolute minimum on an interval *I*. However, if the interval is of the type [*a*,*b*] (which is closed and bounded), then there *must* be an absolute maximum as well as an absolute minimum. This is because we may draw the graph of such a function by starting at (*a*,*f*(*a*)) and proceeding to (*b*,*f*(*b*)) without lifting the pencil in between. It is intuitively clear that there must be a highest point and a lowest point. This observation is precisely stated in the following theorem.

THEOREM 5.11 Let *f* be a continuous function defined on [*a*,*b*]. Then *f* has an absolute maximum and an absolute minimum on [*a*,*b*].

If we *know* that the absolutes exist, we merely need to evaluate the function at the critical values. We don't have to use the first or second derivative test. The largest value will be the absolute maximum, and the smallest the absolute minimum. Let's return to the function in Example 3, $f(x) = x^3 + x^2 - x + 1$, defined on $[-2,0]$, and evaluate it at the critical values -1, -2, and 0. We have

$$f(-1) = 2,$$
$$f(-2) = -1,$$
$$f(0) = 1.$$

Since 2 is the largest value, $(-1,2)$ is the absolute maximum point. Although the example doesn't require it, let's note that the absolute minimum is -1, the smallest of the three values. So $(-2,-1)$ is the absolute minimum point.

EXAMPLE 4

Determine the absolute extreme points of $y = (x - 1)^{2/3}$ on $[0,4]$.

■ **SOLUTION**
Differentiating we get

$$y' = \frac{2}{3}(x - 1)^{-1/3} = \frac{2}{3\sqrt[3]{x - 1}}.$$

Although y' is never zero, it isn't defined at $x = 1$, which is in $[0,4]$. So $x = 1$ is a critical value. Because the function is continuous, and we are dealing with a closed, bounded interval, we may simply evaluate the function at the critical values: 1, 0, and 4.

$$y\big|_{x=1} = 0.$$
$$y\big|_{x=0} = (-1)^{2/3} = 1,$$
$$y\big|_{x=4} = 3^{2/3} = \sqrt[3]{9} \quad (\approx 2.080).$$

5.6 ABSOLUTE EXTREME POINTS

The largest value is $\sqrt[3]{9}$, and the smallest is 0. So $(4,\sqrt[3]{9})$ is the absolute maximum point, and $(1,0)$ is the absolute minimum point.

EXERCISE

Determine the absolute extreme points of $y = (x + 1)^{4/5}$ on $[-3,0]$.

■ ANSWER
$(-1,0)$ is the absolute minimum point; $(-3,\sqrt[5]{16})$ is the absolute maximum point.

EXAMPLE 5

The population density P of bacteria in a culture at temperature t is

$$P = \frac{-1}{8} t^{4/3} + 150t + 3,$$

where $27 \leq t \leq 64$. What is the largest population density in the temperature range?

■ SOLUTION
Differentiation gives

$$\frac{dP}{dt} = \frac{-1}{6} t^{1/3} + 150.$$

Setting this to zero gives

$$\frac{-1}{6} t^{1/3} + 150 = 0$$

$$-t^{1/3} + 900 = 0$$

$$t^{1/3} = 900$$

$$t = 900^3.$$

This value is rejected because it isn't in $[27,64]$. So the only critical values are the endpoints: 27 and 64. Because we have a continuous function and a closed, bounded interval, we may simply evaluate the endpoints:

$$P\Big|_{t=27} = \frac{-1}{8} \cdot 3^4 + 150(27) + 3 = 4042\tfrac{7}{8},$$

$$P\Big|_{t=64} = \frac{-1}{8} \cdot 4^4 + 150(64) + 3 = 9571.$$

So the maximum density is $P = 9571$.

EXERCISE

The population density P of bacteria in a culture at temperature t is

$$P = \frac{-1}{2} t^{3/2} + 125t + 10,$$

where $16 \leq t \leq 49$. What is the largest population density (to the nearest ten) in this temperature range?

■ ANSWER
5960

PROBLEM SET 5.6

In Problems 1–4, determine the absolute extreme points of each function graphed on the specified interval.

1. (a) $[-2,1]$;
   (b) $(1,4]$;
   (c) $(4,7)$.

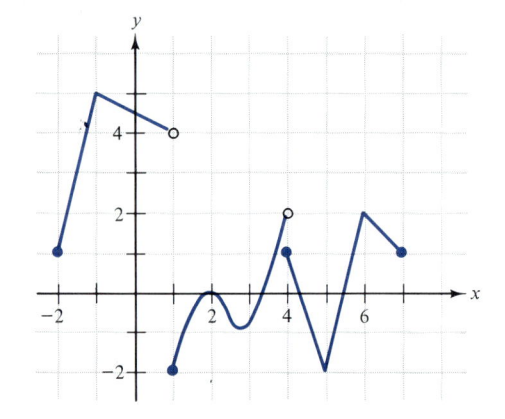

2. (a) $[-4,-1)$;
   (b) $[-1,3]$;
   (c) $(3,5)$.

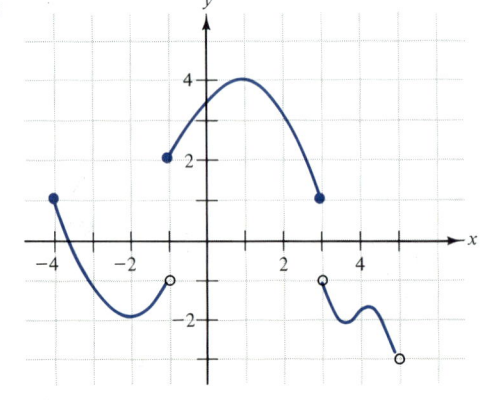

3. (a) $[0,2]$;
   (b) $(2,4]$;
   (c) $(5,7)$.

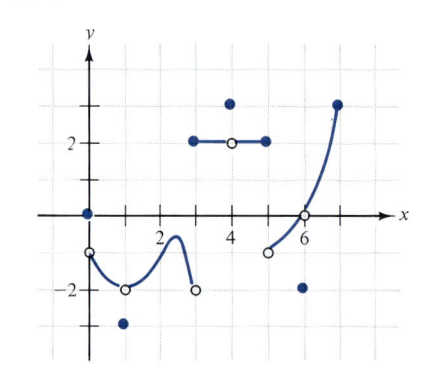

4. (a) $[-7,-5]$;
   (b) $(-5,-3]$;
   (c) $(-2,0)$.

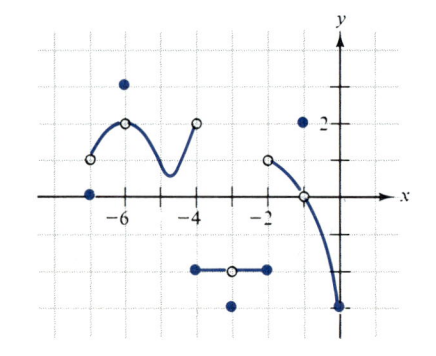

In Problems 5–14, determine the absolute extreme points of f on the given interval.

5. $f(x) = -x^3 + 3x^2$ on $(-2,1)$
6. $f(x) = x^3 - 6x^2 + 9x$ on $(0, \frac{3}{2})$
7. $f(x) = \frac{4}{3}x^3 + 2x^2 - 15x$ on $(-10, -1)$
8. $f(x) = x(1-x)^2$ on $(\frac{1}{2}, 6)$
9. $y = x^2 e^x$ on $[-5, -\frac{1}{2})$
10. $y = x^2 e^{-x/4}$ on $(-2, 7]$
11. $y = 4x^3 - 3x^4$ on $(-1, \infty)$
12. $y = 3 + 10x - 2x^5$ on $(-\infty, 0)$
13. $y = \dfrac{1 + \ln(x-2)}{2 - x}$ on $(2, \infty)$
14. $y = \dfrac{1 + \ln(x+1)}{x + 1}$ on $(-1, \infty)$

15. Find the absolute minimum point of $y = x\sqrt{x+4}$ on $[-3, \infty)$.
16. Find the absolute maximum point of $y = 12/(x^2 + 4)$ on $(-\infty, 5]$.

In Problems 17–28, determine the absolute extreme points of f on the given closed and bounded interval.

17. $f(x) = 7x - 3$ on $[-\pi, \pi]$
18. $f(x) = x^2 - 4x - 5$ on $[0, 6]$
19. $y = e^x + e^{-x}$ on $[-\ln 4, -\ln 2]$
20. $y = e^x - e^{-x}$ on $[-\ln 3, \ln 3]$
21. $f(x) = 3x^4 - 4x^3 - 12x^2$ on $[-2, 3]$
22. $f(x) = (x^2 - 4)^2$ on $[-3, 3]$
23. $f(x) = 1 + (x - 3)^{2/3}$ on $[1, 5]$
24. $f(x) = x/(x - 2)$ on $[-4, 0]$
25. $f(x) = (x^2 + 9)/x$ on $[0.5, 18]$
26. $f(x) = 1/(1 + x^3)$ on $[-\frac{1}{2}, 3]$
27. $y = (\ln x)^2/x$ on $[e, e^4]$
28. $y = (2/x) + \ln x$ on $[e^{-1}, e^2]$

29. Determine the absolute minimum point of $y = x^x$ on $(0, \infty)$.
30. Show that the sum of any positive number and its reciprocal is greater than or equal to 2. [*Hint*: Find the absolute minimum of the function $f(x) = x + (1/x)$ on $(0, \infty)$.]

5.7 MAXIMUM–MINIMUM PROBLEMS

In this section we encounter applied problems in which we must locate extreme points. The problems are identical to those of the preceding section with an important exception: we must determine the function as well as the interval. Before outlining the steps to be followed, let's illustrate the procedure.

Suppose that a long rectangular sheet of metal 10 inches wide is to be bent into a rain gutter by turning up the sides at right angles. What should the height be to maximize the cross-sectional area, and what is the greatest cross-sectional area?

We have infinitely many choices for the height, and they don't all give the same cross-sectional area. In Figure 5.42 we see three different heights that yield three different areas. Our job is to determine the height that makes the cross-sectional area as large as possible.

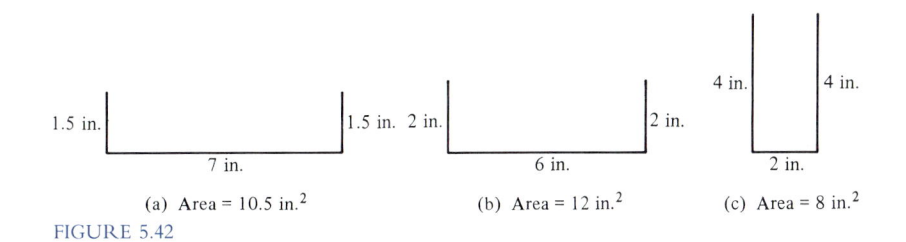

(a) Area = 10.5 in.²   (b) Area = 12 in.²   (c) Area = 8 in.²

FIGURE 5.42

The cross-sectional area is found by multiplying its dimensions; that is,

$$\text{cross-sectional area} = \text{width} \times \text{height}. \tag{5-1}$$

So let's define the following variables:

A = cross-sectional area (in square inches),

w = width (in inches),

h = height (in inches).

With these variables we are able to translate statement (5-1) into an algebraic equation. We have

$$A = wh. \tag{5-2}$$

So A, the quantity to be maximized, is written as a function of *two* variables, w and h. Because we have studied functions of a single variable only, we must substitute for w or h. We search for information that will connect the variables w and h. Because the piece of metal is 10 inches wide,

$$2h + w = 10.$$

Solving this equation for w yields

$$w = 10 - 2h.$$

Returning to Equation (5-2) and replacing w with $10 - 2h$, we get

$$A = (10 - 2h)h = 10h - 2h^2.$$

We have now written the quantity to be maximized as a function of one variable. Our next job is to note any restrictions on this variable. Certainly, h must be positive. (We must bend up something to get the rectangle.) Furthermore, it must be less than 5. (If we bend up 5 we have no rectangle because the width is 0.) Thus $0 < h < 5$. Consequently, the problem is to find the absolute maximum of

$$A = 10h - 2h^2$$

on (0,5). Getting to this stage is the most difficult part. From here on the problem is identical to those of Section 5.6. Differentiating we get

$$\frac{dA}{dh} = 10 - 4h.$$

The only critical value is $h = 2.5$. Let's test it with the second derivative test:

$$\frac{d^2A}{dh^2} = -4,$$

$$\left.\frac{d^2A}{dh^2}\right|_{h=2.5} < 0 \Rightarrow \text{graph is concave down.}$$

So A has a relative maximum at $h = 2.5$. Because A is continuous and has no relative minimum on (0,5), this maximum is absolute (Theorem 5.10). Therefore the cross-sectional area is maximized with a height of

2.5 inches. Since
$$A\Big|_{h=2.5} = 10(2.5) - 2(2.5)^2 = 12.5,$$
the maximum cross-sectional area is 12.5 square inches.

As an aid to solving applied maximum–minimum problems, let's outline the steps we took in the illustration.

1. Identify the quantity to be maximized or minimized and express it in terms of other relevant quantities.
2. Define the necessary variables.
3. Translate the statement of step 1 into an equation.
4. If necessary, substitute so that the quantity to be maximized or minimized is a function of one variable.
5. Note the permissible values of the independent variable.
6. Locate the desired absolute extreme point.
7. Answer the question.

It is essential that you *understand the problem*. Read the problem as many times as necessary to comprehend the information given and requested. Draw a diagram if necessary. Then proceed to step 1.

In step 1, write the function in English. This will tell you exactly which variables need to be defined in step 2. And when this statement is translated into an equation in step 3, we should be able to identify what each term (or group of terms) represents in the problem.

If the variables introduced in step 2 represent measurable quantities (like distance, area, or time), identify the units of measurement.

Step 4 is frequently the most difficult. Generally, the function is in terms of two variables, and you must find and translate a statement connecting the two. Upon doing so, solve this equation (called the **constraint equation**) for one of the variables and then substitute in the formula for the quantity to be maximized or minimized.

In most problems there is some natural interval on which the function is realistic. Step 5 involves finding this interval.

In step 6 determine the value of the independent variable which gives the absolute maximum or minimum.

The final step is simple, but don't overlook it. In the illustration we found the height that maximizes the area and the maximum area. The problem could have asked for the width, or even both dimensions. Just make sure that you supply the requested information.

EXAMPLE 1

A rectangular field along the bank of a river is to be fenced, and no fence is required along the river. The material costs $8 per foot for the two ends and $12 per foot for the side parallel to the river. If $3600 of fence is to be used, what dimensions maximize the area of the field?

■ SOLUTION

We have the situation shown in Figure 5.43.

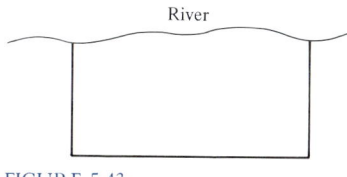

FIGURE 5.43

Step 1. The area of the field is to be maximized, and
$$\text{area} = \text{length} \times \text{width}.$$

Step 2. Let

A = area (in square feet),

x = length, that is, dimension of each end (in feet),

y = width, that is, dimension of side parallel to river (in feet).

Step 3. Thus
$$A = xy. \tag{5-3}$$

Step 4. We need to find an equation that connects x and y. Since $3600 of fence is to be used, with the ends costing $8 per foot and the side costing $12 per foot,
$$8x + 8x + 12y = 3600.$$

We must solve this equation for either x or y. Solving for y gives
$$y = \frac{3600 - 16x}{12} = \frac{900 - 4x}{3}. \tag{5-4}$$

Substituting for y in Equation (5-3) gives
$$A = x\left(\frac{900 - 4x}{3}\right)$$
$$= \frac{900x - 4x^2}{3}$$
$$= 300x - \tfrac{4}{3}x^2.$$

Step 5. Of course, x must be positive. Furthermore, each end must cost less than $1800, so $x < 1800/8 = 225$.

Step 6. We must locate the absolute maximum of A on $(0, 225)$. Differentiation gives
$$\frac{dA}{dx} = 300 - \frac{8}{3}x.$$

Setting this to zero and solving for x, we obtain
$$300 - \frac{8x}{3} = 0$$
$$900 - 8x = 0$$
$$-8x = -900$$
$$x = 112.5.$$

This is the only critical value. We use the second derivative test to test it. We get

$$\frac{d^2A}{dx^2} = \frac{-8}{3},$$

$$\left.\frac{d^2A}{dx^2}\right|_{x=112.5} < 0 \quad \Rightarrow \quad \text{graph is concave down.}$$

Thus A has a relative maximum at $x = 112.5$. Since there are no relative minimums, it is absolute.

Step 7. The problem asked for both dimensions. Using Equation (5-4) we get

$$\left. y \right|_{x=112.5} = \frac{900 - 4(112.5)}{3} = 150.$$

So each end must be 112.5 feet, and the side parallel to the river must be 150 feet.

EXAMPLE 2

A rectangular box, open at the top and with a square base, is to have a volume of 4000 cubic inches. What dimensions minimize the surface area?

■ SOLUTION

The surface area is to be minimized, and

surface area = area of four sides + area of square base
            = 4 × base dimension × height + base dimension squared.

So let

S = surface area (in square inches),

x = dimension of square base (in inches),

h = height of box (in inches).

See Figure 5.44. Thus

$$S = 4xh + x^2. \tag{5-5}$$

Since the volume must be 4000, we have

$$x^2 h = 4000.$$

Solving for h gives

$$h = \frac{4000}{x^2}. \tag{5-6}$$

Substitution into Equation (5-5) gives us

$$S = \frac{16{,}000}{x} + x^2 = 16{,}000 x^{-1} + x^2.$$

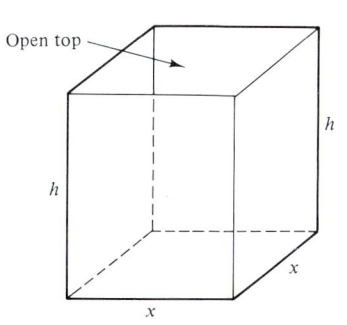

FIGURE 5.44

Since $x > 0$, we must locate the absolute minimum of S on $(0,\infty)$. Differentiation gives

$$\frac{dS}{dx} = -16{,}000x^{-2} + 2x = \frac{-16{,}000}{x^2} + 2x.$$

Setting this to zero and solving for x, we obtain

$$\frac{-16{,}000}{x^2} + 2x = 0$$

$$-16{,}000 + 2x^3 = 0$$

$$2x^3 = 16{,}000$$

$$x^3 = 8000$$

$$x = 20.$$

The only critical value is $x = 20$. Let's test it with the second derivative test. We have

$$\frac{d^2S}{dx^2} = 32{,}000x^{-3} + 2 = \frac{32{,}000}{x^3} + 2,$$

$$\left.\frac{d^2S}{dx^2}\right|_{x=20} > 0 \;\;\Rightarrow\;\; \text{graph is concave up.}$$

Thus S has a relative minimum at $x = 20$. Since there are no relative maximums, it is absolute. From Equation (5-6) we see that

$$\left.h\right|_{x=20} = \frac{4000}{20^2} = 10.$$

So the dimensions are 20 inches for the square base and 10 inches for the height.

EXAMPLE 3

In water, the product of the concentration of hydrogen ions, $[H^+]$, and the concentration of hydroxyl ions, $[H^-]$, remains nearly constant at 10^{-14} mole. Find the ratio $[H^+]/[H^-]$ that minimizes the sum of $[H^+]$ and $[H^-]$.

■ SOLUTION
Let

$S = $ sum of concentrations (in moles),

$x = $ hydrogen ion concentration, $[H^+]$ (in moles),

$y = $ hydroxyl ion concentration, $[H^-]$ (in moles).

Hence we must minimize

$$S = x + y.$$

Since the product of the concentrations is constant at 10^{-14}, we have
$$xy = 10^{-14}$$
$$y = \frac{10^{-14}}{x}.$$

So we must minimize
$$S = x + \frac{10^{-14}}{x}$$

on $(0,\infty)$, Differentiation gives
$$\frac{dS}{dx} = 1 - 10^{-14}x^{-2} = 1 - \frac{10^{-14}}{x^2}.$$

Setting this to zero and solving for x we get
$$1 - \frac{10^{-14}}{x^2} = 0$$
$$x^2 = 10^{-14}$$
$$x = 10^{-7}.$$

Since
$$\frac{d^2S}{dx^2} = 2 \cdot 10^{-14} x^{-3} = \frac{2 \cdot 10^{-14}}{x^3} > 0$$

for all $x > 0$, there is a minimum at $x = 10^{-7}$. Because there are no relative maximums, it is absolute. Further,
$$y = \frac{10^{-14}}{10^{-7}} = 10^{-7}.$$

Hence, the ratio is
$$\frac{[H^+]}{[H^-]} = \frac{x}{y} = \frac{10^{-7}}{10^{-7}} = 1.$$

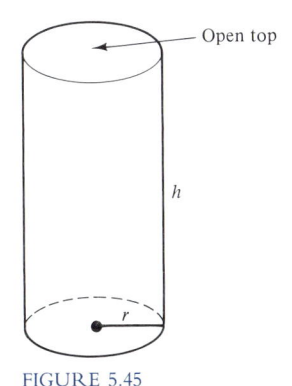

EXAMPLE 4

A right circular cylinder (Figure 5.45) with an open top has a capacity of 24π cubic inches. The cost of the material for the bottom is $\frac{3}{4}$¢ per square inch, and the cost of the side material is $\frac{1}{4}$¢ per square inch. What radius minimizes the total cost?

■ SOLUTION
The total cost is to be minimized, and

$$\text{total cost} = \text{cost of the side} + \text{cost of the bottom}$$
$$= \tfrac{1}{4} \times \text{area of side} + \tfrac{3}{4} \times \text{area of bottom}.$$

FIGURE 5.45

So let

$$C = \text{total cost (in cents)},$$
$$r = \text{radius (in inches)},$$
$$h = \text{height (in inches)}.$$

The area of the side is $2\pi rh$, and its cost is

$$(0.25)2\pi rh.$$

The area of the bottom is πr^2, so its cost is

$$(0.75)\pi r^2.$$

Thus the total cost is

$$C = (0.25)2\pi rh + (0.75)\pi r^2. \tag{5-7}$$

Since the volume is 24π cubic inches, we have

$$\pi r^2 h = 24\pi.$$

Solving for h gives

$$h = \frac{24}{r^2}.$$

Substitution into Equation (5-7) gives

$$C = (0.25)2\pi r \cdot \frac{24}{r^2} + (0.75)\pi r^2$$
$$= \frac{12\pi}{r} + (0.75)\pi r^2.$$

Since $r > 0$, we must locate the absolute minimum on $(0, \infty)$. Differentiating we get

$$\frac{dC}{dr} = \frac{-12\pi}{r^2} + 1.5\pi r. \tag{5-8}$$

Setting Equation (5-8) equal to zero and solving for r we get

$$\frac{-12\pi}{r^2} + 1.5\pi r = 0$$
$$-12\pi + 1.5\pi r^3 = 0$$
$$1.5\pi r^3 = 12\pi$$
$$r^3 = 8$$
$$r = 2.$$

5.7 MAXIMUM–MINIMUM PROBLEMS   255

Test this critical value with the second derivative test:

$$\frac{d^2C}{dr^2} = \frac{24\pi}{r^3} + 1.5\pi,$$

$$\left.\frac{d^2C}{dr^2}\right|_{r=2} > 0 \;\Rightarrow\; \text{graph is concave up.}$$

Thus C has a relative minimum, which is also absolute, at $r = 2$. Hence the cost is minimized with a radius of 2 inches.

EXAMPLE 5

A page of a book is to have an area of 96 square inches. If it must have a 1-inch margin at the top and $\frac{1}{2}$-inch margins at the bottom and sides, what should the dimensions be in order to maximize the area of the printed section?

■ SOLUTION

Let's begin with the diagram in Figure 5.46. The area of the printed section is to be maximized, and

area of printed section
= length of printed section × width of printed section.

So let

A = area of printed section (in square inches),

l = length of printed section (in inches),

w = width of printed section (in inches).

Thus

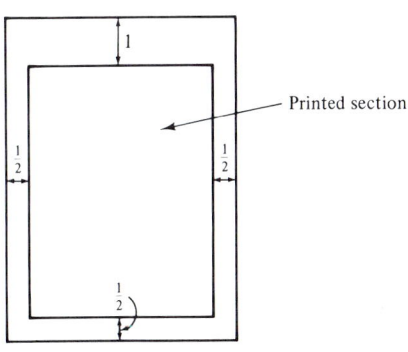

$$A = lw. \qquad (5\text{-}9)$$

FIGURE 5.46

The length of the entire page is l plus the top and bottom margins; that is, $l + \frac{3}{2}$. The width of the entire page is w plus the side margins; that is, $w + 1$. Because the area of the entire page is 96 square inches, we have

$$(l + \tfrac{3}{2})(w + 1) = 96.$$

Solving this for l we get

$$l + \frac{3}{2} = \frac{96}{w+1}$$

$$l = \frac{96}{w+1} - \frac{3}{2}. \tag{5-10}$$

Substitution into Equation (5-9) gives

$$A = \left(\frac{96}{w+1} - \frac{3}{2}\right)w$$

$$= \frac{96w}{w+1} - \frac{3}{2}w.$$

Since $w > 1$ (each side margin is $\frac{1}{2}$ inch), we must locate the absolute maximum of A on $(1, \infty)$. Differentiating we get

$$\frac{dA}{dw} = \frac{(w+1)96 - 96w}{(w+1)^2} - \frac{3}{2}$$

$$= \frac{96}{(w+1)^2} - \frac{3}{2}. \tag{5-11}$$

Setting Equation (5-11) equal to zero and solving for w, we obtain

$$\frac{96}{(w+1)^2} - \frac{3}{2} = 0$$

$$192 - 3(w+1)^2 = 0$$

$$-3(w+1)^2 = -192$$

$$(w+1)^2 = 64$$

$$w + 1 = \pm 8$$

$$w = 7 \quad \text{or} \quad w = -9.$$

Of course, we may exclude the negative value. The only critical value to test is $w = 7$. With the second derivative test we get

$$\frac{d^2A}{dw^2} = \frac{-192}{(w+1)^3},$$

$$\left.\frac{d^2A}{dw^2}\right|_{w=7} < 0 \;\Rightarrow\; \text{graph is concave down.}$$

Thus A has a relative maximum, which is also absolute, at $w = 7$. From Equation (5-10) we get

$$l\Big|_{w=7} = \frac{96}{8} - \frac{3}{2} = \frac{21}{2}.$$

But w and l are the dimensions of the *printed section*. The width of the page is 8 inches, and the length is 12 inches.

■

EXAMPLE 6

A man in a canoe 1 mile from the nearest point P on the shore wishes to go to a point Q 10 miles from P along the straight shoreline. The man can row 3 mph and upon reaching the shore can walk 5 mph. At what point should the man land so as to reach Q in the least amount of time?

■ SOLUTION

We have the situation shown in Figure 5.47. We have let R represent the initial position of the man and S represent the landing site.

We are trying to minimize the time required to go from R to Q. This time is in two parts:

time from R to Q = time from R to S + time from S to Q.

Because

$$\text{time} = \frac{\text{distance}}{\text{rate}}$$

and we know the rates, let

x = distance from R to S (in miles),

y = distance from S to Q (in miles).

In addition, let

T = time from R to Q (in hours).

Therefore

$$T = \frac{x}{3} + \frac{y}{5}. \qquad (5\text{-}12)$$

We must substitute for either x or y, so we are looking for a connection between the two. Note that since $SQ = y$ and $PQ = 10$,

$$PS = 10 - y.$$

By the Pythagorean theorem (using $\triangle RPS$),

$$(10 - y)^2 + 1^2 = x^2.$$

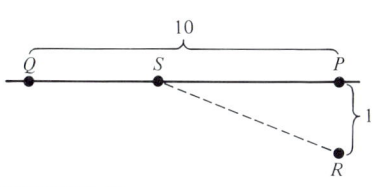

FIGURE 5.47

APPLICATIONS OF THE DERIVATIVE

Solving for x gives

$$x = \sqrt{(10-y)^2 + 1},$$
$$= \sqrt{100 - 20y + y^2 + 1},$$
$$= \sqrt{101 - 20y + y^2}.$$

Substitution for x in Equation (5-12) gives

$$T = \frac{\sqrt{101 - 20y + y^2}}{3} + \frac{y}{5}$$
$$= \frac{1}{3}(101 - 20y + y^2)^{1/2} + \frac{y}{5}.$$

Since the landing site may be at any point between (and including) P and Q, $0 \le y \le 10$. We must minimize T on $[0, 10]$.

Differentiation yields

$$\frac{dT}{dy} = \frac{1}{6}(101 - 20y + y^2)^{-1/2}(-20 + 2y) + \frac{1}{5}$$
$$= \frac{-10 + y}{3\sqrt{101 - 20y + y^2}} + \frac{1}{5}.$$

Setting this to zero and solving for y, we obtain

$$\frac{y - 10}{3\sqrt{101 - 20y + y^2}} + \frac{1}{5} = 0$$
$$5(y - 10) + 3\sqrt{101 - 20y + y^2} = 0$$
$$3\sqrt{101 - 20y + y^2} = -5(y - 10)$$
$$9(101 - 20y + y^2) = 25(y^2 - 20y + 100)$$
$$909 - 180y + 9y^2 = 25y^2 - 500y + 2500$$
$$0 = 16y^2 - 320y + 1591.$$

Using the quadratic formula, we get

$$y = \frac{320 \pm \sqrt{(-320)^2 - (4)(16)(1591)}}{32}$$
$$= \frac{320 \pm \sqrt{576}}{32}$$
$$= \frac{320 \pm 24}{32}$$
$$y = \frac{344}{32} = 10\tfrac{3}{4} \quad \text{or} \quad y = \frac{296}{32} = 9\tfrac{1}{4}.$$

The value $10\frac{3}{4}$ can be ignored because it doesn't lie in [0, 10]. Upon verifying that $y = 9\frac{1}{4}$ is a solution of the original equation (since we squared both sides of an equation to get it), we conclude that it is a critical value.

Any other critical values would result from the derivative being undefined. This requires that $101 - 20y + y^2 \leq 0$. But since $101 - 20y + y^2 = x^2$ and $x \geq 1$, this isn't possible. Thus the only critical values are 0, $9\frac{1}{4}$, and 10.

Because we are dealing with an interval of the type $[a,b]$, we must only evaluate the function at 0, $9\frac{1}{4}$, and 10. We get

$$T\Big|_{y=0} = \frac{1}{3}\sqrt{101} \approx 3.350;$$

$$T\Big|_{y=9.25} = \frac{1}{3}\sqrt{1.5625} + \frac{9.25}{5} \approx 2.267;$$

$$T\Big|_{y=10} = \frac{1}{3}\sqrt{1} + 2 \approx 2.333.$$

The absolute minimum occurs when $y = 9.25$. So the man should land 9.25 miles from Q.

PROBLEM SET 5.7

1. Find two positive numbers whose sum is 30 and whose product is a maximum.
2. Determine two numbers x and y so that $x + 3y = 42$ and xy is as large as possible.
3. Find two positive numbers whose sum is 76 such that the product of one number and the cube of the other number is a maximum.
4. Find two positive numbers whose product is 25 such that the sum of their squares is a minimum.
5. What positive number exceeds its cube by the largest amount?
6. Show that of all rectangles having a fixed area K, the square has the smallest perimeter.
7. A farmer wishes to enclose a rectangular field bordering a straight river with 600 yards of fence. The side along the river requires no fence. Determine the dimensions of the field that maximize the area.
8. A rectangular field is to be enclosed by a fence and then divided into two lots by a fence parallel to one of the sides. If the area of the field is 864 square feet, determine the dimensions of the field that minimize the amount of fence required.
9. A rectangular plot of ground is to be enclosed by a fence and then divided into three smaller rectangles with two parallel fences. If each interior fence costs $2.00 per foot and the other fence costs $3.50 per foot, determine the dimensions of the plot of maximum area that can be enclosed with $2310 worth of fence.
10. An open box is made from a 2 foot square piece of tin by cutting equal squares out of the corners and turning up the sides. Find the dimensions of the box of maximum volume.
11. A rectangular box, open at the top, with a square base is to be constructed using 81 square feet of lumber. Determine the dimensions of the box so that the volume will be a maximum.
12. A rectangular box, open at the top, with a square base, has a volume of 8788 cubic inches. Determine the dimensions of the box that minimize the surface area.
13. Determine the area of the largest rectangle with base on the x-axis and with two vertices on the curve $y = e^{-x^2/2}$.

14. A rectangle in the first quadrant has sides on each of the axes and one vertex on the line segment connecting the points (0,4) and (12,0). Determine the dimensions of the rectangle of maximum area.

15. Determine the area of the largest isosceles triangle that can be inscribed in a circle of radius 10 inches.

16. The legs of an isosceles triangle are each $\sqrt{98}$ inches long. Determine the length of the base so that the triangle has maximum area.

17. A window, of perimeter 33 feet, consists of a rectangular piece of glass topped by an equilateral triangular sheet of glass (see figure below). Determine x and y so that the window will admit the maximum amount of light.

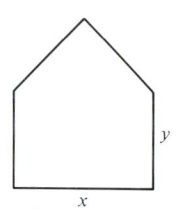

18. A clear rectangular piece of glass is inserted into a colored semicircular glass window (see figure below). The radius of the window is 3 feet. The colored glass admits 50 lumens of light per square foot, and the clear glass passes 100 lumens per square foot. Determine the dimensions of the rectangle so that the maximum amount of light (in lumens) will pass through the entire window.

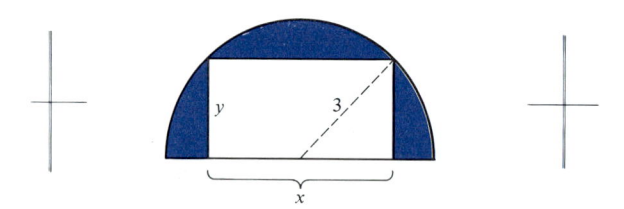

19. Determine the point (x,y), in the first quadrant, on the graph of $xy = 1$ which is closest to the origin.

20. Determine the point (x,y) on the circle $x^2 + y^2 = 4$ which is closest to $(4,0)$.

21. A wire 51 centimeters long is cut into two pieces. One piece is bent into a square and the other into a rectangle whose length is twice its width. How should the wire be cut if the sum of the areas is to be a minimum? A maximum?

22. A box with a square base and a volume of 96 cubic feet is to be constructed. The top is to cost 5 cents per square foot, the bottom 4 cents per square foot, and each side 3 cents per square foot. Find the height of the box that minimizes the cost.

23. The area of the lateral surface of a frustum of a right circular cone is

$$A = \pi(r_1 + r_2)(h^2 + (r_2 - r_1)^2)^{1/2} \quad \text{(see figure below)}.$$

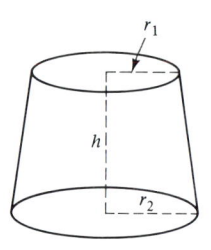

Suppose $h = 2$, $r_2 = 3$, and r_1 is any number in the interval $[0,3]$. Determine the value of r_1 so that the area is a maximum; a minimum.

24. A rectangular field is to be enclosed using an existing 50-foot stone wall plus an additional 100 feet of wire fence (see figure below). Determine the maximum possible area.

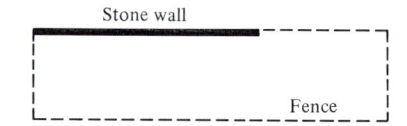

25. A printed page has 3-centimeter margins at the top and bottom and 2-centimeter margins on the sides. The area of the printed portion is 486 square centimeters. Determine the dimensions of the page so that the total area is a minimum. What is the minimum area?

26. The strength of a rectangular beam is proportional to the product of its width and the square of its depth. Determine the dimensions of the strongest rectangular beam that can be cut from a cylindrical log of radius 2 feet.

27. A woman is in a boat 2 miles from the nearest point A on a straight shoreline. She wishes to reach a point

B on the shore 8 miles from A (see figure below). She can row at the rate of 3 mph and walk at the rate of 4 mph. At what point along the shore should she land so as to reach B in the shortest possible time.

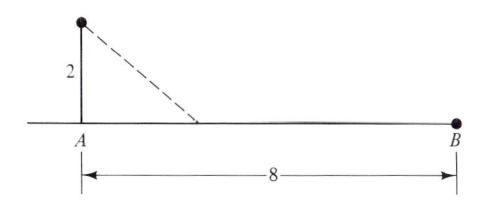

28. Solve Problem 27 if the distance between A and B is 13 miles.
29. Solve Problem 27 if the distance between A and B is 1 mile.
30. Solve Problem 27 if she can row at the rate of 4 mph and walk at the rate of 3 mph.
31. A house at A is in the woods 16 miles north of an east–west road, the nearest point of which is B. At D, 11 miles east of B on the road, is an electric power substation (see figure below). It costs $900 per mile to run a power line through the woods and $300 per mile along the highway. The power line is to be built along the road to a point C part way toward B and then through the woods to A. Find the distance between C and D so that the cost of constructing the power line is a minimum.

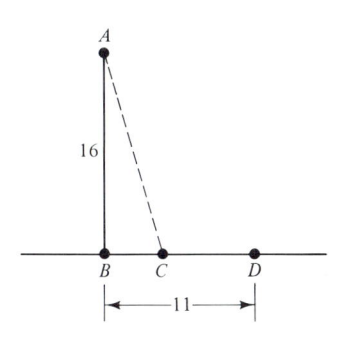

32. Two vertical poles, 20 feet apart and standing on level ground, are 6 feet and 8 feet tall. A cable reaches straight from the top of one pole to some point P on the ground in between and then goes straight to the top of the other pole. Determine the distance between P and the base of the 8-foot pole so that the length of the cable is a minimum.

33. The density d of a population at a distance s from the center of a nonuniform circular town of radius 10 miles is defined by $d = s(10^2 - s^2)$. Determine the value of s for which the population density is a maximum.

34. The specific weight S of water at a temperature t degrees Celsius, where t ranges from 0°C to 100°C, is given by
$$S = (1.4)(10^{-8})t^3 - (6.53)(10^{-6})t^2 + (5.3)(10^{-5})t + 1.$$
Approximate, to the nearest tenth, the value of t so that the water will have maximum specific weight.

35. The velocity V of air through a tube of radius r is given by
$$V = \frac{r^2(r_0 - r)}{\pi ab},$$
where a and b are positive constants and r_0 is the radius of the tube when the pressure is zero. Show that the maximum velocity occurs when $r = \frac{2}{3}r_0$.

36. Find the dimensions of the largest right circular cylinder that can be inscribed in a sphere of radius 15 inches.

37. An apartment complex rents 120 efficiency units. When the rent is $400 per month per unit, the complex is full. If the rent is increased by x dollars per month per unit, the occupancy rate falls to
$$\frac{100{,}000}{100 + \frac{x^2}{2000}} \%.$$
Determine the monthly rent that yields the maximum monthly income.

38. A car rental company has a fleet of 75 cars. When the basic rental charge is $25 per day per car, all cars are rented. If the charge per day per car is increased by x dollars, then
$$\frac{6000}{60 + 0.1x^2} \%$$
of the cars are rented. Determine the daily charge per car which maximizes the daily income.

39. A cylindrical can is to be constructed using sheet metal for the side and bottom and glass for the top. What radius minimizes the total cost if the volume is 32π cubic inches and the glass costs three times as much as the sheet metal?

5.8 BUSINESS APPLICATIONS

In this section we continue our study of maximum–minimum problems, but we concentrate on business applications.

EXAMPLE 1

A manufacturer of vacuum cleaners determines that the weekly revenue R, in dollars, is $R = -0.001x^3 + 0.42x^2 + 18x$, where x is the number of cleaners sold. What output maximizes the weekly revenue?

■ SOLUTION

We want to maximize R on $[0,\infty)$. Differentiation gives

$$\frac{dR}{dx} = -0.003x^2 + 0.84x + 18.$$

We set this to zero to get the critical values:

$$-0.003x^2 + 0.84x + 18 = 0$$
$$3x^2 - 840x - 18{,}000 = 0$$
$$x^2 - 280x - 6000 = 0$$
$$(x - 300)(x + 20) = 0$$
$$x = 300 \quad \text{or} \quad x = -20.$$

The negative value may be rejected because it doesn't lie in $[0,\infty)$. The second derivative test gives us

$$\frac{d^2R}{dx^2} = -0.006x + 0.84,$$

$$\left.\frac{d^2R}{dx^2}\right|_{x=300} = -1.8 + 0.84 < 0 \Rightarrow \text{graph is concave down.}$$

Thus there is a relative maximum at $x = 300$. By Theorem 5.10, it is absolute. Therefore 300 units should be manufactured weekly to maximize revenue.

EXAMPLE 2

A manufacturer determines that the daily cost C, in dollars, of manufacturing and marketing the product is $C = x^3 + 5x^2 + 7x + 30$, where x is the output. If the selling price of the product is $407, how many units should be produced each day to maximize profit?

5.8 BUSINESS APPLICATIONS

■ SOLUTION

We are trying to maximize profit, and

$$\text{profit} = \text{revenue} - \text{cost}.$$

Furthermore, the revenue is the product of the price and number sold. Let

$$P = \text{profit (in dollars)}.$$

Thus

$$P = 407x - C = 407x - (x^3 + 5x^2 + 7x + 30)$$
$$= -x^3 - 5x^2 + 400x - 30,$$

where $x \geq 0$. So we want to maximize P on the interval $[0, \infty)$. Differentiating we get

$$\frac{dP}{dx} = -3x^2 - 10x + 400.$$

Setting this derivative equal to zero gives us the critical values:

$$-3x^2 - 10x + 400 = 0$$
$$3x^2 + 10x - 400 = 0$$
$$(3x + 40)(x - 10) = 0$$
$$x = -\tfrac{40}{3} \quad \text{or} \quad x = 10.$$

Of course, the negative value may be rejected. Using the second derivative test on $x = 10$ we find that

$$\frac{d^2P}{dx^2} = -6x - 10,$$

$$\left.\frac{d^2P}{dx^2}\right|_{x=10} = -60 - 10 < 0 \quad \Rightarrow \quad \text{graph is concave down.}$$

So there is a relative maximum at $x = 10$. By Theorem 5.10, it is absolute. Therefore 10 units should be produced each day to maximize profit.

EXAMPLE 3

The records of a teapot manufacturer indicate that in order to sell x units, the selling price p, in dollars, must be $p = 30 - \sqrt{x}$. What price maximizes revenue?

■ SOLUTION

We are trying to maximize revenue, and

$$\text{revenue} = \text{price} \times \text{number sold}.$$

Letting
$$R = \text{revenue (in dollars)},$$
we have
$$R = px.$$
Substituting for p we get
$$R = (30 - \sqrt{x})x = 30x - x^{3/2}.$$
We must maximize R on $[0, \infty)$. Differentiation gives
$$\frac{dR}{dx} = 30 - \frac{3}{2} x^{1/2},$$
which gives a critical value of $x = 400$. By the second derivative test,
$$\frac{d^2R}{dx^2} = -\frac{3}{4} x^{-1/2} = \frac{-3}{4x^{1/2}},$$
$$\left.\frac{d^2R}{dx^2}\right|_{x=400} < 0 \Rightarrow \text{graph is concave down.}$$

Thus the absolute maximum occurs at $x = 400$. The corresponding price is
$$\left.p\right|_{x=400} = 30 - \sqrt{400} = 10.$$

The maximum revenue is obtained with a selling price of $10.

EXAMPLE 4

A TV manufacturer determines that the demand equation for the product is $p = 450 - x^2$, where p is in dollars. If the total cost C, in dollars, of producing x units is $C = 7.5x^2 + 500$, what price maximizes profit?

■ SOLUTION
We are trying to maximize profit, and
$$\text{profit} = \text{revenue} - \text{cost}.$$
Let
$$P = \text{profit (in dollars)}.$$
Since revenue is price times demand (number sold), we have
$$P = xp - C.$$

5.8 BUSINESS APPLICATIONS

Substitution for p and C gives

$$P = x(450 - x^2) - (7.5x^2 + 500)$$
$$= 450x - x^3 - 7.5x^2 - 500.$$

We must maximize P on $[0, \infty)$. Differentiation gives

$$\frac{dP}{dx} = 450 - 3x^2 - 15x.$$

This gives a critical value of $x = 10$. By the second derivative test,

$$\frac{d^2P}{dx^2} = -6x - 15,$$

$$\left.\frac{d^2P}{dx^2}\right|_{x=10} = -60 - 15 < 0 \;\Rightarrow\; \text{graph is concave down.}$$

Thus the absolute maximum occurs at $x = 10$. The corresponding price is

$$\left. p \right|_{x=10} = 450 - 100 = 350.$$

The maximum profit is obtained with a selling price of $350.

EXAMPLE 5

Until recently hot dogs at a basketball arena sold for $1 each. At that price an average of 10,000 were sold on game nights. When the price was increased to $1.20, the average number sold decreased to 8000. The total cost, in dollars, is $C = 1000 + 0.3x$, where x represents the number sold. If the demand equation is linear, what price maximizes the nightly hot dog profit?

■ SOLUTION
We have

$$\text{profit} = \text{revenue} - \text{cost}.$$

Let

$$P = \text{profit (in dollars)},$$
$$p = \text{price (in dollars)}.$$

So

$$P = xp - C. \tag{5-13}$$

FIGURE 5.48

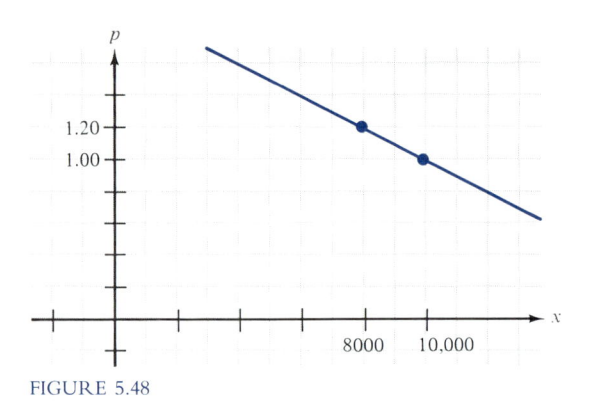

To write this function in terms of x, we need to determine the demand equation. We are told that it is linear and that when $p = 1$, $x = 10{,}000$ and when $p = 1.20$, $x = 8000$. Thus we get the graph in Figure 5.48.

To determine the equation of this line we must first find its slope. We get

$$m = \frac{1.20 - 1}{8000 - 10{,}000} = \frac{0.20}{-2000} = -0.0001.$$

To get the equation we use either point. With $(8000, 1.20)$ we have

$$p - 1.20 = -0.0001(x - 8000).$$

Solving for p gives

$$p = -0.0001x + 2.$$

Upon substituting for p and C in Equation (5-13) we get

$$\begin{aligned} P &= x(-0.0001x + 2) - (1000 + 0.3x) \\ &= -0.0001x^2 + 2x - 1000 - 0.3x \\ &= -0.0001x^2 + 1.7x - 1000. \end{aligned}$$

To locate the maximum on $[0, \infty)$ we differentiate and get

$$\frac{dP}{dx} = -0.0002x + 1.7.$$

This gives a critical value of $x = 8500$. Since

$$\frac{d^2P}{dx^2} = -0.0002 < 0,$$

the second derivative test indicates that the graph of P is concave down and there is a maximum at $x = 8500$. By Theorem 5.10 it is absolute.

5.8 BUSINESS APPLICATIONS

Since
$$p\Big|_{x=8500} = -0.0001(8500) + 2 = 1.15,$$
the price of $1.15 maximizes the profit.

Suppose that a store expects to sell 1000 refrigerators during the next year. All 1000 could, of course, be ordered at the beginning of the year, but this requires significant storage, insurance, and security costs. Therefore, it is decided to place periodic orders of size x (called the lot size). Experience shows that it will cost, on average, $12 per year to hold each refrigerator. Because the refrigerators are sold at a steady rate, the average number being held is $x/2$. Hence, the total holding costs are

$$\text{holding costs} = 12\left(\frac{x}{2}\right) = 6x,$$

in dollars.

Further, each order costs $50 for processing, delivery, and loading. Since there will be $1000/x$ orders, the total ordering costs are

$$\text{ordering costs} = 50\left(\frac{1000}{x}\right) = \frac{50{,}000}{x}.$$

Therefore, the total inventory costs are given by

$$I(x) = 6x + \frac{50{,}000}{x}.$$

We may now determine the lot size that minimizes the total inventory costs. We differentiate to get

$$I'(x) = 6 - 50{,}000x^{-2} = 6 - \frac{50{,}000}{x^2}.$$

Setting $I'(x)$ to zero gives

$$6 - \frac{50{,}000}{x^2} = 0$$

$$6x^2 = 50{,}000$$

$$x \approx 91.$$

By the second derivative test,

$$I''(x) = 100{,}000x^{-3} = \frac{100{,}000}{x^3},$$

$I''(91) > 0 \;\Rightarrow\;$ graph is concave up.

Hence, the inventory cost is minimized by ordering lot sizes of 91.

EXERCISE

A store expects to sell 2000 air conditioners next year, placing periodic orders of lot size x. It will cost, on average, $16 per year, to hold each air conditioner. If the average number being held is $x/2$ and if each order costs $40, what lot size minimizes the total inventory costs?

■ ANSWER
100

PROBLEM SET 5.8

In Problems 1–4, determine the number of units x that should be manufactured in order to maximize the revenue function R.

1. $R = -0.001x^3 + 0.555x^2 + 36x$
2. $R = -0.002x^3 + 0.42x^2 + 9x$
3. $R = 2x\sqrt{120 - x}$
4. $R = 5x\sqrt{2738 - x^2}$

5. A manufacturer of a certain item determines that the cost, in dollars, is $C = x^3 - 9x^2 + 34x + 29$. Find the minimum marginal cost.

6. The cost C, in dollars, of producing x tennis rackets is $C = 0.02x^2 + 6x + 2312$. Determine the minimum average cost. (The average cost of one unit is the total cost divided by the number of units produced.)

In Problems 7 and 8, given the total cost and revenue functions, determine the number of units of a product that should be produced to maximize the profit.

7. $C = 0.025x^2 + 10x + 450$; $R = 73x - 0.045x^2$
8. $C = x^3 - 6x^2 - 40x + 5450$; $R = 1400x$

9. The demand equation, in dollars, for a certain item is $p = 600 - 3x$. Determine the price p so as to maximize the revenue.

10. The relationship between the demand for x units of a specified product and the price p per unit is given by $4x + p^3 - 4000 = 0$.
    (a) Determine the demand equation.
    (b) Determine the revenue function.
    (c) Determine the number of units that will yield the maximum revenue.

11. Records at a travel agency indicate that when the round trip plane fare to Washington, DC from Cincinnati, Ohio is $408, an average of 132 tickets are sold per week and when the price is $288, an average of 192 tickets are sold. If the demand equation is linear, what fare should be charged to maximize revenue?

12. A motel manager determines that when the price for a double room is $81 per night, an average of 65 rooms are occupied, and when the price is $54, an average of 110 rooms are occupied. If the demand equation is linear, what price should be charged to maximize revenue?

In Problems 13 and 14, the demand and cost functions of a product are given. Determine how many units should be produced and the price per unit in order to maximize profit.

13. $p = 30 - \frac{1}{3}x$; $C = 6x + 16$
14. $p = 95 - 5x$; $C = x^3 - 17x^2 + 68x + 300$

In Problems 15 and 16, use the graphs of the linear demand function p and the linear cost function C to determine the selling price p that maximizes the profit.

15.

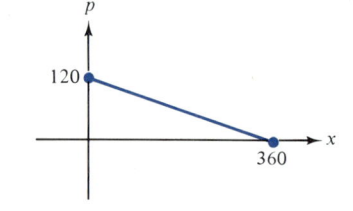

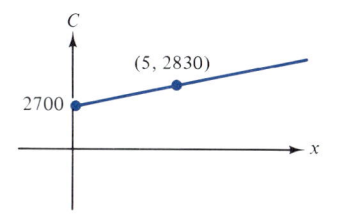

16.

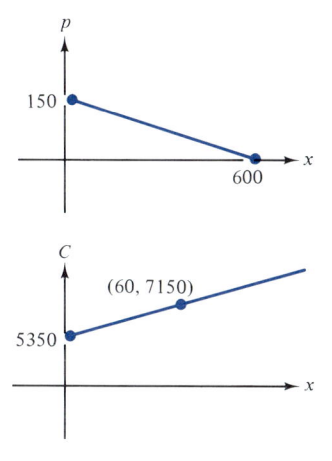

17. A manufacturer determines that the daily cost C, in dollars, of manufacturing and marketing its product is $C = x^3 + 10x^2 - 50x + 1000$, where x is the output. If the selling price is $1550, how many units should be produced each day to maximize profit?

18. The weekly cost, in dollars, of manufacturing and marketing x baskets is $C = 1000 + 0.5x + 0.0005x^2$. If the selling price is $2.50, how many baskets should be produced to maximize profit? What is the maximum profit?

19. Old Mother Hubbard has been selling home made rhubarb pie at $0.50 per slice. At that price an average of 100 slices were sold per day. When she increased the price to $0.60 per slice, the average number of slices sold decreased to 80. Ms. Hubbard estimates it costs her $0.16 a slice in addition to a fixed cost of $20 per day. Assume that the demand equation is linear.
    (a) Determine the revenue function.
    (b) Determine the price per slice that would maximize her revenue.
    (c) Determine the profit function.
    (d) Determine the price per slice that would maximize her profit.

20. A manufacturer determines that 200 units of a product can be sold if the selling price per unit is $15. For each 50-cent decrease in price per unit, the manufacturer can sell an additional 10 units. The fixed costs are $700 and the material and labor costs total $3 per unit. Determine the selling price per unit so as to maximize the profit.

21. Membership at a tennis club ranges from a minimum of 150 to a maximum of 300. Yearly dues are $600 when the membership is 150 and decrease by $2 for each member in excess of 150 (e.g., when the membership is 160, yearly dues are $580). Determine the number of members that yield the maximum yearly dues.

22. Fruit growers estimate that when 26 peach trees are planted per acre, each tree will average $560 in revenue. For each additional peach tree planted per acre, the average revenue per tree is reduced by $14. How many peach trees should be planted per acre in order to maximize the revenue?

23. A book publisher can produce a special paperback edition of a book at $1 per book. It is estimated that if they are sold at x dollars per book, then $400,000e^{-0.4x}$ of them will be sold. Determine the selling price per book so as to maximize the profit.

24. A manufacturer can produce transistor radios at a cost of $2.50 each. It is estimated that if they are sold at x dollars each, then $1000e^{-0.2x}$ of them will be sold each week. Determine the selling price per radio so as to maximize the weekly profit.

25. Show that if the profit is a maximum then the marginal cost is equal to the marginal revenue.

26. Show that if the average cost has a minimum, then it occurs when average cost is equal to the marginal cost. (The average cost of one unit is the total cost divided by the number of units produced.)

27. A computer store expects to sell 750 personal computers during the next year, placing periodic orders of lot size x. It will cost, on average, $9 per year, to stock each personal computer. If the average number being stocked is $x/2$ and if each order costs $35, what lot size minimizes the total inventory costs?

28. An appliance store expects to sell 3000 microwave ovens next year, placing periodic orders of lot size x. It will cost, on average, $15 per year to stock each oven. If the average number being stocked is $x/2$ and if each order costs $30, what lot size minimizes the total inventory costs?

29. A manufacturer of a certain item determines that the revenue, in dollars, is $R = -0.02x^2 + 3x$ and the profit, in dollars, is $P = -0.006x^3 + 0.01x^2 + x - 80$. Determine the minimum marginal cost, in dollars.

CHAPTER 5 REVIEW

1. Determine whether each of the following is true or false.
   (a) If f is increasing on an interval I, then $f'(x) > 0$ for all $x \in I$.
   (b) $f(x) = 1/(-x)^3$ is increasing for all elements in its domain.
   (c) The graph below shows that (1,2) is a relative maximum point and (2,1) is a relative minimum point.

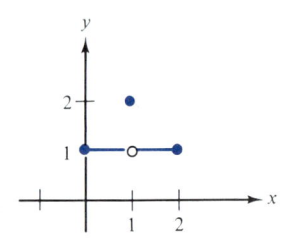

   (d) If f is a continuous function and c is an interior point of the domain and a critical point, then f has a relative maximum or minimum at $x = c$.
   (e) If a is in the domain of f and $f''(a) = 0$, then $(a, f(a))$ is an inflection point.
   (f) A quadratic function can have two critical values.
   (g) The function $f(x) = \frac{1}{32}x^4 - x$ has a minimum at $x = 2$.
   (h) If f is the greatest integer function, then every number is a critical value.
   (i) The graph of $f(x) = x^3 + 3x^2 + 10$ is concave up for $x > -1$.
   (j) The function $f(x) = -3$ defined on $[0,3]$ has one and only one absolute maximum point on $[0,3]$.
   (k) At $x = 1$, the function $f(x) = 1 + 1/(1 + x)$ is increasing.
   (l) If f is a continuous function and has an endpoint in its domain at $x = x_1$, then f has a relative maximum or minimum at $x = x_1$.
   (m) Suppose a function f is differentiable at each point of an interval I and the graph of f is concave down on I. If $a, b \in I$ and $a < b$, then $f'(a) > f'(b)$.
   (n) If $f'(x) > 0$ for all x, then the graph of f is concave up for all x.
   (o) The graph of every polynomial equation of degree 3 (i.e., $y = ax^3 + bx^2 + cx + d$, $a \neq 0$) has one and only one inflection point.
   (p) The function $f(x) = (x + 10)^3$ has at least one relative extreme point.
   (q) The graph below illustrates that the slopes are decreasing on $(\pi, 2\pi)$.

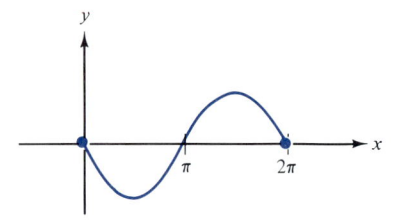

   (r) If the total cost function is $C = 0.07x^2 + 50x + 1000$, then the maginal average cost function is $0.07 - (1000/x^2)$.
   (s) $f'(a) = 0$ implies that f is neither increasing nor decreasing at $x = a$.
   (t) The graph of the function $x + e^x$ is concave up for all x.
   (u) A relative minimum is always less than or equal to a relative maximum.
   (v) For the function graphed below

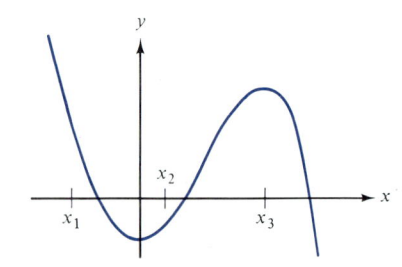

   $f'(x_1) < f''(x_2) - f'(x_3)$.

   (w) At $x = 0$, the function $y = x^3 - 2x^2 + 3x - 10$ is increasing and its graph is concave down.
   (x) If $p = f(x)$ is the demand equation for a certain commodity, then $dp/dx \leq 0$ for all x.

(y) The function $f(x) = (x^2 - 2x)/(x-2)$ has a vertical asymptote $x = 2$.

(z) If f is a continuous function defined on (a,b), then f has an absolute maximum and an absolute minimum on $(a,b,)$.

(aa) The graph of f below depicts that $f'(x_0) < 0$ and $f''(x_0) < 0$.

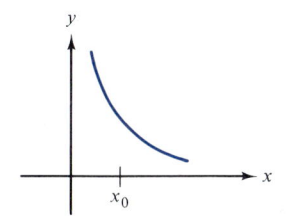

(bb) The graph of a quadratic function never has an inflection point.

(cc) The function $f(x) = \ln \sqrt{x}$ is increasing and its graph is concave up for all $x > 0$.

(dd) The function $f(x) = -e^{-2x}$ is decreasing for all x.

(ee) Let f be a function defined on an interval I. f is decreasing on I provided that for all x_1, $x_1 + h \in I$, where $h > 0$, $f(x_1) - f(x_1 + h) > 0$.

(ff) The minimum value of $f(x) = (49/x) + x + 2$, $x > 0$, is 16.

(gg) If the profit function is $p(x) = x^3 - 30x^2 + 300x$, then the marginal profit is zero when $x = 0$.

(hh) The function $f(x) = x^4 - x^3$ has one and only one inflection point.

(ii) The function graphed below has an absolute maximum at $x = 2$ and an absolute minimum at $x = 4$.

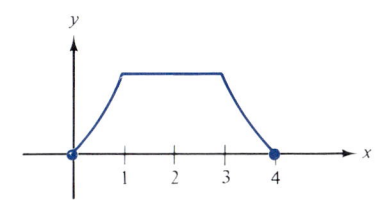

(jj) If it costs a business $C = 2x + 17$ dollars to produce x units and if the sale of x units generates $R = 80x - 0.75x^2$ dollars, then the profit function is $P = -0.75x^2 + 78x - 17$.

(kk) The graph of the function below is concave up at $x = a$.

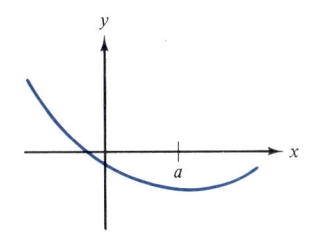

(ll) The horizontal asymptote of $y = 2x(x-1)/(x+2)$ is $y = 2$.

(mm) The function $f(x) = e^x - x$ has a minimum point, but no maximum point.

(nn) For $f(x) = x^{-1/3}$, $x = 0$ is a critical value.

2. One of these functions is increasing at $x = 0$. Which one?
$f(x) = x^2 - 5x + 3$
$g(x) = x^3 - x$
$h(x) = \sqrt{x+1}$
$k(x) = (2x-1)^4$
$u(x) = 6 - x$

3. Below is the graph of a function f. Determine whether the function f, or its graph, exhibits the specified characteristics.

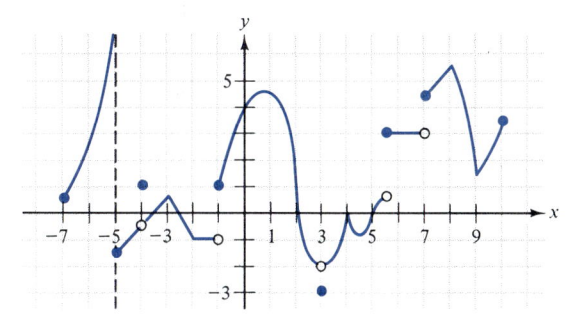

(a) Relative minimum at $x = -7$
(b) Increasing on $(-6, -5)$
(c) Increasing at $x = -4$
(d) Decreasing at $x = -2.5$
(e) Increasing on $(-1, 1)$
(f) Increasing at $x = -1$
(g) Relative maximum at $x = -4$
(h) Relative maximum at $x = -\pi/2$
(i) Concave down on $(-1, 2)$
(j) Concave up at $x = -6$
(k) Absolute minimum at $x = 3$
(l) Inflection point at $x = 5$

(m) Decreasing on (1,3)
(n) Increasing at $x = 5.5$
(o) Relative minimum at $x = 6.3$
(p) Relative maximum at $x = 8$
(q) Inflection point at $x = 9$
(r) Concave up at $x = 10$

4. At which of the six points on the graph below are y' and y'' both negative?

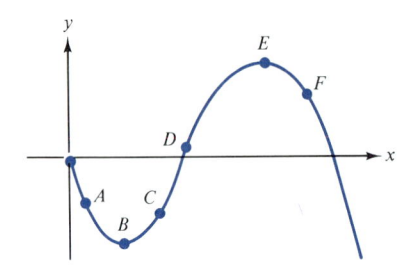

In Problems 5–12, determine all relative extreme points.

5. $f(x) = -x^3 + 3x^2$
6. $f(x) = x^3 + 5x + 3$
7. $f(x) = 3x^5 - 5x^3 + 20$
8. $y = \dfrac{1}{x} - \dfrac{4}{x-1}$
9. $y = x^{3/2} - x^{1/2}$
10. $y = 2x \ln x$
11. $y = (5 - x)/e^x$
12. $y = \dfrac{-\ln(1/x)}{x}$

In Problems 13–18, determine all inflection points of the given function.

13. $f(x) = x^3 - 6x^2 + 9x + 5$
14. $y = \tfrac{1}{4}x^4 - x^3$
15. $y = 1/(1 + x^2)$
16. $y = e^x - e^{-x}$
17. $y = (\ln x)^2$
18. $y = xe^{6x}$

19. The graph of one of these functions is concave up at $x = 0$. Which one?
$f(x) = x^5 - 4x^3 - x^2 + 10$
$g(x) = x^4 + x^3 - 2x^2 - 3$
$h(x) = \sqrt{x + 7}$
$k(x) = 1/(x + 5)$
$u(x) = 1 - (2x - 3)^4$

20. Let $f(x) = 1/(1 + e^{-x})$. Which of the following statements is true?
(a) f is increasing for all values of x.
(b) f is increasing for $x > 0$, decreasing for $x < 0$.
(c) f is decreasing for $x > 0$, increasing for $x < 0$.
(d) f is undefined at $x = \ln 1$.
(e) None of the above is true.

21. Let f be the function with the following graph. Which statement best describes f.

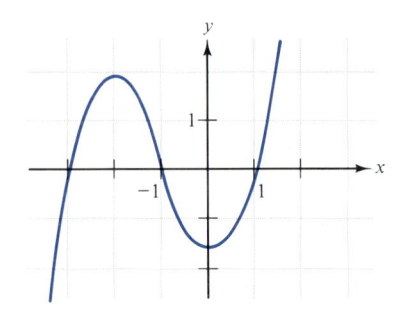

(a) Its second derivative is always positive.
(b) Its second derivative is positive when $x > -1$.
(c) Its first derivative is always positive.
(d) Its first derivative is positive when $x < -1$.
(e) Its first derivative changes sign at $x = -1$.

22. Which of the following statements is true for the function f, graphed below.
(a) $f'(1) < f'(3)$ and $f''(1) < f''(3)$.
(b) $f'(1) > f'(3)$ and $f''(1) < f''(3)$.
(c) $f'(1) < f'(3)$ and $f''(1) > f''(3)$.
(d) $f'(1) > f'(3)$ and $f''(1) > f''(3)$.
(e) None of the above is true.

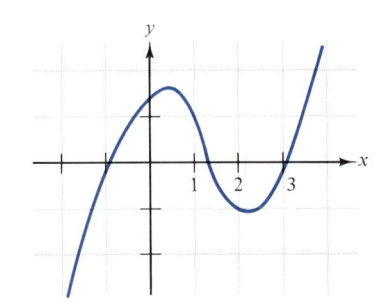

23. Let $f(x) = 4x^5 - 5x^4$. Which of the following is true when $x = -1$?
(a) f is increasing and its graph is concave up.
(b) f is decreasing and its graph is concave up.
(c) f is increasing and its graph is concave down.
(d) f is decreasing and its graph is concave down.
(e) $f'(x)$ does not exist.

24. The function $y = 1/e^{5x}$ is:
(a) increasing and its graph is concave up for all x.
(b) decreasing and its graph is concave up for all x.
(c) increasing and its graph is concave down for all x.

(d) decreasing and its graph is concave down for all x.
(e) none of the above.

25. In each of the following, make one selection from each group so that the resulting statement is true. The function $y = f(x)$ is defined on the interval $(-5,2)$:

(a) If $\begin{pmatrix} f(x) \\ f'(x) \\ f''(x) \end{pmatrix}$ is $\begin{pmatrix} \text{positive} \\ \text{negative} \\ \text{zero} \end{pmatrix}$ for all x in $(-5,2)$, then f is increasing on $(-5,2)$.

(b) If $\begin{pmatrix} f(x) \\ f'(x) \\ f''(x) \end{pmatrix}$ is $\begin{pmatrix} \text{positive} \\ \text{negative} \\ \text{zero} \end{pmatrix}$ for all x in $(-5,2)$, then the graph of f is concave down on $(-5,2)$.

(c) If $\begin{pmatrix} f(1) \\ f'(1) \\ f''(1) \end{pmatrix}$ is $\begin{pmatrix} \text{positive} \\ \text{negative} \\ \text{zero} \end{pmatrix}$ and $\begin{pmatrix} f(1) \\ f'(1) \\ f''(1) \end{pmatrix}$ is $\begin{pmatrix} \text{positive} \\ \text{negative} \\ \text{zero} \end{pmatrix}$, then $(1, f(1))$ is a relative minimum point.

(d) If $\begin{pmatrix} f(x) \\ f'(x) \\ f''(x) \end{pmatrix}$ at $x = 1$ $\begin{pmatrix} \text{is increasing} \\ \text{is zero} \\ \text{changes sign} \end{pmatrix}$, then $(1, f(1))$ is an inflection point.

(e) If $\begin{pmatrix} f(x) \\ f'(x) \\ f''(x) \end{pmatrix}$ is zero at $x = 1$, then $(1, f(1))$ is $\begin{pmatrix} \text{a relative minimum} \\ \text{an inflection point} \\ \text{an } x\text{-intercept} \end{pmatrix}$.

In Problems 26 and 27, sketch a graph of a continuous function f that satisfies the given information.

26. $f(0) = 1$; $f'(x) > 0$ when $-3 < x < 2$.
    $f(2) = 4$; $f'(x) < 0$ when $x < -3$ or $x > 2$.
    $f(-3) = -3$; $f''(x) > 0$ when $x < 0$.
    $f'(-3) = 0$; $f''(x) < 0$ when $x > 0$.
    $f'(2) = 0$.

27. $f(-2) = 0$; $f'(1) = 0$.
    $f(0) = 0$; $f'(x) > 0$ when $x < -1$.
    $f(-1) = 1$; $f'(x) < 0$ when $-1 < x < 1$ or $x > 1$.
    $f(1) = -1$; $f''(x) > 0$ when $0 < x < 1$.
    $f'(-1) = 0$; $f''(x) < 0$ when $x < 0$ or $x > 1$.

28. If $f(x) = 1 + \dfrac{1}{1+x}$, then at $x = 1$ the function or its graph:
(a) is increasing.
(b) has a relative maximum.
(c) is decreasing.
(d) has an inflection point.
(e) none of the above.

In Problems 29–36, determine the absolute extreme points of f on the given interval.

29. $f(x) = x^3 + 3x^2 - 9x$ on $[-6,2]$
30. $y = (4-x)^{1/3}$ on $[3,5]$
31. $y = \dfrac{x+2}{x^2 + 2x + 4}$ on $(-5,0)$
32. $y = \sqrt{25 - 4x^2}$ on $[-2,2]$
33. $y = x - x \ln x$ on $[1/e, e]$
34. $y = xe^{-x}$ on $[-\ln 2, \ln 4]$
35. $y = e^{-x}\sqrt{x}$ on $(0, \infty)$
36. $y = \ln(e^x + e^{-x})$ on $(-\infty, 4)$

37. Determine the absolute maximum of
$$f(x) = \frac{1}{1-x} + \frac{x}{x-1} \text{ on } [2,8].$$

38. Which one of the statements below is true for the function $y = x^4 - 2x^3$.
(a) y has no relative extreme points.
(b) y has one point of inflection and two relative extreme points.
(c) y has two points of inflection and one relative extreme point.
(d) y has two points of inflection and two relative extreme points.
(e) y has two points of inflection and three relative extreme points.

39. Consider the function $f(x) = (x^2 - 2x)^{2/3} + 1$.
(a) Find all critical values of f.
(b) Find the absolute extreme points on $[0,4]$.

40. Find the equation of the tangent line to the graph of $f(x) = x^3 + 3x^2 - 3$ at the inflection point.

41. Below is the graph of f', the derivative of f. Determine the relative extreme points of f.

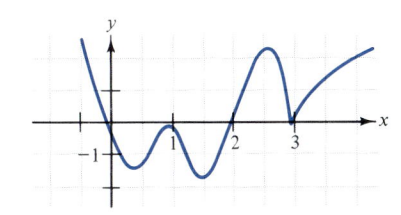

42. Determine the constants a and b so that $f(x) = \frac{1}{6}x^3 + ax^2 + bx - 1$ will have a relative maximum at $x = -2$ and a relative minimum at $x = 6$.

43. Match the graph of each function (left column) with the graph of its derivative (right column).

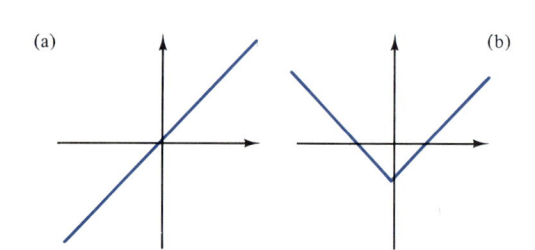

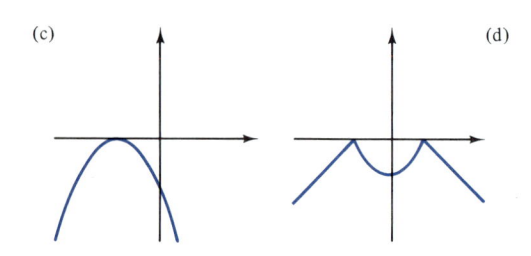

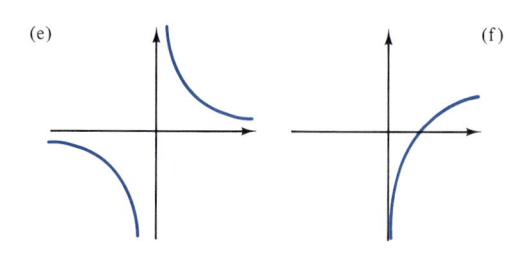

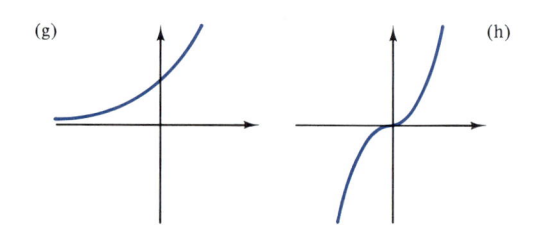

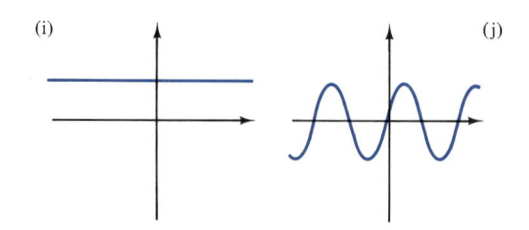

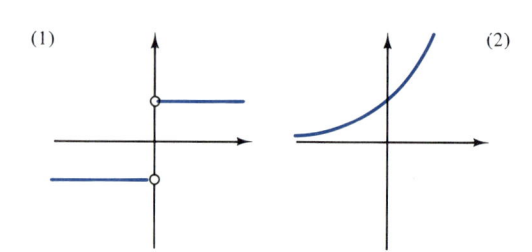

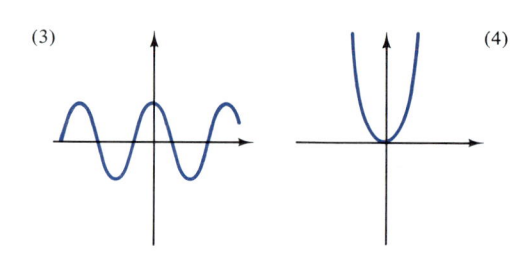

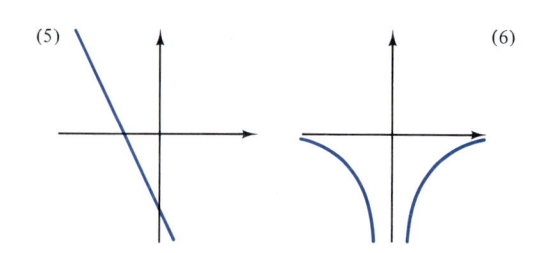

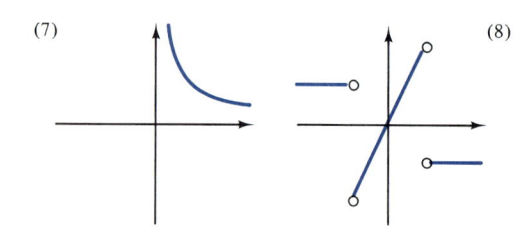

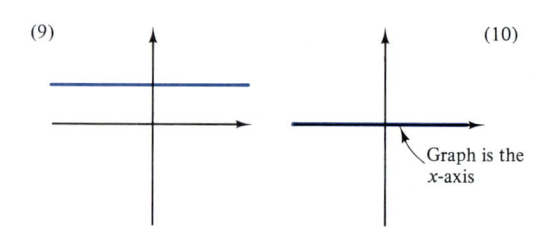

44. Below is the graph of a function f. Sketch the graph of f' and f''.

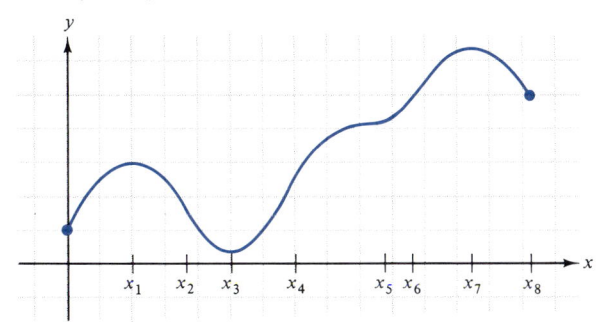

45. Let f be the function with the following graph:

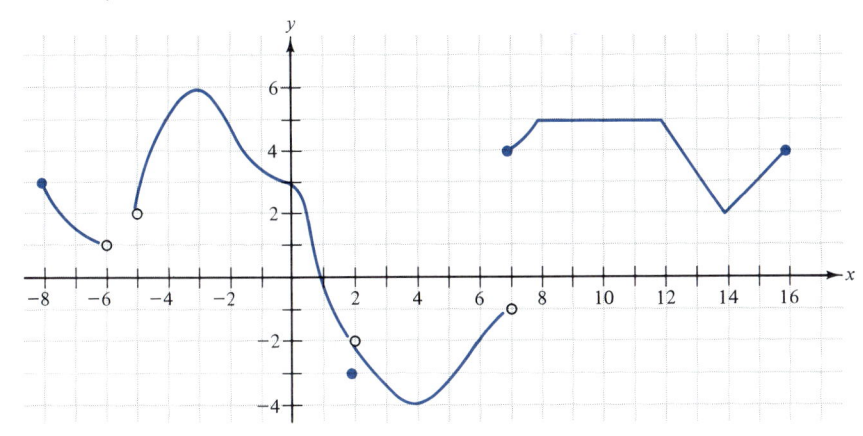

(a) What is the domain of f?
(b) What is the range of f?
(c) $f(0) = ?$
(d) $f(1) = ?$
(e) $f[f(14)] = ?$
(f) $\lim_{x \to 2} f(x) = ?$
(g) $\lim_{x \to 7^-} f(x) = ?$
(h) Is f continuous at $x = 2$?
(i) Is f continuous at $x = 14$?
(j) Is f differentiable at $x = 10$?

Complete (k) through (t) by using one of the following: (1) greater than zero; (2) less than zero; (3) equal to zero; (4) undefined; (5) greater than or equal to zero; (6) less than or equal to zero.

(k) $f''(-5)$ is ?   (l) $f'(-4)$ is ?
(m) $f'(-3)$ is ?   (n) $f'(0)$ is ?
(o) $f'(2)$ is ?   (p) $f''(4)$ is ?
(q) $f(7)$ is ?   (r) $f''(9)$ is ?
(s) $f'(12)$ is ?   (t) $f''(13)$ is ?

46. Find two positive numbers x and y so that $x + y = 50$ and the product $x^2 y^8$ is a maximum.

47. Determine the positive number which when added to the square of its reciprocal yields a minimum sum.

48. Show that of all rectangles with given perimeter K, the square has the largest area.

49. A box (see figure below) with no top and a square base is to be constructed using 50 square feet of material. To determine the maximum volume of the box, we would:

(a) maximize xy^2, where $x^2 + 4xy = 50$.
(b) maximize $x^2 + 4xy$, where $x^2y = 50$.
(c) maximize x^2y, where $2x^2 + 4xy = 50$.
(d) maximize $2x^2 + 4xy$, where $xy^2 = 50$.
(e) none of the above.

50. A field consists of a rectangular region with a semicircular region adjoined at each end. If the perimeter of the field is 1000 feet, determine the maximum possible area of the rectangular part of the field.

51. A rectangular swimming pool with a square base and a volume of 2000 cubic feet is to be built with brick sides and a cement bottom. The cost of the brick is $4 per square foot and the cost of the cement is $2 per square foot. Determine the dimensions of the pool so as to minimize the total cost.

52. Determine the dimensions of the cylinder of maximum volume that can be inscribed in a cone of radius 6 inches and height 21 inches.

53. Determine the area of the largest rectangle with base on the x-axis and with two vertices on the curve $y = 8/(x^2 + 4)$.

54. A computer manufacturer estimates that 2450 computers can be sold per month at $2500 each. For each $100 decrease in price an additional 350 computers can be sold. Determine the price per computer so as to maximize the manufacturer's revenue.

55. A firm's cost function is $C = 5 + 70x$ and its revenue function is

$$R = 225 + 60x - \frac{2250}{x + 10}.$$

How many units should be produced to maximize the firm's profit.

56. The demand equation for a product is $p = 5 - 0.01x$. Determine the value of x that maximizes the revenue.

57. The profit from manufacturing x items is $P = 5x - 400 - 0.01x^2$. If the company is capable of producing at most 300 items, how many should be produced for maximum profit?

58. A manufacturer determines that the weekly revenue R, in dollars, is $R = 3x\sqrt{435 - x}$, where x is the number sold. What output maximizes the weekly revenue?

59. The final cost, in dollars, of constructing an office tower x floors high is $C(x) = 2500x^2 + 190{,}000x + 1{,}440{,}000$. Determine the height of the office tower so as to minimize the average cost per floor. (The average cost of one floor is the total cost divided by the number of floors.)

60. The cost, in dollars, of reproducing x number of copies is $C = 0.004x + (2890/x)$. Determine the value of x that minimizes the cost.

61. A manufacturer of a certain item determines that the demand equation is $p = 10$, and the cost is $C = 0.004x^3 - 0.3x^2 + 10x + 300$. Determine how many units should be produced to maximize profit.

62. Determine the vertical asymptotes (if any) for the following:

(a) $y = \dfrac{3x + 3}{6x + 6}$ (b) $y = \dfrac{x^3 + 1}{x^2 - 9}$

(c) $y = \dfrac{2x^2 + 3x - 2}{2x^2 - 9x + 4}$ (d) $y = \dfrac{1}{(e^x - 4)(\ln x - 5)}$

63. Determine the horizontal asymptotes (if any) for the following:

(a) $y = \dfrac{4x^2 + 1}{x(3x - 1)}$ (b) $y = \dfrac{(x + 4)^5}{(x - 1)^2(x + 2)^4}$

(c) $y = \dfrac{x^4}{5x(x - 3)}$

In Problems 64–77, sketch the graph.

64. $f(x) = \dfrac{2x^2}{x^2 - 4}$

65. $f(x) = \dfrac{1}{(x - 1)(x - 2)}$

66. $f(x) = \dfrac{x^2 + 9}{x}$

67. $f(x) = 2x - \dfrac{1}{x^2}$

68. $f(x) = \tfrac{1}{3}x^3 - x + 1$

69. $f(x) = x^3 + 6x^2 + 9x + 1$

70. $f(x) = \tfrac{3}{4}x^4 - 4x^3 + 6x^2$

71. $f(x) = x^4 - 4x^3$

72. $f(x) = x - e^x$

73. $f(x) = \dfrac{1}{e^x - 1}$

74. $f(x) = \ln(1 + e^x)$

75. $f(x) = \ln(1 + x^2)$

76. $f(x) = \dfrac{1 + \ln x}{x}$

77. $f(x) = x^2 e^{-2x}$

CHAPTER 6

INTEGRATION

CHAPTER OUTLINE
6.1 ANTIDERIVATIVES
6.2 INDEFINITE INTEGRALS CONTINUED
6.3 THE DEFINITE INTEGRAL
6.4 AREA
6.5 THE DEFINITE INTEGRAL AS THE LIMIT OF A SUM

Calculus may be divided into two broad areas—differential calculus and integral calculus. The subject of preceding chapters is differential calculus. This chapter begins the integral calculus. The important concept of the integral is introduced, and the ideas are applied to problems in science and business. Section 6.4 shows how the definite integral is used to calculate area. The last section focuses on the important interpretation of the definite integral as the limit of a special sum.

6.1 ANTIDERIVATIVES

To this point one of our primary concerns has been the question: "Given a function, what is the derivative?" Now we are going to reverse things and ask: "Given a derivative, what is the function?"

Suppose f is a function such that
$$f'(x) = 3x^2.$$

What is $f(x)$? Our first guess is
$$f(x) = x^3.$$

But this isn't the only function that has a derivative of $3x^2$. Indeed, since the derivative of a constant is zero, we could have
$$f(x) = x^3 + 5, \quad \text{or}$$
$$f(x) = x^3 - 1, \quad \text{or}$$
$$f(x) = x^3 + \pi, \quad \text{and so on.}$$

So it appears that our function f is defined by
$$f(x) = x^3 + c$$

for some constant c. But how can we be sure that there is no other function, with a different formula of definition, that has a derivative of $3x^2$? We rely on the following theorem.

THEOREM 6.1 If f and g are functions such that $f'(x) = g'(x)$, then $f(x) - g(x) = c$ for some constant c.

This thoerem says that if two functions have the same derivative, then they must differ only by a constant. It depends on the fact that if the derivative of a function is zero, then it must be constant. Its graph is a horizontal line. If $f'(x) = g'(x)$, then the derivative of the function $h(x) = f(x) - g(x)$ is
$$h'(x) = f'(x) - g'(x) = 0.$$

Hence, h must be a constant function. That is,
$$h(x) = f(x) - g(x) = c.$$

So let's return to the illustration and let
$$g(x) = x^3,$$

a function with the property that $f'(x) = g'(x)$. So f and g must differ by a constant. Thus
$$f(x) - g(x) = c$$

for some constant c. But this gives

$$f(x) = g(x) + c$$
$$= x^3 + c,$$

and we know that any function with a derivative of $3x^2$ has a formula of this type.

Given a function f, an **antiderivative** of f is a function F such that $F'(x) = f(x)$. That is, an antiderivative of a given function is one whose derivative equals the given function. So for $f(x) = 3x^2$, some of the antiderivatives are

$$F_1(x) = x^3,$$
$$F_2(x) = x^3 + 5,$$
$$F_3(x) = x^3 - 1,$$
$$F_4(x) = x^3 + \pi.$$

And we know by Theorem 6.1 that any antiderivatives of a given function will differ by a constant only. The *general antiderivative* is defined by

$$F(x) = x^3 + c,$$

where c is an arbitrary constant. So the general antiderivative is an arbitrary member of an entire family of functions, all differing from one another by constants, whose derivative is the given function. The general antiderivative of $f(x)$ is denoted

$$\int f(x)dx$$

and is more frequently called the **indefinite integral** of $f(x)$. The symbol $\int$ is called the **integral symbol**, $f(x)$ is called the **integrand**, and the dx tells us that the variable is x. Thus

$$\int 3x^2 dx = x^3 + c.$$

As another example, since x^2 is an antiderivative of $2x$, the indefinite integral of $2x$ is

$$\int 2x\, dx = x^2 + c,$$

where c is a constant.

The process of determining the indefinite integral is called **integration**. It is the reverse of differentiation, and the remainder of this section deals with the topic. We begin with the following theorem.

THEOREM 6.2   Let n be any real number such that $n \neq -1$. Then

$$\int x^n dx = \frac{x^{n+1}}{n+1} + c,$$

where c is an arbitrary constant.

INTEGRATION

This theorem says that to integrate x^n, $n \neq -1$, we increase the exponent by one and then divide by the new exponent. It is a direct result of the fact that the derivative of

$$\frac{x^{n+1}}{n+1} + c$$

is

$$\frac{(n+1)x^n}{n+1} + 0 = x^n.$$

Let's see this applied in Example 1.

EXAMPLE 1

Evaluate the following indefinite integrals:

(a) $\int x^5 dx$, (b) $\int \sqrt{x}\, dx$, (c) $\int \frac{1}{x^4} dx$, and (d) $\int 1\, dx$.

■ SOLUTION
(a) By Theorem 6.2 we have

$$\int x^5 dx = \frac{x^{5+1}}{5+1} + c = \frac{x^6}{6} + c.$$

(b) We first rewrite the formula of definition of the function being integrated (the integrand). Using exponential notation instead of a radical, we get

$$\int \sqrt{x}\, dx = \int x^{1/2} dx.$$

Now applying Theorem 6.2 we have

$$\int x^{1/2} dx = \frac{x^{3/2}}{3/2} + c = \frac{2x^{3/2}}{3} + c.$$

(c) Here again we must put the integrand in the appropriate form:

$$\int \frac{1}{x^4} dx = \int x^{-4} dx.$$

Proceeding, we get

$$\int x^{-4} dx = \frac{x^{-3}}{-3} + c = -\frac{1}{3x^3} + c.$$

(d) Since $1 = x^0$, we have

$$\int 1\, dx = \int x^0 dx = \frac{x^1}{1} + c = x + c.$$

6.1 ANTIDERIVATIVES

Is there a way to check our answers? Indeed there is. Because integration is the reverse of differentiation, the derivative of our result should be the function we are integrating. So if we write

$$\int x^{2/3} dx = \frac{x^{5/3}}{5/3} + c = \frac{3x^{5/3}}{5} + c,$$

we may check this by noting that the derivative of

$$\frac{3x^{5/3}}{5} + c$$

is $x^{2/3}$.

EXERCISE

Evaluate the following indefinite integrals:

(a) $\int x^4 dx$, (b) $\int \sqrt[3]{x}\, dx$, and (c) $\int \frac{1}{x^6} dx$.

■ ANSWER

(a) $\frac{x^5}{5} + c$; (b) $\frac{3x^{4/3}}{4} + c$; (c) $\frac{-1}{5x^5} + C$

The next theorem is a direct result of the fact that the derivative of a constant times a function is the constant times the derivative of the function.

THEOREM 6.3 Let k be any constant. Then

$$\int k \cdot f(x) dx = k \cdot \int f(x) dx.$$

This theorem tells us that we may pass constant factors through the integral symbol. Let's apply it to the next example.

EXAMPLE 2

Evaluate the following indefinite integrals:

(a) $\int 2x^4 dx$, (b) $\int \frac{1}{4x^6} dx$, (c) $\int -5\sqrt[3]{x}\, dx$, and (d) $\int -3\, dx$.

■ SOLUTION

(a) According to Theorem 6.3, the integral of $2x^4$ is 2 times the integral of x^4. We get

$$\int 2x^4 dx = 2\int x^4 dx$$
$$= 2\left(\frac{x^5}{5} + c_1\right) = \frac{2x^5}{5} + 2c_1.$$

But $2c_1$ is an arbitrary constant and may just as easily be represented by c. So the result may be written

$$\frac{2x^5}{5} + c.$$

Thus it is not necessary to multiply the arbitrary constant c by the constant passed through the integral symbol.

(b) The integral will be $\frac{1}{4}$ times the integral of $1/x^6$. We get

$$\int \frac{1}{4x^6} = \frac{1}{4}\int \frac{1}{x^6}\,dx$$
$$= \frac{1}{4}\int x^{-6}\,dx$$
$$= \frac{1}{4}\cdot\frac{x^{-5}}{-5} + c = -\frac{1}{20x^5} + c.$$

(c) We have

$$\int -5\sqrt[3]{x}\,dx = -5\int \sqrt[3]{x}\,dx$$
$$= -5\int x^{1/3}\,dx$$
$$= -5\cdot\frac{x^{4/3}}{4/3} + c = \frac{-15x^{4/3}}{4} + c.$$

(d) We have

$$\int -3\,dx = -3\int 1\,dx = -3x + c.$$

EXERCISE

Evaluate the following indefinite integrals:

(a) $\int 5x^3 dx$, (b) $\int \frac{1}{3x^4}\,dx$, (c) $\int -7\sqrt{x}\,dx$, and (d) $\int -7\,dx$.

■ ANSWER

(a) $\frac{5x^4}{4} + c$; (b) $-\frac{1}{9x^3} + c$; (c) $-\frac{14}{3}x^{3/2} + c$; (d) $-7x + c$

6.1 ANTIDERIVATIVES

In Theorem 6.2 we required $n \neq -1$. Otherwise, the denominator $n + 1$ would be zero. This special circumstance is addressed in the next theorem. It is based on the fact that the derivative of $f(x) = \ln|x|$ is $f'(x) = 1/x$.

THEOREM 6.4

$$\int x^{-1} dx = \int \frac{1}{x} dx = \ln|x| + c.$$

We know that the derivative of $f(x) = e^x$ is $f'(x) = e^x$. This gives us Theorem 6.5.

THEOREM 6.5

$$\int e^x \, dx = e^x + c.$$

EXAMPLE 3

Evaluate the following indefinite integrals:

(a) $\int 5e^x dx$ and (b) $\int \frac{-2}{x} dx.$

■ SOLUTION
(a) We have
$$\int 5e^x dx = 5 \int e^x dx = 5e^x + c.$$

(b) We have
$$\int \frac{-2}{x} dx = -2 \int \frac{1}{x} dx = -2 \ln|x| + c.$$

EXERCISE

Evaluate the following indefinite integrals:

(a) $\int \frac{e^x}{3} dx$ and (b) $\int \frac{3}{x} dx.$

■ ANSWER
(a) $\frac{e^x}{3} + c$; (b) $3 \ln|x| + c$

How do we determine the integral of a sum of two functions or the integral of a difference of two functions? It is as easy as we might hope because the derivative of a sum (or difference) is the sum (or difference) of the derivatives.

THEOREM 6.6

$$\int (f(x) + g(x))dx = \int f(x)dx + \int g(x)dx.$$

THEOREM 6.7

$$\int (f(x) - g(x))dx = \int f(x)dx - \int g(x)dx.$$

So we see that the integral of a sum (or difference) is the sum (or difference) of the integrals. And even though the theorems are stated for the sum and difference of only *two* functions, they are nonetheless true for the sum and difference of *any number* of functions.

EXAMPLE 4

Evaluate the following indefinite integrals:

(a) $\int (x^3 + 5x)dx$, (b) $\int \left(x^2 - \dfrac{3}{x^5} + 7x - 2\right)dx$, and

(c) $\int \left(x - e^x + \dfrac{1}{3x}\right)dx$.

■ SOLUTION
(a) We integrate each term and add. We get

$$\int (x^3 + 5x)dx = \int x^3 dx + \int 5x\, dx$$

$$= \frac{x^4}{4} + c_1 + 5\int x\, dx$$

$$= \frac{x^4}{4} + c_1 + \frac{5x^2}{2} + c_2$$

$$= \frac{x^4}{4} + \frac{5x^2}{2} + c_1 + c_2.$$

But $c_1 + c_2$ is an arbitrary constant and may be just as easily represented by c. So the result may be written simply

$$\frac{x^4}{4} + \frac{5x^2}{2} + c.$$

Consequently, we may add the arbitrary constant c in the final step.
(b) We have

$$\int \left(x^2 - \frac{3}{x^5} + 7x - 2\right)dx = \int x^2 dx - 3\int x^{-5}dx + 7\int x\, dx - 2\int 1\, dx$$

$$= \frac{x^3}{3} - 3 \cdot \frac{x^{-4}}{-4} + 7 \cdot \frac{x^2}{2} - 2x + c$$

$$= \frac{x^3}{3} + \frac{3}{4x^4} + \frac{7x^2}{2} - 2x + c.$$

6.1 ANTIDERIVATIVES

(c) We get

$$\int \left(x - e^x + \frac{1}{3x}\right) dx = \int x \, dx - \int e^x \, dx + \frac{1}{3} \int \frac{1}{x} \, dx$$

$$= \frac{x^2}{2} - e^x + \frac{1}{3} \ln|x| + c.$$

EXERCISE

Evaluate the following indefinite integrals:

(a) $\int (x^5 - 2x) dx$, (b) $\int \left(x^3 - \frac{2}{x^4} + 3x - 5\right) dx$, and

(c) $\int \left(e^x - x - \frac{1}{5x}\right) dx$.

■ ANSWER

(a) $\frac{x^6}{6} - x^2 + c$; (b) $\frac{x^4}{4} + \frac{2}{3x^3} + \frac{3x^2}{2} - 5x + c$;

(c) $e^x - \frac{x^2}{2} - \frac{1}{5} \ln|x| + c$

EXAMPLE 5

Determine the equation of the curve $y = f(x)$ that passes through $(2,9)$ if $y' = 3x^2 - 2$.

■ SOLUTION

We are given the derivative and are asked to find the original function. So we must integrate y'. We get

$$y = \int (3x^2 - 2) dx = x^3 - 2x + c.$$

To determine the particular value of c for this function we use the fact that the curve passes through $(2,9)$. Thus $(2,9)$ is a solution of the equation. Replacing x by 2 and y by 9 gives

$$9 = 8 - 4 + c,$$

an equation with only one unknown. Solving for c gives us

$$c = 5.$$

Hence the desired equation is
$$y = x^3 - 2x + 5.$$

EXERCISE

Determine the equation of the curve $y = f(x)$ that passes through $(1, -4)$ if $y' = -6x^2 + 2x$.

■ *ANSWER*
$y = -2x^3 + x^2 - 3$

EXAMPLE 6

Suppose that a manufacturer's marginal cost function (in dollars) is given by
$$C'(x) = 0.06x + 80.$$

What is the total cost of producing 30 units if the cost of producing 20 is $2112?

■ *SOLUTION*
We need to know the cost function to answer the question, so we must integrate the marginal cost function. We get
$$C(x) = \int C'(x)dx = \int (0.06x + 80)dx$$
$$= 0.06 \frac{x^2}{2} + 80x + k$$
$$= 0.03x^2 + 80x + k$$

for some constant k. To determine k we note that $C(20) = 2112$. Thus
$$2112 = 0.03(20)^2 + 80(20) + k.$$

Solving this equation for k gives
$$k = 500.$$

Thus
$$C(x) = 0.03x^2 + 80x + 500.$$

To find the cost of 30 units we compute $C(30)$.
$$C(30) = 0.03(30)^2 + 80(30) + 500 = 2927.$$

The cost of 30 units is $2927.

EXERCISE

Suppose that a manufacturer's marginal cost function (in dollars) is given by

$$C'(x) = 0.04x + 40.$$

What is the total cost of producing 40 units if the cost of producing 30 is $4218?

■ ANSWER
$4632

PROBLEM SET 6.1

In Problems 1–34, evaluate the indefinite integral.

1. $\int x^7 \, dx$
2. $\int x^6 \, dx$
3. $\int x^{2/3} \, dx$
4. $\int x^{5/2} \, dx$
5. $\int \sqrt[4]{x} \, dx$
6. $\int \sqrt[5]{x} \, dx$
7. $\int \frac{1}{x^3} \, dx$
8. $\int \frac{1}{x^{10}} \, dx$
9. $\int 5 \, dx$
10. $\int 8 \, dx$
11. $\int 3x^6 \, dx$
12. $\int 7x^8 \, dx$
13. $\int -x^{-9} \, dx$
14. $\int -x^{-11} \, dx$
15. $\int \pi x^{\pi-1} \, dx$
16. $\int \sqrt{3} \, x^{\sqrt{3}-1} \, dx$
17. $\int \frac{-1}{2\sqrt[3]{x}} \, dx$
18. $\int \frac{1}{-6\sqrt{x}} \, dx$
19. $\int \frac{-x^e}{e} \, dx$
20. $\int \frac{-x^{1.2}}{\ln 3} \, dx$
21. $\int 8e^x \, dx$
22. $\int \frac{-e^x}{5} \, dx$
23. $\int \frac{-4}{x} \, dx$
24. $\int \frac{e}{x} \, dx$
25. $\int \left(\frac{4}{(4x^4)^2} - 4^2 \right) dx$
26. $\int \left(\sqrt{\frac{2}{x^5}} - 2^3 \right) dx$
27. $\int \left(\frac{x^5}{5} - \frac{1}{5x^5} + 5x - 5 \right) dx$
28. $\int \left(\frac{4}{x^4} - 4x^4 + \frac{x}{4} - 4 \right) dx$
29. $\int \left(\frac{1}{x^2} - \frac{1}{2x} + e^x \right) dx$
30. $\int \left(x^3 - \frac{1}{3x} + \frac{1}{e^{-x}} \right) dx$
31. $\int (3x - 4)^2 \, dx$
32. $\int (4x^2 - 3)^2 \, dx$
33. $\int \frac{3x^4 - 4}{x^2} \, dx$
34. $\int \frac{6x^5 - 4}{x^3} \, dx$

35. Determine the equation of the curve $y = f(x)$ that passes through $(-1, -3)$ if $y' = 9x^2 - 4x + 1$.
36. Determine the equation of the curve $y = f(x)$ that passes through $(-2, 2)$ if $y' = -4x^3 + 4x - 3$.
37. Determine the equation of the curve $y = f(x)$ that passes through $(3, 0)$ and has slope $\frac{5}{2}$ at that point if $y'' = x$.
38. Determine the function $f(x)$ such that $f''(x) = 5x^4$, $f'(0) = 0$, and $f(0) = 3$.
39. Suppose that the marginal cost function (in dollars) of a manufacturer is given by $C'(x) = 0.02x + 20$. What is the total cost of producing 50 units if the cost of producing 10 units is $501?
40. Determine the cost function $C(x)$ if the marginal cost function is $C'(x) = 0.3x + 70$ and the initial cost is $C(0) = 600$.
41. Determine the profit function $P(x)$ if the marginal cost is $C'(x) = 3x^2 - 6x - 80$, the marginal revenue is $R'(x) = 2800$, and the initial profit is $P(0) = -500$.
42. Suppose that the marginal revenue (in dollars) of a manufacturer is given by $R'(x) = 560 - 0.08x$. What is the total revenue from selling 25 units?
43. A ball is dropped from the roof of a building 256 feet high. Its velocity t seconds after being dropped is $V(t) = -32t$. Determine the height (in feet) of the ball when $t = 3$.
44. A projectile is fired into the air from the top of a building 176 feet high. Its velocity t seconds after being fired is $V(t) = -32t + 160$. How long does it take the projectile to hit the ground?

6.2 INDEFINITE INTEGRALS CONTINUED

In this section we learn to integrate a few more functions. We begin by noting that, according to the general power rule, the derivative of

$$y = \frac{(f(x))^{n+1}}{n+1}$$

is

$$y' = \frac{n+1}{n+1}(f(x))^n \cdot f'(x)$$
$$= (f(x))^n \cdot f'(x).$$

This gives the following theorem.

THEOREM 6.8   Let f be a differentiable function, and let n be any real number such that $n \neq -1$. Then

$$\int (f(x))^n \cdot f'(x) dx = \frac{(f(x))^{n+1}}{n+1} + c.$$

This theorem says that, to integrate a function raised to a power times its derivative, we increase the exponent by one and divide by the new exponent. Let's use this in Example 1.

EXAMPLE 1

Evaluate the following:

(a) $\int 2x(x^2+1)^3 dx$,   (b) $\int 3x^2 \sqrt{x^3-1}\, dx$,   and   (c) $\int \frac{x}{(x^2-5)^6} dx$.

■ SOLUTION
(a) Theorem 6.8 may be applied directly. We have a function, $x^2 + 1$, raised to a power, 3, being multiplied by the function's derivative, $2x$. We have

$$\int (x^2+1)^3 2x\, dx.$$

Therefore

$$\int 2x(x^2+1)^3 dx = \frac{(x^2+1)^4}{4} + c.$$

We increased the exponent by one and divided by the new exponent.
(b) We first rewrite the function being integrated by using exponential notation instead of a radical. We get

$$\int 3x^2 \sqrt{x^3-1}\, dx = \int 3x^2 (x^3-1)^{1/2} dx.$$

6.2 INDEFINITE INTEGRALS CONTINUED

So we see that we have a function, $x^3 - 1$, raised to a power, $\frac{1}{2}$, multiplied by the function's derivative, $3x^2$. Thus

$$\int 3x^2(x^3 - 1)^{1/2} dx = \frac{(x^3 - 1)^{3/2}}{3/2} + c = \frac{2(x^3 - 1)^{3/2}}{3} + c.$$

(c) We first rewrite the integrand:

$$\int \frac{x}{(x^2 - 5)^6} dx = \int x(x^2 - 5)^{-6} dx.$$

So we have a function, $x^2 - 5$, raised to a power, -6, times x. But the derivative of $x^2 - 5$ is $2x$, not x. We need a factor of 2 in the integrand. We can insert it and simultaneously multiply by $\frac{1}{2}$. We have

$$\int x(x^2 - 5)^{-6} dx = \frac{1}{2} \int 2x(x^2 - 5)^{-6} dx$$

$$= \frac{1}{2} \cdot \frac{(x^2 - 5)^{-5}}{-5} + c = \frac{-1}{10(x^2 - 5)^5} + c.$$

EXERCISE

Evaluate the following indefinite integrals:

(a) $\int 3x^2(x^3 - 1)^5 dx$, (b) $\int 2x\sqrt[3]{x^2 + 1}\ dx$, and (c) $\int \frac{x^2}{(x^3 + 6)^4} dx.$

■ ANSWER

(a) $\frac{(x^3 - 1)^6}{6} + c;$ (b) $\frac{3(x^2 + 1)^{4/3}}{4} + c;$ (c) $\frac{-1}{9(x^3 + 6)^3} + c$

Let's return to Example 1 a moment and look at part (c). To get

$$\int x(x^2 - 5)^{-6} dx$$

in the proper form, we multiplied by 2 on the inside and $\frac{1}{2}$ on the outside to get

$$\frac{1}{2} \int 2x(x^2 - 5)^{-6} dx.$$

This is possible because constants can pass through the integral symbol and, in effect, we have done nothing but multiply by 1. What would we do if we needed to multiply by something other than a constant? For example, suppose we had

$$\int (x^2 - 5)^{-6} dx.$$

First note that we cannot simply integrate by increasing the exponent by one and dividing by the new exponent. This function needs to be multiplied by $2x$. Can we multiply by $2x$ on the inside and $1/(2x)$ on the outside to get

$$\frac{1}{2x}\int 2x(x^2 - 5)^{-6}dx?$$

The answer is *no!* This is because *variables cannot be passed through the integral symbol*. So multiplying by $2x$ on the inside and $1/(2x)$ on the outside is *not* equivalent to multiplying by 1. We have changed the problem. To evaluate

$$\int (x^2 - 5)^{-6}dx,$$

we have to use some techniques developed in the next chapter.

Let's refer again to Theorem 6.8. It stated that for $n \neq -1$,

$$\int (f(x))^n \cdot f'(x)dx = \frac{(f(x))^{n+1}}{n+1} + c.$$

Why do we require $n \neq -1$? The result would have a zero in the denominator if $n = -1$. This special circumstance is addressed in the next theorem.

THEOREM 6.9

$$\int (f(x))^{-1} \cdot f'(x)dx = \ln|f(x)| + c.$$

Theorem 6.9 is a direct result of our work in Chapter 3, where we established that the derivative of $\ln|f(x)|$ is

$$\frac{1}{f(x)} \cdot f'(x) = (f(x))^{-1} \cdot f'(x).$$

Furthermore, we need to recognize the integrand in an alternate form. Theorem 6.9 may also appear as

$$\int \frac{f'(x)}{f(x)} dx = \ln|f(x)| + c.$$

EXAMPLE 2

Evaluate the following indefinite integrals:

(a) $\int \dfrac{2x + 1}{x^2 + x - 3}$ and (b) $\int \dfrac{x^4}{x^5 - 1} dx$.

■ SOLUTION

(a) Because the numerator is the derivative of the denominator, we may apply Theorem 6.9 directly. We get

$$\int \frac{2x + 1}{x^2 + x - 3} dx = \ln|x^2 + x - 3| + c.$$

6.2 INDEFINITE INTEGRALS CONTINUED

(b) The derivative of the denominator is $5x^4$, which is not quite the numerator. We need a factor of 5 in the integrand. We get it by multiplying by 5 on the inside and $\frac{1}{5}$ on the outside. Thus

$$\int \frac{x^4}{x^5 - 1} dx = \frac{1}{5} \int \frac{5x^4}{x^5 - 1} dx = \frac{1}{5} \ln|x^5 - 1| + c.$$

EXERCISE

Evaluate the following indefinite integrals:

(a) $\int \frac{2x - 1}{x^2 - x + 5}$ and (b) $\int \frac{x^3}{x^4 - 2} dx.$

■ ANSWER
(a) $\ln|x^2 - x + 5| + c$; (b) $\frac{1}{4} \ln|x^4 - 2| + c$

Finally, we consider a theorem that deals with integrands containing factors of the type $e^{f(x)}$. Because the derivative of $e^{f(x)}$ is

$$e^{f(x)} \cdot f'(x),$$

we have Theorem 6.10.

THEOREM 6.10

$$\int e^{f(x)} \cdot f'(x) dx = e^{f(x)} + c.$$

Let's apply this theorem in Example 3.

EXAMPLE 3

Evaluate the following indefinite integrals:

(a) $\int e^{x^2} \cdot 2x \, dx$ and (b) $\int x^2 e^{x^3} dx.$

■ SOLUTION
(a) The derivative of the exponent of e is the other factor, $2x$. So Theorem 6.10 may be applied directly. We get

$$\int e^{x^2} \cdot 2x \, dx = e^{x^2} + c.$$

(b) The derivative of the exponent of e is $3x^2$, which is *almost* the other factor. We need a factor of 3. Multiplying by 3 on the inside and $\frac{1}{3}$ on the outside gives

$$\int x^2 e^{x^3} dx = \frac{1}{3} \int 3x^2 e^{x^3} dx = \frac{1}{3} e^{x^3} + c.$$

EXERCISE

Evaluate the following indefinite integrals:

(a) $\int e^{x^4} \cdot 4x^3 \, dx$ and (b) $\int xe^{-x^2} \, dx$.

■ ANSWER

(a) $e^{x^4} + c$; (b) $-\frac{1}{2}e^{-x^2} + c$

EXAMPLE 4

Determine the equation of the curve $y = f(x)$ that passes through $(1, e - 2)$ if

$$y' = 2xe^{x^2} + \frac{1}{x} + 6x(x^2 - 1)^2.$$

■ SOLUTION

We are given the derivative and are asked to find the original function. So we must integrate y'. We get

$$y = \int \left(2xe^{x^2} + \frac{1}{x} + 6x(x^2 - 1)^2\right) dx$$

$$= \int 2xe^{x^2} \, dx + \int \frac{1}{x} \, dx + 6 \int x(x^2 - 1)^2 \, dx$$

$$= e^{x^2} + \ln|x| + 6 \cdot \frac{1}{2} \int 2x(x^2 - 1)^2 \, dx$$

$$= e^{x^2} + \ln|x| + 3 \cdot \frac{(x^2 - 1)^3}{3} + c$$

$$= e^{x^2} + \ln|x| + (x^2 - 1)^3 + c.$$

To determine the particular value of c for this function we use the fact that the curve passes through $(1, e - 2)$. Thus $(1, e - 2)$ is a solution. Replacing x by 1 and y by $e - 2$ gives

$$e - 2 = e^1 + \ln|1| + (1^2 - 1)^3 + c.$$

Solving for c yields

$$e - 2 = e + c$$

$$-2 = c.$$

The desired equation is thus

$$y = e^{x^2} + \ln|x| + (x^2 - 1)^3 - 2.$$

EXERCISE

Determine the equation of the curve $y = f(x)$ that passes through $(0,3)$ if

$$y' = \frac{2x}{x^2 - 1} + e^x + 6x(x^2 + 1)^2.$$

■ ANSWER

$y = \ln|x^2 - 1| + e^x + (x^2 + 1)^3 + 1$

PROBLEM SET 6.2

In Problems 1–46, evaluate each integral.

1. $\int 4x^3(x^4 - 2)^4 dx$

2. $\int 5x^4(x^5 + 2)^5 dx$

3. $\int \left(3 + \frac{x^3}{3}\right)^2 x^2 dx$

4. $\int \left(1 - \frac{x^2}{2}\right)^3 (-x) dx$

5. $\int \frac{6x^2 + 1}{(2x^3 + x)^4} dx$

6. $\int \frac{2x - 1}{(x^2 - x)^3} dx$

7. $\int \frac{(\ln (2x))^7}{x} dx$

8. $\int \frac{-(\ln (1/x))^4}{x} dx$

9. $\int (4x + 5)^7 dx$

10. $\int (1 - 3x)^8 dx$

11. $\int x^3 \sqrt{x^4 + 2}\, dx$

12. $\int x^5 \sqrt[3]{x^6 - 3}\, dx$

13. $\int 5e^{2x}(e^{2x} + 1)^{1/2} dx$

14. $\int \frac{3(1 + \ln x^2)^{10}}{x} dx$

15. $\int x^2(x^3 + 1)^2 \sqrt{3 - (x^3 + 1)^3}\, dx$

16. $\int x^3(x^4 + 3)^4 \sqrt[3]{7 - (x^4 + 3)^5}\, dx$

17. $\int \frac{-3}{x + 1} dx$

18. $\int \frac{2}{x - 3} dx$

19. $\int \frac{2x - 2}{x^2 - 2x + 1} dx$

20. $\int \frac{6x + 1}{3x^2 + x - 7} dx$

21. $\int \frac{x^6}{x^7 + e^7} dx$

22. $\int \frac{x^7}{x^8 - \pi^8} dx$

23. $\int \frac{2x^3 + x}{x^4 + x^2 + 1} dx$

24. $\int \frac{3x^5 - \frac{3}{2}x^2}{x^6 - x^3 - 1} dx$

25. $\int \frac{e^{3x}}{1 + e^{3x}} dx$

26. $\int \frac{x^{-1}}{1 + \ln x^4} dx$

27. $\int \frac{2x^{\pi - 1} + 2}{x^\pi + \pi x} dx$

28. $\int \frac{3x^{e-1} + 3e}{x^e - e^2 x} dx$

29. $\int 3e^{x+1} dx$

30. $\int 5e^{x-2} dx$

31. $\int \frac{e^{5x}}{e^{5x-1}} dx$

32. $\int \frac{e^{-4x}}{e^{-4x-2}} dx$

33. $\int e^{x^7 - 7x}(7x^6 - 7) dx$

34. $\int e^{x^5 + 5x^2}(5x^4 + 10x) dx$

35. $\int e^{ex + \ln x}\left(e + \frac{1}{x}\right) dx$

36. $\int e^{ex + x^e}(e^x + ex^{e-1}) dx$

37. $\int \left(\sqrt{e^x} + \frac{1}{(e^x)^5}\right) dx$

38. $\int \left((e^{2x})^2 + \frac{1}{\sqrt[3]{e^x}}\right) dx$

39. $\int e^x\left(e^x + \frac{1}{e}\right) dx$

40. $\int \frac{1}{e^x}\left(e + \frac{1}{e^x}\right) dx$

41. $\int \left(\frac{x^2}{e^{x^3}} + \frac{e^{\sqrt{x}}}{\sqrt{x}}\right) dx$

42. $\int \left(\frac{x^5}{e^{x^6}} - \frac{e^{1/x}}{x^2}\right) dx$

43. $\int (x - x^3)e^{(x^4/2) - x^2} dx$

44. $\int (5x^{-3} + 10x)e^{4x^2 - 2x^{-2}} dx$

45. $\int \left(\frac{e^{1 + \ln x}}{x} - \frac{e^{-x}}{1 + e^{-x}}\right) dx$

46. $\int \left(\frac{1}{ex + x \ln x} + e^{e^x + x}\right) dx$

47. Determine the equation of the curve $y = f(x)$ that passes through $(1, \frac{5}{6})$ if

$$y' = \frac{3x^2 - 2}{x^3 - 2x} + e^{1-x} - x\sqrt{2x^2 - 1}.$$

48. Determine the equation of the curve $y = f(x)$ that passes through $(2, e + 1)$ if

$$y' = 3x^2 e^{x^3 - 7} + \frac{2}{x - 1} - x^3(x^4 - 16)^3.$$

6.3 THE DEFINITE INTEGRAL

Suppose that a lamp manufacturer has the following weekly marginal cost function:

$$C'(x) = 0.04x + 30.$$

What would be the cost of increasing production from 50 to 60 units per week? What we must compute is

$$C(60) - C(50).$$

Since the cost function is an antiderivative of the marginal cost function,

$$C(x) = \int C'(x)dx = \int (0.04x + 30)dx$$
$$= \frac{0.04x^2}{2} + 30x + k = 0.02x^2 + 30x + k.$$

Even though we don't know the particular value of k for this function, we are still able to compute the cost of increasing production. Indeed,

$$C(60) - C(50) = (0.02(60)^2 + 30(60) + k) - (0.02(50)^2 + 30(50) + k)$$
$$= 0.02(3600) + 1800 + k - 0.02(2500) - 1500 - k$$
$$= 72 + 1800 + k - 50 - 1500 - k = 322.$$

Thus the weekly cost will increase by $322. Note that the k's canceled one another, so the result does not depend on the constant.

The preceding discussion leads us to the following definition. Let f be a continuous function defined on $[a,b]$. Then the **definite integral** from $x = a$ to $x = b$, denoted $\int_a^b f(x)dx$, is

$$\int_a^b f(x)dx = F(b) - F(a),$$

where F is any antiderivative of f. That is, the definite integral from $x = a$ to $x = b$ is the net change in the antiderivatives of f. The constants a and b are called the **limits of integration.**

EXAMPLE 1

Evaluate the definite integral

$$\int_{-1}^{2} (x^2 + 2x - 5)dx.$$

■ SOLUTION

We must compute the net change from $x = -1$ to $x = 2$ in an antiderivative of $x^2 + 2x - 5$. We have

$$\int (x^2 + 2x - 5)dx = \frac{x^3}{3} + x^2 - 5x + c,$$

where c is an arbitrary constant. So let

$$F(x) = \frac{x^3}{3} + x^2 - 5x + c.$$

Thus,

$$\int_{-1}^{2} (x^2 + 2x - 5)dx = F(2) - F(-1)$$
$$= (\tfrac{8}{3} + 4 - 10 + c) - (-\tfrac{1}{3} + 1 + 5 + c)$$
$$= \tfrac{8}{3} + 4 - 10 + c + \tfrac{1}{3} - 1 - 5 - c = -9.$$

Note that the arbitrary constant disappears in the calculation. This will always occur in evaluating a definite integral because $+c$ and $-c$ will sum to 0. Hence the constant doesn't matter for the definite integral, and we may as well choose it to be zero. Thus we could have let

$$F(x) = \frac{x^3}{3} + x^2 - 5x.$$

Before proceeding, let's introduce a notation that will facilitate our work. The net change in $F(x)$ from $x = a$ to $x = b$ will be denoted $F(x)\big|_a^b$. Thus

$$F(x)\Big|_a^b = F(b) - F(a).$$

This notation will streamline the computation. The beginning of Example 1 becomes

$$\int_{-1}^{2} (x^2 + 2x - 5)dx = \left(\frac{x^3}{3} + x^2 - 5x\right)\Big|_{-1}^{2}.$$

The notation tells us that we must evaluate $(x^3/3) + x^2 - 5x$ at the upper limit and subtract its value at the lower limit.

EXAMPLE 2

Evaluate the following definite integrals:

(a) $\int_{-2}^{1} (3x^2 - x + 1)dx$ and   (b) $\int_{0}^{2} e^x dx.$

■ SOLUTION
(a) We have

$$\int_{-2}^{1} (3x^2 - x + 1)dx = \left(x^3 - \frac{x^2}{2} + x\right)\Big|_{-2}^{1}$$
$$= (1 - \tfrac{1}{2} + 1) - (-8 - 2 - 2) = 13\tfrac{1}{2}.$$

(b) We have
$$\int_0^2 e^x dx = e^x \Big|_0^2 = e^2 - e^0 = e^2 - 1 \quad (\approx 6.389).$$

EXERCISE

Evaluate the following definite integrals:

(a) $\int_{-2}^1 (x^2 - 2x - 3)dx$ and (b) $\int_0^1 -e^{-x}dx$.

◧ ANSWER
(a) -3; (b) $(1 - e)/e \; (\approx -0.6321)$

Note that although the definite and indefinite integrals are related, they are fundamentally different. The definite integral is a number. The indefinite integral, however, represents an entire class of functions: antiderivatives that differ by constants.

However, let's also note that the properties of indefinite integrals mentioned in Section 6.1 are shared by definite integrals. That is,

$$\int_a^b k \cdot f(x)dx = k \cdot \int_a^b f(x)dx, \quad \text{where } k \text{ is a constant,}$$

and

$$\int_a^b (f(x) \pm g(x))dx = \int_a^b f(x)dx \pm \int_a^b g(x)dx.$$

EXAMPLE 3

Evaluate the following definite integrals:

(a) $\int_0^{\sqrt{3}} x(x^2 + 1)^{1/2}dx$ and (b) $\int_{-1}^1 (x^2 \sqrt{x^3 + 1} + 3x^2)dx$.

■ SOLUTION
(a) We have
$$\int_0^{\sqrt{3}} x(x^2 + 1)^{1/2}dx = \frac{1}{2}\int_0^{\sqrt{3}} 2x(x^2 + 1)^{1/2}dx$$
$$= \frac{1}{2} \cdot \frac{(x^2 + 1)^{3/2}}{3/2}\Big|_0^{\sqrt{3}}$$
$$= \frac{(x^2 + 1)^{3/2}}{3}\Big|_0^{\sqrt{3}}$$
$$= \frac{4^{3/2}}{3} - \frac{1}{3} = \frac{8}{3} - \frac{1}{3} = \frac{7}{3} = 2\frac{1}{3}.$$

6.3 THE DEFINITE INTEGRAL

(b) We have

$$\int_{-1}^{1} (x^2\sqrt{x^3+1} + 3x^2)dx = \int_{-1}^{1} x^2\sqrt{x^3+1}\, dx + \int_{-1}^{1} 3x^2 dx$$
$$= \tfrac{1}{3}\int_{-1}^{1} 3x^2(x^3+1)^{1/2}dx + 3\int_{-1}^{1} x^2 dx$$
$$= \tfrac{1}{3}(x^3+1)^{3/2}\cdot\tfrac{2}{3}\Big|_{-1}^{1} + x^3\Big|_{-1}^{1}$$
$$= (\tfrac{2}{9}\cdot 2^{3/2} - \tfrac{2}{9}\cdot 0) + (1+1)$$
$$= \frac{2^{5/2}}{9} + 2 \quad (\approx 2.629).$$

EXERCISE

Evaluate the following definite integrals:

(a) $\int_0^2 x^2(x^3+1)^{1/2}dx$ and (b) $\int_1^2 (x\sqrt{x^2-1} + 5x)dx$.

■ ANSWER
(a) $5\tfrac{7}{9}$; (b) $\sqrt{3} + \tfrac{15}{2} \; (\approx 9.232)$

EXAMPLE 4

Suppose that the acceleration of an object (in feet/second^2) is given by

$$a = t^2 - t + 2.$$

What is the net change in velocity from $t = 2$ to $t = 5$?

■ SOLUTION
Because the velocity is an antiderivative of the acceleration, we must compute the definite integral

$$\int_2^5 a\, dt.$$

Substitution for a gives

$$\int_2^5 (t^2 - t + 2)dt = \left(\frac{t^3}{3} - \frac{t^2}{2} + 2t\right)\Big|_2^5$$
$$= (\tfrac{125}{3} - \tfrac{25}{2} + 10) - (\tfrac{8}{3} - 2 + 4)$$
$$= \tfrac{125}{3} - \tfrac{25}{2} + 10 - \tfrac{8}{3} + 2 - 4 = 34\tfrac{1}{2}.$$

The net change is 34.5 feet/second.

EXAMPLE 5

Suppose that the marginal revenue (in thousands of dollars) is given by

$$R'(x) = 0.003x^2 + 0.01x + 0.002.$$

What is the net change in revenue if sales increase from 20 to 25?

■ SOLUTION

Since the revenue is an antiderivative of the marginal revenue, we must compute the definite integral

$$\int_{20}^{25} R'(x)dx.$$

We have

$$\int_{20}^{25} R'(x)dx = \int_{20}^{25} (0.003x^2 + 0.01x + 0.002)dx$$
$$= (0.001x^3 + 0.005x^2 + 0.002x)\Big|_{20}^{25}$$
$$= (0.001(25)^3 + 0.005(25)^2 + 0.002(25))$$
$$\quad - (0.001(20)^3 + 0.005(20)^2 + 0.002(20))$$
$$= 18.8 - 10.04 = 8.76.$$

Since the marginal revenue, and thus revenue, is in thousands of dollars, this gives $8760.

EXERCISE

(a) Suppose that the acceleration of an object (in feet/second^2) is given by

$$a = t^2 - 2t - 3.$$

What is the net change in velocity from $t = 1$ to $t = 4$?

(b) Suppose that the marginal revenue (in thousands of dollars) is given by

$$R'(x) = 0.005x^2 + 0.02x + 0.001.$$

What is the net change in revenue if sales increase from 48 to 60?

■ ANSWER

(a) -3 feet/second;   (b) $188,652

6.3 THE DEFINITE INTEGRAL

The ideal gas law states that

$$PV = nRT,$$

where P is the pressure, V is volume, T is the temperature, R is the "gas constant," and n is the number of moles of the gas present. The work done by an ideal gas in expanding from volume V_0 to volume V_1 is given by

$$W = \int_{V_0}^{V_1} P \, dV.$$

This information is needed for the following example and exercise.

EXAMPLE 6

Assuming that pressure and temperature are constant, find the work done by a gas in expanding from a volume of 1 to a volume of 3.

■ SOLUTION

Solving the ideal gas law for P gives

$$P = \frac{nRT}{V}.$$

Therefore,

$$\begin{aligned} W &= \int_1^3 P \, dV \\ &= \int_1^3 \frac{nRT}{V} \, dV \\ &= nRT \int_1^3 \frac{1}{V} \, dV \\ &= nRT \ln V \Big|_1^3 \\ &= nRT(\ln 3 - \ln 1) \\ &= nRT \ln 3. \end{aligned}$$

EXERCISE

Assuming that pressure and temperature are constant, find the work done by a gas in expanding from a volume of 1 to a volume of 5.

■ ANSWER
$nRT \ln 5$

EXAMPLE 7

The shape of a large tank is such that the volume of the liquid it contains (in cubic feet) is given by

$$V = \pi \int_0^h \sqrt{1 + x^2}\, dx,$$

where h is the depth of the liquid (in feet). If the tank is being filled at the rate of 10 cubic feet per minute, how fast is the depth changing when the depth is 3 feet?

■ SOLUTION

This is a related rates problem in which we are being asked to find

$$\frac{dh}{dt}$$

when $h = 3$, given that

$$\frac{dV}{dt} = 10.$$

So we need an equation connecting h and V. The original equation does this, but we can't evaluate

$$\int \sqrt{1 + x^2}\, dx.$$

But in fact, we don't have to do so. We'll just let

$$F(x) = \int \sqrt{1 + x^2}\, dx.$$

That is, F is an antiderivative of the integrand. Therefore,

$$\begin{aligned} V &= \pi \int_0^h \sqrt{1 + x^2}\, dx \\ &= \pi F(x) \Big|_0^h \\ &= \pi (F(h) - F(0)). \end{aligned}$$

Now we differentiate with respect to t. We get

$$\frac{dV}{dt} = \pi \cdot F'(h) \cdot \frac{dh}{dt}.$$

Note that since $F(0)$ is constant, its derivative is 0. Because $F(x)$ is an antiderivative of $\sqrt{1 + x^2}$, we have

$$F'(x) = \sqrt{1 + x^2},$$
$$F'(h) = \sqrt{1 + h^2}.$$

6.3 THE DEFINITE INTEGRAL

Thus,
$$\frac{dV}{dt} = \pi\sqrt{1+h^2}\,\frac{dh}{dt}.$$

Solving for dh/dt yields
$$\frac{dh}{dt} = \frac{\dfrac{dV}{dt}}{\pi\sqrt{1+h^2}} = \frac{10}{\pi\sqrt{1+h^2}}.$$

When $h = 3$ we get
$$\frac{dh}{dt} = \frac{10}{\pi\sqrt{1+3^2}} = \frac{\sqrt{10}}{\pi} \quad (\approx 1.007).$$

Thus the depth is increasing approximately 1.007 feet per minute.

EXERCISE

The shape of a large tank is such that the volume of liquid it contains (in cubic feet) is given by
$$V = \pi \int_0^h \sqrt{4+x^2}\,dx,$$
where h is the depth of the liquid (in feet). If the tank is being emptied at the rate of 12 cubic feet per minute, how fast is the depth changing when the depth is 2 feet?

■ ANSWER
Decreasing $3\sqrt{2}/\pi$ (≈ 1.350) ft/min.

PROBLEM SET 6.3

In Problems 1–22, evaluate the definite integral.

1. $\int_4^7 3\,dx$
2. $\int_5^{10} 6\,dx$
3. $\int_{-1}^2 (x^2 + 1)\,dx$
4. $\int_{-3}^1 (x^2 - 2)\,dx$
5. $\int_{-3}^3 \left(2x^3 - \dfrac{x}{2}\right)dx$
6. $\int_{-2}^2 (5x^4 + 6x^2 - 1)\,dx$
7. $\int_4^9 \left(\sqrt{x} - \dfrac{1}{\sqrt{x}}\right)dx$
8. $\int_{-8}^{-1} \left(\dfrac{1}{\sqrt[3]{x}} - \sqrt[3]{x}\right)dx$
9. $\int_0^4 \dfrac{-x}{(x^2+1)^2}\,dx$
10. $\int_{-1}^0 \dfrac{x^2}{(x^3-1)^3}\,dx$
11. $\int_{-2}^{-1} \dfrac{1}{x^3}\sqrt{1 - \dfrac{1}{x^2}}\,dx$
12. $\int_{-1/2}^{-1/4} \dfrac{x}{\sqrt{1+8x^2}}\,dx$
13. $\int_{-1}^0 \dfrac{e^{8x}}{e^{5x}}\,dx$
14. $\int_0^{1/5} \dfrac{e^{2x}}{e^{7x+1}}\,dx$
15. $\int_{1/4}^{1/2} \dfrac{e^{1/x}}{x^2}\,dx$
16. $\int_{16}^{25} \dfrac{e^{\sqrt{x}}}{\sqrt{x}}\,dx$
17. $\int_{\sqrt{3}}^{\sqrt{7}} \dfrac{2x}{1+x^2}\,dx$
18. $\int_{\sqrt[3]{10}}^{\sqrt[3]{20}} \dfrac{3x^2}{x^3-5}\,dx$
19. $\int_2^6 \dfrac{4x+2}{x+x^2}\,dx$
20. $\int_{-2}^{-1} \dfrac{9x^2 - 12x}{2x^2 - x^3}\,dx$

21. $\int_1^{e^5} \dfrac{1}{x(1 + \ln x)}\, dx$ 22. $\int_e^{e^2} \dfrac{1}{x(1 + \ln x)^3}\, dx$

23. Determine b if $\int_4^b 3x^2\, dx = 61$.

24. Determine b if $\int_{-1}^b (2x - 6)\, dx = -16$.

25. Determine a if $\int_a^0 e^{-2x}\, dx = \tfrac{5}{2}$.

26. Determine a if $\int_a^0 \dfrac{1}{1 - x}\, dx = 2$.

27. Suppose that the acceleration of an object (in feet/second^2) is given by $a = 2t^2 - 3t + 1$. Determine the net change in velocity from $t = 1$ to $t = 3$.

28. Suppose that the acceleration of an object (in feet/second^2) is given by $a = 6t^2 - 3\sqrt{t} + 2$. Determine the net change in velocity from $t = 4$ to $t = 9$.

29. Suppose that the marginal revenue is given by

$$R'(x) = 60 + \dfrac{2250}{(x + 10)^2}.$$

Determine the net change in revenue if sales increase from 10 to 20.

30. Suppose that the marginal cost and marginal revenue are given by $C'(x) = 0.05x + 10$ and $R'(x) = 73 - 0.09x$. Determine the net change in profit if sales increase from 25 to 30.

31. The shape of an oil tank is such that the volume of the oil it contains (in cubic feet) is given by

$$V = \pi \int_0^h \sqrt{9 + x^3}\, dx,$$

where h is the depth of the oil. If the tank is being filled at the rate of 8 cubic feet per minute, how fast is the depth changing when the depth is 6 feet?

32. The shape of a water tank is such that the volume of water it contains (in cubic feet) is given by

$$V = \pi \int_0^h \sqrt[3]{15 + x^2}\, dx,$$

where h is the depth of the water. If the tank is being emptied at the rate of 5 cubic feet per minute, how fast is the depth changing when the depth is 7 feet?

6.4 AREA

In this section we see how the definite integral may be used to compute the area of a region. We begin by considering a continuous function f, defined on $[a,b]$, such that $f(x) \geq 0$ for all $x \in [a,b]$. What is the area of the region bounded by the curve $y = f(x)$, the x-axis, and the vertical lines $x = a$ and $x = b$? See Figure 6.1.

Let's define a new function, an area function, as follows:

$A(x) =$ area of region from a to x, where $a \leq x \leq b$.

That is, $A(x)$ is the area of the region bounded by the curve $y = f(x)$, the x-axis, and the vertical lines through a and through x. See Figure 6.2.

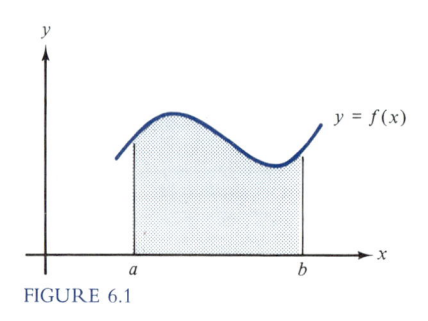

FIGURE 6.1

FIGURE 6.2

6.4 AREA

In terms of this new function, the area we are seeking, which is the area of the region in Figure 6.1, is $A(b)$. And since $A(a) = 0$, the area we are seeking is

$$A(b) - A(a).$$

But this is the net change in $A(x)$ from $x = a$ to $x = b$. It is

$$\int_a^b A'(x)\,dx.$$

So we need to compute $A'(x)$.

From the definition of derivative we have

$$A'(x) = \lim_{h \to 0} \frac{A(x+h) - A(x)}{h}.$$

Consider the expression

$$A(x+h) - A(x).$$

When $h > 0$, this is the area of the region from x to $x + h$, shown in Figure 6.3. (When $h < 0$, it is the area from $x + h$ to x since $x + h < x$.)

When h is small, the area of this region is approximately the area of the rectangle with width h and height $f(x)$. See Figure 6.4. Thus

$$A(x+h) - A(x) \approx h \cdot f(x).$$

Dividing both sides by h gives

$$\frac{A(x+h) - A(x)}{h} \approx f(x).$$

The approximation gets better and better as h gets smaller. Therefore

$$\lim_{h \to 0} \frac{A(x+h) - A(x)}{h} = \lim_{h \to 0} f(x) = f(x).$$

We have shown that

$$A'(x) = f(x).$$

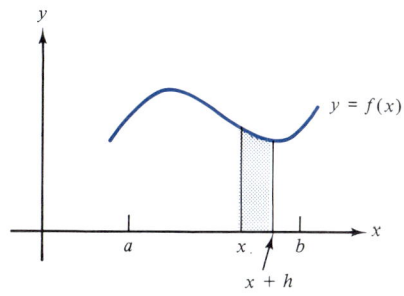

FIGURE 6.3

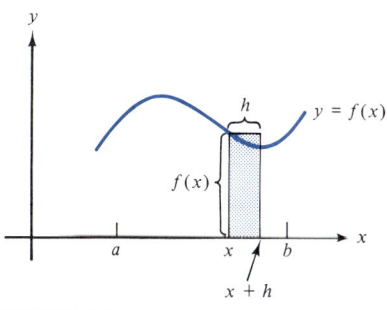

FIGURE 6.4

304   INTEGRATION

The derivative of the area function is $f(x)$. So the area of the region in Figure 6.1 is given by

$$A(b) - A(a) = A(x)\Big|_a^b = \int_a^b f(x)dx.$$

Let's summarize this result in the following theorem.

THEOREM 6.11   Let f be a continuous function defined on $[a,b]$ such that $f(x) \geq 0$ for all $x \in [a,b]$. Then the area of the region bounded by $y = f(x)$, the x-axis, $x = a$, and $x = b$ is

$$\int_a^b f(x)dx.$$

EXAMPLE 1

Determine the area of the region bounded by $f(x) = x^2$, the x-axis, $x = 1$, and $x = 3$.

■ SOLUTION

First, let's sketch the region. See Figure 6.5. Since the function is continuous and $f(x) \geq 0$ for all $x \in [1,3]$ (the graph is *above* the x-axis), the area is the definite integral

$$\int_1^3 x^2 dx.$$

Evaluating, we have

$$\int_1^3 x^2 dx = \frac{x^3}{3}\Big|_1^3 = 9 - \frac{1}{3} = 8\tfrac{2}{3}.$$

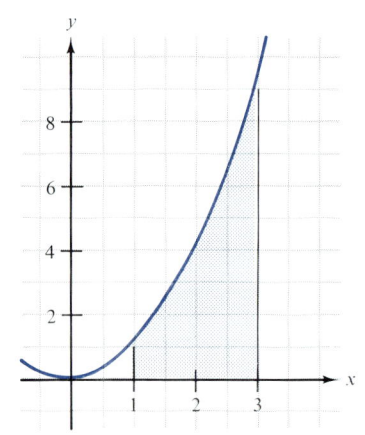

FIGURE 6.5

EXAMPLE 2

Determine the area of the region bounded by $y = (x + 1)^3 + 2$, the x-axis, $x = -2$, and $x = 0$.

■ SOLUTION

A sketch of the region is shown in Figure 6.6. Because the graph is above the x-axis on $[-2,0]$, we evaluate the definite integral

$$\int_{-2}^0 ((x+1)^3 + 2)dx = \left(\frac{(x+1)^4}{4} + 2x\right)\Big|_{-2}^0$$

$$= \tfrac{1}{4} - (\tfrac{1}{4} - 4) = 4.$$

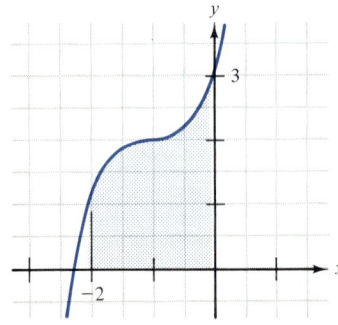

FIGURE 6.6

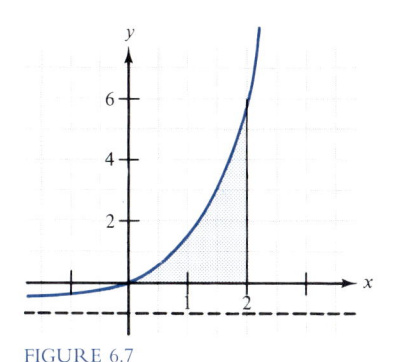

EXAMPLE 3

Determine the area of the region bounded by $y = e^x - 1$, the x-axis, and $x = 2$.

■ SOLUTION

A sketch of the region is shown in Figure 6.7. Since the region is bounded on the left by $x = 0$, we get

$$\int_0^2 (e^x - 1)dx = (e^x - x)\Big|_0^2 = (e^2 - 2) - (1 - 0)$$
$$= e^2 - 3 \quad (\approx 4.389).$$

FIGURE 6.7

EXERCISE

Determine the area of the region (a) bounded by $y = x^2 + 1$, the x-axis, $x = -1$, and $x = 2$; (b) bounded by $y = x^3$, the x-axis, and $x = 2$; and (c) bounded by $y = e^x + 1$, the x-axis, $x = -2$, and $x = 0$.

■ ANSWER
(a) 6;   (b) 4;   (c) $3 - e^{-2}$ (≈ 2.865)

Suppose we must compute the area of a region bounded by a curve that lies *below* the x-axis. That is, suppose that f is a continuous function defined on $[a,b]$ such that $f(x) \leq 0$ for all $x \in [a,b]$. How do we determine the area of the region bounded by $y = f(x)$, the x-axis, $x = a$, and $x = b$? See Figure 6.8.

If we reflect the curve about the x-axis, we get a region that is a mirror image and has the same area. See Figure 6.9.

The equation of the reflected curve is $y = -f(x)$. So the area of the mirrored region, and of the original region as well, is

$$\int_a^b -f(x)dx = -\int_a^b f(x)dx.$$

Thus, when the curve is below the x-axis, we take the negative of the definite integral of the function. See Example 4.

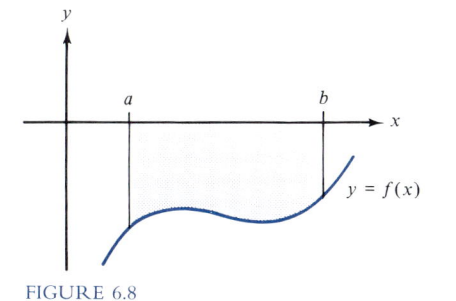

FIGURE 6.8

FIGURE 6.9

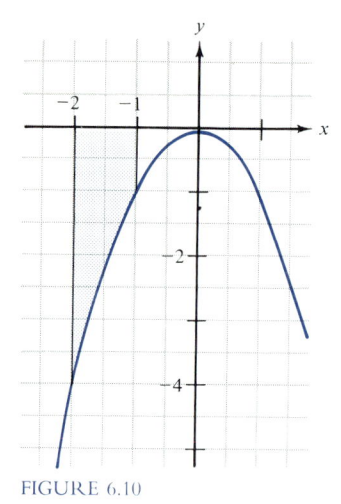

EXAMPLE 4

Determine the area of the region bounded by $y = -x^2$, the x-axis, $x = -2$, and $x = -1$.

■ SOLUTION

Let's sketch the region. See Figure 6.10. We integrate the function $y = -x^2$ from -2 to -1, but because the curve lies below the x-axis, we take the negative. We have

$$-\int_{-2}^{-1}(-x^2)dx = \int_{-2}^{-1} x^2 dx = \left.\frac{x^3}{3}\right|_{-2}^{-1}$$

$$= \frac{-1}{3} - \left(\frac{-8}{3}\right) = \frac{-1}{3} + \frac{8}{3} = \frac{7}{3} = 2\tfrac{1}{3}.$$

FIGURE 6.10

What needs to be done when part of the curve is above the x-axis and part below? See Example 5.

EXAMPLE 5

Determine the area of the region bounded by $y = x^3$, the x-axis, $x = -1$, and $x = 2$.

■ SOLUTION

A sketch of the region is given in Figure 6.11. We have divided the region into two subregions, R_1 and R_2, where R_1 is below the x-axis and R_2 is above. We compute the area of each subregion and add the results. The area of R_1 is

$$-\int_{-1}^{0} x^3 dx = -\left.\frac{x^4}{4}\right|_{-1}^{0} = \frac{1}{4},$$

and the area of R_2 is

$$\int_{0}^{2} x^3 dx = \left.\frac{x^4}{4}\right|_{0}^{2} = 4.$$

So the area of the entire region is $4\tfrac{1}{4}$.

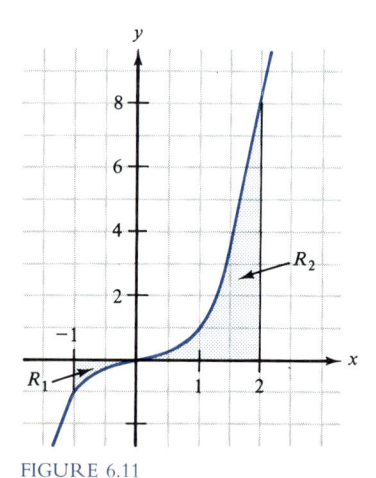

FIGURE 6.11

Note that, in Example 5, we cannot get the area of the region by blindly integrating $y = x^3$ from $x = -1$ to $x = 2$. We would get

$$\int_{-1}^{2} x^3 dx = \left.\frac{x^4}{4}\right|_{-1}^{2} = 4 - \frac{1}{4} = 3\tfrac{3}{4}.$$

We *must* note where the curve is below the x-axis.

EXERCISE

Determine the area of the region (a) bounded by $y = 1/x$, the x-axis, $x = -2$, and $x = -1$; and (b) bounded by $y = -x^3$, the x-axis, $x = -1$, and $x = \frac{1}{2}$.

■ ANSWER

(a) $\ln 2$ (≈ 0.6931); (b) $\frac{17}{64}$

Let's now consider a more general question: How do we compute the area of a region bounded by two curves, as opposed to a curve and the x-axis? Consider the region sketched in Figure 6.12.

If we took the area of the region bounded by $y = f(x)$ and the x-axis and subtracted the area of the region bounded by $y = g(x)$ and the x-axis, we would have the area of the given region. Thus it is

$$\int_a^b f(x)dx - \int_a^b g(x)dx,$$

which equals

$$\int_a^b (f(x) - g(x))dx.$$

It turns out that this same technique may be used regardless of the location of the curves with respect to the x-axis. Both may be below, one may be above and the other below, and so on. What's important is their relationship to one another. Thus, if f and g are continuous functions defined on $[a,b]$, such that $f(x) \geq g(x)$ for all $x \in [a,b]$, then the area of the region bounded by $y = f(x)$, $y = g(x)$, $x = a$, and $x = b$ is given by

$$\int_a^b (f(x) - g(x))dx.$$

FIGURE 6.12

EXAMPLE 6

Determine the area of the region bounded by $f(x) = x^2 + 1$ and $g(x) = x + 3$.

■ SOLUTION

The region is sketched in Figure 6.13. It appears that the line intersects the parabola at $x = -1$ and at $x = 2$. How can we be sure? Well, the two graphs will intersect when $f(x) = g(x)$. So we must solve the following equation for x:

$$x^2 + 1 = x + 3.$$

We get

$$x^2 - x - 2 = 0$$

$$(x - 2)(x + 1) = 0$$

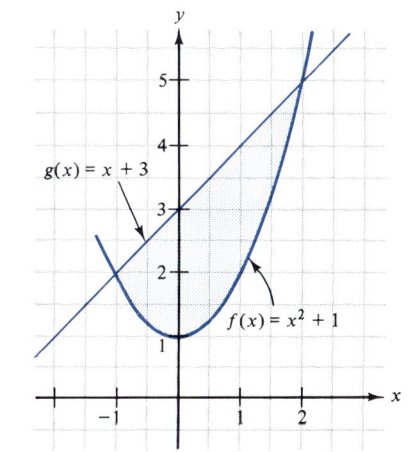

$$x = 2 \quad \text{or} \quad x = -1.$$

FIGURE 6.13

Thus the limits of integration are -1 and 2. Since the line is above the parabola over the region, the integrand is $g(x) - f(x)$. We have

$$\int_{-1}^{2} ((x+3) - (x^2+1))dx = \int_{-1}^{2} (x+2-x^2)dx$$
$$= \left(\frac{x^2}{2} + 2x - \frac{x^3}{3}\right)\Big|_{-1}^{2}$$
$$= (2 + 4 - \tfrac{8}{3}) - (\tfrac{1}{2} - 2 + \tfrac{1}{3})$$
$$= \tfrac{10}{3} - (-\tfrac{7}{6}) = \tfrac{27}{6} = 4\tfrac{1}{2}.$$

EXAMPLE 7

Determine the area of the region bounded by $y = x^3$, $y = x$, $x = 0$, and $x = 2$.

■ SOLUTION

The sketch of the region appears in Figure 6.14. The region has been divided into two subregions. The line $y = x$ lies above the curve $y = x^3$ in R_1, while $y = x$ lies below $y = x^3$ in R_2. The area of R_1 is

$$\int_0^1 (x - x^3)dx.$$

Because x ranges from 0 to 1 over this region, we integrate from 0 to 1. Continuing, we have

$$\int_0^1 (x - x^3)dx = \left(\frac{x^2}{2} - \frac{x^4}{4}\right)\Big|_0^1 = \frac{1}{2} - \frac{1}{4} = \frac{1}{4}.$$

The area of R_2 is

$$\int_1^2 (x^3 - x)dx = \left(\frac{x^4}{4} - \frac{x^2}{2}\right)\Big|_1^2$$
$$= (4 - 2) - (\tfrac{1}{4} - \tfrac{1}{2}) = 2 + \tfrac{1}{4} = 2\tfrac{1}{4}.$$

Hence the area of the entire region is $2\tfrac{1}{4}$.

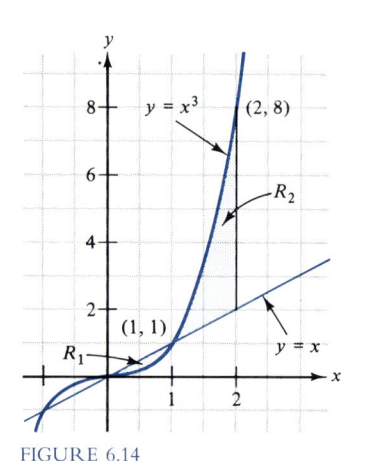

FIGURE 6.14

EXERCISE

Determine the area of the described region (a) bounded by $y = -x^2$ and $y = -x - 2$; and (b) bounded by $y = x^2$, $y = x$, $x = 0$, and $x = 2$.

■ ANSWER
(a) $4\tfrac{1}{2}$; (b) 1

6.4 AREA

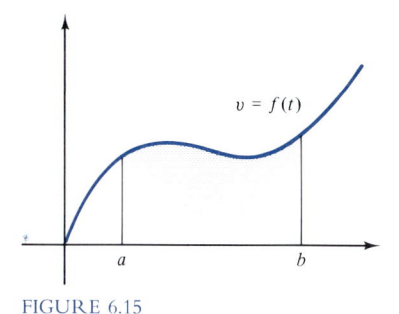

Before leaving this section, let's note that for some functions the area of a region may have an additional meaning. For example, suppose that the function graphed in Figure 6.15 is a velocity function.

The area of the region described is the definite integral

$$\int_a^b f(t)\,dt.$$

But this is the net change in the antiderivative of v, which is a position function. Thus the area of the region represents the net change in the position function from $t = a$ to $t = b$.

In a similar vein, suppose that the experimental data of a biologist indicate that the short-term birth rates and death rates of a population are approximated by $b(t)$ and $d(t)$, respectively. The biologist may use the definite integral to predict population change. The area beneath the birth rate curve will represent the total number of births, and the area beneath the death rate curve will represent the total number of deaths. Hence, the overall population change due to births and deaths from $t = t_1$ to $t = t_2$ will be given by

$$\int_{t_1}^{t_2} b(t)\,dt - \int_{t_1}^{t_2} d(t)\,dt = \int_{t_1}^{t_2} (b(t) - d(t))\,dt.$$

Let's consider another example. Suppose that the two functions graphed in Figure 6.16 are marginal revenue and marginal cost functions. Letting P represent the profit function, we have

$$\begin{aligned}
\text{area } S &= \int_a^b (R'(x) - C'(x))\,dx \\
&= \int_a^b P'(x)\,dx \\
&= P(x)\Big|_a^b \\
&= P(b) - P(a).
\end{aligned}$$

Thus the area of region S is the additional profit generated by increasing production/sales from $x = a$ to $x = b$.

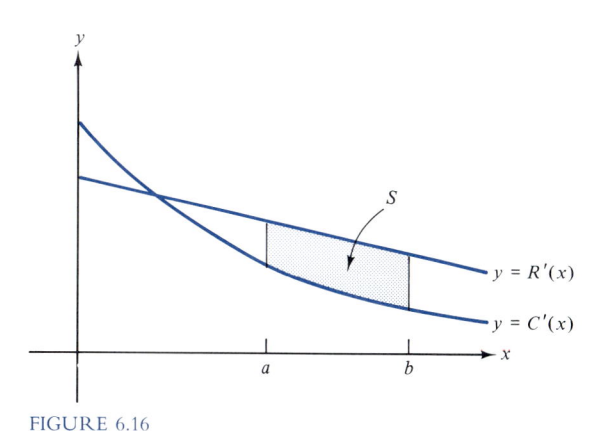

FIGURE 6.15

FIGURE 6.16

INTEGRATION

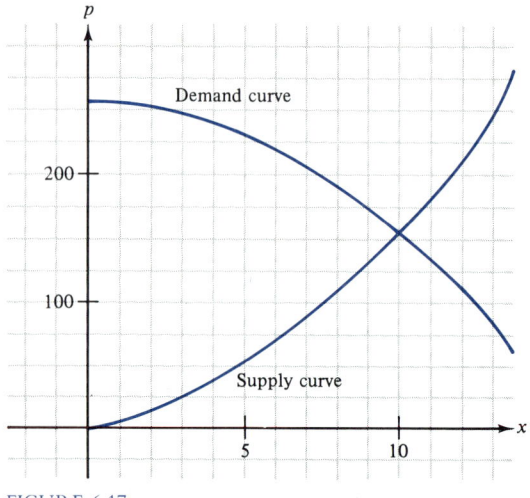

FIGURE 6.17

Finally, suppose that the demand equation for a particular product is given by

$$p = 260 - x^2,$$

where p is the price, in dollars, and x is the demand. Furthermore, suppose that the supply equation is given by

$$p = x^2 + 6x,$$

where p is the price, in dollars, and x is the supply. The graphs of these two functions are shown in Figure 6.17.

The two curves intersect at a point called the equilibrium point, where supply and demand are equal. We find the x-coordinate of the point by equating the expressions for p. We have

$$x^2 + 6x = 260 - x^2$$
$$2x^2 + 6x - 260 = 0$$
$$x^2 + 3x - 130 = 0$$
$$(x + 13)(x - 10) = 0.$$

The only positive solution is 10. When $x = 10$,

$$p = 260 - 10^2 = 160.$$

So the equilibrium point is (10, 160).

As the demand curve shows, there are consumers who are willing to pay more than the equilibrium price, so they benefit from the equilibrium price. The total amount of money saved by consumers because of the

6.4 AREA

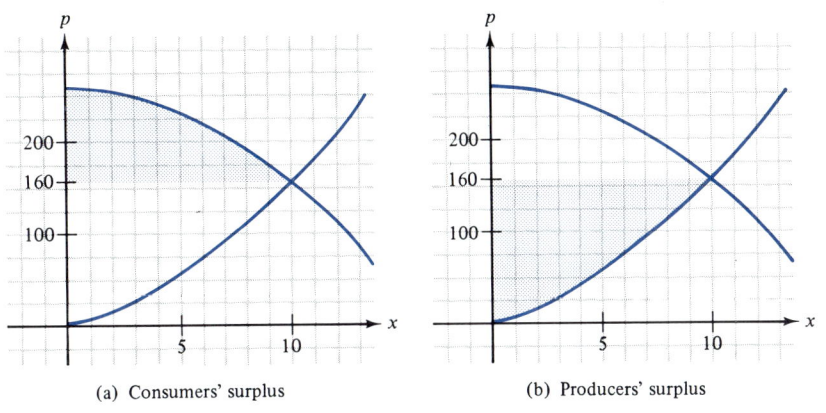

(a) Consumers' surplus
(b) Producers' surplus

FIGURE 6.18

equilibrium price is called the **consumers' surplus**. It is represented by the area shown in Figure 6.18(a).

This area, of course, may be determined by a definite integral. We have

$$\text{consumers' surplus} = \int_0^{10} ((260 - x^2) - 160)dx$$
$$= \int_0^{10} (100 - x^2)dx$$
$$= \left(100x - \frac{x^3}{3}\right)\Big|_0^{10}$$
$$= 1000 - \frac{1000}{3} = \frac{2000}{3} = 666\tfrac{2}{3}.$$

The consumers' surplus is almost $667.

As seen from the supply curve, some producers are willing to offer the product at a price below the equilibrium price, so they benefit from the equilibrium price too. The extra amount of money made by producers because of the equilibrium price is called the **producers' surplus**. It is represented by the area shown in Figure 6.18(b). Using the definite integral we have

$$\text{producers' surplus} = \int_0^{10} (160 - (x^2 + 6x))dx$$
$$= \int_0^{10} (160 - x^2 - 6x)dx$$
$$= \left(160x - \frac{x^3}{3} - 3x^2\right)\Big|_0^{10}$$
$$= 1600 - \frac{1000}{3} - 300 = \frac{2900}{3} = 966\tfrac{2}{3}.$$

The producers' surplus is almost $967.

EXERCISE

Determine the consumers' surplus and the producers' surplus if the demand equation is $p = 525 - x^2$ and the supply equation is $p = x^2 + 5x$, where p is in dollars.

■ ANSWER
Consumers' surplus = $2250; producers' surplus = $2812.50

PROBLEM SET 6.4

In Problems 1–40, determine the area of each region described.

1. Bounded by $y = 5$, the x-axis, $x = -2$, and $x = 4$
2. Bounded by $y = \sqrt{3}$, the x-axis, $x = -\sqrt{3}$, and $x = \sqrt{3}$
3. Bounded by $y = x + 2$, the x-axis, $x = 1$, and $x = 3$
4. Bounded by $y = -x + 5$, the x-axis, $x = 2$, and $x = 5$
5. Bounded by $y = 4 - (x + 2)^2$, the x-axis, $x = -3$, and $x = -1$
6. Bounded by $y = (x + 1)^2 - 1$, the x-axis, $x = -4$, and $x = -3$
7. Bounded by $y = (4 - x)^3$, the x-axis, and $x = 3$
8. Bounded by $y = (-1 - x)^4$, the x-axis, and $x = 1$
9. Bounded by $y = e^{-x} + 2$, the x-axis, the y-axis, and $x = e$
10. Bounded by $y = e^{2x} - e^4$, the x-axis, and $x = e$
11. Bounded by $y = \sqrt{x}$, the x-axis, and $x = 9$
12. Bounded by $y = \sqrt[3]{x}$, the x-axis, and $x = 8$
13. Bounded by $y = 2x - 7$, the x-axis, $x = 0$, and $x = \pi$
14. Bounded by $y = -4x - 6$, the x-axis, $x = -\sqrt{2}$, and $x = 0$
15. Bounded by $y = 1/(x - 6)$, the x-axis, $x = 1$, and $x = 4$
16. Bounded by $y = 1/(x + 5)$, the x-axis, $x = -9$, and $x = -6$
17. Bounded by $y = (x - 2)^2 - 1$, the x-axis, $x = 0$, and $x = 3$
18. Bounded by $y = x(x - 1)$, the x-axis, $x = -1$, and $x = 1$
19. Bounded by $y = 1 - x^4$, the x-axis, $x = -2$, and $x = 2$
20. Bounded by $y = x^2 - 6x + 5$, the x-axis, $x = 0$, and $x = 6$
21. Bounded by $y = 1 - e^{-x}$, the x-axis, $x = -1$, and $x = 3$
22. Bounded by $y = e^{1+x} - 1$, the x-axis, $x = -3$, and $x = 1$
23. Bounded by $y = \begin{cases} -3 & \text{when } x \leq -1 \\ 2x - 1 & \text{when } x > -1 \end{cases}$, the x-axis, $x = -6$, and $x = 2$.
24. Bounded by $y = \begin{cases} -x - 2 & \text{when } x \leq 0 \\ -2 & \text{when } x > 0 \end{cases}$, the x-axis, $x = -6$, and $x = 10$.
25. Bounded by $y = 1 - x^2$ and $y = 2x - 2$
26. Bounded by $y = (x - 3)^2$ and $y = 4x$
27. Bounded by $y = x^2 + 1$ and $y = 9 - x^2$
28. Bounded by $y = x^2 - 2$ and $y = x^3 - 2$
29. Bounded by $y = 3/x$ and $y = -x + 4$
30. Bounded by $y = x^3$ and $y = 4x$
31. Bounded by $y = x/2$, $y = 6 - x$, $x = 0$, and $x = 6$
32. Bounded by $y = 2x + 5$, $y = -x - 1$, $x = -4$, and $x = 0$
33. Bounded by $y = e^{2x}$, $y = 7$, $x = 0$, and $x = 1$
34. Bounded by $y = e^{-x}$, $y = 19$, $x = -3$, and $x = 0$
35. Bounded by $y = -\frac{1}{3}x^3 + x$ and the x-axis
36. Bounded by $y = -x^3 + 12x$ and the x-axis
37. Bounded by $y = \frac{1}{4}x^4 - x^3$ and $y = 0$
38. Bounded by $y = -3x^4 + 4x^3$ and $y = 0$
39. Bounded by $y = x^2(x + 1)(x - 1)$ and the x-axis
40. Bounded by $y = x(x + 1)^2(1 - x)$ and the x-axis

41. A company determines that its marginal revenue is $R'(x) = 125 - 2x$ and its marginal cost is $C'(x) = 0.02x + 24$. Determine the additional profit generated by increasing production and sales from $x = 40$ to $x = 50$.

42. The velocity of a particle is $v = 256 - 32t$. Determine the net change in the position function from $t = 3$ to $t = 4$.

43. The short-term birth and death rates (in hundreds per hour) of a certain strain of bacteria are approximated by
$$b(t) = 2e^{0.3t} - 1 \quad \text{and} \quad d(t) = 2e^{0.2t} - 1.$$
Determine the overall population change (to the nearest hundred) from $t = 2$ to $t = 5$.

44. The short-term birth and death rates (in thousands per day) of a certain species of fly are approximated by
$$b(t) = \sqrt[3]{2t + 3} \quad \text{and} \quad d(t) = \frac{1}{2t + 3}.$$
Determine the overall population change (to the nearest thousand) from $t = 1$ to $t = 12$.

In Problems 45–48, determine the consumers' surplus and the producers' surplus.

45. The demand equation is $p = 30 - x$ and the supply equation is $p = x^2 + 10$.

46. The demand equation is $p = 18 - x$ and the supply equation is $p = x^2 + 2x$.

47. The demand equation is $p = 150 - e^x$ and the supply equation is $p = 50 + e^x$.

48. The demand equation is $p = 40 - \sqrt{x}$ and the supply equation is $p = 10 + 2\sqrt{x}$.

6.5 THE DEFINITE INTEGRAL AS THE LIMIT OF A SUM

We know that the definite integral is the net change in an antiderivative. In this section we develop an entirely different view, one that broadens its applications.

Let's begin by letting $f(x) = (x - 2)^2 + 1$ and considering
$$\int_1^4 ((x - 2)^2 + 1)dx.$$

This has a geometric interpretation; it is the area of the region in Figure 6.19. The area is
$$\int_1^4 ((x - 2)^2 + 1)dx = \left(\frac{(x - 2)^3}{3} + x\right)\Big|_1^4$$
$$= \left(\tfrac{8}{3} + 4\right) - \left(-\tfrac{1}{3} + 1\right) = 6.$$

Now suppose we try to approximate this area by dividing $[1,4]$ into equal subintervals to form bases of rectangles. For example, let's divide $[1,4]$ into six equal subintervals: $[1,1.5]$, $[1.5,2]$, $[2,2.5]$, $[2.5,3]$, $[3,3.5]$, and $[3.5,4]$. Also, let's make the height of each rectangle be the value of the function at the right endpoint of the subinterval. See Figure 6.20.

The sum of the areas of the six rectangles is an approximation of the area of the region. Since the area of each rectangle is its width times its height, we have

approximate area $= (0.5) \cdot f(1.5) + (0.5) \cdot f(2) + (0.5) \cdot f(2.5)$
$\qquad + (0.5) \cdot f(3) + (0.5) \cdot f(3.5) + (0.5) \cdot f(4)$
$= (0.5)(f(1.5) + f(2) + f(2.5) + f(3) + f(3.5) + f(4))$
$= (0.5)(1.25 + 1 + 1.25 + 2 + 3.25 + 5)$
$= 6.875.$

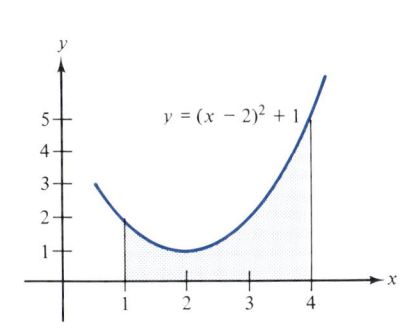

FIGURE 6.19

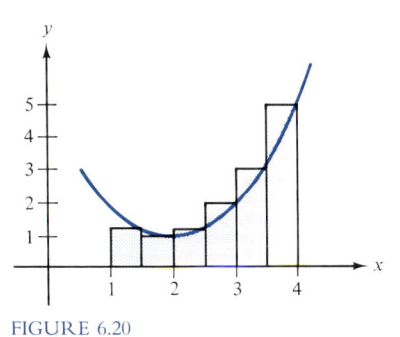

FIGURE 6.20

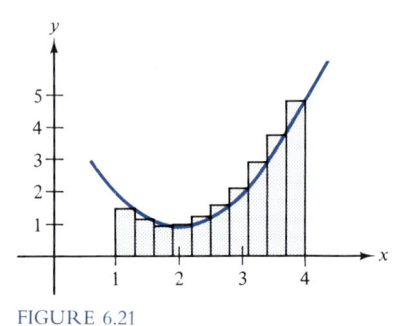

Since the exact area is 6, our approximation is not really good. But we can improve it by using more subintervals. Let's use the same procedure but divide [1,4] into ten subintervals instead of six. See Figure 6.21. Thus

$$\begin{aligned}\text{approximate area} &= (0.3)\cdot f(1.3) + (0.3)\cdot f(1.6) + \cdots + (0.3)\cdot f(4)\\ &= (0.3)(f(1.3) + f(1.6) + \cdots + f(4))\\ &= (0.3)(1.49 + 1.16 + 1.01 + 1.04 + 1.25 + 1.64\\ &\quad + 2.21 + 2.96 + 3.89 + 5)\\ &= 6.495.\end{aligned}$$

FIGURE 6.21

As expected, this approximation is better. Indeed, it can be improved again by increasing the number of subintervals. When $n = 100$, this procedure yields an approximate area that is less than 6.05. How close can we get to the exact value with this procedure? As close as we want. If we let S be our approximation function, such that $S(n)$ represents the approximate area with n subintervals, then

$$\lim_{n\to\infty} S(n) = 6.$$

As n gets larger without bound, $S(n)$ approaches 6, the exact area, which came from a definite integral. This leads to the following important theorem.

THEOREM 6.12

Let f be a continuous function defined on $[a,b]$. If $[a,b]$ is divided into n subintervals of equal length, denoting the ith subinterval as $[x_{i-1},x_i]$,* then

$$\lim_{n\to\infty} S(n) = \int_a^b f(x)\,dx,$$

where

$$S(n) = \frac{b-a}{n}(f(x_1) + f(x_2) + \cdots + f(x_n)).$$

This gives us a very different view of the definite integral. It is the limit of a special approximating sum. It is this special sum that motivates the notation for definite integral. S is frequently written

$$S(n) = \frac{b-a}{n}\sum_{i=1}^{n} f(x_i),$$

where the summation symbol $\sum$ (sigma, Greek S) means

$$\sum_{i=1}^{n} f(x_i) = f(x_1) + f(x_2) + \cdots + f(x_n).$$

Hence,

$$\lim_{n\to\infty} \frac{b-a}{n}\sum_{i=1}^{n} f(x_i) = \int_a^b f(x)\,dx.$$

* Note that $x_{i-1} = a + (i-1)\dfrac{b-a}{n}$ and $x_i = a + i\cdot\dfrac{b-a}{n}$.

6.5 THE DEFINITE INTEGRAL AS THE LIMIT OF A SUM

So we may compute such limits by evaluating a definite integral. (And we see why the definite integral may be thought of as an "infinite sum.") Let's apply this idea to the following problem.

Consider the region bounded by $f(x) = x^3$, the x-axis, $x = 1$, and $x = 2$, shown in Figure 6.22. If this region is rotated about the x-axis, we get the solid pictured in Figure 6.23. What is the volume of this solid? Let's answer this by noting how the volume could be approximated. We could divide the region into rectangles and rotate each rectangle about the x-axis. See Figure 6.24.

When each rectangle is rotated about the x-axis, it forms a disk. What is the volume of such a disk? The volume of a disk is π times radius squared times depth. Let's consider the ith disk, on the subinterval $[x_{i-1}, x_i]$. Its depth is the same as the width of the rectangle that generates it, $(2-1)/n$. Its radius is the same as the height of the rectangle, $f(x_i) = x_i^3$. So its volume is

$$\pi(x_i^3)^2 \cdot \frac{2-1}{n} = \pi x_i^6 \cdot \frac{2-1}{n}.$$

So our approximation $S(n)$ is

$$S(n) = \pi x_1^6 \cdot \frac{2-1}{n} + \pi x_2^6 \cdot \frac{2-1}{n} + \cdots + \pi x_n^6 \cdot \frac{2-1}{n}$$

$$= \pi \cdot \frac{2-1}{n} (x_1^6 + x_2^6 + \cdots + x_n^6),$$

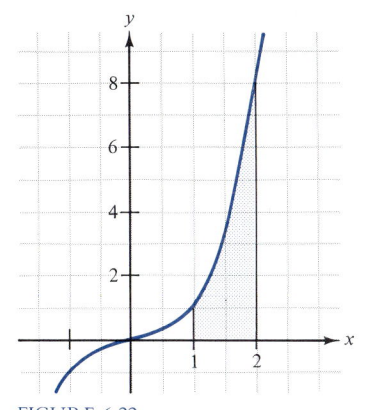

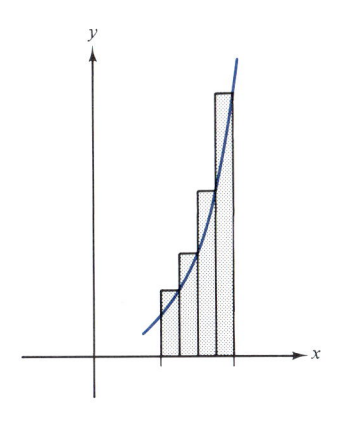

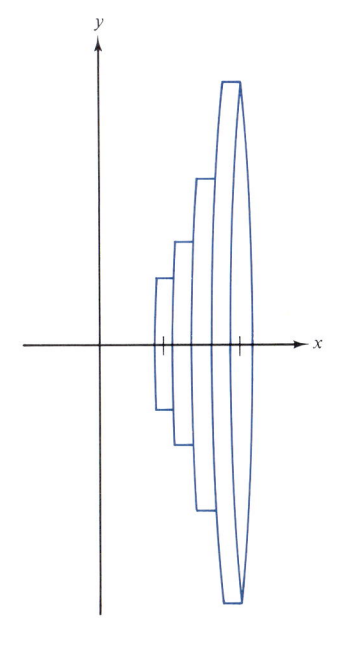

FIGURE 6.22

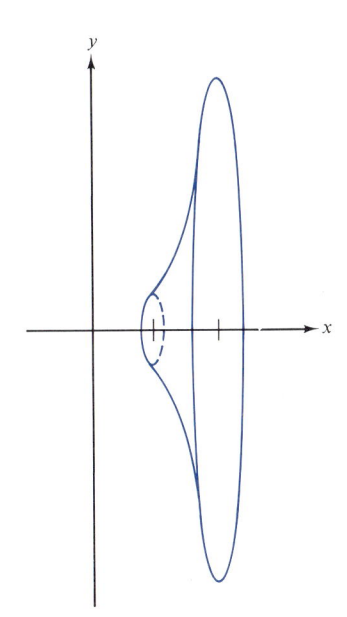

FIGURE 6.23

FIGURE 6.24

and it gets better and better as n gets larger. In fact, the volume is the limit of this approximation:

$$\text{volume} = \lim_{n \to \infty} S(n)$$

$$= \pi \cdot \lim_{n \to \infty} \frac{2-1}{n}(x_1^6 + x_2^6 + \cdots + x_n^6).$$

But this latter limit is just the definite integral

$$\int_1^2 x^6 dx.$$

So the volume is

$$\pi \int_1^2 x^6 dx = \pi \cdot \frac{x^7}{7}\bigg|_1^2 = \pi \left(\frac{128}{7} - \frac{1}{7}\right)$$

$$= \frac{127\pi}{7} \quad (\approx 57.00).$$

We have, in fact, used the following theorem.

THEOREM 6.13 Let f be a continuous function defined on $[a,b]$, and let R be the region bounded by $y = f(x)$, the x-axis, $x = a$, and $x = b$. Then the volume of the solid obtained by rotating R about the x-axis is

$$\pi \int_a^b (f(x))^2 dx.$$

EXAMPLE 1

Let R be the region bounded by $y = 1/x$, the x-axis, $x = 1$, and $x = 3$. Determine the volume of the solid obtained by rotating R about the x-axis.

■ SOLUTION

Let's take a look at the region and the corresponding solid, shown in Figure 6.25. Using Theorem 6.13 we get

$$\pi \int_1^3 (f(x))^2 dx = \pi \int_1^3 \frac{1}{x^2} dx = \pi \int_1^3 x^{-2} dx$$

$$= \pi \cdot \left(\frac{x^{-1}}{-1}\right)\bigg|_1^3 = \pi \left(\frac{-1}{x}\right)\bigg|_1^3$$

$$= \pi \left(\frac{-1}{3} + 1\right) = \tfrac{2}{3}\pi \quad (\approx 2.094).$$

6.5 THE DEFINITE INTEGRAL AS THE LIMIT OF A SUM

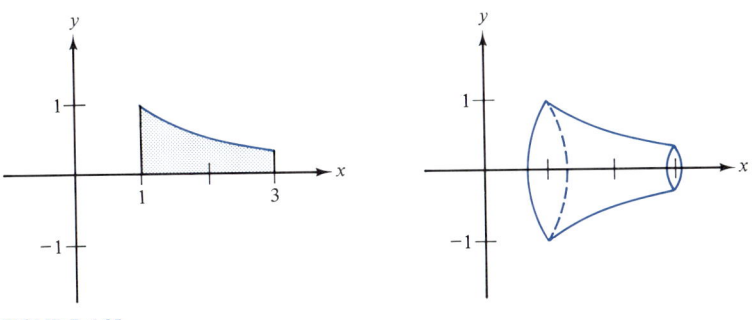

FIGURE 6.25

EXERCISE

Let R be the region bounded by $y = 1/x^2$, the x-axis, $x = -2$, and $x = -1$. Determine the volume of the solid obtained by rotating R about the x-axis.

■ ANSWER
$\frac{7}{24}\pi \ (\approx 0.9163)$

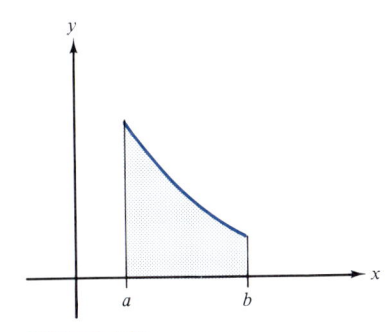

FIGURE 6.26

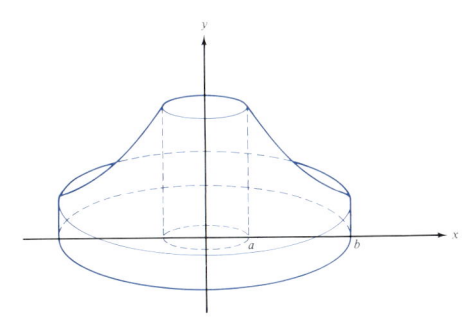

FIGURE 6.27

Let's consider another problem. Suppose that we have the region of Figure 6.26. If the region is rotated about the y-axis, we get a solid (with a hole through the center, Figure 6.27).

What is the volume of the solid? We can approximate it by dividing the region into rectangles and rotating each about the y-axis. When each rectangle is rotated about the y-axis, it forms a shell (like a tin can without top or bottom, Figure 6.28). What is the volume of such a shell? It's the volume of the cylinder determined by the outside surface less the volume of the cylinder determined by the inside surface. The volume of a cylinder

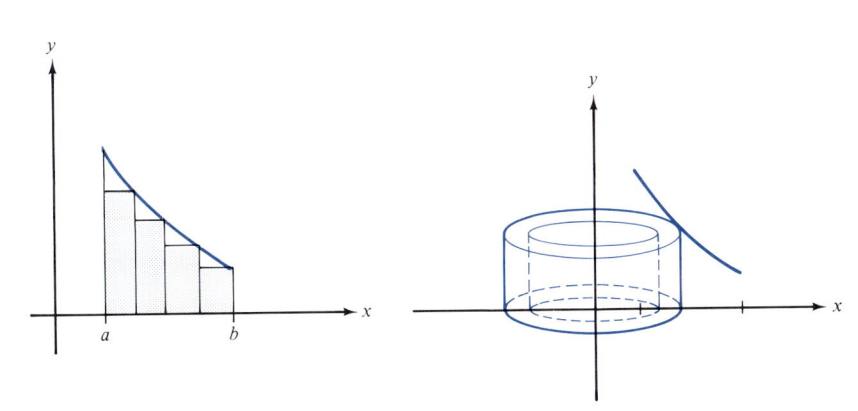

FIGURE 6.28

is π times radius squared times height. Let's consider the ith shell, on the subinterval $[x_{i-1}, x_i]$. Its volume then is

$$\pi x_i^2 \cdot f(x_i) - \pi x_{i-1}^2 \cdot f(x_i) = \pi \cdot f(x_i) \cdot (x_i^2 - x_{i-1}^2)$$
$$= \pi \cdot f(x_i) \cdot (x_i + x_{i-1})(x_i - x_{i-1})$$
$$= 2\pi \cdot f(x_i) \cdot \frac{x_i + x_{i-1}}{2} \cdot \frac{b - a}{n}.$$

But $(x_i + x_{i-1})/2$ is the average of the two radii. If n is large, then this is approximately x_i. So for large n the volume of the ith shell is approximately

$$2\pi \cdot f(x_i) \cdot x_i \cdot \frac{b - a}{n}.$$

Therefore the approximating sum is

$$S(n) = 2\pi \cdot f(x_1) \cdot x_1 \cdot \frac{b - a}{n} + \cdots + 2\pi \cdot f(x_n) \cdot x_n \cdot \frac{b - a}{n}$$
$$= 2\pi \cdot \frac{b - a}{n} (x_1 f(x_1) + x_2 f(x_2) + \cdots + x_n f(x_n)).$$

If we take the limit of $S(n)$ as $n \to \infty$ we get

$$\text{volume} = \lim_{n \to \infty} S(n)$$
$$= 2\pi \cdot \lim_{n \to \infty} \frac{b - a}{n} (x_1 f(x_1) + x_2 f(x_2) + \cdots + x_n f(x_n)).$$

But the latter limit is the definite integral

$$\int_a^b x f(x) \, dx.$$

This is the basis of the following theorem.

THEOREM 6.14

Let f be a continuous function defined on $[a, b]$ such that $f(x) \geq 0$ for all $x \in [a, b]$, and such that $a \geq 0$. Let R be the region bounded by $y = f(x)$, the x-axis, $x = a$, and $x = b$. Then the volume of the solid obtained by rotating R about the y-axis is

$$2\pi \int_a^b x f(x) \, dx.$$

EXAMPLE 2

Let R be the region bounded by $y = x^2$, the x-axis, $x = 1$, and $x = 2$. Determine the volume of the solid obtained by rotating R about the y-axis.

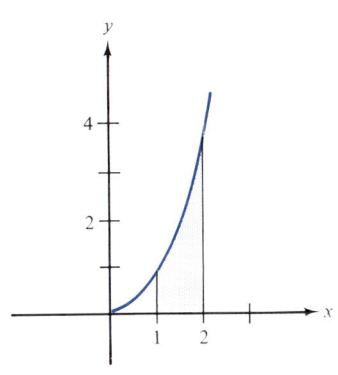

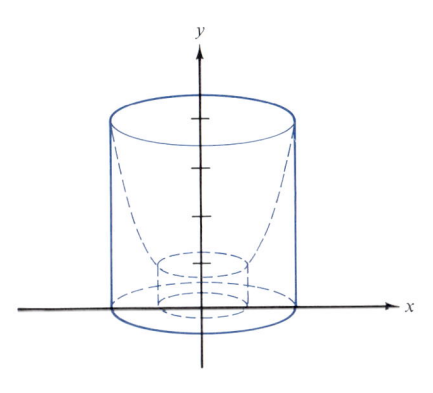

6.5 THE DEFINITE INTEGRAL AS THE LIMIT OF A SUM

FIGURE 6.29

■ SOLUTION

Let's take a look at the region and the corresponding solid, shown in Figure 6.29. Using Theorem 6.14 we get

$$2\pi \int_1^2 xf(x)dx = 2\pi \int_1^2 x \cdot x^2 dx$$
$$= 2\pi \int_1^2 x^3 dx$$
$$= 2\pi \cdot \frac{x^4}{4}\Big|_1^2$$
$$= 8\pi - \frac{\pi}{2} = \frac{15\pi}{2} \quad (\approx 23.56).$$

EXERCISE

Let R be the region bounded by $y = x^3$, the x-axis, $x = 1$, and $x = 2$. Determine the volume of the solid obtained by rotating R about the y-axis.

■ ANSWER
$\frac{62}{5}\pi \; (\approx 38.96)$

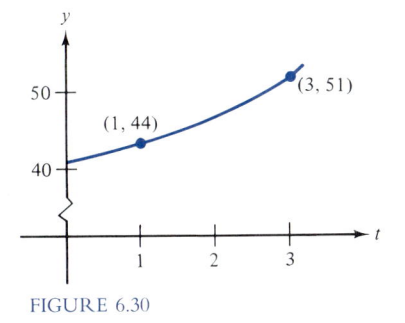

FIGURE 6.30

Let's consider another problem. Suppose $f(t)$ is the temperature, in degrees Fahrenheit, t hours after 12:00 noon on a specified day. If

$$f(t) = \frac{t^2 + 10t + 165}{4},$$

what is the average temperature between 1:00 and 3:00 p.m.?

The graph of this quadratic function is shown in Figure 6.30. We could approximate its average value by dividing [1,3] into equal subintervals and treating the temperature as constant over each subinterval. See Figure 6.31.

In the *i*th subinterval, the temperature is assumed to be $f(t_i)$. So the approximate average temperature $S(n)$ is

$$S(n) = \frac{f(t_1) + f(t_2) + \cdots + f(t_n)}{n}.$$

This approximation would get better and better as n increases. In fact, the average is the limit of this approximation:

$$\text{average} = \lim_{n \to \infty} S(n)$$

$$= \lim_{n \to \infty} \frac{1}{n}(f(t_1) + f(t_2) + \cdots + f(t_n)).$$

To put this limit in a more recognizable form, let's multiply and divide by $3 - 1$. We have

$$\lim_{n \to \infty} \frac{1}{n}(f(t_1) + f(t_2) + \cdots + f(t_n))$$

$$= \lim_{n \to \infty} \frac{1}{3 - 1} \cdot \frac{3 - 1}{n}(f(t_1) + f(t_2) + \cdots + f(t_n))$$

$$= \frac{1}{3 - 1} \lim_{n \to \infty} \frac{3 - 1}{n}(f(t_1) + f(t_2) + \cdots + f(t_n)).$$

This latter limit is a definite integral, so we have

$$\frac{1}{2} \int_1^3 f(t)dt.$$

Thus

$$\text{average} = \frac{1}{2} \int_1^3 f(t)dt$$

$$= \frac{1}{2} \int_1^3 \frac{t^2 + 10t + 165}{4} dt$$

$$= \frac{1}{8}\left(\frac{t^3}{3} + 5t^2 + 165t\right)\bigg|_1^3$$

$$= \frac{1}{8}\left(9 + 45 + 495 - \frac{1}{3} - 5 - 165\right)$$

$$= \frac{1}{8}\left(\frac{1136}{3}\right) = 47\tfrac{1}{3}.$$

The average temperature during the period was $47\tfrac{1}{3}°$F. This example illustrates the following theorem.

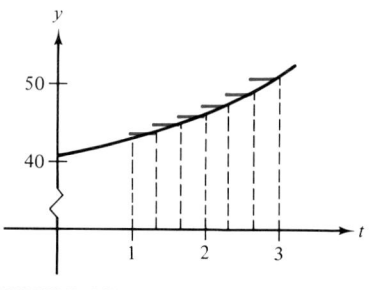

FIGURE 6.31

THEOREM 6.15

Let f be a continuous function defined on $[a,b]$. Then the average value of $f(x)$ on $[a,b]$ is

$$\frac{1}{b-a}\int_a^b f(x)\,dx.$$

EXAMPLE 3

Determine the average value of $f(x) = x\sqrt{x^2+1}$ on $[0,2]$.

■ SOLUTION

Using Theorem 6.15 we get

$$\frac{1}{2-0}\int_0^2 x\sqrt{x^2+1}\,dx = \frac{1}{2}\int_0^2 x(x^2+1)^{1/2}\,dx$$

$$= \frac{1}{4}\int_0^2 2x(x^2+1)^{1/2}\,dx$$

$$= \frac{1}{4}(x^2+1)^{3/2}\cdot\frac{2}{3}\bigg|_0^2$$

$$= \frac{1}{6}(5^{3/2} - 1^{3/2})$$

$$= \frac{5\sqrt{5}-1}{6} \quad (\approx 1.697).$$

EXERCISE

Determine the average value of $f(x) = x^2\sqrt{x^3+1}$ on $[-1,2]$.

■ ANSWER

2

PROBLEM SET 6.5

In Problems 1–12, determine the volume of the solid obtained by rotating the region described about the x-axis.

1. Bounded by $y = 3$, the x-axis, $x = 1$, and $x = 5$
2. Bounded by $y = -5$, the x-axis, $x = -2$, and $x = 3$
3. Bounded by $y = -\frac{1}{2}x$, the x-axis, $x = 0$, and $x = 4$
4. Bounded by $y = 3x$, the x-axis, $x = \sqrt[3]{4}$, and $x = \sqrt[3]{11}$
5. Bounded by $y = 1/\sqrt{x}$, the x-axis, $x = 2$, and $x = 6$
6. Bounded by $y = 1/\sqrt{x+4}$, the x-axis, $x = -3$, and $x = 0$
7. Bounded by $y = 1 - x^2$, the x-axis, $x = -1$, and $x = 1$
8. Bounded by $y = 4 - x^2$, the x-axis, $x = 0$, and $x = 2$
9. Bounded by $y = (x^2 + 2x)^2\sqrt{x+1}$, the x-axis, $x = 0$, and $x = 1$

10. Bounded by $y = \sqrt[3]{2x^3 + 6x}\sqrt{x^2 + 1}$, the x-axis, $x = 0$, and $x = 1$
11. Bounded by $y = e^{-2x}$, the x-axis, $x = -3$, and $x = -2$
12. Bounded by $y = e^{x/3}$, the x-axis, $x = -6$, and $x = 3$
13. Determine the volume of the solid obtained by rotating the line segment with endpoints (1,1) and (3,5) about the x-axis.
14. Determine the volume of the solid obtained by rotating the line segment with endpoints (−3,5) and (6,2) about the x-axis.
15. Determine the volume of the solid obtained by rotating the triangle with vertices (0,0), (2,2), and (6,0) about the x-axis.
16. Determine the volume of the solid obtained by rotating the triangle with vertices (−6,0), (−4,4), and (0,0) about the x-axis.
17. Derive the formula for the volume of a right circular cone of radius r and height h. [*Hint:* Consider the line segment with endpoints (0,0) and (h,r).]
18. Derive the formula for the volume of a right circular cylinder of radius r and height h. [*Hint:* Consider the line segment with endpoints (0,r) and (h,r).]

In Problems 19 and 20, determine the volume of the solid obtained, by rotating about the x-axis, the region bounded by $y = f(x)$, the x-axis, $x = a$ [where a is the x-coordinate of the relative maximum point of $f(x)$], and $x = b$ [where b is the x-coordinate of the inflection point of $f(x)$].

19. $f(x) = \dfrac{x^3}{3} - x$
20. $f(x) = x^3 - 3x^2 + 5$

In Problems 21–28, determine the volume of the solid obtained by rotating the region described about the y-axis.

21. Bounded by $y = 3x$, the x-axis, $x = 2$, and $x = 4$
22. Bounded by $y = 6$, the x-axis, $x = 3$, and $x = 4$
23. Bounded by $y = \sqrt[3]{x}$, the x-axis, $x = 1$, and $x = 8$
24. Bounded by $y = \sqrt{x} + 1$, the x-axis, $x = 0$, and $x = 4$
25. Bounded by $y = e^x/x$, the x-axis, $x = \ln 3$, and $x = \ln 7$
26. Bounded by $y = 1/x^2$, the x-axis, $x = e^3$, and $x = e^8$
27. Bounded by $y = 1 - (x - 3)^2$ and the x-axis
28. Bounded by $y = 4 - (x - 2)^2$ and the x-axis

In Problems 29–38, determine the average value of the function on the indicated interval.

29. $f(x) = 6$, $[2,5]$
30. $f(x) = -7$, $[1,7]$
31. $f(x) = 4x - \pi$, $[-\pi, 2\pi]$
32. $f(x) = \sqrt{3}\,x + \tfrac{3}{2}$, $[-\sqrt{12}, \sqrt{3}]$
33. $f(x) = \sqrt{6x}$, $[6,18]$
34. $f(x) = \sqrt{15x}$, $[15,45]$
35. $f(x) = 1/x$, $[e, e^e]$
36. $f(x) = e^{1 + \ln x}/x$, $[1,e]$
37. $f(x) = x^3/(x^4 + 1)^2$, $[-1,1]$
38. $f(x) = 45x^4(2x^5 - 1)^8$, $[0,1]$

39. The value of a house (in dollars) is given by $f(t) = 60{,}000 e^{0.05t}$, where t is in years. Determine the average value of the house (to the nearest hundred dollars) during the first five years.

40. Two thousand dollars is invested in a savings account paying 8% per year and compounded continuously. Determine the average amount of money in the account (to the nearest dollar) during the first four years.

41. The annual profit (in dollars) of a company is given by $f(t) = 75{,}000 + 4500 e^{0.9t}$, where t is the number of years the company has been in business. Determine the average annual profit (to the nearest thousand dollars) during the first six years.

42. The size of a bacteria population is given by $f(t) = 7000 e^{0.7t}$, where t is elapsed time in hours. Determine the average size (to the nearest thousand) from $t = 1$ to $t = 4$.

The area of the surface generated by rotating $y = f(x)$, $a \leq x \leq b$, about the x-axis is given by

$$\int_a^b 2\pi f(x)\sqrt{1 + (f'(x))^2}\, dx.$$

In Problems 43 and 44, use this information to determine the surface area.

43. $f(x) = \tfrac{1}{3}x^3$, $0 \leq x \leq \sqrt[4]{15}$
44. $f(x) = 3\sqrt{x}$, $0 \leq x \leq 4$

*If P dollars is deposited into an account at regular intervals m times per year for n years at an annual interest rate of r% per year compounded continuously, then the amount of this **annuity** at the end of the n years is a complicated sum that can be approximated by*

$$\int_0^n mP e^{(r/100)(n-t)}\, dt.$$

This integral is needed in Problems 45–50. Approximate (to the nearest dollar) the amount of the annuity described in Problems 45–48.

45. $P = 200$, $m = 4$, $n = 8$, and $r = 10$.
46. $P = 300$, $m = 6$, $n = 11$, and $r = 8$.
47. Bimonthly periodic payments of $500 for four years at a yearly interest rate of 7%.
48. Monthly periodic payments of $500 for four years at a yearly interest rate of 6%.
49. Planning for his 10-year old daughter's college education, a father determines that he will need $50,000 in 8 years. He decides to set up a monthly annuity. Assuming a constant yearly interest rate of 9%, approximate (to the nearest dollar) his monthly payment.
50. A 50-year-old corporate executive planning for retirement would like to have a lump sum of $100,000 available when she retires at age 65. She decides to set up a bimonthly annuity. For estimating purposes she assumes a constant yearly interest rate of 6.5%. Approximate (to the nearest dollar) her bimonthly payment.

Actuaries use a concept called the **force of interest** in cases where it is necessary to measure the intensity with which interest is operating at each moment in time. An important formula is

$$a(n) = Pe^{\int_0^n \delta_t \, dt},$$

where $a(n)$ is the accumulated value after n years of an initial investment of P dollars with a force of interest δ_t. This integral is needed in Problems 51 and 52.

51. Determine the accumulated value of $1 at the end of three years if $\delta_t = 1/(1 + t)$.
52. Determine the accumulated value of $100 at the end of 13 years if $\delta_t = 0.03(1 + t)^{-2}$.
53. A large electric utility company decides to base the design of the cooling tower at one of its nuclear generating plants on the solid obtained by rotating a particular region about the y-axis. The region is bounded by the y-axis, a branch of the hyperbola $x = \sqrt{a^2 + by^2}$ where $a = 147$ and $b = 0.163$, and the horizontal lines $y = 123$ and $y = -442$. Find the total volume (to the nearest thousand) of the cooling tower.

CHAPTER 6 REVIEW

1. Determine whether each of the following is true or false.
   (a) A function F is an antiderivative of a function f if $F'(x) = f(x)$.
   (b) If f and g are functions such that $f'(x) = g'(x)$, then $f(x) = g(x) + c$ for some constant c.
   (c) $\int \pi^3 \, dx = (\pi^4/4) + c$.
   (d) If c_1 and c_2 are any constants, then
   $$\int (c_1 f(x) - c_2 g(x)) \, dx = c_1 \int f(x) \, dx - c_2 \int g(x) \, dx.$$
   (e) $\int x^0 \, dx = \dfrac{x^{0+1}}{0+1} + c$.
   (f) If $\int x(x^2 + 1)^5 \, dx = k(x^2 + 1)^6 + c$, then $k = \frac{1}{6}$.
   (g) If k is any nonzero constant, then
   $$\int_a^b \frac{f(x)}{k} \, dx = \frac{1}{k} \int_a^b f(x) \, dx.$$
   (h) If $\int_a^b 1 \, dx = a - 3b$, then $a = 2b$.
   (i) $\int \ln x \, dx = (x \ln x) - x + c$.
   (j) If $\int_a^b f(x) \, dx = 0$, then either $a = b$ or $f(x) = 0$ on $[a,b]$.
   (k) $\int 2^x \, dx = 2^x + c$.
   (l) The area of the region bounded by $y = x$, the x-axis, $x = -2$, and $x = 2$ is $\int_{-2}^{2} x \, dx$.
   (m) The area of the region bounded by $y = (x - 5)^7$, the x-axis, $x = 2$, and $x = 4$ is $\int_2^4 (x - 5)^7 \, dx$.
   (n) If $\int_1^b 5x^4 = 242$, then $b = \int_{\sqrt{10}}^{\sqrt{13}} 2x \, dx$.
   (o) Let f be any continuous function defined on $[a,b]$. Then the area of the region bounded by $y = f(x)$, the x-axis, $x = a$, and $x = b$ is $\int_a^b |f(x)| \, dx$.
   (p) $\int_{-2}^{-1} |x| \, dx = \frac{3}{2}$.
   (q) If $f(x) = k$ is a constant function on $[a,b]$, then the average value of $f(x)$ on $[a,b]$ is k.
   (r) If the area of R_1 is 3 (see figure below) and the area of R_2 is 7, then $\int_{-2}^{4} f(x) \, dx = 4$.

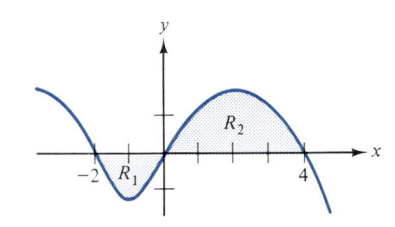

(s) The average value of $f(x) = mx$ on $[-a, a]$ is 0.
(t) The area of the region bounded by $y = x$, $y = x + 1$, $x = -2$, and $x = 5$ is $\int_{-2}^{5} 1 \, dx$.
(u) The area of the region bounded by $y = 2x$, $y = -2x$, $x = -3$, and $x = 3$ is $\int_{0}^{3} 4x \, dx - \int_{-3}^{0} 4x \, dx$.
(v) Let R be the region bounded by $y = \sqrt[4]{x}$, the x-axis, $x = 1$, and $x = 16$. The volume of the solid obtained by rotating R about the x-axis is $\int_{1}^{16} \sqrt{x} \, dx$.
(w) The volume of the solid obtained by rotating the shaded region in the graph below about the x-axis is $\pi \int_{a}^{c} (f(x))^2 \, dx - \pi \int_{c}^{b} (f(x))^2 \, dx$.

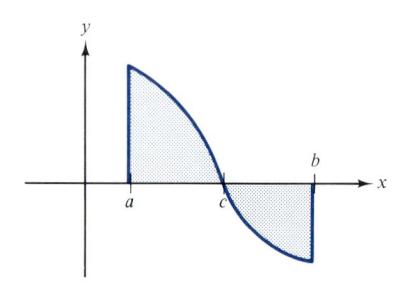

(x) If $y = \sqrt[3]{x^5 + 4x^4 + 3x^3 - 7x^2}$, then $\int_{0}^{1} y' \, dx = 1$.

In Problems 2–25, evaluate the indefinite integral.

2. $\int (4x^3 - 3x^2 + 2x - 1) dx$

3. $\int \sqrt{x} \left(1 - \dfrac{1}{x}\right) dx$

4. $\int \sqrt[3]{3x} \, dx$

5. $\int (x^{3+e} + x^{\log 5}) dx$

6. $\int \dfrac{x^3 - 7x + 4}{x} dx$

7. $\int x(3x + 1)^2 dx$

8. $\int \left(\dfrac{x^4}{4} + 4\right)^8 (x^3) dx$

9. $\int (x^6 - 1)(x^7 - 7x)^7 dx$

10. $\int x^{1/3}(1 + x^{4/3})^{-7} dx$

11. $\int \dfrac{2x}{\sqrt[3]{7 - 5x^2}} dx$

12. $\int \sqrt{\dfrac{e^{2x}}{1 + e^x}} dx$

13. $\int \dfrac{3 + \ln x}{x} dx$

14. $\int (e^x + x^e + e^e) dx$

15. $\int \dfrac{1}{2 + 5x} dx$

16. $\int \dfrac{x^2 e^{x^3}}{e^{x^3} + 7} dx$

17. $\int \dfrac{1}{x \ln x} dx$

18. $\int \dfrac{(\ln(\ln x))^6}{x \ln x} dx$

19. $\int \left(3e^{5-5x} + \dfrac{2}{e^x}\right) dx$

20. $\int \dfrac{e^{x^{1/4}}}{x^{3/4}} dx$

21. $\int \dfrac{1}{1 + e^{-x}} dx$

22. $\int \dfrac{x \ln(1 + x^2)}{1 + x^2} dx$

23. $\int \dfrac{e^x}{e^{2x} + 2e^x + 1} dx$

24. $\int \dfrac{e^x - e^{-x}}{(e^x + e^{-x})^2} dx$

25. $\int \sqrt{3 - (e^{3x} + 1)^2} (e^{6x} + e^{3x}) dx$

In Problems 26–34, evaluate the definite integral.

26. $\int_{-1}^{1} (6x^5 + 5x^4 - 4x^3) dx$

27. $\int_{-1}^{0} (x^3 - x - 1)^4 (3x^2 - 1) dx$

28. $\int_{1}^{4} \dfrac{x^2 - 2x + 3}{\sqrt{x}} dx$

29. $\int_{1}^{2} \dfrac{10(x^3 + 1)^2}{x^2} dx$

30. $\int_{1}^{\sqrt[5]{17}} \dfrac{5^2}{x^5 + 1} dx$

31. $\int_{0}^{\ln 3} \dfrac{e^{2x}}{e^{2x} + 1} dx$

32. $\int_{0}^{12} (e^{x/6} + e^2) dx$

33. $\int_{-2}^{-1} x^2 e^{x^3 - 1} dx$

34. $\int_{0}^{1} e^{e^x} e^x dx$

In Problems 35–44, determine the area of the region described.

35. Bounded by $y = e^3$, the x-axis, $x = 0$, and $x = 3e^{-3}$
36. Bounded by $y = -x$, the x-axis, $x = -1$, and $x = 1$
37. Bounded by $y = 1/x^2$, the x-axis, $x = -\frac{7}{2}$ and $x = -\frac{1}{4}$
38. Bounded by $y = e^{\sqrt{x}}/\sqrt{x}$, the x-axis, $x = 1$, and $x = 4$
39. Bounded by $y = \pi^2 - x^2$ and $y = 0$
40. Bounded by $y = (x - 1)^2 - 1$, the x-axis, $x = -1$, and $x = 1$
41. Bounded by $y = -(x - 2)^2 + 4$ and $y = x$
42. Bounded by $y = 6x - x^2$ and $y = x^2 - 2x$
43. Bounded by $y = x^2 - 2$, $y = x$, $x = -1$, and $x = 3$
44. Bounded by $y = e^{3x}$, $x = 1$, and $y = 1$

In Problems 45–50, determine the volume of the solid obtained by rotating the region described about the x-axis.

45. Bounded by $y = x^3$, the x-axis, $x = 0$, and $x = 1$
46. Bounded by $y = 1/(x - 3)$, the x-axis, $x = -1$, and $x = 1$
47. Bounded by $y = -x^2 - 2x$, the x-axis, $x = -1$, and $x = 0$
48. Bounded by $y = \sqrt{4 - x}$, the x-axis, and $x = 0$
49. Bounded by $y = (e^x + e^{-x})/2$, the x-axis, $x = 0$, and $x = 1$
50. Bounded by $y = x/\sqrt{x^3 + 3}$, the x-axis, $x = 1$, and $x = \sqrt[3]{29}$

In Problems 51–54, determine the volume of the solid obtained by rotating the region described about the y-axis.

51. $y = 1/x$, the x-axis, $x = 4e$, and $x = 6e$
52. $y = 6x - x^2$, the x-axis, $x = 0$, and $x = 2$
53. $y = (\ln x)/x^2$, the x-axis, $x = e$, and $x = e^2$
54. $y = \sqrt{x^2 + 1}$, the x-axis, $x = 0$, and $x = \sqrt{3}$

In Problems 55–58, determine the average value of the function on the indicated interval.

55. $f(x) = x^2 - 1$, $[-2, 0]$
56. $f(x) = x\sqrt{2 - x^2}$, $[-1, 1]$
57. $f(x) = 1/(x - 5)$, $[0, 4]$
58. $f(x) = e^{-2x}$, $[-\frac{1}{2}, \frac{1}{2}]$
59. (a) Sketch the graph of $f(x) = x^3 - x^2 - 2x$.
    (b) Evaluate $\int_{-1}^{2} (x^3 - x^2 - 2x) dx$.
    (c) Determine the area of the region bounded by $f(x) = x^3 - x^2 - 2x$ and the x-axis.
60. Evaluate $\int \dfrac{1}{\sqrt{x+1} - \sqrt{x}} dx$ (Hint: Rationalize the denominator.)
61. Derive the formula for the volume of a sphere of radius r. (Hint: Consider the semicircle $y = \sqrt{r^2 - x^2}$ from $x = -r$ to $x = r$.)
62. Find m if $m > 0$ and the area of the region bounded by $y = mx$ and $y = x^2$ is 288.

63. Show that the average value of $f(x) = mx + b$ on $[-a, a]$ is equal to b.
64. The marginal profit of a manufacturer is given by $P'(x) = -0.06x + 300$. If the profit is $300,000 when 3000 units are sold, determine the maximum profit.
65. The marginal cost of a student's room and board for one academic year is given by $C'(t) = 10t + 50$, where t is in years. Time $t = 0$ corresponds to Fall 1975 when the cost was $1500. Determine the cost for Fall 1990.
66. A company determines that its marginal revenue (in dollars) is $R'(x) = 60 - \frac{1}{2}x$ and its marginal cost is $C'(x) = x + 30$. Determine the additional profit generated by increasing production and sales from $x = 5$ to $x = 15$.
67. A rod 10 inches long has a variable density given by $f(x) = 25 - (x^2/5)$, where x is the distance from one end of the rod. Determine the average density of the rod.
68. A company estimates that the demand for a certain product is given by $f(x) = 3000 - 1100e^{-0.9x}$, where x is the number of years the product has been on the market. Determine the average demand of the product during the first three years.
69. Determine the consumers' surplus and the producers' surplus if the demand equation is $p = 50 - 0.1x^2$ and the supply equation is $p = 10 + 0.3x^2$.

CHAPTER 7

ADDITIONAL TOPICS IN INTEGRATION

CHAPTER OUTLINE
7.1 SUBSTITUTION
7.2 INTEGRATION BY PARTS
7.3 INTEGRATION USING TABLES
7.4 APPROXIMATE INTEGRATION
7.5 LAWS OF GROWTH AND DECAY

The first three sections introduce techniques that substantially increase the number of functions that can be integrated. Section 7.4 focuses on numerical methods that approximate definite integrals. Such methods are ideally suited to computer algorithms and may be used with functions that are difficult or impossible to integrate. The last section introduces some significant applications.

7.1 SUBSTITUTION

In this section we learn to use substitution to transform the function to be integrated from something difficult to something manageable. Suppose that $F(x)$ is an antiderivative of $f(x)$ and that $x = g(u)$ for some function g. By the chain rule, the derivative of $F(g(u))$ with respect to u is

$$F'(g(u)) \cdot g'(u) = f(g(u)) \cdot g'(u).$$

In other words, $F(g(u))$ is an antiderivative of $f(g(u)) \cdot g'(u)$ with respect to u. Since $F(x) = F(g(u))$, the antiderivative of $f(x)$ with respect to x equals the antiderivative of $f(g(u)) \cdot g'(u)$ with respect to u. This is the basis of the integration technique called **substitution.**

THEOREM 7.1 If $x = g(u)$, then

$$\int f(x) dx = \int f(g(u)) \cdot g'(u) du.$$

Let's employ this theorem by considering

$$\int x\sqrt{1 + x}\, dx.$$

In the current form, we are unable to integrate. The power function $(1 + x)^{1/2}$ is not being multiplied by the appropriate derivative 1. So let $f(x) = x\sqrt{1 + x}$, and let $x = g(u) = u^2 - 1$, $u \geq 0$. (We discuss how we selected this function in a moment.) Then

$$\int x\sqrt{1 + x}\, dx = \int f(x) dx$$
$$= \int f(g(u)) \cdot g'(u) du$$
$$= \int (u^2 - 1)\sqrt{1 + u^2 - 1} \cdot 2u\, du$$
$$= \int (u^2 - 1) u \cdot 2u\, du$$
$$= 2 \int (u^4 - u^2) du$$
$$= 2 \left(\frac{u^5}{5} - \frac{u^3}{3} \right) + c$$
$$= \tfrac{2}{15} u^3 (3u^2 - 5) + c.$$

We may write this in terms of x by noting that since

$$x = u^2 - 1,$$

then

$$u^2 = x + 1$$
$$u = \sqrt{x + 1} = (x + 1)^{1/2}.$$

7.1 SUBSTITUTION

Thus

$$\int x\sqrt{1+x}\,dx = \tfrac{2}{15}(x+1)^{3/2}(3x-2) + c.$$

How do we know to let $g(u) = u^2 - 1$? We actually begin by letting

$$u = \sqrt{x+1} \tag{7-1}$$

so that we may eliminate the radical. Since $u \geq 0$, Equation (7-1) is equivalent to

$$u^2 = x + 1$$
$$x = u^2 - 1. \tag{7-2}$$

So Equation (7-2) defines g.

The use of Theorem 7.1 can be clarified by introducing differentials. To this point, the notation dy/dx, representing the derivative of y with respect to x, has been viewed in its entirety. We shall now give a meaning to the individual symbols dy and dx.

Consider the graph of $y = f(x)$ and the tangent line at an arbitrary point $P(x, f(x))$, seen in Figure 7.1. Suppose we let Q represent each other point on the tangent line. We have let dx, called the **differential of x,** represent the change in x from P to Q, and we have let dy, called the **differential of y,** represent the change in y from P to Q. Note that these changes are *along the tangent line*, not along the graph of f.

How are these differentials related? The slope of the tangent line at P is $f'(x)$. Therefore

$$\frac{dy}{dx} = f'(x).$$

FIGURE 7.1

So this ratio of the differentials represents the derivative. But dy/dx is now a fraction, and

$$dy = f'(x)\,dx.$$

The idea behind Theorem 7.1 then is to let x be some function of u and to substitute for x and for dx, the differential of x. This will become clearer in the examples.

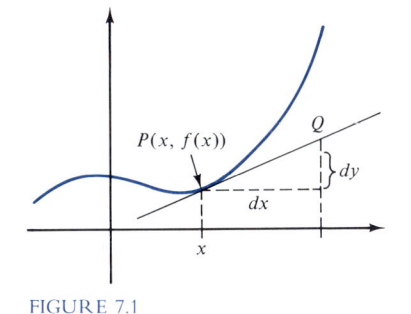

EXAMPLE 1

Evaluate $\int \dfrac{x}{\sqrt{x-1}}\,dx.$

■ SOLUTION
Let

$$u = \sqrt{x-1}$$

because we wish to eliminate the radical. Now let's solve this equation for x. We have

$$u^2 = x - 1$$
$$x = u^2 + 1.$$

Differentiation gives

$$\frac{dx}{du} = 2u.$$

Solving for the differential of x gives

$$dx = 2u\,du.$$

Thus, substituting $u^2 + 1$ for x and $2u\,du$ for dx gives

$$\int \frac{x}{\sqrt{x-1}}\,dx = \int \frac{u^2 + 1}{\sqrt{u^2}} \cdot 2u\,du$$
$$= 2\int (u^2 + 1)\,du$$
$$= 2\left(\frac{u^3}{3} + u\right) + c$$
$$= \tfrac{2}{3}u(u^2 + 3) + c.$$

Since $u = \sqrt{x - 1}$, we have

$$\int \frac{x}{\sqrt{x-1}}\,dx = \tfrac{2}{3}\sqrt{x - 1}\,(x + 2) + c.$$

EXAMPLE 2

Evaluate $\int x^2(2x - 3)^{2/3}\,dx$.

■ SOLUTION
Let

$$u = (2x - 3)^{2/3}.$$

Solving this for x gives

$$u^{3/2} = 2x - 3$$
$$x = \frac{u^{3/2} + 3}{2}.$$

Differentiation gives

$$\frac{dx}{du} = \frac{3}{4}u^{1/2}$$

$$dx = \frac{3}{4}u^{1/2}\,du.$$

Substitution for x and dx gives

$$\int x^2(2x-3)^{2/3}dx$$
$$= \int \frac{(u^{3/2}+3)^2}{4} \cdot u \cdot \frac{3}{4}u^{1/2}du$$
$$= \frac{3}{16}\int u^{3/2}(u^3+6u^{3/2}+9)du$$
$$= \frac{3}{16}\int (u^{9/2}+6u^3+9u^{3/2})du$$
$$= \frac{3}{16}\left(\frac{2u^{11/2}}{11}+\frac{3u^4}{2}+\frac{18u^{5/2}}{5}\right)+c$$
$$= \frac{3}{16}\cdot\frac{1}{110}u^{5/2}(20u^3+165u^{3/2}+396)+c$$
$$= \frac{3}{1760}(2x-3)^{5/3}(20(2x-3)^2+165(2x-3)+396)+c$$
$$= \frac{3}{1760}(2x-3)^{5/3}(80x^2+90x+81)+c.$$

EXERCISE

Evaluate the following indefinite integrals:

(a) $\int \frac{x}{\sqrt{x-2}}\,dx$ and (b) $\int x^2(3x+2)^{2/3}dx.$

■ ANSWER
(a) $\frac{2}{3}\sqrt{x-2}\,(x+4)+c$; (b) $\frac{1}{990}(3x+2)^{5/3}(90x^2-45x+18)+c$

Let's now consider a *definite* integral that requires substitution.

EXAMPLE 3

Evaluate $\int_0^5 x\sqrt{x+4}\,dx.$

■ SOLUTION
We integrate by substitution, letting
$$u = \sqrt{x+4}.$$

Thus, solving for x, we obtain
$$u^2 = x+4$$
$$x = u^2 - 4.$$

Differentiating, we get

$$\frac{dx}{du} = 2u$$

$$dx = 2u\,du.$$

Before substituting, let's note that the limits of integration are for x, not u, and that

$$u\Big|_{x=0} = \sqrt{0+4} = 2,$$

$$u\Big|_{x=5} = \sqrt{5+4} = 3.$$

Thus, when we make the substitutions, we replace the lower and upper limits of integration by 2 and 3, respectively. We get

$$\int_0^5 x\sqrt{x+4}\,dx = \int_2^3 (u^2-4)u \cdot 2u\,du$$

$$= 2\int_2^3 (u^4 - 4u^2)\,du$$

$$= 2\left(\frac{u^5}{5} - \frac{4u^3}{3}\right)\Big|_2^3$$

$$= \frac{2}{15} u^3(3u^2 - 20)\Big|_2^3$$

$$= \frac{2}{15} \cdot 27(27 - 20) - \frac{2}{15} \cdot 8(12 - 20)$$

$$= \tfrac{506}{15} = 33\tfrac{11}{15}.$$

Of course, we could have worked Example 3 by writing the antiderivative in terms of x and using the original limits of integration, but it is generally easier to proceed as we did.

EXAMPLE 4

Evaluate $\int_{-4}^{1} \dfrac{x}{\sqrt{5-x}}\,dx$.

■ **SOLUTION**
Let

$$u = \sqrt{5-x}.$$

Solving for x, we obtain

$$u^2 = 5 - x$$

$$x = 5 - u^2.$$

7.1 SUBSTITUTION

Differentiating, we obtain

$$\frac{dx}{du} = -2u$$

$$dx = -2u\,du.$$

Regarding the limits of integration, we find that

$$u\Big|_{x=-4} = \sqrt{5+4} = 3,$$

$$u\Big|_{x=1} = \sqrt{5-1} = 2.$$

Thus the lower limit is 3 and the upper limit is 2. Although the lower limit is greater than the upper limit, we evaluate in the usual fashion. Making the substitutions, we have

$$\int_{-4}^{1} \frac{x}{\sqrt{5-x}}\,dx = \int_{3}^{2} \frac{5-u^2}{u}(-2u)\,du$$

$$= -2\int_{3}^{2} (5-u^2)\,du$$

$$= -2\left(5u - \frac{u^3}{3}\right)\Big|_{3}^{2}$$

$$= -2(10 - \tfrac{8}{3}) + 2(15 - 9) = -\tfrac{8}{3}.$$

EXERCISE

Evaluate the following definite integrals:

(a) $\int_{3}^{6} x\sqrt{x-2}\,dx$ and (b) $\int_{-1}^{2} \frac{x}{\sqrt{3-x}}\,dx.$

■ ANSWER
(a) $21\tfrac{11}{15}$; (b) $1\tfrac{1}{3}$

EXAMPLE 5

Suppose that the cash reserve of a company, in thousands of dollars, is given by

$$C(x) = x\sqrt{x+1}, \quad 0 \le x \le 12,$$

where x is the number of months since the beginning of the fiscal year. What was the average reserve (to the nearest dollar) during the first quarter?

■ **SOLUTION**

We must compute the average value of this function from $x = 0$ to $x = 3$. Using the formula for average value gives

$$\frac{1}{3-0} \int_0^3 x\sqrt{x+1}\, dx.$$

We use substitution to integrate. Let

$$u = \sqrt{x+1}.$$

Thus

$$u^2 = x + 1$$
$$x = u^2 - 1$$
$$dx = 2u\, du.$$

Substituting and using the new limits of integration, we obtain

$$\frac{1}{3} \int_0^3 x\sqrt{x+1}\, dx = \frac{1}{3} \int_1^2 (u^2 - 1)u \cdot 2u\, du$$

$$= \frac{2}{3} \int_1^2 (u^4 - u^2)\, du$$

$$= \frac{2}{3} \left(\frac{u^5}{5} - \frac{u^3}{3} \right) \Big|_1^2$$

$$= \frac{2}{3} \left(\frac{32}{5} - \frac{8}{3} \right) - \frac{2}{3} \left(\frac{1}{5} - \frac{1}{3} \right)$$

$$= \frac{116}{45} \approx 2.578.$$

Since $C(x)$ is in thousands of dollars, the average cash reserve was $2578.

EXERCISE

Suppose that the cash reserve of a company, in thousands of dollars, is given by

$$C(x) = x\sqrt{2x+1}, \qquad 0 \le x \le 12,$$

where x is the number of months since the beginning of the fiscal year. What was the average reserve (to the nearest dollar) during the first four months?

■ *ANSWER*
$4967

PROBLEM SET 7.1

In Problems 1–24, evaluate the integrals.

1. $\int (x+5)\sqrt{x+6}\, dx$
2. $\int (x-3)\sqrt{x-4}\, dx$
3. $\int x^2 \sqrt{2x-1}\, dx$
4. $\int x^2 \sqrt{x+4}\, dx$
5. $\int \dfrac{x^2 + 8x}{\sqrt{4+x}}\, dx$
6. $\int \dfrac{x^2 - 6x}{\sqrt{x-3}}\, dx$
7. $\int_2^6 \dfrac{x^2}{x+5}\, dx$
8. $\int_4^8 \dfrac{x^2}{x-6}\, dx$
9. $\int \dfrac{e^{2x}}{e^x + 1}\, dx$
10. $\int \sqrt{e^x + 2}\, e^{2x}\, dx$
11. $\int x\sqrt[3]{24 - x}\, dx$
12. $\int x\sqrt[3]{18 - x}\, dx$
13. $\int_0^{e-1} \dfrac{x}{x+1}\, dx$
14. $\int_{1+\sqrt{2}}^{e+\sqrt{2}} \dfrac{x}{x - \sqrt{2}}\, dx$
15. $\int (x^2 - x)(x - 3)^{1/5}\, dx$
16. $\int (x^2 + x)(x + 1)^{1/3}\, dx$
17. $\int_0^1 \dfrac{1}{1 + x^{1/3}}\, dx$
18. $\int_0^1 \dfrac{1}{1 + x^{1/4}}\, dx$
19. $\int_{-1/8}^0 \dfrac{x}{(1+4x)^3}\, dx$
20. $\int_{-1/20}^0 \dfrac{x}{(1+5x)^5}\, dx$
21. $\int \sqrt{5 - \sqrt{x-5}}\, dx$
22. $\int \sqrt{1 + \sqrt{x+1}}\, dx$
23. $\int \dfrac{x}{1 + \sqrt{x}}\, dx$
24. $\int \dfrac{x}{2 - \sqrt{x}}\, dx$

25. Suppose that the cash reserve of a company, in thousands of dollars, is given by $C(x) = x^2\sqrt{4x+1}$, $0 \le x \le 12$, where x is the number of months since the beginning of the fiscal year. What was the average reserve (to the nearest dollar) during the first six months?

26. Suppose that the cash reserve of a company, in thousands of dollars, is given by $C(x) = x^2\sqrt{8x+1}$, $0 \le x \le 12$, where x is the number of months since the beginning of the fiscal year. What was the average reserve (to the nearest dollar) during the second quarter?

27. Determine the area of the region bounded by $y = x/\sqrt{2x+1}$, the x-axis, $x = 0$, and $x = 4$.

28. Let R be the region bounded by $y = x\sqrt[3]{x+6}$, the x-axis, $x = -6$, and $x = -5$. Determine the volume of the solid obtained by rotating R about the x-axis.

7.2 INTEGRATION BY PARTS

In this section we learn to use a powerful technique that will expand the number of functions we can integrate. It is based on the product rule, which tells us that the derivative of

$$f(x)g(x)$$

is

$$f(x)g'(x) + g(x)f'(x).$$

Thus

$$\int (f(x)g'(x) + g(x)f'(x))\, dx = f(x)g(x).$$

Rewriting, we have

$$\int f(x)g'(x)\, dx + \int g(x)f'(x)\, dx = f(x)g(x)$$

$$\int f(x)g'(x)\, dx = f(x)g(x) - \int g(x)f'(x)\, dx.$$

This last formula may be simplified somewhat by letting $u = f(x)$ and $v = g(x)$. It becomes

$$\int uv'\, dx = uv - \int vu'\, dx \qquad (7\text{-}3)$$

and forms the basis of the integration technique known as **integration by parts.**

Integration by parts allows us to integrate certain products by representing one of the functions as u and the other as v'. Of course, after employing the formula, we are still left with an integral:

$$\int vu'dx.$$

However, by correctly choosing u and v', this new integral will be one that we can evaluate. Generally, this means that v' is to be chosen as the more complicated part of the product, provided it can easily be integrated. The following examples clarify this procedure.

EXAMPLE 1

Evaluate $\int xe^x dx$.

■ SOLUTION

The integrand consists of two factors: x and e^x. We want to let u equal one of the factors and v' equal the other. Let

$$u = x \quad \text{and} \quad v' = e^x,$$

so that v' is the more complicated factor, but it can easily be integrated. Thus

$$u' = 1 \quad \text{and} \quad v = \int e^x dx = e^x. \tag{7-4}$$

Using Equation (7-3), we have

$$\int \underset{u\ v'}{xe^x dx} = \underset{u\ v}{xe^x} - \int \underset{v\ u'}{e^x \cdot 1}\, dx.$$

The new integral introduced by the formula is straightforward. We have

$$\int xe^x dx = xe^x - e^x + c.$$

Note in Equation (7-4) that we omitted the arbitrary constant when we wrote

$$v = \int e^x dx = e^x.$$

Actually,

$$v = \int e^x dx = e^x + c.$$

But as you will see, this constant vanishes when we integrate by parts. We have

$$\int \underbrace{x}_{u} \underbrace{e^x}_{v'} dx = \underbrace{x}_{u} \underbrace{(e^x + c)}_{v} - \int \underbrace{(e^x + c)}_{v} \cdot \underbrace{1}_{u'} \, dx$$

$$= xe^x + cx - \int (e^x + c) dx$$
$$= xe^x + cx - e^x - cx + C$$
$$= xe^x - e^x + C.$$

Consequently, in computing v when integrating by parts, the arbitrary constant may be omitted.

Also, note that we might have chosen

$$u = e^x \quad \text{and} \quad v' = x.$$

This gives

$$u' = e^x \quad \text{and} \quad v = \int x \, dx = \frac{x^2}{2}.$$

Under such circumstances, integration by parts yields

$$\int xe^x dx = e^x \cdot \frac{x^2}{2} - \int \frac{x^2}{2} e^x dx.$$

But the new integral introduced here is more difficult than the original! Thus we have made a poor choice for u and v'. Our selection should result in a new integral that is *less* complicated. And as already noted, this generally means letting v' equal the more complicated factor, assuming that it can easily be integrated.

EXAMPLE 2

Evaluate $\int x \ln(3x) dx$.

■ SOLUTION

The first impulse is to let $v' = \ln(3x)$, the more complicated factor. However, we have to integrate $\ln(3x)$ to get v, and we don't know how to do this. So let

$$u = \ln(3x) \quad \text{and} \quad v' = x.$$

Consequently,

$$u' = \frac{1}{3x} \cdot 3 = \frac{1}{x} \quad \text{and} \quad v = \int x \, dx = \frac{x^2}{2}.$$

Therefore

$$\int x \ln(3x)\, dx = \frac{x^2}{2} \ln(3x) - \int \frac{x^2}{2} \cdot \frac{1}{x}\, dx$$

$$= \frac{x^2}{2} \ln(3x) - \frac{1}{2} \int x\, dx$$

$$= \frac{x^2}{2} \ln(3x) - \frac{x^2}{4} + c.$$

EXERCISE

Evaluate (a) $\int xe^{5x}\, dx$ and (b) $\int x \ln x\, dx$.

■ ANSWER

(a) $\dfrac{xe^{5x}}{5} - \dfrac{1}{25} e^{5x} + c$; (b) $\dfrac{x^2 \ln x}{2} - \dfrac{x^2}{4} + c$

The next two examples show that some imagination may be needed in seeing the product.

EXAMPLE 3

Evaluate $\int \ln(5x)\, dx$.

■ SOLUTION

We must view the integrand as $1 \cdot \ln(5x)$ and let

$$u = \ln(5x) \quad \text{and} \quad v' = 1.$$

This gives

$$u' = \frac{1}{5x} \cdot 5 = \frac{1}{x} \quad \text{and} \quad v = \int 1\, dx = x.$$

Therefore

$$\int \ln(5x)\, dx = x \ln(5x) - \int \frac{1}{x} \cdot x\, dx$$

$$= x \ln(5x) - \int 1\, dx$$

$$= x \ln(5x) - x + c.$$

EXAMPLE 4

Evaluate $\int x^5 e^{x^3}\, dx$.

7.2 INTEGRATION BY PARTS

■ SOLUTION

Letting $v' = x^5$ gives us a more complicated integral. If

$$u = e^{x^3} \quad \text{and} \quad v' = x^5,$$

then

$$u' = e^{x^3} \cdot 3x^2 \quad \text{and} \quad v = \frac{x^6}{6}.$$

Thus

$$\int x^5 e^{x^3} dx = e^{x^3} \cdot \frac{x^6}{6} - \int \frac{x^8}{2} e^{x^3} dx.$$

And letting $v' = e^{x^3}$ doesn't help because we can't integrate e^{x^3}. But note that we could easily integrate e^{x^3} if it were multiplied by x^2. Thus we view the integrand as $x^3 \cdot x^2 e^{x^3}$. Let

$$u = x^3 \quad \text{and} \quad v' = x^2 e^{x^3}.$$

Thus

$$u' = 3x^2 \quad \text{and} \quad v = \int x^2 e^{x^3} dx = \tfrac{1}{3} \int 3x^2 e^{x^3} dx = \tfrac{1}{3} e^{x^3}.$$

Therefore

$$\int \ln(5x) dx = x \ln(5x) - \int \frac{1}{x} \cdot x \, dx$$
$$= x \ln(5x) - \int 1 \, dx$$
$$= x \ln(5x) - x + c.$$

EXERCISE

Evaluate (a) $\int \ln(3x) dx$ and (b) $\int x^3 e^{x^2} dx$.

■ ANSWER

(a) $x \ln(3x) - x + c$; (b) $\dfrac{x^2 e^{x^2}}{2} - \dfrac{1}{2} e^{x^2} + c$

EXAMPLE 5

Determine the area of the region bounded by $y = \ln(x + 2)$, the x-axis, and $x = 2$.

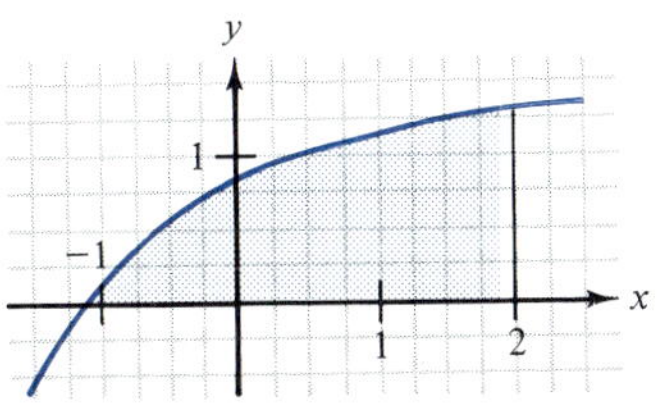

■ SOLUTION

The function $y = \ln(x + 2)$ is the graph of $y = \ln x$ shifted two units to the left. So we get the region shown in Figure 7.2. The area of this region

FIGURE 7.2

is the definite integral

$$\int_{-1}^{2} \ln(x + 2)dx.$$

We integrate by parts. Let

$$u = \ln(x + 2) \quad \text{and} \quad v' = 1.$$

This gives

$$u' = \frac{1}{x + 2} \quad \text{and} \quad v = x + 2.$$

By writing $v = x + 2$ instead of $v = x$, we get a nicer integral. We have

$$\int_{-1}^{2} \ln(x + 2)dx = (x + 2) \ln(x + 2)\Big|_{-1}^{2} - \int_{-1}^{2} \frac{x + 2}{x + 2} dx$$

$$= ((x + 2) \ln(x + 2) - x)\Big|_{-1}^{2}$$

$$= (4 \ln 4 - 2) - (\ln 1 + 1)$$

$$= 4 \ln 4 - 3 \quad (\approx 2.545).$$

EXERCISE

Determine the area of the region bounded by $y = \ln(x - 1)$, the x-axis, and $x = 6$.

■ ANSWER
$5 \ln 5 - 4 \ (\approx 4.047)$

PROBLEM SET 7.2

In Problems 1–22, evaluate the integrals.

1. $\int xe^{-x}dx$
2. $\int xe^{-3x}dx$
3. $\int (1 + x)^{200}x\, dx$
4. $\int (5 - x)^{50}x\, dx$
5. $\int \frac{x}{(2 + 3x)^4} dx$
6. $\int \frac{x}{(5 - 6x)^7} dx$
7. $\int x \ln(6x)dx$
8. $\int x \ln(9x)dx$
9. $\int x^5 \ln(7x)dx$
10. $\int x^{-4} \ln(3x)dx$
11. $\int \ln(ex)dx$
12. $\int \ln(\pi x)dx$
13. $\int x^3 \sqrt{x^2 + 1}\, dx$
14. $\int x^7 \sqrt{x^4 + 1}\, dx$
15. $\int x^{13}e^{x^7 - 3}\, dx$
16. $\int x^{2e-1}e^{x^e}dx$
17. $\int \frac{xe^x}{(1 + x)^2} dx$
18. $\int \frac{\ln(\ln x)}{x} dx$
19. $\int x^2 e^{2x}dx$
20. $\int x(\ln x)^2 dx$
21. $\int \frac{(x + 1)^2}{(x - 1)^4} dx$
22. $\int \frac{x^2}{\sqrt[5]{x + 5}} dx$

In Problems 23 and 24, use integration by parts to derive the reduction formulas.

23. $\int x^n e^x dx = x^n e^x - n \int x^{n-1} e^x dx$
24. $\int (\ln x)^n dx = x(\ln x)^n - n \int (\ln x)^{n-1} dx \quad (n \neq -1)$

In Problems 25 and 26, evaluate the integrals using the reduction formulas derived in Problems 23 and 24.

25. $\int x^4 e^x dx$

26. $\int (\ln x)^4 dx$

27. Use integration by parts to integrate

$$\int \frac{1}{x} \cdot \ln x \, dx.$$

28. Use integration by parts to integrate

$$\int \frac{2x}{1+x^2} \ln(1+x^2) dx.$$

29. Determine the area of the region bounded by $y = \ln x$, $y = 2$, $x = 1/e$, and $x = e^4$.

30. Determine the area of the region bounded by $y = x/e^{2x}$, $y = 1/(2e)$, $x = \frac{1}{2}$, and $x = \frac{3}{2}$.

31. Let R be the region bounded by $y = \ln x$, the x-axis, $x = 1$, and $x = e^3$. Determine the volume of the solid obtained by rotating R about the x-axis.

32. Let R be the region bounded by $y = e^{2x}$, the x-axis, $x = \ln 2$, and $x = \ln 5$. Determine the volume of the solid obtained by rotating R about the y-axis.

Let f be a continuous nonnegative function defined on $[a,b]$. The center of mass of the region bounded by $y = f(x)$, the x-axis, $x = a$, and $x = b$ is defined to be the point $(\bar{x}, \bar{y})$, where

$$\bar{x} = \frac{\int_a^b x \cdot f(x) dx}{\int_a^b f(x) dx} \quad \text{and} \quad \bar{y} = \frac{\int_a^b \frac{1}{2}(f(x))^2 dx}{\int_a^b f(x) dx}.$$

In Problems 33 and 34 use this definition to determine the center of mass of the region described.

33. $y = e^{5x}$, the x-axis, $x = 0$, and $x = 1$

34. $y = \ln(x+1)$, the x-axis, $x = 0$, and $x = e - 1$

7.3 INTEGRATION USING TABLES

As you have probably realized, the process of integration is generally more difficult than differentiation. Many common functions are easy to differentiate but difficult to integrate. In addition to substitution and integration by parts, there are several other techniques that may be used to tackle such functions. However, their study is beyond the scope of this text. Nonetheless, we shall use some of their results in a **table of integrals**. (See inside back cover.) The table includes some integration formulas already studied, as well as other formulas that are derived with advanced techniques. Our table is rather brief. There exist tables that contain hundreds of integrals.

The principal idea is to match the integrand of the problem with one in the table, identifying the relevant constants, as illustrated in Example 1.

EXAMPLE 1

Evaluate the following indefinite integrals:

(a) $\int \frac{x}{3x-2} dx$, (b) $\int \frac{t}{\sqrt{t+5}} dt$, and (c) $\int \frac{1}{x(5-4x)^2} dx$.

■ SOLUTION

(a) This integrand contains the form $ax + b$ and matches number 7 from the table:

$$\int \frac{x}{ax+b} dx = \frac{x}{a} - \frac{b}{a^2} \ln|ax+b| + c,$$

with $a = 3$ and $b = -2$. Substituting 3 for a and -2 for b into the preceding formula gives

$$\int \frac{x}{3x - 2} \, dx = \frac{x}{3} - \frac{-2}{3^2} \ln|3x - 2| + c$$

$$= \frac{x}{3} + \frac{2}{9} \ln|3x - 2| + c.$$

(b) Although the variable here is t instead of x, we see that this integral has the form of number 13:

$$\int \frac{x}{\sqrt{ax + b}} \, dx = \frac{2}{3a^2} (ax - 2b)\sqrt{ax + b} + c,$$

with $a = 1$ and $b = 5$. Thus

$$\int \frac{t}{\sqrt{t + 5}} \, dt = \tfrac{2}{3}(t - 10)\sqrt{t + 5} + c.$$

(c) Let's first note that the binomial $5 - 4x$ may be written $-4x + 5$. So the form involved is $ax + b$. The integrand matches the one numbered 10:

$$\int \frac{1}{x(ax + b)^2} \, dx = \frac{1}{b(ax + b)} + \frac{1}{b^2} \ln\left|\frac{x}{ax + b}\right| + c,$$

with $a = -4$ and $b = 5$. Thus

$$\int \frac{1}{x(5 - 4x)^2} \, dx = \frac{1}{5(5 - 4x)} + \frac{1}{25} \ln\left|\frac{x}{5 - 4x}\right| + c.$$

EXERCISE

Evaluate the following indefinite integrals:

(a) $\int \frac{x}{(5x - 3)^2} \, dx$, (b) $\int t\sqrt{t + 2}$, and (c) $\int \frac{x}{\sqrt{2 - 3x}} \, dx$.

■ ANSWER

(a) $\frac{-3}{25(5x - 3)} + \frac{1}{25} \ln|5x - 3| + c$; (b) $\tfrac{2}{15}(3t - 4)(t + 2)^{3/2} + c$;

(c) $-\tfrac{2}{27}(3x + 4)\sqrt{2 - 3x} + c$

In the next two examples, we see that some algebraic manipulation may be needed to get the integral into the proper form.

7.3 INTEGRATION USING TABLES

EXAMPLE 2

Evaluate $\int \dfrac{1}{3x^2 - 6}\,dx$.

■ SOLUTION

The table doesn't include any forms where the coefficient of x^2 is anything but 1. So we need to factor first. We have

$$\int \dfrac{1}{3x^2 - 6}\,dx = \int \dfrac{1}{3(x^2 - 2)}\,dx$$

$$= \dfrac{1}{3}\int \dfrac{1}{x^2 - 2}\,dx.$$

The form involved is $x^2 - a^2$, and the appropriate integral is number 15:

$$\int \dfrac{1}{x^2 - a^2}\,dx = \dfrac{1}{2a}\ln\left|\dfrac{x - a}{x + a}\right| + c.$$

We have $a^2 = 2$, so choose $a = \sqrt{2}$. Thus

$$\dfrac{1}{3}\int \dfrac{1}{x^2 - a^2}\,dx = \dfrac{1}{3}\left(\dfrac{1}{2\sqrt{2}}\ln\left|\dfrac{x - \sqrt{2}}{x + \sqrt{2}}\right|\right) + c$$

$$= \dfrac{1}{6\sqrt{2}}\ln\left|\dfrac{x - \sqrt{2}}{x + \sqrt{2}}\right| + c.$$

EXAMPLE 3

Evaluate $\int \dfrac{1}{\sqrt{\dfrac{x^2}{5} + 20}}\,dx$.

■ SOLUTION

As in the preceding example, we need to get the coefficient of x^2 to be 1. We have

$$\int \dfrac{1}{\sqrt{\dfrac{x^2}{5} + 20}}\,dx = \int \dfrac{1}{\sqrt{\tfrac{1}{5}(x^2 + 100)}}\,dx$$

$$= \int \dfrac{1}{\sqrt{\tfrac{1}{5}}\sqrt{x^2 + 100}}\,dx$$

$$= \dfrac{1}{\sqrt{\tfrac{1}{5}}}\int \dfrac{1}{\sqrt{x^2 + 100}}\,dx$$

$$= \sqrt{5}\int \dfrac{1}{\sqrt{x^2 + 100}}\,dx.$$

We have an integral with the form $\sqrt{x^2 + a^2}$. The formula to use is number 19:

$$\int \frac{1}{\sqrt{x^2 + a^2}} \, dx = \ln|x + \sqrt{x^2 + a^2}| + c,$$

with $a = 10$. We get

$$\sqrt{5} \int \frac{1}{\sqrt{x^2 + 100}} \, dx = \sqrt{5} \ln|x + \sqrt{x^2 + 100}| + c.$$

EXERCISE

Evaluate the following indefinite integrals:

(a) $\int \frac{1}{20 - 4x^2} \, dx$ and (b) $\int \frac{1}{x\sqrt{8 + \frac{x^2}{2}}} \, dx$.

■ ANSWER

(a) $\frac{1}{8\sqrt{5}} \ln\left|\frac{\sqrt{5} + x}{\sqrt{5} - x}\right| + c;$ (b) $\frac{-\sqrt{2}}{4} \ln\left|\frac{4 + \sqrt{16 + x^2}}{x}\right| + c$

EXAMPLE 4

Determine the producers' surplus (to the nearest dollar) if the demand and supply equations are

$$p = \frac{360}{(x + 3)(x + 1)} \quad \text{and} \quad p = \frac{4x}{x + 3}.$$

respectively, where x is in thousands.

■ SOLUTION

To find the equilibrium point we must solve

$$\frac{360}{(x + 3)(x + 1)} = \frac{4x}{x + 3}.$$

We get

$$360 = 4x(x + 1)$$
$$4x^2 + 4x = 360$$
$$4x^2 + 4x - 360 = 0$$
$$x^2 + x - 90 = 0$$
$$(x - 9)(x + 10) = 0$$
$$x = 9 \quad \text{or} \quad x = -10.$$

7.3 INTEGRATION USING TABLES

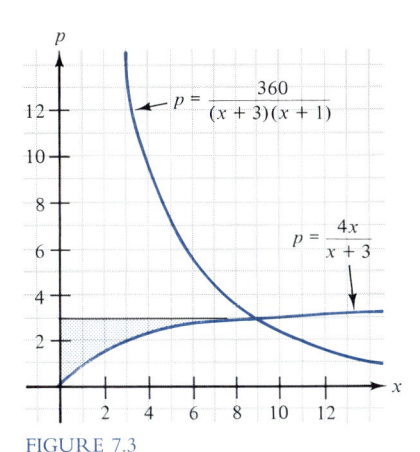

We may ignore the negative value. Thus the equilibrium price occurs when $x = 9$. That price is

$$p = \frac{4(9)}{9 + 3} = 3.$$

To get the producers' surplus we determine the area of the region shown in Figure 7.3. This is

$$\int_0^9 \left(3 - \frac{4x}{x + 3}\right) dx = \int_0^9 3\, dx - 4\int_0^9 \frac{x}{x + 3}\, dx.$$

The last definite integral is determined with the use of tables. In particular, we use number 7:

$$\int_0^9 3\, dx - 4\int_0^9 \frac{x}{x + 3}\, dx = (3x - 4(x - 3\ln|x + 3|))\Big|_0^9$$
$$= (-x + 12\ln|x + 3|)\Big|_0^9$$
$$= -9 + 12\ln 12 - 12\ln 3$$
$$= -9 + 12\ln \tfrac{12}{3} = -9 + 12\ln 4$$
$$\approx 7.636.$$

Since x is in thousands, this is $7636.

FIGURE 7.3

EXERCISE

Determine the producers' surplus (to the nearest dollar) if the demand and supply equations are

$$p = \frac{360}{(x + 2)(x + 1)} \quad \text{and} \quad p = \frac{5x}{x + 2},$$

respectively, where x is in thousands.

■ ANSWER
$8094

PROBLEM SET 7.3

In Problems 1–26, evaluate the integrals.

1. $\int \dfrac{1}{x(5x + 8)}\, dx$

2. $\int x^2 \sqrt{x + 1}\, dx$

3. $\int \dfrac{x}{5 - x^2}\, dx$

4. $\int \sqrt{x^2 - \pi^2}\, dx$

5. $\int \dfrac{1}{x\sqrt{e^2 + x^2}}\, dx$

6. $\int \dfrac{e^{\sqrt{1+x}}}{\sqrt{1 + x}}\, dx$

7. $\int \dfrac{1}{21 - 7t^2}\, dt$

8. $\int \dfrac{1}{6t^2 - 3}\, dt$

9. $\int \dfrac{x}{4x^2 - 4x + 1} \, dx$

10. $\int \dfrac{1}{(3/x) - 2} \, dx$

11. $\int \dfrac{x}{e^{x/2}} \, dx$

12. $\int \ln \dfrac{x}{e} \, dx$

13. $\int \dfrac{4e^{4t} + 2e^{-2t}}{e^{4t} - e^{-2t}} \, dt$

14. $\int \dfrac{2t \sqrt[3]{\ln(t^2 + 1)}}{t^2 + 1} \, dt$

15. $\int \dfrac{1}{\sqrt{25x^2 - 36}} \, dx$

16. $\int \sqrt{\dfrac{x^2}{6} + 5} \, dx$

17. $\int \dfrac{x}{\sqrt{6x^2 - 1}} \, dx$

18. $\int \dfrac{1}{x^3 + 2x^2 + x} \, dx$

19. $\int x(1 - x \ln 2)^{-1/2} \, dx$

20. $\int \dfrac{x}{(9 - x)^{-1/2}} \, dx$

21. $\int \dfrac{(\sqrt{2} \, x)^2}{\sqrt{\sqrt{2} \, x - \sqrt{3}}} \, dx$

22. $\int \dfrac{1}{x}(e^4 - e^2 x^2)^{-1/2} \, dx$

23. $\int_{-5}^{0} x^2 \sqrt{4 - x} \, dx$

24. $\int_{-17}^{-1} \dfrac{x^2}{\sqrt{-x - 1}} \, dx$

25. $\int_{0}^{\sqrt{3}e} \dfrac{1}{\sqrt{(x^2/e^2) + 1}} \, dx$

26. $\int_{1/(e-1)}^{1} \dfrac{1}{ex^2 - x^2 + x} \, dx$

In Problems 27 and 28, determine the producers' surplus (to the nearest dollar).

27. The demand equation is

$$p = \dfrac{504}{(x + 6)(x + 2)}$$

and the supply equation is

$$p = \dfrac{3x}{x + 6},$$

where x is in thousands.

28. The demand equation is

$$p = \dfrac{2400}{(x + 9)(x + 5)}$$

and the supply equation is

$$p = \dfrac{8x}{x + 9},$$

where x is in thousands.

Under suitable conditions, the arc length of the graph of a function f from $(a, f(a))$ to $(b, f(b))$ is given by

$$\int_{a}^{b} \sqrt{1 + (f'(x))^2} \, dx.$$

This information is needed in Problems 29 and 30.

29. Determine the arc length of the graph of $f(x) = x^2$ from $(0,0)$ to $(1,1)$.

30. Determine the arc length of the graph of $f(x) = \tfrac{1}{4}x^2$ from $(0,0)$ to $(\sqrt{5}, \tfrac{5}{4})$.

7.4 APPROXIMATE INTEGRATION

So far we have evaluated a definite integral by computing the net change in an antiderivative. We have already noted that finding the antiderivative can be difficult. In fact, it may be impossible. For example, there is no elementary function whose derivative is

$$e^{-x^2}.$$

Consequently, we cannot evaluate a definite integral like

$$\int_{0}^{1} e^{-x^2} \, dx$$

because we can't find an antiderivative for the integrand. The best we can do is approximate, and this section discusses approximation techniques for definite integrals.

We have already been introduced to one such technique in Section 6.5, where we viewed the definite integral as the limit of a sum. Recall that, given a continuous function defined on $[a, b]$, we divided $[a, b]$ into n

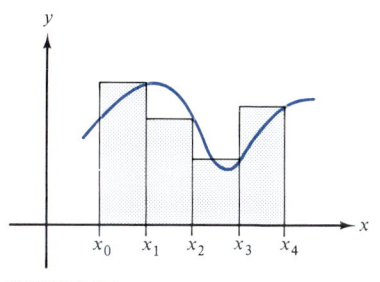

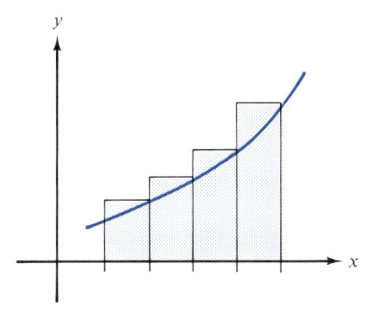

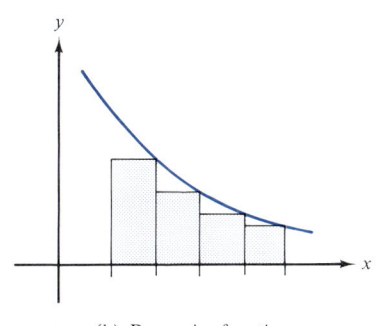

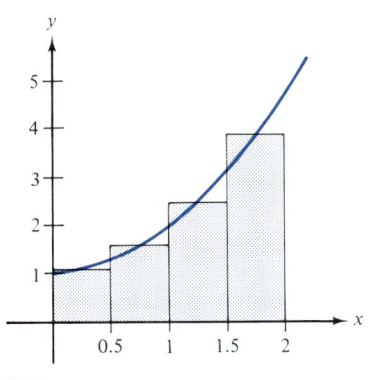

subintervals of equal length, denoting the ith subinterval $[x_{i-1}, x_i]$. Our approximation was

$$S(n) = \frac{b-a}{n}(f(x_1) + f(x_2) + \cdots + f(x_n)).$$

We further noted that the limit of these approximating sums, as n approaches infinity, is indeed

$$\int_a^b f(x)dx.$$

Thus the approximations improve as n gets larger.

In developing the approximation in Section 6.5, recall that we constructed rectangles whose heights were the values of the function at the right endpoints of each subinterval. See Figure 7.4.

Some of the rectangles are too large, some are too small, and some might be about right. If the errors "balance out," our approximation may be pretty good. However, if the function is increasing or decreasing on $[a,b]$, then errors cannot "balance out." See Figure 7.5.

The technique would yield an approximation clearly too large in the situation of Figure 7.5(a) and clearly too small in the situation of Figure 7.5(b).

We can remedy this situation by selecting a point other than the right endpoint to construct the height. A convenient point would be the midpoint of each subinterval (which is the average of its two endpoints).

Let's consider

$$\int_0^2 (x^2 + 1)dx$$

and approximate it with the sum of the four rectangles depicted in Figure 7.6.

The interval $[0,2]$ has been divided into equal fourths. Above each subinterval is a rectangle whose height is the value of the function at the midpoint of the subinterval. Thus

approximate area $= (0.5) \cdot f(0.25) + (0.5) \cdot f(0.75) + (0.5) \cdot f(1.25)$
$\qquad + (0.5) \cdot f(1.75)$
$= (0.5)(f(0.25) + f(0.75) + f(1.25) + f(1.75))$
$= (0.5)(1.0625 + 1.5625 + 2.5625 + 4.0625)$
$= 4.625.$

This approximation is pretty good since

$$\int_0^2 (x^2 + 1)dx = \left(\frac{x^3}{3} + x\right)\Big|_0^2 = \frac{8}{3} + 2 = 4\tfrac{2}{3}.$$

The error is less than 1%, and we are using very few rectangles.

This approximation technique is called the *rectangle rule* and is stated in the following theorem.

THEOREM 7.2 **Rectangle Rule**	Let f be a continuous function defined on $[a,b]$. If $[a,b]$ is divided into n subintervals of equal length, denoting the ith subinterval as $[x_{i-1}, x_i]$ and its midpoint as x_i^*, then $$\int_a^b f(x)dx \approx \frac{b-a}{n}(f(x_1^*) + f(x_2^*) + \cdots + f(x_n^*)).$$

EXAMPLE 1

Use the rectangle rule with $n = 4$ to approximate $\int_0^2 x\sqrt{4 - x^2}\, dx$.

■ SOLUTION

Dividing $[0,2]$ into equal fourths gives

$$x_0 = 0, \quad x_1 = 0.5, \quad x_2 = 1, \quad x_3 = 1.5, \quad x_4 = 2.$$

The midpoints of the four subintervals are

$$x_1^* = 0.25, \quad x_2^* = 0.75, \quad x_3^* = 1.25, \quad x_4^* = 1.75.$$

Thus we have

$$\int_0^2 x\sqrt{4 - x^2}\, dx \approx \frac{b-a}{n}(f(x_1^*) + f(x_2^*) + f(x_3^*) + f(x_4^*))$$

$$= \frac{2-0}{4}(f(0.25) + f(0.75) + f(1.25) + f(1.75))$$

$$\approx 0.5(0.4961 + 1.3905 + 1.9516 + 1.6944)$$

$$= 2.7663,$$

where intermediate results are calculated to the nearest ten thousandth.

Let's note that we can find the exact value of the definite integral in Example 1. Indeed,

$$\int_0^2 x\sqrt{4 - x^2}\, dx = -\tfrac{1}{2}\int_0^2 -2x(4 - x^2)^{1/2} dx$$

$$= -\tfrac{1}{2}(4 - x^2)^{3/2} \cdot \tfrac{2}{3}\Big|_0^2$$

$$= -\tfrac{1}{3}(4 - x^2)^{3/2}\Big|_0^2$$

$$= 0 + \tfrac{1}{3} \cdot 4^{3/2} = \tfrac{8}{3} = 2\tfrac{2}{3}.$$

So the error with the rectangle rule is about 0.0996, slightly less than 4%.
Let's again consider

$$\int_0^2 (x^2 + 1)dx.$$

Let's divide $[0,2]$ into equal fourths again, but instead of building rectangles let's construct trapezoids. See Figure 7.7.

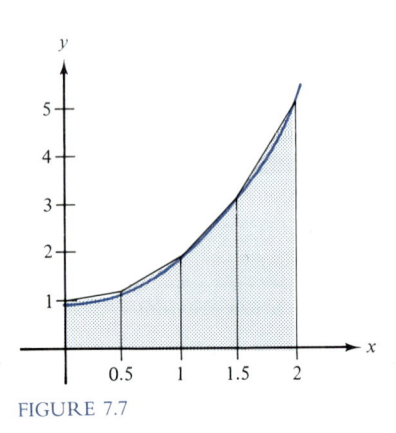

FIGURE 7.7

7.4 APPROXIMATE INTEGRATION

The sum of the areas of the four trapezoids is an approximation of the area of the region. The area of each trapezoid is $\frac{1}{2}$ the sum of the bases times the height. (The bases are the parallel sides. So our trapezoids are turned sideways.) Thus

$$\begin{aligned}\text{approximate area} &= (0.5)(f(0) + f(0.5))(0.5) + (0.5)(f(0.5) + f(1))(0.5) \\ &\quad + (0.5)(f(1) + f(1.5))(0.5) \\ &\quad + (0.5)(f(1.5) + f(2))(0.5) \\ &= (0.5)^2(f(0) + 2f(0.5) + 2f(1) + 2f(1.5) + f(2)) \\ &= (0.25)(1 + 2.5 + 4 + 6.5 + 5) \\ &= 4.75.\end{aligned}$$

Although this approximation is not quite as good as the one obtained with the rectangle rule for this illustration, this is not usually the case. This technique is called the *trapezoid rule*, and for a specified value of n, it generally yields better approximations than the rectangle rule.

THEOREM 7.3
Trapezoid Rule

Let f be a continuous function defined on $[a,b]$. If $[a,b]$ is divided into n subintervals of equal length, denoting the ith subinterval as $[x_{i-1}, x_i]$, then

$$\int_a^b f(x)dx \approx \frac{b-a}{2n}(f(x_0) + 2f(x_1) + 2f(x_2) + \cdots + 2f(x_{n-1}) + f(x_n)).$$

Note that the coefficient of $f(x_i)$ is 2 for all i except $i = 0$ and $i = n$.

EXAMPLE 2

Use the trapezoid rule with $n = 4$ to approximate $\int_0^2 x\sqrt{4 - x^2}\, dx$.

■ SOLUTION
Dividing $[0,2]$ into equal fourths gives

$$x_0 = 0, \quad x_1 = 0.5, \quad x_2 = 1, \quad x_3 = 1.5, \quad x_4 = 2.$$

Thus we have

$$\begin{aligned}\int_0^2 x\sqrt{4-x^2}\, dx &\approx \frac{b-a}{2n}(f(x_0) + 2f(x_1) + 2f(x_2) + 2f(x_3) + f(x_4)) \\ &= \frac{2-0}{2 \cdot 4}(f(0) + 2f(0.5) + 2f(1) + 2f(1.5) + f(2)) \\ &\approx \tfrac{1}{4}(0 + 1.9365 + 3.4641 + 3.9686 + 0) \\ &= 2.3423,\end{aligned}$$

where intermediate results are calculated to the nearest ten thousandth.

FIGURE 7.8

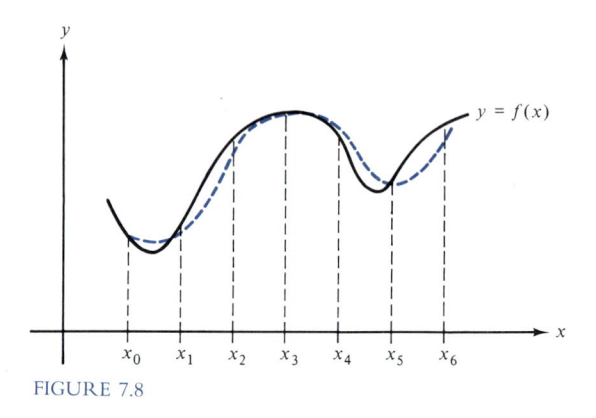

Both the rectangle rule and the trapezoid rule use line segments to connect points on the graph. Another approximation method, called *Simpson's rule* or the *parabolic rule*, uses parabolic curves to connect points. See Figure 7.8.

Each parabolic segment connects three points on the graph. Thus it is necessary to divide the interval into an *even* number of subintervals. The areas of the regions under the parabolas are added to give an approximation of the definite integral.

THEOREM 7.4
Simpson's Rule

Let f be a continuous function defined on $[a,b]$. If $[a,b]$ is divided into n subintervals of equal length (where n is even), denoting the ith subinterval as $[x_{i-1}, x_i]$, then

$$\int_a^b f(x)\,dx \approx \frac{b-a}{3n} (f(x_0) + 4f(x_1) + 2f(x_2) + 4f(x_3) + \cdots + 2f(x_{n-2}) + 4f(x_{n-1}) + f(x_n)).$$

Note that the coefficient of $f(x_i)$ will be 4 when i is odd. When i is even, the coefficient will be 2, except for $i = 0$ and $i = n$, where the coefficient is 1.

EXAMPLE 3

Use Simpson's rule with $n = 4$ to approximate $\int_0^2 x\sqrt{4 - x^2}\, dx$.

■ SOLUTION
Dividing [0,2] into equal fourths gives

$$x_0 = 0, \quad x_1 = 0.5, \quad x_2 = 1, \quad x_3 = 1.5, \quad x_4 = 2.$$

Thus we have

$$\int_0^2 x\sqrt{4-x^2}\,dx \approx \frac{b-a}{3n}(f(x_0)+4f(x_1)+2f(x_2)+4f(x_3)+f(x_4))$$
$$= \tfrac{1}{6}(f(0)+4f(0.5)+2f(1)+4f(1.5)+f(2))$$
$$\approx \tfrac{1}{6}(0+3.8730+3.4641+7.9373+0)$$
$$\approx 2.5457,$$

where intermediate results are calculated to the nearest ten thousandth.

This approximation is even better than the one of Example 2. In general, for a given value of n, Simpson's rule will yield the best approximation.

But regardless of which approximation technique is used, we may make n large enough to get as close as we wish to the exact value. This is because the limit of each approximation as n approaches infinity is the definite integral

$$\int_a^b f(x)\,dx.$$

Note that although the three approximation theorems were motivated by determining the area under a curve, they are stated for any definite integral. They may thus be used to approximate those definite integrals that represent something other than area.

EXERCISE

Approximate $\int_0^2 x\sqrt{9-x^2}\,dx$: (a) using the rectangle rule with $n=4$; (b) using the trapezoid rule with $n=4$; and (c) using Simpson's rule with $n=4$. (d) Evaluate the integral and compare.

■ ANSWER

(a) 5.2996; (b) 5.2203; (c) 5.2723; (d) $9-\dfrac{5^{3/2}}{3}(\approx 5.2732)$

PROBLEM SET 7.4

In Problems 1–18, approximate the definite integral using (a) the rectangle rule, (b) the trapezoid rule, and (c) Simpson's rule. (d) Evaluate the integral and compare.

1. $\int_0^4 (2x-1)\,dx$, $n=4$

2. $\int_{-3}^1 (-3x+1)\,dx$, $n=4$

3. $\int_2^8 \dfrac{1}{x}\,dx$, $n=6$

4. $\int_4^{10} \dfrac{1}{x-2}\,dx$, $n=6$

5. $\int_{-1}^1 (x^2-4)\,dx$, $n=4$

6. $\int_0^{0.8} (x^3+x^2+x)\,dx$, $n=4$

7. $\int_{-6}^{0} \dfrac{x}{\sqrt[5]{5+x^2}}\, dx, \ n=6$

8. $\int_{-1}^{0} 4x^3 \sqrt{1+x^4}\, dx, \ n=2$

9. $\int_{-18}^{-10} \sqrt[4]{10-x}\, dx, \ n=8$

10. $\int_{0}^{1} \sqrt[3]{x+1}\, dx, \ n=4$

11. $\int_{1}^{4} \ln x\, dx, \ n=6$

12. $\int_{-1}^{3} xe^x\, dx, \ n=8$

13. $\int_{0}^{4} f(x)\, dx, \ n=4$, where
$$f(x) = \begin{cases} x+1 & \text{when } 0 \le x < 2 \\ -x+5 & \text{when } 2 \le x \le 4 \end{cases}$$

14. $\int_{-3}^{1} f(x)\, dx, \ n=4$, where
$$f(x) = \begin{cases} 2x+6 & \text{when } x \le -2 \\ x^2 - 2 & \text{when } x > -2 \end{cases}$$

15. $\int_{0.5}^{6.5} (x-3.5)^3\, dx, \ n=6$

16. $\int_{-2.5}^{-1.5} \sqrt[5]{x+2}\, dx, \ n=6$

17. $\int_{\ln 2}^{\ln 6} (x^4 + 1)\, dx, \ n=4$

18. $\int_{-2e^2}^{4+2e^2} (4-x^2)\, dx, \ n=4$

In Problems 19 and 20 use the trapezoid rule with $n=4$ to approximate the definite integral.

19. $\int_{-2e}^{2e} \dfrac{1}{\sqrt{1+x^4}}\, dx$

20. $\int_{\pi}^{5\pi} \dfrac{1}{1+x^3}\, dx$

In Problems 21 and 22 use Simpson's rule with $n=4$ to approximate the definite integral.

21. $\int_{0}^{4} \pi^x\, dx$

22. $\int_{-3.5}^{0.5} 5^x\, dx$

23. Use the trapezoid rule with $n=8$ to approximate $\int_{0}^{0.8} e^{-x^2}\, dx$.

24. Use Simpson's rule with $n=8$ to approximate $\int_{0}^{0.8} e^{-x^2}\, dx$.

25. The area A of a circle of radius r is given by $A = 4\int_{0}^{r} \sqrt{r^2 - x^2}\, dx$. Approximate the area of a circle of radius $r=4$ by using (a) the rectangle rule with $n=4$, (b) the trapezoid rule with $n=4$, and (c) Simpson's rule with $n=4$. (d) Compare the above results with $A = \pi r^2$.

26. It can be shown that the length of the graph of $y = 1/x^2$ between the points $(1,1)$ and $(2,\tfrac{1}{4})$ is given by

$$\int_{1}^{2} \dfrac{\sqrt{4+x^6}}{x^3}\, dx.$$

Approximate this length by using (a) the rectangle rule with $n=4$, (b) the trapezoid rule with $n=4$, and (c) Simpson's rule with $n=4$.

27. It can be shown that

$$4 \int_{0}^{1} \dfrac{1}{1+x^2}\, dx = \pi.$$

Approximate π by using Simpson's rule with $n=10$.

7.5 LAWS OF GROWTH AND DECAY

Suppose that for some function $y = f(x)$, the derivative is proportional to the original function. That is, suppose that

$$y' = ky$$

for some constant $k \ne 0$. This equation is an example of a *differential equation*, an equation that relates y and its derivative. To determine y we divide both sides by y to get

$$\dfrac{y'}{y} = k.$$

Now we integrate both sides with respect to x. We have

$$\int \dfrac{y'}{y}\, dx = \int k\, dx$$

$$\ln|y| + c_1 = kx + c_2$$

7.5 LAWS OF GROWTH AND DECAY

for arbitrary constants c_1 and c_2. Thus
$$\ln|y| = kx + c_2 - c_1.$$
Since $c_2 - c_1$ is an arbitrary constant, we may substitute c and write
$$\ln|y| = kx + c.$$
By the definition of logarithm,
$$|y| = e^{kx+c} = e^{kx} \cdot e^c.$$
Therefore,
$$y = \pm e^c \cdot e^{kx}.$$
Since $\pm e^c$ is also an arbitrary constant, we may substitute C to get
$$y = Ce^{kx}.$$

Thus all functions that satisfy the differential equation $y' = ky$ are defined by $y = Ce^{kx}$. This is the basis of the two formulas in this section.

If a quantity Q increases with time in such a way that its rate of increase is proportional to the value of Q at that time, then
$$Q = Q_0 e^{kt}, \tag{7-5}$$
where Q_0 is the initial value of Q (the value when $t = 0$), k is the constant of proportionality (sometimes called the growth constant) in decimal form, and t represents elapsed time. This may be seen by differentiating Q with respect to t. We have
$$\frac{dQ}{dt} = Q_0 e^{kt} \cdot k$$
$$= k(Q_0 e^{kt})$$
$$= k \cdot Q.$$

Thus the growth rate is indeed proportional to Q. Equation (7-5) is called the **exponential law of growth.**

In a biological experiment it is frequently found that the rate of growth of the population being studied is proportional to the population size. Under such conditions, the relationship between population size and time is described by the law of growth.

EXAMPLE 1

If a bacteria population is 10,000 and the proportionality constant is 0.7 when time is measured in hours, how long will it take for the population to reach 50,000?

■ SOLUTION

Let Q represent the number of bacteria, and let t represent time in hours. Since the initial population is 10,000, we have $Q_0 = 10,000$. Since $k = 0.7$, the law of growth for this problem is
$$Q = 10,000 e^{0.7t}.$$

We want to determine the value of t which makes $Q = 50{,}000$. So we must solve the following exponential equation for t:

$$50{,}000 = 10{,}000 e^{0.7t}.$$

We get

$$5 = e^{0.7t}$$

$$\ln 5 = 0.7t$$

$$t = \frac{\ln 5}{0.7}.$$

This is approximately 2.3 hours.

EXERCISE

If a bacteria population is 5000 and the proportionality constant is 0.5 when time is measured in hours, how long (to the nearest tenth of an hour) will it take for the population to reach 20,000?

■ ANSWER
2.8 hours

EXAMPLE 2

If a bacteria population is initially 1000 and grows to 3000 in 6 hours, what is its law of growth?

■ SOLUTION
The general formula is

$$Q = Q_0 e^{kt}.$$

Since the initial population is 1000, we have

$$Q = 1000 e^{kt}.$$

It remains to find k. Because $Q = 3000$ when $t = 6$,

$$3000 = 1000 e^{6k}.$$

Solving for k yields

$$3 = e^{6k}$$

$$\ln 3 = 6k$$

$$k = \frac{\ln 3}{6} \quad (\approx 0.183).$$

Using the approximation of k gives us

$$Q = 1000 e^{0.183t}.$$

7.5 LAWS OF GROWTH AND DECAY

EXERCISE

If a bacteria population is initially 1000 and grows to 2500 in 7 hours, what is its law of growth?

■ *ANSWER*
$Q = 1000e^{0.131t}$

If a quantity Q *decreases* with time in such a way that its rate of decrease is proportional to the value of Q at that time, then

$$Q = Q_0 e^{-kt}, \qquad (7\text{-}6)$$

where Q_0 is the initial value of Q, k is the constant of proportionality (sometimes called the decay constant), and t represents elapsed time. Equation (7-6) is called the **exponential law of decay.**

In physical chemistry it is found that the rate at which atoms disintegrate is proportional to the number of atoms. Thus the relationship between the amount of a radioactive substance and time is described by the law of decay.

EXAMPLE 3

If the constant of proportionality of a radioactive substance is 0.02 when time is measured in years, how long will it take for the initial amount to decay to one-half its original size?

■ *SOLUTION*
The law of decay for this problem is

$$Q = Q_0 e^{-0.02t}.$$

We want to find the value of t that makes Q equal $Q_0/2$. Thus we have to solve for t in the exponential equation

$$\frac{Q_0}{2} = Q_0 e^{-0.02t}. \qquad (7\text{-}7)$$

We get

$$\tfrac{1}{2} = e^{-0.02t}$$

$$\ln(\tfrac{1}{2}) = -0.02t$$

$$\ln 0.5 = -0.02t$$

$$t = -\frac{\ln 0.5}{0.02}.$$

This is approximately 34.7 years.

EXERCISE

If the constant of proportionality of a radioactive substance is 0.015 when time is measured in years, how long (to the nearest tenth of a year) will it take for the initial amount to decay to one-half its original size?

■ *ANSWER*
46.2 years

In discussing radioactive decay, we customarily work with the **half-life,** which is the length of time it takes for half of a given amount to decay. In Example 3, we actually determined that the half-life of the substance is approximately 34.7 years. Note that in the equation we had to solve, Equation (7-7), there is an unknown constant Q_0, the initial amount. The fact that we were able to solve the equation without knowing the value of Q_0 means that the half-life is independent of the initial amount. Thus the length of time required for 10 grams to disintegrate to 5 is the same as the time it takes for 4 grams to disintegrate to 2. So for a specified substance, the half-life is constant, regardless of the amount.

The law of decay may be used to estimate the age of fossils and ancient artifacts with a procedure called **carbon-14 dating.** All plants and animals contain two forms of carbon: the radioactive isotope carbon-14 and the nonradioactive isotope carbon-12. The ratio of ^{14}C to ^{12}C in living organisms has remained constant throughout history. (This ratio is approximately 1:1 trillion, which is the ratio found in the air.) But when the organism dies, the ^{14}C begins to decay. At a later date, the ratio of ^{14}C to ^{12}C in the dead tissue may be measured to determine how much of the ^{14}C has decayed. With the law of decay for ^{14}C the age may be estimated.

Radioactive carbon-14 has a half-life of about 5730 years. To determine its decay constant we must solve the following equation for k:

$$\frac{Q_0}{2} = Q_0 e^{-k(5730)}.$$

We get

$$\tfrac{1}{2} = e^{-5730k}$$

$$\ln 0.5 = -5730k$$

$$k = \frac{\ln 0.5}{-5730} \approx 0.000121.$$

Thus the law of decay for ^{14}C is

$$Q = Q_0 e^{-0.000121t}.$$

Let's use this in Example 4.

EXAMPLE 4

A piece of human bone was found at an archeological site. If 20% of the original amount of ^{14}C was present, what is the age (to the nearest hundred years) of the bone?

■ SOLUTION
The law of decay for ^{14}C is

$$Q = Q_0 e^{-0.000121t}.$$

We must find the value of t that makes $Q = 0.2Q_0$. Thus we must solve for t:

$$0.2Q_0 = Q_0 e^{-0.000121t}$$

$$0.2 = e^{-0.000121t}$$

$$\ln 0.2 = -0.000121t$$

$$t = \frac{\ln 0.2}{-0.000121} \approx 13{,}300.$$

Thus the bone is approximately 13,300 years old.

EXERCISE

A parchment fragment was discovered in which 70% of the original amount of ^{14}C was present. What is the age (to the nearest hundred years) of the fragment?

■ ANSWER
2900 years

Before leaving this section let's note that certain types of growth that one might expect to be exponential are, in fact, limited by some constraint. For example, available food and water will force a ceiling on the number of deer that might live in a particular forest area. Such growth is called *inhibited* exponential growth and is described by the logistic equation:

$$Q = \frac{L}{1 + Ce^{-Lkt}},$$

where Q is the population at time t, L is the maximum possible population, and k and C are constants.

Let's try to derive the logistic equation for a deer population. Suppose that the forest can support 1000 deer, that the initial population is 200, and that one year later there are 250. Since $L = 1000$, we have

$$Q = \frac{1000}{1 + Ce^{-1000kt}}.$$

We must determine C and k. Because the initial size is 200, $Q = 200$ when $t = 0$. Thus

$$200 = \frac{1000}{1 + Ce^{0}}$$

$$200 = \frac{1000}{1 + C}$$

$$200 + 200C = 1000$$

$$C = 4.$$

So we have

$$Q = \frac{1000}{1 + 4e^{-1000kt}}.$$

It remains to find k. We note that when $t = 1$, $Q = 250$. Hence

$$250 = \frac{1000}{1 + 4e^{-1000k}}$$

$$250 + 1000e^{-1000k} = 1000$$

$$e^{-1000k} = 0.75$$

$$-1000k = \ln 0.75$$

$$k = \frac{\ln 0.75}{-1000} \approx 0.0002877.$$

Therefore, the logistic equation is

$$Q = \frac{1000}{1 + 4e^{-0.2877t}}.$$

This formula could then be used to predict population size. For example, after 5 years the population would be approximately 500.

PROBLEM SET 7.5

1. If a bacteria population is 7000 and grows with a proportionality constant of 0.8 when time is measured in hours, how long will it take the population to reach 42,000?

2. If a bacteria population is 11,000 and grows with a proportionality constant of 0.63 when time is measured in hours, how long will it take the population to triple?

3. If the decay constant of a radioactive substance is 0.04 when time is measured in years, how long will it take for the initial amount to decay to one-half its original size?

4. If the decay constant of a radioactive substance is 0.025 when time is measured in years, how long will it take for the initial amount to decay to one-fourth its original size?

5. Determine the half-life of a radioactive substance which satisfies $Q = Q_0 e^{-0.0035t}$, where time is in years.

6. Determine the half-life of a radioactive substance which satisfies $Q = Q_0 e^{-0.00045t}$, where time is in years.

7. If a bacteria population doubles in 3 hours, what is its constant of proportionality?

8. If a bacteria population grows from 2000 to 9200 in 5.5 hours, what is the constant of proportionality?

9. If the half-life of a radioactive substance is 75 years, how long will it take 4 grams of the substance to disintegrate to $\frac{1}{2}$ gram?

10. If the half-life of a radioactive substance is 300 years, how long will it take 8 grams of the substance to disintegrate to 5 grams?

11. If a bacteria population of 10^6 grows to 2.5×10^6 in 16 hours, how much longer will it take for the population to reach 4×10^6?

12. If a bacteria population of 1000 doubles in 5 hours, how long does it take for the population to triple?

13. A skeleton was uncovered at an archeological site. If 35% of the original amount of ^{14}C was present, what is the age (to the nearest hundred years) of the skeleton?

14. If a tree with 20 grams of ^{14}C died about 13,500 years ago, how much (to the nearest tenth) ^{14}C remains today?

15. Assume that the world's population is growing at a rate of about 2% per year and assume an exponential law of growth. How long will it take for the world's population to double?

16. A town had a population of 14,000 in 1970 and a population of 19,600 in 1980. Assuming an exponential law of growth, determine the population in 1990.

17. If fluid friction is used to slow down a flywheel, then V, the number of revolutions per minute, after t seconds, is given by the formula $V = V_0 e^{-kt}$, where V_0 is the value of V when $t = 0$ and k is a constant. If $k = 0.2$, how long must friction be applied to reduce the number of revolutions from 500 to 100 per minute?

18. The atmospheric pressure P, in pounds per square inch, at a height of z feet is approximately $P = P_0 e^{-kz}$,

where P_0 is the pressure at sea level and k is a constant. If $P_0 = 15$ and $P = 14.5$ at a height of 1100 feet, at what height is the pressure 14?

19. The temperature T (in degrees Celsius) of a body surrounded by cooler air, after t minutes, is given by $T = T_0 + (T_1 - T_0)e^{-kt}$, where T_1 is the initial temperature of the body, T_0 is the temperature of the air, and k is a constant. If $k = 0.13$, $T_1 = 60$, and $T_0 = 20$, how long will it take the body to cool to a temperature of 30°C?

20. If the unhealed area A (in square centimeters) of a skin wound after n days is given by the formula

$$A = A_0 e^{-n/10},$$

where A_0 is the initial area of the wound, how many days will it take for the wound to reduce in area by 75%?

21. The rapid compression or expansion of a gas is very nearly adiabatic. That is, in such a system $P_1 V_1^k = P_2 V_2^k$, where P_1 and V_1 represent the pressure and volume, and k is a constant that depends on the gas. Assume that the compression of a diesel engine is adiabatic. If the compression ratio, V_1/V_2, is 15 and the pressure at the beginning of the stroke is 15 pounds/inch^2 and 663 pounds/inch^2 at the end of the stroke, what is the value of k?

22. A car that costs $12,000 new is expected to have a resale value of $V = 12,000 e^{-0.21t}$ dollars t years from now. Determine the value of t (to the nearest tenth) at which the resale value will be $7500.

23. Determine the age (to the nearest hundred years) of an animal bone if it has lost 40% of its original amount of ^{14}C.

24. Determine the age (to the nearest hundred years) of a skeleton if the ratio of ^{14}C to ^{12}C in the skeleton is one-third the ratio found in the air.

25. Suppose a rabbit population has a birth rate of 0.02 and a death rate of 0.01, when time is measured in weeks. Assuming the population growth is exponential and the growth rate is (birth rate) − (death rate), find how long it will take the population to quadruple?

26. The population of an ant hill is growing exponentially. If there are 10,000 ants in the hill today and there were 1000 ants 30 days ago, how many ants were there 15 days ago?

27. The gross national product (GNP) of a small country was 100 billion dollars in 1975 and 150 billions dollars in 1985. Assuming the GNP grows exponentially, approximately what will the GNP be in 1995?

(a) 225 billion dollars.
(b) 200 billion dollars.
(c) $100e^{10}$ billion dollars.
(d) $100e^{20}$ billion dollars.
(e) More information is required to determine the approximate value.

28. Political scientists study legislatures, and one of the aspects they look at is the length of time a representative stays in office. If we pick a "base-line" year, say 1965, and let $N(t)$ be the number of legislators that have served continuously from 1965 to t ($t > 1965$), then $N(t)$ behaves according to the law of decay. In 1965 there were 434 legislators, and in 1971 only 266 of those 434 legislators were still in office. Predict the number who will still be in office in 1973.

29. In meeting its responsibilities to protect the nation's rivers, forest, and wildlife, the U.S. Department of Interior has placed the bald eagle on its protected species list for a section of western United States. In January of 1987 it was estimated that there were 2000 bald eagles in this area. By January 1988 this number had risen to 3000. The Department of Interior estimates that this area can support a total of 10,000 bald eagles and will take the bald eagle off the list when the number reaches three-quarters of the maximum. Assuming bald eagle populations can be described by the logistic equation, determine the year that the bald eagle will be taken off the list.

30. A year ago, the state department of fish and wildlife stocked a new lake with 500 bass. They now estimate that there are 1500 bass. Assuming that bass population satisfies a logistic equation and that the lake can support 6000 bass in total, predict the bass population (to the nearest hundred) 4 years from now.

CHAPTER 7 REVIEW

1. Determine whether each of the following is true or false.
   (a) If $u = \sqrt[5]{1+x}$, then
   $$\int \frac{x^2 + 2x}{\sqrt[5]{1+x}} dx = 5 \int (u^{13} - u^3) du.$$
   (b) If $u = \sqrt{x+10}$, then
   $$\int_6^{15} x\sqrt{x+10}\, dx = 2 \int_6^{15} (u^4 - 10u^2) du.$$
   (c) When integrating $\int uv'\, dx$ by parts, generally v' is chosen as the more complicated part of the product that can easily be integrated.
   (d) Both the rectangle rule and the trapezoid rule use line segments to connect points on the graph, whereas Simpson's rule uses parabolic curves to connect points.
   (e) For a specified value of n, the trapezoid rule always yields better approximations than the rectangle rule.
   (f) The half-life of C^{14} is 5730 years. Thus, if a fossil contains 50% of its original amount of C^{14}, then its age is 50% (5730) = 2865 years.
   (g) If the half-life of a radioactive substance is 5 years, then it will take 20 years for 40 grams of the substance to distintegrate to 2.5 grams.

In Problems 2–14, evaluate the integrals.

2. $\int \dfrac{x}{x - \pi} dx$

3. $\int (x^2 - 9)(x - 3)^{3/2} dx$

4. $\int x^5 \sqrt{3 - x^3}\, dx$

5. $\int \sqrt{x} \ln x\, dx$

6. $\int \dfrac{x}{\sqrt{8 - 5x}} dx$

7. $\int \dfrac{1}{1 + x^{1/2}} dx$

8. $\int x^7 e^{x^4} dx$

9. $\int \dfrac{1}{x\sqrt{1 + \pi x^2}} dx$

10. $\int xe^{ex} dx$

11. $\int (1 - x)^e x\, dx$

12. $\int \dfrac{3x^2 + 12x + 13}{\sqrt{x + 2}} dx$

13. $\int \dfrac{1}{x(e^2 x^2 - 2ex + 1)} dx$

14. $\int \dfrac{\ln(\ln x)}{x} dx$

In Problems 15–17, approximate the definite integral using (a) the rectangle rule, (b) the trapezoid rule, and (c) Simpson's rule.

15. $\int_2^4 \sqrt{9 + x^3}\, dx$, $n = 4$

16. $\int_{-2\sqrt{3}/3}^{2\sqrt{3}/3} (x^3 - x) dx$, $n = 4$

17. $\int_{-1}^{1} e^{-x^2} dx$, $n = 6$

18. (a) Approximate $\int_1^5 (1/x)dx$ using Simpson's rule with $n = 12$.
    (b) Evaluate the integral and compare.

19. If a bacteria population is 10,000 and grows with a proportionality constant of 0.5 when time is measured in hours, how long will it take the population to double?

20. At the end of 3 hours a bacteria population is 15,000 and at the end of 5 hours the population is 45,000. What was the original size of the population?

21. If the half-life of a radioactive substance is 6000 years, how long will it take 7 grams of the substance to disintegrate to 3 grams?

22. A human skull was recently uncovered in Africa and it was determined that only one-ninth of the original amount of ^{14}C was present. Determine the age (to the nearest hundred years) of the skull.

23. The population of a colony of rats is growing exponentially. Its initial population is 1000 rats, and after 50 days the colony has grown to 2500 rats. Determine the population after 150 days.

24. A colony of Mediterranean fruit flies is growing exponentially. If the size of the colony triples in 15 days, how many days does it take for the colony to double?

25. If 500 grams of a radioactive substance are present initially and 400 grams are left 50 years later, then many grams are left after 150 years?

26. The number of bacteria in a culture at t hours after noon is $25{,}000 - 20{,}000e^{-t}$. Which of the following is not true?
    (a) The number of bacteria at noon is 5000.
    (b) The number of bacteria at 2:00 p.m. is less than 20,000.
    (c) The number of bacteria is eventually more than 24,000.
    (d) The number of bacteria is always less than 25,000.
    (e) The number of bacteria is always increasing.

27. If a and n are constants and $n \neq -1$, use integration by parts to show that

$$\int x^n \ln(ax)\,dx = \frac{x^{n+1}}{n+1} \ln(ax) - \frac{x^{n+1}}{(n+1)^2} + C.$$

CHAPTER 8

MULTIVARIABLE CALCULUS

CHAPTER OUTLINE
8.1 FUNCTIONS OF TWO VARIABLES
8.2 PARTIAL DERIVATIVES
8.3 EXTREME POINTS
8.4 LAGRANGE MULTIPLIERS
8.5 DOUBLE INTEGRALS

The preceding chapters deal with the calculus of functions of one variable. But many quantities depend on more than one other quantity. For example, the volume of a right circular cylinder depends on the radius and the height. This chapter takes a brief look at the calculus of functions of more than one variable. The first section introduces the ideas of equations in three variables, functions in two variables, and their graphs. Sections 8.2–8.4 concern differentiation of such functions, and Section 8.5 covers integration.

8.1 FUNCTIONS OF TWO VARIABLES

This section is a natural extension of Chapter 1. It is the result of introducing a third variable. In Chapter 1 we studied equations in two variables: x and y. In this section we examine equations in three variables, with the additional variable being z. For example,

$$2x - 3y + z = 2 \quad \text{and} \quad x^2 + y^2 + z^2 = 16$$

are equations in x, y, and z. When working with two variables, we use ordered *pairs*. When working with three variables, we use ordered *triples*.

A **solution** of an equation in x, y, and z is an ordered triple (a,b,c) of real numbers that makes the equation true when x is replaced by a, y is replaced by b, and z is replaced by c. Thus $(2,1,1)$ is a solution of $2x - 3y + z = 2$, but $(1,1,2)$ is not.

Given an equation in x and y, we use the xy-plane to give us a "picture" of its solutions. It is formed by *two* perpendicular number lines intersecting at their origins. This gives us a two-dimensional space sometimes called R^2. With equations in x, y, and z, we may also use solutions to give us a picture. To do so we consider *three* perpendicular number lines intersecting at their origins. Such a system, seen in Figure 8.1, is called a *three-dimensional space* and may be denoted R^3.

In this system we have three axes instead of two. They divide the space into eight distinct regions called **octants,** with the first octant being the one where all coordinates are positive. Each pair of axes determines a plane: the xy-plane, the xz-plane, and the yz-plane.

With this system each point in space is associated with a unique ordered triple, and each ordered triple corresponds uniquely to a point in space. Some points and associated ordered triples are indicated in Figure 8.2.

The graph of an equation in x, y, and z is the set of all points in the three-dimensional space which are solutions to the equation. The graphs of equations in three variables are obviously more complex than those in two variables. The graphs of several equations are seen in Figure 8.3.

An equation in x, y, and z is a statement of the relationship between three variables. If the relationship is such that for each permissible value of x and permissible value of y, there corresponds a unique value of z, then we say that **z is a function of x and y.** Examples include

$$x + y + z = 3 \quad \text{and} \quad z = x^2 + y^2.$$

Once we select a value for x and a value for y, the value for z is uniquely determined. We have but one choice for z to make the equation true. In this regard, x and y are referred to as the independent variables, and z is called the dependent variable.

As examples, we note that the area of a rectangle is a function of the length and width. The volume of a right circular cylinder is a function of

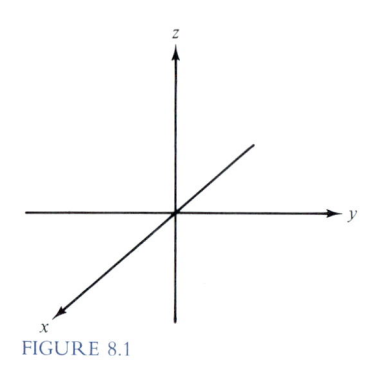

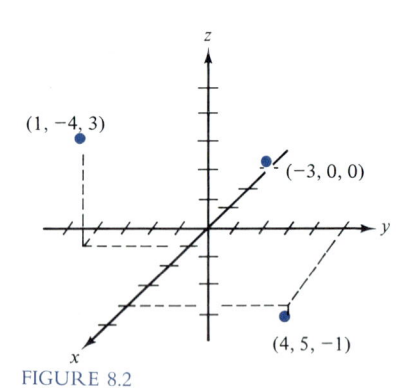

8.1 FUNCTIONS OF TWO VARIABLES

Sphere
$x^2 + y^2 + z^2 = a^2$

Ellipsoid
$\dfrac{x^2}{a^2} + \dfrac{y^2}{b^2} + \dfrac{z^2}{c^2} = 1$

Elliptic paraboloid
$\dfrac{x^2}{a^2} + \dfrac{y^2}{b^2} = \dfrac{z}{c}$

Hyperbolic paraboloid
$\dfrac{x^2}{a^2} - \dfrac{y^2}{b^2} = \dfrac{-z}{c}$

Hyperboloid of two sheets
$\dfrac{x^2}{a^2} + \dfrac{y^2}{b^2} - \dfrac{z^2}{c^2} = -1$

Hyperboloid of one sheet
$\dfrac{x^2}{a^2} + \dfrac{y^2}{b^2} - \dfrac{z^2}{c^2} = 1$

Quadric cone
$\dfrac{x^2}{a^2} + \dfrac{y^2}{b^2} = z^2$

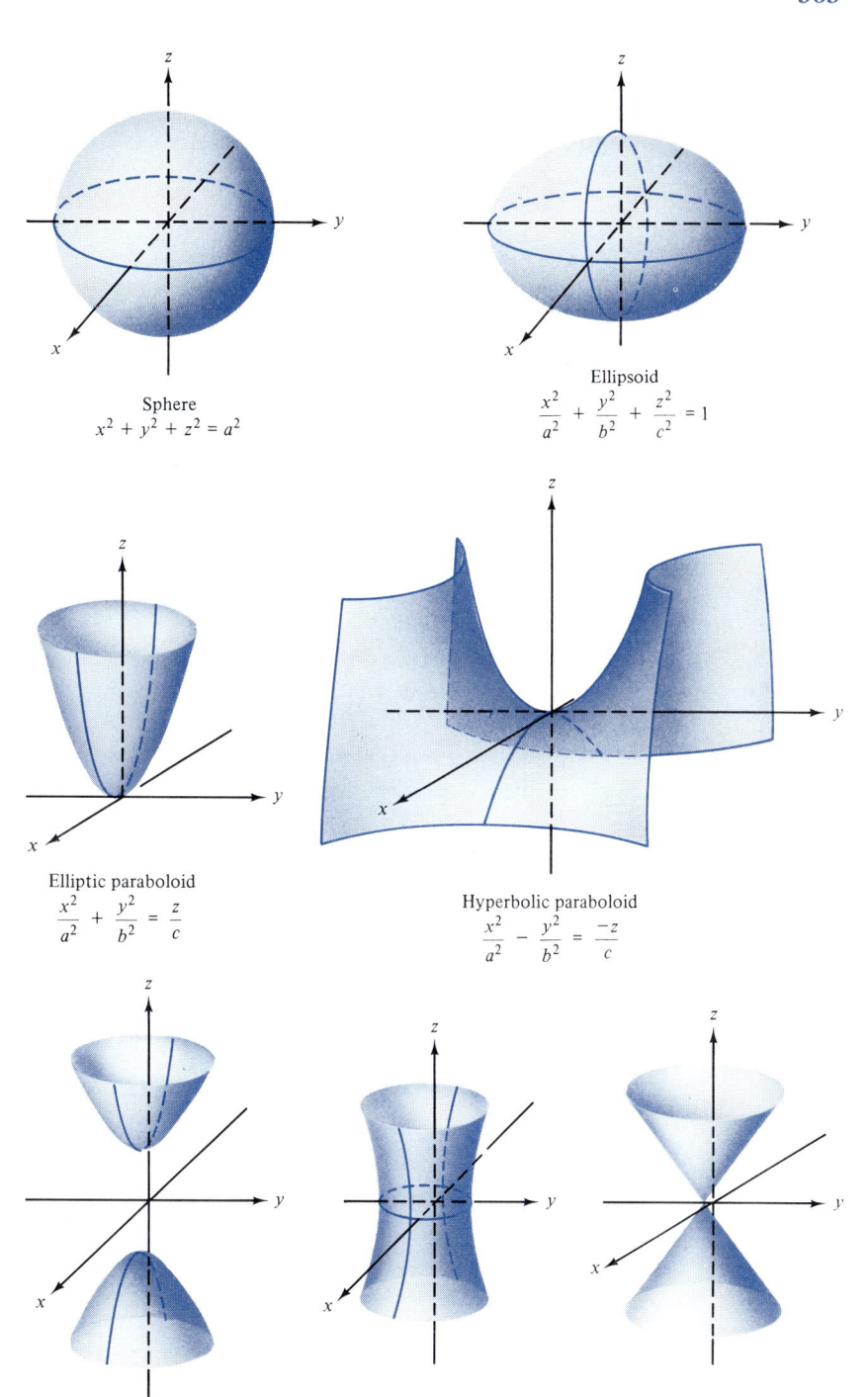

FIGURE 8.3

the radius and height. The effective interest rate is a function of the nominal interest rate and the number of interest periods per year.

On the other hand, z is not a function of x and y if
$$z^2 = x^2 - y^2.$$
When $x = 2$ and $y = 1$, we have $z = \sqrt{3}$ or $z = -\sqrt{3}$. The z-value is *not* uniquely determined.

EXERCISE

Determine whether z is a function of x and y for (a) $x^2 + y^2 + z^2 = 4$; (b) $|z| = x + y$; and (c) $z = x^2 - y^2$.

■ ANSWER
(a) No; (b) no; (c) yes

When working with two variables only, recall that y is a function of x if and only if no vertical line intersects the graph of the equation at more than one point. A vertical line in R^2 is one perpendicular to the x-axis. In R^3, a vertical line is one perpendicular to the xy-plane; and z is a function of x and y provided that no vertical line intersects the graph at more than one point.

EXERCISE

Given the graphs in Figure 8.4, determine whether z is a function of x and y.

■ ANSWER
(a) No; (b) yes; (c) yes; (d) no

A function of a single variable has a domain that is a subset of R, the set of all real numbers. A function of two variables has a domain that is a subset of R^2, the set of all ordered pairs of real numbers. (The *range* will continue to be a subset of R.) For example, if we associate each ordered pair with the sum of its coordinates, then the function's formula of definition is
$$f(x,y) = x + y.$$
The domain is R^2, the xy-plane, and its graph is the graph of
$$z = f(x,y) = x + y,$$
which is a plane. (Its range is R.)

8.1 FUNCTIONS OF TWO VARIABLES

(a)

(b)

(c)

(d)

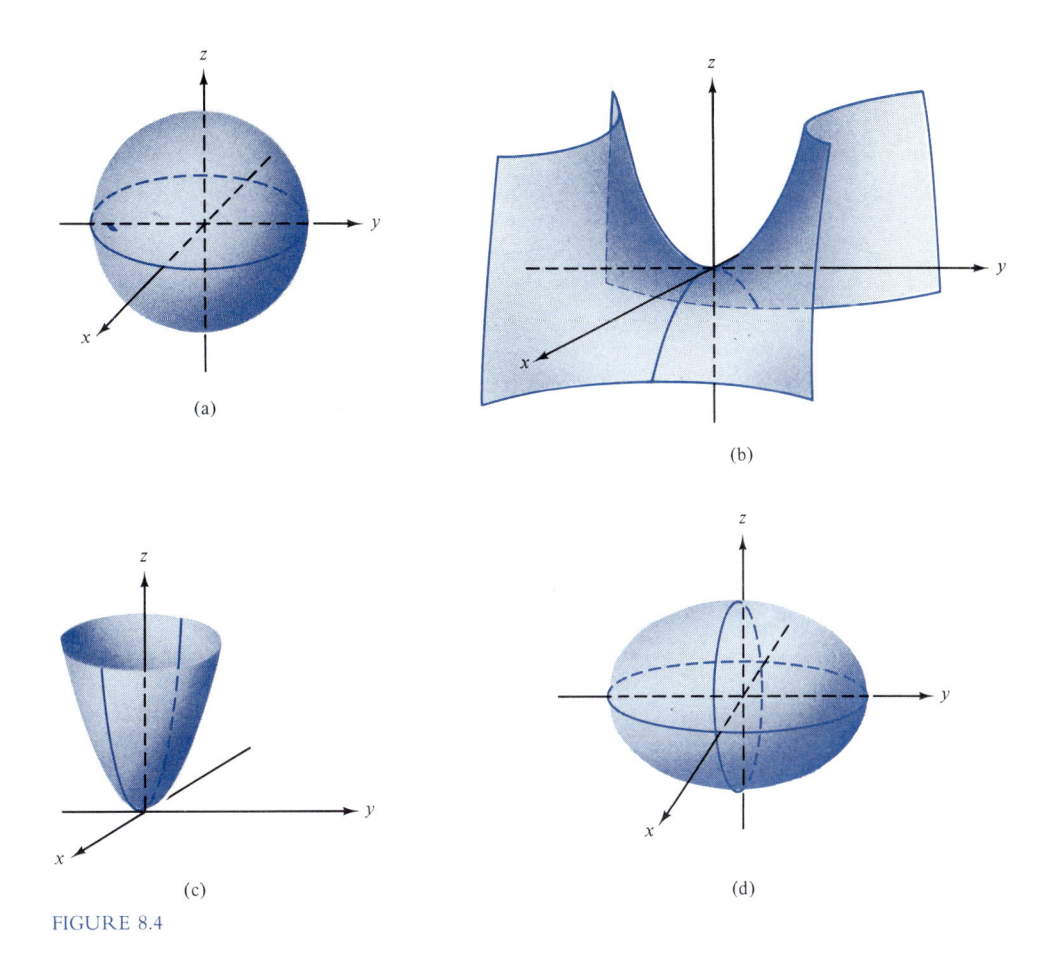

FIGURE 8.4

When the domain is not explicitly specified, it is assumed to be the set of all ordered pairs whose values under the function are defined and real. We made a similar assumption for single-variable functions.

EXAMPLE 1

Determine the domain of each of the following functions:

(a) $f(x,y) = \dfrac{x}{y - x^2}$ and (b) $f(x,y) = \sqrt{xy}$.

■ *SOLUTION*
(a) This function is not defined when
$$y - x^2 = 0.$$
Thus its domain is the set of all points in the xy-plane except those on the parabola $y = x^2$.

(b) This function is not defined when the expression beneath the radical is negative, that is, when

$$xy < 0.$$

This occurs when $x > 0$ and $y < 0$ or when $x < 0$ and $y > 0$. So the domain excludes quadrant IV (when $x > 0$ and $y < 0$) and quadrant II (when $x < 0$ and $y > 0$). The domain is thus the first and third quadrants, plus the axes.

EXERCISE

Determine the domain of each of the following functions:

(a) $f(x,y) = \dfrac{y}{y + x^2}$ and (b) $f(x,y) = \dfrac{1}{\sqrt{xy}}$.

■ ANSWER

(a) All points in R^2 except those on the parabola $y = -x^2$; (b) quadrants I and III only.

EXAMPLE 2

Let f be defined by $f(x,y) = 2xy - y^2$. Determine each of the following:
(a) $f(-1,2)$ and (b) $f(x + h, y) - f(x,y)$.

■ SOLUTION

(a) To calculate $f(-1,2)$, we simply use the formula of definition and replace x by -1 and y by 2. Thus

$$f(-1,2) = 2(-1)(2) - 2^2 = -8.$$

(b) We have

$$f(x + h, y) - f(x,y) = 2(x + h)y - y^2 - (2xy - y^2)$$
$$= 2xy + 2hy - y^2 - 2xy + y^2$$
$$= 2hy.$$

EXERCISE

Let f be defined by $f(x,y) = x^2 - 3xy$. Determine each of the following:
(a) $f(-3,2)$ and (b) $f(x, y + h) - f(x,y)$.

■ ANSWER

(a) 27; (b) $-3xh$

PROBLEM SET 8.1

In Problems 1 and 2, plot the points.

1. $(1,2,4)$, $(3,-4,1)$, $(0,5,-3)$, $(0,0,-4)$, $(-5,-1,-2)$, $(-1,-6,0)$
2. $(2,5,8)$, $(-1,-3,2)$, $(5,0,0)$, $(3,4,-2)$, $(2,0,-3)$, $(0,6,3)$

In Problems 3 and 4 list the ordered triple that corresponds to each of the points in R^3.

3.

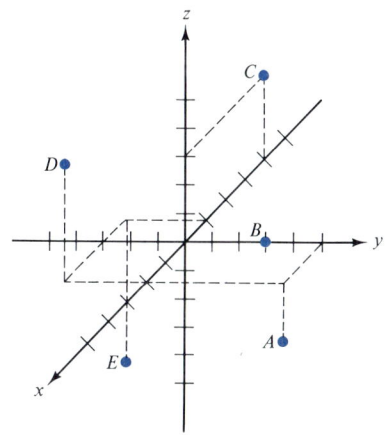

4.

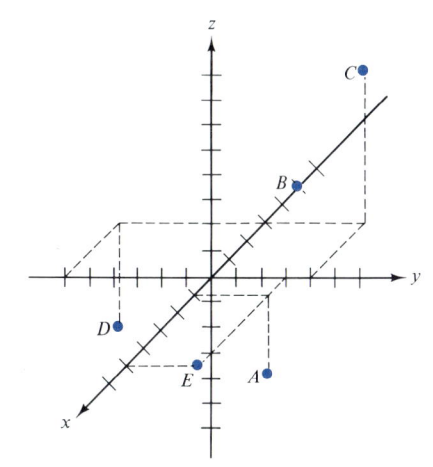

In Problems 5 and 6, determine whether z is a function of x and y.

5. (a) $z = \sqrt{x^2 + y^2}$ (b) $z = e^{x^2 y^2}$
   (c) $x - y^2 - z^2 = 0$ (d) $z + |x| = |y|$
   (e) $\ln z - \ln(xy) = 1$

6. (a) $\dfrac{x^2}{4} + \dfrac{y^2}{4} - \dfrac{z^2}{9} = 1$ (b) $z = 2^{x+y}$
   (c) $z = \sqrt{1 - x^2 - y^2}$ (d) $|z^2| + x^2 = y$
   (e) $z = \ln \sqrt{xy}$

In Problems 7 and 8, given the graph, determine whether z is a function of x and y.

7.

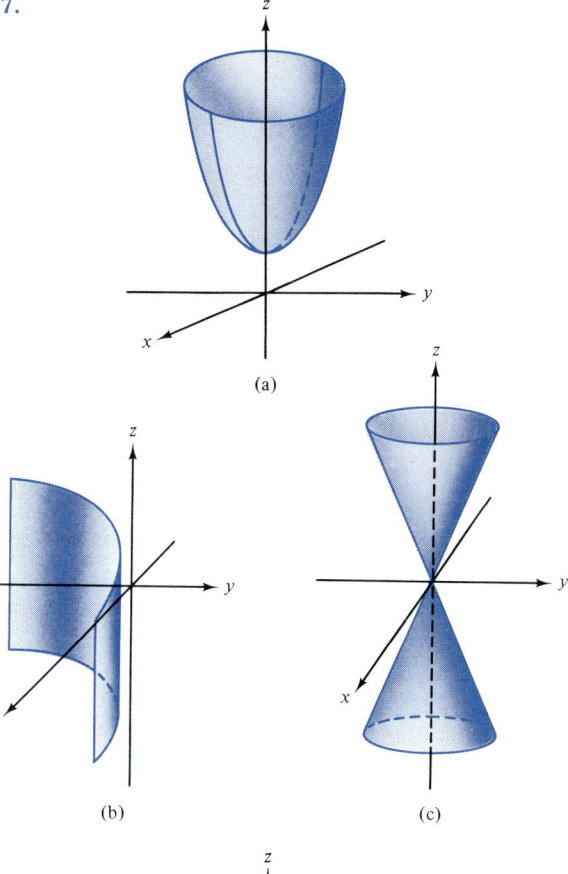

(a)

(b)

(c)

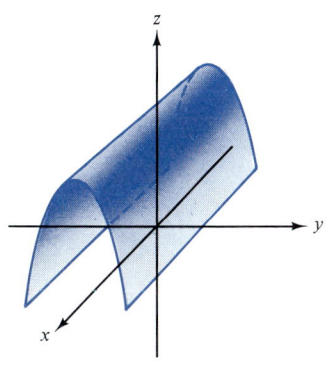

(d)

8.

(a)

(b)

(c)

(d)

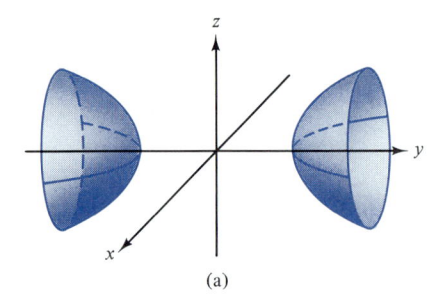

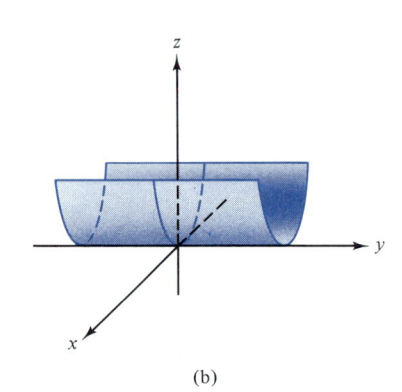

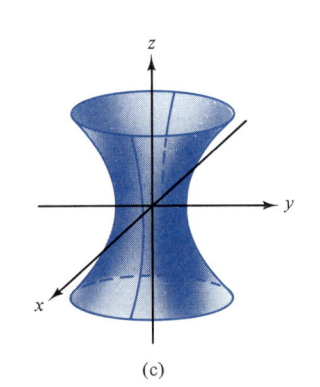

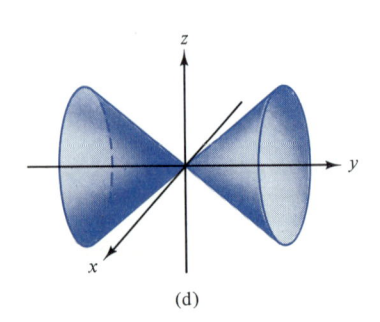

In Problems 9–18, determine the domain for each function.

9. $f(x,y) = x + 3y + 2$
10. $f(x,y) = 5x - y - 6$
11. $f(x,y) = 1/(x^2 + y^2)$
12. $f(x,y) = 1/(x^2 - y^2)$
13. $f(x,y) = e^{y/(x+1)}$
14. $f(x,y) = e^{(x^2-1)/y}$
15. $f(x,y) = \sqrt{x} + \sqrt{1 + y^2}$
16. $f(x,y) = \sqrt{x^2 + 4} - \sqrt{y}$
17. $f(x,y) = \ln(xy)$
18. $f(x,y) = \ln(-x/y)$

In Problems 19–26, determine each of the following for the function f defined.

19. $f(x,y) = x^2 + xy + y^2$: (a) $f(0,0)$, (b) $f(-1,3)$, (c) $f(\sqrt{2}, \sqrt{3})$, (d) $f(a, a^2)$, and (e) $f(x + h, y) - f(x, y)$.

20. $f(x,y) = x^2y + xy^2$: (a) $f(2,2)$, (b) $f(-3,-2)$, (c) $f(\sqrt{5}, 3\sqrt{5})$, (d) $f(b^2, b^3)$, and (e) $f(x + h, y) - f(x, y)$.

21. $f(x,y) = xy/(x^2 + y^2)$: (a) $f(1,0)$, (b) $f(\frac{1}{2}, -2)$, (c) $f(\sqrt{\pi}, \sqrt{\pi})$, (d) $f(a + b, a - b)$, and (e) $f(x^2, y^2)$.

22. $f(x,y) = x^3y^3/(x + y)$: (a) $f(0,1)$, (b) $f(\frac{1}{3}, \frac{2}{3})$, (c) $f(2\sqrt[3]{e}, -\sqrt[3]{e})$, (d) $f(a/(a + 1), 1/(a + 1))$, and (e) $f(x^3, y^3)$.

23. $f(x,y) = xe^y + ye^x$: (a) $f(1,1)$, (b) $f(0,-2) + 1$, (c) $f(0, -2 + 1)$, (d) $f(\ln 2, \ln 3)$, and (e) $f(f(-1,0), f(0,0))$.

24. $f(x,y) = xe^{x+y}$: (a) $f(-3,-3)$, (b) $f(1,2) + 3$, (c) $f(1, 2 + 3)$, (d) $f(\ln 5, \ln \frac{1}{5})$, and (e) $f(f(1,0), f(0,1))$.

25. $f(x,y) = y \ln(x^2/y)$: (a) $f(\sqrt{7}, 1)$, (b) $f(-3, 9)$, (c) $f(e^5, e^9)$, (d) $f(1/x, 1/y)$, and (e) $f(2, 3 + h) - f(2, 3)$.

26. $f(x,y) = \ln y^x + \ln x^y$: (a) $f(2,2)$, (b) $f(\frac{1}{2}, 4)$, (c) $f(e, 1)$, (d) $f(\sqrt{x}, \sqrt{y})$, and (e) $f(1, 4 + h) - f(1, 4)$.

27. If $f(x,y) = x^2 + y^2 + 1$, show that
$$f(a + 4, -2) - f(-4, a + 2) - 4a = 0.$$

28. If $f(x,y) = xy + x^2y^2$, show that
$$f(a - 1, 3) - f(-1, a + 2) - 2(4a - 1)(a - 2) = 0.$$

29. The volume of a right circular cylinder is $V = \pi r^2 h$, where r is the radius of the base and h is the height. The area of the lateral surface of a right circular cylinder is $A = 2\pi rh$. Express V as a function of r and A.

30. The volume of a right circular cone is $V = \frac{1}{3}\pi r^2 h$, where r is the radius of the base and h is the height. The area of the lateral surface of a right circular cone is $A = \pi r \sqrt{r^2 + h^2}$. Express A as a function of r and V.

8.2 PARTIAL DERIVATIVES

In this section we develop the idea of the derivative of a function of two variables. Let's begin by considering the function $f(x,y) = x^2 + y^2$, whose graph is in Figure 8.5.

Consider the curve formed by the intersection of the graph of f with the plane $y = c$, shown in Figure 8.6. In the plane $y = c$ the equation is

$$z = f(x,c) = x^2 + c^2.$$

If we differentiate z with respect to x, we have

$$\frac{dz}{dx} = 2x. \tag{8-1}$$

For the curve this derivative represents the instantaneous rate of change in z with respect to x (in the plane $y = c$). It represents the slope of a line tangent to the curve.

For the surface this derivative represents the instantaneous rate of change in z with respect to x as *x varies and y remains constant*. It represents the slope of a line tangent to the surface *in the x-direction*, that is, parallel to the *xz*-plane.

If we evaluate the derivative at, say, $x = 2$ and $y = 1$, we get the slope of a tangent in the plane $y = 1$ at $x = 2$. See Figure 8.7. We have

$$\left.\frac{dz}{dx}\right|_{\substack{x=2\\y=1}} = 4.$$

Hence the slope of the tangent in the *x*-direction at $(2,1,f(2,1))$ is 4. That is, with y fixed at 1, z is increasing 4 units as x increases 1.

Therefore, given a function f of two variables, the slope of the tangent in the *x*-direction at $(a,b,f(a,b))$ is the derivative of $f(x,b)$ evaluated at a. In limit notation this is

$$\lim_{h \to 0} \frac{f(a+h,b) - f(a,b)}{h}.$$

The slope of the tangent in the *y*-direction is

$$\lim_{h \to 0} \frac{f(a,b+h) - f(a,b)}{h}.$$

Thus, when computing a slope in the *x*-direction, the *x*-values change while the *y*-values remain constant. When determining a slope in the *y*-direction, the *y*-values change while the *x*-values remain constant.

The function f_x defined by

$$f_x(x,y) = \lim_{h \to 0} \frac{f(x+h,y) - f(x,y)}{h}$$

FIGURE 8.5

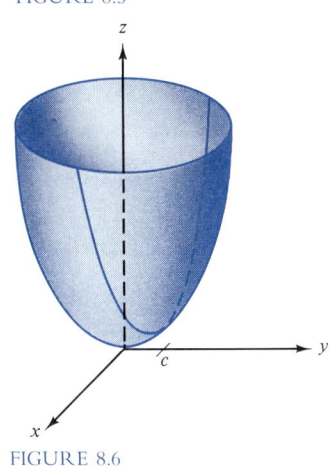

FIGURE 8.6

FIGURE 8.7

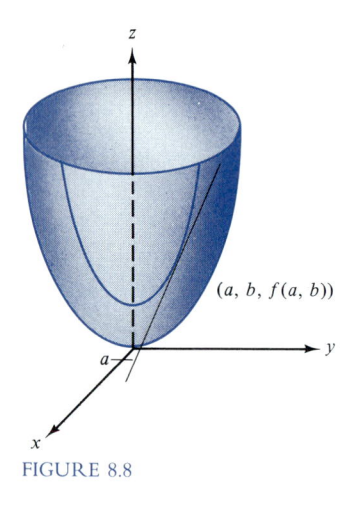

is called the **partial derivative of f with respect to x**. So $f_x(a,b)$ is the slope of the tangent in the x-direction at $(a,b,f(a,b))$.

The function defined by

$$f_y(x,y) = \lim_{h \to 0} \frac{f(x,y+h) - f(x,y)}{h}$$

is called the **partial derivative of f with respect to y**. So $f_y(a,b)$ is the slope of the tangent line in the y-direction at $(a,b,f(a,b))$. See Figure 8.8.

Returning to

$$f(x,y) = x^2 + y^2,$$

let's compute the partial derivative of f with respect to x. We have

$$\begin{aligned} f_x(x,y) &= \lim_{h \to 0} \frac{f(x+h,y) - f(x,y)}{h} \\ &= \lim_{h \to 0} \frac{(x+h)^2 + y^2 - (x^2 + y^2)}{h} \\ &= \lim_{h \to 0} \frac{x^2 + 2xh + h^2 + y^2 - x^2 - y^2}{h} \\ &= \lim_{h \to 0} (2x + h) \\ &= 2x. \end{aligned}$$

FIGURE 8.8

Note that this is exactly the same formula we got in Equation (8-1), which we obtained by differentiating z with respect to x while y was constant. Therefore, to find the partial derivative with respect to x, we differentiate with respect to x while treating y as a constant. To find the partial derivative with respect to y, we differentiate with respect to y while treating x as a constant. Returning to

$$f(x,y) = x^2 + y^2$$

again, we see that

$$f_y(x,y) = 2y.$$

EXAMPLE 1

Determine $f_x(x,y)$ and $f_y(x,y)$ for each function: (a) $f(x,y) = x^2 - xy$ and (b) $f(x,y) = 5x - x^2y^2 + x^3y$.

■ SOLUTION

(a) To determine the partial derivative with respect to x, we differentiate with respect to x, treating y as a constant. We have

$$f_x(x,y) = 2x - y.$$

8.2 PARTIAL DERIVATIVES

To find the partial with respect to y, we regard x as a constant and differentiate with respect to y. We get

$$f_y(x,y) = -x.$$

(b) Treating y as a constant and differentiating with respect to x, we get

$$f_x(x, y) = 5 - 2xy^2 + 3x^2y.$$

Regarding x as a constant and differentiating with respect to y, we have

$$f_y(x,y) = -2x^2y + x^3.$$

EXERCISE

Determine $f_x(x,y)$ and $f_y(x,y)$ for each function: (a) $f(x,y) = y^2 + xy$ and (b) $f(x,y) = x^2y^2 - xy^3 + y^4$

■ ANSWER
(a) $f_x(x,y) = y$; $f_y(x,y) = 2y + x$
(b) $f_x(x,y) = 2xy^2 - y^3$; $f_y(x,y) = 2x^2y - 3xy^2 + 4y^3$

Before proceeding, let's take a moment to introduce an additional notation. If the given function is defined by an equation in x, y, and z instead of by a formula of definition, we use

$$\frac{\partial z}{\partial x} \quad \text{and} \quad \frac{\partial z}{\partial y}$$

to denote the partial derivatives with respect to x and to y. Thus, if

$$z = x^2 + y^2,$$

we write

$$\frac{\partial z}{\partial x} = 2x \quad \text{and} \quad \frac{\partial z}{\partial y} = 2y.$$

EXAMPLE 2

Determine $\partial z/\partial x$ and $\partial z/\partial y$ for each function: (a) $z = (x^2 + xy - y^2)^5$ and (b) $z = e^{x^2 y}$.

■ SOLUTION
(a) We know that to differentiate a power function we multiply exponent by coefficient, reduce exponent by one, and then multiply by the derivative of what's in parentheses. So in computing $\partial z/\partial x$, we must treat

y as a constant in differentiating the expression within parentheses. We get

$$\frac{\partial z}{\partial x} = 5(x^2 + xy - y^2)^4 \cdot (2x + y).$$

Treating x as a constant gives

$$\frac{\partial z}{\partial y} = 5(x^2 + xy - y^2)^4 \cdot (x - 2y).$$

(b) We know that to differentiate e raised to a power, we multiply e to the power by the derivative of the power. So in computing $\partial z/\partial x$, we regard y as a constant in differentiating the exponent. We get

$$\frac{\partial z}{\partial x} = e^{x^2 y} \cdot 2xy = 2xye^{x^2 y}.$$

Viewing x as a constant gives

$$\frac{\partial z}{\partial y} = e^{x^2 y} \cdot x^2 = x^2 e^{x^2 y}.$$

EXERCISE

Determine $\partial z/\partial x$ and $\partial z/\partial y$ for each function: (a) $z = (x^3 + xy^2 - y^2)^4$ and (b) $z = e^{xy^2}$.

■ ANSWER
(a) $\partial z/\partial x = 4(x^3 + xy^2 - y^2)^3 (3x^2 + y^2)$,
$\partial z/\partial y = 4(x^3 + xy^2 - y^2)^3 (2xy - 2y)$; (b) $\partial z/\partial x = y^2 e^{xy^2}$; $\partial z/\partial y = 2xye^{xy^2}$

EXAMPLE 3

Determine the slope of the tangent to the graph of $z = -x^2 + xy + y^2$ at $(1,2,5)$: (a) in the x-direction and (b) in the y-direction.

■ SOLUTION
(a) To compute the slope in the x-direction, we determine the partial derivative with respect to x. We have

$$\frac{\partial z}{\partial x} = -2x + y.$$

Thus

$$\left.\frac{\partial z}{\partial x}\right|_{\substack{x=1 \\ y=2}} = -2 + 2 = 0.$$

The slope is 0 in the x-direction at $(1,2,5)$.

8.2 PARTIAL DERIVATIVES

(b) To compute the slope in the *y*-direction, we calculate the partial derivative with respect to *y*. We have

$$\frac{\partial z}{\partial y} = x + 2y.$$

Thus

$$\left.\frac{\partial z}{\partial y}\right|_{\substack{x=1 \\ y=2}} = 5.$$

In the *y*-direction, the slope is 5 at (1,2,5).

EXERCISE

Determine the slope of the tangent to the graph of $z = x^2 - xy - y^3$ at $(-1, 2, -5)$: (a) in the *x*-direction and (b) in the *y*-direction.

■ ANSWER
(a) -4; (b) -11

Just as with functions of a single variable, we may take second derivatives. But the second derivative is also a partial derivative and is called a **second partial derivative.** The notations and meanings of the second partial derivative follow.

$f_{xx}(x,y)$ $\dfrac{\partial^2 z}{\partial x^2}$ both partial derivatives with respect to *x*

$f_{xy}(x,y)$ $\dfrac{\partial^2 z}{\partial y \, \partial x}$ partial derivative with respect to *x*, then with respect to *y*

$f_{yx}(x,y)$ $\dfrac{\partial^2 z}{\partial x \, \partial y}$ partial derivative with respect to *y*, then with respect to *x*

$f_{yy}(x,y)$ $\dfrac{\partial^2 z}{\partial y^2}$ both partial derivatives with respect to *y*

EXAMPLE 4

Determine all second partial derivatives of $z = x^3 + 2x^2y^2 + 3y^2$.

■ SOLUTION
We begin by finding the partial derivatives:

$$\frac{\partial z}{\partial x} = 3x^2 + 4xy^2 \quad \text{and} \quad \frac{\partial z}{\partial y} = 4x^2y + 6y. \tag{8-2}$$

Taking the two partial derivatives of the first equation in (8-2) gives

$$\frac{\partial^2 z}{\partial x^2} = 6x + 4y^2 \quad \text{and} \quad \frac{\partial^2 z}{\partial y \, \partial x} = 8xy.$$

Taking the two partial derivatives of the second equation in (8-2) gives

$$\frac{\partial^2 z}{\partial y^2} = 4x^2 + 6 \quad \text{and} \quad \frac{\partial^2 z}{\partial x \, \partial y} = 8xy.$$

EXERCISE

Determine all second partial derivatives of $z = x^2 - 2xy + y^3$.

■ ANSWER

$$\frac{\partial^2 z}{\partial x^2} = 2, \quad \frac{\partial^2 z}{\partial y \, \partial x} = -2, \quad \frac{\partial^2 z}{\partial y^2} = 6y, \quad \frac{\partial^2 z}{\partial x \, \partial y} = -2$$

You may have noted in Example 4 and in the Exercise that followed that

$$\frac{\partial^2 z}{\partial x \, \partial y} = \frac{\partial^2 z}{\partial y \, \partial x}.$$

Although this is not true for all functions, it is true for functions whose "mixed" second partial derivatives are *continuous*. What is a continuous function of two variables? We do not give a formal definition in terms of limits. We simply note that a function of two variables is continuous provided that the only breaks in its graph are at breaks in its domain.

The concept of partial derivative may be naturally extended to functions of three or more variables. When computing the partial derivative with respect to one particular variable, the other independent variables are treated as constants. We'll see this when we consider the following function of four variables.

Using data collected prior to World War II, Richard Stone determined that the yearly quantity B of beer consumed in the United Kingdom was approximately

$$B = 1.058 i^{0.136} p^{-0.727} r^{0.914} s^{0.816},$$

where i is the total real income, p is the average retail price of beer, r is the average retail price of all other goods and services, and s is a measure of the strength of the beer.* This information is needed in the following example and exercise.

---

* "The Analysis of Market Demand," *Journal of the Royal Statistical Society*, CVIII, 1945, pages 286–391.

EXAMPLE 5

Using Richard Stone's equation, find $\partial B/\partial p$ and interpret the result.

■ SOLUTION
We have

$$\frac{\partial B}{\partial p} = 1.058 i^{0.136} r^{0.914} s^{0.816} (-0.727) p^{-1.727}.$$

Because this expression is negative, it means that as the average retail price of beer goes up, and real income, prices of other goods and services, and beer strength remain unchanged, beer consumption goes down.

EXERCISE

Using Richard Stone's equation, find $\partial B/\partial r$ and interpret the result.

■ ANSWER

$$\frac{\partial B}{\partial r} = 1.058 i^{0.136} p^{-0.727} s^{0.816} (0.914) r^{-0.086}$$

Because this expression is positive, it means that as the average retail price of all other goods and services goes up, and real income, price of beer, and beer strength remain unchanged, beer consumption goes up.

PROBLEM SET 8.2

In Problems 1–6, determine

(a) $\lim_{h \to 0} \dfrac{f(x+h,y) - f(x,y)}{h}$ and

(b) $\lim_{h \to 0} \dfrac{f(x,y+h) - f(x,y)}{h}$.

1. $f(x,y) = 3x^2 - 2y^2$
2. $f(x,y) = -4x^2 + 5y^2$
3. $f(x,y) = xy^2 + 5x$
4. $f(x,y) = x^2 y - 3y$
5. $f(x,y) = \dfrac{xy}{x+1} + e^3$
6. $f(x,y) = \dfrac{xy}{y-2} + \ln 3$

In Problems 7–14, determine $f_x(x,y)$ and $f_y(x,y)$.

7. $f(x,y) = x^3 + 2y$
8. $f(x,y) = 3x - y^4$
9. $f(x,y) = x^2 y - 3x^3 y^2$
10. $f(x,y) = 2x^4 y^3 - xy^2$
11. $f(x,y) = \dfrac{x^2}{y} + \dfrac{y^2}{x}$
12. $f(x,y) = \dfrac{y}{x^2} + \dfrac{x}{y^2}$
13. $f(x,y) = x^4 (y^2 + 1)^6$
14. $f(x,y) = y^5 (x^3 - 1)^7$

In Problems 15–22, determine $\partial z/\partial x$ and $\partial z/\partial y$.

15. $z = \sqrt{xy^3 - x}$
16. $z = \sqrt{x^5 y + y}$
17. $z = \dfrac{x^2 y^2}{x^2 + y^2}$
18. $z = \dfrac{x^3 y^3}{x^3 - y^3}$
19. $z = \ln(3xy^3 - 1)$
20. $z = \ln(5x^5 y + 7)$
21. $z = xe^{xy}$
22. $z = ye^{x^2 + y^2}$

23. Determine the slope of the tangent to the graph of $z = x^2 - 2xy^2 + 4y^3$ at $(3,1,7)$: (a) in the x-direction and (b) in the y-direction.

24. Determine the slope of the tangent to the graph of $z = x^3 + 3x^2 y^3 - 2y^2$ at $(-2,1,2)$: (a) in the x-direction and (b) in the y-direction.

25. If $f(x,y) = x^3y^3/(x+y)$, show that $xf_x + yf_y = 5f(x,y)$.
26. If $f(x,y) = x^4y^4/(x+y)$, show that $xf_x + yf_y = 7f(x,y)$.

In Problems 27–34, determine

(a) $\dfrac{\partial^2 z}{\partial x^2}$, (b) $\dfrac{\partial^2 z}{\partial y\, \partial x}$, (c) $\dfrac{\partial^2 z}{\partial x\, \partial y}$, and (d) $\dfrac{\partial^2 z}{\partial y^2}$.

27. $z = x^3 - xy$
28. $z = y^3 + xy$
29. $z = \dfrac{x}{y^3} - \dfrac{y}{x^3}$
30. $z = \dfrac{y^3}{x} - \dfrac{x^3}{y}$
31. $z = (x^2 - 2y)^8$
32. $z = (3x - y^2)^{11}$
33. $z = e^{2x} \ln(3y)$
34. $z = e^{-5y} \ln(4x)$

35. If $f(x,y) = x \ln(x/y)$, show that
$$x^2 f_{xx} + 2xy f_{xy} + y^2 f_{yy} = 0.$$

36. If $f(x,y) = e^{-x^2-y^2}$, show that
$$f_{xx} + (y/x)f_{yx} - (x/y)f_{xy} - f_{yy} = 0.$$

A function f with continuous second partial derivatives is said to be harmonic provided
$$\dfrac{\partial^2 f}{\partial x^2} + \dfrac{\partial^2 f}{\partial y^2} = 0.$$

In Problems 37 and 38, show that the function is harmonic.

37. $f(x,y) = 3x^2 y - y^3$
38. $f(x,y) = x^4 - 6x^2 y^2 + y^4$

39. Richard Stone found that the number of automobiles A purchased annually in the United States is given by
$$A = 0.0190 i^{2.932} p^{-3.578} r^{2.865},$$
where i is the total real income, p is the average retail price of automobiles, and r is the average retail price of all other goods and services.
(a) Find $\partial A/\partial i$ and interpret the result.
(b) Find $\partial A/\partial p$ and interpret the result.

40. Richard Stone also found that the annual food consumption F in the United States was approximated by
$$F = 2.186 i^{0.595} p^{-0.543} r^{0.922},$$
where i is the total real income, p is the average retail price of food, and r is the average retail price of all other goods and services.
(a) Find $\partial F/\partial i$ and interpret the result.
(b) Find $\partial F/\partial p$ and interpret the result.

8.3 EXTREME POINTS

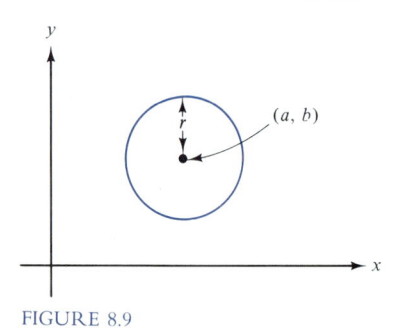

In Chapter 5 we studied extreme points of a function of one variable. We now extend this material to functions of two variables. We begin by defining the two-dimensional counterpart to an open interval. Let $(a,b) \in R^2$, and let $r > 0$. Then the set of all points within the circle centered at (a,b) of radius r is called an **open disk**. See Figure 8.9. So the open disk consists of those points contained *within* the circle.

Two additional concepts needed are those of *interior* and *boundary*. Let D be a subset of R^2. A point $c \in D$ is said to be an **interior point** of D provided that there is an open disk containing c which lies within D. Otherwise, c is called a **boundary point**. See Figure 8.10.

Thus the boundary consists of those points forming the edge of the region. It is the two-dimensional counterpart to endpoint. However, in discussing extreme points, we restrict the study to interior points.

Let f be a function of two variables with domain D, and let (a,b) be an interior point of D. Then we say that f has a **relative maximum at (a,b)** provided that there is an open disk B containing (a,b), such that for all (x,y) in B, $f(a,b) \geq f(x,y)$. Similarly, we say that f has a **relative minimum at (a,b)** provided that there is an open disk B containing (a,b), such that for all (x,y) in B, $f(a,b) \leq f(x,y)$. See Figure 8.11.

In geometric terms, a relative maximum at (a,b) means that *locally* $(a,b,f(a,b))$ is the highest point on the graph. Similarly, a relative mini-

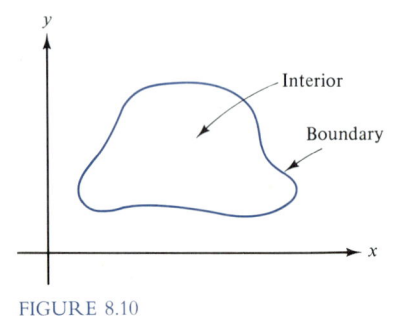

FIGURE 8.9

FIGURE 8.10

8.3 EXTREME POINTS

FIGURE 8.11

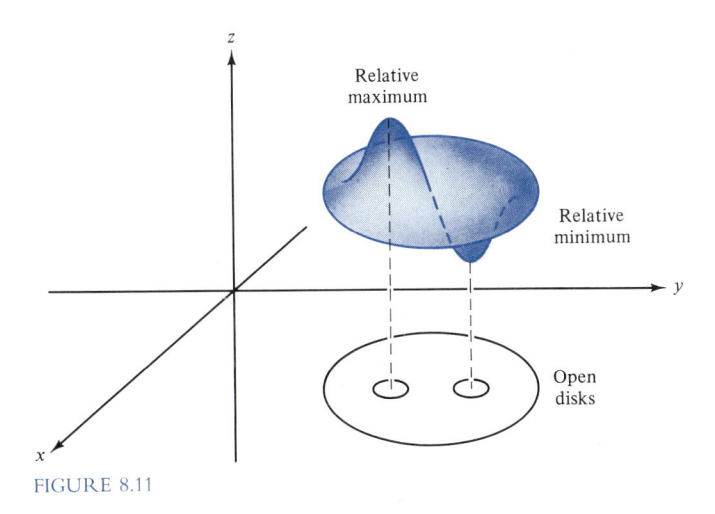

mum at (a,b) means that *locally* $(a,b,f(a,b))$ is the lowest point on the graph.

If f has a relative maximum at (a,b), then the corresponding value $f(a,b)$ is called a **relative maximum**, and $(a,b,f(a,b))$ is called a **relative maximum point**. Analogous definitions are made for **relative minimum** and **relative minimum point**.

The following theorem will help us locate extreme points.

THEOREM 8.1 Let f be a continuous function with domain D. If f has a relative extreme point at (a,b), where (a,b) is in the interior of D, and if f_x and f_y are defined at (a,b), then

$$f_x(a,b) = 0 \quad \text{and} \quad f_y(a,b) = 0.$$

This theorem says that to locate extreme points in the interior, we need to determine where the partial derivatives are zero. A point at which the partial derivatives equal zero is called a **stationary point.** So we need to confine our search to the stationary points. Just as critical values for single-variable functions don't always yield extreme points, stationary points for double-variable functions don't always yield extreme points. See Figure 8.12, which is the graph of $z = y^2 - x^2$.

The point $(0,0)$ is a stationary point. Indeed,

$$\frac{\partial z}{\partial x} = -2x \quad \text{and} \quad \frac{\partial z}{\partial y} = 2y.$$

So

$$\left.\frac{\partial z}{\partial x}\right|_{\substack{x=0 \\ y=0}} = 0 \quad \text{and} \quad \left.\frac{\partial z}{\partial y}\right|_{\substack{x=0 \\ y=0}} = 0.$$

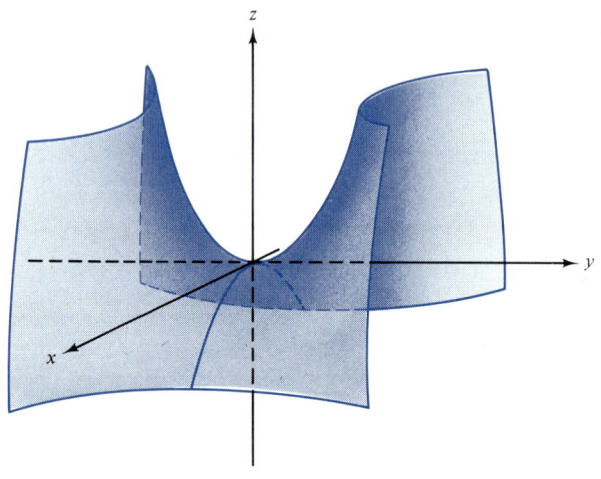

FIGURE 8.12

But there is neither a relative maximum nor minimum at (0,0). In fact, the point (0,0,0) is a maximum point in the x-direction (xz-plane) and a minimum point in the y-direction (yz-plane). Such a point is called a **saddle point**.

Thus we need some method of determining whether a stationary point gives us a relative extreme point. The next theorem, the counterpart to the second derivative test, does this.

THEOREM 8.2
Second Partial Derivatives Test

Let f be a continuous function whose second partial derivatives are continuous, and let (a,b) be a stationary point in the interior of the domain. Let

$$d = f_{xx}(a,b)f_{yy}(a,b) - (f_{xy}(a,b))^2.$$

(i) If $d > 0$ and $f_{xx}(a,b) > 0$, then f has a relative minimum at (a,b).
(ii) If $d > 0$ and $f_{xx}(a,b) < 0$, then f has a relative maximum at (a,b).
(iii) If $d < 0$, then f has neither a maximum nor a minimum at (a,b).
  [If $d < 0$, $(a,b,f(a,b))$ is a saddle point.]

EXAMPLE 1

Determine all relative extreme points of $f(x,y) = x^2 + 4y^2 + x + 8y - 3$.

■ SOLUTION

We must first find the stationary points. We compute the first partial derivatives:

$$f_x(x,y) = 2x + 1 \quad \text{and} \quad f_y(x,y) = 8y + 8.$$

8.3 EXTREME POINTS

Setting each of these to zero gives

$$x = -\tfrac{1}{2} \quad \text{and} \quad y = -1.$$

So the only stationary point is $(-\tfrac{1}{2}, -1)$.

To test it we need to compute the necessary second partial derivatives:

$$f_{xx}(x,y) = 2, \quad f_{yy}(x,y) = 8, \quad f_{xy}(x,y) = 0.$$

Thus

$$\begin{aligned} d &= f_{xx}(-\tfrac{1}{2},-1)f_{yy}(-\tfrac{1}{2},-1) - (f_{xy}(-\tfrac{1}{2},-1))^2 \\ &= 2 \cdot 8 - 0^2 = 16 > 0. \end{aligned}$$

Since $d > 0$ and $f_{xx}(-\tfrac{1}{2},-1) > 0$, f has a relative minimum at $(-\tfrac{1}{2},-1)$. Since $f(-\tfrac{1}{2},-1) = -7\tfrac{1}{4}$, $(-\tfrac{1}{2},-1,-7\tfrac{1}{4})$ is a relative minimum point.

EXERCISE

Determine all relative extreme points of $f(x,y) = 3x^2 + y^2 + 6x - 5y + 1$.

■ ANSWER

$(-1, 2\tfrac{1}{2}, -8\tfrac{1}{4})$ is a relative minimum point.

EXAMPLE 2

Determine all relative extreme points of $z = x^3 - x^2 + y^2 - x + 2y + 2$.

■ SOLUTION

The first partials are

$$\frac{\partial z}{\partial x} = 3x^2 - 2x - 1 \quad \text{and} \quad \frac{\partial z}{\partial y} = 2y + 2.$$

Setting each of these to zero gives

$$3x^2 - 2x - 1 = 0 \quad \text{and} \quad 2y + 2 = 0$$
$$(3x + 1)(x - 1) = 0 \qquad\qquad y = -1.$$
$$x = -\tfrac{1}{3} \text{ or } x = 1$$

Thus the stationary points are $(-\tfrac{1}{3}, -1)$ and $(1, -1)$.
The second partial derivatives needed are

$$\frac{\partial z^2}{\partial x^2} = 6x - 2, \quad \frac{\partial^2 z}{\partial y^2} = 2, \quad \frac{\partial^2 z}{\partial y\, \partial x} = 0.$$

To test $(-\frac{1}{3}, -1)$ we first note that

$$\left.\frac{\partial^2 z}{\partial x^2}\right|_{\substack{x=-1/3 \\ y=-1}} = 6(-\frac{1}{3}) - 2 = -4.$$

Thus

$$d = -4 \cdot 2 - 0^2 = -8 < 0.$$

Because $d < 0$, there is neither a relative maximum nor minimum at $(-\frac{1}{3}, -1)$.

To test $(1, -1)$, we note that

$$\left.\frac{\partial^2 z}{\partial x^2}\right|_{\substack{x=1 \\ y=-1}} = 6(1) - 2 = 4.$$

So

$$d = 4 \cdot 2 - 0^2 = 8 > 0.$$

Because $\partial^2 z/\partial x^2 > 0$, there is a relative minimum at $(1, -1)$. Since $z = 0$ at $(1, -1)$, the relative minimum point is $(1, -1, 0)$.

EXERCISE

Determine all relative extreme points of $z = x^3 + 4x^2 + 2y^2 - 3x - 4y + 1$.

■ ANSWER

$(\frac{1}{3}, 1, -\frac{41}{27})$ is a relative minimum point.

EXAMPLE 3

Determine all relative extreme points of $z = -x^2 + xy - y^2 + 3x$.

■ SOLUTION

The first partial derivatives are

$$\frac{\partial z}{\partial x} = -2x + y + 3 \quad \text{and} \quad \frac{\partial z}{\partial y} = x - 2y.$$

To find the stationary points we must solve simultaneously

$$-2x + y + 3 = 0 \quad \text{and} \quad x - 2y = 0.$$

To do this we solve one of the equations for x or for y and then substitute in the other. If we solve the second for x we get

$$x = 2y. \tag{8-3}$$

Substituting $2y$ for x in the first equation gives
$$-2(2y) + y + 3 = 0$$
$$-3y = -3$$
$$y = 1.$$

Using Equation (8-3) we see that when $y = 1$, $x = 2$. So the only stationary point is $(2,1)$.

The second partial derivatives are
$$\frac{\partial^2 z}{\partial x^2} = -2, \quad \frac{\partial^2 z}{\partial y^2} = -2, \quad \frac{\partial^2 z}{\partial x\, \partial y} = 1.$$

Thus
$$d = (-2)(-2) - 1^2 = 4 - 1 = 3 > 0.$$

Since $\partial^2 z/\partial x^2 < 0$, there is a relative maximum at $(2,1)$. The relative maximum point is $(2,1,3)$.

EXERCISE

Determine all relative extreme points of $z = x^2 - xy + 2y^2 + 7y$.

■ ANSWER

$(-1, -2, -7)$ is a relative minimum point.

Before proceeding, let's note that when using the second partial derivative test, it's possible for the value of d to equal 0. In such a case, the test gives no information, and other methods, beyond the scope of this text, must be used.

EXAMPLE 4

A rectangular box, open at the top, is to have a volume of 4 cubic feet. What dimensions minimize the surface area?

■ SOLUTION
Let
$$S = \text{surface area (in square feet)},$$
$$x = \text{length (in feet)},$$
$$y = \text{width (in feet)},$$
$$z = \text{height (in feet)}.$$

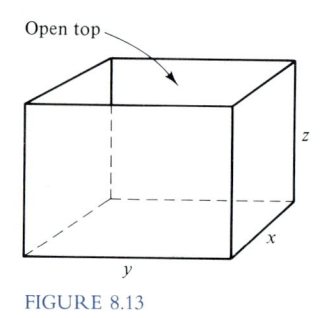

See Figure 8.13. Thus

$$S = xy + 2xz + 2yz. \tag{8-4}$$

But S is a function of three variables, and we need a function of two. Since the volume must be 4 cubic feet, we have

$$xyz = 4.$$

Solving this for z gives

$$z = \frac{4}{xy}.$$

Substituting into Equation (8-4) gives

$$S = xy + 2x \cdot \frac{4}{xy} + 2y \cdot \frac{4}{xy}$$

$$= xy + \frac{8}{y} + \frac{8}{x}.$$

To locate the minimum of S, we compute the partial derivatives:

$$\frac{\partial S}{\partial x} = y - \frac{8}{x^2} \quad \text{and} \quad \frac{\partial S}{\partial y} = x - \frac{8}{y^2}.$$

So we must simultaneously solve

$$y - \frac{8}{x^2} = 0 \quad \text{and} \quad x - \frac{8}{y^2} = 0.$$

Solving the first for y in terms of x gives

$$y = \frac{8}{x^2}.$$

Substituting into the second we get

$$x - \frac{8}{8^2/x^4} = 0$$

$$x - \frac{x^4}{8} = 0$$

$$8x - x^4 = 0$$

$$x(8 - x^3) = 0$$

$$x = 0 \quad \text{or} \quad x^3 = 8$$

$$x = 2.$$

Since x must be positive, we may reject $x = 0$, and because $y = 2$ when $x = 2$, the only stationary point to test is $(2,2)$. The second partial derivatives are

$$\frac{\partial^2 S}{\partial x^2} = \frac{16}{x^3}, \quad \frac{\partial^2 S}{\partial y^2} = \frac{16}{y^3}, \quad \frac{\partial^2 S}{\partial y\, \partial x} = 1.$$

This gives

$$d = \frac{16}{8} \cdot \frac{16}{8} - 1^2 = 3 > 0.$$

Since $\partial^2 S/\partial x^2 > 0$ at the stationary point, we have a minimum. At (2,2),

$$z = \frac{4}{2 \cdot 2} = 1.$$

Thus the dimensions are 2 feet by 2 feet for the base and 1 foot for the height.

Note that in the preceding example we are actually searching for an *absolute* minimum, but our test merely shows that we have a *relative* minimum at (2,2). However, the physical nature of the problem implies that there *must* be an absolute minimum; hence it must be at (2,2). Our word problems will be restricted to those where we shall be able to make this assumption.

EXERCISE

A rectangular box, open at the top, is to have a volume of 32 cubic inches. What dimensions minimize the surface area?

■ ANSWER
Four inches by 4 inches for the base and 2 inches for the height.

PROBLEM SET 8.3

In Problems 1–18, determine all relative extreme points.

1. $f(x,y) = 9 - x^2 - y^2$
2. $f(x,y) = 4 + 2x^2 + 3y^2$
3. $f(x,y) = x^2 + 3y^2 + 3x + 12y + 9$
4. $f(x,y) = -3x^2 - 2y^2 + 6x - 8y - 11$
5. $f(x,y) = \frac{1}{3}x^3 - 9x + y^2$
6. $f(x,y) = x^2 + y^3 - 48y$
7. $f(x,y) = -\pi x^2 + y^5 - 80y$
8. $f(x,y) = x^5 - 5x - ey^2$
9. $z = 2x^3 + \frac{3}{2}x^2 - 3x + y^2 - 4y + 4$
10. $z = -x^2 - 6x + 2y^3 - \frac{1}{2}y^2 - y + \frac{7}{54}$
11. $z = x^2 - 4x - 3y^2 + 6y + 3$

12. $z = 10xy - x^2 - y^2$
13. $z = x^2 - xy + y^2 + 5x + 2y + 11$
14. $z = x^2 - xy + y^2 + 2x - 4y + 4$
15. $z = x^3 - 9xy + y^3$
16. $z = -x^3 + 15xy - y^3$
17. $z = \dfrac{8}{x} + xy + \dfrac{64}{y}$
18. $z = xy - \dfrac{125}{x} - \dfrac{125}{y}$
19. Find three numbers whose sum is 216 and whose product is a maximum.
20. Find three numbers whose sum is 60 such that the sum of their squares is a minimum.
21. Find the point (x,y,z) in the first octant such that $2x + 4y + z = 50$ and x^2y^2z is a maximum.
22. Find the point (x,y,z) in the first octant such that $3x + 2y + 5z = 120$ and x^2yz is a maximum.
23. A rectangular box, open at the top and having a volume of 22.5 cubic feet, is to be constructed. The bottom will cost $5 per square foot, and each side $3 per square foot. Find the dimensions of the box that will minimize the cost.
24. A rectangular box, with a top and a volume of 150 cubic feet, is to be constructed. The bottom will cost $2 per square foot, the top $4 per square foot, and each side $2.50 per square foot. Find the dimensions of the box that will minimize the cost.
25. Determine the volume of the largest rectangular box having one vertex at the origin, three adjacent edges along the coordinate axes, and the vertex opposite the origin lying in the plane $3x + 2y + z = 18$ (see figure below).
26. Determine the volume of the largest rectangular box having one vertex at the origin, three adjacent edges along the coordinate axes, and the vertex opposite the origin lying in the plane $2x + y + 2z = 9$.
27. A company produces two styles of sweater—crew necks and cardigans. The profit on a crew neck sweater is $14 and on a cardigan it is $22. The total cost of producing x crew neck sweaters and y cardigans is $1000 + 7x + (y^2/300)$. If the company's total production budget is $24,775, determine x and y so as to maximize profit.
28. A company manufactures a standard bicycle at a cost of $75 and a deluxe bicycle at a cost of $100. If the standard and deluxe bicycles are priced at $x and $y, respectively, then $2125 - 35x + 25y$ standard bicycles and $4875 + 15x - 40y$ deluxe bicycles are sold. Determine the values of x and y that maximize the profit.

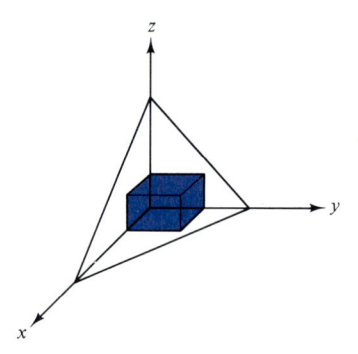

8.4 LAGRANGE MULTIPLIERS

In Section 5.7, concerning maximum–minimum problems, we generally found ourselves trying to find a maximum or minimum of a function of *two* variables, even though we had studied functions of a single variable only. In Example 2, for instance, we had to find the minimum of

$$S = 4xh + x^2. \tag{8-5}$$

To write S as a function of one variable we found an equation connecting x and h. Indeed, we had to minimize S subject to the condition that

$$x^2h = 4000. \tag{8-6}$$

We solved Equation (8-6), the constraint equation, for h in terms of x and substituted into Equation (8-5). This gave us a function of one variable and we were able to proceed.

But what if it is difficult or impossible to solve the constraint equation for one of the variables? For example, what if the constraint equation were

$$x^2 h + x^3 h^3 = 8000?$$

We cannot solve this equation for either one of the variables. In such cases we may use the method of *Lagrange multipliers*, which is based on the following theorem.

THEOREM 8.3 Let f and g be functions of two variables, and let $(a,b) \in$ domain f. If f has a relative maximum or minimum at (a,b), subject to the constraint $g(x,y) = 0$, then there exists a constant λ (lambda) such that

$$f_x(a,b) + \lambda g_x(a,b) = 0$$

and

$$f_y(a,b) + \lambda g_y(a,b) = 0.$$

This theorem says that we may locate the extreme points of f, subject to the constraint, by solving simultaneously three equations:

$$f_x(x,y) + \lambda g_x(x,y) = 0,$$
$$f_y(x,y) + \lambda g_y(x,y) = 0,$$

and

$$g(x,y) = 0.$$

We solve the first two equations for λ (called a **Lagrange multiplier**) and combine them to get an equation in x and y. This new equation, together with the constraint, gives us two equations in x and y, which we may solve.

To illustrate, suppose we wish to find the maximum and minimum of

$$f(x,y) = \frac{12 - 4x - 3y}{4}$$

subject to the constraint

$$x^2 + y^2 = 4.$$

Our first step is to identify the function g. Let

$$g(x,y) = x^2 + y^2 - 4$$

so that $g(x,y) = 0$ is equivalent to the constraint equation. Computing the partial derivatives gives

$$f_x(x,y) = -1, \qquad g_x(x,y) = 2x,$$
$$f_y(x,y) = -\tfrac{3}{4}, \qquad g_y(x,y) = 2y.$$

Thus the equations to be solved are

$$-1 + \lambda \cdot 2x = 0,$$
$$-\tfrac{3}{4} + \lambda \cdot 2y = 0,$$
$$x^2 + y^2 - 4 = 0.$$

Solving the first two equations for λ gives

$$\lambda = \frac{1}{2x} \quad \text{and} \quad \lambda = \frac{3/4}{2y} = \frac{3}{8y}.$$

Combining these gives

$$\frac{1}{2x} = \frac{3}{8y}.$$

Hence we must solve simultaneously

$$\frac{1}{2x} = \frac{3}{8y} \quad \text{and} \quad x^2 + y^2 - 4 = 0.$$

Solving the first equation for y gives

$$y = \frac{3x}{4}.$$

Substitution into the constraint equation gives

$$x^2 + \left(\frac{3x}{4}\right)^2 - 4 = 0$$

$$x^2 + \frac{9x^2}{16} - 4 = 0$$

$$16x^2 + 9x^2 = 64$$

$$25x^2 = 64$$

$$x^2 = \tfrac{64}{25}$$

$$x = \pm \tfrac{8}{5}.$$

Since $y = 3x/4$, $y = \tfrac{6}{5}$ when $x = \tfrac{8}{5}$, and $y = -\tfrac{6}{5}$ when $x = -\tfrac{8}{5}$. Thus the candidates to consider are $(\tfrac{8}{5},\tfrac{6}{5})$ and $(-\tfrac{8}{5},-\tfrac{6}{5})$.

But the Lagrange theorem doesn't provide a test for the candidates. To determine whether we have a maximum, a minimum, or neither at each candidate, we appeal to the geometric nature of the problem. Our consideration is restricted to points in the plane

$$z = \frac{12 - 4x - 3y}{4}$$

which lie on the cylinder

$$x^2 + y^2 = 4.$$

See Figure 8.14.

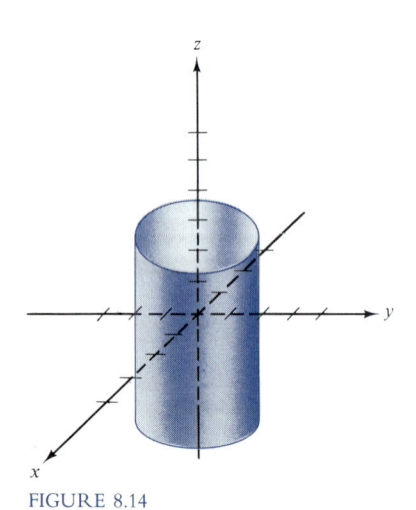

FIGURE 8.14

It is intuitively clear that the intersection of such a plane with a cylinder has a highest and lowest point. That is, there must be an absolute maximum as well as an absolute minimum. Since

$$f(\tfrac{8}{5}, \tfrac{6}{5}) = \tfrac{1}{2} \quad \text{and} \quad f(-\tfrac{8}{5}, -\tfrac{6}{5}) = \tfrac{11}{2},$$

the absolute minimum is $\tfrac{1}{2}$, and the absolute maximum is $5\tfrac{1}{2}$.

Because the Lagrange theorem provides no means of testing the candidates to determine what type (if any) of extreme point exists, we shall consider only those problems where the existence of an absolute maximum or absolute minimum is based on geometric or physical grounds. Under such assumptions, we merely have to evaluate the function at the potential points, with the largest value being the maximum and the smallest being the minimum. We use Lagrange's theorem to determine those potential points.

EXAMPLE 1

Determine the absolute maximum and absolute minimum of $f(x,y) = x^2 y$, subject to the constraint $x^2 + y^2 = 4$.

■ SOLUTION
Let
$$g(x,y) = x^2 + y^2 - 4.$$

Thus the partial derivatives are

$$f_x(x,y) = 2xy, \quad g_x(x,y) = 2x,$$
$$f_y(x,y) = x^2, \quad g_y(x,y) = 2y.$$

The equations to be solved simultaneously are

$$2xy + 2\lambda x = 0$$
$$x^2 + 2\lambda y = 0$$
$$x^2 + y^2 - 4 = 0$$

Solving the first two for λ gives

$$\lambda = -\frac{2xy}{2x} = -y \quad \text{and} \quad \lambda = -\frac{x^2}{2y}.$$

Combining these two gives

$$-y = -\frac{x^2}{2y}$$
$$-2y^2 = -x^2$$
$$2y^2 = x^2.$$

Hence we must simultaneously solve

$$2y^2 = x^2 \quad \text{and} \quad x^2 + y^2 - 4 = 0.$$

Replacing x^2 by $2y^2$ in the constraint equation gives

$$2y^2 + y^2 - 4 = 0$$
$$3y^2 = 4$$
$$y = \pm \frac{2}{\sqrt{3}}.$$

Thus

$$x^2 = 2 \cdot \frac{4}{3} = \frac{8}{3}$$
$$x = \pm \frac{2\sqrt{2}}{\sqrt{3}}.$$

There are four solutions:

$$\left(\frac{2\sqrt{2}}{\sqrt{3}}, \frac{2}{\sqrt{3}}\right), \quad \left(\frac{2\sqrt{2}}{\sqrt{3}}, -\frac{2}{\sqrt{3}}\right), \quad \left(-\frac{2\sqrt{2}}{\sqrt{3}}, -\frac{2}{\sqrt{3}}\right), \quad \text{and} \quad \left(-\frac{2\sqrt{2}}{\sqrt{3}}, \frac{2}{\sqrt{3}}\right).$$

Evaluating the function at the four solutions gives

$$f\left(\frac{2\sqrt{2}}{\sqrt{3}}, \frac{2}{\sqrt{3}}\right) = \frac{8}{3} \cdot \frac{2}{\sqrt{3}} = \frac{16}{3\sqrt{3}},$$
$$f\left(\frac{2\sqrt{2}}{\sqrt{3}}, -\frac{2}{\sqrt{3}}\right) = \frac{8}{3} \cdot \frac{-2}{\sqrt{3}} = -\frac{16}{3\sqrt{3}},$$
$$f\left(-\frac{2\sqrt{2}}{\sqrt{3}}, -\frac{2}{\sqrt{3}}\right) = \frac{8}{3} \cdot \frac{-2}{\sqrt{3}} = -\frac{16}{3\sqrt{3}},$$
$$f\left(-\frac{2\sqrt{2}}{\sqrt{3}}, \frac{2}{\sqrt{3}}\right) = \frac{8}{3} \cdot \frac{2}{\sqrt{3}} = \frac{16}{3\sqrt{3}}.$$

The absolute maximum is

$$\frac{16}{3\sqrt{3}} \quad (\approx 3.079)$$

and the absolute minimum is

$$\frac{-16}{3\sqrt{3}} \quad (\approx -3.079).$$

8.4 LAGRANGE MULTIPLIERS

EXERCISE

Determine the absolute maximum and absolute minimum of $f(x,y) = xy^2$, subject to the constraint $x^2 + y^2 = 9$.

■ ANSWER

Maximum is $6\sqrt{3}$ (≈ 10.39); minimum is $-6\sqrt{3}$ (≈ -10.39).

EXAMPLE 2

A small company manufactures two models of calculators. It makes a profit of $3 on each unit of model A and $4 on each unit of model B. Because of labor and financial constraints, the daily production of x units of model A and y units of model B must satisfy

$$x^2 + 4y^2 = 11{,}700.$$

How should production be allocated between the two models to maximize profit?

■ SOLUTION

We want to maximize profit, which is given by

$$P(x,y) = 3x + 4y,$$

subject to the constraint. Let

$$g(x,y) = x^2 + 4y^2 - 11{,}700.$$

Computing the partial derivatives yields

$$\frac{\partial P}{\partial x} = 3, \qquad \frac{\partial g}{\partial x} = 2x,$$

$$\frac{\partial P}{\partial y} = 4, \qquad \frac{\partial g}{\partial y} = 8y.$$

So the equations to be solved are

$$3 + 2\lambda x = 0,$$
$$4 + 8\lambda y = 0,$$
$$x^2 + 4y^2 - 11{,}700 = 0.$$

Solving the first two for λ gives

$$\lambda = -\frac{3}{2x} \quad \text{and} \quad \lambda = -\frac{1}{2y}.$$

Combining these two yields

$$-\frac{3}{2x} = -\frac{1}{2y}$$

$$2x = 6y$$

$$x = 3y.$$

Substitution into the constraint equation gives

$$9y^2 + 4y^2 - 11{,}700 = 0$$

$$13y^2 = 11{,}700$$

$$y^2 = 900$$

$$y = 30.$$

Since $x = 3y$, the maximum profit occurs when the company produces 90 units of model A and 30 units of model B.

The Lagrange theorem may even be used to verify some business principles. One principle states that maximal output occurs when the ratio between marginal products equals the ratio between corresponding unit prices.

To see this, let's consider a company that produces widgets. The quantity Q that can be produced each year is dependent on the total amount of machine time M and hours of labor L used. That is,

$$Q = f(M,L)$$

for some function f. Let

P_M = hourly cost of machines,

P_L = hourly cost of labor,

C = total dollars available for making widgets.

We need to maximize $Q = f(M,L)$ subject to the constraint

$$P_M M + P_L L = C.$$

Letting $g(M,L) = P_M M + P_L L - C$, we get the following system by the Lagrange theorem:

$$\frac{\partial Q}{\partial M} + \lambda P_M = 0,$$

$$\frac{\partial Q}{\partial L} + \lambda P_L = 0,$$

$$P_M M + P_L L - C = 0.$$

8.4 LAGRANGE MULTIPLIERS

Solving each of the first two for λ gives

$$\lambda = \frac{\partial Q}{\partial M} \cdot \frac{-1}{P_M} \quad \text{and} \quad \lambda = \frac{\partial Q}{\partial L} \cdot \frac{-1}{P_L}.$$

Thus,

$$\frac{\partial Q}{\partial M} \cdot \frac{-1}{P_M} = \frac{\partial Q}{\partial L} \cdot \frac{-1}{P_L}$$

$$\frac{\frac{\partial Q}{\partial M}}{\frac{\partial Q}{\partial L}} = \frac{P_M}{P_L}.$$

Subject to the constraint, the maximal output occurs here. And this equation is the mathematical translation of the principle.

The Lagrange theorem may be extended to functions of three or more variables. See Example 3.

EXAMPLE 3

Determine the absolute maximum and absolute minimum of $f(x,y,z) = 2x + y + z$, subject to the constraint $x^2 + y^2 + z^2 = 6$.

■ SOLUTION

Let
$$g(x,y,z) = x^2 + y^2 + z^2 - 6.$$

So the partial derivatives are

$$\frac{\partial f}{\partial x} = 2, \quad \frac{\partial g}{\partial x} = 2x,$$

$$\frac{\partial f}{\partial y} = 1, \quad \frac{\partial g}{\partial y} = 2y,$$

$$\frac{\partial f}{\partial z} = 1, \quad \frac{\partial g}{\partial z} = 2z.$$

The equations to be solved simultaneously are

$$2 + 2\lambda x = 0,$$
$$1 + 2\lambda y = 0,$$
$$1 + 2\lambda z = 0,$$
$$x^2 + y^2 + z^2 - 6 = 0.$$

Solving the first three for λ gives

$$\lambda = -\frac{1}{x}, \quad \lambda = -\frac{1}{2y}, \quad \text{and} \quad \lambda = -\frac{1}{2z}.$$

We may get y in terms of x by combining the first and second. We have

$$-\frac{1}{x} = -\frac{1}{2y}$$

$$2y = x$$

$$y = \frac{x}{2}.$$

We may get z in terms of x by combining the first and third. We have

$$-\frac{1}{x} = -\frac{1}{2z}$$

$$2z = x$$

$$z = \frac{x}{2}.$$

So the system to be solved is

$$y = \frac{x}{2},$$

$$z = \frac{x}{2},$$

$$x^2 + y^2 + z^2 - 6 = 0.$$

Substituting $x/2$ for y and $x/2$ for z in the constraint equation gives

$$x^2 + \frac{x^2}{4} + \frac{x^2}{4} - 6 = 0$$

$$4x^2 + x^2 + x^2 - 24 = 0$$

$$6x^2 = 24$$

$$x^2 = 4$$

$$x = \pm 2.$$

When $x = 2$, $y = 1$ and $z = 1$, and when $x = -2$, $y = -1$ and $z = -1$. Evaluating the function at the two solutions gives

$$f(2,1,1) = 6,$$

$$f(-2,-1,-1) = -6.$$

The absolute maximum is 6, and the absolute minimum is -6.

EXERCISE

Determine the absolute maximum and absolute minimum of $f(x,y,z) = x - 2y + 2z$, subject to the constraint $x^2 + y^2 + z^2 = 36$.

■ ANSWER
Absolute maximum is 18; absolute minimum is -18.

PROBLEM SET 8.4

In Problems 1–12, determine the absolute maximum and absolute minimum of the function subject to the given constraint. (Assume that the absolutes exist.)

1. $f(x,y) = 6x + 8y - 5$, $x^2 + y^2 = 1$
2. $f(x,y) = 2x - 3y + 4$, $x^2 + y^2 = 13$
3. $f(x,y) = x + y - 3\sqrt{3}$, $\dfrac{x^2}{2} + \dfrac{y^2}{25} = 1$
4. $f(x,y) = x + \tfrac{1}{2}y + 2$, $\dfrac{x^2}{3} + \dfrac{y^2}{4} = 1$
5. $f(x,y) = 2x^2 y$, $x^2 + y^2 = 1$
6. $f(x,y) = 3xy^2$, $x^2 + y^2 = 15$
7. $f(x,y) = x^2 + y^2$, $6x^2 + 4xy + 3y^2 = 70$
8. $f(x,y) = x^2 + y^2$, $13x^2 + 6xy + 5y^2 = 40$
9. $f(x,y,z) = x + z$, $x^2 + y^2 + z^2 = 1$
10. $f(x,y,z) = 2y + z$, $x^2 + y^2 + z^2 = 25$
11. $f(x,y,z) = 4x + y + 4z + 10$, $x^2 + y^2 + z^2 = 132$
12. $f(x,y,z) = 3x - 3y + z + 2$, $3x^2 + y^2 + \tfrac{1}{2}z^2 = 686$
13. Determine the minimum value of $(x-2)^2 + (y-3)^2 + (z-1)^2$ subject to the constraint $2x - 2y + z = -1$.
14. Determine the minimum value of $(x-e)^2 + (y+e^{-1})^2 + (z-e^2)^2$ subject to the constraint $2ex - e^2 y - 2z = e$.
15. Find three positive numbers whose product is as large as possible and such that the first number plus twice the second number plus three times the third number is 45.
16. Find three positive numbers whose sum is as small as possible and such that two times the reciprocal of the first number plus eight times the reciprocal of the second number plus eighteen times the reciprocal of the third number is one.
17. Determine the dimensions of the rectangular box of maximum volume which can be inscribed in the sphere $x^2 + y^2 + z^2 = 75$. What is the maximum volume? (Assume that each edge of the box is parallel to a coordinate axis.)
18. Determine the dimensions of the rectangular box of maximum volume which can be inscribed in the ellipsoid $\tfrac{1}{9}x^2 + \tfrac{1}{36}y^2 + \tfrac{1}{81}z^2 = 1$. What is the maximum volume? (Assume that each edge of the box is parallel to a coordinate axis.)
19. A rectangular box, open at the top, has a surface area of 1083 square inches. Determine the dimensions of the box of maximum volume. What is the maximum volume?
20. A picnic shelter, in the shape of a rectangular box, is to be constructed using 216 square yards of wood for the top, back, and two sides. Determine the dimensions that maximize the volume of the shelter. What is the maximum volume?

8.5 DOUBLE INTEGRALS

Just as the concept of differentiation was extended from one variable to two, the concept of integration may be extended. Given a function f of x and y, an antiderivative with respect to x is a function F such that

$F_x(x,y) = f(x,y)$. That is, it is a function whose partial derivative with respect to x is the given function. So for $f(x,y) = xy$, some of the antiderivatives with respect to x are

$$F_1(x,y) = \frac{x^2 y}{2},$$

$$F_2(x,y) = \frac{x^2 y}{2} + y,$$

$$F_3(x,y) = \frac{x^2 y}{2} + y^3 - 3,$$

$$F_4(x,y) = \frac{x^2 y}{2} - \sqrt{y}.$$

Computing the partial derivative with respect to x of each of these functions will verify the assertion.

Note that any two of these functions differ by a function of y only, which is being treated as a constant. So the general antiderivative with respect to x is

$$F(x,y) = \frac{x^2 y}{2} + C(y),$$

where $C(y)$ is an arbitrary function of y. The general antiderivative with respect to x is denoted

$$\int f(x,y) dx,$$

an indefinite integral. The dx tells us that we are integrating with respect to x; that is, we are treating y as a constant. So

$$\int xy \, dx = \frac{x^2 y}{2} + C(y).$$

In a similar fashion the general antiderivative with respect to y is

$$\int xy \, dy = \frac{xy^2}{2} + C(x),$$

where $C(x)$ is an arbitrary function of x.

EXAMPLE 1

Evaluate the following indefinite integrals: (a) $\int (x^2 + xy - y^2) dx$ and (b) $\int (x^2 + xy - y^2) dy$.

■ SOLUTION

(a) We integrate with respect to x, treating y as a constant. We get

8.5 DOUBLE INTEGRALS

$$\int (x^2 + xy - y^2)dx = \int x^2 dx + \int xy\, dx - \int y^2 dx$$
$$= \int x^2 dx + y\int x\, dx - y^2 \int 1\, dx$$
$$= \frac{x^3}{3} + \frac{yx^2}{2} - y^2 x + C(y),$$

where $C(y)$ is an arbitrary function of y.

(b) We integrate with respect to y, treating the x as a constant. We have

$$\int (x^2 + xy - y^2)dy = \int x^2 dy + \int xy\, dy - \int y^2 dy$$
$$= x^2 \int 1\, dy + x\int y\, dy - \int y^2 dy$$
$$= x^2 y + \frac{xy^2}{2} - \frac{y^3}{3} + C(x),$$

where $C(x)$ is an arbitrary function of x.

EXERCISE

Evaluate the following indefinite integrals: (a) $\int (x^3 - xy + 3y^2)dx$ and (b) $\int (x^3 - xy + 3y^2)dy$.

■ ANSWER

(a) $\dfrac{x^4}{4} - \dfrac{x^2 y}{2} + 3xy^2 + C(y)$; (b) $x^3 y - \dfrac{xy^2}{2} + y^3 + C(x)$

EXAMPLE 2

Evaluate the following indefinite integrals:

$$\text{(a) } \int \frac{x}{x^2 + y}\, dx \quad \text{and} \quad \text{(b) } \int e^{x^2 y}\, dy.$$

■ SOLUTION

(a) If the derivative of the denominator is the numerator, we may integrate using the natural logarithm. In differentiating the denominator, note that we are treating y as a constant. Thus the partial derivative is $2x$, which differs from the numerator by a factor of 2. Therefore

$$\int \frac{x}{x^2 + y}\, dx = \tfrac{1}{2} \int \frac{2x}{x^2 + y}\, dx$$
$$= \tfrac{1}{2} \ln|x^2 + y| + C(y).$$

(b) We may integrate e to a power if it is multiplied by the derivative of the power. The derivative of the exponent with x regarded as a constant is

x^2. Because x is viewed as a constant, it too may be inserted as needed. We have

$$\int e^{x^2 y} dy = \frac{1}{x^2} \int e^{x^2 y} \cdot x^2 dy$$

$$= \frac{1}{x^2} e^{x^2 y} + C(x).$$

EXERCISE

Evaluate the following indefinite integrals:

(a) $\int \dfrac{y^2}{x - y^3} dy$ and (b) $\int e^{xy} dx$.

■ ANSWER

(a) $-\frac{1}{3} \ln|x - y^3| + C(x)$; (b) $\dfrac{e^{xy}}{y} + C(y)$

Not only may the concept of *indefinite* integral be extended, but so may the concept of *definite* integral. The symbol

$$\int_a^b f(x,y) dx$$

denotes the net change in the antiderivative with respect to x, while

$$\int_c^d f(x,y) dy$$

is the net change in the antiderivative with respect to y. For example,

$$\int_{-1}^{2} xy \, dx = \left(\frac{x^2 y}{2} + C(y) \right) \Bigg|_{x=-1}^{x=2}$$

$$= (2y + C(y)) - \left(\frac{y}{2} + C(y) \right)$$

$$= \frac{3y}{2};$$

and

$$\int_{3}^{4} xy \, dy = \left(\frac{xy^2}{2} + C(x) \right) \Bigg|_{y=3}^{y=4}$$

$$= (8x + C(x)) - \left(\frac{9x}{2} + C(x) \right)$$

$$= \frac{7x}{2}.$$

8.5 DOUBLE INTEGRALS

As we noted with previous definite integrals, the constant $C(y)$ or $C(x)$ doesn't influence the result and may thus be omitted.

EXAMPLE 3

Evaluate (a) $\int_{-1}^{2} (x^2 - xy + y)dx$ and (b) $\int_{0}^{1} (x^2 + y^2)^4 y\, dy$.

■ SOLUTION

(a) We integrate with respect to x and then find the difference in the antiderivative at 2 and at -1. We have

$$\int_{-1}^{2} (x^2 - xy + y)dx = \left(\frac{x^3}{3} - \frac{x^2 y}{2} + xy\right)\Bigg|_{x=-1}^{x=2}$$

$$= \left(\frac{8}{3} - 2y + 2y\right) - \left(-\frac{1}{3} - \frac{y}{2} - y\right)$$

$$= \frac{8}{3} + \frac{1}{3} + \frac{y}{2} + y = 3 + \frac{3y}{2}.$$

(b) We get

$$\int_{0}^{1} (x^2 + y^2)^4 y\, dy = \frac{1}{2}\int_{0}^{1} (x^2 + y^2)^4 2y\, dy$$

$$= \frac{(x^2 + y^2)^5}{10}\Bigg|_{y=0}^{y=1}$$

$$= \frac{(x^2 + 1)^5}{10} - \frac{(x^2)^5}{10}$$

$$= \frac{(x^2 + 1)^5 - x^{10}}{10}.$$

EXERCISE

Evaluate (a) $\int_{-2}^{1} (x^2 - xy^2 + y)dx$ and (b) $\int_{-1}^{0} (x^3 + y^3)^3 y^2 dy$.

■ ANSWER

(a) $3 - \dfrac{3y^2}{2} - 3y$; (b) $\dfrac{-x^{12} + (x^3 + 1)^4}{12}$

When we evaluate a definite integral of the type

$$\int_{c}^{d} f(x,y)dy,$$

we get a function of x alone. Thus it makes sense to use this function of x as the integrand of another definite integral. For example, consider

$$\int_0^2 \left(\int_{-1}^2 x^2 y \, dy \right) dx.$$

The inside integral is simply a function of x. Indeed,

$$\int_{-1}^2 x^2 y \, dy = \left. \frac{x^2 y^2}{2} \right|_{y=-1}^{y=2}$$

$$= 2x^2 - \frac{x^2}{2}$$

$$= \frac{3x^2}{2}.$$

Thus

$$\int_0^2 \left(\int_{-1}^2 x^2 y \, dy \right) dx = \int_0^2 \frac{3x^2}{2} dx$$

$$= \left. \frac{x^3}{2} \right|_{x=0}^{x=2}$$

$$= 4.$$

This leads us to the concept of the *double integral*. Let f be a continuous function of x and y defined on a rectangular region

$$R = \{(x,y) \, | \, a \leq x \leq b, \, c \leq y \leq d\}.$$

Then the **double integral of f over R**, denoted

$$\iint_R f(x,y) \, dy \, dx,$$

is

$$\int_a^b \left(\int_c^d f(x,y) \, dy \right) dx.$$

The parentheses are usually omitted, and the preceding integral is written

$$\int_a^b \int_c^d f(x,y) \, dy \, dx.$$

Note that for the inside integral, we are integrating with respect to y so the limits of integration, c and d, are the extreme y-values over the rectangle. The outside integral is with respect to x, so the limits of integration are the extreme values of x over the rectangle.

8.5 DOUBLE INTEGRALS

EXAMPLE 4

Evaluate $\iint_R (x^2 + xy) dy\, dx$, where $R = \{(x,y) \mid 0 \leq x \leq 2,\ -1 \leq y \leq 1\}$.

■ SOLUTION

We have

$$\iint_R (x^2 + xy) dy\, dx = \int_0^2 \int_{-1}^1 (x^2 + xy) dy\, dx$$

$$= \int_0^2 \left(x^2 y + \frac{xy^2}{2} \right) \bigg|_{y=-1}^{y=1} dx$$

$$= \int_0^2 \left(\left(x^2 + \frac{x}{2} \right) - \left(-x^2 + \frac{x}{2} \right) \right) dx$$

$$= \int_0^2 2x^2 dx$$

$$= \frac{2x^3}{3} \bigg|_{x=0}^{x=2}$$

$$= \frac{16}{3} = 5\tfrac{1}{3}.$$

EXERCISE

Evaluate $\iint_R (y^2 - xy) dy\, dx$, where $R = \{(x,y) \mid -2 \leq x \leq 1,\ 0 \leq y \leq 2\}$.

■ ANSWER

11

When dealing with a function of a single variable, we noted that the definite integral could represent area under a curve. A similar situation exists for functions of two variables and double integrals.

THEOREM 8.4 Let f be a continuous function defined on $R = \{(x,y) \mid a \leq x \leq b,\ c \leq y \leq d\}$ such that $f(x,y) \geq 0$ for all $(x,y) \in R$. Then the volume of the solid based on R and bounded above by $z = f(x,y)$, shown in Figure 8.15, is

$$\iint_R f(x,y) dy\, dx.$$

Thus for a nonnegative function, a double integral represents volume just as a single integral represents area.

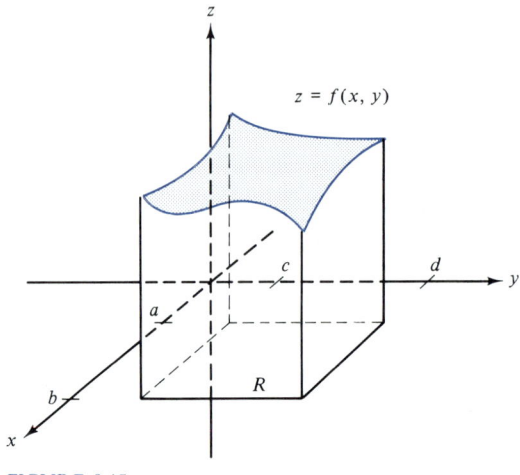

FIGURE 8.15

EXAMPLE 5

Determine the volume of the solid with base $R = \{(x,y) | -2 \leq x \leq 0, 1 \leq y \leq 2\}$, capped by $z = x^2 + y^2$.

■ SOLUTION

We must evaluate the double integral

$$\iint_R (x^2 + y^2) dy\, dx.$$

We have

$$\iint_R (x^2 + y^2) dy\, dx = \int_{-2}^{0} \int_{1}^{2} (x^2 + y^2) dy\, dx$$

$$= \int_{-2}^{0} \left(x^2 y + \frac{y^3}{3} \right) \bigg|_{y=1}^{y=2} dx$$

$$= \int_{-2}^{0} \left(\left(2x^2 + \frac{8}{3} \right) - \left(x^2 + \frac{1}{3} \right) \right) dx$$

$$= \int_{-2}^{0} \left(x^2 + \frac{7}{3} \right) dx$$

$$= \left(\frac{x^3}{3} + \frac{7x}{3} \right) \bigg|_{x=-2}^{x=0}$$

$$= 0 - (-\tfrac{8}{3} - \tfrac{14}{3}) = \tfrac{22}{3} = 7\tfrac{1}{3}.$$

Thus the volume is $7\tfrac{1}{3}$ cubic units.

EXERCISE

Determine the volume of the solid with base $R = \{(x,y) | 0 \leq x \leq 2, -1 \leq y \leq 1\}$, capped by $z = x^2 + 2y^2$.

■ ANSWER

8

PROBLEM SET 8.5

In Problems 1–16, evaluate the integrals.

1. $\int (x^4 - x^2y^2 + y^4)dx$
2. $\int (3x^5 - xy^2 - y^3)dy$
3. $\int \left(\dfrac{x}{y} + \dfrac{y}{x} + \dfrac{1}{x^2}\right)dy$
4. $\int \left(\dfrac{x}{y^2} + \dfrac{y^2}{x} + \dfrac{1}{y}\right)dx$
5. $\int x^4 \sqrt[3]{x^5y - y^5}\, dx$
6. $\int \dfrac{2y - x}{(y^2x - yx^2)^3}\, dy$
7. $\int \dfrac{(\ln(3xy))^5}{y}\, dy$
8. $\int e^{xy}(e^{xy} + y)^6 dx$
9. $\int \dfrac{2x^3 + x}{x^4 + x^2 + e^y}\, dx$
10. $\int \dfrac{y^4}{x^2y^5 + \ln x}\, dy$
11. $\int 3e^{x^3y + x^6}dy$
12. $\int 5e^{xy^5 - 2y^4}dx$
13. $\int_{-1}^{1} (5x^4 + 3x^2y + y)dx$
14. $\int_{-2}^{1} (3y^2 - 2x^2y - 5x^2)dy$
15. $\int_{\sqrt{2}}^{\sqrt{5}} \dfrac{2y}{x + y^2}\, dy$
16. $\int_{1/4}^{1/2} \dfrac{-ye^{y/x}}{x^2}\, dx$

In Problems 17–34, evaluate $\iint_R f(x,y)dy\, dx$.

17. $f(x,y) = -2$, $R = \{(x,y) | -4 \leq x \leq -2, 1 \leq y \leq 5\}$
18. $f(x,y) = -3$, $R = \{(x,y) | 6 \leq x \leq 7, -5 \leq y \leq -1\}$
19. $f(x,y) = x^2 + y$, $R = \{(x,y) | 0 \leq x \leq 2, 0 \leq y \leq 3\}$
20. $f(x,y) = x + y^2$, $R = \{(x,y) | 0 \leq x \leq 6, 0 \leq y \leq 1\}$
21. $f(x,y) = x^2/y^3$, $R = \{(x,y) | \sqrt[3]{2} \leq x \leq \sqrt[3]{10}, 1 \leq y \leq 2\}$
22. $f(x,y) = x^3/y^4$, $R = \{(x,y) | \sqrt[4]{3} < x < \sqrt[4]{15}, \tfrac{1}{2} \leq y \leq 1\}$
23. $f(x,y) = y^2 - x^2$, $R = \{(x,y) | 0 \leq x \leq 5, 0 \leq y \leq 5\}$
24. $f(x,y) = y^2x - x^2y$, $R = \{(x,y) | 0 \leq x \leq 3, 0 \leq y \leq 3\}$
25. $f(x,y) = (3 - y)x^2$, $R = \{(x,y) | 1 \leq x \leq 2, 0 \leq y \leq 3\}$
26. $f(x,y) = (6 - y)x^2$, $R = \{(x,y) | \sqrt[3]{2} \leq x \leq 2\sqrt[3]{2}, 0 \leq y \leq 6\}$
27. $f(x,y) = (x + y)^8$, $R = \{(x,y) | 0 \leq x \leq 6, 2 \leq y \leq 5\}$
28. $f(x,y) = (x + y)^9$, $R = \{(x,y) | 1 \leq x \leq 7, 0 \leq y \leq 3\}$
29. $f(x,y) = x^2y^2 + \dfrac{x}{y}$, $R = \{(x,y) | 0 \leq x \leq 1, 1 \leq y \leq e\}$
30. $f(x,y) = xy + \dfrac{x^2}{y}$, $R = \{(x,y) | -1 \leq x \leq 1, 1 \leq y \leq e^2\}$
31. $f(x,y) = xe^{x+y}$, $R = \{(x,y) | 0 \leq x \leq 1, 0 \leq y \leq 1\}$
32. $f(x,y) = xye^x$, $R = \{(x,y) | 1 \leq x \leq 5, 2 \leq y \leq 4\}$
33. $f(x,y) = \ln y^{2x-1}$, $R = \{(x,y) | 1 \leq x \leq 5, e \leq y \leq e^2\}$
34. $f(x,y) = \ln y^x$, $R = \{(x,y) | 2 \leq x \leq 4, 1 \leq y \leq e^3\}$
35. If $a > 0$ and $b > 0$, show that

$$\int_0^a \int_0^b (xy^2 - x^2y)dy\, dx = \tfrac{1}{6}(a^2b^3 - a^3b^2).$$

36. If $a > 0$ and $b > 0$, show that

$$\int_0^b \int_0^a (y^2 - x^2)dy\, dx = \tfrac{1}{3}(a^3b - ab^3).$$

In Problems 37–42, determine the volume of the solid with base R, capped by $f(x,y)$.

37. $R = \{(x,y) | 0 \leq x \leq 3, -3 \leq y \leq -1\}$, $f(x,y) = x^2 + y^2 + 1$
38. $R = \{(x,y) | -2 \leq x \leq 1, -1 \leq y \leq 2\}$, $f(x,y) = x^2 + 3y^2 + 2$
39. $R = \{(x,y) | 0 \leq x \leq 1, 0 \leq y \leq 1\}$, $f(x,y) = 4x^2 \sqrt[3]{y} + 3y^2 \sqrt[3]{x}$
40. $R = \{(x,y) | 0 \leq x \leq 1, 0 \leq y \leq 1\}$, $f(x,y) = 5x^3 \sqrt[4]{y} + 4y^3 \sqrt[4]{x}$
41. $R = \{(x,y) | \sqrt{2} \leq x \leq \sqrt{6}, 1 \leq y \leq 5\}$, $f(x,y) = xe^{x^2+y}$
42. $R = \{(x,y) | \sqrt[3]{3} \leq x \leq \sqrt[3]{4}, 3 \leq y \leq 6\}$, $f(x,y) = x^2 e^{x^3 + (y/3)}$

CHAPTER 8 REVIEW

1. Determine whether each of the following is true or false.
   (a) $(1,0,-2)$ is a solution of $xe^{x+y} + \ln(z^2 - 3) = e$.
   (b) If $z = x^2 + e^{y^2}$ then z is a function of x and y.
   (c) For the following graph, z is a function of x and y.

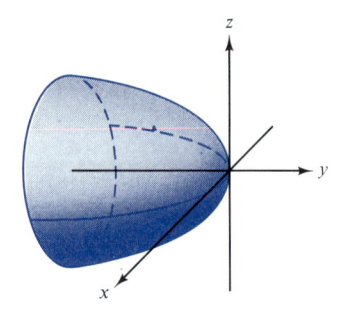

   (d) The domain of $f(x,y) = 1/\sqrt{-xy}$ is quadrants I and III only.
   (e) If $f(x,y) = x^3 + x^2y + y^3$, then $f(\sqrt[3]{2}, \sqrt[3]{-2}) = -2$.
   (f) If $f(x,y) = (x/y) + (y/x)$, then
   $$\frac{f(x+h,y) - f(x,y)}{h} = \frac{1}{y} - \frac{y}{x^2}.$$
   (g) If $z = \ln(xy)^3$, then
   $$x\frac{\partial z}{\partial x} - y\frac{\partial z}{\partial y} = 0.$$
   (h) If $f(x,y) = (x^2 + xy^2)^6$, then $f_x(x,y) = 6(2x + y^2)^5$.
   (i) If $z = x^2 + y^2$, then $\partial^2 z/\partial x^2 = \partial^2 z/\partial y^2$.
   (j) If $f(x,y) = e^x + e^y$, then $f_{xx}(0,0) + f_{xy}(0,0) + f_{yx}(0,0) + f_{yy}(0,0) = 4$.
   (k) A point at which the partial derivatives are equal is called a critical point.
   (l) The function $f(x,y) = 2x^2 - 3y^2$ has no relative extreme points.
   (m) The only critical point of $f(x,y) = x^3 + y^3$ is $(0,0)$.
   (n) $\int_0^1 e^{x/y} dx = ye^{1/y}$.
   (o) $\int_0^1 \int_0^2 1 \, dy \, dx = \int_0^1 \int_0^2 1 \, dx \, dy$.
   (p) If $a > 0$ and $b > 0$, then $\int_0^a \int_0^b 1 \, dy \, dx = ab$.
   (q) $\int_0^3 \int_{-1}^1 (3x^2y^2 + 4y^3) dy \, dx = 18$.

In Problems 2 and 3, determine the domain.

2. $f(x,y) = e^{x^2 - y^2}$
3. $f(x,y) = 1/(\sqrt{x} + \sqrt{y})$

In Problems 4 and 5, determine each of the following for the function f defined.

4. $f(x,y) = x^y + y^x$: **(a)** $f(2,4)$, **(b)** $f(e, \ln 3)$, and **(c)** $f(3, \sqrt[3]{5})$.

5. $f(x,y) = \dfrac{x^2 + y^2}{|x| + |y|}$: **(a)** $f(-2,2)$, **(b)** $f(e^{-1}, -e)$, and **(c)** $f(\pi - 3, 3 - \pi)$.

In Problems 6–9, determine

(a) $\dfrac{\partial^2 z}{\partial x^2}$, (b) $\dfrac{\partial^2 z}{\partial y \, \partial x}$, and (c) $\dfrac{\partial^2 z}{\partial y^2}$.

6. $z = x^4 - xy^2$
7. $z = \dfrac{x}{y^2} + \dfrac{y}{x^2}$
8. $z = \ln \sqrt{x+y}$
9. $z = e^{x + xy + y}$

10. If $f(x,y) = e^x \ln(xy)$, then show that $xf_x - yf_y = xf(x,y)$.
11. If $f(x,y) = \ln \sqrt{x^2 + y^2}$, then show that $f_{xx} + f_{yy} = 0$.

In Problems 12–15, determine all relative extreme points.

12. $f(x,y) = -x^3 + 30xy - y^3$
13. $f(x,y) = x^4 + y^4 + 108x - 4y + 146$
14. $f(x,y) = x^2 - xy + y^2 + 6y + 2$
15. $f(x,y) = x^2 - 8xy + y^2$

In Problems 16 and 17, determine the absolute maximum and absolute minimum of the function subject to the given constraint. (Assume that the absolutes exist.)

16. $f(x,y) = 5x + 12y - 38$, $x^2 + y^2 = 676$
17. $f(x,y,z) = \pi x + 5\pi y - 6\pi z - 17\pi$, $x^2 + \tfrac{5}{2}y^2 + 6z^2 = 17$

18. Find the point (x,y,z) in the first octant such that $x + y + z = 1$ and $xy + xz + yz$ is a maximum.

19. Determine the volume of the largest rectangular box having one vertex at the origin, three adjacent edges along the coordinate axes, and the vertex opposite the origin lying in the plane $x + 2y + 8z = 12$.

20. A rectangular box, closed at the top, is to have a volume of 1000 cubic inches. What dimensions minimize the surface area?

21. A rectangular box, with no top and no front, has a surface area of 150 square feet. Determine the dimensions of the box of maximum volume. What is the maximum volume?

22. Determine the dimensions of the rectangular box of maximum volume that can be inscribed in the ellipsoid $\frac{1}{27}x^2 + \frac{1}{2}y^2 + \frac{1}{50}z^2 = 1$. What is the maximum volume? (Assume that each edge of the box is parallel to a coordinate axis.)

23. If a video store charges $\$x$ for a certain type of VCR and $\$y$ for a maintenance contract, then it can sell $22{,}050 - 25x - 10y$ VCRs and $11{,}300 - 10x - 35y$ maintenance contracts. Determine x and y so as to maximize the store's revenue.

In Problems 24–27, evaluate the integrals.

24. $\int \left(\dfrac{x}{y^3} + \dfrac{y^3}{x} + \dfrac{y}{x^3} \right) dx$

25. $\int (5y^4 + 10xy) e^{y^5 + 5xy^2} dy$

26. $\int \dfrac{2x - 1}{x^2 y^3 - xy^3 + y} dx$

27. $\int_0^1 (x^5 - y^5)^5 x^4 \, dx$

28. Evaluate
$$\iint_R (x^3 y - y^3 x) \, dy \, dx,$$
where $R = \{(x,y) \mid 0 \le x \le 2,\ 2 \le y \le 4\}$.

29. Evaluate
$$\iint_R x e^{xy} \, dy \, dx,$$
where $R = \{(x,y) \mid 0 \le x \le \ln 2,\ 1 \le y \le 3\}$.

30. Determine the volume of the solid with base $R = \{(x,y) \mid 1 \le x \le 2,\ 0 \le y \le 2\}$, capped by $z = 6x^2 + xy + 6y^2$.

TOPICS FOR REVIEW

OUTLINE
A.1 INTERVALS
A.2 EXPONENTS
A.3 POLYNOMIALS
A.4 FACTORING
A.5 RATIONAL EXPRESSIONS
A.6 LINEAR EQUATIONS
A.7 QUADRATIC EQUATIONS

A.1 INTERVALS

An **interval** is a set of real numbers with the property that for any two numbers in the set, all numbers between those two are also in the set. Thus the graph of an interval has no "gaps."

In addition to R, the set of all real numbers, there are eight other types of intervals. They are introduced with interval notation, together with their graphs. The symbols a and b are constants, with $a < b$. The symbols ∞ (**infinity**) and $-\infty$ (**negative infinity**) are *not* numbers. They have meaning only when used in conjunction with other symbols.

Type	Definition	Notation	Graph
Open interval from a to b	$\{x \mid a < x < b\}$	(a,b)	
Closed interval from a to b	$\{x \mid a \leq x \leq b\}$	$[a,b]$	
Half-open (or half-closed) interval from a to b	$\{x \mid a < x \leq b\}$	$(a,b]$	
	$\{x \mid a \leq x < b\}$	$[a,b)$	
Open ray from $-\infty$ to a	$\{x \mid x < a\}$	$(-\infty, a)$	
Closed ray from $-\infty$ to a	$\{x \mid x \leq a\}$	$(-\infty, a]$	
Open ray from a to ∞	$\{x \mid a < x\}$	(a, ∞)	
Closed ray from a to ∞	$\{x \mid a \leq x\}$	$[a, \infty)$	

In this context the constants a and b are called **endpoints.** All other numbers belonging to the interval are called **interior points.** Note that when an endpoint is included in the interval, the notation requires a bracket for that endpoint, and the corresponding point on the graph is a solid dot. When the endpoint is not included, the notation requires a parenthesis, and the graph shows a nonsolid dot for the corresponding point.

A.2 EXPONENTS

Let $a \in R$, and let n be any positive integer. Then we define

(i) $a^1 = a$;
(ii) $a^n = \underbrace{a \cdot a \cdots a}_{n \text{ times}}$ if $n > 1$.

Thus, if $n > 1$, a^n means that n factors of a are multiplied together. Hence $a^2 = a \cdot a$, $a^3 = a \cdot a \cdot a$, and so on. For example, $4^1 = 4$, $4^2 = 16$, and $4^3 = 64$. The number a^n is called the nth power of a, a is called the **base,** and n is called the **exponent** (or **power**). If $a \neq 0$, we define

$$a^0 = 1.$$

The expression 0^0 is *not* defined.

A.2 EXPONENTS

We now summarize the properties of exponents.

Let $a, b \in R$, and let m and n be nonnegative integers. Then

(i) $a^m \cdot a^n = a^{m+n}$;

(ii) $(a^m)^n = a^{mn}$;

(iii) $(ab)^m = a^m b^m$;

(iv) $\left(\dfrac{a}{b}\right)^m = \dfrac{a^m}{b^m}$ $(b \neq 0)$;

(v) $\dfrac{a^m}{a^n} = a^{m-n}$ if $m \geq n$ $(a \neq 0)$;

(vi) $\dfrac{a^m}{a^n} = \dfrac{1}{a^{n-m}}$ if $m < n$ $(a \neq 0)$.

Part (i) says that when multiplying two numbers with the same base, we may *add* the exponents. For example, $2^2 \cdot 2^3 = 2^5$. Part (ii) states that if a number is raised to a power, and then that result is raised to another power, we may *multiply* exponents. Thus $(2^2)^3 = 2^6$. Part (iii) says that if the product of two numbers is raised to a power, we may raise each factor to that power and then multiply. For example, $(2 \cdot 3)^4 = 2^4 \cdot 3^4$. According to part (iv), a quotient raised to a power is equal to the numerator to that power divided by the denominator to that power. Thus $(2/3)^2 = 2^2/3^2$. In dividing two numbers with the same base, we may subtract exponents. According to part (v), $3^3/3^2 = 3^{3-2} = 3^1$, and $2^2/2^2 = 2^{2-2} = 2^0 = 1$. By part (vi) we see that $3^2/3^4 = 1/3^2$.

Let $a \in R$ such that $a \neq 0$, and let n be any positive integer. We define

$$a^{-n} = \dfrac{1}{a^n}.$$

For example, $3^{-2} = 1/3^2 = 1/9$. With this definition, the exponent properties are true even when m and n are negative. In fact, parts (v) and (vi) may be combined:

$$\dfrac{a^m}{a^n} = a^{m-n} = \dfrac{1}{a^{n-m}}.$$

The important thing to remember is that if the exponential form is to be put in the numerator, we must take the exponent in the numerator and subtract the exponent in the denominator. On the other hand, if the exponential form is to be put in the denominator, we must take the exponent in the denominator and subtract the exponent in the numerator.

Furthermore, with negative exponents thus defined, we may move any factor from the numerator to the denominator, or vice versa, provided that we change the sign of the exponent. For example,

$$\frac{a^2 b^{-3}}{c} = \frac{a^2}{b^3 c}, \quad \frac{a^2}{bc^{-2}} = \frac{a^2 c^2}{b}, \quad \text{and} \quad \frac{1+a}{b} = b^{-1}(1+a).$$

Note, however, that we may only move *factors* in such a fashion. Thus

$$\frac{1}{a^{-2} + b^{-2}} \neq a^2 + b^2.$$

EXERCISE

Evaluate (a) $(\frac{1}{2})^3$, (b) $(-3)^4$, (c) $(\frac{2}{3})^{-2}$, (d) 4^{-1}, (e) π^0, and (f) -3^2.

■ ANSWER
(a) $\frac{1}{8}$; (b) 81; (c) $\frac{9}{4}$; (d) $\frac{1}{4}$; (e) 1; (f) -9

Pay particular attention to (f). The exponent is attached to 3, not -3. Thus we square 3 and then take its negative. This is not the same as squaring -3, which is written $(-3)^2$ and equals 9.

EXERCISE

Use properties of exponents to simplify the following: (a) $x^2 \cdot x^3$, (b) $(2a)^3$, (c) a^2/a^3, (d) $(y^2)^3$, (e) $(x/y)^3$, and (f) $y^3/2y^2$.

■ ANSWER
(a) x^5; (b) $8a^3$; (c) $1/a$; (d) y^6; (e) x^3/y^3; (f) $y/2$

Let $a \in R$, and let n be a positive integer. We shall say that b is an **nth root** of a provided that $b^n = a$. For example, a fourth root of 16 is 2 because $2^4 = 16$. Since $(-2)^4 = 16$, -2 is also a fourth root of 16. When $n = 2$ we shall say "square root," and when $n = 3$ we shall say "cube root." Thus 2 and -2 are square roots of 4 because $2^2 = 4$ and $(-2)^2 = 4$. And -3 is a cube root of -27 because $(-3)^3 = -27$. The **principal nth root** of a number is the nth root which agrees with the sign of the number. Thus 2 is the principal square root of 4, and -3 is the principal cube root of -27. When n is even and a is positive, there are two real nth roots, one positive and one negative. The positive one is the principal one. (When n is even and a is negative, the nth roots are *not* real numbers. For example, the fourth roots of -16 are not real.) When n is odd, there is only one real nth root, so it is automatically the principal one. The notation

A.2 EXPONENTS

that refers to the principal nth root of a is

$$\sqrt[n]{a}.$$

The number n is called the **index**, and a is called the **radicand**. When the index is omitted, it is assumed to be 2, and the notation refers to the principal square root. Thus

$$\sqrt{4} = 2 \quad \text{and} \quad \sqrt[3]{-27} = -3.$$

Note that the radicand and the result agree in sign.

Some properties of radicals are as follows.

Let n be an integer greater than 1, and let a and b be real numbers. If $\sqrt[n]{a}$ and $\sqrt[n]{b}$ are real numbers, then

(i) $\sqrt[n]{ab} = \sqrt[n]{a}\sqrt[n]{b}$;

(ii) $\sqrt[n]{\dfrac{a}{b}} = \dfrac{\sqrt[n]{a}}{\sqrt[n]{b}} \quad (b \neq 0).$

For example, $\sqrt{8} = \sqrt{4 \cdot 2} = \sqrt{4}\sqrt{2} = 2\sqrt{2}$ and $\sqrt[3]{2/27} = \sqrt[3]{2}/\sqrt[3]{27} = \sqrt[3]{2}/3$.

EXERCISE

Use properties of radicals to simplify (a) $\sqrt{9}$, (b) $\sqrt[5]{-32}$, (c) $\sqrt{52}$ and (d) $\sqrt{\tfrac{5}{9}}$.

■ ANSWER

(a) 3; (b) -2; (c) $2\sqrt{13}$; (d) $\sqrt{5}/3$.

Let a be any real number and let n be a positive integer. Then we shall define

$$a^{1/n} = \sqrt[n]{a}.$$

For example, $4^{1/2} = \sqrt{4} = 2$ and $(-27)^{1/3} = \sqrt[3]{-27} = -3$.

Let m and n be positive integers and let a be a real number. Then we define

$$a^{m/n} = (a^{1/n})^m = (\sqrt[n]{a})^m.$$

For example,

$$8^{2/3} = (\sqrt[3]{8})^2 = 2^2 = 4$$

and

$$81^{3/4} = (\sqrt[4]{81})^3 = 3^3 = 27.$$

If $\sqrt[n]{a}$ is real, then $a^{m/n} = (a^m)^{1/n} = \sqrt[n]{a^m}$. The two previous examples may be calculated as

$$8^{2/3} = \sqrt[3]{8^2} = \sqrt[3]{64} = 4$$

and

$$81^{3/4} = \sqrt[4]{81^3} = \sqrt[4]{531{,}441} = 27.$$

Let m and n be positive integers, and let a be a nonzero real number. Define

$$a^{-m/n} = \frac{1}{a^{m/n}}.$$

Thus

$$8^{-2/3} = \frac{1}{8^{2/3}} = \frac{1}{(\sqrt[3]{8})^2} = \frac{1}{4}$$

and

$$27^{-1/3} = \frac{1}{27^{1/3}} = \frac{1}{3}.$$

In general, the exponent properties listed on page 409 are true when m and n are rational numbers. The only exception is part (ii), which states that $(a^m)^n = a^{mn}$. By this rule we would get

$$((-2)^2)^{1/2} = (-2)^1 = -2,$$

which is false. We really have

$$((-2)^2)^{1/2} = 4^{1/2} = \sqrt{4} = 2.$$

The exception to part (ii) occurs when a is negative, m is a nonzero even integer, and n is the reciprocal of a nonzero even integer. In such a case we actually get

$$(a^m)^n = |a|^{mn}.$$

In particular, then, $\sqrt{a^2} \neq a$. Rather,

$$\sqrt{a^2} = |a|.$$

EXERCISE

Evaluate (a) $16^{1/2}$, (b) $27^{-2/3}$, (c) $32^{2/5}$, and (d) $8^{-1/3}$.

■ *ANSWER*
(a) 4;   (b) $\frac{1}{9}$;   (c) 4;   (d) $\frac{1}{2}$

We know how to raise a positive number to any rational power. It is also possible to raise a positive number to an irrational power. Although a formal definition is not given, we try to get an intuitive understanding of this concept by considering the meaning of $3^{\sqrt{2}}$. It is possible to obtain a sequence of successively better rational approximations of $\sqrt{2}$:

$$1, \quad 1.4, \quad 1.41, \quad 1.414, \quad 1.4142, \ldots.$$

Because each approximation is rational, each number in the following sequence is defined:

$$3^1, \quad 3^{1.4}, \quad 3^{1.41}, \quad 3^{1.414}, \quad 3^{1.4142}, \ldots.$$

[Note that $3^{1.4} = 3^{14/10} = (\sqrt[10]{3})^{14}$, and so on.] The numbers in this latter sequence get closer and closer to the number that is called $3^{\sqrt{2}}$.

PROBLEM SET A.2

In Problems 1–12, evaluate.

1. 9^2
2. $(-5)^2$
3. 5^{-1}
4. 2^{-3}
5. -5^2
6. $(-4)^0$
7. $(\tfrac{1}{6})^2$
8. $(\tfrac{2}{3})^{-1}$
9. $(\tfrac{2}{5})^{-2}$
10. $5^{-2}/3^{-3}$
11. $3^2 + 3^{-2}$
12. $5 + 5^{-1}$

In Problems 13–22, use the laws of exponents to simplify, expressing your answer with positive exponents.

13. $a^2 a^{-5}$
14. $3x^3 x^{-2}$
15. $(x^2)^5$
16. $(a^{-3})^2$
17. a^3/a^{-4}
18. $2x^{-1}/x^4$
19. $(x^2 y^{-1})^{-3}$
20. $(3a)^2$
21. $(3y^2/x^{-3})^2$
22. $(x^{-1}/(xy^{-1}))^{-3}$

In Problems 23–30, use properties of radicals to simplify.

23. $-\sqrt{16}$
24. $\sqrt[3]{-27}$
25. $\sqrt[3]{16}$
26. $\sqrt{12}$
27. $\sqrt[3]{\tfrac{5}{8}}$
28. $\sqrt{\tfrac{4}{3}}$
29. $\sqrt{4x^2}$
30. $-\sqrt[3]{x^6}$

In Problems 31–38, evaluate.

31. $16^{3/4}$
32. $-25^{3/2}$
33. $(-32)^{2/5}$
34. $27^{-2/3}$
35. $(-27)^{-1/3}$
36. $4^{-1/2}$
37. $(\tfrac{1}{8})^{1/3}$
38. $(\tfrac{1}{4})^{-3/2}$

In Problems 39–44 use the laws of exponents to simplify, expressing your answer with positive exponents.

39. $x^{3/4} \cdot x^{1/4}$
40. $(a^3)^{1/6}$
41. $a^{4/3}/a^{2/3}$
42. $x^{-1/2}/x^{3/2}$
43. $(4a^{2/3})^{-1/2}$
44. $x^2 y^{-1/2}/(x^{1/2} y)$

In Problems 45–48, rewrite each radical by using fractional exponents.

45. $\sqrt{x^3}$
46. $\sqrt[4]{a^3}$
47. $\sqrt{\sqrt{a}}$
48. $\sqrt[3]{\sqrt{x}}$

A.3 POLYNOMIALS

An algebraic expression is a constant, a variable, or any combination of constants and variables made by addition, subtraction, multiplication, division, or extraction of roots. For example,

$$x^2 - 5, \quad \frac{x^2 - y^2}{5xy}, \quad y, \quad \text{and} \quad \frac{x^2 \sqrt{2-x}}{xy - y^2}$$

are algebraic expressions. When an algebraic expression is written as the sum of other expressions, each expression forming the sum is called a **term**. Thus the terms of the expression

$$\frac{x}{y} + x^2 - 5y + 6$$

are x/y, x^2, $-5y$, and 6. When the variable factors of two terms are exactly alike, the terms are said to be **like terms.** Thus $2x^2$ and $-3x^2$ are like terms, whereas $5y$ and $3y^2$ are not.

A **monomial** is an algebraic expression that can be written as the product of a real number and nonnegative integral powers of variables. Thus

$$2x^3, \quad -5xy, \quad 3xy^2, \quad \text{and} \quad -2x^2yz$$

are monomials. The constant of a monomial is called the **numerical coefficient.** For example, 6 is the numerical coefficient of $6x^2$, -2 is the numerical coefficient of $-2xy$, and 1 is the numerical coefficient of y^3.

A **polynomial** is an algebraic expression that may be written as the sum of monomials. Thus

$$x^2 + 5x + 6, \quad 2x^2 - 5xy, \quad \text{and} \quad 5$$

are polynomials. A polynomial that is the sum of two monomials is called a **binomial,** and one that is the sum of three monomials is called a **trinomial.** The largest exponent for a given variable is called the **degree** of the polynomial in that variable. Thus $2x^3 - x^2y + y^2$ is a polynomial of degree 3 in x and of degree 2 in y.

Since the variables of an algebraic expression represent real numbers, the properties of real numbers apply to algebraic expressions. Using these properties, we see that when adding or subtracting polynomials, we can combine like terms by adding or subtracting the numerical coefficients.

EXAMPLE 1

Add $2x^3 + 5x^2 - x + 5$ and $3x^3 - 2x^2 + x + 6$.

■ SOLUTION

Grouping and combining like terms, we have

$$(2x^3 + 5x^2 - x + 5) + (3x^3 - 2x^2 + x + 6)$$
$$= (2x^3 + 3x^3) + (5x^2 - 2x^2) + (-x + x) + (5 + 6)$$
$$= 5x^3 + 3x^2 + 11.$$

EXAMPLE 2

Subtract $2x^2 - 3xy + y^2 - 1$ from $5x^2 - 3y^2 + 2$.

■ SOLUTION

We may proceed as in Example 1 or use a vertical array. Aligning like terms and subtracting the numerical coefficients, we have

$$\begin{array}{r} 5x^2 - 3y^2 + 2 \\ 2x^2 - 3xy + y^2 - 1 \\ \hline 3x^2 + 3xy - 4y^2 + 3. \end{array}$$

EXERCISE

(a) Add $7x^3 - 5x^2y + y^2 + 2$ and $2x^3 + 3x^2y - y^2 + 3$. (b) Subtract $7x^3 - 5x^2 + x + 2$ from $2x^3 - x + 3$.

■ *ANSWER*
(a) $9x^3 - 2x^2y + 5$; (b) $-5x^3 + 5x^2 - 2x + 1$

To find the product of two polynomials, we use the distributive laws, together with the laws of exponents, and then combine like terms.

EXAMPLE 3

Multiply $3x + 5$ by $-2x^2 + x - 1$.

■ *SOLUTION*

$$(3x + 5)(-2x^2 + x - 1) = -6x^3 + 3x^2 - 3x - 10x^2 + 5x - 5$$
$$= -6x^3 - 7x^2 + 2x - 5.$$

Using a vertical array, we could have written

$$
\begin{array}{r}
-2x^2 + x - 1 \\
3x + 5 \\
\hline
-6x^3 + 3x^2 - 3x \qquad [3x(-2x^2 + x - 1)] \\
-10x^2 + 5x - 5 \qquad [5(-2x^2 + x - 1)] \\
\hline
-6x^3 - 7x^2 + 2x - 5. \qquad [\text{sum}]
\end{array}
$$

EXERCISE

Multiply $2x^2 - x$ by $3x^2 + x - 5$.

■ *ANSWER*
$6x^4 - x^3 - 11x^2 + 5x$

Following are some special products that occur frequently. Their validity can be established by actual multiplication.

(i) $(x + y)^2 = x^2 + 2xy + y^2$.
(ii) $(x - y)^2 = x^2 - 2xy + y^2$.
(iii) $(x + y)(x - y) = x^2 - y^2$.
(iv) $(x + a)(x + b) = x^2 + (a + b)x + ab$.
(v) $(x + y)^3 = x^3 + 3x^2y + 3xy^2 + y^3$.
(vi) $(x - y)^3 = x^3 - 3x^2y + 3xy^2 - y^3$.

EXAMPLE 4

Use the rules for special products to perform the indicated operation: (a) $(3x + 2)^2$, (b) $(x + 2y)(x - 2y)$, (c) $(x + 5)(x - 4)$, and (d) $(2x - y)^3$.

■ SOLUTION
(a) $(3x + 2)^2 = (3x)^2 + 2(3x)(2) + 2^2 = 9x^2 + 12x + 4$.
(b) $(x + 2y)(x - 2y) = x^2 - (2y)^2 = x^2 - 4y^2$.
(c) $(x + 5)(x - 4) = x^2 + (5 - 4)x + 5(-4) = x^2 + x - 20$.
(d) $(2x - y)^3 = (2x)^3 - 3(2x)^2 y + 3(2x)y^2 - y^3$
$= 8x^3 - 12x^2 y + 6xy^2 - y^3$.

EXERCISE

Use the rules for special products to perform the indicated operation: (a) $(2x + 3)^2$, (b) $(3x + y)(3x - y)$, (c) $(x + 4)(x - 3)$, and (d) $(x - 2y)^3$.

■ ANSWER
(a) $4x^2 + 12x + 9$; (b) $9x^2 - y^2$; (c) $x^2 + x - 12$;
(d) $x^3 - 6x^2 y + 12xy^2 - 8y^3$

The technique for dividing a polynomial by a monomial is seen in the next example.

EXAMPLE 5

Divide $10x^2 y^2 - 6xy^2 + 5x$ by $2xy$.

■ SOLUTION

$$\frac{10x^2 y^2 - 6xy^2 + 5x}{2xy} = \frac{10x^2 y^2}{2xy} - \frac{6xy^2}{2xy} + \frac{5x}{2xy}$$
$$= 5xy - 3y + \frac{5}{2y}.$$

EXERCISE

Divide $10x^3 y - 5x^2 y^2 + 7y$ by $5xy$.

■ ANSWER

$2x^2 - xy + \dfrac{7}{5x}$

PROBLEM SET A.3

In Problems 1–12, perform the indicated operation.

1. $(2x^2 + x) + (3x^2 - 2x)$
2. $(x^2 - 2xy + 2y^2) + (3x^2 - y^2)$
3. $(y^2 - 5y) - (2y^2 - 3)$
4. $(5x^2 + 6x - 2) - (x^2 + x - 5)$
5. $x(2x - 3y)$
6. $(y^2 - xy + 5x)2xy^2$
7. $(2x - 5)(3x + 2)$
8. $(x - 2y)(3x + 5y)$
9. $(2x - y)(x^2 + xy - 3y^2)$
10. $(x^2 + 3x - 1)(2x^2 - 2x + 5)$
11. $(9x^2y - 6xy + 3x^2y^2) \div 3xy$
12. $(4x^2y - 2x^2y^3 + 4x^4y^2) \div 2x^2y^2$

In Problems 13–24, use the rules for special products to perform the indicated operation.

13. $(2x + 5)^2$
14. $(3x^2y + y^2)^2$
15. $(3y - 2)^2$
16. $(5xy^2 - x^2)^2$
17. $(2x + y)(2x - y)$
18. $(3y^2 + 4xy)(3y^2 - 4xy)$
19. $(x + 3)(x + 5)$
20. $(x - 4)(x + 3)$
21. $(x + 5)(x - 2)$
22. $(x - 4)(x - 6)$
23. $(2x + y)^3$
24. $(x - 3y)^3$

A.4 FACTORING

When a polynomial is written as the product of algebraic expressions, it is said to be **factored.** In this section we study various techniques for factoring polynomials.

A given polynomial may be expressed as a product in more than one way. For example, $x^2 - 1$ may be written

$$(x + 1)(x - 1) \quad \text{or} \quad 4\left(\frac{x + 1}{2}\right)\left(\frac{x - 1}{2}\right) \quad \text{or} \quad x^{-2}(x^4 - x^2).$$

However, in general, we shall want the factors to be polynomials with integer coefficients. Thus, of the preceding three expressions the first is the desired factored form.

A monomial that is a factor of each term of the polynomial to be factored is called a *common* factor. For example, x is a common factor of $x^2 + xy$, and 3 is a common factor of $3y - 9$. By using the distributive property, expressions that have common factors may be factored. Thus

$$x^2 + xy = x(x + y)$$

and

$$3y - 9 = 3(y - 3).$$

Note that the result may be verified by multiplication. If we factor properly, we may multiply the factors and get the original expression.

EXERCISE

Factor (a) $xy + y^3$ and (b) $6x - 2$.

■ *ANSWER*
(a) $y(x + y^2)$; (b) $2(3x - 1)$

EXAMPLE 1

Factor (a) $6x^2y + 4xy^2 - 2x^2y^2$ and (b) $y(x - 2) + z(x - 2) - x + 2$.

■ SOLUTION

(a) This polynomial has several common factors: 2, x, and y. Thus we write the expression as

$$2xy(3x + 2y - xy).$$

(b) These four terms have no common factors. However, we note that the binomial $x - 2$ is a factor of the first two terms and is the negative of the last two terms. Because of this, we may view the given expression as

$$y(x - 2) + z(x - 2) - (x - 2).$$

Appearing as three terms with a common factor of $x - 2$, this expression is factored as

$$(x - 2)(y + z - 1).$$

EXERCISE

Factor (a) $6x^2yz + 3y^2z - 3yz^2$ and (b) $x(y + 1) + y(y + 1) - y - 1$.

■ ANSWER

(a) $3yz(2x^2 + y - z)$; (b) $(y + 1)(x + y - 1)$

The rule for factoring the difference of two squares is expressed as follows:

$$x^2 - y^2 = (x + y)(x - y).$$

This says that the difference of two squares is factored as the product of the sum and difference of the expressions being squared.

EXAMPLE 3

Factor (a) $x^2 - 4$, (b) $9x^2 - 25$, and (c) $x^4 - y^4$.

■ SOLUTION

(a) Recognizing this as the difference of two squares, we get

$$x^2 - 4 = (x + 2)(x - 2).$$

(b) We must first recognize that this is indeed the difference of two squares. The given expression may be written

$$(3x)^2 - 5^2.$$

Thus it factors as
$$(3x + 5)(3x - 5).$$

(c) We have
$$x^4 - y^4 = (x^2)^2 - (y^2)^2 = (x^2 + y^2)(x^2 - y^2).$$

Note that the last factor is again the difference of two squares. By factoring it we get
$$x^4 - y^4 = (x^2 + y^2)(x + y)(x - y).$$

Note that we didn't factor $x^2 + y^2$. In general, we cannot factor the *sum* of two squares.

EXERCISE

Factor (a) $x^2 - 9$, (b) $4x^2 - 49$, and (c) $y^4 - 81$.

■ ANSWER

(a) $(x + 3)(x - 3)$; (b) $(2x + 7)(2x - 7)$; (c) $(y^2 + 9)(y + 3)(y - 3)$

Next we consider factoring trinomials, recalling that $(x + a)(x + b) = x^2 + (a + b)x + ab$. Thus, given a polynomial like the right side of this equation, we know that if it factors, the factors will be binomials with first terms of x and second terms constants. We merely have to find the two numbers whose product equals the constant of the trinomial to be factored, and whose sum equals the coefficient of x of the trinomial. For example, let's factor $x^2 + 5x + 6$. If it factors, it looks like $(x + a)(x + b)$, where a and b are constants whose product is 6 and whose sum is 5. Let's list the pairs of numbers whose product is 6:

a	-1	-2	-3	-6	1	2	3	6
b	-6	-3	-2	-1	6	3	2	1

Checking the possibilities, we find that the desired numbers are 2 and 3 (or 3 and 2, changing the order of the factors). Therefore
$$x^2 + 5x + 6 = (x + 2)(x + 3).$$

Although there are eight pairs of numbers in our list, a couple of observations limit the "real" possibilities to only two. First, four of the pairs are simply a change in order of the other four. For instance, the pair 6 and 1 is just a reversal of 1 and 6. Obviously, switching the numbers around doesn't change their product or sum. Thus our list could have been simplified:

a	-1	-2	1	2
b	-6	-3	6	3

Now a word about the signs. If the constant of the trinomial to be factored is positive (as it is here), then the two constants we are seeking are either both positive or both negative. The sign of the coefficient of x in the trinomial determines which case occurs. If positive (indicating that the sum must be positive), then both constants are positive. If the coefficient of x is negative, then both numbers are negative. So our list can be reduced even more:

a	1	2
b	6	3

If the constant of the trinomial is negative, then one of the numbers is positive and the other is negative. The sign of the coefficient of x matches the sign of the number largest in absolute value.

EXAMPLE 4

Factor (a) $x^2 - 5x + 6$, (b) $x^2 - x - 6$, and (c) $x^2 + x - 6$.

■ SOLUTION

(a) Since the constant is positive and the coefficient of x is negative, we are looking for two negative numbers whose product is 6 and whose sum is -5. The only possibilities are -1 and -6 or -2 and -3. Since the latter pair has the proper sum,

$$x^2 - 5x + 6 = (x - 2)(x - 3).$$

(b) Since the constant is negative, we are looking for a positive and a negative number whose product is -6 and whose sum is -1. Because this sum is negative, we know that the negative number must be larger in absolute value than the positive number. The only possibilities are -6 and 1, and -3 and 2. The latter pair has the proper sum; thus

$$x^2 - x - 6 = (x - 3)(x + 2).$$

(c) We are looking for a positive and a negative number whose product is -6 and whose sum is 1. Thus we know that the positive number is larger in absolute value. We get

$$x^2 + x - 6 = (x + 3)(x - 2).$$

A.4 FACTORING

EXERCISE

Factor (a) $x^2 + 7x + 12$, (b) $x^2 - 8x + 12$, (c) $x^2 - 11x - 12$, and (d) $x^2 + 4x - 12$.

■ *ANSWER*
(a) $(x + 3)(x + 4)$; (b) $(x - 2)(x - 6)$; (c) $(x - 12)(x + 1)$; (d) $(x + 6)(x - 2)$

To factor expressions like $2x^2 + 7x - 4$, where the coefficient of x^2 is not 1, we cannot simply look for numbers whose product equals the constant and whose sum equals the coefficient of x. Instead, we must play a much more complicated guessing game. Let's factor $2x^2 + 7x - 4$. The first terms of the two binomials must have a product of $2x^2$. Thus they must be x and $2x$ (or of course $2x$ and x). Since the product of the last terms of the two binomials must be -4, the factors must be of the form

$$(x + a)(2x - b) \quad \text{or} \quad (x - a)(2x + b) \tag{A-1}$$

for positive constants a and b whose product is 4. To determine which numbers work, we use trial and error. We simply choose factors of 4 and calculate the middle term of the product until we get $7x$. Which form of line (A-1) should we use? Let's not concern ourselves with the signs and use the first. If our middle term turns out to be a $-7x$, we just switch the $+$ and $-$. Using the pairs 1 and 4, 2 and 2, and 4 and 1, we get the following:

$(x + 1)(2x - 4)$ middle term is $-2x$,
$(x + 2)(2x - 2)$ middle term is $+2x$,
$(x + 4)(2x - 1)$ middle term is $+7x$.

Thus we have

$$2x^2 + 7x - 4 = (x + 4)(2x - 1).$$

Note that unlike the case when factoring trinomials whose coefficient of x^2 is 1, the numbers 1 and 4 give us a different set of factors than 4 and 1. This is because the first terms of the binomials are not equal.

EXAMPLE 5

Factor $6x^2 - x - 12$.

■ *SOLUTION*
The first terms of the binomials are x and $6x$ or $2x$ and $3x$, and one of the signs is plus, the other minus. Let's begin by trying numbers whose

product is 12 in the expression
$$(x+\quad)(6x-\quad).$$

We get

$(x + 1)(6x - 12)$ middle term is $-6x$,
$(x + 2)(6x - 6)$ middle term is $6x$,
$(x + 3)(6x - 4)$ middle term is $14x$,
$(x + 4)(6x - 3)$ middle term is $21x$,
$(x + 6)(6x - 2)$ middle term is $34x$,
$(x + 12)(6x - 1)$ middle term is $71x$.

We didn't get a middle term of $-x$. Thus, if the given trinomial is to be factored, the first terms of the binomials must be $2x$ and $3x$. Let's try numbers for
$$(2x+\quad)(3x-\quad).$$

We get

$(2x + 1)(3x - 12)$ middle term is $-21x$,
$(2x + 2)(3x - 6)$ middle term is $-6x$,
$(2x + 3)(3x - 4)$ middle term is x.

We need a middle term of $-x$. By changing the signs of our last guess, we have it. Thus
$$6x^2 - x - 12 = (2x - 3)(3x + 4).$$

In Example 5 we see that several guesses were needed in order to get the result. In general, there is no shortcut to this guessing and calculating the corresponding middle term. However, if we note that there are no common factors in the trinomial, we can eliminate some of the middle-term calculations. Consider the second guess made in Example 5:
$$(x + 2)(6x - 6).$$

Without even calculating the middle term, we can observe that these aren't the proper factors. If these were the correct factors, then 6 would be a common factor of the trinomial, *because* 6 *would be a common factor of the second binomial.* But the trinomial has no common factors. Similarly, we may reject the third, fourth, fifth, seventh, and eighth guesses without calculating the middle term.

EXERCISE

Factor (a) $3x^2 - 7x - 6$, (b) $4x^2 - 5x - 6$, (c) $5x^2 + 27x + 10$, and (d) $10x^2 - 19x + 6$.

■ ANSWER
(a) $(x - 3)(3x + 2)$; (b) $(x - 2)(4x + 3)$; (c) $(5x + 2)(x + 5)$;
(d) $(5x - 2)(2x - 3)$

PROBLEM SET A.4

Factor.
1. $2x + 8$
2. $x^2y + x$
3. $x^2y - 3xy^2 + x^2y^2$
4. $9x^3y^2 + 3xy^2 - 6x^2y^3$
5. $x(y + 1) + y(y + 1)$
6. $2x^2(2y - 3) + 3 - 2y$
7. $4y^2 - 9$
8. $x^4 - 16$
9. $x^2 + 7x + 10$
10. $x^2 + 9x + 20$
11. $x^2 + x - 12$
12. $x^2 - 2x - 15$
13. $x^2 - 7x + 12$
14. $x^2 - 9x + 14$
15. $2x^2 + 11x + 5$
16. $3x^2 - 13x + 12$
17. $3x^2 - 5x - 8$
18. $5x^2 - 7x - 6$
19. $12x^2 + 19x + 4$
20. $6x^2 - 17x + 10$
21. $10x^2 - 7x - 12$
22. $12x^2 + 23x - 2$
23. $2x^3 + 4x^2y + 2xy^2$
24. $6x^4 - 7x^3y - 3x^2y^2$
25. $2x^3 + 7x^2y - 4xy^2$
26. $2x^3 - 8x - 3x^2 + 12$

A.5 RATIONAL EXPRESSIONS

The quotient of two polynomials is called a **rational expression.** Some examples are

$$\frac{x}{2x + 1}, \quad \frac{x^2 + 2xy}{5x + y}, \quad \text{and} \quad \frac{1}{y}.$$

As seen in Example 1, a rational expression may be simplified by canceling common factors.

EXAMPLE 1

Reduce the fraction

$$\frac{x^3 - 3x^2 - 10x}{x^4 - 4x^2}$$

to lowest terms.

■ SOLUTION
Upon factoring both the numerator and denominator, we get

$$\frac{x(x^2 - 3x - 10)}{x^2(x^2 - 4)} = \frac{x(x - 5)(x + 2)}{x^2(x + 2)(x - 2)}.$$

After canceling the common factors of x and $x + 2$, we have

$$\frac{x - 5}{x(x - 2)}.$$

EXERCISE

Reduce the fraction

$$\frac{2x^4 - 2x^2}{3x^3 - 2x^2 - x}$$

to lowest terms.

■ ANSWER

$$\frac{2x(x+1)}{3x+1}$$

We multiply rational expressions the same way we multiply arithmetic fractions. That is, we multiply numerator by numerator and denominator by denominator.

EXAMPLE 2

Evaluate

$$\frac{4x(x-4)}{9(x+4)} \cdot \frac{x^2 - 16}{2x^2}.$$

■ SOLUTION

First we apply the definition and then factor numerator and denominator to see if the result may be reduced: We get

$$\frac{4x(x-4)}{9(x+4)} \cdot \frac{x^2-16}{2x^2} = \frac{4x(x-4)(x^2-16)}{18x^2(x+4)}$$

$$= \frac{4x(x-4)(x+4)(x-4)}{18x^2(x+4)}$$

$$= \frac{2(x-4)^2}{9x}.$$

EXERCISE

Evaluate

$$\frac{x^2 + 4x + 3}{2x^2} \cdot \frac{6x^4}{x^2 - 1}.$$

A.5 RATIONAL EXPRESSIONS

■ ANSWER

$$\frac{3x^2(x+3)}{x-1}$$

When dividing by a rational expression, we invert it and multiply, as seen in Example 3.

EXAMPLE 3

Evaluate

$$\frac{x^2-9}{4x} \div \frac{x^2-x-6}{2x^2}.$$

■ SOLUTION

We invert the divisor and multiply. Then we see if the result may be reduced. We get

$$\frac{x^2-9}{4x} \div \frac{x^2-x-6}{2x^2} = \frac{x^2-9}{4x} \cdot \frac{2x^2}{x^2-x-6}$$
$$= \frac{2x^2(x^2-9)}{4x(x^2-x-6)}$$
$$= \frac{2x^2(x+3)(x-3)}{4x(x-3)(x+2)}$$
$$= \frac{x(x+3)}{2(x+2)}.$$

EXERCISE

Evaluate

$$\frac{3x^2}{2x^2-5x-3} \div \frac{9x^5}{4x^2-1}.$$

■ ANSWER

$$\frac{2x-1}{3x^3(x-3)}$$

To add and subtract rational expressions, we first find a common denominator. Then we write the given expressions as equivalent ones with the common denominator. Finally we combine numerators, keeping the common denominator. See Examples 4 and 5.

EXAMPLE 4

Evaluate
$$\frac{2}{x-3} + \frac{x}{2x+1}.$$

■ SOLUTION

The least common denominator for these two fractions is $(x-3)(2x+1)$. Therefore we have

$$\frac{2}{x-3} + \frac{x}{2x+1} = \frac{2(2x+1)}{(x-3)(2x+1)} + \frac{x(x-3)}{(x-3)(2x+1)}$$
$$= \frac{2(2x+1) + x(x-3)}{(x-3)(2x+1)}$$
$$= \frac{4x + 2 + x^2 - 3x}{(x-3)(2x+1)}$$
$$= \frac{x^2 + x + 2}{(x-3)(2x+1)}.$$

Since the numerator cannot be factored, we know that the last result is in lowest terms.

EXAMPLE 5

Evaluate
$$\frac{2x}{x^2+x-6} - \frac{x+1}{x^2+3x}.$$

■ SOLUTION

Our first task is to find the least common denominator. To this end, it is best to factor the denominators. We get

$$\frac{2x}{(x+3)(x-2)} - \frac{x+1}{x(x+3)}.$$

Thus we see that the least common denominator is $(x+3)(x-2)x$. Proceeding, we get

$$\frac{2x(x)}{(x+3)(x-2)x} - \frac{(x+1)(x-2)}{(x+3)(x-2)x} = \frac{2x^2 - x^2 + x + 2}{(x+3)(x-2)x}$$
$$= \frac{x^2 + x + 2}{(x+3)(x-2)x}.$$

A.6 LINEAR EQUATIONS

EXERCISE

Evaluate the following:

(a) $\dfrac{x}{x+2} + \dfrac{2}{3x-1}$ and (b) $\dfrac{x}{x^2+2x-3} - \dfrac{x+1}{2x^2+5x-3}$.

■ ANSWER

(a) $\dfrac{3x^2+x+4}{(x+2)(3x-1)}$; (b) $\dfrac{x^2-x+1}{(x+3)(x-1)(2x-1)}$

PROBLEM SET A.5

In Problems 1–8, reduce the given fraction to lowest terms.

1. $\dfrac{15x^3}{-3x^2}$

2. $\dfrac{2xy}{6x^2y^3}$

3. $\dfrac{x^2-1}{x-x^2}$

4. $\dfrac{3x-2}{3x^2+x-2}$

5. $\dfrac{2x^2+7x-4}{4x^2-1}$

6. $\dfrac{x^3+4x^2+3x}{3x^2-6x-9}$

7. $\dfrac{x^2+2x-2y-xy}{x^2-y^2}$

8. $\dfrac{2x^4+3x^2-5}{x^4-1}$

In Problems 9–24, evaluate, expressing the result in lowest terms.

9. $\dfrac{x}{x+2} \cdot \dfrac{x}{x-2}$

10. $\dfrac{x+y}{2y} \cdot \dfrac{x-y}{2x}$

11. $\dfrac{y}{x^2-xy} \cdot \dfrac{xy-y^2}{x}$

12. $\dfrac{2x^2+x}{2x-4} \cdot \dfrac{x^2-4}{2xy+y}$

13. $\dfrac{x+5}{2x+5} \div \dfrac{x^2+10x+25}{4x^2+20x+25}$

14. $\dfrac{x^2+4x+4}{x^2+4x+3} \div \dfrac{x+2}{x+1}$

15. $\dfrac{2x^2-3x-5}{2x^3+10x^2+12x} \div \dfrac{x^2-1}{2x}$

16. $\dfrac{x^2-y^2}{3x^2y-5xy^2-2y^3} \div \dfrac{x^2+xy}{y}$

17. $\dfrac{x-1}{7x} + \dfrac{x+2}{7x}$

18. $\dfrac{x+1}{x} - \dfrac{x-1}{x}$

19. $\dfrac{x}{x^2-4x-5} + \dfrac{1}{x^2-4x-5}$

20. $\dfrac{2}{2x^2+x-6} + \dfrac{2x-1}{2x^2+x-6}$

21. $\dfrac{x+1}{x-2} + \dfrac{4}{x+1}$

22. $\dfrac{x-1}{x+5} - \dfrac{2}{x-1}$

23. $\dfrac{x}{2x+2y} + \dfrac{x^2}{x^2-y^2}$

24. $\dfrac{4}{x^2-4} + \dfrac{4}{10-5x} + \dfrac{1}{x+2}$

A.6 LINEAR EQUATIONS

Recall that a **variable** is a symbol that represents each element of a specified set containing more than one element. The symbol is frequently a letter from the end of the alphabet, usually x, y, or z. The specified set is called the **domain** of the variable. When the domain is a subset of R (the set of real numbers), the variable is called a real variable. Unless noted otherwise, the term "variable" will mean "real variable."

Note that a variable represents *two or more elements*. A symbol that represents *one element only* is called a **constant.** When letters of the alphabet are used as constants, we generally use letters from the front of the alphabet, frequently *a, b,* or *c*. In this text each constant, unless noted otherwise, will represent a single *real* number.

Let x be a variable with domain $U = \{1,2,3\}$, and consider the equation $x + 5 = 7$. Because x represents 1, 2, and 3, the equation $x + 5 = 7$ actually stands for three statements: $1 + 5 = 7$, $2 + 5 = 7$, and $3 + 5 = 7$. Thus it is inappropriate to ask whether the equation $x + 5 = 7$ is true or false. Instead, one should ask: "For which elements in the domain is the equation true when the variable is replaced?" In this instance it is clear that the equation is true only when 2 is substituted for x.

A real **root** of an equation in one variable is a real number that makes the equation true when the variable is replaced by that real number. A real **solution** of an equation is a real root that belongs to the domain of the variable. For the equation just considered, 2 is a solution. Because all the variables discussed in this text are real variables, the adjective "real" is frequently omitted when we speak of real roots and real solutions.

Unfortunately, the domain in subsequent problems will not be as simple as that of our example. Frequently, the domain of the variable is not explicitly stated. In such cases we shall assume that the domain is the set of all real numbers for which all terms of the equation are defined and real upon replacement. Given the equation $1/x = \sqrt{x}$, we see that the left side is undefined if x is replaced by 0, and the right side is not real if x is negative. Therefore the domain is the set of all *positive* real numbers.

Usually, the equation will be too complicated to find solutions by observation. In such instances we shall find an *equivalent* equation whose solutions can be easily noted. Two equations are called **equivalent** provided that they have the same solutions. We find equivalent equations by using the following theorem.

Let p_x, q_x, and r_x be algebraic expressions in the variable x. Then the equation

$$p_x = q_x$$

is equivalent to each of the following:

(i) $p_x + r_x = q_x + r_x$.
(ii) $p_x \cdot r_x = q_x \cdot r_x$ when $r_x \neq 0$.

This theorem says that an algebraic expression (including one consisting of a number only) may be added to both sides of an equation, and the resulting equation is equivalent to the beginning equation. Because $p_x - r_x = p_x + (-r_x)$, an algebraic expression may be *subtracted* from

A.6 LINEAR EQUATIONS

both sides of an equation without changing the solutions. Furthermore, the theorem says that both sides of an equation may be multiplied by a *nonzero* algebraic expression, and the resulting equation is equivalent to the initial equation. Since division is the same as multiplication by a reciprocal, both sides of an equation may be *divided* by a *nonzero* algebraic expression without changing the solutions.

The first general type of equation that we study is the linear equation. An equation in a variable x is called **linear** in x provided that it is equivalent to

$$ax + b = 0,$$

where a and b are constants with $a \neq 0$. So linear equations are those in which, when fractions are cleared and like terms are combined, the variable is raised to the first power only. For example,

$$2x - 1 = x + 5 \quad \text{and} \quad \frac{2}{x - 5} = 3$$

are linear equations. But

$$\sqrt{x} + 1 = 4, \quad x^2 - 8 = 0, \quad \text{and} \quad x^2 + 5x = x - 3$$

are *not* linear equations.

To solve a linear equation in x, we get the x terms on one side of the equation and the constants on the other. Then we combine like terms and divide each side by the coefficient of x. This technique is illustrated in Example 1.

EXAMPLE 1

Find the solutions to the following: (a) $3x + 5 = 0$; (b) $2(x - 1) = 3(2x - 1) + 5$; and (c) $3 = 2/(x - 1)$.

■ SOLUTION

(a) Subtracting 5 from each side of the given equation, we get

$$3x = -5.$$

Upon dividing both sides by 3, we have

$$x = -\frac{5}{3}.$$

Thus the solution is $-\frac{5}{3}$.

(b) The given equation is equivalent to each of the following:

$$2x - 2 = 6x - 3 + 5$$
$$2x - 6x = -3 + 5 + 2$$
$$-4x = 4$$
$$x = -1.$$

The solution is -1.

(c) After multiplying both sides by $x - 1$, we have
$$3(x - 1) = 2.$$
This is equivalent to each of the following:
$$3x - 3 = 2$$
$$3x = 5$$
$$x = \frac{5}{3}.$$
Since the root $\frac{5}{3}$ is in the domain $R - \{1\}$, the solution is $\frac{5}{3}$.

EXERCISE

Find the solutions to the following: (a) $2x + 3 = 0$; (b) $3(x + 1) - 2 = -2(2x - 3)$; and (c) $2 = 1/(x + 1)$.

■ ANSWER
(a) $-\frac{3}{2}$; (b) $\frac{5}{7}$; (c) $-\frac{1}{2}$

EXAMPLE 2

Solve $5xy - 3 = 2x - y$ for y, noting any restrictions on x.

■ SOLUTION
When an equation contains other variables in addition to the one for which we are asked to solve, these additional variables may be viewed as constants. Thus, in solving the given equation for y, we shall treat the variable x as a constant. Viewed in this fashion, we see that the equation is linear in y. Hence we want to get the y terms on one side and the remaining terms on the other. We have
$$y + 5xy = 2x + 3.$$
In order to determine the coefficient of y, we may factor the left side. We have
$$y(1 + 5x) = 2x + 3.$$
Dividing both sides by the coefficient of y, we get
$$y = \frac{2x + 3}{1 + 5x}.$$
But this equation makes sense only if the denominator, $1 + 5x$, is not zero. Thus we must have $x \neq -\frac{1}{5}$. (Note that if $x = -\frac{1}{5}$, the given equation reduces to $-3 = -\frac{2}{5}$, a false statement.)

EXERCISE

Solve $3x - 2xy = 5 - 3y$ for y, noting any restrictions on x.

■ ANSWER

$$y = \frac{5 - 3x}{3 - 2x}, \quad x \neq \frac{3}{2}$$

PROBLEM SET A.6

In Problems 1–30, find the solutions.

1. $3x + 10 = 0$
2. $4x - 7 = 0$
3. $4x - 5 = 2x + 3$
4. $6x + 7 = 3x - 5$
5. $4 - 2x = 5x - 2$
6. $2x + 1 = 5x - 6$
7. $3(2 - x) = 2(x - 5)$
8. $4(x - 3) = 3(1 - x)$
9. $3(2x - 5) = 2(4 - 3x) + 1$
10. $5(2x - 1) - 3 = 2(3 - 2x)$
11. $x(x + 1) = x^2 + 3x + 5$
12. $2x^2 + 2x - 1 = x(2x - 3)$
13. $\dfrac{3x + 1}{2x - 3} = \dfrac{1}{8}$
14. $\dfrac{2x - 1}{x + 1} = -\dfrac{2}{3}$
15. $\dfrac{5x + 4}{2 - 3x} + \dfrac{4}{3} = 0$
16. $\dfrac{2 - x}{2x + 3} - \dfrac{1}{2} = 0$
17. $\dfrac{3}{2x - 1} = -\dfrac{5}{x + 3}$
18. $\dfrac{2}{x - 3} = \dfrac{3}{x + 2}$
19. $\dfrac{5}{x + 1} - \dfrac{16}{6 - x} = 0$
20. $\dfrac{1}{x + 6} + \dfrac{5}{x - 3} = 0$
21. $\dfrac{x + 1}{x - 2} - \dfrac{2x + 1}{2x - 2} = 0$
22. $\dfrac{x + 1}{x} + \dfrac{x + 2}{5 - x} = 0$
23. $\dfrac{6}{2x - 1} + \dfrac{x + 1}{2x - 1} = 3$
24. $\dfrac{1}{x + 1} - \dfrac{x}{x + 1} = -2$
25. $\dfrac{x + 1}{x - 2} = 3 + \dfrac{3}{x - 2}$
26. $\dfrac{4x}{2x - 3} = \dfrac{6}{2x - 3} + 2$
27. $\dfrac{x}{x + 3} = 1 - \dfrac{5}{2x - 1}$
28. $\dfrac{2x}{2x + 1} - 1 = \dfrac{3}{x - 2}$
29. $\dfrac{2}{x} = \dfrac{1 + \sqrt{5}}{x - 2}$
30. $\dfrac{\sqrt{3}x}{x + 1} = \dfrac{2}{\sqrt{3} + 1}$

In Problems 31–42, solve for the indicated variable, noting any restrictions on other variables.

31. $\dfrac{x}{3} + a = \dfrac{x - a}{2}$, for x
32. $\dfrac{3}{2x - c} = \dfrac{5}{x + 3}$, for x
33. $d = rt$, for r
34. $v = gt + k$, for t
35. $F = \tfrac{9}{5}C + 32$, for C
36. $A = \dfrac{h}{2}(b + c)$, for c
37. $\dfrac{y - y_1}{x - x_1} = 6$, for y
38. $\dfrac{y - y_1}{x - x_1} = 2$, for x
39. $6x + 5y = 3xy$, for y
40. $2xy - 5 = 3x + y$, for y
41. $2xy' - 3y' + x^2 = 0$, for y'
42. $x^2y' - 3x - 2y^3y' = 1$, for y'

A.7 QUADRATIC EQUATIONS

An equation in a variable x is called **quadratic** in x provided that it is equivalent to

$$ax^2 + bx + c = 0,$$

where a, b, and c are constants with $a \neq 0$. So quadratic equations are those in which, when fractions are cleared and like terms are combined, the variable is raised to the second and first powers only or to the second power only. For example,

$$2x^2 + x + 1 = 0, \quad x^2 - 1 = 0, \quad \text{and} \quad \frac{1}{x+3} = x$$

are quadratic, whereas

$$3x + 2 = 0, \quad x^3 - 2x^2 = 0, \quad \text{and} \quad \sqrt{x} = 4$$

are not.

The method for solving linear equations does not extend to quadratic equations. But one of several other procedures may be used. One technique, called the **method of factoring,** is based on the following theorem.

Let p_x and q_x be algebraic expressions in the variable x. Then the equation

$$p_x \cdot q_x = 0$$

is equivalent to the compound statement

$$p_x = 0 \quad \text{or} \quad q_x = 0.$$

This theorem is a direct result of the fact that if the product of two numbers is zero, then one (or both) of the numbers must be zero. It states that an equation in which the product of two expressions equals zero is equivalent to an "or" statement in which each expression equals zero. Because the solutions of an "or" statement are the union of the solutions of each part, we find the solutions of $p_x = 0$ and unite them with the solutions of $q_x = 0$. This procedure is illustrated in Example 1.

EXAMPLE 1

Find the solutions of the following:
(a) $2x^2 + 5x - 3 = 0$; (b) $(x + 1)(x - 2) = 4$; and (c) $2x - 5 = 12/x$.

■ SOLUTION
(a) Factoring the left side, we get

$$(2x - 1)(x + 3) = 0.$$

This equation is equivalent to the compound statement

$$2x - 1 = 0 \quad \text{or} \quad x + 3 = 0.$$

Upon solving each of these linear equations for x, we have

$$x = \tfrac{1}{2} \quad \text{or} \quad x = -3.$$

Thus the solutions are $\tfrac{1}{2}$ and -3.

(b) Although the left side of this equation is already factored, the right side is not zero. So we must subtract 4 from both sides, multiply the binomials, and combine like terms. We get

$$(x + 1)(x - 2) - 4 = 0$$
$$x^2 - x - 2 - 4 = 0$$
$$x^2 - x - 6 = 0.$$

Factoring the left side, we have

$$(x - 3)(x + 2) = 0.$$

This is equivalent to

$$x - 3 = 0 \quad \text{or} \quad x + 2 = 0$$
$$x = 3 \qquad\qquad x = -2.$$

Thus the solutions are 3 and -2.

(c) After multiplying each side by x, we have

$$2x^2 - 5x = 12.$$

Now we get one side to zero and factor, obtaining

$$2x^2 - 5x - 12 = 0$$
$$(2x + 3)(x - 4) = 0,$$

which is equivalent to

$$2x + 3 = 0 \quad \text{or} \quad x - 4 = 0$$
$$x = -\tfrac{3}{2} \qquad\qquad x = 4.$$

Since both $-\tfrac{3}{2}$ and 4 are in the domain $R - \{0\}$, both are solutions.

EXERCISE

Find the solutions of the following:
(a) $6x^2 + x - 2 = 0$; (b) $(x + 2)(x - 3) = 6$; and (c) $3x + 14 = 5/x$.

■ ANSWER
(a) $-\tfrac{2}{3}, \tfrac{1}{2}$; (b) 4, -3; (c) $\tfrac{1}{3}, -5$

Sometimes the method of factoring cannot be used to find the solutions of a quadratic equation. In such cases we may apply the following theorem.

The equation
$$ax^2 + bx + c = 0,$$
where a, b, and c are constants with $a \neq 0$, is equivalent to the compound statement

$$x = \frac{-b + \sqrt{b^2 - 4ac}}{2a} \quad \text{or} \quad x = \frac{-b - \sqrt{b^2 - 4ac}}{2a}. \tag{A-2}$$

Statement (A-2) is usually abbreviated as

$$x = \frac{-b \pm \sqrt{b^2 - 4ac}}{2a},$$

and is called the **quadratic formula.** It can be used to find the solutions of *any* quadratic equation. It is applied in Example 2.

EXAMPLE 2

Use the quadratic formula to find the solutions of the following:
(a) $12x^2 - 5x - 2 = 0$ and (b) $4x^2 = 8x + 1$.

■ ANSWER
(a) In this problem we have $a = 12$, $b = -5$, and $c = -2$. Substituting these values into the quadratic formula, we get

$$x = \frac{-(-5) \pm \sqrt{(-5)^2 - 4(12)(-2)}}{2(12)}$$

$$= \frac{5 \pm \sqrt{121}}{24} = \frac{5 \pm 11}{24}$$

$$x = \frac{5 + 11}{24} = \frac{2}{3} \quad \text{or} \quad x = \frac{5 - 11}{24} = -\frac{1}{4}.$$

Thus the solutions are $\frac{2}{3}$ and $-\frac{1}{4}$.

(b) Before attempting to apply the quadratic formula, let's put the equation in the form
$$4x^2 - 8x - 1 = 0.$$
Hence we have $a = 4$, $b = -8$, and $c = -1$. After substituting these values into the quadratic formula, we have

$$x = \frac{-(-8) \pm \sqrt{(-8)^2 - 4(4)(-1)}}{2(4)}$$

$$= \frac{8 \pm \sqrt{80}}{8} = \frac{8 \pm 4\sqrt{5}}{8} = \frac{2 \pm \sqrt{5}}{2}.$$

Thus the solutions are $(2 + \sqrt{5})/2$ (≈ 2.118) and $(2 - \sqrt{5})/2$ (≈ -0.1180).

Note that the method of factoring can be used in Example 2(a) because
$$12x^2 - 5x - 2 = (3x - 2)(4x + 1).$$

Factoring will not work in Example 2(b), however.

The number $b^2 - 4ac$, which appears under the radical sign in the quadratic formula, is called the **discriminant** of the quadratic equation. Its value determines the number of real roots as follows:

(i) If the discriminant is positive, then there are two roots.
(ii) If the discriminant is zero, then there is one root.
(iii) If the discriminant is negative, then there are no real roots. (The square root of a negative number isn't real.)

EXAMPLE 3

Find the solutions of $x^2 - 2x + 5 = 0$ by using the quadratic formula.

■ SOLUTION

We have $a = 1$, $b = -2$, and $c = 5$. Substituting, we get
$$x = \frac{2 \pm \sqrt{4 - 20}}{2}.$$

We may stop here. Since the discriminant is negative, there are no real solutions.

EXERCISE

Use the quadratic formula to find the solutions of the following:
(a) $3x^2 + 5x - 2 = 0$; (b) $4x^2 + 2x = 3$; and (c) $2x^2 - x + 1 = 0$.

■ ANSWER

(a) $\frac{1}{3}$, -2; (b) $(-1 + \sqrt{13})/4$ (≈ 0.6514), $(-1 - \sqrt{13})/4$ (≈ -1.151); (c) no solutions

PROBLEM SET A.7

In Problems 1–26, find the solutions by factoring.

1. $x^2 - 3x = 0$
2. $2x^2 + 5x = 0$
3. $x^2 - 5x + 6 = 0$
4. $x^2 + 3x - 10 = 0$
5. $2x^2 - x - 21 = 0$
6. $3x^2 + 10x + 3 = 0$
7. $10x^2 - 3x - 1 = 0$
8. $6x^2 - 23x - 4 = 0$
9. $x^2 + x = 20$
10. $x^2 + 3x = 5x + 15$
11. $x(2x - 1) = 6$
12. $x(3x + 5) = 2$
13. $4x(x + 4) = x + 4$
14. $2x(3x + 1) = 15 + x$
15. $(x - 5)(x + 2) = 8$
16. $(2x + 1)(x + 2) = 5$
17. $(6x + 1)(2x + 3) = 3(x - 1)$
18. $(3x - 5)^2 = x^2 + 5x + 13$
19. $5 = \dfrac{6}{x^2} - \dfrac{7}{x}$
20. $6 + \dfrac{5}{x} = \dfrac{-1}{x^2}$

21. $x + 2 = \dfrac{8}{x}$

22. $x + \dfrac{1}{x} = 2$

23. $x + \dfrac{4}{x-2} = \dfrac{2x}{x-2} - 3$

24. $3x - \dfrac{6x}{2x+1} = \dfrac{14}{2x+1} - 2$

25. $\dfrac{x-2}{2x-5} = \dfrac{x-2}{3x-2}$

26. $3 = \dfrac{2}{x+5} - \dfrac{2}{x+2}$

In Problems 27–40, find the solutions by using the quadratic formula.

27. $2x^2 - 3x - 2 = 0$

28. $3x^2 + 7x = 0$

29. $x^2 - 6x + 6 = 0$

30. $\dfrac{x^2}{24} + \dfrac{x}{2} + 1 = 0$

31. $2x^2 - x = 5$

32. $x^2 + 3x = 5x + 7$

33. $x(3x - 2) = 4$

34. $(2x - 1)(x + 3) = -4$

35. $\dfrac{x}{x^2 + 4} = \dfrac{1}{3}$

36. $\dfrac{2x}{x-1} = \dfrac{3x-1}{x+1}$

37. $\dfrac{5}{x+2} + \dfrac{3}{x-2} = 4 + \dfrac{1}{x^2 - 4}$

38. $\dfrac{1}{x^2 - 1} - \dfrac{x}{x+1} = \dfrac{3}{x-1}$

39. $x^2 - \sqrt{2}x - 12 = 0$

40. $x^2 + 2\sqrt{2}x - 1 = 0$

SELECTED PROOFS

THEOREM 3.5 If $f(x) = e^x$, then $f'(x) = e^x$.

Proof   Using the definition of derivative we get

$$f'(x) = \lim_{h \to 0} \frac{f(x+h) - f(x)}{h}$$

$$= \lim_{h \to 0} \frac{e^{x+h} - e^x}{h}$$

$$= \lim_{h \to 0} \frac{e^x(e^h - 1)}{h}.$$

In computing the limit, x is treated as a constant (since it is the variable h that is approaching 0). Hence, by properties of limits,

$$f'(x) = e^x \lim_{h \to 0} \frac{e^h - 1}{h}.$$

Let us now focus on

$$\lim_{h \to 0} \frac{e^h - 1}{x}.$$

By definition of e,

$$\lim_{h \to 0} (1 + h)^{1/h} = e.$$

Thus, for h close to 0,

$$(1 + h)^{1/h} \approx e$$

$$1 + h \approx e^h$$

$$h \approx e^h - 1$$

$$1 \approx \frac{e^h - 1}{h}.$$

437

Therefore
$$\lim_{h \to 0} \frac{e^h - 1}{h} = 1.$$
Thus
$$f'(x) = e^x \lim_{h \to 0} \frac{e^h - 1}{h}$$
$$= e^x.$$

THEOREM 3.6 If $f(x) = \ln x$, then $f'(x) = 1/x$.

Proof From the definition of derivative we have
$$f'(x) = \lim_{h \to 0} \frac{f(x+h) - f(x)}{h}$$
$$= \lim_{h \to 0} \frac{\ln(x+h) - \ln x}{h}.$$

By properties of logarithms this may be written
$$f'(x) = \lim_{h \to 0} \frac{1}{h} \cdot \ln \frac{x+h}{x}$$
$$= \lim_{h \to 0} \ln \left(\frac{x+h}{x} \right)^{1/h}.$$

Now let's rewrite the argument of the logarithm:
$$\left(\frac{x+h}{x} \right)^{1/h} = \left(1 + \frac{h}{x} \right)^{1/h}$$
$$= \left(1 + \frac{h}{x} \right)^{x/h \cdot 1/x}$$
$$= \left(\left(1 + \frac{h}{x} \right)^{\frac{1}{h/x}} \right)^{1/x}.$$

So we have
$$f'(x) = \lim_{h \to 0} \ln \left(\left(1 + \frac{h}{x} \right)^{\frac{1}{h/x}} \right)^{1/x}$$
$$= \lim_{h \to 0} \frac{1}{x} \cdot \ln \left(1 + \frac{h}{x} \right)^{\overline{h/x}}$$
$$= \frac{1}{x} \lim_{h \to 0} \ln \left(1 + \frac{h}{x} \right)^{\frac{1}{h/x}}. \qquad \textbf{(SP-1)}$$

SELECTED PROOFS

Because the natural logarithmic function is continuous,

$$\lim_{h \to 0} \ln\left(1 + \frac{h}{x}\right)^{\frac{1}{h/x}} = \ln\left(\lim_{h \to 0}\left(1 + \frac{h}{x}\right)^{\frac{1}{h/x}}\right).$$

Since $\lim_{z \to 0} (1 + z)^{1/z} = e$;

$$\lim_{h \to 0}\left(1 + \frac{h}{x}\right)^{\frac{1}{h/x}} = e.$$

Therefore

$$\lim_{h \to 0} \ln\left(1 + \frac{h}{x}\right)^{\frac{1}{h/x}} = \ln e = 1.$$

Equation (SP-1) thus becomes

$$f'(x) = \frac{1}{x}.$$

THEOREM 3.13
Product Rule

If $y = f(x) \cdot g(x)$, where f and g are differentiable functions, then

$$y' = f(x) \cdot g'(x) + g(x) \cdot f'(x).$$

Proof We have

$$y' = \lim_{h \to 0} \frac{f(x + h)g(x + h) - f(x)g(x)}{h}.$$

Upon adding and subtracting $f(x + h)g(x)$ to the numerator, we get

$$y' = \lim_{h \to 0} \frac{f(x + h)g(x + h) - f(x + h)g(x) + f(x + h)g(x) - f(x)g(x)}{h}$$

$$= \lim_{h \to 0} \left(f(x + h) \cdot \frac{g(x + h) - g(x)}{h} + g(x) \cdot \frac{f(x + h) - f(x)}{h} \right)$$

$$= \lim_{h \to 0} f(x + h) \cdot \frac{g(x + h) - g(x)}{h} + \lim_{h \to 0} g(x) \cdot \frac{f(x + h) - f(x)}{h}$$

$$= \lim_{h \to 0} f(x + h) \cdot \lim_{h \to 0} \frac{g(x + h) - g(x)}{h} + \lim_{h \to 0} g(x) \cdot \lim_{h \to 0} \frac{f(x + h) - f(x)}{h}.$$

Since f is differentiable, it is continuous. Thus

$$\lim_{h \to 0} f(x + h) = f(x).$$

Since $g(x)$ does not depend on h,

$$\lim_{h \to 0} g(x) = g(x).$$

And, of course, by definition,

$$\lim_{h \to 0} \frac{g(x+h) - g(x)}{h} = g'(x),$$

$$\lim_{h \to 0} \frac{f(x+h) - f(x)}{h} = f'(x).$$

Therefore

$$y' = f(x) \cdot g'(x) + g(x) \cdot f'(x).$$

ANSWERS TO SELECTED PROBLEMS

CHAPTER 1

PROBLEM SET 1.1, PAGE 6

1.

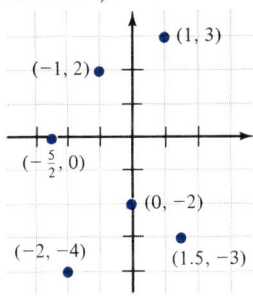

3. $A = (5,1)$, $B = (0,3)$, $C = (-4,4)$, $D = (-3,0)$, $E = (-2,-2)$, $F = (2,-3)$

5. I

7. (a) $\frac{1}{3}$, (b) -4, (c) $1/\pi$, (d) -10

9. (a) 64, (b) 32, (c) -2, (d) 0

11.

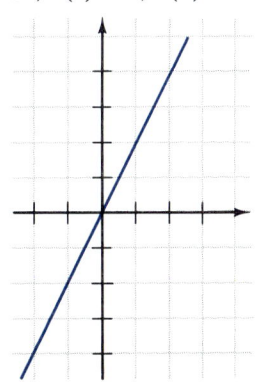

13.

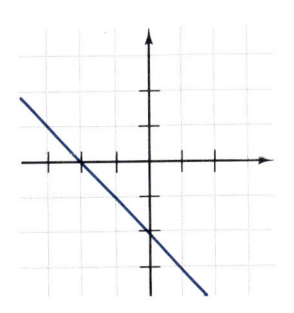

15.

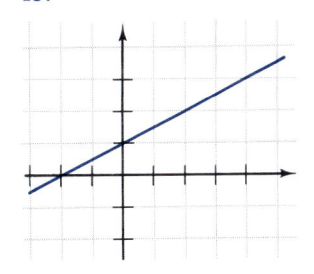

17.

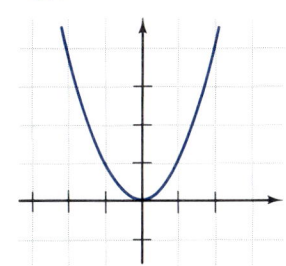

19.

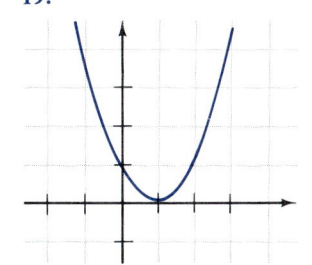

21.

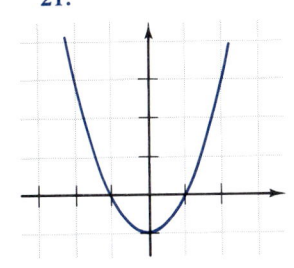

23. $V = \frac{4}{3}\pi\left(\frac{A}{4\pi}\right)^{3/2} = \frac{A^{3/2}}{6\pi^{1/2}}$

25. $A = 4x + 40$

27. $d^2 = 10{,}000t^2 - 30t + \frac{1}{16}$

29. $V = 3\pi h^3$

441

PROBLEM SET 1.2, PAGE 18

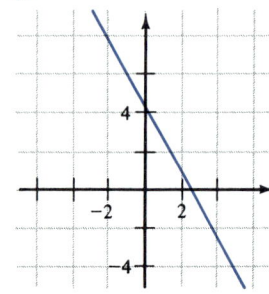

1. [graph]
3. [graph]
5. [graph]
7. [graph]
9. $\frac{1}{2}$
11. $-\frac{5}{11}$
13. 9
15. $-\sqrt{6}/2$
17. 0
19. [graph]
21. [graph]
23. $m\mathcal{A} = 0$, $m\mathcal{B} = \frac{1}{4}$, $m\mathcal{C} = 1$, $m\mathcal{D}$ is undefined, $m\mathcal{E} = 4$, $m\mathcal{F} = -2$
25. $m = 6$, y-intercept $= -7$
27. $m = -\frac{3}{8}$, y-intercept $= 2$
29. $m = 0$, y-intercept $= -4$
31. $m = \frac{4}{3}$, y-intercept $= -\frac{14}{15}$
33. $m = \frac{2}{3}$, y-intercept $= \frac{10}{3}$
35. $y = -5x + \sqrt{2}$
37. $y = \frac{2}{3}x + 4$
39. $y = \frac{3}{2}x - \frac{11}{2}$
41. $y = 3$
43. $y = 2x - 1$
45. $y = \frac{2}{3}x - 2$
47. $y = -\frac{1}{3}x + \frac{11}{3}$
49. -2
51. $y = -\frac{5}{3}x + \frac{8}{3}$
53. (a) $x = 2$, (b) $y = -4$, (c) $y = \frac{1}{2}x + \frac{15}{2}$
55. (a) $C = 75x$, (b) $115,200, (c) 2325
57. (a) $R = 0.18x + 75$, (b) $282.60
59. (a) $C = 22t + 490$, (b) $2800, (c) 135 sec
61. $p = -\frac{7}{3}x + 716$, $191
63. $p = 0.015x - 27$, $36

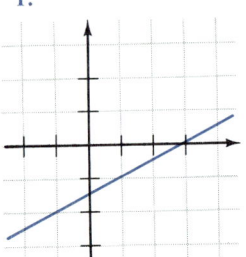

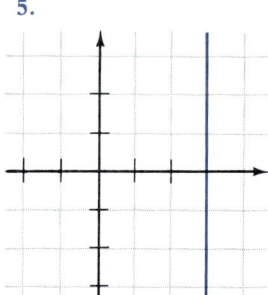

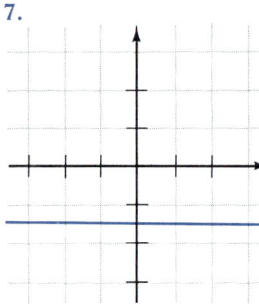

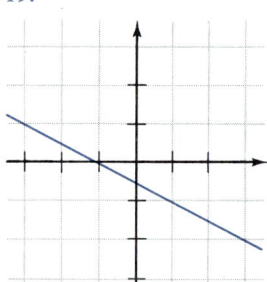

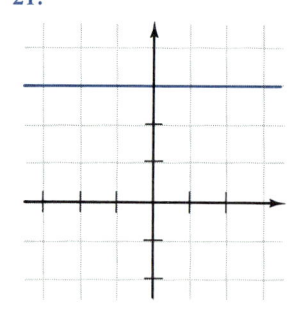

PROBLEM SET 1.3, PAGE 27

1. (a) Yes, (b) yes, (c) no, (d) no, (e) yes, (f) yes
3. (a) Yes, (b) no, (c) no, (d) yes, (e) yes, (f) no
5. (a) Yes, domain = $\{1,3,4,7\}$, range = $\{2,4,8,9\}$; (b) no; (c) yes, domain = $\{1,3,4,7\}$, range = $\{2,4,8\}$; (d) yes, domain = $\{1,3,4,7\}$, range = $\{4\}$
7. (a) 1, (b) 2, (c) 2, (d) 7, (e) 1, (f) -1, (g) -1, (h) $\{0,1,-2,3,4\}$, (i) $\{-1,1,2,7\}$ (j) 0
9. (a) -3, (b) 1, (c) $a - 3$, (d) $x - 1$, (e) $x - 4$, (f) $x - 1$
11. (a) 0, (b) 6, (c) $\dfrac{1+a}{a^2}$, (d) $2xh + h^2 + h$, (e) $x^4 + x^2$
13. (a) $\sqrt{2} + 1$, (b) $\sqrt{2} + 1$, (c) $\sqrt{2} + 1$, (d) $\sqrt{2} + 1$, (e) 0
15. (a) $\dfrac{1}{5}$, (b) $\dfrac{9}{10}$, (c) $\dfrac{t^2}{1+t^2}$, (d) $\dfrac{1}{x^2 - 10x + 26}$, (e) $\dfrac{1}{28}$
17. (a) 2, (b) 0, (c) $2 - \sqrt{3}$, (d) 3, (e) $\frac{1}{2}$
19. R
21. $R - \{2\}$
23. $R - \{2, -2\}$
25. $[-4, \infty)$
27. R
29. $f(x) = 4x + 3$
31. $f(x) = \frac{2}{5}x^2 + 1$
35. $A = P^2/16$
37. $L = 3x + \dfrac{30,000}{x}$
39. $A = 2x^2 + \dfrac{24,000}{x}$
41. $A = 440r - 2\pi r^2$
43. Even
45. Odd
47. Even

PROBLEM SET 1.4, PAGE 40

1. (a) $[-2,3]$; (b) $[-5,6]$; (c) 1; (d) 3; (e) 1; (f) -1; (g) 3; (h) -3, 2, or 5.5; (i) -5 or 4

3.

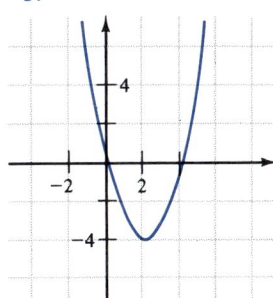

5.

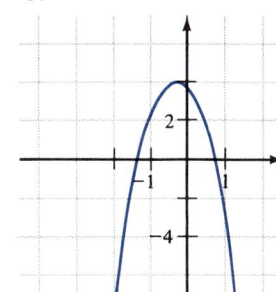

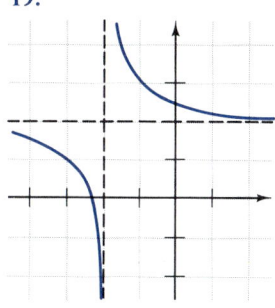

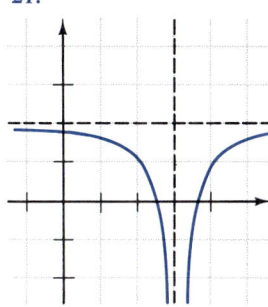

7.

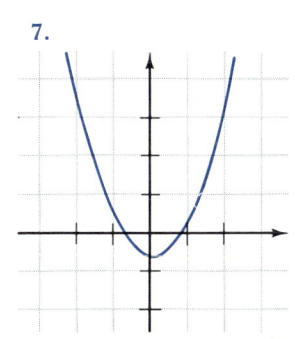

9.

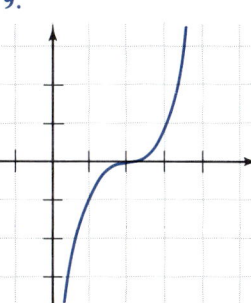

11.

13.

15.

17.

19.

21.

23.

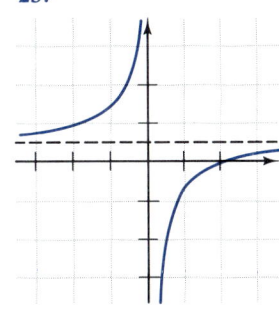

25. c
27. b
29. d

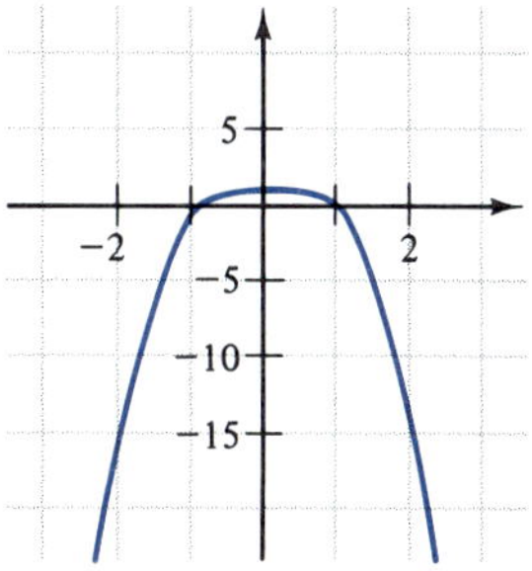

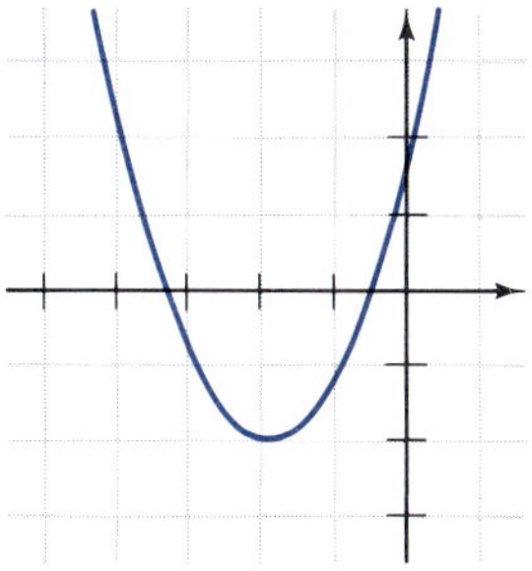

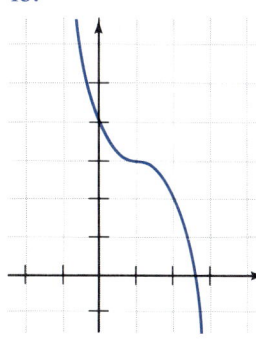

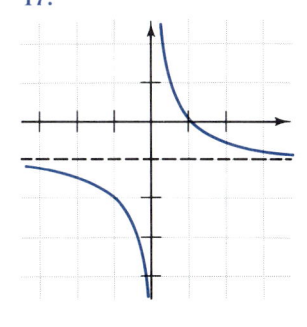

PROBLEM SET 1.5, PAGE 51

1. $4^3 = 64$
3. $(\frac{1}{3})^{-2} = 9$
5. $4^{1/2} = 2$
7. $\log \frac{1}{10} = -1$
9. $\log_{1/3} \frac{1}{27} = 3$
11. $\log_{16} \frac{1}{4} = -\frac{1}{2}$
13. 2
15. -1
17. $\frac{1}{2}$
19. 2
21. $\frac{1}{2}$
23. 1.301
25. -0.693
27. 0.347
29. k^2
31. x
33. $\sqrt{x}$
35. $\log x + \log y - \frac{1}{2} \log z$
37. $\frac{1}{2}(\ln x + \ln y) - 2 \ln z$
39. $\log \dfrac{x\sqrt{z}}{y}$
41. $\ln \dfrac{\sqrt{y}}{x^2 z}$
43. (a) $a - b$, (b) $3b$, (c) $2a + 2b$, (d) $\frac{3}{5}a$, (e) $28(a-b)$
45. $\dfrac{\ln 14}{\ln 6}$
47. $\dfrac{\ln 73}{\ln 64}$
49. $\dfrac{-\ln 2}{\ln 5}$
51. $-\frac{1}{2}$
53. $-\ln 7$
55. $\dfrac{-3 + \ln 15}{2}$
57. $\dfrac{\ln 4}{5}$
59. $\dfrac{3 + \ln \frac{25}{2}}{2}$
61. 4.8 yr
63. $\frac{1}{20}$
65. 10
67. $\frac{25}{2}$
69. $e^2/3$
71. $e^{3/2}$
73. $2e^{3/2}$
75. $\dfrac{-5 + \sqrt{25 + 8e^2}}{4}$

77. (a) 8.2, (b) 10.5, (c) 2.25, (d) $2 - \log 3$,
(e) 10^{-7}, (f) 10^{-3}, (g) $10^{-8.2}$

PROBLEM SET 1.6, PAGE 57

1.

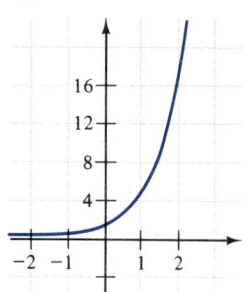

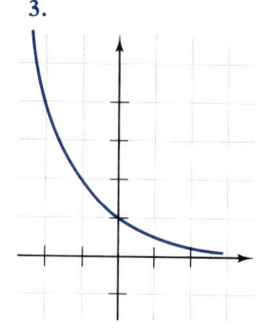

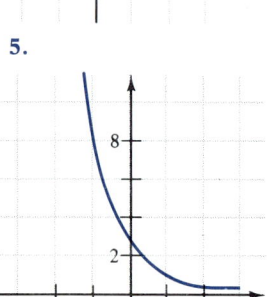

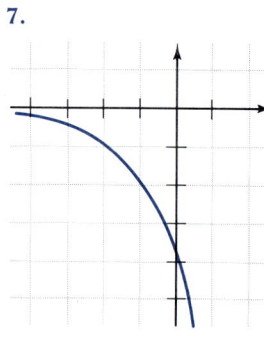

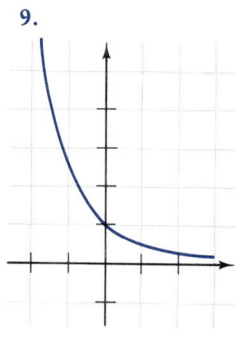

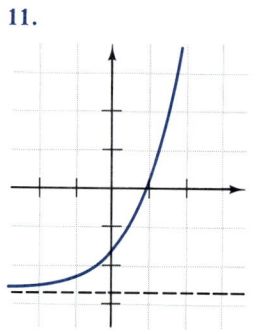

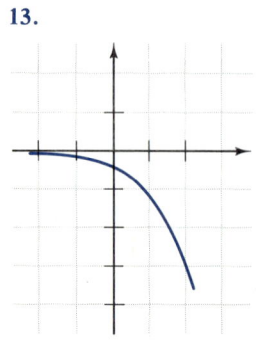

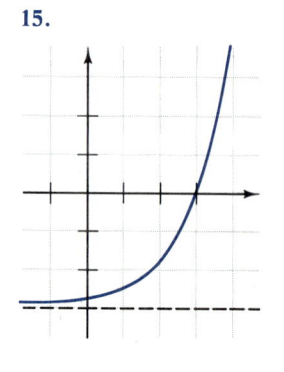

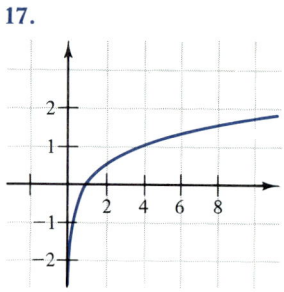

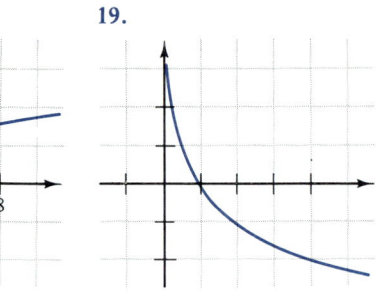

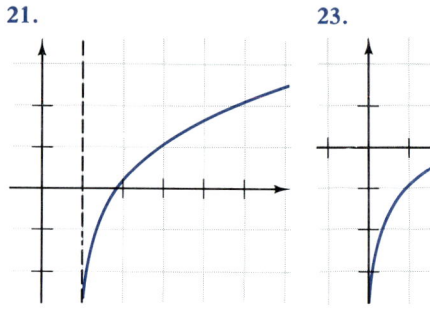

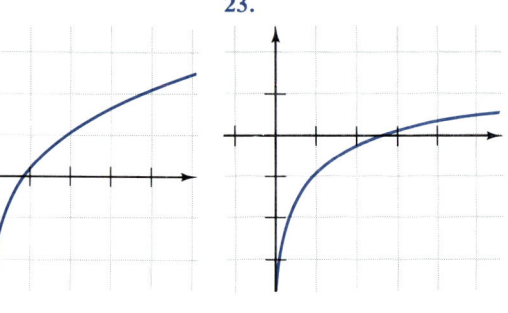

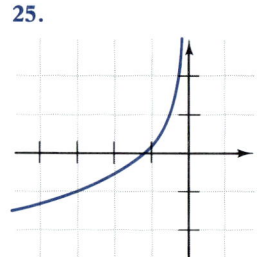

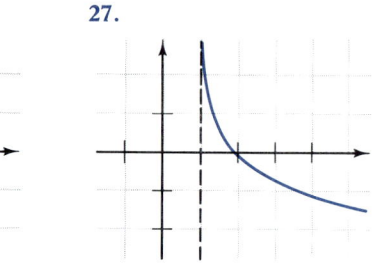

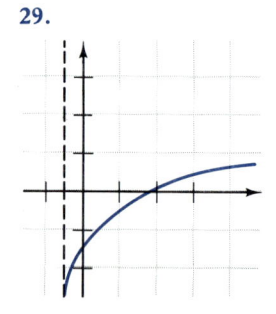

3.

5.

7.

9.

11.

13.

15.

17.

19.

21.

23.

25.

27.

29.

31. x-intercept $= \dfrac{-1 + \ln 5}{3}$ (≈ 0.2031),
y-intercept $= e - 5$ (≈ -2.282)

33. x-intercept $= \dfrac{2e^3 - 4}{1 - e^3}$ (≈ -1.895),
y-intercept $= -3 + \ln 2$ (≈ -2.307)

35. d   **37.** b

PROBLEM SET 1.7, PAGE 62

1. 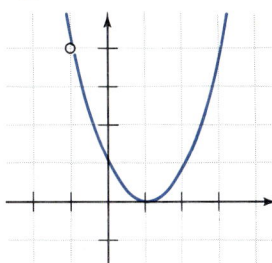
3. 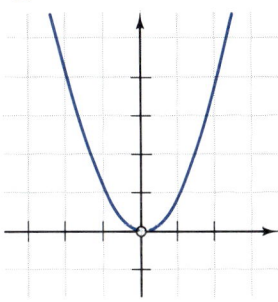
5. 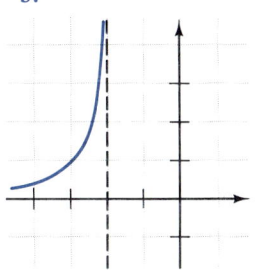
7. 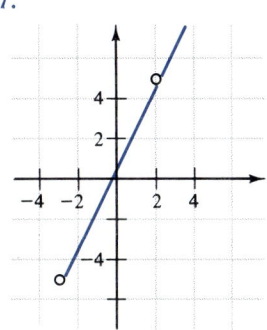
9. 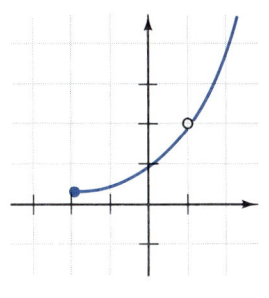
11. 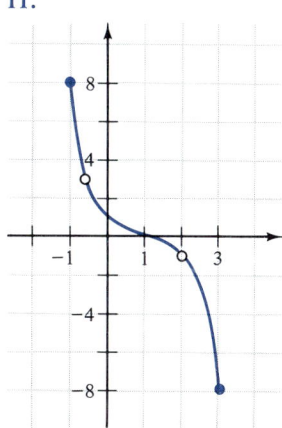
13. 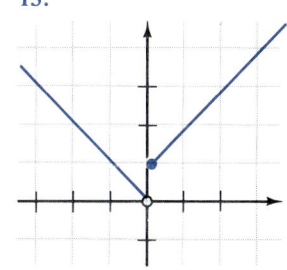
15. 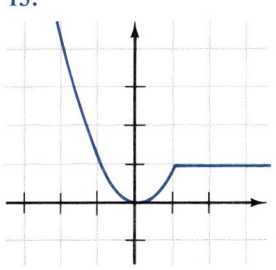
17. 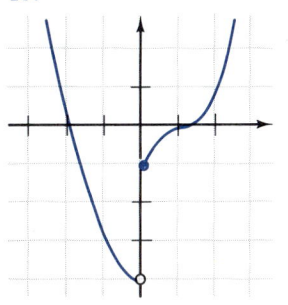
19. 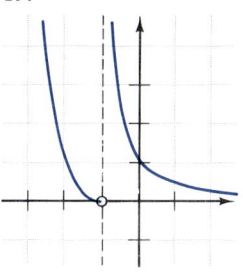
21. 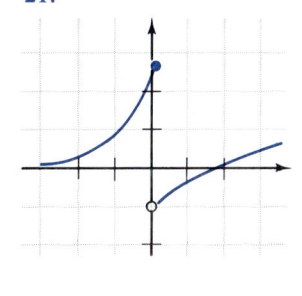
23. 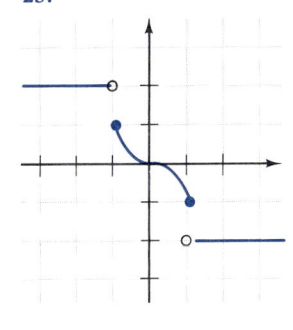
25. 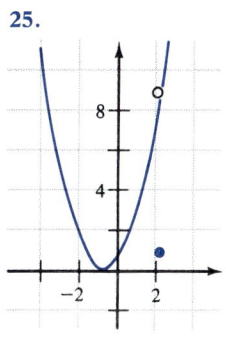
27. 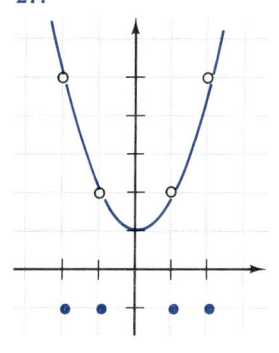
29. 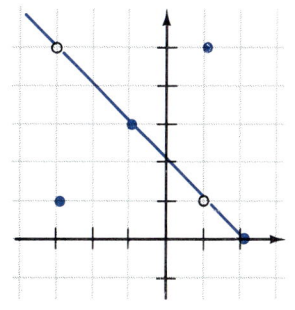
31.

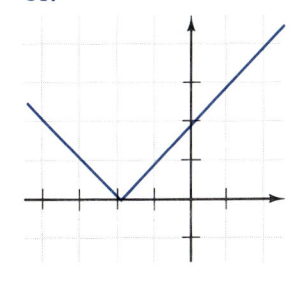

33.

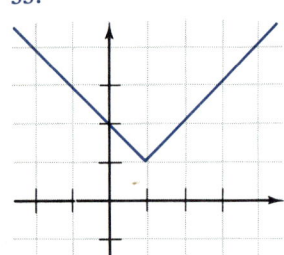

35.

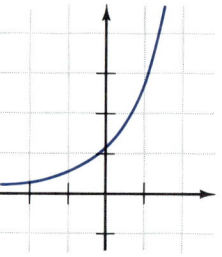

37.

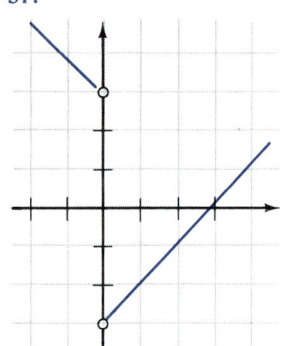

39.

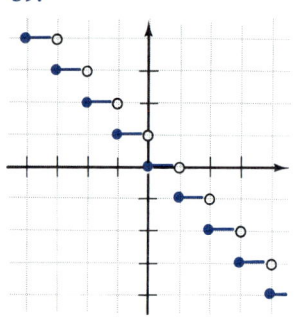

41.

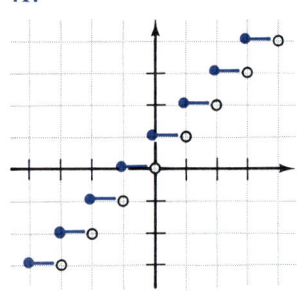

43.

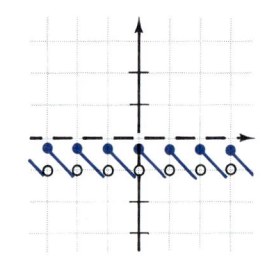

45.

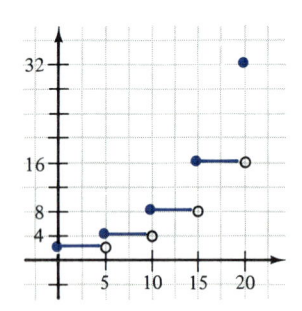

(y) T, (z) F, (aa) T, (bb) T, (cc) F, (dd) F, (ee) T, (ff) F, (gg) F, (hh) T, (ii) T, (jj) T

2. $y = \frac{2}{3}x - \ln 2$ **3.** $y = -3x + 21$
4. $y = (2 + \sqrt{2})x - \sqrt{2}$ **5.** $y = -\frac{1}{5}x - 1$
6. $y = -\frac{3}{2}x - 2$
7. (a) $-\frac{10}{3}$, (b) $\frac{1+a^4}{a^2}$, (c) $\frac{10 + 6h + h^2}{3+h}$, (d) $\frac{x}{1+x^2}$, (e) $\frac{4x-1}{4x}$, (f) $\frac{5}{2}$
8. (a) $2e$, (b) $1/\sqrt[4]{5}$, (c) $\frac{1}{4}$, (d) $\frac{1}{5}$, (e) 6, (f) π
9. R **10.** R
11. $R - \{-4, 3\}$ **12.** $R - \{-1, 1\}$
13. $(-\infty, 5]$ **14.** $(-3, \infty) - \{-1\}$
15. R **16.** $(-e, \infty)$
17. **18.**

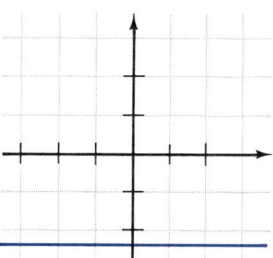

$\left\{\frac{1}{1-\sqrt{2}}\right\}$ R

19.

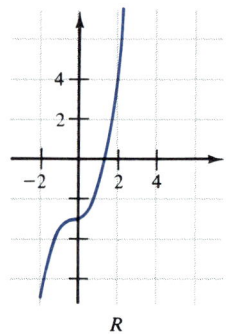

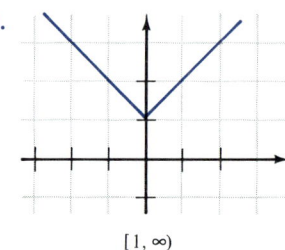

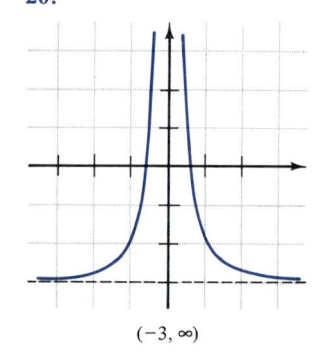

$[1, \infty)$

20. **21.**

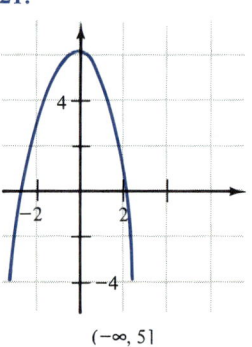

$(-3, \infty)$ $(-\infty, 5]$

■ CHAPTER 1 REVIEW, PAGE 62
1. (a) F, (b) T, (c) T, (d) F, (e) F, (f) F, (g) T, (h) F, (i) T, (j) T, (k) F, (l) T, (m) T, (n) F, (o) T, (p) F, (q) T, (r) T, (s) F, (t) T, (u) T, (v) F, (w) T, (x) T,

ANSWERS TO SELECTED PROBLEMS 447

22. [−11, ∞)

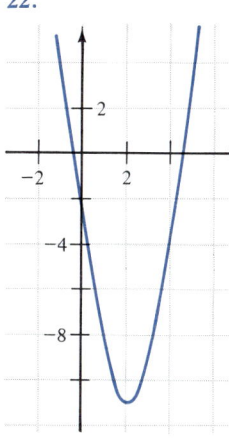

23. (−2, ∞)

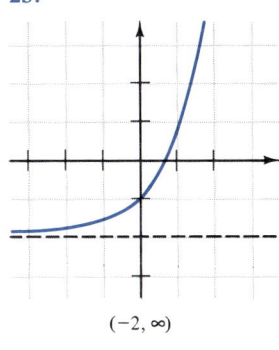

24. R

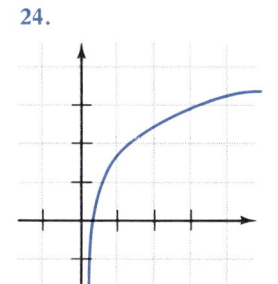

25. [−2,1] ∪ [2,3]
26. {−2,0,2}
27. [−2,0]
28. [0,4] ∪ {−2}

29.

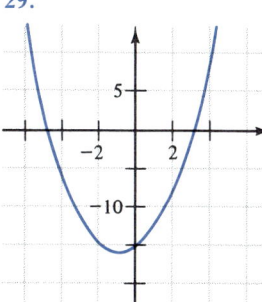

30.

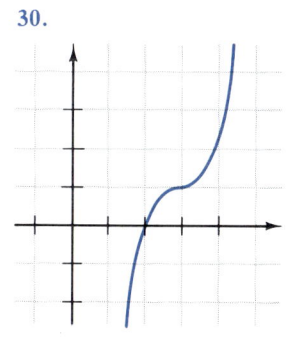

31.

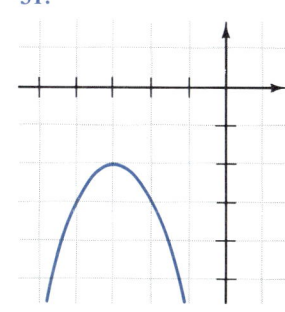

32.

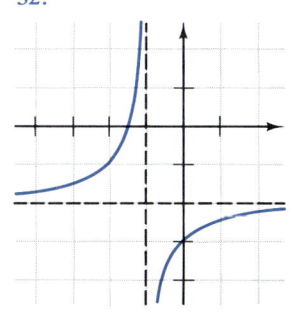

33.

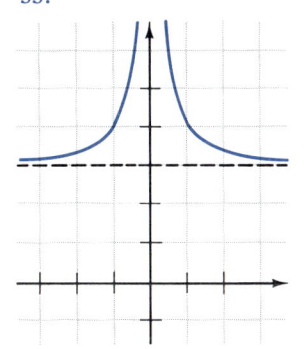

34.

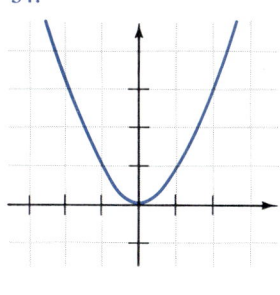

35.

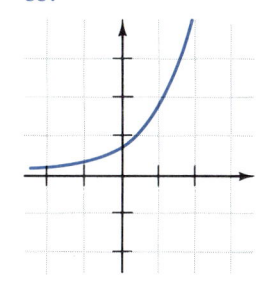

36.

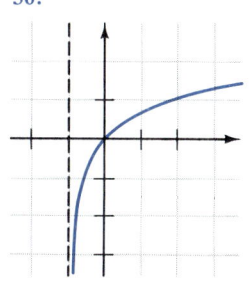

37.

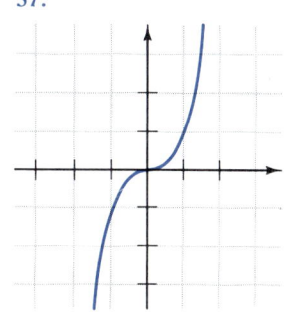

38.

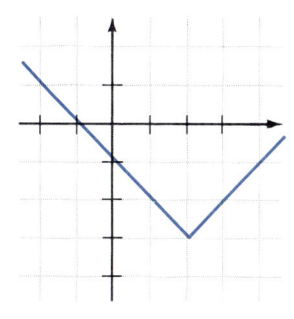

39.

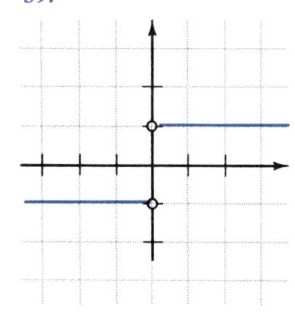

40.

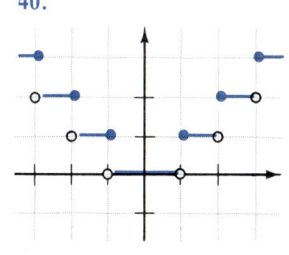

41. [graph] **42.** [graph]

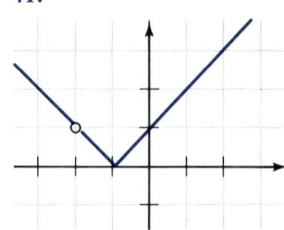

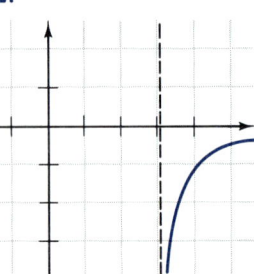

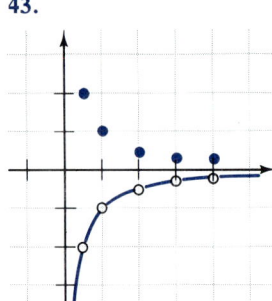

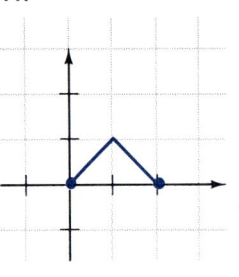

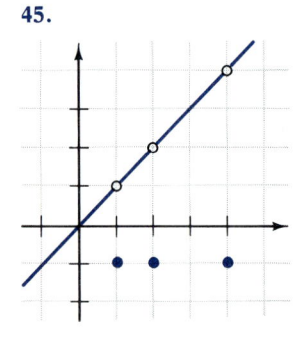

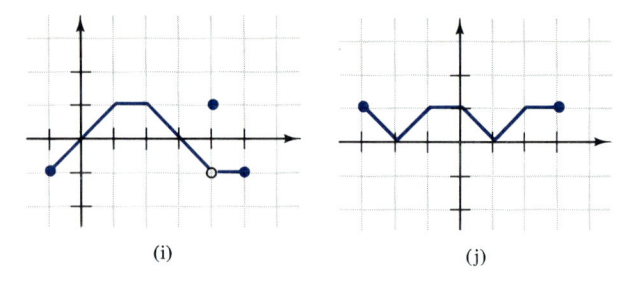

43. [graph] **44.** [graph]

45. [graph] **46.** [graph]

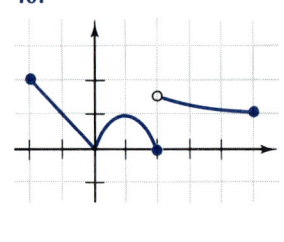

47. (a) $[-3,3]$, (b) $[-1,1]$, (c) 1, (d) -1,
(e) 0, (f) -2 or 1

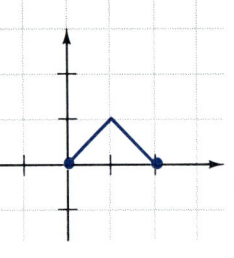

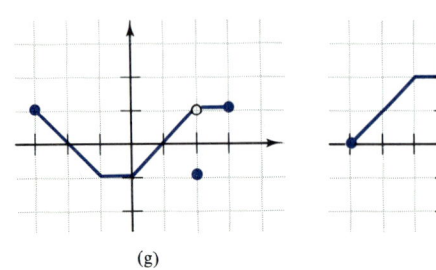

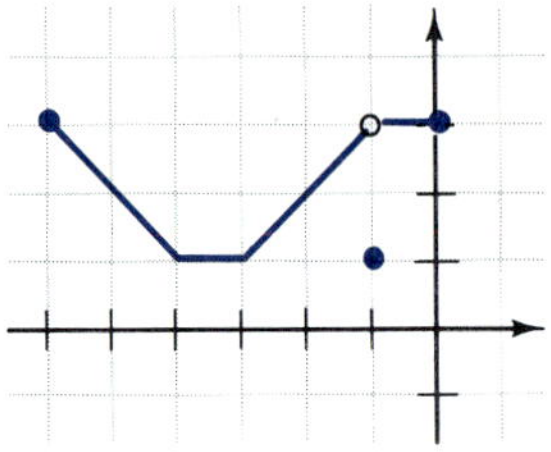

(g) [graph] (h) [graph] (i) [graph] (j) [graph]

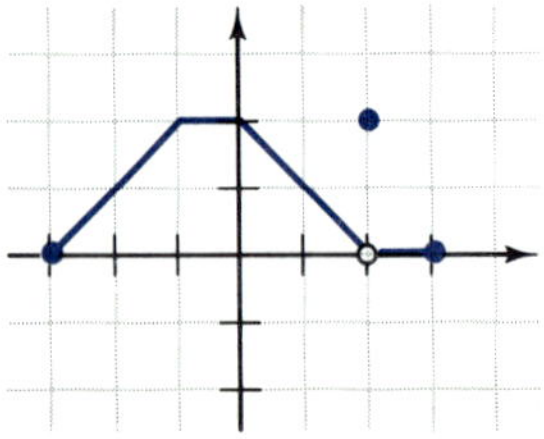

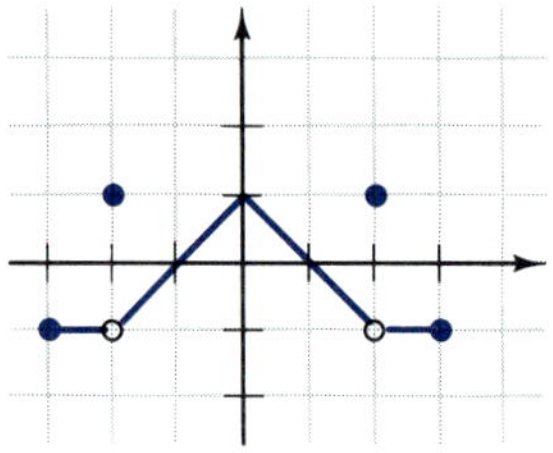

(k) [graph] (ℓ) [graph]

48. [graph]

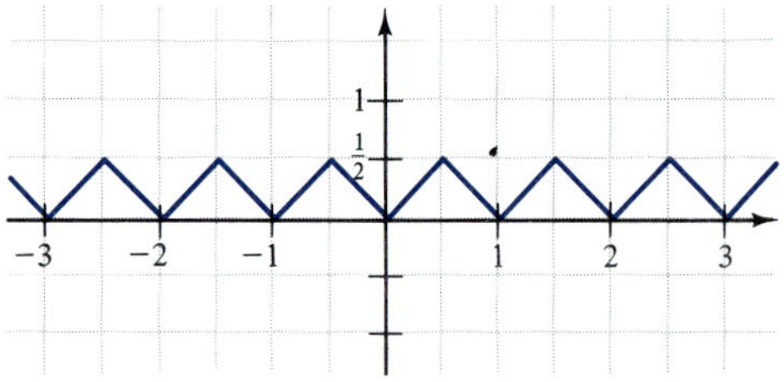

49. (a) G, (b) M, (c) I, (d) A, (e) F, (f) K,
(g) C, (h) O, (i) R, (j) E

50. $\log_{16} 8 = \frac{3}{4}$ **51.** $8^{-5/3} = \frac{1}{32}$

52. $2 \log x + \frac{1}{2} \log y - 3 \log z$

53. $\ln \dfrac{xz^2}{\sqrt[3]{y}}$ **54.** $\dfrac{\ln 20}{\ln 5}$

55. $\sqrt{\dfrac{\ln 20}{\ln 5}}, -\sqrt{\dfrac{\ln 20}{\ln 5}}$ **56.** $\dfrac{1 + \ln 15}{2}$

57. $-\ln 10$ **58.** $\sqrt{\ln 5}, -\sqrt{\ln 5}$

59. $1 + \ln \frac{28}{5}$ **60.** 20

61. $\dfrac{1}{\sqrt{10}}$ (or $\dfrac{\sqrt{10}}{10}$) **62.** 4

63. $1/(5e)$ **64.** $\sqrt{2}/e$

65. $2/e^5$ **66.** $-2e$

67. $\dfrac{e^2 + e\sqrt{e^2 - 4}}{2}, \dfrac{e^2 - e\sqrt{e^2 - 4}}{2}$

68. (a) $I = 1200x + 5000$, (b) $25,400, (c) 31

69. (a) $I = 6x$, (b) $222,000

ANSWERS TO SELECTED PROBLEMS 449

70. (a) $F = \frac{9}{5}C + 32$ or $C = \frac{5}{9}(F - 32)$ **71.** $25.85
(b)

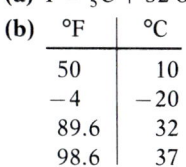

°F	°C
50	10
−4	−20
89.6	32
98.6	37

72. 1104
73. 3.5
74. $T = 125S$

75. $V = \frac{5}{6}\pi r^3$
76. $d^2 = 6100t^2 - 8000t + 11600$
77. $p = -0.0015x + 83$, $51.50
78. $p = 0.2x + 1040$, $2380
79. $A = 500x - \dfrac{x^2}{2}$ **80.** $A = \dfrac{150x}{x-4} + 6x$
81. $C = 15x + \dfrac{1500}{x}$ **82.** $A = 300x - \frac{3}{4}x^2$

CHAPTER 2

PROBLEM SET 2.1, PAGE 77
1. 2
3. 1
5. 2
7. Does not exist
9. 3
11. −1
13. 1, 1, and 1
15. −1, does not exist, and does not exist
17.

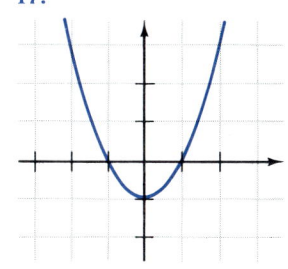

0, 0, 0, −1

19.

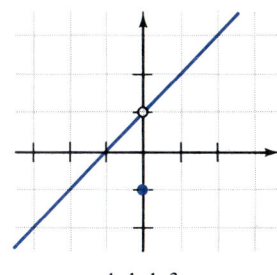

1, 1, 1, 3

21.

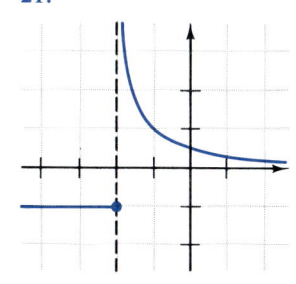

Does not exist, −1, does not exist, −1, $\frac{1}{3}$

23.

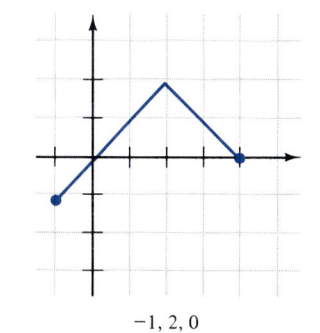

−1, 2, 0

25.

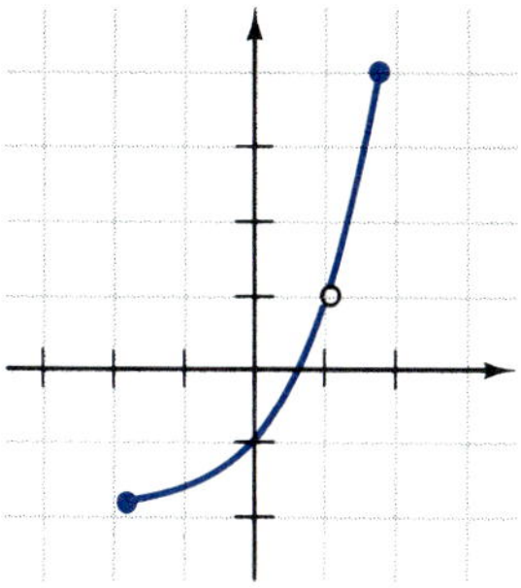

$-\frac{11}{6}$, −1, 0, 1, 4

27. (a) An example is

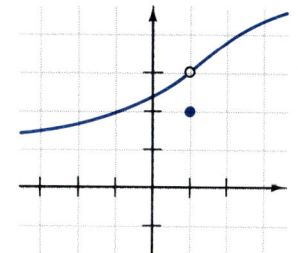

(b) An example is

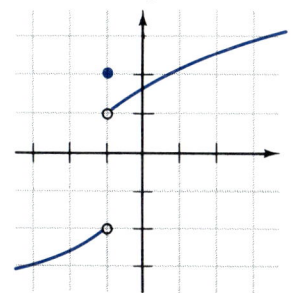

(c) An example is

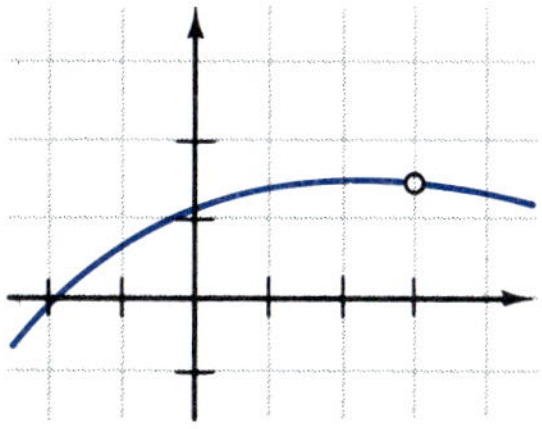

(d) An example is

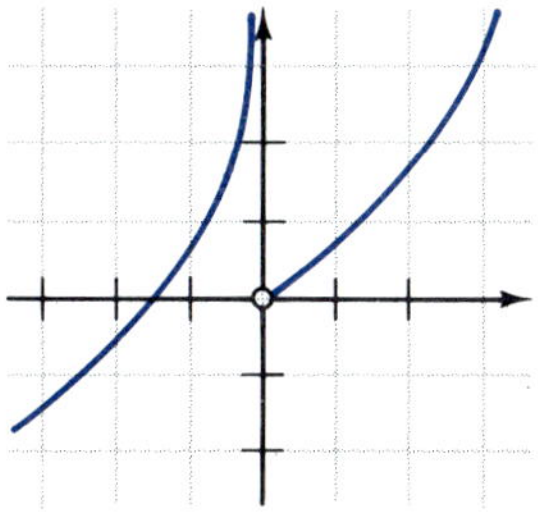

(e) An example is

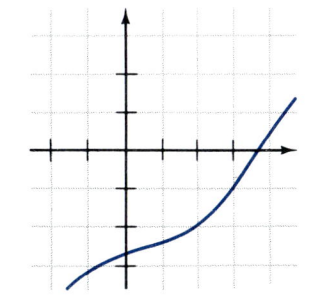

PROBLEM SET 2.2, PAGE 90

1. Continuous
3. Discontinuous
5. Discontinuous
7. Discontinuous
9. Continuous
11. Discontinuous
13. Discontinuous
15. An example is 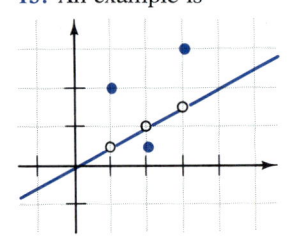
17. Continuous
19. Continuous
21. Discontinuous
23. 5
25. -6
27. 10
29. $4e$
31. 15
33. $-\frac{1}{2}$
35. 0
37. $1/e^3$
39. 0
41. e^5
43. 0
45. 8
47. $\frac{7}{6}$
49. $2a$
51. $\frac{1}{8}$
53. 2
55. $-\frac{3}{16}$
57. 9
59. $4x - 1$
61. $-\frac{1}{16}$
63. $-6a + 2$
65. $-\dfrac{1}{(3+x)^2}$
67. $\dfrac{1-a^2}{(1+a^2)^2}$
69. 0.3679
71. 0.5

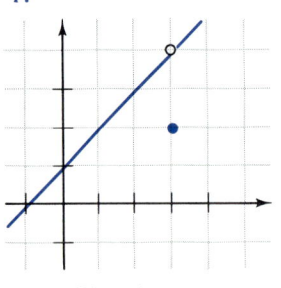

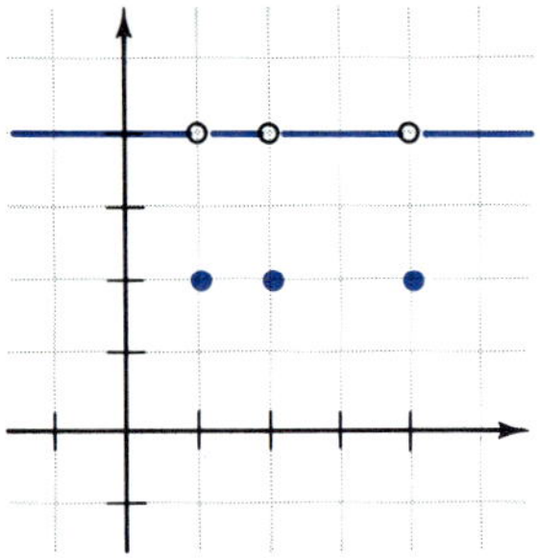

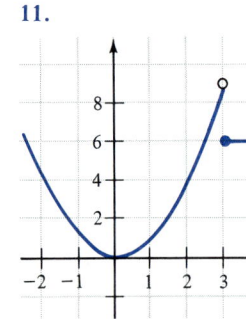

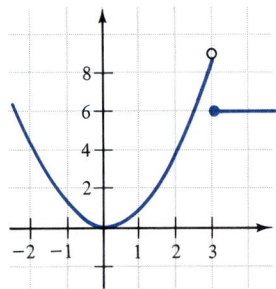

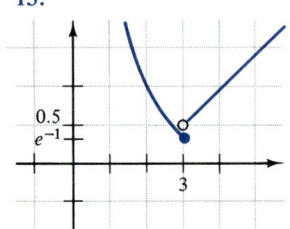

PROBLEM SET 2.3, PAGE 97

1. Tangent line at P is the graph
3. 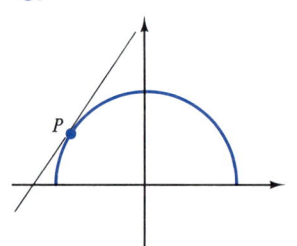
5. 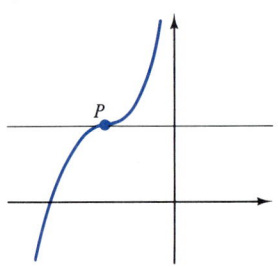
7. No tangent
9. No tangent
11. 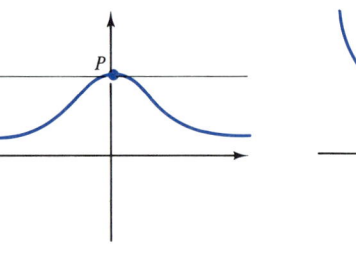
13.

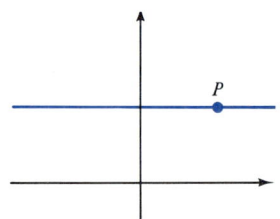

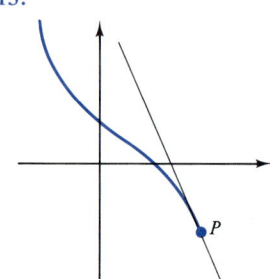

PROBLEM SET 2.4, PAGE 104

1. 2
3. -6
5. 6
7. -1
9. $\frac{3}{4}$
11. $\frac{1}{4}$
13. $y = 3$
15. $y = 4ex + 9e^2$
17. $y = 5$
19. 2
21. 7

CHAPTER 2 REVIEW, PAGE 105

1. (a) T, (b) F, (c) T, (d) F, (e) F, (f) T, (g) T, (h) T, (i) F, (j) T, (k) T, (l) T, (m) F, (n) F, (o) F, (p) T, (q) T, (r) T, (s) T, (t) F, (u) T, (v) T, (w) F, (x) F, (y) F, (z) T, (aa) T

ANSWERS TO SELECTED PROBLEMS 451

2. I. (i) (a) F, (b) T, (c) F, (d) F, (e) F
    I. (ii) (a) T, (b) T, (c) T, (d) F, (e) T
    I. (iii) (a) T, (b) T, (c) F, (d) F, (e) F
    I. (iv) (a) T, (b) T, (c) T, (d) T, (e) T
    II. (i) (a) T, (b) T, (c) F, (d) F, (e) F
    II. (ii) (a) T, (b) T, (c) T, (d) F, (e) T
    II. (iii) (a) T, (b) T, (c) T, (d) T, (e) T
    II. (iv) (a) F, (b) T, (c) F, (d) F, (e) F

3. (a) -2, (b) 2, (c) 2, (d) 4, (e) 4, (f) 4,
   (g) 5, (h) does not exist, (i) does not exist,
   (j) 0, (k) 3, (l) 2, (m) T, (n) T, (o) F,
   (p) T, (q) T, (r) T, (s) F, (t) T, (u) T,
   (v) T, (w) F

4. 8
5. 0
6. 0
7. 0
8. 9
9. 3
10. $\frac{1}{18}$
11. 2
12. $\frac{3}{8}$
13. $\frac{1}{2}$
14. 48
15. 2
16. $\frac{1}{2}$
17. 0
18. -3
19. 3
20. -11
21. $-2/x^3$
22. $-2a - 1$
23. 12
24. $\lim_{x \to 0^+} \frac{|x| - x}{x} = 0$; $\lim_{x \to 0^-} \frac{|x| - x}{x} = -2$

25.

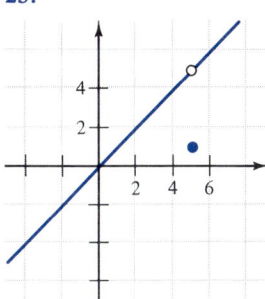

5, 5, 5

26.

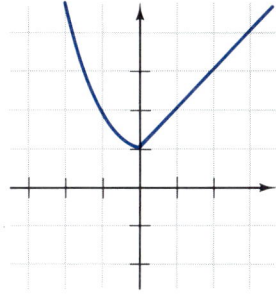

1, 1, 1

27.

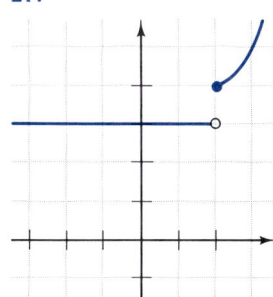

4, 3, does not exist

28.

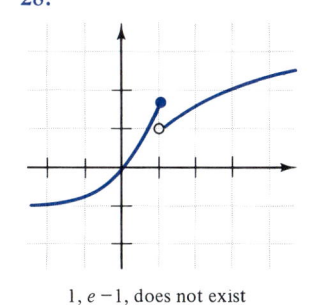

1, $e-1$, does not exist

29. -8
30. 0.36788
31. Continuous
32. Continuous
33. Discontinuous
34. Discontinuous
35. 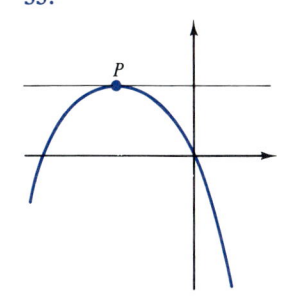
36. 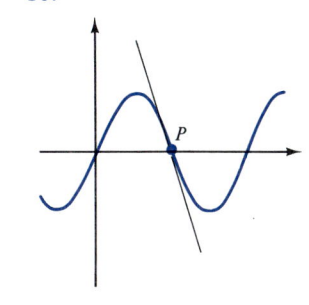
37. 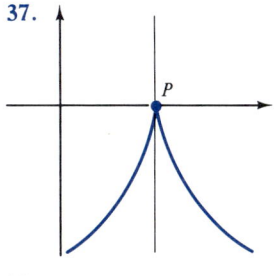
38. No tangent
39. An example is 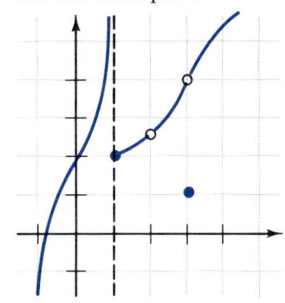
40. An example is

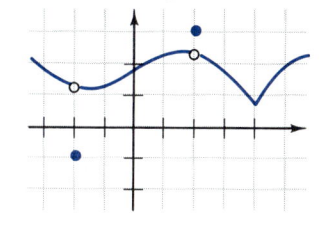

41. -9 and $y = -9x - 8$
42. $-10e$ and $y = -10ex + 12e^2$
43. 0 and $y = 0$
44. 0 and $y = 6$
45. $\frac{1}{3}$ and $y = \frac{1}{3}x + \frac{2}{3}$

CHAPTER 3

PROBLEM SET 3.1, PAGE 118

1. $2x$
3. 3
5. 0
7. $4x + 3$
9. $3x^2 + 1$
11. $-1/x^2$
13. $-\dfrac{1}{(x-3)^2}$
15. $-\dfrac{2}{(x-1)^2}$
17. $\dfrac{-x+4}{x^3}$
19. $\dfrac{1}{2\sqrt{x-3}}$
21. $f'(x) = ex$, $y = -2ex - 2e$
23. $f'(x) = 2$, $y = 2x + 1$
25. $f'(x) = 2x - 6$, $y = 0$

452 ANSWERS TO SELECTED PROBLEMS

27. $f'(x) = \dfrac{-x+4}{x^3}$, $y = -\tfrac{3}{4}x - \tfrac{5}{2}$

29. Differentiable   **31.** Not differentiable
33. Differentiable   **35.** Not differentiable
37. (a) -2, (b) -2, (c) no slope, (d) 0
39. (a) -4, (b) no slope, (c) 0, (d) 2
41. (a) $\tfrac{1}{2}$, (b) 0, (c) -1, (d) 0
43.   **45.** 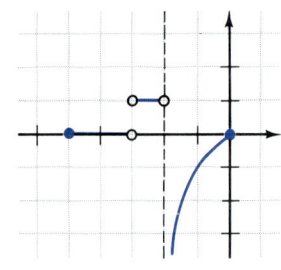
47. 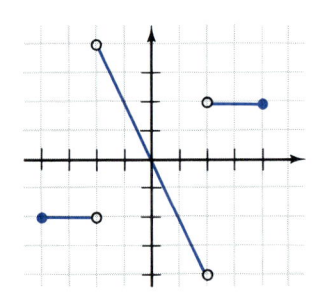
49.
51.

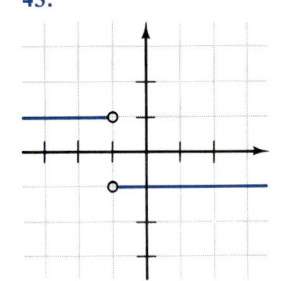

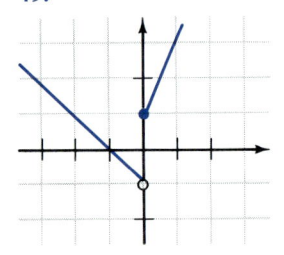

Graph of f 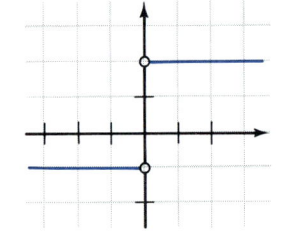   Graph of f'

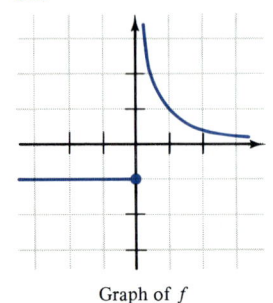

Graph of f 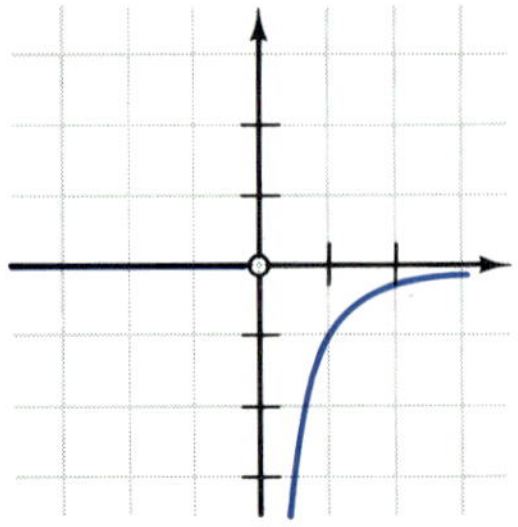   Graph of f'

53. (a) Yes, yes; (b) no, yes; (c) no, yes;
(d) yes, yes; (e) no, no; (f) yes, yes;
(g) yes, yes; (h) yes, yes

PROBLEM SET 3.2, PAGE 131

1. 0   **3.** $13x^{12}$ **5.** $(\pi - 1)x^{\pi-2}$
7. $(\ln 6)x^{(\ln 6)-1}$ **9.** $-4/x^5$ **11.** $\tfrac{5}{3}\sqrt[3]{x^2}$
13. $-\tfrac{9}{4}\sqrt[4]{1/x^{13}}$ **15.** $\tfrac{27}{2}\sqrt{x^7}$ **17.** $\tfrac{11}{5} + \ln 3$
19. x^2 **21.** $-e^2 x^{-e-1}$ **23.** $\dfrac{-1}{x^{8/3}} + e^x$
25. $5e^x$ **27.** $\dfrac{1}{ex}$ **29.** $\dfrac{1}{x^{10}} + 3x^{\sqrt{3}-1}$
31. $100x^9 + 10x^{-11} + \dfrac{1}{x^{11}}$ **33.** $25ex^4 - 5e^x - \dfrac{5e}{x}$
35. $\dfrac{1}{2x} + 3ex^2$ **37.** $8x + 12$
39. $-5x^4 + 2x + 1$ **41.** $\dfrac{3\sqrt{5}}{2}x^{1/2}$
43. $-5, -5, -5$ **45.** $4, 0, 9 + 4\sqrt{3}$
47. $-\tfrac{7}{9}, 53, -3$ **49.** $18, 4, 1\tfrac{1}{9}$
51. $y = -x - 1$ **53.** $(\ln 7, 7 - 7\ln 7)$
55. $(2,8)$ and $(-2,-8)$

PROBLEM SET 3.3, PAGE 140

1. 6
3. (a) 1 sec, 4 sec; (b) -15 cm/sec^2, 15 cm/sec^2
5. (a) 64 ft/sec, (b) -32 ft/sec^2, (c) 5 sec,
 (d) 576 ft, (e) 11 sec, (f) -192 ft/sec
7. $\tfrac{1}{3}$ and 3
9. (a) $\$78$, (b) $C(21) - C(20) = \$78.70$, (c) 37
11. (a) $C'(x) = 0.02x + 20$, $R'(x) = 60$,
 $P'(x) = -0.02x + 40$; (b) 2000
13. (a) 31.5π cm^3/cm, (b) 30.5π cm^3/cm,
 (c) 30.05π cm^3/cm, (d) 30.005π cm^3/cm,
 (e) 30π cm^3/cm
15. (a) 50, (b) 70
17. $A = \pi r^2$ and $\dfrac{dA}{dr} = 2\pi r = C$
19. $\tfrac{1}{3}$ gal/min   **21.** $-\dfrac{B}{16}$ in./hr
23. $32{,}000{,}000 K$

PROBLEM SET 3.4, PAGE 151

1. $3(x^2 + x)^2(2x + 1)$ **3.** 0
5. $\dfrac{-3}{(x-3)^4}$ **7.** $\dfrac{2(\ln x) - 1}{x}$
9. $\dfrac{9(1 + 2\sqrt{x})^8 + 5(1 + 2\sqrt{x})^4}{\sqrt{x}}$

11. $\dfrac{e^{x/2}}{2}$

13. $\dfrac{1}{2\sqrt{x}}$

15. $15(x^3 + x^2)^{14}(3x^2 + 2x)$

17. $7e^x(1 + 4e^x)^{3/4}$

19. $-2/(2x + 1)^2$

21. $\dfrac{6x^5}{\sqrt[3]{(x^6 + 8)^2}}$

23. $\dfrac{-5\left(x + \dfrac{2}{x^3}\right)}{\left(\dfrac{x^2}{2} - x^{-2}\right)^6}$

25. $4e^{4x} - e^{-x}$

27. $(4x^3 + 2x)e^{x^4 + x^2 + e}$

29. $3(x^2 - x)e^{\frac{1}{3}x^3 - \frac{1}{2}x^2}$

31. $(e^x + ex^{e-1})e^{e^x + x^e}$

33. $5(e^{3x} + e^{-4x})^4(3e^{3x} - 4e^{-4x})$

35. $\dfrac{1}{x} + \ln 2$

37. $\dfrac{4}{4x - 7}$

39. $\dfrac{3}{x}(1 + (\ln x)^2)$

41. $\dfrac{1}{x \ln x}$

43. $\dfrac{9e^{9x} + 9e^{-9x}}{e^{9x} - e^{-9x}}$

45. $\dfrac{3(10x^4 - 1)}{2x^5 - x}$

47. -240

49. $\dfrac{1}{x+2} + \dfrac{1}{2(x-3)} - \dfrac{1}{x+5}$

51. $\dfrac{2x^2}{2x^3 - 5} + \dfrac{x^5}{x^6 + 9}$

53. $y = \tfrac{4}{5}x - \tfrac{8}{5} + \ln 5$

55. 768 in.^{3}/sec

57. \$672.08/hr

59. 4 ft^2/hr

61. 28 ft/min

63. $abce^{-be^{-ct} - ct}$

67. 0.2

■ PROBLEM SET 3.5, PAGE 159

1. $(3x + 1) \cdot 2 + (2x - 6) \cdot 3 = 12x - 16$

3. $x^3 \cdot 1 + (x - 1) \cdot 3x^2 = 4x^3 - 3x^2$

5. $e^x \cdot \dfrac{1}{x} + \ln x \cdot e^x = e^x\left(\dfrac{1}{x} + \ln x\right)$

7. $3x \cdot 3(x + 1)^2 + (x + 1)^3 \cdot 3 = 3(x + 1)^2(4x + 1)$

9. $x^2 \cdot \dfrac{1}{2x} \cdot 2 + \ln|2x| \cdot 2x = x(1 + 2\ln|2x|)$

11. $(x + 1)^4 \cdot 2(x - 3) + (x - 3)^2 \cdot 4(x + 1)^3$
$= 2(x + 1)^3(x - 3)(3x - 5)$

13. $x^2 \cdot e^{1/x}\left(\dfrac{-1}{x^2}\right) + e^{1/x} \cdot 2x = e^{1/x}(2x - 1)$

15. $(x^2 - 1)^2 \cdot 4(x^4 + 1)^3 \cdot 4x^3 + (x^4 + 1)^4 \cdot 2(x^2 - 1) \cdot 2x$
$= 4x(x^2 - 1)(x^4 + 1)^3(5x^4 - 4x^2 + 1)$

17. $e^x \cdot 7(e^x + 1)^6 \cdot e^x + (e^x + 1)^7 \cdot e^x = e^x(e^x + 1)^6(8e^x + 1)$

19. $(2x - 7)^{1/2} \cdot 3(x^2 - 7)^2 \cdot 2x + (x^2 - 7)^3$
$\cdot \tfrac{1}{2}(2x - 7)^{-1/2} \cdot 2 = \dfrac{(x^2 - 7)^2(13x^2 - 42x - 7)}{\sqrt{2x - 7}}$

21. $(x^3 + 1)^3(-3)\left(\dfrac{x}{3} - 1\right)^{-4} \cdot \dfrac{1}{3} + \left(\dfrac{x}{3} - 1\right)^{-3}$
$\cdot 3(x^3 + 1)^2 \cdot 3x^2 = (x^3 + 1)^2\left(\dfrac{x}{3} - 1\right)^{-4}(2x^3 - 9x^2 - 1)$

23. $\dfrac{1}{x^2 \ln x^2}\left(x^2 \cdot \dfrac{1}{x^2} \cdot 2x + \ln x^2 \cdot 2x\right) = \dfrac{1 + \ln x^2}{x \ln x}$

25. $(x + 1)((x - 2)^8 \cdot 7(x + 3)^6 + (x + 3)^7 \cdot 8(x - 2)^7) +$
$(x - 2)^8(x + 3)^7 \cdot 1 = (x - 2)^7(x + 3)^6(16x^2 + 26x + 4)$

27. $\dfrac{(2 + x^2 + x^4) \cdot 0 - 2(2x + 4x^3)}{(2 + x^2 + x^4)^2} = \dfrac{-4x - 8x^3}{(2 + x^2 + x^4)^2}$

29. $\dfrac{\ln x \cdot 1 - x \cdot \dfrac{1}{x}}{(\ln x)^2} = \dfrac{(\ln x) - 1}{(\ln x)^2}$

31. $\dfrac{(x + 1)(2x) - (x^2 - 1)(1)}{(x + 1)^2} = 1$

33. $\dfrac{(x - 1) \cdot 1 - (x + 1) \cdot 1}{(x - 1)^2} = -\dfrac{2}{(x - 1)^2}$

35. $\dfrac{e^{x+1} \cdot 2x - x^2 \cdot e^{x+1}}{(e^{x+1})^2} = \dfrac{x(2 - x)}{e^{x+1}}$

37. $\dfrac{(x^4 - \pi x)(1) - (x + \pi)(4x^3 - \pi)}{(x^4 - \pi x)^2} = \dfrac{-3x^4 - 4\pi x^3 + \pi^2}{(x^4 - \pi x)^2}$

39. $\dfrac{(e^x - e)^4 \cdot e^x - e^x \cdot 4(e^x - e)^3 \cdot e^x}{(e^x - e)^8} = \dfrac{e^x(-3e^x - e)}{(e^x - e)^5}$

41. $\dfrac{(x^5 + 1)^5 \cdot 1 - x \cdot 5(x^5 + 1)^4 \cdot 5x^4}{(x^5 + 1)^{10}} = \dfrac{1 - 24x^5}{(x^5 + 1)^6}$

43. $\dfrac{(3 + x) \cdot x^{-1/2} - 2x^{1/2} \cdot 1}{(3 + x)^2} = \dfrac{3 - x}{\sqrt{x}(3 + x)^2}$

45. $\dfrac{(e^{2x} - e)(2e^{2x}) - (e^{2x} + e)(2e^{2x})}{(e^{2x} - e)^2} = \dfrac{-4e^{2x+1}}{(e^{2x} - e)^2}$

47. $\dfrac{(2x^2 + x) \cdot 4x^3 - (x^4 - 1)(4x + 1)}{(2x^2 + x)^2} = \dfrac{4x^5 + 3x^4 + 4x + 1}{(2x^2 + x)^2}$

49. $\dfrac{1}{\dfrac{e^x}{e^x + 1}}\left(\dfrac{(e^x + 1) \cdot e^x - e^x \cdot e^x}{(e^x + 1)^2}\right) = \dfrac{1}{e^x + 1}$

51. $\dfrac{\ln x(x \cdot e^x + e^x \cdot 1) - xe^x \cdot \dfrac{1}{x}}{(\ln x)^2} = \dfrac{e^x(\ln x(x + 1) - 1)}{(\ln x)^2}$

53. $\tfrac{40}{3}$

55. $y = -x + 7$

57. $(1, 0)$ and $(e^2, 4/e^2)$

59. $\dfrac{47\pi}{3}(\approx 49.22)$ in.^{2}/in.

61. $y = -\tfrac{1}{10}x - \tfrac{11}{10}$

63. Both sides of the equation are equal to $16x^3(4 - x)^{-5}$

65. $10 - e^{-2}(\approx 9.865)$ ft/sec

CHAPTER 3 REVIEW, PAGE 161

1. (a) T, (b) T, (c) F, (d) F, (e) T, (f) T, (g) T, (h) F, (i) T, (j) (1) T (2) T (3) F (4) T (5) F (6) F (7) T, (k) T, (l) T, (m) F, (n) T, (o) F, (p) F, (q) F, (r) T, (s) T, (t) F, (u) T, (v) T, (w) F, (x) T, (y) F, (z) T, (aa) F, (bb) F, (cc) F, (dd) T

2. $8x - 1$

3. $-10x + 2$

4. $-\dfrac{3}{(x-3)^2}$

5. $-\dfrac{5}{(x-2)^2}$

6. $2x - \dfrac{1}{x^2}$

7. $\dfrac{2 - x^2}{(x^2 + 2)^2}$

8. $-25,\ y = -25x + 25$

9. $-4,\ y = -4x + 6$

10. $-\dfrac{3}{x^4}$

11. $x^4 + \dfrac{25}{x^6} + 5$

12. $-\dfrac{2}{x^3} - \dfrac{1}{4\sqrt[4]{x^3}}$

13. $x^{e-1} - \dfrac{e^x}{e}$

14. $4x - 7$

15. $5x^4 - 2x + \dfrac{1}{2\sqrt{x^3}} - \dfrac{1}{x^2}$

16. $50x - 25$

17. $-\dfrac{2(3x^2 + 1)}{(x^3 + x)^2}$

18. $e^{1 + \frac{1}{2}x} + 2xe^{1 - x^2}$

19. $\dfrac{e}{1 + ex}$

20. $7(3x^3 - x)^6(9x^2 - 1) + \dfrac{2}{(10x)^{4/5}}$

21. $40x^3(2x^4 - 6)^4 - \left(\dfrac{x}{\sqrt{3} + 1}\right)^{\sqrt{3}}$

22. $(x^2 + 1)^3 \cdot 4(x^2 - 1)^3 \cdot 2x + (x^2 - 1)^4 \cdot 3(x^2 + 1)^2 \cdot 2x$
    $= 2x(x^2 + 1)^2(x^2 - 1)^3(7x^2 + 1)$

23. $(x^3 + x)^2 \cdot 5(x^3 - x)^4(3x^2 - 1) + (x^3 - x)^5$
    $\cdot 2(x^3 + x)(3x^2 + 1)$
    $= (x^3 + x)(x^3 - x)^4(21x^5 + 6x^3 - 7x)$

24. $x(-5)(x^2 + 1)^{-6}(2x) + (x^2 + 1)^{-5} \cdot 1 = \dfrac{-9x^2 + 1}{(x^2 + 1)^6}$

25. $x^4 \cdot e^{x^4} \cdot 4x^3 + e^{x^4} \cdot 4x^3 = 4x^3 e^{x^4}(x^4 + 1)$

26. $\dfrac{(x^2 - 1)\left(\dfrac{1}{x^2 - 1}\right)(2x) - (\ln(x^2 - 1))(2x)}{(x^2 - 1)^2}$
    $= \dfrac{2x(1 - \ln(x^2 - 1))}{(x^2 - 1)^2}$

27. $\dfrac{(x^4 - x^2)(4x^3 + 2x) - (x^4 + x^2)(4x^3 - 2x)}{(x^4 - x^2)^2}$
    $= -\dfrac{4x^5}{(x^4 - x^2)^2}$

28. $\dfrac{(1 - x^3)(4x^3) - (x^4 + 4)(-3x^2)}{(1 - x^3)^2} = \dfrac{-x^6 + 4x^3 + 12x^2}{(1 - x^3)^2}$

29. $4\left(\dfrac{x + 2}{x - 4}\right)^3 \left(\dfrac{(x - 4)(1) - (x + 2)(1)}{(x - 4)^2}\right) = \dfrac{-24(x + 2)^3}{(x - 4)^5}$

30. $2\left(\dfrac{x^2 - 1}{x + 1}\right)\left(\dfrac{(x + 1)(2x) - (x^2 - 1)(1)}{(x + 1)^2}\right) = 2(x - 1)$

31. $\dfrac{9(\ln(\ln x))^8}{x \ln x}$

32. $-1/e^x$

33. $\dfrac{1}{4\sqrt{x}\sqrt{1 + \sqrt{x}}}$

34. (a) -1, (b) no slope, (c) 2, (d) 2

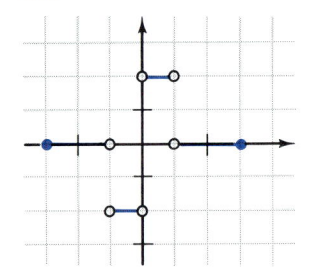

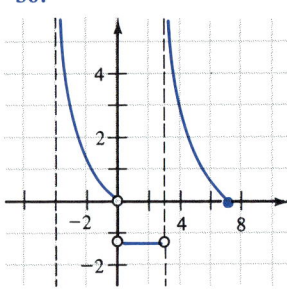

35.

36.

37. 10

38. 192

39. $\dfrac{13}{2}$

40. $\left(\dfrac{\sqrt{3}}{3}, \dfrac{3\sqrt{3}}{16}\right), \left(-\dfrac{\sqrt{3}}{3}, -\dfrac{3\sqrt{3}}{16}\right)$

41. $y = \dfrac{1}{e}x$

42. $(1, -1),\ (3, 9)$

43. (a) $4x^6$, (b) $8x^7$

44. (a) 144 ft, (b) 96 ft/sec

45. (a) 120 ft, (b) $43\frac{1}{3}$ ft/sec, (c) $5\frac{5}{27}$ ft/sec^2

46. (a) 32 ft, (b) -16 ft/sec, (c) -32 ft/sec^2, (d) 36 ft, (e) -48 ft/sec

47. 150

48. $a = -4,\ b = 8,\ c = 4$

49. $\dfrac{xc' - c}{x^2},\ \dfrac{x^2c'' - 2xc' + 2c}{x^3}$

50. (a) \$93.30, (b) \$93.33

51. (a) $\dfrac{dV}{dh} = \dfrac{\pi}{3}(r_1^2 + r_1 r_2 + r_2^2)$,
    (b) $\dfrac{dV}{dr_1} = \dfrac{\pi h}{3}(2r_1 + r_2)$

52. (a) 18.93 cm^2/cm, (b) 19.09 cm^2/cm, (c) 19.23 cm^2/cm, (d) 19.25 cm^2/cm, (e) 19.25 cm^2/cm

53. An example is

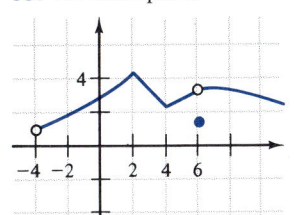

54. 0

13. $\dfrac{y - 8x^3}{3y^2 - x}$

15. $\dfrac{-y(y + x \ln y)}{x(x + y \ln x)}$

17. $\dfrac{(x - y)^{3/4}}{1 + (x - y)^{3/4}}$

19. $\dfrac{-(3x^2 + 4xy^2 + y)}{4x^2y + x}$

21. $ye^x + y \ln y$

23. 1

25. $\tfrac{1}{3}$

27. $-e$

29. -1

31. $y = -\tfrac{3}{4}x + \tfrac{13}{2}$

33. $y = -2x - 1$

35. $\dfrac{3y^2 - x^2}{9y^3} = -\dfrac{4}{9y^3}$

37. $-\dfrac{y}{4x^2}$

39. $\dfrac{90y^2 - 6}{(3y^2 + 1)^5}$

CHAPTER 4

PROBLEM SET 4.1, PAGE 169

1. 6

3. $48x^2 - e^2(e - 1)x^{e-2} + 1$

5. $\dfrac{12}{x^5} - \dfrac{12}{x^4} + \dfrac{1}{x^3}$

7. $36/e^{6x}$

9. $-5/x^2$

11. $2592(6x - 5)^7$

13. $-18(x^2(-7)(x^3 - 7)^{-8}(3x^2) + (x^3 - 7)^{-7}(2x))$
$= \dfrac{18x(19x^3 + 14)}{(x^3 - 7)^8}$

15. $3 + 2 \ln x$

17. $x(-\tfrac{1}{2})(x^2 + 4)^{-3/2}(2x) + (x^2 + 4)^{-1/2}(1) = \dfrac{4}{(x^2 + 4)^{3/2}}$

19. $-\dfrac{36}{(3x + 1)^3}$

21. $\dfrac{(1 + x^3)^2(-6x^2) - (1 - 2x^3)(2)(1 + x^3)(3x^2)}{(1 + x^3)^4}$
$= \dfrac{6x^2(x^3 - 2)}{(1 + x^3)^3}$

23. $-1/x^2$

25. $\tfrac{1}{4}$

27. 2

29. $-\tfrac{1}{96}$

31. $2r^{-3} - \tfrac{3}{16}r^{-7/4}$

33. $29{,}160(3x - 7)^2$

35. $-\dfrac{6}{(x + 1)^4}$

39. -3 and 5

41. 13

43. 0.1

PROBLEM SET 4.2, PAGE 176

1. $\dfrac{16x}{9y}$

3. $-\dfrac{\sqrt{y}}{\sqrt{x}}$

5. $-\dfrac{y}{2x}$

7. $\dfrac{1 - e^{3x}}{e^{3y}}$

9. $\dfrac{1 - 4x^3}{4y^3 - 1}$

11. $\dfrac{2xy}{1 + 3y^3}$

41. $3x^{3x}(1 + \ln x)$

43. $(\ln x)^x \left(\dfrac{1}{\ln x} + \ln(\ln x) \right)$

45. $e^x x^{e^x}\left(\dfrac{1}{x} + \ln x\right)$

47. $\dfrac{1}{xe^y}$

49. At $(0,0)$ the slopes are $\tfrac{3}{4}$ and $-\tfrac{4}{3}$

51. $\dfrac{-2xC^3}{3x^2C^2 - 4C^3}$

53. $e^{2At}(A - I)^2$

PROBLEM SET 4.3, PAGE 187

1. -6

3. $\tfrac{1}{20}$ ft/sec

5. 0.0013 in./sec

7. $\dfrac{186}{\sqrt{369}}$ (≈ 9.683) mph

9. 4.5 ft/sec

11. $3\tfrac{1}{4}$ ft/sec

13. $\dfrac{9\sqrt{5}}{5}$ (≈ 4.025) ft/sec

15. $\dfrac{8}{25\pi}$ (≈ 0.1019) ft/sec

17. $-\sqrt{3}$ (≈ -1.732) in./sec

19. $\dfrac{\sqrt{3}}{5}$ (≈ 0.3464) cm/sec

21. Decreasing at 2 cm/min

23. $\dfrac{\pi}{320}$ (≈ 0.0098) m/sec

CHAPTER 4 REVIEW, PAGE 188

1. (a) T, **(b)** F, **(c)** F, **(d)** T, **(e)** T, **(f)** F, **(g)** T, **(h)** T, **(i)** T, **(j)** T, **(k)** T, **(l)** F, **(m)** T, **(n)** T, **(o)** F, **(p)** F

2. $60x^4 + \tfrac{1}{4}x^{-3/2}$

3. $\dfrac{90}{x^7} + \dfrac{4}{9x^{7/3}}$

4. $9e^{3x}$

5. $-\dfrac{1}{x^2}$

6. $10e^x(1+e^x)^8(1+10e^x)$

7. $-\dfrac{12}{(x+3)^3}$

8. $e^{e^x+x}(1+e^x)$

9. $\dfrac{-1-\ln x}{(x \ln x)^2}$

10. $\dfrac{-e}{x^2}$

11. $\dfrac{xe^x - e^x}{x^2} + \dfrac{e^x}{x} + e^x \ln x$

12. $4x^3 e^{x^4}(4x^4+5)$

13. $-\dfrac{y^{1/3}}{x^{1/3}}$

14. $\dfrac{y^2 - xy}{xy - x^2} = \dfrac{y}{x}$

15. $\dfrac{-x^3 - 2xy^2}{2x^2 y + y^3}$

16. $\dfrac{e^{x-y} - e^x}{e^{x-y} - e^y}$

17. $e^{5y}(2 - x^4)$

18. $\dfrac{1+y^3}{3y^2}$

19. $\dfrac{y}{x}(e^x - \ln y)$

20. $\dfrac{e^x - \dfrac{1}{x}}{\dfrac{1}{y} - e^y}$

21. $\dfrac{\sqrt{x^x}}{2}(1 + \ln x)$

22. $5\left(\dfrac{3}{x}\right)^{5x}\left(\ln\left(\dfrac{3}{x}\right) - 1\right)$

23. $(e^x)^{\ln x}(1 + \ln x)$

24. $(\ln x)^{x^2}\left(\dfrac{x}{\ln x} + 2x \ln(\ln x)\right)$

25. $\dfrac{e^{1/2}}{2x^{3/2}}$

26. $\dfrac{-42y^5 - 6y}{(7y^6 + 3y^2)^3}$

27. $\dfrac{-1 + 2y^2}{4x^2 y^3}$

28. $\dfrac{3}{(2x+y)^3}$

29. $-122{,}880(4x-1)^{-6}$

30. $\dfrac{24}{(1-x)^5}$

31. $\dfrac{(1-2y)y}{(1+y)^5}$

33. $-\dfrac{7}{3}$

34. $\dfrac{8075}{\sqrt{14{,}125}}$ (≈ 67.94) mph

35. $(2,10)$

36. $\dfrac{9}{10}$ ft/min

37. Decreasing at 1950π (≈ 6126) cm³/sec

CHAPTER 5

PROBLEM SET 5.1, PAGE 196

1. Decreasing on $(-\infty, 1)$
3. Increasing on $(-\infty, -3)$ and on $(\tfrac{1}{2}, 4)$, decreasing on $(-3, \tfrac{1}{2})$ and on $(4, \infty)$
5. Increasing on $(-\infty, -1)$, on $(-1, 5)$, and on $(5, \infty)$
7. There are no intervals on which f is increasing or decreasing
9. Increasing at 0 and at 1, decreasing at -2 and at 3, neither at -1 and at 2
11. Neither at -2, at -1, at 0, at 1, at 2, and at 3
13. Increasing at 0, decreasing at -2 and at 2, neither at -1, at 1, and at 3
15. Increasing at -2 and at -1, decreasing at 1 and at 2, neither at 0 and at 3
17. Increasing at -4 and at 5, decreasing at 1.99
19. Increasing at -5 and at $\sqrt{4.5}$, decreasing at -0.1
21. Increasing at $\tfrac{9}{10}$, decreasing at -6 and at -1
23. Increasing at 0 and at $\ln 2$, decreasing at -2
25. Decreasing at $-\sqrt[3]{11}$, at 0, and at 10
27. Increasing at e^{-1} and at $\tfrac{1}{2}$, decreasing at 2
29. Increasing at $-\sqrt{11}$ and at 1, decreasing at -6
31. Decreasing at -5.2, at -1, and at 5
33. Increasing on $(1, \infty)$, decreasing on $(-\infty, 1)$
35. Increasing on R
37. Increasing on $(-\infty, -1)$ and on $(2, 4)$, decreasing on $(-1, 2)$ and on $(4, \infty)$
39. (a), (c), (d)

PROBLEM SET 5.2, PAGE 209

1. Relative maximum points: $(-5, 4)$ and $(0, 3)$; relative minimum point: $(-3, -2)$
3. Relative maximum points: $(2, 2)$ and $(5, 1)$; relative minimum points: $(0, -3)$ and $(4, -4)$
5. Relative maximum points: $(-1, -1)$, $(1, 3)$, and $(4, 0)$; relative minimum points: $(-4, 0)$, $(-3, 1)$, and $(3, -3)$
7. $(3, 12)$ is a relative maximum point
9. $(\ln 3, 3(\ln 3) - 3)$ is a relative maximum point
11. $(-3, 20)$ is a relative maximum point, $(1, -12)$ is a relative minimum point
13. $(3, \tfrac{9}{2} - 6 \ln 2)$ is a relative minimum point
15. No relative extreme points
17. $(0, 1)$ is a relative maximum point, $(\sqrt{6}, -8)$ and $(-\sqrt{6}, -8)$ are relative minimum points
19. $(2, 1)$ is a relative maximum point, $(-1, 4)$ is a relative minimum point
21. $(\tfrac{7}{3}, \tfrac{1}{3} e^7)$ is a relative maximum point
23. $(\tfrac{7}{2}, -4)$ is a relative maximum point
25. $(0, 0)$ is a relative maximum point, $(1, -2)$ is a relative minimum point
27. $(-3, 20)$ is a relative maximum point, $(0, -25)$ is a relative minimum point

29. $(1, e^{1/2})$ is a relative maximum point, $(-2, -2/e)$ is a relative minimum point
31. $(-5, -\frac{1}{130})$ is a relative maximum point
33. $t = 1/R$

■ PROBLEM SET 5.3, PAGE 218
1. Concave down on $(-\infty, \infty)$
3. Concave up on $(-4, -2)$ and on $(2, \infty)$; concave down on $(-2, 2)$
5. There are no intervals on which the graph of the function is concave up or concave down
7. Concave up on $(1, 3)$ and on $(5, \infty)$; concave down on $(-\infty, 1)$ and on $(3, 5)$
9. Concave up on $(1, \infty)$; concave down on $(-\infty, 1)$
11. Concave up on $(-\infty, -3)$ and on $(-1, \infty)$; concave down on $(-3, -1)$
13. Concave up at -1 and at 3; concave down at 1; neither at -2, 0, and 2
15. Concave up at $-2, -1, 0, 1, 2,$ and 3
17. Concave up at $-2, -1, 0,$ and 3; neither at 1 and 2
19. Concave up at -2 and 1; concave down at -1 and 2; neither at 0 and 3
21. Concave down at -4, 0, and 5
23. Concave up at $\frac{1}{2}$; concave down at $\frac{4}{5}$ and 1
25. Concave up at 17; concave down at -2 and 0
27. Concave up at -10, 0, and 100
29. Concave up at $\ln 8$; concave down at -1 and $e - 1$
31. Concave up at -5 and 6; concave down at $\sqrt{3} + \pi$
33. Concave up on $(-\infty, \infty)$
35. Concave up on $(-\infty, -3)$; concave down on $(-3, \infty)$
37. $(-1, -9)$ is a relative minimum point
39. $(1, 6)$ is a relative maximum point, $(-1, 2)$ is a relative minimum point
41. $(-2, 8)$ and $(2, 8)$ are relative minimum points
43. $\left(\frac{1}{2e}, \frac{1}{2e}\right)$ is a relative maximum point
45. $(-1, -2)$ is a relative minimum point, $(0, 2)$ is a relative maximum point
47. $(0, -2)$ is a relative maximum point, $(2, -e^2 - e^{-2})$ is a relative minimum point
49. No relative extreme points
51. $(-\frac{1}{2}, \frac{5}{6})$ and $(3, 9)$ are relative maximum points, $(-3, -45)$ and $(\frac{3}{2}, -\frac{9}{2})$ are relative minimum points
53. $(3, 7)$ is a relative maximum point
57. (d)

■ PROBLEM SET 5.4, PAGE 227
1. $(0, -1)$
3. $(-1, -2), (0, 0),$ and $(1, 2)$
5. $(-1, 1)$ and $(4, 1)$
7. $(-2, 0), (0, 0),$ and $(2, 0)$
9. $(0, 0)$
11. No inflection points
13. $(2, -7)$
15. $(1, -5)$ and $(-1, -5)$
17. $(-3, 5)$
19. $(-\sqrt{3}/3, 7\sqrt{3}/54), (0, 0),$ and $(\sqrt{3}/3, -7\sqrt{3}/54)$
21. $(\frac{1}{2}, e^{-2})$
23. $(e^{3/2}, -\frac{3}{2}e^{-3/2})$
25. $(-6, -6/e^2)$
27. $a = -6$ and $b = 9$
29. -3 and 5

■ PROBLEM SET 5.5, PAGE 239
1. $x = -4$
3. $x = \ln 7$
5. $x = -2$ and $x = 2$
7. $x = -3$ and $x = \dfrac{\ln 3}{4}$
9. No vertical asymptotes
11. No horizontal asymptote
13. $y = 0$
15. $y = \frac{1}{2}$
17. $y = \frac{1}{10}$
19. Vertical: $x = \frac{3}{2}, x = -\frac{4}{3}$; horizontal: $y = \frac{1}{6}$
21. An example is $y = \dfrac{2x^2}{(x+1)(x-3)}$

23.

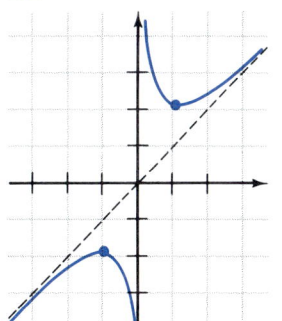

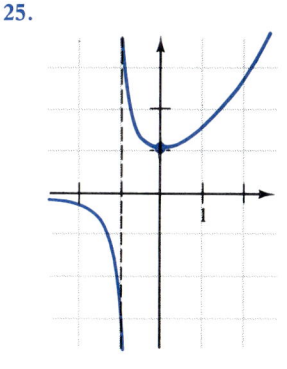

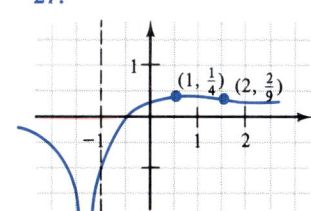

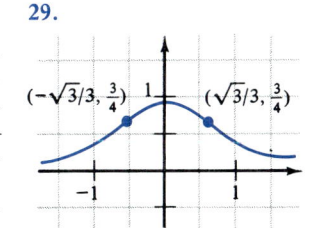

25.

27.

29.

31.

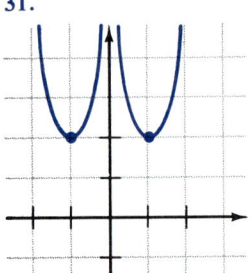

33. $(0, -\frac{1}{9})$

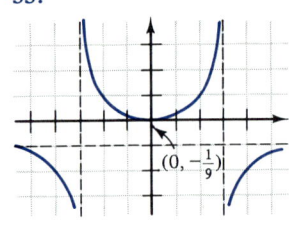

35.

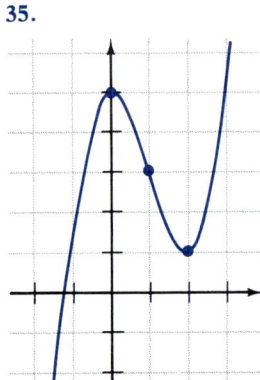

37.

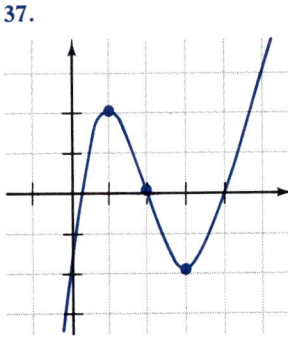

39. $(1, \frac{2}{3})$, $(-1, -\frac{2}{3})$

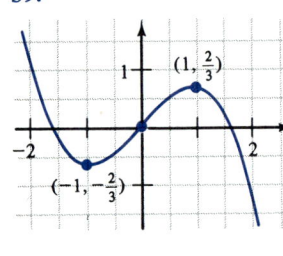

41. $(\frac{2}{3}, \frac{16}{27})$

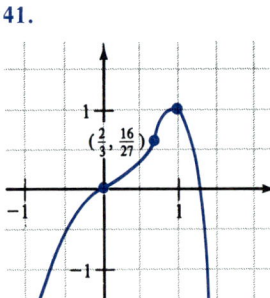

43. $(0, \ln 4)$

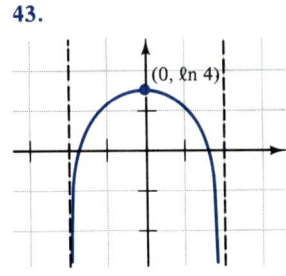

45. $(-2, 4e^{-2})$, $-2 - \sqrt{2}$, $-2 + \sqrt{2}$

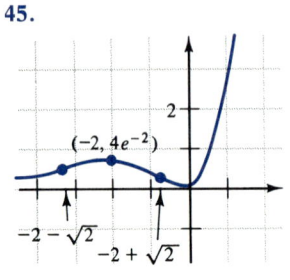

47. $(1/e, -1/e)$

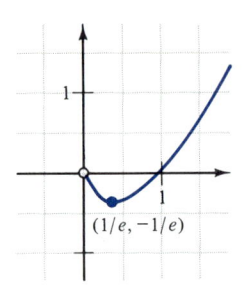

49. $(\sqrt{2}/2, \sqrt{2}e^{-1/2}/2)$, $(\sqrt{3}/2, \sqrt{3}e^{-3/4}/2)$, $(-\sqrt{3}/2, -\sqrt{3}e^{-3/4}/2)$, $(-\sqrt{2}/2, -\sqrt{2}e^{-1/2}/2)$

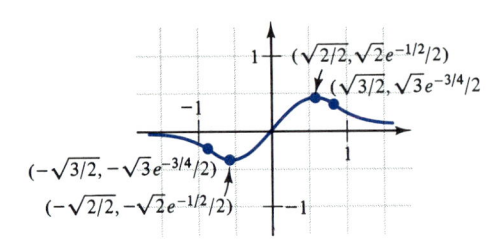

51. (c)

PROBLEM SET 5.6, PAGE 246

1. (a) $(1, -2)$ is the absolute minimum point, $(-1, 5)$ is the absolute maximum point
(b) No absolute extreme points
(c) $(5, -2)$ is the absolute minimum point, $(6, 2)$ is the absolute maximum point

3. (a) $(1, -3)$ is the absolute minimum point, $(0, 0)$ is the absolute maximum point
(b) No absolute minimum point, $(4, 3)$ is the absolute maximum point
(c) $(6, -2)$ is the absolute minimum point, no absolute maximum point

5. $(0, 0)$ is the absolute minimum point, no absolute maximum point

7. $(-\frac{5}{2}, \frac{175}{6})$ is the absolute maximum point, no absolute minimum point

9. $(-2, 4e^{-2})$ is the absolute maximum point, no absolute minimum point

11. $(1, 1)$ is the absolute maximum point, no absolute minimum point

13. $(0, 1)$ is the absolute maximum point, no absolute minimum point

15. $(-\frac{8}{3}, -\frac{16}{9}\sqrt{3})$

17. $(-\pi, -7\pi - 3)$ is the absolute minimum point, $(\pi, 7\pi - 3)$ is the absolute maximum point

19. $(-\ln 2, 2\frac{1}{2})$ is the absolute minimum point, $(-\ln 4, 4\frac{1}{4})$ is the absolute maximum point

21. $(2, -32)$ is the absolute minimum point, $(-2, 32)$ is the absolute maximum point

23. (3,1) is the absolute minimum point, $(1, 1+(-2)^{2/3})$ and $(5, 1+2^{2/3})$ are the absolute maximum points
25. (3,6) is the absolute minimum point, (0.5,18.5) and (18,18.5) are the absolute maximum points
27. $(e^4, 16/e^4)$ is the absolute minimum point, $(e^2, 4/e^2)$ is the absolute maximum point
29. $(e^{-1}, e^{-1/e})$

PROBLEM SET 5.7, PAGE 259
1. 15 and 15
3. 19 and 57
5. $\sqrt{3}/3$
7. 150 yd by 300 yd
9. 105 ft by 165 ft
11. $3\sqrt{3} (\approx 5.196)$ ft by $3\sqrt{3} (\approx 5.196)$ ft by $\frac{3}{2}\sqrt{3} (\approx 2.598)$ ft
13. $2e^{-1/2} (\approx 1.213)$
15. $75\sqrt{3} (\approx 129.9)$ in.^{2}
17. $x = 6 + \sqrt{3} (\approx 7.732)$ ft and $y = \dfrac{15 - 3\sqrt{3}}{2} (\approx 4.902)$ ft
19. (1,1)
21. For a minimum, use 24 cm for the square and 27 cm for the rectangle; there is no maximum
23. Maximum at $r_1 = 3$; minimum at $r_1 = 0$
25. 22 cm by 33 cm; minimum area = 726 cm^2
27. $6\sqrt{7}/7 (\approx 2.268)$ miles from A
29. Row directly to B
31. $11 - 4\sqrt{2} (\approx 5.343)$ mi
33. $10\sqrt{3}/3 (\approx 5.774)$ mi
37. $600
39. 2 in.

PROBLEM SET 5.8, PAGE 268
1. 400
3. 80
5. $7
7. 450
9. $300
11. $336
13. 36, $18
15. $73
17. 20
19. (a) $-0.005x^2 + x$, (b) $0.50, (c) $-0.005x^2 + 0.84x - 20$, (d) $0.58
21. 225
23. $3.50
27. 76
29. $1.95

CHAPTER 5 REVIEW, PAGE 270
1. (a) F, (b) T, (c) T, (d) F, (e) F, (f) F, (g) T, (h) T, (i) T, (j) F, (k) F, (l) T, (m) T, (n) F, (o) T, (p) F, (q) T, (r) T, (s) F, (t) T, (u) F, (v) T, (w) T, (x) T, (y) F, (z) F, (aa) F, (bb) T, (cc) F, (dd) F, (ee) T, (ff) T, (gg) F, (hh) F, (ii) T, (jj) T, (kk) T, (ll) F, (mm) T, (nn) F
2. h

3. (a) yes, (b) yes, (c) no, (d) yes, (e) no, (f) no, (g) yes, (h) yes, (i) yes, (j) yes, (k) yes, (l) yes, (m) yes, (n) no, (o) yes, (p) yes, (q) no, (r) yes
4. F
5. (0,0) is a relative minimum point, (2,4) is a relative maximum point
6. No extreme points
7. (1,18) is a relative minimum point, $(-1,22)$ is a relative maximum point
8. $(\frac{1}{3}, 9)$ is a relative minimum point, $(-1, 1)$ is a relative maximum point
9. $(\frac{1}{3}, -\frac{2}{9}\sqrt{3})$ is a relative minimum point, (0,0) is a relative maximum point
10. $(1/e, -2/e)$ is a relative minimum point
11. $(6, -1/e^6)$ is a relative minimum point
12. $(e, 1/e)$ is a relative maximum point
13. (2,7)
14. (0,0) and $(2,-4)$
15. $(\sqrt{3}/3, \frac{3}{4})$ and $(-\sqrt{3}/3, \frac{3}{4})$
16. (0,0)
17. $(e, 1)$
18. $(-\frac{1}{3}, -\frac{1}{3}e^{-2})$
19. k
20. (a)
21. (b)
22. (a)
23. (c)
24. (b)
25. (a) $f'(x)$, positive; (b) $f''(x)$, negative; (c) $f'(1)$, zero, $f''(1)$, positive; (d) $f''(x)$, changes sign; (e) $f(x)$, an x-intercept

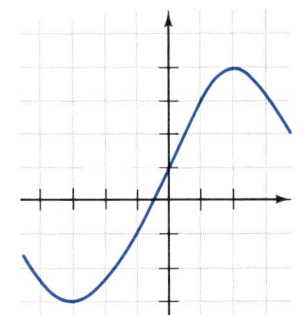

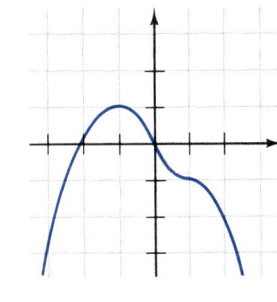

26.
27.

28. (c)
29. $(-6, -54)$ is the absolute minimum point, $(-3, 27)$ is the absolute maximum point
30. $(5, -1)$ is the absolute minimum point, (3,1) is the absolute maximum point
31. $(-4, -\frac{1}{6})$ is the absolute minimum point, no absolute maximum point
32. (2,3) and $(-2, 3)$ are the absolute minimum points, (0,5) is the absolute maximum point

33. $(e, 0)$ is the absolute minimum point, $(1,1)$ is the absolute maximum point

34. $(-\ln 2, -2\ln 2)$ is the absolute minimum point, $(1, 1/e)$ is the absolute maximum point

35. $(\frac{1}{2}, 1/\sqrt{2e})$ is the absolute maximum point

36. $(0, \ln 2)$ is the absolute minimum point, no absolute maximum point

37. 1   **38.** (c)

39. (a) 0, 1, and 2;
(b) (0,1) and (2,1) are the absolute minimum points, (4,5) is the absolute maximum point

40. $y = -3x - 4$

41. Relative minimum point at $(2, f(2))$, relative maximum point at $(0, f(0))$

42. $a = -1$, $b = -6$

43. (a) (9), (b) (1), (c) (5), (d) (8), (e) (6), (f) (7), (g) (2), (h) (4), (i) (10), (j) (3)

44.

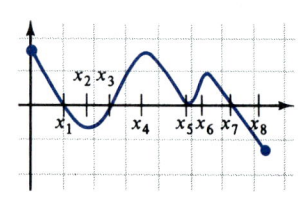

Graph of f'

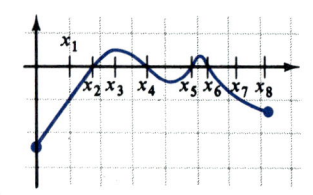

Graph of f''

45. (a) $[-8, -6) \cup (-5, 16]$, (b) $[-4, 6]$, (c) 3, (d) 0, (e) -3, (f) -2, (g) -1, (h) no, (i) yes, (j) yes, (k) undefined, (l) greater than zero, (m) equal to zero, (n) less than zero, (o) undefined, (p) greater than or equal to zero, (q) greater than zero, (r) equal to zero, (s) undefined, (t) equal to zero

46. $x = 10$, $y = 40$ **47.** $\sqrt[3]{2}$

49. (e)

50. $125,000/\pi$ ($\approx 39,790$) ft^2

51. 20 ft $\times$ 20 ft $\times$ 5 ft

52. Radius = 4 in., height = 7 in.

53. 4   **54.** $1600   **55.** 5

56. 250   **57.** 250   **58.** 290

59. 24 floors   **60.** 850   **61.** 50

62. (a) No vertical asymptotes; (b) $x = 3$, $x = -3$; (c) $x = 4$; (d) $x = \ln 4$, $x = e^5$

63. (a) $y = \frac{4}{3}$, (b) $y = 0$, (c) no horizontal asymptote

64.

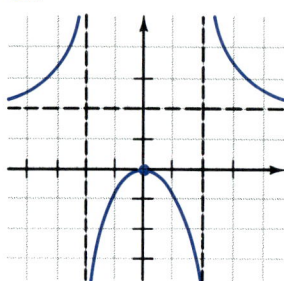

65.

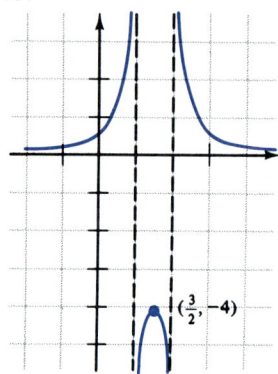

66.

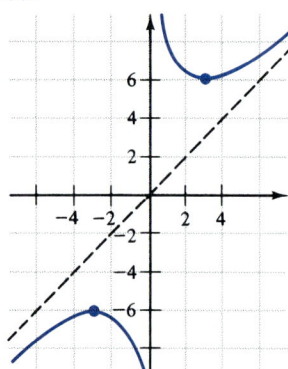

67.

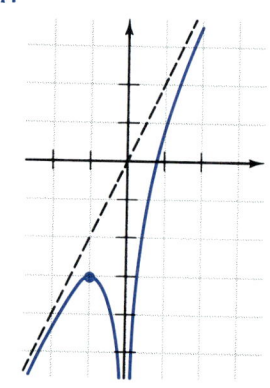

68.

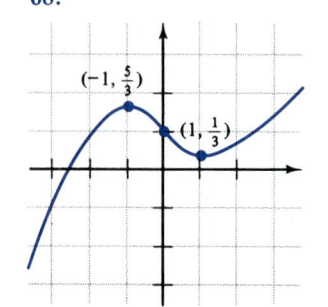

69.

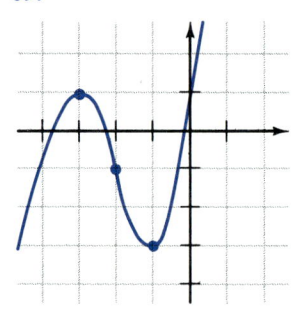

ANSWERS TO SELECTED PROBLEMS

70. (graph with point $(\tfrac{2}{3}, \tfrac{44}{27})$)

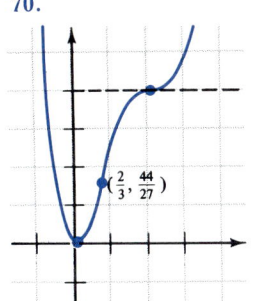

71. (graph with points $(2, -16)$ and $(3, -27)$)

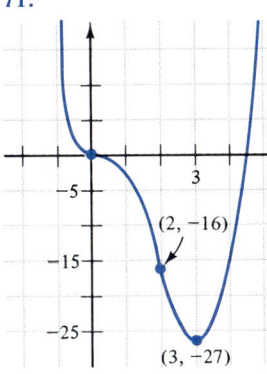

72. (graph)

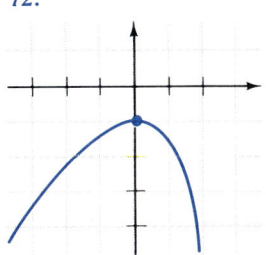

73. (graph)

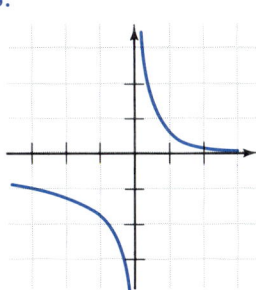

74. (graph)

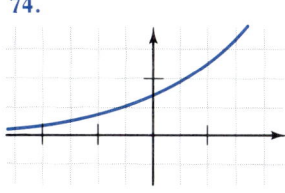

75. (graph with points $(-1, \ln 2)$ and $(1, \ln 2)$)

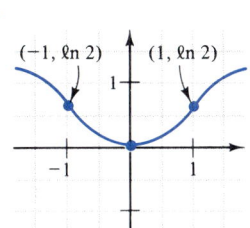

76. (graph with point $(e^{1/2}, \tfrac{3}{2e^{1/2}})$)

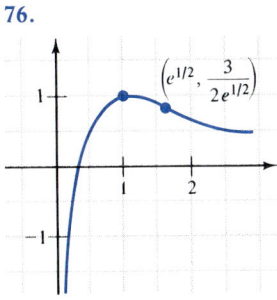

77. (graph with points $(1, e^{-2})$ and $(\tfrac{1}{2}, \tfrac{1}{4e})$)

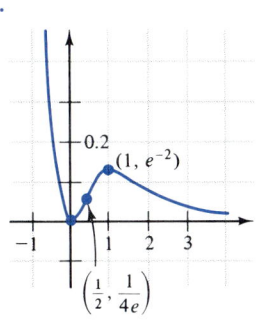

CHAPTER 6

PROBLEM SET 6.1, PAGE 287

1. $\dfrac{x^8}{8} + C$ **3.** $\dfrac{3x^{5/3}}{5} + C$ **5.** $\dfrac{4x^{5/4}}{5} + C$

7. $\dfrac{x^{-2}}{-2} + C$ **8.** $5x + C$ **11.** $\dfrac{3x^7}{7} + C$

13. $\dfrac{1}{8x^8} + C$ **15.** $x^\pi + C$ **17.** $\dfrac{-3x^{2/3}}{4} + C$

19. $\dfrac{-x^{e+1}}{e^2 + e} + C$ **21.** $8e^x + C$ **23.** $-4\ln|x| + C$

25. $-\dfrac{1}{28x^7} - 16x + C$

27. $\dfrac{x^6}{30} + \dfrac{1}{20x^4} + \dfrac{5x^2}{2} - 5x + C$

29. $-\dfrac{1}{x} - \dfrac{1}{2}\ln|x| + e^x + C$

31. $3x^3 - 12x^2 + 16x + C$

33. $x^3 + \dfrac{4}{x} + C$

35. $y = 3x^3 - 2x^2 + x + 3$

37. $y = \dfrac{x^3}{6} - 2x + \dfrac{3}{2}$ **39.** $1325

41. $-x^3 + 3x^2 + 2880x - 500$

43. 112 ft

PROBLEM SET 6.2, PAGE 293

1. $\dfrac{(x^4 - 2)^5}{5} + C$ **3.** $\dfrac{(3 + \tfrac{1}{3}x^3)^3}{3} + C$

5. $\dfrac{1}{-3(2x^3 + x)^3} + C$ **7.** $\dfrac{(\ln(2x))^8}{8} + C$

9. $\dfrac{(4x + 5)^8}{32} + C$ **11.** $\dfrac{(x^4 + 2)^{3/2}}{6} + C$

13. $\tfrac{5}{3}(e^{2x+1})^{3/2} + C$

15. $-\tfrac{2}{27}(3 - (x^3 + 1)^3)^{3/2} + C$

17. $-3\ln|x + 1| + C$ **19.** $\ln|x^2 - 2x + 1| + C$

21. $\tfrac{1}{7}\ln|x^7 + e^7| + C$ **23.** $\tfrac{1}{2}\ln|x^4 + x^2 + 1| + C$

25. $\tfrac{1}{3}\ln|1 + e^{3x}| + C$ **27.** $\dfrac{2}{\pi}\ln|x^\pi + \pi x| + C$

29. $3e^{x+1} + C$ **31.** $ex + C$

33. $e^{x^7 - 7x} + C$ **35.** $e^{ex + \ln x} + C$

37. $2e^{x/2} - \dfrac{1}{5e^{5x}} + C$ **39.** $\tfrac{1}{2}e^{2x} + e^{x-1} + C$

41. $-\dfrac{1}{3e^{x^3}} + 2e^{\sqrt{x}} + C$ **43.** $-\tfrac{1}{2}e^{(1/2)x^4 - x^2} + C$
45. $e^{1 + \ln x} + \ln|1 + e^{-x}| + C$
47. $y = \ln|x^3 - 2x| - e^{1-x} - \tfrac{1}{6}(2x^2 - 1)^{3/2} + 2$

PROBLEM SET 6.3, PAGE 301
1. 9   **3.** 6   **5.** 0
7. $10\tfrac{2}{3}$ **9.** $-\tfrac{8}{17}$ **11.** $-\dfrac{\sqrt{3}}{8}$
13. $\tfrac{1}{3}\left(1 - \dfrac{1}{e^3}\right)$ **15.** $e^4 - e^2$ **17.** $\ln 2$
19. $2 \ln 7$ **21.** $\ln 6$ **23.** 5
25. $\dfrac{\ln 6}{-2}$ **27.** $7\tfrac{1}{3}$ ft/sec   **29.** \$637.50
31. Increasing $\dfrac{8}{15\pi}$ (≈ 0.1698) ft/min

PROBLEM SET 6.4, PAGE 312
1. 30   **3.** 8   **5.** $7\tfrac{1}{3}$
7. $\tfrac{1}{4}$ **9.** $\dfrac{-1}{e^e} + 2e + 1$ **11.** 18
13. $7\pi - \pi^2$ **15.** $\ln \tfrac{5}{2}$ **17.** $2\tfrac{2}{3}$
19. 12   **21.** $e + \dfrac{1}{e^3}$ **23.** $19\tfrac{1}{2}$
25. $10\tfrac{2}{3}$ **27.** $21\tfrac{1}{3}$ **29.** $4 - 3\ln 3$
31. 15   **33.** $7\ln 7 + \tfrac{1}{2}e^2 - 13\tfrac{1}{2}$
35. $1\tfrac{1}{2}$ **37.** $12\tfrac{4}{5}$
39. $\tfrac{4}{15}$ **41.** 101
43. The population increased by 500
45. Consumers' surplus = 8; producers' surplus = $42\tfrac{2}{3}$
47. Consumers' surplus = $50(\ln 50) - 49$; producers' surplus = $50(\ln 50) - 49$

PROBLEM SET 6.5, PAGE 321
1. 36π **3.** $\tfrac{16}{3}\pi$ **5.** $\pi \ln 3$
7. $\tfrac{16}{15}\pi$ **9.** 24.3π **11.** $\dfrac{\pi}{4}(e^{12} - e^8)$
13. $20\tfrac{2}{3}\pi$ **15.** 8π **17.** $\tfrac{1}{3}\pi r^2 h$
19. $\tfrac{68}{315}\pi$ **21.** 112π **23.** $108\tfrac{6}{7}\pi$
25. 8π **27.** 8π **29.** 6
31. π **33.** $6\sqrt{3} - 2$ **35.** $\dfrac{e - 1}{e^e - e}$
37. 0   **39.** \$68,200   **41.** \$259,000

43. 7π **45.** \$9804   **47.** \$13,848
49. \$356   **51.** \$4.00   **53.** \$53,413,000

CHAPTER 6 REVIEW, PAGE 323
1. (a) T, (b) T, (c) F, (d) T, (e) T, (f) F, (g) T, (h) T, (i) T, (j) F, (k) F, (l) F, (m) F, (n) T, (o) T, (p) T, (q) T, (r) T, (s) T, (t) T, (u) T, (v) F, (w) F, (x) T

2. $x^4 - x^3 + x^2 - x + C$ **3.** $\tfrac{2}{3}x^{3/2} - 2x^{1/2} + C$
4. $\tfrac{1}{4}(3x)^{4/3} + C$ **5.** $\dfrac{x^{4+e}}{4+e} + \dfrac{x^{1+\log 5}}{1 + \log 5} + C$
6. $\dfrac{x^3}{3} - 7x + 4\ln|x| + C$ **7.** $\dfrac{9x^4}{4} + 2x^3 + \dfrac{x^2}{2} + C$
8. $\dfrac{1}{9}\left(\dfrac{x^4}{4} + 4\right)^9 + C$ **9.** $\tfrac{1}{56}(x^7 - 7x)^8 + C$
10. $-\tfrac{1}{8}(1 + x^{4/3})^{-6} + C$ **11.** $-\tfrac{3}{10}(7 - 5x^2)^{2/3} + C$
12. $2\sqrt{1 + e^x} + C$ **13.** $\dfrac{(3 + \ln x)^2}{2} + C$
14. $e^x + \dfrac{x^{e+1}}{e+1} + e^e x + C$ **15.** $\tfrac{1}{5}\ln|2 + 5x| + C$
16. $\tfrac{1}{3}\ln|e^{x^3} + 7| + C$ **17.** $\ln|\ln x| + C$
18. $\tfrac{1}{7}(\ln(\ln x))^7 + C$ **19.** $-\tfrac{3}{5}e^{5-5x} - 2e^{-x} + C$
20. $4e^{x^{1/4}} + C$ **21.** $\ln|1 + e^x| + C$
22. $\tfrac{1}{4}(\ln(1 + x^2))^2 + C$ **23.** $-\dfrac{1}{e^x + 1} + C$
24. $\dfrac{-1}{e^x + e^{-x}} + C$
25. $-\tfrac{1}{9}(3 - (e^{3x} + 1)^2)^{3/2} + C$
26. 2   **27.** 0   **28.** $9\tfrac{1}{15}$
29. 97   **30.** $\ln 9$ **31.** $\tfrac{1}{2}\ln 5$
32. $18e^2 - 6$ **33.** $\tfrac{1}{3}(e^{-2} - e^{-9})$ **34.** $e^e - e$
35. 3   **36.** 1   **37.** $3\tfrac{5}{7}$
38. $2(e^2 - e)$ **39.** $\tfrac{4}{3}\pi^3$ **40.** 2
41. $4\tfrac{1}{2}$ **42.** $21\tfrac{1}{3}$ **43.** $6\tfrac{1}{3}$
44. $\tfrac{1}{3}(e^3 - 1)$ **45.** $\pi/7$ **46.** $\pi/4$
47. $\tfrac{8}{15}\pi$ **48.** 8π
49. $\dfrac{\pi}{8}(e^2 - e^{-2}) + \dfrac{\pi}{2}$
50. $\dfrac{\pi}{3}\ln 8$ **51.** $4\pi e$ **52.** 24π
53. 3π **54.** $\dfrac{14\pi}{3}$ **55.** $\tfrac{1}{3}$
56. 0   **57.** $-\dfrac{\ln 5}{4}$ **58.** $\tfrac{1}{2}\left(e - \dfrac{1}{e}\right)$

59. (a) [graph] **(b)** $-2\frac{1}{4}$ **(c)** $3\frac{1}{12}$

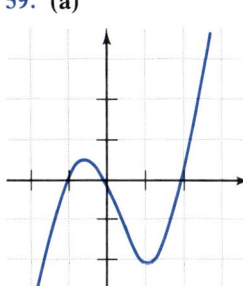

60. $\frac{2}{3}(x+1)^{3/2} + \frac{2}{3}x^{3/2} + C$ **61.** $\frac{4}{3}\pi r^3$
62. 12 **64.** $420,000 **65.** $3375
66. $150 **67.** $18\frac{1}{3}$ **68.** 2620
69. Consumers' surplus $= \frac{200}{3}$; producers' surplus $= 200$

CHAPTER 7

PROBLEM SET 7.1, PAGE 335

1. $\frac{2}{5}(x+6)^{5/2} - \frac{2}{3}(x+6)^{3/2} + C$
3. $\frac{1}{28}(2x-1)^{7/2} + \frac{1}{10}(2x-1)^{5/2} + \frac{1}{12}(2x-1)^{3/2} + C$
5. $\frac{2}{5}(4+x)^{5/2} - 32(4+x)^{1/2} + C$
7. $-4 + 25\ln\frac{11}{7}$ **9.** $e^x - \ln|e^x + 1| + C$
11. $\frac{3}{7}(24-x)^{7/3} - 18(24-x)^{4/3} + C$
13. $e - 2$
15. $\frac{5}{16}(x-3)^{16/5} + \frac{25}{11}(x-3)^{11/5} + 5(x-3)^{6/5} + C$
17. $-\frac{3}{2} + 3\ln 2$ **19.** $-\frac{1}{32}$
21. $\frac{4}{5}(5-(x-5)^{1/2})^{5/2} - \frac{20}{3}(5-(x-5)^{1/2})^{3/2} + C$
23. $\frac{2}{3}x^{3/2} - x + 2\sqrt{x} - 2\ln(1+\sqrt{x}) + C$
25. $51,835   **27.** $3\frac{1}{3}$

PROBLEM SET 7.2, PAGE 340

1. $-xe^{-x} - e^{-x} + C$
3. $\dfrac{x(1+x)^{201}}{201} - \dfrac{(1+x)^{202}}{(201)(202)} + C$
5. $\dfrac{-x(2+3x)^{-3}}{9} - \dfrac{(2+3x)^{-2}}{54} + C$
7. $\dfrac{x^2}{2}\ln(6x) - \dfrac{x^2}{4} + C$ **9.** $\dfrac{x^6\ln(7x)}{6} - \dfrac{x^6}{36} + C$
11. $x\ln(ex) - x + C$
13. $\dfrac{x^2}{3}(x^2+1)^{3/2} - \dfrac{2}{15}(x^2+1)^{5/2} + C$
15. $\dfrac{x^7}{7}e^{x^7-3} - \dfrac{1}{7}e^{x^7-3} + C$ **17.** $\dfrac{e^x}{1+x} + C$

19. $\frac{1}{2}x^2e^{2x} - \frac{1}{2}xe^{2x} + \frac{1}{4}e^{2x} + C$
21. $-\frac{1}{3}(x+1)^2(x-1)^{-3} - \frac{1}{3}(x+1)(x-1)^{-2} - \frac{1}{3}(x-1)^{-1} + C$
25. $x^4e^x - 4x^3e^x + 12x^2e^x - 24xe^x + 24e^x + C$
27. $\frac{1}{2}(\ln x)^2 + C$ **29.** $e^4 + 2e^2 - \dfrac{4}{e}$
31. $\pi(5e^3 - 2)$
33. $\bar{x} = \dfrac{4e^5+1}{5(e^5-1)}$, $\bar{y} = \dfrac{1}{4}(e^5+1)$

PROBLEM SET 7.3, PAGE 345

1. $\dfrac{1}{8}\ln\left|\dfrac{x}{5x+8}\right| + C$ **3.** $-\frac{1}{2}\ln|5-x^2| + C$
5. $-\dfrac{1}{e}\ln\left|\dfrac{e+\sqrt{e^2+x^2}}{x}\right| + C$
7. $\dfrac{1}{14\sqrt{3}}\ln\left|\dfrac{\sqrt{3}+t}{\sqrt{3}-t}\right| + C$
9. $-\dfrac{1}{4(2x-1)} + \frac{1}{4}\ln|2x-1| + C$
11. $4e^{-x/2}\left(-\dfrac{x}{2}-1\right) + C$
13. $\ln|e^{4t} - e^{-2t}| + C$
15. $\frac{1}{5}\ln|x + \frac{1}{5}\sqrt{25x^2-36}| + C$
17. $\frac{1}{6}(6x^2-1)^{1/2} + C$
19. $\dfrac{2}{3(\ln 2)^2}(-x(\ln 2) - 2)\sqrt{1 - x\ln 2} + C$
21. $\dfrac{2\sqrt{2}}{15}(3x^2 + 2\sqrt{6}x + 12)\sqrt{\sqrt{2}x - \sqrt{3}} + C$
23. $115\frac{79}{105}$
25. $e(\ln|\sqrt{3}e + 2e| - 1) = e\ln(\sqrt{3}+2)$
27. $7775   **29.** $\dfrac{\sqrt{5}}{2} + \dfrac{1}{4}\ln(2+\sqrt{5})$

PROBLEM SET 7.4, PAGE 351

1. (a) 12, (b) 12, (c) 12, (d) 12
3. (a) 1.3768, (b) 1.4054, (c) 1.3877, (d) $\ln 4 \approx 1.3863$
5. (a) -7.375, (b) -7.25, (c) -7.3333, (d) $-7\frac{1}{3}$
7. (a) -9.9456, (b) -9.8931, (c) -9.9293, (d) $\frac{5}{8}((5)^{4/5} - (41)^{4/5}) (\approx -9.9279)$
9. (a) 17.6916, (b) 17.6909, (c) 17.6914, (d) $-\frac{4}{5}((20)^{5/4} - (28)^{5/4}) (\approx 17.6914)$
11. (a) 2.5529, (b) 2.5297, (c) 2.5447, (d) $4(\ln 4) - 3 (\approx 2.5452)$
13. (a) 8, (b) 8, (c) 8, (d) 8

15. (a) 0, (b) 0, (c) 0, (d) 0
17. (a) 4.6921, (b) 4.8961, (c) 4.7609,
(d) $\dfrac{(\ln 6)^5 - (\ln 2)^5}{5} + \ln 3 \ (\approx 4.7600)$
19. 3.5392   **21.** 84.9133   **23.** 0.6570
25. (a) 50.9428, (b) 47.9314, (c) 49.3375,
(d) $16\pi \ (\approx 50.2655)$
27. 3.1416

PROBLEM SET 7.5, PAGE 358

1. $\dfrac{5 \ln 6}{4} \ (\approx 2.240)$ hr   **3.** $\dfrac{\ln 2}{0.04} \ (\approx 17.33)$ yr

5. $\dfrac{\ln 2}{0.0035} \ (\approx 198.0)$ yr   **7.** $\dfrac{\ln 2}{3} \ (\approx 0.2310)$

9. 225 yr   **11.** $\dfrac{16 \ln 1.6}{\ln 2.5} \ (\approx 8.207)$ hr

13. 8700 yr   **15.** 35.00 yr

17. $5 \ln 5 \ (\approx 8.047)$ sec   **19.** $\dfrac{100 \ln 4}{13} \ (\approx 10.66)$ min

21. $\dfrac{\ln \frac{221}{5}}{\ln 15} \ (\approx 1.399)$ **23.** 4200 yr

25. $\dfrac{\ln 4}{0.01} \ (\approx 138.6)$ wk   **27.** (a) 225 billion dollars

29. 1991

CHAPTER 7 REVIEW, PAGE 360

1. (a) T, (b) F, (c) T, (d) T, (e) F, (f) F, (g) T
2. $x + \pi \ln|x - \pi| + C$
3. $\frac{2}{9}(x-3)^{9/2} + \frac{12}{7}(x-3)^{7/2} + C$
4. $-\frac{2}{9}x^3(3 - x^3)^{3/2} - \frac{4}{45}(3 - x^3)^{5/2} + C$
5. $\dfrac{2x^{3/2}}{3}(\ln x) - \frac{4}{9}x^{3/2} + C$
6. $\frac{2}{75}(-5x - 16)\sqrt{8 - 5x} + C$
7. $2x^{1/2} - 2\ln(1 + x^{1/2}) + C$
8. $\frac{1}{4}x^4 e^{x^4} - \frac{1}{4}e^{x^4} + C$
9. $-\ln\left|\dfrac{\frac{1}{\sqrt{\pi}} + \sqrt{\frac{1}{\pi} + x^2}}{x}\right| + C$
10. $\dfrac{e^{ex}}{e^2}(ex - 1) + C$
11. $\dfrac{-x(1-x)^{e+1}}{e+1} - \dfrac{(1-x)^{e+2}}{(e+1)(e+2)} + C$
12. $\frac{6}{5}(x+2)^{5/2} + 2(x+2)^{1/2} + C$

13. $-\dfrac{1}{ex - 1} + \ln\left|\dfrac{x}{ex - 1}\right| + C$
14. $\ln x(\ln(\ln x) - 1) + C$
15. (a) 12.2069, (b) 12.2491, (c) 12.2210
16. (a) 0, (b) 0, (c) 0
17. (a) 1.5005, (b) 1.4800, (c) 1.4938
18. (a) 1.6098, (b) $\ln 5 \ (\approx 1.6094)$
19. $\dfrac{\ln 2}{0.5} \ (\approx 1.386)$ hr   **20.** 2887
21. $\dfrac{-6000 \ln \frac{3}{7}}{\ln 2} \ (\approx 7334)$ yr   **22.** 18,200 yr
23. $1000e^{3 \ln 2.5} = 15{,}625$ **24.** $\dfrac{15 \ln 2}{\ln 3} \ (\approx 9.464)$ days
25. $500e^{3 \ln(4/5)} = 256$ **26.** (b)

CHAPTER 8

PROBLEM SET 8.1, PAGE 369

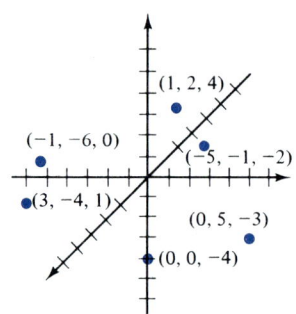

1.

3. $A \ (2,5,-2), \ B \ (0,3,0), \ C \ (-4,0,3), \ D \ (2,-3,4),$
$E \ (-1,-3,-5)$
5. (a) Yes, (b) yes, (c) no, (d) yes, (e) yes
7. (a) Yes, (b) no, (c) no, (d) yes
9. R^2
11. All points in R^2 except $(0,0)$
13. All points in R^2 except the line $x = -1$
15. Quadrants I and IV plus $(0,0)$, the positive x-axis, and the y-axis
17. Quadrants I and III
19. (a) 0, (b) 7, (c) $5 + \sqrt{6}$, (d) $a^2 + a^3 + a^4$,
(e) $2xh + h^2 + hy$
21. (a) 0, (b) $-\frac{4}{17}$, (c) $\frac{1}{2}$, (d) $\dfrac{a^2 - b^2}{2(a^2 + b^2)}$,
(e) $\dfrac{x^2 y^2}{x^4 + y^4}$

23. (a) $2e$, (b) -1, (c) -1, (d) $\ln 72$, (e) -1

25. (a) $\ln 7$, (b) 0, (c) e^9, (d) $\dfrac{1}{y}\ln\dfrac{y}{x^2}$,

(e) $3\ln\left(\dfrac{3}{3+h}\right) + h\ln\dfrac{4}{3+h}$

29. $V = rA/2$

PROBLEM SET 8.2, PAGE 377

1. (a) $6x$, (b) $-4y$ **3.** (a) $y^2 + 5$, (b) $2xy$

5. (a) $\dfrac{y}{(x+1)^2}$, (b) $\dfrac{x}{x+1}$

7. $f_x(x,y) = 3x^2$, $f_y(x,y) = 2$

9. $f_x(x,y) = 2xy - 9x^2y^2$, $f_y(x,y) = x^2 - 6x^3y$

11. $f_x(x,y) = \dfrac{2x}{y} - \dfrac{y^2}{x^2}$, $f_y(x,y) = -\dfrac{x^2}{y^2} + \dfrac{2y}{x}$

13. $f_x(x,y) = 4x^3(y^2+1)^6$, $f_y(x,y) = 12x^4y(y^2+1)^5$

15. $\dfrac{\partial z}{\partial x} = \dfrac{y^3-1}{2\sqrt{xy^3-x}}$, $\dfrac{\partial z}{\partial y} = \dfrac{3xy^2}{2\sqrt{xy^3-x}}$

17. $\dfrac{\partial z}{\partial x} = \dfrac{2xy^4}{(x^2+y^2)^2}$, $\dfrac{\partial z}{\partial y} = \dfrac{2x^4y}{(x^2+y^2)^2}$

19. $\dfrac{\partial z}{\partial x} = \dfrac{3y^3}{3xy^3-1}$, $\dfrac{\partial z}{\partial y} = \dfrac{9xy^2}{3xy^3-1}$

21. $\dfrac{\partial z}{\partial x} = e^{xy}(xy+1)$, $\dfrac{\partial z}{\partial y} = x^2e^{xy}$

23. (a) 4, (b) 0

27. (a) $6x$, (b) -1, (c) -1, (d) 0

29. (a) $-\dfrac{12y}{x^5}$, (b) $-\dfrac{3}{y^4} + \dfrac{3}{x^4}$, (c) $-\dfrac{3}{y^4} + \dfrac{3}{x^4}$,

(d) $\dfrac{12x}{y^5}$

31. (a) $16(x^2-2y)^6(15x^2-2y)$,
(b) $-224x(x^2-2y)^6$, (c) $-224x(x^2-2y)^6$,
(d) $224(x^2-2y)^6$

33. (a) $4e^{2x}\ln(3y)$, (b) $\dfrac{2e^{2x}}{y}$, (c) $\dfrac{2e^{2x}}{y}$, (d) $-\dfrac{e^{2x}}{y^2}$

39. (a) $\partial A/\partial i = (2.932)(0.0190)i^{1.932}p^{-3.578}r^{2.865}$; automobile consumption increases as real income increases
(b) $\partial A/\partial p = 0.0190i^{2.932}r^{2.865}(-3.578)p^{-4.578}$; automobile consumption decreases as the price of automobiles increase.

PROBLEM SET 8.3, PAGE 385

1. $(0,0,9)$ is a relative maximum point

3. $(-\frac{3}{2}, -2, -5\frac{1}{4})$ is a relative minimum point

5. $(3,0,-18)$ is a relative minimum point

7. $(0,-2,128)$ is a relative maximum point

9. $(\frac{1}{2},2,-\frac{7}{8})$ is a relative minimum point

11. No relative extreme points

13. $(-4,-3,-2)$ is a relative minimum point

15. $(3,3,-27)$ is a relative minimum point

17. $(1,8,24)$ is a relative minimum point

19. 72, 72, and 72   **21.** $(10,5,10)$

23. 3 ft by 3 ft for the base, 2.5 ft for the height

25. 36   **27.** $x = 2100$, $y = 1650$

PROBLEM SET 8.4, PAGE 395

1. Absolute maximum is 5, absolute minimum is -15

3. Absolute maximum is 0, absolute minimum is $-6\sqrt{3}$

5. Absolute maximum is $\dfrac{4}{3\sqrt{3}}$, absolute minimum is $\dfrac{-4}{3\sqrt{3}}$

7. Absolute maximum is 35, absolute minimum is 10

9. Absolute maximum is $\sqrt{2}$, absolute minimum is $-\sqrt{2}$

11. Absolute maximum is 76, absolute minimum is -56

13. 0   **15.** 15, $\frac{15}{2}$, and 5

17. 10 by 10 for the base, 10 for the height; volume $= 1000$

19. 19 in. by 19 in. for the base, 9.5 in. for the height; volume $= 3429.5$ in.^{3}

PROBLEM SET 8.5, PAGE 403

1. $\dfrac{x^5}{5} - \dfrac{x^3y^2}{3} + y^4x + C(y)$

3. $x\ln|y| + \dfrac{y^2}{2x} + \dfrac{y}{x^2} + C(x)$

5. $\dfrac{3}{20y}(x^5y - y^5)^{4/3} + C(y)$

7. $\dfrac{(\ln(3xy))^6}{6} + C(x)$

9. $\frac{1}{2}\ln|x^4 + x^2 + e^y| + C(y)$

11. $\dfrac{3}{x^3}e^{x^3y+x^6} + C(x)$

13. $2 + 4y$ **15.** $\ln\left|\dfrac{x+5}{x+2}\right|$ **17.** -16

19. 17   **21.** 1   **23.** 0

25. $\frac{21}{2}$

27. $\frac{1}{90}(11^{10} - 8^{10} - 5^{10} + 2^{10})$

29. $\frac{e^3}{9} + \frac{7}{18}$ 31. $e - 1$ 33. $20e^2$ 37. 50

39. $\frac{7}{4}$ 41. $\frac{1}{2}(e^{11} - 2e^7 + e^3)$

CHAPTER 8 REVIEW, PAGE 404

1. (a) T, (b) T, (c) F, (d) F, (e) T, (f) F, (g) T, (h) F, (i) T, (j) F, (k) F, (l) T, (m) T, (n) F, (o) T, (p) T, (q) T
2. R^2
3. Quadrant I plus the positive x-axis and the positive y-axis
4. (a) 32, (b) $3 + (\ln 3)^e$, (c) $3^{\sqrt[3]{5}} + 5$
5. (a) 2, (b) $\dfrac{1 + e^4}{e(1 + e^2)}$, (c) $\pi - 3$
6. (a) $12x^2$, (b) $-2y$, (c) $-2x$
7. (a) $\dfrac{6y}{x^4}$, (b) $-\dfrac{2}{y^3} - \dfrac{2}{x^3}$, (c) $\dfrac{6x}{y^4}$
8. (a) $-\dfrac{1}{2(x+y)^2}$, (b) $-\dfrac{1}{2(x+y)^2}$, (c) $-\dfrac{1}{2(x+y)^2}$
9. (a) $(1 + y)^2 e^{x+xy+y}$, (b) $(2 + x + y + xy)e^{x+xy+y}$, (c) $(1 + x)^2 e^{x+xy+y}$
12. $(10, 10, 1000)$ is a relative maximum point
13. $(-3, 1, -100)$ is a relative minimum point
14. $(-2, -4, -10)$ is a relative minimum point
15. No relative extreme points
16. Absolute maximum is 300, absolute minimum is -376
17. Absolute maximum is 0, absolute minimum is -34π
18. $(\frac{1}{3}, \frac{1}{3}, \frac{1}{3})$ 19. 4
20. 10 in. by 10 in. by 10 in.
21. 10 ft by 5 ft for the base, 5 ft for the height; volume is 250 ft³
22. 6 by $\frac{2}{3}\sqrt{6}$ for the base, $\frac{10}{3}\sqrt{6}$ for the height; volume is 80
23. $x = 425$, $y = 40$
24. $\dfrac{x^2}{2y^3} + y^3 \ln|x| - \dfrac{y}{2x^2} + C(y)$
25. $e^{y^5 + 5xy^2} + C(x)$
26. $\dfrac{1}{y^3} \ln|x^2 y^3 - xy^3 + y| + C(y)$
27. $\dfrac{(1 - y^5)^6 - y^{30}}{30}$ 28. -96
29. $\frac{4}{3}$ 30. 47

APPENDIX

PROBLEM SET A.2, PAGE 413

1. 81 2. 25 3. $\frac{1}{5}$ 4. $\frac{1}{8}$
5. -25 6. 1 7. $\frac{1}{36}$ 8. $\frac{3}{2}$
9. $\frac{25}{4}$ 10. $\frac{27}{25}$ 11. $\frac{82}{9}$ 12. $\frac{26}{5}$
13. $1/a^3$ 14. $3x$ 15. x^{10} 16. $1/a^6$
17. a^7 18. $2/x^5$ 19. y^3/x^6 20. $9a^2$
21. $9x^6 y^4$ 22. x^6/y^3 23. -4 24. -3
25. $2\sqrt[3]{2}$ 26. $2\sqrt{3}$
27. $\sqrt[3]{5}/2$ 28. $2/\sqrt{3}$ (or $2\sqrt{3}/3$)
29. $2|x|$ 30. $-x^2$ 31. 8 32. -125
33. 4 34. $\frac{1}{9}$ 35. $-\frac{1}{3}$ 36. $\frac{1}{2}$
37. $\frac{1}{2}$ 38. 8 39. x 40. $a^{1/2}$
41. $a^{2/3}$ 42. $1/x^2$ 43. $\dfrac{1}{2a^{1/3}}$ 44. $(x/y)^{3/2}$
45. $x^{3/2}$ 46. $a^{3/4}$ 47. $a^{1/4}$ 48. $x^{1/6}$

PROBLEM SET A.3, PAGE 417

1. $5x^2 - x$ 2. $4x^2 - 2xy + y^2$
3. $-y^2 - 5y + 3$ 4. $4x^2 + 5x + 3$
5. $2x^2 - 3xy$ 6. $2xy^4 - 2x^2y^3 + 10x^2y^2$
7. $6x^2 - 11x - 10$ 8. $3x^2 - xy - 10y^2$
9. $2x^3 + x^2y - 7xy^2 + 3y^3$
10. $2x^4 + 4x^3 - 3x^2 + 17x - 5$
11. $3x - 2 + xy$ 12. $\dfrac{2}{y} - y + 2x^2$
13. $4x^2 + 20x + 25$ 14. $9x^4y^2 + 6x^2y^3 + y^4$
15. $9y^2 - 12y + 4$ 16. $25x^2y^4 - 10x^3y^2 + x^4$
17. $4x^2 - y^2$ 18. $9y^4 - 16x^2y^2$
19. $x^2 + 8x + 15$ 20. $x^2 - x - 12$
21. $x^2 + 3x - 10$ 22. $x^2 - 10x + 24$
23. $8x^3 + 12x^2y + 6xy^2 + y^3$
24. $x^3 - 9x^2y + 27xy^2 - 27y^3$

PROBLEM SET A.4, PAGE 423

1. $2(x + 4)$ 2. $x(xy + 1)$
3. $xy(x - 3y + xy)$ 4. $3xy^2(3x^2 + 1 - 2xy)$
5. $(y + 1)(x + y)$ 6. $(2y - 3)(2x^2 - 1)$
7. $(2y - 3)(2y + 3)$ 8. $(x^2 + 4)(x + 2)(x - 2)$
9. $(x + 5)(x + 2)$ 10. $(x + 4)(x + 5)$
11. $(x + 4)(x - 3)$ 12. $(x - 5)(x + 3)$
13. $(x - 4)(x - 3)$ 14. $(x - 2)(x - 7)$
15. $(2x + 1)(x + 5)$ 16. $(x - 3)(3x - 4)$

17. $(x + 1)(3x − 8)$
18. $(x − 2)(5x + 3)$
19. $(3x + 4)(4x + 1)$
20. $(6x − 5)(x − 2)$
21. $(2x − 3)(5x + 4)$
22. $(12x − 1)(x + 2)$
23. $2x(x + y)^2$
24. $x^2(3x + y)(2x − 3y)$
25. $x(2x − y)(x + 4y)$
26. $(x + 2)(x − 2)(2x − 3)$

PROBLEM SET A.5, PAGE 427

1. $-5x$
2. $\dfrac{1}{3xy^2}$
3. $\dfrac{-x-1}{x}$
4. $\dfrac{1}{x+1}$
5. $\dfrac{x+4}{2x+1}$
6. $\dfrac{x(x+3)}{3(x-3)}$
7. $\dfrac{x+2}{x+y}$
8. $\dfrac{2x^2+5}{x^2+1}$
9. $\dfrac{x^2}{x^2-4}$
10. $\dfrac{x^2-y^2}{4xy}$
11. $\dfrac{y^2}{x^2}$
12. $\dfrac{x(x+2)}{2y}$
13. $\dfrac{2x+5}{x+5}$
14. $\dfrac{x+2}{x+3}$
15. $\dfrac{2x-5}{(x+2)(x+3)(x-1)}$
16. $\dfrac{x-y}{x(3x+y)(x-2y)}$
17. $\dfrac{2x+1}{7x}$
18. $\dfrac{2}{x}$
19. $\dfrac{1}{x-5}$
20. $\dfrac{2x+1}{(2x-3)(x+2)}$
21. $\dfrac{(x-1)(x+7)}{(x-2)(x+1)}$
22. $\dfrac{x^2-4x-9}{(x+5)(x-1)}$
23. $\dfrac{x(3x-y)}{2(x+y)(x-y)}$
24. $\dfrac{1}{5(x-2)}$

PROBLEM SET A.6, PAGE 431

1. $-\tfrac{10}{3}$
2. $\tfrac{7}{4}$
3. 4
4. -4
5. $\tfrac{6}{7}$
6. $\tfrac{7}{3}$
7. $\tfrac{16}{5}$
8. $\tfrac{15}{7}$
9. 2
10. 1
11. $-\tfrac{5}{2}$
12. $\tfrac{1}{5}$
13. $-\tfrac{1}{2}$
14. $\tfrac{1}{8}$
15. $-\tfrac{20}{3}$
16. $\tfrac{1}{4}$
17. $-\tfrac{4}{13}$
18. 13
19. $\tfrac{2}{3}$
20. $-\tfrac{9}{2}$
21. 0
22. $-\tfrac{5}{6}$
23. 2
24. -3
25. No solutions
26. All reals $\neq \tfrac{3}{2}$
27. 18
28. $-\tfrac{1}{7}$
29. $-\sqrt{5}-1$
30. $\sqrt{3}-1$
31. $x = 9a$
32. $x = \dfrac{5c+9}{7}$
33. $r = d/t,\ t \neq 0$
34. $t = \dfrac{v-k}{g},\ g \neq 0$
35. $C = \tfrac{5}{9}(F-32)$
36. $C = \dfrac{2A - hb}{h},\ h \neq 0$
37. $y = 6x - 6x_1 + y_1,\ x \neq x_1$
38. $x = \dfrac{y - y_1 + 2x_1}{2},\ y \neq y_1$
39. $y = \dfrac{6x}{3x-5},\ x \neq \tfrac{5}{3}$
40. $y = \dfrac{3x+5}{2x-1},\ x \neq \tfrac{1}{2}$
41. $y' = \dfrac{x^2}{3-2x},\ x \neq \tfrac{3}{2}$
42. $y' = \dfrac{1+3x}{x^2 - 2y^3},\ x^2 \neq 2y^3$

PROBLEM SET A.7, PAGE 435

1. $0, 3$
2. $0, -\tfrac{5}{2}$
3. $2, 3$
4. $-5, 2$
5. $-3, \tfrac{7}{2}$
6. $-3, -\tfrac{1}{3}$
7. $\tfrac{1}{2}, -\tfrac{1}{5}$
8. $4, -\tfrac{1}{6}$
9. $-5, 4$
10. $-3, 5$
11. $2, -\tfrac{3}{2}$
12. $-2, \tfrac{1}{3}$
13. $-4, \tfrac{1}{4}$
14. $-\tfrac{5}{3}, \tfrac{3}{2}$
15. $6, -3$
16. $\tfrac{1}{2}, -3$
17. $-\tfrac{2}{3}, -\tfrac{3}{4}$
18. $4, \tfrac{3}{8}$
19. $-2, \tfrac{3}{5}$
20. $-\tfrac{1}{3}, -\tfrac{1}{2}$
21. $-4, 2$
22. 1
23. -1
24. $\tfrac{4}{3}, -\tfrac{3}{2}$
25. $2, -3$
26. $-3, -4$
27. $2, -\tfrac{1}{2}$
28. $0, -\tfrac{7}{3}$
29. $3 + \sqrt{3},\ 3 - \sqrt{3}$
30. $-6 + 2\sqrt{3},\ -6 - 2\sqrt{3}$
31. $\dfrac{1+\sqrt{41}}{4},\ \dfrac{1-\sqrt{41}}{4}$
32. $1 + 2\sqrt{2},\ 1 - 2\sqrt{2}$
33. $\dfrac{1+\sqrt{13}}{3},\ \dfrac{1-\sqrt{13}}{3}$
34. $\dfrac{-5+\sqrt{17}}{4},\ \dfrac{-5-\sqrt{17}}{4}$
35. No solutions
36. $3 + 2\sqrt{2},\ 3 - 2\sqrt{2}$
37. $\dfrac{2+\sqrt{15}}{2},\ \dfrac{2-\sqrt{15}}{2}$
38. No solutions
39. $3\sqrt{2},\ -2\sqrt{2}$
40. $-\sqrt{2}+\sqrt{3},\ -2\sqrt{2}-\sqrt{3}$

INDEX

Absolute maximum, 240, 389
   at $x = c$, 240
   point, 240
Absolute minimum, 240, 389
   at $x = c$, 240
   point, 240
Absolute value function, 61
Acceleration, 133
Antiderivative, 279
Area
   between two curves, 307
   under a curve, 302–304
Argument, 24
Asymptote, 39
Average value, 319–321
Axis, 4, 32
   x-, 4
   y-, 4
   z-, 364

Base, 408
Binomial, 414
Boundary point, 378
Branch, 39

Carbon-14 dating, 356
Cartesian coordinate system, 3
Cartesian plane, 4
Chain rule, 142
Change of base formulas, 55
Common logarithm, 43
Compound interest, 47–48
Concavity
   at $x = a$, 211
   on an interval, 210–211
Constant, 428
Constant function, 31
Constraint equation, 249

Consumers' surplus, 310–311
Continuous at $x = a$, 80
Continuous function, 82
Coordinate plane, 4
Cost function, 136
Critical value, 202

Decay constant, 355
Decreasing
   at $x = a$, 193
   on an interval, 192
Definite integral, 294
   approximation of, 346–351
   as a limit of sums, 313–314
   as area, 302–304
Degree, 31, 414
Demand, 15
Demand equation, 15–16
Dependent variable, 22
Derivative, 112–113
   of a constant, 123
   of a constant times a function, 124–125
   of a general power function, 145
   notation, 137–138, 166, 168, 375
   nth, 168
   partial, 371–372
   of a product, 153
   of a quotient, 156–157
   second, 166
   second partial, 375
   of a simple power function, 123
   of a sum or difference, 128
   of $f(g(x))$, 141–142
   of the exponential function with base e, 126
   of the natural logarithmic function, 126
Differentiable at $x = a$, 114–115
Differentiable function, 115

Differential, 329
Differential equation, 352
Differentiate, 114
Differentiation
   implicit, 172
   logarithmic, 175
Discontinuous at $x = a$, 80
Discontinuous function, 82
Discriminant, 435
Domain
   of a function, 24
   of a variable, 427
Double integral, 400

e, 43, 72
Endpoint, 408
Equation
   constraint, 249
   demand, 15–16
   equivalent, 428
   exponential, 46
   in x and y, 3
   in x, y, and z, 364
   linear, 8
   logarithmic, 48
   quadratic, 431
   supply, 17
Equivalent equations, 428
Exponent, 408
Exponents, properties of, 409
Exponential equation, 46
Exponential function, 52
Exponential law of decay, 355
Exponential law of growth, 353
Extreme points, 201

Factored, 417
First derivative rule, 194–195

INDEX

First derivative test, 203
Formula of definition, 25
Function, 24
  absolute value, 61
  argument of, 24
  constant, 31
  continuous, 82
  cost, 136
  domain of, 24
  exponential, 52
  formula of definition of, 25
  graph of, 31
  greatest integer, 61
  linear, 31
  logarithmic, 54
  marginal cost, 136
  marginal profit, 136
  marginal revenue, 136
  polynomial, 31
  position, 133
  power, 86
  profit, 136
  quadratic, 31
  range of, 24
  rational, 38
  revenue, 136
  value of, 24

General power rule, 145
Graph
  of a function, 31
  of an equation, 4
Greatest integer function, 61
Growth constant, 353

Half-life, 356

Implicit differentiation, 172
Increasing
  at $x = a$, 193
  on an interval, 192
Indefinite integral, 279, 395–396
Independent variable, 22
Index, 411
Infinite limit, 229–230
Infinity, 407–408
Inflection point, 223
Inflection point test, 225
Inhibited exponential growth, 357
Integral
  definite, 294
  double, 400
  indefinite, 279, 395–396
  symbol, 279
Integrand, 279

Integration, 279
Integration by parts, 335–336
Interior point, 408
Interval, 407–408
Interval notation, 408
Inverse, 56

Lagrange multiplier, 387
Leading coefficient, 31
Leading term, 31
Like terms, 414
Limit, 70–71
  infinite, 229–230
  at infinity, 231
  one-sided, 73
  point, 70
  properties, 83–84
Limits of integration, 294
Linear equation, 8, 429
Linear function, 31
Logarithm, 42–43
  common, 43
  natural, 43
Logarithms, laws of, 44–45
Logarithmic differentiation, 175
Logarithmic equation, 48
Logarithmic function, 54
Lot size, 267

Marginal cost function, 136
Marginal profit function, 136
Marginal revenue function, 136
Maxima and minima
  absolute, 240, 389
  relative, 201, 378–379
Method of factoring, 432
Monomial, 414

Natural logarithm, 43
Negative infinity, 407–408
nth derivative, 168
nth root, 410
Numerical coefficient, 414

Octant, 364
One-sided limit, 73
Open disk, 378
Ordered pair, 3
Origin, 4

Parabola, 31–33
Partial derivative, 371–372
Parts, integration by, 335–336
Point–slope form, 14

Polynomial, 414
Polynomial function, 31
Position function, 133
Power, 408
Power function, 86
Principal nth root, 410
Producers' surplus, 311
Product rule, 153
Profit function, 136

Quadrant, 4
Quadratic equation, 431
Quadratic formula, 434
Quadratic function, 31
Quotient rule, 156–157

Radicand, 411
Range, 24
Rational expression, 423
Rational function, 38
Rectangle rule, 346–348
Relative extreme point, 201, 378–379
Relative maximum, 201
  at $x = c$, 201
  at (a, b), 378
  point, 201
Relative minimum, 201
  at $x = c$, 201
  at (a, b), 378–379
  point, 201
Revenue function, 136
Root, 410, 428

Saddle point, 380
Secant line, 93
Second derivative, 166
Second derivative rule, 213
Second derivative test, 215
Second partial derivative, 375
Second partial derivative test, 380
Simple power rule, 123
Simpson's rule, 350
Slope
  of a curve, 103–104
  of a line, 9–11
Slope–intercept form, 12
Solution
  of an equation in one variable, 428
  of an equation in x and y, 3
  of an equation in x, y, and z, 364
Stationary point, 379
Substitution, 328
Supply, 17
Supply equation, 17
Symmetry, 32

Table of integrals, 341, inside back cover
Tangent line, 93
Term, 413
Transformation, 35
Trapezoid rule, 348–349
Trinomial, 414

Value of f at a, 24
Variable, 428
  dependent, 22
  independent, 22

Velocity, 133
Vertex, 32
Volume
  of a region rotated about the x-axis, 315–316
  of a region rotated about the y-axis, 317–318

x-axis, 4
x-coordinate, 4

x-intercept, 8
xy-plane, 4

y-axis, 4
y-coordinate, 4
y-intercept, 8
y is a function of x, 22

z-axis, 364
z-coordinate, 364
z is a function of x and y, 364

TABLE OF INTEGRALS

Elementary Forms

1. $\int x^n dx = \dfrac{x^{n+1}}{n+1} + c \quad (n \neq -1)$

2. $\int \dfrac{1}{x} dx = \ln|x| + c$

3. $\int (f(x))^n \cdot f'(x) dx = \dfrac{[f(x)]^{n+1}}{n+1} + c \quad (n \neq -1)$

4. $\int \dfrac{f'(x)}{f(x)} dx = \ln|f(x)| + c$

5. $\int e^x dx = e^x + c$

6. $\int e^{f(x)} \cdot f'(x) dx = e^{f(x)} + c$

Forms Containing $ax + b$

7. $\int \dfrac{x}{ax+b} dx = \dfrac{x}{a} - \dfrac{b}{a^2} \ln|ax+b| + c$

8. $\int \dfrac{x}{(ax+b)^2} dx = \dfrac{b}{a^2(ax+b)} + \dfrac{1}{a^2} \ln|ax+b| + c$

9. $\int \dfrac{1}{x(ax+b)} dx = \dfrac{1}{b} \ln\left|\dfrac{x}{ax+b}\right| + c$

10. $\int \dfrac{1}{x(ax+b)^2} dx = \dfrac{1}{b(ax+b)} + \dfrac{1}{b^2} \ln\left|\dfrac{x}{ax+b}\right| + c$

Forms Containing $\sqrt{ax+b}$

11. $\int x\sqrt{ax+b}\, dx = \dfrac{2}{15a^2}(3ax-2b)(ax+b)^{3/2} + c$

12. $\int x^2\sqrt{ax+b}\, dx = \dfrac{2}{105a^3}(15a^2x^2 - 12abx + 8b^2)(ax+b)^{3/2} + c$

13. $\int \dfrac{x}{\sqrt{ax+b}} dx = \dfrac{2}{3a^2}(ax-2b)\sqrt{ax+b} + c$

14. $\int \dfrac{x^2}{\sqrt{ax+b}} dx = \dfrac{2}{15a^3}(3a^2x^2 - 4abx + 8b^2)\sqrt{ax+b} + c$

Forms Containing $\pm(x^2 - a^2)$

15. $\int \dfrac{1}{x^2 - a^2} dx = \dfrac{1}{2a} \ln\left|\dfrac{x-a}{x+a}\right| + c$

16. $\int \dfrac{1}{a^2 - x^2} dx = \dfrac{1}{2a} \ln\left|\dfrac{a+x}{a-x}\right| + c$

Forms Containing $\sqrt{x^2 \pm a^2}$ or $\sqrt{a^2 \pm x^2}$

17. $\int \sqrt{x^2 + a^2}\, dx = \dfrac{x}{2}\sqrt{x^2+a^2} + \dfrac{a^2}{2} \ln\left|x + \sqrt{x^2+a^2}\right| + c$

18. $\int \sqrt{x^2 - a^2}\, dx = \dfrac{x}{2}\sqrt{x^2-a^2} - \dfrac{a^2}{2} \ln\left|x + \sqrt{x^2-a^2}\right| + c$